CORPORATE FINANCE

CFA Institute is the premier association for investment professionals around the world, with more than 150,000 CFA charterholders worldwide in 165+ countries and regions. Since 1963 the organization has developed and administered the renowned Chartered Financial Analyst® Program. With a rich history of leading the investment profession, CFA Institute has set the highest standards in ethics, education, and professional excellence within the global investment community and is the foremost authority on investment profession conduct and practice. Each book in the CFA Institute Investment Series is geared toward industry practitioners along with graduate-level finance students and covers the most important topics in the industry. The authors of these cutting-edge books are themselves industry professionals and academics and bring their wealth of knowledge and expertise to this series.

CORPORATE FINANCE

Economic Foundations and Financial Modeling

Third Edition

Michelle R. Clayman, CFA

Martin S. Fridson, CFA

George H. Troughton, CFA

WILEY

Published by John Wiley & Sons, Inc., Hoboken, New Jersey
Published simultaneously in Canada

For general information on our other products and services or for technical support, please contact our Customer Care Department within the United States at (800) 762-2974, outside the United States at (317) 572-3993 or fax (317) 572-4002.

Wiley also publishes its books in a variety of electronic formats. Some content that appears in print may not be available in electronic formats. For more information about Wiley products, visit our web site at www.wiley.com.

Library of Congress Cataloging-in-Publication Data:

    Corporate finance : a practical approach / [edited by] Michelle R. Clayman, Martin S. Fridson, George H. Troughton. — 2nd ed.
      p. cm. — (CFA Institute investment series ; 42)
    Includes index.
    ISBN 978-1-119-74376-7 (cloth); ISBN 978-1-119-74377-4 (ebk);
    ISBN 978-1-119-74380-4 (ebk)
      1. Corporations—Finance. I. Clayman, Michelle R. II. Fridson, Martin S. III. Troughton, George H.
HG4026.C67   2022
658.15—dc23

                                                                         2011039258

Printed in the United States of America

SKY10036084_091522

CONTENTS

Foreword   xv
Acknowledgments   xix
About the CFA Institute Investment Series   xxi

CHAPTER 1
Corporate Structures and Ownership   1

Learning Outcomes   1
1. Introduction   1
2. Business Structures   2
   2.1. Sole Proprietorship (Sole Trader)   2
   2.2. General Partnership   3
   2.3. Limited Partnership   4
   2.4. Corporation (Limited Companies)   5
3. Public and Private Corporations   12
   3.1. Exchange Listing and Share Ownership Transfer   13
   3.2. Share Issuance   15
   3.3. Going Public from Private—IPO, Direct Listing, Acquisition   18
   3.4. Life Cycle of Corporations   20
4. Lenders and Owners   23
   4.1. Equity and Debt Risk–Return Profiles   25
   4.2. Equity vs. Debt Conflicts of Interest   31
5. Summary   31
6. Practice Problems   32

CHAPTER 2
Introduction to Corporate Governance and Other ESG Considerations   35

Learning Outcomes   35
1. Introduction   36
2. Stakeholder Groups   36
   2.1. Shareholder vs. Stakeholder Theory   37
   2.2. Shareholders   38
   2.3. Creditors/Debtholders   38
   2.4. Board of Directors   38
   2.5. Managers   39
   2.6. Employees   40
   2.7. Customers   40
   2.8. Suppliers   40
   2.9. Governments   40

3. Principal–Agent and Other Relationships   41
   3.1. Shareholder and Manager/Director Relationships   42
   3.2. Controlling and Minority Shareholder Relationships   44
   3.3. Manager and Board Relationships   49
   3.4. Shareholder vs. Creditor (Debtholder) Interests   49
4. Corporate Governance and Mechanisms to Manage Stakeholder Risks   51
   4.1. Shareholder Mechanisms   52
   4.2. Creditor Mechanisms   55
   4.3. Board of Director and Management Mechanisms   56
   4.4. Employee Mechanisms   60
   4.5. Customer and Supplier Mechanisms   60
   4.6. Government Mechanisms   61
5. Corporate Governance and Stakeholder Management Risks and Benefits   63
   5.1. Operational Risks and Benefits   63
   5.2. Legal, Regulatory, or Reputational Risks and Benefits   65
   5.3. Financial Risks and Benefits   66
6. ESG Considerations in Investment Analysis   69
   6.1. Introduction to Environmental and Social Factors   70
   6.2. Evaluating ESG-Related Risks and Opportunities   72
7. Environmental, Social, and Governance Investment Approaches   73
   7.1. ESG Investment Approaches   73
   7.2. ESG Market Overview   77
8. Summary   77
9. Practice Problems   79

CHAPTER 3
Working Capital & Liquidity   81

   Learning Outcomes   81
1. Introduction   81
2. Financing Options   82
   2.1. Internal Financing   83
   2.2. External Financing: Financial Intermediaries   85
   2.3. External Financing: Capital Markets   87
3. Working Capital, Liquidity, and Short-Term Funding Needs   89
4. Liquidity and Short-Term Funding   95
   4.1. Primary Sources of Liquidity   96
   4.2. Secondary Sources of Liquidity   96
   4.3. Drags and Pulls on Liquidity   98
5. Measuring Liquidity   99
6. Evaluating Short-Term Financing Choices   103
7. Summary   105
8. Practice Problems   105

CHAPTER 4
Capital Investments   109

   Learning Outcomes   109
1. Introduction   109
2. Types of Capital Investments   110

    2.1. Business Maintenance   111
    2.2. Business Growth   112
  3. The Capital Allocation Process   114
  4. Investment Decision Criteria   119
    4.1. Net Present Value   119
    4.2. Internal Rate of Return   122
  5. Common Capital Allocation Pitfalls   125
  6. Corporate Use of Capital Allocation   126
  7. Real Options   129
    7.1. Timing Options   130
    7.2. Sizing Options   131
    7.3. Flexibility Options   131
    7.4. Fundamental Options   131
  8. Summary   132
  9. Practice Problems   133

CHAPTER 5
Capital Structure   **139**

  Learning Outcomes   139
  1. Introduction   139
  2. Factors Affecting Capital Structure   140
    2.1. Internal Factors Affecting Capital Structure   141
    2.2. Existing Leverage   144
    2.3. External Factors Affecting Capital Structure   149
  3. Capital Structure and Company Life Cycle   151
    3.1. Background   151
    3.2. Start-Ups   152
    3.3. Growth Businesses   153
    3.4. Mature Businesses   154
    3.5. Unique Situations   156
  4. Modigliani–Miller Propositions   157
    4.1. MM Proposition I without Taxes: Capital Structure Irrelevance   159
    4.2. MM Proposition II without Taxes: Higher Financial Leverage
        Raises the Cost of Equity   160
    4.3. MM Propositions with Taxes: Firm Value   163
    4.4. MM Propositions with Taxes: Cost of Capital   163
    4.5. Costs of Financial Distress   165
  5. Optimal and Target Capital Structures   167
    5.1. Market Value vs. Book Value   169
    5.2. Target Weights and WACC   170
    5.3. Pecking Order Theory and Agency Costs   172
  6. Stakeholder Interests   174
    6.1. Debt vs. Equity Conflict   175
    6.2. Preferred Shareholders   180
    6.3. Management and Directors   181
  7. Summary   183
  8. Practice Problems   183

CHAPTER 6

Measures of Leverage   **189**

    Learning Outcomes   189
  1. Introduction   189
  2. Leverage   190
  3. Business and Sales Risks   192
    3.1. Business Risk and Its Components   192
    3.2. Sales Risk   193
  4. Operating Risk and the Degree of Operating Leverage   194
  5. Financial Risk, the Degree of Financial Leverage and the Leveraging Role of Debt   201
  6. Total Leverage and the Degree of Total Leverage   205
  7. Breakeven Points and Operating Breakeven Points   208
  8. The Risks of Creditors and Owners   211
  9. Summary   213
 10. Practice Problems   214

CHAPTER 7

Cost of Capital: Foundational Topics   **219**

    Learning Outcomes   219
  1. Introduction   219
  2. Cost of Capital   220
    2.1. Taxes and the Cost of Capital   222
  3. Costs of the Various Sources of Capital   223
    3.1. Cost of Debt   223
    3.2. Cost of Preferred Stock   226
    3.3. Cost of Common Equity   228
  4. Estimating Beta   232
    4.1. Estimating Beta for Public Companies   232
    4.2. Estimating Beta for Thinly Traded and Nonpublic Companies   233
  5. Flotation Costs   237
  6. Methods in Use   239
  7. Summary   240
  8. Practice Problems   241

CHAPTER 8

Cost of Capital: Advanced Topics   **249**

    Learning Outcomes   249
  1. Introduction   249
  2. Cost of Capital Factors   250
    2.1. Top-Down External Factors   251
    2.2. Bottom-Up Company-Specific Factors   254
    2.3. Cost of Capital Factors Summary   259
  3. Estimating the Cost of Debt   261
    3.1. Traded Debt   262
    3.2. Non-Traded Debt   262
    3.3. Bank Debt   263
    3.4. Leases   264
    3.5. International Considerations   266
  4. The ERP   268

	4.1. Historical Approach	268
	4.2. Forward-Looking Approach	272
5.	The Cost of Equity (Required Return on Equity)	279
	5.1. DDMs	279
	5.2. Bond Yield Plus Risk Premium Approach	280
	5.3. Risk-Based Models	281
	5.4. Estimating the Cost of Equity for Private Companies	284
	5.5. International Considerations	287
	5.6. Required Return on Equity Summary	290
6.	Mini-Case 1	293
	6.1. Gretna Engines	293
7.	Mini-Case 2	299
	7.1. Precision Irrigation	299
8.	Practice Problems	300

CHAPTER 9
Analysis of Dividends and Share Repurchases   303

	Learning Outcomes	303
1.	Dividends: Forms and Effects on Shareholder Wealth and Financial Ratios	304
	1.1. Dividends: Forms and Effects on Shareholder Wealth and Issuing Company's Financial Ratios	305
2.	Dividend Policy and Company Value: Theories	311
	2.1. Dividend Policy Does Not Matter	311
	2.2. Dividend Policy Matters: The Bird in the Hand Argument	312
	2.3. Dividend Policy Matters: The Tax Argument	313
3.	Other Theoretical Issues: Signaling	313
	3.1. The Information Content of Dividend Actions: Signaling	313
	3.2. Agency Costs and Dividends as a Mechanism to Control Them	317
4.	Other Theoretical Issues: Summary	320
5.	Factors Affecting Dividend Policy in Practice	320
	5.1. Investment Opportunities	320
	5.2. The Expected Volatility of Future Earnings	321
	5.3. Financial Flexibility	321
	5.4. Tax Considerations	322
	5.5. Flotation Costs	324
	5.6. Contractual and Legal Restrictions	325
	5.7. Factors Affecting Dividend Policy: Summary	326
6.	Payout Policies	327
	6.1. Stable Dividend Policy	327
	6.2. Constant Dividend Payout Ratio Policy	329
	6.3. Global Trends in Payout Policy	331
7.	Share Repurchases	332
	7.1. Share Repurchase Methods	332
	7.2. Financial Statement Effects of Repurchases	334
8.	Valuation Equivalence of Cash Dividends and Share Repurchase	338
9.	The Dividend versus Share Repurchase Decision	339
10.	Analysis of Dividend Safety	347
11.	Summary	351
12.	Practice Problems	353

CHAPTER 10
Business Models & Risks   **359**

   Learning Outcomes   359
  1. Introductory Context/Motivation   359
  2. What Is a Business Model?   359
    2.1. Business Model Features   361
    2.2. Customers, Market: Who   361
    2.3. Firm Offering: What   362
    2.4. Channels: Where   362
    2.5. Pricing: How Much   365
    2.6. Value Proposition (Who + What + Where + How Much)   368
    2.7. Business Organization, Capabilities: How   370
    2.8. Profitability and Unit Economics   372
  3. Business Model Types   373
    3.1. Business Model Innovation   374
    3.2. Business Model Variations   374
    3.3. E-Commerce Business Models   375
    3.4. Network Effects and Platform Business Models   375
    3.5. Crowdsourcing Business Models   376
    3.6. Hybrid Business Models   376
  4. Business Models: Financial Implications   378
    4.1. External Factors   378
    4.2. Firm-Specific Factors   380
  5. Business Risks   383
    5.1. Summary   383
  6. Macro Risk, Business Risk, and Financial Risk   384
    6.1. Risk Impacts Are Cumulative   386
  7. Business Risk: A Closer Look   386
    7.1. Industry Risks   386
    7.2. Industry Definition   387
    7.3. Company-Specific Risks   387
  8. Financial Risk   389
    8.1. Measuring Operating and Financial Leverage   390
  9. Summary   392
 10. Practice Problems   392

CHAPTER 11
The Firm and Market Structures   **395**

   Learning Outcomes   395
  1. Analysis of Market Structures   395
    1.1. Analysis of Market Structures   396
  2. Perfect Competition   401
    2.1. Demand Analysis in Perfectly Competitive Markets   401
  3. Elasticity of Demand   403
  4. Other Factors Affecting Demand   406
  5. Consumer Surplus: Value Minus Expenditure   408
  6. Supply Analysis, Optimal Price, and Output in Perfectly Competitive Markets   410
    6.1. Optimal Price and Output in Perfectly Competitive Markets   411

7. Long-Run Equilibrium In Perfectly Competitive Markets   416
8. Monopolistic Competition   418
   8.1. Demand Analysis in Monopolistically Competitive Markets   419
   8.2. Supply Analysis in Monopolistically Competitive Markets   420
   8.3. Optimal Price and Output in Monopolistically Competitive Markets   420
9. Long-Run Equilibrium in Monopolistic Competition   421
10. Oligopoly and Pricing Strategies   422
    10.1. Demand Analysis and Pricing Strategies in Oligopoly Markets   423
11. The Cournot Assumption   425
12. The Nash Equilibrium   428
13. Oligopy Markets: Optimal Price, Output, and Long-Run Equilibrium   431
    13.1. Optimal Price and Output in Oligopoly Markets   432
    13.2. Factors Affecting Long-Run Equilibrium in Oligopoly Markets   433
14. Monopoly Markets: Demand/Supply and Optimal Price/Output   434
    14.1. Demand Analysis in Monopoly Markets   435
    14.2. Supply Analysis in Monopoly Markets   436
    14.3. Optimal Price and Output in Monopoly Markets   438
15. Price Discrimination and Consumer Surplus   440
16. Monopoly Markets: Long-Run Equilibrium   442
17. Identification of Market Structure   443
    17.1. Econometric Approaches   444
    17.2. Simpler Measures   444
18. Summary   446
19. Practice Problems   447

CHAPTER 12
Introduction to Industry and Company Analysis   **451**

Learning Outcomes   451
1. Introduction   452
2. Uses of Industry Analysis   452
3. Approaches to Identifying Similar Companies   453
   3.1. Products and/or Services Supplied   453
   3.2. Business-Cycle Sensitivities   454
   3.3. Statistical Similarities   455
4. Industry Classification Systems   457
   4.1. Commercial Industry Classification Systems   457
   4.2. Constructing a Peer Group   462
5. Describing and Analyzing an Industry and Principles of Strategic Analysis   465
   5.1. Principles of Strategic Analysis   467
   5.2. Barriers to Entry   468
   5.3. Industry Concentration   470
   5.4. Industry Capacity   472
   5.5. Market Share Stability   474
   5.6. Price Competition   475
   5.7. Industry Life Cycle   476
6. External Influences on Industry   480
   6.1. Macroeconomic Influences   480
   6.2. Technological Influences   480
   6.3. Demographic Influences   482

    6.4. Governmental Influences   482
    6.5. Social Influences   483
    6.6. Environmental Influences   483
    6.7. Industry Comparison   486
  7. Company Analysis   489
    7.1. Elements That Should Be Covered in a Company Analysis   490
    7.2. Spreadsheet Modeling   492
  8. Summary   493
  9. Practice Problems   496

CHAPTER 13
Financial Statement Modeling   **501**

  Learning Outcomes   501
  1. Introduction   502
    1.1. Financial Statement Modeling: An Overview   502
  2. Income Statement Modeling: Operating Costs   508
  3. Modeling Operating Costs: Cost of Goods Sold and SG&A   512
    3.1. SG&A Expenses   514
  4. Modeling Non-operating Costs and Other Items   520
    4.1. Financing Expenses   520
    4.2. Corporate Income Tax   521
    4.3. Income Statement Modeling: Other Items   525
  5. Balance Sheet and Cash Flow Statement Modeling   525
  6. Building a Financial Statement Model   531
    6.1. Company Overview   531
    6.2. Revenue Forecast   533
    6.3. COGS   534
    6.4. SG&A Expenses and Other Operating Expense   534
    6.5. Operating Profit by Segment   535
    6.6. Non-Operating Items   537
    6.7. Corporate Income Tax Forecast   537
    6.8. Shares Outstanding   537
    6.9. Pro Forma Income Statement   538
    6.10. Pro Forma Statement of Cash Flows   540
    6.11. Capital Investments and Depreciation Forecasts   541
    6.12. Working Capital Forecasts   542
    6.13. Forecasted Cash Flow Statement   542
    6.14. Forecasted Balance Sheet   543
    6.15. Valuation Model Inputs   544
  7. Behavioral Finance and Analyst Forecasts   545
    7.1. Overconfidence in Forecasting   545
    7.2. Illusion of Control   547
    7.3. Conservatism Bias   548
    7.4. Representativeness Bias   549
    7.5. Confirmation Bias   551
  8. The Impact of Competitive Factors in Prices and Costs   551
    8.1. Cognac Industry Overview   552
  9. Inflation and Deflation   561
    9.1. Sales Projections with Inflation and Deflation   561

    9.2. Cost Projections with Inflation and Deflation   567

10. Technological Developments   570

11. Long-Term Forecasting   580

    11.1. Case Study: Estimating Normalized Revenue   580

12. Summary   584

13. Practice Problems   585

CHAPTER 14

Corporate Restructurings   **593**

    Learning Outcomes   593

1. Introduction   593

2. Corporate Evolution, Actions, and Motivations   594

    2.1. Corporate Life Cycle and Actions   594

    2.2. Motivations for Corporate Structural Change   595

    2.3. Types of Corporate Restructurings   597

3. Evaluating Corporate Restructurings   611

    3.1. Initial Evaluation   612

    3.2. Preliminary Valuation   614

4. Modeling and Valuation   620

    4.1. Pro Forma Weighted Average Cost of Capital   622

5. Evaluating Investment Actions   628

    5.1. Equity Investment   628

    5.2. Joint Venture   632

    5.3. Acquisition   636

6. Evaluating Divestment Actions   640

7. Evaluating Restructuring Actions   647

8. Summary   653

9. Practice Problems   654

CHAPTER 15

Environmental, Social, and Governance (ESG) Considerations in
Investment Analysis   **659**

    Learning Outcomes   659

1. Introduction   659

2. Ownership Structures and Their Effects on Corporate Governance   660

    2.1. Dispersed vs. Concentrated Ownership   660

    2.2. Conflicts within Different Ownership Structures   662

    2.3. Types of Influential Shareholders   663

    2.4. Effects of Ownership Structure on Corporate Governance   665

3. Evaluating Corporate Governance Policies and Procedures   666

    3.1. Board Policies and Practices   667

    3.2. Executive Remuneration   669

    3.3. Shareholder Voting Rights   669

4. Identifying ESG-Related Risks and Opportunities   670

    4.1. Materiality and Investment Horizon   670

    4.2. Relevant ESG-Related Factors   670

5. Evaluating ESG-Related Risks and Opportunities   676

5.1. ESG Integration   676
5.2. Examples of ESG Integration   677
6. Summary   685
7. Practice Problems   686

CHAPTER 16
Intercorporate Investments   **689**

Learning Outcomes   689
1. Introduction   689
2. Basic Corporate Investment Categories   690
3. Investments In Financial Assets: IFRS 9   692
   3.1. Classification and Measurement   692
   3.2. Reclassification of Investments   694
4. Investments in Associates and Joint Ventures   695
   4.1. Equity Method of Accounting: Basic Principles   696
5. Amortization of Excess Purchase Price, Fair Value Option, and Impairment 700
   5.1. Amortization of Excess Purchase Price   701
   5.2. Fair Value Option   704
   5.3. Impairment   704
6. Transactions with Associates and Disclosure   705
   6.1. Disclosure   708
   6.2. Issues for Analysts   708
7. Acquisition Method   709
   7.1. Acquisition Method   711
   7.2. Impact of the Acquisition Method on Financial Statements, Post-Acquisition 713
8. The Consolidation Process   716
   8.1. Business Combination with Less Than 100% Acquisition   716
   8.2. Non-controlling (Minority) Interests: Balance Sheet   716
   8.3. Non-controlling (Minority) Interests: Income Statement   719
   8.4. Goodwill Impairment   720
9. Financial Statement Presentation   722
10. Variable Interest and Special Purpose Entities   725
    10.1. Securitization of Assets   727
11. Additional Issues in Business Combinations That impair Comparability   729
    11.1. Contingent Assets and Liabilities   729
    11.2. Contingent Consideration   729
    11.3. In-Process R&D   730
    11.4. Restructuring Costs   730
12. Summary   730
13. Practice Problems   731

Glossary   **743**
References   **757**
About the Authors   **763**
About the CFA Program   **769**
Index   **771**

FOREWORD

I am honored to introduce this second edition of *Corporate Finance: A Practical Approach*, which promises to be an important and comprehensive discourse on corporate financial management. The significant additions in this edition and revisions to the first edition build on the topic areas introduced in 2008. Furthermore, they bring much-needed practical dimensions to the complex and dynamic aspects of corporate finance.

Certainly, the global financial landscape has changed dramatically since the release of the first edition of this work. The economic drama and financial carnage injected into the marketplace starting in late 2007 have penetrated the very core of financial thought and practice and have challenged long-standing economic beliefs and relationships. The effects on corporate governance, capital structure, and budgeting caused by this extreme market volatility and economic upheaval have moved corporate treasurers and chief financial officers to the front lines in their companies' continuing pursuits of profitability and financial security. Only those institutions that can quickly adapt their financial management and corporate structure to this "new normal" will survive well into the future. The chapters in this edition have been revised to take into consideration some of the profound changes that have affected this new global financial setting. Yet, it is refreshing to note that no matter what economic environment exists in the future, sound, traditional financial management practices will always be essential to the long-term success of any entity.

The authors of these chapters are leading industry practitioners and recognized academic thought leaders. Their unique perspectives and thorough understanding of their respective topic areas are invaluable in providing readers with a factual exposition of the subject matter. In addition, their commonsense approach of highlighting important learning outcomes and incorporating practical problem-solving tools gives readers techniques they can apply in real-world financial settings.

Like the original text, this edition is assembled from readings used in the CFA Program curriculum. The CFA Program is a comprehensive, self-directed, distance learning program administered by CFA Institute. Since the early 1960s, the attainment of the CFA designation has been viewed as a significant achievement in the realm of finance and investment management. Those who enter the CFA Program sit for three consecutive and rigorous examinations that cover a broad range of important financial topics, including accounting, quantitative methods, equity and fixed-income analysis, portfolio management, and ethics. Most who enter this program already possess a strong record of achievement in the financial industry, as well as advanced business degrees, but welcome the additional focus and comprehensive curriculum of this designation program. I am fortunate to have earned the CFA charter and am proud to serve on the Board of Governors of CFA Institute.

WHY THIS TEXT IS IMPORTANT

Competing in the global financial arena has been a far more daunting challenge during this decade than in earlier periods. The scarcity of credit and risk capital following the global financial challenges of the past few years, along with the evolution of emerging economies as formidable players on the world financial stage, demands that businesses operate at utmost efficiency. Optimal financial management and peak operating effectiveness are prerequisites not only for success but also for survival. And in order to successfully commit risk capital, companies must incorporate disciplined, systematic capital-budgeting techniques so as to allocate capital to only those projects with optimal returns. Furthermore, companies must be able to understand the life spans of projects, effectively anticipate cash flow needs, and accurately forecast lean periods in their liquidity to avoid potentially devastating shocks to their financial and market health. Also critical in this new financial environment is the ability to properly analyze the effects of inflation, disinflation, foreign currency shocks, and regulatory risk on existing projects, as well as the ability to recognize capital-budgeting biases and errors. This book offers comprehensive insights into avoiding these common pitfalls.

In particular, the chapter on capital budgeting is instrumental in instilling in the reader the discipline to anticipate extraneous influences on capital planning. Another critical section of the book concerns forecasting and evaluating the weighted average cost of capital that an entity faces. Recent as well as long-term financial history has taught everyone the importance of properly analyzing this crucial financial component. The degree of assumed leverage, tax benefits and implications of using debt over other forms of capitalization, the cost of debt versus common and preferred equity, and the impact of changes in debt ratings—all are essential areas of knowledge for company leaders. The ability to use the cost of capital as an effective discipline in organizational budgeting is yet another key component of continued financial stability.

In addition to the tools and techniques for measuring the cost of capital, the appropriate use of financial leverage is an important topic in this text. Clearly, increased leverage heightens the level of earnings volatility and, ultimately, the cost of equity and the overall risk attached to any company. Properly understanding the prudent use of financial leverage as an earnings-enhancement vehicle is essential. Furthermore, examining the degree of operating leverage and the impact of cost structure on production is a vital component of measuring and evaluating the operating efficiency of any organization. And last but not least, an incredibly large part of ultimately determining the financial competitiveness of a company is successfully anticipating and accounting for the effect of taxes.

A key element of attracting investors and maintaining adequate sources of capital is fully understanding how an entity manages its own equity in the context of dividends and share repurchases. In addition, I cannot overstate the advantages of having a technical grasp of the effects on financial statements of altering dividend policy or engaging in share buybacks or secondary offerings, nor can I overemphasize the commensurate impacts on a company's effective cost of capital and overall financial flexibility. In this environment of heightened investor focus on liquidity and financial health, effective working capital management is a necessity. The text walks the reader through the important steps in successfully monitoring an optimal cash balance, contains a primer on short-term investment instruments, and delves into accounts receivable and inventory management. It also examines the benefits of short-term borrowing versus cash disbursements and other accounts payable strategies.

Finally, the critical steps in a merger and acquisition strategy are defined and analyzed. This segment of the text highlights the effects of the successful use of these approaches on firm competitiveness, scale, and market power and addresses the potential pitfalls of integration and cost management. Finally, this section examines the impact of taxes and regulatory challenges on a potentially successful business combination tactic, as well as discussing when an acquisition posture makes sense.

WHAT HAS CHANGED SINCE THE FIRST EDITION

This second edition provides the reader with comprehensive updates on all topics, especially where new techniques or technologies have emerged, and gears the learning outcomes, descriptions, and end-of-chapter exercises to the new economic realities of this decade. The sections on dividend policy, share repurchases, and capital structure have also been revised and reconstructed. These chapters contain significantly new content as well as updated exercises.

No book can provide a practitioner or student with a no-fail recipe for comprehensive success in financial management, and most entities have discovered that challenges and impacts generally appear from unexpected sources and directions. The authors have tried to create a substantial taxonomy of corporate financial topics with real-world, commonsense applications as well as rigorous problems and exercises that allow readers to test their comprehension of the subjects covered.

This book will become an important resource for a wide array of individuals. Some may ask whether the intricacies of capital budgeting, corporate liquidity, and dividend policy are of interest to a cross section of practitioners, but as many have discovered over the past five years, ignoring the key building blocks of an optimal corporate financial structure and a lean, competitive, and well-capitalized organization can be perilous. Today's corporate landscape, with all its volatility and high barriers to entry, requires that most members of a corporate entity be well schooled in the fundamentals of financial management. Organizations today must deal with formidable foreign competition, an older workforce, and significant capital investments in order to achieve critical scale. A sound understanding of the capital management techniques needed to maintain competitiveness and innovation is a necessity. Students will use this book either as a resource to gain a broad understanding of corporate financial practice or as a useful reference tool for quickly comprehending specific areas of the financial domain.

The long-term performance of all organizations is based on sound decision making by their constituents, whose decisions have wide-ranging implications for the future soundness of their companies. I hope this book will prove to be a valuable resource for present and future members of these organizations.

Matthew Scanlan, CFA
President and CEO
Renaissance Institutional Management LLC
CFA Institute Board of Governors

ACKNOWLEDGMENTS

We would like to thank the many individuals who played important roles in producing this book.

The standards and orientation of the second edition are a continuation of those set for the first edition. Robert R. Johnson, CFA, former senior managing director of CFA Institute, supported the creation of custom curriculum readings in this area and their revision. Dennis W. McLeavey, CFA, initiated the project during his term as head of Curriculum Development. Christopher B. Wiese, CFA, oversaw final organization, writing, and editing of the first edition for the CFA curriculum.

First edition manuscript reviewers were Jean-Francois Bureau, CFA, Sean D. Carr, Rosita P. Chang, CFA, Jacques R. Gagné, CFA, Gene C. Lai, Asjeet S. Lamba, CFA, Piman Limpaphayom, CFA, and Zhiyi Song, CFA. Chapter authors Pamela P. Drake, CFA, and John D. Stowe, CFA, provided notable assistance at critical junctures. We thank all of the above for their excellent and detailed work.

For this second edition, Gregory Noronha, CFA, was added to the author lineup. Second edition manuscript reviewers were Evan Ashcraft, CFA, David K. Chan, CFA, Lee Dunham, CFA, Philip Fanara, CFA, Usman Hayat, CFA, William Jacobson, CFA, Frank Laatsch, CFA, Murli Rajan, CFA, Knut Reinertz, CFA, Sanjiv Sabherwal, Sandeep Singh, CFA, Frank Smudde, CFA, and Peter Stimes, CFA. Jerald E. Pinto, CFA, director, Curriculum Projects, had primary responsibility for the delivery of the revised chapters.

ABOUT THE CFA INSTITUTE SERIES

CFA Institute is pleased to provide you with the CFA Institute Investment Series, which covers major areas in the field of investments. We provide this series for the same reason we have been chartering investment professionals for more than 50 years: to lead the investment profession globally by promoting the highest standards of ethics, education, and professional excellence for the ultimate benefit of society.

The books in the CFA Institute Investment Series contain practical, globally relevant material. They are intended both for those contemplating entry into the extremely competitive field of investment management as well as for those seeking a means of keeping their knowledge fresh and up to date. This series was designed to be user friendly and highly relevant.

We hope you find this series helpful in your efforts to grow your investment knowledge, whether you are a relatively new entrant or an experienced veteran ethically bound to keep up to date in the ever-changing market environment. As a long-term, committed participant in the investment profession and a not-for-profit global membership association, CFA Institute is pleased to provide you with this opportunity.

THE TEXTS

Alternative Investments is the definitive guide to help students and professionals understand non-traditional asset classes, including real estate, commodities, infrastructure, private equity, private credit, and hedge funds. This book provides readers the foundational knowledge to recognize the many distinguishing characteristics of alternative investments—higher fees, less regulation than traditional investments, concentrated portfolios, unique legal and tax considerations, and more. Through a series of strategically designed learning objectives and high-level chapter summaries, learners will develop an understanding of the value, risks, and processes associated with non-traditional investments.

Derivatives is a key resource for anyone interested in the role of derivatives within comprehensive portfolio management. Via accessible prose and real-world examples, a general discussion of the types of derivatives leads to a detailed examination of each market and its contracts—including forwards, futures, options and swaps, and a look at credit derivative markets and their instruments. This vital text offers a conceptual framework for understanding the fundamentals of derivatives. By the end of the book, readers will recognize the different types of derivatives, their characteristics, and how and why derivatives are essential to risk management.

The Portfolio Management in Practice three-volume set meets the needs of a wide range of individuals, from graduate-level students focused on finance to practicing investmentpro-fessionals. This set within the CFA Institute Investment Series delivers complete coverage of the foundational issues surrounding modern portfolio management, examining everything from asset allocation strategies to risk management frameworks. Readers are guided through the full portfolio management process with accessible chapters that distill the knowledge, skills, and abilities needed to succeed in today's fast-paced financial world. Key topics outlined in this set include forming capital market expectations, principles and processes of asset allocation, considerations specific to high-net-worth individuals and institutions, ESG inte-gration, and more. Discover the most comprehensive overview of portfolio management on the market with *Portfolio Management in Practice, Volume 1: Investment Management, Portfolio Management in Practice, Volume 2: Asset Allocation, and Portfolio Management in Practice, Volume 3: Equity Portfolio Management.*

Quantitative Investment Analysis, 4th Edition focuses on the primary quantitative tools needed by today's professional investor. Readers begin with classic time value of money, discounted cash flow applications, and probability models applied to investment management problems. The text then develops a critical skill that challenges many professionals—the ability to distinguish useful information from the overwhelming quantity of available data. Chapters dealing with correlation and hypothesis testing lead into regression modeling and machine learning that ultimately demonstrates how to extract insights from Big Data found in investment management. The final chapter of *Quantitative Investment Analysis* covers port-folio concepts and takes the reader beyond the traditional capital asset pricing model (CAPM) type of tools and into the more practical world of multifactor models and arbitrage pricing theory.

International Financial Statement Analysis, 4th Edition is designed to address the ever-increasing need for investment professionals and students to think about financial statement analysis from a global perspective. The text is a practically oriented introduction to financial statement analysis that is distinguished by its combination of a true international orienta-tion, a structured presentation style, and abundant illustrations and tools covering concepts as they are introduced. The authors cover this discipline comprehensively and with an eye to ensuring the reader's success at all levels in the complex world of financial statement analysis.

Equity Asset Valuation, 4th Edition integrates accounting and finance concepts to deliver a comprehensive collection of valuation models and guide novice investors and experienced practitioners alike in determining which models are appropriate for specific situations. This updated edition of the *Equity Asset Valuation* text blends theory and practice, details con-temporary techniques used to determine the intrinsic value of an equity security and demonstrates how these techniques are applied in both foreign and domestic markets. Readers will find clear, example-driven coverage of technical analysis, fundamental analysis, and an array of valuation techniques.

All titles in the Investment Series are also available on https://www.wiley.com/ for purchase directly from the publisher in print and eBook formats.

Qualified instructors may request evaluation copies for university classroom use at https://secure.wiley.com/digitalevaluationcopyrequest/. *Restrictions apply.*

CHAPTER 1

CORPORATE STRUCTURES AND OWNERSHIP

Vahan Janjigian, PhD, CFA

Greenwich Wealth Management, LLC (Greenwich, CT, USA)

LEARNING OUTCOMES

The candidate should be able to:

- compare business structures and describe key features of corporate issuers
- compare public and private companies
- compare the financial claims and motivations of lenders and owners

1. INTRODUCTION

In 1997, Martin Eberhard and Marc Tarpenning, an engineer and a computer scientist, started a company called NuvoMedia to make an electronic book reader they called the Rocket eBook, a precursor to the Kindle eBook popularized by Amazon. Three years after it was founded, NuvoMedia was sold for USD187 million.

Soon after, the two entrepreneurs decided to form a new company, this one focused on making electric cars. They named this company in honor of the inventor Nikola Tesla. Because this was a high-risk, capital-intensive endeavor, they used only some of their newfound wealth and sought other investors with expertise in electric vehicles and fundraising capabilities. Elon Musk, an entrepreneur with a shared vision in the commercialization of electric sports cars, joined the team.

In addition to making an initial investment of USD6.3 million in Tesla, Musk also helped raise more money from other venture capitalists. Due to conflicts that were not disclosed, Eberhard and Tarpenning resigned just before Tesla came out with its first vehicle, the Roadster, in 2008. Musk took over as CEO and led Tesla's initial public offering in 2010, which raised USD226 million.

In many ways, Tesla's story is typical of how businesses begin and succeed. They are often started by founders with significant knowledge or technical expertise but who may lack the skills required to manage a business as it grows larger. Capital is needed to fund growth and is initially raised through private channels. Private investors often get involved in the management of the company, especially if they have a large investment at stake. Eventually, even larger amounts of capital are required, and the company is acquired or taken public.

Here we examine different forms of business structures, focusing on corporations and the securities they issue to capital providers.

2. BUSINESS STRUCTURES

While the focus here is on corporations, it is important to recognize that other business structures exist and to understand how they compare with one another. Our focus here is on four areas:

1. **Legal Relationship**—the legal relationship between the owner(s) and the business.
2. **Owner–Operator Relationship**—the relationship between the owner(s) of the business and those who operate the business.
3. **Business Liability**—the extent to which individuals have liability for actions undertaken by the business or its business debts. Liability can be unlimited or limited in nature.
4. **Taxation**—the treatment of profits or losses generated by the business for tax purposes.

While there are numerous forms of business structures, some with variations, we discuss only the more common forms shown in Exhibit 1.

EXHIBIT 1: Common Business Structures

- Sole Proprietorship
- General Partnership
- Limited Partnership
- Corporation

2.1. Sole Proprietorship (Sole Trader)

The simplest business structure is the sole proprietorship, also called the sole trader, shown in Exhibit 2. In a sole proprietorship, the owner personally funds the capital needed to operate the business and retains full control over the operations of the business while participating fully in the financial returns and risks of the business.

EXHIBIT 2: Sole Proprietorship

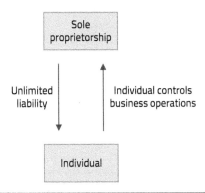

An example of a sole proprietorship is a family-owned store. To start the business and run daily operations, the owner would likely use personal savings, credit card debt, and loans from banks or other family and friends. The owner retains full control over the business, including how it will operate and what products to sell at what price. If the business does well, the owner retains all return (profits), which are taxed as personal income. At the same time, the owner has unlimited liability and retains all risk associated with the business, meaning she can be held financially responsible for all debt the business owes.

While sole proprietorships are preferred for small-scale businesses given their simplicity and flexibility, the business is constrained by the owner's ability to access capital and assume risk.

In summary, key features of sole proprietorships include the following:

- No legal identity; considered extension of owner
- Owner-operated business
- Owner retains all return and assumes all risk
- Profits from business taxed as personal income
- Operational simplicity and flexibility
- Financed informally through personal means
- Business growth is limited by owner's ability to finance and personal risk appetite

What if more resources are needed than can be provided by an individual owner?

2.2. General Partnership

A general partnership, shown in Exhibit 3, has two or more owners called partners whose roles and responsibilities in the business are outlined in a **partnership agreement**. General partnerships are like sole proprietorships with the important distinction that they allow for additional resources to be brought into the business along with the sharing of business risk among a larger group of individuals.

EXHIBIT 3: General Partnership

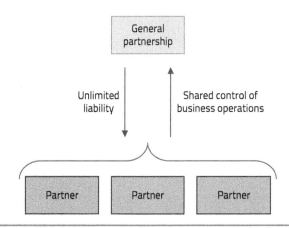

Examples of general partnerships are professional services businesses (e.g., law, accounting, medicine) and small financial or financial advisory firms. Such businesses have a small number of partners who establish the business by contributing equal amounts of capital. The partners bring complementary expertise, such as business development, financial acumen, operations, or legal/compliance, and share responsibility in running the business. All profits, losses, and risks of the business are collectively assumed and shared by the partners. If one partner is unable to pay their share of the business's debts, the remaining partners are fully liable. Like a sole proprietorship, potential for growth is limited by the partners' ability to source capital and expertise and their collective risk tolerance.

In summary, key features of general partnerships include the following:

- No legal identity; partnership agreement sets ownership
- Partner-operated business
- Partners share all risk and business liability
- Partners share all return, with profits taxed as personal income
- Contributions of capital and expertise by partners
- Business growth is limited by partner resourcing capabilities and risk appetite

2.3. Limited Partnership

Exhibit 4 shows a special type of partnership called the **limited partnership**. A limited partnership must have at least one **general partner** with unlimited liability who is responsible for the management of the business. Remaining partners, called **limited partners**, have limited liability, meaning they can lose only up to the amount of their investment in the limited partnership. With limited liability, personal assets are considered separate to, and thus protected from, the liabilities of the business. All partners are entitled to a share of the profits, with general partners typically getting a larger portion given their management responsibility for the business.

An example of a limited partnership is a private equity fund, which operates with a general partner (GP) who assumes responsibility for business operations and liabilities.

Remaining partners are called limited partners (LPs), who have limited liability to business risk but may provide capital or expertise. Limited partners have no control over the operation of the business and no way to replace the GP in the event the GP runs the business poorly or fails to act in the interest of the LPs.

EXHIBIT 4: Limited Partnership

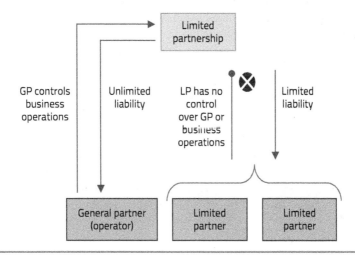

Other examples of limited partnerships include real estate and professional services businesses (e.g., law, accounting, medicine), small financial firms, and hedge funds.

In summary, key features of limited partnerships include the following:

- No legal identity; partnership agreement sets ownership
- GP operates the business, having unlimited liability
- LPs have limited liability but lack control over business operations
- All partners share in return, with profits taxed as personal income
- Contributions of capital and expertise by partners
- Business growth is limited by GP/LP financing capabilities and risk appetite and GP competence and integrity in running the business

In a limited partnership, while financial risk and reward are shared, such resources as capital and expertise are limited to what the partners can personally contribute. Limited partners ultimately grant control to the GP, which entails risk.

What if a business requires greater resources than can be provided by either an individual or small group of individuals?

2.4. Corporation (Limited Companies)

An evolved model of the limited partnership is the corporation, known as a limited liability company (LLC) in many countries or as a limited company in others, such as the United Kingdom. In the United States, while similar, an LLC and a corporation are not the same. The main difference being with a US LLC, taxation occurs at the personal level, whereas with a US corporation, taxation takes place at both the personal level (distributions to owners) and corporate level (profits).

Like a limited partnership, owners in a corporation (and US LLC) have limited liability; however, corporations have greater access to the capital and expertise required to fuel growth. As a result, the corporation is the preferred form for larger companies and the dominant business structure globally by revenues and asset values.

Examples of corporations are national or multinational conglomerates, global asset managers, and regional stock exchanges. As shown in Exhibit 5, the three main types of corporations are public for-profit, private for-profit, and nonprofit.

EXHIBIT 5: Types of Corporations

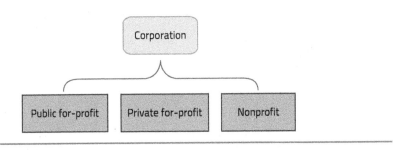

2.4.1. Nonprofits

While corporations are typically created to return profits, some corporations are formed with the specific purpose of promoting a public benefit, religious benefit, or charitable mission. These are known as **nonprofit corporations (nonprofits)** or nonprofit organizations and include private foundations. Like for-profit corporations, nonprofits have a board of directors and can have paid employees.

Unlike for-profit corporations, nonprofits do not have shareholders and do not distribute dividends. Nonprofits typically are exempt from paying taxes. If they are run well, nonprofits can generate profits; however, all profits must be reinvested in promoting the mission of the organization. Well-known nonprofits include Harvard University, Ascension (a large nonprofit private health care provider in the United States), and the Asian Development Bank (regional development bank based in the Philippines).

2.4.2. For-Profits

Most corporations are "for profit," or motivated to make money (profits) for the owners of the business. While corporations can engage in any kind of legal business, they are usually created with a profit motive and specific purpose at inception.

Prior Example: In the introduction, the two entrepreneurs formed Tesla with the belief they had the expertise to design and produce an electric sports car at a price that high-end consumers would pay. Over time, Tesla expanded its manufacturing to other electric models, including sedans and SUVs, and later entered the solar power market with a product line of solar panels and batteries for homes and businesses. As is often the case with companies, over time Tesla pursued growth unrelated to its original product and purpose—that of manufacturing a viable electric sports car for a targeted customer segment.

2.4.3. For-Profits: Public vs. Private

For-profit corporations can be public or private. Primary distinctions are the number of shareholders that exist and whether the company has a stock exchange listing. In some countries, such as the United Kingdom and Australia, if there are a large number of shareholders (usually greater than 50), the company is categorized as a public company and subject to more onerous regulatory requirements whether or not it is listed on a stock exchange. In numerous other countries like the United States, the distinction of being public is defined by a stock exchange listing. Terms and names for business entities vary at the local country level, such as the use of Plc, AG, or SA extensions for public limited liability companies, or GmbH, Pte/Pty Ltd, or SARL for private limited liability companies.

For remaining coverage, we focus on for-profit corporations given their overriding importance within the investor community.

2.4.4. Legal Identity

A corporation is formed through the filing of articles of incorporation with a regulatory authority. A corporation is therefore considered a legal entity separate and distinct from its owners. As far as the law is concerned, a corporation has many of the rights and responsibilities of an individual and can engage in many of the same activities. For example, a corporation can enter into contracts, hire employees, sue and be sued, borrow and lend money, make investments, and pay taxes.

Large corporations frequently have business operations in many different geographic regions and are subject to regulatory jurisdictions where either:

- the company is incorporated,
- business is conducted, or
- the company's securities are listed

for such activities as:

- registration (for public companies),
- financial and non-financial reporting and disclosure, or
- capital market activities (e.g., security issuance, trading, investment).

2.4.5. Owner–Operator Separation

A key feature of most corporations is the separation between those who own the business, the owners, and those who operate it, as represented by the board of directors and company management. In a corporation, owners are largely removed from the day-to-day operations of the business. This owner–operator separation of capital and business capabilities enables owners to create businesses by leveraging greater resources to run the business while allowing for shared business risk and return.

In a corporation, owners elect a board of directors to oversee business operations. The directors hire the CEO and senior leaders responsible for management and day-to-day operations of the company. Directors and officers have a responsibility to act in the best interest of the owners. The separation of operating control from ownership enables the corporation to finance itself from a larger universe of potential investors who are not required to have expertise in operating the business.

Should the board or management not conduct business in line with owner interests, owners have the ability to enact change through voting rights attached to their shares. In this way, owners can ensure those operating the business are aligned with owners' interests to maximize their return on investment in the company. The ability to influence or change operational control through the use of their voting rights as corporate owners is a key difference from the limited partnership model. Note, however, that shares can differ in their voting rights and not all shares have voting rights.

At the same time, corporations are also expected to consider the interests of other stakeholders, including employees, creditors, customers, suppliers, regulators, and members of the communities in which they operate and conduct business. While the appointed board of directors and company officers are obligated to act in the best interests of shareholders, conflicts of interest do occur when management acts to place their interests, or the interests of other stakeholders, above those of the owners. To prevent conflicts and mismanagement of the business, corporate governance policies and practices are in place to oversee business operations and ensure sound management practices.

2.4.6. Business Liability

In a corporation, risk is shared across all owners and owners have limited liability. The maximum amount owners can lose is what they invested in the company. Owners also share in the returns of the company through their equity claim as represented by their shares. No contractual obligation exists for the company to repay ownership capital. Instead, owners have a residual claim to the company's net assets after its liabilities have been paid. Exhibit 6 shows the relationship between owners and the corporation.

EXHIBIT 6: Corporation

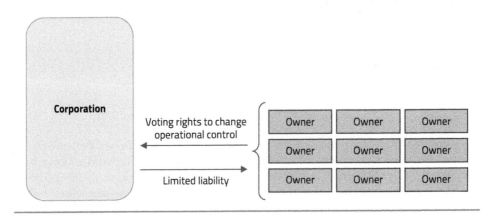

2.4.7. Capital Financing

The separation between ownership and management allows corporations to access capital more easily than other business structures because capital is the only requirement for owners to join the business. While more expensive to form and operate than other business structures, the corporate structure is typically preferred when capital requirements for a business overwhelm what could be raised by an individual or limited number of individuals.

Corporations are able to raise the financing they need from **capital providers**, who include those individuals and entities willing to provide capital to the company in return for the corporation's issued securities, which may be equity securities (stocks) or debt securities (bonds). Other capital providers are financial institutions, such as banks who lend corporations capital in the form of loans.

Types of capital providers include the following:

- Individuals
- Institutions
- Corporations
- Family offices
- Government

Corporations can raise two types of capital: **ownership capital (equity)**, and **borrowed capital (debt)**. Shareholders have exchanged their capital for issued equity securities, while bondholders have exchanged their capital for issued debt securities. Both are investors in the corporation's securities.

Ownership capital, or equity, refers to money invested by the owners of the corporation. In return for capital provided, the company grants the equity investor ownership in the company. Owners are also called shareholders (or stockholders) because they are issued shares, with each share representing an ownership interest. The more shares an investor owns, the greater their ownership stake in the corporation.

Exhibit 7 highlights the exchange of capital and issued security by type between the corporation and investor.

EXHIBIT 7: Corporate Financing—Ownership Capital (Equity) vs. Borrowed Capital (Debt)

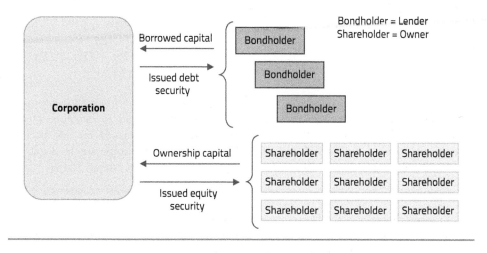

2.4.8. Taxation

While taxation for corporations can differ greatly from country to country, the corporation is ultimately subject to the tax authority and tax code governing the issuer's tax reporting, payment, and status. In most countries, corporations are taxed directly on their profits. In many countries, shareholders pay an additional tax on distributions (dividends) that are passed on to them. Economists refer to this as the double taxation of corporate profits. In some countries, shareholders do not pay a personal tax on dividends if the corporation has paid tax previously on the earnings distributed to shareholders; or, shareholders receive a personal tax credit for their proportional share of taxes paid by the corporation. Still in other countries, corporations pay no tax at all or may face different tax regimes within one country.

KNOWLEDGE CHECK   Double Taxation of Corporate Profits

1. The French company Elo (previously known as Auchan Holding) generated operating income of €838 million and paid corporate taxes of €264 million. Investors in France also pay a 30% tax on dividends received. If Elo had distributed all of its after-tax income to investors as a dividend, what would have been the effective tax rate on each euro of operating earnings?

Solution:

Operating Income	**€838**
Corporate Taxes (31.5%)	**€264**
After-Tax Income	(€838 − €264)
	= €574
Distributed Dividend	€574
Investor Dividend Tax **(30%)**	€574 × 0.3
	= €172.2
Effective Tax Rate	(€264 + €172.2) / €838
	= 52.1%

If the remaining after-tax income of €574 million was paid to investors as a dividend, investors would pay €172.2 million in taxes on the dividends received. Total taxes paid would be €436.2 million (€264 million at the corporate level plus €172.2 million at the personal level), resulting in an effective tax rate of 52.1%.

In many countries, a tax disadvantage is associated with the corporate business structure because shareholders must pay a tax on distributions that have already been taxed at the corporate level. Despite this disadvantage, the corporate business structure remains attractive because corporations have the potential capability to raise large amounts of capital from a disparate group of investors.

While shareholders may be taxed on distributions, owners in other business structures are taxed on profits, regardless of distribution. This difference makes the corporate structure attractive to businesses that require significant amounts of capital and/or anticipate retaining earnings for future investment. In addition, where corporate tax rates are lower than personal income tax rates, it can be advantageous in some jurisdictions to "store" profits or capital in the business.

2.4.9. Corporation Key Features Summary

In summary, key features of corporations include the following:

- Separate legal identity
- Owner–operator separation allowing for greater, more diverse resourcing with some risk control
- Business liability is shared across multiple, limited liability owners with claims to return and financial risk of their equity investment
- Shareholder tax disadvantage in countries with double taxation
- Distributions (dividends) taxed as personal income
- Unbounded access to capital and unlimited business potential

---

KNOWLEDGE CHECK

1. Which of the following are shared similarities among the four major business structure types?
   A. Sole proprietorships and general partnerships lack legal identity.
   B. Corporate shareholders and general partners have limited liability.
   C. The taxation of sole proprietorships and limited partnerships is comparable.

Solution:

A and C are correct.

Both sole proprietorships and general partnerships have no legal identity, with the business considered an extension of the owner in a sole proprietorship and the partnership agreement setting ownership in a general partnership. Both sole proprietorships and limited partnerships have similar tax structures, with all profits taxed as personal income. But in relation to liability, while general partners have unlimited liability, shareholders of corporations are granted limited liability.

2. State one condition that would make a corporation subject to a regulatory jurisdiction.

Solution:

Large corporations frequently have business operations in many different geographic regions and are subject to regulatory jurisdictions where either:
   • the company is incorporated,
   • business is conducted, or
   • the company's securities are listed.

3. True or false: A primary advantage of the separation of ownership from control in corporations is that it improves management by preventing conflicts of interest.

A. True.
B. False.

Solution:

B is correct; the statement is false.

A major benefit of the separation between ownership and management is that it allows corporations to access capital more easily than other business structures because capital is the only requirement for owners to join the business. While the appointed board of directors and company officers are obligated to act in the best interests of shareholders, that does not eliminate conflicts of interest, which occur when management acts to place their interests, or the interests of other stakeholders, above those of the owners. To prevent conflicts and mismanagement of the business, corporate governance policies and practices are in place to oversee business operations and ensure sound management practices.

4. What is the primary distinction between corporate bondholders and shareholders?

Solution:

Both bondholders and shareholders are capital providers and thus investors in the corporation's securities. However, in exchanging their capital for issued equity securities, shareholders purchase an ownership stake that entitles them to a residual claim in the corporation. Bondholders, or debtholders, have exchanged their capital for issued debt securities and are lenders to the corporation with no ownership entitlement.

3. PUBLIC AND PRIVATE CORPORATIONS

The word "public" can be misleading because it typically implies government involvement. However, when it comes to corporations, "public" and "private" are typically defined by whether the company's equity is listed on a stock exchange, although in some countries whether a company is considered public or not may depend on its number of shareholders, irrespective of whether it is listed.

Shares of public companies are most often listed on a stock exchange and thereafter trade on the exchange in the open market, also known as the secondary market. Listed companies have undergone a "go public" event, such as an **initial public offering (IPO)** in the primary market. An IPO is a process in which shares in the company are offered to the public for the first time in an exchange listing. Primary differences between public and private companies relate to the following:

- Exchange listing and share ownership transfer
- Share issuance
- Registration and disclosure requirements

We discuss each of these.

3.1. Exchange Listing and Share Ownership Transfer

In most cases, public companies have their shares listed and traded on an exchange. An exchange listing allows ownership to be more easily transferred because buyers and sellers transact directly with one another in the secondary market, on the exchange. An investor with a brokerage account can become a shareholder in a public company simply by executing a buy order. Similarly, a shareholder can reduce or liquidate her ownership position by executing a sell order. This can be done in a matter of seconds if the number of shares involved in the transaction is relatively small and trading of the stock is liquid (i.e., a large number of shares trade on a daily basis). It can take longer, however, if the investor is trying to buy or sell a large amount of stock in a company whose shares trade infrequently.

Each trade between buyer and seller can cause a change in the share price. By plotting share price over time, we can see how the company's value changes. We can also see how significant news, either about the company specifically or about the general state of the economy, impacts the value of the shares.

Exhibit 8 and Exhibit 9 highlight differences in share ownership transfer between public and private companies.

EXHIBIT 8: Public Companies—Share Ownership Transfer

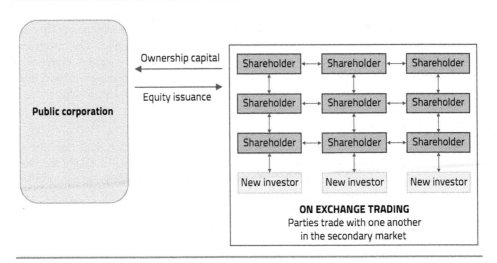

In contrast, private company shares do not trade on an exchange, so no visible valuation or price transparency exists for the company and shares are not easily bought and sold. This makes ownership transfers between seller and buyer much more difficult than for a public company. If an owner of a private company wants to sell shares, he must find a willing buyer and the two parties must agree on a price. Even then, the company may refuse the transfer of ownership. Shareholders in private companies must exercise patience. Their investment is usually locked up until the company is acquired for cash or shares by another company, or it goes public.

EXHIBIT 9: Private Companies—Share Ownership Transfer

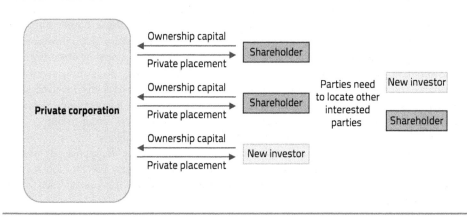

So why invest in a private company if you cannot readily sell the shares when you want to?

Because the potential returns in private companies can be much larger than those earned from investing in public companies. This is because investors in private companies are usually joining early in the company's life cycle when there is little assurance of success. They are often buying shares in a company that has little more than a business plan. The investment risks are great, but the potential rewards can be great too. With often smaller numbers of shareholders in private companies, investors have greater control over management and there may be greater chance of ownership overlaps between management and shareholders.

3.1.1. Market Capitalization and Enterprise Value

Because shares in (most) public companies are traded on an exchange, it is also easy to determine what the company's equity is worth at any moment in time. By taking the most recent stock price and multiplying it by the number of shares outstanding, we can calculate the company's market capitalization. That is,

$$\textbf{Market Capitalization} = \text{Current Stock Price} \times \text{Total Shares Outstanding.}$$

In theory, this is what someone would have to pay to acquire ownership of the entire corporation. In reality, a premium over this amount would have to be offered to convince enough shareholders to agree to an acquisition.

While market capitalization represents the market value of the company's shares in aggregate, enterprise value represents the total market value of the corporation, net of cash held by the company (i.e., the sum of the market value of the equity and the market value of debt, net of cash). Acquirers are often more interested in enterprise value because it's a better representation of what it would cost to own the company free and clear of all debt.

$$\textbf{Market Capitalization} = \text{Market Value of Shares}$$

$$\textbf{Enterprise Value} = \text{Market Value of Shares} + \text{Market Value of Debt} - \text{Cash}$$

KNOWLEDGE CHECK   Market Capitalization vs. Enterprise Value

8Tera Therapeutics is a hypothetical, public company with 15.2 million shares outstanding, no short-term debt, and USD200 million of long-term debt. The company also has USD20 million in cash and a recent stock price of USD120 per share.

1. What is 8Tera's market capitalization?

Solution:

   Market capitalization is the total market value of the equity, which is determined by multiplying the most recent stock price by the number of shares outstanding.

Market Capitalization = (USD120 per share) × (15.2 million shares) = USD1.824 billion

2. What is 8Tera's enterprise value?

Solution:

   Enterprise value (EV) is equal to market capitalization plus net debt.

EV = USD1.824 billion + USD200 million − USD20 million = USD2.004 billion

   EV tells us what it would cost to own the entire company free and clear of all debt.

3.2. Share Issuance

To raise more capital after listing, public companies may issue additional shares in the capital markets, typically raising very large amounts from many investors who may then actively trade shares among themselves in the secondary market. In contrast, private companies finance much smaller amounts in the primary market (private debt or equity) with far fewer investors who have much longer holding periods.

   Exhibit 10 and Exhibit 11 illustrate differences in public vs. private company share issuance and relative size of capital accessed.

EXHIBIT 10: Public Companies—Share Issuance and Capital Access

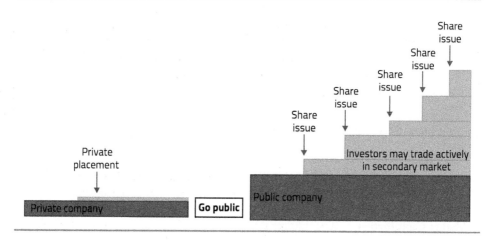

EXHIBIT 11: Private Companies—Share Issuance and Capital Access

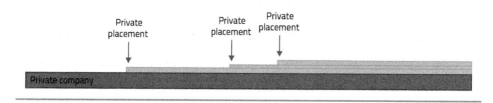

Investors in private companies are typically invited to purchase shares in the company through a private placement whose terms are outlined in a legal document called a **private placement memorandum (PPM)**. The PPM, also termed the offering memorandum, describes the business, the terms of the offering, and most importantly, the risks involved in making an investment in the company. Because private securities are generally not registered with a regulatory authority, investors may be restricted to accredited investors, also termed "eligible" or "professional" investors depending on the jurisdiction.

Accredited investors are those who are sophisticated enough to take greater risks and to have a reduced need for regulatory oversight and protection. To be considered accredited, an investor must have a certain level of income or net worth or possess a certain amount of professional experience or knowledge. Given the lower levels of disclosure required of private companies, regulators want to make sure that investors understand the associated risks and can afford the possibility of losing their entire investment.

3.2.1. Registration and Disclosure Requirements

Public companies are required to register with a regulatory authority. As a result, they are subject to greater compliance and reporting requirements. In the United States, for example, public companies must disclose certain kinds of financial information on a quarterly basis through the filing of documents with the Securities and Exchange Commission (SEC) on the system known as EDGAR (Electronic Data Gathering, Analysis, and Retrieval). In the European Union, listed companies must disclose on a semi-annual basis providing such information as their financial reports, major changes in the holding of voting rights, and other inside information that might be expected to affect security price.

Public companies must also disclose other kinds of information, such as any stock transactions made by officers and directors. These documents are made available to the general public, not just the investors in the company. The primary purpose of this kind of disclosure is to make it easier for investors and analysts to assess the risks that might impact the company's business strategy and its ability to generate profits or meet its financial obligations in the future.

In contrast, private companies are generally not subject to the same level of regulatory oversight. While many of the rules that pertain to the regulation of public companies (for example, prohibitions against fraud and the obligation to produce a corporate tax return) also apply to private companies, private companies have no obligation to disclose certain information to the public.

Of course, they willingly disclose pertinent information directly to their investors, especially if they hope to be able to raise additional capital in the future, but private companies are typically not required to file documents with the regulatory authority that oversees public companies. Exhibit 12 and Exhibit 13 compare typical entity relationships for public and private companies.

EXHIBIT 12: Public Companies—Typical Entity Relationships

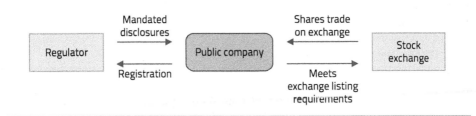

EXHIBIT 13: Private Companies—Typical Entity Relationships

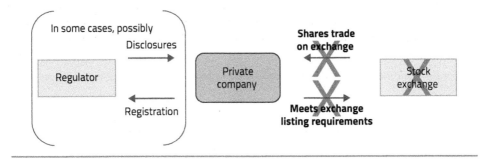

KNOWLEDGE CHECK

1. Match the applicable company characteristic with its most correct category (Publicly-held, Privately-held, Both).

Company characteristic:

	Publicly-Held	Privately-Held	Both
Exchange listed			
Shareholder–management ownership overlaps			
Registered			
Share liquidity			
Non-financial disclosure required			
Negotiated sales of debt and equity			

Solution:

	Publicly-Held	Privately-Held	Both
Exchange listed	X		
Shareholder–management ownership overlaps		X	
Registered	X		
Share liquidity	X		
Non-financial disclosure required			X
Negotiated sales of debt and equity		X	

Publicly-held companies are most often listed on exchanges and required to register shares. Their shares are typically liquid with minor ownership overlap between management and shareholders. These companies must make both financial and non-financial disclosures, and both their debt and equity are typically traded on exchanges.

Privately-held companies are not exchange listed nor usually subject to registration requirements. Share issuance is smaller in nature, creating a greater chance of ownership overlap between management and shareholders. Private company shares are illiquid. Generally, these companies are required to make only non-financial disclosures. The sale of their equity and debt is privately negotiated between company insiders and capital providers.

3.3. Going Public from Private—IPO, Direct Listing, Acquisition

So how exactly do private companies become public companies? A private company can go public in the following ways:

- IPO
- Direct listing
- Acquisition
  - Special Purpose Acquisition Company

As noted earlier, many companies choose to use the IPO process to list on an exchange. To complete an IPO, companies must meet specific listing requirements required by the exchange. The IPO involves the participation of investment banks who underwrite, or guarantee, the offering or sale of new (or existing) shares. Proceeds from the sale of new shares go to the issuing corporation, which can use the proceeds to finance new investments. Once the IPO process is completed, the company is public and its shares begin trading on an exchange.

A private company can also go public through a **direct listing (DL)**, which differs from an IPO in two key ways. A DL does not involve an underwriter, and no new capital is raised. Instead, the company is simply listed on an exchange and shares are sold by existing shareholders. Major benefits of a DL are the speed of going public and the lower costs involved.

Often, a company may go public through acquisition. For example, this may occur indirectly when the company is acquired by another company that is public. In such cases, the acquiring company is usually larger. As a result, a share in the combined entity might represent only a small interest in the company that was acquired.

Another means of acquisition is through a **special purpose acquisition company (SPAC)**. A SPAC is a shell company, often called a "blank check" company, because it exists solely for the purpose of acquiring an unspecified private company sometime in the future.

SPACs raise capital through an IPO. Proceeds are placed in a trust account and can only be disbursed to complete the acquisition or for return back to investors. SPACs are publicly listed and may specialize in a particular industry. SPACs have a finite time period, such as 18 months, to complete a deal; otherwise, proceeds are returned to investors. While investors in a SPAC might not know with certainty what the SPAC will buy, they might make an educated guess based on the backgrounds of the SPAC executives or comments these individuals have made in the media.

Once the SPAC completes the purchase of a private company, that company becomes public. SPACs are replacing the formerly used reverse merger process of going public, which used a listed company shell with a previous business and trading history.

KNOWLEDGE CHECK

1. Match the method by which a private company can go public with the most closely related term from corporate finance.

Going Public Method:

	"Blank Check"	Existing Shareholder	Underwriter
IPO			
DL			
SPAC			

Solution:

	"Blank Check"	Existing Shareholder	Underwriter
IPO			X
DL		X	
SPAC	X		

An IPO is facilitated by investment banks who underwrite, or guarantee, the offering. A direct listing does not involve an underwriter, and no new capital is raised. Instead, the company is simply listed on an exchange and shares are sold by existing shareholders. A SPAC is a shell company, often called a "blank check" company, because it exists solely for the purpose of acquiring an unspecified private company sometime in the future.

2. True or false: Accredited investors are the capital providers qualified by regulators to invest in public companies.
   A. *True. Statement to support this option on why it's true.*
   B. *False. Statement to support this option on why it's false.*

Solution:

B is correct; the statement is false. Accredited investors are perceived by regulators to have the sophistication for understanding and assuming the risks that come with investing in private, not public, companies.

3.4. Life Cycle of Corporations

Whether a company is public or private often depends on where it is in its life cycle. As shown in Exhibit 14, companies begin life as start-ups, then enter growth, maturity, and lastly decline. During their life cycle, companies access different types of financing.

EXHIBIT 14: Life Cycle and Financing

Life cycle stage	Start-up	Growth	Maturity	Decline
Revenues	Low to none	Increasing	Positive & Predictable	Deteriorating
Cash flow	Negative	Increasing	Positive & Predictable	Deteriorating
Business risk	High	Moderate	Low	Increasing
Financing need	Proof of concept	Scale	Business as usual	Shortfalls
Financing difficulty	Very high	Very high to high	Moderate to low	Increasing

3.4.1. Start-Ups

3.4.1.1. Start-ups are a little more than an idea and a business plan. They are initially funded by the founders. If more capital is needed, the founders might turn to friends and family, who may buy an ownership interest or make a loan to the company. At this stage, the company lacks revenues and cash flows. Business risk is extremely high, making financing challenging.

As the company grows, more capital will be needed. The founders might hire an investment banker who specializes in helping private companies raise capital from private equity or private debt investors. Early-stage equity investors are sometimes referred to as venture capitalists, or Series A investors.

3.4.1.2. Growth As the company progresses through the growth stage, even greater amounts of capital will be needed. Most likely, while revenues and cash flows may be improving, the company is still not profitable; so, it cannot yet rely on internally generated earnings to fund growth. It might raise more capital through a Series B or even a Series C issuance (i.e., additional rounds of capital raises). This is also the time the company might consider "going public" in an IPO.

Despite the desire to go public, some companies might remain private for many years. In some cases, the founder(s) may not be willing to give up ownership or control, while in other cases, this may be partly due to stock exchange listing requirements. Depending on the exchange, to qualify for listing a company must be able to pay the listing fees, have a minimum number of shareholders, and meet a minimum valuation requirement. If the company can meet the listing requirements, the decision to go public may depend on its ability to access capital.

Rapidly growing companies may find that their capital needs are too great for private investors to meet. In such cases, going public could make sense because it is usually easier to raise large amounts of capital in the public markets than in the private markets. In many developed countries, however, it has become easier for companies to access needed capital in the private market and the number of companies choosing to go public has been decreasing.

3.4.1.3. Maturity Once a company reaches the maturity stage of the life cycle, its external financing needs diminish and business risk is much less. Companies in this stage are usually profitable, cash flow generative, and can fund growth internally with retained earnings. In addition, these companies find it easier to borrow money at reasonable terms because their cash flows are more predictable with "business-as-usual" (BAU) operations. A mature company that is public can borrow money either in the public or private markets.

3.4.1.4. Decline When a company is in decline it may have little need for additional financing. However, companies in this stage may try to reinvent themselves either by developing new lines of business or by acquiring other companies that are growing rapidly. Either way, additional financing can be useful in such circumstances, but companies may find the cost of financing increasingly expensive as their financials and cash flows deteriorate.

Exhibit 15 illustrates the sources of financing typically available to a company during its life cycle, given characteristics of its revenues, cash flows, and business risk.

EXHIBIT 15: Type of Financing by Firm Life Cycle

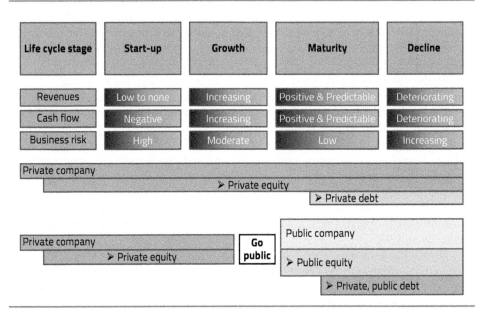

3.4.2. Public to Private—LBO, MBO

Public companies can also end up going private. This happens when an investor (or group of investors) acquires all of the company's shares and delists it from the exchange. This is done through a **leveraged buyout (LBO)** or **management buyout (MBO)**. Both processes involve borrowing large amounts of money to finance the acquisition. An LBO occurs when the investors are not affiliated with the company they are buying. An MBO occurs when the investors are members of the company's current management team.

LBOs and MBOs are initiated when the investors believe the public market is undervaluing the shares and financing costs are sufficiently low and attractive. Even though they must pay a premium to convince shareholders to tender (sell) their shares, the investors believe the transaction is worth it due to synergies or cost savings they believe can be realized by taking the company private. These companies are often taken public again several years later if the investors believe they can get a good valuation price at that time.

Exhibit 16 shows the interchange that can occur between private and public companies. Private companies can go public by being acquired by a company that is already public or through an IPO, DL, or SPAC. A private company could also remain private if it is acquired by another private company. Public companies may be taken private and delisted in an LBO or MBO.

EXHIBIT 16: Interchange between Private and Public Companies

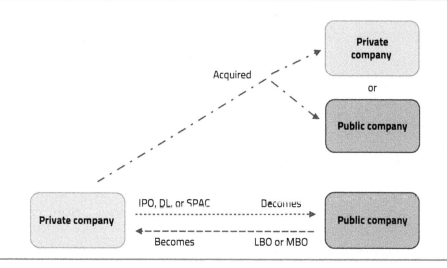

It is interesting to note the trends in public and private companies over time. In many emerging economies, the number of public companies is rising, while the opposite is happening in developed economies. Emerging economies are typically characterized by higher rates of growth and are transitioning from closed to open market structures. Therefore, it makes sense that the number of public companies would increase as these emerging economies grow larger.

What explains the decline in public companies in developed markets?

Mergers and acquisitions are partly responsible. When a public company is acquired by a private company or by another public company, one less public company exists. LBOs and MBOs are also responsible since they are structured to take public companies private. Still another factor is that many private companies simply choose to remain private. This is due, in part, to the greater ease of accessing capital in the private markets. Due to the burgeoning venture capital, private equity, and private debt markets, companies often find that they can get the capital they need in these markets while avoiding the regulatory burdens and associated compliance costs of going public. In addition, companies may choose to remain private to avoid the short-term focus many investors in listed companies have. Remaining private can also provide leadership with greater flexibility and responsiveness in decision making.

4. LENDERS AND OWNERS

As shown in Exhibit 17, a key difference between the debt and equity financing used by corporations is the binding contract the company has with its debtholders, or lenders. The contract requires their claims be fully paid before the company can make distributions to equity owners. In other words, debtholders have a prior legal claim on the company's cash flows and assets over the claims of equity owners. Equityholders are therefore residual claimants to the company after all other stakeholders have been paid, including creditors (interest/principal), suppliers (accounts payable), government (taxes), and employees (wages).

EXHIBIT 17: Debt vs. Equity Claim Difference

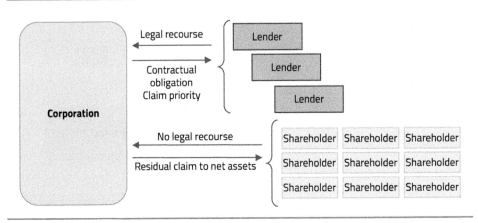

Another difference is that interest payments to debtholders are generally treated as a tax-deductible expense for the company, while dividend payments to shareholders are not. Finally, equityholders represent a more permanent source of capital and have voting rights to elect the board of directors, which oversees the management of the company. In contrast, debt represents a cheaper financing source for companies and a lower risk for investors.

KNOWLEDGE CHECK

1. Match/choose the applicable financing feature with its correct form (Debt or Equity).

	Debt	Equity
Legal repayment obligation		
Residual asset claim		
Discretionary payments		
Tax-deductible expenses		
Finite term commitments		
Voting rights		

Solution:

	Debt	Equity
Legal repayment obligation	X	
Residual asset claim		X
Discretionary payments		X
Tax-deductible expenses	X	
Finite term commitments	X	
Voting rights		X

> Similar to a loan agreement, debt involves a contractual obligation with priority for interest and principal payments. Equity has no contractual commitment and involves a residual claim to assets. Equity features discretionary payments like dividends, which are not tax deductible. Debt requires contractual interest and principal payments, with interest expense being tax deductible to the issuer. Debt has a stated, finite term with generally no voting rights, while equity has no finite term and includes voting rights.

4.1. Equity and Debt Risk–Return Profiles

Risk is an important issue to consider for both the issuing corporation and the investors. From an investor's perspective, stocks are riskier than bonds because shareholders are residual claimants on the firm. Thus, bonds having predictable coupon payments are less risky than a stock that may, or may not, receive dividends or experience a capital gain. The opposite is true from the corporate issuer's perspective. Bonds require the corporate issuer to have the funds available for the payments—or face default—while payments to shareholders are at the discretion of the issuer's management team.

4.1.1. Investor Perspective

The maximum loss equity owners face is limited to the amount of their equity investment. However, an equity owner has the potential for significant upside gain, dependent on future share price increases. If the corporation is successful, there is theoretically no limit to how much equity owners could make from their investment. As residual claimants, after a profitable corporation meets its other obligations, shareholders are entitled to the full remaining value of assets and distributions.

Stocks are considered riskier for investors, however, because the company has no contractual obligation to distribute funds to shareholders or repay their capital investment. In the worst-case scenario, the company might go bankrupt and owners may lose their entire investment. Due to their limited liability with the corporation, however, shareholders cannot lose more than their investment.

Exhibit 18 shows this asymmetry in shareholder's downside losses versus potential upside gains. The value of equity is determined as the residual of the future value of the firm less the value of its debt. In theory, the market value of debt should be used; however, book value is often used as a proxy since market values for bonds are often unavailable or unreliable. Potential upside gains to shareholders are limited only by the future value of the firm, while shareholder losses are limited to their initial investment. If the value of the firm falls below the book value of debt, debtholders experience losses.

EXHIBIT 18: Equityholder—Upside and Downside

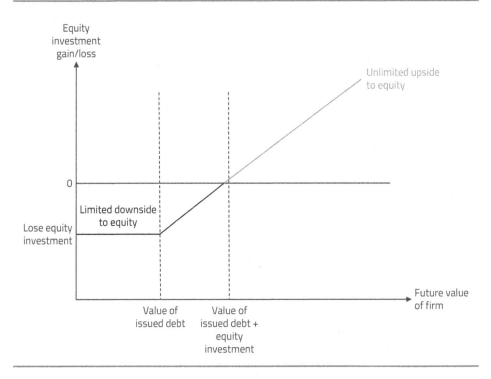

Equity owners, therefore, have an interest in the ongoing maximization of company value (net assets less liabilities), which directly corresponds to the value of their shareholder wealth. Cash flows to equityholders include such distributions as dividends, share repurchases and buybacks, and proceeds from the sale of the company.

Investor Perspective	Equity	Debt
Return potential	Unlimited	Capped
Maximum loss	Initial investment	Initial investment
Investment risk	Higher	Lower
Investment interest	Max (Net assets − Liabilities)	Timely repayment

With a fixed priority claim, bondholders are contractually promised priority in receiving their specified interest payment with return of principal. No matter how profitable the company becomes, however, bondholders will never receive more than their interest and principal repayment. When the company is financially healthy and able to service its debt commitments from cash flows, or has sufficient assets to serve as collateral to debt, debt offers predictable returns for investors. There is no residual claim value for bondholders, only a priority claim.

Exhibit 19 shows this asymmetry in downside losses versus potential upside gains to debtholders. Potential upside gains to debtholders are limited to interest plus principal repayment regardless of how high the future value of the firm rises. In contrast, if the value of the firm falls below the book value of debt, debtholders experience losses in direct relationship to the decrease in firm value.

EXHIBIT 19: Debtholder—Upside and Downside

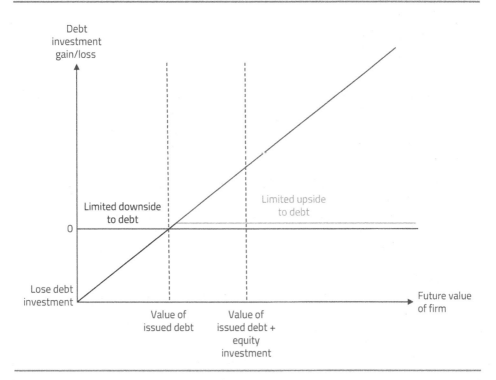

Bondholders are thus interested in assessing the likelihood of timely debt repayment and the risk associated with the company's ability to meet its debt obligations. This assessment includes the following:

- Assessing issuer cash flows and collateral/security
- Evaluating issuer creditworthiness and willingness to pay its debt
- Estimating the probability of default and amount of loss given a default

Downside risk increases to bondholders as a company takes on more debt. Debt becomes increasingly unattractive and risky to investors when the company's cash flows fail to comfortably cover its debt obligations.

If the company is struggling, unlike equity holders, bondholders do have some recourse. While bondholders could lose their entire investment as well, they receive priority in the event of financial distress. If necessary, bondholders can force the company through the contractual agreement in place to liquidate assets and return to them as much of their money as possible, reducing the likelihood that bondholders lose their entire investment. Additionally, the company cannot legally make dividend payments to shareholders until it first meets its bondholder obligations.

KNOWLEDGE CHECK

1. Equity and debtholders share the same investor perspective in regard to _____.
   A. maximum loss
   B. investment risk
   C. return potential

Solution:

A is correct. For both equityholders and debtholders, their initial investment represents their maximum possible loss. The return potential is theoretically unlimited for equityholders while it is capped for debtholders. Equityholders are exposed to a higher level of investment risk given no contractual obligation exists between them and the company.

2. True or false: Debtholders, unlike equityholders, have symmetric potential downside losses and upside gains.
   A. True. Both are at risk of losing the full amount of their investment.
   B. False. Debtholders' upside gains are capped in contrast to those of equityholders.

Solution:

B is correct; the statement is false. Both debtholders and equityholders have asymmetries between their downside losses and upside gains. For debtholders, potential upside gains are limited to interest plus principal repayment regardless of how high the future value of the firm rises. In contrast, if the value of the firm falls below the book value of debt, debtholders experience losses in direct relationship to the fall in firm value.

For equityholders, equity value is determined as the residual of the future value of the firm less the value of its debt. Potential upside gains to shareholders are limited only by the future value of the firm, while shareholder losses are limited to their initial investment.

4.1.2. Issuer Perspective

Because the returns to lenders are capped and because the cost of debt is lower than the cost of equity, corporations with predictable cash flows may prefer to borrow money rather than sell an ownership stake to raise the capital they need to finance their investments. This is because issuing more equity dilutes upside return for existing equity owners given that residual value must be shared across more owners.

From the issuer's perspective, bonds are riskier than stocks for the same reason bonds are safer than stocks for investors. Bonds increase risk to the corporation by increasing leverage. If the company is struggling and cannot meet its promised obligations to bondholders, bondholders have the legal standing to force certain actions upon the corporation, such as bankruptcy and liquidation.

Issuer Perspective	Equity	Debt
Capital cost	Higher	Lower
Attractiveness	Creates dilution, may be only option when issuer cash flows are absent or unpredictable	Preferred when issuer cash flows are predictable
Investment risk	Lower, holders cannot force liquidation	Higher, adds leverage risk
Investment interest	Max (Net assets − Liabilities)	Debt repayment

In contrast, shareholders have no such contractual rights. Issuing equity dilutes ownership, but equity is less risky to the corporation than debt because shareholders do not have the same incentive to force the company into bankruptcy or liquidation proceedings. In fact, early-stage companies or companies with unpredictable cash flows may not be able to borrow even if they wanted to.

If the company fails to meet its obligation to bondholders, it does have some options to try and avoid bankruptcy. For example, it can try to renegotiate more favorable terms with the bondholders or bank lenders. If the bondholders refuse, it can petition the courts for bankruptcy protection. In such cases, the company may be forced to suspend certain other payments, such as dividend payments on the stock. Eventually, however, the assets might have to be liquidated to raise as much money as possible to return to the bondholders. Alternatively, the business might be reorganized, with shareholders getting wiped out and bondholders becoming the new shareholders of the reorganized company.

KNOWLEDGE CHECK   Biotech Startup

A scientist discovers and patents a medical compound that shows promise for curing a debilitating disease. This scientist soon realizes that significant capital will be required to run the clinical trials demanded by the national public health authority before approval for the medication can be granted. If approval is granted, more money will be required for manufacturing, marketing, and distribution. Laboratory space and state-of-the-art equipment must be purchased or leased, contracts will have to be signed with suppliers, and other scientists and administrative personnel will have to be hired.

1. What form of business structure is most appropriate for this business, and why?

Solution:
   The corporate form of business structure would be most suitable for the scientist's biotechnology business. Because the corporation is a legal entity, it can engage in all of the activities mentioned and is better suited to handle the financing of the anticipated growth needs of the business in addition to providing risk protection to the scientist and other future investors.

2. Will the scientist be able to borrow the money she needs to get the business started?

Solution:

This early-stage start-up company has no revenues or profits; therefore, it will be almost impossible to borrow money. Lenders are more risk averse than equity investors and tend to avoid businesses that do not have sufficient cash flows to make the contractual payments on a loan. Furthermore, lenders have a limited upside payoff profile. No matter how successful the company becomes, lenders receive only a fixed return. This start-up company would seek to avoid debt at this stage as missing an interest payment could result in bankruptcy, putting an end to the business.

The more realistic solution for raising capital at this stage is to sell an ownership stake to others. Venture capitalists might find this start-up an attractive investment because they specialize in taking greater risks than lenders, in exchange for an unlimited upside payoff profile. By selling an ownership interest to equity investors, the scientist can raise the capital required to begin the process of running the trials and securing approval to manufacture and market the medication.

The scientist, as founder of the company, starts off as the sole investor and full owner. She owns all of the equity, or shares, in the company. To raise significant amounts of capital for the clinical trials, she agrees to sell some of her ownership stake to others. With the help of skilled advisers, the business is valued at ¥100 million based on its potential and shares are offered to investors.

To maintain control over the company, the scientist/founder decides to keep half the shares for herself and make the other half available to others. Suppose one investor invests ¥20 million and three other investors invest ¥10 million each.

3. Who are the likely investors, and why?

Solution:

In this case, the money will be raised in the private market. Potential investors are likely to be venture capitalists who specialize in investing in risky biotechnology startups.

4. What percentage ownership stake and share amount does each investor have after the equity raise if there are 10 shares in total?

Solution:

Given the company has a valuation of ¥100 million, ¥50 million will have to be raised from other investors. After the capital is raised, the founder owns 50% (¥50 million /¥100 million) and 5 shares of the company, one investor owns 20% (¥20 million / ¥100 million) and 2 shares, and the three remaining investors own 10% (¥10 million / ¥100 million) and 1 share each in the company.

Note that the number of shares is arbitrary and can change by splitting the shares or by raising more capital in the future. The more important issues are the overall valuation of the company and the proportional ownership stake each investor has.

4.2. Equity vs. Debt Conflicts of Interest

Potential conflict can occur between the interests of shareholders and bondholders. Because shareholders have limited downside liability, equal to the amount of their investment, and unlimited return potential, they prefer management to invest in projects that involve greater calculated risks and potential returns. At the extreme, shareholders would like the company to simply increase dividend payments and share repurchases with debt proceeds.

For bondholders, the upside return is capped or limited to the face value of debt plus the coupon. Bondholders receive no financial benefit or reward from issuer investment decisions that increase risk. As a result, bondholders prefer management to invest in less risky projects that increase cash flow certainty, even if those cash flows are relatively small, to increase the likelihood of timely interest and principal repayment by the company. Because bondholders do not have control over management decisions, they often rely on covenants to protect them against exploitive actions that compromise the safety of their investment.

5. SUMMARY

- Common forms of business structures include sole proprietorships, general and limited partnerships, and corporations.
- Sole proprietorships and partnerships are considered extensions of their owner or partner(s). This largely means that profits are taxed at the individual's personal rates and individuals are fully liable for all of the business's debts.
- Limited partnerships and corporations allow for the specialization of expertise in operator roles, in addition to the re-distribution of risk and return sharing between owners, partners, and operators.
- The corporate form of business structure is preferred when capital requirements are greater than what could be raised through other business structures.
- A corporation is a legal entity separate and distinct from its owners. Owners have limited liability, meaning that only their investment is at risk of loss.
- Corporations raise capital by selling an ownership interest and by borrowing money. They issue stocks, or shares, to equity investors who are owners. Debt represents money borrowed from lenders. Long-term lenders are issued bonds.
- Nonprofit corporations are formed to promote a public benefit, religious benefit, or charitable mission. They do not have shareholders, they do not distribute dividends, and they generally do not pay taxes.
- For-profit corporations can be public or private.
- In many jurisdictions, corporate profits are taxed twice: once at the corporate level and again at the individual level when profits are distributed as dividends to the owners.
- Public corporations are usually listed on an exchange and ownership is easily transferable.
- Private corporations are not listed on an exchange and, therefore, have no observable stock price, making their valuation more challenging. Transactions between buyers and sellers are negotiated privately, and ownership transfer is much more difficult.
- The market capitalization of a public company is equal to share price multiplied by number of shares outstanding.
- Enterprise value represents the total value of the company and is equal to the sum of the market capitalization and the market value of net debt. (Net debt is debt less cash.)

- Public companies are subject to greater regulatory and disclosure requirements—most notably, the public disclosure of financial information through periodic filings with their regulator. Private companies are not required to make such disclosures to the public.
- Given greater risks, only accredited investors are permitted to invest in private companies.
- Corporations have a life cycle with four distinct stages: start-up, growth, maturity, and decline.
- Although corporations begin as private companies, many eventually choose to go public or are acquired by public companies. IPOs typically occur in the growth phase and are usually driven by capital needs to fund growth.
- In many developed countries, it has become easier for private companies to access the capital they need without having to go public. As a result, the number of listed (public) companies in developed countries has been trending downwards. The number of listed companies in emerging economies continues to grow.
- Debt (bonds) represents a contractual obligation on the part of the issuing company. The corporation is obligated to make the promised interest payments to the debtholders and to return the principal. Equity (stocks) does not involve a contractual obligation.
- Interest payments on debt are typically a tax-deductible expense for the corporation. Dividend payments on equity are not tax deductible.
- Debtholders have claim priority, but they are entitled only to the interest payments and the return of principal. Equityholders have no priority in claims.
- Therefore, from the investor's perspective, investing in equity is riskier than investing in debt. Equityholders do have a residual claim, meaning that they are entitled to whatever firm value remains after paying off the priority claim holders, which grants them unlimited upside potential.
- From the corporation's perspective, issuing debt is riskier than issuing equity. A corporation that cannot meet its contractual obligations to the debtholders can be forced into bankruptcy and liquidation.
- Potential conflicts can occur between debtholders and equityholders. Debtholders would prefer the corporation to invest in safer projects that produce smaller, more certain cash flows that are large enough to service the debt. Equityholders would prefer riskier projects that have much larger return potential, which they do not share with the debtholders.

6. PRACTICE PROBLEMS

1. Describe the process of going public by a private company.

2. Describe the process of going private by a public company.

3. Identify the true statement(s) about corporation types from among the following:
   A. Nonprofit corporations by definition cannot generate profits.
   B. Transferring ownership from seller to buyer is more difficult for a private company than for a public company.
   C. Companies are categorized as public when they have greater than a minimum number of shareholders.

4. From the corporate issuer's perspective, the risk level of bonds compared to stocks is
   _____.
   A. lower
   B. higher
   C. the same

5. True or false: Bondholders can become shareholders through non-market-based means.
   Justify your answer.
   A. True.
   B. False.

6. Explain potential conflicts of interest between debtholders and equityholders.

7. State a reason for the declining number of public companies in developed markets.

CHAPTER 2

INTRODUCTION TO CORPORATE GOVERNANCE AND OTHER ESG CONSIDERATIONS

Young Lee, JD, CFA
MacKay Shields LLC (USA and Europe),
MacKay Shields Europe Investment Management Ltd. (Ireland),
and MacKay Shields UK LLP (United Kingdom)

Assem Safieddine, PhD
Suliman Olayan Business School, American University of Beirut (Lebanon)

Donna F. Anderson, CFA
(USA)

Deborah S. Kidd, CFA
CFA Institute (USA)

Hardik Sanjay Shah, CFA
GMO LLC (Singapore)

LEARNING OUTCOMES

The candidate should be able to:

- describe a company's stakeholder groups and compare their interests
- describe the principal-agent relationship and conflicts that may arise between stakeholder groups
- describe corporate governance and mechanisms to manage stakeholder relationships and mitigate associated risks

- describe both the potential risks of poor corporate governance and stakeholder management and the benefits from effective corporate governance and stakeholder management
- describe environmental, social, and governance considerations in investment analysis
- describe environmental, social, and governance investment approaches

1. INTRODUCTION

All companies operate in a complex ecosystem composed of interested stakeholder groups that are dependent on the company as well as each other for economic success. Key stakeholder groups include the company's capital providers, otherwise referred to as its debt and equity holders. In addition, companies have a number of other interested parties.

These stakeholder groups do not necessarily share the same goals for, nor seek the same ends from, the company. The interests of any one stakeholder group may diverge or conflict with that of others and, in some cases, with the interests of the company itself. A company's ability to maximize long-term value for shareholders and generate sufficient profitability to make its debt obligations is compromised if one stakeholder group is able to consistently extract benefits to the detriment of another group. Therefore, the controls and mechanisms to harmonize and safeguard the interests of the company's stakeholders are key areas of both interest and risk for financial analysts.

2. STAKEHOLDER GROUPS

A stakeholder is any individual or group that has a vested interest in a company. The primary stakeholder groups and their roles are listed below.

In a typical company,

- the shareholders and creditors provide the capital and financial resources to finance the company's activities;
- the board of directors serves as the steward of the company;
- the managers execute the strategy set by the board and run day-to-day operations;
- the employees provide the human capital for the company's day-to-day operations;
- the customers provide the demand for the company's products and services;
- the suppliers provide the raw inputs and the goods and services that cannot be efficiently generated internally, including functions that are outsourced; and
- the government and regulators dictate the rules and regulations governing the corporate entity.

Exhibit 1 illustrates the primary stakeholder groups and their interests, showing what each group provides and, in turn, receives in their relationship with the company.

EXHIBIT 1: Key Stakeholder Groups

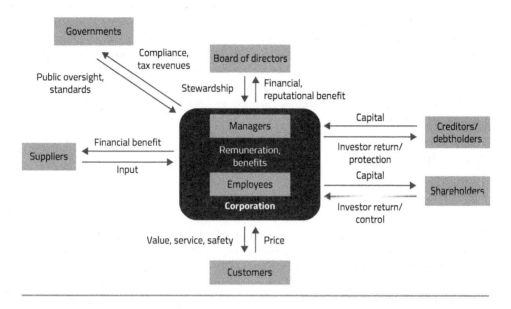

2.1. Shareholder vs. Stakeholder Theory

In the traditional corporate governance framework, shareholders elect a board of directors, which in turn hires managers to serve the interests of shareholders. The interests of other stakeholders—such as creditors, employees, customers, and society more broadly—are considered only to the extent that they affect shareholder value. This is referred to as the "shareholder theory" model.

Advocates for what is known as "stakeholder theory" argue that corporate governance should consider the interests of all stakeholders, not just shareholders. Stakeholder theory gives more prominence to **ESG** (environmental, social, and governance) considerations by making them an explicit objective for the board of directors and management. Doing this, however, involves certain challenges:

- the complexity of balancing multiple objectives
- a lack of clarity on how non-shareholder objectives are defined, measured, and balanced
- the challenges of competing globally when competitors may not face similar constraints
- the direct costs of adhering to higher ESG standards

Here we consider a corporation's primary stakeholder groups, such as its capital providers (e.g., shareholders and debtholders), as well as other groups. A discussion of principal-agent considerations and the conflicts that may arise among the groups also follows.

2.2. Shareholders

Shareholders, also called equity holders, own shares of stock, or equity, in a corporation. In terms of capital structure, they are residual claim holders, which means that if the company defaults or goes bankrupt, shareholders receive proceeds, if any, only after all other claims are paid. Shares typically entitle their owners to certain rights, including the exclusive right to vote on important matters, such as the composition of the board of directors, mergers, and the liquidation of assets.

A shareholder's interests are typically focused on growth in corporate profitability that maximizes the value of the company's share price and dividends.

2.3. Creditors/Debtholders

2.3.1. Banks and Private Lenders

Banks and private lenders generally hold a company's debt to maturity. They typically have direct access to company management and non-public information about the company; in principle, this reduces information asymmetries that exist between the company and these groups. Since an individual bank or private lender can be a critical source of capital, particularly for a small- or mid-sized company, this type of lender has a degree of influence on the company. These lenders can decide to relax debt restrictions or extend more credit, or it can refuse to do either of these, which is typically more difficult in the case of public debt held by many parties.

With banks and private lenders, the general perspective of debtholders applies: less financial leverage implies less risk and is therefore preferred. Among private lenders, however, there is wide variation in their risk appetite, approach, behavior, and relationships with companies to whom they have provided capital. Some focus mainly on asset value, such as the collateral supporting their loan; some hold both debt and equity positions in the same company; some have an equity-like focus on the cash flows, value, and prospects of the business; and some lend to businesses they would be interested in owning if the borrowing company were to default on its payments.

2.3.2. Public Debtholders

Public debtholders (or bondholders) rely on public information and credit rating agency determinations to make their investment decisions. In return for their capital, debtholders expect to receive interest payments on a regular basis and a return of their principal at the maturity of the bond. Unlike shareholders, debtholders do not hold voting power, and they typically have limited influence over a company's day-to-day operations.

Debtholders generally seek to minimize downside risk, preferring stability in company operations and performance, which contrasts with the interests of shareholders, who are inclined to tolerate higher risks in return for higher return potential from strong company performance.

2.4. Board of Directors

A company's board of directors is elected by shareholders to protect shareholders' interests and provide strategic direction, taking into consideration the company's risk appetite, which it defines for the company. The board is also responsible for hiring the CEO and monitoring the performance of the company and management. A board is often composed of both inside and independent directors. Inside directors are major shareholders, founders, and senior managers, whereas independent directors do not have a material relationship with the company with regard to employment, ownership, or remuneration and are chosen because of their experience managing or directing other companies. (The terms *remuneration* and *compensation* are typically interchangeable, with *compensation* generally used in North America and *remuneration* generally used outside North America. In this chapter, unless specifically identified with North America, we primarily use *remuneration*.)

There is no single or optimal board structure, and the number of directors may differ depending on the company's size, structure, and complexity of operations. However, most codes addressing corporate governance standards (known as "corporate governance codes") require that board members represent a diverse mix of expertise, backgrounds, and competencies, with best practice generally dictating at least one-third of the board be independent. The duties of directors are mandated by law in many countries and vary across jurisdictions. Directors are required under law to display a high standard of prudence, care, and loyalty to the company.

STAGGERED BOARDS

The general practice for boards is that elections occur simultaneously and for specified terms (three years, for example). Some companies, however, have **staggered boards**, whereby directors are typically divided into three classes that are elected separately in consecutive years—that is, one class every year. Because shareholders would need several years to replace a full board, this election process limits their ability to effect a major change of control at the company. The positive aspect of a staggered board, though, is that it provides continuous implementation of strategy and oversight without constantly being reassessed by new board members, which otherwise risks bringing short-termism into company strategy. This practice is common in Australia and a number of European countries, including Belgium, France, the Netherlands, and Spain.

2.5. Managers

Managers, led by the chief executive officer of the company, are responsible for determining and implementing the corporation's strategy under the oversight of the board of directors. In addition, they are responsible for the smooth function of day-to-day operations.

Senior executives and other high-level managers are normally compensated through a base salary, a short-term bonus usually delivered in the form of cash, and a multi-year incentive plan delivered in one or more forms of equity (options, time-vested shares, and/or performance-vested shares). As a result, in addition to acting to protect their employment status, managers may be motivated to maximize the value of their total remuneration.

2.6. Employees

A company relies on the labor and skill, or human capital, of its employees to provide its goods and services. In return, employees typically seek fair remuneration, good working conditions, access to promotions, career development opportunities, training, job security, and a safe and healthy work environment.

Employees may have both a direct financial stake in their employer company through equity-oriented participation plans (such as profit-sharing, share purchase, or stock option plans) and a broader interest in the company's long-term stability, survival, and growth. For employees in most businesses, equity ownership is a minor part of compensation and thus less important than interest in the company's stability and growth.

2.7. Customers

Customers expect a company's products or services to satisfy their needs and provide appropriate benefits given the price paid, while meeting applicable standards of safety. Depending on the type of product or service and the duration of their relationship with the company, customers may desire ongoing support, product guarantees, and after-sale service. Given its potential correlation with sales revenue and profit, customer satisfaction is a key concern for most companies. Brand boycotts by consumers and shareholder actions in response to adverse environmental and social impacts and controversies caused by their products and services are also increasingly concerning for companies.

2.8. Suppliers

A company's suppliers are typically short-term creditors who have a primary interest in being paid as contracted in a timely manner for products or services delivered to the company. These include outsourced services provided to the company, such as information technology and payroll. When companies are in financial distress, the financial position of its suppliers may be affected, as might suppliers' willingness to extend additional credit to the company. However, suppliers' interest in the financial health of a customer company is often broad because suppliers often seek to build long-term relationships with companies for the benefit of both parties and because suppliers aim for these relationships to be fair and transparent. Like customers, suppliers typically have an interest in the company's long-term stability, particularly in the case when products are specialized and the customer or supplier has made a significant investment in the relationship—for example, through product design, retooling, training, or software customization.

2.9. Governments

Governments seek to protect the interests of the general public and ensure the well-being of their nations' economies. Because corporations have a significant effect on a nation's economic output, capital flows, employment, social welfare, and environment, for instance, regulators have an interest in ensuring that corporations behave in a manner that is consistent with applicable laws. Moreover, as the collector of tax revenues from companies and their employees, a government can also be considered one of the company's major stakeholders.

STAKEHOLDERS IN NON-PROFIT ORGANIZATIONS

The stakeholders of a non-profit organization tend to differ from those of for-profit companies. Non-profit organizations do not have shareholders. Their stakeholders most commonly include board directors or trustees, employees, clients, regulators, society, patrons of the organization, donors, and volunteers. The stakeholders of non-profit organizations are generally focused on ensuring that the organization is serving the intended cause and that donated funds are used as promised.

EXAMPLE 1   Stakeholder Groups

1. Which stakeholders would *most likely* realize the greatest benefit from a significant increase in the market value of the company?
   A. Creditors
   B. Customers
   C. Shareholders

Solution:

C is correct. Shareholders own shares of stock in the company, and their wealth is directly related to the market value of the company. A is incorrect because creditors are usually not entitled to any additional cash flows (beyond interest and debt repayment) if the company's value increases. B is incorrect because while customers may have an interest in the company's stability and long-term viability, they do not benefit directly from an increase in a company's value.

3. PRINCIPAL–AGENT AND OTHER RELATIONSHIPS

A **principal–agent relationship** (also known as an agency relationship) is created when a principal hires an agent to perform a particular task or service. Because the agent is expected to act in the best interests of the principal, the principal-agent relationship involves obligations, trust, and expectations of loyalty and diligence.

The relationship between shareholders and managers/directors is a classic example of a principal-agent relationship, whereby shareholders (the principal in this case) elect directors (an agent) who are expected to protect their interests by appointing senior managers (another agent) to run the company. Exhibit 2 illustrates the principal-agent relationship.

EXHIBIT 2: Principal–Agent and Other Relationships

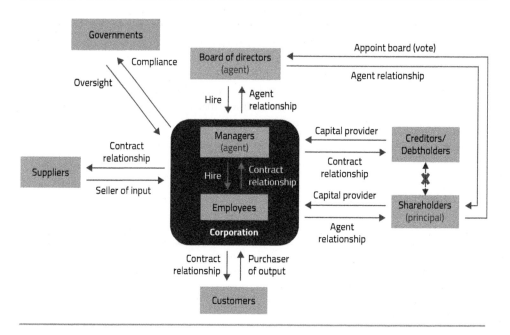

Asymmetric information (an unequal distribution of information) arises from the fact that managers have more information about a company's performance and prospects (including future investment opportunities) than is made available to outsiders, such as owners and creditors. Such information asymmetry decreases the ability of shareholders to assess the true performance of manager and directors, thereby weakening their ability to vote out poor performers.

Whereas all companies have a certain level of asymmetric information, companies with comparatively high asymmetry in information include those with complex products. These include high-tech companies, companies with little transparency in financial accounting information, and companies with lower levels of institutional ownership. Providers of both debt and equity capital demand higher risk premiums and returns from companies with higher asymmetry in information because there is greater potential for conflicts of interest.

Examples of principal-agent relationships and potential conflicts between the principal and agent are discussed in the following sections. Other conflicts among stakeholder groups not involving principal-agent relationships are also discussed.

3.1. Shareholder and Manager/Director Relationships

Conflicts arise where the interests of a principal and an agent diverge. In practice, compensation is the main tool used to create alignment of interests between management and board directors on the one hand and shareholders on the other. In principle, management compensation (which may include grants of shares and options to purchase shares in the company) is intended to motivate managers to work hard to maximize shareholder value. However, the alignment of interests between managers and shareholders is rarely perfect. If we consider the typical elements of management compensation, we can identify common examples of misalignment or conflicts.

3.1.1. Entrenchment

When the overall level of board director or manager compensation, or tenure, is excessive, the result may lead to the avoidance of risk motivated by a vested interest in keeping one's position. In such a scenario, directors may avoid speaking out against management in the interest of shareholders or other stakeholders.

3.1.2. Empire Building

When director and management compensation are high and tied to the size of the business, it can also lead to "growth for growth's sake" in which managers are motivated to pursue acquisitions and expansion that might not increase shareholder value.

3.1.3. Excessive Risk Taking

A compensation package relying too heavily on stock grants and options can motivate risk-taking behavior by management, since option holders participate only in upside share price moves. Similarly, too little or no use of stock grants and options awarded to managers can lead to the opposite result. However, managers and directors without a meaningful equity stake in the company are typically more risk averse in their corporate decision making so they can better protect their long-term engagement by the company. This misalignment may be at odds with the company's value creation objective or with shareholder's desire for higher-risk, higher-reward endeavors.

EXAMPLE 2   Shareholder and Manager/Director Relationships

1. A construction company has the opportunity to invest in a high-risk but high-reward capital infrastructure project. Which of the following could be a reason why the company decides not to pursue the project?
   A. The compensation of managers is closely tied to the size of the company's business.
   B. The directors receive excessive all-cash compensation.
   C. The managers have recently been awarded a generous amount of options to purchase shares in the company.

Solution:

   B is correct. Where compensation, particularly if it is excessive, does not include an adequate amount of stock grants or options, the risk tolerance of directors and managers may be low because directors and managers may be inclined to give up taking risks that create value for the company so as to not jeopardize the compensation they have been receiving. Choice A is incorrect because this describes the "empire building" phenomenon that would likely result in the decision to grow the company at any cost in order to attempt to secure higher compensation. Choice C would likely lead to an alignment of interests similar to that of shareholders and thus to a tolerance for risk.

Under the agency theory, managers are expected to undertake their duties with a central goal of serving shareholders' best interests and maximizing firm value. (Agency theory considers the problems that can arise in a business relationship when one person delegates decision-making authority to another. The traditional view in the investment community is that directors and managers are agents of shareholders. More recently, however, many legal experts have argued that in several countries, corporations are separate "legal persons"; thus, directors and managers are agents of the corporations rather than shareholders (or a subset of shareholders). (See https://themoderncorporation.wordpress.com/company-law-memo.) The separation of ownership and control in corporations, however, creates diverging interests for shareholders and managers and gives rise to agency problems. Managers may attempt to exploit the firm's resources and direct its operations so as to maximize their personal benefits—not limited to financial compensation, perquisites, job safety, and other benefits—to the detriment of shareholders' interests. Managers can do so through various means such as making value-destroying decisions, granting themselves excessive benefits, exploiting the company's assets and resources for their own gain, misappropriating funds, or committing other forms of fraudulent behavior.

Agency costs—the incremental costs arising from conflicts of interest when an agent makes decisions for a principal—are associated with the fact that all public companies and the larger private companies are managed by non-owners. In the context of a corporation, agency costs arise from conflicts of interest between managers, shareholders, and bondholders. "Perquisite consumption" refers to items that executives may legally authorize for themselves that have a cost to shareholders, such as subsidized dining, a corporate jet fleet, and chauffeured limousines.

The smaller the stake managers have in the company, the less their share in bearing the cost of excessive perquisite consumption—and, consequently, the less their desire to give their best efforts in running the company to maximize shareholder wealth. The costs arising from this conflict of interest have been called the agency costs of equity. Given that outside shareholders are aware of this conflict, they will monitor activities by management and the board that incur costs by taking actions such as requiring audited financial statements and holding annual meetings. Management will also take actions to assure owners they are working in the owners' best interest—actions such as using noncompete employment contracts and insurance to guarantee performance.

The better the company governance, the lower the agency costs. Good governance practices translate into higher shareholder value because managers' interests are better aligned with those of shareholders.

3.2. Controlling and Minority Shareholder Relationships

Corporate ownership structures are generally classified as dispersed, concentrated, or a hybrid of the two. Dispersed ownership reflects the existence of many shareholders, none of which have the ability to individually exercise control over the corporation. Exhibit 3 illustrates a scenario in which each of the four shareholders has 25% share ownership and voting rights and none has control.

EXHIBIT 3: Dispersed Ownership

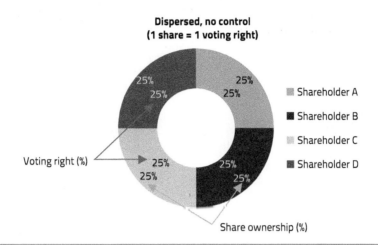

In contrast, concentrated ownership reflects an individual shareholder or a group (called **controlling shareholders**) with the ability to exercise control over the corporation. In this context, a group is typically a family, another company (or companies), or a sovereign entity.

Share ownership alone may not necessarily reflect whether the control of a company is dispersed or concentrated. This is because controlling shareholders may be either majority shareholders (i.e., own more than 50% of a corporation's shares) or **minority shareholders** (i.e., own less than 50% of shares). In some ownership structures, shareholders may have disproportionately high control of a corporation relative to their ownership stakes.

Exhibit 4 illustrates controlling majority versus minority shareholder scenarios. In the controlling majority shareholder scenario, Shareholder A holds 70% (greater than 50%) share ownership and voting rights, and where decisions are based on a majority vote, Shareholder A will always control the outcome.

In the controlling minority shareholder scenario, Shareholder A has significant influence but not the same degree of control as in the controlling majority scenario where a majority vote is required. Nevertheless, in the controlling minority shareholder scenario, Shareholder A has control. With 40% (less than 50%) share ownership and voting rights, Shareholder A only needs to ensure that it has the support of anything over 10% of the voting shareholders.

EXHIBIT 4: Concentrated Ownership — Controlling Majority and Controlling Minority Shareholder

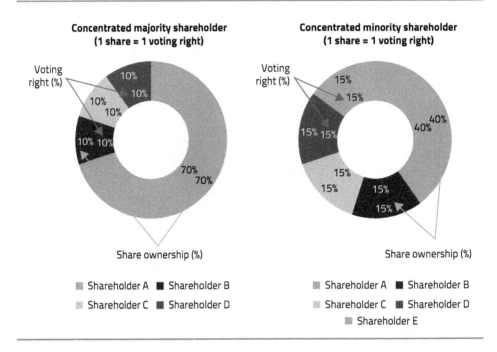

Clearly, not all shareholders have identical financial interests, and where there are one or more large shareholders, the issuance or retirement of common shares affects voting control of the company.

In companies in which a particular shareholder holds a controlling stake, conflicts of interest may arise among the controlling and minority (without control) shareholders. In such ownership structures, the opinions of minority shareholders are often outweighed or overshadowed by the influence of the controlling shareholders. Minority shareholders often have limited or no control over management and limited or no voice in director appointments or in major transactions that could have a direct effect on the value of their shares.

For instance, in companies that adopt **straight voting** (i.e., one vote for each share owned), controlling shareholders clearly wield the most influence in board of director elections, leaving minority shareholders with much less representation on the board.

The decisions made by controlling shareholders, or their board representatives, could also have an effect on corporate performance and, consequently, on minority shareholders' wealth. Takeover transactions are notable situations in which controlling shareholders typically have greater influence than minority shareholders have with regard to the consideration received and other deal terms.

QTEL CONSORTIUM ACQUISITION

In 2007 Qtel, Qatar's largest telecommunications company, executed a deal with a select consortium of the shareholders of Wataniya (excluding from the deal shareholders that were not part of the consortium), Kuwait's telecommunications company, to acquire the consortium's shares in Wataniya (representing a 51% stake in the target). This consortium of Wataniya's shareholders sold their shares to Qtel at a premium of 48% on the stock price to the exclusion of minority shareholders.

In addition, concentrated ownership may lead to any of the following situations:

- Where controlling shareholders have multiple voting shares, they can pursue expansion strategies and acquisitions that may not increase shareholder value and can issue shares to do so, with no risk that minority shareholders or other stakeholders will block their actions. An example might be the acquisition of a sports team by a company in an unrelated business.
- A controlling shareholder (such as a private equity backer) seeking to sell its stake might take a very short-term view on financing—for example, resisting actions by the company to raise new capital by issuing new shares that might result in dilution of its equity stake.
- Conversely, some companies that are founder-led and founder-controlled benefit from the fact that founders often take a very long-term perspective on their business, while minority shareholders might not. Amazon is a high-profile example since it has consistently sacrificed short-term profitability in favor of long-term growth and market share. Founder Jeff Bezos has allowed his ownership stake to be diluted as the company has grown.

Generally speaking, corporations with publicly traded equity have a voting structure that involves one vote for each share; that is, any shareholder's voting power is equal to the percentage of the company's outstanding shares owned by that shareholder. When there are exceptions to this norm and economic ownership becomes separated from control, investors can face significant potential risks.

In a small number of markets, the local regulatory framework or exchange rules allows other alternative share-class structures, which are the most common way that voting power is decoupled from ownership. An equity structure with multiple share classes in which one class is non-voting or has limited voting rights creates a divergence between the ownership and control rights of different classes of shareholders.

3.2.1. Dual-Share Classes

Under a multiple-class structure (traditionally called a dual-class structure when there are two share classes), a common arrangement has one share class (for example, Class A) that carries one vote per share and those shares are publicly traded while another share class (for example, Class B) carries several votes per share and those shares are held exclusively by company insiders or family members. The company's founders, executives, and other key insiders control the company by virtue of ownership of a share class with superior voting powers.

In this situation, shareholders have unequal voting rights. For example while Shareholder A holds 55% of shares (a majority), this represents only 10% of the voting rights. Exhibit 5 illustrates this scenario of unequal voting rights where one share may have greater or less than one voting right attached to it.

EXHIBIT 5: Unequal Voting Rights

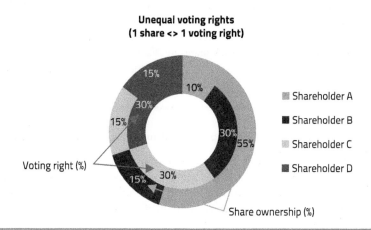

The multiple-class structure enables controlling shareholders, usually founders or insiders, to mitigate dilution of their voting power when new shares are issued and to continue to control board elections, strategic decisions, and all other significant voting matters for a long period—even once their ownership level declines to less than 50% of the company's shares. Examples of companies that have adopted multiple-class stock structures are Alibaba and Facebook (each with two share classes).

EXAMPLE 3   Dual-Share Class Structure

1. Which of the following *best* describes dual-class share structures?
   A. Dual-class share structures can be easily changed over time.
   B. Company insiders can maintain significant power over the organization.
   C. Conflicts of interest between management and stakeholder groups are less likely than with single-share structures.

Solution:

B is correct. Under dual-class share systems, company founders or insiders may control board elections, strategic decisions, and other significant voting matters. A is incorrect because dual-share systems are virtually impossible to dismantle once adopted. C is incorrect because conflicts of interest between management and stakeholders are more likely than with single-share structures because of the potential control element under dual systems.

3.3. Manager and Board Relationships

Conflicts of interest between the management and the board of directors can occur in cases where managers seek to extract private benefits or where they tend to increase information asymmetries by withholding relevant information from the board with the purpose of hindering its ability to exercise proper monitoring.

3.4. Shareholder vs. Creditor (Debtholder) Interests

The conflict between shareholders and creditors, or debtholders, reflects their different positions in the capital structure and the different structure of risks and returns for each. Debtholders have a contractual and prior claim to cash flows and firm assets over shareholders. For a holder of debt to maturity, the return or upside is prescribed and limited, while the risk, or downside, is not. In other words, the risk–return profile for debtholders is very asymmetric.

In contrast, shareholders typically have more downside risk but much higher upside return potential. As a result, debtholders favor decisions that reduce a company's leverage and financial risk, whereas shareholders often prefer higher leverage levels that offer them greater return potential. A divergence in risk tolerance regarding the company's investments thus exists between shareholders and debtholders. The potential debt/equity conflict is greater in the case of long-term rather than short-term debt because the passage of time exposes debtholders to possible changes in business conditions, strategy, and management behavior.

Debtholders may also find their interests jeopardized when the company attempts to increase its borrowings to a level that would increase default risk. If the company's operations and investments fail to generate sufficient returns required to repay the increased interest and debt obligations, creditors will be increasingly exposed to default risk. The distribution of excessive dividends to shareholders might also conflict with debtholders' interests if it impairs the company's ability to pay interest and principal. To prevent this, creditors may require covenants to limit increased leverage or dividend payouts.

The company's activities may also deviate from creditors' interests when it attempts to increase its borrowings to a level that would drive default risk upward. In some cases, the excessive borrowings might be driven by fraudulent behavior by shareholders or managers. In other cases, it might aim at financing risky operations or investments. If such investments fail to generate the returns required to pay the large interest and debt obligations, creditors will be exposed to default risk.

EXAMPLE 4   Stakeholder Relationships

1. A controlling shareholder of XYZ Company owns 55% of XYZ's shares, and the remaining shares are spread among a large group of shareholders. In this situation, conflicts of interest are *most likely* to arise between:
   A. shareholders and bondholders.
   B. the controlling shareholder and managers.
   C. the controlling shareholder and minority shareholders.

Solution:

C is correct. In this ownership structure, the controlling shareholder's power is likely more influential than that of minority shareholders. Thus, the controlling shareholder may be able to exploit its position to the detriment of the interests of the remaining shareholders. Choices A and B are incorrect because the ownership structure in and of itself is unlikely to create material conflicts between shareholders and regulators or shareholders and managers.

EXAMPLE 5   Leverage and Other Stakeholders—Mainly Metal Boats, Inc.

Mainly Metal Boats is a small, debt-free manufacturer of welded metal boats and is located in a remote small town. It sells both domestically and internationally in a market that is highly competitive and cyclical. Sales are conducted through a network of dealers, who typically sell three or four different boat brands. Of the company's 50 employees, about half are specialized aluminum welders, with most others in sales and management. The primary purchased input for Mainly's boat production is sheet aluminum. Mainly's sole aluminum supplier is a large multinational company that has many clients. Mainly has not paid dividends previously and now has substantial retained earnings that finance the company's working capital. Mainly's owners have recently decided to borrow heavily to finance working capital so they can pay a large, one-time dividend from the retained earnings.

1. Which of the following stakeholder groups is likely to be most negatively affected by the increase in leverage?
   A. The welders employed by the company
   B. The company's dealers
   C. The supplier of aluminum to the business

Solution:

A is correct. As employees, the welders could face loss of employment if the company were to become financially distressed with the increase in leverage, and since their skills are very specialized, they would probably have difficulty finding another job locally. In a small and remote town, employment opportunities are likely to be limited for specialized workers.

B is incorrect. The dealers might suffer lost sales if Mainly were to fail, but they could likely replace Mainly with a competing brand.

C is incorrect. The aluminum supplier would probably suffer the least impact since it is large and Mainly is not likely a large proportion of its sales.

2. Is it likely that any of these groups would be impacted positively?

Solution:

In all cases, impacts are negative. Note that for modest borrowing, these effects would be very minor.

4. CORPORATE GOVERNANCE AND MECHANISMS TO MANAGE STAKEHOLDER RISKS

Corporate governance practices differ among countries and jurisdictions, and even within countries different corporate governance systems may coexist. These differences reflect unique economic, political, social, legal, and other forces in each country and/or region. Notwithstanding these variations or the lack of a common definition, there is universal consensus that effective corporate governance is essential for the proper functioning of a market economy. There is evidence that some movement toward a global convergence of corporate governance systems is underway. One trend is the increased acceptance and adoption of corporate governance regulations with similar principles from one jurisdiction to another.

Notably, the Organisation for Economic Co-operation and Development (OECD) affirmed that "The presence of an effective corporate governance system, within an individual company and across an economy as a whole, helps to provide a degree of confidence that is necessary for the proper functioning of a market economy. As a result, the cost of capital is lower and firms are encouraged to use resources more efficiently, thereby underpinning growth" (OECD 2004).

Corporate governance is the arrangement of checks, balances, and incentives that exists to manage conflicting interests among a company's management, board, shareholders, creditors, and other stakeholders. Sound corporate governance practices are essential to ensuring sound capital markets and the stability of the financial system; weak corporate governance is a common thread found in many company failures. The assessment of a company's corporate governance system, including consideration of conflicts of interest and transparency of operations, has increasingly become an essential factor in the investment decision-making process.

EXAMPLE 6   Corporate Governance Overview

1. Which statement regarding corporate governance is *most* accurate?
   A. Most countries have similar corporate governance regulations.
   B. A single definition of corporate governance is widely accepted in practice.
   C. Both shareholder theory and stakeholder theory consider the needs of a company's shareholders.

Solution:

C is correct. Both shareholder and stakeholder theories consider the needs of shareholders, with the latter extending to a broader group. A is incorrect because corporate governance regulations differ across countries, although there is a trend

> toward convergence. B is incorrect because a universally accepted definition of corporate governance remains elusive.

Given differences in the interests of stakeholder groups, a company's governance and stakeholder management practices attempt to manage these interests to minimize potential stakeholder conflict and risk to the organization. **Stakeholder management** involves identifying, prioritizing, and understanding the interests of stakeholder groups, and it aims at laying the framework through which they can exercise adequate levels of influence and control and protect their interests in the company. For such balance to be maintained, corporate governance sets upon an underlying legal, contractual, and organizational infrastructure that defines the rights, responsibilities, and powers of each group and employs specific stakeholder management mechanisms.

4.1. Shareholder Mechanisms

As residual owners of the company, shareholders have legal and contractual rights in the company (ownership rights) and are driven to secure those rights through a variety of mechanisms (control rights) to protect their ownership interest and control in the company.

A prescribed, or standard, set of rights and mechanisms does not exist across all companies, and the principles vary across countries and jurisdictions. Yet there are some basic ownership rights granted to shareholders and common control rights and mechanisms available to them in corporations around the globe. These are presented in this section but should not be viewed as comprehensive or standard.

4.1.1. Corporate Reporting and Transparency

Shareholders have access to a range of financial and non-financial information concerning the company, typically through annual reports, proxy statements, disclosures on the company's website, the investor relations department, and other means of communication (e.g., social media). This information may relate to the company's operations, its strategic direction or objectives, audited financial statements, governance structure, ownership structure, remuneration policies, related-party transactions, and risk factors. Such information is essential for shareholders to

- reduce the extent of information asymmetry between shareholders and managers;
- assess the performance of the company and that of its directors and managers;
- make informed decisions in valuing the company and deciding to purchase, sell, or transfer shares; and
- vote on key corporate matters or changes.

4.1.2. Shareholder Meetings

General meetings, also termed annual general meetings (AGMs) because they are typically held once a year, enable shareholders to participate in discussions and vote on major corporate matters and transactions that are not delegated to the board of directors. An extraordinary general meeting (EGM) can be called by the company or shareholders throughout the year when other resolutions requiring shareholder approval are proposed. Companies are required to give shareholders the right to call a general meeting, subject to conditions of a specified minimum number of calling shareholders or a minimum proportion of outstanding stock held by these shareholders.

The matters present for shareholder vote vary across jurisdictions and companies, but the most basic and common ones relate to

- election of board members,
- approval of annual financial statements,
- approval of proposed dividend distributions,
- approval of director compensations,
- approval of independent auditor and auditor compensation, and
- material corporate changes, such as the following:
    - amendments to the company's by-laws and articles of association
    - transactions, mergers and acquisitions, takeovers, sale of significant corporate assets
    - increases in the company's capital
    - implementation of shareholder rights plans
    - voluntary liquidation of the firm

Proxy voting is a process that enables shareholders who are unable to attend a meeting to authorize another individual to vote on their behalf. Proxy voting is the most common form of investor participation in general meetings. Although most resolutions at most companies pass without controversy, sometimes minority shareholders attempt to strengthen their influence at companies via proxy voting. Several shareholders might opt to use this process to collectively vote their shares in favor of or in opposition to a certain resolution.

Cumulative voting (as opposed to straight voting) enables shareholders to accumulate and vote all their shares for a single candidate in an election involving more than one director. This voting process raises the likelihood that minority shareholders are represented by at least one director on the board, but it may not be compatible with majority voting standards for director elections in which share ownership is widely dispersed. In terms of worldwide practice, the existence of cumulative voting varies; for example, it is mandated in Spain but not allowed in several countries, such as Germany, Japan, Singapore, and Turkey.

EXAMPLE 7   Shareholder Meetings

1. Which of the statements about extraordinary general meetings (EGMs) of shareholders is true?
   A. The appointment of external auditors occurs during the EGM.
   B. A corporation provides an overview of corporate performance at the EGM.
   C. An amendment to a corporation's bylaws typically occurs during the EGM.

Solution:

C is correct. An amendment to corporate bylaws would normally take place during an EGM, which covers significant changes to a company, such as bylaw amendments. A and B are incorrect because the appointment of external auditors and a corporate performance overview would typically take place during the AGM, not the EGM.

4.1.3. Shareholder Activism

Shareholder activism refers to strategies used by shareholders to attempt to compel a company to act in a desired manner. Although shareholder activism can focus on a range of issues, including those involving social, political, or environmental considerations, the primary motivation of activist shareholders is to increase shareholder value. Activism can also take the form of direct corporate engagement and stewardship to promote positive corporate action. Activist shareholders often pressure management through such tactics as initiating proxy battles (fights), proposing shareholder resolutions, and publicly raising awareness on issues of contention.

Hedge funds are among the most predominant shareholder activists. Unlike most traditional institutional investors, hedge funds have a fee structure that often provides a significant stake in the financial success of any activist campaign. Furthermore, unlike regulated investment entities, such as mutual funds, that are typically subject to restrictions on their investments (e.g., limitations on leverage or ownership of distressed or illiquid securities), hedge funds are more lightly regulated and can thus pursue a greater range of activist opportunities.

EXAMPLE 8   Activist Shareholders

1. Which of the following *best* describes activist shareholders?
   A. Activist shareholders help stabilize a company's strategic direction.
   B. Activist shareholders have little effect on the company's long-term investors.
   C. Activist shareholders can alter the composition of a company's shareholder base.

Solution:
   C is correct. The presence of activist shareholders can create substantial turnover in the company's shareholder composition. A is incorrect because the presence of activist shareholders can materially change a company's strategic direction. B is incorrect because long-term investors in a company need to consider how activist shareholders affect the company.

4.1.4. Shareholder Derivative Lawsuits

Shareholder activists may pursue additional tactics, such as shareholder derivative lawsuits, which are legal proceedings initiated by one or more shareholders against board directors, management, and/or controlling shareholders of the company. The theory behind this type of lawsuit is that the plaintiff shareholder is deemed to be acting on behalf of the company in place of its directors and officers, who have failed to adequately act for the benefit of the company and its shareholders. With shareholder derivative lawsuits, minority shareholders have some protection in a dual-share class structure. However, in markets with dual-share classes where derivative lawsuits are illegal, minority shareholders have little protection.

In many countries, however, the law restricts shareholders from pursuing legal action via the court system—in some cases, by imposing thresholds that enable only shareholders with interests above a minimum amount to pursue legal actions or by denying legal action altogether.

4.1.5. Corporate Takeovers

The traditional view of the market for corporate control (often known as the takeover market) is one in which shareholders of a company hire and fire management to achieve better resource utilization. Corporate takeovers can be pursued in several different ways. One mechanism is the **proxy contest** (or proxy fight). In a proxy contest, shareholders are persuaded to vote for a group seeking a controlling position on a company's board of directors.

Managerial teams can also be displaced through **tender offers** and **hostile takeovers**, which seek to control a company through control of the board and thus management. A tender offer involves an offer to shareholders to sell their interests directly to the group seeking to gain control. A contest for corporate control may attract arbitrageurs and takeover specialists, who facilitate transfers of control by accumulating long positions from existing shareholders in the target company and later selling the positions to the highest bidder. A **hostile takeover** is an attempt to acquire the company without consent of the company's management.

Preservation of their employment status serves as an incentive for board members and managers to focus on shareholder wealth maximization. This threat of removal, however, can also have negative implications for a company's corporate governance practices if the company chooses to adopt anti-takeover measures, such as a staggered board or a shareholder rights plan (also known as a poison pill) to reduce the likelihood of an unwanted takeover. Staggering director elections can dilute the value of shareholder voting rights by extending the term that each director serves and eliminating the ability of shareholders to replace the entire board at any given election. Shareholder rights plans enable shareholders to buy additional shares at a discount if another shareholder purchases a certain percentage of the company's shares. These plans are designed to increase the cost to any bidder seeking to take over a company.

4.2. Creditor Mechanisms

To protect their economic interests in a company, creditors have a number of available mechanisms. The rights of creditors are established by laws and according to contracts executed with the company. Laws vary by jurisdiction but commonly contain provisions to protect creditors' interests and provide legal recourse.

4.2.1. Bond Indenture

The rights of bondholders are established through contracts executed with the company. A bond **indenture** is a legal contract that describes the structure of a bond, the obligations of the company, and the rights of the bondholders. To limit bondholders' risk during the term of a bond (or loan), the bond indenture typically contains **covenants**, which are the terms and conditions of lending agreements, enabling creditors to specify the actions an issuer is obligated to perform or prohibited from performing. Affirmative, or positive, covenants require the company to perform certain actions or meet certain requirements, such as maintaining adequate levels of insurance. Restrictive, or negative, covenants require bond issuers to not perform certain actions, such as allowing the company's liquidity level to fall below a minimum coverage ratio. **Collaterals** are another tool often used by bondholders to guarantee repayment, representing assets or financial guarantees that are pledged by an issuer to secure its promise to repay its obligations.

4.2.2. Corporate Reporting and Transparency

To further protect their rights, bondholders usually require the company to provide periodic information (including financial statements) to ensure that covenants are not violated and thus potential default risk is not increased. Because it is usually impractical and costly for individual bondholders to fully scrutinize a bond issue, companies often hire a financial institution to act as a trustee and monitor the company on behalf of the bondholders.

4.2.3. Creditor Committees

In some countries, official creditor committees—particularly for unsecured bondholders—are established once a company files for bankruptcy. Such committees are expected to represent bondholders throughout the bankruptcy proceedings and protect bondholder interests in any restructuring or liquidation.

Where a company is struggling to meet its obligations under an indenture, ad-hoc committees may be formed by a group of bondholders to discuss with the company potential options to restructure their bonds. While members of the ad-hoc committees are not representative of the other bondholders as a whole, their interests are often aligned with the broader bondholder group.

4.3. Board of Director and Management Mechanisms

The board is a central component of a company's governance structure. In addition to ensuring the company has appropriate audit control and enterprise risk management systems in place, the board also has the responsibility to review any proposals for corporate transactions or changes—such as major capital acquisitions, divestments, mergers, and acquisitions—before they are referred to shareholders for approval, if applicable.

4.3.1. Board Committees

To fulfill their duties, boards establish committees to which they delegate specific functions within their areas of specialization. The committees are responsible for thoroughly considering, reviewing, monitoring, and following up on matters falling within their mandates, which may require specific expertise or independence. The committees provide recommendations and reporting to the board on a regular basis. When establishing committees, boards do not delegate their ultimate responsibility, nor are they discharged of their liabilities. The board is required to review, challenge, and assure the content of any reports raised to it by the committees and make the proper decisions or actions.

The most commonly established board committees are shown in Exhibit 6.

EXHIBIT 6: Common Board Committees and Key Oversight Functions

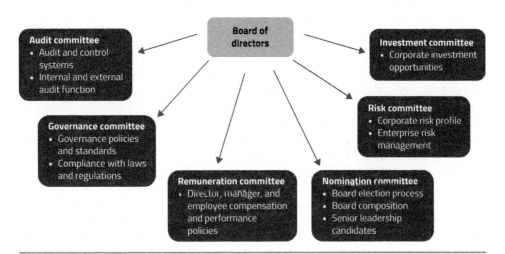

4.3.1.1. Audit Committee The audit committee is the most widely required and most commonly established committee of the board. The audit committee plays a key role in overseeing the audit and control systems at the company and ensuring their effectiveness. Best practice for audit committee composition is for all members to be independent.

The audit committee monitors the financial reporting process, including the application of high standard accounting policies, and ensures the integrity of the financial statements. It supervises the internal audit function or department and ensures its independence and competence. It presents an annual audit plan to the board and monitors its implementation by the internal audit function. It examines an annual review of the audit and control systems, ensures their effectiveness, and proposes necessary actions.

The audit committee is also responsible for recommending the appointment of a competent and independent external auditor and proposing its remuneration. It interacts and holds meetings with the external auditor. It receives the reports raised to it by the internal and external auditors, proposes remedial action for highlighted issues or matters, and follows up on them. In some cases, the audit committee may also oversee information technology security.

In summary, key oversight functions of the audit committee include

- monitoring the financial reporting process;
- supervising the internal audit function, annual audit plan, and annual review; and
- appointing and interacting with an external auditor as well as implementing remediation per that auditor.

4.3.1.2. Governance Committee The main role of the board's governance committee is to ensure that the company adopts good corporate governance structures and practices. For this purpose, it oversees the development of the governance policies at the company such as

- the corporate governance code,
- the charter of the board and its committees,
- the code of ethics, and
- the conflict of interest policy, among others.

The committee reviews these policies on a regular basis to incorporate any new regulatory requirements or relevant developments in the field. Most importantly, it monitors implementation of the governance policies standards and compliance with the applicable laws and regulations throughout the firm and then recommends proper action if any flaws or breaches are identified.

Developing and implementing policies for related-party transactions and other conflicts of interest are increasingly common among companies. These policies establish the procedures for mitigating, managing, and disclosing such cases. Typically, directors and managers are required to disclose any actual or potential, or direct or indirect, conflict of interest they have with the company, as well as any material interests in a transaction that may affect the company.

In addition to overseeing the board election process, the governance committee may also oversee an annual evaluation of the board to ensure that its functioning and activities are aligned with the governance principles. In terms of the governance structure, the committee ensures that the company's organizational structure clarifies the distribution of responsibilities and authorities and that it allows for smoothness and efficiency in operations while maintaining adequate levels of control. The committee ensures that the composition of the board and its committees is aligned with the governance principles and that new board members receive appropriate training to fulfill their roles effectively.

In summary, key oversight functions of the governance committee include

- developing and monitoring corporate governance policies and practices,
- ensuring organizational compliance and remediation with applicable laws and regulations, and
- aligning organizational structure with governance principles.

4.3.1.3. Remuneration or Compensation Committee The remuneration committee of the board specializes in compensation matters. It develops and proposes the remuneration policies for the directors and key executives. It may also be involved in handling the contracts of managers and directors, as well as in setting performance criteria and evaluating the performance of managers. The responsibilities of the remuneration committee may extend to setting the company's human resources policies, particularly those policies related to pay packages and compensations of employees.

Remuneration Plans
Executive remuneration plans have gained significant attention in the investment world, with a primary goal of aligning the interests of managers with those of shareholders. For this purpose, incentive plans increasingly include a variable component—typically profit sharing, stocks, or stock options—that is contingent on corporate or stock price performance. The granting of stock-based remuneration does not serve its purpose, however, if managers can improve their personal gains at the expense of the company while limiting their exposure to weak stock performance.

As a result, companies are increasingly designing incentive plans that discourage either "short-termism" or excessive risk taking by managers. Some incentive plans include granting shares, rather than options, to managers and restricting their vesting or sale for several years or until retirement. A long-term incentive plan delays the payment of remuneration, either partially or in total, until company strategic objectives (typically performance targets) are met. Overall, remuneration packages that are designed to prevent managers from chasing short-term profits are likely to be most effective and aligned with long-term shareholder interests.

Given the role of remuneration plans in aligning the interests of executives with those of shareholders, both regulators and companies are increasingly seeking shareholder views on pay. The concept of **say on pay** enables shareholders to vote on executive remuneration matters. By allowing shareholders to express their views on remuneration, companies can limit the discretion of directors and managers in granting themselves excessive or inadequate remuneration. Best practice is for the majority of remuneration committee members to be independent.

In summary key oversight functions of the remuneration committee include

- developing director and executive remuneration policies,
- overseeing performance policy management and evaluation, and
- setting human resources (HR) policies relating to employee compensation.

4.3.1.4. Nomination Committee The nomination committee is concerned with the nomination of directors to the board and the election process. This committee may also identify candidates for senior leadership roles, such as the CEO. It sets the nomination procedures and policies, including the criteria for board directorship, the search for and identification of qualified candidates for board directorships, and the election process by shareholders. Most importantly, it oversees the complete election process and ensures its transparency.

In designing its policies and nominating candidates to the board, the committee ensures that the structure of the board is balanced and maintains alignment with the governance principles. It recommends a definition for director independence and ensures on a continuous basis that the independent members of the board remain so.

In summary, key oversight functions of the nomination committee include

- overseeing the director nomination and board election process,
- identifying senior leadership candidates, and
- maintaining board composition and independence.

4.3.1.5. Risk Committee The risk committee assists the board in determining the risk profile and appetite of the company and in ensuring the company has an appropriate enterprise risk management system in place whereby risks are identified, mitigated, assessed, and managed appropriately. Accordingly, it oversees the setting of the risk policy and risk management annual plans and monitors their implementation. It supervises the risk management and control functions in the company, receives regular reports, and reports on its findings and recommendations to the board. In fulfilling its responsibilities, the committee ensures that the company's activities are aligned with its risk profile and that risks are mitigated or identified and well managed.

In summary, key oversight functions of the risk committee include

- determining company risk profile,
- ensuring appropriate enterprise risk management, and
- aligning corporate activities with risk appetite.

4.3.1.6. Investment Committee The investment committee of the board reviews the major investment opportunities proposed by the management and considers their viability. Such opportunities may include large projects, acquisitions, and expansion plans, as well as divestures or major asset disposals, among others. In studying an opportunity and making its recommendations to the board, the committee investigates and considers such factors as the projected financials and the expected value creation to the company, the alignment of the investment with the company's strategic direction and its risk profile, the underlying risks, the proposed financing of the project, and other quantitative and qualitative factors. In doing so, the committee challenges, where necessary, the management assumptions underlying the investment prospects.

In summary, key oversight functions of the investment committee include

- assessing of major investment opportunities, and
- evaluating board investment recommendations.

4.4. Employee Mechanisms

By managing its relationships with its employees, a company seeks to comply with employees' rights and mitigate legal or reputational risks in violation of these rights. Managing employee relationships also helps ensure that employees are fulfilling their responsibilities toward the company and are qualified and motivated to act in the company's best interests.

4.4.1. Labor Laws

Employee rights are primarily secured through labor laws, which define the standards for employees' rights and responsibilities and cover such matters as labor hours, pension and retirement plans, hiring and firing, and vacation and leave. In most countries, employees have the right to create unions. Unions seek to influence certain matters affecting employees. Although this not a common practice in many other parts of the world, in some countries (e.g., Germany, Austria, and Luxembourg) employees are sometimes represented on the board of directors—or on supervisory boards—of companies meeting certain size or ownership criteria.

4.4.2. Employment Contracts

At the individual level, employment contracts specify an employee's various rights and responsibilities. Some companies have employee stock ownership plans (ESOPs) to help retain employees and further align their interests with that of the company. As part of an ESOP, a company establishes a fund consisting of cash and/or company shares. The shares, which have designated vesting periods, are granted to employees who, because of their compensation package, have economic interests similar to that of shareholders.

4.5. Customer and Supplier Mechanisms

A company's customers and suppliers enter into contractual agreements that specify the products and services underlying the relationship, the prices or fees and the payment terms, the rights and responsibilities of each party, the after-sale relationship, and any guarantees. Contracts also specify actions to be taken and recourse available if either party breaches the terms of the contract.

Social media has become a powerful tool that customers, owners, and other stakeholders have increasingly used to voice or protect their interests or to enhance their influence on corporate matters. For example, negative media attention can adversely affect the reputation or public perception of a company or its managers and directors. Through social media, these stakeholders can instantly broadcast information with little cost or effort and are thus better able to compete with company management in influencing public sentiment.

4.6. Government Mechanisms

4.6.1. Regulations

As part of their public service roles, governments and regulatory authorities develop laws that companies must follow and monitor companies' compliance with these laws. Such laws may address or protect the rights of a specific group, such as consumers or the environment. Industries or sectors whose services, products, or operations are more likely to endanger the public or specific stakeholders' interests are usually subject to a more rigorous regulatory framework. Examples of these industries are banks, food manufacturers, and health care companies.

4.6.2. Corporate Governance Codes

Many regulatory authorities have also adopted corporate governance codes that consist of guiding principles for publicly traded companies. These codes require companies to disclose their adoption of recommended corporate governance practices or explain why they have not done so. In some jurisdictions, companies are required to go beyond this "comply or explain" approach. In Japan, for example, companies with no outside directors must justify why appointing outside directors is not appropriate. Some jurisdictions do not have national corporate governance codes but make use of company law or regulation (e.g., Chile) or stock exchange listing requirements (e.g., India) to achieve similar objectives.

EXAMPLE 9   Stakeholder Management

1. Which of the following is **not** typically used to protect creditors' rights?
   A. Proxy voting
   B. Collateral to secure debt obligations
   C. The imposition of a covenant to limit a company's debt level

Solution:

A is correct. Proxy voting is a practice adopted by shareholders, not creditors. B and C are incorrect because both collateral and covenants are used by creditors to help mitigate the default risk of a company.

EXAMPLE 10   Responsibilities of Board Committees

1. A primary responsibility of a board's audit committee does **not** include:
   A. the proper application of accounting policies.
   B. the adoption of proper corporate governance.
   C. the recommendation of remuneration for external auditors.

Solution:

B is correct. The adoption of proper corporate governance is the responsibility of a corporation's governance committee. Both A and C are incorrect because proper application of accounting policies and the remuneration of external auditors fall under the domain of the audit committee.

EXAMPLE 11   Shareholder Activism

1. Which of the following is true of shareholder activism?
   A. Shareholder activists rarely include hedge funds.
   B. Regulators play a prominent role in shareholder activism.
   C. A primary goal of shareholder activism is to increase shareholder value.

Solution:

C is correct. Although the subject of shareholder activism may involve social and political issues, activist shareholders' primary motivation is to increase shareholder value. A is incorrect because hedge funds commonly serve as shareholder activists. B is incorrect because regulators play a prominent role in setting standards, not shareholder activism.

4.6.3. Common Law vs. Civil Law Systems

The legal environment in which a company operates can significantly influence the rights and remedies of stakeholders. Countries that have a common law system (such as the United Kingdom, the United States, India, and Canada) are generally considered to offer superior protection of the interests of shareholders and creditors relative to those that have adopted a civil law system (such as France, Germany, Italy, and Japan).

The key difference between the two systems lies in the ability of a judge to create laws. In civil law systems, laws are created primarily through statutes and codes enacted by the legislature. The role of judges is generally limited to rigidly applying the statutes and codes to the specific case brought before the court.

In contrast, in common law systems, laws are created both from statutes enacted by the legislature and by judges through judicial opinions. In common law systems, shareholders and creditors have the ability to appeal to a judge to rule against management actions and decisions that are not expressly forbidden by statute or code, whereas in civil law systems this option is generally not possible.

Regardless of a country's legal system, creditors are generally more successful in seeking remedies in court to enforce their rights than shareholders are because shareholder disputes often involve complex legal theories, such as whether a manager or director breached a duty owed to shareholders. In contrast, disputes involving creditors, such as whether the terms of an indenture or other debt contract have been breached, are more straightforward and therefore more easily determinable by a court.

5. CORPORATE GOVERNANCE AND STAKEHOLDER MANAGEMENT RISKS AND BENEFITS

Depending on their nature and magnitude, unmanaged conflicts of interest with weaknesses in stakeholder management mechanisms or the adoption of poor governance structures with weak control over a company's operations can create various risks for a company and its stakeholders. These include legal, regulatory, reputational, and financial default risks. A weak control environment can encourage misconduct and hinder the ability of the company to identify and manage its risks.

In contrast, the development of good governance practices can play a vital role in both aligning the interests of managers and the board of directors with those of shareholders and balancing the interests of the company's other stakeholders. By adopting effective guidelines and instituting adequate levels of control, corporate governance can be reflected in better company relationships, operational efficiency, improved control processes, better financial performance, and lower levels of risk.

5.1. Operational Risks and Benefits

5.1.1. Weak Control Systems, Ineffective Decision-Making

Organizations with higher inherent risks—financial institutions, for example—require stronger controls so that residual risks are low or moderate. In a company with weak control systems or inefficient monitoring tools, such as poor audit procedures or insufficient scrutiny by the board, one stakeholder group may benefit at the expense of the company or other stakeholders. This can result in an adverse effect on the company's resources, performance, and value.

When the quality and quantity of information available to managers are superior to those available to the board or shareholders and sufficient monitoring tools are absent, managers have an opportunity to make decisions that benefit themselves relative to the company or shareholders. Without proper scrutiny, such practices might go unnoticed. Deficient decisions could include managing the company with a lower risk profile relative to shareholders' tolerance, thus avoiding investment opportunities that could create value for the company. Conversely, manager overconfidence may result in poor investment decisions without proper examination of their effect on the company or on shareholders' wealth.

EXAMPLE 12   Theranos Inc.

The rise and fall of Theranos Inc., a US-based blood testing technology company, is illustrative of numerous corporate governance failures. The company and its founder and CEO, Elizabeth Holmes, hoped to revolutionize the health care industry with breakthrough technology that could cheaply and rapidly identify numerous human conditions based on a simple blood test.

In 2014 Theranos was valued at US$10 billion. Its board was composed of highly recognizable and influential directors (including former US Secretaries of State and former directors of the US Centers for Disease Control and Prevention), giving the company and Holmes the credibility to raise hundreds of millions of dollars from investors.

In 2015, questions began to surface publicly around the company's blood testing technology. Whistleblowers came forward voicing concerns about questionable testing practices within the company. Soon after, it became clear that the technology and results promoted by the company and Holmes had serious issues. In 2018, the company, its CEO (Holmes), and its COO (Ramesh Balwani) were charged with "massive fraud" by the US Securities and Exchange Commission (SEC). Facing numerous criminal investigations and civil lawsuits, Theranos closed down.

The numerous corporate governance failures at Theranos largely relate to inadequate board composition and oversight.

- While the board was composed of highly accomplished and well-known individuals, most had little to no knowledge of medical technology and were therefore not able to detect the fraud being perpetuated by Holmes.
- Given the lack of medical technology understanding, the board should have hired an independent consultant to validate the innovative technology being promoted, but it failed to do so.
- The board failed to raise conflict of interest concerns regarding both Holmes' romantic relationship with Balwani and his senior position at the company despite his lack of relevant industry experience.
- The board dismissed fraud allegations brought forward by whistleblowers and remained silent even after these whistleblowers were fired soon after making their allegations.

In addition, the company failed to have individuals operating in crucial roles such as chief financial officer, global compliance officer, and other key positions for most of its life.

5.1.1.1. (Adequate) Scrutiny and Control

Strong governance practices institute more efficient procedures for scrutiny and control at all corporate levels, starting at the level of shareholders and moving up to management and the board of directors. These mechanisms allow for the mitigation of risk factors as well as fraudulent activities or for their identification and control at early stages, thus preventing them from hindering corporate performance and reputation. The control is enhanced by the proper functioning of the audit committee and the effectiveness of the audit systems in ensuring the accuracy and fairness of financial reporting at the company, promoting transparency, and resolving any matters of concern. By having procedures for monitoring compliance with internal and external policies and regulations and for reporting any violations, the firm can mitigate the risks of being exposed to regulatory questioning or legal proceedings and their associated costs.

Additionally, the adoption of formal procedures for dealing with conflict of interest and related party transactions allows the company to ensure fairness in the deal terms and avoid the hidden costs that could be associated with any preferential or unfair treatment in favor of the related party.

5.1.1.2. (Improved) Operating Performance

In a good governance setting, an organizational structure would clarify the delegation of authorities and reporting lines across the company and ensure that all employees have a clear understanding of their respective responsibilities. In addition, the governance, risk, and compliance (GRC) functions in the organization would work together to ensure an effective alignment of interests. These arrangements lead to smoother and improved decision-making processes and provide managers with the flexibility they need when responding to opportunities and challenges in a constantly changing environment.

Nonetheless, the adequate internal control mechanisms are an equally important pillar of the organizational and governance structures as they aim at ensuring that decisions and activities are properly monitored and controlled to prevent risks from arising and to circumvent misconduct or abusive behaviors. These mechanisms improve the operational efficiency of the company. Similarly, when the board exercises its role in defining the risk profile of the firm, setting its strategic direction, and supervising its implementation, then the managerial decisions and the firm operations will be better aligned with the interests of shareholders, thus paving the way for better operational results.

5.2. Legal, Regulatory, or Reputational Risks and Benefits

Compliance weaknesses in the implementation of regulatory requirements or lack of proper reporting practices may expose the company to legal, regulatory, or reputational risks. In such cases, the company may become subject to investigation by government or regulatory authorities for violation of applicable laws. A company could also be vulnerable to lawsuits filed by shareholders, employees, creditors, or other parties for breach of contractual agreements or company bylaws or for violation of stakeholders' legal rights. Improperly managed conflicts of interest or governance failures could bring reputational damage to the company, and its associated costs could be significant. Such risks are particularly acute for publicly listed companies subject to scrutiny by investors, analysts, and other market participants.

EXAMPLE 13   Diesel Emissions ("Dieselgate")

The diesel emissions scandal in 2014 involved a number of global car manufacturers, including Volkswagen and Audi, who were caught using "cheat" software. When the software detected that a car was being tested for compliance with nitrous oxide emissions requirements, it automatically provided a result that significantly under-reported the actual level of pollutants emitted.

Whether company executives were aware of the cheat software codes remains unanswered. However, concerns about board independence, proper governance and oversight of the employees who installed the codes, and the blatant disregard for the health of the communities in which the cars were sold significantly damaged the reputation of the companies involved. At the time the scandal became public, these companies experienced significant stock price declines. A number of companies have since paid billions in fines and penalties.

The commitment to governance and the corporate initiatives to better balance the interests of its various stakeholders can be reflected in the company's reputation. Employees, creditors, customers, and suppliers would more likely strive to build long-term relationships with a company that has a reputation for respecting the rights of its constituents and stakeholders. This would likely improve the company's ability to attract talent, secure capital, improve sales, or reach better terms with suppliers. In addition, ethics education and training for key stakeholders help support good governance practices. Good governance enables a company to mitigate the various risks underlying conflict of interest and agency problems and to maintain stability in operations.

5.3. Financial Risks and Benefits

5.3.1. Debt Default and Bankruptcy

Poor corporate governance, including weak management of creditors' interests, can affect the company's financial position and hinder its ability to honor its debt obligations. To the extent that the deterioration of corporate performance results in a debt default, the company may be exposed to bankruptcy risk if creditors choose to take legal action. The adverse consequences of corporate failures are not limited to the company's shareholders; they extend to other stakeholders, such as managers and employees, creditors, and even society and the environment.

5.3.2. (Lower) Default Risk and Cost of Debt

Good corporate governance contributes to maximizing shareholder value, and investors reward those companies that have sound governance, social, and environmental practices. Additionally, good corporate governance is associated with lower levels of business and investment risk, which limit the likelihood of unfavorable incidents affecting the company and reduce their impact. Governance arrangements that seek to manage creditor conflicts of interest restrict those corporate actions that would hinder the company's ability to repay its debt and therefore reduce its default risk. Default risks are also mitigated by properly functioning audit systems, transparent and better reporting of earnings, and controlling information asymmetries between the company and its capital providers. Lower default risks are associated with better credit ratings for the company and lower costs of debt borrowing, given that creditors typically require a lower return when their funds are better secured and their rights protected.

5.3.3. (Enhanced) Valuation and Stock Performance

Governance mechanics practiced at shareholders' meetings and maintained by internal corporate mechanisms, such as the board of directors and its committees, grant investors the assurance as to protection of their capital. These mechanisms help ensure investors that their rights to participate in discussions, vote on important matters in general meetings, and to enjoy fair and equal treatment are well protected. Investor confidence and the company's credibility in the marketplace are also enhanced by the appropriate and timely disclosure of material information concerning operating, financial, and governance activities. The improved transparency, the integrity of financial reporting processes, and the independent audit promote shareholders' and market participants' trust in the quality of reported earnings and their fair representation of the firm's financial position. This enables investors to make educated investment decisions and to reduce their risk perception of well-governed firms and therefore of the return required on capital invested in these firms. Consequently, good governance enhances the attractiveness of firms to investors, improves their valuations and stock performance, and reduces their cost of equity. Studies have found that

- improvements in corporate governance practices increase the likelihood of upgrading a company's credit rating from speculative to investment grade, resulting in a significant decrease in the cost of debt;
- a positive impact associated with experienced audit committees' possessing financial expertise whereby listed firms with such committees are more likely to have positive market performance during times of crisis; and
- board independence and diversity appear to be key factors in firm valuation—particularly for initial public offerings—and play an important role in value creation and value protection for firms.

EXAMPLE 14   Benefits of Corporate Governance

1. Which of the following is **not** a benefit of an effective corporate governance structure?
   A. Operating performance can be improved.
   B. A corporation's cost of debt can be reduced.
   C. Corporate decisions and activities require less control.

Solution:

C is correct. A benefit of an effective corporate governance structure is to enable adequate scrutiny and control over operations. B is incorrect because an effective governance structure can reduce investors' perceived credit risk of a corporation, thus potentially lowering the corporation's cost of debt. A is incorrect because operating efficiency may indeed be a benefit of an effective corporate governance structure.

Key questions analysts should consider about a company's corporate governance or stakeholder management include the following:

- What is the company's ownership and voting structure?
  - Analysts should evaluate whether separations exist between ownership and control or whether unusual structures are in place that favor certain shareholders, creating potential risks.

- Do the skill sets and experience of the board representatives match the current and future needs of the company?
  - Analysts should look at aspects such as director independence, tenure, experience, board size, and board diversity for investment insights.

- How closely does the management team's remuneration and incentive structure align with factors expected to drive overall company results?
  - While the availability and quality of information about executive remuneration plans vary widely across markets, analysts should assess whether misalignments in interests, which create risk, exist.

- Who are the significant investors in the company?
  - Analysts should assess the composition and behavior of major investors in a company to identify limitations and catalysts with regard to future changes in the company.

- Are shareholder rights at the company strong, weak, or average compared with peers?
  - Within a framework of regional regulations and corporate governance codes, analysts should evaluate how strong shareholder rights are relative to the company's competitors.

- How effectively is the company managing long-term risks and strengthening long-term sustainability?
  - Management's consideration of, or response to, environmental risks, human capital, corporate transparency, treatment of investors, and other stakeholders can provide analysts with important information or insights.

These questions and an analysis of these areas—typically provided by a company's proxy statements, annual reports, and sustainability reports, if available—can provide important insights about the quality of management and sources of potential risk.

EXAMPLE 15   Analyst Considerations

1. An investment analyst would likely be *most* concerned with an executive remuneration plan that:
   A. varies each year.
   B. is consistent with a company's competitors.
   C. is cash-based only, without an equity component.

Solution:

C is correct. If an executive remuneration plan offers cash only, the incentives between management and investors and other stakeholders may be misaligned. A is incorrect because a plan that varies over time would typically be of less concern to an analyst compared with one that did not change. B is incorrect because an analyst would likely be concerned if a company's executives were excessively compensated relative to competitors.

6. ESG CONSIDERATIONS IN INVESTMENT ANALYSIS

The inclusion of governance factors in investment analysis has evolved considerably. Management and accountability structures are relatively transparent, and information regarding them is widely available. Many performance indicators can help evaluate risks arising from governance issues, such as ownership structure, board independence and composition, and compensation. Also, the risks of poor corporate governance have long been understood by analysts and shareholders.

In contrast, the practice of considering environmental and social factors (which collectively with governance are known by the commonly used acronym ESG) has evolved more slowly. A large number of environmental and social issues exist, and identifying which factors are likely to affect company performance is not an easy task.

ESG considerations have become increasingly relevant for two key reasons. First, ESG issues are having more material financial impacts on a company's fair value. Many investors have suffered substantial losses due to mismanagement of ESG issues by corporations, which resulted in environmental disasters, social controversies, or governance deficiencies. Second, a greater number of younger investors are increasingly demanding that their inherited wealth or their pension contributions be managed using investment strategies that systematically consider material ESG risks as well as negative environmental and societal impacts of their portfolio investments.

Historically, environmental and social issues such as climate change, air pollution, and societal impacts of a company's products and services have been treated as negative externalities—ones whose costs are not borne by the concerned company. However, increased stakeholder awareness and strengthening regulations are internalizing environmental and societal costs into the company's income statement either explicitly or implicitly by responsible investors.

Although ESG factors were once regarded as intangible or qualitative information, refinements in the identification and analysis of such factors, as well as increased corporate disclosures, have resulted in increasingly quantifiable information.

EXAMPLE 16   ESG Relevancy

1. ESG considerations have become increasingly relevant for which of the following reasons?
   A. Many in the new generation of investors are demanding that investment strategies incorporate ESG factors.

B. ESG issues are having more material financial impacts on a company's fair value.
C. Environmental and social issues are being treated as negative externalities.

Solution:

A and B are correct.

A is correct because a greater number among the new generation of investors are increasingly demanding that their inherited wealth or their pension contributions be managed using investment strategies that systematically consider material ESG risks as well as negative environmental and societal impacts of their portfolio investments.

B is correct because ESG issues are having more material impacts on a company's fair value. Many investors have suffered substantial losses due to mismanagement of ESG issues by corporations, which resulted in environmental disasters, social controversies, or governance deficiencies.

C is incorrect. Environmental and social issues are not being treated as negative externalities as much as they were previously. Historically, environmental and social issues such as climate change, air pollution, and societal impacts of a company's products and services have been treated as negative externalities—ones whose costs are not borne by the concerned company. However, increased stakeholder awareness and strengthening regulations are internalizing environmental and societal costs into the company's income statement either explicitly or implicitly by responsible investors.

6.1. Introduction to Environmental and Social Factors

The materiality of ESG factors, particularly environmental and social factors, in investment analysis often differs meaningfully among sectors. An ESG factor is considered to be material when that factor is believed to have an impact on a company's long-term business model. For example, environmental factors such as emissions and water usage will likely be significant for utilities or mining companies, yet these are relatively inconsequential for financial institutions.

Overall, environmental factors that are generally considered material in investment analysis include natural resource management, pollution prevention, water conservation, energy efficiency and reduced emissions, the existence of carbon assets, adherence to environmental safety and regulatory standards, and the humane treatment of animals.

A specific concern among investors of energy companies is also the existence of "stranded assets"—carbon-intensive assets that are at risk of no longer being economically viable because of changes in regulation or investor sentiment. Analysts may find it difficult to assess potentially significant financial risks of energy companies because of limited information on the existence of these companies' carbon assets and because of the difficulty in determining political and regulatory risks.

Material environmental effects can arise from strategic or operational decisions based on inadequate governance processes or errors in judgment. For example, oil spills, industrial waste contamination events, and local resource depletion can result from poor environmental standards, breaches in safety standards, or unsustainable business models. Such events can be costly in terms of regulatory fines, litigation, clean-up costs, reputational risk, and resource management.

TOXIC EMISSIONS AND WASTE AS AN ENVIRONMENTAL RISK

Environmental issues such as toxic emissions and waste have historically been treated as externalities and thus not fully provisioned for in a company's financial reporting. However, with growing awareness among stakeholders, including regulators, companies may face financial liabilities associated with pollution, contamination, and the emission of toxic or carcinogenic substances and therefore must manage these risks. Gross mismanagement of these risks could result not only in a permanent loss of a company's license to operate but also in severe financial penalties.

In 2019, the collapse of Dam I of the Córrego do Feijão Mine in Brumadinho, Brazil, resulted in the spillage of millions of tons of nontoxic mud. Two hundred seventy lives were lost, and the nearby Paraopeba River was contaminated. The mine was owned and operated by Vale, multinational Brazilian mining corporation. Vale has since been accused of hiding information about the dam's instability for years to avoid damaging its reputation. Several employees from the company, including its former CEO, and its auditor, TÜV SÜD, were charged with murder and environmental crimes. Vale was fined millions of dollars in addition to bearing clean-up costs.

Social factors considered in ESG implementation generally pertain to the management of a business's human capital, including human rights and welfare concerns in the workplace; product development; and, in some cases, community impact. Staff turnover, worker health, training and safety, employee morale, ethics policies, employee diversity, and supply chain management can all affect a company's ability to sustain its competitive advantage.

In addition, minimizing social risks can lower a company's costs (e.g., through higher employee productivity, lower employee turnover, and reduced litigation potential) and reduce its reputational risk.

DATA PRIVACY AND SECURITY AS A SOCIAL RISK

Data privacy and security focus on how companies gather, use, and secure personally identifiable information and other metadata collected from individuals. In some industries, such as internet software and services, this includes managing the risks associated with government requests that may result in violations of civil and political rights.

With the proliferation of the internet, more services are being offered online, and consumers of these services are leaving a large digital footprint behind, often unknowingly. Some of this information may be personally identifiable in nature, leaving users vulnerable in the case of theft or misuse. As per the *2019 Cost of a Data Breach Report* released by IBM and the Ponemon Institute, the average cost of a data breach is US$3.9 million. (IBM 2021)

Given the large amounts of sensitive data being managed by some of the largest internet and financial services companies today, mismanagement of data privacy and security risk can have materially damaging consequences for both a company's business model and its financial performance. For example, lax cybersecurity measures at Equifax Inc. led to a data breach and the theft of identity and financial data belonging to more than 140 million US citizens in 2017. Equifax has incurred hundreds of millions of dollars in expenses resulting from the breach and faced numerous lawsuits and investigations.

Another example is the scandal involving Facebook and Cambridge Analytica, in which the personal data of over 80 million Facebook users were allegedly shared without consent and used in influencing voters, leading to one of the largest US government fines (US$5 billion) ever imposed in the technology sector and to a significant drop in user trust.

6.2. Evaluating ESG-Related Risks and Opportunities

A typical starting point for evaluating ESG-related risks and opportunities is the identification of material qualitative and quantitative ESG factors that pertain to a company or its industry. For this, a company's annual and sustainability reports can be good sources of information. An analyst may evaluate these factors on a historical basis and make appropriate forecasts, as well as evaluate these factors with respect to a specific company relative to its peers.

A non-exhaustive list of environmental, social, and governance factors is shown in Exhibit 7. Typically, a smaller set of ESG factors are material for each company, influenced by the business segments it operates in and its geography of operation.

EXHIBIT 7: Examples of Environmental, Social, and Governance Factors

Environmental	Social	Governance
• Climate change and carbon emissions	• Human rights	• Bribery and corruption
	• Labor standards	• Shareholder rights
• Air and water pollution	• Data security and privacy	• Board composition (independence and diversity)
• Biodiversity	• Occupational health and safety	
• Deforestation		• Audit committee structure
• Energy efficiency	• Customer satisfaction and product responsibility	• Executive compensation
• Waste management		• Lobbying and political contributions
• Water scarcity	• Treatment of workers	
	• Equity and diversity	• Whistleblower schemes
	• Community relations and charitable activities	

From a risk/reward perspective, the use of qualitative and quantitative ESG factors in traditional security and industry analysis typically differs for equity and fixed-income (debt) analysis. In equity analysis, ESG considerations are used to both identify potential opportunities and mitigate downside risk, whereas in fixed-income analysis, ESG considerations are generally focused on mitigating downside risk.

The process of identifying and evaluating relevant ESG-related factors is reasonably similar for both equity and corporate credit analysis. However, ESG integration differs considerably between equities and fixed income with respect to valuation. In equity security analysis, ESG-related factors are often analyzed in the context of forecasting financial metrics and ratios, adjusting valuation model variables (e.g., discount rate), or using sensitivity and/or scenario analysis.

For example, an analyst might increase the forecast of a hotel company's operating costs because of the impacts of excessive employee turnover—lost productivity, reduced customer satisfaction, and increased expenses for employee searches, temporary workers, and training programs. As another example, an analyst might choose to lower the discount rate for a snack food company that is expected to gain a competitive advantage by transitioning to a sustainable source of a key ingredient in its products.

In credit analysis, ESG factors may be integrated by using internal credit assessments, forecasting financial ratios, and ranking the relative credit of companies (or governments). In terms of valuation, relative value, spread, duration, and sensitivity/scenario analysis is often used. For example, an analyst may include the effect of lawsuits on the credit ratios, cash flow, or liquidity of a toy company. The same analyst may also estimate the potential for the credit spreads of the company's bonds to widen from these lawsuits.

Generally speaking, the effect on the credit spreads of an issuer's debt obligations or its credit default swaps (CDSs) may differ depending on maturity. As a different example, consider an analyst who believes that a coal company faces long-term risk from potential asset write-downs—that is, for assets that are obsolete or no longer economically viable, owing to changes in regulatory or government policy or shifts in demand. In this case, the analyst may believe that valuation of the coal company's 10-year maturity notes would be considerably more negatively affected than its 1-year maturity notes.

7. ENVIRONMENTAL, SOCIAL, AND GOVERNANCE INVESTMENT APPROACHES

There is a lack of consensus on ESG-related terms used in the investment community. For the purposes of this chapter, we define ESG investing terminology as follows:

Responsible investing is the broadest (umbrella) term used in ESG investing coverage. Responsible investing incorporates ESG factors into investment decisions with the objective of mitigating risk and protecting asset value while avoiding negative environmental or social consequences.

Sustainable investing selects assets and companies based on their perceived ability to deliver value by advancing economic, environmental, and social sustainability. Sustainable investing seeks to promote positive ESG practices that may enhance returns.

Socially responsible investing (SRI) incorporates environmental and social factors into the investment decision-making process, selecting those investments and companies with favorable profiles or attributes based on the investor's social, moral, or faith-based beliefs.

ESG investing ranges from being *value*-based to *values*-based. The objective of *value*-based investing is to incorporate material ESG considerations and traditional financial metrics into investment analysis while mitigating risk. The objective of *values*-based investing is to select investments that express, or align with, the moral or faith-based beliefs of an investor.

7.1. ESG Investment Approaches

Below we discuss six common ESG investment approaches:

- Negative screening
- Positive screening
- ESG integration

- Thematic investing
- Engagement/active ownership
- Impact investing

Negative screening excludes certain sectors, companies, or practices from investment using criteria based on the investor's values, ethics, or preferences. Examples of a negative screen are excluding from a portfolio the fossil fuel extraction/production sector or those companies underperforming globally accepted standards in areas such as human rights or environmental management. Companies producing controversial products such as weapons or tobacco can also be excluded as part of a negative screening approach. Many negative screens use a specific set of standards, such as the UN Global Compact's Ten Principles on human rights, labor, the environment, and corruption.

Positive screening includes certain sectors, companies, or practices for investment using criteria based on the investor's values, ethics, or preferences. A positive screening approach is typically implemented using an ESG ranking or scoring methodology. Positive screening targets investments in companies with well-managed material ESG risks relative to peers that rank highest according to the selected criteria. For example, a positive screening approach may include seeking companies that promote employee rights, exhibit diversity in the workplace and board rooms, or perform well in customer safety.

ESG integration entails the systematic consideration of material ESG factors in asset allocation, security selection, and portfolio construction decisions to achieve the product's or portfolio's stated investment objectives. ESG factors are explicitly included in the financial analysis of individual stocks or bonds as inputs into cash flow forecasts, credit/default risk forecasts, and/or cost-of-capital estimates. The focus of an ESG integration approach is to identify risks and opportunities arising from material ESG factors and to determine how well a company may be managing them.

Thematic investing refers to investing in assets related to ESG factors or themes, such as clean energy, green technology, sustainable agriculture, gender diversity, and affordable housing. This approach is often based on needs arising from economic or social trends. Two common investment themes focus on growing demand for energy and water and on the availability of alternative sources for each. Global economic development has increased the demand for energy at the same time that rising greenhouse gas emissions are widely believed to be negatively affecting Earth's climate. Similarly, increasing global living standards and industrial needs have created greater demands for water along with the need to prevent drought or increase access to clean drinking water in certain regions of the world. While these themes are based on trends related to environmental issues, social issues—such as access to affordable health care and nutrition, especially in the poorest countries in the world—are also of great interest to thematic investors.

Engagement/active ownership uses shareholder or bondholder rights and mechanisms to influence corporate behavior through direct corporate engagement (i.e., communicating with senior management and/or boards of companies), the filing or co-filing of shareholder proposals, and proxy voting directed by ESG guidelines. Engagement/active ownership seeks to achieve targeted social or environmental objectives in addition to financial returns. Engagement/active ownership can be implemented through various asset classes and investment vehicles and often through direct transactions, such as venture capital investing.

Collaborative engagement initiatives entail multiple investors collectively engaging with company management to influence positive action in managing their material ESG risks. Climate Action 100+, backed by more than 450 investors with over US$40 trillion in assets collectively under management (as of July 2020), is one such widely supported initiative that aims to influence the world's largest corporate greenhouse gas emitters to take necessary action on climate change (Climate Action). Other key ESG initiatives include air pollution, plastic waste management, human and labor rights in the supply chain, and executive remuneration.

Impact investing, which represents a smaller segment of the sustainable and responsible investing market, is investing "with the intention to generate positive, measurable social and environmental impact alongside a financial return," according to the Global Impact Investing Network (GIIN). An example is investing in products or services that help achieve one (or more) of the 17 Sustainable Development Goals (SDGs) launched by the United Nations in 2015, such as SDG 6: Clean Water and Sanitation ("Ensure availability and sustainable management of water and sanitation for all") or SDG 11: Sustainable Cities and Communities ("Make cities and human settlements inclusive, safe, resilient, and sustainable").

EXAMPLE 17   ESG Investment Approach

1. The ESG investment approach that is *most* associated with excluding certain sectors or companies is:
   A. thematic investing.
   B. negative screening.
   C. positive screening.

Solution:

B is correct. Negative screening entails excluding certain companies or sectors, such as fossil fuel extraction, from a portfolio. A is incorrect because thematic investing typically focuses on investing in companies within a specific sector or following a specific theme, such as energy efficiency or climate change, as opposed to merely excluding a set of companies or industries from a portfolio. Likewise, C is incorrect because positive screening focuses on including companies that rank (or score) most favorably compared to their peers with regard to ESG factors.

GREEN FINANCE

Green finance is a responsible investing approach that uses financial instruments that support a green economy. According to the Organisation for Economic Co-Operation and Development (OECD), green finance relates to "achieving economic growth while reducing pollution and greenhouse gas emissions, minimizing waste, and improving efficiency in the use of natural resources."

The primary investment vehicles used in green finance are **green bonds**, in which issuers earmark the proceeds toward environmental-related projects. To meet investor ESG requirements and thus increase issue appeal to a broader investor audience, companies often will issue their bonds in compliance with voluntary standards such as the Green Bond Principles developed by the International Capital Market Association (ICMA). In addition to green bonds, **sustainability linked loans** (including **green**

loans) are also used in green finance investing. Sustainability linked loans are types of loan instruments and/or contingent facilities (such as bonding lines, guarantee lines, or letters of credit) that incentivize the borrower's achievement of ambitious, predetermined sustainability performance objectives.

A summary of the six investment approaches along with a mapping to other classifications is shown in Exhibit 8.

EXHIBIT 8: ESG Investment Approaches

ESG Investment Approach	Description	Mapping to Other Classifications	
		Financial Analysts Journal	*Global Sustainable Investment Review*
Negative screening	Excludes companies or sectors based on business activities or environmental or social concerns	Negative screening	Negative/ Exclusionary screening Norms-based screening
Positive screening	Includes sectors or companies based on specific ESG criteria, typically ESG performance relative to industry peers	Positive screening Relative/ Best-in-class screening	Positive/ Best-in-class screening
ESG integration	Systematically considers material ESG factors in asset allocation, security selection, and portfolio construction decisions to achieve or exceed the product's stated investment objectives	Full integration Overlay/ Portfolio tilt Risk factor/Risk premium	ESG integration
Thematic investing	Invests in themes or assets related to ESG factors	Thematic investing	Sustainability-themed investing
Engagement/Active ownership	Uses shareholder power to influence corporate behavior to achieve targeted ESG objectives along with financial returns	Engagement/ Active ownership	Corporate engagement/ Shareholder action
Impact investing	Invests with the intention to generate positive, measurable social and environmental impact alongside a financial return	N/A	Impact/ Community investing

Note: For information on the *Financial Analysts Journal* column under "Mapping to Other Classifications," see www.tandfonline.com/doi/full/10.2469/faj.v74.n3.2. For the *Global Sustainable Investment Review* column, see www.gsi-alliance.org/wp-content/uploads/2021/08/GSIR-20201.pdf.

7.2. ESG Market Overview

Reflecting the growth of ESG-related information available, global assets dedicated to ESG investments have increased substantially. According to the Global Sustainable Investment Alliance (GSIA), a collaboration of organizations dedicated to advancing sustainable investing in the financial markets, Europe and the United States account for the vast majority of these assets. China and India are leading emerging markets for green bond issuance. Given differences in the way managers and investors define and implement sustainable and ESG mandates, however, determining the exact size of the ESG investment universe is challenging.

Increased interest in sustainable investing has also led to increased corporate disclosures of ESG issues and to a growing number of entities that collect and analyze ESG data. In addition to the GSIA, other organizations have formed to monitor and advance the mission of sustainable investing. These include

- the Global Reporting Initiative (GRI), a non-profit organization that produces a sustainability reporting framework to measure and report sustainability-related issues and performance,
- a collaboration between the United Nations and a consortium of institutional investors that launched the Principles for Responsible Investment (PRI) Initiative, and
- the Sustainability Accounting Standards Board (SASB), a non-profit organization that supports sustainability accounting standards for companies disclosing material ESG information.

In 2018, to help educate investors, the CFA Institute and the PRI published *Guidance and Case Studies for ESG Integration: Equities and Fixed Income* (www.cfainstitute.org/-/media/documents/survey/guidance-case-studies-esg-integration.ashx).

One area of continuing debate is whether the consideration of ESG factors is consistent with fiduciary duty—particularly in the oversight and management of pension fund assets. While pension fund regulation regarding ESG considerations varies globally, the PRI and the United Nations Environment Programme Finance Initiative (UNEP FI) promote the belief that ESG integration is a key part of investment analysis, stating, "Investors that fail to incorporate ESG issues are failing their fiduciary duties and are increasingly likely to be subject to legal challenge" (UNEPFI and PRI 2019).

8. SUMMARY

The investment community is increasingly recognizing and quantifying environmental and social considerations and the impacts of corporate governance in the investment process. Analysts who understand these considerations can better evaluate their associated implications and risks for an investment decision. The core concepts covered are listed here:

- The primary stakeholder groups of a corporation consist of shareholders, creditors, the board of directors, managers and employees, customers, suppliers, and government/regulators.
- A principal–agent relationship (or agency relationship) entails a principal hiring an agent to perform a particular task or service. In a company, both the board of directors and management act in agent capacity to represent the interests of shareholder principals.

- Conflicts occur when the interests of various stakeholder groups diverge and when the interests of one group are compromised for the benefit of another.
- Stakeholder management involves identifying, prioritizing, and understanding the interests of stakeholder groups and managing the company's relationships with stakeholders.
- Mechanisms to mitigate shareholder risks include company reporting and transparency, general meetings, investor activism, derivative lawsuits, and corporate takeovers.
- Mechanisms to mitigate creditor risks include bond indenture(s), company reporting and transparency, and committee participation.
- Mechanisms to mitigate board risks include board/management meetings and board committees.
- Remaining mechanisms to mitigate risks for other stakeholders (employees, customers, suppliers, and regulators) include policies, laws, regulations, and codes.
- Executive (internal) directors are employed by the company and are typically members of senior management. Non-executive (external) directors have limited involvement in daily operations but serve an important oversight role.
- Two primary duties of a board of directors are duty of care and duty of loyalty.
- A company's board of directors typically has several committees that are responsible for specific functions and report to the board. Although the types of committees may vary across organization, the most common are the audit committee, governance committee, remuneration (compensation) committee, nomination committee, risk committee, and investment committee.
- Shareholder activism encompasses a range of strategies that may be used by shareholders when seeking to compel a company to act in a desired manner.
- From a corporation's perspective, risks of poor governance include weak control systems; ineffective decision making; and legal, regulatory, reputational, and default risk. Benefits include better operational efficiency, control, and operating and financial performance, as well as lower default risk (or cost of debt), which enhances shareholder value.
- Key analyst considerations in corporate governance and stakeholder management include economic ownership and voting control, board of directors' representation, remuneration and company performance, investor composition, strength of shareholders' rights, and the management of long-term risks.
- Environmental and social issues, such as climate change, air pollution, and societal impacts of a company's products and services, have historically been treated as negative externalities. However, increased stakeholder awareness and strengthening regulations are internalizing environmental and societal costs into the company's income statement by responsible investors.
- ESG investment approaches are *value*-based or *values*-based. There are six common ESG investment approaches: negative screening, positive screening, ESG integration, thematic investing, engagement/active ownership, and impact investing.

9. PRACTICE PROBLEMS

1. Which group of company stakeholders would be *least* affected if the firm's financial position weakens?
   A. Suppliers
   B. Customers
   C. Managers and employees

2. Which of the following represents a principal-agent conflict between shareholders and management?
   A. Risk tolerance
   B. Multiple share classes
   C. Accounting and reporting practices

3. Which of the following statements regarding stakeholder management is *most* accurate?
   A. Company management ensures compliance with all applicable laws and regulations.
   B. Directors are excluded from voting on transactions in which they hold material interest.
   C. The use of variable incentive plans in executive remuneration is decreasing.

4. Which of the following issues discussed at a shareholders' general meeting would *most likely* require only a simple majority vote for approval?
   A. Voting on a merger
   B. Election of directors
   C. Amendments to bylaws

5. Which of the following statements about environmental, social, and governance (ESG) in investment analysis is correct?
   A. ESG factors are strictly intangible in nature.
   B. ESG terminology is easily distinguishable among investors.
   C. Environmental and social factors have been adopted in investment analysis more slowly than governance factors.

6. The existence of "stranded assets" is a specific concern among investors of:
   A. energy companies.
   B. health care companies.
   C. property companies.

7. An investor concerned about clean-up costs resulting from breaches in a publicly traded company's safety standards would *most likely* consider which factors in her investment analysis?
   A. Social factors
   B. Governance factors
   C. Environmental factors

8. _____ investing is the umbrella term used to describe investment strategies that incorporate environmental, social, and governance (ESG) factors into their approaches.
   A. ESG
   B. Sustainable
   C. Responsible

9. An investor concerned about a publicly traded company's data privacy and security practices would *most likely* incorporate which type of ESG factors in an investment analysis?
   A. Social
   B. Governance
   C. Environmental

10. Which of the following statements regarding ESG investment approaches is *most accurate*?
    A. Negative screening excludes industries and companies that do not meet the investor's ESG criteria.
    B. Thematic investing considers multiple factors.
    C. Positive screening excludes industries with unfavorable ESG aspects.

11. Which of the following stakeholders are *least likely* to be positively affected by increasing the proportion of debt in the capital structure?
    A. Senior management
    B. Non-management employees
    C. Shareholders

12. Which statement correctly describes corporate governance?
    A. Corporate governance complies with a set of global standards.
    B. Corporate governance is independent of both shareholder theory and stakeholder theory.
    C. Corporate governance seeks to minimize and manage conflicting interests between insiders and external shareholders.

13. Which of the following represents a responsibility of a company's board of directors?
    A. Implementation of strategy
    B. Enterprise risk management
    C. Considering the interests of shareholders only

14. Which of the following statements concerning the legal environment and shareholder protection is *most* accurate?
    A. A civil law system offers better protection of shareholder interests than does a common law system.
    B. A common law system offers better protection of shareholder interests than does a civil law system.
    C. Neither system offers an advantage over the other in the protection of shareholder interests.

CHAPTER 3

WORKING CAPITAL & LIQUIDITY

LEARNING OUTCOMES

The candidate should be able to:

- compare methods to finance working capital
- explain expected relations between working capital, liquidity, and short-term funding needs (NEW)
- describe sources of primary and secondary liquidity and factors affecting a company's liquidity position
- compare a company's liquidity position with that of peers
- evaluate short-term funding choices available to a company

1. INTRODUCTION

Working capital (also called net working capital) is defined simply as current assets minus current liabilities or

$$(\text{Net}) \text{ Working capital} = \text{Current assets} - \text{Current liabilities}$$

and includes both operating assets and liabilities, such as accounts receivable, accounts payable, and inventory, as well as financial assets and liabilities, such as short-term investments and short-term debt. **Working capital management** is the management of a firm's short-term assets and liabilities and an important aspect of a firm's operations. The goal of working capital management is to ensure the company has adequate, ready access to funds necessary for day-to-day operations, while avoiding excess reserves that can be a costly drag on the business' profitability and returns. Having excess levels of working capital can have a harmful effect on shareholder returns. At the same time, insufficient levels of working capital can harm a company if it cannot meet its short-term obligations, leading to product shortages, sales slowdowns, and, in the extreme, bankruptcy.

An analyst should carefully evaluate the working capital position of the firm to make an informed decision about the firm's ability to meet its short-term needs as it works to implement its long-term plans. To assess whether a firm is operating at an optimal level of working capital, financed at the lowest possible cost, an analyst should begin by asking two fundamental questions:

- What are the required investments in working capital for the firm?
- How should those investments be financed?

Understanding this provides the analyst with a basis for sound valuation analysis.

2. FINANCING OPTIONS

A firm typically has a number of options to finance itself, and how a firm chooses to finance itself can determine whether the firm stays liquid long enough to see its long-term plans materialize. Given the complex nature of a firm's assets and liabilities, understanding the financing options available to a firm is important. Companies make their decisions based on the costs and risks to the company and the returns and risks to the creditor or investor, in addition to market conditions, regulatory requirements, and the services of agents, brokers, dealers, and financial intermediaries working in the market.

It can be helpful to think of working capital from the perspective of uses and sources of funding for the firm. Cash, accounts receivable, inventory, and short-term investments, also termed marketable securities, represent uses of working capital because they must be financed.

Funds from operating activities such as accounts payable, credit lines, short-term loans, and short-term instruments sold (or issued) by the company, such as commercial paper, represent sources of short-term financing. Long-term debt and common equity issued by a company represent other sources of financing that can also be used to fund working capital needs.

Exhibit 1 shows a firm's financing alternatives by source and funding duration. A company can finance its working capital internally, through operating activities, or externally, through financial intermediaries and the capital markets. We discuss each of these in turn.

EXHIBIT 1: Internal vs. External Financing Alternatives

	Internal	External	
		Financial intermediaries	Capital markets
Short-term	• After-tax operating cash flows • Accounts payable • Accounts receivable • Inventory • Marketable securities	• Uncommitted lines of credit • Committed lines of credit • Revolving credit • Secured loans • Factoring	• Commercial paper
Long-term			• Long-term debt • Equity

2.1. Internal Financing

Companies of varying sizes and profitability can, in principle, generate internal financing and liquidity from their short-term operating activities in several ways. These include

- generating more after-tax operating cash flow;
- increasing working capital efficiency, such as extending a company's payables period, reducing its receivables period, or shortening its cash conversion cycle; and
- converting liquid assets such as receivables, inventories, and marketable securities to cash.

2.1.1. Operating Cash Flows

Operating cash flows—which are the company's after-tax operating cash flows less interest and dividend payments (adjusted for taxes)—can be used to invest in assets and are equal to net income plus depreciation minus dividend payments. A company with higher, more predictable after-tax operating cash flows has greater ability to finance itself using internal means.

2.1.2. Working Capital Efficiency: Accounts Payable and Accounts Receivable

Accounts payable are amounts due to the company's suppliers of goods and services that have not been paid. They arise from **trade credit**, which is a spontaneous form of credit in which the company, as buyer of the goods or service, is financing its purchase by delaying the date on which payment is made.

Trade credit might involve a delay of payment with a discount for early payment. The terms of trade credit are generally stated in the discount form: A discount from the purchase price is given by the supplier if payment by the firm is received within a specified number of days; otherwise, the full amount is due by a specified date. For example, the terms "2/10, net 30" indicate that a 2% discount is available if the account is paid within 10 days; otherwise, the full amount is due by the 30th day. While terms differ by industry—influenced by tradition within the industry, terms of competitors, and current interest rates—often accounts payable costs are high. Having market power, however, can help a company dictate more favorable terms for accounts payable, allowing it to delay payments without having to forgo discounts.

EXAMPLE 1   Keown Corporation—Internal Financing Decision

Keown Corp. is an established manufacturer of custom paddleboards for whitewater expeditions operating in the North American market. Keown, which operates its own manufacturing plant in Canada, sells its paddleboards exclusively through its website to avoid the overhead costs of retail locations.

The bulk of Keown's sales takes place during the North American summer season from May to August. Its customers want instant order fulfillment when they go to the site, so Keown must have substantial inventory on hand to start the summer season or risk losing sales to competitors who can provide prompt delivery if Keown cannot. Given the seasonality of the business, Keown is particularly focused on working capital management to ensure it can continue to operate and meet customers' needs.

Keown has had a target capital structure of 60% equity and 40% debt. The business is profitable and has generated positive net income and free cash flow for the past five years. Keown's payout ratio is targeted at 40% of net income, allowing the firm to retain 60% for reinvestment. As the firm is considered mature by the market, the CEO feels it is critical to finance any working capital needs through the use of debt rather than equity to avoid diluting existing shareholders.

As the CFO of Keown, you are deciding whether you should draw down your external line of credit to take the discount offered by your suppliers (standard terms in the industry are 2/10, net 30). The CEO has argued that she would rather not utilize the external line of credit for a 2% supplier discount. Keown can borrow through its line of credit at an effective annual rate of 7.7%.

1. Is the CEO correct? Should you forego the 2% supplier discount rather than drawing on the line of credit?

Solution:

No. Keown should not forego the 2% discount offered by its supplier and should instead use its external credit line for financing. This is because the effective annual rate (EAR) on the foregone trade credit is 44.6%, or

$$= [(1+(2/98))\wedge(365/20)] - 1$$

$$= [(1+0.02041)\wedge(18.25)] - 1$$

$$= 44.6\%,$$

which is significantly higher than the 7.7% rate Keown would pay on proceeds drawn from the external credit line.

Accounts receivable are the opposite of accounts payable and represent amounts owed by the firm's customers. In general, businesses prefer to delay paying what they owe but prefer to receive what is owed to them as quickly as possible. One company's accounts payable represent another company's accounts receivable. The sooner a company can collect what it is owed, the lesser its need to finance its operations in some other way.

2.1.3. Liquid Assets: Inventory and Marketable Securities

Like accounts receivable, inventory is a current asset on the balance sheet. These include raw materials and work-in-progress in production as well as finished goods waiting to be sold. Investing in and holding inventory cost money. Companies would prefer not to put a lot of money into inventory when that money could be used for more productive means. The longer the inventory remains unsold, the longer that money is tied up and not usable for other purposes. There may also be costs associated with maintaining or insuring inventory, and inventory can become obsolete the longer it is held, resulting in costly write-downs. As a result, an efficient company holds as little inventory as is necessary and sells or turns over the inventory as quickly as possible. If a company holds too little inventory, however, it risks resulting shortfalls and lost sales. Companies must therefore manage the tradeoff between the costs of holding too much inventory and the benefits of avoiding inventory shortfalls. Once inventory is sold, the purchase amount moves into accounts receivable, and the cash becomes available when the customer makes payment.

Marketable securities are financial instruments, such as stocks and bonds, that can be quickly sold and converted to cash. They are listed as a current asset if the company intends to liquidate them within a year or if the security has less than a year in maturity, earmarking them for the company's working capital needs. These securities could be short-term debt that matures within a year, long-term debt, and even common stocks (which have no maturity date) that will be sold within a year. Companies often invest in marketable securities to earn a rate of return greater than what they would earn by holding cash. Companies can sell marketable securities if they need funds for any reason, such as when making a capital expenditure.

2.2. External Financing: Financial Intermediaries

Financial intermediaries, such as bank and non-bank lenders, can also be a means to finance working capital. The main types of short-term bank financing include

- uncommitted bank lines of credit,
- committed bank lines of credit, and
- revolving credit agreements, or revolvers.

The latter two types can be unsecured or secured, depending on the company's financial strength and the general credit situation, which can vary from country to country. Uncommitted lines and revolvers are more common in the United States, whereas regular committed lines are more common in other parts of the world. Lines of credit represent flexible and immediate funding access.

2.2.1. Lines of Credit

Uncommitted lines of credit are, as the name suggests, the least reliable form of bank borrowing. A bank can offer an uncommitted line of credit but reserves the right to refuse to honor any request for use of the line. Given this, companies should not rely on uncommitted lines as banks are often unwilling to lend at the time the lines are most needed, such as during times of financial market stress. The primary attraction of uncommitted lines is that they do not require the company to pay any compensation other than interest.

Committed (regular) lines of credit are the form of bank line of credit, up to a pre-specified amount, that most companies refer to as regular lines of credit. They are more reliable than uncommitted lines because of the bank's formal commitment, which can be verified through an acknowledgment letter as part of the annual financial audit and can be footnoted in the company's annual report. These lines of credit are in effect for 364 days. This term length benefits companies by minimizing amounts needed to meet bank capital requirements. For commitments of a year or longer, banks require more capital. This term length also effectively ensures that, when drawn, these are short-term liabilities, usually classified as notes payable or the equivalent.

Regular lines are unsecured and pre-payable without penalty. The borrowing rate paid by the company is negotiated, with the most common rate being the bank's prime rate or a money market rate plus a spread. The spread is dependent on the firm's **creditworthiness**, which is the perceived willingness and ability of the firm to pay its debt obligations in a timely manner and represents the ability of a company to withstand adverse impacts on its cash flows. Unlike uncommitted lines, regular lines require compensation, usually in the form of a commitment fee to the lender. The fee is typically a fractional percent (e.g., 0.50%) of the full amount or the unused amount of the line, depending on bank–company negotiations.

Revolving credit agreements, also referred to as "revolvers" (or "operating lines of credit"), are the most reliable form of short-term bank borrowing. They involve formal legal agreements that define the aspects of the agreement. These agreements are similar to those for regular lines with respect to borrowing rates, compensation, and being unsecured. Revolvers differ in that they are in effect for multiple years and can have optional medium-term loan features. In addition, they are often used for larger amounts than a regular line would cover, and these larger amounts are spread out among more than one bank. With revolvers, companies draw down and pay back amounts periodically.

2.2.2. Loans and Factoring

Secured ("asset-based") loans are loans in which the lender requires the company to provide collateral in the form of an asset, such as a fixed asset that the company owns or high-quality receivables, inventory, or marketable securities. These assets are pledged against the loan, and the lender files a lien against them. This lien becomes part of the borrowing company's financial record and is shown on its credit report. Companies that lack sufficient credit quality to qualify for unsecured loans might arrange for secured loans.

A company can use its accounts receivable to generate cash flow through the **assignment of accounts receivable**, which is the use of these receivables as collateral for a loan. A company can securitize its receivables by selling its accounts receivable to a special purpose vehicle (SPV), which in turn issues a bond, backed by the receivables as collateral, that is sold to investors. A company can also sell its accounts receivable to a lender, called a factor, typically at a substantial discount. In an assignment arrangement, the company remains responsible for the collection of the accounts, whereas in a **factoring arrangement**, the company shifts the credit-granting and collection process to the lender or factor. The cost of this credit (i.e., the amount of the discount) depends on the credit quality of the accounts and the costs of collection. Similarly, inventory can be used in different ways as collateral for a loan.

Web-based lenders and **non-bank lenders** are recent innovations not typically used by larger companies. Web-based lenders operate primarily on the internet, offering loans in relatively small amounts, typically to small businesses in need of cash. Non-bank lenders also lend to businesses, but unlike typical banks, which make loans and take deposits, these lenders only make loans and may provide specific financial services to targeted consumers and firms such as mortgage services, lease financing, and venture capital.

Many short-term loans have historically been tied to Libor (London Interbank Offered Rate), such as Libor plus 0.50% (50 basis points). However, in 2021, Libor and other similar global benchmark rates were replaced with alternative reference rates in the United States, Europe, Switzerland, Great Britain, and Japan. Both bank and non-bank lenders often charge companies commitment fees, or additional commissions and fees beyond the quoted interest rate.

2.3. External Financing: Capital Markets

2.3.1. *Short-Term Commercial Paper*

Commercial paper is a short-term, unsecured instrument typically issued by large, well-rated companies. A company sells, or issues, commercial paper (also referred to as promissory notes or bills of exchange) directly to investors or through dealers. To avoid registration costs with national regulatory agencies, maturities for commercial paper are typically a few days or up to 270 days. Although a significant amount of asset-backed commercial paper exists, most commercial paper is unsecured, with no specific collateral. Issuers of commercial paper are often required to have a backup line of credit. The short-term nature of commercial paper, along with the creditworthiness of the borrower and the backup line of credit, generally make commercial paper a low-risk investment for investors.

2.3.2. *Long-Term Debt and Equity*

Depending on a firm's particular risk objectives, it may choose to finance its working capital with longer-term securities. By their nature, these securities are generally more costly to the firm, but they can provide the firm with increased financial flexibility. Borrowing long-term capital, such as debt or equity, removes pressure on the firm to find ways to repeatedly refinance needs in the near term. In addition, most bonds only require semiannual interest payments until maturity, reducing cash needs for the firm in the interim.

2.3.2.1. *Long-Term Debt* Long-term debt has a maturity of at least one year. Because of their long maturities, bonds are riskier than shorter-term notes or money market instruments from an interest rate and credit risk perspective. Hence, bond lenders (investors) and borrowers (companies) agree to bond covenants that are detailed contracts specifying the rights of the lender and restrictions on the borrower. These covenants regulate the company's use and nature of assets, restrict its ability to pay dividends, and limit the issuance of additional debt that might dilute the value of a bond.

Public debt is negotiable and approved for sale on open markets. In this context, a negotiable instrument is a written document describing the promise to pay that is transferable and can be sold to another party. Private debt can also be negotiable; however, private debt does not trade on a market and, therefore, is less liquid and more difficult for the holder to sell. While some private debt instruments, such as savings bonds and certificates of deposit, are not negotiable, private debt issued by businesses can usually be sold by one party to another.

2.3.2.2. *Common Equity* Common equity, or common shares, represents ownership in a company and is considered a more permanent source of capital. Owners, or shareholders, have residual claim on the company's profits after its obligations under other contractual claims are satisfied. In some instances—more likely when debt is not available—companies may issue common equity to fund growth in working capital.

EXAMPLE 2   Keown Corporation—External Financing Decision

Keown Corp. is planning its financing for a substantial investment of C$30 million next year. The assumptions for Keown's plan are the following:

- The total investment of C$30 million will be distributed as follows: C$5 million in receivables, C$5 million in inventory, and fixed capital investments of C$20 million, including C$5 million to replace depreciated equipment and C$15 million of net new investments.
- Projections include a net income of C$10 million, depreciation charges of C$5 million, and dividend payments of C$4 million.
- Short-term financing from accounts payable of C$3 million is expected. The company will use receivables as collateral for another C$3 million loan. The company will also issue a C$4 million short-term note to a commercial bank.
- Any additional external financing needed can be raised from an increase in long-term bonds. If additional financing is not needed, any excess funds will be used to repurchase common shares.

1. Describe how Keown would determine its financing needs.

Solution:

Keown should begin by considering its various sources of net cash to determine whether its net cash is sufficient to meet its investment needs. The facts state that the company will generate net income and will also have depreciation charges and make dividend payments. Because depreciation is a non-cash expense, it should be added to net income as a source of cash. Dividends, however, are paid from net income, are a use of cash, and reduce the net cash available for funding. Other sources of cash include the amounts generated from accounts payable, accounts receivable, and the short-term note from the bank.

2. How much, if any, does Keown need to issue in long-term bonds?
   A. Keown does not need to issue any bonds.
   B. Keown will need to issue C$4 million of bonds.
   C. Keown will need to issue C$9 million of bonds.

Solution:

C is correct. Keown must issue C$9 million of bonds.

Source	Amount (C$, millions)
Internal Financing	
Operating cash flow (Net income + Depreciation – Dividends)	11
Accounts payable	3
Short-Term Intermediary Financing	
Bank loan against receivables	3
Short-term note	4
Total Sources	21

> Since Keown requires C$30 million of financing and the planned sources total C$21 million, Keown will need to issue C$9 million of new bonds.

3. WORKING CAPITAL, LIQUIDITY, AND SHORT-TERM FUNDING NEEDS

Companies require sufficient resources to meet day-to-day obligations—such as paying suppliers and employees as well as meeting lease terms and other financial commitments—and to continue operations as a going concern. Successful companies seek to balance funds dedicated to current assets (most of which earn minimal returns or even decline in value as inventory becomes increasingly obsolete) against the risk of shortages in current assets negatively impacting day-to-day operations, while keeping focus on longer-term goals.

Working capital requirements are often a function of a firm's particular business model. Some businesses require heavy investment in inventory and receivables, while others do not. Retail businesses—particularly those with physical ("brick and mortar") locations or significant inventory and those operating more heavily on credit (vs. cash)—require substantially more working capital to fund their day-to-day operations. In contrast, technology businesses—such as software companies or online-only businesses with large amounts of intangible assets and few physical assets—have far lower working capital needs. There are wide variations, however, in working capital needs even among firms in the same industry or segment.

Companies typically determine their required working capital investment by first identifying their optimal levels of inventory, receivables, and payables, as function of sales, and then modeling those assumptions forward for the business. In establishing what is "optimal," a company's management usually evaluates some trade-off between costs, both the cost of capital for the company and obsolescence risks with its inventory, and benefits, such as fewer inventory shortfalls (or stockouts) and more accommodative credit policies, which management believes will translate to higher sales or revenues.

After determining its working capital requirements, a firm then identifies the optimal mix of short- and long-term financing to acquire necessary current assets while providing sufficient financial flexibility in times of stress. The analyst's job is to measure the efficacy of the firm's current approach and to understand its inherent risk.

Companies take different approaches to working capital management, ranging from conservative to moderate to aggressive.

> Conservative: In a conservative approach the firm holds a larger position in cash, receivables, and inventories, relative to sales. This provides the firm with the financial flexibility to manage and respond to unforeseen events that might disrupt supply chains and customer payments, such as during a regional or global crisis.
> Aggressive: In an aggressive approach the firm has substantially less committed to current assets, thereby reducing the company's short-term financial flexibility in exchange for higher equity returns.
> Moderate: In a moderate approach the firm holds a position somewhere between the two approaches.

EXAMPLE 3   Keown Corporation—Approach to Working Capital Management

As the CFO of Keown Corp., you would like recommendations on which approach to working capital (conservative, aggressive, moderate) makes the most sense for the business. You note that Keown has base levels of inventory, staffing, and receivables that are considered permanent current assets because they remain relatively constant during the year, while its higher levels of inventory and labor needed during the company's peak production and sales periods are considered variable current assets.

What factors should be considered and what approach should the company take?

Scenario 1 (Conservative)

Keown finances its current assets with long-term debt or equity financing.

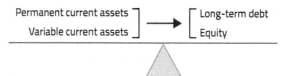

What are the pros and cons of a conservative approach for Keown?

Pros	Cons
Stable, more permanent financing that does not require regular refinancing; reduced rollover risk	Higher debt financing cost with an upward-sloping yield curve
Financing costs are known upfront	High cost of equity
Certainty of working capital needed to purchase the necessary paddleboard inventory	Permanent financing dismisses the opportunity to borrow only as needed (increasing ongoing financing costs)
Extended payment term reduces short-term cash needs for debt service	A longer lead time is required to establish the financing position
Improved flexibility during times of stress, with excess liquidity in marketable securities	Long-term debt may require more covenants that restrict business operations

Choosing to finance Keown's current assets with fixed-rate long-term debt, given a normal (upward-sloping) yield curve, or equity will have a higher associated cost. At the same time, using longer-term financing will provide Keown with more stability in funding, even during periods of market stress, by reducing the firm's need to regularly roll its debt and reducing short-term debt service requirements.

Why might Keown choose this conservative funding approach?

Reasons Keown might choose a conservative approach include the following:

- Reduced need to access the capital markets in times of stress
- Keown anticipates a flat to rising interest rate environment
- Preference for long-term cash flow stability over the risk inherent in available short-term, unsecured financing options
- Benefits of increased certainty and access to permanent sources of capital are perceived to offset the higher associated financing cost
- CEO's preference for long-term debt (over equity) to reduce shareholder dilution

Scenario 2 (Aggressive)

Keown finances the majority of its current assets with short-term debt or payables.

What are the pros and cons of an aggressive approach for Keown?

Pros	Cons
Lower cost of financing than conservative approach, given a normal upward-sloping yield curve	Interest expense could fluctuate as rates change on short-term financing
Short-term lines of credit provide the flexibility to access financing only when needed—particularly appropriate for seasonality—reducing overall interest expense	Higher levels of short-term cash may be needed to meet short-term debt maturities
Short-term loans involve less rigorous credit analysis, as the lender has greater clarity as to the short-term operations of the firm	Potential difficulty in rolling the short-term loans, thus increasing bankruptcy risk, particularly during times of stress
Flexibility to refinance if rates decline	Greater reliance on trade credit (expensive financing) may be necessary if the business is unable to refinance at favorable terms
	Tighter customer credit standards may be required, thereby reducing sales, if the business is unable to access the necessary financing to support credit terms to its customers

An increased reliance on short-term financing (short-term debt, accounts payable, accruals) would reduce the cost of financing relative to a conservative approach in exchange for greater risk if short-term financing sources dry up, which would make the rolling of short-term debt difficult, or even impossible, during economic downturns. Such a phenomenon did occur during the financial crisis in 2008–2009 and during the initial phases of the pandemic crisis in 2020.

Why might Keown choose this aggressive funding approach?

Reasons Keown might choose an aggressive approach include the following:

- Keown is confident in its ability to forecast upcoming sales and produce a detailed cash budget with a high degree of precision. Doing so would provide Keown with improved clarity and certainty as to its working capital needs.
- Keown anticipates a stable to falling interest rate environment.
- Keown anticipates shortening its cash conversion cycle, which would be achieved by reducing its account receivable and inventory period and lengthening its accounts payable period.
- In this case, moving to a model whereby customers pay cash at the time of order would be useful for Keown, allowing it to minimize its accounts receivable.

The challenge for Keown is that it must purchase its inventory well in advance. In this scenario, Keown is confident it can forecast near term sales and produce an accurate cash budget. Assuming this is the case, Keown would have a high degree of clarity and certainty as to its working capital needs to make the paddleboards, which requires a significant investment. Given the seasonal nature of the business, losing access to financing at the wrong time of the year could have a significantly negative impact for Keown.

Scenario 3 (Moderate)

Keown employs a moderate strategy, using short- and long-term financing methods, focusing on a liability-matching approach.

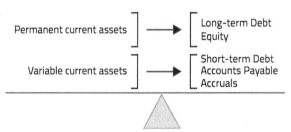

In this approach, Keown uses long-term financing as a baseline for financing its permanent level of current assets, such as year-round staffing needs and demo models needed for trade shows, and uses short-term financing for variable current assets, such as increased inventory and staffing during its seasonally busy periods.

What are the pros and cons of a moderate approach for Keown?

Pros	Cons
Lower cost of financing than conservative approach	Access to short-term capital may be restricted when needed for inventory build
Flexibility to increase financing for seasonal spikes while maintaining a base level for ongoing needs	Potential difficulty in rolling the short-term loans, thus increasing bankruptcy risk, particularly during times of stress
Diversifying sources of funding with a more disciplined approach to balance sheet management	Greater reliance on trade credit (expensive financing) may be necessary if the business is unable to refinance at favorable terms
	Tighter customer credit standards may be required, thereby reducing sales, if the business is unable to access the necessary financing to support credit terms to its customers

> Why might Keown choose this moderate funding approach? Reasons Keown might choose a moderate approach include the following:
>
> - Reduced risk with having to repeatedly access the equity markets for additional financing, given that Keown's core level of financing is established in accordance with its target capital structure
> - Reduced financing costs relative to a conservative approach while taking less risk and receiving greater financial flexibility than the aggressive approach
> - Preference to balance the benefits of lower-cost short-term financing with the increased stability and certainty of having its permanent working capital financed with long-term options
>
> Given Keown's business, taking a moderate approach to working capital would likely be appropriate for Keown. Due to the firm's seasonality, having a baseline level of long-term funding available for inventory, receivables, and permanent staffing makes sense. Keown could then look to control financing costs by using short-term financing for its seasonal periods. Keown's approach, however, will likely vary over time and be based on the preferences of firm management at the time.
>
> For example, a more risk-averse manager would take a more conservative approach, opting for reduced risk and greater financial flexibility at the expense of higher financing costs, whereas a more aggressive manager, in relying more heavily on short-term financing solutions, would be choosing lower financing costs at the expense of greater risk and reduced financial flexibility.

One way to evaluate the financial impact of a firm's working capital approach is to use the DuPont equation where

$$\text{Return on equity (ROE)} = \frac{\text{Net income}}{\text{Average shareholder's equity}}$$

$$\text{ROE} = (\text{Net profit margin}) \times (\text{Total asset turnover}) \times (\text{Leverage})$$

$$\text{ROE} = \frac{\text{Net income}}{\text{Revenue}} \times \frac{\text{Revenue}}{\text{Average total assets}} \times \frac{\text{Average total assets}}{\text{Average shareholder's equity}}$$

To assess the impact on returns, an analyst should focus on the total asset turnover component of the DuPont equation:

$$\text{Total asset turnover} = \frac{\text{Revenue}}{\text{Average total assets}}$$

As a company reduces its investment in working capital, its total asset turnover will increase, driving higher returns on equity, all else being equal. A company can reduce its working capital, for example, by using just-in-time inventory management, allowing it to reduce its investment into inventory on hand. Similarly, by requiring faster payment from customers and accelerating cash collections, a company can reduce its working capital. To help ensure appropriate financing to meet day-to-day liabilities, companies may use daily or monthly cash budgets.

A company that can generate high levels of sales with minimal asset levels can provide outsized returns to shareholders. Examples of this are the rapid growth and strong returns of large global technology companies such as Alibaba, Apple, Google, Microsoft, and Tencent. A common characteristic of these "asset light" companies is their reduced level of investment in long-term assets, leading to higher margins and cash flow generation.

Exhibit 2 summarizes the relationship between financing requirements, costs, risks, and return on equity based on funding approach.

EXHIBIT 2: Working Capital: Financing, Costs, and Returns

Funding approach	Current asset level	Financing required	Financing cost	Financial flexibility	Financial risk	Equity return
Conservative	↑ Higher	↑ Higher	↑ Higher	↑ Higher	Lower ↓	Lower ↓
Moderate	Moderate ↔	Moderate ↔	Moderate ↔	Moderate ↔	Moderate ↔	Moderate ↔
Aggressive	Lower ↓	Lower ↓	Lower ↓	Lower ↓	↑ Higher	↑ Higher

Looking more closely at the components of working capital helps an analyst to better understand the liquidity position of the firm and its likelihood of financial distress. While cash, accounts receivable, inventory, and marketable securities have different liquidity characteristics for a firm, the commonality between them is that higher levels of each provide the firm with increased financial flexibility, reducing the risk of financial distress while simultaneously leading to lower equity returns for the firm.

Complicating the working capital decision further is the interaction between working capital policies and firm marketing efforts. Extending additional credit, or more generous credit terms, can lead to increased sales for the company. Such changes result in larger accounts receivable balances and increases in uncollectible receivables, both of which require additional financing by the firm. In this case, the increased borrowing cost must be weighed against the profit generated from the higher level of sales and the firm's ability to access incremental financing needed to support higher levels of current assets.

Effective management of liquidity is a core finance function in most firms. Even profitable companies can encounter financial difficulties by failing to ensure they have sufficient liquidity to meet current liabilities.

EXAMPLE 4   A Change in Credit Policy

1. Keown Corp. is considering increasing the line of credit it offers to new customers because its sales manager believes this will lead to increased sales. What would be the expected impact on Keown's working capital if this change were made?
   A. The company would reduce its inventory levels.
   B. The company would likely collect faster, reducing its receivables.
   C. The company would have an increased need for working capital.
   D. The company could pay its suppliers sooner, reducing its accounts payable.
   E. The company would not see any impact to its net working capital needs as a result of the change.

Solution:
   C is correct. The company would likely need more working capital to support the expected increase in required inventory and accounts receivable resulting from an increase in sales.

---

4. LIQUIDITY AND SHORT-TERM FUNDING

Liquidity is the extent to which a company is able to meet its short-term obligations using cash flows and those assets that can be readily transformed into cash. Liquidity refers to the cash balances, borrowing capacity, and ability to convert other assets or extend other liabilities into cash, enabling the business to pay its short-term obligations when due and continue its operations. The liquidity of an asset can be evaluated along two dimensions:

- the type of asset
- the speed at which the asset can be converted to cash, either by sale or financing

For companies that have large excesses of cash, liquidity is typically taken for granted, and their focus is on putting the excess liquidity to its most productive use. In the event that no productive use can be identified, shareholders will pressure companies to return this cash to owners in the form of share buybacks or dividends.

Liquidity management refers to the company's ability to generate cash when needed, at the lowest possible cost. For the most part, liquidity is associated with short-term assets and liabilities, yet longer-term assets such as marketable securities can be converted into cash to provide liquidity. In addition, companies can also renegotiate longer-term liabilities. These last two methods might be costly for a company because they tend to reduce the company's overall financial strength. When a company faces tighter financial situations, having effective liquidity management is important to ensure solvency.

The challenges of managing liquidity include developing, implementing, and maintaining a liquidity policy. To do this effectively, a company must manage its key sources of liquidity efficiently. While these sources vary by company, they generally include

- primary sources of liquidity, such as cash balances
- secondary sources of liquidity, such as selling assets

4.1. Primary Sources of Liquidity

Primary sources of liquidity represent the most readily accessible resources available to the company. These can be cash held or near-cash securities and include the following:

- *Free cash flow*, which is the firm's after-tax operating cash flow less planned short- and long-term investments. For a profitable firm, free cash flow provides substantial liquidity. A rapidly growing firm has less free cash flow because of the investments required to facilitate the firm's growth.
- *Ready cash balances*, which is cash available in bank accounts, resulting from the firm's payment collections, investment income, liquidation of near-cash securities (those with maturities of fewer than 90 days), and other cash flows.
- *Short-term funds*, which can include items such as trade credit, bank lines of credit, and short-term investment portfolios of the firm.
- *Cash management*, which is the company's effectiveness in its cash management system and practices and the degree of decentralization of the collections or payments processes. The more decentralized the system of collections, for example, the more likely the company will be to have cash tied up in the system and not available for use. The use of technology has enabled companies to make significant improvements in the timeliness, efficiency, and accuracy of their cash management functions.

These sources represent the liquidity that is typical for most companies and readily accessible at relatively low cost.

4.2. Secondary Sources of Liquidity

The main difference between primary and secondary sources of liquidity is that using a primary source is not likely to affect the normal operations of the company, whereas using a secondary source might result in a change in the company's financial and operating positions. Secondary sources used by companies include

- *negotiating debt contracts*, such as relieving pressures from high interest payments or principal repayments, waiving debt covenants or suspending dividends, and negotiating contracts with customers and suppliers;
- *liquidating assets*, which depends on the degree to which short-term and/or long-term assets can be liquidated and converted into cash without substantial loss in value; and
- *filing for bankruptcy* protection and reorganization.

The use of secondary sources might signal a company's deteriorating financial health and provide liquidity at a high price—the cost of giving up a company asset to produce emergency cash. This last source, reorganization through bankruptcy, can also be considered a liquidity tool because a company under bankruptcy protection that generates operating cash will be liquid and generally able to continue business operations until a restructuring has been devised and approved. However, this option is likely to be at a significant cost, or disadvantage, to existing debt and equity holders, the company's employees, and other stakeholders.

Example 5 shows the net proceeds from the primary and secondary sources of liquidity for Keown Corp. in a liquidity crisis. It also shows the liquidation costs incurred by the company when these sources are used to raise funds. These costs can include the fees and commissions involved with the asset sale as well as any discount in asset value due to liquidity issues.

EXAMPLE 5   Keown Corporation: Estimating Costs of Liquidity

Keown Corp. is having a liquidity crisis. You have identified four potential actions that Keown could take to raise funds. Your estimates of fair value for Keown's assets and liquidation costs are shown below.

Source of Funds	Fair Value (C$, millions)	Liquidation Costs (%)
Sell short-term marketable securities	10	0
Sell select inventories and receivables	20	10
Sell excess real estate property	50	15
Sell a subsidiary of the firm	30	20

The liquidation costs include the fees and commissions of selling an asset as well as any reduction in the value of the asset because it is an illiquid asset being sold quickly. In this case, liquidation costs for marketable securities are rounded to 0%.

1. Net of liquidation costs, how much liquidity can Keown raise if all four sources of funds are used, and what are the total liquidation costs incurred by Keown? In local currency, these amounts are:
   A. 110 million, 9.5 million
   B. 94.5 million, 15.5 million
   C. 125.5 million, 15.5 million

Solution:
The costs and net funds raised are summarized in this table:

Source of Funds	Fair Value (C$, millions)	Liquidation Costs %	Liquidation Costs (C$, millions)	Net Proceeds (C$, millions)
Marketable securities	10	0	0	10
Inventories and receivables	20	10	2	18
Real estate property	50	15	7.5	42.5
Subsidiary of the firm	30	20	6	24
Total			15.5	94.5

B is correct. Shown in the table above in local currency terms, the total net proceeds are C$94.5 million, and the total liquidation costs incurred are C$15.5 million.

4.3. Drags and Pulls on Liquidity

A company's cash flow transactions—that is, cash receipts and disbursements—have significant effects on its liquidity position. These effects are known as drags and pulls on liquidity. A **drag on liquidity** is when receipts (inflows) lag, creating pressure from the decreased available funds; a **pull on liquidity** is when disbursements (outflows) are paid too quickly by the company or trade credit availability is limited, requiring companies to expend funds before they receive funds from sales that could cover the liability.

Major drags on receipts involve pressures from credit management and deterioration in other assets and include the following:

- *Uncollected receivables.* The longer these are outstanding, the greater the risk that they will not be collected at all. They are indicated by the large number of days of receivables and high levels of bad debt expenses.
- *Obsolete inventory.* If inventory stands unused for long periods, it might be an indication that it is no longer usable.
- *Tight credit.* When economic conditions make capital scarcer, short-term debt becomes more expensive to access.

In many cases, drags can be reduced by stricter enforcement of credit and collection practices, but this can also lead to lower sales. (Customers may be unwilling or unable to make a purchase if cash payment is required, for example.)

Managing cash outflows is as important as managing the inflows. If suppliers and other vendors who offer credit terms perceive the company to be in a weakened financial position or are unfamiliar with the company, they might restrict payment terms so much that the company's liquidity reserves are stretched thin. Major pulls on payments include the following:

- *Making payments early.* By paying vendors, employees, or others before the due dates, companies forgo the use of those funds. Effective payment management means not making early payments.
- *Reduced credit limits.* If a company has a history of making late payments, suppliers might cut the amount of credit they will allow to be outstanding at any time.
- *Limits on short-term lines of credit.* If a company's bank reduces the line of credit it offers the company, a liquidity squeeze might result. Credit line restrictions can be government mandated, market related, or simply company specific.
- *Low liquidity positions.* Many companies face chronic liquidity shortages, often because of their industry or from their weaker financial position. This risk is enhanced when the firm takes an aggressive approach to working capital management.

In Example 6, you are an analyst trying to identify changes that are affecting Keown's liquidity position.

EXAMPLE 6　Drags and Pulls on Liquidity

Keown Corp. is experiencing liquidity challenges. Several things might be contributing to this. Three notable changes have been suggested as drags or pulls on liquidity:

1. The increasing days in receivables is a drag on liquidity.
2. Lower inventory turnover is a drag on liquidity.
3. Increase in credit limits by lenders is a pull on liquidity.

1. Which of these does not contribute to the firm's liquidity issue?
   A. The change in days in receivables
   B. The change in inventory turnover
   C. The change in credit limits

Solution:
   C is correct. The increase in credit limits is not a pull on liquidity but is in fact the opposite: it provides liquidity.

5. MEASURING LIQUIDITY

Liquidity contributes to a company's creditworthiness, and the latter allows the company to obtain lower borrowing costs and better trade credit terms, giving the company greater flexibility and enabling it to exploit profitable opportunities.

The less liquid the company, the greater the risk it will experience financial distress or, in the extreme, insolvency or bankruptcy. Because debt obligations are paid with cash, the company's cash flows ultimately determine solvency. Immediate sources of funds for paying bills are cash on hand, proceeds from the sale of marketable securities, and the collection of accounts receivable. Additional liquidity comes from inventory that can be sold and thus converted into cash, either directly through cash sales or indirectly through credit sales (i.e., accounts receivable).

At some point, however, a company might have too much invested in low- and non-earning assets. Cash, marketable securities, accounts receivable, and inventory represent a company's liquidity position, but these investments are low-earning relative to the long-term, capital investment opportunities that companies might have available.

Various financial ratios can be used to assess a company's liquidity as well as its management of assets over time. Here we look at a number of liquidity and activity ratios in more detail, which are summarized in Exhibit 3.

EXHIBIT 3: Ratios Used for Assessing Company Liquidity

5.1. Liquidity Ratios

$$\text{Current ratio} = \frac{\text{Current assets}}{\text{Current liabilities}}$$

$$\text{Quick ratio} = \frac{\text{Cash} + \text{Short-term marketable instruments} + \text{Receivables}}{\text{Current liabilities}}$$

$$\text{Cash ratio} = \frac{\text{Cash + Short-term marketable instruments}}{\text{Current liabilities}}$$

5.2. Activity Ratios

$$\text{Accounts receivable turnover} = \frac{\text{Credit sales}}{\text{Average receivables}}$$

$$\text{Inventory turnover} = \frac{\text{Cost of goods sold}}{\text{Average inventory}}$$

$$\text{Number of days of receivables ("Days sales outstanding")} = \frac{\text{Average accounts receivable}}{\text{Average day's sales on credit}}$$

$$= \frac{\text{Average accounts receivable}}{\text{Sales on credit}/365}$$

$$\text{Number of days of inventory}$$

$$\text{("Days inventory outstanding")} = \frac{\text{Average inventory}}{\text{Average day's cost of goods sold}}$$

$$= \frac{\text{Average inventory}}{\text{Cost of goods sold}/365}$$

$$\text{Number of days of payables ("Days payable outstanding")} = \frac{\text{Average accounts payable}}{\text{Average day's purchases}}$$

$$= \frac{\text{Average accounts payable}}{\text{Purchases}/365}$$

$$\text{Cash conversion cycle} = \text{Days of inventory} + \text{Days of receivables} - \text{Days of payables}$$

We calculate **liquidity ratios** to measure a company's ability to meet short-term obligations to creditors as they mature or come due. This form of liquidity analysis focuses on the relationship between current assets and current liabilities and the rapidity with which receivables and inventory can be converted into cash during normal business operations. The levels of these ratios, and their trends, or changes over time, in addition to comparisons with competitors or the industry, are used to judge a firm's liquidity position.

In addition to looking at the relationships among these balance sheet accounts, we can also estimate **activity ratios**, which measure how well key current assets and working capital are managed over time. These key activity ratios use information from the income statement and the balance sheet to help tell the story of how well a company is managing its liquid assets.

Some of the major applications of this type of analysis include performance evaluation, monitoring, creditworthiness assessment, and financial projections. But ratios are useful only when they can be compared. This should be done in two ways:

- comparisons over time for the same company, and
- comparisons over time for the company compared with its peer group. Peer groups can include competitors from the same industry as well as other companies of comparable size with comparable financial situations.

Consider Daimler AG, a producer of cars, trucks, and vans. We can see the change in the company's current, quick, and cash ratios over a decade (2010–2019) in Panel A of Exhibit 4. Here, we see that the current ratio and the quick ratio increased over the time period. However, the cash ratio did not show the upward trend that the quick and current ratios exhibited over the decade.

We can see what is driving these trends in the calculation of the cash conversion cycle in Panel B of the exhibit. Over the 10 years, the cash conversion cycle increased by more than 40 days. The slight increase in days of payables outstanding would have decreased the cash conversion cycle slightly. The days of inventory increased by approximately nine days, and the days of receivables increased by approximately 37 days. Although the increase in inventory certainly puts a demand on liquidity, for Daimler the impact of the increase in receivables was more dramatic. Over the decade, however, based on the liquidity and activity ratios, this company seemed to have good control of its liquidity position.

EXHIBIT 4: Liquidity Analysis of Daimler AG, 10 Years Ending December 2019

	2019	2018	2017	2016	2015	2014	2013	2012	2011	2010
Panel A: Current, Quick, and Cash Ratios, December 2010–2019										
Current ratio	1.21	1.24	1.22	1.21	1.19	1.15	1.19	1.15	1.11	1.07
Quick ratio	0.93	0.94	0.93	0.91	0.88	0.84	0.90	0.85	0.80	0.80
Cash ratio	0.25	0.25	0.26	0.25	0.23	0.23	0.30	0.26	0.20	0.25
Panel B: Days of Inventory, Receivables, Payables, and Cash Conversion Cycle, December 2010–2019										
Days of inventory on hand	75.2	74.9	71.6	73.9	69.1	68.5	69.2	71.5	71.2	66.6
+ Days of receivables	136.8	127.9	118.8	118.4	104.6	102.6	105.5	104.6	104.2	100.0
– Days of payables outstanding	34.1	35.2	33.6	32.8	31.3	33.4	35.5	37.4	37.5	31.6
= Cash conversion cycle	177.9	167.6	156.8	159.5	142.4	137.7	139.2	138.7	137.9	135.0

Now consider Walmart, Target Corporation, Kohl's Corporation, and Costco Wholesale Corporation. Selected ratios for these large US discount retailers are shown in Exhibit 5. The data are from the fiscal year ending January 2020, except for Costco, whose fiscal year ended in August 2019.

We see some differences among these four competitors. These differences can be explained, in part, by the retailers' different product mixes (e.g., Walmart and Costco have more sales from grocery lines than the other two) as well as by their different inventory management systems and different inventory suppliers. None of the four firms invests heavily in accounts receivable, and customers generally pay with credit cards. The different need for liquidity can also be explained, in part, by the companies' different operating cycles.

The most striking difference is for Kohl's. Walmart, Target, and Costco have investments in inventory that are largely matched and paid for by accounts payable. Kohl's, notably, has the highest investment in inventory, which is not financed by payables. Because it includes more of such items as clothing, Kohl's inventory is also more seasonal than that of the other companies. Hence, Kohl's has the highest current ratio because much of its inventory must be financed by non-current liabilities.

EXHIBIT 5: Liquidity Ratios among Discount Retailers

Ratio for January 2020 Fiscal Year	Walmart	Target	Kohl's	Costco
Current ratio	0.79	0.89	1.68	1.01
Quick ratio	0.22	0.27	0.40	0.52
Days of inventory on hand	41.0	59.1	98.0	30.8
Days of receivables	4.4	4.5	0.4	3.8
Days of payables outstanding	43.5	56.2	33.3	31.4
Cash conversion cycle	1.9	7.4	65.1	3.2

EXAMPLE 7   Measuring Liquidity

Given the following ratios, how well has Company X been managing its liquidity?

Ratio	Current Fiscal Year Company X	Industry	Average for the Previous Five Fiscal Years Company X	Industry
Current ratio	1.9	2.5	1.1	2.3
Quick ratio	0.7	1.0	0.4	0.9
Days of receivables	39.0	34.0	44.0	32.5
Days of inventory on hand	41.0	30.3	45.0	27.4
Days of payables outstanding	34.3	36.0	29.4	35.5

Solution:
The ratios should be compared in two ways: for Company X over time (which would typically be examined) and for Company X over time vis-à-vis the trend in the industry. In all ratios shown here, the current year shows improvement over the previous years in terms of increased liquidity. In each case, however, Company X remains behind the industry average in terms of liquidity. A brief snapshot such as this example could be the starting point in assessing management's ability to deliver future improvement and reach or beat the industry standards.

6. EVALUATING SHORT-TERM FINANCING CHOICES

Companies may find themselves with liquidity issues if they fail to sufficiently explore their available options or take advantage of cost savings that some forms of financing, or borrowing, offer. If a company lacks a sound short-term financing strategy, it may find itself stuck in an uneconomical situation or, in the extreme, facing a crisis in which it cannot borrow from any source.

To avoid this, companies seek to implement a short-term financing strategy that achieves a number of objectives:

- Ensure the company has sufficient funding capacity to handle peak cash needs.
- Maintain sufficient and diversified sources of credit to fund ongoing cash needs. While many companies use one alternative primarily, although often with more than one provider, a company should ideally ensure it has adequate alternatives and is not overly reliant on one lender or form of lending, particularly if the amount of their borrowing is large.
- Ensure the rates paid for financing are competitive.
- Ensure both implicit and explicit funding costs are considered in the company's effective cost of borrowing. This becomes more challenging for complex instruments such as convertibles and other derivatives.

In addition, several other factors, such as the following, influence a company's short-term borrowing strategy:

- *Size and creditworthiness*. A company's size can dictate the financing options available to it. Larger companies can take advantage of economies of scale to access commercial paper, banker's acceptances, and so on. The lender's size is also an important criterion, because larger banks have higher house or legal lending limits. The company's creditworthiness will determine the rate it will pay, the compensation amount, and even whether the loan will be approved by the lender.
- *Legal and regulatory considerations*. Some countries impose constraints on how much a company can borrow and the terms under which it can borrow. Such constraints are usually greater for companies operating in developed countries with well-defined legal systems than for those operating in countries with emerging economies. In developed countries, some industries are highly regulated. Companies in these industries, such as utilities and banks, might be restricted in how much they can borrow and the kind of borrowing they can engage in. Banks, additionally, are required to have minimum levels of equity capital.
- *Asset nature*. Depending on their business model, companies may have assets considered attractive as collateral for secured loans.
- *Flexibility of financing options*. Flexibility enables a company to manage its debt maturities more efficiently. Cash budgeting exercises can help companies avoid issues when tight credit markets restrict a firm's ability to roll a particular maturity. In addition, the proper spacing of debt maturities through effective maturity management can also be critical for companies.

EXAMPLE 8   Evaluating Short-Term Choices

1. When contemplating choices for short-term financing, which of the following should a company consider?
   A.   The cost of the funds borrowed
   B.   The flexibility offered by the source
   C.   The ease with which the funds can be accessed
   D.   Any legal or regulatory constraints that might favor one source over another
   E.   All of the above

Solution:
   The correct answer is E. The cost of funds for a company is the most obvious item to consider, but it may choose to borrow at a slightly higher cost after taking all the other items into consideration.

EXAMPLE 9   Meeting Short-Term Financing Need

1. Keown Corp. has accounts payable of C$2 million with terms of 2/10, net 30. Accounts receivable also stands at C$2 million. In addition, the company has C$5 million in marketable securities. Keown has a short-term need of C$200,000 to meet payroll. Which of the following options makes the most sense for raising the C$200,000?
   A.   The company should issue long-term debt.
   B.   The company should issue common stock.
   C.   The company should delay paying accounts payable and forgo the 2% discount.
   D.   The company should sell some of its accounts receivable to a factor at a 10% discount.
   E.   The company should sell some of its marketable securities at a 0.5% brokerage cost.

Solution:
   A and B would not be appropriate for raising C$200,000 for a short-term need. These options take time to arrange, and they are more appropriate for long-term capital needs and for much larger financing amounts.
   C, D, and E are all appropriate options for meeting short-term financing needs. However, C and D are costly.
   The options for raising C$200,000 are summarized in this table:

		Liquidation Costs	
Source of Funds	Action	%	C$
C. Accounts payable (2/10, net 30)	Delay C$200,000 in payment and forgo 2% discount	2.0	4,000
D. Accounts receivable	Sell C$222,222 in value at 10% discount to raise CA$200,000	10.0	22,222
E. Marketable securities	Sell C$200,000 in value	0.5	1,000

Choosing C means forgoing a 2% discount, which on C$200,000 amounts to a cost of C$4,000. To net C$200,000 using option D, the company would have to sell C$222,222 of accounts receivable to a factor, representing a cost of C$22,222. E appears to be the best choice. Marketable securities are liquid and can be easily sold for market value, less the relatively minor brokerage cost of C$1,000.

7. SUMMARY

Here we considered key aspects of short-term financial management: the choices available to fund a company's working capital needs and effective liquidity management. Both are critical in ensuring a company's day-to-day operations and ability to remain in business.

Key points of coverage included the following:

- Internal and external sources available to finance working capital needs and considerations in their selection
- Working capital approaches, their considerations, and their impact on the funding needs of the company
- Primary and secondary sources of liquidity and factors that can enhance a company's liquidity position
- The evaluation of a company's liquidity position and comparison to peers
- The evaluation of short-term financing choices based on their characteristics and effective costs

8. PRACTICE PROBLEMS

1. Two analysts are discussing the costs of external financing sources. The first states that the company's bonds have a known interest rate but that the interest rate on accounts payable and the interest rate on equity financing are not specified. They are implicitly zero. Upon hearing this, the second analyst advocates financing the firm with greater amounts of accounts payable and common shareholders equity. Is the second analyst correct in his analysis?

    A. He is correct in his analysis of accounts payable only.

    B. He is correct in his analysis of common equity financing only.

    C. He is not correct in his analysis of either accounts payable or equity financing.

2. A company has arranged a $20 million line of credit with a bank, allowing the company the flexibility to borrow and repay any amount of funds as long as the balance does not exceed the line of credit. These arrangements are called:

    A. convertibles.

    B. factoring.

    C. revolvers.

3. The SOA Company needs to raise 75 million, in local currency, for substantial new investments next year. Specific details, all in local currency, are as follows:

- Investments of 10 million in receivables and 15 million in inventory will be made. Fixed capital investments of 50 million, including 10 million to replace depreciated equipment and 40 million of net new investments, will also be made.
- Net income is expected to be 30 million, and dividend payments will be 12 million. Depreciation charges will be 10 million.
- Short-term financing from accounts payable of 6 million is expected. The firm will use receivables as collateral for an 8 million loan. The firm will also issue a 14 million short-term note to a commercial bank.
- Any additional external financing needed can be raised from an increase in long-term bonds. If additional financing is not needed, any excess funds will be used to repurchase common shares.

What additional financing does SOA require?

    A. SOA will need to issue 19 million of bonds.

    B. SOA will need to issue 26 million of bonds.

    C. SOA can repurchase 2 million of common shares.

4. XY1 Corporation's CFO has decided to pursue a moderate approach to funding the firm's working capital. Which of the following methods would best fit that particular approach?

    A. Finance permanent and variable current assets with long-term financing.

    B. Finance permanent and variable current assets with short-term financing.

    C. Finance permanent current assets with long-term financing and variable current assets with short-term financing.

5. Kwam Solutions must raise €120 million. Kwam has two primary sources of liquidity: €60 million of marketable securities (which can be sold with minimal liquidation/brokerage costs) and €30 million of bonds (which can be sold with 3% liquidation costs). Kwam can sell some or all of either of these portfolios. Kwam has a secondary source of liquidity, which would be to sell a large piece of real estate valued at €70 million (which would incur 10% liquidation costs). If Kwam sells the real estate, it must be sold entirely. (A fractional sale is not possible.) What is the lowest cost strategy for raising the needed €120 million?

    A. Sell €60 million of the marketable securities, €30 million of the bonds, and €34.3 million of the real estate property.

    B. Sell the real estate property and €50 million of the marketable securities.

    C. Sell the real estate property and €57 million of the marketable securities.

6. A company increasing its credit terms for customers from 1/10, net 30 to 1/10, net 60 will *most likely* experience:
    A. an increase in cash on hand.
    B. a lower level of uncollectible accounts.
    C. an increase in the average collection period.

7. Paloma Villarreal has received three suggestions from her staff about how to address her firm's liquidity problems.

    Suggestion 1. Reduce the firm's inventory turnover rate.

    Suggestion 2. Reduce the average collection period on accounts receivable.

    Suggestion 3. Accelerate the payments on accounts payable by paying invoices before their due dates.

    Which suggestion should Villarreal employ to improve the firm's liquidity position?
    A. Suggestion 1
    B. Suggestion 2
    C. Suggestion 3

8. Selected liquidity ratios for three firms in the leisure products industry are given in the table below. The most recent fiscal year ratio is shown along with the average of the previous five years.

	Company H		Company J		Company S	
	Most Recent	Five-Year Average	Most Recent	Five-Year Average	Most Recent	Five-Year Average
Current ratio	5.37	2.51	3.67	3.04	3.05	2.53
Quick ratio	5.01	2.19	2.60	2.01	1.78	1.44
Cash ratio	3.66	0.97	1.96	1.28	0.96	0.67

Relative to its peers and relative to its own prior performance, which company is in the most liquid position?
A. Company H
B. Company J
C. Company S

9. An analyst is examining the cash conversion cycles and their components for three companies that she covers in the leisure products industry. She believes that changes in the investments in these working capital accounts can reveal liquidity stresses on a company.

	2021	2020	2019	2018	2017	2016
Company H						
Days of inventory on hand	68.4	70.5	60	57.8	59.8	59.8
+ Days of receivables	101.8	103.4	95.6	92.4	94.7	93.3

	2021	2020	2019	2018	2017	2016
– Days of payables outstanding	52.1	54.6	48	41.9	36.8	35.9
= Cash conversion cycle	118.1	119.3	107.6	108.3	117.7	117.2
Company J						
Days of inventory on hand	105.6	101.4	96.3	105.2	103.2	101.4
+ Days of receivables	27.7	29.4	32.9	36.3	37.8	38
– Days of payables outstanding	36.6	38.5	35.3	39.3	37.8	40.2
= Cash conversion cycle	96.7	92.3	93.9	102.2	103.2	99.2
Company S						
Days of inventory on hand	135.8	131	118.9	69.2	63.4	81.7
+ Days of receivables	49.1	42.5	54.2	36.2	29.1	38.3
– Days of payables outstanding	30.9	27.9	34.6	29.8	31.8	35.9
= Cash conversion cycle	154.0	145.6	138.5	75.6	60.7	84.1

Which company's operating cycle appears to have caused the most liquidity stress?

A. Company H's

B. Company J's

C. Company S's

10. Which of the following are considered internal sources of financing for a company's working capital management?

A. Committed and uncommitted lines of credit

B. Accounts receivable and inventory

C. Accounts payable and accruals

CHAPTER 4

CAPITAL INVESTMENTS

John D. Stowe, PhD, CFA
Ohio University (USA)

Jacques R. Gagné, FSA, CFA, CIPM
ENAP (Canada)

LEARNING OUTCOMES

The candidate should be able to:

- describe types of capital investments made by companies
- describe the capital allocation process and basic principles of capital allocation
- demonstrate the use of net present value (NPV) and internal rate of return (IRR) in allocating capital and describe the advantages and disadvantages of each method
- describe common capital allocation pitfalls
- describe expected relations among a company's investments, company value, and share price
- describe types of real options relevant to capital investment

1. INTRODUCTION

Capital investments, also referred to here as capital projects, are investments with a life of one year or longer made by corporate issuers. Issuers make capital investments to generate value for their stakeholders by returning long-term benefits and future cash flows greater than the associated funding cost of the capital invested. How companies allocate capital between competing priorities and the resulting capital investment portfolio are central to a company's success and together constitute a fundamental area for analysts to understand. Given that corporate disclosure of capital investments is typically very high level and lacking in specifics, the evaluation of a company's capital investments is often challenging for analysts.

Capital investments describe a company's future prospects better than its working capital or capital structure, which are often similar for companies, and provide insight into the quality of management's decisions and how the company is creating value for stakeholders.

While the focus of this coverage is on capital investments, it is important to note that companies also make other investments in increased working capital, information technology (IT), and/or human resources projects that might not be capitalized and therefore affect near-term operating profit, but that are made for similar longer-term benefit as capital investments.

2. TYPES OF CAPITAL INVESTMENTS

The types of capital investments made by companies vary considerably and often span the full spectrum of risk and return. Some are less risky and fairly easy to evaluate, such as the replacement of depreciated equipment, while others, such as the development of a new product or an acquisition of another company, are riskier and far more complex.

Capital investments are undertaken for two primary purposes—to maintain the existing business and to grow it—and can generally be classified into four types of projects. The first two types,

1. going concern (or maintenance) projects and
2. regulatory/compliance projects,

ensure business-as-usual continuity while the latter two investment types,

3. expansion projects and
4. other projects,

are made to expand the business in some strategic manner. Each of these is highlighted in Exhibit 1 with a brief explanation and examples.

EXHIBIT 1: Types of Capital Projects

Business Maintenance	Business Growth
1. Going concern	**3. Expansion**
Projects necessary to continue current operations and maintain existing size of the business or to improve business efficiencies	Projects that expand business size and typically involve greater degrees of risk and uncertainty than going concern projects
Example:	**Example:**
machine replacement, infrastructure improvement	new product or service development, merger, acquisition
2. Regulatory/Compliance	**4. Other**
Projects typically required by a third party, such as the government regulatory body, to meet specified safety and compliance standards	Projects, which should include high-risk investments and new growth initiatives, that are outside the company's conventional business lines
Example:	**Example:**
factory pollution control installation, performance bond posting to guarantee satisfactory project completion	exploration investment into a new innovation, business model, or idea

2.1. Business Maintenance

2.1.1. Going Concern Projects

Going concern projects are those investments needed to continue the company's current operations and maintain the existing size of the business. The most common going concern projects are replacements of assets that reach the end of their useful life and spending to maintain IT hardware and software. For example, a company might elect to replace older infrastructure in its production facilities (light fixtures, heating and cooling units, etc.) with more modern and efficient alternatives. Going concern projects do not typically yield incremental revenue but might benefit the company through improved efficiencies and cost savings over time.

Going concern projects are fairly easy for management to evaluate because their costs are typically small relative to the production or business interruption costs that could result from not making the investment. In addition, the analyses of going concern projects often benefit from having readily available data from existing business operations to use in the decision-making process. The time length for these projects can vary, with some projects expected to span several years.

To fund these projects, managers will often try to match the financing with the life-span of the asset. For example, a company might issue a 20-year bond to finance replacement equipment with an expected useful life of 20 years. In matching the cash flows and maturity structures of their assets and liabilities, companies reduce risk. A company financing long-term assets with short-term obligations faces rollover risk, which could threaten profitability if short-term financing costs go up over the financing period.

Similarly, a company financing short-term assets with long-term financing beyond the term needed faces the risk that the company overpays in financing costs. Asset liability misalignment increases the risk of default and cost of capital for companies as capital suppliers demand higher returns in compensation.

Corporate issuers typically do not disclose the amount of capital spending associated with going concern projects, or any other type of capital investment, on financial statements or elsewhere. A common, but imperfect, estimate for going concern capital spending used by analysts is the amount of depreciation and amortization expense reported on the income statement. The accuracy of this estimate depends on how closely the accounting useful life of assets approximates the actual useful life and whether the historical cost of an asset approximates its replacement cost; both assumptions are likely to be more accurate for shorter-lived assets.

2.1.2. Regulatory/Compliance Projects

Unlike going concern and expansion projects, for which management has discretion in deciding whether or not to invest, regulatory and compliance projects are required by third parties, such as government regulatory bodies, to meet safety and regulatory compliance standards. These projects might be driven by public or private mandates, such as a government agency's newly enacted requirement to install pollution control technologies, the need to secure a surety performance bond to guarantee satisfactory completion of a project, or the requirement of financial institutions to meet capital adequacy requirements and perform stress tests to assess their ability to withstand economic shocks.

Regulatory/compliance projects might not generate revenue and might not otherwise be undertaken by a company but are required to continue operations. However, there can be a potential benefit to industry incumbents, as regulatory/compliance costs can serve as barriers to industry entry, thereby increasing or protecting incumbents' profitability. Additionally, in some instances when a company is able to work directly with regulators to develop the prescribed standards, those standards can be tailored to best suit the company's compliance capabilities, thereby reducing the compliance burden.

When a company is faced with having to invest in a new regulatory/compliance project—perhaps due to a new regulatory requirement—management will have to decide whether the economics of the underlying business are still favorable after consideration of the additional costs associated with the regulatory/compliance project. In many cases, the company will accept the required investment and continue to operate, passing the added cost on to consumers, in full or in part, in the form of higher prices. Occasionally, however, the cost of such projects is sufficiently high that the company would be better off ceasing to operate altogether or shutting down any part of the business that is related to the new regulatory/compliance project. "Stranded assets," or assets at risk of no longer being economically feasible because of changes in regulation (or investor sentiment), such as carbon-intensive assets, are an example of this; their "costs" of production, inclusive of greenhouse emissions, are seen as being higher than their realizable value.

2.2. Business Growth

2.2.1. Expansion Projects

An important value driver for companies is growth in profits, which can be achieved by companies expanding the scale of existing activities or extending their reach into new product or service categories and markets. Expansion projects are those that increase business size, usually by investing in the development of new products or services and/or acquiring other companies.

Expansion projects typically involve greater uncertainty, time, and amounts of capital than going concern projects. Some industries, such as pharmaceuticals and oil and gas, spend heavily on expansion projects. Companies in these two industries often invest over 10% of annual revenues per year in pursuit of new medications and energy reserves, respectively. Similarly, technology companies typically invest heavily in expansion projects to accelerate product development cycles, maintain competitiveness, and stay ahead of rivals.

When internal opportunities for expansion appear to be limited, or when a rapid integration of new capabilities is preferred to building from within the company, a common strategic response by management is to look to acquisitions. Acquisitions can take a variety of forms, with special tax, financial accounting, and market regulation considerations. Two serious risks, however, are the difficulty in integrating the business operations of the acquirer and the target and the risk of overpaying. Often, stakeholders are better off if management returns capital through dividends and share repurchases rather than expanding through acquisitions.

Analysts should carefully examine the issuer's level and trend of expansion capital investment overall, as well as by segment or line of business if it is disclosed, to analyze growth prospects, management's priorities, and the rates of return on the investment relative to alternatives. The level and trend of expansion capital spending can be estimated by subtracting non-expansion capital investment from total capital spending, often estimated using depreciation and amortization expense.

2.2.2. Other Projects

Sometimes, a company's management will decide to invest in a unique activity outside, or only minimally related to, the company's strategy. This happens more often with firms that are privately held or under the control of a founding owner or significant shareholder. Whether these projects are seen as special situations offering atypical growth or investment opportunities or innovation opportunities for the company's business or business model, these projects are likely to be at the riskier end of capital investments. In some cases, these might be projects driven by a founding owner or controlling shareholder who feels strongly about the investment. Such projects might be approved without going through the customary analysis normally undertaken for the other types of capital investments.

These other projects often have a venture capital element to them, such as investing some capital to explore a new technology or a business idea/model for sources of new business growth. The probable outcome might be a complete loss of investment, but the attraction is that the project could be highly profitable if successful.

EXAMPLE 1   Types of Capital Investment

Paladote Company is a mid-sized, financially sound, and profitable supplier of food service packaging, based in Canada. Paladote produces its products in a variety of new and established facilities throughout the world and distributes these to a globally diverse customer base. At Paladote's annual Investor and Analyst Day, management describes four capital investment priorities for the next one to three years:

1. Investment to develop new customized packaging products for new customers in India.
2. Funding of an extensive study on edible food packaging. During the presentation, the investment is positioned as an initiative that will reshape the industry. Similar efforts by several other companies have been unsuccessful to date.
3. Investment to modify production processes in its Latin American production plant in response to a recent regional ban on the use of certain food contact substances that becomes effective next year.
4. Investments in Paladote's older production facilities to lower production costs.

1. Which project would *most likely* be classified as an "other" project?

Solution:

Project 2. The funding of an extensive study on edible food packaging appears to be a project that is likely to be classified as an "other" project. While the project is unlikely to be successful, the company's management believes that making the investment could potentially reshape the food packaging industry.

2. Which project would *most likely* be classified as a going concern project?

Solution:

Project 4. Investments in Paladote's older production facilities to lower production costs would be classified as a going concern project, which are projects generally focused on asset replacement, either to replace assets at the end of their useful lives or to replace older, inefficient assets with newer and more efficient assets.

3. Which project would *most likely* be classified as an expansion project?

Solution:

Project 1. An investment to develop new customized packaging products for new customers in India would be classified as an expansion project, which are those projects that increase business size, usually by investing in the development of new products or services and/or by the acquisition of other companies.

4. Which project would *most likely* be classified as a regulatory/compliance project?

Solution:

Project 3. An investment to modify production processes in Paladote's Latin American production plant in response to a recent regional ban on the use of certain food contact substances would be classified as a regulatory/compliance project. The project would be required to comply with the new ban that goes into effect next year.

3. THE CAPITAL ALLOCATION PROCESS

Capital allocation is the process used by an issuer's management to make capital investment decisions. Given that corporations exist to deliver competitive risk-adjusted returns for stakeholders, capital allocation is the most important job of management and is typically done by those at the executive and board level. In general, the process undertaken by a corporate issuer is substantially the same as the process undertaken by portfolio managers and analysts of an investment manager; both entities are allocating stakeholder capital in pursuit of competitive risk-adjusted returns. However, most corporate managers do not have a background in capital allocation; it is an uncommon skill that analysts must actively identify in corporate issuers' management.

As Warren Buffett, CEO of Berkshire Hathaway, said: "[CEOs] get to the top of a corporation in various ways. [They] may come through sales or engineering. And all of a sudden, [they're] in a different job…. because now [they're] involved in allocating capital. That's something many CEOs haven't done, and yet they're expected to do it and some of them think they can do it that aren't really very good at it."

The steps that management should take in the capital allocation process are shown in Exhibit 2.

EXHIBIT 2: Steps in the Capital Allocation Process

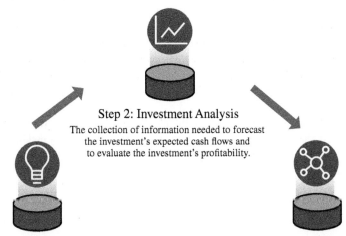

Step 2: Investment Analysis
The collection of information needed to forecast the investment's expected cash flows and to evaluate the investment's profitability.

Step 1: Idea Generation
The generation of investment ideas can originate from anywhere within the organization or from outside the company. Having good investment ideas for management consideration is the most important step in the capital allocation process.

Step 3: Capital Allocation Planning
The organization of the profitable proposals that together best fit the company's strategy. Financial and real resource constraints mean the scheduling and prioritizing of capital investments are key considerations.

Step 4: Monitoring and Post-Audit
The comparison of actual results to planned or predicted results to assess execution to date and plan for the future.

Following the generation of investment ideas, management should forecast the amount, timing, duration, and volatility of an investment's expected cash flows in addition to the probability of the cash flows' occurrence. Capital allocation planning then involves the selection and prioritization of profitable investment opportunities that, when considered together, are most value enhancing on a risk-adjusted return basis. Opportunities that fail to generate returns sufficient to cover their associated cost of funding should not be pursued. Additionally, some projects that look attractive in isolation might be undesirable strategically. Rather than investing in unprofitable or strategically unwise projects, management is better off returning capital to shareholders as dividends or share repurchases.

Post-auditing capital projects and monitoring an investment's realized revenues, expenses, and cash flows against expectations are important for several reasons. First, these steps help review assumptions that underlie the capital allocation process. Systematic errors, such as overly optimistic forecasts, become apparent. Second, they might help improve business operations. If sales or costs are out of line, the monitoring and post-auditing processes will focus management's attention on bringing performance closer to expectations, if at all possible. Finally, monitoring and post-auditing recent capital investments could produce concrete ideas for future investments. Managers should invest more heavily in profitable areas and scale down or dispose of assets in areas that are disappointing or are worth more in the hands of others. In practice, the post-auditing and monitoring of projects is difficult given the challenges in the accurate measurement of expected and realized benefits, costs, and revenues, data availability (which in some cases could take years), organizational politics, and so on.

Like other business activities, the capital allocation activity is a cost–benefit exercise for the company. At the margin, the benefits from the improved decision making should exceed the costs of the capital allocation efforts. The primary principles underlying capital allocation are shown in Exhibit 3.

EXHIBIT 3: Capital Allocation Principles

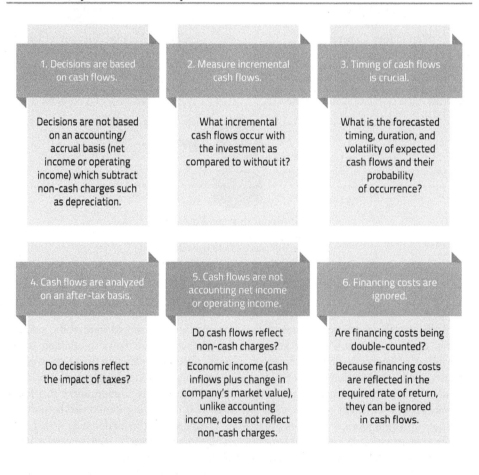

In ignoring financing costs, we referred to the rate used in discounting the cash flows as the "required rate of return." The required rate of return is the discount rate that the issuer's suppliers of capital require given the riskiness of the project. This discount rate is frequently called the "opportunity cost of funds" or the "**cost of capital**." A company's weighted average cost of capital (WACC) is its cost of capital at the enterprise level, based on its average-risk investment and capital sources used to finance its assets.

If the company can invest elsewhere and earn a return of *r*, or if the company can repay its sources of capital and save a cost of *r*, then *r* is the company's opportunity cost of funds. If the company cannot earn more than its opportunity cost of funds on an investment, it should not undertake that investment. Regardless of what it is called, an economically sound discount rate is essential for making capital allocation decisions.

EXAMPLE 2   Required Rate of Return for Capital Investments

At its Capital Markets Day, the management of Ørsted, a listed renewable energy company headquartered in Denmark, shared the following information concerning the company's required rate of return on capital investments.

Ørsted uses a WACC plus a 150–300 basis point spread as the required rate of return for each project. The WACC reflects the required rate of return of Ørsted's capital providers, while the 150–300 basis point spread, which varies by project, reflects risks associated with a specific project, such as technology (solar versus wind, hydrogen, etc.), its counterparties, and the country in which the project is located.

The achievement of rates of return at or above the WACC plus the 150–300 basis point spread on investments depends on the achievement of after-tax project cash flows at or above the estimate used at the time of the project bid.

Although the principles of capital allocation are simple, they are easily confused in practice, leading to poor decisions made by companies. The following are important capital allocation principles.

- A **sunk cost** is one that has already been incurred. One cannot change a sunk cost. Management's decisions should be based on current and future cash flows and should not be affected by prior, or sunk, costs.
- An **incremental cash flow** is the cash flow that is realized because of an investment decision: the cash flow *with* a decision minus the cash flow *without* that decision. Only incremental cash flows are relevant for capital allocation.
- An **externality** is the effect of an investment on things other than the investment itself. Frequently, an investment affects the cash flows of other parts of the company, and these externalities can be positive or negative. A positive externality occurring within the company would be expected synergies with existing projects or business activities that result from making the investment. The production and sale of a new complementary product or service might increase demand or lower costs for an existing product or service the company offers. **Cannibalization** is an example of a negative externality occurring within the company. Cannibalization occurs when an investment takes customers and sales away from another part of the company. If possible, companies should consider

externalities in the investment decision. Often the adjustments are subjective, such as the anticipated competitor response to a new product feature or price change, because the company cannot derive a precise estimate. Sometimes externalities occur outside the company that require evaluation of economic, social, or environmental considerations. An investment might benefit (or harm) other companies or society at large, yet the company is not compensated for these benefits (or charged for the costs).

- **Conventional cash flow pattern** versus **nonconventional cash flow pattern**: A conventional cash flow pattern is one with an initial outflow followed by a series of inflows. In a nonconventional cash flow pattern, the initial outflow is not followed by inflows only, but the cash flows can flip from being positive (inflows) to negative (outflows) again or possibly change signs several times. An investment that involved outlays (negative cash flows) for the first couple of years that were followed by positive cash flows would be considered to have a conventional pattern. If cash flows change signs once, the pattern is conventional. If cash flows change signs two or more times, the pattern is nonconventional. Exhibit 4 shows a conventional cash flow pattern followed by an unconventional cash flow pattern.

EXHIBIT 4: Cash Flow Patterns

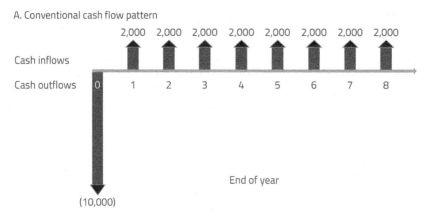

A. Conventional cash flow pattern

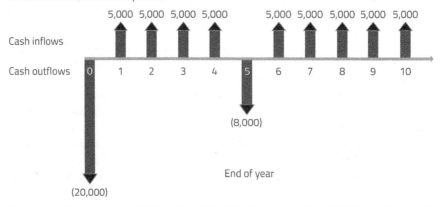

B. Unconventional cash flow pattern

For example, a crude oil refining facility might require an initial investment outlay that produces positive cash flows for several years followed by additional outlays to refurbish the facilities needed to produce additional positive cash flows. Or an investment in a nuclear power facility that generates electricity for a number of years might be followed by another cash outlay to decommission the power plant.

In assessing potential investment opportunities, several types of project interactions make the incremental cash flow analysis challenging for companies. The following are some of these interactions:

- **Independent projects** versus **mutually exclusive projects**: Independent projects are capital investments whose cash flows are independent of each other. Mutually exclusive projects compete directly with each other. For example, if Projects A and B are mutually exclusive, the company can choose to invest in A or B but cannot choose both. Sometimes management might be presented with a group of several mutually exclusive projects and can choose only one project from the group.

  While some investments require relatively little management effort ("order the new plane"), others are extremely management intensive, require other resources that are very scarce (e.g., skilled IT personnel), or create a significant level of organization disruption that limits the company's ability to take on additional projects. Given that all management teams have limits on their execution capability, to help resolve these challenges, management will create and compare "menus" of projects ("we can do A, C, and D or C, E, and F").

- **Project sequencing**: Many capital projects are sequenced over time, so that investing in a project creates the option to invest in future projects. For example, the company might invest in a project today and one year later invest in a second project if the financial results of the first project or new economic conditions are favorable. If the results of the first project or new economic conditions are not favorable, the company would not invest in the second project. Another example might be a strategically important investment, such as investment in a new capability, system, or platform, that enables follow-on investments. While these projects can be difficult to evaluate because their benefits could be hard to predict, they can be extremely valuable for companies.
- Management principles such as "fail fast," "minimum viable product," and prototyping are concepts associated with project sequencing. These are intended to take a potentially large project and break it up into smaller successive "projects" that enable management to make go/no-go decisions in a faster, more agile timeframe based on intelligence gleaned in early stages.

4. INVESTMENT DECISION CRITERIA

Management uses several criteria to make capital investment decisions. The two most comprehensive measures to assess whether an investment is profitable or unprofitable are the **net present value** and **internal rate of return**. An analyst should understand the economic logic behind each of these investment decision criteria, as well as their strengths and limitations in practice.

4.1. Net Present Value

For a capital investment with one investment outlay, made initially, the net present value (NPV) is the present value of the future after-tax cash flows minus the investment outlay, or

$$NPV = \sum_{t=1}^{n} \frac{CF_t}{(1+r)^t} - \text{Outlay},$$ (1)

where

CF_t = After-tax cash flow at time t
r = Required rate of return for the investment
Outlay = Investment cash flow at time zero

To illustrate the NPV criterion, we will consider a simple example.

EXAMPLE 3   Gerhardt Corporation NPV

1. Assume that Gerhardt Corporation is considering a capital investment of EUR50 million that will return after-tax cash flows of EUR16 million per year for the next four years, plus another EUR20 million in Year 5.

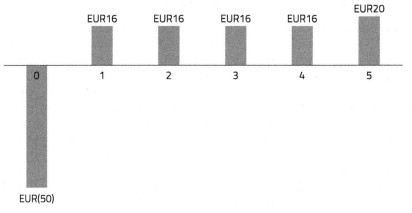

Gerhardt corporation after-tax cash flows

If the company's required rate of return is 10%, what is the associated NPV of this investment?

Solution:

The NPV would be

$$NPV = \frac{16}{1.10^1} + \frac{16}{1.10^2} + \frac{16}{1.10^3} + \frac{16}{1.10^4} + \frac{20}{1.10^5} - 50.$$

$$NPV = 14.545 + 13.223 + 12.021 + 10.928 + 12.418 - 50.$$

$$NPV = 63.135 - 50 = €13.135 \text{ million.}$$

> The investment has a total value, or present value of future cash flows, of EUR63.135 million. Because this investment can be acquired at a cost of EUR50 million, the company is giving up EUR50 million of its wealth in exchange for an investment worth EUR63.135 million. The investment increases the wealth of the company by a net amount of EUR13.135 million.

Because the NPV is the amount by which the company's wealth increases as a result of the investment, the decision rule for the NPV is as follows:

Invest if	NPV > 0.
Do not invest if	NPV < 0.

Positive-NPV investments are wealth increasing for the company and its shareholders, whereas negative-NPV investments are wealth decreasing for the company and its shareholders. In the rare case that NPV turns out to be zero, the project could be accepted because it meets the required rate of return. Keep in mind, however, that NPV analysis relies on estimated future cash flows. A zero-NPV project leaves no room for error.

Many investments have unconventional cash flow patterns in which outflows might occur not only at time zero but also at future dates. NPV is still calculated as the present value of all future cash inflows and outflows:

$$\text{NPV} = \text{CF}_0 + \frac{\text{CF}_1}{(1+r)^1} + \frac{\text{CF}_2}{(1+r)^2} + \ldots + \frac{\text{CF}_n}{(1+r)^n}, \text{ or}$$
$$\text{NPV} = \sum_{t=0}^{n} \frac{\text{CF}_t}{(1+r)^t}. \tag{2}$$

In Equation 2, the investment outlay, CF_0, is simply a negative cash flow. Future cash flows can also be negative.

Microsoft Excel functions can be used to quickly solve for the NPV, regardless of the cash flow pattern. Two functions are available: NPV and XNPV.

NPV takes the form of =NPV(rate, values), where "rate" is the discount rate and "values" are the cash flows. By default, the NPV function assigns the first cash flow t=1, so a t=0 cash flow must be entered outside the NPV function and assumes equal periods between cash flows.

The XNPV function is more flexible and takes the form of =XNPV(rate, values, dates), where "rate" is the discount rate, "values" are the cash flows, and "dates" are the dates of each of the cash flows, which must be in the form of dates (not periods like 0, 1, 2, etc.).

Both NPV and XNPV functions assume a constant discount rate; for varying discount rates, the analyst must enter the discounting algebra manually. The spreadsheet shows the operation of the NPV and XNPV functions for the Gerhardt example.

NPV function

	t	0	1	2	3	4	5
	EUR Cash flow	€(50)	€16	€16	€16	€16	€20
NPV	€13.14						

XNPV function

	assumed date of CF	01/01/00	31/12/00	31/12/01	31/12/02	30/12/03	30/12/04
	EUR cash flow	€(50)	€16	€16	€16	€16	€20
XNPV	€13.14						

4.2. Internal Rate of Return

The internal rate of return (IRR) is one of the most frequently used concepts in capital allocation and security analysis. For a capital investment with a conventional cash flow pattern, the IRR is the discount rate that makes the present value of the future after-tax cash flows equal to the investment outlay. Expressed in equation form, the IRR solves the following equation:

$$\sum_{t=1}^{n} \frac{CF_t}{(1+IRR)^t} = \text{Outlay},$$

where IRR is the internal rate of return. The left-hand side of this equation is the present value of the capital investment's future cash flows, which, discounted at the IRR, equals the investment outlay. This equation will also be seen rearranged as

$$\sum_{t=1}^{n} \frac{CF_t}{(1+IRR)^t} - \text{Outlay} = 0. \tag{3}$$

In this form, Equation 3 looks like the NPV equation, Equation 1, except that the discount rate is the IRR instead of r (the required rate of return). Discounted at the IRR, the NPV is equal to zero.

It is also common to define the IRR as the discount rate that makes the present values of all cash flows sum to zero:

$$\sum_{t=0}^{n} \frac{CF_t}{(1+IRR)^t} = 0. \tag{4}$$

$$0 = \text{Outlay}_0 + \sum_{t=1}^{n} \frac{CF_t}{(1+IRR)^t} = CF_0 + \sum_{t=1}^{n} \frac{CF_t}{(1+IRR)^t} = \sum_{t=0}^{n} \frac{CF_t}{(1+IRR)^t} \tag{new 3}$$

Equation 4 is a more general version of Equation 3.

In the Gerhardt Corporation example, we want to find a discount rate that makes the total present value of all cash flows, the NPV, equal zero.

In equation form, the IRR is the discount rate that solves the following equation:

$$-50 + \frac{16}{(1+\text{IRR})^1} + \frac{16}{(1+\text{IRR})^2} + \frac{16}{(1+\text{IRR})^3} + \frac{16}{(1+\text{IRR})^4} + \frac{20}{(1+\text{IRR})^5} = 0.$$

Algebraically, this equation would be difficult to solve. Without the use of a financial calculator or functions, we would have to resort to trial and error, systematically choosing various discount rates until we find one, the IRR that satisfies the equation.

Fortunately, software such as Microsoft Excel can derive the IRR quickly using the IRR function, which takes the form of =IRR(values, guess), where "values" are the cash flows and "guess" is an optional user-specified guess that defaults to 10%. Importantly, the Microsoft Excel IRR function assumes that cash flows are received, or paid, at the end of each period and that each period is evenly spaced.

The XIRR function, which takes the form of =XIRR(values, dates, guess) grants flexibility on the periods, with the "dates" arguments being a specification of the date of each cash flow. The following spreadsheet shows the IRR of the Gerhardt examples using both the IRR and XIRR functions, as well as the IRR using the XIRR function if the date of each cash inflow is moved forward by six months.

IRR function							
	t	0	1	2	3	4	5
	EUR cash flow	€(50)	€16	€16	€16	€16	€20
IRR	19.52%						

XIRR function							
	Assumed date of cash flow	01/01/00	12/31/00	12/31/01	12/31/02	12/31/03	12/31/04
	EUR cash flow	€(50)	€16	€16	€16	€16	€20
XIRR	19.52%						
		01/01/00	30/06/00	30/06/01	30/06/02	30/06/03	30/06/04
XIRR	24.55%	€(50)	€16	€16	€16	€16	€20

The decision rule for the IRR is to invest if the IRR exceeds the required rate of return for a capital investment:

Invest if	IRR > r.
Do not invest if	IRR < r.

The required rate of return is often called the **hurdle rate**, the rate that a project's IRR must exceed for the project to be accepted by the company. In the unlikely event that the IRR is equal to r, the project is theoretically acceptable because it meets the required return. In fact,

NPV equals zero when IRR equals *r*. In the Gerhardt example, because the IRR of 19.52% exceeds the project's required rate of return of 10%, Gerhardt should invest.

NPV and IRR criteria will usually indicate the same investment decision for a given capital investment. In the case of mutually exclusive investment projects, a company could, on occasion, face the following situation: Project A might have a larger NPV than Project B, but Project B has a higher IRR than Project A. Because the company can invest in only one project, which should it be—Project A or Project B?

The correct choice is Project A, the one with the higher NPV. To understand why, consider this simple example. Suppose you could choose just one of two investments. The first allows you to double your initial outlay of USD100 in just one year. The second requires an investment of USD100,000, which will grow by 20% in a year. Which should you choose? The first investment gives you a profit of USD100. The second gives you a USD20,000 profit. Assuming you can access the required funds, the second choice is preferred. Even though it offers a smaller percentage return, it increases your wealth by much more.

When the choice is between two mutually exclusive projects and the NPV and IRR rank the two projects differently, the NPV criterion is strongly preferred. There are good reasons for this preference. The NPV shows the amount of gain, or wealth increase in company value, as a currency amount. The NPV assumes reinvestment of cash flows at the required rate of return, while the IRR assumes reinvestment at the IRR. In using the opportunity cost of funds, the reinvestment assumption of the NPV is the more economically realistic measure. Mathematically, whenever you discount a cash flow at a particular discount rate, you are implicitly assuming that you can reinvest a cash flow at that same discount rate. It is more realistic to assume reinvestment at a lower rate. The IRR does give a rate of return, but the IRR could be for a small investment size or for only a short period of time. As a practical matter, once a corporation has the data to calculate the NPV, it is fairly trivial to then calculate the IRR and other capital allocation criteria. However, the most appropriate and theoretically sound criterion is the NPV.

Another issue is that when the cash flows are nonconventional (i.e., they change sign more than once), there are multiple IRRs. We can illustrate this problem with the following nonconventional cash flow pattern:

Time	0	1	2
Cash flow	−1,000	5,000	−6,000

The IRR for these cash flows satisfies this equation:

$$-1,000 + \frac{5,000}{(1+\text{IRR})^1} + \frac{-6,000}{(1+\text{IRR})^2} = 0.$$

It turns out that two values of IRR satisfy the equation: IRR = 1 = 100% and IRR = 2 = 200%. As a result, the IRR is not useful for nonconventional cash flow projects.

This brings up the following question: If NPV is always preferred over IRR for selecting projects, why do companies even bother with IRR? The answer is that many people find a rate of return easy to understand. If they know that the required return is 10%, they can easily understand that a project returning more than 10% is desirable. If they are simply told the NPV amount, they might not find it as meaningful. In practice, most companies use both metrics. They typically use NPV to make the investment decisions, but they also report the IRR to help their audience understand.

5. COMMON CAPITAL ALLOCATION PITFALLS

Although the principles of capital allocation might be easy to understand, applying the principles to real-world investment opportunities can be challenging for companies. Some of the common capital allocation pitfalls, or mistakes, that companies make are listed here.

- **Inertia**. In a study of more than 1,600 US listed companies, McKinsey research found a 0.92 correlation between capital investment in a business segment or unit from one year to the next. This is the result of management anchoring their capital investment budgets to prior year amounts.

  Analysts can identify the presence of inertia by examining the level of capital investment in total, by segment, or by business line, if disclosed, and comparing it to the prior year level and the return on investment. If capital investment each year is static or increasing despite falling returns on investment, the analyst should question the issuer's justification for its capital investment and whether management should be considering alternative uses.

- **Source of capital bias**. The primary source of capital for investments by corporate issuers is cash flows from operations. Many management teams behave as though this internally generated capital is "free" but scarce and allocate it according to a budget that is heavily anchored to prior period amounts. Externally raised capital, from debt or equity issuance, however, is treated differently: it is used less often, typically for larger investments such as acquisitions, and is treated as "expensive."

  Instead, management teams should view all capital as having an opportunity cost, regardless of source, and use the capital allocation process for all capital investments.

  This pitfall might be identified by analysts in examining the issuer's capital structure and its capital return history in addition to inquiring about the capital allocation process. If the issuer has significantly lower leverage than peers, a high cash balance, and stated return hurdles for acquisitions but not for internal investments, then management might potentially be affected by this bias.

- **Failing to consider investment alternatives or alternative states.** While generating good investment ideas is the most basic step in the capital allocation process, many good alternatives are never even considered at some companies. Many companies also fail to consider differing states of the world, which can and should be incorporated through breakeven, scenario, and simulation analyses. This pitfall could be in effect if an issuer has had limited capital investment activity, such as not making divestitures or acquisitions, or not having a failed investment; while failure is obviously undesirable, the lack of having any failed investments over time could indicate a management team that is not taking enough risk.

- **Pushing "pet" projects.** Often, **pet projects** are selected at companies without undergoing normal capital allocation analysis. Or the pet project receives the analysis, but overly optimistic projections are used to inflate the investment's profitability. As Warren Buffett noted in the 1989 Berkshire Hathaway Shareholder Letter, "Any business craving of the leader, however foolish, will be quickly supported by detailed rate-of-return and strategic studies."

  Observing pet projects, or management's penchant for them, is difficult to do quantitatively because financial statements are at a high level of aggregation and the projects might not meet the threshold of materiality. Instead, analysts should look to the corporate governance structure for warning signs that increase the chances of misallocation of capital: controlled companies or significant ownership concentration by a single individual or group, weak oversight by the board of directors, and executive compensation that is not aligned with stakeholders' interests.

- **Basing investment decisions on EPS, net income, or ROE.** Companies sometimes have incentives to increase earnings per share, net income, or return on equity and to do so in the short run. Many capital investments, even those with high NPVs, do not increase these accounting numbers in the short run and often reduce them, as opposed to reducing costs or repurchasing shares, which can be done quickly and can positively affect those measures. Paying too much attention to short-run accounting numbers can result in a company choosing investments that are not in the long-run economic interests of its shareholders. Analysts can observe this behavior first by examining the direct financial incentives of management: the structure and composition of their compensation. Second, analysts can compare the level of capital spending to historical and peer levels to judge whether management has prioritized shorter-term, accounting-based measures. However, a decline in capital investment can be a sign of a lack of investment opportunities, in which case allocating capital to alternative uses is wise.

- **Internal forecasting errors.** In addition, companies might make errors in their internal forecasts, which could be difficult, if not impossible, for external analysts to identify. However, if significant enough, the incorrect or flawed analysis will ultimately manifest itself in failed, or underperforming, investment outcomes. These errors include incorrect cost or discount rate inputs. For example, overhead costs such as management time, IT support, and financial systems can be challenging to estimate. The incorrect treatment of sunk costs, missed real opportunity costs, and the use of the company's overall cost of capital, **cost of debt**, or **cost of equity**, rather than the investment's required rate of return, are also common mistakes by companies. Finally, companies often fail to incorporate market responses into the analysis of a planned investment.

6. CORPORATE USE OF CAPITAL ALLOCATION

Analysts should understand the basic logic of the various capital allocation criteria as well as the practicalities involved in their use at corporations. The usefulness of any analytical tool always depends on the specific application.

If a company can make an investment that earns more than its opportunity cost of funds, then the investment is creating value for stakeholders and should be undertaken. Conversely, if a potential investment is expected to earn less than the company's opportunity cost of funds, or an existing investment is already underperforming the hurdle rate, the investment decreases stakeholder value, and alternative uses should be considered.

The **return on invested capital** (ROIC) is a measure of the profitability of a company or business segment relative to the amount of capital invested by the equity- and debtholders. ROIC reflects how effectively a company's management is able to convert capital into after-tax operating profits. The ratio is calculated by dividing the after-tax operating profit by the average book value of invested capital: common equity, preferred equity, and debt, or

$$ROIC = After\text{-}Tax\ Operating\ Profit/Average\ Book\ Value\ of\ Invested\ Capital$$

The numerator does not expense the cost of financing (e.g., interest expense) because it represents a source of return for providers of debt capital, and the denominator includes sources of capital from all providers. Example 4 illustrates an example where ROIC might provide important insights into a company's situation.

EXAMPLE 4   Valeant ROIC

In September 2010, Valeant Pharmaceuticals International, Inc., a TSX and NYSE listed pharmaceutical company, embarked on an acquisitions-focused growth strategy. This strategy was quite different from the R&D-driven strategies used by most pharmaceutical companies at the time. Valeant would selectively acquire companies with approved products and pursue opportunities to increase revenues, by launching in new geographies, and profitability, by reducing overhead and R&D expenses. Valeant completed dozens of acquisitions between 2010 and 2015, using debt to finance a large portion of its purchases.

From September 2010 to mid-2015, Valeant's share price increased from CAD26 per share to over CAD330 per share, as the company increased revenues and adjusted net income rapidly, largely as a result of its acquisitions. However, looking at the company's ROIC told a different story. Calculating the measure from reported (US GAAP) figures showed that the company's ROIC was lackluster, never rising above 8%. Even when using the company's adjusted (non GAAP) earnings figures, ROIC was in the low double-digit percentages. In most years, Valeant's free cash flow significantly lagged adjusted earnings significantly, casting doubt as to the relevance of its adjusted earnings figures. These measures are shown in the following chart.

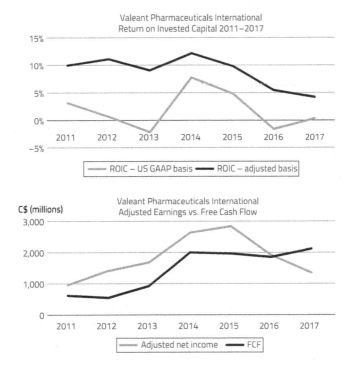

In 2015, problems began to surface for Valeant when an activist investor published a report detailing significant problems with Valeant's business model and pointing to price increases as being responsible for a significant percentage of the company's growth. The report also alleged accounting misstatements of transactions with one of Valeant's subsidiaries.

In response to these damaging allegations, the company restated its financial statements, began a restructure of its business model, and made numerous divestments to ensure it would not default on its debt. Valeant's share price reaction was swift and severe; by year-end 2016, Valeant shares had fallen to CAD18 per share, down 95% from 18 months earlier.

While some of the problems with Valeant would not be visible in its ROIC, an important takeaway for analysts is to closely scrutinize issuer claims of value creation associated with acquisition activity when ROIC is low and falling. Secondly, it is important to prioritize cash flow measures such as free cash flow over accounting measures, especially adjusted accounting measures, in evaluating capital investments.

The ROIC measure is often compared with the associated company cost of capital (COC), the required return used in the NPV calculation, and the company's associated cost of funds. If the ROIC measure is higher than the COC, the company is generating a higher return for investors compared with the required return, thereby increasing the firm's value for shareholders. The inverse is true if the COC is higher than the ROIC.

If management has undertaken investments with a positive NPV and/or an IRR greater than its COC, the ROIC for the issuer overall will generally exceed the COC as well, and value will be created for shareholders.

Example 5 illustrates this scenario for a company making a new investment.

EXAMPLE 5   NPVs and Stock Prices

1. Paladote is investing CAD600 million in distribution facilities. The present value of the future after-tax cash flows is estimated to be CAD850 million. Paladote has 200 million outstanding shares with a current market price of CAD32.00 per share. This investment is new information, and it is independent of other expectations about the company. What should be the investment's effect on the value of the company and the stock price?

Solution:

The NPV of the investment is CAD850 million – CAD600 million = CAD250 million. The total market value of the company prior to the investment is CAD32.00 × 200 million shares = CAD6,400 million. The value of the company should increase by CAD250 million, to CAD6,650 million. The price per share should increase by the NPV per share, or CAD250 million/200 million shares = CAD1.25 per share. The share price should increase from CAD32.00 to CAD33.25.

The effect of a capital investment's positive or negative NPV on share price is more complicated than in Example 3, in which the value of the stock increased by the investment's NPV. The value of a company is the value of its existing investments plus the NPVs of all its future investments, accounting for any externalities. If an analyst learns of an investment, the impact of that investment on the company's stock price will depend on whether the investment's profitability is more or less than expected.

For example, an analyst could learn of a positive-NPV project, but if the project's profitability is less than expected, the company's stock price might drop because of this news. Alternatively, news of a particular capital project might be considered a signal about other capital investments under way or in the future. An investment that by itself might add EUR0.25, for example, to the value of the stock might signal the existence of other profitable projects. News of this investment might increase the stock price by far more than EUR0.25.

Inflation affects a company's capital allocation analysis in several ways. The first is whether the investment analysis is done in "nominal" terms or in "real" terms. Nominal cash flows include the effects of inflation, whereas real cash flows are adjusted downward to remove the effects of inflation. Companies might choose to do the analysis in either nominal or real terms, and sound decisions can be made either way, but irrespective of choice, the cash flows and discount rate used by the company should be consistent. That is, nominal cash flows should be discounted at a nominal discount rate, and real cash flows should be discounted at a real rate.

Inflation reduces the value of depreciation tax savings to the company (unless the tax system adjusts depreciation for inflation), effectively increasing its real taxes. The effect of expected inflation is captured in the discounted cash flow (DCF) analysis. If inflation is higher than expected, the profitability of the investment is correspondingly lower than expected. Inflation essentially shifts wealth from the taxpayer (i.e., company) to the government. Conversely, lower-than-expected inflation reduces real taxes for the company (the depreciation tax shelters are more valuable than expected) and results in higher-than-expected profitability of the investment and a corresponding wealth increase for the company.

Finally, inflation does not affect all revenues and costs uniformly. The company's after-tax cash flows will be better or worse than expected depending on how particular sales outputs or cost inputs are affected.

7. REAL OPTIONS

Real options are options that allow companies to make decisions in the future that alter the value of capital investment decisions made today. Instead of making all capital investment decisions now, at time zero, a company can wait and make additional decisions at future dates when these future decisions are contingent on future economic events or information. It is more reasonable to assume that a company is making decisions sequentially, some now and some in the future, rather than one-time decisions. A combination of optimal current and future decisions is what will maximize company value. Real options, by providing future decision-making flexibility to companies, can be an important piece of the value in many capital investments.

Real options are like financial options except that they deal with real assets instead of financial assets.

EXAMPLE 6   Financial Option Similarity

A simple financial option could be a call option on a share of stock. Suppose Paladote stock is selling for CAD50, you own a call option with an exercise (strike) price of CAD50, and the option expires in one year.

1. What action should you take if Paladote's stock price increases to CAD60?

Solution:

   Because Paladote's stock price (CAD60) is greater than the option exercise price (CAD50), you should exercise the option, which allows you to buy Paladote stock, worth CAD60, for a price of CAD50. In effect, you have a CAD10 gain less what you paid for the option.

2. What action should you take if Paladote's stock price falls to CAD40?

Solution:

   Because Paladote's stock price (CAD40) is less than the option exercise price (CAD50), you should not exercise the option. After all, why would you pay CAD50 for Paladote when it is only worth CAD40? If you really want to own the stock, it would be cheaper to buy Paladote in the market for CAD40.

Real options, like financial options, grant companies the right to make a decision but do not impose an obligation to do so. A company should exercise a real option it holds only if it is value enhancing.

Just as financial options are contingent on an underlying asset, real options are contingent on future events for a company. The flexibility that real options give to companies can greatly enhance the NPV of the companies' capital investments. The following are four types of real options used by companies:

- Timing options
- Sizing options
- Flexibility options
- Fundamental options

7.1. Timing Options

Instead of investing now, the company can choose to delay its investing decision. In doing so, the company hopes to obtain improved information for the NPV of the projects selected. Project sequencing options allow the company to defer the decision to invest in a future investment until the outcome of some or all of a current investment is known. Investments can be sequenced over time so that investing in a project creates the option to make future investments.

7.2. Sizing Options

An **abandonment option** allows a company to abandon the investment after it is undertaken, if the financial results are disappointing. At some future date, if the cash flow from abandoning an investment exceeds the present value of the cash flows from continuing the investment, the company should exercise the abandonment option. Conversely, if the company can make additional investments when future financial results are strong, the company has a **growth option**, or an expansion option. When estimating the cash flows from an expansion, the analyst must also be wary of cannibalization.

7.3. Flexibility Options

Companies might also have other options for operational flexibilities, besides abandonment or expansion, once an investment is made. For example, suppose the company finds itself in a situation where demand for its product or service exceeds capacity. Management might be able to exercise a **price-setting option**. By increasing prices, the company could benefit from the excess demand, which it cannot do by increasing production.

There are also **production-flexibility options**, which offer the company the operational flexibility to alter production when demand varies from what is forecast. The company can profit from working overtime or from adding shifts, which in this case makes economic sense, even though it is expensive.

7.4. Fundamental Options

In such cases as the aforementioned, options are embedded in a project that can raise its value. In other cases, the whole investment is essentially an option. The payoffs from the investment are contingent on an underlying asset, just like most financial options.

For example, the value of an oil well or refinery investment is contingent on the price of oil. The value of a gold mine is contingent on the price of gold. If oil prices were low, the company likely would not choose to drill a well. If oil prices were high, it would go ahead and drill. Many R&D projects also look like options.

Companies use the following approaches in evaluating capital investments with real options:

1. DCF analysis without considering options. If the NPV is positive to the company without considering real options and the project has real options that would add more value, the company should simply make the investment.
2. Project NPV = NPV (based on DCF alone) − Cost of options + Value of options. In this approach, the company determines the project NPV based on expected cash flows, then subtracts the incremental cost of the real options and adds back their associated value.
3. Decision trees and option pricing models. Both of these can be used by companies to assess the value associated with future sequential decisions a company might have for its business.

Example 7 illustrates a production-flexibility option for a company, in which an additional investment outlay gives the company an option to use alternative fuel sources.

EXAMPLE 7   Production-Flexibility Option

1. Auvergne AquaFarms has estimated the NPV of the expected cash flows from a new processing plant to be –EUR0.40 million. Auvergne is evaluating an incremental investment of EUR0.30 million that would give the company the flexibility to switch among coal, natural gas, and oil as energy sources. The original plant relied only on coal. The option to switch to cheaper sources of energy when they are available has an estimated value of EUR1.20 million. What is the value of the new processing plant including this real option to use alternative energy sources?

Solution:
The NPV, including the real option, should be

Project NPV = NPV (based on DCF alone) – Cost of options + Value of options.

Project NPV = –0.40 million – 0.30 million + 1.20 million

= EUR0.50 million.

Without the flexibility offered by the real option, the plant is unprofitable. The real option to adapt to cheaper energy sources adds enough to the value of this investment to give it a positive NPV. The company should undertake the investment, which would add to its value.

---

8. SUMMARY

Capital investments—those investments with a life of one year or longer—are key in determining whether a company is profitable and generating value for its shareholders. Capital allocation is the process companies use to decide their capital investment activity. This chapter introduces capital investments, basic principles underlying the capital allocation model, and the use of NPV and IRR decision criteria.

- Companies invest for two reasons: to maintain their existing businesses and to grow them. Projects undertaken by companies to maintain a business including operating efficiencies are (1) going concern projects and (2) regulatory/compliance projects, while (3) expansion projects and (4) other projects are undertaken by companies to strategically expand or grow their operations.
- Capital allocation supports the most critical investments for many corporations—their investments in long-term assets. The principles of capital allocation are also relevant and can be applied to other corporate investing and financing decisions and to security analysis and portfolio management.
- The typical steps companies take in the capital allocation process are (1) idea generation, (2) investment analysis, (3) capital allocation planning, and (4) post-audit/monitoring.
- Companies should base their capital allocation decisions on the investment project's incremental after-tax cash flows discounted at the opportunity cost of funds. In addition,

companies should ignore financing costs because both the cost of debt and the cost of other capital are captured in the discount rate used in the analysis.
- The NPV of an investment project is the present value of its after-tax cash flows (or the present value of its after-tax cash inflows minus the present value of its after-tax outflows) or

$$\text{NPV} = \sum_{t=0}^{n} \frac{\text{CF}_t}{(1+r)^t},$$

where the investment outlays are negative cash flows included in CF_t and r is the required rate of return for the investment.
- Microsoft Excel functions to solve for the NPV for both conventional and unconventional cash flow patterns are

  - NPV or =NPV(rate, values) and
  - XNPV or =XNPV(rate, values, dates),

where "rate" is the discount rate, "values" are the cash flows, and "dates" are the dates of each of the cash flows.
- The IRR is the discount rate that makes the present value of all future cash flows of the project sum to zero. This equation can be solved for the IRR:

$$\sum_{t=0}^{n} \frac{\text{CF}_t}{(1+\text{IRR})^t} = 0.$$

- Using Microsoft Excel functions to solve for IRR, the functions are

  - IRR or =IRR(values, guess) and
  - XIRR or =XIRR(values, dates, guess),

where "values" are the cash flows, "guess" is an optional user-specified guess that defaults to 10%, and "dates" are the dates of each cash flow.
- Companies should invest in a project if the NPV > 0 or if the IRR > r.
- For mutually exclusive investments that are ranked differently by the NPV and IRR, the NPV criterion is the more economically sound and the approach companies should use.
- The fact that projects with positive NPVs theoretically increase the value of the company and the value of its stock could explain the use and popularity of the NPV method by companies.
- Real options allow companies to make future decisions contingent on future economic information or events that change the value of capital investment decisions the company has made today. These can be classified as (1) timing options; (2) sizing options, which can be abandonment options or growth (expansion) options; (3) flexibility options, which can be price-setting options or production-flexibility options; and (4) fundamental options.

9. PRACTICE PROBLEMS

1. With regard to capital allocation, an appropriate estimate of the incremental cash flows from an investment is *least likely* to include:
   A. externalities.
   B. interest costs.
   C. opportunity costs.

2. The NPV of an investment is equal to the sum of the expected cash flows discounted at the:
    A. internal rate of return.
    B. risk-free rate.
    C. opportunity COC.

3. A USD2.2 million investment will result in the following year-end cash flows:

Year	1	2	3	4
Cash flow (millions)	USD1.3	USD1.6	USD1.9	USD0.8

Using an 8% opportunity COC, the investment's NPV is *closest* to:
    A. USD2.47 million.
    B. USD3.40 million.
    C. USD4.67 million.

4. The IRR is *best* described as the:
    A. opportunity COC.
    B. time-weighted rate of return.
    C. discount rate that makes the NPV equal to zero.

5. A three-year investment requires an initial outlay of GBP1,000. It is expected to provide three year-end cash flows of GBP200 plus a net salvage value of GBP700 at the end of three years. Its IRR is *closest* to:
    A. 10%.
    B. 11%.
    C. 20%.

6. Given the following cash flows for a capital investment, calculate the NPV and IRR. The required rate of return is 8%.

Year	0	1	2	3	4	5
Cash flow	−50,000	15,000	15,000	20,000	10,000	5,000

	NPV	IRR
A	USD1,905	10.9%
B	USD1,905	26.0%
C	USD3,379	10.9%

7. An investment of USD100 generates after-tax cash flows of USD40 in Year 1, USD80 in Year 2, and USD120 in Year 3. The required rate of return is 20%. The NPV is *closest* to:
    A. USD42.22.
    B. USD58.33.
    C. USD68.52.

8. An investment of USD150,000 is expected to generate an after-tax cash flow of USD100,000 in one year and another USD120,000 in two years. The COC is 10%. What is the IRR?
   A. 28.39%
   B. 28.59%
   C. 28.79%

9. Kim Corporation is considering an investment of KRW750 million with expected after-tax cash inflows of KRW175 million per year for seven years. The required rate of return is 10%. What is the investment's:

	NPV?	IRR?
A.	KRW102 million	14.0%
B.	KRW157 million	23.3%
C.	KRW193 million	10.0%

10. Erin Chou is reviewing a profitable investment that has a conventional cash flow pattern. If the cash flows for the initial outlay and future after-tax cash flows all double, Chou would predict that the IRR would:
    A. increase and the NPV would increase.
    B. stay the same and the NPV would increase.
    C. stay the same and the NPV would stay the same.

11. Catherine Ndereba is an energy analyst tasked with evaluating a crude oil exploration and production company. The company previously announced that it plans to embark on a new project to drill for oil offshore. As a result of this announcement, the stock price increased by 10%. After conducting her analysis, Ms. Ndereba concludes that the project does indeed have a positive NPV. Which statement is true?
    A. The stock price should remain where it is because Ms. Ndereba's analysis confirms that the recent run-up was justified.
    B. The stock price should go even higher now that an independent source has confirmed that the NPV is positive.
    C. The stock price could remain steady, move higher, or move lower.

12. The Bearing Corp. invests only in positive-NPV projects. Which of the following statements is true?
    A. Bearing's ROIC is greater than its COC.
    B. Bearing's COC is greater than its ROIC.
    C. We cannot reach any conclusions about the relationship between the company's ROIC and COC.

13. Investments 1 and 2 have similar outlays, although the patterns of future cash flows are different. The cash flows, as well as the NPV and IRR, for the two investments are shown below. For both investments, the required rate of return is 10%.

	Cash Flows						
Year	0	1	2	3	4	NPV	IRR (%)
Investment 1	−50	20	20	20	20	13.40	21.86
Investment 2	−50	0	0	0	100	18.30	18.92

The two projects are mutually exclusive. What is the appropriate investment decision?
A. Invest in both investments.
B. Invest in Investment 1 because it has the higher IRR.
C. Invest in Investment 2 because it has the higher NPV.

14. Consider the two investments below. The cash flows, as well as the NPV and IRR, for the two investments are given. For both investments, the required rate of return is 10%.

	Cash Flows						
Year	0	1	2	3	4	NPV	IRR (%)
Investment 1	−100	36	36	36	36	14.12	16.37
Investment 2	−100	0	0	0	175	19.53	15.02

What discount rate would result in the same NPV for both investments?
A. A rate between 0.00% and 10.00%
B. A rate between 10.00% and 15.02%
C. A rate between 15.02% and 16.37%

15. Wilson Flannery is concerned that the following investment has multiple IRRs.

Year	0	1	2	3w
Cash flows	−50	100	0	−50

How many discount rates produce a zero NPV for this investment?
A. One, a discount rate of 0%
B. Two, discount rates of 0% and 32%
C. Two, discount rates of 0% and 62%

16. What type of project is *most likely* to yield new revenues for a company?
A. Regulatory/compliance
B. Going concern
C. Expansion

The following information relates to questions 17–19

Bouchard Industries is a Canadian company that manufactures gutters for residential houses. Its management believes it has developed a new process that produces a superior product. The company must make an initial investment of CAD190 million to begin production. If demand is high, cash flows are expected to be CAD40 million per year. If demand is low, cash flows will be only CAD20 million per year. Management believes there is an equal chance that demand will be high or low. The investment, which has an investment horizon of ten years, also gives the company a production-flexibility option allowing the company to add shifts at the end of the first year if demand turns out to be high. If the company exercises this option, net cash flows would increase by an additional CAD5 million in Years 2–10. Bouchard's opportunity cost of funds is 10%.

The internal auditor for Bouchard Industries has made two suggestions for improving capital allocation processes at the company. The internal auditor's suggestions are as follows:

Suggestion 1: "In order to treat all capital allocation proposals in a fair manner, the investments should all use the risk-free rate for the required rate of return."

Suggestion 2: "When rationing capital, it is better to choose the portfolio of investments that maximizes the company NPV than the portfolio that maximizes the company IRR."

17. What is the NPV (CAD millions) of the original project for Bouchard Industries without considering the production-flexibility option?
    A. –CAD6.11 million
    B. –CAD5.66 million
    C. CAD2.33 million

18. What is the NPV (CAD millions) of the optimal set of investment decisions for Bouchard Industries including the production-flexibility option?
    A. –CAD6.34 million
    B. CAD7.43 million
    C. CAD31.03 million

19. Should the capital allocation committee accept the internal auditor's suggestions?
    A. No for Suggestions 1 and 2
    B. No for Suggestion 1 and yes for Suggestion 2
    C. Yes for Suggestion 1 and no for Suggestion 2

CHAPTER 5

CAPITAL STRUCTURE

Raj Aggarwal, PhD, CFA
Kent State University Foundation Board (USA)

Glen D. Campbell, MBA
(Canada)

Lee M. Dunham, PhD, CFA
Creighton University (USA)

Pamela Peterson Drake, PhD, CFA
James Madison University (USA)

Adam Kobor, PhD, CFA
New York University (USA)

LEARNING OUTCOMES

The candidate should be able to:

- explain factors affecting capital structure
- describe how a company's capital structure may change over its life cycle
- explain the Modigliani–Miller propositions regarding capital structure
- describe the use of target capital structure in estimating WACC, and calculate and interpret target capital structure weights
- describe competing stakeholder interests in capital structure decisions

1. INTRODUCTION

Capital structure refers to the specific mix of debt and equity used to finance a company's assets and operations. From a corporate perspective, equity represents a more expensive, permanent source of capital with greater financial flexibility. Financial flexibility allows a company to raise capital on reasonable terms when capital is needed. Debt, on the other hand, represents a cheaper, finite-to-maturity capital source that legally obligates a company

139

to make promised cash outflows on a fixed schedule with the need to refinance at some future date at an unknown cost.

As we will show, debt is an important component in the "optimal" capital structure. The trade-off theory of capital structure tells us that managers should seek an optimal mix of equity and debt that minimizes the firm's weighted average cost of capital, which in turn maximizes company value. That optimal capital structure represents a trade-off between the cost-effectiveness of borrowing relative to the higher cost of equity and the costs of financial distress.

In reality, many practical considerations affect capital structure and the use of leverage by companies, leading to wide variation in capital structures even among otherwise similar companies. Practical considerations impacting capital structure include:

- *business characteristics:* features associated with a company's business model, operations, or maturity;
- *capital structure policies and leverage targets:* guidelines set by management and the board that seek to establish sensible borrowing limits for the company based on the company's risk appetite and ability to support debt; and
- *market conditions:* current share price levels and market interest rates for a company's debt. The prevalence of low interest rates increases the debt-carrying capacity of businesses and the use of debt by companies.

Since we are considering how a company minimizes its overall cost of capital, the focus here is on the market values of debt and equity. Therefore, capital structure is also affected by changes in the market value of a company's securities over time.

While we tend to think of capital structure as the result of a conscious decision by management, it is not that simple. For example, unmanageable debt, or financial distress, can arise because a company's capital structure policy was too aggressive, but it can also occur because operating results or prospects deteriorate unexpectedly.

Finally, in seeking to maximize shareholder value, company management may make capital structure decisions that are not in the interests of other stakeholders, such as debtholders, suppliers, customers, or employees.

2. FACTORS AFFECTING CAPITAL STRUCTURE

Many factors influence a company's capital structure and its ability to support debt, including the nature and stability of its business, its maturity, capital intensity, and the strength of its market position. In addition, there is significant variation in capital structures across industries. What causes the capital structures of companies to differ, in some cases, so significantly from one another?

The primary factors, both internal and external, that affect a company's capital structure and differences in capital structures across companies and industries are summarized in Exhibit 1. Note that the discussion on company maturity, or life-cycle stage, is covered in a following section.

EXHIBIT 1: Key Determinants of Capital Structure

Internal	External
▪ Business model characteristics ▪ Existing leverage ▪ Corporate tax rate ▪ Capital structure policies, guidelines ▪ Company life cycle stage	▪ Market conditions/Business cycle ▪ Regulatory constraints ▪ Industry/Peer firm leverage

2.1. Internal Factors Affecting Capital Structure

2.1.1. Business Model Characteristics

The risk inherent in a company's business model can greatly impact the company's capital structure by influencing its ability to service debt. Key factors that differ among business models include differences in:

- revenue, earnings, and cash flow sensitivity,
- asset type, and
- asset ownership.

2.1.1.1. Revenue, Earnings, and Cash Flow Sensitivity Some companies, such as Vodafone in the telecom industry or Microsoft in the software industry, generally have very stable revenue streams resulting from a large proportion of their revenues being subscription-like, recurring revenues. A high proportion of recurring revenues for a company is generally viewed as a positive for its ability to support debt, because the company's revenue stream is likely to be more predictable and less sensitive to the ups and downs of the macro economy.

In contrast, companies in cyclical industries, such as Toyota in the automobile industry and Komatsu in the construction equipment industry, typically have more volatile revenue streams that are highly sensitive to the macroeconomic environment. Revenue streams subject to relatively high volatility, and consequently less predictability, are less favorable for supporting debt in the capital structure. Further, companies with pay-per-use business models, rather than subscription-based models, are likely to have a lower degree of revenue predictability and a lower ability to support debt in the capital structure.

Stable revenue streams can also lead to earnings and cash flow streams being relatively more stable. However, the company's cost structure—the proportions of fixed costs and variable costs—will impact the degree of stability and predictability in earnings and cash flows.

One measure of business risk is a company's degree of operating leverage, measured as the proportion of fixed costs to total costs:

$$\text{Operating leverage} = \text{Fixed costs/Total costs}$$

Companies with higher operating leverage experience a greater change in earnings and cash flows for a given change in revenue than firms with low operating leverage. Companies with low volatility in their revenue, earnings, and cash flow streams can support higher levels of debt in their capital structures than firms with high volatility in these streams. For a given level of debt, firms with low revenue, earnings, and cash flow volatility are likely to have a lower probability of default and be able to access debt at lower cost than firms with high volatility in these streams.

Exhibit 2 presents a summary of the relationships between these business model characteristics and a firm's ability to support debt.

EXHIBIT 2: Relationships between Business Model Factors and Ability to Support Debt

Business Model Factor	Ability to Support Debt
High (low) revenue, cash flow volatility	Reduced (increased)
High (low) earnings predictability	Increased (reduced)
High (low) operating leverage	Reduced (increased)

2.1.1.2. Asset Type A company's assets can be broadly categorized as tangible or intangible, fungible or non-fungible, and liquid or illiquid. Tangible assets are identifiable, physical assets like property, plant and equipment, inventory, cash, and marketable securities, whereas intangible assets do not exist in physical form, such as goodwill and patents/intellectual property rights. It should be noted that under most accounting standards, intangible assets on the balance sheet reflect only acquired intangible assets, such as goodwill, and not internally generated intangible assets.

Generally speaking, assets supporting the use of debt include those that are typically considered strong collateral by creditors, cash generative, and relatively easy to market (i.e., liquid). From a creditor's perspective, tangible assets are deemed safer than intangible assets and can better serve as debt collateral. Therefore, companies with mostly tangible assets, such as those in the oil and gas, infrastructure, and real estate industries, are likely to be able to operate with greater amounts of debt in their capital structures than companies with a high proportion of intangible assets, such as those in the software industry, due to their ability to pledge such assets as collateral for debt.

Fungible assets are those assets that are interchangeable with, or substitutable for, another of similar identity. Money, for example, represents a fungible asset. In contrast, non-fungible assets are unique assets, such as art pieces, that are not mutually interchangeable or substitutable. Asset liquidity refers to the ability to convert an asset into cash without losing a substantial amount of its value. Marketable securities are very liquid, given the ease with which they can be converted into cash. On the other hand, real estate and property as well as plant and equipment are fairly illiquid assets that are not easily convertible into cash at their market values. Companies with mostly fungible and highly liquid assets are likely to support greater debt capacity than firms with mostly non-fungible, illiquid assets. That said, illiquid assets can serve as debt collateral given their tangible nature. Exhibit 3 presents a summary of the relationships between a firm's asset type and its cost of capital ability/ability to support debt.

EXHIBIT 3: Relationships between Asset Type and Ability to Support Debt

Asset Type	Ability to Support Debt
Greater (fewer) fungible, tangible, liquid, or marketable assets	Increased (reduced)

2.1.1.3. Asset Ownership For some companies, management may choose not to own assets but instead "outsource" asset ownership to other parties, thereby reducing balance sheet assets. Outsourcing of assets can allow the company to move to a variable cost structure, resulting in lower business risk as measured by lower operating leverage. By minimizing the costs and risks associated with owning and operating a significant amount of fixed assets, these "asset-light" companies can maximize their flexibility and ability to scale quickly.

For example, Uber is a global taxi company that does not actually own its fleet of automobiles, and Airbnb is a global accommodations company that does not actually own the underlying real estate. Parent companies of major restaurant chains like McDonald's that choose to sell some franchises to individuals rather than own all of their physical locations also fit into this classification of asset-light companies. Companies like Uber, Airbnb, and McDonald's still benefit from these tangible assets by having control over them—they just do not own them.

In one respect, the lower asset base allows these asset-light companies to operate with lower operating leverage, which, all else equal, can support high debt capacities. On the other hand, asset-light companies often have a lower proportion of tangible assets that better serve as collateral for debt. This characteristic of asset-light companies suggests a lower ability to support debt in the capital structure than their asset-heavy counterparts, such as real estate and hotel companies, that own the underlying tangible assets.

EXAMPLE 1   Business Model Characteristics and Capital Structure

An analyst is reviewing the business characteristics of two companies in different industries to assess their ability to support debt in their capital structures. The analyst gathers the following common-size balance sheet information and other information on the two companies:

	Company A	Company B
Common-size balance sheet		
Cash and equivalents	7%	2%
Accounts receivable	8%	2%
Inventory	1%	1%
Other current assets	2%	0%
Property, plant, and equipment (net)	30%	72%
Operating leases—right to use assets	7%	18%
Intangible assets and goodwill	41%	2%
Other assets	4%	43%

	Company A	Company B
Other Selected Information:		
% of total revenue that is recurring	10%	90%
Operating leverage	Low	High

1. Discuss two characteristics of either company that would support a relatively low proportion of debt in its capital structure. Discuss one characteristic of either company that would support a relatively high proportion of debt in its capital structure.

Solution:

Two characteristics of Company A that would support a relatively low proportion of debt are (1) its large proportion of intangible assets and (2) its low proportion of recurring revenues.

First, from a creditor's perspective, tangible assets are often deemed safer than intangible assets and can better serve as debt collateral. Therefore, companies like Company A with a high proportion of intangible assets (41%) have less ability to pledge such assets as collateral for debt. Another 7% of assets are leased, and these assets are also unlikely to be usable as debt collateral. Second, companies with a low percentage of recurring revenues (10% for Company A) are likely to have a lower degree of revenue predictability and a relatively lower ability to support debt in the capital structure.

In contrast, a large majority of Company B's assets (72%) are tangible property, plant, and equipment and most of the company's revenues are recurring (90%), suggesting a subscription-based business model with more predictable revenues, earnings streams, and cash flow streams. Companies like Company B are likely to be able to support greater amounts of debt.

One characteristic of Company A that would support a relatively high proportion of debt is its low operating leverage. Companies with lower variability in earnings and cash flows can achieve greater results with a higher ability to support debt in their capital structures. In contrast, Company B operates with much higher operating leverage and would likely experience greater earnings and cash flow volatility for a given change in revenue.

2.2. Existing Leverage

When a company elects to raise capital, whether it be debt or equity, the cost of that capital is highly dependent on the firm's existing financial leverage (debt level relative to total assets or total equity) and capital structure. A company's debt capacity is the total amount of debt that the company can take on and repay without causing insolvency. In general, firms with higher proportions of debt in their capital structures face a higher probability of default and have less ability to service additional debt than underleveraged firms.

If a company wants to raise debt capital, an important question is whether the company can service the additional debt. An analysis of a few financial ratios can help answer this question. Commonly used ratios for this exercise are presented in Exhibit 4.

EXHIBIT 4: Metrics Used to Assess a Company's Ability to Service Debt

Liquidity	Profitability	Leverage	Interest Coverage
Current assets/ Current liabilities	EBIT/Revenue	Total debt (or net debt)/ EBITDA	EBIT/Interest expense
	EBITDA/Revenue	Total debt (or net debt)/ Total assets (or total equity)	(EBIT + lease payments)/ (Interest expense + lease payments)
	Operating income/ Revenue		EBITDA/Interest expense

Notes:

Net debt = Interest-bearing debt – cash and cash equivalents
EBIT = Net income + interest expense + taxes = EBITDA – depreciation and amortization expenses
Operating income = Operating revenue – operating expenses = EBIT – non-operating profit + non-operating expenses

A starting point for determining a company's debt capacity is its current ratio, equal to current assets divided by current liabilities. The current ratio provides an indication of the ability of the firm to meet its short-term debt obligations. The higher the ratio, the greater the ability of the company to repay its debt. Similarly, a higher level of profitability—usually measured in terms of operating income or EBIT or EBITDA divided by revenue—implies greater amounts of earnings available to service the company's debt obligations. In general, companies with higher liquidity and profitability have a greater ability to support greater use of debt in their capital structures.

A common leverage ratio used by analysts to assess a firm's debt capacity is the ratio of total (or net) debt to EBITDA. This ratio provides an estimate of how many years it would take to pay off the company's debt. In general, ratio values of 3 or less are considered acceptable; values higher than 3 start to raise concerns about the company's ability to service its debt obligations. Finally, interest coverage ratios are also commonly used to assess companies' debt capacities. Generally, these ratios provide an estimate of how many times a company can cover its interest expense (or interest expense plus lease payments) with current earnings (usually measured as EBIT or EBITDA). In other words, interest coverage ratios provide an indication of a company's financial cushion in meeting its debt service obligations. The larger the interest coverage ratio, the larger the financial cushion and the greater the company's ability to service its debt obligations.

For example, an interest coverage ratio of 4 would indicate that the company's earnings could fall by as much as 75% before the company would be unable to meet interest payments and/or lease obligations. In general, an interest coverage ratio of 2 is deemed the minimum acceptable level, as values less than 2 imply little financial cushion and cast doubt on the company's ability to service its debt obligations.

Exhibit 5 presents a summary of these relationships.

EXHIBIT 5: Relationships between Selected Financial Ratio Types and Ability to Support Debt

Financial Ratio Type	Ability to Support Debt
Higher (lower) liquidity	Increased (reduced)
Higher (lower) profitability	Increased (reduced)
Higher (lower) leverage	Reduced (increased)
Higher (lower) interest coverage	Increased (reduced)

2.2.1. Corporate Tax Rate

Another important factor in the determination of a firm's capital structure is its marginal income tax rate. In many countries and jurisdictions, interest expense is a tax-deductible expense in the income statement. Therefore, a company's after-tax cost of debt will be lower than the actual cost due to this tax savings. The higher (lower) the firm's marginal income tax rate, the greater (lower) the tax benefit of using debt in the firm's capital structure.

EXAMPLE 2   Changes in the US Corporate Tax Rate

In 2017, the US corporate income tax system changed from a progressive tax rate ranging from 15% to 35% (depending on taxable income) to a flat rate of 21%.

1. Discuss the implications of this change in the tax system on the capital structures of companies subject to corporate tax rates well above 21% before the change.

Solution:

Companies subject to income tax rates well above 21% before the change benefited from a higher tax savings per dollar of interest expense after the change. For firms facing the top tax rate of 35%, the change in the tax system reduced the tax savings associated with debt capital from USD0.35 per dollar of interest expense to USD0.21. The reduction in the tax rate for these companies had the effect of raising the after-tax cost of debt, thereby making debt capital less attractive than before the change. Despite this increase in the after-tax cost of debt making debt capital more costly, it is important to note that these companies would have benefited from the tax rate reduction by paying less income tax on their pre-tax earnings.

2.2.2. Capital Structure Policies/Guidelines

The capital structures of some companies are often also guided and influenced by firm-specific policies relating to financing decisions. Given the difficulty of estimating a company's cost of equity capital or potential costs of financial distress, it is common for companies to establish capital structure policies that are debt-oriented, defining acceptable levels of debt in the capital structure. Such policies might contain directives such as "debt/equity less than 0.5 times"; "debt to operating cash flow less than 2.0 times"; or "debt as a maximum of X% of total capital."

Companies differ in the measures and thresholds used, but they frequently start with debt covenants or rating agency thresholds to which they add a cushion, or "margin of safety," to ensure that the debt limits or covenants are not breached or to avoid a rating downgrade.

Having explicit capital structure policies is important for companies that are significant and frequent borrowers, since the risks associated with too much leverage can be severe while the risks associated with too little leverage generally are not. Companies with little to no debt, such as start-ups or some technology companies, may not have capital structure policies or targets. In certain industries such as banking and utilities, capital structures are evaluated by regulators, and thus capital structure policies are determined accordingly.

Another important consideration for corporate issuers is whether their debt or equity issuances meet index provider requirements that allow inclusion in a benchmark index, as such inclusion affects the demand for their securities by major investors. Companies reaching a certain market capitalization size in addition to meeting specific index provider requirements may qualify for index membership. Similarly, whether a specific debt issue meets the requirements—including issuance size, in particular—for inclusion in an index is a key factor in debt-financing decisions.

EXAMPLE 3   Capital Structure Policy: Abha Software

1. Abha Software's management believes the company can obtain attractive borrowing terms if debt/EBITDA (earnings before interest, taxes, depreciation, and amortization) is at 2 times or less, which for Abha is the primary criterion used by lenders to assess borrowing capacity and terms. Abha's EBITDA for the latest year is USD50 million, and it has a total capitalization of USD1.0 billion. Management and the board have agreed that Abha should use leverage if the company can borrow easily at attractive rates. They are seeking a capital structure policy that reflects this objective. Which of the following is *most likely* to be an appropriate capital structure policy for Abha?
   A. Debt should be a maximum of 25% of total capital in book value terms.
   B. Debt should be a maximum of 10% of total capital in market value terms.
   C. The debt-to-EBITDA ratio should be no more than 2 times.

Solution:

C is correct. It is the most appropriate capital structure policy, since the debt-to-EBITDA ratio is the primary criterion that lenders and management are using to determine Abha's debt capacity. Note that lending criteria vary by sector, by market, and over time, including the ratios used (as well as the threshold ratios for those ratios).

B is least likely to be appropriate. While useful in calculating the cost of capital for Abha, market value weights are less practical and less commonly used in capital structure targets. Market values of equity can fluctuate a great deal without a corresponding change in the company's borrowing capacity. Increases or decreases in the company's share price would imply increases or decreases in maximum debt that are unlikely to be appropriate.

A's policy, with 25% debt/capital, implies up to USD250 million in debt. This ratio, unlike B's policy, is unaffected by fluctuations in the share price. However, the implied debt capacity of USD250 million and 5.0 times debt/EBITDA (USD250 million/ USD50 million) is greater than the cap of 2 times established by management and identified as the primary criterion by Abha's lenders.

Finally, a company's cash flow generation is almost never entirely predictable and is likely to deviate from management's plan, which will affect the company's borrowing capacity and its financing plans. As management consider their financing plans, they will continually refine their views on the company's cash flow generation as well as its investment needs.

2.2.2.1. Third-Party Debt Ratings Debt ratings, also called credit ratings, are independent, third-party measures of the quality and safety of a company's debt based on an analysis of the company's ability to pay the promised cash flows. Debt ratings are an important consideration in the practical management of leverage and a primary factor underlying a company's capital structure policies. For example, maintaining the company's rating at a certain level, such as investment-grade or above, may be an explicit policy target for management.

Most large companies pay one or more rating services to provide debt ratings for their bonds. Debt issues are rated for creditworthiness by these credit-rating agencies after they perform a financial analysis of the company's ability to pay the promised cash flows as well as an analysis of the bond's indenture (i.e., the set of complex legal documents associated with the issuance of debt instruments). These agencies evaluate a wealth of information about the issuer and the bond, including the bond's characteristics and indenture agreement, and provide investors with an assessment of the company's ability to pay the interest and principal on the bond as promised. Both the issuer, or company, and the issuance, or security, are rated by these agencies.

As leverage rises, rating agencies tend to lower the ratings of the company's debt to reflect the higher credit risk and probability of default arising from the increase in leverage. Lower ratings signify higher risk to both equity and debt capital providers, who demand higher returns for supplying capital to the company.

Most managers consider the company's debt rating in their capital structure policies because the cost of capital is tied so closely to bond ratings. Some companies explicitly target a certain debt rating in their capital structure policies. For example, a company might target an S&P debt rating of A or higher, which is one level above BBB, the minimum investment-grade rating on S&P's scale. The cost of debt increases significantly when a bond's rating drops below investment-grade. In economic recessions, these spreads may widen significantly, and borrowing can become more difficult for companies with non-investment-grade ratings.

Firms that have more stable revenues, earnings, and cash flows as well as greater profitability, a higher proportion of tangible assets, shorter asset conversion cycles, and/or more liquid assets can support more debt and tend to receive higher debt ratings and have lower borrowing costs. These companies are often in stable and defensive sectors, such as utilities and consumer staples, and enjoy strong market positions.

Companies with a high proportion of intangible assets require relatively heavy investment in inventory or specialized equipment—with long asset conversion cycles and cyclical or less stable cash flows and/or profitability—have a reduced ability to consistently meet fixed debt payments over time, and thus face lower ratings and higher borrowing costs.

Highly rated companies have greater borrowing flexibility, better terms, and lower borrowing costs. They can borrow in debt markets for "general corporate purposes" on an unsecured basis, with very few debt covenants. Similarly, lower-rated, non-investment-grade companies have higher borrowing costs, more restrictive debt covenants, liens on assets, and differing subordination levels.

2.3. External Factors Affecting Capital Structure

2.3.1. Market Conditions/Business Cycle

A company's capital structure is highly influenced by market conditions—namely, interest rates and the current macroeconomic environment. A company's use of debt capital is driven by its costs, which are driven by interest rates and credit spreads. A company's cost of debt is equal to a benchmark risk-free rate (r_f) plus a credit spread specific to the company.

The credit spread above the benchmark risk-free rate reflects issuer-specific risks that influence the company's probability of default, such as business model characteristics, earnings predictability, and the company's existing debt level. The greater these company-specific risks, the higher the credit spread and the cost of debt capital.

Macroeconomic and country-specific factors are also reflected in the benchmark rate and in the overall level of credit spreads, which widen during recessions and tighten during expansionary times. When borrowing is less costly due to low interest rates and/or tight credit spreads, companies may increase their use of debt and vice versa. The macroeconomic conditions over the longer term—as measured by business cycles—may also affect firms' capital structures. Some firms tend to borrow more during expansionary times as credit spreads tighten and borrow less during recessionary times as credit spreads widen.

In cyclical sectors, such as mining and materials and many industrials, revenues and cash flows vary widely through the economic cycle, which limits debt capacity. As a result, businesses in cyclical sectors may have less debt in their capital structures than companies in other, less cyclical industries.

EXAMPLE 4   Changes in Capital Structure during the COVID-19 Pandemic

The airline industry was one of the hardest-hit industries during the COVID-19 pandemic. Exhibit 6 presents selected data on leverage-related ratios for American Airlines, Southwest Airlines, and Lufthansa AG for 2018–2020.

EXHIBIT 6: Selected Leverage Ratios for American Airlines, Southwest Airlines, and Lufthansa AG

	2018	2019	2020
Total debt to total assets			
American Airlines	0.43	0.43	0.55
Southwest Airlines	0.13	0.12	0.31
Lufthansa AG	0.04	0.04	0.08

	2018	2019	2020
Total debt to equity			
American Airlines	1.80	2.21	4.49
Southwest Airlines	0.13	0.11	0.27
Lufthansa AG	0.16	0.19	0.40
EBITDA to interest expense			
American Airlines	3.66	4.61	(7.94)
Southwest Airlines	33.64	35.39	(7.34)
Lufthansa AG	23.61	11.33	(6.47)

Notes: Equity is measured as calendar year-end market capitalization. Total debt includes the current portion of long-term debt, operating lease liabilities, and long-term debt.

1. Compare and contrast the capital structures of these three companies over 2018–2020.

Solution:

In the two years before the COVID-19 pandemic, which started in early 2020, Southwest Airlines and Lufthansa AG had very little debt in their capital structures, as indicated by very low ratios of total debt to total assets and total debt to equity. As a result, the interest coverage ratio (EBITDA to interest expense) was very high for both companies before the pandemic.

In contrast, American Airlines had significantly more debt in its capital structure heading into the pandemic, as indicated by much higher ratios of debt to total assets and total debt to equity. American's interest coverage of less than 5× heading into the pandemic provided little financial cushion in meeting its debt service obligations.

During the pandemic year of 2020, all three companies experienced a sharp decrease in profitability. EBIT and EBITDA were negative for all three firms in 2020, resulting in negative interest coverage ratios, and leverage ratios significantly worsened for all three companies.

2.3.2. Regulatory Constraints

The capital structures of some firms are regulated by government or other regulators. Some key financial decisions of financial firms, utility firms, and property developers, such as those relating to capital structure, payout policy, and pricing, are often subject to guidelines set by regulatory bodies. For example, financial institutions must generally maintain certain levels of solvency or capital adequacy, as defined by regulators. Similarly, regulatory oversight of public utility companies by local governments can often influence their capital structures through rules and regulations relating to setting pricing/rates.

2.3.3. Industry/Peer Firm Leverage

The industry in which a firm operates is likely to have a significant effect on its capital structure. It is not uncommon for companies in the same industry to have fairly similar capital structures. One explanation for this result is that companies in the same industry are likely to have common asset types and business model characteristics, among other commonalities. For instance, companies in the automobile industry tend to own large proportions of tangible, non-fungible fixed assets in the form of property, plant, and equipment, with significant proportions of debt in their capital structures.

3. CAPITAL STRUCTURE AND COMPANY LIFE CYCLE

This section discusses the typical changes in a company's capital structure as it evolves over time, from a start-up to a growth business to a mature business. It will also highlight key variations.

3.1. Background

Many financial transactions can be seen in simple terms as the trading of money across time: A party with surplus cash today provides it to another party requiring cash in exchange for payments in the future. This statement is true of not only everyday personal banking activities but also companies accessing the capital markets over their life cycle, from start-up through maturity. Typically, companies begin life as consumers of capital. As they mature, cash flows turn from negative to positive. Capital markets connect them to investors with the opposite requirement: those with surplus cash to invest today in exchange for future payments.

The framework in Exhibit 7 describes the relationship between a company's life-cycle stage and its cash flow characteristics and ability to support debt. Life-cycle stage is a principal factor in determining capital structure. Capital not sourced through borrowing must come from equity, either from retained earnings or from issuing/selling shares. The framework in Exhibit 7 categorizes the stages in life-cycle development as start-up, growth, and mature and shows typical revenue and cash flow characteristics of companies in each stage. As companies mature, business risk typically declines, and their cash flows turn positive and become increasingly predictable, allowing for greater use of leverage on more attractive (less costly) financing terms. Debt then becomes a larger component of their capital structures.

Note that the framework references cash flow, which is net of investment. Profitable, high-growth businesses may have negative cash flow once investment is taken into account. Investment includes spending on property, plant, and equipment and other fixed assets as well as the expansion of working capital to support and grow the business over time.

Note also that the stages of a company's life cycle—start-up, growth, and maturity—are similar to the evolutionary stages of an industry. However, start-ups and growth companies can often be found in mature industries. Examples include restaurants and apparel (with new concepts, formats, and fashions appearing regularly) and technology-driven disruption of established industries, such as advertising (e.g., Google and Facebook) and even automobiles (e.g., Tesla and BYD). This framework is a very general one, and there are wide variations between and within sectors.

EXHIBIT 7: Capital Structure and Company Life Cycle

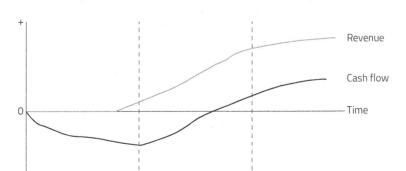

Stage in life cycle	Start-up	Growth	Mature
Financial management			
Revenue growth	Beginning	Rising	Slowing
Cash flow	Negative	Improving	Positive/Predictable
Business risk	High	Medium	Low
Debt capital/leverage			
Availability	Very limited	Limited/improving	High
Cost	High	Medium	Low
Typical cases	N/A	Secured (by receivables, fixed assets)	Unsecured (bank and public debt)
Typical % of capital structure[1]	Close to 0%	0%–20%	20% +

[1]These ratios are calculated based on the market values of equity and debt.

3.2. Start-Ups

Early in its life, a company is typically a cash consumer. Investment is required to advance concepts through the prototype stage and into commercial production. Revenues are zero or minimal, and risk of business failure is high. The company must raise capital, and since the timing and potential for cash flow generation are highly uncertain, it will generally raise equity rather than debt. Equity for start-ups is usually sourced privately (e.g., through venture capital rather than in public markets through an IPO), in part because many stock exchange listing requirements include minimum profitability levels, which most start-ups have yet to achieve.

At this early stage, debt capital is typically not available or available only at a high cost. Most lenders require stable and positive cash flow to service debt and/or collateral to secure it. An early-stage company often has neither, making it a high-risk prospect to lenders.

From the perspective of an early-stage issuer, debt may be an attractive way to reduce or avoid the dilution associated with equity issuance. However, with cash flows that are negative and unpredictable, a typical start-up would have difficulty making regular debt payments, or "servicing the debt." Even if debt is available, the cost, inflexibility, and risk associated with borrowing are often unattractive to a start-up. As a result, debt is a negligible component of the capital structures of most start-up companies.

EXAMPLE 5   Start-Up Financing

1. Which of the following are limiting factors in the ability of a start-up company to take on debt?
   A. Lender requirement for positive cash flows
   B. Few to no assets that can be used as collateral
   C. Exchange listing requirements for minimum levels of profitability
   D. A and B only
   E. All of the above

Solution:

D is correct. Most lenders require positive and stable cash flows and/or collateral for servicing debt payments. Start-ups often have neither, given their early stage in development. With expenditures outpacing revenues, a start-up company's cash flow is negative and unpredictable.

For equity financing, most start-ups fail to meet minimum profitability requirements for an exchange listing in public markets and thus source their capital needs through private equity markets. Therefore, C is incorrect, since an exchange listing relates to equity and is not a debt-financing limiting factor.

3.3. Growth Businesses

As a company exits the start-up stage, it is typically generating revenues, providing confirmation of the product concept and evidence of demand. Revenue growth may be rising and/or high, but investment is needed to achieve this growth and scale. This spending includes operating expenses, such as sales and marketing expenses, growth-related capital expenditures, and working capital investment. Operating cash flow is still likely to be negative but may be improving and becoming more predictable. The company begins to establish a customer and supplier base.

As the business progresses through the growth stage, execution and competitive risks decline. Operating cash flow typically turns positive and then becomes more stable and predictable as the business grows. As a result, the business becomes more attractive to lenders. Depending on the business model, there may also be assets that can be used to secure debt, such as receivables, inventory, or fixed assets. Both the availability and the terms of debt financing improve for the company during this stage.

Many growth companies use debt conservatively in order to preserve operational and financial flexibility and minimize the risk of financial distress. Equity remains the predominant source of capital. Some business models are inherently **capital light**; that is, they require little incremental investment in fixed assets or working capital to enable revenue growth. As a result, they have minimal need to borrow or otherwise raise capital to grow, even though they could easily support debt. Software businesses often fit this description.

EXAMPLE 6   Growth Company Financing

1. A growth retail business that is expected to generate positive operating cash flows in the next 3–5 years would normally be financed with:
   A. little or no debt.
   B. significant debt to minimize equity dilution.
   C. significant debt to minimize its weighted average cost of capital.

Solution:

A is correct. A growth retail business expected to generate positive operating cash flows in the next 3–5 years would normally be financed with little or no debt.

While one can often find exceptions, the standard approach to financing a business in such a highly competitive sector as retail, with negative and/or unpredictable cash flows, is to rely primarily on equity. Using predominantly equity financing to meet capital needs allows management to preserve operational and financial flexibility while minimizing the risk of financial distress associated with debt.

3.4. Mature Businesses

At the maturity stage, a company's revenue growth may slow or even begin to decline. At this stage, however, a successful business generates reliable and positive cash flow and likely has an established customer and supplier base. There is typically a decline or a deceleration in growth-related investment spending. The company becomes able to support low-cost debt, often on an unsecured basis. From the company's perspective, debt financing is likely to be more attractive than higher-cost equity financing.

In practice, large, mature public companies commonly use significant debt in their capital structures, although many seek to maintain an investment-grade rating in order to preserve maximum financial flexibility. An investment-grade rating enables a company to access a very wide pool of potential investors on an unsecured basis without onerous debt covenants, and it minimizes the risk that financing might become unavailable.

Mature businesses often de-leverage over time, experiencing a reduction in debt as a proportion of total capital. De-leveraging occurs due to continuing cash flow generation and because equity values commonly rise over time from share price appreciation. To offset this de-leveraging, companies may elect to pay more cash dividends or conduct share buybacks. By using cash to buy back shares, a company reduces its outstanding share count, thereby reducing equity in its capital structure.

Share buybacks, also called stock repurchases, are attractive to companies because, compared with dividends, they offer greater flexibility and are generally a more tax-efficient means of distributing cash to taxable investors. Particularly in North America, investors typically expect dividend levels to be maintained once established, but that is not their expectation for share buybacks. Buybacks can, therefore, be conducted when cash is available and when the share price is seen by management to be undervalued.

Investors generally respond favorably to share buyback announcements, which may lead to increases in share price and in share option values. The share count reduction caused by buybacks can enhance per-share metrics, such as EPS or EPS growth, which in turn can enhance management compensation and also lead to potential conflicts of interest with other stakeholders.

EXAMPLE 7   Mature Business Capital Structure Considerations

Sleepy Mattress Company went public 10 years ago. Since then, the company has seen its revenues and cash flows increase every year. This growth is expected to continue for the foreseeable future. No dividends have ever been paid. All cash flow has gone toward debt reduction (strongly preferred by the prior CEO), and the company has recently become debt-free. The shares are trading at 10× trailing cash flow.

There is now a lively debate within the board about the company's capital structure. Board members agree that the company's capital structure should include debt in order to minimize its overall cost of capital, but they do not agree on how to achieve this goal. We consider each board member's recommendation, its associated scenario, the likely impact on Sleepy's capital structure, and what is most likely the best course of action:

A. Director A has argued that the company should pay a one-time special dividend equal to last year's after-tax cash flow, drawing down its unused line of credit to do so.

B. Director B recommends that the company borrow an amount equal to two years' cash flow and then seek an appropriate acquisition.

C. Director C advocates making a tender offer to buy back 50% of the company's shares at a 50% premium to market price and issuing debt to finance the offer. Since this would be a very large tender offer (equal to 75% of the company's equity market capitalization), it would be financed using a combination of senior and high-yield debt, carrying a relatively high 6% average interest rate. The company's cash flow will cover the projected interest payments, with operating cash flow equal to 1.1 times interest, and the surplus available for debt reduction. Projected debt/capital would be above 75%.

D. Director D favors a smaller share buyback: 20% of the company's shares at a 20% premium to market price, financed by issuing investment-grade debt with a 3% coupon. The company's cash flow will cover the projected interest payments, with operating cash flow equal to 6.9 times interest, and the surplus available for share repurchases. Projected debt/capital would be 20% to 25%.

Discussion

Sleepy Mattress is a mature and stable business. It should therefore be able to support significant debt. The optimal capital structure for such a company would normally include debt, with the firm's value enhanced by the tax-deductibility of interest expense. But the company is now debt-free, generating cash flow and paying no dividend. If no action is taken, cash will accumulate on the company's balance sheet. We look at each recommendation in turn:

A. A's recommendation to pay a special cash dividend is reasonable. However, the size of the proposed dividend and associated borrowing ($1\times$ after-tax cash flow) is small, leaving Sleepy with a balance sheet that has very little debt (and likely no debt within a year).

B. B's recommendation is not appropriate unless the company has already identified an acquisition that would create value for the business. Even then, it would be prudent to look at the capital structure of the target company (and the pro forma combined capital structures) before determining how to finance the acquisition.

C. C's recommendation to buy back shares with debt would increase the debt and reduce the equity in the capital structure. This recapitalization plan is a step in the right direction; however, the resulting interest coverage of 1.1 times is extremely low, so taking this action would likely be too aggressive for the company. Any profit deterioration could easily cause the company to fail to meet its interest obligations. While we are assuming that Sleepy Mattress could raise the debt, the company could find it challenging to do so. At over 75%, pro forma debt as a percentage of total capital is very high. For companies with more stable and predictable cash flows, such as regulated utilities or REITs, higher percentages (i.e., above 60%) are common, but they are not common in consumer or industrial companies. Percentages above 75% often indicate that a company may be in financial distress.

D. D's recommendation is a superior course of action. It is a more balanced version of C, resulting in a manageable level of debt in the capital structure (under 25%), with a strong projected interest coverage ratio (6.9 times). It would be reasonable for the board to recommend this recapitalization to address the all-equity capital structure and, in addition, to initiate a cash dividend. Conducting a regular share buyback combined with a cash dividend would increase debt relative to equity in the capital structure and help counteract the de-leveraging in the business over time.

3.5. Unique Situations

In our discussion of the general relationship between company maturity and capital structure, there are important exceptions to note.

3.5.1. Capital-Intensive Businesses with Marketable Assets

Some businesses use high levels of leverage regardless of their development stage. For example, in real estate, utilities, shipping, airlines, and certain other highly capital-intensive businesses, the underlying assets can be bought and sold fairly easily, tend to retain their value regardless of who owns them, and can therefore support substantial debt secured by those assets. This would be true of a downtown office building, for example, but would not be true of a highly specialized factory in a remote location.

Note that in some cases, business models have evolved to take advantage of this fact. What were once highly capital-intensive and vertically integrated businesses (e.g., trucking, hotels, retailers, restaurants) have evolved to the point that many major brands are now owned by marketing or service businesses, which in turn have contractual relationships with the owners of real estate or other fixed assets used in the business. For example, Hilton Worldwide, one of the world's largest hotel companies, operates almost all its hotel rooms through long-term franchise or management agreements; the hotels themselves are owned by others. Conversely, some relatively large and mature businesses use little debt.

3.5.2. "Capital-Light" Businesses

Some business models—notably, software-based technology businesses—regardless of their development stage, have minimal fixed investments or working capital needs. They tend to have little debt in their capital structures and in many cases have substantial net cash, reflecting several factors:

- With little or no fixed assets or capital expenditure required to support growth, these businesses are often cash flow positive from an early stage, never needing to raise large amounts of capital.
- Many companies in rapidly evolving industries see the need to accumulate cash for potential acquisitions.
- If they are rapidly growing and successful, companies may not face typical pressure to pay dividends or repurchase shares.
- A rapidly rising share price can cause the market value of a company's equity to significantly outpace the value of any debt that might have been raised.

EXAMPLE 8   Debt Use: Industry Variations

1. Green Company and Black Company are each achieving 15% annual revenue growth and have recently started to generate positive cash flow. Green Company owns and acquires renewable energy generation projects. Black Company is a cloud-based software company with a dominant market position, serving auto dealers. Which company is more likely to have greater debt in its capital structure, and why?
   A. Black Company, because it serves a cyclical business
   B. Black Company, because of the strength of its market position
   C. Green Company, because its underlying assets can be financed with debt

Solution:

C is correct. Green Company has fixed assets, for which there is likely to be a ready and liquid market, and stable cash flows, which are supportive of debt financing. Black Company, a cloud-based software technology company, is a "capital-light" business, with few fixed assets. Its assets are likely to consist of mostly human capital. Additionally, servicing a cyclical industry is also likely to lead to Black Company having low debt.

---

4. MODIGLIANI–MILLER PROPOSITIONS

In a classic paper, Nobel Prize–winning economists Franco Modigliani and Merton Miller (1958) argued that, given certain assumptions, a company's choice of capital structure does not affect (or is "irrelevant" in determining) its value, where firm value is equal to the present value of the firm's expected future cash flows, discounted by the firm's weighted average cost of capital. In short, managers cannot change firm value simply by changing the company's capital structure.

Let's begin by imagining a company's capital structure as a pie, with each slice of the pie representing a specific type of capital (e.g., common equity or debt) and the size of the pie representing the company's total value. We can slice the pie in any number of ways, yet the total size remains the same. This is equivalent to saying that a company's value, or present value of expected cash flows, remains the same no matter how the capital slices are allocated, so long as the future cash flow stream is expected to remain the same and the risk of that cash flow stream, as reflected by the company's weighted average cost of capital, remains the same.

In their work, Modigliani and Miller (MM) used simplifying assumptions to show the irrelevance of capital structure to firm value, and then they relaxed the assumptions to show the impact of taxes and financial distress costs on capital structure. In their theoretical framework, MM assumed that all investors have homogeneous expectations about expected future corporate earnings and the riskiness of those earnings. Their assumptions, including a world of **perfect capital markets**—in which there are no taxes, no transaction costs, and no bankruptcy costs, and all investors have equal ("symmetric") information—are shown in Exhibit 8.

EXHIBIT 8: Modigliani–Miller Assumptions

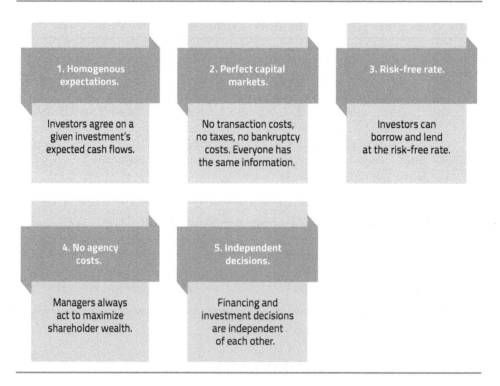

1. Homogenous expectations.	2. Perfect capital markets.	3. Risk-free rate.
Investors agree on a given investment's expected cash flows.	No transaction costs, no taxes, no bankruptcy costs. Everyone has the same information.	Investors can borrow and lend at the risk-free rate.

4. No agency costs.	5. Independent decisions.
Managers always act to maximize shareholder wealth.	Financing and investment decisions are independent of each other.

Modigliani and Miller's seminal work provides us with a starting point and allows us to examine what happens when the assumptions are relaxed to reflect real-world considerations.

While these assumptions do not hold in practice—which ultimately does alter MM's original conclusion of capital structure irrelevance—the MM theoretical framework remains a popular starting point for thinking about the strategic use of debt in a company's capital structure.

4.1. MM Proposition I without Taxes: Capital Structure Irrelevance

Given their assumptions, Modigliani and Miller proved that changing the capital structure does not affect firm value, in part because individual investors can create any capital structure they prefer for the company by borrowing and lending in their own accounts in addition to holding shares in the company. This "homemade" leverage argument relies on the MM assumption that investors can lend and borrow at the risk-free rate.

Example: Suppose that a company has a capital structure consisting of 50% debt and 50% equity and that an individual investor would prefer that the company's capital structure be 70% debt and 30% equity. The investor could borrow money to finance their share purchases so that their ownership of company assets would reflect their preferred 70% debt financing. This action would be equivalent to buying stock on margin and would have no effect on either the company's expected operating cash flows or company value.

Modigliani and Miller used the concept of arbitrage to demonstrate their point: If the value of an unlevered company (i.e., a company without any debt) is not equal to that of a levered company, investors could make a riskless arbitrage profit at no cost by selling shares of the overvalued company and using the proceeds to buy shares of the undervalued company, forcing their values to become equal. The value of a firm is thus determined not by the securities it issues but, rather, by its expected future cash flows. Their conclusion is summarized below.

MM PROPOSITION I WITHOUT TAXES

The market value of a company is not affected by the company's capital structure.

Implications:

1. The value of the levered company (V_L) = the value of the unlevered company (V_U), or: $V_L = V_U$
2. The value of a company is determined solely by its expected future cash flows (not its relative reliance on debt and equity capital).
3. In the absence of taxes, the weighted average cost of capital (WACC), or

$$\text{WACC} = w_d\, r_d + w_p r_p + w_e r_e,$$

is unaffected by capital structure.

4.2. MM Proposition II without Taxes: Higher Financial Leverage Raises the Cost of Equity

Debt capital is cheaper than equity capital because debtholders have a priority in claims. Therefore, one might expect a company's weighted average cost of capital to decline by adding debt capital to its capital structure. However, adding leverage to a company's capital structure increases the risk to equityholders because greater debt increases the probability of bankruptcy. As a result, equityholders will demand a higher return on their equity investment as leverage increases in order to offset the increase in risk.

MM Proposition II without taxes tells us that adding any amount of lower-cost debt capital to the capital structure is always perfectly offset by an increase in the cost of equity, resulting in no change to the company's overall weighted average cost of capital. MM Proposition II explains why investors require higher returns on levered equity; their required returns should match the increased risk from leverage. Specifically, MM Proposition II without taxes tells us that a company's cost of equity is a linear function of its debt-to-equity ratio:

$$r_e = r_0 + (r_0 - r_d)\frac{D}{E}, \tag{1}$$

where r_e is the cost of equity, r_o is the cost of capital for a company financed only with equity (i.e., an all-equity company), r_d is the cost of debt, D is the market value of debt, and E is the market value of equity. Equation 1 is a linear function with the intercept equal to r_0 and the slope equal to the quantity $(r_0 - r_d)$.

Given that capital structure changes do not affect the company's future cash flow stream and the company's weighted average cost of capital remains unchanged for any chosen capital structure, there is no change in the value of the company. Note that Modigliani and Miller did not assume away the possibility of bankruptcy. They simply assumed there was no cost to bankruptcy.

MM PROPOSITION II WITHOUT TAXES

The cost of equity is a linear function of the company's debt-to-equity ratio.

Implications:

1. Higher leverage raises the cost of equity but does not change firm value or WACC.
2. The increase in the cost of equity must exactly offset the greater use of lower-cost debt.

Example: Consider the Leverkin Company, which currently has an all-equity capital structure. Leverkin has expected annual cash flows to equityholders (which we denote "CF_e") of USD5,000 and a cost of equity of 10%, which is also its WACC since equity is the firm's only source of capital. For simplicity, we assume that all cash flows are perpetual. Therefore, Leverkin's value is equal to:

$$V = \frac{CFe}{r_{wacc}} = \frac{\$5,000}{0.10} = \$50,000$$

Now suppose that Leverkin plans to issue USD15,000 in debt at a cost of 5% and use the proceeds to buy back and reduce its outstanding equity by USD15,000. This action leaves the total invested capital unchanged at USD50,000.

Under MM Proposition I, $V_L = V_U$, the value of Leverkin must remain the same at USD50,000 after the change in capital structure. Under MM Proposition II, after the change in capital structure, the cost of equity for Leverkin—now with USD15,000 in debt capital and USD35,000 in equity capital—increases to 12.143%:

$$r_e = 0.10 + (0.10 - 0.05)\frac{\$15,000}{\$35,000} \approx 0.12143 = 12.143\%$$

To prove that Leverkin's firm value does not change after the change in capital structure, we need to show that its WACC remains unchanged at 10%. With the new cost of equity, Leverkin's WACC is now calculated as:

$$r_{wacc} = \left(\frac{\$15,000}{\$50,000}\right)0.05 + \left(\frac{\$35,000}{\$50,000}\right)0.12143 = 0.10 = 10\%$$

Leverkin's WACC is still 10%, as the move to cheaper debt was perfectly offset by an increase in the cost of equity. Thus, consistent with MM Proposition I, the value of the firm remains unchanged at USD50,000. Furthermore, the value of Leverkin must equal the sum of the present values of cash flows to debtholders (which we denote "CF$_d$") and equityholders. With USD15,000 debt at a cost of 5% (r$_d$), Leverkin makes annual interest payments of USD750 to debtholders, leaving USD5,000 - USD750 = USD4,250 remaining for equityholders. Therefore, the total value of the company can also be expressed as:

$$V = D + E$$
$$V = \frac{CF_d}{r_d} + \frac{CF_e}{r_e}$$
$$V = \frac{\text{USD750}}{0.05} + \frac{\text{USD4,250}}{0.12143} = \text{USD50,000}$$

As the level of debt rises, the risk of the company defaulting on its debt increases. This risk is borne by the equity holders. So, as the proportionate use of debt rises, the equity's beta, β_e, also rises.

Now let's consider a company's systematic risk. Portfolio managers know that the beta of an investment portfolio is a market-value-weighted average of the betas of the investments in that portfolio. Similarly, the beta (or systematic risk) of a company's assets is a weighted average of the systematic risks of its sources of capital. This concept is explained by the Hamada equation, which does not account for default risk (see Hamada 1972):

$$\beta_a = \left(\frac{D}{V}\right)\beta_d + \left(\frac{E}{V}\right)\beta_e, \qquad\qquad (2)$$

where β_a is the asset's systematic risk, or **asset beta**, β_d is the beta of debt, and β_e is the equity beta. According to Modigliani and Miller, the company's cost of capital depends not on its capital structure but, rather, on its business risk as reflected in the firm's WACC. As the level of debt rises, however, the risk of the company defaulting on its debt increases. This risk is borne by the equityholders. So, as the proportionate use of debt rises, the equity's beta, β_e, also rises. By reordering the terms of Equation 2, we get

$$\beta_e = \beta_a + (\beta_a - \beta_d)\left(\tfrac{D}{E}\right). \tag{3}$$

Conclusion: We have learned that under Modigliani and Miller's restrictive assumptions, when there are no taxes, leverage does not affect the value of the company or its weighted average cost of capital. However, leverage does cause the risk of equity to increase and thus the cost of equity to increase as well.

EXAMPLE 9   Value of Firm in Perfect Capital Markets

1. Company A has 25% debt and 75% equity in its capital structure. Management decides to increase leverage, so it issues more debt and buys back company stock. As a result, the new capital structure is 50% debt and 50% equity. Which of the following statements is true in perfect capital markets?
   A. After refinancing, the company is worth more because leverage has increased.
   B. After refinancing, the company is worth less because there is a greater chance of bankruptcy.
   C. Neither is true.

Solution:
   Neither answer is correct. In perfect capital markets, a change in capital structure has no impact on the value of the company.

EXAMPLE 10   Effect of Leverage on Equity Beta

1. The Chang Shou Noodle Company is financed with 10% debt and 90% equity.

   If the asset beta is 0.8 and the debt beta is 0.2, what is the equity beta?

Solution:
   We use Equation 3 to solve this problem.
   Prior to the change in capital structure, the equity beta is

$$\beta_e = 0.8 + (0.8 - 0.2)(10/90) = 0.87.$$

2. How does the equity beta change if management increases leverage to 30% debt?

Solution:
   After the capital structure change, the equity beta is higher because more debt increases the risk to equityholders. The new equity beta is

$$\beta_e = 0.8 + (0.8 - 0.2)(30/70) = 1.06.$$

4.3. MM Propositions with Taxes: Firm Value

Now let's explore what happens to the two MM propositions when we relax the assumption of no corporate taxes.

In most countries, interest expense is deductible from income for tax purposes. In other words, debt provides a tax shield for companies that are earning profits, and the money saved in taxes enhances the value of the company. If we ignore other realities for now, such as the costs of financial distress and bankruptcy, the value of the company increases with increasing levels of debt. The actual cost of debt is reduced by the amount of the tax benefit:

After-tax cost of debt = Before-tax cost of debt × (1 − marginal tax rate)

Modigliani and Miller's Proposition I with corporate taxes states that in the presence of corporate taxes (but not personal taxes), the value of the levered company is greater than that of the all-equity company by an amount equal to the tax rate multiplied by the value of the debt, defined as the present value of the **debt tax shield**:

$$V_L = V_U + tD, \tag{4}$$

where t is the marginal tax rate and tD is the present value of the debt tax shield. When there are corporate taxes, a profitable company can increase its value by using debt financing. Taken to the extreme, Equation 4 predicts a value-maximizing capital structure of 100% debt.

MM PROPOSITION I WITH CORPORATE TAXES

The market value of a levered company is equal to the value of an unlevered company plus the value of the debt tax shield.

Implications:

1. In the presence of taxes, a profitable company can increase its value (V) by using debt.
2. The higher the tax rate, the greater the benefit of using debt in the capital structure.

4.4. MM Propositions with Taxes: Cost of Capital

If the value of the company increases as it uses more debt, the company's weighted average cost of capital must decrease as it uses more debt. That is, in the earlier propositions without corporate taxes, the lower cost of debt was perfectly offset by an increase in the cost of equity. Now, in the presence of corporate taxes, the cost of debt is further lowered by the tax benefit such that the lower debt cost outweighs the increase in the cost of equity and results in a lower WACC.

To demonstrate this idea, let's begin with the revised cost of equity under MM Proposition II with corporate taxes:

$$r_e = r_0 + (r_0 - r_d)(1 - t)\frac{D}{E} \tag{5}$$

Notice that the only difference between Equation 5 and Equation 1 (MM Proposition II with no taxes) is the presence of the term $(1 - t)$. When t is zero, the two equations are identical. When t is not zero, the term $(1 - t)$ is less than 1 and serves to reduce the cost of levered equity. The cost of equity still rises as the company increases the amount of debt in its capital structure, but it rises at a slower rate than in the no-tax case.

Consequently, as debt increases, the company's WACC decreases and the company's value increases. This result implies that when there are taxes (and no financial distress or bankruptcy costs), debt financing is highly advantageous. Taken to an extreme, this result also suggests that a company's optimal capital structure is all debt—a conclusion that is at odds with reality and a direct result of Modigliani and Miller's restrictive assumptions.

MM PROPOSITION II WITH CORPORATE TAXES

The cost of equity is a linear function of the company's debt-to-equity ratio with an adjustment for the tax rate.

Implications:

1. In the presence of taxes, the cost of equity rises as the company uses more debt but at a slower rate than in the no-tax case.
2. As the company's use of debt increases, its WACC decreases and its value increases.
3. In the presence of taxes (but no financial distress or bankruptcy costs), the use of debt is value enhancing and, at the extreme, 100% debt is optimal.

Example: Referring back to the previous example involving the Leverkin Company, recall that annual cash flows to equityholders were USD5,000 and the cost of equity (and WACC) was 10%. As before, Leverkin is planning to issue USD15,000 of 5% debt in order to buy back an equivalent amount of equity. Now, however, assume that Leverkin pays corporate taxes at a rate of 25%.

Since the company does not currently have debt, the after-tax cash flows are now USD5,000(1 - 0.25), or USD3,750. Because the cash flows are assumed to be perpetual, the value of the company is USD37,500 (= USD3,750/0.10), considerably less than it was when there were no corporate taxes.

Now, suppose Leverkin proceeds to issue USD15,000 of debt and uses the proceeds to repurchase equity. According to MM Proposition I with corporate taxes (i.e., Equation 4), the value of the company is

$$V_L = V_U + tD = \text{USD37,500} + 0.25(\text{USD15,000}) = \text{USD41,250}.$$

The total company value is now USD41,250, consisting of debt of USD15,000 and equity of USD26,250 (= USD41,250 - USD15,000).

According to MM Proposition II with corporate taxes (Equation 5), the new cost of equity for Leverkin is

$$r_e = 0.10 + (0.10 - 0.05)(1 - 0.25)\tfrac{\$15,000}{\$26,250} = 0.12143 = 12.143\%$$

Using this new cost of equity, we can compute the new WACC:

$$r_{wacc} = \tfrac{\$15,000}{\$41,250}(0.05)(1 - 0.25) + \tfrac{\$26,250}{\$41,250}(0.12143)$$
$$= 0.09091 = 9.091\%$$

Unlike the previous example where Leverkin's WACC did not change with the change in capital structure, Leverkin's WACC decreased in this example from 10% to 9.091%. This reduction in WACC resulted in an increase in company value to USD41,250:

$$V_L = \tfrac{\text{CFe}(1-t)}{\text{WACC}} = \tfrac{\$5,000(1-0.25)}{0.09091} \approx \$41,250$$

As shown in the previous example, the value of the company must also equal the present value of cash flows to debtholders and equityholders:

$$V_L = D + E = \tfrac{r_d D}{r_d} + \tfrac{(\text{CFe}-r_d D)(1-t)}{r_e}$$
$$= \tfrac{\$750}{0.05} + \tfrac{(\$5,000-\$750)(1-0.25)}{0.12143} \approx \$41,250$$

Exhibit 9 summarizes the results using formulae.

EXHIBIT 9: **Modigliani and Miller Propositions**

	Without Taxes	With Taxes
Proposition I	$V_L = V_U$	$V_L = V_U + tD$
Proposition II	$r_e = r_0 + (r_0 - r_d)\tfrac{D}{E}$	$r_e = r_0 + (r_0 - r_d)(1 - t)\tfrac{D}{E}$

Of course, in the real world, taxes are not the only factor that affects the value of a levered company. The analysis gets more complicated when we allow for such things as the costs of financial distress and other real-world considerations. We consider costs of financial distress next.

4.5. Costs of Financial Distress

Operating and financial leverage can magnify profits and losses. Losses can put companies into **financial distress**, the costs of which can be explicit or implicit. Financial distress refers to the heightened uncertainty regarding a company's ability to meet its various obligations because of diminished earnings power or actual current losses. Even before filing for bankruptcy, companies under financial distress may lose customers, creditors, suppliers, and valuable employees.

EXAMPLE 11   Costs of Financial Distress

The Carillion PLC was a UK-based entity with revenues of almost GBP4.4 billion in 2016. It had a number of contracts with the UK government for the maintenance of roads and for catering and cleaning at hundreds of schools. Its share price was GBP308 at the end of 2015 and GBP236 at the end of 2016.

In mid-2017, Carillion warned that profits would fall short of expectations due to problems collecting on several construction contracts. Soon after, its share price fell by 30%. Even as it faced collection problems, the company was awarded more contracts, including contracts for railway and military projects.

Subsequent profit warnings sent the share price further downward. The second profit warning of that year was followed by new credit facilities and deferrals of debt repayments. The third profit warning, which included concerns over violating debt covenants, caused the share price to fall to around GBP21.

Discussions with creditors in December 2017 and January 2018 did not result in an agreement. Carillion was put in compulsory liquidation on 15 January 2018, and share trading was suspended.

The primary causes of Carillion's problems were its many overreaching, unprofitable projects and its inability to collect payments quickly.

The costs of financial distress included:

- the loss of all shareholder value;
- GBP44.2 million paid to an accounting firm to manage the insolvency;
- costs to the UK government as it grappled with nationalizing contracts; and
- creditors getting paid only a fraction of what they were owed.

The direct costs of financial distress include actual cash expenses associated with the bankruptcy process, such as legal and administrative fees. Indirect costs include forgone investment opportunities, reputational risk, impaired ability to conduct business, and costs arising from conflicts of interest between managers and debtholders, known as **agency costs** of debt, during periods in which the company is near or in bankruptcy.

The costs associated with financial distress are lower for companies whose assets have a ready secondary market. Airlines, shipping companies, and steel manufacturers typically have tangible assets that can be easily sold. High-tech growth companies, pharmaceutical companies, information technology companies, and companies in the services industry typically have fewer tangible assets that can be sold. These companies have higher costs associated with financial distress.

The probability of financial distress and bankruptcy increases when there is a greater amount of debt in the capital structure, a greater amount of business risk, and fewer reserves available to delay bankruptcy. Other factors that affect the probability of bankruptcy include diminished earnings power, unprofitable capital investments, the company's corporate governance structure, and the quality of the management team.

5. OPTIMAL AND TARGET CAPITAL STRUCTURES

Thus far in our discussion of the MM propositions, we have relaxed only the assumption of no corporate taxes. We now consider a scenario with both corporate taxes and bankruptcy/financial distress costs. The value-enhancing effects of leverage from the tax-deductibility of interest must now be weighed against the value-reducing impact of the present value of expected (or probability-weighted) costs of financial distress or bankruptcy, debt agency costs, debt restructuring and issuance fees, etc. Formally, we can modify MM Proposition I with corporate taxes to incorporate a deduction in firm value for the present value of financial distress costs:

$$V_L = V_U + tD - PV \text{ (Costs of financial distress)} \tag{6}$$

Equation 6 represents the **static trade-off theory of capital structure**, which is illustrated in Exhibit 10. The point V_U represents the value of an unlevered or all-equity firm. Moving to the right from this starting point, debt is added to the capital structure, and the new levered firm value shown by the green line is derived from Equation 6. At low levels of debt (x-axis), the tax benefit of debt typically outweighs the present value of financial distress costs, resulting in a higher firm value.

However, as more and more debt is added to the capital structure (moving farther to the right on the graph), the company's financial distress costs begin to rise substantially and eventually equal the tax benefit of debt at the point D*. Taking on debt beyond this point begins to reduce firm value because the substantial present value of financial distress costs now outweighs the tax benefit of debt. The theoretical point D*, the point at which the value of the company is maximized, is referred to as the **optimal capital structure**.

EXHIBIT 10: Static Trade-Off Theory with Taxes and Costs of Financial Distress: Firm Value and the Debt-to-Equity Ratio

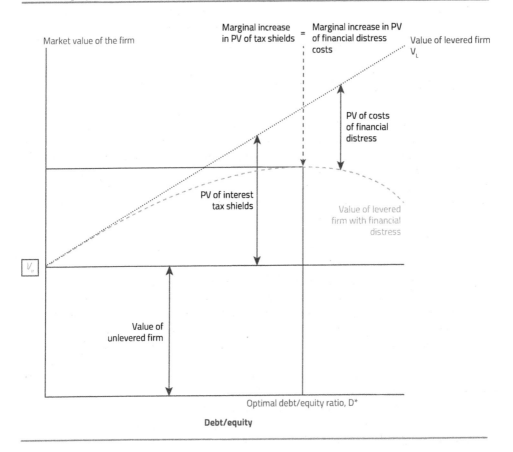

The static trade-off theory of capital structure suggests that managers should seek the optimal capital structure (D*) mix, the mix at which the marginal increase in the present value of interest tax shields is perfectly offset by the increase in the present value of financial distress costs. However, in practice, managers cannot precisely identify D*. But, by considering the company's business risk, tax situation, corporate governance, financial accounting information, probable bankruptcy costs, and other factors, management should be able to identify a range, or **target capital structure**, to strive for that is fairly close to the optimal capital structure. In addition, defining the company's optimal capital structure may vary according to economic conditions, industry sector, line of business, firm maturity, and regulatory environment.

There are a few reasons why a company's actual capital structure may differ from its target capital structure. For example, management may be able to exploit short-term opportunities in a particular financing source. A company issuing high-grade debt at attractive rates, for instance, may choose to increase deal size in response to strong investor demand. Or, fluctuations in the market values of the company's debt and equity securities can cause the company's actual capital structure to deviate from the target. In addition, flotation costs, which are the costs incurred by a publicly traded company when it issues new debt or equity securities, may make it impractical for a company to continually adjust its capital structure to keep it on target. In any case, while optimal capital structure may exist as a specific point in theory, it cannot be exactly determined because it is difficult to precisely estimate some costs, such as financial distress costs.

In practice, the optimal capital structure should be thought of as being within a range rather than a precise ratio. For example, it would be impossible to determine with certainty that the optimal amount of debt in the capital structure should be exactly 40%. Yet, the company should be able to determine that its target capital structure should be in the range of 30% to 50% debt.

The starting MM capital structure framework, even with its unrealistic assumptions, is appealing for understanding the strategic use of debt by companies. While its original predictions of capital structure irrelevance and a firm-value-maximizing capital structure of 100% debt do not hold when the assumptions are relaxed, the resulting static trade-off theory of capital structure still provides a thoughtful framework for using debt in the capital structure from a cost-benefit perspective.

One prediction of the trade-off theory is that highly profitable firms will use more debt than firms with lower profits to increase the tax-deductibility benefit of using debt. That is, the marginal benefit of using debt for highly profitable firms is often quite high as reflected in a high marginal corporate income tax rate, and these high-profit firms also tend to benefit from relatively lower costs of financial distress.

However, in practice, numerous studies have documented a negative relationship between debt use and profit levels. Even though this empirical finding does suggest that firm managers do not subscribe to the trade-off theory in setting their firms' capital structures, surveys have shown that managers do indeed manage their capital structures with a target capital structure in mind. Regardless of the empirical shortcomings of the trade-off theory, it is still a common starting point for understanding the strategic use of debt and has led to other possible capital structure theories, such as the pecking order theory and the market timing theory. A detailed discussion of these competing theories of capital structure is beyond the scope of this coverage.

5.1. Market Value vs. Book Value

While an optimal capital structure is calculated using the market value of equity and debt, a company's capital structure targets often use book value instead for the following reasons:

1. *Market values can fluctuate substantially and seldom impact the appropriate level of borrowing.* On the contrary, a company that has seen a rapid increase in its share price might opportunistically decide to raise equity capital rather than debt to maintain a certain debt-to-equity ratio.
2. *For management, the primary concern is the amount and types of capital invested* by *the company, not in the company.* This perspective includes how future investments will be funded. It is different, for example, from that of a shareholder who has purchased shares at the prevailing market price and is concerned with generating a return on that investment.
3. *Capital structure policy ensures management's ability to borrow easily and at low cost.* Since lenders, debt investors, and rating agencies generally focus on the book value of debt and equity for their calculation measures, companies and their managers will take this fact into account in determining their capital structure policies.

Although it is common for target capital structures to be expressed in terms of book values, managers pay close attention to both the price of their companies' shares and the market interest rates for their debt in deciding when, how much, and what type of capital to raise. For this reason, financings are often opportunistic to some degree, explaining why capital structures often deviate from target levels defined by management.

5.2. Target Weights and WACC

When conducting an analysis, how do we determine what WACC weights to use? Ideally, we want to use the proportion of each source of capital that the company would use in the project or company. If we assume that a company has a target capital structure and raises capital consistent with this target, we should use this target capital structure—the capital structure that the company is striving to obtain. If we know the company's target capital structure, then of course we should use it in our analysis. Analysts outside the company, however, would not know the target capital structure if not disclosed by the company and must estimate it using one of several methods:

1. Assume the company's current capital structure, at market value weights for the components, represents the company's target capital structure.
2. Examine trends in the company's capital structure or statements by management regarding capital structure policy to infer the target capital structure.
3. Use averages of comparable companies' capital structures as the target capital structure.

In the absence of knowledge of a company's target capital structure, it may be best to rely on the first method as the baseline. Note that in applying the third method, it is common, for simplicity, to use an unweighted, arithmetic average. An alternative is to calculate a weighted average, which would give more weight to larger companies.

Suppose we are using a company's current capital structure as a proxy for the target capital structure. In this case, we use the market values of the different capital sources in calculating the proportions. For example, suppose a company has the following capital structure based on market values:

Bonds outstanding	USD5 million
Preferred stock	1 million
Common stock	14 million
Total capital	USD20 million

The weights that we use would be as follows:

	Weights
Debt	0.25
Preferred equity	0.05
Common equity	0.70

Example 12 illustrates the estimation of weights. Note that a simple way of transforming a debt-to-equity ratio (D/E) into a weight—that is, $D/(D + E)$—is to divide D/E by $1 + D/E$.

EXAMPLE 12   Estimating the Proportions of Capital

Fin Anziell is a financial analyst with Analytiker Firma. Anziell is in the process of estimating the cost of capital of Gewicht GmbH. The following information is provided:
   Market value of debt: EUR50 million
   Market value of equity: EUR60 million
   Primary competitors and their capital structures (in millions):

Competitor	Market Value of Debt	Market Value of Equity
A	EUR25	EUR50
B	EUR101	EUR190
C	GBP40	GBP60

   What are Gewicht's proportions of debt and equity that Anziell would use in his analysis if he estimates these proportions using the company's:

1. Current capital structure?

Solution:
   Current capital structure:

$$w_d = \frac{€50 \text{ million}}{€50 \text{ million} + €60 \text{ million}} = 0.4545$$

$$w_e = \frac{€60 \text{ million}}{€50 \text{ million} + €60 \text{ million}} = 0.5454$$

2. Competitors' capital structure?

Solution:
   Competitors' capital structure:

$$w_d = \frac{\left(\frac{€25}{€25+€50}\right) + \left(\frac{€101}{€101+€190}\right) + \left(\frac{£40}{£40+£60}\right)}{3} = 0.3601$$

$$w_e = \frac{\left(\frac{€50}{€25+€50}\right) + \left(\frac{€190}{€101+€190}\right) + \left(\frac{£60}{£40+£60}\right)}{3} = 0.6399$$

3. Suppose Gewicht announces that a debt-to-equity ratio of 0.7 reflects its target capital structure. What weights should Anziell use in the cost of capital calculations?

Solution:

A debt-to-equity ratio of 0.7 represents a weight on debt of 0.7/1.7 = 0.4118, so $w_d = 0.4118$ and $w_e = 1 - 0.4118 = 0.5882$. These would be the preferred weights to use in a cost of capital calculation.

5.3. Pecking Order Theory and Agency Costs

Investors understand that management has access to more information about a business and its prospects than they do—known as **asymmetric information** (or information asymmetry) —and that management will take this information into account when raising capital. Providers of both equity and debt capital demand higher returns from companies with higher information asymmetry and will be concerned either that a company will issue shares when its shares are expensive or that it will issue debt when its creditworthiness is about to deteriorate —for example, due to higher investment or acquisitions.

Some degree of asymmetric information always exists because investors never know as much as managers and other insiders do. Consequently, investors often closely watch manager behavior for insight into insider opinions on the company's prospects. Aware of this scrutiny, managers consider how their actions might be interpreted by outsiders. The signaling model of capital structure suggests a hierarchy ("pecking order") to managers' selection of methods for financing new investments.

The **pecking order theory**, developed by Myers and Majluf (1984), suggests that managers choose methods of financing according to a hierarchy that gives first preference to methods with the least potential information content (internally generated funds) and lowest preference to methods with the most potential information content (public equity offerings). Public equity offerings are often closely scrutinized because investors are typically skeptical that existing owners would share ownership of a company that has a great future with other investors. In brief, managers prefer internal financing. If internal financing is insufficient, managers next prefer debt, then equity.

Another implication of the work of Myers and Majluf is that financial managers tend to issue equity when they believe the stock is overvalued, but they are reluctant to issue equity if they believe the stock is undervalued, potentially choosing instead to buy back shares. Thus, additional issuance of equity is often interpreted by investors as a negative signal.

We can read the signals that managers provide in their choice of financing method. Managers can signal to the market their confidence in a company's prospects through the issuance of debt, which commits the company to future obligations (so-called debt signaling). For example, commitments to fixed payments, such as dividends and debt service payments, may be interpreted as the company's management having confidence in the company's future ability to make payments. Such signals are considered too costly for poorly performing companies to afford.

Alternatively, the signal of raising money at the top of the pecking order and issuing equity at the bottom of the pecking order holds other clues. If, for instance, the company's cost of capital increases after an equity issuance, we can interpret this effect as an indication that management needs capital beyond what comes cheaply; in other words, this is a negative signal regarding the company's prospects. Managers may hesitate to issue new equity when they believe the company's shares are underpriced, because they wish to avoid signaling that they believe the shares are overpriced and also to avoid the cost and effort involved with new equity issuance.

Information asymmetry and "signaling" about the value of a company's shares can also become important factors when there are share sales in a company that has a controlling shareholder. Investors will look for signals about the controlling shareholder's confidence in the value of the shares and reasons for selling shares. For instance, if the company is issuing new equity, is the controlling shareholder participating? If there is no new equity being issued, what is the stated reason for the sale and how convincing is that reason?

When a private equity owner takes a portfolio company public, it is typically assumed that it will eventually sell, often in stages over time. With companies controlled by founders or their families, this is less likely to be the case, although it is common for founders to seek to reduce their stake in order to decrease their exposure to a single business or for succession management reasons. In any case, public investors will assume that controlling shareholders will sell their shares at opportune times, taking advantage of favorable market conditions and/ or their superior knowledge of the business.

Agency costs are the incremental costs that arise from conflicts of interest between managers, shareholders, and bondholders. Additionally, agency theory predicts that a reduction in net agency costs of equity results from an increase in the use of debt versus equity. That is, there are savings in the agency costs of equity associated with the use of debt. Similarly, the more financially leveraged a company, the less freedom for managers to either take on more debt or spend cash unwisely. This is the foundation of Michael Jensen's (1986) **free cash flow hypothesis**: higher debt levels discipline managers by forcing them to manage the company efficiently so the company can make its interest and principal payments and by reducing the company's free cash flow and thus managers' opportunities to misuse cash.

EXAMPLE 13 Agency Costs, Asymmetric Information, and Signaling

Cloudy Prospects PLC, a small pharmaceutical company, is testing the potential for its primary drug, which is already in commercial production, to be used in a new application for which it was not originally intended: treatment of patients with a widespread virus. The company is managed by a team of medical scientists. Management hopes this new application for the drug will result in a big increase in sales and the value of the company. The company has been consistently profitable and debt-free.

Over the course of three months, the following events occur:

In June, management monitors test results closely. Results are promising; the share price is stable.

In July, test results continue to look promising. Anticipating that it might have to scale up production quickly, the company negotiates and announces a large increase in its credit line.

In August, Cloudy announces successful test results. The CEO receives a call from a headhunter, who thinks the CEO might be a good candidate to lead a larger competitor. The CEO takes the call and decides to meet the headhunter.

Which, if any, of the following are represented here, and by which event and when?

1. Agency costs

Solution:

Agency costs. The CEO's decision in August to take the headhunter meeting about a possible opportunity with a competitor was unwise. If the CEO were acting solely in the interests of the shareholders of Cloudy Prospects, he would not take the meeting.

2. Asymmetric information

Solution:

Asymmetric information. Management had knowledge of the positive test results in June and July, before they were publicly announced in August.

3. Signaling

Solution:

Signaling. The company's announcement in July that it was increasing its credit line could reasonably be taken as a signal of its confidence that test results will be positive and that it will need to expand production capacity. Note: This is true whether or not the signaling is intentional.

6. STAKEHOLDER INTERESTS

We now look at how and why stakeholder interests are affected when specific capital structure decisions are made by management. Stakeholder groups that we will consider include providers of capital, such as shareholders and debtholders, as well as others, such as management and the board. Key stakeholder groups are shown in Exhibit 11.

EXHIBIT 11: Key Stakeholder Groups

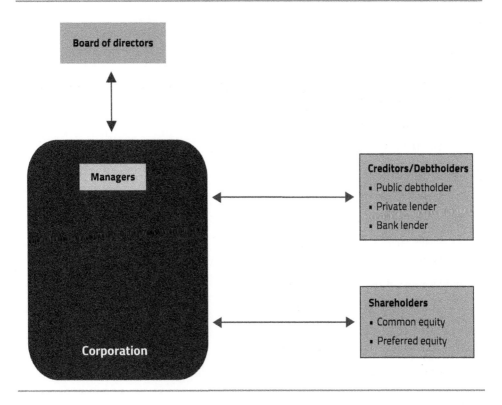

  Capital structure decisions impact stakeholder groups differently. In general, higher financial leverage increases risk for all stakeholders to varying degrees. However, the benefits of increased leverage, primarily through higher returns, accrue almost entirely to shareholders, often including senior management and the board. As a result, shareholders seeking higher returns from the company—and managers acting on their behalf—might prefer decisions that increase the company's financial leverage, while debtholders and other stakeholders in the company generally will not.

6.1. Debt vs. Equity Conflict

High leverage increases the potential conflict of interest between debtholders and shareholders. At high levels of leverage, the risk–return profile of shareholders becomes more asymmetric. The downside for equity investors is never more than 100%, or the full value of their investment, assuming no leverage or shorting. For highly leveraged companies, the upside reward for shareholders can be multiples of their initial investment. Meanwhile, for a holder of debt to maturity, the return, or upside, remains the face value of the debt plus the coupon. However, downside risk for a debtholder increases with higher leverage and the increased probability that the company will be unable to meet its outstanding debt obligations. Similarly, lower leverage levels decrease downside risk for a debtholder as the probability that the company can meet its debt obligations increases.

Let's look at a case study.

EXAMPLE 14   Acme Holdings Case Study

Acme Holdings (Acme), a hypothetical company, is planning to make an investment. Details are below.

Acme business valuation

> USD1 billion

New investment

> USD500 million

New investment financing

> Debt: 50% = USD250 million
> Equity: 50% = USD250 million

Ending value of new investment, T1

> USD1.2 billion (50% probability)
> USD0 (50% probability)

Expected value of new investment, E(V)

> USD600 million or

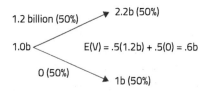

NPV of new investment

> USD100 million = (USD600 million − USD500 million)

Post-investment Acme valuation

> USD2.2 billion (50% probability) = (USD1.0 billion + USD1.2 billion)
> USD1.0 billion (50% probability) = (USD1.0 billion + USD0)

Three capital structure scenarios, each with a different starting leverage for Acme, are compared for their impact on Acme's shareholders and debtholders.

The scenarios are as follows:

Scenario 1. Normal leverage

Acme has a modest amount of debt (USD250 million), consistent with an investment-grade rating and composing a minority (25%) of its capital structure, with equity worth USD750 million.

Scenario 2. High leverage

Acme is highly leveraged, with debt composing the majority (USD900 million, or 90%) of its capital structure and equity of USD100 million (10%).

Scenario 3. Financial distress

Acme has debt of USD1.5 billion, exceeding the value of its business; the intrinsic value of its equity is therefore zero.

Discussion

This case illustrates how the outcomes for shareholders and debtholders are different in each scenario and how management decisions may or may not compromise the interests of debtholders.

It is not necessary that you memorize or be able to replicate the calculations in this example. The purpose is simply to illustrate a debt-equity conflict of interest numerically.

All values are shown in millions.

Scenario 1 (normal leverage)

	Debt	Equity
Value T_0	250	750
+ New Financing	250	250
= Value T_1	500	1,000

1. Normal leverage	Outcome	ACME T_1	Debtholder T_1	Equityholder T_1
Debt: .25 billion	Upside	2,200	500	1,700 (or 2,200 − 500)
Equity: .75 billion	Downside	1,000	500	500 (or 1,000 − 500)
	E(*V*)		500	1,100 (or .5(1,700) + .5(500))
	E(Impact on value)		0	100 (or 1,100 − 750 − 250)

In Scenario 1, the value of the business in both the upside outcome (2.2 billion) and the downside outcome (1.0 billion) is sufficient to easily repay debtholder value, or post-investment debt, of 500 million. Debtholders are not disadvantaged by the investment since they will receive proceeds regardless of whether the investment fails or succeeds. The expected impact on value is equal to (E(V) − Debt value T_1), or (500 − 500) = 0, or neutral for debtholders.

For equityholders, the expected return is positive. The expected value remaining for equityholders is 1.1 billion. Equityholders benefit because this expected value is higher than it would be, by 100 million, if the investment were not made (750 million) plus the 250 million of new investment (1.1 billion – 1.0 billion). In this scenario, there is no debt-equity conflict.

Scenario 2 (high leverage)

	Debt	Equity
Value T_0	900	100
+ New Financing	250	250
= Value T_1	1,150	350

2. High leverage	Outcome	ACME T_1	Debtholder T_1	Equityholder T_1
Debt: .9 billion	Upside	2,200	1,150	1,050 (or 2,200 – 1,150)
Equity: .1 billion	Downside	1,000	1,000 (loss)	0 (loss)
	$E(V)$		1075	525 (or .5(1,050) + 0)
	E(Impact on value)		–75	175 (or 525 – 100 – 250)

For Scenario 2 (high leverage), we calculate the results the same way, but a conflict arises. In this scenario, post-investment debt equals 1,150 million. In the upside outcome, debtholders are fully covered; however, in the downside outcome, there is more debt to repay (1,150 million) than the business is worth (1.0 billion). This potential for loss makes the investment negative from a debtholder perspective, given that debtholders do not participate in any upside. Reducing the expected value of 1,075 by the post-investment value of 1,150, or Debt value T_1, results in an expected impact on value of –75.

From an equityholder perspective, the investment is positive. Although there is a 50% chance equityholders will receive nothing, given that debt exceeds the value of the business in the downside outcome, they have a 50% chance that the business will be worth 2.2 billion, making their equity worth 800 million (2.2 billion – 1.15 billion debt – 250 million equity investment), which compares very favorably with the 100 million starting equity value without the investment. Expected value is positive at 525 million, and after reducing this amount by the starting equity value and the investment, the expected impact on value is 175. If management and the board do what maximizes value for equity, they would make the investment—to the detriment of debtholders. In this case, there is a debt-equity conflict.

Scenario 3 (financial distress)

	Debt	Equity
Value T_0	1,500	0
+ New Financing	250	250
= Value T_1	1,750	250

3. Financial distress	Outcome	ACME T_1	Debtholder T_1	Equityholder T_1
Debt: 1.5 billion	Upside	2,200	1,750	450 (or 2,200 − 1,750)
Equity: 0	Downside	1,000	1,000 (loss)	0 (loss)
	$E(V)$		1,375	225 (or .5(450) + 0))
	E(Impact on value)		125	−25 (or 225 − 250)

For Scenario 3, the impacts are again different. The value of the business before the proposed investment (1.0 billion) is so much less than the amount of debt outstanding (1.5 billion) that equityholders would not see an increase in value, despite the fact that the investment would have a positive 100 million NPV. However, netting the expected value of 225 for the equity investment results in a negative impact on value of −25. For debtholders, the expected impact on value is positive at 125 (or 1,375 − 1,000 − 250). In this case, making the investment would create positive value for Acme, but in seeking to maximize equity value, management would not make the investment because the return to equityholders is negative. Management's decision compromises the interests of its bondholders for the interests of its equityholders. In this case, there is a debt-equity conflict.

In summary, management is likely to make the investment when equityholders are expected to benefit, even if the impact on debtholders is negative, resulting in a debt-equity conflict. Management is unlikely to make the investment when the impact on equityholders is negative, even if the impact on bondholders and the project's NPV is positive.

6.1.1. Distressed Debt: Observations

The Acme Holdings example shows a distress scenario: The value of debt outstanding exceeds the value of the enterprise, and the company's equity has negative intrinsic value. Given this scenario, it would be difficult for Acme to raise new equity capital, and management might decline to make investments that would increase enterprise value.

In this situation, a financial restructuring is often a logical course of action. Restructuring can be involuntary, such as when the company is in default, or voluntary. In either case, by exchanging debt for equity, the company's capital structure can be repaired, new investments can be financed, and the company can avoid liquidation—which is a very costly type of financial distress.

When leverage and financial risk are high, the perspective of debtholders becomes more like that of equityholders. Normally, debt has low default risk and is priced to provide a modest yield to maturity. Return, or upside, is limited, unless the general level of interest rates declines. A holder of debt to maturity will be very focused on minimizing downside risk. However, with higher-risk debt and particularly with distressed debt, the potential upside can be substantial if the company does not default or if recoveries in default are higher than expected. In these circumstances, the return profile (and thus the perspective) of the debtholder becomes closer to that of an equity investor.

6.1.2. Other Debt Considerations

6.1.2.1. Seniority and Security Debtholder returns are influenced not only by the probability of default but also by the likely recoveries in the event of default. In a default scenario, secured lenders are likely to recover more of their principal than unsecured lenders; likewise, senior debt is likely to recover more than subordinated debt. Recall that senior debt is often secured, but not always. As a result, secured and senior lenders can better tolerate actions by management that increase the probability of default, such as new investment by the company or increasing the level of unsecured or subordinated debt.

6.1.2.2. Safeguards for Debtholders Management generally seeks to maximize equity value and thus may take actions that are unfavorable to debtholders. However, debtholders have the following safeguards to protect their interests:

- Debt covenants can be used to put contractual limits on future borrowing by the company and can limit other management actions that would increase risk to debtholders. Positive covenants state what the borrower must do, such as maintaining financial ratios within certain thresholds. Ratios commonly used in debt covenants are drawn from the income and cash flow statements (cash coverage of interest or fixed charges), the balance sheet (minimum tangible net worth, debt-to-equity ratio), or both (debt-to-EBITDA ratio). Negative covenants state what the borrower cannot do, such as additional secured borrowing or dividend payments.
- Companies generally want to preserve access to credit on favorable terms and so will act accordingly to maintain or improve their creditworthiness, since they may need to borrow in the future. Management's track record—its statements and actions with respect to capital structure, investment, M&A, dividends, and strategy—will impact the company's future credit rating, banking relationships, and cost of borrowing.
- Financial distress costs can be substantial. Even with a primary focus on maximizing common share value, management will generally seek to keep default risk—and other stakeholder impacts from high leverage—at very low levels.

6.2. Preferred Shareholders

As with common shareholders, preferred shareholders provide long-term capital, with no maturity (repayment) date. The issuance of preferred equity, therefore, creates less risk for the company's debtholders and common shareholders than if the company were to issue debt. From a common shareholder perspective, whether issuing preferred equity is more attractive than issuing debt depends on the relative after-tax borrowing cost for the company.

Since they are providers of permanent capital and lack covenant protection, preferred shareholders are vulnerable to decisions that increase financial leverage and risk over the long term. For example, a company in a mature business might commit to a long-term policy of dividend growth and share repurchases. This strategy would result in higher financial leverage over the long term. Existing senior secured debtholders might be unconcerned, particularly for debt maturing relatively soon, since there is minimal default risk. However, preferred shareholders might be concerned that the new policy could gradually erode the company's capacity to pay preferred dividends.

6.3. Management and Directors

It is critical to consider the interests of management and the board since they make capital structure and business strategy decisions. In practice, compensation is the principal tool used to create alignment of interests between management and directors and shareholders. Equity compensation can be a substantial portion of management's total compensation.

In principle, management compensation is intended to motivate managers to work hard to maximize long-term shareholder value. However, the alignment of interests between managers and shareholders is never perfect. For example, the interests of owners are not necessarily identical to the interests of managers, who happen to receive shares and options as part of their compensation.

The following highlights this aspect of management compensation.

EXAMPLE 15   Management Stock Options and Leverage

The company Binary Outcomes Ltd. is debt-free and has a share price of USD100, with 1 million shares outstanding. Its intrinsic value is USD100 million (USD100 × 1 million), which is based on a 50% probability of a USD110/share value and a 50% probability of a USD90/share value. If management has options exercisable at USD100, their current expected value is USD5.

Is it in management's interest to increase leverage at the company, such as by issuing USD50 million of debt to buy back shares?

Discussion

As shown in Exhibit 12, it would be in management's interest to increase leverage, such as by issuing debt to buy back 50% of the company's shares at USD100 per share. This action would increase debt by USD50 million (purchase of 0.5 million shares at USD100 per share) and reduce equity value by an equivalent amount, creating a 50% probability of a USD120/share value and a 50% probability of an USD80/share value. Although there is no change in shareholder value, the leverage results in an increase in share value (USD120) and corresponding option value (USD20) in the upside scenario, while the downside option value remains USD0, with an average expected option value of USD10. The use of leverage doubles the average expected value of management's options from USD5 to USD10.

EXHIBIT 12: Binary Outcomes Leverage Scenario

Scenario	Upside	Downside	Expected Value
Probability	50%	50%	
Firm value	USD110,000,000	USD90,000,000	USD100,000,000
No leverage			
Debt	—	—	
Equity value	USD110,000,000	USD90,000,000	
Shares outstanding	1,000,000	1,000,000	
Share price	USD110	USD90	USD100
Option exercise price	USD100	USD100	

Scenario	Upside	Downside	Expected Value
Option value	USD10	—	USD5
With leverage			
Debt	USD50,000,000	USD50,000,000	
Equity value	USD60,000,000	USD40,000,000	
Shares outstanding	500,000	500,000	
Share price	USD120	USD80	USD100
Option exercise price	USD100	USD100	
Option value	USD20	—	USD10

With typical management share option schemes, rather than paying dividends, management will be motivated to buy back shares with excess cash. This strategy benefits them by increasing the value of their share options. Similarly, management would be incentivized to retain profits rather than distribute them as a dividend to shareholders.

Continuing this example, if Binary Outcomes earns a profit of USD10/share and adds USD10/share in cash, retaining that profit would increase its intrinsic value from USD100/share to USD110/share, thus increasing the intrinsic value of management's options by USD5 (from USD5 to USD10). If the entire profit is instead distributed as a dividend, however, there would be no increase in intrinsic value for the shares or management's options.

To mitigate this issue, some companies pay executive performance bonuses in shares rather than in options or have minimum share ownership requirements for senior managers and, in some cases, directors.

In mature or stable businesses, compensation can skew heavily toward salaries and bonuses tied to "easy" targets, and management complacency can be a risk. The business may not have enough upside to attract highly talented managers or enough influence to make management aggressively pursue incremental sales or cost efficiencies. In these cases, adding financial leverage is a common strategy, increasing both the incentive for and the pressure on management to maximize value.

When managers stay in their positions for only a few years, they may be motivated to pursue short-term rather than long-term objectives: They want to demonstrate success and keep their jobs, and they are unsure whether they will be with the company long enough to benefit from longer-term initiatives. From a shareholder perspective, the solution is not to avoid management turnover but, rather, to ensure that it is based on performance (i.e., evaluated objectively and carefully) instead of on non-performance-related reasons.

Some of these misalignments offset each other. For example, stock options motivate risk-taking, while high cash compensation can create excessive caution and entrenchment.

7. SUMMARY

- Financing decisions are typically tied to investment spending and are based on the company's ability to support debt given the nature of its business model, assets, and operating cash flows.
- A company's stage in the life cycle, its cash flow characteristics, and its ability to support debt largely dictate its capital structure, since capital not sourced through borrowing must come from equity (including retained earnings).
- Generally speaking, as companies mature and move from start-up through growth to maturity, their business risk declines as operating cash flows turn positive with increasing predictability, allowing for greater use of leverage on more attractive terms.
- Modigliani and Miller's work, with its simplifying assumptions, provides a starting point for thinking about the strategic use of debt and shows us that managers cannot change firm value simply by changing the firm's capital structure. Firm value is independent of capital structure decisions.
- Given the tax-deductibility of interest, adding leverage increases firm value up to a point but also increases the risk of default for capital providers who demand higher returns in compensation.
- To maximize firm value, management should target the optimal capital structure that minimizes the company's weighted average cost of capital.
- "Optimal capital structure" involves a trade-off between the benefits of higher leverage, which include the tax-deductibility of interest and the lower cost of debt relative to equity, and the costs of higher leverage, which include higher risk for all capital providers and the potential costs of financial distress.
- Managers may provide investors with information ("signaling") through their choice of financing method. For example, commitments to fixed payments may signal management's confidence in the company's prospects.
- Managers' capital structure decisions impact various stakeholder groups differently. In seeking to maximize shareholder wealth or their own, managers may create conflicts of interest in which one or more groups are favored at the expense of others, such as a debt-equity conflict.

8. PRACTICE PROBLEMS

1. Which of the following is *least* likely to affect the capital structure of Longdrive Trucking Company? Longdrive has moderate leverage today.
   A. The acquisition of a major competitor for shares
   B. A substantial increase in share price
   C. The payment of a stock dividend

2. Which of these statements is *most* accurate with respect to the use of debt by a start-up fashion retailer with negative cash flow and uncertain revenue prospects?
   A. Debt financing will be unavailable or very costly.
   B. The company will prefer to use equity rather than debt given its uncertain cash flow outlook.
   C. Both A and B.

3. Which of the following is true of the growth stage in a company's development?
   A. Cash flow is negative, by definition, with investment outlays exceeding cash flow from operations.
   B. Cash flow may be negative or positive.
   C. Cash flow is positive and growing quickly.

4. Which of the following mature companies is *most* likely to use a high proportion of debt in its capital structure?
   A. A mining company with a large, fixed asset base
   B. A software company with very stable and predictable revenues and an asset-light business model
   C. An electric utility

5. Which of the following is *most* likely to occur as a company evolves from growth stage to maturity and seeks to optimize its capital structure?
   A. The company relies on equity to finance its growth.
   B. Leverage increases as the company needs more capital to support organic expansion.
   C. Leverage increases as the company is able to support more debt.

6. If investors have homogeneous expectations, the market is efficient, and there are no taxes, no transaction costs, and no bankruptcy costs, Modigliani and Miller's Proposition I states that:
   A. bankruptcy risk rises with more leverage.
   B. managers cannot change the value of the company by changing the amount of debt.
   C. managers cannot increase the value of the company by using tax-saving strategies.

7. According to Modigliani and Miller's Proposition II without taxes:
   A. the capital structure decision has no effect on the cost of equity.
   B. investment and capital structure decisions are interdependent.
   C. the cost of equity increases as the use of debt in the capital structure increases.

8. The weighted average cost of capital (WACC) for Van der Welde is 10%. The company announces a debt offering that raises the WACC to 13%. The *most* likely conclusion is that for Van der Welde:
   A. the company's prospects are improving.
   B. equity financing is cheaper than debt financing.
   C. the company's debt/equity has moved beyond the optimal range.

9. According to the static trade-off theory:
   A. debt should be used only as a last resort.
   B. companies have an optimal level of debt.
   C. the capital structure decision is irrelevant.

The following information relates to questions 10–12

Nailah Mablevi is an equity analyst who covers the entertainment industry for Kwame Capital Partners, a major global asset manager. Kwame owns a significant position, with a large unrealized capital gain, in Mosi Broadcast Group (MBG). On a recent conference call, MBG's management stated that they plan to increase the proportion of debt in the company's capital structure. Mablevi is concerned that any changes in MBG's capital structure will negatively affect the value of Kwame's investment.

To evaluate the potential impact of such a capital structure change on Kwame's investment, she gathers the information about MBG given in Exhibit 1.

EXHIBIT 1: Current Selected Financial Information on MBG

Yield to maturity on debt	8.00%
Market value of debt	USD100 million
Number of shares of common stock	10 million
Market price per share of common stock	USD30
Cost of capital if all equity-financed	10.3%
Marginal tax rate	35%

10. MBG is *best* described as currently:
   A. 25% debt-financed and 75% equity-financed.
   B. 33% debt-financed and 66% equity-financed.
   C. 75% debt-financed and 25% equity-financed.

11. Holding operating earnings constant, an increase in the marginal tax rate to 40% would:
   A. result in a lower cost of debt capital.
   B. result in a higher cost of debt capital.
   C. not affect the company's cost of capital.

12. Which of the following is *least* likely to be true with respect to optimal capital structure?
   A. The optimal capital structure minimizes WACC.
   B. The optimal capital structure is generally close to the target capital structure.
   C. Debt can be a significant portion of the optimal capital structure because of the tax-deductibility of interest.

13. Other factors being equal, in which of the following situations are debt-equity conflicts likely to arise?
   A. Financial leverage is low.
   B. The company's debt is secured.
   C. The company's debt is long-term.

14. Which of the following is an example of agency costs? In each case, management is advocating a substantial acquisition and management compensation is heavily composed of stock options.
   A. Management believes the acquisition will be positive for shareholder value but negative for the value and interests of the company's debtholders.
   B. Management's stock options are worthless at the current share price. The acquisition has a high (50%) risk of failure (with zero value) but substantial (30%) upside if it works out.
   C. The acquisition is positive for equityholders and does not significantly impair the position of debtholders. However, the acquisition puts the company into a new business where labor practices are harsh and the production process is environmentally damaging.

15. Which of the following is *least* accurate with respect to debt-equity conflicts?
    A. Equityholders focus on potential upside and downside outcomes, while debtholders focus primarily on downside risk.
    B. Management attempts to balance the interests of equityholders and debtholders.
    C. Debt covenants can mitigate the conflict between debtholders and equityholders.

16. Which of the following is *least* likely to be true with respect to agency costs and senior management compensation?
    A. Equity-based incentive compensation is the primary method to address the problem of agency costs.
    B. A well-designed compensation scheme should eliminate agency costs.
    C. High cash compensation for senior management, without significant equity-based performance incentives, can lead to excessive caution and complacency.

17. Integrated Systems Solutions Inc. (ISS) is a technology company that sells software to companies in the building construction industry. The company's assets consist mostly of intangible assets. Although the company is profitable, revenue growth and earnings growth have been slowing in recent years. The company's business model is a pay-per-use model, and given the cyclical nature of the construction industry, the company's revenues and earnings vary considerably over the business cycle.

    Describe two factors that would point to ISS having a relatively high cost of borrowing and low proportion of debt in its capital structure.

18. Tillett Technologies is a manufacturer of high-end audio and video (AV) equipment. The company, with no debt in its capital structure, has experienced rapid growth in revenues and improved profitability in recent years. About half of the company's revenues come from subscription-based service agreements. The company's assets consist mostly of inventory and property, plant, and equipment, representing its production facilities. Now, the company seeks to raise new capital to finance additional growth.

    Describe two factors that would support Tillett being able to access debt capital at a reasonable cost to finance the additional growth. Justify your response.

19. Discuss two financial metrics that can be used to assess a company's ability to service additional debt in its capital structure.

20. Identify two market conditions that can be characterized as favorable for companies wishing to add debt to their capital structures.

21. Which of the following is *least* accurate with respect to the market value and book value of a company's equity?
    A. Market value is more relevant than book value when measuring a company's cost of capital.
    B. Book value is often used by lenders and in financial ratio calculations.
    C. Both market value and book value fluctuate with changes in the company's share price.

22. Fran McClure of Alba Advisers is estimating the cost of capital of Frontier Corporation as part of her valuation analysis of Frontier. McClure will be using this estimate, along with projected cash flows from Frontier's new projects, to estimate the effect of these new projects on the value of Frontier. McClure has gathered the following information on Frontier Corporation:

	Current Year (USD)	Forecasted for Next Year (USD)
Book value of debt	50	50
Market value of debt	62	63
Book value of shareholders' equity	55	58
Market value of shareholders' equity	210	220

The weights that McClure should apply in estimating Frontier's cost of capital for debt and equity are, respectively:
A. $w_d = 0.200$; $w_e = 0.800$.
B. $w_d = 0.185$; $w_e = 0.815$.
C. $w_d = 0.223$; $w_e = 0.777$.

23. Which of the following is *not* a reason why target capital structure and actual capital structure tend to differ?
    A. Financing is often tied to a specific investment.
    B. Companies raise capital when the terms are attractive.
    C. Target capital structure is set for a particular project, while actual capital structure is measured at the consolidated company level.

24. According to the pecking order theory:
    A. new debt is preferable to new equity.
    B. new debt is preferable to internally generated funds.
    C. new equity is always preferable to other sources of capital.

25. Vega Company has announced that it intends to raise capital next year, but it is unsure as to the appropriate method of raising capital. White, the CFO, has concluded that Vega should apply the pecking order theory to determine the appropriate method of raising capital. Based on White's conclusion, Vega should raise capital in the following order:
    A. debt, internal financing, equity.
    B. equity, debt, internal financing.
    C. internal financing, debt, equity.

CHAPTER 6

MEASURES OF LEVERAGE

Pamela Peterson Drake, PhD, CFA
James Madison University (USA)

Raj Aggarwal, PhD, CFA
Kent State University Foundation Board (USA)

Cynthia Harrington, CFA
teamyou.co (USA)

Adam Kobor, PhD, CFA
New York University (USA)

LEARNING OUTCOMES

The candidate should be able to:

- define and explain leverage, business risk, sales risk, operating risk, and financial risk and classify a risk
- calculate and interpret the degree of operating leverage, the degree of financial leverage, and the degree of total leverage
- analyze the effect of financial leverage on a company's net income and return on equity
- calculate the breakeven quantity of sales and determine the company's net income at various sales levels
- calculate and interpret the operating breakeven quantity of sales

1. INTRODUCTION

This chapter presents elementary topics in leverage. **Leverage** is the use of fixed costs in a company's cost structure. Fixed costs that are operating costs (such as depreciation or rent) create operating leverage. Fixed costs that are financial costs (such as interest expense) create financial leverage.

Analysts refer to the use of fixed costs as leverage because fixed costs act as a fulcrum for the company's earnings. Leverage can magnify earnings both up and down. The profits of highly leveraged companies might soar with small upturns in revenue. But the reverse is also true: Small downturns in revenue may lead to losses.

Analysts need to understand a company's use of leverage for three main reasons. First, the degree of leverage is an important component in assessing a company's risk and return characteristics. Second, analysts may be able to discern information about a company's business and future prospects from management's decisions about the use of operating and financial leverage. Knowing how to interpret these signals also helps the analyst evaluate the quality of management's decisions. Third, the valuation of a company requires forecasting future cash flows and assessing the risk associated with those cash flows. Understanding a company's use of leverage should help in forecasting cash flows and in selecting an appropriate discount rate for finding their present value.

The chapter is organized as follows: Section 2 introduces leverage and defines important terms. Section 3 illustrates and discusses measures of operating leverage and financial leverage, which combine to define a measure of total leverage that gauges the sensitivity of net income to a given percent change in units sold. This section also covers breakeven points in using leverage and corporate reorganization (a possible consequence of using leverage inappropriately). A summary and practice problems conclude this chapter.

2. LEVERAGE

Leverage increases the volatility of a company's earnings and cash flows and increases the risk of lending to or owning a company. Additionally, the valuation of a company and its equity is affected by the degree of leverage: The greater a company's leverage, the greater its risk and, hence, the greater the discount rate that should be applied in its valuation. Further, highly leveraged (levered) companies have a greater chance of incurring significant losses during downturns, thus accelerating conditions that lead to financial distress and bankruptcy.

Consider the simple example of two companies, Impulse Robotics, Inc., and Malvey Aerospace, Inc. These companies have the following performance for the period of study:[1]

EXHIBIT 1: Impulse Robotics and Malvey Aerospace

	Impulse Robotics	Malvey Aerospace
Revenues	$1,000,000	$1,000,000
Operating costs	700,000	750,000
Operating income	$300,000	$250,000
Financing expense	100,000	50,000
Net income	$200,000	$200,000

These companies have the same net income, but are they identical in terms of operating and financial characteristics? Would we appraise these two companies at the same value? Not necessarily.

---

[1]We are ignoring taxes for this example, but when taxes are included, the general conclusions remain the same.

The risk associated with future earnings and cash flows of a company are affected by the company's cost structure. The **cost structure** of a company is the mix of variable and fixed costs. **Variable costs** fluctuate with the level of production and sales. Some examples of variable costs are the cost of goods purchased for resale, costs of materials or supplies, shipping charges, delivery charges, wages for hourly employees, sales commissions, and sales or production bonuses. **Fixed costs** are expenses that are the same regardless of the production and sales of the company. These costs include depreciation, rent, interest on debt, insurance, and wages for salaried employees.

Suppose that the cost structures of the companies differ in the manner shown in Exhibit 2.

EXHIBIT 2: Impulse Robotics and Malvey Aerospace

	Impulse Robotics	Malvey Aerospace
Number of units produced and sold	100,000	100,000
Sales price per unit	$10	$10
Variable cost per unit	$2	$6
Fixed operating cost	$500,000	$150,000
Fixed financing expense	$100,000	$50,000

The risk associated with these companies is different, although, as we saw in Exhibit 1, they have the same net income. They have different operating and financing cost structures, resulting in differing volatility of net income.

For example, if the number of units produced and sold is different from 100,000, the net income of the two companies diverges. If 50,000 units are produced and sold, Impulse Robotics has a loss of $200,000 and Malvey Aerospace has $0 earnings. If, on the other hand, the number of units produced and sold is 200,000, Impulse Robotics earns $1 million whereas Malvey Aerospace earns $600,000. In other words, the variability in net income is greater for Impulse Robotics, which has higher fixed costs in terms of both fixed operating costs and fixed financing costs.

Impulse Robotics' cost structure results in more leverage than that of Malvey Aerospace. We can see this effect when we plot the net income of each company against the number of units produced and sold, as in Exhibit 3. The greater leverage of Impulse Robotics is reflected in the greater slope of the line representing net income. This means that as the number of units sold changes, Impulse Robotics experiences a greater change in net income than does Malvey Aerospace for the same change in units sold.

EXHIBIT 3: Net Income for Different Numbers of Units Produced and Sold

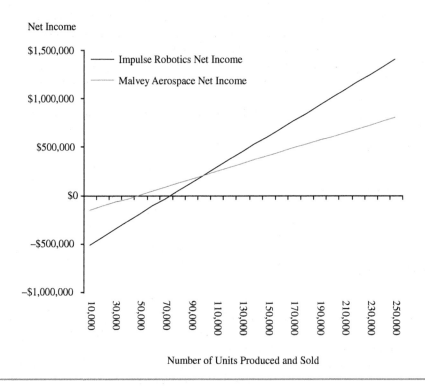

Companies that have more fixed costs relative to variable costs in their cost structures have greater variation in net income as revenues fluctuate and, hence, more risk.

3. BUSINESS AND SALES RISKS

Risk arises from both the operating and financing activities of a company. In the following, we address how that happens and the measures available to the analyst to gauge the risk in each case.

3.1. Business Risk and Its Components

Business risk is the risk associated with operating earnings. Operating earnings are risky because total revenues are risky, as are the costs of producing revenues. Revenues are affected by a large number of factors, including economic conditions, industry dynamics (including the actions of competitors), government regulation, and demographics. Therefore, prices of the company's goods or services or the quantity of sales may be different from what is expected. We refer to the uncertainty with respect to the price and quantity of goods and services as **sales risk**.

Operating risk is the risk attributed to the operating cost structure, in particular the use of fixed costs in operations. The greater the fixed operating costs relative to variable operating costs, the greater the operating risk. Business risk is therefore the combination of sales risk and operating risk. Companies that operate in the same line of business generally have similar business risk.

3.2. Sales Risk

Consider Impulse Robotics once again. Suppose that the forecasted number of units produced and sold in the next period is 100,000 but that the standard deviation of the number of units sold is 20,000. And suppose the price that the units sell for is expected to be $10 per unit but the standard deviation is $2. Contrast this situation with that of a company named Tolley Aerospace, Inc., which has the same cost structure but a standard deviation of units sold of 40,000 and a price standard deviation of $4.

If we assume, for simplicity's sake, that the fixed operating costs are known with certainty and that the units sold and price per unit follow a normal distribution, we can see the impact of the different risks on the operating income of the two companies through a simulation; the results are shown in Exhibit 4. Here, we see the differing distributions of operating income that result from the distributions of units sold and price per unit. So, even if the companies have the same cost structure, differing *sales risk* affects the potential variability of the company's profitability. In our example, Tolley Aerospace has a wider distribution of likely outcomes in terms of operating profit. This greater volatility in operating earnings means that Tolley Aerospace has more sales risk than Impulse Robotics.

EXHIBIT 4: Operating Income Simulations for Impulse Robotics and Tolley Aerospace

Panel A: Impulse Robotics

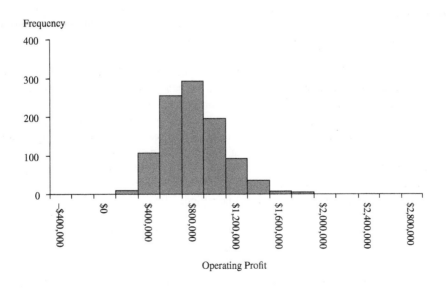

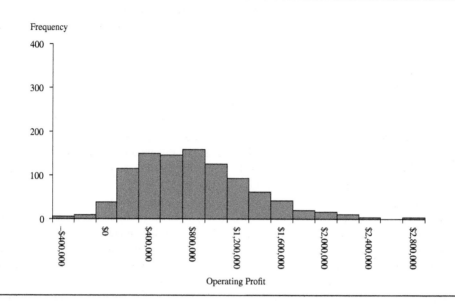

4. OPERATING RISK AND THE DEGREE OF OPERATING LEVERAGE

The greater the fixed component of costs, the more difficult it is for a company to adjust its operating costs to changes in sales. The mixture of fixed and variable costs depends largely on the type of business. Even within the same line of business, companies can vary their fixed and variable costs to some degree. We refer to the risk arising from the mix of fixed and variable costs as **operating risk**. The greater the fixed operating costs relative to variable operating costs, the greater the operating risk.

Next, we look at how operating risk affects the variability of cash flows. A concept taught in microeconomics is **elasticity**, which is simply a measure of the sensitivity of changes in one item to changes in another. We can apply this concept to examine how sensitive a company's operating income is to changes in demand, as measured by unit sales. We will calculate the operating income elasticity, which we refer to as the **degree of operating leverage** (DOL). DOL is a quantitative measure of operating risk as it was defined earlier.

The degree of operating leverage is the ratio of the percentage change in operating income to the percentage change in units sold. We will simplify things and assume that the company sells all that it produces in the same period. Then,

$$DOL = \frac{\text{Percentage change in operating income}}{\text{Percentage change in units sold}} \qquad (1)$$

For example, if DOL at a given level of unit sales is 2.0, a 5 percent increase in unit sales from that level would be expected to result in a $(2.0)(5\%) = 10$ percent increase in operating income. As illustrated later in relation to Exhibit 5, a company's DOL is dependent on the level of unit sales being considered.

Returning to Impulse Robotics, the price per unit is $10, the variable cost per unit is $2, and the total fixed operating costs are $500,000. If Impulse Robotics' output changes from 100,000 units to 110,000 units—an increase of 10 percent in the number of units sold—operating income changes from $300,000 to $380,000:[2]

EXHIBIT 5: Operating Leverage of Impulse Robotics

Item	Selling 100,000 Units	Selling 110,000 Units	Percentage Change
Revenues	$1,000,000	$1,100,000	+10.00
Less variable costs	200,000	220,000	+10.00
Less fixed costs	500,000	500,000	0.00
Operating income	$300,000	$380,000	+26.67

Operating income increases by 26.67 percent when units sold increases by 10 percent. What if the number of units *decreases* by 10 percent, from 100,000 to 90,000? Operating income is $220,000, representing a *decline* of 26.67 percent.

What is happening is that for a 1 percent change in units sold, the operating income changes by 2.67 times that percentage, in the same direction. If units sold increases by 10 percent, operating income increases by 26.7 percent; if units sold decreased by 20 percent, operating income would decrease by 53.3 percent.

We can represent the degree of operating leverage as given in Equation 1 in terms of the basic elements of the price per unit, variable cost per unit, number of units sold, and fixed operating costs. Operating income is revenue minus total operating costs (with variable and fixed cost components):

$$\begin{aligned} \text{Operating income} = &\left[\left(\begin{array}{c} \text{Price} \\ \text{per unit} \end{array} \right) \left(\begin{array}{c} \text{Number of} \\ \text{units sold} \end{array} \right) \right] \\ &- \left[\left(\begin{array}{c} \text{Variable cost} \\ \text{per unit} \end{array} \right) \left(\begin{array}{c} \text{Number of} \\ \text{units sold} \end{array} \right) \right] - \left[\begin{array}{c} \text{Fixed operating} \\ \text{costs} \end{array} \right] \end{aligned}$$

or

$$\text{Operating income} = \left(\begin{array}{c} \text{Number of} \\ \text{units sold} \end{array} \right) \underbrace{\left[\left(\begin{array}{c} \text{Price} \\ \text{per unit} \end{array} \right) - \left(\begin{array}{c} \text{Variable cost} \\ \text{per unit} \end{array} \right) \right]}_{\text{Contribution margin}} - \left[\begin{array}{c} \text{Fixed operating} \\ \text{costs} \end{array} \right]$$

---

[2]We provide the variable and fixed operating costs for our sample companies used in this chapter to illustrate the leverage and breakeven concepts. In reality, however, the financial analyst does not have these breakdowns but rather is faced with interpreting reported account values that often combine variable and fixed costs and costs for different product lines.

The **per unit contribution margin** is the amount that each unit sold contributes to covering fixed costs—that is, the difference between the price per unit and the variable cost per unit. That difference multiplied by the quantity sold is the **contribution margin**, which equals revenue minus variable costs.

How much does operating income change when the number of units sold changes? Fixed costs do not change; therefore, operating income changes by the contribution margin. The percentage change in operating income for a given change in units sold simplifies to

$$\text{DOL} = \frac{Q(P - V)}{Q(P - V) - F} \tag{2}$$

where Q is the number of units, P is the price per unit, V is the variable operating cost per unit, and F is the fixed operating cost. Therefore, $P - V$ is the per unit contribution margin and $Q(P - V)$ is the contribution margin.

Applying the formula for DOL using the data for Impulse Robotics, we can calculate the sensitivity to change in units sold from 100,000 units:

$$\text{DOL @ 100,000 units} = \frac{100,000(\$10 - \$2)}{100,000(\$10 - \$2) - \$500,000} = 2.67$$

A DOL of 2.67 means that a 1 percent change in units sold results in a $1\% \times 2.67 = 2.67\%$ change in operating income; a DOL of 5 means that a 1 percent change in units sold results in a 5 percent change in operating income, and so on.

Why do we specify that the DOL is at a particular quantity sold (in this case, 100,000 units)? Because the DOL is different at different numbers of units produced and sold. For example, at 200,000 units,

$$\text{DOL @ 200,000 units} = \frac{200,000(\$10 - \$2)}{200,000(\$10 - \$2) - \$500,000} = 1.45$$

We can see the sensitivity of the DOL for different numbers of units produced and sold in Exhibit 6. When operating profit is negative, the DOL is negative. At positions just below and just above the point where operating income is $0, operating income is at its most sensitive on a percentage basis to changes in units produced and sold. At the point at which operating income is $0 (at 62,500 units produced and sold in this example), the DOL is undefined because the denominator in the DOL calculation is $0. After this point, the DOL gradually declines as more units are produced and sold.

EXHIBIT 6: Impulse Robotics' Degree of Operating Leverage for Different Number of Units Produced and Sold

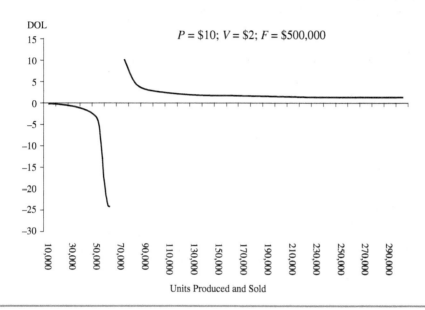

Units Produced and Sold

We will now look at a similar situation in which the company has shifted some of the operating costs away from fixed costs and into variable costs. Malvey Aerospace has a unit sales price of $10, a variable cost of $6 a unit, and $150,000 in fixed costs. A change in units sold from 100,000 to 110,000 (a 10 percent change) changes operating profit from $250,000 to $290,000, or 16 percent. The DOL in this case is 1.6:

$$\text{DOL @ 100,000 units} = \frac{100,000(\$10 - \$6)}{100,000(\$10 - \$6) - \$150,000} = 1.6$$

and the change in operating income is 16 percent:

$$\text{Percentage change in operating income} = (\text{DOL})\left(\text{Percentage change in units sold}\right) = (1.6)(10\%) = 16\%$$

We can see the difference in leverage in the case of Impulse Robotics and Malvey Aerospace companies in Exhibit 7. In Panel A, we see that Impulse Robotics has higher operating income than Malvey Aerospace when both companies produce and sell more than 87,500 units, but lower operating income than Malvey when both companies produce and sell less than 87,500 units.[3]

---

[3]We can calculate the number of units that produce the same operating income for these two companies by equating the operating incomes and solving for the number of units. Let X be the number of units. The X at which Malvey Aerospace and Impulse Robotics generate the same operating income is the X that solves the following: $10X - 2X - 500,000 = 10X - 6X - 150,000$; that is, $X = 87,500$.

EXHIBIT 7: Profitability and the DOL for Impulse Robotics and Malvey Aerospace

Impulse Robotics: $P = \$10; \; V = \$2; \; F = \$500,000$
Malvey Aerospace: $P = \$10; \; V = \$6; \; F = \$150,000$

Panel A: Operating Income and Number of Units Produced and Sold

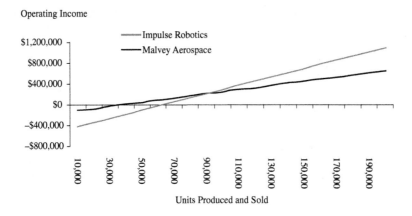

Panel B: Degree of Operating Leverage (DOL)

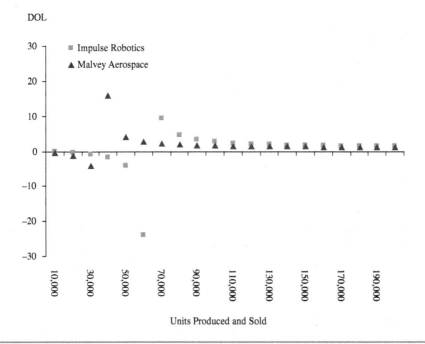

This example confirms what we saw earlier in our reasoning of fixed and variable costs: The greater the use of fixed, relative to variable, operating costs, the more sensitive operating income is to changes in units sold and, therefore, the more operating risk. Impulse Robotics has more operating risk because it has more operating leverage. However, as Panel B of Exhibit 7 shows, the degrees of operating leverage are similar for the two companies for larger numbers of units produced and sold.

Both sales risk and operating risk influence a company's business risk. And both sales risk and operating risk are determined in large part by the type of business the company is in. But management has more opportunity to manage and control operating risk than sales risk.

Suppose a company is deciding which equipment to buy to produce a particular product. The sales risk is the same no matter what equipment is chosen to produce the product. But the available equipment may differ in terms of the fixed and variable operating costs of producing the product. Financial analysts need to consider how the operating cost structure of a company affects the company's risk.

EXAMPLE 1   Calculating the Degree of Operating Leverage

1. Arnaud Kenigswald is analyzing the potential impact of an improving economy on earnings at Global Auto, one of the world's largest car manufacturers. Global is headquartered in Berlin. Global Auto manufactures passenger cars and produces revenues of €168 billion. Kenigswald projects that sales will improve by 10 percent due to increased demand for cars. He wants to see how Global's earnings might respond given that level of increase in sales. He first looks at the degree of leverage at Global, starting with operating leverage.

   Global sold 6 million passenger cars in 2017. The average price per car was €28,000, fixed costs associated with passenger car production total €15 billion per year, and variable costs per car are €20,500. What is the degree of operating leverage of Global Auto?

Solution:

$$\text{DOL @ 6 million units} = \frac{6\text{ million }(€28,000 - €20,500)}{6\text{ million }(€28,000 - €20,500) - €15\text{ billion}} = 1.5$$

Operating income is [6 million × (€28,000 − €20,500)] − €15 billion = €30 billion

For a 10 percent increase in cars sold, operating income increases by 1.50 × 10% = 15.0%.

Industries that tend to have high operating leverage are those that invest up front to produce a product but spend relatively little on making and distributing it. Software developers and pharmaceutical companies fit this description. Alternatively, retailers have low operating leverage because much of the cost of goods sold is variable.

Because most companies produce more than one product, the ratio of variable to fixed costs is difficult to obtain. We can get an idea of the operating leverage of a company by looking at changes in operating income in relation to changes in sales for the entire company. This relation can be estimated by regressing changes in operating income (the variable to be explained) on changes in sales (the explanatory variable) over a recent time period.[4] Although this approach does not provide a precise measure of operating risk, it can help provide a general idea of the amount of operating leverage present. For example, compare the relation between operating earnings and revenues for Delta Air Lines, a transportation company, and Wal-Mart Stores, a discount retailer, as shown in Exhibit 8. Note that the slope of the least-squares regression line is greater for Delta Air Lines (with a slope coefficient of 0.1702) than for Wal-Mart (with a slope coefficient of 0.0493). (A visual comparison of slopes should not be relied upon because the scales of the *x*- and *y*-axes are different in diagrams for the two regressions.) We can see that operating earnings are more sensitive to changes in revenues for the higher-operating-leveraged Delta Air Lines as compared to the lower-operating-leveraged Wal-Mart Stores.

EXHIBIT 8: Relation between Operating Earnings and Revenues

Panel A: Delta Airlines Operating Earnings and Revenues, 1990–2017

Estimated regression: Operating earnings = −$2,249 + 0.1702 Revenues
    $R^2 = 64.73\%$

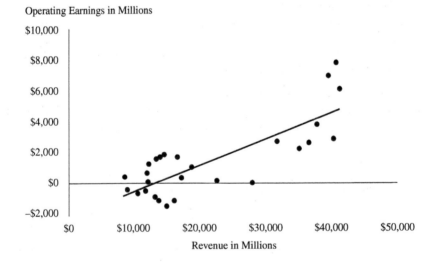

---

[4]A least-squares regression is a procedure for finding the best-fitting line (called the least squares regression line) through a set of data points by minimizing the squared deviations from the line.

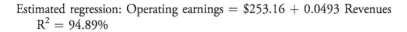

Panel B: Wal-Mart Stores Operating Earnings and Revenues, 1990–2017

Estimated regression: Operating earnings = $253.16 + 0.0493 Revenues
$R^2 = 94.89\%$

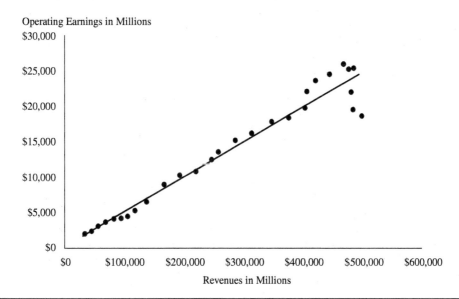

5. FINANCIAL RISK, THE DEGREE OF FINANCIAL LEVERAGE AND THE LEVERAGING ROLE OF DEBT

We can expand on the concept of risk to accommodate the perspective of owning a security. A security represents a claim on the income and assets of a business; therefore, the risk of the security goes beyond the variability of operating earnings to include how the cash flows from those earnings are distributed among the claimants—the creditors and owners of the business. The risk of a security is therefore affected by both business risk and financial risk.

Financial risk is the risk associated with how a company finances its operations. If a company finances with debt, it is legally obligated to pay the amounts that make up its debts when due. By taking on fixed obligations, such as debt and long-term leases, the company increases its financial risk. If a company finances its business with common equity, generated either from operations (retained earnings) or from issuing new common shares, it does not incur fixed obligations. The more fixed-cost financial obligations (e.g., debt) incurred by the company, the greater its financial risk.

We can quantify this risk in the same way we did for operating risk, looking at the sensitivity of the cash flows available to owners when operating income changes. This sensitivity, which we refer to as the **degree of financial leverage** (DFL), is

$$DFL = \frac{\text{Percentage change in net income}}{\text{Percentage change in operating income}} \tag{3}$$

For example, if DFL at a given level of operating income is 1.1, a 5 percent increase in operating income would be expected to result in a (1.1)(5%) = 5.5 percent increase in net income. A company's DFL is dependent on the level of operating income being considered.

Net income is equal to operating income, less interest and taxes.[5] If operating income changes, how does net income change? Consider Impulse Robotics. Suppose the interest payments are $100,000 and, for simplicity, the tax rate is 0 percent: If operating income changes from $300,000 to $360,000, net income changes from $200,000 to $260,000:

EXHIBIT 9: Financial Risk of Impulse Robotics (1)

	Operating Income of $300,000	Operating Income of $360,000	Percentage Change
Operating income	$300,000	$360,000	+20
Less interest	100,000	100,000	0
Net income	$200,000	$260,000	+30

A 20 percent increase in operating income increases net income by $60,000, or 30 percent. What if the fixed financial costs are $150,000? A 20 percent change in operating income results in a 40 percent change in the net income, from $150,000 to $210,000:

EXHIBIT 10: Financial Risk of Impulse Robotics (2)

	Operating Income of $300,000	Operating Income of $360,000	Percentage Change
Operating income	$300,000	$360,000	+20
Less interest	150,000	150,000	0
Net income	$150,000	$210,000	+40

Using more debt financing, which results in higher fixed costs, increases the sensitivity of net income to changes in operating income. We can represent the sensitivity of net income to a change in operating income, continuing the notation from before and including the fixed financial cost, C, and the tax rate, t, as

$$\text{DFL} = \frac{[Q(P-V)-F](1-t)}{[Q(P-V)-F-C](1-t)} = \frac{[Q(P-V)-F]}{[Q(P-V)-F-C]} \qquad (4)$$

As you can see in Equation 4, the factor that adjusts for taxes, $(1-t)$, cancels out of the equation. In other words, the DFL is not affected by the tax rate.

In the case in which operating income is $300,000 and fixed financing costs are $100,000, the degree of financial leverage is

---

[5]More complex entities than we have been using for our examples may also need to account for other income (losses) and extraordinary income (losses) together with operating income as the basis for earnings before interest and taxes.

$$\text{DFL } @\atop \$300,000 \text{ operating income} = \frac{\$300,000}{\$300,000 - \$100,000} = 1.5$$

If, instead, fixed financial costs are $150,000, the DFL is equal to 2.0:

$$\text{DFL } @\atop \$300,000 \text{ operating income} = \frac{\$300,000}{\$300,000 - \$150,000} = 2.0$$

Again, we need to qualify our degree of leverage by the level of operating income because DFL is different at different levels of operating income.

The greater the use of financing sources that require fixed obligations, such as interest, the greater the sensitivity of net income to changes in operating income.

EXAMPLE 2   Calculating the Degree of Financial Leverage

Global Auto also employs debt financing. If Global can borrow at 8 percent, the interest cost is €18 billion. What is the degree of financial leverage of Global Auto if 6 million cars are produced and sold?

Solution:

At 6 million cars produced and sold, operating income = €30 billion. Therefore:

$$\text{DFL @}\atop \text{€30 billion operating income} = \frac{\text{€30 billion}}{\text{€30 billion} - \text{€18 billion}} = 2.5$$

For every 1 percent change in operating income, net income changes 2.5 percent due to financial leverage.

Unlike operating leverage, the degree of financial leverage is most often a choice by the company's management. Whereas operating costs are very similar among companies in the same industry, competitors may decide on differing capital structures.

Companies with relatively high ratios of tangible assets to total assets may be able to use higher degrees of financial leverage than companies with relatively low ratios because the claim on the tangible assets that lenders would have in the event of a default may make lenders more confident in extending larger amounts of credit. In general, businesses with plants, land, and equipment that can be used to collateralize borrowings and businesses whose revenues have below-average business cycle sensitivity may be able to use more financial leverage than businesses without such assets and with relatively high business cycle sensitivity.

Using financial leverage generally increases the variability of return on equity (net income divided by shareholders' equity). In addition, its use by a profitable company may increase the level of return on equity. Example 3 illustrates both effects.

EXAMPLE 3   The Leveraging Role of Debt

Consider the Capital Company, which is expected to generate $1,500,000 in revenues and $500,000 in operating earnings next year. Currently, the Capital Company does not use debt financing and has assets of $2,000,000.

Suppose Capital were to change its capital structure, buying back $1,000,000 of stock and issuing $1,000,000 in debt. If we assume that interest on debt is 5 percent and income is taxed at a rate of 30 percent, what is the effect of debt financing on Capital's net income and return on equity if operating earnings may vary as much as 40 percent from expected earnings?

EXHIBIT 11: Return on Equity of Capital Company

No Debt (Shareholders' Equity = $2 million)	Expected Operating Earnings, Less 40%	Expected Operating Earnings	Expected Operating Earnings, Plus 40%
Earnings before interest and taxes	$300,000	$500,000	$700,000
Interest expense	0	0	0
Earnings before taxes	$300,000	$500,000	$700,000
Taxes	90,000	150,000	210,000
Net income	$210,000	$350,000	$490,000
Return on equity[1]	10.5%	17.5%	24.5%

Debt to Total Assets = 50%; (Shareholders' Equity = $1 million)	Expected Operating Earnings, Less 40%	Expected Operating Earnings	Expected Operating Earnings, Plus 40%
Earnings before interest and taxes	$300,000	$500,000	$700,000
Interest expense	50,000	50,000	50,000
Earnings before taxes	$250,000	$450,000	$650,000
Taxes	75,000	135,000	195,000
Net income	$175,000	$315,000	$455,000
Return on equity	17.5%	31.5%	45.5%

[1] Recall that ROE is calculated as net income/shareholders' equity.

Depicting a broader array of capital structures and operating earnings, ranging from an operating loss of $500,000 to operating earnings of $2,000,000, Exhibit 12 shows the effect of leverage on the return on equity for Capital Company:

EXHIBIT 12: Return on Equity of Capital Company for Different Levels of Operating
Earnings and Different Financing Choices

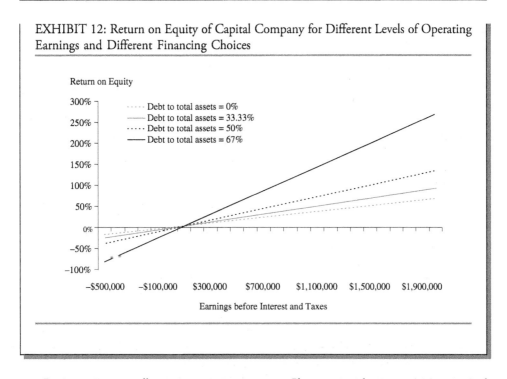

Business is generally an uncertain venture. Changes in the macroeconomic and
competitive environments that influence sales and profitability are typically difficult to discern
and forecast. The larger the proportion of debt in the financing mix of a business, the greater
is the chance that it will face default. Similarly, the greater the proportion of debt in the
capital structure, the more earnings are magnified upward in improving economic times. The
bottom line? Financial leverage tends to increase the risk of ownership for shareholders.

6. TOTAL LEVERAGE AND THE DEGREE OF TOTAL LEVERAGE

The degree of operating leverage gives us an idea of the sensitivity of operating income to
changes in revenues. And the degree of financial leverage gives us an idea of the sensitivity of
net income to changes in operating income. But often we are concerned about the combined
effect of both operating leverage and financial leverage. Owners are concerned about the
combined effect because both factors contribute to the risk associated with their future cash
flows. And financial managers, making decisions intended to maximize owners' wealth, need
to be concerned with how investment decisions (which affect the operating cost structure)
and financing decisions (which affect the capital structure) affect lenders' and owners' risk.

Look back at the example of Impulse Robotics. The sensitivity of owners' cash flow to a
given change in units sold is affected by both operating and financial leverage. Consider using
100,000 units as the base number produced and sold. A 10 percent increase in units sold
results in a 27 percent increase in operating income and a 40 percent increase in net income; a
like decrease in units sold results in a similar decrease in operating income and net income.

EXHIBIT 13: Total Leverage of Impulse Robotics

	Units Produced and Sold		
	90,000	100,000	110,000
Revenues	$900,000	$1,000,000	$1,100,000
Less variable costs	180,000	200,000	220,000
Less fixed costs	500,000	500,000	500,000
Operating income	$220,000	$300,000	$380,000
Less interest	100,000	100,000	100,000
Net income	$120,000	$200,000	$280,000
Relative to 100,000 units produced and sold			
Percentage change in units sold	−10%		+10%
Percentage change in operating profit	−27%		+27%
Percentage change in net income	−40%		+40%

Combining a company's degree of operating leverage with its degree of financial leverage results in the **degree of total leverage** (DTL), a measure of the sensitivity of net income to changes in the number of units produced and sold. We again make the simplifying assumption that a company sells all that it produces in the same period:

$$DTL = \frac{\text{Percentage change in net income}}{\text{Percentage change in the number of units sold}} \qquad (5)$$

or

$$DTL = \frac{Q(P - V)}{Q(P - V) - F} \times \frac{[Q(P - V) - F]}{[Q(P - V) - F - C]}$$

$$DOL \times DFL \qquad (6)$$

$$= \frac{Q(P - V)}{Q(P - V) - F - C}$$

Suppose

Number of units sold = Q = 100,000

Price per unit   = P = $10

Variable cost per unit = V = $2

Fixed operating cost = F = $500,000

Fixed financing cost = C = $100,000

Then,

$$DTL = \frac{100,000(\$10 - \$2)}{100,000(\$10 - \$2) - \$500,000 - \$100,000} = 4.0$$

which we could also have determined by multiplying the DOL, 2.67, by the DFL, 1.5. This means that a 1 percent increase in units sold will result in a 4 percent increase in net income; a 50 percent increase in units produced and sold results in a 200 percent increase in net income; a 5 percent decline in units sold results in a 20 percent decline in income to owners; and so on.

Because the DOL is relative to the base number of units produced and sold and the DFL is relative to the base level of operating earnings, DTL is different depending on the number of units produced and sold. We can see the DOL, DFL, and DTL for Impulse Robotics for different numbers of units produced and sold, beginning at the number of units for which the degrees are positive, in Exhibit 14.

EXHIBIT 14: DOL, DFL, and DTL for Different Numbers of Units Produced and Sold

$P = \$10$, $V = \$2$, $F = \$500,000$, $C = \$100,000$

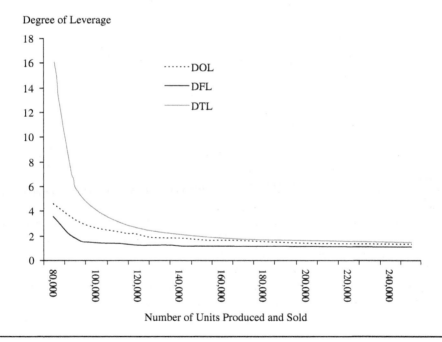

In the case of operating leverage, the fixed operating costs act as a fulcrum. The greater the proportion of operating costs that are fixed, the more sensitive operating income is to changes in sales. In the case of financial leverage, the fixed financial costs, such as interest, act as a fulcrum. The greater the proportion of financing with fixed cost sources, such as debt, the more sensitive cash flows available to owners are to changes in operating income. Combining the effects of both types of leverage, we see that fixed operating and financial costs together increase the sensitivity of earnings to owners.

EXAMPLE 4   Calculating the Degree of Total Leverage

Continuing from Examples 1 and 2, Global Auto's total leverage is

$$\frac{\text{DTL @}}{6 \text{ million units}} = \frac{\text{DOL @}}{6 \text{ million units}} \times \frac{\text{DFL @}}{\text{€30 billion}}$$

$$\frac{\text{DTL @}}{6 \text{ million units}} = \frac{6 \text{ million}(\text{€28,000} - \text{€20,500})}{[6 \text{ million}(\text{€28,000} - \text{€20,500}) - \text{€15 billion}] - \text{€18 billion}}$$

$$= \frac{\text{€45 billion}}{\text{€12 billion}} = 3.75$$

$$\frac{\text{DTL @}}{6 \text{ million units}} = 1.5 \times 2.5 = 3.75$$

Given Global Auto's operating and financial leverage, a 1 percent change in unit sales changes net income by 3.75 percent.

---

7. BREAKEVEN POINTS AND OPERATING BREAKEVEN POINTS

Looking back at Exhibit 3, we see that there is a number of units at which the company goes from being unprofitable to being profitable—that is, the number of units at which the net income is zero. This number is referred to as the breakeven point. The **breakeven point**, Q_{BE}, is the number of units produced and sold at which the company's net income is zero— the point at which revenues are equal to costs.

Plotting revenues and total costs against the number of units produced and sold, as in Exhibit 15, indicates that the breakeven is at 75,000 units. At this number of units produced and sold, revenues are equal to costs and, hence, profit is zero.

EXHIBIT 15: Impulse Robotics Breakeven

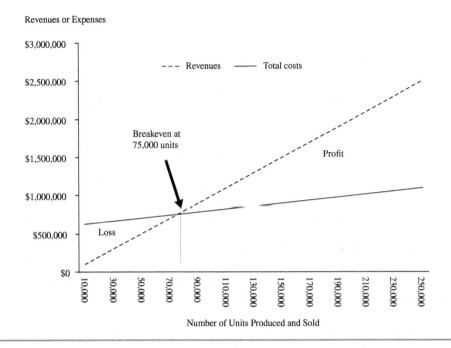

We can calculate this breakeven point for Impulse Robotics and Malvey Aerospace. Consider that net income is zero when the revenues are equal to the expenses. We can represent this equality of revenues and costs (summing variable operating costs, fixed operating costs, and fixed financing costs) by the following equation:

$$PQ = VQ + F + C$$

where
      P = the price per unit
      Q = the number of units produced and sold
      V = the variable cost per unit
      F = the fixed operating costs
      C = the fixed financial cost

Therefore,

$$PQ_{BE} = VQ_{BE} + F + C$$

and the breakeven number of units, Q_{BE}, is[6]

---

[6]You will notice that we did not consider taxes in our calculation of the breakeven point. This is because at the point of breakeven, taxable income is zero.

$$Q_{BE} = \frac{F + C}{P - V} \qquad (7)$$

In the case of Impulse Robotics and Malvey Aerospace, Impulse Robotics has a higher breakeven point. Using numbers taken from Exhibit 2:

$$\text{Impulse Robotics}: \quad Q_{BE} = \frac{\$500{,}000 + \$100{,}000}{\$10 - \$2} = 75{,}000 \text{ units}$$

$$\text{Malvey Aerospace}: \quad Q_{BE} = \frac{\$150{,}000 + \$50{,}000}{\$10 - \$6} = 50{,}000 \text{ units}$$

This means that Impulse Robotics must produce and sell more units to achieve a profit. So, while the higher-leveraged Impulse Robotics has a greater breakeven point relative to Malvey Aerospace, the profit that Impulse Robotics generates beyond this breakeven point is greater than that of Malvey Aerospace. Therefore, leverage has its rewards in terms of potentially greater profit, but it also increases risk.

In addition to the breakeven point specified in terms of net income, Q_{BE}, we can also specify the breakeven point in terms of operating profit, which we refer to as the **operating breakeven** point, Q_{OBE}. Revenues at the operating breakeven point are set equal to operating costs at the operating breakeven point to solve for the operating breakeven number of units, Q_{OBE}. The expression shows Q_{OBE} as equal to fixed operating costs divided by the difference between price per unit and variable cost per unit:

$$PQ_{OBE} = VQ_{OBE} + F$$
$$Q_{OBE} = \frac{F}{P - V}$$

For the two companies in our example, Impulse Robotics and Malvey Aerospace, the operating breakevens are 62,500 and 37,500 units, respectively:

$$\text{Impulse Robotics}: \quad Q_{OBE} = \frac{\$500{,}000}{\$10 - \$2} = 62{,}500 \text{ units}$$

$$\text{Malvey Aerospace}: \quad Q_{OBE} = \frac{\$150{,}000}{\$10 - \$6} = 37{,}500 \text{ units}$$

Impulse Robotics has a higher operating breakeven point in terms of the number of units produced and sold.

EXAMPLE 5   Calculating Operating Breakeven and Breakeven Points

Continuing with his analysis, Kenigswald considers the effect of a possible downturn on Global Auto's earnings. He divides the fixed operating costs of €15 billion by the per unit contribution margin:

$$Q_{OBE} = \frac{€15 \text{ billion}}{€28,000 - €20,500} = 2 \text{ million cars}$$

The operating breakeven for Global is 2,000,000 cars, or €56 billion in revenues. We calculate the breakeven point by dividing fixed operating costs, plus interest costs, by the contribution margin:

$$Q_{BE} = \frac{€15 \text{ billion} + €18 \text{ billion}}{€28,000 - €20,500} = 4,400,000$$

Considering the degree of total leverage, Global's breakeven is 4.4 million cars, or revenues of €123.2 billion.

We can verify these calculations by constructing an income statement for the breakeven sales (in € billions):

	2,000,000 Cars	4,400,000 Cars
Revenues ($= P \times Q$)	€56.0	€123.2
Variable operating costs ($= V \times Q$)	41.0	90.2
Fixed operating costs (F)	15.0	15.0
Operating income	€0	€18.0
Fixed financial costs (C)	18.0	18.0
Net income	−€18.0	€0

As business expands or contracts beyond or below breakeven points, fixed costs do not change. The breakeven points for companies with low operating and financial leverage are less important than those for companies with high leverage. Companies with greater total leverage must generate more revenue to cover fixed operating and financing costs. The farther unit sales are from the breakeven point for high-leverage companies, the greater the magnifying effect of this leverage.

8. THE RISKS OF CREDITORS AND OWNERS

As we discussed earlier, business risk refers to the effect of economic conditions as well as the level of operating leverage. Uncertainty about demand, output prices, and costs are among the many factors that affect business risk. When conditions change for any of these factors, companies with higher business risk experience more volatile earnings. Financial risk is the additional risk that results from the use of debt and preferred stock. The degree of financial risk grows with greater use of debt. Who bears this risk?

The risk for providers of equity and debt capital differs because of the relative rights and responsibilities associated with the use of borrowed money in a business. Lenders have a prior claim on assets relative to shareholders, so they have greater security. In return for lending money to a business, lenders require the payment of interest and principal when due. These contractual payments to lenders must be made regardless of the profitability of the business. A business must satisfy these claims in a timely fashion or face the pain of bankruptcy should it default. In return for their higher priority in claims, lenders get predefined yet limited returns.

In contrast, equity providers claim whatever is left over after all expenses, including debt service, have been paid. So, unlike the fixed and known commitments to the lenders, what is left over for the owners may be a great deal or may be nothing. In exchange for this risk, providers of equity capital exercise the decision-making power over the business, including the right to hire, guide, and if necessary, fire managers. In public companies, ownership rights are usually exercised through an elected board of directors. They undertake the decisions over what portion of the business's earnings should be paid out as dividends for common shareholders.

Legal codes in most countries provide for these rights, as well as conditions for companies to file for bankruptcy (with reference to businesses, often called insolvency). A number of bankruptcy codes provide in some form for two categories of bankruptcies. One form provides for a temporary protection from creditors so that a viable business may reorganize. In the United States, the US Bankruptcy Code sets the terms for the form of negotiated **reorganization** of a company's capital structure that allows it to remain a going concern in Chapter 11.[7] For businesses that are not viable, the second form of bankruptcy process allows for the orderly satisfaction of the creditors' claims. In the United States, this form of bankruptcy is referred to as **liquidation**.[8] Whereas both types of bankruptcy lead to major dislocations in the rights and privileges of owners, lenders, employees, and managers, it is in this latter category of bankruptcy that the original business ceases to exist.

The difference between a company that reorganizes and emerges from bankruptcy and one that is liquidated is often the difference between operating and financial leverage. Companies with high operating leverage have less flexibility in making changes, and bankruptcy protection does little to help reduce operating costs. Companies with high financial leverage use bankruptcy laws and protection to change their capital structure and, once the restructuring is complete, can emerge as ongoing concerns.

---

[7] US Code, Title 11—Bankruptcy, Chapter 11—Reorganization. Companies filing for bankruptcy under this code are referred to as having filed for Chapter 11 bankruptcy.
[8] US Code, Title 11—Bankruptcy, Chapter 7—Liquidation.

EXAMPLE 6   Dow Corning: In and Out of Chapter 11 Bankruptcy

Dow Corning, a leading silicone producer, was a joint venture of Dow Chemical and Corning Inc. Dow Chemical filed for bankruptcy protection using Chapter 11 in 1995 as a result of the lawsuits related to silicone implants. The company was profitable at the time of filing, with more than $500 million in net income in 1994, but the potential liability from lawsuits, initially estimated around $2 billion, was significant when compared to its $4 billion in total assets. In 2004, Dow Corning emerged from bankruptcy, and in 2016 Dow Chemical completed the acquisition of 100 percent of Dow Corning, which currently operates as a wholly owned subsidiary of Dow Chemical Company.

EXAMPLE 7   Retailers Do Not Deliver

Traditional brick-and-mortar retail stores have been challenged with competition from online retailers. Whereas some retailers successfully added online access, others have struggled to compete effectively. A number of US retail stores filed for bankruptcy protection in 2017 and 2018, including Radio Shack, Nine West, Toys R Us, Brookstone, Payless, and hhgregg. Though some of these retailers were "reborn" online (e.g., hhgregg.com), others liquidated (e.g., Toys R Us), and many are closing stores and working closely with creditors to stave off liquidation.

Whereas the ability to file for bankruptcy is important to the economy, the goal of most investors is to avoid ownership of companies that are heading toward this extreme step, as well as to be able to evaluate opportunities among companies already in bankruptcy. Under both Chapter 7 and Chapter 11, providers of equity capital generally lose all value during the bankruptcy. On the other hand, debtholders typically receive at least a portion of their capital, but the payments of principal and interest are delayed during the period of bankruptcy protection.

9. SUMMARY

In this chapter, we have reviewed the fundamentals of business risk, financial risk, and measures of leverage.

- Leverage is the use of fixed costs in a company's cost structure. Business risk is the risk associated with operating earnings and reflects both sales risk (uncertainty with respect to the price and quantity of sales) and operating risk (the risk related to the use of fixed costs in operations). Financial risk is the risk associated with how a company finances its operations (i.e., the split between equity and debt financing of the business).

- The degree of operating leverage (DOL) is the ratio of the percentage change in operating income to the percentage change in units sold. We can use the following formula to measure the degree of operating leverage:

$$\text{DOL} = \frac{Q(P-V)}{Q(P-V)-F}$$

- The degree of financial leverage (DFL) is the percentage change in net income for a one percent change in operating income. We can use the following formula to measure the degree of financial leverage:

$$\text{DFL} = \frac{[Q(P-V)-F](1-t)}{[Q(P-V)-F-C](1-t)} = \frac{[Q(P-V)-F]}{[Q(P-V)-F-C]}$$

- The degree of total leverage (DTL) is a measure of the sensitivity of net income to changes in unit sales, which is equivalent to $\text{DTL} = \text{DOL} \times \text{DFL}$.
- The breakeven point, Q_{BE}, is the number of units produced and sold at which the company's net income is zero, which we calculate as

$$Q_{BE} = \frac{F+C}{P-V}$$

- The operating breakeven point, Q_{OBE}, is the number of units produced and sold at which the company's operating income is zero, which we calculate as

$$Q_{OBE} = \frac{F}{P-V}$$

10. PRACTICE PROBLEMS

The following information relates to questions 1–9

Mary Benn, CFA, is a financial analyst for Twin Fields Investments, located in Storrs, Connecticut, USA. She has been asked by her supervisor, Bill Cho, to examine two small Japanese cell phone component manufacturers: 4G, Inc. and Qphone Corp. Cho indicates that his clients are most interested in the use of leverage by 4G and Qphone. Benn states, "I will have to specifically analyze each company's respective business risk, sales risk, operating risk, and financial risk." "Fine, I'll check back with you shortly," Cho, answers.

Benn begins her analysis by examining the sales prospects of the two firms. The results of her sales analysis appear in Exhibit 1. She also expects very little price variability for these cell phones. She next gathers more data on these two companies to assist her analysis of their operating and financial risk.

When Cho inquires as to her progress Benn responds, "I have calculated Qphone's degree of operating leverage (DOL) and degree of financial leverage (DFL) at Qphone's 2009 level of unit sales. I have also calculated Qphone's breakeven level for unit sales. I will have 4G's leverage results shortly."

Cho responds, "Good, I will call a meeting of some potential investors for tomorrow. Please help me explain these concepts to them, and the differences in use of leverage by these two companies. In preparation for the meeting, I have a number of questions":

- "You mentioned business risk; what is included in that?"
- "How would you classify the risk due to the varying mix of variable and fixed costs?"
- "Could you conduct an analysis and tell me how the two companies will fare relative to each other in terms of net income if their unit sales increased by 10 percent above their 2009 unit sales levels?"
- "Finally, what would be an accurate verbal description of the degree of total leverage?"

The relevant data for analysis of 4G is contained in Exhibit 2, and Benn's analysis of the Qphone data appears in Exhibit 3:

EXHIBIT 1: Benn's Unit Sales Estimates for 4G, Inc. and Qphone Corp.

Company	2009 Unit Sales	Standard Deviation of Unit Sales	2010 Expected Unit Sales Growth Rate (%)
4G, Inc.	1,000,000	25,000	15
Qphone Corp.	1,500,000	10,000	15

EXHIBIT 2: Sales, Cost, and Expense Data for 4G, Inc. (At Unit Sales of 1,000,000)

Number of units produced and sold	1,000,000
Sales price per unit	¥108
Variable cost per unit	¥72
Fixed operating cost	¥22,500,000
Fixed financing expense	¥9,000,000

EXHIBIT 3: Benn's Analysis of Qphone (At Unit Sales of 1,500,000)

Degree of operating leverage	1.40
Degree of financial leverage	1.15
Breakeven quantity (units)	571,429

1. Based on Benn's analysis, 4G's sales risk relative to Qphone's is *most likely* to be:
   A. lower.
   B. equal.
   C. higher.

2. What is the *most appropriate* response to Cho's question regarding the components of business risk?
   A. Sales risk and financial risk.
   B. Operating risk and sales risk.
   C. Financial risk and operating risk.

3. The *most appropriate* response to Cho's question regarding the classification of risk arising from the mixture of variable and fixed costs is:
   A. sales risk.
   B. financial risk.
   C. operating risk.

4. Based on the information in Exhibit 2, the degree of operating leverage (DOL) of 4G, Inc., at unit sales of 1,000,000, is *closest* to:
   A. 1.60.
   B. 2.67.
   C. 3.20.

5. Based on the information in Exhibit 2, 4G, Inc.'s degree of financial leverage (DFL), at unit sales of 1,000,000, is *closest* to:
   A. 1.33.
   B. 2.67.
   C. 3.00.

6. Based on the information in Exhibit 1 and Exhibit 3, Qphone's expected percentage change in operating income for 2010 is *closest* to:
   A. 17.25%.
   B. 21.00%.
   C. 24.30%.

7. 4G's breakeven quantity of unit sales is *closest* to:
   A. 437,500 units.
   B. 625,000 units.
   C. 875,000 units.

8. In response to Cho's question regarding an increase in unit sales above 2009 unit sales levels, it is *most likely* that 4G's net income will increase at:
   A. a slower rate than Qphone's.
   B. the same rate as Qphone's.
   C. a faster rate than Qphone's.

9. The *most appropriate* response to Cho's question regarding a description of the degree of total leverage is that degree of total leverage is:
   A. the percentage change in net income divided by the percentage change in units sold.
   B. the percentage change in operating income divided by the percentage change in units sold.
   C. the percentage change in net income divided by the percentage change in operating income.

10. If two companies have identical unit sales volume and operating risk, they are *most likely* to also have identical:
    A. sales risk.
    B. business risk.
    C. sensitivity of operating earnings to changes in the number of units produced and sold.

11. Degree of operating leverage is *best* described as a measure of the sensitivity of:
    A. net earnings to changes in sales.
    B. fixed operating costs to changes in variable costs.
    C. operating earnings to changes in the number of units produced and sold.

12. The Fulcrum Company produces decorative swivel platforms for home televisions. If Fulcrum produces 40 million units, it estimates that it can sell them for $100 each. Variable production costs are $65 per unit and fixed production costs are $1.05 billion. Which of the following statements is *most accurate*? Holding all else constant, the Fulcrum Company would:
    A. generate positive operating income if unit sales were 25 million.
    B. have less operating leverage if fixed production costs were 10 percent greater than $1.05 billion.
    C. generate 20 percent more operating income if unit sales were 5 percent greater than 40 million.

13. The business risk of a particular company is *most accurately* measured by the company's:
    A. debt-to-equity ratio.
    B. efficiency in using assets to generate sales.
    C. operating leverage and level of uncertainty about demand, output prices, and competition.

14. Consider two companies that operate in the same line of business and have the same degree of operating leverage: the Basic Company and the Grundlegend Company. The Basic Company and the Grundlegend Company have, respectively, no debt and 50 percent debt in their capital structure. Which of the following statements is *most accurate*? Compared to the Basic Company, the Grundlegend Company has:
    A. a lower sensitivity of net income to changes in unit sales.
    B. the same sensitivity of operating income to changes in unit sales.
    C. the same sensitivity of net income to changes in operating income.

15. Myundia Motors now sells 1 million units at ¥3,529 per unit. Fixed operating costs are ¥1,290 million and variable operating costs are ¥1,500 per unit. If the company pays ¥410 million in interest, the levels of sales at the operating breakeven and breakeven points are, respectively:

    A. ¥1,500,000,000 and ¥2,257,612,900.
    B. ¥2,243,671,760 and ¥2,956,776,737.
    C. ¥2,975,148,800 and ¥3,529,000,000.

16. Juan Alavanca is evaluating the risk of two companies in the machinery industry: The Gearing Company and Hebelkraft, Inc. Alavanca used the latest fiscal year's financial statements and interviews with managers of the respective companies to gather the following information:

	The Gearing Company	Hebelkraft, Inc.
Number of units produced and sold	1 million	1.5 million
Sales price per unit	$200	$200
Variable cost per unit	$120	$100
Fixed operating cost	$40 million	$90 million
Fixed financing expense	$20 million	$20 million

Based on this information, the breakeven points for The Gearing Company and Hebelkraft, Inc. are:
A. 0.75 million and 1.1 million units, respectively.
B. 1 million and 1.5 million units, respectively.
C. 1.5 million and 0.75 million units, respectively.

CHAPTER 7

COST OF CAPITAL: FOUNDATIONAL TOPICS

Yves Courtois, CMT, MRICS, CFA
KPMG (Luxembourg)

Gene C. Lai, PhD
University of North Carolina at Charlotte (USA)

Pamela Peterson Drake, PhD, CFA
James Madison University (USA)

LEARNING OUTCOMES

The candidate should be able to:

- calculate and interpret the weighted average cost of capital (WACC) of a company
- describe how taxes affect the cost of capital from different capital sources
- calculate and interpret the cost of debt capital using the yield-to-maturity approach and the debt-rating approach
- calculate and interpret the cost of noncallable, nonconvertible preferred stock
- calculate and interpret the cost of equity capital using the capital asset pricing model approach and the bond yield plus risk premium approach
- explain and demonstrate beta estimation for public companies, thinly traded public companies, and nonpublic companies
- explain and demonstrate the correct treatment of flotation costs

1. INTRODUCTION

A company grows by making investments that are expected to increase revenues and profits. It acquires the capital or funds necessary to make such investments by borrowing (i.e., using debt financing) or by using funds from the owners (i.e., equity financing). By applying this capital to investments with long-term benefits, the company is producing value today. How much value? The answer depends not only on the investments' expected future cash flows but also on the cost of the funds. Borrowing is not costless, nor is using owners' funds.

The cost of this capital is an important ingredient in both investment decision making by the company's management and the valuation of the company by investors. If a company invests in projects that produce a return in excess of the cost of capital, the company has created value; in contrast, if the company invests in projects whose returns are less than the cost of capital, the company has destroyed value. Therefore, the estimation of the cost of capital is a central issue in corporate financial management and for an analyst seeking to evaluate a company's investment program and its competitive position.

Cost of capital estimation is a challenging task. As we have already implied, the cost of capital is not observable but, rather, must be estimated. Arriving at a cost of capital estimate requires a multitude of assumptions and estimates. Another challenge is that the cost of capital that is appropriately applied to a specific investment depends on the characteristics of that investment: The riskier the investment's cash flows, the greater its cost of capital. In reality, a company must estimate project-specific costs of capital. What is often done, however, is to estimate the cost of capital for the company as a whole and then adjust this overall corporate cost of capital upward or downward to reflect the risk of the contemplated project relative to the company's average project.

This chapter is organized as follows: In Section 2, we introduce the cost of capital and its basic computation. Section 3 presents a selection of methods for estimating the costs of the various sources of capital: debt, preferred stock, and common equity. For the latter, two approaches for estimating the equity risk premium are mentioned. Section 4 discusses beta estimation, a key input in using the CAPM to calculate the cost of equity, and Section 5 examines the correct treatment of flotation, or capital issuance, costs. Section 6 highlights methods used by corporations, and a summary and practice problems conclude the chapter.

2. COST OF CAPITAL

The **cost of capital** is the rate of return that the suppliers of capital—lenders and owners—require as compensation for their contribution of capital. Another way of looking at the cost of capital is that it is the opportunity cost of funds for the suppliers of capital: A potential supplier of capital will not voluntarily invest in a company unless its return meets or exceeds what the supplier could earn elsewhere in an investment of comparable risk. In other words, to raise new capital, the issuer must price the security to offer a level of expected return that is competitive with the expected returns being offered by similarly risky securities.

A company typically has several alternatives for raising capital, including issuing equity, debt, and hybrid instruments that share characteristics of both debt and equity, such as preferred stock and convertible debt. Each source selected becomes a component of the company's funding and has a cost (required rate of return) that may be called a **component cost of capital**. Because we are using the cost of capital in the evaluation of investment opportunities, we are dealing with a *marginal* cost—what it would cost to raise additional funds for the potential investment project. Therefore, the cost of capital that the investment analyst is concerned with is a marginal cost, and the required return on a security is the issuer's marginal cost for raising additional capital of the same type.

The cost of capital of a company is the required rate of return that investors demand for the average-risk investment of a company. A company with higher-than-average-risk investments must pay investors a higher rate of return, competitive with other securities of similar risk, which corresponds to a higher cost of capital. Similarly, a company with lower-than-average-risk investments will have lower rates of return demanded by investors, resulting in a lower associated cost of capital. The most common way to estimate this required rate of return is to calculate the marginal cost of each of the various sources of capital and then calculate a weighted average of these costs. You will notice that the debt and equity costs of capital and the tax rate are all understood to be "marginal" rates: the cost or tax rate for additional capital.

The weighted average is referred to as the **weighted average cost of capital** (WACC). The WACC is also referred to as the marginal cost of capital (MCC) because it is the cost that a company incurs for additional capital. Further, this is the current cost: what it would cost the company today.

The weights are the proportions of the various sources of capital that the company uses to support its investment program. It is important to note that the weights should represent the company's **target capital structure**, not the current capital structure. A company's target capital structure is its chosen (or targeted) proportions of debt and equity, whereas its current capital structure is the company's actual weighting of debt and equity. For example, suppose the current capital structure is one-third debt, one-third preferred stock, and one-third common stock. Now suppose the new investment will be financed by issuing more debt so that capital structure changes to one-half debt, one-fourth preferred stock, and one-fourth common stock. Those new weights (i.e., the target weights) should be used to calculate the WACC.

Taking the sources of capital to be common stock, preferred stock, and debt and allowing for the fact that in some jurisdictions, interest expense may be tax deductible, the expression for WACC is

$$\text{WACC} = w_d r_d (1 - t) + w_p r_p + w_e r_e, \tag{1}$$

where

w_d = the target proportion of debt in the capital structure when the company raises new funds

r_d = the before-tax marginal cost of debt

t = the company's marginal tax rate

w_p = the target proportion of preferred stock in the capital structure when the company raises new funds

r_p = the marginal cost of preferred stock

w_e = the target proportion of common stock in the capital structure when the company raises new funds

r_e = the marginal cost of common stock

Note that preferred stock is also referred to as preferred equity, and common stock is also referred to as common equity, or equity.

EXAMPLE 1   Computing the Weighted Average Cost of Capital

1. Assume that ABC Corporation has the following capital structure: 30% debt, 10% preferred stock, and 60% common stock, or equity. Also assume that interest expense is tax deductible. ABC Corporation wishes to maintain these proportions as it raises new funds. Its before-tax cost of debt is 8%, its cost of preferred stock is 10%, and its cost of equity is 15%. If the company's marginal tax rate is 40%, what is ABC's weighted average cost of capital?

Solution:
The weighted average cost of capital is

$$\text{WACC} = (0.3)(0.08)(1 - 0.40) + (0.1)(0.1) + (0.6)(0.15)$$

$$= 11.44\%.$$

The cost for ABC Corporation to raise new funds while keeping its current capital structure is 11.44%.

Self reflection:
   Maintaining its current capital structure, what happens to ABC's weighted average cost of capital if component costs increase or decrease? What happens if the company's marginal tax rate increases or decreases?

There are important points concerning the calculation of the WACC as shown in Equation 1 that the analyst must be familiar with. The next section addresses the key issue of taxes.

2.1. Taxes and the Cost of Capital

The marginal cost of debt financing is the cost of debt after considering the allowable deduction for interest on debt based on the country's tax law. If interest cannot be deducted for tax purposes, the tax rate applied is zero, so the effective marginal cost of debt is equal to r_d in Equation 1. If interest can be deducted in full, the tax deductibility of debt reduces the effective marginal cost of debt to reflect the income shielded from taxation (often referred to as the tax shield) and the marginal cost of debt is $r_d(1 - t)$. For example, suppose a company pays €1 million in interest on its €10 million of debt. The cost of this debt is not €1 million, because this interest expense reduces taxable income by €1 million, resulting in a lower tax. If the company has a marginal tax rate of 40%, this €1 million of interest costs the company (€1 million)(1 - 0.4) = €0.6 million because the interest reduces the company's tax bill by €0.4 million. In this case, the before-tax cost of debt is 10%, whereas the after-tax cost of debt is (€0.6 million)/(€10 million) = 6%, which can also be calculated as 10%(1 - 0.4).

   In jurisdictions in which a tax deduction for a business's interest expense is allowed, there may be reasons why additional interest expense is not tax deductible (e.g., not having sufficient income to offset with interest expense). If the above company with €10 million in debt were in that position, its effective marginal cost of debt would be 10% rather than 6% because any additional interest expense would not be deductible for tax purposes. In other words, if the limit on tax deductibility is reached, the marginal cost of debt is the cost of debt without any adjustment for a tax shield.

EXAMPLE 2   Incorporating the Effect of Taxes on the Costs of Capital

Jorge Ricard, a financial analyst, is estimating the costs of capital for the Zeale Corporation. In the process of this estimation, Ricard has estimated the before-tax costs of capital for Zeale's debt and equity as 4% and 6%, respectively. What are the after-tax costs of debt and equity if there is no limit to the tax deductibility of interest and Zeale's marginal tax rate is:

1. 30%?
2. 48%?

	Marginal Tax Rate	After-Tax Cost of Debt	After-Tax Cost of Equity
Solution to 1:	30%	0.04(1 − 0.30) = 2.80%.	6%
Solution to 2:	48%	0.04(1 − 0.48) = 2.08%.	6%

Note: There is no adjustment for taxes in the case of equity; the before-tax cost of equity is equal to the after-tax cost of equity.

3. COSTS OF THE VARIOUS SOURCES OF CAPITAL

Each source of capital has a different cost because of the differences among the sources, such as risk, seniority, contractual commitments, and potential value as a tax shield. We focus on the costs of three primary sources of capital: debt, preferred stock, and common equity.

3.1. Cost of Debt

The **cost of debt** is the cost of debt financing to a company when it issues a bond or takes out a bank loan. That cost is equal to the risk-free rate plus a premium for risk. A company that is perceived to be very risky would have a higher cost of debt than one that presents little investment risk. Factors that might affect the level of investment risk include profitability, stability of profits, and the degree of financial leverage. In general, the cost of debt would be higher for companies that are unprofitable, whose profits are not stable, or that are already using a lot of debt in their capital structure. We discuss two methods to estimate the before-tax cost of debt, r_d: the yield-to-maturity approach and debt-rating approach.

3.1.1. Yield-to-Maturity Approach

The before-tax required return on debt is typically estimated using the expected **yield to maturity** (YTM) of the company's debt based on current market values. YTM is the annual return that an investor earns on a bond if the investor purchases the bond today and holds it until maturity. In other words, it is the yield, r_d, that equates the present value of the bond's promised payments to its market price:

$$P_0 = \frac{PMT_1}{\left(1 + \frac{r_d}{2}\right)} + \cdots + \frac{PMT_n}{\left(1 + \frac{r_d}{2}\right)^n} + \frac{FV}{\left(1 + \frac{r_d}{2}\right)^n} = \left[\sum_{t=1}^{n} \frac{PMT_t}{\left(1 + \frac{r_d}{2}\right)^t}\right] + \frac{FV}{\left(1 + \frac{r_d}{2}\right)^n}, \quad (2)$$

where

P_0 = the current market price of the bond

PMT_t = the interest payment in period t

r_d = the yield to maturity

n = the number of periods remaining to maturity

FV = the maturity value of the bond

In this valuation equation, the constant 2 reflects the assumption that the bond pays interest semi-annually (which is the case in many but not all countries) and that any intermediate cash flows (i.e., the interest payments prior to maturity) are reinvested at the rate $r_d/2$ semi-annually.

Example 3 illustrates the calculation of the after-tax cost of debt.

EXAMPLE 3   Calculating the After-Tax Cost of Debt

Valence Industries issues a bond to finance a new project. It offers a 10-year, $1,000 face value, 5% semi-annual coupon bond. Upon issue, the bond sells at $1,025. What is Valence's before-tax cost of debt? If Valence's marginal tax rate is 35%, what is Valence's after-tax cost of debt?

Solution:

The following are given:

$$PV = \$1,025.$$

$$FV = \$1,000.$$

$$PMT = 5\% \quad \text{of} \quad 1,000 \div 2 = \$25.$$

$$n = 10 \times 2 = 20.$$

$$\$1,025 = \left[\sum_{t=1}^{20} \frac{\$25}{(1+i)^t}\right] + \frac{\$1,000}{(1+i)^{20}}.$$

Before proceeding to solve the problem, we already know that the before-tax cost of debt must be less than 5% because the present value of the bond is greater than the face value. We can use a financial calculator to solve for i, the six-month yield. Because $i = 2.342\%$, the before-tax cost of debt is $r_d = 2.342\% \times 2 = 4.684\%$, and Valence's after-tax cost of debt is $r_d(1 - t) = 0.04684(1 - 0.35) = 0.03045$, or 3.045%.

3.1.2. Debt-Rating Approach

When a reliable current market price for a company's debt is not available, the **debt-rating approach** can be used to estimate the before-tax cost of debt. Based on a company's debt rating, we estimate the before-tax cost of debt by using the yield on comparably rated bonds for maturities that closely match that of the company's existing debt.

Suppose a company's capital structure includes debt with an average maturity of 10 years and the company's marginal tax rate is 35%. If the company's rating is AAA and the yield on debt with the same debt rating and similar maturity is 4%, the company's after-tax cost of debt is

$$r_d(1 - t) = 0.04(1 - 0.35) = 2.6\%.$$

EXAMPLE 4   Calculating the After-Tax Cost of Debt

1. Elttaz Company's capital structure includes debt with an average maturity of 15 years. The company's rating is A1, and it has a marginal tax rate of 18%. If the yield on comparably rated A1 bonds with similar maturity is 6.1%, what is Elttaz's after-tax cost of debt?

Solution:

Elttaz's after-tax cost of debt is

$$r_d(1 - t) = 0.061(1 - 0.18) = 5.0\%.$$

A consideration when using this approach is that debt ratings are ratings of the debt issue itself, with the issuer being only one of the considerations. Other factors, such as debt seniority and security, also affect ratings and yields, so care must be taken to consider the likely type of debt to be issued by the company in determining the comparable debt rating and yield. The debt-rating approach is a simple example of pricing on the basis of valuation-relevant characteristics, which in bond markets has been known as evaluated pricing or **matrix pricing**.

3.1.3. Issues in Estimating the Cost of Debt

There are other issues to consider when estimating the cost of debt. Among these are whether the debt is fixed rate or floating rate, whether it has option-like features, whether it is unrated, and whether the company uses leases instead of typical debt.

3.1.3.1. Fixed-Rate Debt vs. Floating-Rate Debt Up to now, we have assumed that the interest on debt is a fixed amount each period. We can observe market yields of the company's existing debt or market yields of debt of similar risk in estimating the before-tax cost of debt. However, the company may also issue floating-rate debt, in which the interest rate adjusts periodically according to a prescribed index, such as the prime rate, over the life of the instrument.

Estimating the cost of a floating-rate security is difficult because the cost of this form of capital over the long term depends not only on the current yields but also on the future yields. The analyst may use the current term structure of interest rates and term structure theory to assign an average cost to such instruments.

3.1.3.2. Debt with Optionlike Features How should an analyst determine the cost of debt when the company uses debt with option-like features, such as call, conversion, or put provisions? Clearly, options affect the value of debt. For example, a callable bond would have a yield greater than a similar noncallable bond of the same issuer because bondholders want to be compensated for the call risk associated with the bond. In a similar manner, the put feature of a bond, which provides the investor with an option to sell the bond back to the issuer at a predetermined price, has the effect of lowering the yield on a bond below that of a similar nonputable bond. Likewise, convertible bonds, which give investors the option of converting the bonds into common stock, lower the yield on the bonds below that of similar nonconvertible bonds.

If the company already has debt outstanding incorporating optionlike features that the analyst believes are representative of the future debt issuance of the company, the analyst may simply use the yield to maturity on such debt in estimating the cost of debt.

If the analyst believes that the company will add or remove option features in future debt issuance, the analyst can make market value adjustments to the current YTM to reflect the value of such additions or deletions. The technology for such adjustments is an advanced topic that is outside the scope of this coverage.

3.1.3.3. Nonrated Debt If a company does not have any debt outstanding or if the yields on the company's existing debt are not available, the analyst may not always be able to use the yield on similarly rated debt securities. It may be the case that the company does not have rated bonds. Although researchers offer approaches for estimating a company's "synthetic" debt rating based on financial ratios, these methods are imprecise because debt ratings incorporate not only financial ratios but also information about the particular bond issue and the issuer that are not captured in financial ratios. A further discussion of these methods is outside the scope of this chapter.

3.1.3.4. Leases A lease is a contractual obligation that can substitute for other forms of borrowing. This is true whether the lease is an **operating lease** or a **finance lease** (also called a capital lease). If the company uses leasing as a source of capital, the cost of these leases should be included in the cost of capital. The cost of this form of borrowing is similar to that of the company's other long-term borrowing.

3.2. Cost of Preferred Stock

The **cost of preferred stock** is the cost that a company has committed to pay preferred stockholders as a preferred dividend when it issues preferred stock. In the case of nonconvertible, noncallable preferred stock that has a fixed dividend rate and no maturity date (**fixed-rate perpetual preferred stock**), we can use the formula for the value of a preferred stock:

$$P_p = \frac{D_p}{r_p},$$

where
P_p = the current preferred stock price per share
D_p = the preferred stock dividend per share
r_p = the cost of preferred stock

We can rearrange this equation to solve for the cost of preferred stock:

$$r_p = \frac{D_p}{P_p}. \tag{3}$$

Therefore, the cost of preferred stock is the preferred stock's dividend per share divided by the current preferred stock's price per share. Unlike interest on debt, the dividend on preferred stock is not tax-deductible by the company; therefore, there is no adjustment to the cost for taxes.

A preferred stock may have a number of features that affect its yield and hence its cost. These features include a call option, cumulative dividends, participating dividends, adjustable-rate dividends, and convertibility into common stock. When estimating a yield based on current yields of the company's preferred stock, we must make appropriate adjustments for the effects of these features on the yield of an issue. For example, if the company has callable, convertible preferred stock outstanding yet it is expected that the company will issue only noncallable, nonconvertible preferred stock in the future, we would have to either use the current yields on comparable companies' noncallable, nonconvertible preferred stock or estimate the yield on preferred equity using methods outside the scope of this coverage.

EXAMPLE 5   Calculating the Cost of Preferred Stock

1. Consider a company that has one issue of preferred stock outstanding with a $3.75 cumulative dividend. If the price of this stock is $80, what is the estimate of its cost of preferred stock?

Solution:
  Cost of preferred stock = $3.75/$80 = 4.6875%.

EXAMPLE 6   Choosing the Best Estimate of the Cost of Preferred Stock

1. Wim Vanistendael is finance director of De Gouden Tulip N.V., a leading Dutch flower producer and distributor. He has been asked by the CEO to calculate the cost of preferred stock and has recently obtained the following information:

   - The issue price of preferred stock was €3.5 million, and the preferred dividend is 5%.
   - If the company issued new preferred stock today, the preferred dividend yield would be 6.5%.
   - The company's marginal tax rate is 30.5%.

What is the cost of preferred stock for De Gouden Tulip N.V.?

Solution:
  If De Gouden Tulip were to issue new preferred stock today, the dividend yield would be close to 6.5%. The current terms thus prevail over the past terms when evaluating the actual cost of preferred stock. The cost of preferred stock for De Gouden Tulip is, therefore, 6.5%. Because preferred dividends offer no tax shield, there is no adjustment made on the basis of the marginal tax rate.

3.3. Cost of Common Equity

The cost of common equity, r_e, usually referred to simply as the **cost of equity**, is the rate of return required by a company's common stockholders. A company may increase common equity through the reinvestment of earnings—that is, retained earnings—or through the issuance of new shares of stock.

The estimation of the cost of equity is challenging because of the uncertain nature of the future cash flows in terms of the amount and timing. Commonly used approaches for estimating the cost of equity include the capital asset pricing model (CAPM) method and the bond yield plus risk premium (BYPRP) method. In practice, analysts may use more than one approach to develop the cost of equity. A survey of analysts showed that the CAPM approach is used by 68% of respondents, whereas a build-up approach (bond yield plus a premium) is used by 43% of respondents (Pinto, Robinson, and Stowe 2019).

3.3.1. Capital Asset Pricing Model Approach

In the CAPM approach, we use the basic relationship from the capital asset pricing model theory that the expected return on a stock, $E(R_i)$, is the sum of the risk-free rate of interest, R_F, and a premium for bearing the stock's market risk, $\beta_i(R_M - R_F)$. Note that this premium incorporates the stock's return sensitivity to changes in the market return, or market-related risk, known as β_i, or beta:

$$E(R_i) = R_F + \beta_i[E(R_M) - R_F], \qquad (4)$$

where

$$\beta_i = \text{the return sensitivity of stock } i \text{ to changes in the market return}$$
$$E(R_M) = \text{the expected return on the market}$$
$$E(R_M) - R_F = \text{the expected market risk premium}$$

A risk-free asset is defined here as an asset that has no default risk. A common proxy for the risk-free rate is the yield on a default-free government debt instrument. In general, the selection of the appropriate risk-free rate should be guided by the duration of projected cash flows. For example, for the evaluation of a project with an estimated useful life of 10 years, the rate on the 10-year Treasury bond would be an appropriate proxy to use.

EXAMPLE 1   Using the CAPM to Estimate the Cost of Equity

1. Valence Industries wants to know its cost of equity. Its chief financial officer (CFO) believes the risk-free rate is 5%, the market risk premium is 7%, and Valence's equity beta is 1.5. What is Valence's cost of equity using the CAPM approach?

Solution to 1:

   The cost of equity for Valence is 5% + 1.5(7%) = 15.5%.

2. Exxon Mobil Corporation, BP p.l.c., and Total S.A. are three "super major" integrated oil and gas companies headquartered, respectively, in the United States, the United Kingdom, and France. An analyst estimates that the market risk premium

in the United States, the United Kingdom, and the eurozone are, respectively, 4.4%, 5.5%, and 5.9%. Other information is summarized in Exhibit 1.

EXHIBIT 1: ExxonMobil, BP, and Total

Company	Beta	Estimated Market Risk Premium (%)	Risk-Free Rate (%)
Exxon Mobil Corporation	0.90	4.4	2.8
BP p.l.c.	0.78	5.5	2.0
Total S.A.	0.71	5.9	1.7

Source: Bloomberg; Fernandez, Pershn, and Acin (2018) survey.

Using the capital asset pricing model, calculate the cost of equity for:

1. Exxon Mobil Corporation.
2. BP p.l.c.
3. Total S.A.

Solution to 2:

1. The cost of equity for ExxonMobil is 2.8% + 0.90(4.4%) = 6.76%.
2. The cost of equity for BP is 2.0% + 0.78(5.5%) = 6.29%.
3. The cost of equity for Total is 1.7% + 0.71(5.9%) = 5.89%.

The expected market risk premium, or $E(R_M - R_F)$, is the premium that investors demand for investing in a market portfolio relative to the risk-free rate. When using the CAPM to estimate the cost of equity, in practice we typically estimate beta relative to an equity market index. In that case, the market premium estimate we are using is actually an estimate of the **equity risk premium** (ERP). Therefore, we are using the terms market risk premium and equity risk premium interchangeably.

An alternative to the CAPM to accommodate risks that may not be captured by the market portfolio alone is a multifactor model that incorporates factors that may be other sources of **priced risk** (risk for which investors demand compensation for bearing), including macroeconomic factors and company-specific factors. In general,

$$E(R_i) = R_F + \beta_{i1}(\text{Factor risk premium})_1$$
$$+ \beta_{i2}(\text{Factor risk premium})_2 + \dots \qquad (5)$$
$$+ \beta_{ij}(\text{Factor risk premium})_j,$$

where

β_{ij} = stock i's sensitivity to changes in the jth factor
(Factor risk premium)$_j$ = expected risk premium for the jth factor

The basic idea behind these multifactor models is that the CAPM beta may not capture all the risks, especially in a global context, which include inflation, business-cycle, interest rate, exchange rate, and default risks.

There are several ways to estimate the equity risk premium, although there is no general agreement as to the best approach. The two we discuss are the historical equity risk premium approach and the survey approach.

The **historical equity risk premium approach** is a well-established approach based on the assumption that the realized equity risk premium observed over a long period of time is a good indicator of the expected equity risk premium. This approach requires compiling historical data to find the average rate of return of a country's market portfolio and the average rate of return for the risk-free rate in that country. For example, an analyst might use the historical returns to the TOPIX Index to estimate the risk premium for Japanese equities. The exceptional bull market observed during the second half of the 1990s and the bursting of the technology bubble that followed during 2000–2002 remind us that the time period for such estimates should cover complete market cycles.

Elroy Dimson, Paul Marsh, and Mike Staunton (2018) conducted an analysis of the equity risk premiums observed in markets located in 21 countries, including the United States, over the period 1900–2017. These researchers found that the annualized US equity risk premium relative to US Treasury bills was 5.6% (geometric mean) and 7.5% (arithmetic mean). They also found that the annualized US equity risk premium relative to bonds was 4.4% (geometric mean) and 6.5% (arithmetic mean). Jeremy Siegel (2005), covering the period from 1802 through 2004, observed an equity return of 6.82% and an equity risk premium in the range of 3.31%–5.36%. Note that the arithmetic mean is greater than the geometric mean as a result of the significant volatility of the observed market rate of return and the observed risk-free rate. Under the assumption of an unchanging distribution of returns over time, the arithmetic mean is the unbiased estimate of the expected single-period equity risk premium, but the geometric mean better reflects the growth rate over multiple periods. In Exhibit 2, we provide historical estimates of the equity risk premium for a few of the developed markets from Dimson et al. (2018).

EXHIBIT 2: Selected Equity Risk Premiums Relative to Bonds (1900–2017)

	Mean	
	Geometric	Arithmetic
Australia	5.0%	6.6%
Canada	3.5	5.1
France	3.1	5.4
Germany	5.1	8.4
Japan	5.1	9.1
South Africa	5.3	7.1
Switzerland	2.2	3.7
United Kingdom	3.7	5.0
United States	4.4	6.5

Note: Germany excludes 1922–1923.
Source: Dimson, Marsh, and Staunton (2018).

To illustrate the historical method as applied in the CAPM, suppose that we use the historical geometric mean for US equity of 4.4% to value Apple Computer as of early August 2018. According to Yahoo Finance, Apple had a beta of 1.14 at that time. Using a 10-year US Treasury bond yield of 3.0% to represent the risk-free rate, the estimate of the cost of equity for Apple Computer is 3.0% + 1.14(4.4%) = 8.02%.

In general, the equity risk premium can be written as

$$\text{ERP} = \overline{R}_M - \overline{R}_F,$$

where ERP is the equity risk premium, $\overline{R}_M$ is the mean return for equity, and $\overline{R}_F$ the risk-free rate.

The historical premium approach has several limitations. One limitation is that the level of risk of the stock index may change over time. Another is that the risk aversion of investors may change over time. A third limitation is that the estimates are sensitive to the method of estimation and the historical period covered.

EXAMPLE 7   Estimating the Equity Risk Premium Using Historical Rates of Return

1. Suppose that the arithmetic average T-bond rate observed over the last 90 years is an unbiased estimator for the risk-free rate and is 4.88%. Likewise, suppose the arithmetic average of return on the market observed over the last 90 years is an unbiased estimator for the expected return for the market. The average rate of return of the market was 9.65%. Calculate the equity risk premium.

Solution:

$$\text{ERP} = \overline{R}_M - \overline{R}_F = 9.65\% - 4.88\% = 4.77\%.$$

Another approach to estimate the equity risk premium is quite direct: Ask a panel of finance experts for their estimates, and take the mean response. This is the **survey approach**. For example, a survey of US CFOs in December 2017 found that the average expected US equity risk premium over the next 10 years was 4.42% and the median was 3.63% (Graham and Harvey 2018).

Once we have an estimate of the equity risk premium, we fine-tune this estimate for the particular company or project by adjusting it for the specific systematic risk of the project. We adjust for the specific systematic risk by multiplying the market risk premium by beta to arrive at the company's or project's risk premium, which we then add to the risk-free rate to determine the cost of equity within the framework of the CAPM.

3.3.2. Bond Yield plus Risk Premium Approach

For companies with publicly traded debt, the **bond yield plus risk premium approach** provides a quick estimate of the cost of equity. The BYPRP approach is based on the fundamental tenet in financial theory that the cost of capital of riskier cash flows is higher than that of less risky cash flows. In this approach, we sum the before-tax cost of debt, r_d, and a risk premium that captures the additional yield on a company's stock relative to its bonds. The estimate is, therefore,

$$r_e = r_d + \text{Risk premium}. \tag{6}$$

The risk premium compensates for the additional risk of the equity issue compared with the debt issue (recognizing that debt has a prior claim on the cash flows of the company). This risk premium is not to be confused with the equity risk premium. The equity risk premium is the difference between the cost of equity and the risk-free rate of interest. The risk premium in the bond yield plus risk premium approach is the difference between the cost of equity and the cost of debt of the company. Ideally, this risk premium is forward looking, representing the additional risk associated with the equity of the company as compared with the company's debt. However, we often estimate this premium using historical spreads between bond yields and stock yields. In developed country markets, a typical risk premium added is in the range of 3%–5%.

Looking again at Apple Computer, as of early August 2018, the yield to maturity of Apple's 3.35% coupon bonds maturing in 2027 was approximately 3.56%. Adding an arbitrary risk premium of 4.0% produces an estimate of the cost of equity of 3.56% + 4.0% = 7.56%. This estimate contrasts with the higher estimate of 8.026% from the CAPM approach. Such disparities are not uncommon and reflect the difficulty of cost of equity estimation.

4. ESTIMATING BETA

Beta is an estimate of the company's systematic or market-related risk. It is a critical component of the CAPM, and it can be used to calculate a company's WACC. Therefore, it is essential to have a good understanding of how beta is estimated.

4.1. Estimating Beta for Public Companies

The simplest estimate of beta results from an ordinary least squares regression of the return on the stock on the return on the market. The result is often called an unadjusted or "raw" historical beta. The actual values of beta estimates are influenced by several choices:

- *The choice of the index used to represent the market portfolio*: For US equities, the S&P 500 Index and NYSE Composite have been traditional choices. In Japan, analysts would likely use the Nikkei 225 Index.
- *The length of the data period and the frequency of observations*: The most common choice is five years of monthly data, yielding 60 observations.

Researchers have observed that beta tends to regress toward 1.0. In other words, the value of a stock's beta in a future period is likely to be closer to the mean value of 1.0, the beta of an average-systematic-risk security, than to the value of the calculated raw beta. Because valuation is forward looking, it is logical to adjust the raw beta so that it more accurately predicts a future beta. The most commonly used adjustment was introduced by Blume (1971):

$$\text{Adjusted beta} = (2/3)(\text{Unadjusted beta}) + (1/3)(1.0). \tag{7}$$

For example, if the beta from a regression of an asset's returns on the market return is 1.30, adjusted beta is (2/3)(1.30) + (1/3)(1.0) = 1.20. Equation 7 acts to "smooth" raw betas by adjusting betas above and below 1.0 toward 1.0. Vendors of financial information, such as Bloomberg, often report both raw and adjusted betas.

EXAMPLE 8   Estimating the Adjusted Beta for a Public Company

1. Betty Lau is an analyst trying to estimate the cost of equity for Singapore Telecommunications Limited. She begins by running an ordinary least squares regression to estimate the beta. Her estimated value is 0.4, which she believes needs adjustment. What is the adjusted beta value she should use in her analysis?

Solution:

$$\text{Adjusted beta} = (2/3)(0.4) + (1/3)(1.0) = 0.6.$$

Arriving at an estimated beta for publicly traded companies is generally not a problem because of the accessibility of stock return data, the ease of use of estimating beta using simple regression, and the availability of estimated betas on publicly traded companies from financial analysis vendors.

The challenge comes in estimating a beta for a company that is thinly traded or nonpublic or for a project that is not the average or typical project of a publicly traded company. Estimating beta in these cases requires proxying for the beta by using information on the project or company combined with the beta of a publicly traded company.

4.2. Estimating Beta for Thinly Traded and Nonpublic Companies

It is not possible to run an ordinary least squares regression to estimate beta if a stock is thinly traded or a company is nonpublic. When a share issue trades infrequently, the most recent transaction price may be stale and may not reflect underlying changes in value. If beta is estimated on the basis of, for example, a monthly data series in which missing values are filled with the most recent transaction price, the estimated beta will be too small. This is because this methodology implicitly assumes that the stock's price is more stable than it really is. As a result, the required return on equity will be understated.

In these cases, a practical alternative is to base the beta estimate on the betas of comparable companies that are publicly traded. A **comparable company**, also called a **peer company**, is a company that has similar business risk. A comparable, or peer, company can be identified by using an industry classification system, such as the MSCI/Standard & Poor's Global Industry Classification Standard (GICS) or the FTSE Industry Classification Benchmark (ICB). The analyst can then indirectly estimate the beta on the basis of the betas of the peer companies.

Because financial leverage can affect beta, an adjustment must be made if the peer company has a substantially different capital structure. First, the peer company's beta must be unlevered to estimate the beta of the assets—reflecting only the systematic risk arising from the fundamentals of the industry. Then, the unlevered beta, often referred to as the **asset beta** because it reflects the business risk of the assets, must be re-levered to reflect the capital structure of the company in question.

Let β_E be the equity beta of the peer company before removing the effects of leverage. Assuming the debt of the peer company is of high quality—so that the debt's beta, or β_D, is approximately equal to zero (that is, it is assumed to have no market risk)—analysts can use the following expression to unlever the beta:

$$\beta_U = \beta_E \left[\frac{1}{1 + (1 - t)\frac{D}{E}} \right], \tag{8}$$

where β_U is the unlevered beta, t is the marginal tax rate of the peer company, and D and E are the market values of debt and equity, respectively, of the peer company.

Now we can re-lever the unlevered beta by rearranging the equation to reflect the capital structure of the thinly traded or nonpublic company in question:

$$\beta_E = \beta_U \left[1 + (1 - t)\frac{D}{E} \right]. \tag{9}$$

where β_E is now the equity beta of the thinly traded or nonpublic company, t is the marginal tax rate of the thinly traded or nonpublic company, and D and E are the debt-to-equity values, respectively, of the thinly traded or nonpublic company.

EXAMPLE 9   Estimating the Adjusted Beta for a Nonpublic Company

1. Raffi Azadian wants to determine the cost of equity for Elucida Oncology, a privately held company. Raffi realizes that he needs to estimate Elucida's beta before he can proceed. He determines that Merck & Co. is an appropriate publicly traded peer company. Merck has a beta of 0.7, it is 40% funded by debt, and its marginal tax rate is 21%. If Elucida is only 10% funded by debt and its marginal tax rate is also 21%, what is Elucida's beta?

Solution:

Since Merck is 40% funded by debt, it is 60% funded by equity. Therefore,

$$\text{Unlevered beta} = (0.7)\left[\frac{1}{1 + (1 - 0.21)\left(\frac{0.4}{0.6}\right)} \right] = 0.46.$$

Now we re-lever the unlevered beta using Elucida's tax rate and capital structure:

$$\text{Elucida's beta} = 0.46\left[1 + (1 - 0.21)\left(\frac{0.1}{0.9}\right) \right] = 0.50.$$

The following table and figure show how Elucida's beta increases as leverage rises.

Debt-to-Equity Ratio	Equity Beta
0.00	0.46
0.11	0.50
0.25	0.55
0.43	0.62
0.67	0.70
1.00	0.82
1.50	1.01
2.33	1.31
4.00	1.91
9.00	3.73

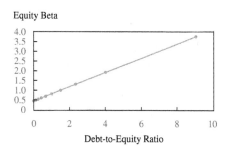

The beta estimate can then be used to determine the component cost of equity and combined with the cost of debt in a weighted average to provide an estimate of the cost of capital for the company.

EXAMPLE 10   Estimating the Weighted Average Cost of Capital

Georg Schrempp is the CFO of Bayern Chemicals KgaA, a German manufacturer of industrial, commercial, and consumer chemical products. Bayern Chemicals is privately owned, and its shares are not listed on an exchange. The CFO has appointed Markus Meier, CFA, a third-party valuator, to perform a stand-alone valuation of Bayern Chemicals. Meier has access to the following information to calculate Bayern Chemicals' weighted average cost of capital:

- The nominal risk-free rate, represented by the yield on the long-term 10-year German bund, was 4.5% at the valuation date.
- The average long-term historical equity risk premium in Germany is assumed to be 5.7%.
- Bayern Chemicals' corporate tax rate is 38%.
- Bayern Chemicals' target debt-to-equity ratio is 0.7. Its capital structure is 41% debt.
- Bayern Chemicals' cost of debt has an estimated spread of 225 bps over the 10-year bund.
- Exhibit 3 supplies additional information on comparables for Bayern Chemicals.

EXHIBIT 3: Information on Comparables

Comparable Companies	Country	Tax Rate (%)	Market Capitalization in Millions	Net Debt in Millions	D/E	Beta
British Chemicals Ltd.	United Kingdom	30.0	4,500	6,000	1.33	1.45
Compagnie Petrochimique S.A.	France	30.3	9,300	8,700	0.94	0.75
Rotterdam Chemie N.V.	Netherlands	30.5	7,000	7,900	1.13	1.05
Average					1.13	1.08

Based only on the information given, calculate Bayern Chemicals' WACC.

Solution:

To calculate the cost of equity, the first step is to "unlever" the betas of the comparable companies and calculate an average for a company with business risk similar to the average of these companies:

Comparable Companies	Unlevered Beta
British Chemicals Ltd.	$0.75 = \left[\dfrac{1.45}{1+(1-0.30)(1.33)}\right]$
Compagnie Petrochimique S.A.	$0.45 = \left[\dfrac{0.75}{1+(1-0.303)(0.94)}\right]$
Rotterdam Chemie N.V.	$0.59 = \left[\dfrac{1.05}{1+(1-0.305)(1.13)}\right]$
Average*	0.60

*An analyst must apply judgment and experience to determine a representative average for the comparable companies. This example uses a simple average, but in some situations a weighted average based on some factor, such as market capitalization, may be more appropriate.

Levering the average unlevered beta for the peer group average, applying Bayern Chemicals' target debt-to-equity ratio and marginal tax rate, results in a beta of 0.86:

$$\beta_{BayernChemicals} = 0.60\{1 + [(1 - 0.38)0.7]\} = 0.86.$$

Using CAPM, the cost of equity of Bayern Chemicals (r_e) can be calculated as follows:

$$r_e = 4.5\% + (0.86)(5.7\%) = 9.4\%.$$

The weights for the cost of debt and cost of equity may be calculated as follows:

$$w_d = 0.41, \text{ and } w_e = (1 - 0.41) = 0.59.$$

The before-tax cost of debt of Bayern Chemicals (r_d) is 6.75%:

$$r_d = 4.5\% + 2.25\% = 6.75\%.$$

As a result, Bayern Chemicals' WACC is 7.26%:

$$\text{WACC} = (0.41)(0.0675)(1 - 0.38) + (0.59)(0.094)$$

$$= 0.0726, \text{ or } 7.26\%.$$

5. FLOTATION COSTS

When a company raises new capital, it generally seeks the assistance of investment bankers. Investment bankers charge the company a fee based on the size and type of offering. This fee is referred to as the **flotation cost**. In general, flotation costs are higher in percentage terms for equity issuances than they are for debt. They are also higher for smaller issuance amounts or for issuances that are perceived to be riskier. In the case of debt and preferred stock, we do not usually incorporate flotation costs in the estimated cost of capital because the amount of these costs is quite small, often less than 1% of the value of the offering.

However, with equity issuance, the flotation costs may be substantial, so we should consider these when estimating the cost of external equity capital. Average flotation costs for new equity have been estimated at 7.11% of the value of the offering in the United States,[1] 1.65% in Germany,[2] 5.78% in the United Kingdom,[3] and 4.53% in Switzerland.[4] A large part of the differences in costs among these studies is likely attributed to the type of offering; cash underwritten offers, typical in the United States, are generally more expensive than rights offerings, which are common in Europe.

How should flotation costs be accounted for? There are two views on this topic. One view, which you can find often in textbooks, is to directly incorporate the flotation costs into the cost of capital. The other view is that flotation costs should be incorporated into the valuation analysis as an additional cost. We will argue that the second view is preferred.

Consistent with the first view, we can specify flotation costs in monetary terms as an amount per share or as a percentage of the share price. With flotation costs specified in monetary terms on a per share basis, the cost of external equity is

$$r_e = \left(\frac{D_1}{P_0 - F} \right) + g, \tag{10}$$

where

r_e is the cost of equity
D_1 is the dividend expected at the end of Period 1
P_0 is the current stock price
F is the monetary per share flotation cost
g is the growth rate

As a percentage applied against the price per share, the cost of external equity is

$$r_e = \left[\frac{D_1}{P_0(1 - f)} \right] + g, \tag{11}$$

where f is the flotation cost as a percentage of the issue price.

[1]Inmoo Lee, Scott Lochhead, Jay R. Ritter, and Quanshui Zhao, "The Costs of Raising Capital," *Journal of Financial Research* 19 (Spring 1996): 59–71.

[2]Thomas Bühner and Christoph Kaserer, "External Financing Costs and Economies of Scale in Investment Banking: The Case of Seasoned Equity Offerings in Germany," *European Financial Management* 9 (June 2002): 249.

[3]Seth Armitage, "The Direct Costs of UK Rights Issues and Open Offers," *European Financial Management* 6 (2000): 57–68.

[4]Christoph Kaserer and Fabian Steiner, "The Cost of Raising Capital—New Evidence from Seasoned Equity Offerings in Switzerland," working paper, Technische Universität München (February 2004).

EXAMPLE 11   Estimating the Cost of Equity with Flotation Costs

A company has a current dividend of $2 per share, a current price of $40 per share, and an expected growth rate of 5%.

1. What is the cost of internally generated equity (i.e., stock is not issued and flotation costs are not incurred)?

Solution to 1:

$$r_e = \left[\frac{\$2(1+0.05)}{\$40}\right] + 0.05 = 0.0525 + 0.05 = 0.1025, \text{ or } 10.25\%.$$

2. What is the cost of external equity (i.e., new shares are issued and flotation costs are incurred) if the flotation costs are 4% of the issuance?

Solution to 2:

$$r_e = \left[\frac{\$2(1+0.05)}{\$40(1-0.04)}\right] + 0.05 = 0.05469 + 0.05 = 0.1047, \text{ or } 10.47\%.$$

Many experts object to this methodology. Flotation costs are a cash flow that occurs at issue and they affect the value of the project only by reducing the initial cash flow. However, by adjusting the cost of capital for flotation costs, we apply a higher cost of capital to determine the present value of the future cash flows. The result is that the calculated net present value of a project is less than its true net present value. As a result, otherwise profitable projects may get rejected when this methodology is used.

An alternative and preferred approach is to make the adjustment for flotation costs to the cash flows in the valuation computation. For example, consider a project that requires a €60,000 initial cash outlay and is expected to produce cash flows of €10,000 each year for 10 years. Suppose the company's marginal tax rate is 40%, the before-tax cost of debt is 5%, and the cost of equity is 10%. Assume the company will finance the project with 40% debt and 60% equity. Exhibit 4 summarizes the information on the component costs of capital.

EXHIBIT 4: After-Tax Costs of Debt and Equity

Source of Capital	Amount Raised (€)	Proportion	Marginal After-Tax Cost
Debt	24,000	0.40	0.05(1 – 0.4) = 0.03
Equity	36,000	0.60	0.10

The weighted average cost of capital is 7.2%, calculated as 0.40(3%) + 0.60(10%). Ignoring flotation costs for the moment and using a financial calculator, we find that the net present value (NPV) of this project can be expressed as

$$NPV = \text{Present value of inflows} - \text{Present value of the outflows,}$$

or

$$NPV = €69,591 - €60,000 = €9,591,$$

where €69,591 is the present value of €10,000 per year for 10 years at 7.2%. Now suppose flotation costs amount to 5% of the new equity capital: $(0.05)(€36,000) = €1,800$. If flotation costs are not tax deductible, the net present value considering flotation costs is

$$NPV = €69,591 - €60,000 - €1,800 = €7,791.$$

If flotation costs are tax deductible, the net present value considering flotation costs is

$$NPV = €69,591 - €60,000 - €1,800(1-0.4) = €8,511.$$

Suppose instead of considering the flotation costs as part of the cash flows, we made an adjustment to the cost of equity. Without showing the calculations, the cost of equity increases from 10% to 10.2632%, the cost of capital increases from 7.22% to 7.3579%, and the NPV decreases from €9,591 to €9,089. As you can see, we arrive at different assessments of value using these two methods.

If the preferred method is to deduct the flotation costs as part of the net present value calculation, why do many textbooks highlight the adjustment to the cost of capital? One reason is that it is often difficult to identify specific financing associated with a project. Making the adjustment for flotation costs to the cost of capital is most useful if specific project financing cannot be identified. A second reason is that by adjusting the cost of capital for the flotation costs, it is easier to demonstrate how the costs of financing a company change as a company exhausts internally generated equity (i.e., retained earnings) and switches to externally generated equity (i.e., a new stock issue).

6. METHODS IN USE

We have introduced methods that may be used to estimate the cost of capital for a company or a project, but which methods do companies actually use when making investment decisions? John Graham and Campbell Harvey (2002) surveyed a large number of CFOs to find out which methods they prefer. Their survey revealed the following:

- The most popular method for estimating the cost of equity is the capital asset pricing model.
- Few companies use the dividend discount model (which we did not cover) to estimate the cost of equity.
- Publicly traded companies are more likely to use the capital asset pricing model than are private companies.
- In evaluating projects, the majority of CFOs use a single company cost of capital, but a large portion apply some type of risk adjustment for individual projects.

Their survey also revealed that the single-factor capital asset pricing model is the most popular method for estimating the cost of equity. The second and third most popular methods, respectively, are average stock returns and multifactor return models. The lack of popularity of the dividend discount model indicates that this approach, although once favored, has lost its appeal in practice.

In a survey of publicly traded multinational European companies, Franck Bancel and Usha Mittoo (2004) provided evidence consistent with the Graham and Harvey (2002) survey. They found that over 70% of companies use the CAPM to determine the cost of equity; this finding is similar to the 73.5% of US companies that use the CAPM. In a survey of both publicly traded and private European companies, Dirk Brounen, Abe de Jong, and Kees Koedijk (2004) confirmed the result of Graham and Harvey that larger companies are more likely to use the more sophisticated methods, such as CAPM, in estimating the cost of equity. Brounen, de Jong, and Koedijk found that the use of the CAPM was less popular for their sample (ranging from 34% to 55.6%, depending on the country) than for the other two surveys, which may reflect the inclusion of smaller, private companies in their sample.

We learn from the survey evidence that the CAPM is a popular method for estimating the cost of equity capital and that it is used less often by smaller, private companies. The latter result is not surprising, because of the difficulty in estimating systematic risk in cases in which the company's equity is not publicly traded.

7. SUMMARY

In this chapter, we provided an overview of the techniques used to calculate the cost of capital for companies and projects. We examined the weighted average cost of capital, discussing the methods commonly used to estimate the component costs of capital and the weights applied to these components.

- The weighted average cost of capital is a weighted average of the after-tax marginal costs of each source of capital: $\text{WACC} = w_d r_d (1 - t) + w_p r_p + w_e r_e$.
- The before-tax cost of debt is generally estimated by either the yield-to-maturity method or the bond rating method.
- The yield-to-maturity method of estimating the before-tax cost of debt uses the familiar bond valuation equation. Assuming semi-annual coupon payments, the equation is

$$P_0 = \frac{PMT_1}{\left(1 + \frac{r_d}{2}\right)} + \dots + \frac{PMT_n}{\left(1 + \frac{r_d}{2}\right)^n} + \frac{FV}{\left(1 + \frac{r_d}{2}\right)^n} = \left[\sum_{t=1}^{n} \frac{PMT_t}{\left(1 + \frac{r_d}{2}\right)^t}\right] + \frac{FV}{\left(1 + \frac{r_d}{2}\right)^n}.$$

We solve for the six-month yield ($r_d/2$) and then annualize it to arrive at the before-tax cost of debt, r_d.
- Because interest payments are generally tax deductible, the after-tax cost is the true, effective cost of debt to the company. If a yield to maturity or bond rating is not available, such as in the case of a private company without rated debt or a project, the estimate of the cost of debt becomes more challenging.
- The cost of preferred stock is the preferred stock dividend divided by the current preferred stock price:

$$r_p = \frac{D_p}{P_p}.$$

- The cost of equity is the rate of return required by a company's common stockholders. We estimate this cost using the CAPM (or its variants).
- The CAPM is the approach most commonly used to calculate the cost of equity. The three components needed to calculate the cost of equity are the risk-free rate, the equity risk premium, and beta:

$$E(R_i) = R_F + \beta_i[E(R_M) - R_F].$$

- In estimating the cost of equity, an alternative to the CAPM is the bond yield plus risk premium approach. In this approach, we estimate the before-tax cost of debt and add a risk premium that reflects the additional risk associated with the company's equity.
- When estimating the cost of equity capital using the CAPM, if we do not have publicly traded equity, we may be able to use a comparable company operating in the same business line to estimate the unlevered beta for a company with similar business risk, β_U:

$$\beta_U = \beta_E \left[\frac{1}{1 + (1 - t)\frac{D}{E}} \right].$$

Then, we lever this beta to reflect the financial risk of the project or company:

$$\beta_E = \beta_U \left[1 + (1 - t)\frac{D}{E} \right].$$

- Flotation costs are costs incurred in the process of raising additional capital. The preferred method of including these costs in the analysis is as an initial cash flow in the valuation analysis.
- Survey evidence tells us that the CAPM method is the most popular method used by companies in estimating the cost of equity. The CAPM method is more popular with larger, publicly traded companies, which is understandable considering the additional analyses and assumptions required in estimating systematic risk for a private company or project.

8. PRACTICE PROBLEMS

The following information relates to questions 1–5
Jurgen Knudsen has been hired to provide industry expertise to Henrik Sandell, CFA, an analyst for a pension plan managing a global large-cap fund internally. Sandell is concerned about one of the fund's larger holdings, auto parts manufacturer Kruspa AB. Kruspa currently operates in 80 countries, with the previous year's global revenues at €5.6 billion. Recently, Kruspa's CFO announced plans for expansion into Trutan, a country with a developing economy. Sandell worries that this expansion will change the company's risk profile and wonders if he should recommend a sale of the position.

Sandell provides Knudsen with the basic information. Kruspa's global annual free cash flow to the firm is €500 million, and earnings are €400 million. Sandell estimates that cash flow will level off at a 2% rate of growth. Sandell also estimates that Kruspa's after-tax free cash flow to the firm on the Trutan project for the next three years is, respectively, €48 million, €52 million, and €54.4 million. Kruspa recently announced a dividend of €4.00 per share of stock. For the initial analysis, Sandell requests that Knudsen ignore possible currency fluctuations. He expects the Trutanese plant to sell only to customers within Trutan for the first three years. Knudsen is asked to evaluate Kruspa's planned financing of the required €100 million in Sweden with an €80 million public offering of 10-year debt and the remainder with an equity offering.

Additional Information	
Equity risk premium, Sweden	4.82%
Risk-free rate of interest, Sweden	4.25%
Industry debt-to-equity ratio	0.3
Market value of Kruspa's debt	€900 million
Market value of Kruspa's equity	€2.4 billion
Kruspa's equity beta	1.3
Kruspa's before-tax cost of debt	9.25%
Trutan credit A2 country risk premium	1.88%
Corporate tax rate	37.5%
Interest payments each year	Level

1. Using the capital asset pricing model, Kruspa's cost of equity capital for its typical project is *closest* to:
   A. 7.62%.
   B. 10.52%.
   C. 12.40%.

2. Sandell is interested in the weighted average cost of capital of Kruspa AB prior to its investing in the Trutan project. This weighted average cost of capital is *closest* to:
   A. 7.65%.
   B. 9.23%.
   C. 10.17%.

3. In his estimation of the project's cost of capital, Sandell would like to use the asset beta of Kruspa as a base in his calculations. The estimated asset beta of Kruspa prior to the Trutan project is *closest* to:
   A. 1.053.
   B. 1.110.
   C. 1.327.

4. Sandell is performing a sensitivity analysis of the effect of the new project on the company's cost of capital. If the Trutan project has the same asset risk as Kruspa, the estimated project beta for the Trutan project, if it is financed 80% with debt, is *closest* to:
   A. 1.300.
   B. 2.635.
   C. 3.686.

5. As part of the sensitivity analysis of the effect of the new project on the company's cost of capital, Sandell is estimating the cost of equity of the Trutan project considering that the Trutan project requires a country equity premium to capture the risk of the project. The cost of equity for the project in this case is *closest* to:
    A. 10.52%.
    B. 19.91%.
    C. 28.95%.

6. Which of the following statements is correct?
    A. The appropriate tax rate to use in the adjustment of the before-tax cost of debt to determine the after-tax cost of debt is the average tax rate because interest is deductible against the company's entire taxable income.
    B. For a given company, the after-tax cost of debt is generally less than both the cost of preferred equity and the cost of common equity.
    C. For a given company, the after-tax cost of debt is generally higher than both the cost of preferred equity and the cost of common equity.

7. The Gearing Company has an after-tax cost of debt capital of 4%, a cost of preferred stock of 8%, a cost of equity capital of 10%, and a weighted average cost of capital of 7%. Gearing intends to maintain its current capital structure as it raises additional capital. In making its capital-budgeting decisions for the average-risk project, the relevant cost of capital is:
    A. 4%.
    B. 7%.
    C. 8%.

8. Fran McClure, of Alba Advisers, is estimating the cost of capital of Frontier Corporation as part of her valuation analysis of Frontier. McClure will be using this estimate, along with projected cash flows from Frontier's new projects, to estimate the effect of these new projects on the value of Frontier. McClure has gathered the following information on Frontier Corporation:

	Current Year ($)	Forecasted for Next Year ($)
Book value of debt	50	50
Market value of debt	62	63
Book value of equity	55	58
Market value equity	210	220

The weights that McClure should apply in estimating Frontier's cost of capital for debt and equity are, respectively:
A. $w_d = 0.200$ and $w_e = 0.800$.
B. $w_d = 0.185$ and $w_e = 0.815$.
C. $w_d = 0.223$ and $w_e = 0.777$.

9. An analyst assembles the following facts concerning a company's component costs of capital and capital structure. Based on the information given, calculate the company's WACC.

Facts	(%)
Cost of equity based on the CAPM	15.60
Pretax cost of debt	8.28
Corporate tax rate	30.00
Capital structure weight	Equity 80, Debt 20

10. The cost of equity is equal to the:
    A. expected market return.
    B. rate of return required by stockholders.
    C. cost of retained earnings plus dividends.

11. Dot.Com has determined that it could issue $1,000 face value bonds with an 8% coupon paid semi-annually and a five-year maturity at $900 per bond. If Dot.Com's marginal tax rate is 38%, its after-tax cost of debt is *closest* to:
    A. 6.2%.
    B. 6.4%.
    C. 6.6%.

12. The cost of debt can be determined using the yield-to-maturity and bond rating approaches. If the bond rating approach is used, the:
    A. coupon is the yield.
    B. yield is based on the interest coverage ratio.
    C. company is rated and the rating can be used to assess the credit default spread of the company's debt.

13. Morgan Insurance Ltd. issued a fixed-rate perpetual preferred stock three years ago and placed it privately with institutional investors. The stock was issued at $25 per share with a $1.75 dividend. If the company were to issue preferred stock today, the yield would be 6.5%. The stock's current value is:
    A. $25.00.
    B. $26.92.
    C. $37.31.

14. Two years ago, a company issued $20 million in long-term bonds at par value with a coupon rate of 9%. The company has decided to issue an additional $20 million in bonds and expects the new issue to be priced at par value with a coupon rate of 7%. The company has no other debt outstanding and has a tax rate of 40%. To compute the company's weighted average cost of capital, the appropriate after-tax cost of debt is *closest* to:
    A. 4.2%.
    B. 4.8%.
    C. 5.4%.

15. At the time of valuation, the estimated betas for JPMorgan Chase & Co. and the Boeing Company were 1.50 and 0.80, respectively. The risk-free rate of return was 4.35%, and the equity risk premium was 8.04%. Based on these data, calculate the required rates of return for these two stocks using the CAPM.

16. An analyst's data source shows that Newmont Mining (NEM) has an estimated beta of –0.2. The risk-free rate of return is 2.5%, and the equity risk premium is estimated to be 4.5%.
    A. Using the CAPM, calculate the required rate of return for investors in NEM.
    B. The analyst notes that the current yield to maturity on corporate bonds with a credit rating similar to NEM is approximately 3.9%. How should this information affect the analyst's estimate?

17. Wang Securities had a long-term stable debt-to-equity ratio of 0.65. Recent bank borrowing for expansion into South America raised the ratio to 0.75. The increased leverage has what effect on the asset beta and equity beta of the company?
    A. The asset beta and the equity beta will both rise.
    B. The asset beta will remain the same, and the equity beta will rise.
    C. The asset beta will remain the same, and the equity beta will decline.

18. Brandon Wiene is a financial analyst covering the beverage industry. He is evaluating the impact of DEF Beverage's new product line of flavored waters. DEF currently has a debt-to-equity ratio of 0.6. The new product line would be financed with $50 million of debt and $100 million of equity. In estimating the valuation impact of this new product line on DEF's value, Wiene has estimated the equity beta and asset beta of comparable companies. In calculating the equity beta for the product line, Wiene is intending to use DEF's existing capital structure when converting the asset beta into a project beta. Which of the following statements is correct?
    A. Using DEF's debt-to-equity ratio of 0.6 is appropriate in calculating the new product line's equity beta.
    B. Using DEF's debt-to-equity ratio of 0.6 is not appropriate; rather, the debt-to-equity ratio of the new product, 0.5, is appropriate to use in calculating the new product line's equity beta.
    C. Wiene should use the new debt-to-equity ratio of DEF that would result from the additional $50 million debt and $100 million equity in calculating the new product line's equity beta.

19. Happy Resorts Company currently has 1.2 million common shares of stock outstanding, and the stock has a beta of 2.2. It also has $10 million face value of bonds that have five years remaining to maturity and an 8% coupon with semi-annual payments and are priced to yield 13.65%. If Happy issues up to $2.5 million of new bonds, the bonds will be priced at par and will have a yield of 13.65%; if it issues bonds beyond $2.5 million, the expected yield on the entire issuance will be 16%. Happy has learned that it can issue new common stock at $10 a share. The current risk-free rate of interest is 3%, and the expected market return is 10%. Happy's marginal tax rate is 30%. If Happy raises $7.5 million of new capital while maintaining the same debt-to-equity ratio, its weighted average cost of capital will be *closest* to:
    A. 14.5%.
    B. 15.5%.
    C. 16.5%.

The following information relates to questions 20–23

Boris Duarte, CFA, covers initial public offerings for Zellweger Analytics, an independent research firm specializing in global small-cap equities. He has been asked to evaluate the upcoming new issue of TagOn, a US-based business intelligence software company. The industry has grown at 26% per year for the previous three years. Large companies dominate the market, but sizable comparable companies, such as Relevant Ltd., ABJ Inc., and Opus Software Pvt. Ltd., also compete. Each of these competitors is domiciled in a different country, but they all have shares of stock that trade on the US NASDAQ. The debt ratio of the industry has risen slightly in recent years.

Company	Sales in Millions ($)	Market Value Equity in Millions ($)	Market Value Debt in Millions ($)	Equity Beta	Tax Rate (%)	Share Price ($)
Relevant Ltd.	752	3,800	0.0	1.702	23	42
ABJ Inc.	843	2,150	6.5	2.800	23	24
Opus Software Pvt. Ltd.	211	972	13.0	3.400	23	13

Duarte uses the information from the preliminary prospectus for TagOn's initial offering. The company intends to issue 1 million new shares. In his conversation with the investment bankers for the deal, he concludes the offering price will be between $7 and $12. The current capital structure of TagOn consists of a $2.4 million five-year noncallable bond issue and 1 million common shares. The following table includes other information that Duarte has gathered:

Currently outstanding bonds	$2.4 million five-year bonds, coupon of 12.5% paying semi-annually with a market value of $2.156 million
Risk-free rate of interest	5.25%
Estimated equity risk premium	7%
Tax rate	23%

20. The asset betas for Relevant, ABJ, and Opus, respectively, are:
    A. 1.70, 2.52, and 2.73.
    B. 1.70, 2.79, and 3.37.
    C. 1.70, 2.81, and 3.44.

21. The average asset beta for comparable players in this industry, Relevant, ABJ, and Opus, weighted by market value of equity is *closest* to:
    A. 1.67.
    B. 1.97.
    C. 2.27.

22. Using the capital asset pricing model, the cost of equity capital for a company in this industry with a debt-to-equity ratio of 0.01, an asset beta of 2.27, and a marginal tax rate of 23% is *closest* to:
    A. 17%.
    B. 21%.
    C. 24%.

23. The marginal cost of capital for TagOn, based on an average asset beta of 2.27 for the industry and assuming that new stock can be issued at $8 per share, is *closest* to:
    A. 20.5%.
    B. 21.0%.
    C. 21.5%.

24. An analyst gathered the following information about a private company and its publicly traded competitor:

Comparable Companies	Tax Rate (%)	Debt/Equity	Equity Beta
Private company	30.0	1.00	na
Public company	35.0	0.90	1.75

The estimated equity beta for the private company is *closest* to:
    A. 1.029.
    B. 1.104.
    C. 1.877.

25. Which of the following statements is *most accurate*? If two equity issues have the same market risk but the first issue has higher leverage, greater liquidity, and a higher required return, the higher required return *is most likely* the result of the first issue's:
    A. greater liquidity.
    B. higher leverage.
    C. higher leverage and greater liquidity.

26. SebCoe plc, a British firm, is evaluating an investment in a £50 million project that will be financed with 50% debt and 50% equity. Management has already determined that the NPV of this project is £5 million if it uses internally generated equity. However, if the company uses external equity, it will incur flotation costs of 5.8%. Assuming flotation costs are not tax deductible, the NPV using external equity would be:
    A. less than £5 million because we would discount the cash flows using a higher weighted average cost of capital that reflects the flotation costs.
    B. £3.55 million because flotation costs reduce NPV by $1.45 million.
    C. £5 million because flotation costs have no impact on NPV.

CHAPTER 8

COST OF CAPITAL: ADVANCED TOPICS

Lee M. Dunham, PhD, CFA
Creighton University (USA)

Pamela Peterson Drake, PhD, CFA
James Madison University (USA)

LEARNING OUTCOMES

The candidate should be able to:

- explain top-down and bottom-up factors that impact the cost of capital
- compare methods used to estimate the cost of debt
- explain historical and forward-looking approaches to estimating an equity risk premium
- compare methods used to estimate the required return on equity
- estimate the cost of debt or required return on equity for a public company and a private company
- evaluate a company's capital structure and cost of capital relative to peers

1. INTRODUCTION

A company's **weighted average cost of capital (WACC)** represents the cost of debt and equity capital used by the company to finance its assets. The **cost of debt** is the after-tax cost to the issuer of debt, based on the return that debt investors require to finance a company. The **cost of equity** represents the return that equity investors require to own a company, also referred to as the **required rate of return on equity** or the required return on equity.

A company's WACC is used by the company's internal decision makers to evaluate capital investments. For analysts and investors, it is a critical input used in company valuation.

Equation 1 reminds us that a company's WACC is driven by the proportions, or weights (the w_i), of the different capital sources used in its capital structure, applied to the costs of each source (the r_i), with d, p, and e subscripts denoting debt, preferred equity, and common equity, respectively:

$$\text{WACC} = w_d r_d (1 - t) + w_p r_p + w_e r_e. \tag{1}$$

(These weights are all non-negative and sum to 1.0.)

Determining a company's WACC is an important, albeit challenging, task for an analyst given the following:

- Many different methods can be used to calculate the costs of each source of capital; there is no single, "right" method.
- Assumptions are needed regarding long-term **target capital structure**, which might or might not be the current capital structure.
- The company's marginal tax rate must be estimated and might be different than its average or effective tax rate.

Estimating the cost of capital for a company thus involves numerous, sometimes complex, assumptions and choices, all of which affect the resulting investment conclusion.

2. COST OF CAPITAL FACTORS

Financial theory argues that companies should seek the optimal mix of debt and equity that results in the lowest WACC and maximizes shareholder wealth. Given differences in risk and financial risk tolerances across companies, the capital structure, cost of debt, and costs of equity vary across companies.

A company's cost of capital is influenced by the type of capital the company seeks. Because of its lower risk relative to equity, debt capital typically has a lower cost than equity capital. A company's cost of debt, before considering the tax deductibility of interest, can be represented as the sum of the benchmark **risk-free rate** and a **credit spread** that compensates investors for the risk inherent in the company's debt security:

$$r_d = r_f + \text{Credit spread}. \tag{2}$$

The credit spread reflects company-specific factors such as the riskiness of the company's business model, future profitability and growth prospects, applicable tax rates, the protective covenants in the debt securities, the company's policy regarding debt leverage—and possible changes thereto, the maturity and callability of the debt, and the nature and liquidity of the company's assets and operations.

A company's cost of equity can be represented by the sum of the benchmark risk-free rate and an equity risk premium that compensates investors for the risk inherent in the company's equity securities, or

$$r_e = r_f + (\text{ERP} + \text{IRP}), \tag{3}$$

where the **equity risk premium (ERP)** is a market risk premium for bearing the systematic risk of investing in equities in general, and the **idiosyncratic risk premium (IRP)** is a company-specific risk premium for bearing the company-specific risks of investing in the subject company's equity securities.

Because preferred equity typically has a stated dividend rate and a higher claim on assets than common equity, the ERP for a company's preferred equity is likely to be smaller than the ERP for its common equity, resulting in preferred equity having a lower cost than common equity.

Factors influencing a company's cost of capital can either be top-down (i.e., external or systematic) or bottom-up (i.e., company specific or idiosyncratic). Exhibit 1 summarizes these key factors.

EXHIBIT 1: Cost of Capital Factors

Top-Down, External	Bottom-Up, Company Specific
• Capital availability	• Revenue, earnings, and cash flow volatility
• Market conditions	• Asset nature and liquidity
• Legal and regulatory considerations/country risk	• Financial strength, profitability, and leverage
• Tax jurisdiction	• Security features

2.1. Top-Down External Factors

Top-down factors include macroeconomic factors such as risk-free rates, aggregate credit spreads, and the ERP.

2.1.1. Capital Availability

One cost of capital determinant is the general availability of capital in the company's market, region, or country. Greater capital availability typically leads to more favorable terms for corporate issuers and lower associated costs of capital.

Developed economies typically have more established, liquid capital markets with greater capital availability, more stable currencies, better property protection, and a greater strength in the rule of law than those of developing economies. Consequently, the perceived risk associated with investing in companies in more mature capital markets is lower than for companies in less mature economies. Lower perceived risk translates into lower credit spreads, ERPs, and costs of capital for companies in more mature, or developed, economies.

In regions with less developed capital markets, a lack of corporate debt markets could require companies to rely on other means for funding, such as bank loans or the shadow banking system. **Shadow banking** refers to any type of lending by financial institutions not regulated as banks.

2.1.2. Market Conditions

A company's cost of capital is also highly influenced by **market conditions** such as interest rates, inflation rates, and the macroeconomic environment. The credit spreads and ERPs demanded by debt and equity investors reflect overall credit and equity market conditions in addition to issuer-specific risk factors. Higher credit spreads and ERPs signify higher risk to potential new debt and equity capital providers, respectively, who demand higher returns for supplying capital.

Macroeconomic and country-specific economic factors, such as inflation rates, are reflected in benchmark interest rates and the overall level of credit spreads, which tend to widen during recessions and tighten during expansionary times. When interest rates are relatively low and credit spreads are tight, the costs of debt and equity capital are lower. Higher relative rates of inflation, represented in a higher risk-free rate, increase the cost of capital for companies.

Similarly, the ERP demanded by investors tends to increase during recessions and decrease during expansionary times. In developed economies, more predictable and transparent monetary policy contributes to greater certainty and lower volatility in interest rates and inflation rates, lowering the cost of capital for companies.

Macroeconomic conditions over the longer term—as measured by business cycles—also affect companies' costs of capital. During expansionary times, as credit spreads narrow, or tighten, companies tend to borrow more, to fund growth and expansion or refinance existing debt, as their cost of debt becomes cheaper. Similarly, during recessionary times when credit spreads can widen, companies tend to borrow less. Finally, exchange rates also affect the cost of capital. In countries with greater exchange rate volatility and higher associated currency risk, companies have higher costs of capital.

2.1.3. Legal and Regulatory Considerations, Country Risk

Empirical evidence suggests a strong relationship between capital market conditions in different countries and the legal traditions followed by those countries. Countries with common law–based legal systems tend to be more mature and have stronger legal systems, as measured by greater enforceability of investor rights, than countries with civil law–based legal systems. Legal systems with greater investor protections often support more developed capital markets, providing investors with a greater sense of security with respect to their investments. Investors in mature regulatory environments offering greater investor protections typically demand lower credit spreads and ERPs, leading to lower costs of capital for corporate issuers.

Companies' costs of capital are also influenced by regulatory policies and guidelines set by government or other related entities, which can drive key financial decisions such as those related to capital structure, payout policy, and pricing. Financial institutions and utility companies, for instance, are examples of entities in highly regulated industries.

2.1.4. Tax Jurisdiction

Another factor in cost of capital determination is the company's marginal income tax rate. In many countries and jurisdictions, interest expense is a tax-deductible expense, effectively reducing a company's after-tax cost of debt due to associated tax savings. The higher a company's marginal income tax rate, the greater the tax benefit associated with using debt in the capital structure.

EXAMPLE 1   External Factors and Cost of Capital

GW is a junior analyst researching two companies that are in the same industry but headquartered, and seeking to raise capital, in different countries. GW gathers the following information on each country's capital market:

Feature	Country A	Country B
Credit spreads	Wide	Narrow
Volatility in interest rates	High	Low

Feature	Country A	Country B
Inflation rate	High	Low
Capital availability	Low	High
Corporate tax rate	15%	25%

1. Which country is more likely to have lower costs of capital for corporate issuers, and why?

Solution:

Country B is more likely to have lower costs of capital for corporate issuers. All else equal, given a higher corporate income tax rate in Country B, corporate issuers in that country would benefit from a lower after-tax cost of debt. The higher the company's marginal income tax rate, the greater the attractiveness of using debt in the company's capital structure because of the associated tax savings benefit, assuming interest expense is tax deductible and the company has taxable income.

Additionally, corporate issuers in Country B benefit from narrow credit spreads, low volatility in interest rates, and a low inflation rate, all of which contribute to lower costs of capital for corporate issuers. When interest rates and volatility are relatively low and/ or credit spreads are narrow, the cost of debt and equity capital is lower than in periods of high interest rates and volatility and wide credit spreads.

Further, the higher supply of capital available in a given market often leads to more favorable terms for corporate issuers, resulting in a lower cost of capital.

2. Country A is considering tax legislation that, if passed, would raise the corporate income tax rate from 15% to 25%. What effect is this likely to have on the cost of debt for corporate issuers in Country A?

Solution:

The tax legislation under consideration would raise the corporate income tax rate in Country A from 15% to 25% and have the effect of lowering the after-tax cost of debt for corporate issuers in that country. As long as a company has the taxable income before interest available to offset the interest on debt, there is a benefit to the tax deductibility of interest and, therefore, a lower cost of debt.

3. What assumption are you making in drawing conclusions regarding the effect of tax legislation in Country A?

Solution:

The assumption necessary for the tax legislation to have an effect on companies' costs of capital depends on whether the interest is deductible for tax purposes. If interest is not deductible, there would be no effect on the WACC; if interest is deductible and the company has taxable earnings, the effect is to reduce the WACC.

2.2. Bottom–Up Company Specific Factors

In addition to the external environment, a company's business model influences its cost of capital. Analysts must assess company-specific characteristics such as revenue sensitivity, earnings volatility, the nature and liquidity of assets owned or used, current and anticipated financial leverage, and features embedded in the company's debt and equity securities to determine their impact on the company's cost of capital.

A company's WACC should ultimately reflect the riskiness of the company's expected cash flow streams. Key factors that drive differences in WACC across companies include

- revenue, earnings, and cash flow volatility;
- asset nature and liquidity;
- financial strength, profitability, and leverage; and
- security features.

2.2.1. Revenue, Earnings and Cash Flow Volatility

Some companies, such as telecom companies and companies in the media streaming business, have subscription-based, recurring revenue that leads to fairly stable earnings and cash flow streams. A high proportion of recurring revenues for a company is generally viewed as a positive by investors because the company's revenue stream is likely to be more stable and predictable and less sensitive to the ups and downs of the macroeconomy. In contrast, companies in cyclical industries, such as those in the industrial equipment industry and companies with pay-per-use models, typically have more volatile revenues, earnings, and cash flow streams with greater sensitivity to the macroeconomic environment.

A company's business and financial risks affect the volatility of its revenues, earnings, and cash flow in that

- companies with greater **sales risk** (that is, uncertainty regarding the price and number of units sold) have greater potential revenue volatility;
- companies that generate a majority of their revenues from a few customers, and thus face **customer concentration risk**, also have higher sales risk; and
- companies with higher operating and **financial leverage** (or a higher proportion of fixed costs and debt burden) have greater earnings volatility.

For a given level of debt, a company with greater predictability and lower associated volatility in its revenues, earnings, and cash flow streams is likely to have a lower probability of default and a narrower credit spread, resulting in a lower cost of debt and equity capital.

Additionally, a company with higher environmental, social, and governance (ESG) risk is likely to have a higher cost of capital. Suppose a company is in an industry that has a significant carbon footprint, yet the company does not appear to be taking sufficient action to mitigate its environmental impact. Investors could demand a higher cost of capital for this company given the perceived financial risk from the externality, which might include mitigation costs, consumer preferences or boycotts that lower sales, and litigation costs.

Similarly, a company with known employee safety concerns is likely to be viewed as having a greater risk of lawsuits and negative customer perception, which would increase its associated risk and cost of capital demanded by investors. Companies with weak governance practices typically face higher costs of capital because of the inherent risks and costs associated with inadequate systems and poor oversight. For example, a company that has anti-takeover provisions might deter takeovers but increase management entrenchment. Rather than reflecting these ESG risks in the cost of capital, analysts can choose to adjust the future cash flow forecasts in their valuation models.

Exhibit 2 presents a summary of the relationships between business model characteristics and a company's cost of capital.

EXHIBIT 2: Revenues, Earnings, and Cash Flow Volatility and Cost of Capital

Revenue, Earnings, Cash Flow Volatility	Effect on Cost of Capital	
	Lower	Higher
Higher stability of revenues earnings, and cash flows	✓	
Higher revenue concentration		✓
Higher earnings predictability	✓	
Higher operating leverage		✓
Higher financial leverage		✓
Higher ESG risks		✓

2.2.2. Asset Nature and Liquidity

The type and nature of a company's assets also determines its cost of capital. **Tangible assets** are physical assets such as property, plant, and equipment, and inventory, whereas **intangible assets**, such as goodwill, patents, intellectual property rights, and an educated and stable employee workforce, do not exist in physical form. In general, companies with primarily tangible assets are likely to be able to access debt capital at lower cost than companies with a high proportion of intangible assets because they have the ability to pledge these assets as collateral.

Companies with primarily fungible, (i.e., interchangeable into other units of the same identity) and highly liquid assets, such as cash and marketable securities, are likely to have access to lower-cost capital than companies with mostly non-fungible, illiquid assets such as specialized property, plant, and equipment. Another factor to consider is whether the tangible assets are collateralized, supporting debt; this will have the effect of lowering the issuer's cost of debt but potentially increasing its cost of equity, given that creditors could have a prior claim on assets in the event of liquidation.

Exhibit 3 presents a summary of the relationships between a company's asset liquidity and its cost of capital.

EXHIBIT 3: Asset Type and Cost of Capital

Asset Type	Effect on Cost of Capital	
	Lower	Higher
Higher proportion of fungible, tangible assets	✓	
Higher proportion of liquid assets	✓	

2.2.3. Financial Strength, Profitability, and Financial Leverage

Another cost of capital determinant is the company's projected financial strength. Companies with weakening profitability, poor cash flow generation, low IC, or tight liquidity typically face higher costs of capital because their credit spreads widen and idiosyncratic ERPs increase to account for their deteriorating characteristics.

When a company elects to raise debt or equity capital, the cost of that capital is highly dependent on the company's existing debt level and capital structure. Holding business risk constant, companies with higher proportions of debt in their capital structure, typically measured by leverage ratios such as a higher total debt-to-EBITDA ratio, higher debt-to-equity (D/E) ratio, or a lower interest coverage (IC) ratio, could face higher costs of capital in the form of higher credit spreads and a higher probability of default arising from a reduced ability to service additional debt.

EXHIBIT 4: Financial Strength and Cost of Capital

	Effect on Cost of Capital	
Financial Strength	Lower	Higher
Higher profitability	✓	
Higher cash flow generation	✓	
Higher IC, liquidity	✓	
Higher leverage ratios		✓

2.2.4. Security Features

A company's cost of capital is also affected by the features embedded in the debt and equity securities it issues. An issuer's debt securities might have various features, such as a call, put, and convertible feature. These features can increase or decrease the cost of capital for an issuer depending on what benefits they offer to the investor or the company.

- **Callability.** Call features on debt provide a benefit to the corporate issuer. When interest rates fall, the issuer can issue new, lower-cost debt at the prevailing lower interest rates and use the proceeds to buy or "call" back the existing higher-cost debt from investors. Because investors are disadvantaged by the call feature, they demand a higher yield on a callable bond at issuance than they would on an otherwise similar option-free bond. Corporate issuers who issue callable bonds thus incur an initial higher cost or yield on debt capital than if they issued option-free bonds. However, this higher cost at issuance could be reduced in the future if interest rates fall and the issuer is able to issue new debt and call back the existing debt.
- **Putability.** In contrast, investors benefit from a put feature that grants them the option to sell or "put" the bond back to the issuer prior to maturity. When rates rise, this is a valuable option because investors holding the issuer's putable bond can sell the bond back to the issuer before maturity and reinvest the proceeds at the higher prevailing yields. By permitting investors to sell their bonds to the issuer before maturity, put features also allow investors to avoid the effects of company-related events, such as a leveraged buyout or an acquisition, that could increase the risk of the bond and negatively affect its price. In

exchange for putability, investors accept a lower yield on a putable bond at issuance than they would receive on an otherwise similar option-free bond. However, this lower cost could increase in the future if interest rates rise and the issuer is forced to refinance at higher rates to buy back the bonds put back to the company.

- **Convertibility.** The conversion feature benefits investors by granting them the option to convert the bond into shares of the issuer's common stock at a specified ratio. Investors accept a lower rate of return on bonds with convertibility features than on option-free bonds.

Thus, corporate issuers who issue putable or convertible bonds will have a lower initial cost of debt capital than if they issued option-free bonds. It is important to note, however, that this lower cost at issuance can lead to higher costs later either in the form of having to issue higher-cost debt later if the bonds are put back to the issuer or, in the case of a convertible debt, in the form of equity dilution if investors ultimately convert the bonds into equity.

- **Cumulative versus Non-cumulative.** Preferred stock can differ with respect to the policy on missed dividends. **Cumulative preferred stock** requires that the company pay in full any missed dividends (that is, dividends promised but not paid) before paying dividends to common shareholders. In contrast, non-cumulative preferred stock does not require that missed dividends be paid before dividends are paid to common shareholders; the only requirement is that dividends to common shares cannot be reinstated unless preferred stock dividends are currently being paid. In a liquidation, preferred shareholders could have a claim for any unpaid dividends before distributions are made to common shareholders. Thus, investors accept a lower rate of return on cumulative preferred share compared to otherwise similar non-cumulative preferred shares.

- **Share Class.** Finally, some companies might issue different classes of common stock that provide different cash flow and voting rights. In general, an arrangement in which a company offers multiple classes of common stock (e.g., Class A and Class B) typically provides one class of shareholders with superior voting or cash flow rights, or both. The cost of common equity capital can be higher for shares with inferior cash flow or voting rights.

Exhibit 5 presents a summary of the relationships between the features of a corporate issuer's securities and the company's cost of capital.

EXHIBIT 5: Security Features and Cost of Capital

		Effect on Cost of Capital	
	Feature	Lower	Higher
Debt			
	Callability		✓
	Putability	✓	
	Convertibility	✓	
Equity			
Preferred	Cumulative	✓	
Common	Inferior cash flow or voting rights		✓

EXAMPLE 2   Company-Specific Factors and Cost of Capital

GW next gathers the following common size balance sheet and other selected information on the two companies:

	Company 1	Company 2
Cash and equivalents	5%	10%
Marketable securities	15%	7%
Accounts receivable	12%	19%
Inventory	3%	2%
Other current assets	4%	4%
Property, plant, and equipment (net)	46%	29%
Intangible assets and goodwill	10%	24%
Other assets	5%	5%
Other Selected Information:		
Net debt/EBITDA	2.1	2.5
IC ratio	12.6	7.9
Operating leverage	Low	High
% Sales from top five customers	15%	27%
Features in existing debt securities	Put	Call

1. Which company is more likely to have a lower cost of capital? Justify your response.

Solution:

   Company 1 is likely to have a lower cost of capital. It has a larger percentage of cash and equivalents and marketable securities (20%) than Company 2 (17%). Company 1 also has a much lower percentage of intangible assets (10%) than Company 2 (24%). In general, companies with primarily tangible and liquid assets are likely to be able to access debt and equity capital at lower cost than companies with a high proportion of intangible assets. Company 1's higher proportion of tangible property, plant, and equipment (46%) might also allow the company to access debt capital at lower cost because of its ability to pledge these assets as collateral.

   Company 1 also operates with lower financial leverage, as indicated by a lower net debt-to-EBITDA ratio (2.1 versus 2.5) and a higher IC ratio (12.6 versus 7.9). Companies with lower levels of debt, typically measured by leverage ratios such as a lower net debt-to-EBITDA ratio or a higher IC ratio, will have lower capital costs. Company 1 also operates with lower operating leverage, reflecting a cost structure that includes a lower percentage of fixed costs and a more diversified customer base (top five customers accounting for 15% of total sales versus 27% for Company 2). Companies with lower operating leverage and lower customer concentration risk tend to have greater stability in their earnings and cash flow streams and thus are likely to have lower costs of capital than companies with high volatility in these streams.

   Finally, the existing debt securities of Company 1 have embedded put options that allow investors to sell the securities back to the company prior to maturity if interest rates rise. In contrast, the existing debt securities of Company 2 have embedded call options that allow the company to call the securities prior to maturity if interest rates rise. The put option is a benefit to investors, whereas the call feature is a benefit to the issuer, which leads to putable bonds having a lower cost or yield than otherwise comparable callable bonds.

2.3. Cost of Capital Factors Summary

- The costs of debt and equity capital are influenced by both top-down and bottom-up factors.
- Top-down factors include macroeconomic and political factors such as capital availability and market conditions (risk-free rates, credit spreads, and the ERP), legal and regulatory considerations such as the maturity of the regulatory environment in the country in which the company operates, and the company's tax jurisdiction.
- Key bottom-up factors include issuer-specific characteristics such as revenue and earnings volatility, the nature and liquidity of assets owned or used, financial leverage, and firm-specific risks.
- Features of debt securities, including callability, putability, and convertibility, affect the cost of debt. Features of equity securities, such as cumulative dividends, affect the costs of equity.
- Whether an analyst's approach to estimating WACC is top-down, bottom-up, or a combination, the analyst must make a number of assumptions and estimates to derive a company's WACC.

Exhibit 6 presents a summary of factors analysts should consider in determining WACC.

EXHIBIT 6: Analyst Checklist for WACC Determination

- **Top-down, external factors**
- Availability of debt and equity capital
- Debt market conditions (e.g., credit spreads)
- Equity market conditions (e.g., ERP)
- Business cycle (e.g., expansion versus recession)
- Legal and regulatory environment (e.g., country risk, common law versus civil law basis, maturity of regulatory environments)
- Tax jurisdiction

- **Bottom-up, company-specific factors**
- Sales risk
- Operating and financial leverage
- Debt features: type of interest, collateral, embedded options
- Equity features: seniority, voting rights
- ESG risks
- Asset tangibility and liquidity
- Tax deductibility of interest expense

KNOWLEDGE CHECK

1. Identify whether each of the following factors would positively or negatively affect an issuer's cost of capital. An issuer

   I. with a high degree of operating leverage.

   II. with relatively high earnings predictability.

   III. seeking capital in a region with a high supply of available capital.

   IV. seeking capital in a region with weak legal and regulatory systems.

Solution:

Factors I and IV would likely lead to an issuer having a higher cost of capital. Companies with higher operating leverage will experience greater earnings volatility for a given change in revenue than companies operating with lower operating leverage. Higher earnings volatility leads to lower earnings predictability, which typically leads to a higher cost of capital. Further, issuers seeking capital in regions with weak legal and regulatory environments will face higher costs of capital to compensate investors for the weak investor protections.

Factors II and III would likely lead to an issuer having a lower cost of capital. Higher earnings predictability typically leads to a lower cost of capital. Further, a high supply of capital available in a given market often leads to more favorable terms for corporate issuers, also resulting in a lower cost of capital.

2. Identify which issuer, based solely on its given business model characteristics, would likely have a lower cost of capital and be able to support a higher proportion of debt in its capital structure. Justify your selection.

Company 1	Company 2
Pay-per-use model	Subscription model
Asset base consists largely of intangible assets	Assets base consists largely of tangible assets
60% of revenues come from largest five customers	No more than 1% of revenues come from a single customer

Solution:

Company 2 is correct. Companies with subscription-based business models are typically characterized by fairly predictable revenues and earnings than companies with pay-per-use models. Further, companies with asset bases consisting primarily of tangible assets are likely to access debt and equity capital at lower costs than companies with a high proportion of intangible assets because of the lower risk inherent in tangible assets. Finally, companies that generate their revenues from highly diversified customer bases (low customer concentration risk) are likely to have lower costs of capital than companies that generate a majority of their revenues from a very few customers.

3. Identify two market conditions that are most likely favorable for companies to issue debt securities. Justify your response.

Solution:

A company's cost of debt is equal to a risk-free rate plus a credit spread specific to the company. Lower interest rates, for example arising from expansionary monetary policy, and tighter credit spreads, as during periods of economic expansion, would make borrowing less costly and debt financing relatively more attractive for companies.

In contrast, when interest rates are relatively high and/or more restrictive monetary policy is expected, or when spreads are wider because of weak or worsening overall economic conditions, borrowing would be more expensive for companies.

4. Describe two embedded debt features that would most likely result in a lower cost of debt capital at issuance.

Solution:

Bonds issued with either a put feature or a convertible feature offer a benefit to investors. Putable bonds offer investors the option to sell the bond back to the company prior to maturity when interest rates rise. Convertible bonds provide investors with the option of converting the bonds into shares of the issuer's common stock prior to maturity. Consequently, bonds with these features will typically be issued at a lower initial cost or yield relative to option-free bonds.

3. ESTIMATING THE COST OF DEBT

Analysts have several methods available to estimate the cost of debt, and the use of those methods depends on a number of factors, namely the following:

* *Type of debt*: Is the company's debt publicly traded? Non-traded or private? Bank debt? A lease?
* *Debt liquidity*: How liquid or marketable is the issued debt?
* *Credit rating*: Does the debt have a credit rating?
* *Debt currency*: In what currency is the debt denominated?

In the following sections, we examine these factors and the methods an analyst can use to estimate the cost of debt.

3.1. Traded Debt

If a company has publicly traded debt with no embedded options, otherwise known as **straight debt**, the yield to maturity (YTM) on the company's existing debt with the longest maturity could be a reasonable estimate of the company's cost of issuing straight debt. If the company has shorter-term bonds that are more liquid and trade more frequently than its longest dated bond, the YTM on the shorter-term debt might be a more reliable estimate of the company's cost of debt. Effectively, the YTM reflects the current market interest rate on the debt, which can be interpreted as the current cost of issuing new debt with similar features.

3.2. Non-Traded Debt

Most private companies, and some public companies, have non-traded or illiquid debt securities. In these cases, a quoted YTM either does not exist or is an unreliable estimate of the cost of debt because of the presence of a large liquidity premium embedded in the yield.

In such scenarios, an analyst can check whether credit ratings exist for the company's debt securities. If so, one approach to estimating a company's cost of debt is to use the yields to maturity of bonds of other companies with the same or similar maturities and credit ratings and apply matrix pricing to estimate a YTM for the subject company's bonds.

If no credit rating exists, an alternative is to use fundamental characteristics of the company, such as IC ratios or other financial leverage ratios, to deduce the likely bond rating, or a synthetic credit rating, of the company's outstanding debt. This approach requires a model that estimates a bond's rating class. Using proprietary information, bond ratings, features, and rating classes, it is possible to model the ratings classifications using statistical models.

Once a credit rating has been inferred, an analyst can use the YTM on bonds with a similar maturity and the inferred credit rating to estimate a cost of debt. Alternatively, the analyst can determine the current credit spread for that credit rating and maturity of the company's debt. This credit spread is then added to the benchmark risk-free rate to arrive at an estimate of the cost of debt for the subject company.

EXAMPLE 3   Synthetic Credit Ratings

After examining a large number of companies in the manufacturing industry with rated debt, analysts at the Brunswix Firm developed the likely range of ratios for each credit rating class, which are presented in Exhibit 7.

EXHIBIT 7: Rating Classes and Leverage Ratios

Rating class	IC	D/E
AAA	IC > 10 times	D/E < 35%
AA	8 < IC < 10	35% < D/E < 40%
A	5 < IC < 8	40% < D/E < 42%
BBB	3 < IC < 5	42% < D/E < 44%
BB	2 < IC < 3	44% < D/E < 50%

Rating class	IC	D/E
B	1.4 < IC < 2.0	50% < D/E < 60%
CCC	1.0 < IC < 1.4	60% < D/E < 70%
CC	0.6 < IC < 1.0	70% < D/E < 80%
C	0.3 < IC < 0.6	80% < D/E <100%
D	IC < 0.3	D/E > 100%

A Lee, an analyst at the firm, would like to use this proprietary model to predict the debt rating for Gamma Company, a manufacturing company with non-traded debt. Gamma has an IC ratio of 1.5 and a D/E ratio of 43%.

1. What rating class should Lee assign to Gamma Company's debt and why?

Solution:

Given a conflict in potential rating that exists for Gamma, it is not clear which rating class the company should be assigned. This is because even though Gamma's IC ratio indicates that the company aligns with a B rating, its D/E ratio indicates that a BBB rating is more appropriate.

2. What else should Lee do to estimate the synthetic rating?

Solution:

Lee should attempt to look at these ratios historically for Gamma and examine whether trends appear in these ratios that might indicate future increases or decreases. For example, if the IC ratio has been trending upward, Lee might want to use personal judgment to suggest a BB rating for Gamma rather than the current synthetic B rating.

It should be noted that the issuer's overall credit rating might be different than the credit ratings on its issued securities. Further, some companies have different credit ratings for their own different outstanding debt issues, based on bond features. For instance, a company could have both AA- and A-rated debt, with the AA debt granting more protection to the investor through collateral, seniority, convertibility, or other features. The analyst's challenge is to estimate a cost of debt that best reflects the company's risk profile.

3.3. Bank Debt

In some countries, bank financing is a primary source of debt financing for companies and the primary source of funding for small businesses. Fixed-rate and floating-rate bank debt can be fully amortizing, partially amortizing, or non-amortizing. In general, amortizing loans typically have a lower cost of debt because of their lower default risk, given that some portion of principal is being repaid over the loan term. In contrast, non-amortizing loans, where the entire principal is repaid at maturity, similar to a bullet bond, typically have higher default risk and a higher cost of debt.

An analyst should attempt to determine the interest rate paid by the company on new bank debt financing to estimate the cost of bank debt. If a company has recently taken on new bank debt, the interest rate on that loan could be a good estimate of the company's cost of debt if the analyst believes the interest rate reflects current market conditions and the company's risk profile has not materially changed since issuance.

Again, it is important to note that an estimate of the cost of debt should be used with caution if there is any belief that market conditions or the company's risk profile has substantially changed since its issuance.

3.4. Leases

Some companies use lease financing to acquire assets such as property, aircraft, and other large-ticket capital assets. A **finance (or capital) lease** is an example of an amortized loan. In contrast, operating leases involve expenses, and the property is not capitalized on the lessee's financial statement. A finance lease has properties similar to the ownership of the leased asset: use of the asset, payment(s), and the lessee owns the asset at the end of the lease term or has an option for asset purchase. The interest rate or the implicit lease rate in a finance lease can be inferred from the lease payments and the fair value of the leased asset, considering the residual value of the asset and direct costs of the lessor. As a type of secured loan, leases often have lower associated borrowing costs for a company than if the company were to borrow in the capital markets on an unsecured basis to purchase the asset outright.

According to IFRS-16 and ASC-842, the interest rate, or the **rate implicit in the lease (RIIL)** is the discount rate that equates the sum of the present value of the lease payments and the present value of the residual value with the sum of the fair value of the leased asset and the lessor's direct costs (e.g., legal fees) such that:

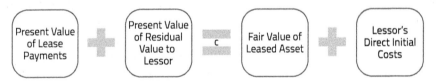

However, the present value of the residual value and the lessor's direct initial costs are often not known to the lessee (company) or analyst. If unknown, the **incremental borrowing rate (IBR)**, which is the rate of interest the company would pay to borrow using a collateralized loan over the same term, might be used. If this rate is not known, the analyst might use the non-traded debt estimation method. In most public company filings, however, lessees will disclose the interest rates for their lease liabilities.

Under some tax jurisdictions, a finance lease is considered a purchase (and therefore, a sale from the point of view of the lessor), and interest expense is tax deductible. In this case, an adjustment is made to the cost of debt to put it on an after-tax basis.

EXAMPLE 4   Leasing Costs

G&S Airlines is considering whether to borrow money or use cash on hand (equity) to purchase or lease a new aircraft needed for its business. The company's unsecured IBR is 6%, and its cost of equity is 11%.

The lease terms the company has negotiated are for a 15-year lease with annual payments (PMT) of EUR9.0 million at the end of each year. The leased asset has a fair value (FV) of EUR100 million. The lessor would incur a cost of €5 million at the time of the lease agreement. The residual value of the leased asset at the end of 15 years is EUR10 million.

1. What is the implied interest cost of this lease?

Solution:
The cash flows associated with the lease are as follows:

	0	1	2	3	...	15
Lease PMT		€9.0	€9.0	€9.0		€9.0
Residual value						€10.0
FV of leased asset	−€100.0					
Lessor direct costs	−€5.0					
Net cash flows	−€105.0	€9.0	€9.0	€9.0		€19.0

Solving for the discount rate that equates the initial net cash outflow of €105.0 million to the present value (PV) of the net cash flows beyond the initial year results in a rate of 4.08%.

Using a calculator,

PMT = 9.0, PV = −105.0, N = 15, FV = 10.0

Using Microsoft Excel,

RATE(15,9.0,-105.0,10.0,0)

Using Python,

import numpy_financial as npf

r = npf(15,9.0,-105.0,10.0,0)
print(r)

Using R,

library(FinCal)

discount.rate(15,-105.0,10.0,9.0,0)

2. What factors should G&S consider in the decision to buy outright versus leasing?

Solution:
    At 4.08%, the leasing option is lower cost and lower risk than the company's unsecured IBR of 6%. It is also lower in cost than issuing equity, which would be dilutive. Leasing avoids the risks associated with ownership. However, G&S would have increased leverage as a result of the lease transaction.

3.5. International Considerations

When being estimated for international markets, the cost of debt should reflect the currency in which the company's cash flows occur. One approach to estimating the cost of debt for an entity in a less mature, foreign market is to add a country risk premium to the debt's yield. In this case, a **country risk rating (CRR)** can be used.

A CRR is a rating applied to a country based on the assessment of risk pertaining to that country, in areas such as

- economic conditions,
- political risk,
- exchange rate risk, and
- securities market development and regulation.

    Risks are often assessed relative to a country's sovereign debt risk. Sovereign risk is a component of country risk and relates to a country's likelihood of defaulting on its debt obligations, whereas country risk includes the factors beyond the sovereign risk, such as political stability, economic competitiveness, and human development. This information is then used to adjust the cost of debt for a subject company. The ratings can be similar to credit ratings—that is, AAA, AA, and so on—or might have a numeric range (e.g., 0 to 10, 0 to 100) using a benchmark country. For each rating class or numeric score, the median interest rate can be calculated. By comparing the median interest rate with the benchmark country's rate, the country risk premium can be derived.

    Consider the chart of rates and country risk premiums in Exhibit 8, using Country A as the benchmark (therefore, a 0% country risk premium). Country C has a risk rating of 2 and a median interest rate of 4.5%. Country C's country risk premium is therefore 0.5% (or 4.5% – 4.0%).

EXHIBIT 8: Country Risk Premiums

Country	Rating (1 = least risk, 10 = most risk)	Median Interest Rate	Country Risk Premium
A	1	4.0%	0.0%
B	5	7.0%	3.0%
C	2	4.5%	0.5%
D	8	15.5%	11.5%
E	7	9.5%	5.5%
F	6	7.5%	3.5%

EXAMPLE 5   Cost of Debt Summary

- The cost of debt is affected by the type of debt, the liquidity of the debt issue, the debt's credit rating, and the currency in which the debt is issued.
- Calculating the cost of traded debt is relatively uncomplicated, especially for straight debt, but determining the cost of non-traded debt requires using approaches such as a synthetic credit rating.
- Determining the cost of bank debt and leasing requires information for the calculation of the effective cost of this financing.
- The cost of debt in international markets can be estimated using CRRs that reflect economic, political, and exchange rate risk, as well as information about the financial markets and regulation.

1. An analyst is estimating the cost of debt for a company that leases its assets. What information does the analyst need to estimate the company's cost of debt?

Solution:

To estimate the cost of debt, the analyst will need to know, or estimate
- lease payments,
- the residual value of the leased asset,
- the fair value of the leased asset,
- lessor direct costs, and
- the term of the lease.

2. If there is a limit on the monetary amount of the interest deduction for tax purposes, how would this affect a company's cost of debt?

Solution:

If a company has already reached the limit on interest that might be tax deductible, the cost of debt is not adjusted for the tax rate. This is because the cost of debt is the cost of raising additional debt, and no further tax benefit can be realized by the company.

3. An analyst is estimating the cost of debt for a company with outstanding debt that is not traded. Which methods, if any, can be considered for estimating the company's cost of debt?

Solution:

Potential methods include the following:

Matrix pricing – Identifying other debt that is publicly traded with similar features in maturity, features, and credit quality.

Synthetic rating – Using the companies' fundamentals, such as IC ratios and other leverage ratios, to estimate a credit rating class. Once a credit rating has been inferred, an analyst can simply use the YTM on bonds with a similar maturity and credit rating to estimate a cost of debt.

4. THE ERP

The ERP represents the expected incremental return that investors demand as compensation for holding risky equity securities rather than a risk-free asset. It is the difference between the expected return on equities and a benchmark risk-free rate.

Analysts estimate a company-specific ERP to calculate the company's cost of equity capital, or r_e, as

$$\text{Company i } r_e = E(r_f) + (\text{Systematic market ERP} + \text{Company i IRP})$$

$$= E(r_f) + (\text{ERP} + \text{IRP}). \tag{4}$$

The focus here is on estimating the size of the ERP rather than the IRP for the company. Even for long-established developed markets, estimating the size of the ERP is challenging and subject to estimation error, resulting in differing investment conclusions among analysts.

Two broad approaches used to estimate the ERP are

- the *historical approach (ex-post)*, which uses backward-looking historical data to estimate the ERP, and
- the *forward-looking approach (ex-ante)*, which uses forward-looking expectational data.

Given that both methods are used in practice, analysts should be aware of their limitations and how their conclusions can be affected by estimation error.

4.1. Historical Approach

A historical approach is often used when reliable long-term equity return data are available. A historical ERP estimate is typically calculated as the mean value of the difference between a broad-based equity market index return and a government debt return, as a proxy for the risk-free rate, over some sample period.

In using a historical estimate to represent the ERP going forward, the analyst is assuming that returns are stationary and that markets are relatively efficient, so over the long term, average returns should be an unbiased estimate of what investors expected to earn. An analyst therefore must assess whether historical returns in the market of interest provide useful information about future expectations before using the historical approach.

An analyst has four key decisions in the development of a historical ERP:

1. What equity index best represents equity market returns?
2. What time period is best to calculate the estimate?
3. What measure for mean returns should be used?
4. Which proxy for the risk-free rate is best?

4.1.1. Equity Index Selection

The analyst should select an equity index that accurately represents the typical returns earned by equity investors in the market. Broad-based, market-value-weighted indexes are typically chosen as representative. Examples include the S&P 500 Index, Russell 3000 Index, MSCI EAFE Index, Australia All Ordinaries, and the Shanghai Composite Index.

4.1.2. Time Period

Deciding on the best estimation time period will involve trade-offs. One method uses the longest reliable return series available, but this is problematic because the distant past might not be representative of the current market environment. In addition, research shows significant evidence of non-constant underlying return volatility in many equity markets. This fluctuating volatility has less of an effect on estimates from a long data series; however, this assumes the ERP has not experienced any permanent changes in its level.

Using a shorter data period avoids using less-representative periods contained in longer data series and makes it more likely that the ERP estimate is representative of the current market environment. The trade-off, however, is that using a shorter time period increases the likelihood of greater noise in the ERP estimate. More specifically, a shorter estimation period, such as one covering only a portion of a business cycle or a period of disruption such as the global financial crisis or the COVID-19 pandemic, might not be sufficiently robust to forecast future returns. In the case of the latter, a time period that does not include the market disruption is needed.

A similar issue arises when a series of strong market returns has increased historical mean ERP estimates, making it likely that the historical estimate could be overestimating the forward-looking ERP. In general, analysts tend to favor the use of a longer time period, given the reduction in the standard error of the ERP estimate that occurs as the estimation period lengthens.

4.1.3. Selection of the Mean Type

An analyst using the historical approach must also decide on the mean type to use in the estimation, the choices being to use either a geometric mean or an arithmetic mean in calculating the average difference between the equity market return and the benchmark risk-free rate. Exhibit 9 summarizes the advantages and disadvantages of each.

EXHIBIT 9: Arithmetic Mean Return versus Geometric Mean Return

Mean Type	Advantages	Disadvantages
Arithmetic Mean	• Easy to calculate • Considers all observations in the time series	• Sensitive to extreme values • Overestimates the expected terminal value of wealth
Geometric Mean	• Considers all observations in the time series • Gives outliers less weight • Estimates the expected terminal value of wealth	

The arithmetic mean return as the average one-period return best represents the mean return in a single period. Popular models for estimating required return—the capital asset pricing model and multifactor models—are single-period models, so the arithmetic mean, with its focus on single-period returns, is a model-consistent choice.

The geometric mean return represents the compound rate of growth that equates the beginning value to the ending value of one unit of money initially invested in an asset.

The geometric mean is generally preferred because it is less sensitive to outliers and is also consistent with expected terminal wealth estimates. However, both mean types are used in practice.

4.1.4. Selection of the Risk-Free Rate Proxy

Lastly, the analyst must decide on a proxy for the risk-free return. Choices include a short-term government debt rate, such as a USD or EUR Treasury-bill rate, or the YTM on a long-term government bond. Given that they have less (near zero) default risk, government bonds are preferred over even the highest-rated corporate bonds. Exhibit 10 summarizes the advantages and disadvantages of using a short-term rather than long-term proxy.

EXHIBIT 10: Short- versus Long-Term Risk-Free Rate Proxy

Risk-Free Proxy	Advantages	Disadvantages
Short-term government bill rate	• The rate is an exact estimate of the risk-free rate, assuming no default.	• The rate does not closely match the duration of an infinite-life equity security.
Long-term government bond YTM	• The YTM more closely matches the duration of an infinite-life equity security.	• The YTM is not a completely risk-free return at the time of purchase because of unknown coupon reinvestment rates.

Some analysts prefer to use a very short-term government bond rate as a proxy, such as a three-month benchmark government bond rate, with the rationale being that a short-term government bond is typically a zero-coupon bond with a return known up front (at the time of purchase) that is not dependent on the reinvestment of coupons. The stated yield is truly the return received by the investor, assuming no default. The disadvantage of using the short-term government bond is that it does not closely match the duration of an infinite-life equity security or most investment horizons.

Industry practice has tended to favor the use of a long-term government bond yield as the risk-free rate proxy. The actual return an investor receives from owning the long-term government bond is not known up front at the time of purchase; the actual return depends, in part, on the rates of return earned from coupon reinvestment during the life of the bond. This is a disadvantage of using the YTM on a long-term government bond as a proxy: it is not a risk-free, known return at the time of purchase. Regardless, the current YTM on a long-term government bond is still used by analysts as an approximation for the bond's expected return.

4.1.5. Limitations of the Historical Approach

Although popular in practice, the historical approach is subject to several limitations, including the following:

• ERPs can vary over time. If the ERP has shifted to a permanently different level in recent years, estimates based on a long time series of historical data are not representative of the future ERP.

- **Survivorship bias** tends to inflate historical estimates of the ERP. This bias is present in equity market data when poorly performing or defunct companies are removed from index membership, so that only relative winners remain represented in index performance.

EXAMPLE 6   ERP Estimation Using the Historical Approach

1. Identify a reason why using a very short-term government bond rate to estimate a historical ERP might be justified. Explain its disadvantage.

Solution:

The justification for using a very short-term government bond to estimate an ERP using the historical approach is that unlike a long-term government bond, a short term government bond is typically a zero coupon bond with a return known up front and is not dependent on the reinvestment of coupons. Thus, its stated yield is truly the return that the investor receives, assuming no default; this is not the case for the YTM on a long-term government bond. The disadvantage of using the short-term government bond is that it does not match the duration of an infinite-life equity security.

2. Describe a key assumption an analyst must make to justify the use of a historical ERP to estimate a required return using an asset pricing model.

Solution:

An analyst who uses a historical ERP to estimate a required return using an asset pricing model is assuming that returns are stationary—that is, the parameters that describe the return-generating process are the same in the future as they were in the past.

3. Explain why using the geometric mean might be preferred over the arithmetic mean in the historical approach to estimating the ERP.

Solution:

Estimated ERPs using geometric means are less sensitive to outliers than those using the arithmetic mean. Further, using the geometric mean to compound wealth forward estimates the expected terminal value of wealth.

D Smith and J Müller are equity analysts at Odyssey Investments. Smith and Müller estimate different ERPs using the following assumptions:

	Smith	Müller
Benchmark index	Russell 3000	S&P 500
Sample time period	35 years	65 years
Risk-free rate proxy	30-year Treasury bond	3-month Treasury bill
Mean measure used	Arithmetic	Geometric
Average benchmark index return	12.96%	11.23%
Average risk-free rate over sample period	6.25%	3.11%

4. Calculate two estimates of the ERP using both sets of assumptions.

Solution:
The estimate of the ERP using Smith's assumptions is

$$12.96\% - 6.25\% = 6.71\%.$$

The estimate of the ERP using Müller's assumptions is

$$11.23\% - 3.11\% = 8.12\%.$$

5. Explain why both estimates could be valid.

Solution:
Even though the two estimates of the ERP are different, they might both be valid. The two analysts simply made different choices of the four key decisions in estimating the historical ERP to arrive at their different estimates. This example demonstrates that differences in underlying analyst assumptions can yield different ERP estimates with corresponding valuation implications.

4.2. Forward-Looking Approach

A forward-looking approach is consistent with the idea that the ERP depends strictly on future expectations, given that an investor's returns depend only on the investment's expected future cash flows. The ERP should therefore be based only on expectations for economic and financial variables that affect future cash flows. In a forward-looking approach, the ERP is estimated using current information and expectations concerning such variables. These estimates are often called **forward-looking estimates** or ex ante estimates. We provide an overview of three forward-looking estimation methods:

- Survey-based estimates
- Dividend discount models
- Macroeconomic modeling

4.2.1. Survey-Based Estimates

One forward-looking approach is to gauge expectations by asking people what they expect. Survey estimates of the ERP involve asking a sample of people—frequently, experts—about their expectations for the ERP, or for capital market expectations from which the ERP can be inferred. In general, such surveys reveal that the ERP is much higher in developing markets when compared to developed markets. One issue with using surveys to estimate the ERP is that these estimates tend to be sensitive to recent market returns.

4.2.2. Dividend Discount Model Estimates

The second approach involves use of a **dividend discount model (DDM)**, which expresses the value of a stock, V_0, as the present value of future expected dividends. A simplified form of a DDM used to estimate a forward-looking ERP is based on an expected constant earnings growth rate and known as the **Gordon growth model**:

$$V_o = \frac{D_1}{r_e - g}. \tag{5}$$

Solving for the required return on equity (r_e) yields

$$r_e = \frac{D_1}{V_0} + g, \tag{6}$$

where $\frac{D_1}{V_0}$ is an expected dividend yield, and g is the expected earnings growth rate.

Broad-based equity indexes typically have an associated dividend yield, and the year-ahead dividend (D_1) for the index might be fairly predictable. In addition, the expected earnings growth rate, g, can be inferred based on expectations such as consensus analyst expectations of the earnings growth rate for an equity market index. These expectations can be top-down or bottom-up generated forecasts.

Subtracting the current risk-free rate from this expected market equity return from Equation 6 yields a forward-looking ERP estimate:

$$\text{ERP} = E\left(\frac{D_1}{V_0}\right) + E(g) - r_f. \tag{7}$$

Note that an underlying assumption of the constant growth DDM is that earnings, dividends, and prices will grow at the same rate, resulting in a constant P/E. If, however, the analyst believes this is not likely to be the case going forward, an adjustment would be needed that reflects anticipated P/E multiple expansion or contraction. This is because from a given starting market level associated with a given level of earnings and P/E, the return from capital appreciation cannot be greater (or less than) than the earnings growth rate unless the P/E increases (or decreases). P/E increases (or decreases) can result from an increase (or decrease) in the earnings growth rate or a decrease (or increase) in risk. Some analysts also include the aggregate amount spent on buybacks by the index constituent companies in the dividend yield term to reflect total payout. When doing so, an analyst should also consider the degree to which buybacks might alter growth rates in earnings and dividends.

EXAMPLE 7   ERP Estimation Using the Constant Growth DDM

An analyst is estimating a forward-looking ERP for the UK market using the FTSE 100 Index. The analyst gathers the following information:

Market Index	FTSE 100 Index	Analyst Forecast Range
FTSE 100 Index forward dividend yield, $E\left(\frac{D_1}{V_0}\right)$	1.94%	1.5% to 3.5%
FTSE 100 Index expected long-term earnings growth rate, $E(g)$	5.0%	4.0% to 6.0%
Long-term Gilt bond yield, (r_f)	1.63%	1.5% to 2.5%

1. Calculate an estimate of the ERP using the constant growth DDM.

Solution:

The UK ERP estimate is 5.31%, or

$$ERP = 1.94\% + 5.0\% - 1.63\% = 5.31\%.$$

2. The analyst is developing a sensitivity analysis for the ERP. What is the effect of allowing for the variations in analyst forecasts in a simulation of the ERP?

Solution:

At the forecast extremes, the ERP ranges from $1.5\% + 4\% - 2.5\% = 3\%$ to $3.5\% + 6\% - 1.5\% = 8\%$. The analyst might want to simulate the dividend yield and the long-term bond yield based on this range, using information about distribution among the analysts as part of the simulation.

For rapidly growing economies, an analyst might assume multiple earnings growth stages. Applying the constant growth DDM in this situation, the analyst might forecast

1. a *fast growth stage* for the aggregate of companies included in the subject country equity index, followed by
2. a *transition growth stage* in which growth rates decline, and
3. a *mature growth stage* characterized by growth at a moderate, sustainable rate.

The required rate of return, r_e, is calculated as the rate that equates the sum of the present values for each stage to the equity index price, or

$$\text{Equity index price} = PV_{0,Stage1} + PV_{0,Stage2} + PV_{0,Stage3}, \tag{8}$$

where the $PV_{0,Stage1}$ is the value at time 0 (that is, today) of the Stage 1 dividends, and $PV_{0,Stage2}$ and $PV_{0,Stage3}$ are similarly for the other two stages. The calculation requires solving for the internal rate of return. Once we have this rate, the chosen proxy for the risk-free rate is then subtracted to arrive at the ERP.

4.2.3. Macroeconomic Modeling

ERP estimates derived from macroeconomic models rely on a number of forecasted economic variables such as inflation and expected growth in real earnings per share. Using relationships between macroeconomic and financial variables in equity valuation models, analysts can develop ERP estimates. These models might be more reliable when public equities represent a relatively large share of the economy, as in many developed markets.

One such model is the Grinold-Kroner (2001) decomposition of the return on equity:

$$ERP = [\text{Dividend yield} + \text{Expected capital gain}] - E(r_f)$$

or

$$\text{ERP} = [\text{DY} + \text{Expected repricing} + \text{Earnings growth per share}] - E(r_f). \tag{9}$$

Dividend yield, DY, reflects the expected income component of the equity investment. The expected repricing term relates to expected changes in P/E ratios within the market being evaluated. Earnings growth per share can be expressed as

Earnings growth per share

$$= \text{Expected inflation} + \text{Real economic growth} + \text{Change in shares outstanding}$$

$$= i + g + \Delta S. \tag{10}$$

Empirical studies suggest that ΔS, the change in shares outstanding or the dilution effect, varies significantly across countries for a variety of reasons. We assume that $\Delta S = 0$ here, but there is a further discussion in the economic growth module regarding ways to model this for a particular market.

$$\text{ERP} = [\text{DY} + \Delta(\text{P/E}) + i + g + \Delta S] - E(r_f). \tag{11}$$

The Grinold-Kroner model effectively builds the expected market equity return as a function of five factors. Note that this model explicitly considers expected changes in the P/E ratio of the market mentioned in our discussion of the DDM. The following table summarizes the factors, and their common proxies, in the Grinold-Kroner (2001) decomposition of the return on equity.

Factor	Symbol	Common Proxy
Expected income component	DY	Broad-based market index dividend yield
Expected growth rate in the P/E	ΔP/E	Analyst adjustment for market over or under valuation (commonly $= 0$)
Expected inflation	i	(nominal yield less real yield) for similar maturity security
Expected growth rate in real earnings per share	g	Real GDP growth
Expected change in shares outstanding	ΔS	Depends on market and time period

An analyst can compare the nominal and real yields for similar-maturity government benchmark bonds to estimate the expected inflation rate. For example, expected inflation can be estimated as the ratio of the yield on a US Treasury bond and a similar maturity Treasury Inflation-Protected Security (TIPS):

$$i = \frac{1+\text{YTM}_{Treasury\,bond}}{1+\text{YTM}_{TIPS}} - 1 \approx \text{YTM}_{Treasury\,bond} - \text{YTM}_{TIPS}. \tag{12}$$

EXAMPLE 8   ERP Estimation Using the Forward-Looking Approach

1. If the yield on a 10-year Treasury bond is 2.3% and the yield on a similar maturity, inflation-protected Treasury bond is 0.66%, what is the implied inflation rate?

Solution:

$$i = \frac{1.023}{1.0066} - 1 = 0.016, \text{ or } 1.6\%.$$

An analyst is estimating a forward-looking ERP for a market based on the following information:

Input	Scenario 1	Scenario 2
r_f	2.5%	3%
i	1.6%	3%
g	3%	2%
Δ(P/E)	0	1%
DY	2.2%	2%
ΔS	−0.7%	0

2. Using the Grinold-Kroner model, calculate estimates of the ERP under Scenarios 1 and 2.

Solution:

Using the Grinold-Kroner forward-looking approach, in Scenario 1, the ERP estimate is 3.6%, or

$$\text{ERP} = \{2.2 + 0 + [1.6 + 3.0 + (- 0.7)]\} - 2.5 = 3.6\%.$$

Using the Grinold-Kroner model, the ERP estimate in Scenario 2 is 5.0%, or

$$\text{ERP} = \{2.0 + 1.0 + [3.0 + 2.0 + 0.0)]\} - 3.0 = 5.0\%.$$

The premiums of 3.6% or 5.0%, respectively, compensate investors for average market risk, given expectations for inflation, real earnings growth, P/E growth, and anticipated income depending on the scenario.

3. How does the ERP change when expected inflation increases? When expected income declines?

Solution:

Increases in the inflation rate increase the ERP because expectations are revised upward to compensate for the increased inflation. In contrast, decreases in the expected income decrease the ERP as expectations are adjusted downward given lower expected income.

4. Under what circumstances is it not appropriate to use the Grinold-Kroner model?

Solution:

The model is not appropriate for estimating the ERP in a developing country where the stock market is not a sufficiently large portion of the economy.

4.2.4. Limitations of the Forward-Looking Approach

Relative to historical estimates, ex ante estimates are likely to be less subject to non-stationarity or data biases. Limitations of forward-looking approaches are listed in the following table:

Forward-Looking Approach	Limitation
Surveys	• Estimate data can be subject to sampling and response biases, and to behavioral biases such as **recency bias** (placing more relevance on recent events) and **confirmation bias** (paying more attention to information that supports one's opinions and ignoring the rest).
DDM	• Assumes constant P/E. where growth in earnings, dividends, and prices are different from one another; an adjustment is needed to reflect P/E multiple expansion or contraction.
Macroeconomic models	• Financial and economic models could have modeling errors or behavioral biases in forecasting.

EXAMPLE 9   ERP Summary

- The ERP represents the expected incremental return that investors demand as compensation for holding risky equity securities rather than a risk-free asset.
- Two broad approaches are used to estimate the ERP: the historical approach, which uses backward-looking historical data to estimate the ERP, and the forward-looking approach, which uses forward-looking, expectational data to estimate the ERP.
- When estimating the ERP using the historical approach, an analyst has four key decisions to make regarding the following choices: (1) equity index, (2) estimation time period, (3) mean measure, and (4) proxy for the risk-free rate.
- Care must be taken in using historical estimates because the ERP can vary over time, and there is a possibility of survivorship bias in the estimate.
- ERP using the forward-looking approach include (1) survey-based estimates, (2) DDM-based estimates, and (3) estimates derived from macroeconomic models.
- Limitations to using forward-looking approaches include sampling, response, and behavioral biases (recency and confirmation biases) associated with survey estimates, the assumption of a constant P/E in DDM estimates, and modeling errors and behavioral biases in macroeconomic estimates.

1. Discuss the four key decisions that an analyst must make to estimate an ERP using the historical approach.

Solution:

The four key decisions that an analyst must make to use the historical approach are as follows:

- Which equity index to use to represent equity market returns
- What time period to use for estimating the ERP
- Which mean measure to use
- What proxy to use for the risk-free return

2. Justify the use of a long-term government bond yield as a proxy for the risk-free rate in estimating an ERP using the historical approach.

Solution:

Even though the YTM on a long-term government bond yield is not in fact risk free because of the coupon reinvestment risk over the life of the bond, the current YTM on a long-term government bond can still be used as an approximation for the expected return on the bond.

3. Calculate estimates of the ERP for a particular market using both the historical approach and the forward-looking approach using the following information:

Expected inflation	1.9%
Expected growth in the P/E	−1.2%
Expected income component	1.8%
Expected growth in real earnings per share	2.7%
Expected change in shares outstanding	0.0%
Current three-month government bond yield	0.96%
Long-term geometric average return of market equity index	9.96%
Long-term geometric average return of short-term government bond	3.15%

Solution:

The ERP using the historical approach is calculated as the mean value of the difference between a broad-based equity market index return and a government debt return. Therefore, the ERP using the historical approach is calculated as 9.96% − 3.15% = 6.81%.

The ERP using the forward-looking approach is calculated as

$$ERP = \{1.8 - 1.2 + (1.9 + 2.7 + 0.0)\} - 0.96$$
$$ERP = 5.20 - 0.96 = 4.24\%.$$

4. Discuss limitations of using macroeconomic models to estimate a forward-looking ERP.

Solution:

ERPs derived from macroeconomic models rely on a number of forecasts of economic variables such as inflation and expected growth in real earnings per share. These forecasts are often generated using financial and economic models that can be subject to potential modeling errors or behavioral biases in forecasting.

5. THE COST OF EQUITY (REQUIRED RETURN ON EQUITY)

Upon determining an ERP, analysts can then go on to estimate a company's required rate of return for use in a WACC calculation. To estimate the required rate of return on equity, analysts have a variety of methods available, which include

- DDMs,
- the bond yield plus risk premium build-up method, and
- risk-based models.

Estimating the required rate of return for private and international companies adds further complexity for an analyst.

5.1. DDMs

One method of estimating a company's required return on equity is to apply the constant growth DDM used earlier in estimating a forward-looking ERP. That is, we apply this model to a particular subject company given a forecast of its expected future dividend D_1, expected growth rate in dividends g, and current share price

$$P_0, \text{ or } r_e = \frac{D_1}{P_0} + g. \tag{13}$$

For example, using the constant growth model and given the following inputs for Company X,

Company X	Definition	Value
Current share price	P_0	€40
Expected future dividend	D_1	€1.04
Expected (perpetual) growth rate in dividends	g	4%

the cost of equity estimate is 6.6%, or

$$r_e = \frac{€1.04}{€40.00} + 0.04 = 0.066.$$

Using a DDM for r_e estimation is straightforward and based on the logic that the share price of stock reflects the present value of future dividends and the relevant cash flow to equity holders is the dividend payment. However, it requires that the company's shares be publicly traded and that the company pays dividends that are stable and predictable.

In equity valuation, it is common to build a multiyear financial forecast inclusive of a forecasted share price at the end of the forecast period. Using the DDM, a company's required return on equity can also be estimated by solving the following equation for r_e:

$$P_0 = \left[\sum_{t=1}^{n} \frac{D_t}{(1+r_e)^t} \right] + \frac{P_n}{(1+r_e)^n}. \tag{14}$$

For example, suppose we have the following information:

Year	0	1	2	3	4
Dividend		$1.00	$1.25	$1.35	$1.50
Stock price	$40.00				$45.00

Given a current share price of USD40, the required rate of equity can be solved for by using a calculator or software tools to arrive at a rate of 6.015%. This calculation incorporates not only the near-term dividend forecast but also the forecast of the share price at some period into the future (i.e., USD45).

Toolkit

Using Microsoft Excel,

  =IRR({-40,1,1.25,1.35,46.5})

Using Python,

  import numpy as np
  irr = np.irr([-40,1,1.25,1.35,46.5])

Using R,

  library(jrvFinance)
  irr(c(-40,1,1.25,1.35,46.5))

5.2. Bond Yield Plus Risk Premium Approach

Recall that the **bond yield plus risk premium (BYPRP) approach** is another means of estimating the required return on equity for a company that has public debt. The BYPRP approach estimates a company's required return on equity as:

$$r_e = r_d + \text{RP}, \tag{15}$$

where r_d is the company's cost of debt (typically proxied by the YTM on the company's long-term debt), and RP is a risk premium to compensate equity investors for additional risk relative to the risk of investing in the company's debt securities.

The challenge to the BYPRP approach is in estimating RP. One common approach to estimating this risk premium involves using the historical mean difference in returns between an equity market index and a corporate bond index, similar to the process of estimating a historical ERP estimate. This difference yields a historical estimate of the average extra return earned by equity investors relative to corporate bond investors.

Exhibit 11 summarizes key advantages and disadvantages of the BYPRP approach.

EXHIBIT 11: BYPRP Approach: Advantages and Disadvantages.

Advantages	Disadvantages
• Estimating a company's cost of debt provides a starting point estimate of the return demanded by that company's debt investors.	• Determination of RP is relatively arbitrary. • Approach requires company to have traded debt. • If the company has multiple traded debt securities, each with different features, there is no prescription regarding which bond yield to select. Common practice is to use the company's long-term bond YTM.

EXAMPLE 10   Cost of Equity Estimation using the BYPRP Approach

An analyst estimates a required return on equity for a company using the BYPRP approach. The analyst estimates the yield on the company's bonds as 4.3% and a historical risk premium of 6.1% earned by equity investors relative to long-term corporate bond yields.

1. Calculate an estimate of the required return on equity for the company using the BYPRP approach.

Solution:
   The required return on equity for the company using the BYPRP approach is estimated at 10.40%, calculated as $r_e = 0.043 + 0.061 = 0.1040$.

2. What are potential considerations associated with this method?

Solution:
   Considerations include the following:

• Using historical data might not be appropriate if the risk premiums are not stationary.
• The company might have no traded debt or might have multiple issues of traded debt with different yields.

5.3. Risk-Based Models

Risk-based models estimate the required return on equity as the sum of the compensation for the time value of money and compensation for bearing risk, or

$$r_e = \begin{array}{c}\text{Compensation for}\\\text{the time value of money}\end{array} + \begin{array}{c}\text{Compensation for}\\\text{bearing risk.}\end{array}$$

Several types of risk models are used to develop estimates for r_e, their primary difference being how they model compensation for bearing risk. One class of risk models is factor models, such as the **capital asset pricing model (CAPM)** and the Fama–French models we discuss here. Other factor models include theoretically derived models, statistical factor models, fundamental factor models, and macroeconomic factor models.

5.3.1. CAPM

Recalling the single-factor CAPM, given an estimate of a company's beta (β), the risk-free rate, and the ERP, a company's required return on equity can be estimated as

$$r_e = r_f + \widehat{\beta}(\text{ERP}), \tag{16}$$

where $\widehat{\beta}$ is a measure of the sensitivity of the company's stock's returns to changes in the ERP.

The **market model**, which replaces expected returns on the company and market with their actual historic returns, is commonly used to estimate the company's beta, regressing the company i's equity excess returns, $r_{i,t}$, over the risk-free rate, $r_{f,t}$, against the excess returns of an equity market index, $r_{m,t}$:

$$(r_{i,t} - r_{f,t}) = b_0 + b_1(r_{m,t} - r_{f,t}) + \varepsilon_t. \tag{17}$$

The estimate of b_1, $\widehat{b}_1$, is used as a proxy for β_i in Equation 17. A variation of the market model is to not subtract the risk-free rate from the stock's returns and the market returns.

Using this approach, the analyst should consider the following:

- What is the most appropriate equity market index?
- What period was used to estimate beta? As with choosing the time period when estimating a historical ERP, the analyst should seek a balance between sufficient data to develop a robust forecast and using data from too far back in time that might not be representative for the company's stock going forward.
- What proxy was used for the risk-free rate? In an environment of a normal upward-sloping yield curve, using the short-term benchmark government bill rate will yield a meaningfully lower cost of equity estimate than if the long-term government bond YTM is used, particularly if the yield curve is steep.

Even if a company is not publicly traded, it is still possible to estimate the cost of equity using CAPM. Recall that the beta of a comparable, publicly traded company with similar business risk can be estimated and then adjusted for the differing financial leverage of the company to arrive at a beta estimate for the subject company. This is done by "unlevering" the beta of the comparable company to arrive at a beta for a company with no debt in its capital structure and then "re-levering" it to adjust for the debt of the subject company. The estimated beta is then used in the CAPM to estimate a cost of equity for the subject company.

5.3.2. Fama–French Models

The **Fama–French models** are an alternative set of factor models to estimate a company's required return on equity. In the Fama–French three-factor model, in addition to the single market factor, equity returns can be explained by the size of the company—a size factor measured by market capitalization—and the relationship between the book value and equity value of a company's equity, termed the value factor. Using this three-factor model, a company's excess return on equity is calculated as

$$r_e = r_f + \beta_1 \text{ERP} + \beta_2 \text{SMB} + \beta_3 \text{HML}, \tag{18}$$

where SMB is the size premium, equal to the average difference in equity returns between companies with small and large capitalizations, and HML is the value premium, equal to the average difference in equity returns between companies with high and low book-to-market ratios.

The five-factor Fama–French model adds two other factors—a profitability factor (RMW) and an investment factor (CMA):

$$r_e = r_f + \beta_1 \text{ERP} + \beta_2 \text{SMB} + \beta_3 \text{HML} + \beta_4 \text{RMW} + \beta_5 \text{CMA}, \tag{19}$$

where RMW is the profitability premium, equal to the average difference in equity returns between companies with robust and weak profitability, and CMA is the investment premium, equal to the average difference in equity returns between companies with conservative and aggressive investment portfolios.

In essence, the Fama–French models are an extension of the CAPM that add additional factors to explain excess returns. Like in the CAPM, the estimated slope coefficients in the Fama–French models represent the sensitivity of a stock's returns to the factors. Estimating the Fama–French models is similar to the CAPM: the company's excess equity returns are regressed on the factors to generate estimates of the three betas, referred to as **factor betas**. The required return on equity is then estimated using the factor betas and estimates of the **factor risk premiums**.

EXAMPLE 11   Cost of Equity Estimation using the Fama–French Five-Factor Model

An analyst estimates the required return on equity for a company using the Fama–French five-factor model. The analyst must estimate risk premiums for each factor and run a regression of the company's excess stock returns on the five factors to estimate the factor betas. The premiums and betas are presented in the following table:

Factor	Estimated Beta	Risk Premium
Market	1.2	6.5%
Size (SMB)	0.10	1.8%
Value (HML)	−0.20	4.0%
Profitability (RMW)	0.5	2.0%
Style (CMA)	0.2	1.0%

The risk-free rate is 3.82%.

1. Calculate an estimate of the required return on equity for the company using the Fama–French five-factor model.

Solution:

Using the model, the required return on equity for the company is estimated at 12.2%, or

$$r_e = 0.0382 + (1.2 \times 0.065) + (0.10 \times 0.018) + (-0.2 \times 0.04)$$
$$+ (0.5 \times 0.02) + (0.2 \times 0.01)$$

$$r_e = 0.0382 + 0.078 + 0.0018 - 0.008 + 0.01 + 0.002 = 0.1220, \text{ or } 12.2\%$$

The use of these risk-based models is similar:

- Historical returns are used to estimate the relationship between a company's stock's excess returns and these factors.
- Slope coefficients from the estimated regression, along with expectations for the factor risk premiums and the risk-free rate, are used to calculate an estimate of the company's required return on equity.

However, analysts should be aware of the following:

- Estimates from the different risk factor models often yield different results.
- The beta coefficient on the market factor (ERP) normally differs between the single-factor CAPM and multifactor models such as the Fama–French models because of the presence of the additional factors in the models.
- Analysts often use a short-term risk-free rate when computing excess returns to estimate the factor betas in these risk-based models. In an environment with an upward-sloping yield curve, doing so can result in the understatement of the risk-free rate. However, this understatement can be remedied by using a different time series for the risk-free rate, properly adjusted for periodicity, when regressing historical stock returns against these different factors.

5.4. Estimating the Cost of Equity for Private Companies

Estimating the required return on equity for a privately held company is more challenging for analysts, given the following:

- Security prices and returns are not readily available for private companies, so risk factor models such as the CAPM and Fama–French models cannot be directly applied to privately held companies. However, these models can be adapted and applied indirectly to private companies.
- Unlike public companies, private companies might be smaller, earlier in the company life cycle, have owners as managers, and have ownership structures with greater concentration of control.
- Private companies are less liquid and might disclose less investor relevant information than public companies.

The required return on equity for private companies often includes

- a **size premium (SP)**,
- an **industry risk premium (IP)**, and
- a **specific-company risk premium (SCRP)**.

A smaller company size is typically associated with greater company risk, which can arise from greater difficulty in securing capital, more uncertain growth prospects, and riskier business operations. Collectively, these can result in higher risk and required returns on equity for private companies. An IP can be added for private companies in relatively riskier industries.

The SCRP is a general risk premium that reflects factors such as geographic risk, key-person risk, or other firm-specific factors that might not be easy to diversify away. Another key risk factor inherent in private companies is their illiquidity. However, the higher illiquidity risk is typically not reflected in the required return as an additional risk premium but rather as a reduction in the estimated value for an equity interest, referred to as a discount for lack of marketability.

To estimate the required return on equity for a private company, analysts commonly have two choices, namely,

- the expanded CAPM and
- the build-up approach.

5.4.1. Expanded CAPM

To estimate r_e for non-publicly traded or private companies, analysts can use an adaptation of the CAPM called the expanded CAPM, which adds a premium for small company size and other company-specific risks. The expanded CAPM requires estimation of a beta from a peer group of publicly traded companies, with r_e calculated as

$$r_e = r_f + \beta_{peer}(\text{ERP}) + \text{SP} + \text{IP} + \text{SCRP}. \tag{20}$$

We use the following steps in the estimation:

1. Estimate an industry beta, β_{peer}, from a peer group of publicly traded companies in the same industry as the subject private company.
2. Given an estimate of the risk-free rate r_f and the ERP, compute a CAPM estimate for r_e.
3. Determine whether additional risk premia for company size and other company-specific risk factors are warranted.
4. If warranted, add relevant size and company-specific risk premia to arrive at a final estimate of r_e for the subject company.

Analysts typically add an SP to the required return on equity for smaller, privately held companies. The amount of the SP is often assumed to be inversely related to the size of the company being valued. When the SP estimate is appropriately based on the lowest market-cap decile of public companies—frequently the case because many private businesses are small relative to publicly traded companies—the result corresponds to the return on an average-systematic-risk micro-cap public equity issue.

An analyst should exercise caution when using historical measures of the SP. The population of small capitalization companies likely includes previously larger capitalization companies in financial distress. If this is the case, a historical risk premium estimate could require a downward adjustment for estimating the required return for a small, but financially healthy, private company.

The estimation of a company-specific risk premium is varied in practice and based on both qualitative and quantitative factors. These factors are summarized in Exhibit 12.

EXHIBIT 12: Company-Specific Premium: Qualitative versus Quantitative Factors

Qualitative Factors	Quantitative Factors
• The industry in which the business operates • Competitive position within the industry • Management's experience and expertise • Customer and supplier concentration • Geographic concentration of the business • Governance model of the company • Asset nature and type (tangible vs. intangible)	• Financial and operational leverage • Volatility in cash flows and earnings • Earnings predictability • Pricing power

These factors can be analyzed relative to those of a peer group of publicly traded or other privately held companies in the same industry. The larger the company-specific risks identified by the analyst, the larger the company-specific risk premium.

5.4.2. Build-Up Approach

A second approach analysts use for estimating a private company's r_e is the build-up approach. This approach involves "building up" the required return on equity, beginning with the risk-free rate, and then adding relevant risk premia to account for various risk considerations, or

$$r_e = r_f + \text{ERP} + \text{SP} + \text{SCRP}, \qquad (21)$$

where SP is a size premium and SCRP is a specific-company risk premium.

The ERP is often estimated with reference to equity indexes of publicly traded companies and is not beta adjusted. The largest market-capitalization companies typically constitute a large fraction of these indexes' value. With a beta of 1.0 implicitly multiplying the ERP, the sum of the risk-free rate and the ERP is effectively the required return on equity for an average-systematic-risk large-cap public equity issue. The build-up approach starts with this and then adjusts for additional size and company-specific premia as shown in Exhibit 13.

EXHIBIT 13: Build-Up Approach for Private Companies

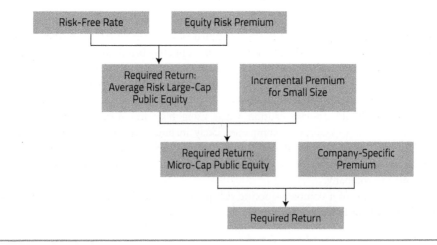

As with the extended CAPM method, analysts often add an SP to account for the smaller size of most privately held companies, again where the premium is typically after adjustment for the differences in the betas of small- and large-cap stocks to isolate the effect of size—a beta-adjusted SP.

Finally, an analysis of risk factors incremental to those captured by the previously included premia might lead the analyst to also add a specific-company premium to arrive at a final estimate of the subject company's required return on equity. The build-up approach might be appropriate when a set of comparable public companies are unavailable or of questionable comparability.

5.5. International Considerations

Exchange rates, inflation, data, and models in emerging markets are possible considerations for an analyst when estimating r_e for international companies. For example, factor models, such as the locally focused CAPM, might not work well for an emerging market.

5.5.1. Country Spread and Country Risk Rating Models

Risk premium estimation for emerging markets is particularly challenging. Of the numerous approaches that have been proposed to supplement or replace traditional historical and forward-looking methods, we look at two:

- the country spread model
- the country risk rating model

Using the country spread model for ERP estimation, an additional risk premium—the **country risk premium (CRP)** or country spread premium—is required by investors for the added risk of investing in another country, often referred to as the "local" country. The added risk could be due to economic conditions, risk of expropriation, political risk, or other risk.

For an emerging equity market, this model is

$$\text{ERP} = \begin{array}{c} \text{ERP for a} \\ \text{developed market} \end{array} + (\lambda \times \text{Country risk premium}), \tag{22}$$

where λ is the level of exposure of the company to the local country.

The CRP represents a premium associated with the anticipated greater risk of a market compared with the benchmark developed market. One method for calculating this premium is to use the **sovereign yield spread**, or a comparison of the yield on a local country, denominated in the benchmark developed country's currency, with the yield on a similar maturity sovereign bond in the developed country.

Typically, analysts hope that a sovereign bond yield spread is adequate for approximating this premium. Thus, the country premium is often estimated as the yield on emerging market bonds (denominated in the currency of the developed market) minus the yield on developed market government bonds.

Consider the sovereign risk ratings in Exhibit 14 and the corresponding CRPs. These CRPs are estimated using the sovereign yield spread relative to a benchmark country's yield.

The problem with this method is that we are using a bond yield spread to estimate a country's ERP. Because of differences in legal and market environments among countries, using the yield spread on sovereign bonds might not be appropriate for a cost of equity.

EXHIBIT 14: CRPs by Country Based on the Sovereign Yield Spread

Country	Sovereign Risk Rating (10 = Most risk)	CRP
A	6	3.90%
B	2	0.50%
C	5	2.75%
D	7	5.40%
E	4	1.75%
F	10	19.50%
G	9	14.50%
H	1	0.0%
I	3	1.0%
J	8	9.20%

Aswath Damodaran (2021) refined the CRP estimation by modifying the sovereign yield spread for the relative volatility between equity versus bond returns, where

$$\text{Country risk premium} = \text{Sovereign yield spread} \times \frac{\sigma_{Equity}}{\sigma_{Bond}}, \tag{23}$$

where

σ_{Equity} is the volatility of the local country's equity market
σ_{Bond} is the volatility of the local country's bond market

This method, however, requires that the local country have both historical equity and bond returns.

5.5.2. Extended CAPM

In cases where there is exposure to a country's risk, a country risk adjustment should be made to r_e. Several approaches are used in estimating r_e for companies operating internationally. These include the following:

- global CAPM
- international CAPM
- country spread and risk rating models

In the **global CAPM (GCAPM)**, where a global market index is the single factor, there are no assumed significant risk differences across countries. The issue is that a likely result is a low, or even negative, slope coefficient because of the correlation between emerging and developed market returns being quite low in general. Expanding this model to include a second factor, such as domestic market index returns, mitigates this to a degree but depends on the availability of reliable financial data in the emerging market.

Another approach is the **international CAPM (ICAPM)**, where the returns on a stock in an emerging market are regressed against the risk premium of a global index (r_{gm}) in addition to that of wealth-weighted foreign currency index (r_c):

$$E(r_e) = r_f + \beta_G\left(E\left(r_{gm}\right) - r_f\right) + \beta_C\left(E(r_c) - r_f\right). \tag{24}$$

Proxies for the global index *(gm)* include the MSCI All Country World Index (MSCI ACWI) and the FTSE All-World Index. The foreign currency index, r_c, aggregates the return from investing in the foreign currency relative to the company's domestic currency using country relative wealth, not market capitalization, weightings. The return to each currency consists of the expected change in the exchange rate plus the risk-free return of that country.

The sensitivity to the global index, β_G, depends on the company's relationship with its local economy versus the global economy. Lower values of β_G are associated with companies that are less connected to the global economy. The sensitivity to the foreign currency index, β_C, depends on whether the company's cash flows are sensitive to exchange rates through its imports, exports, and investments.

5.5.3. Comparison of International Adjustment Methods

Analysts face challenges in estimating the cost of equity for cross-border valuations, given that there is no generally accepted methodology for estimating the CRP for companies with operations in a developing country.

- If the company's operations are global, but limited to developed countries, the GCAPM and ICAPM are reasonable methods to apply.
- If however, the company's operations extend to developing countries, the methodology is less clear. The estimation of the CRP using the sovereign yield approach might be appropriate, but these estimations are based on historical rates and might not reflect the risk premium going forward.

EXAMPLE 12   CRP

An analyst is estimating the CRP for the Makinassi Company headquartered in Country X that has 40% of its sales in Country Y. The analyst gathers the following information:

Country	Sovereign Country Yield Spread	Standard Deviation of Equity Returns	Standard Deviation of Bond Returns
X (Headquarters)	1.5%	2.0%	1.0%
Y (Local)	3.2%	4.0%	2.5%

1. Using the Damodaran model, calculate the CRP that the analyst should use for the Makinassi Company.

Solution:

From the perspective of a company operating in Country X, the relevant sovereign yield spread is 3.2% − 1.5% = 1.7%. Adjusting this spread for the relative volatility of the equity and bond returns in the local market, the premium is

$$CRP = 0.017 \times 0.04/0.025 = 0.0272$$

Adjusting this premium for the exposure that Makinassi has to Country Y,

$$\text{Premium} = 0.40 \times 0.0272 = 0.01088$$

Therefore, when the analyst calculates the cost of equity for Makinassi, he should add a CRP of 1.088% to the cost of equity for the company.

5.6. Required Return on Equity Summary

- Models used to estimate the cost of equity include (1) the DDM, (2) the BYPRP model, and (3) risk-based models.
- Risk-based models for estimating the cost of equity include the CAPM and factor models, such as the Fama–French models.
- Estimating the cost of equity for a private company using risk-based models requires adjusting the premiums for company size, the industry in which it operates, and any specific company premium. A method that can be used to estimate the cost of equity for private companies is the expanded CAPM.
- The build-up method for the cost of equity starts with the risk-free rate and the ERP, then adjusts this cost for any other premia.
- The cost of equity can be adjusted for additional risk related to international considerations using the CRP or the ICAPM.

KNOWLEDGE CHECK

1. What are the primary differences between the CAPM and the Fama–French models for estimating the cost of equity?

Solution:

The CAPM is a one-factor model—the market factor, that is, the primary driver of security returns in the market. The Fama–French models allow for more factors to influence security returns beyond the market factor.

2. Classify each of the following elements of the DDM based on the effect on the cost of equity using the DDM.

Change, holding all other factors constant	No Effect	Increase	Decrease
Increase in the current dividend			
Increase in the expected growth rate of dividends			
Increase in the share price			
Decrease in the current dividend			
Decrease in the expected growth rate of dividends			
Decrease in the share price			

Effect on Cost of Equity

Solution:

Change, holding all other factors constant	No Effect	Positive	Negative
Increase in the current dividend		✓	
Increase in the expected growth rate of dividends		✓	
Increase in the share price			✓
Decrease in the current dividend			✓
Decrease in the expected growth rate of dividends			✓
Decrease in the share price		✓	

3. An analyst is using a three-factor model with factors F1, F2, and F3 to estimate the risk premium for an individual stock. The results of the regression are

   $$r_i - r_f = 0.003 + 1.2\,F1 - 0.4\,F2 + 0.2\,F3.$$

   If the expected risk-free rate is 2%, and the three factor risk premiums are

   F1 = 0.05,

   F2 = 0.01, and

   F3 = 0.04,

   what is the expected cost of equity?

Solution:

   The required return on equity for the stock is
   $r_e - r_f = 0.003 + (1.2 \times 0.05) - (0.4 \times 0.01) + (0.2 \times 0.04) = 0.067.$
   The estimate of the cost of equity is $0.067 + 0.02 = 0.087$, or 8.7%.

Consider a company that currently pays a dividend of USD2.50. The current price of the stock is USD50, and the dividend is expected to grow at a rate of 5% per year into perpetuity. Using the DDM, determine the following:

4. What is the company's required rate of return on equity?

Solution:

   $r_e = \frac{\$2.5(1+0.05)}{\$50} + 0.05 = \frac{\$2.625}{\$50} + 0.05 = 0.0525 + 0.05 = 0.1025$, or 10.25%.

5. If the growth rate of dividends is revised upward, what effect does this have on the required rate of return on equity?

Solution:

   If the growth rate is revised upward, both the dividend yield (D_1/P_0) and the growth rate (g) increase, increasing the required rate of return on equity.

6. If the price of the stock declines, but expectations regarding dividends and dividend growth remain the same, what effect does this have on the required rate of return on equity?

Solution:

If the stock price declines, the dividend yield (D_1/P_0) increases, resulting in the increased required rate of return on equity.

An analyst is estimating the required return on equity for a company and has gathered the following information:

Estimated risk-free rate (10-year government bond)	6%
Estimated equity market return	10%
Estimated ERP beta	0.8
Estimated SMB premium	5%
Estimated HML premium	2%
Fama–French three-factor regression estimation:	
Intercept	0.01
Coefficient on market factor	0.75
Coefficient on SMB factor	0.15
Coefficient on HML factor	0.05

The Fama–French three-factor model coefficients were estimated using the same risk-free rate that is used in the CAPM.

7. What is the required rate of return based on the CAPM?

Solution:
$r_e = 0.06 + 0.8(0.10 - 0.06) = 0.092$, or 9.2%

8. What is the required rate of return based on the Fama–French model?

Solution:
$r_e - 0.06 = 0.01 + [0.75(0.10 - 0.06)] + [0.15(0.05)] + [0.05(0.02)]$
$r_e - 0.06 = 0.0485$
$r_e = 0.1085$, or 10.85%

9. Why do these required rates of return on equity differ between these two models?

Solution:

The Fama–French model allows more factors or drivers of returns, whereas the CAPM limits the factors to the single market factor. In this case, the SMB and HML factors increase the required return on equity by $[0.15(0.05)] + [0.05(0.02)] = 0.0085$, or 0.85%.

6. MINI-CASE 1

6.1. Gretna Engines

KM is a junior analyst at Atla Investments. KM meets with her manager to discuss a possible investment in Gretna Engines. KM's manager tasks her with estimating Gretna's cost of debt and equity as a starting point for determining Gretna's WACC and related valuation. KM notes some of Gretna's key information:

Company: Gretna Engines	Small capitalization, publicly traded company
Business Model	Manufacturer of small engines for boats and recreational all-terrain vehicles (ATVs). Operates with a relatively high proportion of fixed costs in its cost structure.
Industry	Industrial equipment (cyclical)
Revenues, Earnings, Cash Flows	All have been trending upward in recent years but vary considerably over the business cycle.
Nature of Assets	Assets consist primarily of inventory and property, plant, and equipment representing its engine production facilities.

Gretna has recently been performing well in terms of sales and profitability. However, several years back, because of a significant decline in sales of boats and ATVs, the company found itself in a liquidity crisis. At that time, the company issued redeemable, preferred stock to improve its liquidity position, albeit at a rather high cost.

In recent financial filings, Gretna's management has indicated that given favorable market conditions, they are seeking to issue new, unsecured debt to retire the preferred shares at par value. Exhibit 15 presents Gretna's current capital structure and selected information about each capital type.

EXHIBIT 15: Gretna's Current Capital Structure and Related Information

Capital Type	Current Capital Structure	Selected Capital Type Information
Debt	20%	Single debt issue: 7% coupon rate; remaining maturity of seven years; semiannual payments. Straight unsecured debt; BBB credit rating; thinly traded issue—no reliable YTM available.
Preferred Equity	15%	Dividend rate of 7%, currently redeemable at par value of 1,000 per share Trades frequently; current share price is 980
Common Equity	65%	Actively traded

Next, KM gathers information on four liquid, semiannual-pay corporate bonds with the same BBB rating as Gretna, shown in Exhibit 16.

EXHIBIT 16: Selected Information on Liquid, BBB-Rated Bonds

	Coupon Rate	Remaining Maturity	Current Price (per 100 of par value)
Bond 1	5%	4 years	99.50
Bond 2	7%	4 years	106.46
Bond 3	6%	8 years	100
Bond 4	8%	8 years	112.42

Using the CAPM and the Fama–French five-factor (FF5) model, KM estimates Gretna's cost of equity by regressing Gretna's excess returns on the relevant risk factors using the most recent 60 months of returns. Factor betas from the CAPM and the FF5 model, along with her estimated factor risk premiums, are shown in Exhibit 17. She decides to use the 20-year government benchmark rate of 2.1% as the risk-free proxy.

EXHIBIT 17: CAPM and FF5 Factor Beta and Risk Premiums

	Factor	Factor Beta	Risk Premium
A. CAPM Factor Beta and Risk Premium			
	Market (ERP)	0.91	5.5%
B. FFM5 Factor Betas and Risk Premiums			
	Market (ERP)	0.95	5.5%
	Size (SMB)	0.45	1.8%
	Value (HML)	0.14	3.9%
	Profitability (RMW)	−0.19	3.1%
	Investment (CMA)	0.30	3.7%

Finally, KM also estimates Gretna's cost of equity using the BYPRP approach. For this estimate, she assumes a historical risk premium of 6.2% earned by equity investors relative to long-term corporate bond yields.

KM reports back to her manager with her estimates of Gretna's costs of debt and equity. Her manager asks how she arrived at the ERP of 5.5% in her cost of equity estimates. KM tells her manager that she estimated it using the historical approach, electing to use the short-term government bill rate and an arithmetic mean in the estimation.

KNOWLEDGE CHECK

1. Identify two characteristics of Gretna's business model that might cause the firm to have a relatively higher cost of capital.

Solution:

One characteristic would be relatively high volatility (less stability) in revenues and earnings, given the cyclical nature of the industry in which Gretna operates. Such firms are likely to face a higher cost of capital than firms with low volatility in revenues and earnings. Another factor could be the relative illiquidity of the firm's assets. All else equal, firms with asset bases comprising relatively low (high) proportions of liquid assets are more likely to have higher (lower) costs of capital. A third factor would be that Gretna currently operates with high operating leverage (a high proportion of fixed costs in its cost structure).

2. How might KM estimate a current cost of debt given Gretna's current capital structure? What is Gretna's current cost of debt?

Solution:

   In the absence of a reliable YTM, given the debt's illiquidity, KM could use matrix pricing to estimate Gretna's current cost of debt. The current market prices for each of the four similarly rated bonds in Exhibit 16 are presented in the following matrix:

Price Matrix: BBB-Rated Bonds

Remaining Maturity	5% Coupon	6% Coupon	7% Coupon	8% Coupon
4 Years	99.5		106.46	
5 Years				
6 Years				
7 years				
8 years		100		112.42

Step 1 Calculate the YTM for each bond based on its market price.

Bond 1 YTM: N = 8; PV= –99.5; PMT = 2.5; FV = 100; CPT I/Y
   = 2.570% × 2 = <u>5.140%</u>

Bond 2 YTM: N = 8; PV= –106.46; PMT = 3.5; FV = 100; CPT I/Y
   = 2.595% × 2 = <u>5.191%</u>

Bond 3 YTM: N = 16; PV= –100; PMT = 3; FV = 100; CPT I/Y
   = 3.000% × 2 = <u>6.000%</u>

Bond 4 YTM: N = 16; PV= –112.42; PMT = 4; FV = 100; CPT I/Y
   = 3.010% × 2 = <u>6.021%</u>

Step 2 Calculate the average YTM for each maturity (i.e., 4-year and 8-year). This can be done by placing the YTM and price for each bond into a similar matrix form.

Price and YTM Matrix: BBB-Rated Bonds

Remaining Maturity	5% Coupon	6% Coupon	7% Coupon	8% Coupon	Average YTM
4 Years	99.5 (5.140%)		106.46 (5.191%)		5.165%
5 Years					

Remaining Maturity	5% Coupon	6% Coupon	7% Coupon	8% Coupon	Average YTM
6 Years					
7 years					
8 years		100 (6.000%)		112.42 (6.021%)	6.010%

Average YTM (4-year maturity) = (5.140% + 5.191%)/2 = 5.166%

Average YTM (8-year maturity) = (6.000% + 6.021%)/2 = 6.011%

Step 1: Use linear interpolation to estimate the average YTMs for the 5-year, 6-year, and 7-year maturities by first computing the difference in YTMs between the 8-year average YTM and the 4-year average YTM (linear interpolation assumes that the yields between the two known yields are equal distance apart).

8-year average YTM − 4-year average YTM = 6.011% − 5.166% = 0.845%
Divide this difference by the difference in years between the known yields (in this case, 8 − 4 = 4): 0.845%/4 = 0.211%.

Step 2: Use this 0.211% as the estimated annual incremental in average yield as the term to maturity increases after year 4:

Estimated average YTM for 5-year maturity =
4-year average YTM + 0.211% = 5.166% + 0.211% = 5.377%
Estimated average YTM for 6-year maturity =
5-year average YTM + 0.211% = 5.377% + 0.211% = 5.588%
Estimated average YTM for 7-year maturity =
6-year average YTM + 0.211% = 5.588% + 0.211% = 5.799%

Based on matrix pricing, Gretna's debt would likely have a YTM of approximately 5.799%, or 5.8%. However, given that this YTM was derived from more liquid bonds than Gretna's thinly traded bond, Gretna's debt would likely have a slightly higher YTM to compensate investors for liquidity risk.

3. What is Gretna's current cost of preferred equity?

Solution:

Gretna's preferred equity is actively traded and is currently trading at a price of 980. Given its annual dividend rate of 7% and par value of 1,000, the annual dividend amount is 70. Therefore, the cost of the preferred issue can be estimated at 7.14%, calculated using the perpetuity formula (which is the DDM formula, solving for r_e, with a growth rate equal to 0):

Cost of preferred equity = 70/980 = 7.14%.

4. How might KM estimate Gretna's cost of debt should management execute its plan to redeem its preferred equity?

Solution:

Currently, debt and preferred equity represent 35% of Gretna's capital structure. If Gretna's management follows through with its plan to issue new debt to redeem its preferred equity, the company's new capital structure would be 35% debt and 65% common equity. A starting point for KM to estimate a new cost of debt would be to look at the current estimated cost of debt of 5.8% and cost of preferred equity of 7.14%. Given that debtholders have a higher claim on assets than preferred shareholders, the additional debt would likely have a slightly higher cost than the current estimated cost of debt of 5.8% but lower cost than the current 7.14% cost of preferred equity.

5. Describe the market conditions that would lead Gretna's management team to reach its conclusion about the timing of issuing the new debt.

Solution:

Favorable market conditions for issuing the new debt would be a relatively low risk-free rate and/or relatively tighter credit spreads. Such conditions would likely lead to a relatively lower cost of debt for Gretna. At the current price of 980, the preferred is trading at a slight discount to par. The fact that management believes current market conditions to issue the debt are favorable, even when the company would have to redeem the preferred equity at par value (a slight premium to the current price), suggests that the risk-free rate is relatively low and/or credit spreads are relatively tight.

6. What actions could Gretna's management team take to further lower the cost of issuing the new debt?

Solution:

To further lower its debt cost at issuance, Gretna's management could consider (1) issuing secured debt, secured by some of its property, plant, and equipment; (2) issuing the debt with a put option; or (3) issuing the debt with a conversion feature. First, issuing secured debt will typically be cheaper than issuing unsecured debt because the bondholder now has collateral to lessen the risk of loss given default. Second, issuing debt with a put or conversion feature provides investors with valuable rights that also serve to lower the initial yield on the new debt at issuance.

7. What is Gretna's cost of common equity using the (1) CAPM, (2) FF5 model, and (3) BYPRP model?

Solution:

Gretna's estimated cost of common equity using the CAPM is 7.11%, calculated as
$r_e = r_f + \beta(\text{ERP})$
$r_e = 0.021 + 0.91\,(0.055) = 0.0711$, or 7.11%.

Gretna's estimated cost of common equity using the FF5 model is 9.20%, calculated as

$$r_e = r_f + \beta_1(\text{ERP}) + \beta_2\text{SMB} + \beta_3\text{HML} + \beta_4\text{RMW} + \beta_5\text{CMA}$$
$$r_e = 0.021 + 0.95(0.055) + 0.45(0.018) + 0.14(0.0390) - 0.19(0.031)$$
$$+ 0.30(0.037) = 0.0920, \text{ or } 9.20\%$$

Gretna's estimated cost of common equity using the BYPRP model can be calculated by adding the estimated cost of debt of 5.8% derived from matrix pricing and KM's estimated premium of 6.2% earned by equity investors relative to long-term corporate bond yields:

$$r_e = r_d + \text{RP}$$
$$r_e = 0.058 + 0.062 = 0.12, \text{ or } 12\%$$

8. Explain why, given the data from Panel A of Exhibit 17, the CAPM estimate of Gretna's cost of common equity might not be a reasonable estimate.

Solution:
The three estimates of the cost of common equity, based on the information given, are as follows:

- CAPM: 7.11%
- FF5 model: 9.20%
- BYPRP estimate: 12.00%

The cost of preferred equity is 7.14%. Given that common shareholders have a residual claim on assets below that of preferred shareholders, they will demand a higher required return on equity. Thus, the CAPM estimate of 7.11% does not appear to be a realistic estimate, given the estimated cost of preferred shareholders of 7.14%.

9. Explain why KM's estimate of the ERP might be relatively high or low, given her two choices in the estimation.

Solution:
Two of the four key assumptions an analyst must make in estimating the ERP using the historical approach are (1) which proxy to use for the risk-free return and (2) which mean measure to use. KM estimated the ERP using the short-term government bill rate and an arithmetic mean.

Assuming a typical normal yield curve for most of the estimation period where short-term government bond yields were lower than longer-term government bond yields, the use of the short-term bill rate in the estimation would lead to a higher estimate of the ERP. Further, using an arithmetic mean rather than a geometric mean would very likely lead to a higher estimate of the ERP. Thus, KM's estimate of the ERP under her chosen assumptions is likely to be high relative to another estimate that uses other choices (long-term government bond YTM, geometric mean) for those two key assumptions.

7. MINI-CASE 2

7.1. Precision Irrigation

LM is an analyst in the corporate development group at Hydrocrop Ltd, a company that manufactures and sells irrigation equipment. Management is considering the acquisition of Precision Irrigation, a private company that offers software solutions aimed at increasing irrigation efficiency. Precision is located in an emerging-market country with higher sovereign risk. LM has been tasked with estimating Precision's WACC.

LM gathers financial information on Precision and publicly traded software companies in the emerging country. The information is presented in Exhibit 18.

EXHIBIT 18: Selected Information for Precision and Peer Companies

	Precision Irrigation	Software Industry Average
A. Common-Sized Balance Sheet		
Cash and equivalents	9%	14%
Accounts receivable	10%	12%
Inventory	4%	3%
Other current assets	5%	4%
Property, plant, and equipment (net)	21%	30%
Intangible assets and goodwill	47%	32%
Other assets	4%	5%
B. Other Information		
Total debt (millions)	18.4	296.4
Total assets (millions)	105.2	1,276.2
EBITDA (millions)	12.2	177.4
Interest expense (millions)	1.6	23.5
Beta	N/A	1.25
Marginal tax rate	20%	25%

Other notes about Precision are as follows:

- The company's founder and CEO continues to be highly involved in all aspects of the company's operations, with no clear succession plan in place.
- Approximately 60% of the company's revenues come from software subscriptions, and 70% come from five major customers within close geographic proximity of each other.

LM estimates a cost of debt by estimating a synthetic bond yield on the company's 10-year non-traded bonds. He relies on an internally developed schedule of synthetic credit ratings driven by companies' leverage ratios. A portion of the schedule is presented in Exhibit 19.

EXHIBIT 19: Synthetic Credit Rating Schedule

Credit Rating	IC	D/E	Credit Spread
AAA	IC > 11 times	D/E < 15%	0.82%
AA	9 < IC < 11	15% < D/E < 20%	1.09%
A	7 < IC < 9	20% < D/E < 25%	1.46%
BBB	5 < IC < 7	25% < D/E < 30%	2.15%
BB	3 < IC < 1.4	30% < D/E < 40%	2.88%

The YTM on the emerging country's 10-year benchmark government bond is 5.41%. Interest expense is fully tax deductible.

LM also estimates a cost of equity for Precision using both the extended CAPM and the build-up approach. The corporate development team typically assigns an SP in the range of 3%–6% and an SCRP of 4%–8% for private companies, depending on company size and characteristics, respectively. After consulting with colleagues, LM assigns the relevant risk premiums presented in Exhibit 20.

EXHIBIT 20: Factor Risk Premiums

Factor	Risk Premium
Market (ERP)	6%
Size (SP)	5%
Industry (IP)	1%
Specific-company (SCRP)	6%

In arriving at a final cost of debt and equity for Precision, LM believes a CRP of 2% is warranted to compensate for the higher sovereign risk. In estimating Precision's WACC, LM assumes that the company's current capital structure is its long-term, target capital structure.

8. PRACTICE PROBLEMS

1. Calculate an estimate of Precision's after-tax cost of debt.

2. Explain why the SP LM chose for estimating Precision's cost of equity is likely justified in being near the high end of the range.

3. Discuss company characteristics of Precision that would justify a higher or lower SCRP.

4. Calculate estimates of Precision's cost of equity using the (1) extended CAPM and the (2) build-up approach.

5. Calculate an estimate of Precision's WACC using the build-up approach estimate of the cost of equity.

The following information relates to questions 6–10

An equity index is established in Year 1 for a country that has recently moved to a market economy. The index vendor constructed returns for the four years prior to Year 1 based on the initial group of companies constituting the index in Year 1. From Year 12 to Year 16, a series of military confrontations concerning a disputed border disrupted the economy and financial markets. The dispute is conclusively arbitrated at the end of Year 16. In total, 20 years of equity market return history is available. Other selected data are in the following tables.

Selected Data

Geometric mean return relative to 10-year government bond returns (over a 20-year period)	2% per year
Arithmetic mean return relative to 10-year government bond returns (over a 20-year period)	2.3% per year
Index forward dividend yield	1%
Forecasted public company earnings growth	5% per year
Forecasted market P/E growth	1% per year
Forecasted real GDP growth rate (by Year 19)	4%
Current vs. long-term inflation forecast	6% vs. 4% per year
Current yield curve (inversion)	Short maturities: 9%
	10-year maturities: 7%

6. The inclusion of index returns prior to Year 1 would be expected to:
   A. bias the historical ERP estimate upward.
   B. bias the historical ERP estimate downward.
   C. have no effect on the historical ERP estimate.

7. The events of 2012 to 2016 would be expected to:
   A. bias the historical ERP estimate upward.
   B. bias the historical ERP estimate downward.
   C. have no effect on the historical ERP estimate.

8. In the current interest rate environment, using a required return on equity estimate based on the short-term government bond rate and a historical ERP defined in terms of a short-term government bond rate would be expected to:
   A. bias long-term required return on equity estimates upward.
   B. bias long-term required return on equity estimates downward.
   C. have no effect on long-term required return on equity estimates.

9. An estimate of the ERP consistent with the Grinold-Kroner model is *closest* to:
   A. 2.7%.
   B. 3.0%.
   C. 4.3%.

10. Common stock issues in the aforementioned market with average systematic risk are *most likely* to have required rates of return of:

    A. between 2% and 7%.

    B. between 7% and 9%.

    C. 9% or greater.

CHAPTER 9

ANALYSIS OF DIVIDENDS AND SHARE REPURCHASES

Gregory Noronha, PhD, CFA
University of Washington, Tacoma (USA)

George H. Troughton, PhD, CFA
(USA)

LEARNING OUTCOMES

The candidate should be able to:

- describe the expected effect of regular cash dividends, extra dividends, liquidating dividends, stock dividends, stock splits, and reverse stock splits on shareholders' wealth and a company's financial ratios
- compare theories of dividend policy and explain implications of each for share value given a description of a corporate dividend action
- describe types of information (signals) that dividend initiations, increases, decreases, and omissions may convey
- explain how agency costs may affect a company's payout policy
- explain factors that affect dividend policy in practice
- calculate and interpret the effective tax rate on a given currency unit of corporate earnings under double taxation, dividend imputation, and split-rate tax systems
- compare stable dividend with constant dividend payout ratio, and calculate the dividend under each policy
- describe broad trends in corporate payout policies
- compare share repurchase methods
- calculate and compare the effect of a share repurchase on earnings per share when 1) the repurchase is financed with the company's surplus cash and 2) the company uses debt to finance the repurchase
- calculate the effect of a share repurchase on book value per share
- explain the choice between paying cash dividends and repurchasing shares

- calculate and interpret dividend coverage ratios based on 1) net income and 2) free cash flow
- identify characteristics of companies that may not be able to sustain their cash dividend

1. DIVIDENDS: FORMS AND EFFECTS ON SHAREHOLDER WEALTH AND FINANCIAL RATIOS

This chapter covers the features and characteristics of dividends and share repurchases as well as the theory and practice of corporate payout policy. A **dividend** is a distribution paid to shareholders. Dividends are declared (i.e., authorized) by a corporation's board of directors, whose actions may require approval by shareholders (e.g., in most of Europe) or may not require such approval (e.g., in the United States). Shares trading **ex-dividend** refers to shares that no longer carry the right to the next dividend payment. The **ex-dividend date** is the first date that a share trades without (i.e., "ex") this right to receive the declared dividend for the period. All else holding constant, on the ex-dividend date the share price can be expected to drop by the amount of the dividend. In contrast to the payment of interest and principal on a bond by its issuer, the payment of dividends is discretionary rather than a legal obligation and may be limited in amount by legal statutes and debt contract provisions. Dividend payments and interest payments in many jurisdictions are subject to different tax treatment at both the corporate and personal levels.

In this chapter, we focus on dividends on common shares (as opposed to preferred shares) paid by publicly traded companies. A company's **payout policy** is the set of principles guiding cash dividends and the value of shares repurchased in any given year. Payout policy (also called distribution policy) is more general than dividend policy because it reflects the fact that companies can return cash to shareholders by means of share repurchases and cash dividends. One of the longest running debates in corporate finance concerns the impact of a company's payout policy on common shareholders' wealth. Payout decisions, along with financing (capital structure) decisions, generally involve the board of directors and senior management and are closely watched by investors and analysts.

Dividends and share repurchases concern analysts because, as distributions to shareholders, they affect investment returns and financial ratios. The contribution of dividends to total return for stocks is formidable. For example, the total compound annual return for the S&P 500 Index with dividends reinvested from the beginning of 1926 to the end of 2018 was 10.0%, as compared with 5.9% on the basis of price alone. Similarly, from 1950 to 2018 the total compound annual return for the Nikkei 225 Index with dividends reinvested was 11.1%, as compared with 8.0% on the basis of price alone. Dividends also may provide important information about future company performance and investment returns. Analysts should strive to become familiar with all investment-relevant aspects of dividends and share repurchases.

This chapter is organized as follows. Section 2 reviews the features and characteristics of cash dividends, liquidating dividends, stock dividends, stock splits, and reverse stock splits and describes their expected effect on shareholders' wealth and a company's financial ratios. Section 3 presents theories of the effects of dividend policy on company value. In Section 4, we discuss factors that affect dividend policy in practice. In Section 5, we cover three major types of dividend policies. Section 6 presents share repurchases, including their income statement and balance sheet effects and equivalence to cash dividends (under certain assumptions). Section 7 presents global trends in payout policy. Section 8 covers analysis of dividend safety. The chapter concludes with a summary and practice problems.

1.1. Dividends: Forms and Effects on Shareholder Wealth and Issuing Company's Financial Ratios

Companies can pay dividends in a number of ways. Cash dividends can be distributed to shareholders through regular, extra (also called special or irregular), or liquidating dividends. Other forms of dividends include stock dividends and stock splits. In this section, we review the different forms that dividends can take and explain their impact on both the shareholder and the issuing company.

1.1.1. Regular Cash Dividends

Many companies choose to distribute cash to their shareholders on a regular schedule. The customary frequency of payment, however, may vary among markets. In the United States and Canada, most companies that pay dividends choose a quarterly schedule of payments, whereas in Europe and Japan, the most common choice is to pay dividends twice a year (i.e., semiannually). Elsewhere in Asia, companies often favor paying dividends once a year (i.e., annually). Exhibit 1 summarizes typical dividend payment schedules for selected markets.

EXHIBIT 1: Geographic Differences in Frequency of Payment of Cash Dividends

Market	Most Common Frequency
Canada, United States	Quarterly
Australia, Japan, Saudi Arabia	Semiannually
Egypt, Germany, Thailand	Annually

Most companies that pay cash dividends strive to maintain or increase their dividends. A record of consistent dividends over a long period of time is important to many companies and shareholders because it is widely interpreted as evidence of consistent profitability. At a minimum, most dividend-paying companies strive not to reduce dividends when they are experiencing temporary problems.

Regular dividends, and especially increasing regular dividends, also signal to investors that their company is growing and will share profits with its shareholders. Perhaps more importantly, management can use dividend announcements to communicate confidence in the company's future. Accordingly, an increase in the regular dividend (especially if it is unexpected) often has a positive effect on share price.

1.1.2. Extra or Special (Irregular) Dividends

An **extra dividend** or **special dividend** (also known as an irregular dividend) is either a dividend paid by a company that does not pay dividends on a regular schedule or a dividend that supplements regular cash dividends with an extra payment. These extra dividend payments may be brought about by special circumstances. For example, in December 2018 Hong Kong Stock Exchange (HKEX)-listed Tencent Holdings, a leading provider of internet value-added services, declared a special dividend of HKD250 million to its shareholders after its spin-off Tencent

Music went public in New York. This special dividend was approximately 3.5% of Tencent's annual dividend. Like many high-growth technology companies, Tencent had a history of paying very low dividends—with a yield of just 0.26% for 2018 (compared to an average of 4.6% for all stocks listed on the Hong Kong Stock Exchange).

Companies, particularly in cyclical industries, have sometimes chosen to use special dividends as a means of distributing more earnings only during strong earnings years. During economic downturns, when earnings are low or negative, cash that might otherwise be used for dividends is conserved. For example, a company may choose to declare a small regular dividend, and then when operating results are good, it may declare an extra dividend at the end of the year. In May 2018, Mumbai-listed Ingersoll-Rand (India) Ltd, a diversified industrial manufacturer, declared a special "second interim" dividend of Rs202 in addition to the regular annual Rs6 dividend, whereas for the prior 2 decades, the company had paid only the regular Rs6 dividend (excepting a special 2011 Rs24 dividend). The 2018 second interim dividend was paid out of current year profits and accumulated surpluses from earlier years. At the time, the company's reported year-on-year net profit growth was 25%.

Example 1 concerns a hypothetical company with a stated **dividend policy**—the strategy a company follows to determine the amount and timing of dividend payments—regarding the payment of extra dividends. In the example, the **dividend payout ratio** refers to common share cash dividends divided by net income available to common shares over the same time period.

EXAMPLE 1   AfriSage Technologies' Dividend Policy

AfriSage Technologies (AST), a hypothetical company, is a leading provider of commercial and enterprise software solutions in Southern African Development Community (SADC) countries. AST's financial data are reported in South African Rand (ZAR). In November 2017, AfriSage's board of directors modified its dividend policy, stating:

The company will target an investment-grade, long-term credit rating to secure strategic financial flexibility for investments in future growth. The ordinary dividend shall be at least 35% of net income. Excess capital will be returned to shareholders after the board has taken into consideration the company's cash at hand, projected cash flow, and planned investment from a medium-term perspective as well as capital market conditions.

Selected AfriSage Financial per Share Data

	2018	2017
Shares outstanding	632.5 million	632.5 million
Earnings per share	ZAR14.23	ZAR12.65
Cash dividends per share	ZAR7.61	ZAR10.68

1. Calculate the cash dividend payout ratio for 2018 and 2017.

Solution:

With the same number of shares outstanding, the dividend payout ratio on a per share basis is dividends per share divided by earnings per share.

> For 2018: ZAR7.61/ZAR14.23 = 53.5%.
>
> For 2017: ZAR10.68/ZAR12.65 = 84.4%.
>
> 2. Assuming the board's new dividend policy became effective in 2018, calculate the amount of the annual ordinary dividend on the basis of AfriSage's minimum payout policy in 2018 and the amount that could be considered an extra dividend.
>
> *Solution:*
>
> Under a policy of 35% of earnings, the minimum amount of dividends would be ZAR14.23 × 0.35 = ZAR4.98. The amount of the extra dividend would then be ZAR7.61 − ZAR4.98 = ZAR2.63.

1.1.3. Liquidating Dividends

A dividend may be referred to as a **liquidating dividend** when a company:

- goes out of business and the net assets of the company (after all liabilities have been paid) are distributed to shareholders;
- sells a portion of its business for cash and the proceeds are distributed to shareholders; or
- pays a dividend that exceeds its accumulated retained earnings (impairs stated capital).

These points illustrate that a liquidating dividend is a return of capital rather than a distribution from earnings or retained earnings.

1.1.4. Stock Dividends

Stock dividends are a non-cash form of dividends. With a **stock dividend** (also known as a **bonus issue of shares** or a scrip dividend), the company distributes additional shares (typically 2–10% of the shares then outstanding) of its common stock to shareholders instead of cash. Although the shareholder's total cost basis remains the same, the cost per share held is reduced. For example, if a shareholder owns 100 shares with a purchase price of US$10 per share, the total cost basis would be US$1,000. After a 5% stock dividend, the shareholder would own 105 shares of stock at a total cost of US$1,000. However, the cost per share would decline to US$9.52 (US$1,000/105).

Superficially, the stock dividend might seem an improvement on the cash dividend from both the shareholders' and the company's point of view. Each shareholder ends up with more shares, which did not have to be paid for, and the company did not have to spend any actual money issuing a dividend. Furthermore, stock dividends are generally not taxable to shareholders because a stock dividend merely divides the "pie" (the market value of shareholders' equity) into smaller pieces. The stock dividend, however, does not affect the shareholder's proportionate ownership in the company because other shareholders receive the same proportionate increase in shares. Additionally, the stock dividend does not change the value of each shareholder's ownership position because the increase in the number of shares held is accompanied by an offsetting decrease in earnings per share, and other measures of value per share, resulting from the greater number of shares outstanding.

The second point is illustrated in Exhibit 2, which shows the impact of a 3% stock dividend to a shareholder who owns 10% of a company with a market value of US $20 million. As one can see, the market value of the shareholder's wealth does not change, assuming an unchanged **price-to-earnings ratio** (the ratio of share price, P, to earnings per share, E, or P/E). That assumption is reasonable because a stock dividend does not alter a company's asset base or earning power. (As the reader will see shortly, the same is true of a stock split.) The total market value of the company is unaffected by the stock dividend because the decrease in the share price is exactly offset by the increase in the number of shares outstanding.

EXHIBIT 2: Illustration of the Effect of a Stock Dividend

	Before Dividend	After Dividend
Shares outstanding	1,000,000	1,030,000
Earnings per share	US$1.00	US$0.97 (1,000,000/1,030,000)
Stock price	US$20.00	US$19.4175 (20 × 0.9709)
P/E	20	20
Total market value	US$20 million	US$20 million (1,030,000 × US$19.4175)
Shares owned	100,000 (10% × 1,000,000)	103,000 (10% × 1,030,000)
Ownership value	US$2,000,000 (100,000 × US$20)	US$2,000,000 (103,000 × US$19.4175)

Note: The exhibit shows intermediate results rounded to four decimal places, but final results are based on carrying intermediate results at full precision.

Companies that regularly pay stock dividends see some advantages to this form of dividend payment. It favors long-term investors, which, in turn, may lower the company's cost of equity financing. The payment of a stock dividend also helps increase the stock's float, which improves the liquidity of the shares and dampens share price volatility.

A traditional belief is that a lower stock price will attract more investors, all else equal. US companies often view the optimal share price range as US$20 to US$80. For a growing company, payment of a regular stock dividend is more likely to help keep the stock in the "optimal" range. In February 2019, for example, Massmart—the second-largest distributor of consumer goods in Africa—changed its established policy of paying interim and final dividends in cash and instead declared a scrip dividend for the 2018 final dividend. When the company pays the same dividend rate on the new shares as it did on the old shares, a shareholder's dividend income increases; however, the company could have accomplished the same result by increasing the cash dividend.

From a company's perspective, the key difference between a stock dividend and a cash dividend is that a cash dividend affects a company's capital structure, whereas a stock dividend has no economic impact on a company. Cash dividends reduce assets (because cash is being paid out) and shareholders' equity (by reducing retained earnings). All else equal, liquidity ratios, such as the cash ratio (cash and short-term marketable securities divided by current liabilities) and current ratio (current assets divided by current liabilities), should decrease, reflecting the reduction in cash. Financial leverage ratios, such as the debt-to-equity ratio (total debt divided by total shareholders' equity) and debt-to-assets ratio (total debt divided by total assets), should also increase. Stock dividends, on the other hand, do not affect assets or shareholders' equity. Although retained earnings are reduced by the value of the stock dividends paid (i.e., by the number of shares issued × price per share), contributed capital increases by the same amount (i.e., the value of the shares issued). As a result, total shareholders' equity does not change. Neither stock dividends nor stock splits (which are discussed in the next section) affect liquidity ratios or financial leverage ratios.

1.1.5. Stock Splits

Stock splits are similar to stock dividends in that they have no economic effect on the company, and the shareholders' total cost basis does not change. For example, if a company announces a two-for-one stock split, each shareholder will be issued an additional share for each share currently owned. Thus, a shareholder will have twice as many shares after the split as before the split. Therefore, earnings per share (and all other per share data) will decline by half, leaving the P/E and equity market value unchanged. Assuming the corporation maintains the same dividend payout ratio as before the split, **dividend yield** (annual dividends per share divided by share price) will also be unchanged. Apart from the effect of any information or benefit that investors perceive a stock split to convey, stock splits (like stock dividends) should be neutral in their effect on shareholders' wealth.

Although two-for-one and three-for-one stock splits are the most common, such unusual splits as five-for-four or seven-for-three sometimes occur. It is important for shareholders to recognize that their wealth is not changed by the stock split (just as it was not changed for a stock dividend, all else equal). Exhibit 3 shows an example of a two-for-one split and its impact on stock price, earnings per share, dividends per share, dividend payout ratio, dividend yield, P/E, and market value.

EXHIBIT 3: Before and After a Two-for-One Stock Split

	Before Split	After Split
Number of shares outstanding	4 million	8 million
Stock price	€40.00	€20.00 (€40/2)
Earnings per share	€1.50	€0.75 (€1.50/2)
Dividends per share	€0.50	€0.25 (€0.50/2)
Dividend payout ratio	1/3	1/3
Dividend yield	1.25%	1.25% (€0.25/€20.00)
P/E	26.7	26.7 (€20.00/€0.75)
Market value of equity	€160 million	€160 million (€20.00 × 8 million)

As can be seen, a two-for-one stock split is basically the same as a 100% stock dividend because all per share data have been reduced by 50%. The only difference is in the accounting treatment: Although both stock dividends and stock splits have no effect on total shareholders' equity, a stock dividend is accounted for as a transfer of retained earnings to contributed capital. A stock split, however, does not affect any of the balances in shareholder equity accounts.

A company may announce a stock split at any time. Typically, a split is announced after a period in which the stock price has risen. Many investors view the announcement of a stock split as a positive sign pointing to future stock price increases. More often, however, announced stock splits merely recognize that the stock has risen enough to justify a stock split to return the stock price to a lower, more marketable price range.

Several of the largest companies in the world (as measured by market value) had stock splits in the last decade. For example, Schneider Electric SA (France) had a two-for-one split in 2011; Whole Foods Market (United States) had a two-for-one split in 2013. In each case, the stock split came after a significant rise in stock price but was not, in and of itself, a meaningful predictor of future price action. However, data show that stock splits have been on the decline in the United States. Although S&P 500 constituent stock splits averaged 45 per year between 1980 and 2017, they reached the maximum of 114 splits in 1986 and have steadily declined since 2015 (e.g., only 5 splits in 2017). This decline in stock splits has been attributed to greater use of funds and exchange-traded funds (ETFs) by individual investors and to changes in market microstructure that have de-linked such transaction costs as commissions paid to number of shares traded. Thus, the concept of a "marketable price range" of a company's stock has become less important.

Much less common than stock splits are reverse stock splits. A **reverse stock split** increases the share price and reduces the number of shares outstanding—again, with no effect on the market value of a company's equity or on shareholders' total cost basis. Just as a high stock price might lead a company to consider a stock split, so too a low stock price may lead a company to consider a reverse stock split. The objective of a reverse stock split is to increase the price of the stock to a higher, more marketable range. As reported in *Barron's*, companies execute reverse splits "to attract institutional investors and mutual funds that often shy from buying stocks trading below US$5." Reverse stock splits are perhaps most common for companies in, or coming out of, financial distress. Kitov Pharma, an Israeli drug developer, announced a 1-for-20 reverse split in December 2018, reducing its issued shares to 16 million, in order to meet minimum share price listing criteria to begin trading on the Tel Aviv Stock Exchange and to begin the trading of its ADRs on the NASDAQ in January 2019.

Reverse splits, historically less common in Asia, are becoming more popular. For example, reverse stock splits were not permitted in Japan under Corporation Law until 2001, but since 2007, they have been actively encouraged by the Tokyo Stock Exchange to meet the Exchange's objective of standardizing trading lot size to 100 shares for listed companies by 1 October 2018. While most companies were compliant by the deadline, on that date 23 companies reduced their trading lot size to 100 shares by carrying out reverse stock splits. As an example, in May 2018 Fuji Electric Co. Ltd announced that it would conduct a 5-for-1 reverse stock split on 1 October 2018 to adjust the unit of investment in the company to a level deemed desirable by the TSE (between ¥50,000 and ¥500,000).

EXAMPLE 2   Globus Maritime Announces a Reverse Split

In May 2018, Globus Maritime Ltd, a Greek dry bulk shipping company providing worldwide maritime transportation services, was warned by NASDAQ that it no longer met the continuing listing requirements once its share price had traded below the US$1 a share minimum price requirement for 30 consecutive business days. Globus was given until the end of October 2018 to regain compliance. Globus announced a 1 for 10 reverse split to occur on 15 October. On 12 October, shares were trading at US$4.25 before the reverse split had taken place.

1. If the reverse split were to take place when the share price was US$4.25, find the expected stock price after a 1-for-10 reverse split, assuming no other factors affect the split.

Solution:

If the price was US$4.25 before the reverse split, for every 10 shares, a shareholder would have 1 share priced at 10 × US$4.25 = US$42.50.

2. Comment on the following statement: "Shareholder wealth is negatively affected by a reverse stock split."

Solution:

The statement is not generally correct. Considering the reverse split on its own, the market capitalization of the common equity would be unchanged. If the reverse split was interpreted as a good decision (e.g., because the company will be able to retain the advantages of being listed on the NASDAQ), its price and thus market capitalization might increase. But other factors—such as continued limited growth of its operations or continued small share float and turnover—could drive down the stock's value.

2. DIVIDEND POLICY AND COMPANY VALUE: THEORIES

Since the early 1960s, financial theorists have debated the extent to which dividend policy (decisions about whether, when, and in what amount to pay dividends) should and does matter to a company's shareholders. One group of theorists believes that dividend policy is irrelevant to shareholders. This group typically holds that only the decisions of the company that are directly related to investment in working and fixed capital affect shareholders' wealth. A second group holds that dividend policy does matter to investors, for one or more reasons, and that a company can affect shareholders' wealth through its dividend policy. Typically, dividend relevance is attributed to either the belief that investors value a unit of dividends more highly than an equal amount of uncertain capital gains or to one or more market imperfections. Such imperfections include taxes (because dividends may be taxed differently than capital gains), asymmetric information (corporate insiders are better informed about their company's prospects than outside investors), and agency costs (management has a tendency to squander extra cash). We examine these positions and the assumptions that underlie them in the following subsections.

2.1. Dividend Policy Does Not Matter

In a 1961 paper, Miller and Modigliani ("MM") argued that in a world without taxes, transaction costs, and equal ("symmetric") information among all investors—that is, under **perfect capital market** assumptions—a company's dividend policy should have no impact on its cost of capital or on shareholder wealth. Their argument begins by assuming a company has a given capital budget (e.g., it accepts all projects with a positive net present value, or NPV) and that its current capital structure and debt ratio are optimal. Another way of stating this argument is that the dividend decision is independent of a company's investment and financing decisions. For example, suppose that an all-equity financed company decided to pay as a dividend the investment amount it required for its capital budget. To finance capital projects, the company could issue additional common shares in the amount of its capital budget (such financing would leave its capital structure unchanged). The value of the newly issued shares would exactly offset the value of the dividend. Thus, if a company paid out a dividend that represented 5% of equity, its share price would be expected to drop by 5%. If a common stock in Australia is priced at A\$20 before an A\$1 per share dividend, the implied new price would be A\$19. The shareholder has assets worth A\$20 if the dividend is not paid or assets worth A\$20 if the stock drops to A\$19 and an A\$1 dividend is paid.

Note that under the MM assumptions, there is no meaningful distinction between dividends and share repurchases (repurchases of outstanding common shares by the issuing company): They are both ways for a company to return cash to shareholders. If a company had few investment opportunities such that its current cash flow was more than that needed for positive NPV projects, it could distribute the excess cash flow via a dividend or a share repurchase. Shareholders selling shares would receive A\$20 a share, and shareholders not selling would hold shares whose value continued to be A\$20. To see this, suppose the company being discussed has 10,000 shares outstanding, a current free cash flow of A\$10,000, and a present value of future cash flows of A\$190,000. Thus, the share price is (A\$10,000 + A\$190,000)/10,000 = A\$20. Now if the company uses the free cash flow to repurchase shares, in lieu of paying a dividend of A\$1, it will repurchase 500 shares (A\$10,000/A\$20 = 500). The 9,500 shares left outstanding have a claim on the A\$190,000 future cash flow, which results in a share price of A\$20 (A\$190,000/9,500 = A\$20).

An intuitive understanding of MM dividend irrelevance also follows from the concept of a "homemade dividend." In a world with no taxes or transaction costs, if shareholders wanted or needed income, they could construct their own dividend policy by selling sufficient shares to create their desired cash flow stream. Using the example above, assume the company did not pay the A\$1 dividend and the stock remained at A\$20. A holder of 1,000 shares who desired A\$1,000 in cash could sell 50 shares at A\$20, thus reducing his or her holdings to 950 shares. Note that by reducing share holdings, second-period dividend income is reduced; higher dividend income in one period is at the expense of exactly offsetting lower dividend income in subsequent periods. The irrelevance argument does not state that dividends per se are irrelevant to share value but that dividend *policy* is irrelevant. By taking the earning power of assets as a given and assuming perfect capital markets, policy alternatives merely involve tradeoffs of different dividend streams of equal present value.

In the real world, market imperfections create some problems for MM's dividend policy irrelevance propositions. First, both companies and individuals incur transaction costs. A company issuing new shares incurs **flotation costs** (i.e., costs in selling shares to the public that include underwriters' fees, legal costs, registration expenses, and possible negative price effects) often estimated to be as much as 4% to 10% of the capital raised, depending on the size of the company and the size of the issue. Shareholders selling shares to create a "homemade" dividend would incur transaction costs and, in some countries, capital gains taxes (of course, cash dividends incur taxes in most countries). Furthermore, selling shares on a periodic basis to create an income stream of dividends can be problematic over time if share prices are volatile. If share prices decline, shareholders have to sell more shares to create the same dividend stream.

2.2. Dividend Policy Matters: The Bird in the Hand Argument

Financial theorists have argued that, even under perfect capital markets assumptions, investors prefer a dollar of dividends to a dollar of potential capital gains from reinvesting earnings because they view dividends as less risky. A related viewpoint is that "the typical dollar of reinvestment has less economic value to the shareholder than a dollar paid in dividends" (Graham, Dodd, Cottle, and Tatham 1962). These arguments are similar and have sometimes been called the "bird in the hand" argument, a reference to the proverb "a bird in the hand is worth two in the bush." By assuming that a given amount of dividends is less risky than the same amount of capital gains, the argument is that a company that pays dividends will have a lower cost of equity capital than an otherwise similar company that does not pay dividends; the lower cost of equity should result in a higher share price. MM contend that this argument is incorrect because, under their assumptions, paying or increasing the dividend today does not affect the risk of future cash flows. Such actions only lower the ex-dividend price of the share.

2.3. Dividend Policy Matters: The Tax Argument

In some countries, dividend income has traditionally been taxed at higher rates than capital gains. In the United States since 2012, for instance, dividends on shares held at least 60 days have been taxed at a maximum rate of 20%, which exceeds the long-term capital gains tax rate of 15%. In mainland China, there is no capital gains tax on shares; however, dividend income is taxed at 20% for shares held less than a month, 10% for shares held between one month and a year, and since 2015 at 0% for shares held longer than a year.

An argument could be made that in a country that taxes dividends at higher rates than capital gains, taxable investors should prefer companies that pay low dividends and reinvest earnings in profitable growth opportunities. Presumably, any growth in earnings in excess of the opportunity cost of funds would translate into a higher share price. If, for any reason, a company lacked growth opportunities sufficient to consume its annual retained earnings, it could distribute such funds through share repurchases (again, the assumption is that capital gains are taxed more lightly than dividends). Taken to its extreme, this argument would advocate a *zero* dividend payout ratio. Real-world market considerations may complicate the picture. For example, in some jurisdictions governmental regulation may require companies to distribute excess earnings as dividends or to classify share repurchases as dividends if the repurchases appear to be ongoing in lieu of dividend payments.

3. OTHER THEORETICAL ISSUES: SIGNALING

In the following section, we present additional perspectives related to the theory of dividend policy.

3.1. The Information Content of Dividend Actions: Signaling

MM assumed that all investors—including outside investors—have the same information about the company: a situation of symmetric information. In reality, corporate managers typically have access to more detailed and extensive information about the company than do outside investors.

A situation of asymmetric information raises the possibility that dividend increases or decreases may affect share price because they may convey new information about the company. A company's board of directors and management, having more information than outside investors, may use dividends to signal to investors about (i.e., convey information on) the company's prospects. A company's decision to initiate, maintain, increase, or cut a dividend may convey more credible information than positive words from management because cash is involved. For a signal to be effective, it must be difficult or costly to mimic by another entity without the same attributes. Dividend increases are costly to mimic because a company that does not expect its cash flows to increase will not be able to maintain the dividend at increasingly high levels in the long run. (In the short run, a company may be able to borrow to fund dividends.)

Empirical studies broadly support the thesis that dividend initiations or increases convey positive information and are associated with future earnings growth, whereas dividend omissions or reductions convey negative information and are associated with future earnings problems. A dividend declaration can help resolve some of the information asymmetry between insiders and outsiders and help close any gap between the market price of shares and their intrinsic value. Evidence in both developed and emerging market equities suggests the presence of an earnings and return effect following dividend initiation announcements. In general, company earnings increase in the year of dividend initiation and in the following several years, and then the announcement of the initiation of a regular cash dividend is accompanied by an excess return. By looking at two historical examples of signaling, Example 3 provides further support for the idea that dividend initiations contain value-relevant information.

EXAMPLE 3   Historical Examples: Information on Dividend Initiations

Following are two examples of the information content of dividend initiations following the 2008 global financial crisis.

A. Oracle Corporation, a leading business software maker, initiated a US$0.05 quarterly dividend in May 2009. Oracle's annual US$0.20 dividend amounts to about US$1 billion, a relatively small amount compared with operating cash flow of US$8 billion and another US$9 billion in cash and cash-equivalent assets on its balance sheet at the end of fiscal year 2009. An analyst who follows Oracle for institutional investors saw the Oracle announcement as a signal that the company was well positioned to ride out the downturn and also gain market share.

B. In mid-2009, Paris-based Groupe Eurotunnel announced its first ever dividend after it completed a debt restructuring and received insurance proceeds resulting from a fire that had closed the Channel Tunnel. In a 2 June 2009 press release, Eurotunnel's CEO said that this "marked a turning point for the company as its business has returned to the realm of normality; the company anticipated a return to profitability."

Some researchers have argued that a company's dividend initiation or increase tends to be associated with share price increases because it attracts more attention to the company. Managers have an incentive to increase the company's dividend if they believe the company to be undervalued because the increased scrutiny will lead to a positive price adjustment. In contrast, according to this line of reasoning, managers of overvalued companies have little reason to mimic such a signal because increased scrutiny would presumably result in a downward price adjustment to their shares.

EXAMPLE 4   Signaling with Dividends and the Costs of Mimicking

Suppose that the management of a company with poor future prospects recommends to the board of directors an increase in its dividend. Management explains to the board that investors may then believe that the company has positive future prospects, leading to an increase in share value and shareholder wealth.

1. State whether such imitation is likely to achieve the stated objective over the long term.

Solution:

No, such dividend increases are not likely to achieve the stated objective over the long term for the company described.

2. Justify your answer to Question 1.

Solution:

Dividend increases are costly to mimic because a company that does not expect its cash flows to increase will not be able to maintain the increased dividend. The company will have to either cut the dividend in the future or go to the market to obtain new equity or debt funding to pay the dividend. Both these alternatives are costly for the company because they result in downward revisions, on average, to the stock price.

Many companies take pride in their record of consistently increasing dividends over a long period of time. Standard & Poor's, for example, identifies companies in its US-based S&P 500 Index, Europe 350 Index, Pan Asia Index, and S&P/TSX Canadian Index that have increased their dividend for a number of consecutive years (at least 25 years in the case of the S&P 500, at least 10 years in the case of the Europe 350, at least 7 years in the case of Pan Asia Index, and at least 5 years in the case of the S&P/TSX). These companies are in various industries. When a company's earnings and cash flow outlook has been and continues to be positive, it often views a policy of increasing dividends as an important tool to convey that information to existing and potential shareholders. Companies that consistently increase their dividends seem to share certain characteristics:

- Dominant or niche positions in their industry
- Global operations
- Relatively less volatile earnings
- Relatively high returns on assets
- Relatively low debt ratios (dividend payouts unlikely to be affected by restrictions in debt covenants)

Dividend cuts or omissions, in contrast, present powerful and often negative signals. For companies under financial or operating stress, the dividend declaration date may be viewed with more than usual interest. Will they cut the dividend? Will they omit the dividend altogether? In these instances, merely maintaining the dividend or not cutting it as much as expected is usually viewed as good news (i.e., that current difficulties are transitory and manageable), unless investors view managers as trying to convey erroneous information to the market.

In principle, although difficult in practice, management can attempt to send a positive signal by cutting the dividend. Telstra, a major Australian telecoms company with an enviable record of paying close to 90% of profits as dividends, announced in 2017 a 30% cut in its dividend—its first cut in more than 20 years. Telstra's management explained it intended to use the funds conserved to reinvest in the business. It was planning for the longer term and retaining financial flexibility as a priority because the company faced significant challenges from rising competition and competing technologies. Although management's message was met with an initial 12% share price decline as disappointed yield-focused investors exited the stock, it was, in retrospect, a positive signal. Telstra was viewed by institutional investors as successfully using its cash flow to reorganize to meet business challenges, and it was regarded as one of the few cases in which a large Australian dividend payer was not cutting payouts as a result of extreme financial pressure.

EXAMPLE 5   Dividend Reductions and Price Increases

In November 2018, BT Group Plc, one of the world's largest providers of communication services and solutions operating in over 170 countries, announced it would cut its interim dividend from 4.85 pence a share to 4.62 pence a share. The company also revealed that net cash flow from operating activities had plunged 71% to £754 million and that revenue had fallen 2% to £11.6 billion, with declines across all divisions.

All this despite the fact that in the first six months of the year, the company reported a pretax profit increase to £1.3 billion from £1.1 billion a year prior and a 2% increase in adjusted earnings (EBITDA) to £3.7 billion from £3.6 billion as the telecoms giant cut costs as part of its restructuring. One analyst commented that while the dividend decrease was an "unwelcome surprise," it was also a "prudent move" given the 71% decline in net cash and thus "should not take too much sheen on a dividend yield, which previously stood at an attractive 6.4%." It was also noted that BT Group was replacing its chief executive in February 2019; thus, future dividends would depend on decisions made by the new leadership. As the market digested this information, the telecoms company's share price rose 6.9% to 257 pence per share.

Source: Renae Dyer, "BT Shares Surge Despite Dividend Cut as It Expects Earnings to Hit Top End of Guidance," Proactive Investors (1 November 2018).

Another example of the signaling content of dividends can be found in the actions of eBay, the e-commerce multinational corporation, and its initial dividend declaration in 2019 (24 years after the online retailer was established in 1995 during the dot-com boom). Technology companies have among the lowest dividend yields and below-average dividend payout ratios. This is because most technology companies have high R&D requirements, and some (e.g., integrated circuit manufacturers) are capital intensive. Those that are profitable often achieve returns on assets and owners' equity that are well above average. In addition, business risk is considerable as discoveries and unforeseen advances change the product landscape. All of these considerations would suggest a policy of low (or no) dividend payments so that internally generated funds are directed toward new product development and capital investment that will maintain high growth and returns. Some companies in the technology sector, however, do mature. Legacy tech companies that initiated dividends as their businesses matured and growth slowed include Apple in 2012, Cisco in 2011, Oracle in 2009, and Microsoft in 2003. At the time of eBay's dividend initiation, such non-dividend-paying tech companies as Alibaba, Weibo, Baidu, and JD.com remained the norm in markets where the technology sector was still growing.

In early 2019, eBay declared its first-ever dividend and announced that it would begin paying quarterly dividends of US$0.14 a share, which represented a yield of 1.6% (for comparison, Microsoft's dividend yield at the time was 1.9% and Cisco's was 2.9%). At the same time, eBay announced an increase in its existing share repurchase program to US$4 billion. Investor reaction was mixed. Some believed that eBay was signaling an interest in broadening its investor focus by attracting a new group of shareholders focused on income over growth while refraining from undertaking unprofitable expansion. Others viewed the dividend declaration as an admission that it was becoming a mature company—that it could no longer deliver high returns from reinvesting its earnings. The future growth prospects for the stock, they would argue, had been diminished. In other words, although the dividend initiation showed confidence in eBay's cash flow generation, investors preferred for management's use of internal investments to regenerate eBay's core business. Regardless, few could argue that eBay's dividend initiation declaration in 2019 was not a corporate event of some importance.

3.2. Agency Costs and Dividends as a Mechanism to Control Them

Large, publicly traded corporations typically have a substantial separation between the professional managers who control the corporation's operations and the outside investors who own it. When agents (the managers) and owners (the shareholders) are two separate parties, managers may have an incentive to maximize their own welfare at the company's expense because they own none or relatively small percentages of the company for which they work and thus do not bear all the costs of such actions. This incentive is ultimately also a problem of unequal (asymmetric) information between managers and outside investors because if outside investors could perfectly observe managers, managers would be dissuaded from such actions. One managerial incentive of particular concern is the potential private benefit managers may obtain from investment in negative net present value (NPV) projects. Such projects will generate negative economic returns; but because they may grow the size of the company (measured in sales or assets) and thus enlarge the manager's span of control, the manager may have the incentive to invest in them. This is a particular problem when management's compensation is tied to assets or sales rather than value enhancement, a flaw in the firm's corporate governance. The potential overinvestment agency problem might be alleviated by the payment of dividends. In particular, by paying out all free cash flow to equity in dividends, managers would be constrained in their ability to overinvest by taking on negative NPV projects. This concern or hypothesis that management may create an overinvestment agency cost is known as Jensen's free cash flow hypothesis.

The potential for managers to squander free cash flow by undertaking unprofitable projects is a consideration to be evaluated on a case-by-case basis. Prior to initiating its dividend in 2003, for example, Microsoft accumulated increasingly large cash positions but was not observed to squander monies on unprofitable projects. In some cases, such cash positions may provide financial flexibility to respond quickly to changes in the environment, to grasp unforeseen opportunities, or to survive periods of restricted credit, as in the case of Ford Motor Company's accumulation of cash during profitable years in the 1990s and similarly by Japanese automotive parts manufacturer Denso Corporation in the late 2000s and 2010s. Clearly, there are industry-specific and life-cycle conditions to consider. In general, it makes sense for growing companies in industries characterized by rapid change to hold cash and pay low or no dividends, but it does not make sense for large, mature companies in relatively non-cyclical industries. In general, there is empirical support for the market reaction to dividend change announcements to be stronger for companies with greater potential for overinvestment than for companies with lesser potential for overinvestment.

Another concern when a company is financed by debt as well as equity is that paying dividends can exacerbate the agency conflict between shareholders and bondholders. When a company has debt outstanding, the payment of dividends reduces the cash cushion available to the company for the disbursement of fixed required payments to bondholders. The payment of large dividends, with the intention of transferring wealth from bondholders to shareholders, could lead to underinvestment in profitable projects. All else equal, both dividends and share repurchases increase the default risk of debt. Reflecting bondholders' concern, the bond **indenture** (contract) often includes a covenant restricting distributions to shareholders that might impair the position of bondholders. A typical form of this restriction is to define the maximum allowable amount of distributions to shareholders during the life of the bond. This amount of funds is usually a positive function of the company's current and past earnings and issues of new equity and a negative function of dividends paid since the bonds were issued. Such covenants often do not really restrict the level of dividends as long as those dividends come from new earnings or from new issues of stock. What the covenant attempts to do is prevent the payment of dividends financed by the sale of the company's existing assets or by the issuance of new debt. Covenants that specify minimum levels of EBITDA and/or EBIT coverage of interest charges are frequently used as well. These covenants provide some assurance that operating earnings include a cushion for the payment of fixed charges. Other covenants focus on balance sheet strength—for example, by specifying a maximum value for the ratio of debt to tangible net worth.

EXAMPLE 6   Agency Issues and Dividends

1. Two dividend-paying companies A and B directly compete with each other. Both companies are all-equity financed and have recent dividend payout ratios averaging 35%. The corporate governance practices at Company B are weaker than at Company A. For example, at B but not A, the chief executive officer is also chair of the board of directors. Recently, profitable investment opportunities for B have become fewer, although operating cash flow for both A and B is strong.

   Based only on the information given, investors who own shares in both A and B are *most likely* to press for a dividend increase at:

A.   Company A, because it has better growth prospects than Company B.

B.   Company B, because a dividend increase may mitigate potential overinvestment agency problems.

C.   Company B, because a dividend increase may mitigate potential underinvestment agency problems.

Solution:

B is correct. Company B's strong operating cash flow in an environment of fewer profitable growth opportunities may tempt Company B's management to overinvest. The concern is increased because of Company B's relatively weak corporate governance.

The final example in this section illustrates the complex agency considerations that may affect dividend policy.

EXAMPLE 7   Electric Utilities, Agency Costs, and Dividends

Electric utilities often have above average dividend yields. A distinctive characteristic of many utility companies is that they pay a high percentage of earnings as dividends, while periodically issuing new equity to invest in the many projects necessitated by the capital-intensive nature of their business. This practice of financing dividends with new equity appears unwise because new equity is expensive. Researchers examining a set of US-based electric utilities, however, have demonstrated that there may be a good reason for paying dividends and then issuing equity: the mitigation of the agency problems between managers and shareholders and between utility regulators and utility shareholders.

Because electric utilities are typically monopolies in the sense that they are usually the only providers of electricity in a given area, they are regulated so they are not able to set electricity rates at monopolistically high levels. The regulators are expected to set rates such that the company's operating expenses are met and investors are provided with a fair return. The regulators, however, are usually elected, or are political appointees, and view ratepayers as potential voters. Thus, utility shareholders, in addition to facing potential manager–shareholder agency issues because managers have incentives to consume perquisites or to overinvest, also face a regulator–shareholder conflict in which regulators set rates low to attract the votes of individuals being served by the utility.

In the utility industry, therefore, dividends and the subsequent equity issue are used as mechanisms to monitor managers and regulators. The company pays high dividends and then goes to the capital markets to issue new equity. If the market does not think that shareholders are getting a fair return because regulators are setting rates too low, or because managers are consuming too many perks, the price at which new equity can be sold will fall until the shareholder expectations for returns are met. As a result, the company may not be able to raise sufficient funds to expand its plant to meet increasing electricity demand—the electric utility industry is very capital intensive—and, in the extreme, customer needs may not be met. Faced with this possibility, and potentially angry voters, regulators have incentives to set rates at a fair level. Thus, the equity market serves to monitor and arbitrate conflicts between shareholders and both managers and regulators.

4. OTHER THEORETICAL ISSUES: SUMMARY

What can we conclude about the link between dividends and valuation? In theory, in the absence of market imperfections Miller and Modigliani (1961) find that dividend policy is irrelevant to the wealth of a company's investors. But in reality, the existence of market imperfections makes matters more complicated. In addition, some investors are led, by logic or custom, to prefer dividends.

Unfortunately, in the search for the link between dividend policy and value, the evidence is inconclusive. It is difficult to show an exact relationship between dividends and value because so many variables affect value. We have presented factors that would seem to explain why some companies put emphasis on dividends and others do not. Financial theory predicts that reinvestment opportunities should be the dominant factor. Indeed, no matter where they are located in the world, small, fast-growing companies pay out little or none of their earnings. Regardless of jurisdiction, more mature companies with fewer reinvestment opportunities tend to pay dividends. For these mature companies, taxes, regulations/laws, tradition, signaling, ownership structure, and attempts to reconcile agency conflicts all seem to play a role in determining the dividend payout ratio. At a minimum, in looking at a company an analyst should evaluate whether a given company's dividend policy matches its reinvestment opportunities and legal/financial environment.

5. FACTORS AFFECTING DIVIDEND POLICY IN PRACTICE

In Section 3 we discussed theories of dividend policy and value and concluded that the issue is, at best, unresolved. In this section we explore six factors that affect a company's dividend policy, which we defined earlier as decisions about whether, when, and in what amount to pay dividends:

- Investment opportunities
- The expected volatility of future earnings
- Financial flexibility
- Tax considerations
- Flotation costs
- Contractual and legal restrictions

Boards of directors and managers spend considerable time setting dividend policy despite the lack of clear guidance from theory to inform their deliberations. The factors listed are, however, often mentioned by managers themselves as relevant to dividend policy selection in practice. Some of the factors we explore, such as taxation, are not company-specific, whereas other factors, such as possible contractual restrictions on dividend payments and the expected volatility of future earnings, are more company-specific. The factors may be interrelated, and the presence of one may enhance or diminish the effect of another. Importantly, the independence between the investment, financing, and dividend decisions assumed by MM may no longer hold when such market imperfections as information effects, agency problems, and taxes are recognized.

5.1. Investment Opportunities

All else equal, a company with many profitable investment opportunities will tend to pay out less in dividends than a company with fewer opportunities because the former company will have more uses for internally generated cash flows. Internally generated cash flow is generally a cheaper source of equity funding than new equity issuance. Opportunities for new investments, and the speed with which a company needs to respond to them, are influenced by the industry in which the company operates. A company with the ability to delay the initiation of projects without penalty may be willing to pay out more in dividends than a company that needs to act immediately to exploit profitable investment opportunities. Technology companies tend to have much lower average dividend yields than utilities. The chief explanation may be the size and time horizon of profitable investment opportunities in relation to annual operating cash flow generated. For technology companies, the pace of change is rapid, so having internally generated funds available to react to profitable opportunities affords them valuable flexibility. For utility companies, for which there are typically fewer such opportunities and for which change is much slower, higher dividend payouts are indicated.

5.2. The Expected Volatility of Future Earnings

Several important factors in the dividend payout decision have been identified as important to managers. Most managers

- had a target payout ratio based on long-run sustainable earnings;
- focused more on dividend changes (increases or decreases) than on dividend levels; and
- were reluctant to increase the dividend if the increase might soon need to be reversed.

Findings in the United States, United Kingdom, and other countries suggest that managers are reluctant to cut dividends—preferring to smooth them over time. Smoothing takes the form of relating dividend increases to the long-term earnings growth rate, even if short-term earnings are volatile. All else equal, the more volatile earnings are, the greater the risk that a given dividend increase may not be covered by earnings in a future time period. Thus, when earnings are volatile, we expect companies to be more cautious in the size and frequency of dividend increases. These findings also hold for other countries, although variation between countries has been noted in managers' willingness to decrease dividends based on available investment opportunities.

5.3. Financial Flexibility

Companies may not initiate, or may reduce or omit, dividends to obtain the financial flexibility associated with having substantial cash on hand. A company with substantial cash holdings is in a relatively strong position to meet unforeseen operating needs and to exploit investment opportunities with minimum delay. Having a strong cash position can be particularly valuable during economic contractions when the availability of credit may be reduced. Financial flexibility may be viewed as a tactical consideration that is of greater importance when access to liquidity is critical and when the company's dividend payout is relatively large.

A classic example of explaining a dividend decision in terms of the need to preserve financial flexibility occurred with Skanska AB, based in Sweden. On 8 February 2019, Skanska AB, one of the world's biggest construction and development companies, announced its board's suggestion to cut Skanska's dividend going forward by 30% to SKr6.00. This would allow for continued expansion of its project development business while maintaining its financial ability to deliver sustainable shareholder returns. Skanska's Chief Executive Anders Danielsson stated:

As we enter 2019, there are political and macroeconomic uncertainties which are likely to increase further. In many of our home geographies and sectors, the markets are levelling out and it is difficult to predict how long this relatively favourable environment will last.

Source: "Skanska Warns of 'Increasing Uncertainties' and Proposes Dividend Cut," *Financial Times* (8 February 2019): https://www.ft.com/content/9201486e-2b81-11e9-a5ab-ff8ef2b976c7.

The cut was expected to conserve SKr920 million on an annual basis. With approximately SKr19 billion of cash on hand at the time of the statement and with operating cash flows at least covering the previous dividend, the dividend reduction appeared to be accurately characterized as "precautionary." Although the dividend cut announcement was accompanied by a 9% decline in Skanska's share price, the share price quickly recovered. Within two months, it had risen 7% above its pre-dividend cut announcement value, indicating the market's favorable response to Skanska's decision to cut the dividend arising from uncertainty in its operating environment and the desire to maintain financial flexibility.

When increasing financial flexibility is an important consideration, a company may decide to distribute money to shareholders primarily by means of share repurchases (covered in Section 6) rather than regular dividends. A program to repurchase shares in the open market does not involve a formal requirement that any repurchases be executed, and share repurchases in general do not establish the same expectations for continuation in the future as regular dividends.

5.4. Tax Considerations

Taxation is an important factor that affects investment decisions for taxable investors, in particular, because it is the after-tax return that is most relevant to investors. Different jurisdictions tax corporate dividends in a wide variety of ways. Some tax both capital gains and dividend income. Others tax dividends but not capital gains. Even within a given country, taxation can be quite complex. In addition, because taxation is a major fiscal policy tool that is subject to politics, governments have a tendency to "re-address" tax issues, sometimes with great frequency. As with other aspects of taxation, governments use the taxation of dividends to address a variety of goals: to encourage or discourage the retention or distribution of corporate earnings; to redistribute income; or to address other political, social, and/or investment goals.

For the global investor, foreign taxes can be as important as domestic taxes. Foreign tax credits in the investor's home country also may figure importantly into the overall taxation issue. For example, France requires companies domiciled in France to withhold dividends paid to foreign investors at the corporate tax rate (reduced to 25% by 2022), but investors in other countries can usually claim a tax credit on their home country tax return for the amount of that tax, especially where a double tax agreement exists.

5.4.1. Taxation Methods

We look at three main systems of taxation that determine dividends: double taxation, imputation, and split-rate. Other tax systems can be a combination of these.

In a **double taxation system**, corporate pretax earnings are taxed at the corporate level and then taxed again at the shareholder level if they are distributed to taxable shareholders as dividends. Exhibit 4 illustrates double taxation, where the individual tax rate on dividends is an assumed maximum of 15%.

EXHIBIT 4: Double Taxation of Dividends at 15% Personal Tax Rate (per US$100)

	15.0%
Net income before taxes	US$100
Corporate tax rate	35%
Net income after tax	US$65
Dividend assuming 100% payout	US$65
Shareholder tax on dividend	US$9.75
Net dividend to shareholder	US$55.25
Double tax rate on dividend distributions*	44.8%

* Based on pretax income.

Investors will clearly prefer a lower tax rate on dividends, but it is not clear whether they prefer a higher or lower payout. Payout preferences will depend on whether there is a tax on long-term capital gains for shareholders in their country and whether the tax rate on capital gains is higher or lower than the tax rate on dividends. Later, we will discuss a company's decision with respect to the dividend payout ratio.

A second major taxation system is the **dividend imputation tax system**, which effectively ensures that corporate profits distributed as dividends are taxed just once, at the shareholder's tax rate. Australia and New Zealand use a dividend imputation tax system. Under this system, a corporation's earnings are first taxed at the corporate level. When those earnings are distributed to shareholders in the form of dividends, however, shareholders receive a tax credit, known as a **franking credit**, for the taxes that the corporation paid on those distributed earnings (i.e., corporate taxes paid are imputed to the individual shareholder). If the shareholder's marginal tax rate is higher than the company's, the shareholder pays the difference between the two rates. Exhibit 5 shows one variation of a tax imputation system in which a shareholder with a lower marginal tax bracket than the company's actually receives a tax credit for the difference between the corporate rate and his own rate.

EXHIBIT 5: Taxation of Dividends Based on Tax Imputation System (A$)

	Marginal Shareholder Tax Rate	
	15%	47%
Pretax income	A$100	A$100
Taxes at 30% corporate tax rate	30	30
Net income after tax	70	70
Dividend assuming 100% payout	70	70
Shareholder tax on pretax income	15	47
Less tax credit for corporate payment	30	30
Tax due from shareholder	(15)	17
Effective tax rate on dividend	15/100	47/100
	= 15%	= 47%

A **split-rate tax system** is a third taxation system of greater historical than current importance. Under this system, corporate earnings that are distributed as dividends are taxed at a lower rate at the corporate level than earnings that are retained. At the level of the individual investor, dividends are taxed as ordinary income. Earnings distributed as dividends are still taxed twice, but the relatively low corporate tax rate on earnings mitigates that penalty. Exhibit 6 depicts this split-rate tax system for dividends.

EXHIBIT 6: Taxation of Dividends Based on Split-Rate System (per €100)

Pretax earnings	€200
Pretax earnings retained	100
35% tax on retained earnings	35
Pretax earnings allocated to dividends	100
20% tax on earnings allocated to dividends	20
Dividends distributed	80
Shareholder tax rate	35%
After tax dividend to shareholder	$[(1 - 0.35) \times 80] = 52$
Effective tax rate on dividend	$[20\% + (80 \times 0.35)\%] = 48\%$

5.4.2. Shareholder Preference for Current Income versus Capital Gains

All other things being equal, one could expect that the lower an investor's tax rate on dividends relative to his or her tax rate on capital gains, the stronger the investor's preference for dividends. But other issues also impinge on this preference. The investor may buy high-payout shares for a tax-exempt retirement account. Even if dividends are taxed at a lower rate than capital gains, it is not clear that shareholders will necessarily prefer higher dividends. After all, capital gains taxes do not have to be paid until the shares are sold, whereas taxes on dividends must be paid in the year received even if reinvested. In addition, in some countries, such as the United States and Australia, shares held at the time of death benefit from a step-up valuation or tax exemption as of the death date. Finally, tax-exempt institutions, such as pension funds and endowment funds, are major shareholders in most industrial countries. Such institutions are typically exempt from both taxes on dividends and taxes on capital gains. Hence, all other things being equal, they are indifferent as to whether their return comes in the form of current dividends or capital gains.

5.5. Flotation Costs

Another factor that affects a company's dividend policy is flotation cost. Flotation costs include 1) the fees that the company pays (to investment bankers, attorneys, securities regulators, auditors, and others) to issue shares and 2) the possible adverse market price impact from a rise in the supply of shares outstanding. Aggregate flotation costs are proportionally higher (in terms of percentage of gross proceeds) for smaller companies (which issue fewer shares) than for larger companies. Flotation costs make it more expensive for companies to raise new equity capital than to use their own internally generated funds. As a result, many companies try to avoid establishing a level of dividends that would create the need to raise new equity to finance positive NPV projects.

EXAMPLE 8   A Company That Needs to Reinvest All Internally Generated Funds

1. Boar's Head Spirits Ltd., based in the United Kingdom, currently does not pay a dividend on its common shares. Boar's Head has an estimated operating cash flow of £500 million. The company's financial analyst has calculated its cost of capital as 12%. The same analyst has evaluated modernization and expansion projects with a positive NPV that would require £800 million. The cost of positive NPV projects exceeds estimated operating cash flow by £300 million (£800 million – £500 million). Having an above average debt ratio for its industry, Boar's Head is reluctant to increase its long-term debt in the next year. Discuss whether you would expect Boar's Head to initiate a dividend based on the above facts.

Solution:

One would expect Boar's Head would not initiate a dividend. As things stand, internally generated funds, as represented by operating cash flow, are not sufficient to fund positive NPV projects. So, payment of a dividend would be at the expense of rejecting positive NPV projects unless the balance of such projects and the dividend were both financed by debt. Given its concern about debt levels, the company would not be expected to pay a dividend that needs to be financed by debt. Because the company has unfunded positive NPV projects, it could consider issuing new shares to fund those projects. The company, however, would not be expected to issue shares solely for the purpose of paying dividends.

5.6. Contractual and Legal Restrictions

The payment of dividends is often affected by legal or contractual restrictions or rules. In some countries, such as Brazil, the distribution of dividends is legally mandated (with certain exceptions). In other countries (e.g., Canada and the United States) the payment of a dividend not specifically indicated to be a liquidating dividend may be restricted by an **impairment of capital rule**. Such a rule requires that the net value of the remaining assets as shown on the balance sheet be at least equal to some specified amount (related to the company's capital).

Contractual restrictions on the amount of dividends that can be paid are often imposed by bondholders in bond indentures. These restrictions require that the company maintain certain ratios (interest coverage ratios, current ratio, etc.) or fulfill certain conditions before dividend payments can be made. Debt covenants in a bond indenture are a response to the agency problems that exist between shareholders and bondholders and are put in place to limit the ability of the shareholders to expropriate wealth from bondholders. As an extreme example, in the absence of covenants or legal restrictions management could liquidate the company's assets and pay the proceeds to the shareholders as a liquidating dividend, leaving the bondholders with nothing to settle their claims.

If a company has issued preference shares, dividends on common shares may not be paid until preference share dividends are paid. In addition, if the preference dividends are cumulative, then preference dividends that are in arrears must be paid before any common dividend can be paid.

5.7. Factors Affecting Dividend Policy: Summary

Several factors of varying degrees of importance can affect a company's dividend policy. In the following example, we explore how these factors affect the dividend policy of a hypothetical company named Makinasi Appliances Company.

EXAMPLE 9   Makinasi Appliances Company Cuts Its Dividend

1. In September 2018, Makinasi Appliances Company, a hypothetical global home appliances manufacturer, announced it would cut its dividend for the first time in its history. The company, which pays quarterly dividends, said the dividend would be reduced to US$0.70 a share from the US$1.60 paid a year earlier. The 2017 total dividend was US$6.50 a share. The dividend cut ends a 400% cumulative increase in the dividend over 10 years. Faced with plunging global demand for appliances (Makinasi's sales were forecasted to fall 19%) and ongoing competition in the white goods industry, Makinasi was expecting a loss as high as US$32.5 million (operating loss of US$46 million) for fiscal year ending March 2019, compared with the analyst forecasted loss of US$18.3 million for the same period. The company already had a loss of US$28.6 million in fiscal year 2018 (the operating loss was US$30.4 million). Makinasi's plans are to aggressively cut costs: It plans to cut production-related costs by US$18 million and fixed costs by US$21 million. The company has said that the lower dividend is because of the difficulty in maintaining the dividend at its previous level. Board member bonuses have been eliminated, and manager bonuses have been reduced by 40%. Capital spending will be cut by 30% to US$27 million, and R&D spending will be cut by 13.5% to US$24 million.

   The company announced plans to raise capital via a bond issue for up to US$50 million. The national credit rating agency has cut Makinasi's bond rating from A to A–.

   Discuss Makinasi's decision to cut its dividend in light of the factors affecting dividend policy covered in this section.

Solution:
Of the six factors discussed in this section, the *volatility of future earnings* and preservation of *financial flexibility* are the major factors influencing Makinasi's decision to cut its dividend. Paying the full dividend would have lowered Makinasi's liquidity ratios and forced it to raise even more external capital. In addition, paying the full dividend probably would likely have resulted in a more severe downgrade in its bond rating and an increase in the cost of debt financing. Paying the full dividend when faced with huge, larger than expected operating losses also might have sent a signal to

investors that Makinasi was not serious about cutting costs and curtailing losses. *Flotation costs* could also play a role in Makinasi's case. Flotation costs on new equity are typically higher than those on new debt; it is possible that if it paid a dividend of more than US$0.70 a share, it would have to issue new equity in addition to the US $50 million in debt.

6. PAYOUT POLICIES

In the following sections we discuss two types of dividend policies: stable dividend and constant dividend payout ratio policies. A **stable dividend policy** is one in which regular dividends are paid that generally do not reflect short-term volatility in earnings. This type of dividend policy is the most common because managers are very reluctant to cut dividends, as discussed earlier. A **constant dividend payout ratio policy** is the policy of paying out a constant percentage of net income in dividends. In Section 6, we discuss share repurchases as an alternative to the payment of cash dividends.

6.1. Stable Dividend Policy

This dividend policy is the most common. Companies that use a stable dividend policy base dividends on a long-term forecast of sustainable earnings and increase dividends when earnings have increased to a sustainably higher level. Thus, if the long-term forecast for sustainable earnings is slow growth, the dividends would be expected to grow slowly over time, more or less independent of cyclical upward or downward spikes in earnings. If sustainable earnings were not expected to grow over time, however, the corresponding dividends would be level (i.e., not growing). Compared with the constant payout ratio policy, a stable dividend policy typically involves less uncertainty for shareholders about the level of future dividends. This is so because the constant payout ratio policy reflects to a higher degree short-term volatility in earnings and/or in investment opportunities.

Many companies pride themselves on a long record of gradually and consistently increasing dividends. Exhibit 7 shows the record of Gruppo Hera (Hera), an Italian multi-utility company that operates in waste management, water, gas, electricity and central heating distribution, and energy trading and electricity generation. Between 2003 and 2018, dividends per share (DPS) show an upward trajectory. Earning declines during this period were accompanied by stable or increasing dividends, underscoring the company's longer-term stated policy of a stable and growing dividend, irrespective of yearly earnings. Consequently, Hera's payout ratio varies widely, between 52% to 125%, over the period shown. For the long term, Hera's management appeared notably optimistic about earnings prospects. In 2019, they committed to a continuing increase in annual dividends per share from €0.10 up to €0.11 by 2022.

EXHIBIT 7:   Gruppo Hera Earnings and Dividends

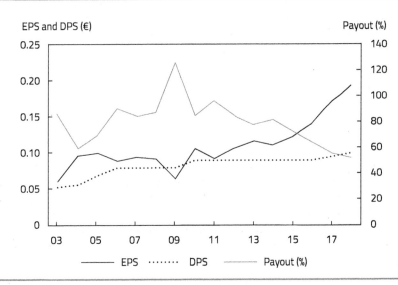

Source: https://eng.gruppohera.it/group/investor_relations/investor_proposition/hera_share/dividends/

As the example shows, dividends over the period were either stable or rising—even while earnings experienced considerable variability.

A stable dividend policy can be modeled as a process of gradual adjustment toward a target payout ratio based on long-term sustainable earnings. A **target payout ratio** is a goal that represents the proportion of earnings that the company intends to distribute (pay out) to shareholders as dividends over the long term.

A model of gradual adjustment (which may be called a "target payout adjustment model") was developed by John Lintner (1956). The model reflects three basic conclusions from his study of dividend policy: 1) Companies have a target payout ratio based on long-term, sustainable earnings; 2) managers are more concerned with dividend changes than with the level of the dividend; and 3) companies will cut or eliminate a dividend only in extreme circumstances or as a last resort.

A simplified version of Lintner's model can be used to show how a company can adjust its dividend. For example, suppose that the payout ratio is below the target payout ratio and earnings are expected to increase. The expected increase in the dividend can be estimated as a function of four variables: expected earnings next year, the target payout ratio, the previous dividend, and the adjustment factor (one divided by the number of years over which the adjustment in dividends should take place). Suppose that the current dividend is US$0.40, the target payout ratio is 50%, the adjustment factor is 0.2 (i.e., the adjustment is to occur over five years), and expected earnings are US$1.50 for the year ahead (an increase from the US$1 value of last year). The expected increase in dividends is US$0.07, as shown here:

Expected increase in dividends
= (Expected earnings × Target payout ratio − Previous dividend) × Adjustment factor
= (US$1.50 × 0.5 − US$0.40) × 0.2
= US$0.07

Therefore, even though earnings increased 50% from US$1.00 to US$1.50, the dividend would only incrementally increase by about 17.5% from US$0.40 to US$0.47.

By using this model, note that if in the following year earnings temporarily fell from US$1.50 to US$1.34, the dividend might well be increased by up to US$0.04 [(US$1.34 × 0.5 – US$0.47) × 0.2 = US$0.04] a share, because the implied new dividend of US$0.51 would still be moving the company toward its target payout ratio of 50%. Even if earnings were to fall further or even experience a loss, the company would be reluctant to cut or eliminate the dividend (unless its estimate of sustainable earnings or target payout ratio were lowered); instead, it would rather opt to maintain the current dividend until future earnings increases justified an increase in the dividend.

EXAMPLE 10   Determining Dividends by Using a Target Payout Adjustment Model

1. Last year Luna Inc. had earnings of US$2.00 a share and paid a regular dividend of US$0.40. For the current year, the company anticipates earnings of US$2.80. It has a 30% target payout ratio and uses a 4-year period to adjust the dividend. Compute the expected dividend for the current year.

Solution:

Expected dividend = Previous dividend + [(Expected earnings × Target payout ratio – Previous dividend) × Adjustment factor)]

  = US$0.40 + [(US$2.80 × 0.3 – US$0.40) × (1/4)]
  = US$0.40 + [(US$0.84 – US$0.40) × (1/4)]
  = US$0.51 dividend, a US$0.11 increase

Thus, although earnings are expected to increase by 40%, the increase in the dividend would be 27.5%. Despite the adjustment process, the payout ratio would fall from 20% (US$0.40/US$2.00) to 18.2% (US$0.51/US$2.80). The firm would move toward its target payout ratio if earnings growth were slower and the adjustment time period were shorter (i.e., the adjustment factor higher).

6.2. Constant Dividend Payout Ratio Policy

In this type of policy, a dividend payout ratio decided on by the company is applied to current earnings to calculate the dividend. With this type of dividend policy, dividends fluctuate with earnings in the short term. Constant dividend payout ratio policies are infrequently adopted in practice. Example 11 illustrates this type of policy with Pampas Fertilizer, a hypothetical company.

EXAMPLE 11   Pampas Fertilizer Changes from a Stable to a Constant Dividend Payout Ratio Policy

Pampas Fertilizer, a hypothetical company, is the leading fertilizer producer in Argentina. Its earnings tend to be highly volatile. Demand for fertilizer is seasonal, typically being higher in summer than in winter. On the supply side, costs are primarily driven by ammonia prices that are subject to business cycle influences and are thus very volatile. In consideration of earnings volatility, Pampas might have difficulty sustaining a steadily rising dividend level. In view of such considerations, Pampas changed its dividend policy from a stable dividend policy to a constant dividend payout ratio policy (called a "variable dividend policy" by management) in its fiscal year 2018. The following is the explanation by the company:

Pampas has paid cash dividends on our common stock since 2003. The annual dividend rate of ARS0.50 per share of common stock, or ARS1.50 per quarter, was paid each fiscal quarter, as shown in the following table, through the second quarter of fiscal year 2018.

Effective 30 November 2017, the company's board of directors approved the use of a variable dividend policy to replace the company's fixed dividend policy. Beginning with the third quarter of fiscal year 2018, Pampas began to pay a dividend to shareholders of its common stock on a quarterly basis for each quarter for which the company reports net income in an amount equal to 25% of such quarterly income.

The board of Pampas implemented the variable dividend policy to more accurately reflect the results of the company's operations while recognizing and allowing for the cyclicality of the fertilizer industry.

Exhibit 8 shows quarterly data for fiscal years 2019 and 2018 in Argentine pesos (ARS).

EXHIBIT 8: Earnings per Share (EPS) and Dividends per Share (DPS) for Pampas Fertilizer (Fiscal Years Ending 31 March)

Fiscal Period	EPS(ARS)	DPS(ARS)
2019:Q4	9.32	2.350
2019:Q3	4.60	1.152
2019:Q2	15.41	3.852
2019:Q1	10.53	2.636
2018:Q4	7.84	1.961
2018:Q3	18.65	4.660
2018:Q2	26.30	1.500
2018:Q1	21.22	1.500

1. From the table, identify the fiscal quarter when Pampas first applied a constant dividend payout ratio policy.

Solution:
Pampas first used that policy in the third quarter of fiscal year 2018. Until then, a quarterly dividend of ARS1.500 was paid irrespective of quarterly earnings. The payout ratios in all subsequent quarters round to approximately 25%.

> 2. Demonstrate that the dividend for 2019:Q4 reflects the stated current dividend policy.
>
> *Solution:*
> (EPS ARS9.32)/4 = ARS2.330, which differs only slightly from the reported dividend of ARS2.350 (EPS are rounded to two decimal places, so rounding error is expected).

6.3. Global Trends in Payout Policy

An interesting question is whether corporations are changing their dividend policies in response to changes in the economic environment and in investor preferences. Dividend policy practices have international differences and change through time, even within one market, consistent with the idea that companies adapt their dividend policy over time to changing investor tastes. Typically, fewer companies in a given US stock market index have paid dividends than have companies in a comparable European stock market index. In some Asian markets, companies have significantly increased their dividend payouts, albeit from a lower base, as these companies and markets mature. In addition, the following broad trends in dividend policy have been observed:

- The fraction of companies paying cash dividends has been in long-term decline in most developed markets (e.g., the United States, Canada, the European Union overall, the United Kingdom, and Japan). In Asia-Pacific, however, the value paid out in annual dividends tripled from 2009 to 2019. In the rest of the world, the value of annual dividend payouts only doubled over the same period.
- Since the early 1980s in the United States and the early 1990s in the United Kingdom and continental Europe, the fraction of companies engaging in share repurchases has trended upward. Since the late 2010s, share repurchases by major companies in Asia, particularly in mainland China and Japan, have been substantial (following a history of little to no prior share repurchase activity).

Research on dividend behavior globally shows that aggregate dividend amounts as well as payout ratios have generally increased over time, although the fraction of dividend payers has decreased. For example, studies using data from around the world substantiate the proportion of cash dividend paying firms declining over the long term, with aggregate dividend payments concentrated in a relatively small number of firms. Post-global financial crisis, there has been some reversal in the long-term downward trend in the fraction of dividend payers and payout ratios. The dividend payers are, on average, larger, more profitable, have fewer growth opportunities, and spend less on R&D compared to the non-dividend payers.

Moreover, researchers have documented internationally a negative relationship between dividend initiations/increases and enhanced corporate governance and transparency (such as mandatory adoption of IFRS rules and enforcement of new insider trading laws). This is consistent with the notion of the decreasing information content of dividends and their reduced signaling role as governance and transparency of markets improves. Similarly, findings show less generous dividend payout policies in countries requiring detailed corporate disclosures and having strong investor protection. The reduction in both information asymmetry and agency issues resulting from improved corporate governance, along with the flexibility offered by share repurchases, appear to explain the long-term decline in dividend payers.

7. SHARE REPURCHASES

A **share repurchase** (or **buyback**) is a transaction in which a company buys back its own shares. Unlike stock dividends and stock splits, share repurchases use corporate cash. Hence, share repurchases can be viewed as an alternative to cash dividends. Shares that have been issued and subsequently repurchased are classified as **treasury shares/stock** if they may be reissued or **canceled shares** if they will be retired; in either case, they are not then considered for dividends, voting, or computing earnings per share.

In contrast to the case of cash dividends, usage or growth in usage of share repurchases has historically required enabling regulation. In the United Kingdom, share repurchases became legal in 1981. They were never explicitly illegal in the United States, but usage became substantial only subsequent to US Securities and Exchange Commission rule 10b–18 in 1982. (That rule protected repurchasing companies from charges of share manipulation if repurchases were conducted consistent with the terms of the rule.) Other markets in continental Europe and Asia have also followed with enabling regulation (e.g., 1995 for Japan, 1998 for Germany and Singapore, 1999 for India and Norway, 2000 for Denmark and Sweden). Share repurchases in many markets remain subject to more restrictions than in the United States. Restrictions include requiring shareholder approval of share repurchase programs, limiting the percent of share repurchases to a certain fraction (often 10%) of outstanding shares, allowable repurchase mechanisms, and other restrictions to protect creditors. In many markets, use of share repurchases is becoming increasingly common.

In general, when an amount of share repurchases is authorized, the company is not strictly committed to following through with repurchasing shares. This situation contrasts with the declaration of dividends, where that action does commit the company to pay the dividends. Another contrast with cash dividends is that whereas cash dividends are distributed to shareholders proportionally to their ownership percentage, share repurchases in general do not distribute cash in such a proportionate manner. For example, if repurchases are executed by a company via buy orders in the open market, cash is effectively being received by only those shareholders with concurrent sell orders.

The next section presents the means by which a company may execute a share repurchase program.

7.1. Share Repurchase Methods

Following are the four main ways that companies repurchase shares, listed in order of importance.

1. **Buy in the open market.** This method of share repurchase is the most common, with the company buying its own shares as conditions warrant in the open market. The open market share repurchase method gives the company maximum flexibility. Open market repurchases are the most flexible option for a company because there is no legal obligation to undertake or complete the repurchase program; a company may not follow through with an announced program for various reasons, such as unexpected cash needs

for liquidity, acquisitions, or capital expenditures. In the United States, open market transactions do not require shareholder approval, whereas in Europe, shareholder approval is required for buybacks. After studying buybacks in 32 countries, findings by Manconi, Peyer, and Vermaelen (2015) suggest that all companies have shareholder authorization in place to allow management the opportunity to buy back undervalued shares in the future. They conclude that the need for shareholder approval does not compensate for poor corporate governance and instead limits management's flexibility to time buybacks to create long-term shareholder value. Authorizations to repurchase stock can last for years. In many shareholders' minds, the announcement of a repurchase policy provides support for the share price. If the share repurchases are competently timed to minimize price impact and to exploit perceived undervaluation in the marketplace, this method is also relatively cost effective.

2. **Buy back a fixed number of shares at a fixed price.** Sometimes a company will make a **fixed price tender offer** to repurchase a specific number of shares at a fixed price that is typically at a premium to the current market price. For example, in Australia, if a stock is selling at A\$37 a share, a company might offer to buy back 5 million shares from current shareholders at A\$40. If shareholders are willing to sell more than 5 million shares, the company will typically buy back a pro rata amount from each shareholder. By setting a fixed date, such as 30 days in the future, a fixed price tender offer can be accomplished quickly.

3. **Dutch auction.** A Dutch auction is also a tender offer to existing shareholders, but instead of specifying a fixed price for a specific number of shares, the company stipulates a range of acceptable prices. A Dutch auction uncovers the minimum price at which the company can buy back the desired number of shares with the company paying that price to all qualifying bids. For example, if the stock price is A\$37 a share, the company would offer to buy back 5 million shares in a range of A\$38 to A\$40 a share. Each shareholder would then indicate the number of shares and the lowest price at which he or she would be willing to sell. The company would then begin to qualify bids beginning with those shareholders who submitted bids at A\$38 and continue to qualify bids at higher prices until 5 million shares had been qualified. In our example, that price might be A\$39. Shareholders who bid between A\$38 and A\$39, inclusive, would then be paid A\$39 per share for their shares. Like Method 2, Dutch auctions can be accomplished in a short time period.

4. **Repurchase by direct negotiation.** In some markets, a company may negotiate with a major shareholder to buy back its shares, often at a premium to the market price. The company may do this to keep a large block of shares from overhanging the market (and thus acting to dampen the share price). A company may try to prevent an "activist" shareholder from gaining representation on the board of directors. In some of the more infamous cases, unsuccessful takeover attempts have ended with the company buying back the would-be suitor's shares at a premium to the market price, referred to as a **greenmail** transaction, often to the detriment of remaining shareholders. Private repurchases can also be made at discounts to the market price, reflecting the relatively weaker negotiating position of large investors with liquidity needs.

Outside the United States and Canada, almost all share repurchases occur in the open market (Method 1). Note that not all the methods listed may be permissible according to local regulations.

EXAMPLE 12   BCII Considers Alternative Methods of Share Repurchase

The board of directors of British Columbia Industries, Inc. (BCII) is considering a 5 million common share repurchase program. BCII has a sizable cash and marketable securities portfolio. BCII's current stock price is C$37. The company's chief financial officer wants to accomplish the share repurchases in a cost-effective manner. Some board members want repurchases accomplished as quickly as possible, whereas other board members mention the importance of flexibility. Discuss the relative advantages of each of the following methods with respect to cost, flexibility, and speed:

1. Open market share repurchases.

Solution:
Open market share repurchases give the company the most flexibility. BCII can time repurchases, making repurchases when the market prices its stock below its perceived intrinsic value. BCII can also change amounts repurchased or even not execute the repurchase program. Open market repurchases are typically made opportunistically, with cost a more important consideration than speed. Because open market repurchases can be conducted so as to minimize any effects on price and can be timed to exploit prices that are perceived to be below intrinsic value, this method is also relatively cost effective.

2. A fixed price tender offer.

Solution:
A fixed price tender offer can be accomplished quickly, but the company usually has to offer a premium. Obviously, this raises the cost of the buyback; however, the premium may provide a positive signal to investors regarding management's view of the value of the stock.

3. Dutch auction tender offer.

Solution:
Dutch auctions generally enable a company to do the buyback at a lower price than with a fixed price tender offer. For example, a fixed price tender offer for 5 million shares at C$40 would cost BCII C$200 million. If the Dutch auction were successful at C$38, the cost would be C$190 million, a savings of C$10 million. Dutch auctions can be accomplished quickly, though usually not as quickly as fixed price tender offers

7.2. Financial Statement Effects of Repurchases

Share repurchases affect both the balance sheet and income statement. Both assets and shareholders' equity decline if the repurchase is made with surplus cash. As a result, leverage increases. Debt ratios (leverage) will increase even more if the repurchase is financed with debt.

On the income statement, fewer shares outstanding could increase earnings per share (i.e., by reducing the denominator) depending on how and at what cost the repurchase is financed. We discuss the effects on the income statement and balance sheet in the following sections.

7.2.1. Changes in Earnings per Share

One rationale for share repurchases often cited by corporate financial officers and some investment analysts is that reducing the number of shares outstanding can increase earnings per share (EPS). Assuming a company's net income does not change, a smaller number of shares after the buyback will produce a higher EPS. If a company's share repurchase is financed by high-cost borrowing, the resulting lower net income can offset the effect of the reduced shares outstanding, producing a lower EPS.

Example 13 and Example 14 show changes in EPS resulting from alternative methods of financing a share repurchase.

EXAMPLE 13   Share Repurchase Using Surplus Cash

1. Takemiya Industries, a Japanese company, has been accumulating cash in recent years with a plan of expanding in emerging Asian markets. Takemiya's management and directors believe that such expansion is no longer practical, and they are considering a share repurchase using surplus cash. Takemiya has 10 million shares outstanding, and its net income is ¥100 million. Takemiya's share price is ¥120. Cash not needed for operations totals ¥240 million and is invested in Japanese government short-term securities that earn close to zero interest. For a share repurchase program of the contemplated size, Takemiya's investment bankers think the stock could be bought in the open market at a ¥20 premium to the current market price, or ¥140 a share. Calculate the impact on EPS if Takemiya uses the surplus cash to repurchase shares at ¥140 per share.

Solution:
First, note that current EPS = (¥100 million net income)/(10 million shares) = ¥10.00. If Takemiya repurchases shares, net income is unchanged at ¥100 million. A share repurchase at ¥140 a share reduces share count by approximately 1.7 million shares (¥240,000,000/¥140) so that 8.3 million shares remain outstanding. Thus, after the share repurchase, EPS should be (¥100 million)/(8.3 million shares) = ¥12.00, approximately. EPS would increase by 20% as a result of the share repurchase. Note that EPS would increase even more if the open market purchases were accomplished at the prevailing market price without the premium.

In the absence of surplus cash and equivalents, companies may fund share repurchases by using long-term debt. Example 14 shows that any increase in EPS is dependent on the company's after-tax borrowing rate on the funds used to repurchase stock.

EXAMPLE 14   Share Repurchases Using Borrowed Funds

Selamat Plantations, Inc., plans to borrow Malaysian ringgit (MYR)12 million, which it will use to repurchase shares. The following information is given:

- Share price at time of share repurchase = MYR60
- Earnings after tax = MYR6.6 million
- EPS before share repurchase = MYR3
- Price/Earnings (P/E) = MYR60/MYR3 = 20
- Earnings yield (E/P) = MYR3/MYR60 = 5%
- Shares outstanding = 2.2 million
- Planned share repurchase = 200,000 shares

1. Calculate the EPS after the share repurchase, assuming the after-tax cost of borrowing is 5%.

Solution:
EPS after buyback = (Earnings – After-tax cost of funds)/Shares outstanding after buyback

   = [MYR6.6 million – (MYR12 million × 0.05)]/2 million shares
   = [MYR6.6 million – (MYR0.6 million)]/2 million shares
   = MYR6.0 million/2 million shares
   = MYR3.00

With the after-tax cost of borrowing at 5%, the share repurchase has no effect on the company's EPS. Note that the stock's earnings yield, the ratio of earnings per share to share price or E/P, was MYR3/MYR60 = 0.05 or 5%, equal to the after-tax cost of debt.

2. Calculate the EPS after the share repurchase, assuming the company's borrowing rate increases to 6% because of the increased financial risk of borrowing the MYR12 million.

Solution:
EPS after buyback = (Earnings – After-tax cost of funds)/Shares outstanding after buyback

   = [MYR6.6 million – (MYR12 million × 0.06)]/2 million shares
   = [MYR6.6 million – (MYR0.72 million)]/2 million shares
   = MYR5.88 million/2 million shares
   = MYR2.94

Note that in this case, the after-tax cost of debt, 6%, is greater than the 5% earnings yield; thus, a reduction in EPS resulted.

In summary, a share repurchase may increase, decrease, or have no effect on EPS. The effect depends on whether the repurchase is financed internally or externally. In the case of internal financing, a repurchase increases EPS only if the funds used for the repurchase would *not* earn their cost of capital if retained by the company. In the case of external financing, the effect on EPS is positive if the earnings yield exceeds the after-tax cost of financing the repurchase. In Example 14, when the after-tax borrowing rate equaled the earnings yield of 5%, EPS was unchanged as a result of the buyback. Any after-tax borrowing rate above the earnings yield would result in a decline in EPS, whereas an after-tax borrowing rate less than the earnings yield would result in an increase in EPS.

These relationships should be viewed with caution so far as any valuation implications are concerned. Notably, to infer that an increase in EPS indicates an increase in shareholders' wealth would be incorrect. For example, the same surplus cash could also be distributed as a cash dividend. Informally, if one views the total return on a stock as the sum of the dividend yield and a capital gains return, any capital gains as a result of the boost to EPS from the share repurchase may be at the expense of an offsetting loss in dividend yield.

7.2.2. Changes in Book Value per Share

Price-to-book value per share is a popular ratio used in equity valuation. The following example shows the impact of a share repurchase on book value per share (BVPS).

EXAMPLE 15   The Effect of a Share Repurchase on Book Value per Share

The market price of both Company A's and Company B's common stock is US$20 a share, and each company has 10 million shares outstanding. Both companies have announced a US$5 million buyback. The only difference is that Company A has a market price per share greater than its book value per share, whereas Company B has a market price per share less than its book value per share:

- Company A has a book value of equity of US$100 million and BVPS of US$100 million/10 million shares = US$10. *The market price per share of US$20 is greater than BVPS of US$10.*
- Company B has a book value of equity of US$300 million and BVPS of US$300 million/10 million shares = US$30. *The market price per share of US$20 is less than BVPS of US$30.*

Both companies:

- buy back 250,000 shares at the market price per share (US$5 million buyback/ US$20 per share = 250,000 shares) and
- are left with 9.75 million shares outstanding (10 million pre-buyback shares – 0.25 million repurchased shares = 9.75 million shares).

After the share repurchase:

- Company A's shareholders' equity at book value falls to US$95 million (US$100 million – US$5 million), and its *book value per share decreases* from US $10 to US$9.74 (shareholders' equity/shares outstanding = US$95 million/ 9.75 million shares = US$9.74).
- Company B's shareholders' equity at book value falls to US$295 million (US$300 million – US$5 million), and its *book value per share increases* from US $30 to US$30.26 (shareholders' equity/shares outstanding = US$295 million/ 9.75 million = US$30.26).

This example shows that when the market price per share is greater than its book value per share, BVPS will decrease after the share repurchase. When the market price per share is less than BVPS, however, BVPS will increase after a share repurchase.

8. VALUATION EQUIVALENCE OF CASH DIVIDENDS AND SHARE REPURCHASE

A share repurchase should be viewed as equivalent to the payment of cash dividends of equal amount in terms of the effect on shareholders' wealth, all other things being equal. "All other things being equal" in this context is shorthand for assumptions that the taxation and information content of cash dividends and share repurchases do not differ. Understanding this baseline equivalence result permits more advanced analysis for when taxation and/or information content do differ between cash dividends and share repurchases. Example 16 demonstrates the claim of equivalence in the "all other things being equal" case.

EXAMPLE 16   The Equivalence of Share Repurchases and Cash Dividends

1. Rohit Chemical Industries, Inc. (RCII) has 10 million shares outstanding with a current market value of Rs200 per share. WCII's board of directors is considering two ways of distributing RCII's current Rs500 million free cash flow to equity. The first method involves paying an irregular or special cash dividend of Rs500 million/10 million = Rs50 per share. The second method involves repurchasing Rs500 million worth of shares. For simplicity, we make the assumptions that dividends are received when the shares go ex-dividend and that any quantity of shares can be bought at the market price of Rs200 per share. We also assume that the taxation and information content of cash dividends and share repurchases, if any, do not differ. How would the wealth of a shareholder be affected by RCII's choice of method in distributing the Rs500 million?

Solution:

Cash Dividend
After the shares go ex-dividend, a shareholder of a single share would have Rs50 in cash (the dividend) and a share worth Rs200 – Rs50 = Rs150. The ex-dividend value of Rs150 can be demonstrated as the market value of equity after the distribution of Rs500 million divided by the (unchanged) number of shares outstanding after the dividend payment, or [(10 million)(Rs200) – Rs500 million]/10 million = Rs1,500 million/10 million = Rs150. Total wealth from ownership of one share is, therefore, Rs50 + Rs150 = Rs200.

Share Repurchase
With Rs500 million, RCII could repurchase Rs500 million/Rs200 = 2.5 million shares. The post-repurchase share price would be unchanged at Rs200, which can be calculated as the market value of equity after the Rs500 million share repurchase divided by the shares outstanding after the share repurchase, or [(10 million) (Rs200) – Rs500 million]/(10 million – 2.5 million) = Rs1,500 million/7.5 million = Rs200. Total wealth from ownership of one share is, therefore, Rs200—exactly the same as in the case of a cash dividend. Whether the shareholder actually sold the share back to RCII in the share repurchase is irrelevant for a shareholder's wealth: If the share was sold, Rs200 in cash would be realized; if the share was not sold, its market value of Rs200 would count equally toward the shareholder's wealth.

The theme of Example 16 is that a company should not expect to create or destroy shareholder wealth merely by its method of distributing money to shareholders (i.e., by share repurchases as opposed to cash dividends). Example 17 illustrates that if a company repurchases shares from an individual shareholder at a negotiated price representing a premium over the market price, the remaining shareholders' wealth is reduced.

EXAMPLE 17   Direct Negotiation: A Share Repurchase That Transfers Wealth

1. AfriCitrus (AC) common shares sell at South African rand (ZAR)200, and there are 10 million shares outstanding. Management becomes aware that Kirk Mzazi recently purchased a major position in its outstanding shares with the intention of influencing the business operations of AC in ways the current board does not approve. An adviser to the board has suggested approaching Mzazi privately with an offer to buy back ZAR500 million worth of shares from him at ZAR250 per share, which is a ZAR50 premium over the current market price. The board of AC declines to do so because of the effect of such a repurchase on AC's other shareholders. Determine the effect of the proposed share repurchase on the wealth of shareholders other than Mzazi.

Solution:
With ZAR500 million, AC could repurchase ZAR500 million/ZAR250 = 2 million shares from Mzazi. The post-repurchase share price would be ZAR187.50, which can be calculated as the market value of equity after the ZAR500 million share repurchase divided by the shares outstanding after the share repurchase, or [(10 million) (ZAR200) - ZAR500 million]/(10 million - 2 million) = ZAR1,500 million/8 million = ZAR1875.50. Shareholders other than Mzazi would lose ZAR200 - ZAR187. 50 = ZAR12.50 for each share owned. Although this share repurchase would conserve total wealth (including Mzazi's), it effectively transfers wealth to Mzazi from the other shareholders.

---

9. THE DIVIDEND VERSUS SHARE REPURCHASE DECISION

The question of the valuation implications of share repurchases and dividends is of great interest to investors. Many investors and corporate managers believe that share repurchases have, on average, a net positive effect on shareholder value Studies have found that share repurchase announcements are accompanied by significant positive excess returns both around the announcement date and for the next two years—and in some studies, five years. An explanation consistent with that finding is that managements tend to buy back their stock when it is undervalued in the marketplace and issue stock when it is overvalued.

Theory concerning the dividend–share repurchase decision generally concludes that share repurchases are equivalent to cash dividends of equal amount in their effect on shareholders' wealth, all other things being equal. Further discussion about the choice revolves around what might not "be equal" and what might cause one distribution mechanism to be preferred over the other. The use of share repurchases also may be legally restricted.

In general, share repurchases can be considered part of a company's broad policy on distributing earnings to shareholders. Also, a company may engage in share repurchases for reasons similar to those mentioned in connection with cash dividends—for example, to distribute free cash flow to equity to common shareholders. A number of additional reasons for share repurchases include the following:

- Potential tax advantages
- Share price support/signaling that the company considers its shares a good investment
- Added managerial flexibility
- Offsetting dilution from employee stock options
- Increasing financial leverage

In jurisdictions that tax shareholder dividends at higher rates than capital gains, share repurchases have a tax advantage over cash dividends. Even if the two tax rates are equal, the option to defer capital gains taxes—by deciding not to participate in the share repurchase—will be valuable to many investors.

Management of a company may view its own shares as undervalued in the marketplace and hence a good investment. Although management's stock market judgment can be just as good or bad as that of any other market participant, corporate management typically does have more information about the company's operation and future prospects than does any outside investor or analyst. Furthermore, share repurchases via open market purchase, the dominant repurchase mechanism, allow management to time share repurchases with respect to market price. The announcement of a share repurchase program is often understood as a positive signal about the company's prospects and attractiveness as an investment. An unexpected announcement of a meaningful share repurchase program can often have the same positive impact on share price as would a better-than-expected earnings report or similar positive event. In the days following the global stock market crash of October 1987, a number of prominent companies announced huge buybacks in an effort to halt the slide in the price of their shares and show confidence in the future. It may have been an important aspect in the stock market recovery that followed. Some investment analysts, however, take issue with the notion that initiation of share repurchases is a positive signal, because a repurchase program could mean that the company has no new profitable investment opportunities and is thus returning cash to shareholders.

Unlike regular cash dividends, share repurchase programs appear not to create the expectation among investors of continuance in the future. Furthermore, in contrast to an announced dividend, the announcement of a share repurchase by open market purchase does not typically create an obligation to follow through with repurchases. Additionally, the timing of share repurchases via open market activity is at managers' discretion. Share repurchases also afford shareholders flexibility because participation is optional, which is not the case with the receipt of cash dividends.

For some companies, share repurchases are used to offset the possible dilution of earnings per share that may result from the exercise of employee stock options. Whether stated or not, many companies try to repurchase at least as many shares as were issued in the exercise of stock options—even though the options are typically exercised at lower prices than the repurchase price.

Another reason for repurchasing shares is to modify the company's capital structure because share repurchases can be used to increase leverage. Share buybacks funded by newly issued debt increase leverage more than those funded by surplus cash.

Among other reasons mentioned for share repurchases by corporate managers is the objective of increasing EPS. This objective, however, is problematic for two reasons. First, even when share repurchases result in an EPS increase, the required rate of return will likely increase, reflecting higher leverage. Second, according to finance theory, changing EPS by changing the number of shares outstanding does not affect shareholder wealth given that total free cash flow is unchanged.

EXAMPLE 18   Share Repurchase to Increase Financial Leverage

Deira Oasis Holdings Inc. (DOHI), with debt and a debt ratio of United Arab Emirates durham (AED)30 million and 30%, respectively, plans a share repurchase program involving AED7 million or 10% of the market value of its common shares.

1. Assuming nothing else changes, what debt ratio would result from financing the repurchases using cash on hand?

Solution:
Assuming nothing else changes, if DOHI uses cash on hand to make the share repurchase, the debt ratio would increase to 32% (AED30 million/AED93 million = 0.3226 or 32.3%).

2. Assuming nothing else changes, what debt ratio would result from financing the repurchases using new debt?

Solution:
Assuming nothing else changes, if DOHI uses debt to finance the share repurchase, the debt ratio would increase to 37% (AED37 million/AED100 million = 0.3700 or 37.0%).

3. Discuss the effect on value of equity from financing the repurchases using cash on hand, assuming DOHI's net income and P/E remain the same.

Solution:
After repurchase, DOHI's equity stands at AED63 million. However, with the same net income and fewer shares outstanding, its EPS would increase. Then, with the same P/E, DOHI's market value of equity would be expected to increase above AED63 million.

4. Discuss the effect on value of equity from financing the repurchases using new debt, assuming DOHI's after-tax cost of debt is greater than its E/P, which remains the same.

Solution:
After repurchase, DOHI's equity stands at AED63 million. However, with the after-tax cost of debt exceeding the E/P, its EPS would decrease. Then, with the same P/E, DOHI's market value of equity would be expected to decrease below AED63 million.

5. Discuss the effect on value of debt from financing the repurchases using new debt, assuming the conditions in question 4 and knowing that DOHI is in imminent danger of a credit rating downgrade.

Solution:
After repurchase, DOHI's debt stands at AED37 million. However, with the real threat of a credit rating downgrade, spreads for DOHI's debt versus government treasuries would widen. Then, DOHI's market value of debt would be expected to decrease below AED37 million.

Note that with the assumptions in questions 4 and 5, the post-repurchase market values of both equity and debt would be expected to decrease. Therefore, the proportion of each in DOHI's post-repurchase capital structure is indeterminate based on the information given.

Exhibit 9 shows the results. By either means of financing the share repurchase, financial leverage increases.

EXHIBIT 9: Estimated Impact on Capital Structure (AED millions)

| | Before Buyback | | After Buyback | | | |
| | | | All Cash | | All Debt | |
	AED	%	AED	%	AED	%
Debt	30	30	30	32	37	37
Equity (at market)	70	70	63	68	63	63
Total Cap	100	100	93	100	100	100

Deira Oasis Holdings' beginning debt ratio was 30%. If Deira Oasis Holdings uses borrowed funds to repurchase equity, the debt ratio at market value will increase to 37%, which is significantly more than if it used excess cash (32%).

EXAMPLE 19   ITOCHU Corporation Announces Share Buyback to Improve ROE

1. In October 2018, ITOCHU Corporation, a leading Japanese *sogo shosha* (general trading company), reported that in order to improve its return on equity (ROE) it would repurchase shares by fiscal year-end March 2019 to achieve a target medium-to-long-term ROE of 13% or higher. Accordingly, ITOCHU said it could repurchase shares in the amount up to ¥30 billion. In February 2019, ITOCHU announced it was increasing its share repurchase target up to ¥100 billion. ITOCHU repurchases in these first two tranches are shown in Exhibit 10.

EXHIBIT 10: Share Buyback Activities, October 2018 to March 2019

Period	Shares Repurchased	Average Price (¥)	Total Value (¥)
December 2018–January 2019	15,097,200	1,987	30 billion
February–March 2019	19,024,200	1.997	38 billion
Sum	**34,121,400**	**1,993**	**68 billion**

Source: Annual Report 2019 (online version), ITOCHU Corporation: https://www.itochu.co.jp/en/ir/ financial_statements/2020/__icsFiles/afieldfile/2019/08/09/20_1st_03_e.pdf.

ITOCHU was followed by many other large Japanese companies—including SoftBank, Sony, Haseko, Tokyo Tatemono, and Toppan Printing. Also in February 2019, these companies announced large share buyback programs to improve ROE in response to shareholder activist pressure to improve shareholder returns and governance.

A company can use both special cash dividends and share repurchases as a supplement to regular cash dividends. These means of distributing cash are often used in years when there are large and extraordinary increases in cash flow that are not expected to continue in future years. In making these types of payments, the company essentially communicates that the distribution, like the increase in cash flow, should not be expected to continue in the future. In this context, a share repurchase is effectively an alternative to paying a special cash dividend.

Some companies initiate payouts to shareholders using share repurchases rather than cash dividends. As with the case of a share repurchase substituting for a special cash dividend, the use of share repurchases is again with the expectation that it will not be viewed as creating a fixed commitment.

Although all of the preceding can be the stated or unstated reasons for share repurchases, in general, share repurchases increase when the economy is strong and companies have more cash. During recessions, when cash is often short, share repurchases typically fall. From the fourth quarter of 2004 to the fourth quarter of 2008, the 500 companies in the S&P 500 spent US $1.8 trillion on share repurchases as compared with US$2 trillion on capital expenditures and US$1 trillion on cash dividends. In the market crash of 2008–2009, share repurchases plummeted. Major companies (particularly in the global financial sector) that had made large share repurchases encountered challenges to their financial viability in 2008 and 2009. This caused them to abandon their share repurchases and then to drastically curtail, or even eliminate, their dividends. The predominance of large US banks abandoning their share repurchase programs following the 2008 global financial crisis is shown in Exhibit 11.

EXHIBIT 11: Historical Example: Share Repurchases and Dividends for Several Large US Banks

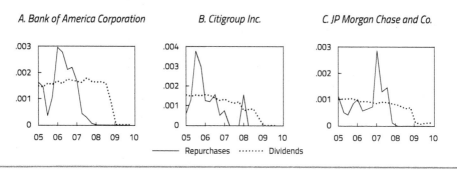

Source: Hirtle (2016).

The curtailing of share repurchases following the 2008 global financial crisis was a general occurrence; it was not restricted to the banking sector. As can be seen in Exhibit 12, data for the companies in the Russell 1000 Index, a broader US stock index than the S&P 500, show that share repurchases grew at almost twice the rate of cash dividends between 2000 and 2007, 25.0% compared to 13.0%. However, during the financial crisis of 2008–2009, companies cut back sharply on their discretionary share repurchases, from US$680 billion to US$223 billion, because many faced shrinking operating cash flows or even financial distress. Although cash dividends were also cut, the decline was much less considerable (US$286 billion to US$262 billion). By 2015, corporate operating cash flows had recovered to the point where total distributions (cash dividends plus share repurchases) reached US$1,102 billion, surpassing their previous peak of US$966 billion in 2007. Share repurchases increased nearly three times from their 2009 levels to reach US$650 billion. However, cash dividends reached US$452 billion, or over 40% of total distributions; this compares to slightly less than 30% of total distributions (US$286 billion/US$966 billion) in 2007. The higher proportion of dividends in total distributions may reflect investors' increased appetite for dividend yield during the extended period of low (or even negative) interest rates on many fixed-income securities that has prevailed in many developed countries since the end of the financial crisis.

EXHIBIT 12: Historical Example: Share Repurchases and Cash Dividends: Russell 1000 Companies (2000 to 2015)

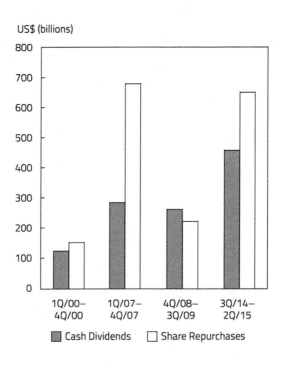

Time Period	Cash Dividends*	Share Repurchases	CAGR Cash Dividends	CAGR Repurchases
	(US$ billions)		(Base Year is 2000)	
1Q2000–4Q2000	126	152	—	—
1Q2007–4Q2007	286	680	13.0%	25.0%
4Q2008–3Q2009	262	223	9.0%	4.0%
3Q2014–2Q2015	452	650	10.0%	11.0%

* Includes special dividends.
Source: JP Morgan, "2015 Distribution Policy" (September 2015).

Example 20, in which a hypothetical company's board of directors initiates a cash dividend, integrates a number of themes related to cash dividends, stock dividends (in which additional shares are distributed to shareholders instead of cash), and share repurchases.

EXAMPLE 20   Shenzhen Medical Devices' Dividend Policy Decision

Shenzhen Medical Devices Ltd. (SMDL) is a hypothetical company based in Shenzhen, China. SMDL is emerging as a leader in providing medical testing equipment to the pharmaceutical and biotechnology industries. SMDL's primary markets are growing, and the company is spending ¥100 million a year on research and development to enhance its competitive position. SMDL is highly profitable and has substantial positive free cash flow after funding positive NPV projects. During the past three years, SMDL has made significant share repurchases. Subsequent to the removal of tax on cash dividends from shares held more than a year in mainland China, SMDL management is proposing the initiation of a cash dividend. The first dividend is proposed to be an annual dividend of ¥0.40 a share to be paid during the next fiscal year. Based on estimated earnings per share of ¥3.20, this dividend would represent a payout ratio (DPS/EPS) of 0.125 or 12.5%. The proposal that will be brought before the board of directors is the following:

"Proposed: Shenzhen Medical Devices Ltd. will institute a program of cash dividends. The first dividend will be an annual dividend of ¥0.40 a share, to be paid at a time to be determined during the next fiscal year. Thereafter, an annual dividend will be paid, equal to or above this amount, consistent with the intention of reaching a target payout ratio of 25% in line with management's expectation for long-term sustainable earnings—thereby retaining funds sufficient to finance profitable capital projects."

The company's board of directors will formally consider the dividend proposal at its next meeting in one month's time. Although some directors favor the dividend initiation proposal, other directors, led by Director Z, are skeptical of it. Director Z has stated:

"The initiation of a cash dividend will suggest to investors that SMDL is no longer a growth company."

As a counterproposal, Director Z has offered his support for the initiation of an annual 2% stock dividend. Director W, a director who is neutral to both the cash dividend and stock dividend ideas, has told Director Z the following:

"A 2% stock dividend will not affect the wealth of our shareholders."

Exhibit 13 presents selected *pro forma* financials of SMDL, if the directors approve the initiation of a cash dividend.

EXHIBIT 13: Shenzhen Medical Devices Ltd. Pro Forma Financial Data Assuming Cash Dividend (¥ millions)

Income Statement		Statement of Cash Flows	
Sales	1,200	Cash flow from operations	135
Earnings before taxes	155	Cash flow from investing activities	(84)
Taxes	35	Cash flow from financing activities	
Net income	120	Debt repayment	(4)
		Share repurchase	(32)
		Proposed dividend	(15)
		Estimated change in cash	0

Ratios		Five-Year Forecasts	
Current ratio	2.1	Sales growth	8% annually
Debt/Equity (at market)	0.27	Earnings growth	11% annually
Interest coverage	10.8x	Projected cost of capital	10%
ROA	10.0%		
ROE	19.3%		
P/E	20x		
E/P	5.0%		

Using the information provided, address the following:

1. Critique Director Z's statement.

Solution:
The following points argue against the thesis of Director Z's statement:

- As discussed in the text, dividend initiations and increases are on average associated with higher future earnings growth.
- Forecasted sales and earnings growth rates are relatively high.
- SMDL still has considerable positive NPV projects available to it, as shown by the cash flow from investing activities of negative ¥84 million. This fact is consistent with SMDL being a company with substantial current growth opportunities.
- For the past three years, SMDL has been making share repurchases, so investors are already cognizant that management is distributing cash to shareholders. The initiation of a dividend as a continuation of that policy is less likely to be interpreted as an information signaling event.

2. Justify Director W's statement.

Solution:

A stock dividend has no effect on shareholder wealth. A shareholder owns the same percentage of the company and its earnings as it did before the stock dividend. All other things being equal, the price of a stock will decline to reflect the stock dividend, but the decline will be exactly offset by the greater number of shares owned.

3. Identify and explain the dividend policy that the proposed ¥0.40 a share cash dividend reflects.

Solution:

As shown in the statement of cash flows, the ¥0.40 a share annual dividend reflects a total amount of ¥15 million, fully using SMDL's free cash flow after acceptance of positive NPV projects. However, the proposal brought before the board also states a commitment to maintain the annual dividend at ¥0.40 a share (or greater), as a stable dividend policy would typically imply. Further, the proposal refers to a target payout ratio based on long-term sustainable earnings. These facts taken together are most consistent with a stable dividend policy based on a target payout adjustment model. (The relatively low target payout ratio of 25% of long-term sustainable earnings allows for sufficient funding of profitable capital projects, suitable for maintaining growth as a pharmaceutical company.)

10. ANALYSIS OF DIVIDEND SAFETY

The global recession that began in late 2007 gave rise to the largest number of dividend cuts and suspensions since the Great Depression of the 1930s. By mid-2009, S&P 500 dividends for US companies were down by 25% from the prior year, and, as indicated earlier in Exhibit 13, by 3Q 2009 dividends for companies in the broader Russell 1000 index declined by over 8% from 2007 levels. Other markets experienced similar dividend cuts following the global financial crisis; for example, UK companies reduced dividends by 15% and Australian companies by 9% in 2009. In this section, we discuss how an analyst can form a judgment on the likelihood that a company's cash dividend may be cut.

The traditional way of looking at dividend safety is the dividend payout ratio (dividends/ net income) and its inverse, the **dividend coverage ratio** (net income/dividends). A higher dividend payout ratio or a lower dividend coverage ratio tends to indicate, all else equal, higher risk of a dividend cut. The logic is that with a relatively high dividend payout ratio, a relatively small percentage decline in earnings could cause the dividend not to be payable out of earnings.

EXAMPLE 21   Traditional Measures of Dividend Safety

1. Given the following data, calculate the dividend payout and coverage ratios:

Mature European SA	FY2019
Net income available for common stock	€100 million
Dividends paid	€40 million

Solution:

Dividend payout ratio	40/100 = 40%
Dividend coverage ratio	100/40 = 2.5x

In judging these ratios, various generalizations may be stated based on observed practice. In stating these generalizations, we emphasize that they should be confirmed for the particular market and time period being addressed.

Small, young companies generally do not pay dividends, preferring to reinvest internally for growth. However, as such companies grow, they typically initiate dividends and their payout ratios tend to increase over time. Large mature companies often target dividend payout ratios of 40% to 60% so that dividend coverage ratios range from about 1.7x to 2.5x, excluding "extra" payments. Mature companies are expected to be in this range over the course of a 5- to 10-year business cycle. Higher dividend payout ratios (or lower dividend coverage ratios) often constitute a risk factor that a dividend may be cut if earnings decline. High dividend payout ratios in relation to those of peer group companies may also point to dividend safety concerns. When a dividend coverage ratio drops to 1.0, the dividend is considered to be in jeopardy unless non-recurring events, such as an employee strike or a typhoon, are responsible for a temporary decline in earnings. In judging safety, qualitative pluses are awarded for companies that have had stable or increasing dividends, while minuses accrue to companies that have reduced their dividend in the past. Indeed, concerning this issue, Graham et al. (1962) stated that "[t]he absence of rate reduction in the past record is perhaps as important as the presence of numerous rate advances."

Free cash flow to equity represents the cash flow available for distribution as dividends after taking account of working and fixed capital expenditure needs. If those needs are ignored, distribution of dividends may be at cross-purposes with shareholder wealth maximization. Cash flow—specifically, free cash flow to equity (FCFE)—not reported net income, should be viewed as the source of cash dividend payments from that perspective. Thus, analysis of dividend safety can properly include payout and coverage ratios based on FCFE rather than net income. Other cash flow definitions besides FCFE have also been used in such ratios. Examining the correlation of dividends with cash flow measures may also provide insights.

Payouts should be considered in terms of share repurchases as well as dividends because they both represent cash distributions to shareholders. Arguably, a comprehensive measure of dividend safety would relate FCFE to both cash dividends and share repurchases:

FCFE coverage ratio = FCFE/[Dividends + Share repurchases].

If that ratio is 1, the company is returning all available cash to shareholders. If it is significantly greater than 1, the company is improving liquidity by using funds to increase cash and/or marketable securities. A ratio significantly less than 1 is not sustainable because the company is paying out more than it can afford by drawing down existing cash/marketable securities, thereby decreasing liquidity. At some point the company will have to raise new equity or cut back on capital spending.

Fundamental risk factors with regard to dividend safety include above-average financial leverage. Additional issuance of debt, whether to fund projects or to finance the dividend, may be restricted during business downturns.

Example 22 shows an analysis of dividend sustainability for Lygon Resources Ltd. (Lygon), a hypothetical company that is one of the world's largest producers of fertilizer products. The analysis includes the traditional earnings/dividend coverage approach and an alternative FCFE approach that considers total cash payouts to shareholders—dividends and share repurchases.

EXAMPLE 22   Lygon's Coverage Ratios

Lygon Resources Ltd. is a lithium miner and producer with operations in Australia, South America, and South Africa, and export markets worldwide. The company has paid dividends since 1995. Exhibit 14 shows financial information for the company.

EXHIBIT 14: Lygon Resources

Years Ending 31 December (A$ millions)	2015	2016	2017	2018
Net income (earnings)	540	458	399	341
Cash flow from operations	837	824	679	628
FCInv (capital expenditures)	554	417	296	327
Net borrowing	(120)	(39)	79	(7)
Dividends paid	121	256	277	323
Stock repurchases	0	105	277	0

1. Using the above information, calculate the following for 2015, 2016, 2017, and 2018:
   A. Dividend/earnings payout ratio.
   B. Earnings/dividend coverage ratio.
   C. Free cash flow to equity (FCFE).
   D. FCFE/[Dividend + Stock repurchase] coverage ratio.

Solution:

A. Dividend/earnings payout = A\$121/A\$540 = 0.224 or 22.4% in 2015; A\$256/A\$458 = 0.559 or 55.9% in 2016; 0.694 or 69.4% in 2017; and 0.947 or 94.7% in 2018.

B. Earnings/dividend coverage = A$540/A$121 = 4.46x in 2015; A$458/A$256 = 1.79x in 2016; 1.44x in 2017; and 1.06x in 2018.

C. FCFE = Cash flow from operations (CFO) – FCInv + Net borrowing = A$837 – A$554 + (A$120) = A$163 in 2015; A$824 – A$417 + (A$39) = A$368 in 2016; A$462 in 2017; and A$294 in 2018.

D. FCFE coverage of dividends + Share repurchases = FCFE/[Dividends + Stock repurchases] = A$163/(A$121 + 0) = 1.35x in 2015, and A$368/(A$256 + A$105) = 1.02x in 2016. Similar calculations result in 0.83x in 2017 and 0.91x in 2018.

These results are summarized in Exhibit 15.

EXHIBIT 15: Lygon Resources Coverage Ratios

Years Ending 31 December	2015	2016	2017	2018
A. Dividend-to-earnings payout ratio	22.4%	55.9%	69.4%	94.7%
B. Earnings-to-dividend coverage ratio (x)	4.46	1.79	1.44	1.06
C. Free cash flow to equity (FCFE) (mil.)	163	368	462	294
D. FCFE/[div. + stock repurch.] cover. (x)	1.35	1.02	0.83	0.91

2. Discuss the trends in earnings/dividend coverage and in FCFE/[Dividend + Stock repurchase] coverage.

Solution:
Although earnings/dividend coverage was nearly 4.5x in 2015, it declined steadily over the four years. By 2018, accounting earnings were just sufficient to pay the dividend (1.06x earnings-to-dividend coverage ratio). An analyst who looked at this metric should have suspected problems.

The FCFE coverage ratio was 1.35x in 2015, a year before the stock repurchase program began. In 2016, the FCFE coverage of dividends and stock repurchases declined to 1.02x. Lower capital expenditures were offset by increased dividends and the new stock repurchase program. Despite declining capital expenditures and positive net borrowings, the FCFE coverage ratio continued to fall substantially to 0.83x in 2017 as the company elected to increase distributions to shareholders. Despite completing the stock repurchase program the previous year, by 2018 FCFE had deteriorated so much that FCFE coverage of dividends was still less than 1.0x (0.91x).

3. Comment on the sustainability of Lygon's dividend and stock repurchase policy after 2017/2018.

Solution:
With the FCFE coverage ratio falling to 0.83x in 2017, management likely realized that it was not prudent to undertake any new discretionary stock repurchases. By 2018, net income was still declining and FCFE coverage of the dividend at less than 1.0x meant that management should probably consider cutting the dividend.

The deterioration over time of Lygon's earnings/dividend coverage and FCFE coverage (of dividends and stock repurchases) was clear. There may be other instances when the earnings-to-dividend coverage ratio declines but still appears healthy. This is why it is important for analysts to closely examine the level and trend of the FCFE coverage ratio and the components of FCFE. Analysts should be particularly alert to companies that support their dividends and stock repurchases by reducing productive capital spending or by adding net debt or by some combination of the two because these neither are sustainable policies.

Whether based on a company's net income or free cash flow, past financial data do not always predict dividend safety. Surprise factors and other unexpected events can confound the most rigorous analysis of past data. Equity and debt markets were shaken in 2008–2009 by the losses taken by almost all US and European banks. These losses led to the cutting and, in some cases, virtual elimination of cash dividends. Not all 21st century investors would agree with Graham et al.'s 1962 assertion that "for the vast majority of common stocks, the dividend record and prospects have always been the most important factor controlling investment quality and value." But most investors would agree that when the market even begins to suspect a decrease or suspension of a company's cash dividend, that expectation is likely to weigh unfavorably on that company's common stock valuation. Therefore, many analysts look for external stock market indicators of market expectations of dividend cuts.

Extremely high dividend yields in comparison with a company's past record and forward-looking earnings is often another warning signal that investors are predicting a dividend cut. For example, the dividend yield on Singapore-listed telecoms company StarHub shares was 9.4% just prior to its fixed-to-variable dividend cut in 2019. After the announced dividend cut to a variable 80% of net profit for 2019 onwards, StarHub shares were still projected to yield about 5.6%, relatively high compared to its yield in recent years prior to the fixed dividend (which were generally about 5%). At the time, shareholder equity value was anticipated to go to zero by 2020 if the fixed dividend continued. In such cases, investors bid down the price of shares such that after the expected cut the expected total return on the shares remains adequate.

The observations of Madden (2008) support an attitude of caution with respect to very high dividend yields. Madden examined yields for the 1,963 stocks in the MSCI World Index. His company classified 865 companies out of the 1,963 companies as a "High Dividend Universe" (HDU). In the early months of the economic decline, Madden found that 78.6% of the companies in the HDU had questionable ability to maintain their dividend payments as compared with 30.7% of all the companies in the MCSI World Index. This point is supported by more recent evidence. Research using data for the S&P 500 Index stocks from 2005 to 2015 shows that the top 5% of dividend-yielding stocks accounted for over 8% of the bottom decile of performance. This over-representation of very high dividend-yielding stocks in the bottom decile of performance is likely attributable to deteriorating corporate fundamentals resulting in non-sustainable dividends. Similarly, in 2016 analysts became concerned that many European companies' dividends were unsustainable because they were paying out the highest proportion of their earnings as dividends in decades (a 60% payout ratio) at a time when their earnings were declining. This caused some companies to change their policies and cut dividends for future reinvestment and balance sheet improvement.

11. SUMMARY

A company's cash dividend payment and share repurchase policies constitute its payout policy. Both entail the distribution of the company's cash to its shareholders affect the form in which shareholders receive the return on their investment. Among the points this chapter has made are the following:

- Dividends can take the form of regular or irregular cash payments, stock dividends, or stock splits. Only cash dividends are payments to shareholders. Stock dividends and splits merely carve equity into smaller pieces and do not create wealth for shareholders. Reverse stock splits usually occur after a stock has dropped to a very low price and do not affect shareholder wealth.
- Regular cash dividends—unlike irregular cash dividends, stock splits, and stock dividends—represent a commitment to pay cash to stockholders on a quarterly, semiannual, or annual basis.
- There are three general theories on investor preference for dividends. The first, MM, argues that given perfect markets dividend policy is irrelevant. The second, "bird in hand" theory, contends that investors value a dollar of dividends today more than uncertain capital gains in the future. The third theory argues that in countries in which dividends are taxed at higher rates than capital gains, taxable investors prefer that companies reinvest earnings in profitable growth opportunities or repurchase shares so they receive more of the return in the form of capital gains.
- An argument for dividend irrelevance given perfect markets is that corporate dividend policy is irrelevant because shareholders can create their preferred cash flow stream by selling the company's shares ("homemade dividends").
- Dividend declarations may provide information to current and prospective shareholders regarding management's confidence in the prospects of the company. Initiating a dividend or increasing a dividend sends a positive signal, whereas cutting a dividend or omitting a dividend typically sends a negative signal. In addition, some institutional and individual shareholders see regular cash dividend payments as a measure of investment quality.
- Payment of dividends can help reduce the agency conflicts between managers and shareholders, but it also can worsen conflicts of interest between shareholders and debtholders.
- Empirically, several factors appear to influence dividend policy, including investment opportunities for the company, the volatility expected in its future earnings, financial flexibility, tax considerations, flotation costs, and contractual and legal restrictions.
- Under double taxation systems, dividends are taxed at both the corporate and shareholder level. Under tax imputation systems, a shareholder receives a tax credit on dividends for the tax paid on corporate profits. Under split-rate taxation systems, corporate profits are taxed at different rates depending on whether the profits are retained or paid out in dividends.
- Companies with outstanding debt often are restricted in the amount of dividends they can pay because of debt covenants and legal restrictions. Some institutions require that a company pay a dividend to be on their "approved" investment list. If a company funds capital expenditures by borrowing while paying earnings out in dividends, it will incur flotation costs on new debt issues.
- Using a stable dividend policy, a company tries to align its dividend growth rate to the company's long-term earnings growth rate. Dividends may increase even in years when earnings decline, and dividends will increase at a lower rate than earnings in boom years.
- A stable dividend policy can be represented by a gradual adjustment process in which the expected dividend is equal to last year's dividend per share plus [(Expected earnings × Target payout ratio - Previous dividend) × Adjustment factor].

- Using a constant dividend payout ratio policy, a company applies a target dividend payout ratio to current earnings; therefore, dividends are more volatile than with a stable dividend policy.
- Share repurchases, or buybacks, most often occur in the open market. Alternatively, tender offers occur at a fixed price or at a price range through a Dutch auction. Shareholders who do not tender increase their relative position in the company. Direct negotiations with major shareholders to get them to sell their positions are less common because they could destroy value for remaining stockholders.
- Share repurchases made with excess cash have the potential to increase earnings per share, whereas share repurchases made with borrowed funds can increase, decrease, or not affect earnings per share depending on the company's after-tax borrowing rate and earnings yield.
- A share repurchase is equivalent to the payment of a cash dividend of equal amount in its effect on total shareholders' wealth, all other things being equal.
- If the buyback market price per share is greater (less) than the book value per share, then the book value per share will decrease (increase).
- Companies can repurchase shares in lieu of increasing cash dividends. Share repurchases usually offer company management more flexibility than cash dividends by not establishing the expectation that a particular level of cash distribution will be maintained.
- Companies can pay regular cash dividends supplemented by share repurchases. In years of extraordinary increases in earnings, share repurchases can substitute for special cash dividends.
- On the one hand, share repurchases can signal that company officials think their shares are undervalued. On the other hand, share repurchases could send a negative signal that the company has few positive NPV opportunities.
- Analysts are interested in how safe a company's dividend is, specifically whether the company's earnings and, more importantly, its cash flow are sufficient to sustain the payment of the dividend.
- Early warning signs of whether a company can sustain its dividend include the dividend coverage ratio, the level of dividend yield, whether the company borrows to pay the dividend, and the company's past dividend record.

12. PRACTICE PROBLEMS

1. The payment of a 10% stock dividend by a company will result in an increase in that company's:
   A. current ratio.
   B. financial leverage.
   C. contributed capital.

2. If a company's common shares trade at very low prices, that company would be *most likely* to consider the use of a:
   A. stock split.
   B. stock dividend.
   C. reverse stock split.

3. In a recent presentation, Doug Pearce made two statements about dividends:

Statement 1   "A stock dividend will increase share price on the ex-dividend date, all other things being equal."

Statement 1   "One practical concern with a stock split is that it will reduce the company's price-to-earnings ratio."

Are Pearce's two statements about the effects of the stock dividend and stock split correct?
A. No for both statements.
B. Yes for Statement 1, and no for Statement 2.
C. No for Statement 1, and yes for Statement 2.

4. All other things being equal, the payment of an internally financed cash dividend is *most likely* to result in:
A. a lower current ratio.
B. a higher current ratio.
C. the same current ratio.

The following information relates to questions 5–9

John Ladan is an analyst in the research department of an international securities firm. Ladan is currently analyzing Yeta Products, a publicly traded global consumer goods company located in the United States. Selected data for Yeta are presented in Exhibit 1.

EXHIBIT 1: Selected Financial Data for Yeta Products

Most Recent Fiscal Year		Current	
Pretax income	US$280 million	Shares outstanding	100 million
Net income after tax	US$182 million	Book value per share	US$25.60
Cash flow from operations	US$235 million	Share price	US$20.00
Capital expenditures	US$175 million		
Earnings per share	US$1.82		

Yeta currently does not pay a dividend, and the company operates with a target capital structure of 40% debt and 60% equity. However, on a recent conference call, Yeta's management indicated that they are considering four payout proposals:

Proposal #1: Issue a 10% stock dividend.
Proposal #2: Repurchase US$40 million in shares using surplus cash.
Proposal #3: Repurchase US$40 million in shares by borrowing US$40 million at an after-tax cost of borrowing of 8.50%.
Proposal #4: Initiate a regular cash dividend.

5. The implementation of Proposal #1 would generally lead to shareholders:
A. having to pay tax on the dividend received.
B. experiencing a decrease in the total cost basis of their shares.
C. having the same proportionate ownership as before implementation.

6. If Yeta's management implemented Proposal #2 at the current share price shown in Exhibit 1, Yeta's book value per share after implementation would be *closest* to:
   A. US$25.20.
   B. US$25.71.
   C. US$26.12.

7. Based on Exhibit 1, if Yeta's management implemented Proposal #3 at the current share price, earnings per share would:
   A. decrease.
   B. remain unchanged.
   C. increase.

8. Based on Yeta's target capital structure, Proposal #4 will *most likely:*
   A. increase the default risk of Yeta's debt.
   B. increase the agency conflict between Yeta's shareholders and managers.
   C. decrease the agency conflict between Yeta's shareholders and bondholders.

9. The implementation of Proposal #4 would *most likely* signal to Ladan and other investors that future earnings growth can be expected to:
   A. decrease.
   B. remain unchanged.
   C. increase.

10. Match the phrases in Column A with the corresponding dividend theory in Column B. Note that you may use the answers in Column B more than once.

Column A	Column B
1. Bird in the hand	a) Dividend policy matters
2. Homemade dividends	b) Dividend policy is irrelevant
3. High tax rates on dividends	

11. Which of the following assumptions is *not* required for Miller and Modigliani's (MM) dividend theory?
    A. Shareholders have no transaction costs when buying and selling shares.
    B. There are no taxes.
    C. Investors prefer dividends over uncertain capital gains.

12. Sophie Chan owns 100,000 shares of PAT Company. PAT is selling for €40 per share, so Chan's investment is worth €4,000,000. Chan reinvests the gross amount of all dividends received to purchase additional shares. Assume that the clientele for PAT shares consists of tax-exempt investors. If PAT pays a €1.50 dividend, Chan's new share ownership after reinvesting dividends at the ex-dividend price is *most likely* to be closest to:
    A. 103,600.
    B. 103,750.
    C. 103,900.

13. Which of the following is *most likely* to signal negative information concerning a company?
    A. Share repurchase.
    B. Decrease in the quarterly dividend rate.
    C. A two-for-one stock split.

14. WL Corporation is located in a jurisdiction that has a 40% corporate tax rate on pretax income and a 30% personal tax rate on dividends. WL distributes all its after-tax income to shareholders. What is the effective tax rate on WL pretax income distributed in dividends?
    A. 42%.
    B. 58%.
    C. 70%.

15. Which of the following factors is *least likely* to be associated with a company having a low dividend payout ratio?
    A. High flotation costs on new equity issues.
    B. High tax rates on dividends.
    C. Low growth prospects.

16. The dividend policy of Berkshire Gardens Inc. can be represented by a gradual adjustment to a target dividend payout ratio. Last year Berkshire had earnings per share of US$3.00 and paid a dividend of US$0.60 a share. This year it estimates earnings per share will be US$4.00. Find its dividend per share for this year if it has a 25% target payout ratio and uses a five-year period to adjust its dividend.
    A. US$0.68.
    B. US$0.80.
    C. US$0.85.

17. Beta Corporation is a manufacturer of inflatable furniture. Which of the following scenarios best reflects a stable dividend policy for Beta?
    A. Maintaining a constant dividend payout ratio of 40–50%.
    B. Maintaining the dividend at US$1.00 a share for several years given no change in Beta's long-term prospects.
    C. Increasing the dividend 5% a year over several years to reflect the two years in which Beta recognized mark-to-market gains on derivatives positions.

18. A company has 1 million shares outstanding and earnings are £2 million. The company decides to use £10 million in surplus cash to repurchase shares in the open market. The company's shares are trading at £50 per share. If the company uses the entire £10 million of surplus cash to repurchase shares at the market price, the company's earnings per share will be *closest* to:
    A. £2.00.
    B. £2.30.
    C. £2.50.

19. Devon Ltd. common shares sell at US$40 a share, and their estimated price-to-earnings ratio (P/E) is 32. If Devon borrows funds to repurchase shares at its after-tax cost of debt of 5%, its EPS is *most likely* to:

A. increase.

B. decrease.

C. remain the same.

20. A company can borrow funds at an after-tax cost of 4.5%. The company's stock price is US$40 per share, earnings per share is US$2.00, and the company has 15 million shares outstanding. If the company borrows just enough to repurchase 2 million shares of stock at the prevailing market price, that company's earnings per share is *most likely* to:

A. increase.

B. decrease.

C. remain the same.

21. Crozet Corporation plans to borrow just enough money to repurchase 100,000 shares. The following information relates to the share repurchase:

Shares outstanding before buyback	3.1 million
Earnings per share before buyback	US$4.00
Share price at time of buyback	US$50
After-tax cost of borrowing	6%

Crozet's earnings per share after the buyback will be *closest* to:

A. US$4.03.

B. US$4.10.

C. US$4.23.

22. A company with 20 million shares outstanding decides to repurchase 2 million shares at the prevailing market price of €30 per share. At the time of the buyback, the company reports total assets of €850 million and total liabilities of €250 million. As a result of the buyback, that company's book value per share will *most likely*:

A. increase.

B. decrease.

C. remain the same.

23. An analyst gathered the following information about a company:

Number of shares outstanding	10 million
Earnings per share	US$2.00
P/E	20
Book value per share	US$30

If the company repurchases 1 million shares at the prevailing market price, the resulting book value per share will be *closest* to:

A. US$26.

B. US$27.

C. US$29.

24. If a company's objective is to support its stock price in the event of a market downturn, it would be advised to authorize:
    A. an open market share repurchase plan to be executed over the next five years.
    B. a tender offer share repurchase at a fixed price effective in 30 days.
    C. a Dutch auction tender offer effective in 30 days.

25. A company has positive free cash flow and is considering whether to use the entire amount of that free cash flow to pay a special cash dividend or to repurchase shares at the prevailing market price. Shareholders' wealth under the two options will be equivalent unless the:
    A. company's book value per share is less than the prevailing market price.
    B. company's book value per share is greater than the prevailing market price.
    C. tax consequences and/or information content for each alternative is different.

26. Assume that a company is based in a country that has no taxes on dividends or capital gains. The company is considering either paying a special dividend or repurchasing its own shares. Shareholders of the company would have:
    A. greater wealth if the company paid a special cash dividend.
    B. greater wealth if the company repurchased its shares.
    C. the same wealth under either a cash dividend or share repurchase program.

27. Investors may prefer companies that repurchase their shares instead of paying a cash dividend when:
    A. capital gains are taxed at lower rates than dividends.
    B. capital gains are taxed at the same rate as dividends.
    C. the company needs more equity to finance capital expenditures.

The following information relates to questions 28–29

Janet Wu is treasurer of Wilson Chemical Company, a manufacturer of specialty chemicals used in industrial manufacturing and increasingly in technology applications. Wilson Chemical is selling one of its older divisions for US$70 million cash. Wu is considering whether to recommend a special dividend of US$70 million or a repurchase of 2 million shares of Wilson common stock in the open market. She is reviewing some possible effects of the buyback with the company's financial analyst. Wilson has a long-term record of gradually increasing earnings and dividends.

28. Wilson's share buyback could be a signal that the company:
    A. is decreasing its financial leverage.
    B. views its shares as undervalued in the marketplace.
    C. has more investment opportunities than it could fund internally.

29. The most likely tax environment in which Wilson Chemical's shareholders would prefer that Wilson repurchase its shares (share buybacks) instead of paying dividends is one in which:
    A. the tax rate on capital gains and dividends is the same.
    B. capital gains tax rates are higher than dividend income tax rates.
    C. capital gains tax rates are lower than dividend income tax rates.

CHAPTER 10

BUSINESS MODELS & RISKS

Glen D. Campbell, MBA (Canada)

LEARNING OUTCOMES

The candidate should be able to:

- describe key features and types of business models
- describe expected relations between a company's external environment, business model, and financing needs
- explain and classify types of business and financial risks for a company

1. INTRODUCTORY CONTEXT/MOTIVATION

A clearly described business model helps the analyst understand a business: how it operates, its strategy, target customers, key partners, prospects, risks, and financial profile. Rather than rely on management's description of its business model, analysts should develop their own understanding.

Many firms have conventional business models that are easily understood and described in simple terms, such as manufacturer, wholesaler, retailer, professional firm, or restaurant chain. However, many business models are complex, specialized, or new. Digital technology in particular has enabled significant business model innovation, bringing business models into the spotlight. It has spawned new services and markets and has also changed the way most businesses operate. In many cases, technology has enabled the disruption of existing business models, allowing new players to win against large and well-established players who lack the capabilities or agility to respond.

2. WHAT IS A BUSINESS MODEL?

Successful new businesses may be based on a new product or technology, but there are many success stories based on familiar products or services and a new business model. For example,

IKEA successfully combines existing business concepts—low-cost self-assembly furniture, modernist Scandinavian design, and big box retailing—in a uniquely successful way. Similarly, Google did not invent online search but found a way to generate revenues through online advertising based on user search data.

Often, successful business models are not new or unique. Many businesses, such as wholesalers, retailers, law firms, building contractors, banks, and insurers, have conventional business models. Success for these firms hinges not on business model innovation but on superior execution, skill, proprietary technology, a strong brand, scale, or other factors.

So what is a business model? There is no precise definition, but a business model essentially describes how a business is organized to deliver value to its customers:

- who its customers are,
- how the business serves them,
- key assets and suppliers, and
- the supporting business logic.

A business model makes it clear what the business does, how it operates, and how it generates revenue and profits, as well as how it differs in these respects from its competitors. It provides enough detail so that the basic relationships between the key elements are clear, but it does not provide a full description that we would expect to see in a business plan, such as detailed financial forecasts.

A business model should have a value proposition and a value chain as illustrated in Exhibit 1. In addition, an analyst must also assess the profitability and risk of the firm's business model.

EXHIBIT 1: Firm Business Model

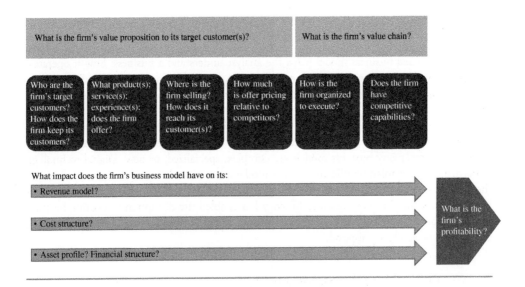

2.1. Business Model Features

Key features of a public company's business model are often provided in annual reports or other disclosure documents. For example, the "Business Description" in Tesla's annual report starts as follows:

> We design, develop, manufacture, sell and lease high-performance fully electric vehicles and energy generation and storage systems, and offer services related to our products. We are the world's first vertically integrated sustainable energy company, offering end-to-end clean energy products, including generation, storage and consumption. We generally sell our products directly to customers, including through our website and retail locations. We also continue to grow our customer-facing infrastructure through a global network of vehicle service centers, Mobile Service technicians, body shops, Supercharger stations and Destination Chargers to accelerate the widespread adoption of our products. We emphasize performance, attractive styling and the safety of our users and workforce in the design and manufacture of our products, and are continuing to develop full self-driving technology for improved safety. We also strive to lower the cost of ownership for our customers through continuous efforts to reduce manufacturing costs and by offering financial services tailored to our vehicles. Our sustainable energy products, engineering expertise, intense focus to accelerate the world's transition to sustainable energy and achieve the benefits of autonomous driving, and business model differentiate us from other companies.

In this paragraph, the company describes numerous features, including its products and their attributes, key channels, and its emphasis on innovation and vertical integration. An analyst's focus is understanding a company's business model to evaluate how effectively it has been implemented and the related impact on the return and risk of the company. Let's explore the features further.

2.2. Customers, Market: Who

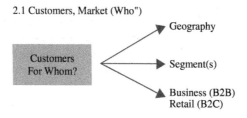

2.1 Customers, Market (Who")

The business model should identify the firm's target customers:

- What geographies will be served?
- What market segments will be served?
- What customer segments will be served? Is this a business (B2B) or consumer (B2C) market?

It is common in consumer markets to think of target demographic segments as defined by marketers (e.g., high-income suburban families). In many cases, segmentation is unique to the product or service category (e.g., affluent early adopters of technology with homes that support plug-in charging in countries with EV [electric vehicles] subsidies). Business opportunities often arise because established firms may not effectively serve (or even recognize) particular customer segments. At the same time, choices made concerning a firm's business model may introduce other related considerations or risks to the firm. For example, the firm might face high barriers to entry, changes in customer segment(s), or increased market competition.

In the Tesla example, the description is silent on which customer segments Tesla is targeting. The likely reason is that Tesla's target market is shifting over time toward the mass market, as costs and prices decline. As an analyst, this type of inference and evaluation can be used to guide your financial modeling and to produce forecasts that reflect key aspects of the firm's business model.

2.3. Firm Offering: What

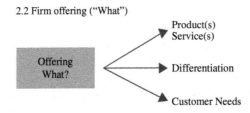

2.2 Firm offering ("What")

The business model should define what the firm offers (what product or service), in terms that differentiate it from competitor offerings, and with reference to the needs of its target customers. This helps the analyst to understand the addressable market for the business and to identify key competitors and associated risks. For example, there may be high risk of imitation or substitution if no "moat," or barriers to competition, exists for the product or service offered by the firm and the level of differentiation is low, or there may be changes in target customer needs and preferences for the firm's offer.

Using the Tesla example, "electric car" is too broad a description of its product offering. Tesla's description of "high-performance fully electric vehicles and energy generation and storage systems" is more precise and useful to the analyst.

It is common for companies to use overly broad terms in describing their offerings or addressable markets, to overstate differentiation, or to reference platforms or networks that may be very weakly developed—all in an attempt to convince the analyst or investor of the value of the business. It is important for analysts to understand and assess the business independently.

2.4. Channels: Where

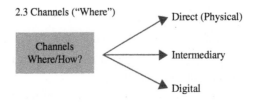

2.3 Channels ("Where")

A firm's channel strategy refers to "where" the firm is selling its offering; that is how it is reaching its customers. Channel strategy usually involves two main functions:

1.   Selling the firm's products and services
2.   Delivering them to customers

In assessing a firm's channel strategy, it is important to distinguish the functions performed from the assets that might be involved and different firms that might be involved in performing those functions or owning those facilities. Exhibit 2 provides examples of the functions, assets, and firms that may be part of the channel strategy for a firm.

EXHIBIT 2: Channel Strategy: Functions vs. Assets vs. Firms

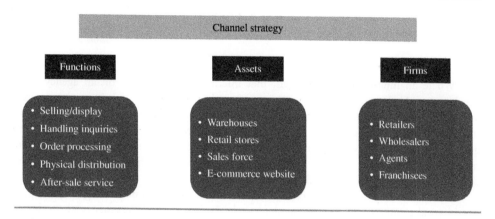

For "product" businesses, the traditional channel strategy is typically reflected in the flow of finished goods (e.g., from manufacturer to wholesaler, retailer, and end customer), each with its own physical facilities and with the product sold and purchased at each stage.

In some categories, manufacturers employ a **direct sales** strategy, selling directly to the end customer. Direct sales to the end customer bypass ("disintermediate") the distributor or retailer. Typically, this involves the company's own sales force, which in some cases represents a significant business investment and carrying cost for the firm. Large retailers often purchase directly from manufacturers, bypassing wholesalers. Direct sales is a common and longstanding channel strategy for complex or high-margin products or services, such as industrial equipment, pharmaceuticals, and life insurance. It is also a common strategy in B2B markets where the universe of potential customers is relatively small and easily reached. With e-commerce, however, direct sales have become a cost-effective strategy across many business and consumer markets.

Exhibit 3 contrasts the interactions of a traditional channel strategy versus a direct sales strategy.

EXHIBIT 3: Traditional Channel Strategy (Product) vs. Direct Sales Strategy

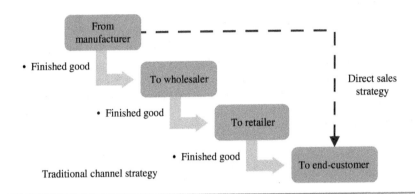

Where an intermediary is involved, that intermediary may work on an agency basis, earning commissions, rather than taking ownership of the goods. Examples include auctioneers, such as Sotheby's (fine art) and Ritchie Bros. (industrial equipment). Using an intermediary may be a good business model solution for the firm, but it requires the firm to give up a degree of control to the intermediary. In the e-commerce realm, the **drop shipping** model enables an online marketer to have goods delivered directly from manufacturer to end customer without taking the goods into inventory.

Often, channels are used in combination. With an **omnichannel** strategy, both digital and physical channels are used to complete a sale. For example, a customer might order an item online and pick it up in a store ("click and collect") or select an item in a store and have it delivered. The use of a digital channel strategy introduces potential cybersecurity and access risks, while having a physical location might introduce substantially greater financial risk.

EXAMPLE 1   Adidas Business Model

Adidas is the world's second largest sportswear brand. The following excerpt from the 2019 Adidas annual report (www.adidas-group.com/media/filer_public/a8/5c/a85c9b8e-865b-4237-8def-8574be243577/annual_report_gb-2019_en.pdf) provides a brief summary of its channel strategy:

> With more than 2,500 own-retail stores, more than 15,000 mono-branded franchise stores and more than 150,000 wholesale doors, we have an unrivaled network of consumer touchpoints within our industry. In addition, through our own e-commerce channel, our single biggest store available to consumers in over 40 countries, we are leveraging a consistent global framework.

List and number the channels used by the Adidas business model.

Solution:
Retail, franchise, wholesale, e-commerce; 4.

The channels used by a business can influence a firm's revenues, cost structure, profitability, and sensitivity to internal and external risk factors.

For some businesses, channel strategy is of critical importance and a key competitive advantage. For example, large firms in such sectors as life insurance, pharmaceuticals, film/music production, and food/beverages have often made a large investment in their sales force or distribution network, one that is not easily replicated by competitors.

It is important to recognize how a firm's channel strategy differs from those of its competitors. For example, Tesla references its direct sales strategy, which differs from the franchised dealer model used by most automakers. Hyundai's Genesis luxury car division also uses a no-dealer model, making visits to the customer's home for test drive appointments and for after-sale service appointments.

KNOWLEDGE CHECK

The Tesla and Hyundai no-dealer models are examples of _____ an established distribution channel.

Solution:
The Tesla and Hyundai no-dealer models are examples of *disintermediating (bypassing)* an established distribution channel.

1. A customer looking to buy a new car might do research online and enter her contact details in order to obtain product information; those details are a "customer lead" that is forwarded to a nearby dealer who might offer a test drive. Identify the channel strategy used in this business model.
    A.   "Bricks and mortar"
    B.   Third party
    C.   Omnichannel

Solution:
C is correct. The business model employs an omnichannel strategy in which both digital and physical channels are used in combination to complete a sale.

2.5. Pricing: How Much

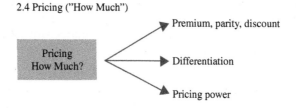

2.4 Pricing ("How Much")

Pricing How Much? → Premium, parity, discount

Pricing How Much? → Differentiation

Pricing How Much? → Pricing power

A business model needs to provide sufficient pricing detail so that the logic of the business is clear.

- Does the firm price at a premium, parity, or discount relative to competitors?
- How is the firm's pricing justified in its business model?

For a producer of a commodity, pricing is usually not an essential part of the business model. Companies with little differentiation are "commodity" producers that must accept market prices dictated to them ("price taker"), whereas companies with high differentiation can command premium pricing ("price setter") and face much less pricing risk from competitors. It is important for an analyst to assess whether the firm requires access to specific capital, labor, or inputs to maintain its level of differentiation.

When a business lacks pricing power, demand is highly price-elastic, with small price changes by the company causing very large changes in demand. A business model in a commodity market is likely to emphasize other sources of value, such as a cost advantage. That said, a discounting strategy might be employed in order to build scale and a cost advantage. The retail sector provides ready examples of this, including Walmart, Carrefour, and Tesco.

More commonly, firms attempt to differentiate their offerings in some way, in order to achieve some degree of pricing power. Using our Tesla example, rather than providing details on price points, the annual report references "**total cost of ownership**," reflecting the importance of government subsidies and lower operating costs for electric vehicles as an offset to higher purchase prices. Total cost of ownership refers to the aggregate direct and indirect costs associated with owning an asset over its life span. Tesla's pricing could be in line with other high-volume luxury cars but with a lower "total cost of ownership." This value proposition (reduced total cost of ownership through some combination of product capabilities, reliability, ease of maintenance and operation, training, etc.) is common to business models in many sectors.

2.5.1. Pricing and Revenue Models

Pricing approaches are typically value or cost based. **Value-based pricing** attempts to set pricing based on the value received by the customer. As noted earlier, Tesla's cars command a premium price in part because they have low operating costs, which are a source of value to their owners. **Cost-based pricing** attempts to set pricing based on costs incurred. An environmental law firm might opt to charge clients by the hour, given the difficulties in estimating how many hours might be required or in measuring the benefit to the client. In contrast, a law firm handling personal injury claims can more easily assess these factors and might charge clients a percentage of the award received. The latter is an example of success-based or contingency billing, a type of value-based pricing.

2.5.1.1. Price Discrimination Economists use the term "**price discrimination**" when firms charge different prices to different customers. In theory, the objective of price discrimination is to maximize revenues in a situation where different customers have different willingness to pay. It may also be less costly to serve certain customer segments, such as large-volume buyers. Common pricing strategies in this category include the following:

- **Tiered pricing** charges different prices to different buyers, most commonly based on volume purchased. Note that volume discounts achieve a similar result.

- **Dynamic pricing** charges different prices at different times. Specific examples include off-peak pricing (e.g., for hotel rooms, advertising, airline tickets, electricity, or matinee movie tickets), "surge" pricing, and "congestion" pricing (e.g., for ride sharing and toll roads). Digital technology can make dynamic pricing models easier to implement and manage.
- **Auction/reverse auction models** establish prices through bidding (by sellers in the case of reverse auctions). Digital technology enables this process to be automated, making these models feasible in new categories (e.g., eBay for consumer merchandise and Google and Amazon for digital advertising).

2.5.1.2. Pricing for Multiple Products Some pricing models are used by firms selling multiple or complex products:

- **Bundling** refers to combining multiple products or services so that customers are incentivized, or required, to buy them together. Bundling can be effective, particularly for products that are complementary, with high incremental margins and high marketing costs relative to the cost of the product itself. Examples include hotel rooms with free breakfast; furnished rental apartments; cable TV and internet services; pre-packaged sets of toys, tools, or kitchen utensils; and cloud-based software combining an application, processing power, storage, and support services.
- **Razors-and-blades pricing** combines a low price on a piece of equipment (e.g., razor, printer, water purifier, or gaming console) and high-margin pricing on repeat-purchase consumables (blades, printer ink, filter cartridges, software).
- **Optional product pricing** applies when a customer buys additional services or product features, either at the time of purchase (e.g., a deluxe interior for a car or a side order with a restaurant meal) or afterward (e.g., change orders in a construction contract). A common strategy is to seek higher margins on the optional features or services, when the customer is "captive" (i.e., the initial purchase decision has already been made), although firms that take this strategy too far can damage customer goodwill and their reputation.

2.5.1.3. Pricing for Rapid Growth **Penetration pricing** is an example of discount pricing and is used when a firm willingly sacrifices margins in order to build scale and market share. Examples include Netflix (subscription video), Huawei (telecom equipment), and Amazon (tablets, e-readers, Alexa speakers).

For digital businesses, growing a user base is often a critical objective, since the incremental costs associated with one more customer subscription are often minimal and the benefits can be enormous, including promotion through word of mouth and, potentially, network effects. Trial and adoption can be encouraged through pricing strategies, which include the following:

- **Freemium pricing** allows customers a certain level of usage or functionality at no charge—for example, with news content, a software application, or a game. This model is widely used in digital content and services, such as periodicals, video games, software/apps, and cloud storage, where the provider stands to benefit from wide adoption (often via network effects).
- **Hidden revenue business models** provide services to users at no charge and generate revenues elsewhere. This is a common feature of both legacy and digital business models in the media sector, with "free" content and paid advertising. Examples can also be found

in online marketplaces (e.g., where sellers pay and buyers do not) and financial services (e.g., free checking accounts, free stock trading).

2.5.1.4. Alternatives to Ownership Some business models create value by providing an alternative to purchasing an asset or product, such as the following:

- **Recurring revenue/subscription pricing** ("product as a service") enables customers to "rent" a product or service for as long as they need it. The subscription model is traditionally associated with the media sector, where firms provide access to standardized content that has a low marginal cost (e.g., TV channels, magazines, streaming services, consumer software). Subscription models can also tie revenues to customer needs or usage, as we see in utilities, telecommunication services, real estate, and many business services. The simplicity of electronic invoicing and payments and the value that businesses and investors place on predictable, recurring revenue streams have driven the introduction of subscription pricing models in new areas. Wealth management is a good example, with fees increasingly based on assets managed rather than commissions charged for each stock or bond trade. Subscription models have also been extended broadly to enterprise software ("software as a service"); computing power, storage, and other technology business; charitable giving; and even consumer staples, such as printer ink and disposable razors (Dollar Shave Club).
- **Fractionalization** creates value by selling an asset in smaller units or through the use of an asset at different times. Examples include web hosting, which enables sharing of server capacity, office sub-leasing/co-working (WeWork), vacation property time shares (Marriott), and private jets (NetJets).
- **Leasing** involves shifting the ownership of an asset from the firm using it to an entity that has lower costs for capital and maintenance. Common examples include real estate, automobiles, aircraft, and specialized equipment.
- *Licensing* typically gives a firm access to intangible assets (e.g., a brand name or intellectual property, such as a film library, song, or patented formula) in return for royalty payments (often a percentage of revenues).
- **Franchising** is a more comprehensive form of licensing, in which the franchisor typically gives the franchisee the right to sell or distribute its product or service in a specified territory and to receive marketing and other support.

2.6. Value Proposition (Who + What + Where + How Much)

A firm's **value proposition** refers to the product or service attributes valued by a firm's target customer that lead those customers to prefer a firm's offering over those of its competitors, given relative pricing. Value propositions vary greatly and relate to

- the product itself (e.g., capability, performance, features, style),
- service and support (e.g., "high-touch" or "low-touch" customer service, depending on the requirements of the customer and the type of product or service, access to repairs, spare parts, etc.),
- the sale process (e.g., purchasing convenience, no-hassle returns), and
- pricing relative to competitors.

Crafting a value proposition requires management to consider carefully which customers it is targeting and through which channels; their wants, needs, and "pain points" being addressed; and competitor product/service offerings and pricing.

Tesla's electric car value proposition emphasizes the benefits of its electric propulsion system: zero emissions and high performance (strong and silent acceleration) and technological sophistication (e.g., self-driving capabilities, frequent enhancements via software upgrades). Low operating costs result in a total cost of ownership below that of other luxury cars. Its direct sales approach helps keep unit costs down without creating inconvenience for customers or limiting sales volume.

EXAMPLE 2   HD Tools Business Model

Let's consider a fictional firm, HD Tools, that wants to sell common hand tools, such as wrenches, screwdrivers, and pliers. The firm is considering which one of two business models it should pursue in the market. Elements of the business models are presented below.

	Business Model A	Business Model B
Customer Segment	• apartment dwellers and new homeowners	• do-it-yourself/professional trades market
Product	• a simple, low-priced set (kit) of tools	• a full assortment of high-quality tools for individual purchase
Channel	• they do not shop at home improvement stores and are likely to buy a kit online or from a mass retailer	• they frequent large home improvement stores and specialty trade distributers
Customer Profile, Need	• they may not know what tools they need and may have none to start with • occasional use to do everyday repairs • tools do not have to be heavy duty	• their time is extremely valuable • know and differentiate between tool brands • heavy use, high-quality requirement
Relative Pricing	• low and affordable price point	• premium priced tools
Customer Value	• a kit that contains several tools they are likely to need • a simple and compact toolbox given limited storage space	• will pay a premium for a tool that they are confident will be durable and will perform
Service Expectations	• after-sales support is not critical, provided there is an acceptable return policy	• demand high-quality tools that will perform flawlessly

Each of these business models is valid for its respective customer segment. Which one makes the most sense for HD Tools to pursue?

Discussion

Both require significant scale to gain distribution in large retailers. However, Model A (low-priced kits) could potentially be established at a smaller scale online.

With Model A, the challenge will be to have a low enough product cost, or cost of goods sold (COGS), to generate an acceptable margin for the business. Differentiation against other "kit" providers might be achievable through superior toolbox design or construction, a better selection of tools, or perhaps an extra feature not offered by competitors—for example, including a selection of common fasteners, aimed at maximizing customer convenience at a low price point.

With Model B, the more critical factor is likely to be product cost and quality. The do-it-yourself (DIY)/professional market requires tools that are of demonstrably high quality so that their customers, who are knowledgeable, will choose them over established rival brands upon seeing them in the store. This might be difficult for a new brand, such as HD Tools. However, HD Tools might be able to overcome this, with objective statements about the quality of materials used in making the tools, their strength and durability, a lifetime warranty, or a "no questions" return policy.

Business models can be viewed in terms of level of product or service differentiation and potential for scale or scope. For example, businesses with "commodity" type offerings that are thus limited to no pricing power might face constraining factors that limit potential scale and growth, such as a regional (regulated) energy provider subject to price caps, or they might have few constraining factors and be relatively unconstrained in growth prospects, such as a mass-market consumer goods manufacturer.

Businesses with high levels of differentiation in their products or services and strong pricing power can set their desired prices given a unique value proposition. Similarly, these businesses might have specific market segments and face scale or scope constraints, such as a luxury watch brand specializing in limited edition time pieces for wealthy consumers, or they might have few constraints on scale or scope with much larger markets, such as a technology platform business. It is important to note that growth business models can also exist in mature markets or industries—for example, fintech firms.

2.7. Business Organization, Capabilities: How

Evaluating a firm's business model requires consideration of not only the value proposition (who it is targeting, what and where the firm is selling, and for how much) but also "how" the firm is structured to deliver that value:

- What assets and capabilities (e.g., skilled personnel, technologies) does the firm require to execute on its business model?
- Will these be owned/insourced or rented/outsourced?

If a firm is renting or purchasing critical resources from other firms, those supplier relationships can become key elements of its strategy and a potential risk.

The auto business has traditionally been organized with automakers supplied by networks of parts manufacturers. Parts manufacturers might supply very specific components (e.g., tires) or complete assemblies (e.g., seats, engines). In some cases, automakers outsource vehicle production entirely. There is generally a very tight working relationship between automakers and their suppliers. Parts or assemblies are often custom designed for a particular vehicle, with the supplier involved from the design stage and throughout the production stage. In these cases, it becomes critical to the automaker to avoid quality issues or supply interruptions at its suppliers.

In contrast, Tesla's business model emphasizes vertical integration, with in-house development and production of key components, such as batteries and software/electronics. This requires substantial capital and effort and is therefore an unusual choice for a new company but is consistent with Tesla's strategy of maintaining a competitive advantage in product technology.

2.7.1. Value Chain

The "how" aspect of a business model is also referred to as a firm's **value chain**:

*   the systems and processes within a firm that create value for its customers.

A value chain includes only those functions performed by a single firm, which may be functions that are valued by customers but do not involve physical transformation or handling the product.

Note that a firm's value chain is different from a **supply chain**, which refers to the sequence of processes involved in the creation of a product, both within and external to a firm. A supply chain includes all the steps involved in producing and delivering a physical product to the end customer, regardless of whether those steps are performed by a single firm.

For some businesses, marketing and sales are strategically critical functions. The "value proposition" addresses what channels are used to reach customers and what value the firm might deliver through the sales and service functions; how to make that happen becomes an important business organization issue.

Tesla's vertical integration strategy extends to distribution, with its company-owned network of stores. It was a major undertaking for Tesla to build this network in multiple countries and to ensure that it achieved the level of sales support and service expected by luxury car buyers. In Tesla's value proposition, the "where" (distribution) element is less critical than the "what" (product features), but it has a significant impact on the company's economics and is a significant part of the "how" (business organization) part of its strategy.

Value chain analysis provides a link between the firm's value proposition for customers and its profitability. It involves:

1. identifying the specific activities carried out by the firm,
2. estimating the value added and costs associated with each activity, and
3. identifying opportunities for competitive advantage.

Michael Porter's 1985 book *Competitive Advantage* defined five primary activities:

*   inbound logistics,
*   operations,
*   outbound logistics,
*   marketing, and
*   sales and service.

In addition, a firm's four primary "support" activities are procurement, human resources, technology development, and firm infrastructure. This is a useful starting point for an analyst evaluating the value chain of a company, although dramatic advances in digital technology have radically changed the way that some of these functions are carried out in many businesses.

2.8. Profitability and Unit Economics

When examined, a business model should also reveal how the firm expects to generate its profit. An analyst will want to examine margins, break-even points, and **unit economics**, which is expressing revenues and costs on a per-unit basis. For example:

- A producer of bottle caps might sell its product at 2.5 cents per unit, with direct costs for material and labor of 2.0 cents per unit and a contribution margin (selling price per unit minus variable cost per unit) of 0.5 cents per unit. If the firm has fixed costs of USD500,000 per year, what is its unit break-even point?

$$\text{Break-even point (unit)} = \text{Fixed costs/Contribution margin}$$

$$= \text{USD500,000/0.5 cents}$$

$$= 100 \text{ million units.}$$

- A restaurant chain might have an average order of EUR50, with ingredient costs equal to 50% of sales. If fixed costs are EUR250,000 annually per outlet, what is the firm's unit break-even point and operating margin at 20,000 orders per year?

$$\text{Break-even point (order)} = \text{Fixed costs/Contribution margin}$$

$$= \text{EUR250,000/EUR25}$$

$$= 10,000 \text{ orders/year.}$$

$$\text{Operating margin} = 20,000 \text{ orders} \times \text{EUR50}$$

$$= \text{EUR1,000,000 revenues} - \text{EUR500,000 ingredient costs} (= 50\% \text{ of sales}) - \text{EUR50,000 fixed costs}$$

$$= \text{EUR250,000 operating profit, or}$$

$$= \text{EUR250,000/EUR1,000,000} = 25\%.$$

- A custom homebuilder might price its services at cost plus a 20% markup. In this case, there is no simple way to express output in terms of units, but it is not necessary to do so.

Tesla's business model is based on a *decline over time* in unit revenues and costs as volumes increase and technology improves. This would be expected to create a virtuous circle: Lower prices enable Tesla to expand its addressable market and its market share, while lower costs allow profits to rise and create a barrier to competition.

Exhibit 4 summarizes key business model features for analyst consideration.

EXHIBIT 4: Business Model Features for Analysis

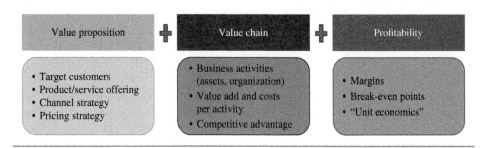

3. BUSINESS MODEL TYPES

Each industry tends to have its own established business models. In goods-producing sectors, it is generally easy to classify firms based on how they fit into the supply chain, such as manufacturers, wholesalers, retailers, and various suppliers of raw materials, components, equipment, and services. Describing a firm as a "plumbing supplies wholesaler," for example, gives an analyst a good starting point in understanding the business model of a typical company in that business.

Service businesses are more diverse. Some target consumers (B2C); some sell to other businesses (B2B). Some involve physical products (e.g., importing, selling, testing, repairs); most do not. There are service business models specific to each sector. For example, the financial services sector includes many established business models, as shown in Exhibit 5.

EXHIBIT 5: Financial Services Business Models

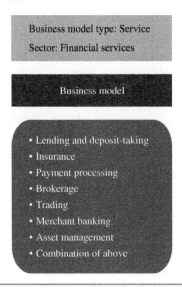

Some firms combine these ("universal banks"), while some specialize. The same is true for other service sectors, such as health care, transportation, real estate, lodging, and entertainment.

3.1. Business Model Innovation

Most discussion of business models focuses on innovation: how new business models can be introduced in conjunction with new businesses or adapted to existing markets. Digital technology has spawned many new businesses, such as

- software,
- content,
- digital advertising,
- data and related services, and
- a wide array of internet-based communities and marketplaces.

These services are not entirely new. There was linear television before streaming video and classified advertising before online marketplaces. But digital technology has changed these services—and the economics of delivering them—almost unrecognizably.

More specifically, digital technology has transformed the "where" and the "how" elements of business models in established markets, by radically reducing the cost of communicating, exchanging information, and transacting between businesses.

- *Location matters less*; digital communications and, in particular, e-commerce enable customers to shop and purchase more easily from firms having no local physical presence.
- *Outsourcing is easier*, for similar reasons.
- *Digital marketing* makes it easy and cost-effective to reach very specific groups of customers, regardless of location, and to engage more deeply with them than was possible with traditional advertising.
- *Network effects*, discussed below, have become more powerful and accessible to more firms.

The rate of innovation itself creates pressure on firms to be agile and adapt, to avoid disruption. In some cases, this can lead them to outsource, in order to focus on what they do best (e.g., apparel companies); in other cases, firms will "insource" in order to strengthen their competitive position, rather than relying on outside suppliers (think Apple with processor chips, Tesla with batteries). While large-scale business model innovation did not start with digital technology, the rapid and open-ended advance of digital technology has dramatically changed how businesses operate.

3.2. Business Model Variations

However, there are still many business model variations, such as the following:

- **Private label or "contract" manufacturers** that produce goods to be marketed by others. This is an extremely common arrangement, particularly for offshore production.
- **Licensing arrangements** in which a company will produce a product using someone else's brand name in return for a royalty. This is common in toys and apparel, for example, when manufacturers might pay for the right to use the name of a famous film character, a

sports team, or a brand that has become popular in a related category (e.g., sporting goods).

- **Value added resellers** that not only distribute a product but also handle more complex aspects of product installation, customization, service, or support. This is common with complex, service-intensive products, such as construction machinery, heating/air conditioning systems, and other specialized equipment.
- *Franchise models* in which distributers or retailers have a tightly defined and often exclusive relationship with the parent company. Franchising is typically used in multi-location service-intensive businesses, where the franchisee handles sales and service and uses the parent (franchisor) business model and brand. Compensation is usually via a royalty arrangement and/or a markup on products sold.

3.3. E-Commerce Business Models

E-commerce is a very broad category, encompassing a variety of internet-based direct sales models. The following are a few key business model variations within e-commerce:

- **Affiliate marketing** generates commission revenues for sales generated on others' websites. It is a specific type of "performance marketing," which refers to an arrangement in which a marketer or agency is paid to achieve defined results (leads, clicks, or actual sales). Examples include CJ Affiliate, Awin, and Leadbit.
- **Marketplace businesses** create networks of buyers and sellers without taking ownership of the goods during the process. Examples include Alibaba, eBay, Mercado Libre, and Etsy.
- **Aggregators** are similar to marketplaces, but the aggregator re-markets products and services under its own brand. Examples include Uber and Spotify.

3.4. Network Effects and Platform Business Models

Network effects refer to the increase in value of a network to its users as more users join. Many internet-based businesses are built on network effects. For example, China's WeChat messaging and payments platform is valuable to its users in large part because it is used by so many people. Other examples can be found in such internet businesses as online classifieds, social media, and ride-sharing services.

Network effects are also at work in many older, non-internet businesses, such as telephone service, credit cards, real estate agencies, and stock exchanges. In some cases, network effects apply to two or more groups of users, such as buyers and sellers in an online marketplace, and can be described as "two-sided" or "multi-sided." "One-sided" network effects apply in the case when users are a single, homogeneous group.

A platform business is based on a network and can be distinguished from a traditional or "linear" business that adds value to something that is sold to customers in a linear supply chain. Software companies for example, often have an essentially linear business model. With a linear business, value is added by the firm; with a platform business, value is created in the network, outside the firm.

3.5. Crowdsourcing Business Models

Crowdsourcing business models enable users to contribute directly to a product, service, or online content. Examples include contests and competitions; online gaming; product development, such as open source software; knowledge aggregation, such as Wikipedia and Waze/Google Maps; fan or hobbyist clubs; and networks of tradespersons or professionals. Other examples include customer reviews and feedback, such as Amazon and Tripadvisor. Many of these examples involve "user communities" that enable voluntary collaboration between users of a product or service, typically with little to no oversight.

3.6. Hybrid Business Models

Hybrid models, combining platform and traditional "linear" businesses, are also common. For example, Amazon's core business has both traditional elements (goods distribution) and platform elements (online marketing and advertising). Tesla sells cars (via a linear model), but its customers benefit from an expanding network of charging stations. Intuit sells QuickBooks accounting software (a linear business) but benefits from the fact that many accountants know how to use it.

EXAMPLE 3   Business Model Evolution in the Hotel and Travel Industry

The hotel industry provides a good illustration of business model evolution over time and the emergence of different business models with varying financial characteristics.

The hotel industry has ancient origins, likely based on an early version of home sharing. The world's oldest operating hotel, Nishiyama Onsen Keiunkan in Japan, is over 1,000 years old and has been in the same family for 52 generations. Until the 20th century, business model evolution was slow. In response to increasing scale and specialization demanded by a growing market, hotels became larger and more numerous but with little change in the basic business model.

The 20th century brought major changes to business models in the industry. The single-property hotel business remained a relevant business model due to the inherent uniqueness of hotel properties. However, with a much larger and highly mobile customer base, hotel operators saw an opportunity and a need to

- serve a growing corporate travel market,
- increase the scale and footprint of their businesses,
- provide convenience and consistency, and
- increase operating efficiency.

The results of this change were the following:

Scale: The emergence of large hotel chains with multiple locations to serve highly mobile customers and brands to serve numerous market segments.

> Example: InterContinental Hotels & Resorts has more than 15 brands in approximately 6,000 locations whose markets range from basic to luxury and extended stay.

Specialization: The emergence of specialized lodging businesses to serve specific market segments.

Example: Resort hotels, vacation packages (bundled flights plus lodging plus meals), casinos, weekly/monthly accommodation (for out-of-town executives).

Franchising: The application of franchising to the hotel business.

Example: Hilton Hotels & Resorts. The vast majority of Hilton properties are not owned or leased by Hilton but instead are operated by franchisees who pay fees.

Functional separation: A move to specialized businesses handling such functions as branding and marketing, property ownership, management, and development.

Example: REITs and property ownership. The largest hotel companies seldom own all of their hotels; some own none. Host Hotels & Resorts, the world's largest hotel REIT and the only investment-grade-rated lodging REIT, owns close to 100 hotel properties and is the largest third-party owner of Marriott and Hyatt hotels.

Fractionalized ownership: The introduction of fractionalized ownership in the form of time-sharing, creating a new lodging category between the hotel and the vacation home.

Example: Wyndham Destinations is the largest vacation ownership company. The company develops, sells, and manages time-share properties under various vacation ownership clubs.

Loyalty programs: The introduction of programs to increase brand loyalty among high-value, frequent travelers.

Example: Hotel loyalty programs first introduced by Holiday Inn and Marriott in 1983.

Online travel agency (OTA): The emergence of the online travel agency business to address the complexities of travel planning and bookings. Digital technology has accelerated changes in hotel business models. The most important single change has been in the agency business, with the rise of the online travel agency business model. In both its traditional and online forms, the travel agency business is a two-sided network.

Like a traditional travel agent, the OTA assists travelers with research and planning, price comparisons, bookings, and logistics. For hotels, it provides exposure, leads, bookings, customer information, feedback, and competitive intelligence. Automating these functions and delivering them as a web-based service so greatly improved their convenience, speed, and efficiency that the business model was transformed, shifting the relationship and the balance of power between agencies and their hotel customers.

Examples of differing OTA business models are shown in the following table.

OTA Business Model	Description	Example(s)
Price-comparison "aggregators"	These network-based businesses offer buyers and sellers within the hotel and travel community travel-related price comparison services and bookings.	Booking.com, Expedia, Trip.com, eDreams
Crowdsourcing	These platform businesses provide crowdsourced reviews and information on hotels and other travel services.	Tripadvisor.com
Home sharing/ short-term rental service	These platform businesses have challenged and disrupted the traditional hotel model by supplying a variety of temporary, often unique, accommodations.	Airbnb; Vrbo (acquired in 2006 by HomeAway, which, in turn, was acquired by Expedia in 2015)

Hotel operators have responded to these challenges by investing in their own websites, customer data, and direct booking capabilities. In response to competition from alternative accommodations, traditional hotel chains, which have historically emphasized consistency, have launched so-called soft brands, which are hotels that operate under their own name with a greater degree of local operator autonomy.

4. BUSINESS MODELS: FINANCIAL IMPLICATIONS

Businesses have very different financing needs and risk profiles, driven by their business model and other factors. Whether capital is readily available to finance a business and what type of capital depends on these factors, which may be external or firm specific.

Lenders in particular look closely at the predictability and stability of demand, revenue and margins of the business (whether there are cash flows to support the servicing and repayment of the debt), and whether the assets in the business can be resold if the business fails (whether there is collateral to secure the debt). Equity analysts and investors also consider these factors but focus more on the long-term potential of the business.

4.1. External Factors

External factors include the following:

- *Economic conditions* affect almost all businesses. In addition to GDP growth, other macroeconomic variables, such as exchange rates, interest rates, the credit environment, unemployment, and inflation, can also be important, depending on the sector. While security markets and the financial press focus on short-term movements in economic data, most businesses are concerned with longer-term trends. There are important variations by sector. For example, a consumer credit business is likely to be highly sensitive to fluctuations in unemployment and GDP growth, while the economics of a wind farm business are likely to be very sensitive to interest rates and the long-term outlook for alternative energy costs and less sensitive to overall GDP growth. In addition, a country's level of economic development is also important when assessing market potential.

- *Demographic trends* influence the overall economy, but in certain markets, they are important in their own right. Mature, urbanized economies are increasingly characterized by aging and, in some cases, declining populations, with growing labor shortages. In most emerging markets, notably in Latin America and Africa, population growth and labor availability remain high. Unlike economic forecasting, long-term demographic forecasting can be done with relatively high accuracy since the underlying drivers (birth, death, and immigration rates) change very slowly.

- *Sector demand* characteristics vary by industry. Some industries, such as consumer staples, have very stable and predictable demand, while others, such as industrial machinery, are more cyclical. The business cycle tends to have less effect on demand for products that are non-discretionary and consumed immediately than on demand for long-lived products or assets. For example, toothpaste and breakfast cereal would be classified as consumer staples, with less cyclicality than clothing, autos, housing, or the commodities that go into making autos or housing. The machinery used to make cars or other "capital goods" are also long-lived assets, with cyclical demand. For long-lived goods, the timing of their replacement is often somewhat discretionary, even if the goods themselves are not.

- *Industry cost characteristics,* such as capital intensity and operating leverage, are also important. Some industries are inherently capital intensive, such as hotels, utilities, and airlines, while others tend to require very little capital, such as many internet-based and service businesses. In addition, the degree of operating leverage differs by business. Businesses with low variable costs and high contribution margins have high "operating leverage" and are said to be "scalable," with operating margins expanding rapidly as business revenues grow. Examples of operations that may scale in this manner include many software, media, and online marketplace businesses.

- The *political, legal, and regulatory environment* is also a key "external" factor for many businesses. It includes the institutions, laws, regulations, and policies that affect the business. Some aspects are background factors that affect business generally, with businesses preferring an environment in which laws and regulations are stable, predictable, and consistently applied and where contracts are easily enforceable. Some regulations create constraints or support for specific industries or businesses. Examples include licensing, environmental, product safety, and trade regulations. While businesses often balk at regulation, keep in mind that regulations that constrain businesses, such as the requirement to obtain a license or to adhere to product standards, can also create barriers to competition. Such barriers can protect a firm's profit margins and add value to the business.

- *Social and political trends:* Shifts in public opinion and tastes often precede changes in consumer buying behavior or the political/legal environment. Examples include consumer preferences for green products, the shift to renewable energy, healthy e-living, and remote learning/working. That said, it can be risky for analysts to generalize broadly from trends or headlines.

4.2. Firm-Specific Factors

Firm-specific factors include the following:

- *Firm maturity* or stage of development of the business: A startup or early-stage business typically requires more capital, such as that needed to finance new facilities or for "investment spending" on product development, marketing/sales, working capital, and/or startup losses, and presents more business risk than a more mature business.
- *Competitive position:* A company with strong barriers to competition, also referred to as a "wide moat," will have lower business and financial risk than one that does not, other things being equal. Companies that are leaders in their markets often enjoy scale and brand advantages over smaller players.
- *Business model:* Some businesses are inherently capital intensive, requiring investment for facilities, productive capacity, and/or working capital, while others are more human capital intensive. A firm's decisions about which assets and resources to "own" rather than "rent" are often driven by its business model and will greatly affect its financial profile. For instance:
  - **Asset-light business models** shift the ownership of high-cost assets to other firms. Examples can be found in traditionally capital-intensive businesses, such as hotels, restaurants, and retailing, where the physical assets are owned by the franchisee rather than the parent company.
  - **Lean startups** extend this logic to human resources, outsourcing as many functions as possible. Technology companies frequently adopt this approach, to accelerate their development and to increase their agility. Note that Tesla has embraced the opposite approach: Whereas most automakers rely on networks of parts suppliers, Tesla has chosen to vertically integrate in order to control and accelerate product development. Apple has embraced a similar strategy.
  - **Pay-in-advance** business models reduce or eliminate the need for working capital. Companies that can generate cash from sales before paying suppliers can operate with minimal or even negative working capital. As the business grows, working capital can become a source of cash. Examples include Amazon (e-commerce) and Berkshire Hathaway Specialty Insurance (insurance).

EXAMPLE 4   Three Ways to Sell Cars

In this example, we consider the business of selling used cars. While the underlying product is the same—used cars—we show that each business has a different underlying business model, resulting in different assets, financing requirements, and expected profitability.

Consider the three following businesses.

- **D Cars (D):** A traditional dealership buys and resells vehicles, which are cleaned, inspected, and held as inventory on its balance sheet between purchase and resale.
- **C Cars (C):** A consignment dealer sells vehicles on behalf of their owners from its own premises but without taking ownership. The seller receives funds only when the car is sold to the new owner, and the consignment dealer, C, then receives a

commission. In this transaction, C is essentially a broker or agent and does not take ownership of the vehicle, and so the seller might receive a higher net price.

- **O Cars (O):** A two-sided online marketplace that allows owners to list vehicles for sale and has no physical premises. As with the consignment model, the transaction between seller and buyer does not directly involve O, but O receives a listing fee from the seller. This is less convenient for both buyer and seller, but both should benefit financially by avoiding the dealer profit or commission.

These three models offer different value propositions for buyers and sellers of used vehicles. The two customer groups in this market are shown in the following table.

Value Proposition Summary

	D Cars	C Cars	O Cars
	Traditional Dealer	Consignment Sales	Online Marketplace
	Dealer pays seller	Buyer pays seller	Buyer pays seller
	Buyer pays dealer	Seller pays dealer commission	Seller pays dealer fee
Buyer Value Proposition			
Vehicle selection	Good	Good	Better
Compare cars in one place	Yes	Yes	No
Vehicle inspected and cleaned	Yes	Yes	No
Assistance with licensing and paperwork	Yes	Yes	No
Price paid	Average	Better	Best
Seller Value Proposition			
Convenience/one-stop shop	Yes	Yes	No
Time to transact	Fast	Slower	Slower
Price realized	Average	Better	Best

The three businesses also have differing assets and cost structures. The costs for D and C are fairly similar because both require a physical showroom/lot to sell cars and involve on-site vehicle inspections, sales, and operations. C, however, does not have to finance or bear the risk associated with inventory.

O's business costs are significantly lower since sales occur online, with no physical premises or on-premise sales staff. D's assets include cars held as inventory between purchase and resale. Both D and C require physical premises with employees to sell cars, while O requires neither inventory nor a physical sales lot, reducing its asset base and financing need. It does, however, require a supported website.

Business Costs and Capital Summary

	D Cars	C Cars	O Cars
	Traditional Dealer	Consignment Sales	Online Marketplace
	Dealer pays seller	Buyer pays seller	Buyer pays seller
	Buyer pays dealer	Seller pays commission	Seller pays fee
Business Cost Structure	**High**	**High/medium**	**Low**
Advertising	Yes	Yes	Yes
Vehicle inspection and cleaning	Yes	Yes	No
Showroom operations	Yes	Yes	No
On-premise sales force	Yes	Yes	No
Website maintenance	No	No	Yes
Capital Required	**High**	**Medium**	**Low**
Showroom/Lot	Yes	Yes	No
Inventory	Yes	No	No

Let's consider an example involving the sale of a vehicle with a standard retail value of 20,000.

D Cars: If the dealer earns a margin of 20% or 4,000 and incurs direct costs of 1,000 to inspect, clean, and advertise the vehicle, it would have a contribution margin of 3,000 to cover the cost of its facilities, the cost of sales staff, the cost of capital required by the business, and the risk that it has misjudged the market value of the car.

C Cars: While the process would be similar to D Cars, the seller in this case would set an asking price in consultation with C to ensure that the car is marketable. The final price would be negotiated between seller and buyer, and C would charge a commission on the final sale. The commission might be a flat fee, a percentage of the negotiated price, a cost-plus arrangement that reimburses C for its direct costs, or some combination thereof. Since C does not have to bear the inventory risk or provide capital on the transaction, it is likely to earn less than if it did do these things. If we assume a commission of 3,000, by dealing with C the seller receives 17,000.

O Cars: With O Cars, the sale process is markedly different. The seller would list her vehicle for a fixed fee; prospective buyers would then arrange to meet to see it, test-drive it, and arrange for their own inspection. This process is more time consuming for both buyer and seller. The seller is likely to demand a higher net price (say, 18,000). If we assume a listing fee paid by the seller of, say, 100, then the buyer would pay less than by going to C or D, compensating for the additional effort involved. For O, the listing fee of 100 is a fraction of the 3,000 commission that C would receive and the 4,000 gross margin that D would receive; however, O has much lower operating costs and capital need than C or D.

The following table summarizes this information for each business.

	D Cars	C Cars	O Cars
Buyer pays	20,000	20,000	18,000
Margin/commission/fee	4,000	3,000	100
Seller receives	16,000	17,000	17,900

Looking at the three business models:

- With D Cars, the dealer adds more value and requires a higher gross profit per vehicle.
- With C Cars, the seller bears more risk but receives a higher net price.
- With O Cars, both seller and buyer receive a better price, reflecting the effort and inconvenience of having to transact without a dealer to facilitate, O earns a relatively low fee but has a very low cost structure.

In practice, the used vehicle market includes all three of these business models, which cater to different buyer and seller preferences. New car dealers are also active in the used car market. Like all marketplace businesses, buying and selling used cars requires a critical mass of buyers and sellers in order to succeed and become an effective two-sided network.

In the case of the D and C businesses operating from a single lot, this can be difficult to achieve since the addressable market includes only buyers and sellers who are within a convenient distance of their lot. The online model of O has a similar challenge: It may attract buyers and sellers from anywhere, but they will be willing to transact only if they are convenient to each other.

5. BUSINESS RISKS

5.1. Summary

- Risk factors with a direct influence on the long-term financial viability of a business are macro risks, business risks, and financial risks.
- Business risk is the risk that the firm's operating results will be different from expectations, independently of how the business is financed, and includes both industry risk and company-specific risk.
- Main industry risk factors include cyclicality, industry structure and concentration, competitive intensity, competitive dynamics in the value chain, long-term growth, and demand outlook.
- Main company-specific risk factors include competitive position, product market risk, execution risk, and operating leverage.
- These risk factors and risks are cumulative and often multiplicative.

Financial analysts and investors need to consider risk factors that might cause investment returns to be different from expectations. Business risk encompasses factors related to the business itself and the industry in which it operates. We distinguish business risk from macro risk, which relates to the overall environment in which the business operates, and financial risk, which relates to how the business is financed.

The perspective of debt and equity investors is different but has many common elements. Debtholders expect the timely repayment of principal and interest, with interest paid timely at an agreed-on rate. They must consider the risk that the borrower will default and if that occurs, the likely magnitude of their loss. For equity investors, the potential for loss is more complicated. Their returns consist of dividends received and changes in the value of the business, which, in turn, hinge not only on how the business performs but also on changes in expectations for future performance. Both consider the cash flow–generating ability of the business as an indicator of future performance.

It is also worth noting that investors who buy and sell investments face risk from security price fluctuations. The price fluctuations reflect not only changes to the fundamentals of the business but also changes in investor sentiment, expectations, and market conditions.

The risk framework presented here classifies risks by type and source. Investors cannot influence the company's business, so their goals are to understand and evaluate those risks and underlying risk factors and risk drivers. Business risks are in the domain of management, who do influence the business and whose risk framework would typically distinguish between preventable risks (to be avoided), strategic risks (consciously taken to achieve business benefits), and external risks (outside management control, to be monitored and mitigated).

6. MACRO RISK, BUSINESS RISK, AND FINANCIAL RISK

Risk that management, debtholders, and equity investors consider arises from the economic environment in which a business operates (macro risk), the business itself (business risk), and the way the business is financed (financial risk), as Exhibit 6 shows.

EXHIBIT 6: Risks Impacting the Business

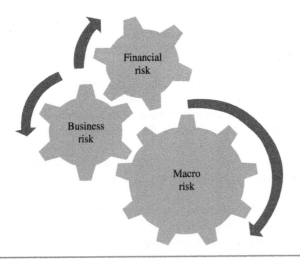

Macro risk refers to the risk from political, economic, legal, and other institutional risk factors that impact all businesses in an economy, a country, or a region. In most situations, the principal macro risk is the potential for a slowdown or a decline in economic activity (measured by changes in GDP) and associated demand. Depending on the geographic location of the business, other country risk factors, such as exchange rates, political instability, or gaps in the legal or financial framework, may also be important. Some firms sell to customers in multiple countries, which can reduce country risk (although not necessarily macro risk).

While macro risks apply to essentially all businesses in the country, some industries are relatively insensitive to economic activity levels (e.g., utilities, consumer staples), whereas others are more sensitive (e.g., capital goods and consumer discretionary goods, such as jewelry and vacation travel).

Business risk is the risk that the firm's operating results will be different from expectations, independently of how the business is financed. In accounting terms, business risk reflects the risk at the operating profit (EBIT) level. Business risk can be seen as the risk of a revenue shortfall and/or higher-than-expected costs, potentially magnified by operating leverage.

Business risk includes both industry risk and company-specific risk, as Exhibit 7 shows. Some risk frameworks would distinguish "external" and "internal" risk factors, with external risks including both macro and industry risks.

EXHIBIT 7: Business Risk and Its Components

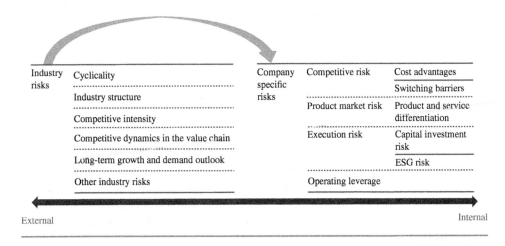

Financial risk refers to the risk arising from a company's capital structure and, specifically, from the level of debt and debt-like obligations (such as leases and pension obligations) involving fixed contractual payments. These fixed financial charges cause net profit and cash flow to vary by more than operating profit, on both the upside and the downside—hence the term *financial leverage*. They also create the possibility that the firm will be unable to secure needed financing on competitive terms: "financing risk." Default risk is also a result of financial leverage. As we will see, even without a default, excessive financial leverage can lead a firm to operate in a sub-optimal manner, as it struggles to conserve cash, key customers, and employees.

Debtholders' perspective on risk differs from that of the company and its equity investors. Debt covenants and collateral reduce risk to the lender but increase risk for equityholders. Long-term fixed-coupon debt reduces interest rate and refinancing risk for the borrower but exposes the holder to risk from interest rate fluctuations (relative to short-term or floating-rate debt). Exchange rate risk arises for the borrower when debt and revenues are denominated in a different currency; for lenders, exchange rate risk can also arise when debt is in a different currency than their own reference currency. In addition, firms will often have multiple loans or debt issues outstanding, with differences in seniority, covenants, collateral, and other terms. These differences create differences in risk faced by the firm's debt investors.

6.1. Risk Impacts Are Cumulative

The impact of risks on a business and the returns debtholders and equity investors earn from the business is cumulative. While we make a distinction between macro risks and business risks, both affect a company's operating results. When we look to measure business risk, it will reflect the impact of macro risk. Likewise, we make a distinction between business risk and financial risk, but both (together with macro risk) affect the company's cash flow, net earnings, and ability to service debt. Financial risk will reflect the combined impacts of macro issues, business risks, and financial leverage.

7. BUSINESS RISK: A CLOSER LOOK

Business risk includes both industry risk and company-specific risk, which we now will examine.

7.1. Industry Risks

Industry risks apply to all competitors in the same industry and include risk factors likely to affect the overall level of demand, pricing, and profitability in the industry.

- *Cyclicality* is a feature of many industries, particularly discretionary goods; housing; durable goods, such as autos and appliances; and capital equipment. These products are generally long lived, giving the buyer flexibility as to when to replace them. Inputs to those industries—including commodities, such as lumber, steel, and copper, and certain business services (e.g., heavy equipment rentals)—also face cyclical demand. For cyclical businesses, revenue fluctuations generally cause even larger fluctuations in operating profit, due to the impact of fixed costs.

  Firms attempt to mitigate the impact of cyclicality in different ways. Some firms try to stabilize revenues by entering long-term customer or hedging contracts. Some attempt to minimize fixed operating costs—for example, through outsourcing or flexible contracts with workers and suppliers. Generally, firms with cyclical (or otherwise unpredictable) revenues will tend to have more conservative capital structure policies, with relatively little debt and therefore smaller fixed financing obligations, compared with less cyclical firms.

- *Industry structure* has an impact on the overall risk of the industry. Lower concentration (i.e., the presence of many small competitors) is generally associated with a high degree of competitive intensity, although the presence of many small players is also a feature of sectors that are very service oriented, are local in nature, or have high product differentiation. Examples include law firms, electrical contracting, boutique hotels, and niche software providers.

A common measure of industry concentration is the Herfindahl–Hirschman Index (HHI), calculated as the sum of the squares of competitor market shares. The HHI would be 1.00 for a one-player market, 0.50 for a market with two equal players, 0.33 if there are three equal players, and so on. (Index values are different when competitors have unequal market shares, as is normally the case.)

- *Competitive intensity* influences overall industry profitability. If the data are available, one can measure industry profitability directly. Return on invested capital (ROIC) and operating profit margins (EBIT/revenue) are common measures. Analysts look at the absolute levels for these measures and changes over time (correcting for cyclical variations). They also seek to understand the factors that influence competitive intensity for an industry and how those factors are changing.
- *Competitive dynamics within the value chain*—that is, potential profitability pressures from the interaction of buyers, suppliers, current and potential competitors, and suppliers of substitute goods. Michael Porter's "five forces" model (mentioned previously) describes these factors in detail.
- *Long-term growth and demand outlook* are more a determinant of industry attractiveness than of risk, but an unexpected falloff (or absolute decline) in growth can result in excess capacity and more aggressive competition. Long-term growth trends are determined by the level of innovation, the pervasive and dominating business models, and the age/ maturity of the industry. Long-term growth can contribute to long-term profitability, although it can also attract more competition.
- *Other industry risks* include regulatory and other potential external risks to industry demand and profitability.

7.2. Industry Definition

Care must be taken to define the industry appropriately when evaluating risk and more generally when analyzing a business. If the analyst defines an industry too broadly, conclusions about the market and competitive conditions may be too broad to be useful. Within the auto parts sector, for example, the markets for brakes, tires, and entertainment systems are very different, with different competitors. Within the lodging sector, there are wide variations between geographic markets (e.g., Paris versus Rio de Janeiro) and across segments (e.g., beach hotels versus corporate extended-stay lodging). In general, a more precise (i.e., narrower) industry definition is preferable, since it enables the analyst to focus on the specific factors affecting the firm. However, if the industry is defined too narrowly, it can become difficult to obtain accurate data on demand and competition and to give appropriate emphasis to trends, issues, or risks affecting the industry as a whole.

7.3. Company-Specific Risks

Company-specific risks vary based on the nature, scale, and maturity of the business. They are often closely related to the company's market position and business model. Generally speaking, these risks are likely to be greater for businesses that are smaller, less dominant in their industry, or at an early stage of development (i.e., when their profit potential or even the revenue potential is not yet proven). Company-specific risk categories include the following:

- **Competitive risk** can be defined as the risk of a loss of market share or pricing power to competitors and often reflects a lack of competitive advantage. Pricing power is analogous to the price elasticity of demand: the likely decline in demand if the company were to raise its prices (e.g., by 10%) and competitors did not follow. When market share and pricing power are low or declining, the level of competitive pressure and risk is generally high. Typically, companies with strong competitive positions in attractive industries tend to have high margins and, other things being equal, lower business risk.

   Competitive risk also arises from the potential for **disruption**: when new or potential competitors using new technology or business models take market share, rather than known or established competitors using established business models.

- **Product market risk** is the risk that the market for a new product or service will fall short of expectations. It is not generally a consideration for mature or well-established businesses. But for an early-stage startup, this is often the single largest source of business risk. Risk is typically very high for pre-revenue companies; it declines as the firm progresses from concept development through product testing and market testing (still with no revenues) to commercial launch, revenue generation, and then larger-scale roll-out. Analysts should also consider the possibility that product life cycles may be cut short, by such factors as changing consumer preferences, product obsolescence, or the end of patent protection.

   Product mix and diversity can reduce risk for large firms that sell multiple products to diverse customers and markets. At the same time, a broad product portfolio can reduce the ability of the business to address problems across its product portfolio.

Much has been written on the sources of competitive advantage. Companies can benefit from the following:

- *Cost advantages,* which can be based on scale, a superior production process, proprietary technology, or other factors.
- *Product or service differentiation,* which creates value for customers. This could be based on traditional attributes, such as reliability, durability, and performance; on how the product is sold, bundled, or serviced; on branding; or on network effects.
- *Network effects,* which refer to the increase in utility for some services and products when they are widely adopted. Examples include social media networks, Airbnb, or companies marketing construction equipment that rely on having a trained network of qualified mechanics.
- **Switching barriers** are factors that make it more difficult or more costly to switch suppliers. These can derive from long-term supply contracts, the need for the customer to invest in training or new systems when changing suppliers, or other factors.

The larger and more durable these advantages, the lower the level of competitive risk. Note that these factors affect competitive risk for a particular firm; they are in addition to the factors discussed earlier that are applicable to the industry as a whole.

- **Execution risk** arises from the possibility that management will be unable to do what is needed to deliver the expected results. Execution risk tends to be accentuated by other business risks: A small or early-stage business with a weak or deteriorating market position and/or in a highly competitive industry is likely to have higher operational risk than a large, established, stable business. For such a business, there is likely to be less room for management error and more work to do in order for the business to achieve its plan. Analysts should also look for specific issues that could create operational risk, such as reliance on key suppliers or personnel, challenging turnarounds or IT platform migrations, or high-risk new product launches.

- **Capital investment risk** is the potential for sub-optimal investment by a firm. This tends to be a bigger concern for mature businesses that generate cash flow but lack natural reinvestment opportunities in their current business and in firms where management has shown a propensity to make high-profile ego-driven investments. While some companies have diversified successfully, either organically or through mergers and acquisition, many have not.

- **ESG risk** traditionally focuses on governance risk: the potential misalignment of objectives between shareholders focused on value maximization and management (who might pursue growth for its own sake or resist necessary major changes to the business). It is impossible to eliminate governance risk completely, but analysts generally look for strong independent directors, separation of the CEO and chairman roles, executive compensation that properly incentivizes shareholder value creation, and significant share ownership by the board and senior management. Analysts must also consider the risks arising from potential failure of the business to meet society's expectations for environmental and social responsibility.

- **Operating leverage** refers to the sensitivity of a firm's operating profit to a change in revenues. For businesses with low variable costs (e.g., software, media), operating leverage is high. For successful, growing businesses, high operating leverage can have a very positive influence on profitability and value. For businesses that are struggling or facing declining demand, high operating leverage can be problematic and is a source of business risk. We discuss the calculation of operating leverage below.

8. FINANCIAL RISK

Financial risk (as distinguished from business risk) refers to the risk arising from a company's capital structure and, specifically, from the level of debt (and other debt-like obligations, such as leases and pension obligations) involving fixed contractual payments. These fixed financial charges cause net profit and cash flow to vary by more than operating profit, on both the upside and the downside—hence the term "financial leverage." They also create the possibility that the firm will be unable to secure needed financing (financing risk) or that it will fail to meet its financial obligations (default risk). Default can be expensive and traumatic. But even without a default, excessive financial leverage impacts the firm's financial capacity and leads a firm to become financially distressed—to operate in a sub-optimal manner as it struggles to conserve cash, key customers, and employees.

Financial risk is closely related to the variability of profits and cash flows. These, in turn, depend on the predictability, or volatility, of the revenues and operating cash flow (i.e., business risk). Financial risk thus reflects the cumulative impacts of macro and business risk. Consider an example: Uncertainty about sales to a key customer would be considered a business risk, not a financial risk. But when we measure financial risk, we would normally capture all the sources of uncertainty about financial results, including risks to revenues.

Businesses vary widely in their ability and capacity to support debt, depending on their industry, competitive position, and stage of maturity. A business with a low level of business risk can typically support a high level of financial leverage and is generally one with demand that is predictable and stable, a strong and durable competitive position, and high operating margins and that does not require large amounts of investment to maintain its position. For example, an electric utility—a regulated monopoly with very stable revenues and operating cash flows—can typically maintain a high proportion of debt in its capital structure.

EXHIBIT 8: Components of Leverage

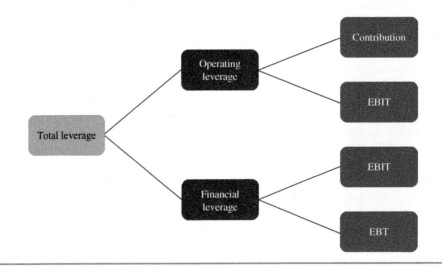

8.1. Measuring Operating and Financial Leverage

Financial risk is closely related to the variability of profits and cash flows. These, in turn, depend on the predictability, or volatility, of the business revenues but also on the sensitivity of profits to changes in revenue. There are several different approaches we can use to quantify this risk. An approach is to consider profit sensitivity by looking at the change in net income in relation to change in revenues to capture total leverage of the business. Specifically, total leverage can be broken down to several components:

$$\text{Total leverage} = \text{Operating leverage} \times \text{Financial leverage}. \quad (1)$$

Here, operating leverage captures the sensitivity of operating profit, proxied by EBIT, to a change in revenues and can also be calculated as follows:

$$\text{Operating leverage} = \text{Contribution/EBIT}. \quad (2)$$

Financial leverage reflects the variability of profits introduced by interest charges—that is, the sensitivity of net profit to a change in operating profit. It can also be calculated as

$$\text{Financial leverage} = \text{EBIT/EBT}. \tag{3}$$

Note that this approach refers to EBT rather than net income, since taxes fluctuate but would normally be a stable percentage of EBT. For this reason, we can also measure financial leverage as the percentage change in EBIT divided by the percentage change in earnings or EPS.

In accounting terms, "business risk" can be seen as the risk of a revenue shortfall, which is, in turn, magnified by operating leverage. (Note that when demand is weak, revenue shortfalls are also accompanied by pricing and margin weakness, which causes operating leverage to increase.) Financial risk is the magnification of business risk through financial leverage (i.e., the magnification of an EBIT shortfall at the EBT or EPS line).

Business Risk in Three Hotel Businesses

This example compares three typical but distinctly different hotel businesses and how their strategy impacts their business risk and consequently their financial risk. Hotels cater to essentially three different types of customers: corporate customers on business trips, leisure customers on holidays, and temporary accommodations. As such, hotels offer a broad range of services, at different prices, and different experiences. Economic factors tend to influence all hotel businesses in largely a similar manner.

- MegaChain Hotel owns and operates a multi-hotel franchise and has a very well-established brand. It does not own any physical hotel properties outright but provides marketing, management, and booking services to all its franchisees, who pay 10% of revenues as a franchise fee. Operating expenses are about 75% of revenues. MegaChain Hotel has no debt.
- Hotel OwnCo, a MegaChain Hotel franchisee, owns five well-located large hotel properties catering to a mix of business and leisure costumers. The company has mortgages outstanding for about 40% of property value. Its operating expenses are about 50% of revenues.
- BCHZ Hotel is a small, family-run hotel catering to backpackers, surfers, and local families. It sits on a location comparable to other similar properties in the area: near a beach among other similar businesses. BCHZ is known for excellent food and service, and demand for its rooms is not sensitive to overall economic activity. Operating expenses are about 35% of revenues. The business owns the hotel property outright with no debt.

Comparing these three hotels, MegaChain has a high level of operating leverage and no financial leverage. Its franchisee, Hotel OwnCo, has lower operating leverage but high financial leverage. BCHZ Hotel has low operating leverage and no financial leverage. BCHZ Hotel presents the lowest level of financial risk. However, it appears that its success is based on food quality and service, presumably reflecting the effort and skill of the family who runs it. This is a significant source of business-specific risk that is not present with MegaChain Hotel or Hotel OwnCo.

9. SUMMARY

- A business model describes how a business is organized to deliver value to its customers:
  - who its customers are,
  - how the business serves them,
  - key assets and suppliers, and
  - the supporting business logic.
- The firm's "value proposition" refers to the product or service attributes valued by a firm's target customer that lead those customers to prefer a firm's offering over those of its competitors, given relative pricing.
- Channel strategy may be a key element of a business model, and it addresses how the firm is reaching its customers.
- Pricing is often a key element of the business model. Pricing approaches are typically value or cost based.
- In addition to the value proposition, a business model should address the "value chain" and "how" the firm is structured to deliver that value.
- While many firms have conventional business models that are easily understood and described in simple terms, many business models are complex, specialized, or new.
- Digital technology has enabled significant business model innovation, often based on network effects.
- To understand the profitability of a business, the analyst should examine margins, break-even points, and "unit economics."
- Businesses have very different financing needs and risk profiles, depending on both external and firm-specific factors, which will determine the ability of the firm to raise capital.

10. PRACTICE PROBLEMS

1. Which of the following is *least likely* to be a key feature of a business model?
   A. Unit economics
   B. Channel strategy
   C. Financial forecasts
   D. Customer cost of ownership
   E. Target customer identification

2. When should an analyst expect a business model to employ premium pricing? When:
   A. the company is a price taker.
   B. the firm is small and returns are highly scale sensitive.
   C. significant differentiation is possible in the product category.
   D. the firm is a market leader and demand is very price sensitive.

3. Which is the *most accurate* statement about a platform business?
   A. A platform business is based on network effects.
   B. A platform business can be a non-technology business.

C. Value creation for customers for a platform business occurs externally.

D. It can be difficult to attract users in the beginning to a platform business.

E. All of the above

4. Which of the following businesses is *least likely* to have network effects?

   A. A stock exchange

   B. A telephone company

   C. A classified advertising website

   D. A price comparison website for travel airfares

   E. A resume preparation service for online job seekers

5. A flower shop has preferred supplier arrangements with an answering service, to take orders after hours, and a bicycle delivery service, to ensure that it can make deliveries quickly, reliably, and at a reasonable cost. Which of the following statements is *most accurate* for the flower shop?

   A. The answering service is part of its supply chain.

   B. The bicycle delivery service is part of its value chain.

   C. The bicycle delivery service is part of its supply chain.

   D. The bicycle delivery service is not a part of the value proposition for the flower shop.

6. Which of the following is the *closest* example of a one-sided network?

   A. An online employment website

   B. A dating website for men and women

   C. A social network for model train collectors

   D. A website for home improvement contractors

7. Which of the following statements is not representative of unit costs?

   A. Unit costs generally exclude labor costs.

   B. Business models generally consider unit costs.

   C. Unit costs are used to calculate break-even points.

   D. If a lemonade stand uses 5 cents worth of lemons, 2 cents worth of sugar, and a cup costing 3 cents for each glass of lemonade, it has a unit cost of 10 cents.

8. Which of the following companies would *most likely* have a high level of macro risk?

   A. A coffee plantation in Brazil

   B. A Swedish mining equipment manufacturer

   C. A call center outsourcing business based in India

9. Which of the following is *most likely* to have a high level of industry risk?

   A. Toll road

   B. Pest control services company

   C. Oil well drilling service company

10. For a newly launched clothing company in Japan that uses offshore production in Malaysia, classify each of the following impacts:

1. Demand falls gradually due to a declining population	A. Company-specific risk
2. Consumer tastes shift to favor locally manufactured apparel	B. Macro risk
3. The company faces uncertainty about future demand as it hires a new chief designer and makes changes to its top-selling products	C. Industry risk

11. Which of the following is an example of significant execution risk?
    A. A manufacturer replaces aging factory machinery with similar but more efficient equipment.
    B. A marketer of high-fashion pet accessories tests the market to see if there is demand for glamourous dog harnesses made with faux fur.
    C. A company with consistent operating margins of about 5% with stable market share of 5% for swimming pool chemicals plans to double its margins and triple its market share over the next five years.

12. Which of the following is *most likely* to increase a business's operating leverage?
    A. Reducing prices
    B. Borrowing rather than issuing equity
    C. Using casual labor rather than a salaried work force

13. Which of the following is *most likely* to increase financial leverage?
    A. Cutting prices
    B. Replacing short-term debt with long-term debt
    C. Entering a sale-leaseback transaction for the company's head office building

THE FIRM AND MARKET STRUCTURES

Richard Fritz, PhD
School of Economics at Georgia Institute of Technology (USA)

Michele Gambera, PhD, CFA
UBS Asset Management and University of Illinois at Urbana-Champaign (USA)

LEARNING OUTCOMES

The candidate should be able to:

- describe characteristics of perfect competition, monopolistic competition, oligopoly, and pure monopoly
- explain relationships between price, marginal revenue, marginal cost, economic profit, and the elasticity of demand under each market structure
- describe a firm's supply function under each market structure
- describe and determine the optimal price and output for firms under each market structure
- describe pricing strategy under each market structure
- explain factors affecting long-run equilibrium under each market structure
- describe the use and limitations of concentration measures in identifying market structure
- identify the type of market structure within which a firm operates

1. ANALYSIS OF MARKET STRUCTURES

The purpose of this chapter is to build an understanding of the importance of market structure. As different market structures result in different sets of choices facing a firm's decision makers, an understanding of market structure is a powerful tool in analyzing issues such as a firm's pricing of its products and, more broadly, its potential to increase profitability. In the long run, a firm's profitability will be determined by the forces associated with the market structure within which it operates. In a highly competitive market, long-run profits will be driven down by the forces of competition. In less competitive markets, large profits are possible even in the long run; in the short run, any outcome is possible. Therefore, understanding the forces behind the market structure will aid the financial analyst in determining firms' short- and long-term prospects.

Section 2 introduces the analysis of market structures. The section addresses questions such as: What determines the degree of competition associated with each market structure? Given the degree of competition associated with each market structure, what decisions are left to the management team developing corporate strategy? How does a chosen pricing and output strategy evolve into specific decisions that affect the profitability of the firm? The answers to these questions are related to the forces of the market structure within which the firm operates.

Sections 3, 4, 5, and 6 analyze demand, supply, optimal price and output, and factors affecting long-run equilibrium for perfect competition, monopolistic competition, oligopoly, and pure monopoly, respectively.

Section 7 reviews techniques for identifying the various forms of market structure. For example, there are accepted measures of market concentration that are used by regulators of financial institutions to judge whether or not a planned merger or acquisition will harm the competitive nature of regional banking markets. Financial analysts should be able to identify the type of market structure a firm is operating within. Each different structure implies a different long-run sustainability of profits. A summary and practice problems conclude the chapter.

1.1. Analysis of Market Structures

Traditionally, economists classify a market into one of four structures: perfect competition, monopolistic competition, oligopoly, and monopoly. Section 2.1 explains that four-way classification in more detail. Section 2.2 completes the introduction by providing and explaining the major points to evaluate in determining the structure to which a market belongs.

1.1.1. Economists' Four Types of Structure

Economists define a market as a group of buyers and sellers that are aware of each other and can agree on a price for the exchange of goods and services. While the internet has extended a number of markets worldwide, certain markets are limited by geographic boundaries. For example, the internet search engine Google operates in a worldwide market. In contrast, the market for premixed cement is limited to the area within which a truck can deliver the mushy mix from the plant to a construction site before the compound becomes useless. Thomas L. Friedman's international best seller *The World Is Flat*[1] challenges the concept of the geographic limitations of the market. If the service being provided by the seller can be digitized, its market expands worldwide. For example, a technician can scan your injury in a clinic in Switzerland. That radiographic image can be digitized and sent to a radiologist in India to be read. As a customer (i.e., patient), you may never know that part of the medical service provided to you was the result of a worldwide market.

Some markets are highly concentrated, with the majority of total sales coming from a small number of firms. For example, in the market for internet search, three firms controlled 98.9 percent of the US market (Google 63.5 percent, Microsoft 24 percent, and Oath

---

[1]Friedman (2006).

[formerly Yahoo] 11.4 percent) as of January 2018.[2] Other markets are very fragmented, such as automobile repairs, where small independent shops often dominate and large chains may or may not exist. New products can lead to market concentration: It is estimated that the Apple iPod had a world market share of over 70 percent among MP3 players in 2009.

THE IMPORTANCE OF MARKET STRUCTURE

Consider the evolution of television broadcasting. As the market environment for television broadcasting evolved, the market structure changed, resulting in a new set of challenges and choices. In the early days, there was only one choice: the "free" analog channels that were broadcast over the airwaves. In most countries, there was only one channel, owned and run by the government. In the United States, some of the more populated markets were able to receive more channels because local channels were set up to cover a market with more potential viewers. By the 1970s, new technologies made it possible to broadcast by way of cable connectivity and the choices offered to consumers began to expand rapidly. Cable television challenged the "free" broadcast channels by offering more choice and a better-quality picture. The innovation was expensive for consumers and profitable for the cable companies. By the 1990s, a new alternative began to challenge the existing broadcast and cable systems: satellite television. Satellite providers offered a further expanded set of choices, albeit at a higher price than the free broadcast and cable alternatives. In the early 2000s, satellite television providers lowered their pricing to compete directly with the cable providers.

Today, cable program providers, satellite television providers, and terrestrial digital broadcasters that offer premium and pay-per-view channels compete for customers who are increasingly finding content on the internet and on their mobile devices. Companies like Netflix, Apple, and Amazon offered alternative ways for consumers to access content. By 2018, these companies had moved beyond the repackaging of existing shows to developing their own content, mirroring the evolution of cable channels such as HBO and ESPN a decade earlier.

This is a simple illustration of the importance of market structure. As the market for television broadcasting became increasingly competitive, managers have had to make decisions regarding product packaging, pricing, advertising, and marketing in order to survive in the changing environment. In addition, mergers and acquisitions as a response to these competitive pressures have changed the essential structure of the industry.

Market structure can be broken down into four distinct categories: perfect competition, monopolistic competition, oligopoly, and monopoly.

We start with the most competitive environment, **perfect competition**. Unlike some economic concepts, perfect competition is not merely an ideal based on assumptions. Perfect competition is a reality—for example, in several commodities markets, where sellers and buyers have a strictly homogeneous product and no single producer is large enough to

---

[2]Source: www.statista.com/statistics/267161/market-share-of-search-engines-in-the-united-states/.

influence market prices. Perfect competition's characteristics are well recognized and its long-run outcome unavoidable. Profits under the conditions of perfect competition are driven to the required rate of return paid by the entrepreneur to borrow capital from investors (so-called normal profit or rental cost of capital). This does not mean that all perfectly competitive industries are doomed to extinction by a lack of profits. On the contrary, millions of businesses that do very well are living under the pressures of perfect competition.

Monopolistic competition is also highly competitive; however, it is considered a form of imperfect competition. Two economists, Edward H. Chamberlin (US) and Joan Robinson (UK), identified this hybrid market and came up with the term because there are not only strong elements of competition in this market structure but also some monopoly-like conditions. The competitive characteristic is a notably large number of firms, while the monopoly aspect is the result of product differentiation. That is, if the seller can convince consumers that its product is uniquely different from other, similar products, then the seller can exercise some degree of pricing power over the market. A good example is the brand loyalty associated with soft drinks such as Coca-Cola. Many of Coca-Cola's customers believe that their beverages are truly different from and better than all other soft drinks. The same is true for fashion creations and cosmetics.

The **oligopoly** market structure is based on a relatively small number of firms supplying the market. The small number of firms in the market means that each firm must consider what retaliatory strategies the other firms will pursue when prices and production levels change. Consider the pricing behavior of commercial airline companies. Pricing strategies and route scheduling are based on the expected reaction of the other carriers in similar markets. For any given route—say, from Paris, France, to Chennai, India—only a few carriers are in competition. If one of the carriers changes its pricing package, others will likely retaliate. Understanding the market structure of oligopoly markets can help in identifying a logical pattern of strategic price changes for the competing firms.

Finally, the least competitive market structure is **monopoly**. In pure monopoly markets, there are no other good substitutes for the given product or service. There is a single seller, which, if allowed to operate without constraint, exercises considerable power over pricing and output decisions. In most market-based economies around the globe, pure monopolies are regulated by a governmental authority. The most common example of a regulated monopoly is the local electrical power provider. In most cases, the monopoly power provider is allowed to earn a normal return on its investment and prices are set by the regulatory authority to allow that return.

1.1.2. Factors That Determine Market Structure

Five factors determine market structure:

1. The number and relative size of firms supplying the product;
2. The degree of product differentiation;
3. The power of the seller over pricing decisions;
4. The relative strength of the barriers to market entry and exit; and
5. The degree of non-price competition.

The number and relative size of firms in a market influence market structure. If there are many firms, the degree of competition increases. With fewer firms supplying a good or service, consumers are limited in their market choices. One extreme case is the monopoly market structure, with only one firm supplying a unique good or service. Another extreme is perfect competition, with many firms supplying a similar product. Finally, an example of relative size is the automobile industry, in which a small number of large international producers (e.g., Volkswagen and Toyota) are the leaders in the global market, and a number of small companies either have market power because they are niche players (e.g., Ferrari or McLaren) or have little market power because of their narrow range of models or limited geographical presence (e.g., Mazda or Fiat-Chrysler).

In the case of monopolistic competition, there are many firms providing products to the market, as with perfect competition. However, one firm's product is differentiated in some way that makes it appear better than similar products from other firms. If a firm is successful in differentiating its product, the differentiation will provide pricing leverage. The more dissimilar the product appears, the more the market will resemble the monopoly market structure. A firm can differentiate its product through aggressive advertising campaigns; frequent styling changes; the linking of its product with other, complementary products; or a host of other methods.

When the market dictates the price based on aggregate supply and demand conditions, the individual firm has no control over pricing. The typical hog farmer in Nebraska and the milk producer in Bavaria are **price takers**. That is, they must accept whatever price the market dictates. This is the case under the market structure of perfect competition. In the case of monopolistic competition, the success of product differentiation determines the degree with which the firm can influence price. In the case of oligopoly, there are so few firms in the market that price control becomes possible. However, the small number of firms in an oligopoly market invites complex pricing strategies. Collusion, price leadership by dominant firms, and other pricing strategies can result.

The degree to which one market structure can evolve into another and the difference between potential short-run outcomes and long-run equilibrium conditions depend on the strength of the barriers to entry and the possibility that firms fail to recoup their original costs or lose money for an extended period of time and are therefore forced to exit the market. Barriers to entry can result from very large capital investment requirements, as in the case of petroleum refining. Barriers may also result from patents, as in the case of some electronic products and drug formulas. Another entry consideration is the possibility of high exit costs. For example, plants that are specific to a special line of products, such as aluminum smelting plants, are non-redeployable, and exit costs would be high without a liquid market for the firm's assets. High exit costs deter entry and are therefore also considered barriers to entry. In the case of farming, the barriers to entry are low. Production of corn, soybeans, wheat, tomatoes, and other produce is an easy process to replicate; therefore, those are highly competitive markets.

Non-price competition dominates those market structures where product differentiation is critical. Therefore, monopolistic competition relies on competitive strategies that may not include pricing changes. An example of non-price competition is product differentiation through marketing. In other circumstances, non-price competition may occur because the few firms in the market feel dependent on each other. Each firm fears retaliatory price changes that would reduce total revenue for all of the firms in the market. Because oligopoly industries have so few firms, each firm feels dependent on the pricing strategies of the others. Therefore, non-price competition becomes a dominant strategy.

EXHIBIT 1: Characteristics of Market Structure

Market Structure	Number of Sellers	Degree of Product Differentiation	Barriers to Entry	Pricing Power of Firm	Non-price Competition
Perfect competition	Many	Homogeneous/ Standardized	Very Low	None	None
Monopolistic competition	Many	Differentiated	Low	Some	Advertising and Product Differentiation
Oligopoly	Few	Homogeneous/ Standardized	High	Some or Considerable	Advertising and Product Differentiation
Monopoly	One	Unique Product	Very High	Considerable	Advertising

From the perspective of the owners of the firm, the most desirable market structure is that with the most control over price, because this control can lead to large profits. Monopoly and oligopoly markets offer the greatest potential control over price; monopolistic competition offers less control. Firms operating under perfectly competitive market conditions have no control over price. From the consumers' perspective, the most desirable market structure is that with the greatest degree of competition because prices are generally lower. Thus, consumers would prefer as many goods and services as possible to be offered in competitive markets.

As often happens in economics, there is a trade-off. While perfect competition gives the largest quantity of a good at the lowest price, other market forms may spur more innovation. Specifically, there may be high costs in researching a new product, and firms will incur such costs only if they expect to earn an attractive return on their research investment. This is the case often made for medical innovations, for example—the cost of clinical trials and experiments to create new medicines would bankrupt perfectly competitive firms but may be acceptable in an oligopoly market structure. Therefore, consumers can benefit from less-than-perfectly-competitive markets.

PORTER'S FIVE FORCES AND MARKET STRUCTURE

A financial analyst aiming to establish market conditions and consequent profitability of incumbent firms should start with the questions framed by Exhibit 1: How many sellers are there? Is the product differentiated? and so on. Moreover, in the case of monopolies and quasi monopolies, the analyst should evaluate the legislative and regulatory framework: Can the company set prices freely, or are there governmental controls? Finally, the analyst should consider the threat of competition from potential entrants.

This analysis is often summarized by students of corporate strategy as "Porter's five forces," named after Harvard Business School professor Michael E. Porter. His book, *Competitive Strategy*, presented a systematic analysis of the practice of market strategy. Porter (2008) identified the five forces as:

- Threat of entry;
- Power of suppliers;
- Power of buyers (customers);
- Threat of substitutes; and
- Rivalry among existing competitors.

It is easy to note the parallels between four of these five forces and the columns in Exhibit 1. The only "orphan" is the power of suppliers, which is not at the core of the theoretical economic analysis of competition, but which has substantial weight in the practical analysis of competition and profitability.

Some stock analysts (e.g., Dorsey 2004) use the term "economic moat" to suggest that there are factors protecting the profitability of a firm that are similar to the moats (ditches full of water) that were used to protect some medieval castles. A deep moat means that there is little or no threat of entry by invaders, i.e. competitors. It also means that customers are locked in because of high switching costs.

2. PERFECT COMPETITION

Perfect competition is characterized by the five conditions presented in Exhibit 1, above:

1. There are a large number of potential buyers and sellers.
2. The products offered by the sellers are virtually identical.
3. There are few or easily surmountable barriers to entry and exit.
4. Sellers have no market-pricing power.
5. Non-price competition is absent.

While few markets achieve the distinction of being perfectly competitive, it is useful to establish the outcome associated with this market structure as a benchmark against which other market structures can be compared. The most typical example of perfect competition is found in certain aspects of the agriculture industry, such as the large number of farmers growing corn for animal feed. Corn is a primary source of food for pork, beef, and poultry production. A bushel of corn from Farmer Brown is virtually identical to a bushel of corn from Farmer Lopez. If a hog farmer needs corn to feed his hogs, it does not matter whether the corn comes from Farmer Brown or Farmer Lopez. Furthermore, the aggregate corn market is well defined, with active futures and spot markets. Information about the corn market is easy and inexpensive to access, and there is no way to differentiate the product, such as by advertising. Agribusiness is capital intensive, but where arable land is relatively abundant and water is available, the barriers to entry (e.g., capital and expertise) for corn production are relatively low.

2.1. Demand Analysis in Perfectly Competitive Markets

The price of a homogeneous product sold in a competitive market is determined by the demand and supply in that market. Economists usually represent demand and supply in a market through demand and supply curves in a two-axis plane, where quantity and price are shown on the *x*-axis and *y*-axis, respectively. Economists believe that demand functions have negative slopes, as shown in Exhibit 2. That is, at high prices, less is demanded. For normal goods and services, as the price declines, the quantity demanded increases. This concept is based on two effects: the income effect and the substitution effect. The income effect results from the increased purchasing power the consumer has when prices fall. With lower prices, the consumer can afford to purchase more of the product. The substitution effect comes from the increasing attractiveness of the lower-priced product. If soybean prices are unchanged and corn prices decrease, hog farmers will substitute corn for soybeans as feed for their animals.

EXHIBIT 2: Market Demand in Perfect Competition

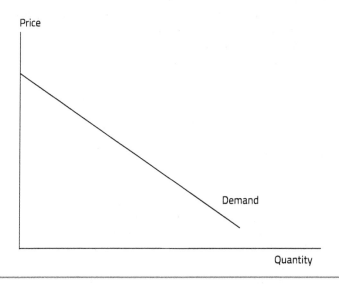

Assume the demand for this product can be specified as

$$Q_D = 50 - 2P$$

where Q_D is the quantity of demand and P is the product's price. This demand function can be rearranged in terms of price:

$$P = 25 - 0.5Q_D$$

In this form, total revenue (TR) is equal to price times quantity, or $P \times Q_D$. Thus,

$$\text{TR} = PQ_D = 25Q_D - 0.5Q_D^2$$

Average revenue (AR) can be found by dividing TR by Q_D. Therefore,

$$\text{AR} = \text{TR}/Q_D = (25Q_D - 0.5Q_D^2)/Q_D = 25 - 0.5Q_D$$

Note that the AR function is identical to the market demand function. The assumption here is that the relationship between price and quantity demanded is linear. Clearly, that may not be the case in the real market. Another simplifying assumption made is that the price of the product is the only determinant of demand. Again, that is not likely in the real market. For example, economic theory suggests that consumer income is another important factor in determining demand. The prices of related goods and services, such as substitutes and complements, are also considered factors affecting demand for a specific product.

Marginal revenue (MR) is the change in total revenue per extra increment sold when the quantity sold changes by a small increment, Q_D. Substituting ($Q_D + Q_D$) into the total revenue (TR) equation, marginal revenue can be expressed as:

$$MR = \frac{\Delta TR}{\Delta Q_D} = \frac{[25(Q_D + \Delta Q_D) - 0.5(Q_D^2 + 2Q_D\Delta Q_D + \Delta Q_D^2)] - [25Q_D - 0.5Q_D^2]}{\Delta Q_D}$$

$$= \frac{25\Delta Q_D - Q_D\Delta Q_D - 0.5\Delta Q_D^2}{\Delta Q_D} = 25 - Q_D - 0.5\Delta Q_D$$

For example, suppose $Q_D = 5$ and $Q_D = 1$, then total revenue increases from 112.50 [$= 25$ (5) $- 0.5$ (5^2)] to 132 [$= 25(6) - 0.5(6^2)$], and marginal revenue is 19.5 = (132 – 112.5)/1. Note that marginal revenue is equal to (25 – Q_D – 0.5 Q_D). Now suppose that Q_D is much smaller, for example $Q_D = 0.1$. In this case, total revenue increases to 114.495 [$= 25(5.1) - 0.5(5.1^2)$], and marginal revenue is 1.995/0.1 = 19.95. It is straightforward to confirm that as Q_D gets smaller marginal revenue gets closer to 20 = 25 – Q_D. So, for very small changes in the quantity sold we can write marginal revenue as[3]

$$MR = 25 - Q_D$$

Although we have introduced the concept of marginal revenue in the context of the demand curve for the market as a whole, its usefulness derives from its role in the output and pricing decisions of individual firms. As we will see, marginal revenue and an analogous concept, marginal cost, are critical in determining firms' profit-maximizing strategies.

3. ELASTICITY OF DEMAND

Consumers respond differently to changes in the price of different kinds of products and services. The quantity demanded for some products is very price sensitive, while for other products, price changes result in little change in the quantity demanded. Economists refer to the relationship between changes in price and changes in the quantity demanded as the price elasticity of demand. Therefore, the demand for the former group of products—those that are very price sensitive—is said to have high price elasticity, whereas the demand for the latter group is said to have low price elasticity. Understanding the sensitivity of demand changes to changes in price is critical to understanding market structures.

Price elasticity of demand measures the percentage change in the quantity demanded given a percentage change in the price of a given product. Because the relationship of demand to price is negative, the price elasticity of demand would be negative. *Many economists, however, present the price elasticity as an absolute value, so that price elasticity has a positive sign.*

---

[3]Readers who are familiar with calculus will recognize this as the derivative of total revenue with respect to the quantity sold.

We will follow that convention. Higher price elasticity indicates that consumers are very responsive to changes in price. Lower values for price elasticity imply that consumers are not very responsive to price changes. Price elasticity can be measured with the following relationship:

$$\varepsilon_P = -(\% \text{ change in } Q_D) \div (\% \text{ change in } P)$$

where ε_P is price elasticity of demand, Q_D is the quantity demanded, and P is the product's price.

Price elasticity of demand falls into three categories. When demand is very responsive to price change, it is identified as *elastic*. When demand is not responsive to price change, it is identified as *inelastic*. When the percentage change in quantity demanded is exactly the same as the percentage change in price, the demand is called *unitary elastic*.

$$\varepsilon_P > 1 \text{ Demand is elastic}$$

$$\varepsilon_P = 1 \text{ Demand is unitary elastic}$$

$$\varepsilon_P < 1 \text{ Demand is inelastic}$$

Price elasticity of demand depends on several factors. *Price elasticity will be higher if there are many close substitutes for the product.* If a product has many good alternatives, consumers will be more sensitive to price changes. For example, carbonated beverages ("soft drinks") have many close substitutes. It takes strong brand loyalty to keep customer demand high in the soft drink market when one brand's price is strategically lowered; the price elasticity of demand for Coca-Cola has been estimated to be 3.8. For products with numerous close substitutes, demand is highly elastic. For products with few close substitutes, demand is lower in price elasticity and would be considered price inelastic. The demand for first-class airline tickets is often seen as inelastic because only very wealthy people are expected to buy them; the demand for economy-class tickets is elastic because the typical consumer for this product is more budget-conscious. Consumers do not consider economy-class airline tickets a close substitute for first-class accommodations, particularly on long flights.

The airline ticket example introduces another determinant of price elasticity of demand. *The greater the share of the consumer's budget spent on the item, the higher the price elasticity of demand.* Expensive items, such as durable goods (e.g., refrigerators and televisions), tend to have higher elasticity measures, while less expensive items, such as potatoes and salt, have lower elasticity values. Consumers will not change their normal salt consumption if the price of salt decreases by 10 percent. Instead, they will buy their next package of salt when they run out, with very little regard to the price change.

The airline ticket also makes a good example for the final factor determining price elasticity. *Price elasticity of demand also depends on the length of time within which the demand schedule is being considered.* Holiday airline travel is highly price elastic. Consumers shop vigorously for vacation flights because they have time to plan their holiday. Business airline travelers typically have less flexibility in determining their schedules. If your business requires a face-to-face meeting with a client, then the price of the ticket is somewhat irrelevant. If gasoline prices increase, there is very little you can do in the short run but pay the higher price. However, evidence of commuter choices indicates that many use alternative transportation methods after the gasoline price spikes. In the long run, higher gasoline prices will lead consumers to change their modes of transportation, trading in less efficient vehicles for automobiles with higher gas mileage or public transit options where available.

There are two extreme cases of price elasticity of demand. One extreme is the **horizontal demand schedule**. This term implies that at a given price, the response in the quantity demanded is infinite. *This is the demand schedule faced by a perfectly competitive firm because it is a price taker*, as in the case of a corn farmer. If the corn farmer tried to charge a higher price than the market price, nobody would buy her product. On the other hand, the farmer has no incentive to sell at a lower price because she can sell all she can produce at the market price. In a perfectly competitive market the quantity supplied by an individual firm has a negligible effect on the market price. In the case of *perfect price elasticity*, the measure is $\varepsilon_P = \infty$.

The other extreme is the **vertical demand schedule**. The vertical demand schedule implies that some fixed quantity is demanded, regardless of price. An example of such demand is the diabetic consumer with the need for a certain amount of insulin. If the price of insulin goes up, the patient will not consume less of it. The amount desired is set by the patient's medical condition. The measure for *perfect price inelasticity* is $\varepsilon_P = 0$.

The nature of the elasticity calculation and consumer behavior in the marketplace imply that for virtually any product (excluding cases of perfect elasticity and perfect inelasticity), demand is more elastic at higher prices and less elastic (more inelastic) at lower prices. For example, at current low prices, the demand for table salt is very inelastic. However, if table salt increased in price to hundreds of dollars per ounce, consumers would become more responsive to its price changes. Exhibit 3 reports several empirical estimates of price elasticity of demand.

EXHIBIT 3: Empirical Price Elasticities

Commodity (Good/Service)	Price Elasticity of Market Demand
Alcoholic beverages consumed at home	
Beer	0.84
Wine	0.55
Liquor	0.50
Coffee	
Regular	0.16
Instant	0.36
Credit charges on bank cards	2.44
Furniture	3.04
Glassware/china	1.20
International air transportation United States/Europe	1.20
Shoes	0.73
Soybean meal	1.65
Tomatoes	2.22

Note: Various sources, as noted in McGuigan, Moyer, and Harris (2008), p. 95. These are the elasticities with respect to the product's own price; by convention, they are shown here as positive numbers.

4. OTHER FACTORS AFFECTING DEMAND

There are two other important forces that influence shifts in consumer demand. One influential factor is consumer income and the other is the price of a related product. For normal goods, as consumer income increases, the demand increases. The degree to which consumers respond to higher incomes by increasing their demand for goods and services is referred to as income elasticity of demand. **Income elasticity of demand** measures the responsiveness of demand to changes in income. The calculation is similar to that of price elasticity, with the percentage change in income replacing the percentage change in price. Note the new calculation below:

$$\varepsilon_Y = (\% \text{ change in } Q_D) \div (\% \text{ change in } Y)$$

where ε_Y is income elasticity of demand, Q_D is the quantity demanded, and Y is consumer income. For normal goods, the measure ε_Y will be a positive value. That is, as consumers' income rises, more of the product is demanded. For products that are considered luxury items, the measure of income elasticity will be greater than one. There are other goods and services that are considered inferior products. For inferior products, as consumer income rises, less of the product is demanded. Inferior products will have negative values for income elasticity. For example, a person on a small income may watch television shows, but if this person had more income, she would prefer going to live concerts and theater performances; in this example, television shows would be the inferior good.

As a technical issue, the difference between price elasticity of demand and income elasticity of demand is that the demand adjustment for price elasticity represents a movement *along the demand schedule* because the demand schedule represents combinations of price and quantity. The demand adjustment for income elasticity represents a *shift in the demand curve* because with a higher income one can afford to purchase more of the good at any price. For a normal good, an increase in income would shift the demand schedule out to the right, away from the origin of the graph, and a decrease in income would shift the demand curve to the left, toward the origin.

The final factor influencing demand for a product is the change in price of a related product, such as a strong substitute or a complementary product. If a close competitor in the beverage market lowers its price, consumers will substitute that product for your product. Thus, your product's demand curve will shift to the left, toward the origin of the graph. **Cross-price elasticity of demand** is the responsiveness of the demand for product A that is associated with the change in price of product B:

$$\varepsilon_X = (\% \text{ change in } Q_{DA}) \div (\% \text{ change in } P_B)$$

where ε_X is cross-price elasticity of demand, Q_{DA} is the quantity demanded of product A, and P_B is the price of product B.

When the cross-price elasticity of demand between two products is *positive*, the two products are considered to be **substitutes**. For example, you may expect to have positive cross-price elasticity between honey and sugar. If the measure of cross-price elasticity is *negative*, the two products are referred to as **complements** of each other. For example, if the price of DVDs goes up, you would expect consumers to buy fewer DVD players. In this case, the cross-price elasticity of demand would have a negative value.

Reviewing cross-price elasticity values provides a simple test for the degree of competition in the market. The more numerous and the closer the substitutes for a product, the lower the pricing power of firms selling in that market; the fewer the substitutes for a product, the greater the pricing power. One interesting application was a US Supreme Court case involving the production and sale of cellophane by DuPont.[4] The court noted that the relevant product market for DuPont's cellophane was the broader flexible packaging materials market. The Supreme Court found the cross-price elasticity of demand between cellophane and other flexible packaging materials to be sufficiently high and exonerated DuPont from a charge of monopolizing the market.

Because price elasticity of demand relates changes in price to changes in the quantity demanded, there must be a logical relationship between marginal revenue and price elasticity. Recall that marginal revenue equals the change in total revenue given a change in output or sales. An increase in total revenue results from a decrease in price that results in an increase in sales. In order for the increase in the quantity demanded to be sufficient to offset the decline in price, the percentage change in quantity demanded must be greater than the percentage decrease in price. The relationship between TR and price elasticity is as follows:

$$\varepsilon_P > 1 \text{ Demand is elastic} \uparrow P \rightarrow \text{TR} \downarrow \text{ and } \downarrow P \rightarrow \text{TR} \uparrow$$

$$\varepsilon_P = 1 \text{ Demand is unitary elastic} \updownarrow P \rightarrow \text{ no change in TR}$$

$$0 < \varepsilon_P < 1 \text{ Demand is inelastic} \uparrow P \rightarrow \text{TR} \uparrow \text{ and } \downarrow P \rightarrow \text{TR} \downarrow$$

Total revenue is maximized when marginal revenue is zero. The logic is that as long as marginal revenue is positive (i.e., each additional unit sold contributes to additional total revenue), total revenue will continue to increase. Only when marginal revenue becomes negative will total revenue begin to decline. Therefore, the percentage decrease in price is greater than the percentage increase in quantity demanded. The relationship between marginal revenue (MR) and price elasticity can be expressed as

$$\text{MR} = P[1 - (1/\varepsilon_P)]$$

An understanding of price elasticity of demand is an important strategic tool. It would be very useful to know in advance what would happen to your firm's total revenue if you increased the product's price. If you are operating in the inelastic portion of the demand curve, increasing the price of the product will increase total revenue. On the other hand, if you are operating in the elastic portion of the product's demand curve, increasing the price will decrease total revenue.

Decision makers can also use the relationship between marginal revenue and price elasticity of demand in other ways. For example, suppose you are a farmer considering planting soybeans or some other feed crop, such as corn. From Exhibit 3, we know that

[4]*US v. DuPont*, 351 US 377 (1956), as noted in McGuigan, Moyer, and Harris (2008).

soybean meal's price elasticity of demand has been estimated to be 1.65. We also know that the current (May 2018) soybean meal price is $465.00 per metric ton.[5] Therefore, by solving the equation above, we find that the expected marginal revenue per metric ton of soybean meal is $183.16. Soybeans may prove to be a profitable crop for the farmer. Just a few years earlier, in May of 2014, the price of a metric ton of soybean meal was $578.75. Given the crop's price elasticity of demand, the estimated marginal revenue per metric ton was then $227.97. The higher price translates into higher marginal revenue and might have induced the farmer to plant even more soybeans rather than another feed crop instead.

How do business decision makers decide what level of output to bring to the market? To answer that question, the firm must understand its cost of resources, its production relations, and its supply function. Once the supply function is well defined and understood, it is combined with the demand analysis to determine the profit-maximizing levels of output.

5. CONSUMER SURPLUS: VALUE MINUS EXPENDITURE

To this point, we have discussed the fundamentals of supply and demand curves and explained a simple model of how a market can be expected to arrive at an equilibrium combination of price and quantity. While it is certainly necessary for the analyst to understand the basic workings of the market model, it is also crucial to have a sense of why we might care about the nature of the equilibrium. In this section we review the concept of **consumer surplus**, which is helpful in understanding and evaluating business pricing strategies. Consumer surplus is defined as the difference between the value that a consumer places on the units purchased and the amount of money that was required to pay for them. It is a measure of the value gained by the buyer from the transaction.

To get an intuitive feel for the concept of consumer surplus, consider the last thing you purchased. Whatever it was, think of how much you paid for it. Now contrast that price with the maximum amount you *would have been willing to pay* rather than go without the item altogether. If those two numbers are different, we say you received some consumer surplus from your purchase. You got a "bargain" because you would have been willing to pay more than you had to pay.

Earlier, we referred to the law of demand, which says that as price falls, consumers are willing to buy more of the good. This observation translates into a negatively sloped demand curve. Alternatively, we could say that the highest price that consumers are willing to pay for an additional unit declines as they consume more and more of a good. In this way, we can interpret their *willingness to pay* as a measure of how much they *value* each additional unit of the good. This is a very important point: To purchase a unit of some good, consumers must give up something else they value. So, the price they are willing to pay for an additional unit of a good is a measure of how much they value that unit, in terms of the other goods they must sacrifice to consume it.

If demand curves are negatively sloped, it must be because the value of each additional unit of the good falls as more of the good is consumed. We shall explore this concept further below, but for now, it is enough to recognize that the demand curve can therefore be

---

[5]Source: World-Bank Commodity Market Report 2018.

considered a **marginal value curve**, because it shows the highest price consumers would be willing to pay for each additional unit. In effect, the demand curve is the willingness of consumers to pay for each additional unit.

This interpretation of the demand curve allows us to measure the total value of consuming any given quantity of a good: It is the sum of all the marginal values of each unit consumed, up to and including the last unit. Graphically, this measure translates into the area under the consumer's demand curve, up to and including the last unit consumed, as shown in Exhibit 4, where the consumer is choosing to buy Q_1 units of the good at a price of P_1. The marginal value of the Q_1^{th} unit is clearly P_1 because that is the highest price the consumer is willing to pay for that unit. Importantly, however, the marginal value of each unit *up to* the Q_1^{th} is greater than P_1.

EXHIBIT 4: Consumer Surplus

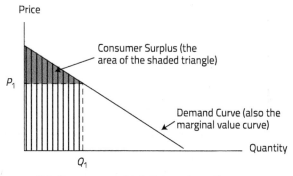

Note: Consumer surplus is the area beneath the demand curve and above the price paid.

Because the consumer would have been willing to pay more for each of those units than she paid (P_1), we can say she received more value than the cost to her of buying them. This extra value is the buyer's consumer surplus. The *total value* of quantity Q_1 to the buyer is the area of the vertically crosshatched trapezoid in Exhibit 4. The *total expenditure* is only the area of the rectangle with height P_1 and base Q_1 (bottom section). The total consumer surplus received from buying Q_1 units at a level price of P_1 per unit is the difference between the area under the demand curve and the area of the rectangle $P_1 \times Q_1$. The resulting area is shown as the lightly shaded triangle (upper section).

EXAMPLE 1   Consumer Surplus

A market demand function is given by the equation $Q_D = 180 - 2P$. Find the value of consumer surplus if price is equal to 65.

Solution:
    First, input 65 into the demand function to find the quantity demanded at that price: $Q_D = 180 - 2(65) = 50$. Then, to make drawing the demand curve easier, invert the demand function by solving for P in terms of Q_D: $P = 90 - 0.5Q_D$. Note that the price intercept is 90 and the quantity intercept is 180. Draw the demand curve:

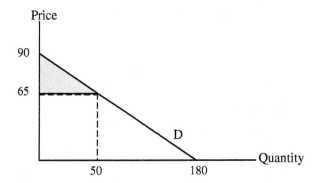

Find the area of the triangle above the price of 65 and below the demand curve, up to quantity 50: Area $= \frac{1}{2}$ (Base)(Height) $= \frac{1}{2}$ (50)(25) = 625.

6. SUPPLY ANALYSIS, OPTIMAL PRICE, AND OUTPUT IN PERFECTLY COMPETITIVE MARKETS

Consider two corn farmers, Mr. Brown and Ms. Lopez. They both have land available to them to grow corn and can sell at one price, say 3 currency units per kilogram. They will try to produce as much corn as is profitable at that price. If the price is driven up to 5 currency units per kilogram by new consumers entering the market—say, ethanol producers—Mr. Brown and Ms. Lopez will try to produce more corn. To increase their output levels, they may have to use less productive land, increase irrigation, use more fertilizer, or all three. Their production costs will likely increase. They will both still try to produce as much corn as possible to profit at the new, higher price of 5 currency units per kilogram. Exhibit 5 illustrates this example. Note that the supply functions for the individual firms have positive slopes. Thus, as prices increase, the firms supply greater quantities of the product.

EXHIBIT 5: Firm and Market Supply in Perfect Competition

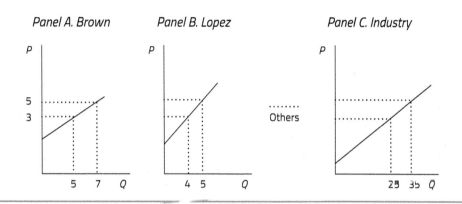

Notice that the market supply curve is the sum of the supply curves of the individual firms—Brown, Lopez, and others—that make up the market. Assume that the supply function for the market can be expressed as a linear relationship, as follows:

$$Q_S = 10 + 5P, \text{ or } P = -2 + 0.2Q_S,$$

where Q_S is the quantity supplied and P is the price of the product.

Before we analyze the optimal supply level for the firm, we need to point out that economic costs and profits differ from accounting costs and profits in a significant way. **Economic costs** include all the remuneration needed to keep the productive resource in its current employment or to acquire the resource for productive use.

To evaluate the remuneration needed to keep the resource in its current use and attract new resources for productive use, economists refer to the resource's **opportunity cost**. Opportunity cost is measured by determining the resource's next best opportunity. If a corn farmer could be employed in an alternative position in the labor market with an income of 50,000, then the opportunity cost of the farmer's labor is 50,000. Similarly, the farmer's land and capital could be leased to another farmer or sold and reinvested in another type of business. The return foregone by not doing so is an opportunity cost. In economic terms, total cost includes the full normal market return on all the resources utilized in the business. **Economic profit** is the difference between TR and total cost (TC). Economic profit differs from accounting profit because accounting profit does not include opportunity cost. Accounting profit includes only explicit payments to outside providers of resources (e.g. workers, vendors, lenders) and depreciation based on the historic cost of physical capital.

6.1. Optimal Price and Output in Perfectly Competitive Markets

Carrying forward our examples from Sections 3.1 and 3.2, we can now combine the market supply and demand functions to solve for the equilibrium price and quantity, where Q^* represents the equilibrium level of both supply and demand.

$$P = 25 - 0.5Q_D = -2 + 0.2Q_S = P$$
$$25 - 0.5Q_D = -2 + 0.2Q_S$$
$$27 = 0.7Q^*$$
$$Q^* = 38.57$$

According to the market demand curve, the equilibrium price is

$$P = 25 - 0.5Q^* = 25 - 0.5(38.57) = 25 - 19.29 = 5.71.$$

With many firms in the market and total output in the market of almost 39 units of the product, the effective market price would be 5.71. This result becomes the demand function for each perfectly competitive firm. Even if a few individual producers could expand production, there would not be a noticeable change in the market equilibrium price. In fact, if any one firm could change the equilibrium market price, the market would not be in perfect competition. Therefore, the demand curve that each perfectly competitive firm faces is a horizontal line at the equilibrium price, as shown in Exhibit 6, even though the demand curve for the whole market is downward sloping.

EXHIBIT 6: Individual Firm's Demand in Perfect Competition

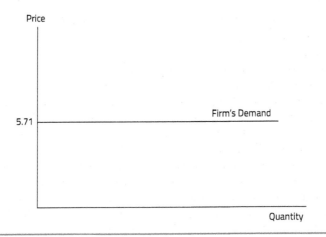

EXAMPLE 2   Demand Curves in Perfect Competition

1. Is it possible that the demand schedule faced by Firm A is horizontal while the demand schedule faced by the market as a whole is downward sloping?
   A. No, because Firm A can change its output based on demand changes.
   B. No, because a horizontal demand curve means that elasticity is infinite.

> C. Yes, because consumers can go to another firm if Firm A charges a higher price, and Firm A can sell all it produces at the market price.
>
> *Solution:*
>   C is correct. Firm A cannot charge a higher price and has no incentive to sell at a price below the market price.

To analyze the firm's revenue position, recall that average revenue is equivalent to the firm's demand function. Therefore, the horizontal line that represents the firm's demand curve is the firm's AR schedule.

Marginal revenue is the incremental increase in total revenue associated with each additional unit sold. For every extra unit the firm sells, it receives 5.71. Thus, the firm's MR schedule is also the horizontal line at 5.71. TR is calculated by multiplying AR by the quantity of products sold. Total revenue is the area under the AR line at the point where the firm produces the output. In the case of perfect competition, the following conditions hold for the individual firm:

$$\text{Price} = \text{Average revenue} = \text{Marginal revenue}$$

The next step is to develop the firm's cost functions. The firm knows that it can sell the entire product it produces at the market's equilibrium price. How much should it produce? That decision is determined by analysis of the firm's costs and revenues. A corn farmer uses three primary resources: land, labor, and capital. In economics, capital is any man-made aid to production. For the corn farmer, his or her capital includes the irrigation system, tractors, harvesters, trucks, grain bins, fertilizer, and so forth. The labor includes the farmer, perhaps members of the farmer's family, and hired labor. In the initial stages of production, only the farmer and the farmer's family are cultivating the land, with a significant investment in capital. They have a tractor, fertilizer, irrigation equipment, grain bins, seed, and a harvester. The investment in land and capital is relatively high compared with the labor input. In this production phase, the average cost of producing a bushel of corn is high. As they begin to expand by adding labor to the collection of expensive land and capital, the average cost of producing corn begins to decline—for example, because one tractor can be used more intensively to plow a larger amount of land. When the combination of land, labor, and capital approaches an efficient range, the average cost of producing a bushel of corn declines.

Given a certain level of technology, there is a limit to the increase in productivity. Eventually something begins to cause declining marginal productivity. That is, each additional unit of input produces a progressively smaller increase in output. This force is called the **law of diminishing returns**. This "law" helps define the shape of the firm's cost functions. Average cost and marginal cost will be U-shaped. Over the initial stages of output, average and marginal costs will decline. At some level of output, the law of diminishing returns will overtake the efficiencies in production and average and marginal costs will increase.

Average cost (AC) is Total cost (TC) divided by Output (Q). Therefore,

$$\text{AC} = \text{TC}/Q$$

Note that we have defined average cost (AC) in terms of total costs. Many authors refer to this as "average total cost" to distinguish it from a related concept, "average variable cost," which omits fixed costs. In the remainder of this chapter, *average cost should be understood to mean average total cost.*

Marginal cost (MC) is the change in TC associated with an incremental change in output:

$$MC = TC/Q$$

By definition, fixed costs do not vary with output, so marginal cost reflects only changes in variable costs.[6] MC declines initially because processes can be made more efficient and specialization makes workers more proficient at their tasks. However, at some higher level of output, MC begins to increase (e.g., must pay workers a higher wage to have them work overtime and, in agriculture, less fertile land must be brought into production). MC and AC will be equal at the level of output where AC is minimized. This is a mathematical necessity and intuitive. If you employ the least expensive labor in the initial phase of production, average and marginal cost will decline. Eventually, additional labor will be more costly. For example, if the labor market is at or near full employment, in order to attract additional workers, you must pay higher wages than they are currently earning elsewhere. Thus, the additional (marginal) labor is more costly, and the higher cost increases the overall average as soon as MC exceeds AC. Exhibit 7 illustrates the relationship between AC and MC.

EXHIBIT 7: Individual Firm's Short-Run Cost Schedules

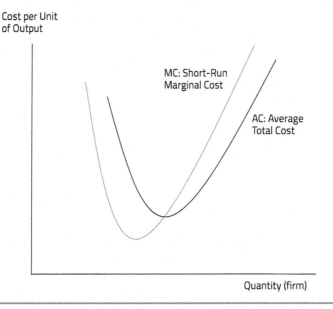

<hr>

[6]Readers who are familiar with calculus will recognize that MC is simply the derivative of total cost with respect to quantity produced.

Now combine the revenue and cost functions from Exhibit 6 and Exhibit 7. In short-run equilibrium, the perfectly competitive firm can earn an economic profit (or an economic loss). In this example, the equilibrium price, 5.71, is higher than the minimum AC. The firm will always maximize profit at an output level where MR = MC. Recall that in perfect competition, the horizontal demand curve is the marginal revenue and average revenue schedules. By setting output at point A in Exhibit 8, where MR = MC, the firm will maximize profits. Total revenue is equal to $P \times Q$—in this case, 5.71 times Q_C. Total cost is equal to Q_C times the average cost of producing Q_C, at point B in Exhibit 8. The difference between the two areas is economic profit.

EXHIBIT 8: Perfectly Competitive Firm's Short-Run Equilibrium

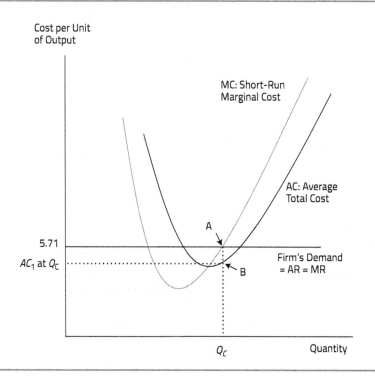

7. LONG-RUN EQUILIBRIUM IN PERFECTLY COMPETITIVE MARKETS

In the long run, economic profit will attract other entrepreneurs to the market, resulting in the production of more output. The aggregate supply will increase, shifting the industry supply (S_1) curve to the right, away from the origin of the graph. For a given demand curve, this increase in supply at each price level will lower the equilibrium price, as shown in Exhibit 9.

EXHIBIT 9: Perfectly Competitive Market with Increased Supply

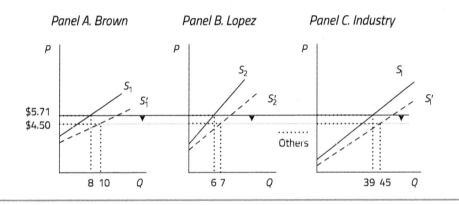

In the long run, the perfectly competitive firm will operate at the point where marginal cost equals the minimum of average cost, because at that point, entry is no longer profitable: In equilibrium, price equals not only marginal cost (firm equilibrium) but also minimum average cost, so that total revenues equal total costs. This result implies that the perfectly competitive firm operates with zero economic profit. That is, the firm receives its normal profit (rental cost of capital), which is included in its economic costs. Recall that economic profits occur when total revenue exceeds total cost (and therefore differ from accounting profits). With low entry cost and homogeneous products to sell, the perfectly competitive firm earns zero economic profit in the long run.

Exhibit 10 illustrates the long-run equilibrium position of the perfectly competitive firm. Note that total revenue equals price ($4.50) times quantity ($Q_E$) and total cost equals average cost ($4.50) times quantity ($Q_E$).

EXHIBIT 10: Perfectly Competitive Firm's Long-Run Equilibrium

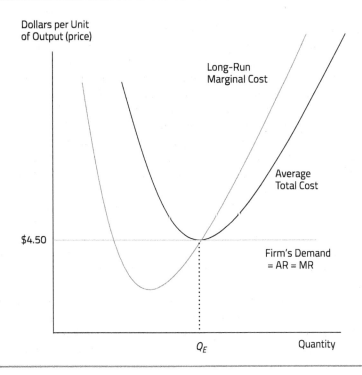

The long-run marginal cost schedule is the perfectly competitive firm's supply curve. The firm's demand curve is dictated by the aggregate market's equilibrium price. The basic rule of profit maximization is that MR = MC, as is the case in long-run equilibrium. The firm's demand schedule is the same as the firm's marginal revenue and average revenue. Given its cost of operation, the only decision the perfectly competitive firm faces is how much to produce. The answer is the level of output that maximizes its return, and that level is where MR = MC. The demand curve is perfectly elastic. Of course, the firm constantly tries to find ways to lower its cost in the long run.

SCHUMPETER ON INNOVATION AND PERFECT COMPETITION

The Austrian-American economist Joseph A. Schumpeter[7] pointed out that technical change in economics can happen in two main ways:

1.   Innovation of process: a new, more efficient way to produce an existing good or service.

[7] See part 2 of Schumpeter (1942) for the famous "creative destruction" process.

2.   Innovation of product: a new product altogether or an innovation upon an existing product.

Innovation of process is related to production methods. For example, instead of mixing cement by hand, since the invention of the electric engine it has been possible to use electric mixers. A more recent innovation has been to use the internet to provide technical support to personal computer users: A technician can remotely log on to the customer's PC and fix problems instead of providing instructions over the phone. The result is likely the same, but the process is more efficient.

Innovation of product is related to the product itself. MP3 players, smart phones, robot surgery, and GPS vehicle monitoring have existed only for a few years. They are new products and services. While portable music players existed before the MP3 player, no similar service existed before GPS monitoring of personal vehicles and freight trucks was invented.

How does the reality of continuous innovation of product and process, which is a characteristic of modern economies, fit into the ideal model of perfect competition, where the product is made by a huge number of tiny, anonymous suppliers? This seems a contradiction because the tiny suppliers cannot all be able to invent new products— and indeed, the markets for portable music players and smart phones do not look like perfect competition.

Schumpeter suggested that perfect competition is more of a long-run type of market. In the short run, a company develops a new process or product and is the only one to take advantage of the innovation. This company likely will have high profits and will outpace any competitors. A second stage is what Schumpeter called the swarming (as when a group of bees leaves a hive to follow a queen): In this case, some entrepreneurs notice the innovation and follow the innovator through imitation. Some of them will fail, while others will succeed and possibly be more successful than the initial innovator. The third stage occurs when the new technology is no longer new because everyone has imitated it. At this point, no economic profits are realized, because the new process or product is no longer a competitive advantage, in the sense that everyone has it—which is when perfect competition prevails and we have long-run equilibrium until a new innovation of process or product is introduced.

8. MONOPOLISTIC COMPETITION

Early in the 20th century, economists began to realize that most markets did not operate under the conditions of perfect competition.[8] Many market structures exhibited characteristics of strong competitive forces; however, other distinct non-competitive factors played important roles in the market. As the name implies, monopolistic competition is a hybrid market. *The most distinctive factor in monopolistic competition is product differentiation.* Recall the characteristics from Exhibit 1:

---

[8]Chamberlin (1933).

1. There are a large number of potential buyers and sellers.
2. The products offered by each seller are close substitutes for the products offered by other firms, and each firm tries to make its product look different.
3. Entry into and exit from the market are possible with fairly low costs.
4. Firms have some pricing power.
5. Suppliers differentiate their products through advertising and other non-price strategies.

While the market is made up of many firms that compose the product group, each producer attempts to distinguish its product from that of the others. Product differentiation is accomplished in a variety of ways. For example, consider the wide variety of communication devices available today. Decades ago, when each communication market was controlled by a regulated single seller (the telephone company), all telephones were alike. In the deregulated market of today, the variety of physical styles and colors is extensive. All versions accomplish many of the same tasks.

The communication device manufacturers and providers differentiate their products with different colors, styles, networks, bundled applications, conditional contracts, functionality, and more. Advertising is usually the avenue pursued to convince consumers there is a difference between the goods in the product group. Successful advertising and trademark branding result in customer loyalty. A good example is the brand loyalty associated with Harley-Davidson motorcycles. Harley-Davidson's customers believe that their motorcycles are truly different from and better than all other motorcycles. The same kind of brand loyalty exists for many fashion creations and cosmetics.

The extent to which the producer is successful in product differentiation determines pricing power in the market. Very successful differentiation results in a market structure that resembles the single-seller market (monopoly). However, because there are relatively low entry and exit costs, competition will, in the long run, drive prices and revenues down toward an equilibrium similar to perfect competition. Thus, the hybrid market displays characteristics found in both perfectly competitive and monopoly markets.

8.1. Demand Analysis in Monopolistically Competitive Markets

Because each good sold in the product group is somewhat different from the others, the demand curve for each firm in the monopolistic competition market structure is downward sloping to the right. Price and the quantity demanded are negatively related. Lowering the price will increase the quantity demanded, and raising the price will decrease the quantity demanded. There will be ranges of prices within which demand is elastic and (lower) prices at which demand is inelastic. Exhibit 11 illustrates the demand, marginal revenue, and cost structures facing a monopolistically competitive firm in the short run.

EXHIBIT 11: Short-Run Equilibrium in Monopolistic Competition

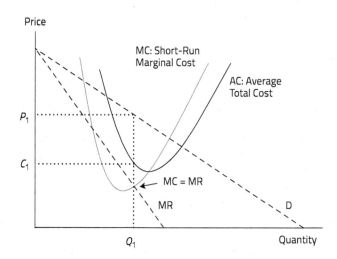

In the short run, the profit-maximizing choice is the level of output where MR = MC. Because the product is somewhat different from that of the competitors, the firm can charge the price determined by the demand curve. Therefore, in Exhibit 11, Q_1 is the ideal level of output and P_1 is the price consumers are willing to pay to acquire that quantity. Total revenue is the area of the rectangle $P_1 \times Q_1$.

8.2. Supply Analysis in Monopolistically Competitive Markets

In perfect competition, the firm's supply schedule is represented by the marginal cost schedule. In monopolistic competition, there is no well-defined supply function. The information used to determine the appropriate level of output is based on the intersection of MC and MR. However, the price that will be charged is based on the market demand schedule. The firm's supply curve should measure the quantity the firm is willing to supply at various prices. That information is not represented by either marginal cost or average cost.

8.3. Optimal Price and Output in Monopolistically Competitive Markets

As seen in Section 4.1, in the short run, the profit-maximizing choice is the level of output where MR = MC and total revenue is the area of the rectangle $P_1 \times Q_1$ in Exhibit 11.

The average cost of producing Q_1 units of the product is C_1, and the total cost is the area of the rectangle $C_1 \times Q_1$. The difference between TR and TC is economic profit. The profit relationship is described as

$$\pi = TR - TC$$

where π is total profit, TR is total revenue, and TC is total cost.

THE BENEFITS OF IMPERFECT COMPETITION

Is monopolistic competition indeed imperfect—that is, is it a bad thing? At first, one would say that it is an inefficient market structure because prices are higher and the quantity supplied is less than in perfect competition. At the same time, in the real world, we see more markets characterized by monopolistic competition than markets meeting the strict conditions of perfect competition. If monopolistic competition were that inefficient, one wonders, why would it be so common?

A part of the explanation goes back to Schumpeter. Firms try to differentiate their products to meet the needs of customers. Differentiation provides a profit incentive to innovate, experiment with new products and services, and potentially improve the standard of living.

Moreover, because each customer has differing tastes and preferences, slight variations of each good or service are likely to capture the niche of the market that prefers them. An example is the market for candy, where one can find chocolate, licorice, mint, fruit, and many other flavors.

A further reason why monopolistic competition may be good is that people like variety. Traditional economic theories of international trade suggested that countries should buy products from other countries that they cannot produce domestically. Therefore, Norway should buy bananas from a tropical country and sell crude oil in exchange. But this is not the only kind of exchange that happens in reality: For example, Germany imports Honda, Subaru, and Toyota cars from Japan and sells Volkswagen, Porsche, Mercedes, and BMW cars to Japan. In theory, this should not occur because each of the countries produces good cars domestically and does not need to import them. The truth, however (see, for example, Krugman 1989), is that consumers in both countries enjoy variety. Some Japanese drivers prefer to be at the steering wheel of a BMW; others like Hondas, and the same happens in Germany. Variety and product differentiation, therefore, are not necessarily bad things.

9. LONG-RUN EQUILIBRIUM IN MONOPOLISTIC COMPETITION

Because TC includes all costs associated with production, including opportunity cost, economic profit is a signal to the market, and that signal will attract more competition. Just as with the perfectly competitive market structure, with relatively low entry costs, more firms will enter the market and lure some customers away from the firm making an economic profit. The loss of customers to new entrant firms will drive down the demand for all firms producing similar products. In the long run for the monopolistically competitive firm, economic profit will fall to zero. Exhibit 12 illustrates the condition of long-run equilibrium for monopolistic competition.

EXHIBIT 12: Long-Run Equilibrium in Monopolistic Competition

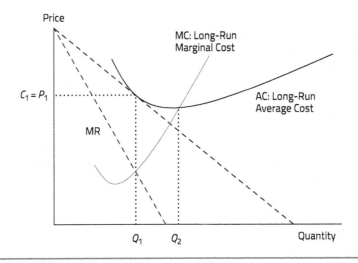

In long-run equilibrium, output is still optimal at the level where MR = MC, which is Q_1 in Exhibit 12. Again, the price consumers are willing to pay for any amount of the product is determined from the demand curve. That price is P_1 for the quantity Q_1 in Exhibit 12, and total revenue is the area of the rectangle $P_1 \times Q_1$. Notice that unlike long-run equilibrium in perfect competition, in the market of monopolistic competition, the equilibrium position is at a higher level of average cost than the level of output that minimizes average cost. Average cost does not reach its minimum until output level Q_2 is achieved. Total cost in this long-run equilibrium position is the area of the rectangle $C_1 \times Q_1$. Economic profit is total revenue minus total cost. In Exhibit 12, economic profit is zero because total revenue equals total cost: $P_1 \times Q_1 = C_1 \times Q_1$.

In the hybrid market of monopolistic competition, zero economic profit in long-run equilibrium resembles perfect competition. However, the long-run level of output, Q_1, is less than Q_2, which corresponds to the minimum average cost of production and would be the long run level of output in a perfectly competitive market. In addition, the economic cost in monopolistic competition includes some cost associated with product differentiation, such as advertising. In perfect competition, there are no costs associated with advertising or marketing because all products are homogeneous. Prices are lower, but consumers may have little variety.

10. OLIGOPOLY AND PRICING STRATEGIES

An oligopoly market structure is characterized by only a few firms doing business in a relevant market. The products must all be similar and generally be substitutes for one another. In some oligopoly markets, the goods or services may be differentiated by marketing and strong brand recognition, as in the markets for breakfast cereals and for bottled or canned beverages. Other examples of oligopoly markets are made up of homogeneous products with little or no attempt at product differentiation, such as petroleum and cement. *The most distinctive characteristic of oligopoly markets is the small number of firms that dominate the market. There are so few firms in the relevant market that their pricing decisions are interdependent.* That is, each firm's pricing decision is based on the expected retaliation by the other firms. Recall from Exhibit 1 the characteristics of oligopoly markets:

1. There are a small number of potential sellers.
2. The products offered by each seller are close substitutes for the products offered by other firms and may be differentiated by brand or homogeneous and unbranded.
3. Entry into the market is difficult, with fairly high costs and significant barriers to competition.
4. Firms typically have substantial pricing power.
5. Products are often highly differentiated through marketing, features, and other non-price strategies.

Because there are so few firms, each firm can have some degree of pricing power, which can result in substantial profits. Another by-product of the oligopoly market structure is the attractiveness of price collusion. Even without price collusion, a dominant firm may easily become the price maker in the market. Oligopoly markets without collusion typically have the most sophisticated pricing strategies. Examples of non-colluding oligopolies include the US tobacco market and the Thai beer market. In 2004, four firms controlled 99 percent of the US tobacco industry.[9] Brands owned by Singha Co. and by ThaiBev controlled over 90 percent of the Thai beer market in 2009. (This situation is expected to change soon, as the Association of Southeast Asian Nations trade agreement will open the doors to competition from other ASEAN producers.) Perhaps the most well-known oligopoly market with collusion is the OPEC cartel, which seeks to control prices in the petroleum market by fostering agreements among oil-producing countries.

10.1. Demand Analysis and Pricing Strategies in Oligopoly Markets

Oligopoly markets' demand curves depend on the degree of pricing interdependence. In a market where collusion is present, the aggregate market demand curve is divided up by the individual production participants. Under non-colluding market conditions, each firm faces an individual demand curve. Furthermore, non-colluding oligopoly market demand characteristics depend on the pricing strategies adopted by the participating firms. There are three basic pricing strategies: pricing interdependence, the Cournot assumption, and the Nash equilibrium.

The first pricing strategy is to assume pricing interdependence among the firms in the oligopoly. A good example of this situation is any market where there are "price wars," such as the commercial airline industry. For example, flying out of their hubs in Atlanta, both Delta Air Lines and AirTran Airways jointly serve several cities. AirTran is a low-cost carrier and typically offers lower fares to destinations out of Atlanta. Delta tends to match the lower fares for those cities also served by AirTran when the departure and arrival times are similar to its own. However, when Delta offers service to the same cities at different time slots, Delta's ticket prices are higher.

---

[9]These examples are based on "Industry Surveys," Net Advantage Database, Standard & Poor's; and Market Share Reports, Gale Research, annual issues, as noted in McGuigan, Moyer, and Harris (2016).

The most common pricing strategy assumption in these price war markets is that competitors will match a price reduction and ignore a price increase. The logic is that by lowering its price to match a competitor's price reduction, the firm will not experience a reduction in customer demand. Conversely, by not matching the price increase, the firm stands to attract customers away from the firm that raised its prices. The oligopolist's demand relationship must represent the potential increase in market share when rivals' price increases are not matched and no significant change in market share when rivals' price decreases are matched.

Given a prevailing price, the price elasticity of demand will be much greater if the price is increased and less if the price is decreased. The firm's customers are more responsive to price increases because its rivals have lower prices. Alternatively, the firm's customers are less responsive to price decreases because its rivals will match its price change.

This implies that the oligopolistic firm faces two different demand structures, one associated with price increases and another relating to price reductions. Each demand function will have its own marginal revenue structure as well. Consider the demand and marginal revenue functions in Exhibit 13. The functions $D_{P\uparrow}$ and $MR_{P\uparrow}$ represent the demand and marginal revenue schedules associated with higher prices, while the functions $D_{P\downarrow}$ and $MR_{P\downarrow}$ represent the lower prices' demand and marginal revenue schedules. The two demand schedules intersect at the prevailing price (i.e., the price where price increase and price decrease are both equal to zero).

EXHIBIT 13: Kinked Demand Curve in Oligopoly Market

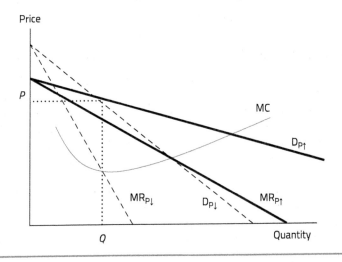

This oligopolistic pricing strategy results in a kinked demand curve, with the two segments representing the different competitor reactions to price changes. The kink in the demand curve also yields a discontinuous marginal revenue structure, with one part associated with the price increase segment of demand and the other relating to the price decrease segment. Therefore, the firm's overall demand equals the relevant portion of $D_{P\uparrow}$ and the relevant portion of $D_{P\downarrow}$. Exhibit 14 represents the firm's new demand and marginal revenue schedules. The firm's demand schedule in Exhibit 14 is segment $D_{P\uparrow}$ and $D_{P\downarrow}$, where overall demand $D = D_{P\uparrow} + D_{P\downarrow}$.

EXHIBIT 14: Kinked Demand Curve in Oligopoly Market

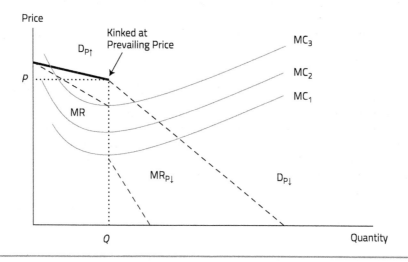

Notice in Exhibit 14 that a wide variety of cost structures are consistent with the prevailing price. If the firm has relatively low marginal costs, MC_1, the profit-maximizing pricing rule established earlier, $MR = MC$, still holds for the oligopoly firm. Marginal cost can rise to MC_2 and MC_3 before the firm's profitability is challenged. If the marginal cost curve MC_2 passes through the gap in marginal revenue, the most profitable price and output combination remains unchanged at the prevailing price and original level of output.

Criticism of the kinked demand curve analysis focuses on its inability to determine what the prevailing price is from the outset. The kinked demand curve analysis does help explain why stable prices have been observed in oligopoly markets and is therefore a useful tool for analyzing such markets. However, because it cannot determine the original prevailing price, it is considered an incomplete pricing analysis.

11. THE COURNOT ASSUMPTION

The second pricing strategy was first developed by French economist Augustin Cournot in 1838. In the **Cournot assumption**, each firm determines its profit-maximizing production level by assuming that the other firms' output will not change. This assumption simplifies pricing strategy because there is no need to guess what the other firm will do to retaliate. It also provides a useful approach to analyzing real-world behavior in oligopoly markets. Take the most basic oligopoly market situation, a two-firm duopoly market.[10] In equilibrium,

---

[10]The smallest possible oligopoly market is a duopoly, which is made up of only two sellers.

neither firm has an incentive to change output, given the other firm's production level. Each firm attempts to maximize its own profits under the assumption that the other firm will continue producing the same level of output in the future. The Cournot strategy assumes that this pattern continues until each firm reaches its long-run equilibrium position. In long-run equilibrium, output and price are stable: There is no change in price or output that will increase profits for either firm.

Consider this example of a duopoly market. Assume that the aggregate market demand has been estimated to be

$$Q_D = 450 - P$$

The supply function is represented by constant marginal cost MC = 30.

The Cournot strategy's solution can be found by setting $Q_D = q_1 + q_2$, where q_1 and q_2 represent the output levels of the two firms. Each firm seeks to maximize profit, and each firm believes the other firm will not change output as it changes its own output (Cournot's assumption). The firm will maximize profit where MR = MC. Rearranging the aggregate demand function in terms of price, we get:

$$P = 450 - Q_D = 450 - q_1 - q_2, \text{ and MC} = 30$$

Total revenue for each of the two firms is found by multiplying price and quantity:

$$TR_1 = Pq_1 = (450 - q_1 - q_2)q_1 = 450q_1 - q_1^2 - q_1q_2, \text{ and}$$
$$TR_2 = Pq_2 = (450 - q_1 - q_2)q_2 = 450q_2 - q_2q_1 - q_2^2$$

Marginal revenue is defined as the change in total revenue, given a change in sales (q_1 or q_2).[11] For the profit-maximizing output, set MR = MC, or

$$450 - 2q_1 - q_2 = 30$$

and

$$450 - q_1 - 2q_2 = 30$$

Find the simultaneous equilibrium for the two firms by solving the two equations with two unknowns:

$$450 - 2q_1 - q_2 = 450 - q_1 - 2q_2$$

---

[11]The marginal revenue formulas can be obtained using the technique introduced in Section 3.1. For the market demand function, total revenue is $P \times Q = 450Q - Q^2$ and our technique yields MR = $\Delta TR/\Delta Q = 450 - 2Q$. For the individual firms in the Cournot duopoly, $MR_1 = TR_1/q_1 = 450 - 2q_1 - q_2$, and $MR_2 = TR_2/q_2 = 450 - q_1 - 2q_2$. Each of these marginal revenue formulas is, of course, the derivative of the relevant total revenue formula with respect to the relevant quantity.

Because $q_2 = q_1$ under Cournot's assumption, insert this solution into the demand function and solve as

$$450 - 2q_1 - q_1 = 450 - 3q_1 = 30$$

Therefore, $q_1 = 140$, $q_2 = 140$, and $Q = 280$.
The price is $P = 450 - 280 = 170$.

In the Cournot strategic pricing solution, the market equilibrium price will be 170 and the aggregate output will be 280 units. This result, known as the Cournot equilibrium, differs from the perfectly competitive market equilibrium because the perfectly competitive price will be lower and the perfectly competitive output will be higher. In general, non-competitive markets have higher prices and lower levels of output in equilibrium when compared with perfect competition. In competition, the equilibrium is reached where price equals marginal cost.

$$P_C = MR_C = MC, \text{ so } 450 - Q = 30$$

where P_C is the competitive firm's equilibrium price.

$$Q = 420, \text{ and } P_C = 30.$$

Exhibit 15 describes the oligopoly, competitive, and monopoly market equilibrium positions, where P_M is the monopoly optimum price, P_C is the competitive price, and $P_{Cournot}$ is the oligopoly price under the Cournot assumption.

EXHIBIT 15: Cournot Equilibrium in Duopoly Market

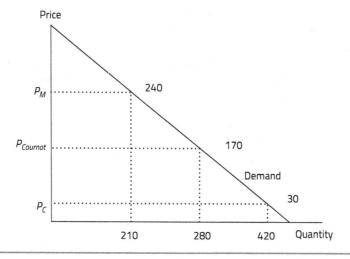

In the later discussion regarding monopoly market structure, equilibrium will be established where MR = MC. That solution is also shown in Exhibit 15. The monopoly firm's demand schedule is the aggregate market demand schedule. Therefore, the solution is

$$MR = MC$$

From Footnote 10, $MR = 450 - 2Q$; therefore,

$$450 - 2Q = 30 \quad \text{and} \quad Q = 210$$

From the aggregate demand function, solve for price:

$$P_M = 450 - 210 = 240$$

Note that the Cournot solution falls between the competitive equilibrium and the monopoly solution.

It can be shown that as the number of firms increases from two to three, from three to four, and so on, the output and price equilibrium positions move toward the competitive equilibrium solution. This result has historically been the theoretical basis for the antitrust policies established in the United States.

12. THE NASH EQUILIBRIUM

The third pricing strategy is attributed to one of the 1994 Nobel Prize winners, John Nash, who first developed the general concepts. In the previous analysis, the concept of market equilibrium occurs when firms are achieving their optimum remuneration under the circumstances they face. In this optimum environment, the firm has no motive to change price or output level. Existing firms are earning a normal return (zero economic profit), leaving no motive for entry to or exit from the market. All firms in the market are producing at the output level where price equals the average cost of production.

In **game theory** (the set of tools that decision makers use to consider responses by rival decision makers), the **Nash equilibrium** is present when two or more participants in a non-cooperative game have no incentive to deviate from their respective equilibrium strategies after they have considered and anticipated their opponent's rational choices or strategies. In the context of oligopoly markets, the Nash equilibrium is an equilibrium defined by the characteristic that none of the oligopolists can increase its profits by unilaterally changing its pricing strategy. The assumption is made that each participating firm does the best it can, given the reactions of its rivals. Each firm anticipates that the other firms will react to any change made by competitors by doing the best they can under the altered circumstances. The firms in the oligopoly market have interdependent actions. The actions are non-cooperative, with each firm making decisions that maximize its own profits. The firms do not collude in an effort to maximize joint profits. The equilibrium is reached when all firms are doing the best they can, given the actions of their rivals.

Exhibit 16 illustrates the duopoly result from the Nash equilibrium. Assume there are two firms in the market, ArcCo and BatCo. ArcCo and BatCo can charge high prices or low prices for the product. The market outcomes are shown in Exhibit 16.

EXHIBIT 16: Nash Equilibrium in Duopoly Market

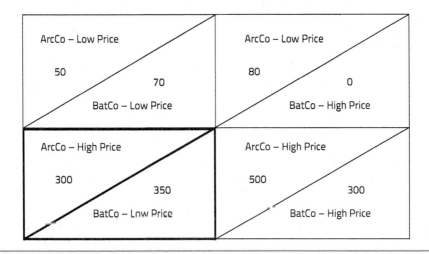

For example, the top left solution indicates that when both ArcCo and BatCo offer the product at low prices, ArcCo earns a profit of 50 and BatCo earns 70. The top right solution shows that if ArcCo offers the product at a low price, BatCo earns zero profits. The solution with the maximum joint profits is the lower right equilibrium, where both firms charge high prices for the product. Joint profits are 800 in this solution.

However, the Nash equilibrium requires that each firm behaves in its own best interest. BatCo can improve its position by offering the product at low prices when ArcCo is charging high prices. In the lower left solution, BatCo maximizes its profits at 350. While ArcCo can earn 500 in its best solution, it can do so only if BatCo also agrees to charge high prices. This option is clearly not in BatCo's best interest because it can increase its return from 300 to 350 by charging lower prices.

This scenario brings up the possibility of collusion. If ArcCo agrees to share at least 51 of its 500 when both companies are charging high prices, BatCo should also be willing to charge high prices. While, in general, such collusion is unlawful in most countries, it remains a tempting alternative. Clearly, conditions in oligopolistic industries encourage collusion, with a small number of competitors and interdependent pricing behavior. Collusion is motivated by several factors: increased profits, reduced cash flow uncertainty, and improved opportunities to construct barriers to entry.

When collusive agreements are made openly and formally, the firms involved are called a **cartel**. In some cases, collusion is successful; other times, the forces of competition overpower collusive behavior. There are six major factors that affect the chances of successful collusion.[12]

---

[12]McGuigan, Moyer, and Harris (2016).

1. *The number and size distribution of sellers.* Successful collusion is more likely if the number of firms is small or if one firm is dominant. Collusion becomes more difficult as the number of firms increases or if the few firms have similar market shares. When the firms have similar market shares, the competitive forces tend to overshadow the benefits of collusion.

2. *The similarity of the products.* When the products are homogeneous, collusion is more successful. The more differentiated the products, the less likely it is that collusion will succeed.

3. *Cost structure.* The more similar the firms' cost structures, the more likely it is that collusion will succeed.

4. *Order size and frequency.* Successful collusion is more likely when orders are frequent, received on a regular basis, and relatively small. Frequent small orders, received regularly, diminish the opportunities and rewards for cheating on the collusive agreement.

5. *The strength and severity of retaliation.* Oligopolists will be less likely to break the collusive agreement if the threat of retaliation by the other firms in the market is severe.

6. *The degree of external competition.* The main reason to enter into the formal collusion is to increase overall profitability of the market, and rising profits attract competition. For example, in 2016 the average extraction cost of a barrel of crude oil from Saudi Arabia was approximately $9, while the average cost from United States shale oil fields was roughly $23.50. The cost of extracting oil from the Canadian tar sands in 2016 was roughly $27 per barrel. It is more likely that crude oil producers in the gulf countries will successfully collude because of the similarity in their cost structures (roughly $9–$10 per barrel). If OPEC had held crude oil prices down below $30 per barrel, there would have been a viable economic argument to develop US shale oil fields through fracking or expand extraction from Canada's tar sands. OPEC's successful cartel raised crude oil prices to the point where outside sources became economically possible and in doing so increased the competition the cartel faces.[13]

There are other possible oligopoly strategies that are associated with decision making based on game theory. The Cournot equilibrium and the Nash equilibrium are examples of specific strategic games. A strategic game is any interdependent behavioral choice employed by individuals or groups that share a common goal (e.g., military units, sports teams, or business decision makers). Another prominent decision-making strategy in oligopolistic markets is the first-mover advantage in the **Stackelberg model**, named after the economist who first conceptualized the strategy.[14] The important difference between the Cournot model and the Stackelberg model is that Cournot assumes that in a duopoly market, decision making is simultaneous, while Stackelberg assumes that decisions are made sequentially. In the Stackelberg model, the leader firm chooses its output first and then the follower firm chooses after observing the leader's output. It can be shown that the leader firm has a distinct

---

[13]"Barrel Breakdown," *Wall Street Journal*, April 15, 2016.
[14]Von Stackelberg (1952). See also Kelly (2011) for a comparison between the Cournot and Stackelberg equilibriums.

advantage, being a first mover.[15] In the Stackelberg game, the leader can aggressively overproduce to force the follower to scale back its production or even punish or eliminate the weaker opponent. This approach is sometimes referred to as a "top dog" strategy.[16] The leader earns more than in Cournot's simultaneous game, while the follower earns less. Many other strategic games are possible in oligopoly markets. The important conclusion is that the optimal strategy of the firm depends on what its adversary does. The price and marginal revenue the firm receives for its product depend on both its decisions and its adversary's decisions.

13. OLIGOPY MARKETS: OPTIMAL PRICE, OUTPUT, AND LONG-RUN EQUILIBRIUM

As in monopolistic competition, the oligopolist does not have a well-defined supply function. That is, there is no way to determine the oligopolist's optimal levels of output and price independent of demand conditions and competitor's strategies. However, the oligopolist still has a cost function that determines the optimal level of supply. Therefore, the profit-maximizing rule established earlier is still valid: The level of output that maximizes profit is where MR = MC. The price to charge is determined by what price consumers are willing to pay for that quantity of the product. Therefore, the equilibrium price comes from the demand curve, while the output level comes from the relationship between marginal revenue and marginal cost.

Consider an oligopoly market in which one of the firms is dominant and thus able to be the price leader. Dominant firms generally have 40 percent or greater market share. When one firm dominates an oligopoly market, it does so because it has greater capacity, has a lower cost structure, was first to market, or has greater customer loyalty than other firms in the market.

Assuming there is no collusion, the dominant firm becomes the price maker, and therefore its actions are similar to monopoly behavior in its segment of the market. The other firms in the market follow the pricing patterns of the dominant firm. Why wouldn't the price followers attempt to gain market share by undercutting the dominant firm's price? The most common explanation is that the dominant firm's supremacy often stems from a lower cost of production. Usually, the price followers would rather charge a price that is even higher than the dominant firm's price choice. If they attempt to undercut the dominant firm, the followers risk a price war with a lower-cost producer that can threaten their survival. Some believe that one explanation for the price leadership position of the dominant firm is simply convenience. Only one firm has to make the pricing decisions, and the others can simply follow its lead.

Exhibit 17 establishes the dominant firm's pricing decision. The dominant firm's demand schedule, D_L, is a substantial share of the total market demand, D_T. The low-cost position of the dominant firm is represented by its marginal cost, MC_L. The sum of the marginal costs of the price followers is established as ΣMC_F and represents a higher cost of production than that of the price leader.

---

[15]Nicholson and Snyder (2016).
[16]Fudenberg and Tirole (1984).

EXHIBIT 17: Dominant Oligopolist's Price Leadership

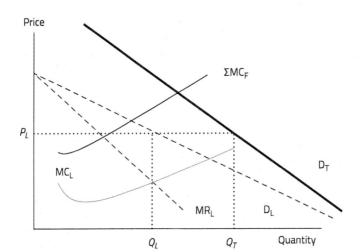

There is an important reason why the total demand curve and the leader demand curve are not parallel in Exhibit 17: Remember that the leader is the low-cost producer. Therefore, as price decreases, fewer of the smaller suppliers will be able to profitably remain in the market, and several will exit because they do not want to sell below cost. Therefore, the leader will have a larger market share as P decreases, which implies that Q_L increases at a low price, exactly as shown by a steeper D_T in the diagram.

The price leader identifies its profit-maximizing output where $MR_L = MC_L$, at output Q_L. This is the quantity it wants to supply; however, the price it will charge is determined by its segment of the total demand function, D_L. At price P_L, the dominant firm will supply quantity Q_L of total demand, D_T. The price followers will supply the difference to the market, $(Q_T - Q_L) = Q_F$. Therefore, neither the dominant firm nor the follower firms have a single functional relationship that determines the quantity supplied at various prices.

13.1. Optimal Price and Output in Oligopoly Markets

From the discussion above, clearly there is no single optimum price and output analysis that fits all oligopoly market situations. The interdependence among the few firms that make up the oligopoly market provides a complex set of pricing alternatives, depending on the circumstances in each market. In the case of the kinked demand curve, the optimum price is the prevailing price at the kink in the demand function. However, as previously noted, the kinked demand curve analysis does not provide insight into what established the prevailing price in the first place.

Perhaps the case of the dominant firm, with the other firms following the price leader, is the most obvious. In that case, the optimal price is determined at the output level where $MR = MC$. The profit-maximizing price is then determined by the output position of the segment of the demand function faced by the dominant firm. The price followers have little incentive to change the leader's price. In the case of the Cournot assumption, each firm assumes that the other firms will not alter their output following the dominant firm's selection of its price and output level.

Therefore, again, the optimum price is determined by the output level where MR = MC. In the case of the Nash equilibrium, each firm will react to the circumstances it faces, maximizing its own profit. These adjustments continue until there are stable prices and levels of output. Because of the interdependence, there is no certainty as to the individual firm's price and output level.

13.2. Factors Affecting Long-Run Equilibrium in Oligopoly Markets

Long-run economic profits are possible for firms operating in oligopoly markets. However, history has shown that, over time, the market share of the dominant firm declines. Profits attract entry by other firms into the oligopoly market. Over time, the marginal costs of the entrant firms decrease because they adopt more efficient production techniques, the dominant firm's demand and marginal revenue shrink, and the profitability of the dominant firm declines. In the early 1900s, J.P. Morgan, Elbert Gary, Andrew Carnegie, and Charles M. Schwab created the United States Steel Corporation (US Steel). When it was first formed in 1901, US Steel controlled 66 percent of the market. By 1920, US Steel's market share had declined to 46 percent, and by 1925 its market share was 42 percent.

In the long run, optimal pricing strategy must include the reactions of rival firms. History has proven that pricing wars should be avoided because any gains in market share are temporary. Decreasing prices to drive competitors away lowers total revenue to all participants in the oligopoly market. Innovation may be a way—though sometimes an uneconomical one—to maintain market leadership.

OLIGOPOLIES: APPEARANCE VERSUS BEHAVIOR

When is an oligopoly not an oligopoly? There are two extreme cases of this situation. A normal oligopoly has a few firms producing a differentiated good, and this differentiation gives them pricing power.

At one end of the spectrum, we have the oligopoly with a credible threat of entry. In practice, if the oligopolists are producing a good or service that can be easily replicated, has limited economies of scale, and is not protected by brand recognition or patents, they will not be able to charge high prices. The easier it is for a new supplier to enter the market, the lower the margins. In practice, this oligopoly will behave very much like a perfectly competitive market.

At the opposite end of the spectrum, we have the case of the cartel. Here, the oligopolists collude and act as if they were a single firm. In practice, a very effective cartel enacts a cooperative strategy. As shown in Section 5.1, instead of going to a Nash equilibrium, the cartel participants go to the more lucrative (for them) cooperative equilibrium.

A cartel may be explicit (that is, based on a contract) or implicit (based on signals). An example of signals in a duopoly would be that one of the firms reduces its prices and the other does not. Because the firm not cutting prices refuses to start a price war, the firm that cut prices may interpret this signal as a "suggestion" to raise prices to a higher level than before, so that profits may increase for both.

14. MONOPOLY MARKETS: DEMAND/SUPPLY AND OPTIMAL PRICE/OUTPUT

Monopoly market structure is at the opposite end of the spectrum from perfect competition. For various reasons, there are significant barriers to entry such that a single firm produces a highly specialized product and faces no threat of competition. There are no good substitutes for the product in the relevant market, and the market demand function is the same as the individual firm's demand schedule. *The distinguishing characteristics of monopoly are that a single firm represents the market and significant barriers to entry exist.* Exhibit 1 identified the characteristics of monopoly markets:

1. There is a single seller of a highly differentiated product.
2. The product offered by the seller has no close substitute.
3. Entry into the market is very difficult, with high costs and significant barriers to competition.
4. The firm has considerable pricing power.
5. The product is differentiated through non-price strategies such as advertising.

Monopoly markets are unusual. With a single seller dominating the market, power over price decisions is significant. For a single seller to achieve this power, there must be factors that allow the monopoly to exist. One obvious source of monopoly power would be a patent or copyright that prevents other firms from entering the market. Patent and copyright laws exist to reward intellectual capital and investment in research and development. In so doing, they provide significant barriers to entry.

Another possible source of market power is control over critical resources used for production. One example is De Beers Consolidated Mines Limited. De Beers owned or controlled all diamond mining operations in South Africa and established pricing agreements with other important diamond producers. In doing so, De Beers was able to control the prices for cut diamonds for decades. Technically, De Beers was a near-monopoly dominant firm rather than a pure monopoly, although its pricing procedure for cut diamonds resembled monopoly behavior.

Perhaps the most common form of monopolistic market power occurs as the result of government-controlled authorization. In most urban areas, a single source of water and sewer services is offered. In some cases, these services are offered by a government-controlled entity. In other cases, private companies provide the services under government regulation. Such "natural" monopolies require a large initial investment that benefits from economies of scale; therefore, government may authorize a single seller to provide a certain service because having multiple sellers would be too costly. For example, electricity in most markets is provided by a single seller. Economies of scale result when significant capital investment benefits from declining long-run average costs. In the case of electricity, a large gas-fueled power plant producing electricity for a large area is substantially more efficient than having a small diesel generator for every building. That is, the average cost of generating and delivering a kilowatt of electricity will be substantially lower with the single power station, but the initial fixed cost of building the power station and the lines delivering electricity to each home, factory, and office will be very high.

In the case of natural monopolies, limiting the market to a single seller is considered beneficial to society. One water and sewer system is deemed better for the community than dozens of competitors because building multiple infrastructures for running water and sewer service would be particularly expensive and complicated. One electrical power grid supplying electricity for a community can make large capital investments in generating plants and lower the long-run average cost, while multiple power grids would lead to a potentially dangerous maze of wires. Clearly, not all monopolies are in a position to make significant economic profits. Regulators, such as public utility commissions in the United States, attempt to determine what a normal return for the monopoly owners' investment should be, and they set prices accordingly. Nevertheless, monopolists attempt to maximize profits.

Not all monopolies originate from "natural" barriers. For some monopolists, barriers to entry do not derive from increasing returns to scale. We mentioned that marketing and brand loyalty are sources of product differentiation in monopolistic competition. In some highly successful cases, strong brand loyalty can become a formidable barrier to entry. For example, if the Swiss watchmaker Rolex is unusually successful in establishing brand loyalty, so that its customers think there is no close substitute for its product, then the company will have monopoly-like pricing power over its market.

The final potential source of market power is the increasing returns associated with network effects. Network effects result from synergies related to increasing market penetration. By achieving a critical level of adoption, Microsoft was able to extend its market power through the network effect—for example, because most computer users know how to use Microsoft Word. Therefore, for firms, Word is cheaper to adopt than other programs because almost every new hire will be proficient in using the software and will need no further training. At some level of market share, a network-based product or service (think of Facebook or eBay) reaches a point where each additional share point increases the probability that another user will adopt.[17] These network effects increase the value to other potential adopters. In Microsoft's case, the network effects crowded out other potential competitors, including Netscape's internet browser, that might have led to applications bypassing Windows. Eventually, Microsoft's operating system's market share reached 92 percent of the global market. Similar situations occur in financial markets: If a publicly listed share or a derivative contract is more frequently traded on a certain exchange, market participants wishing to sell or buy the security will go to the more liquid exchange because they expect to find a better price and faster execution there.

14.1. Demand Analysis in Monopoly Markets

The monopolist's demand schedule is the aggregate demand for the product in the relevant market. Because of the income effect and the substitution effect, demand is negatively related to price, as usual. The slope of the demand curve is negative and therefore downward sloping. The general form of the demand relationship is

$$Q_D = a - bP \qquad \text{or, rewritten,} \qquad P = a/b - (1/b)Q_D$$

Therefore, total revenue = $\text{TR} = P \times Q = (a/b)Q_D - (1/b)Q_D^2$

Marginal revenue is the change in revenue given a change in the quantity demanded. Because an increase in quantity requires a lower price, the marginal revenue schedule is

---

[17]When a network-based device reaches a 30 percent share, the next 50 percentage points are cheaper to promote, according to McGuigan, Moyer, and Harris (2016).

steeper than the demand schedule. If the demand schedule is linear, then the marginal revenue curve is twice as steep as the demand schedule.[18]

$$MR = TR/Q = (a/b) - (2/b)Q_D$$

The demand and marginal revenue relationship is expressed in Exhibit 18.

EXHIBIT 18: Monopolist's Demand and Marginal Revenue

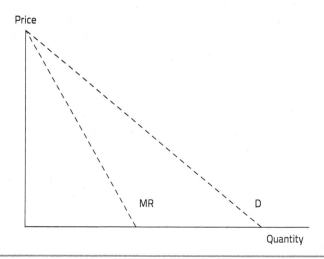

Suppose a company operating on a remote island is the single seller of natural gas. Demand for its product can be expressed as

$Q_D = 400 - 0.5P$, which can be rearranged as

$P = 800 - 2Q_D$

Total revenue is $P \times Q = TR = 800Q_D - 2Q_D^2$, and marginal revenue is $MR = 800 - 4Q_D$.[19]

In Exhibit 18, the demand curve's intercept is 800 and the slope is −2. The marginal revenue curve in Exhibit 18 has an intercept of 800 and a slope of −4.

Average revenue is TR/Q_D; therefore, $AR = 800 - 2Q_D$, which is the same as the demand function. In the monopoly market model, average revenue is the same as the market demand schedule.

14.2. Supply Analysis in Monopoly Markets

A monopolist's supply analysis is based on the firm's cost structure. As in the market structures of monopolistic competition and oligopoly, the monopolist does not have a well-defined supply function that determines the optimal output level and the price to charge. The

---

[18]Marginal revenue can be found using the technique shown in Section 3.1 or, for readers who are familiar with calculus, by taking the derivative of the total revenue function: $MR = TR/Q = (a/b) - (2/b)Q_D$.
[19]$MR = \Delta TR/\Delta Q = 800 - 4Q$.

optimal output is the profit-maximizing output level. The profit-maximizing level of output occurs where marginal revenue equals marginal cost, MR = MC.

Assume the natural gas company has determined that its total cost can be expressed as

$$TC = 20{,}000 + 50Q + 3Q^2$$

Marginal cost is $TC/Q = MC = 50 + 6Q$.[20]

Supply and demand can be combined to determine the profit-maximizing level of output. Exhibit 19 combines the monopolist's demand and cost functions.

EXHIBIT 19: Monopolist's Demand, Marginal Revenue, and Cost Structures

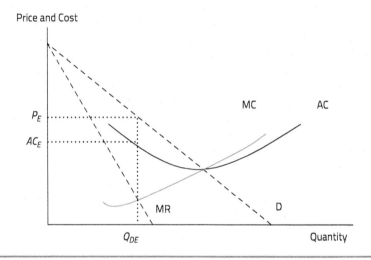

In Exhibit 19, the demand and marginal revenue functions are clearly defined by the aggregate market. However, the monopolist does not have a supply curve. The quantity that maximizes profit is determined by the intersection of MC and MR, Q_{DE}.

The price consumers are willing to pay for this level of output is P_E, as determined by the demand curve, P_E.

The profit-maximizing level of output is MR = MC: $800 - 4Q_D = 50 + 6Q_D$; therefore, $Q_D = 75$ when profit is maximized.

Total profit equals total revenue minus total cost:

$$\pi = 800Q - 2Q_D^2 - (20{,}000 + 50Q_D + 3Q_D^2) = -20{,}000 + 750Q_D - 5Q_D^2$$

Profit is represented by the difference between the area of the rectangle $Q_{DE} \times P_E$, representing total revenue, and the area of the rectangle $Q_{DE} \times AC_E$, representing total cost.

---

[20]The marginal cost equation can be found in this case by applying the technique used to find the marginal revenue equation in Section 3.1, or by taking the derivative of the total cost function.

MONOPOLISTS AND THEIR INCENTIVES

In theoretical models, which usually take product quality and technology as given, monopolists can choose to vary either price or quantity. In real life, they also can vary their product.

A monopolist can choose to limit quality if producing a higher-quality product is costly and higher quality does not increase profits accordingly. For example, the quality of domestically produced cars in most developed countries improved dramatically once imports became more available. Before the opening of borders to imports, the single incumbent that dominated the market (for example, Fiat in Italy) or the small group of incumbents acting as a collusive oligopoly (such as the Detroit "Big Three" in the United States) were the effective monopolists of their domestic automobile markets. Rust corrosion, limited reliability, and poor gas mileage were common.[21]

Similarly, regulated utilities may have limited incentives to innovate. Several studies, including Gómez-Ibáñez (2003), have found that state-owned and other monopoly telephone utilities tended to provide very poor service before competition was introduced. Poor service may not be limited to poor connection quality but may also include extensive delays in adding new users and limited introduction of new services, such as caller ID or automatic answering services.

Intuitively, a monopolist will not spend resources on quality control, research and development, or even customer relations unless there is a threat of entry of a new competitor or unless there is a clear link between such expenses and a profit increase. In contrast, in competitive markets, including oligopoly, innovation and quality are often ways to differentiate the product and increase profits.

14.3. Optimal Price and Output in Monopoly Markets

Continuing the natural gas example from above, the total profit function can be solved using the quadratic formula.[22] Another method to solve the profit function is to evaluate π/Q_D and set it equal to zero. This identifies the point at which profit is unaffected by changes in output.[23] Of course, this will give the same result as we found by equating marginal revenue with marginal cost. The monopoly will maximize profits when $Q^* = 75$ units of output and the price is set from the demand curve at 650.

$$P^* = 800 - 2(75) = 650 \text{ per unit}$$

To find total maximum profits, substitute these values into the profit function above:

$$\pi = -20{,}000 + 750Q_D - 5Q_D^2 = -20{,}000 + 750(75) - 5(75^2) = 8{,}125$$

---

[21]For more on this topic, see Banker, Khosla, and Sinha (1998).

[22]The quadratic formula, where $aQ^2 + bQ + c = 0$, is $Q = \{-b \pm \sqrt{(b^2 - 4ac)}\}/2a$.

[23]Maximum profit occurs where $\pi/Q_D = 0 = 750 - 10Q_D$. Therefore, profits are maximized at $Q_D = 75$.

Note that the price and output combination that maximizes profit occurs in the elastic portion of the demand curve in Exhibit 19. This must be so because marginal revenue and marginal cost will always intersect where marginal revenue is positive. This fact implies that quantity demanded responds more than proportionately to price changes, i.e. demand is elastic, at the point at which MC = MR. As noted earlier, the relationship between marginal revenue and price elasticity, E_P, is:

$$MR = P[1 - 1/E_P]$$

In monopoly, MR = MC; therefore,

$$P[1 - 1/E_P] = MC$$

The firm can use this relationship to determine the profit-maximizing price if the firm knows its cost structure and the price elasticity of demand, E_P. For example, assume the firm knows that its marginal cost is constant at 75 and recent market analysis indicates that price elasticity is estimated to be 1.5. The optimal price is solved as

$$P[1 - 1/1.5] = 75 \text{ and}$$

$$P = 225$$

Exhibit 19 indicated that the monopolist wants to produce at Q_E and charge the price of P_E. Suppose this is a natural monopoly that is operating as a government franchise under regulation. Natural monopolies are usually found where production is based on significant economies of scale and declining cost structure in the market. Examples include electric power generation, natural gas distribution, and the water and sewer industries. These are often called public utilities. Exhibit 20 illustrates such a market in long-run equilibrium.

EXHIBIT 20: Natural Monopoly in a Regulated Pricing Environment

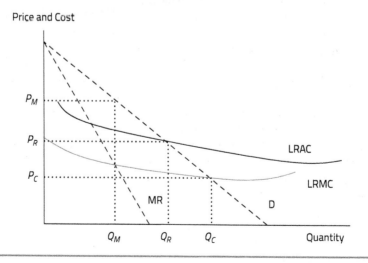

In Exhibit 20, three possible pricing and output solutions are presented. The first is what the monopolist would do without regulation: The monopolist would seek to maximize profits by producing Q_M units of the product, where long-run marginal cost equals marginal revenue, LRMC = MR. To maximize profits, the monopolist would raise the price to the level the demand curve will accept, P_M.

In perfect competition, the price and output equilibrium occurs where price is equal to the marginal cost of producing the incremental unit of the product. In a competitive market, the quantity produced would be higher, Q_C, and the price lower, P_C. For this regulated monopoly, the competitive solution would be unfair because at output Q_C, the price P_C would not cover the average cost of production. One possibility is to subsidize the difference between the long-run average cost, LRAC, and the competitive price, P_C, for each unit sold.

Another solution is for the regulator to set the price at the point where long-run average cost equals average revenue. Recall that the demand curve represents the average revenue the firm receives at each output level. The government regulator will attempt to determine the monopolistic firm's long-run average cost and set the output and price so that the firm receives a fair return on the owners' invested capital. The regulatory solution is output level Q_R, with the price set at P_R. Therefore, the regulatory solution is found between the unregulated monopoly equilibrium and the competitive equilibrium.

15. PRICE DISCRIMINATION AND CONSUMER SURPLUS

Monopolists can either be more or less effective in taking advantage of their market structure. At one extreme, we have a monopolist that charges prices and supplies quantities that are the same as they would be in perfect competition; this scenario may be a result of regulation or threat of entry (if the monopolist charged more, another company could come in and price the former monopolist out of the market). At the opposite extreme, hated by all consumers and economists, is the monopolist that extracts the entire consumer surplus. This scenario is called **first-degree price discrimination**, where a monopolist can charge each customer the highest price the customer is willing to pay. This is called price discrimination because the monopolist charges a different price to each client. How can this be? For example, if the monopolist knows the exact demand schedule of the customer, then the monopolist can capture the entire consumer surplus. In practice, the monopolist can measure how often the product is used and charges the customer the highest price the consumer is willing to pay for that unit of good. Another possibility is that public price disclosure is non-existent, so that no customer knows what the other customers are paying. Interestingly, not every consumer is worse off in this case, because some consumers may be charged a price that is below that of a monopoly, as long as the marginal revenue exceeds the marginal cost.

In **second-degree price discrimination** the monopolist offers a menu of quantity-based pricing options designed to induce customers to self-select based on how highly they value the product. Such mechanisms include volume discounts, volume surcharges, coupons, product bundling, and restrictions on use. In practice, producers can use not just the quantity but also the quality (e.g., "professional grade") to charge more to customers that value the product highly.

Third-degree price discrimination happens when customers are segregated by demographic or other traits. For example, some econometric software is licensed this way:

A student version can handle only small datasets and is sold for a low price; a professional version can handle very large datasets and is sold at a much higher price because corporations need to compute the estimates for their business and are therefore willing to pay more for a license. Another example is that airlines know that passengers who want to fly somewhere and come back the same day are most likely business people; therefore, one-day roundtrip tickets are generally more expensive than tickets with a return flight at a later date or over a weekend.

Price discrimination has many practical applications when the seller has pricing power. The best way to understand how this concept works is to think of consumer surplus: As seen in this chapter, a consumer may be willing to pay more for the first unit of a good, but to buy a second unit she will want to pay a lower price, thus getting a better deal on the first unit. In practice, sellers can sometimes use income and substitution effects to their advantage. Think of something you often buy, perhaps lunch at your favorite café. How much would you be willing to pay for a "lunch club membership card" that would allow you to purchase lunches at, say, half price? If the café could extract from you the maximum amount each month that you would be willing to pay for the half-price option, then it would successfully have removed the income effect from you in the form of a monthly fixed fee. Notice that a downward-sloping demand curve implies that you would end up buying more lunches each month than before you purchased the discount card, even though you would be no better or worse off than before. This is a way that sellers are sometimes able to extract consumer surplus by means of creative pricing schemes. It's a common practice among big-box retailers, sports clubs, and other users of what is called "two-part tariff pricing," as in the example below.

EXAMPLE 3   Price Discrimination

Nicole's monthly demand for visits to her health club is given by the following equation: $Q_D = 20 - 4P$, where Q_D is visits per month and P is euros per visit. The health club's marginal cost is fixed at €2 per visit.

1. Draw Nicole's demand curve for health club visits per month.

Solution to 1:
   $Q_D = 20 - 4P$, so when $P = 0$, $Q_D = 20$. Inverting, $P = 5 - 0.25Q_D$, so when $Q = 0$, $P = 5$.

2. If the club charged a price per visit equal to its marginal cost, how many visits would Nicole make per month?

Solution to 2:
   $Q_D = 20 - 4(2) = 12$. Nicole would make 12 visits per month at a price of €2 per visit.

3. How much consumer surplus would Nicole enjoy at that price?

Solution to 3:
   Nicole's consumer surplus can be measured as the area under her demand curve and above the price she pays for a total of 12 visits, or $(0.5)(12)(3) = 18$. Nicole would enjoy a consumer surplus of €18 per month.

4. How much could the club charge Nicole each month for a membership fee?

Solution to 4:

The club could extract all of Nicole's consumer surplus by charging her a monthly membership fee of €18 plus a per-visit price of €2. This pricing method is called a two-part tariff because it assesses one price per unit of the item purchased plus a per-month fee (sometimes called an "entry fee") equal to the buyer's consumer surplus evaluated at the per-unit price.

16. MONOPOLY MARKETS: LONG-RUN EQUILIBRIUM

The unregulated monopoly market structure can produce economic profits in the long run. In the long run, all factors of production are variable, while in the short run, some factors of production are fixed. Generally, the short-run factor that is fixed is the capital investment, such as the factory, machinery, production technology, available arable land, and so forth. The long-run solution allows for all inputs, including technology, to change. In order to maintain a monopoly market position in the long run, the firm must be protected by substantial and ongoing barriers to entry. If the monopoly position is the result of a patent, then new patents must be continuously added to prevent the entry of other firms into the market.

For regulated monopolies, such as natural monopolies, there are a variety of long-run solutions. One solution is to set the price equal to marginal cost, $P = MC$. However, that price will not likely be high enough to cover the average cost of production, as Exhibit 19 illustrated. The answer is to provide a subsidy sufficient to compensate the firm. The national rail system in the United States, Amtrak, is an example of a regulated monopoly operating with a government subsidy.

National ownership of the monopoly is another solution. Nationalization of the natural monopoly has been a popular solution in Europe and other parts of the world. The United States has generally avoided this potential solution. One problem with this arrangement is that once a price is established, consumers are unwilling to accept price increases, even as factor costs increase. Politically, raising prices on products from government-owned enterprises is highly unpopular.

Establishing a governmental entity that regulates an authorized monopoly is another popular solution. Exhibit 19 illustrated the appropriate decision rule. The regulator sets price equal to long-run average cost, $P_R = LRAC$. This solution assures that investors will receive a normal return for the risk they are taking in the market. Given that no other competitors are allowed, the risk is lower than in a highly competitive market environment. The challenge facing the regulator is determining the authentic risk-related return and the monopolist's realistic long-run average cost.

The final solution is to franchise the monopolistic firm through a bidding war. Again, the public goal is to select the winning firm based on price equaling long-run average cost. Retail outlets at rail stations and airports and concession outlets at stadiums are examples of government franchises. The long-run success of the monopoly franchise depends on its ability to meet the goal of pricing its products at the level of its long-run average cost.

EXAMPLE 4   Monopolies and Efficiency

1. Are monopolies *always* inefficient?
   A. No, because if they charge more than average cost they are nationalized.
   B. Yes, because they charge all consumers more than perfectly competitive markets would.
   C. No, because economies of scale and regulation (or threat of entry) may give a better outcome for buyers than perfect competition.

Solution:

C is correct. Economies of scale and regulation may make monopolies more efficient than perfect competition.

---

17. IDENTIFICATION OF MARKET STRUCTURE

Monopoly markets and other situations where companies have pricing power can be inefficient because producers constrain output to cause an increase in prices. Therefore, there will be less of the good being consumed and it will be sold at a higher price, which is generally inefficient for the overall market. As a result, many countries have introduced competition law to regulate the degree of competition in many industries.

Market power in the real world is not always as clear as it is in textbook examples. Governments and regulators often have the difficult task of measuring market power and establishing whether a firm has a dominant position that may resemble a monopoly. A few historical examples of this are as follows:

1. In the 1990s, US regulators prosecuted agricultural corporation Archer Daniels Midland for conspiring with Japanese competitors to fix the price of lysine, an amino acid used as an animal feed additive. The antitrust action resulted in a settlement that involved over US$100 million in fines paid by the cartel members.
2. In the 1970s, US antitrust authorities broke up the local telephone monopoly, leaving AT&T the long-distance business (and opening that business to competitors), and required AT&T to divest itself of the local telephone companies it owned. This antitrust decision brought competition, innovation, and lower prices to the US telephone market.
3. European regulators (specifically, the European Commission) have affected the mergers and monopoly positions of European corporations (as in the case of the companies Roche, Rhone-Poulenc, and BASF, which were at the center of a vitamin price-fixing case) as well as non-European companies (such as Intel) that do business in Europe. Moreover, the merger between the US company General Electric and the European company Honeywell was denied by the European Commission on grounds of excessive market concentration.

Quantifying excessive market concentration is difficult. Sometimes, regulators need to measure whether something that has not yet occurred might generate excessive market power. For example, a merger between two companies might allow the combined company to be a monopolist or quasi monopolist in a certain market.

A financial analyst hearing news about a possible merger should always consider the impact of competition law (sometimes called antitrust law)—that is, whether a proposed merger may be blocked by regulators in the interest of preserving a competitive market.

17.1. Econometric Approaches

How should one measure market power? The theoretical answer is to estimate the elasticity of demand and supply in a market. If demand is very elastic, the market must be very close to perfect competition. If demand is rigid (inelastic), companies *may* have market power. This is the approach taken in the cellophane case mentioned in Section 3.1.2.

From the econometric point of view, this estimation requires some attention. The problem is that observed price and quantity are the equilibrium values of price and quantity and do not represent the value of either supply or demand. Technically, this is called the problem of endogeneity, in the sense that the equilibrium price and quantity are jointly determined by the interaction of demand and supply. Therefore, to have an appropriate estimation of demand and supply, we will need to use a model with two equations, namely, an equation of demanded quantity (as a function of price, income of the buyers, and other variables) and an equation of supplied quantity (as a function of price, production costs, and other variables). The estimated parameters will then allow us to compute elasticity.

Regression analysis is useful in computing elasticity but requires a large number of observations. Therefore, one may use a time-series approach and, for example, look at 20 years of quarterly sales data for a market. However, the market structure may have changed radically over those 20 years, and the estimated elasticity may not apply to the current situation. Moreover, the supply curve may change due to a merger among large competitors, and the estimation based on past data may not be informative regarding the future state of the market post merger.

An alternative approach is a cross-sectional regression analysis. Instead of looking at total sales and average prices in a market over time (the time-series approach mentioned above), we can look at sales from different companies in the market during the same year, or even at single transactions from many buyers and companies. Clearly, this approach requires substantial data-gathering effort, and therefore, this estimation method can be complicated. Moreover, different specifications of the explanatory variables (for example, using total GDP rather than median household income or per-capita GDP to represent income) may sometimes lead to dramatically different estimates.

17.2. Simpler Measures

Trying to avoid the above drawbacks, analysts often use simpler measures to estimate elasticity. The simplest measure is the concentration ratio, which is the sum of the market shares of the largest N firms. To compute this ratio, one would, for example, add the sales values of the largest 10 firms and divide this figure by total market sales. This number is always between zero (perfect competition) and 100 percent (monopoly).

The main advantage of the concentration ratio is that it is simple to compute, as shown above. The disadvantage is that it does not directly quantify market power. In other words, is a high concentration ratio a clear signal of monopoly power? The analysis of entry in Section 2 explains clearly that this is not the case: A company may be the only incumbent in a market, but if the barriers to entry are low, the simple presence of a *potential* entrant may be sufficient to convince the incumbent to behave like a firm in perfect competition. For example, a sugar wholesaler may be the only one in a country, but the knowledge that other large wholesalers in the food industry might easily add imported sugar to their range of products should convince the sugar wholesaler to price its product as if it were in perfect competition.

Another disadvantage of the concentration ratio is that it tends to be unaffected by mergers among the top market incumbents. For example, if the largest and second-largest incumbents merge, the pricing power of the combined entity is likely to be larger than that of the two pre-existing companies. But the concentration ratio may not change much.

CALCULATING THE CONCENTRATION RATIO

Suppose there are eight producers of a certain good in a market. The largest producer has 35 percent of the market, the second largest has 25 percent, the third has 20 percent, the fourth has 10 percent, and the remaining four have 2.5 percent each. If we computed the concentration ratio of the top three producers, it would be 35 + 25 + 20 = 80 percent, while the concentration ratio of the top four producers would be 35 + 25 + 20 + 10 = 90 percent.

If the two largest companies merged, the new concentration ratio for the top three producers would be 60 (the sum of the market shares of the merged companies) + 20 + 10 = 90 percent, and the concentration ratio for the four top producers would be 92.5 percent. Therefore, this merger affects the concentration ratio very mildly, even though it creates a substantial entity that controls 60 percent of the market.

For example, the effect of consolidation in the US retail gasoline market has resulted in increasing degrees of concentration. In 1992, the top four companies in the US retail gasoline market shared 33 percent of the market. By 2001, the top four companies controlled 78 percent of the market (Exxon Mobil 24 percent, Shell 20 percent, BP/Amoco/Arco 18 percent, and Chevron/Texaco 16 percent).

To avoid the known issues with concentration ratios, economists O.C. Herfindahl and A.O. Hirschman suggested an index where the market shares of the top N companies are first squared and then added. If one firm controls the whole market (a monopoly), the Herfindahl–Hirschman index (HHI) equals 1. If there are M firms in the industry with equal market shares, then the HHI equals $(1/M)$. This provides a useful gauge for interpreting an HHI. For example, an HHI of 0.20 would be analogous to having the market shared equally by 5 firms.

The HHI for the top three companies in the example in the box above would be $0.35^2 + 0.25^2 + 0.20^2 = 0.225$ before the merger, while after the merger, it would be $0.60^2 + 0.20^2 + 0.10^2 = 0.410$, which is substantially higher than the initial 0.225. The HHI is widely used by competition regulators; however, just like the concentration ratio, the HHI does not take the possibility of entry into account, nor does it consider the elasticity of demand. Therefore, the HHI has limited use for a financial analyst trying to estimate the potential profitability of a company or group of companies.

EXAMPLE 5   The Herfindahl–Hirschman Index

1. Suppose a market has 10 suppliers, each of them with 10 percent of the market.
   What are the concentration ratio and the HHI of the top four firms?
   A.   Concentration ratio 4 percent and HHI 40
   B.   Concentration ratio 40 percent and HHI 0.4
   C.   Concentration ratio 40 percent and HHI 0.04

Solution:
   C is correct. The concentration ratio for the top four firms is $10 + 10 + 10 + 10 = 40$ percent, and the HHI is $0.10^2 \times 4 = 0.01 \times 4 = 0.04$.

---

18. SUMMARY

In this chapter, we have surveyed how economists classify market structures. We have analyzed the distinctions between the different structures that are important for understanding demand and supply relations, optimal price and output, and the factors affecting long-run profitability. We also provided guidelines for identifying market structure in practice. Among our conclusions are the following:

- Economic market structures can be grouped into four categories: perfect competition, monopolistic competition, oligopoly, and monopoly.
- The categories differ because of the following characteristics: The number of producers is many in perfect and monopolistic competition, few in oligopoly, and one in monopoly. The degree of product differentiation, the pricing power of the producer, the barriers to entry of new producers, and the level of non-price competition (e.g., advertising) are all low in perfect competition, moderate in monopolistic competition, high in oligopoly, and generally highest in monopoly.
- A financial analyst must understand the characteristics of market structures in order to better forecast a firm's future profit stream.
- The optimal marginal revenue equals marginal cost. However, only in perfect competition does the marginal revenue equal price. In the remaining structures, price generally exceeds marginal revenue because a firm can sell more units only by reducing the per unit price.
- The quantity sold is highest in perfect competition. The price in perfect competition is usually lowest, but this depends on factors such as demand elasticity and increasing returns to scale (which may reduce the producer's marginal cost). Monopolists, oligopolists, and producers in monopolistic competition attempt to differentiate their products so that they can charge higher prices.
- Typically, monopolists sell a smaller quantity at a higher price. Investors may benefit from being shareholders of monopolistic firms that have large margins and substantial positive cash flows.

- Competitive firms do not earn economic profit. There will be a market compensation for the rental of capital and of management services, but the lack of pricing power implies that there will be no extra margins.
- While in the short run firms in any market structure can have economic profits, the more competitive a market is and the lower the barriers to entry, the faster the extra profits will fade. In the long run, new entrants shrink margins and push the least efficient firms out of the market.
- Oligopoly is characterized by the importance of strategic behavior. Firms can change the price, quantity, quality, and advertisement of the product to gain an advantage over their competitors. Several types of equilibrium (e.g., Nash, Cournot, kinked demand curve) may occur that affect the likelihood of each of the incumbents (and potential entrants in the long run) having economic profits. Price wars may be started to force weaker competitors to abandon the market.
- Measuring market power is complicated. Ideally, econometric estimates of the elasticity of demand and supply should be computed. However, because of the lack of reliable data and the fact that elasticity changes over time (so that past data may not apply to the current situation), regulators and economists often use simpler measures. The concentration ratio is simple, but the HHI, with little more computation required, often produces a better figure for decision making.

19. PRACTICE PROBLEMS

1. A market structure characterized by many sellers with each having some pricing power and product differentiation is *best* described as:
   A. oligopoly.
   B. perfect competition.
   C. monopolistic competition.

2. A market structure with relatively few sellers of a homogeneous or standardized product is *best* described as:
   A. oligopoly.
   B. monopoly.
   C. perfect competition.

3. The demand schedule in a perfectly competitive market is given by $P = 93 - 1.5Q$ (for $Q \leq 62$) and the long-run cost structure of each company is:

$$\text{Total cost: } 256 + 2Q + 4Q^2$$
$$\text{Average cost: } 256/Q + 2 + 4Q$$
$$\text{Marginal cost: } 2 + 8Q$$

   New companies will enter the market at any price greater than:
   A. 8.
   B. 66.
   C. 81.

4. If companies earn economic profits in a perfectly competitive market, over the long run the supply curve will *most likely*:
   A. shift to the left.
   B. shift to the right.
   C. remain unchanged.

5. A company doing business in a monopolistically competitive market will *most likely* maximize profits when its output quantity is set such that:
   A. average cost is minimized.
   B. marginal revenue equals average cost.
   C. marginal revenue equals marginal cost.

6. Oligopolistic pricing strategy *most likely* results in a demand curve that is:
   A. kinked.
   B. vertical.
   C. horizontal.

7. Collusion is *less likely* in a market when:
   A. the product is homogeneous.
   B. companies have similar market shares.
   C. the cost structures of companies are similar.

8. In an industry comprised of three companies, which are small-scale manufacturers of an easily replicable product unprotected by brand recognition or patents, the *most* representative model of company behavior is:
   A. oligopoly.
   B. perfect competition.
   C. monopolistic competition.

9. Deep River Manufacturing is one of many companies in an industry that makes a food product. Deep River units are identical up to the point they are labeled. Deep River produces its labeled brand, which sells for $2.20 per unit, and "house brands" for seven different grocery chains, which sell for $2.00 per unit. Each grocery chain sells both the Deep River brand and its house brand. The *best* characterization of Deep River's market is:
   A. oligopoly.
   B. perfect competition.
   C. monopolistic competition.

10. SigmaSoft and ThetaTech are the dominant makers of computer system software. The market has two components: a large mass-market component in which demand is price sensitive, and a smaller performance-oriented component in which demand is much less price sensitive. SigmaSoft's product is considered to be technically superior. Each company can choose one of two strategies:

- *Open architecture (Open):* Mass market focus allowing other software venders to develop products for its platform.
- *Proprietary (Prop):* Allow only its own software applications to run on its platform.

    Depending upon the strategy each company selects, their profits would be:

Chapter 11   The Firm and Market Structures

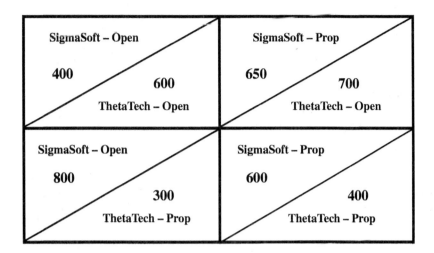

The Nash equilibrium for these companies is:
A. proprietary for SigmaSoft and proprietary for ThetaTech.
B. open architecture for SigmaSoft and proprietary for ThetaTech.
C. proprietary for SigmaSoft and open architecture for ThetaTech.

11. Companies *most likely* have a well-defined supply function when the market structure is:
    A. oligopoly.
    B. perfect competition.
    C. monopolistic competition.

12. Aquarius, Inc. is the dominant company and the price leader in its market. One of the other companies in the market attempts to gain market share by undercutting the price set by Aquarius. The market share of Aquarius will *most likely*:
    A. increase.
    B. decrease.
    C. stay the same.

13. Over time, the market share of the dominant company in an oligopolistic market will *most likely*:
    A. increase.
    B. decrease.
    C. remain the same.

14. Market competitors are *least likely* to use advertising as a tool of differentiation in an industry structure identified as:
    A. monopoly.
    B. perfect competition.
    C. monopolistic competition.

15. Upsilon Natural Gas, Inc. is a monopoly enjoying very high barriers to entry. Its marginal cost is $40 and its average cost is $70. A recent market study has determined the price elasticity of demand is 1.5. The company will *most likely* set its price at:

    A. $40.

    B. $70.

    C. $120.

16. A government entity that regulates an authorized monopoly will *most likely* base regulated prices on:

    A. marginal cost.

    B. long run average cost.

    C. first degree price discrimination.

17. An analyst gathers the following market share data for an industry:

Company	Sales (in millions of €)
ABC	300
Brown	250
Coral	200
Delta	150
Erie	100
All others	50

    The industry's four-company concentration ratio is *closest* to:

    A. 71%.

    B. 86%.

    C. 95%.

18. An analyst gathered the following market share data for an industry comprised of five companies:

Company	Market Share (%)
Zeta	35
Yusef	25
Xenon	20
Waters	10
Vlastos	10

    The industry's three-firm Herfindahl–Hirschmann Index is *closest* to:

    A. 0.185.

    B. 0.225.

    C. 0.235.

19. One disadvantage of the Herfindahl–Hirschmann Index is that the index:

    A. is difficult to compute.

    B. fails to reflect low barriers to entry.

    C. fails to reflect the effect of mergers in the industry.

CHAPTER 12

INTRODUCTION TO INDUSTRY AND COMPANY ANALYSIS

Patrick W. Dorsey, CFA
Dorsey Asset Management (USA)

Anthony M. Fiore, CFA
Silvercrest Asset Management (USA)

Ian Rossa O'Reilly, CFA
(Canada)*

LEARNING OUTCOMES

The candidate should be able to:

- explain uses of industry analysis and the relation of industry analysis to company analysis
- compare methods by which companies can be grouped
- explain the factors that affect the sensitivity of a company to the business cycle and the uses and limitations of industry and company descriptors such as "growth," "defensive," and "cyclical"
- describe current industry classification systems, and identify how a company should be classified, given a description of its activities and the classification system
- explain how a company's industry classification can be used to identify a potential "peer group" for equity valuation
- describe the elements that need to be covered in a thorough industry analysis
- describe the principles of strategic analysis of an industry
- explain the effects of barriers to entry, industry concentration, industry capacity, and market share stability on pricing power and price competition

*CFA Institute would like to thank Katy Zhao, at the Whitman Group, Morgan Stanley, (USA), for the revision of Introduction to Industry and Company Analysis chapter.

- describe industry life-cycle models, classify an industry as to life-cycle stage, and describe limitations of the life-cycle concept in forecasting industry performance
- describe macroeconomic, technological, demographic, governmental, social, and environmental influences on industry growth, profitability, and risk
- compare characteristics of representative industries from the various economic sectors
- describe the elements that should be covered in a thorough company analysis

1. INTRODUCTION

Understanding how industries and companies operate, together with an analysis of financial statements, provides a basis for forecasting company performance and allows analysts to determine the value of an investment in a company or its securities. **Industry analysis** is the analysis of a specific branch of manufacturing, service, or trade. Understanding the industry in which a company operates provides an essential framework for the analysis of the individual company—that is, **company analysis**. Equity analysis and credit analysis are often conducted by analysts who concentrate on one or several industries, which results in synergies and efficiencies in gathering and interpreting information.

In this chapter, we will address the following questions:

- What are the similarities and differences among industry classification systems?
- How does an analyst go about choosing a peer group of companies?
- What are the key factors to consider when analyzing an industry?
- What advantages are enjoyed by companies in strategically well-positioned industries?
- How should an analyst approach research and analysis of new industries?
- What are the factors that influence individual companies?

2. USES OF INDUSTRY ANALYSIS

Industry analysis is useful in a number of investment applications that make use of fundamental analysis. Its uses include the following:

- *Understanding a company's business and business environment.* Industry analysis is often a critical early step in stock selection and valuation because it provides insights into the issuer's growth opportunities, competitive dynamics, and business risks. For a credit analyst, industry analysis provides insights into the appropriateness of a company's use of debt financing and into its ability to meet its promised payments.
- *Identifying active equity investment opportunities.* Investors taking a top-down investing approach use industry analysis to identify industries with positive, neutral, or negative outlooks for profitability and growth. Generally, investors will then position their portfolios accordingly—by overweighting, market weighting, or underweighting those industries relative to the investor's benchmark if the investor judges that the industry's perceived prospects are not fully incorporated in market prices. In fact, some investors base their investment process on attempting to outperform their benchmarks or deliver absolute returns by industry rotation—that is, timing investments in industries in relation

to an analysis of industry fundamentals and/or business-cycle conditions (technical analysis may also play a role in such strategies).

- *Portfolio performance attribution.* The purpose of performance attribution is to identify and understand the sources of portfolio return. Portfolio attribution output will show any positive or negative contribution to returns from the fund manager's choice of industries and/or sectors in the portfolio. Industry classification schemes play a role in such performance attribution.

EXAMPLE 1

1. Which of the following information about a company would *most likely* depend on an industry analysis? The company's:
   A. dividend distribution policy.
   B. competitive environment.
   C. trends in personnel expenses.

Solution:
B is correct. To understand the competitive environment, analysts need to understand the industry as a whole. A and C are incorrect because both are specific to the company.

We will next explore how companies may be grouped into industries.

3. APPROACHES TO IDENTIFYING SIMILAR COMPANIES

Industry classification attempts to place companies into groups on the basis of commonalities. In the following sections, we discuss the three major approaches to industry classification:

- products and/or services supplied,
- business-cycle sensitivities, and
- statistical similarities.

3.1. Products and/or Services Supplied

Modern classification schemes are most commonly based on grouping companies by similar products and/or services. According to this perspective, an **industry** is defined as a group of companies offering similar products and/or services. For example, major companies in the global technology industry include Microsoft, Apple, Alphabet (owner of Google), Tencent, and Samsung Electronics. Although those companies are known to belong to the technology industry, they differ from one another in numerous ways. This is an issue that analysts should be aware of and take into consideration when making recommendations and investment decisions.

Industry classification schemes typically provide multiple levels of aggregation. The term **sector** is often used to refer to a group of related industries. The health care sector, for example, consists of a number of related industries, including the pharmaceutical, biotechnology, medical device, medical supply, hospital, and managed care industries.

These classification schemes typically place a company in an industry on the basis of a determination of its principal business activity. A company's **principal business activity** is the source from which the company derives a majority of its revenues and/or earnings. For example, companies that derive a majority of their revenues from the sale of pharmaceuticals include Novartis AG, Pfizer Inc., Roche Holding AG, GSK plc, and Sanofi S.A., all of which could be grouped together as part of the global pharmaceutical industry. Companies that engage in more than one significant business activity usually report the revenues (and, in many cases, operating profits) of the different business segments in their financial statements.

Examples of classification systems based on products and/or services include the commercial classification systems that will be discussed later—namely, the Global Industry Classification Standard (GICS) and the Industry Classification Benchmark (ICB). In addition to grouping companies by products and/or services, some of the major classification systems group consumer-related companies into cyclical and non-cyclical categories depending on a company's sensitivity to the business cycle. The next section addresses how companies can be categorized on the basis of economic sensitivity.

3.2. Business-Cycle Sensitivities

Companies are sometimes grouped on the basis of their relative sensitivity to the business cycle. This method often results in two broad groupings of companies:

- A **cyclical** company is one whose profits are strongly correlated with the strength of the overall economy. Such companies experience wider-than-average fluctuations in demand— high demand during periods of economic expansion and low demand during periods of economic contraction—and/or are subject to greater-than-average profit variability related to high operating leverage (i.e., high fixed costs). Concerning demand, cyclical products and services are often relatively expensive and represent purchases that can be delayed if necessary (e.g., because of declining disposable income). Examples of cyclical industries and broader sectors are autos, housing, basic materials, industrials, and technology.
- A **non-cyclical** company is one whose performance is largely independent of the business cycle. Non-cyclical companies produce goods or services for which demand remains relatively stable throughout the business cycle. Examples of non-cyclical industries are food and beverage, household and personal care products, health care, and utilities.

Although the classification systems we will discuss do not label their categories as cyclical or non-cyclical, certain sectors tend to experience greater economic sensitivity than others. Sectors that tend to exhibit a relatively high degree of economic sensitivity include consumer discretionary, energy, financials, industrials, technology, and materials. In contrast, sectors that exhibit relatively less economic sensitivity include consumer staples, health care, telecommunications, and utilities.

DESCRIPTIONS RELATED TO THE CYCLICAL/NON-CYCLICAL DISTINCTION

Analysts commonly encounter a number of labels related to the cyclical/non-cyclical distinction. For example, non-cyclical industries have sometimes been sorted into defensive (or stable) versus growth. Defensive industries and companies are those whose revenues and profits are least affected by fluctuations in overall economic activity.

These industries/companies tend to produce staple consumer goods (e.g., bread), provide basic services (grocery stores, drug stores, fast food outlets), or have their rates and revenues determined by contracts or government regulation (e.g., cost-of-service, rate-of-return regulated public utilities). Growth industries include industries with specific demand dynamics that are so strong that they override the significance of broad economic or other external factors and generate growth regardless of overall economic conditions, although their rates of growth may slow during an economic downturn.

The usefulness of industry and company labels, such as cyclical, growth, and defensive, is limited. Cyclical industries often have growth companies within them. A cyclical industry itself, although exposed to the effects of fluctuations in overall economic activity, may grow at an above-average rate for periods spanning multiple business cycles. The label "**growth cyclical**" is sometimes used to describe companies that are growing rapidly on a long-term basis but that still experience above-average fluctuation in their revenues and profits over the course of a business cycle.

Furthermore, when fluctuations in economic activity are large, as in the deep recession of 2008–2009, few companies escape the effects of the cyclical weakness in overall economic activity.

The defensive label is also problematic. Industries may include both companies that are growth and companies that are defensive in character, making the choice between a "growth" and a "defensive" label difficult. Moreover, "defensive" cannot be understood as necessarily being descriptive of investment characteristics. Food supermarkets, for example, would typically be described as defensive but can be subject to profit-damaging price wars. So-called defensive industries/companies may sometimes face industry dynamics that make them far from defensive in the sense of preserving shareholders' capital.

One limitation of the cyclical/non-cyclical classification is that business-cycle sensitivity is a continuous spectrum rather than an "either/or" issue, so placement of companies in one of the two major groups is somewhat arbitrary. The impact of severe recessions usually reaches all parts of the economy, so non-cyclical is better understood as a relative term.

Another limitation of a business-cycle classification for global investing is that different countries and regions of the world frequently progress through the various stages of the business cycle at different times. While one region of the world may be experiencing economic expansion, other regions or countries may be in recession, which complicates the application of a business-cycle approach to industry analysis. For example, a jewelry retailer (i.e., a cyclical company) that is selling domestically in a weak economy will exhibit markedly different fundamental performance relative to a jewelry company operating in an environment where demand is robust. Comparing these two companies—that is, similar companies that are currently exposed to different demand environments—could suggest investment opportunities. Combining fundamental data from such companies, however, to establish industry benchmark values would be misleading.

3.3. Statistical Similarities

Statistical approaches to grouping companies are typically based on the correlations of past securities' returns. For example, using the technique known as cluster analysis, companies are separated (on the basis of historical correlations of stock returns) into groups *in which* correlations are relatively high but *between which* correlations are relatively low. Clustering algorithms can be based on a range of financial characteristics (e.g., total assets, total revenue, profitability, leverage) and operating characteristics (e.g., R&D intensity, employee headcount). This method of aggregation often results in non-intuitive groups of companies, and the composition of the groups may vary significantly by time period and region of the world. Moreover, statistical approaches rely on historical data, but analysts have no guarantee that past correlation values will continue in the future. In addition, such approaches carry the inherent dangers of all statistical methods—namely, (1) falsely indicating a relationship that arose by chance and is not supported by plausible economic basis or (2) falsely excluding a relationship that actually is significant.

EXAMPLE 2

1. Which of the following is the *least likely* to be a method for grouping companies?
   A. Statistical approaches that assess past correlations of securities' returns
   B. Similarity of products and services
   C. Similarity of operating profit margins

Solution to 1:
   C is correct. Profit margins are not used as a method for grouping companies. Companies with similar profit margins may have little in common. A is incorrect because it describes the statistical similarities approach, which is a method for grouping companies. B is incorrect because similarity of products and services is one of the most common ways of grouping companies.

2. Companies are classified as cyclical or non-cyclical (defensive) on the basis of the exposure of their business to:
   A. their industry life cycle.
   B. the business cycle of the economy.
   C. the credit cycle, which affects their ability to borrow.

Solution to 2:
   B is correct. The cyclical/non-cyclical grouping reflects companies' sensitivity to the economy's business cycle. A is incorrect because the industry life cycle describes how the industry evolves over time, not how it relates to economic fluctuations. C is incorrect because the credit cycle explains the availability and cost of credit, not the fluctuations of output of the economy to which cyclical or non-cyclical companies are exposed.

4. INDUSTRY CLASSIFICATION SYSTEMS

A well-designed classification system often serves as a useful starting point for industry analysis. It allows analysts to compare industry trends and relative valuations among companies in a group. Classification systems that take a global perspective enable portfolio managers and research analysts to make global comparisons of companies in the same industry. For example, given the global nature of the automobile industry, a thorough analysis of the industry would include auto companies from many different countries and regions of the world. Classification systems are developed and used by both commercial entities and various governmental agencies. Most government and commercial classification systems are reviewed and, if necessary, updated from time to time. Generally, commercial classification systems are adjusted more frequently than government classification systems, which may be updated only every five years or so. We focus on the commercial systems because they are more commonly used in the investment industry.

4.1. Commercial Industry Classification Systems

Major index providers, including Standard & Poor's, MSCI, Russell Investments, Dow Jones, and FTSE Russell, classify companies in their equity indexes into industry groupings. Most classification schemes used by these index providers contain multiple levels of classification that start at the broadest level with a general sector grouping and then, in several further steps, subdivide or disaggregate the sectors into more granular, narrowly defined sub-industry groups.

4.1.1. Global Industry Classification Standard

GICS, jointly developed by Standard & Poor's and MSCI, was designed to facilitate global comparisons of industries. It classifies companies in both developed and developing economies. In June 2020, the GICS classification structure comprised four levels of detail consisting of 11 sectors, 24 industry groups, 69 industries, and 158 sub-industries. The composition of GICS historically has been adjusted over time to reflect changes in the global equity markets. One of the most significant changes happened in 2018 when GICS launched the new Communication Services sector to expand beyond simply the Telecommunication Services sector to incorporate many information technology and internet-related companies that offer communication platforms, content, and information.

4.1.2. Industry Classification Benchmark

The Industry Classification Benchmark (ICB), which was jointly developed by Dow Jones and FTSE, uses a four-tier structure to categorize companies globally on the basis of the source from which a company derives the majority of its revenue. In June 2020, the ICB classification system consisted of 11 industries, 20 supersectors, 45 sectors, and 173 subsectors. Although the ICB is similar to GICS in the number of tiers and the method by which companies are assigned to particular groups, the two systems use significantly different nomenclature. For example, whereas GICS uses the term "sector" to describe its broadest grouping of companies, ICB uses the term "industry" to describe the broadest category. The ICB is used by many global stock exchanges to categorize listed companies, including the

London Stock Exchange, Euronext, and NASDAQ OMX. In addition, all Russell Indexes are set to adopt a newly enhanced ICB structure after the market close on 18 September 2020.

Exhibit 1 provides examples of how several companies are classified. Note how differently the systems classify PayPal, Uber, and Activision Blizzard.

EXHIBIT 1: Industry Classification Examples

Stock Examples	Global Industry Classification Standard	Industry Classification Benchmark
PayPal	Information Technology > Software & Services > IT Services > Data Processing & Outsourced Services	Industrials > Industrial Goods & Services > Support Services > Financial Administration
Peloton Interactive	Consumer Discretionary > Consumer Durables & Apparel > Leisure Products > Leisure Products	Consumer Services > Travel & Leisure > Travel & Leisure > Recreational Services
Uber	Industrials > Transportation > Road & Rail > Trucking	Consumer Services > Retail > General Retailers > Specialized Consumer Services
Activision Blizzard	Communication Services > Media & Entertainment > Entertainment > Interactive Home Entertainment	Consumer Goods > Personal & Household Goods > Leisure Goods > Toys

Despite the fact that some companies are assigned to different broader sectors and industries by the different systems, the two commercial classification systems use common methodologies for assigning companies to groups. Also, the broadest level of grouping for GICS and the ICB is quite similar. Specifically, GICS and the ICB each identify 11 broad groupings below which all other categories reside. Next, we describe sectors that are fairly representative of how the broadest level of classification is viewed by GICS (into "sectors") and the ICB (into "industries").

4.1.3. Description of Representative Sectors/Industries

Exhibit 2 provides a description of each of the 11 broad sectors.

EXHIBIT 2: Sector Descriptions

Materials	Companies engaged in the production of building materials, chemicals, paper and forest products, and containers and packaging, as well as metal, mineral, and mining companies.
Consumer Discretionary	Companies that derive a majority of revenue from the sale of consumer-related products or services for which demand tends to exhibit a relatively high degree of economic sensitivity. Examples of business activities that frequently fall into this category are automotive, apparel, hotel, and restaurant businesses.
Consumer Staples	Consumer-related companies whose business tends to exhibit less economic sensitivity than other companies—for example, manufacturers of food, beverages, tobacco, and personal care products.

Energy	Companies whose primary line of business involves exploring for, production of, or refining of natural resources used to produce energy; companies that derive a majority of revenue from the sale of equipment or through the provision of services to energy companies also fall into this category.
Financials	Companies whose primary line of business involves banking, finance, insurance, asset management, and/or brokerage services.
Health Care	Manufacturers of pharmaceutical and biotech products, medical devices, health care equipment, and medical supplies and providers of health care services.
Industrials	Manufacturers of capital goods and providers of commercial services; for example, business activities would include heavy machinery and equipment manufacture, aerospace and defense, transportation services, and commercial services and supplies.
Real Estate	Companies engaged in the development and operation of real estate. This includes companies offering real estate–related services and equity real estate investment trusts (REITs).
Information Technology	Manufacture or sale of computers, software, semiconductors, and communications equipment; other business activities that frequently fall into this category are electronic entertainment, internet services, and technology consulting and services.
Communication Services/ Telecommunications	This sector includes traditional telecommunication companies that provide fixed line and wireless communication services, with media, entertainment, and interactive media and services, such as video gaming companies.
Utilities	Electric, gas, and water utilities; telecommunication companies are sometimes included in this category.

To classify a company accurately in a particular classification scheme requires definitions of the classification categories, a statement about the criteria used in classification, and detailed information about the subject company. Example 3 introduces an exercise in such classification. In addressing the question, the reader can make use of the widely applicable sector descriptions just given and familiarity with available business products and services.

EXAMPLE 3   Classifying Companies into Industries

1.   Exhibit 2 defines 11 representative sectors, repeated here in Exhibit 3. Assume the classification system is based on the criterion of a company's principal business activity as judged primarily by source of revenue.

EXHIBIT 3: List of Sectors

Sector
Materials
Consumer Discretionary
Consumer Staples
Energy

Sector
Financials
Health Care
Industrials
Real Estate
Information Technology
Communication Services/ Telecommunications
Utilities

Based on the information given, determine an appropriate sector membership for each of the following hypothetical companies:

1. An operator of shopping malls
2. A natural gas transporter and marketer
3. A manufacturer of heavy construction equipment
4. A provider of regional telephone services
5. A semiconductor company
6. A manufacturer of medical devices
7. A video conference provider
8. A manufacturer of chemicals and plastics
9. A manufacturer of automobiles
10. A cloud computing service provider
11. A food delivery company
12. A regulated supplier of electricity
13. A provider of wireless broadband services
14. A manufacturer of soaps and detergents
15. A software development company
16. An insurer
17. A regulated provider of water/wastewater services
18. A robotic-assisted surgery company
19. A manufacturer of pharmaceuticals
20. A provider of rail transportation services
21. A data center real estate investment trust
22. A developer of residential housing

Solution:

Sector	Company Number
Materials	7
Consumer Discretionary	8, 10
Consumer Staples	13
Energy	1
Financials	15
Health Care	5, 17, 18
Industrials	2, 19

Sector	Company Number
Real Estate	0, 20, 21
Information Technology	4, 9, 14
Communication Services/	3, 6, 12
Telecommunications	
Utilities	11, 16

EXAMPLE 4   Industry Classification Schemes

1. The GICS classification system classifies companies on the basis of a company's primary business activity as measured primarily by:
   A. assets.
   B. income.
   C. revenue.

Solution to 1:
   C is correct.

2. Which of the following is *least likely* to be accurately described as a cyclical company?
   A. An automobile manufacturer
   B. A producer of breakfast cereals
   C. An apparel company producing new, trendy clothes for teenage girls

Solution to 2:
   B is correct. A producer of staple foods, such as cereals, is a classic example of a non-cyclical company. Demand for automobiles is cyclical—that is, relatively high during economic expansions and relatively low during economic contractions. Also, demand for teenage fashions is likely to be more sensitive to the business cycle than demand for standard food items, such as breakfast cereals. When budgets have been reduced, families may try to avoid expensive clothing or may try to extend the life of existing clothing.

3. Which of the following is the *most accurate* statement? A statistical approach to grouping companies into industries:
   A. is based on historical correlations of the securities' returns.
   B. frequently produces industry groups whose composition is similar worldwide.
   C. emphasizes the descriptive statistics of industries consisting of companies producing similar products and/or services.

Solution to 3:
   A is correct.

4.2. Constructing a Peer Group

A **peer group** is a group of companies engaged in similar business activities whose economics and valuation are influenced by closely related factors. Comparisons of a company in relation to a well-defined peer group can provide valuable insights into the company's performance and its relative valuation.

The construction of a peer group is a subjective process; the result often differs significantly from even the most narrowly defined categories given by the commercial classification systems. However, commercial classification systems do provide a starting point for the construction of a relevant peer group because by using such systems, an analyst can quickly discover the public companies operating in the chosen industry.

In fact, one approach to constructing a peer group is to start by identifying other companies operating in the same industry. Analysts who subscribe to one or more of the commercial classification systems can quickly generate a list of other companies in the industry in which the company operates according to that particular service provider's definition of the industry. An analyst can then investigate the business activities of these companies through a range of sources, such as companies' public disclosures or industry trade publications, and confirm that each comparable company derives a significant portion of its revenue and operating profit from a business activity similar to the primary business of the subject company.

The following questions may improve the list of peer companies:

- *What proportion of revenue and operating profit is derived from business activities similar to those of the subject company?* In general, a higher percentage results in a more meaningful comparison.
- *Does a potential peer company face a demand environment similar to that of the subject company?* For example, a comparison of growth rates, margins, and valuations may be of limited value when comparing companies that are exposed to different stages of the business cycle. (As mentioned, such differences may be the result of conducting business in geographically different markets.)
- *Does the peer company have a significant business segment(s) that is comparable to other companies even if they are not in the same commercial classification system?* For example, Amazon Web Services' business (cloud computing) is more comparable to that of such peers as Microsoft and Cisco than to that of its e-commerce peers.

Although companies with limited lines of business may be neatly categorized into a single peer group, companies with multiple divisions may be included in more than one category. For example, US-based Hewlett-Packard Company (HP), a global provider of technology and software solutions, used to be included in more than one peer group before it separated its business into HP Inc., which sells hardware, and Hewlett-Packard Enterprise (HPE), which sells software and services. Investors interested in the personal computer (PC) industry, for example, used to include HP in their peer group, but investors constructing a peer group of providers of information technology services also included HP in that group.

Example 5 illustrates the process of identifying a peer group of companies and shows some of the practical hurdles to determining a peer group.

EXAMPLE 5   An Analyst Researches the Peer Group of Novartis

Suppose that an analyst needs to identify the peer group of companies for Novartis for use in the valuation section of a company report. Novartis develops and produces branded pharmaceuticals and operates globally. The analyst starts by looking at Novartis's industry classification according to GICS. The most narrowly defined category that GICS uses is the sub-industry level, and in July 2020, Novartis was in the GICS sub-industry called Pharmaceuticals, together with the companies listed in Exhibit 4 (a sample of companies is shown).

Exhibit 4: GICS Industry Classification: Pharmaceuticals

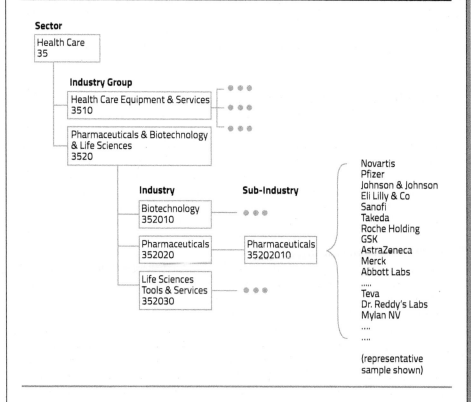

After looking over the list of companies, the analyst quickly realizes that some adjustments need to be made to the list to end up with a peer group of companies that are comparable to Novartis.

Research of the companies' disclosures, websites, and company descriptions provided by electronic data/information vendors reveals that Novartis focuses on research, development, and production of branded, patent-protected original products. Such products account for 79% of the company's revenues (source: "Novartis Annual

Report 2019"). The business model is, therefore, distinct from that of companies that focus on the production of generic pharmaceuticals that do not benefit from patent protection the way branded original products do. For example, Teva and Dr. Reddy's main business is in the generic pharmaceuticals space, so those companies would not fit Novartis's peer group. In contrast, Novartis's business is subject to similar drivers and external influences that apply to a narrow range of companies, such as Roche, Pfizer, GSK, and Sanofi. The peer group that the analyst should use is, therefore, narrower than what the GICS Pharmaceuticals sub-industry would suggest.

In summary, analysts must distinguish between a company's industry—as defined by one or more of the various classification systems—and its peer group. A company's peer group should consist of companies with similar business activities whose economic activity depends on similar drivers of demand and similar factors related to cost structure and access to financial capital. In practice, these necessities frequently result in a smaller group (even a different group) of companies than the most narrowly defined categories used by the common commercial classification systems. Example 6 illustrates various aspects of developing and using peer groups.

EXAMPLE 6   The Semiconductor Industry: Business-Cycle Sensitivity and Peer-Group Determination

The GICS semiconductor and semiconductor equipment industry (453010) has two sub-industries—the semiconductor equipment sub-industry (45301010) and the semiconductors sub-industry (45301020). Members of the semiconductor equipment sub-industry include equipment suppliers, such as Lam Research Corporation and ASML Holdings NV; the semiconductors sub-industry includes integrated circuit manufacturers Intel Corporation and Taiwan Semiconductor Manufacturing Company Ltd.

Lam Research is a leading supplier of wafer fabrication equipment and services to the world's semiconductor industry. Lam also offers wafer-cleaning equipment that is used after many of the individual steps required to manufacture a finished wafer. Often, the technical advances that Lam introduces in its wafer-etching and wafer-cleaning products are also available as upgrades to its installed base. This benefit provides customers with a cost-effective way to extend the performance and capabilities of their existing wafer fabrication lines.

ASML describes itself as the world's leading provider of lithography systems (etching and printing on wafers) for the semiconductor industry. ASML manufactures complex machines that are critical to the production of integrated circuits or microchips. ASML designs, develops, integrates, markets, and services these advanced systems, which help chip makers reduce the size and increase the functionality of microchips and consumer electronic equipment. The machines are costly and thus represent a substantial capital investment for a purchaser.

Based on revenue, Intel is the world's largest semiconductor chip maker and has a dominant share of microprocessors for the personal computer market. Intel designs and produces its own proprietary semiconductors for direct sale to customers, such as personal computer makers. Intel has made significant investments in research and development (R&D) to introduce and produce new chips for new applications.

Established in 1987, Taiwan Semiconductor Manufacturing (TSMC) is the world's largest dedicated semiconductor foundry company (dedicated semiconductor foundries are semiconductor fabrication plants that execute the designs of other companies). TSMC describes itself as offering cutting-edge process technologies, pioneering design services, manufacturing efficiency, and product quality. TSMC provides design and production services to a diverse group of integrated circuit suppliers that generally do not have their own in-house manufacturing capabilities. The company's revenues represented more than 50% of the dedicated foundry segment in the semiconductor industry.

The questions that follow take the perspective of a recession similar to that of early 2009, when many economies around the world were in a recession. Based only on the information given, answer the following questions:

1. If the weak economy, similar to that of early 2009, were to recover within the next 12–18 months, which of the two sub-industries of the semiconductor and semiconductor equipment industry would most likely be the first to experience a positive improvement in business?

Solution to 1:
In the most likely scenario, improvement in the business of the equipment makers (Lam and ASML) would lag that of semiconductor companies (Intel and TSMC). Because of the weak economy, excess manufacturing capacity should be available to meet increased demand for integrated circuits in the near term without additional equipment, which is a major capital investment. When semiconductor manufacturers believe the longer-term outlook has improved, they should begin to place orders for additional equipment.

2. Explain whether Intel and TSMC should be considered members of the same peer group.

Solution to 2:
Intel and TSMC are not likely to be considered comparable members of the same peer group because they have different sets of customers and different business models. Intel sells its proprietary semiconductors directly to customers, whereas TSMC provides design and production services to circuit suppliers that do not have their own in-house manufacturing capabilities. Standard & Poor's does not group Intel and TSMC in the same peer group; Intel was in the Semiconductors, Logic, Larger Companies group, and TSMC was in the Semiconductors, Foundry Services group.

3. Explain whether Lam Research and ASML should be considered members of the same peer group.

Solution to 3:
Both Lam Research and ASML are leading companies that design and manufacture equipment to produce semiconductor chips. The companies are comparable because they both depend on the same economic factors that drive demand for their products. Their major customers are the semiconductor chip companies. Standard & Poor's grouped both companies in the same peer group—Semiconductor Equipment, Larger Front End.

5. DESCRIBING AND ANALYZING AN INDUSTRY AND PRINCIPLES OF STRATEGIC ANALYSIS

In their work, analysts with superior knowledge about an industry's characteristics, conditions, and trends have a competitive edge in evaluating the investment merits of the companies in the industry. Analysts attempt to develop practical, reliable industry forecasts by using various approaches to forecasting. They often estimate a range of projections for a variable reflecting various possible scenarios. In order to conduct this analysis, analysts can study a wide range of factors, including but not limited to the following:

1. Statistical relationships between industry trends
2. Economic and business variables
3. Information from industry associations, from the individual subject companies they are analyzing, and from these companies' competitors, suppliers, and customers
4. Relevant industry trends and metrics to help understand and forecast trends

Investment managers and analysts also examine industry performance (1) in relation to other industries to identify industries with superior/inferior returns and (2) over time to determine the degree of consistency, stability, and risk in the returns in the industry over time. The objective of this analysis is to identify industries that offer the highest potential for investment returns on a risk-adjusted basis. The investment time horizon can be either long or short, as is the case for a rotation strategy in which portfolios are rotated into the industry groups that are expected to benefit from the next stage in the business cycle.

Analysts may also seek to compare their assumptions and projections with those made by other analysts. Doing so enables them to identify and understand any differences in methodology and any differences between their forecasts and consensus forecasts.

Exhibit 5 provides a framework designed to help analysts check that they have considered the range of forces that may affect the evolution of an industry. It shows, at the macro level, macroeconomic, demographic, environmental, governmental, social, and technological influences affecting the industry. It also depicts how an industry is affected by the forces driving industry competition (threat of new entrants, substitution threats, customer and supplier bargaining forces), the competitive forces in the industry (rivalry), life-cycle issues, and business-cycle considerations. Exhibit 5 summarizes and brings together visually the topics and concepts discussed in this section.

Exhibit 5: A Framework for Industry Analysis

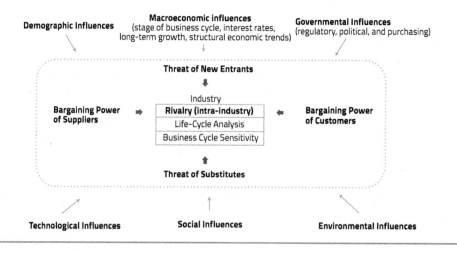

5.1. Principles of Strategic Analysis

When analyzing an industry, the analyst must recognize that the economic fundamentals can vary markedly among industries. Some industries are highly competitive, with most players struggling to earn adequate returns on capital, whereas other industries have attractive characteristics that allow almost all industry participants to generate healthy profits.

Differing competitive environments are often tied to the structural attributes of an industry, which is one reason industry analysis is a vital complement to company analysis. To thoroughly analyze a company itself, the analyst needs to understand the context in which the company operates. As analysts examine the competitive structure of an industry, they should always be thinking about what attributes could change in the future. Needless to say, industry analysis must be forward looking and could ultimately help determine an overweight or underweight to sector positioning.

Analysis of the competitive environment with an emphasis on the implications of the environment for corporate strategy is known as **strategic analysis**. Michael Porter's "five forces" framework is the classic starting point for strategic analysis; although it was originally aimed more at internal managers of businesses than at external security analysts, the framework is useful to both.

Porter (2008) identified five determinants of the intensity of competition in an industry: The threat of entry, the power of suppliers, the power of buyers, the threat of substitutes, and rivalry among existing competitors. Exhibit 6 illustrates the Porter framework.

Exhibit 6: Porter's Five Forces

Threat of New Entrants
Depends on the existence and extent of barriers to enter the industry.
Q: How difficult would it be for new competitors to enter the industry? Industries that are easy to enter will generally be more competitive than industries with high barriers to entry.

Bargaining Power of Suppliers
Affected by:
- concentration of industry is,
- switching costs of suppliers' customers,
- supply substitutes.
Q: Are suppliers able to increase prices, restrict supply, or pass on rising input costs?
Suppliers of scarce or limited parts or elements often possess significant pricing power.

Rivalry (intra-industry)
Rivalry among existing competitors; price discipline. Depends on:
- Industry structure and concentration/fragmentation
- Product or service differentiation
- Industry exit barriers

Bargaining Power of Customers
Affected by:
- size and concentration of customers,
- costs of switching to other suppliers,
- customers' ability to produce the product or service themselves.
Are customers able to force price reductions or better payment terms?

Threat of Substitutes (products or services)
Affected by the availability of (alternative) product categories that can satisfy customer needs
Q: Are lower-priced brands close substitutes for premium brands and vice versa?

Addressing the following questions should help the analyst evaluate the threat of new entrants and the level of competition in an industry and thereby provide an effective base for describing and analyzing the industry:

- What are the barriers to entry? Is it difficult or easy for a new competitor to challenge incumbents? Relatively high (low) barriers to entry imply that the threat of new entrants is relatively low (high).
- How concentrated is the industry? Do a small number of companies control a relatively large share of the market, or does the industry have many players, each with a small market share?
- What are capacity levels? That is, based on existing investment, how much of the goods or services can be delivered in a given time frame? Does the industry suffer chronic over- or undercapacity, or do supply and demand tend to come into balance reasonably quickly in the industry?
- How stable are market shares? Do companies tend to rapidly gain or lose share, or is the industry stable?
- How important is price to the customer's purchase decision?
- Where is the industry in its life cycle? Does it have meaningful growth prospects, or is demand stagnant/declining?

The answers to these questions are elements of any thorough industry analysis. They are explored each in turn in the sections that follow.

5.2. Barriers to Entry

When a company is earning economic profits, the chances that it will be able to sustain them over time are greater, all else being equal, if the industry has high barriers to entry. The ease with which new competitors can challenge incumbents is often an important factor in determining the competitive landscape of an industry. If new competitors can easily enter the industry, the industry is likely to be highly competitive because high returns on invested capital will quickly be competed away by new entrants eager to grab their share of economic profits. As a result, industries with low barriers to entry often have little pricing power because price increases that raise companies' returns on capital will eventually attract new competitors to the industry.

If incumbents are protected by barriers to entry, the threat of new entrants is lower and incumbents may enjoy a more benign competitive environment. Often, these barriers to entry can lead to greater pricing power, because potential competitors would find it difficult to enter the industry and undercut incumbents' prices. Of course, high barriers to entry do not guarantee pricing power, because incumbents may compete fiercely among each other.

A classic example of an industry with low barriers to entry is restaurants. Anyone with a modest amount of capital and some culinary skill can open a restaurant, and popular restaurants quickly attract competition. As a result, the industry is very competitive, and many restaurants fail in their first few years of business.

At the other end of the spectrum of barriers to entry are the global credit card networks, such as MasterCard and Visa, both of which often post operating margins greater than 30%. Such high profits should attract competition, but the barriers to entry are extremely high. Capital costs are one hurdle; also, building a massive data-processing network would not be cheap. Imagine for a moment that a venture capitalist were willing to fund the construction of a network that would replicate the physical infrastructure of the incumbents; the new card-processing company would have to convince millions of consumers to use the new card and convince thousands of merchants to accept the card. Consumers would not want to use a card that merchants did not accept, and merchants would not want to accept a card that few consumers carried. This problem would be difficult to solve, which is why the barriers to entering this industry are quite high. The barriers help preserve the profitability of the incumbent players.

One way of understanding barriers to entry is simply by thinking about what it would take for new players to compete in an industry. How much money would they need to spend? What kind of intellectual capital would they need to acquire? How easy would it be to attract enough customers to become successful?

Another way to investigate the issue is by looking at historical data. How often have new companies tried to enter the industry? Is a list of industry participants today markedly different from what it was 5 or 10 years ago? These kinds of data can be very helpful because the information is based on the real-world experience of many entrepreneurs and businesses making capital allocation decisions. If an industry has seen a flood of new entrants over the past several years, the odds that the barriers are low are good; conversely, if the same 10 companies that dominate an industry today dominated it 10 years ago, barriers to entry are probably fairly high.

Do not confuse barriers to *entry*, however, with barriers to *success*. In some industries, entering may be easy but becoming successful enough to threaten the incumbents might be quite hard.

Also, high barriers to entry do not automatically lead to good pricing power and attractive industry economics. Consider the cases of the auto manufacturing, commercial aircraft manufacturing, and oil refining industries. Starting up a new company in any of these industries is very difficult. Aside from the massive capital costs, there would be significant other barriers to entry: A new automaker would need manufacturing expertise and a dealer network, an aircraft manufacturer would need a significant amount of intellectual capital, and a refiner would need process expertise and regulatory approvals. Despite the high barriers to entry, the industries are all quite competitive with limited pricing power. Very few industry participants reliably generate returns on capital in excess of their costs of capital. Exiting the industries and re-deploying capacity to other uses when demand conditions worsen are also difficult, meaning that the industries can be prone to overcapacity.

A final consideration when analyzing barriers to entry is that they can change over time as new technologies or ways of conducting business become available. For example outsourcing of some activities means that companies can focus on product or service design, without the need to build and own production capacity.

Exhibit 7 provides an overview of barriers to entry for three representative industries.

EXHIBIT 7: Elements of a Strategic Analysis for Three Industries: Barriers to Entry

	Branded Pharmaceuticals	Oil Services	Confections/Candy
Major Companies	Pfizer, Novartis, Merck, GSK plc	Schlumberger, Baker Hughes, Halliburton	Hershey, Mars/Wrigley, Nestle
Barriers to Entry	*Very High*: Substantial financial and intellectual capital required to compete effectively. A potential new entrant would need to create a sizable R&D operation, a global distribution network, and large-scale manufacturing capacity.	*High*: Technological expertise is required, but a high level of innovation allows niche companies to enter the industry and compete in specific areas.	*Medium/Low*: Low financial or technological hurdles, but new players would lack the established brands that drive consumer purchase decisions and potential supply chain operations.

5.3. Industry Concentration

Much like industries with barriers to entry, industries that are concentrated among a relatively small number of players often experience relatively less price competition. Again, there are important exceptions, so the reader should not automatically assume that concentrated industries always have pricing power or that fragmented industries do not. The degree of concentration is often measured using the Herfindahl–Hirschman Index.

An analysis of industry concentration should start with market share: What percentage of the market does each of the largest players have, and how large are those shares relative to each other and relative to the remainder of the market? Often, the *relative* market shares of competitors matter as much as their *absolute* market shares.

For example, the global market for commercial aircraft (for 100 or more passengers) is extremely concentrated; only Boeing and Airbus manufacture this type of plane on significant scale. The two companies tend to have broadly similar market shares, however, and control essentially the entire market. Because neither enjoys a scale advantage relative to its competitor and because any business gained by one is lost by the other, competition tends to be fierce.

This situation contrasts with the market for home improvement products in the United States, which is dominated by Home Depot and Lowe's. These two companies had about 11% and 7% market shares for the decade up to 2020, respectively, which does not sound very large. However, the next largest competitor had only 2% of the market, and most market participants are tiny, with miniscule market shares. Both Home Depot and Lowe's have historically posted high returns on invested capital, in part because they could profitably grow by squeezing out smaller competitors rather than engaging in fierce competition with each other.

Fragmented industries tend to be highly price competitive for several reasons. First, the large number of companies makes coordination difficult because there are too many competitors for each industry member to monitor effectively. Second, each player has such a small piece of the market that even a small gain in market share can make a meaningful difference to its fortunes, which increases the incentive of each company to undercut prices and attempt to steal market share. Finally, the large number of players encourages industry members to think of themselves individualistically rather than as members of a larger group, which can lead to fierce competitive behavior.

In concentrated industries, in contrast, each player can relatively easily keep track of what its competitors are doing, which makes tacit coordination much more feasible. Also, leading industry members are large, which means they have more to lose—and proportionately less to gain—by destructive price behavior. Large companies are also more tied to the fortunes of the industry as a whole, making them more likely to consider the long-run effects of a price war on overall industry economics.

As with barriers to entry, the level of industry concentration is a guideline rather than a hard-and-fast rule when thinking about the level of pricing power in an industry. For example, Exhibit 8 shows a rough classification of industries based on analysis by Morningstar after asking its equity analysts whether industries were characterized by strong or weak pricing power and whether those industries were concentrated or fragmented. Examples of companies in industries are included in parentheses. In the upper right quadrant ("concentrated with weak pricing power"), those industries that are capital intensive and/or sell commodity-like products are shown in boldface.

EXHIBIT 8: A Two-Factor Analysis of Industries

Concentrated with Strong Pricing Power	Concentrated with Weak Pricing Power
Orthopedic Devices (Zimmer, Smith & Nephew)	**Commercial Aircraft** (Boeing, Airbus)
Biotech (Amgen, Genzyme)	**Automobiles** (General Motors, Toyota,
Pharmaceuticals (Merck & Co., Novartis)	Daimler)
Industrial Gases (Praxair, Air Products and Chemicals)	**Memory** (DRAM & Flash Product, Samsung,
Enterprise Networking (Cisco Systems)	Hynix)
US Defense (General Dynamics)	**Semiconductor Equipment** (Applied Mate-
Heavy Construction Equipment (Caterpillar, Komatsu)	rials, Tokyo Electron)
Credit Card Networks (MasterCard, Visa)	Generic Drugs (Teva Pharmaceutical Indus-
Investment Banking/Mergers & Acquisitions (Gold-	tries, Sandoz)
man Sachs, UBS)	Printers/Office Machines (HP, Lexmark)
Futures Exchanges (Chicago Mercantile Exchange,	**Refiners** (Valero, Marathon Oil)
Intercontinental Exchange)	**Major Integrated Oil** (BP, ExxonMobil)
Tobacco (Philip Morris, British American Tobacco)	
Alcoholic Beverages (Diageo, Pernod Ricard)	

Fragmented with Strong Pricing Power	Fragmented with Weak Pricing Power
For-Profit Education (Apollo Group, DeVry	Consumer Packaged Goods (Procter & Gamble,
University)	Unilever)
Analog Chips (Texas Instruments, STMicroelec-	Retail (Walmart, Carrefour Group)
tronics)	Marine Transportation (Maersk Line, Frontline)
Industrial Distribution (Fastenal, W.W. Grain-	Solar Panels
ger)	Airlines
Propane Distribution (AmeriGas, Ferrellgas)	Restaurants
Private Banking (Northern Trust, Credit Suisse)	Life Insurance

Source: Adapted from Morningstar Equity Research.

The industries in the top right quadrant defy the "concentration is good for pricing" guideline. When we examine these concentrated-yet-competitive industries, a clear theme emerges: Many industries in this quadrant (the boldface ones) are highly capital intensive and sell commodity-like products. Exiting the industries and re-deploying capacity to other uses when demand conditions worsen are also difficult, meaning that the industries can be prone to overcapacity. Also, if the industry sells a commodity product that is difficult—or impossible—to differentiate, the incentive to compete on price increases because a lower price frequently results in greater market share.

Generally, industry concentration is a good indicator that an industry has pricing power and rational competition, but other factors may override the importance of concentration. Industry fragmentation is a much stronger signal that the industry is competitive with limited pricing power.

The industry characteristics discussed here are guidelines meant to steer the analyst in a particular direction, not rules that should cause the analyst to ignore other relevant analytical factors.

EXHIBIT 9: Elements of a Strategic Analysis for Three Industries: Levels of Concentration

	Branded Pharmaceuticals	Oil Services	Confections/Candy
Major Companies	Pfizer, Novartis, Merck, GSK plc	Schlumberger, Baker Hughes, Halliburton	Hershey, Mars/Wrigley, Nestle
Level of Concentration	*Concentrated*: A small number of companies control the bulk of the global market for branded drugs. Recent mergers have increased the level of concentration.	*Fragmented*: Although only a small number of companies provide a full range of services, many smaller players compete effectively in specific areas. Service arms of national oil companies may control significant market share in their own countries, and some product lines are concentrated in the mature US market.	*Very Concentrated*: The top four companies have a large proportion of global market share. Recent mergers have increased the level of concentration.

5.4. Industry Capacity

The effect of industry capacity (the maximum amount of a good or service that can be supplied in a given time period) on pricing is clear: Tight, or limited, capacity gives participants more pricing power because demand for the product or service exceeds supply, whereas overcapacity leads to price cutting and a very competitive environment because excess supply chases demand. An analyst should think about not only current capacity conditions but future changes in capacity levels. How quickly can companies in the industry adjust to fluctuations in demand? How flexible is the industry in bringing supply and demand into balance? What will be the effect of that process on industry pricing power or on industry margins?

5.4.1. Capacity: Short Term vs. Long Term

Generally, capacity is fixed in the short term and variable in the long term because capacity can be increased (e.g., new factories can be built) if time is sufficient. What is considered "sufficient" time—and, therefore, the duration of the short term, in which capacity cannot be increased—may vary dramatically among industries. Sometimes, adding capacity takes years to complete, as in the case of the construction of a new manufacturing plant for pharmaceuticals, which is complex and subject to regulatory requirements. In other situations, capacity may be added or reduced relatively quickly, as in the case of service industries, such as advertising. In cyclical markets, such as commercial paper and paperboard, capacity conditions can change rapidly. Strong demand in the early stages of an economic recovery can result in the addition of supply. Given the long lead times to build manufacturing plants, new supply may reach the market just as demand slows, rapidly changing capacity conditions from tight to loose. Such considerations underscore the importance of forecasting long-term industry demand in evaluating industry investments in capacity.

5.4.2. Physical Capacity

Generally, if new capacity is physical—for example, an auto manufacturing plant or a massive cargo ship—it will take longer for new capacity to come on line to meet an increase in demand, resulting in a longer period of tight conditions. Unfortunately, capacity additions frequently overshoot long-run demand, and because physical capital is often hard to re-deploy, industries reliant on physical capacity may get stuck in conditions of excess capacity and diminished pricing power for an extended period.

Note that capacity need not be physical. After Hurricane Katrina caused enormous damage to the southeastern United States in 2005, reinsurance rates quickly spiked as customers sought to increase their financial protection from future hurricanes. However, these high reinsurance rates enticed a flood of fresh capital into the reinsurance market, and a number of new reinsurance companies were founded, which brought rates back down.

Financial and human capital, in contrast, can be quickly shifted to new uses. In the reinsurance example, for instance, financial capital was quick to enter the reinsurance market and take advantage of tight capacity conditions, but if too much capital had entered the market, some portion of that capital could easily have left to seek higher returns elsewhere. Money can be used for many things, but massive bulk cargo vessels are not useful for much more than transporting heavy goods across oceans. Exhibit 10 shows the elements of a strategic analysis relating to industry capacity.

EXHIBIT 10: Elements of a Strategic Analysis: Industry Capacity

	Branded Pharmaceuticals	Oil Services	Confections/Candy
Major Companies	Pfizer, Novartis, Merck, GSK plc	Schlumberger, Baker Hughes, Halliburton	Hershey, Mars/Wrigley, Nestle
Impact of Industry Capacity	*Not Applicable*: Pharmaceutical pricing is primarily determined by patent protection and regulatory issues, including government approvals of drugs and of manufacturing facilities. Manufacturing capacity is of little importance.	*Medium/High*: Demand can fluctuate quickly depending on commodity prices, and industry players often find themselves with too few (or too many) employees on the payroll.	*Not Applicable*: Pricing is driven primarily by brand strength. Manufacturing capacity has little effect.

EXAMPLE 7

1. Which of the following companies is *most likely* to have the greatest ability to quickly increase capacity?
   A. Legal services provider
   B. Manufacturing company producing heavy machinery
   C. Company operating cargo ships

Solution:

   A is correct. Capacity increases in providing legal services would not require significant fixed capital investments. B and C are incorrect because the companies would require capital investments, and capacity expansion would take time to implement.

5.5. Market Share Stability

Examining the stability of industry market shares over time is similar to thinking about barriers to entry and the frequency with which new players enter an industry. In fact, barriers to entry and the frequency of new product introductions, together with such factors as product differentiation, affect market shares. Stable market shares typically indicate less competitive industries; unstable market shares often indicate highly competitive industries that have limited pricing power. Exhibit 11 illustrates the development of market shares in two medical devices markets.

EXHIBIT 11: Market Shares in Orthopedic and Metal Mesh Devices

Over 2010–2020, the orthopedic device industry—mainly artificial hips and knees—has been a relatively stable global oligopoly led by Stryker, Zimmer Biomet, Smith & Nephew, and Johnson & Johnson, which jointly control about three quarters of the global market.

In contrast, the market for stents—small metal mesh devices used to prop open blocked arteries—while controlled by a handful of companies, has seen market shares change from being very stable to being marked by rapid change. Johnson & Johnson, which together with Boston Scientific, dominated the US stent market for many years, went from having about half the market in 2007 to having only 15% in early 2009 and exited the market in 2011; over the same period, Abbott Laboratories increased its market share from 0% to around 30%. The reason for this change was the launch of new stents by Abbott and Medtronic, which took market share from Johnson & Johnson's and Boston Scientific's established stents.

Orthopedic device companies have experienced more stability in their market shares for two reasons. First, artificial hips and knees are complicated to implant, and each manufacturer's products are slightly different. As a result, orthopedic surgeons become proficient at using one or several companies' devices and may be reluctant to incur the time and cost of learning how to implant products from a competing company. The second reason is the relatively slow pace of innovation in the orthopedic device industry, making the benefit of switching among product lines relatively low. In addition, the number of orthopedic device companies has remained fairly static over many years.

In contrast, the US stent market has experienced rapid shifts in market shares because of several factors. First, interventional cardiologists seem to be more open to implanting stents from different manufacturers; that tendency may reflect lower switching costs for stents relative to orthopedic devices and the interchangeability of stents. More importantly, however, the pace of innovation in the stent market has become quite rapid, giving cardiologists added incentive to switch to newer stents, with potentially better patient outcomes, as they became available.

Low switching costs plus a relatively high benefit from switching caused market shares to change quickly in the stent market. High switching costs for orthopedic devices coupled with slow innovation resulted in a lower benefit from switching, which led to greater market share stability in orthopedic devices.

Exhibit 12 briefly describes market share stability in the three representative industries.

EXHIBIT 12: Elements of a Strategic Analysis: Market Share

	Branded Pharmaceuticals	Oil Services	Confections/Candy
Major Companies	Pfizer, Novartis, Merck, GSK plc	Schlumberger, Baker Hughes, Halliburton	Hershey, Mars/ Wrigley, Nestle
Industry Stability	*Stable*: The branded pharmaceutical market is dominated by major companies and consolidation via mega-mergers. Market shares shift quickly, however, as new drugs are approved and gain acceptance or lose patent protection.	*Unstable*: Market shares may shift frequently depending on technology offerings and demand levels.	*Very Stable*: Market shares change glacially slowly.

5.6. Price Competition

A useful tool for analyzing an industry is attempting to think like a customer of the industry. Whatever factor most influences customer purchase decisions is likely to also be the focus of competitive rivalry in the industry. In general, industries for which price is a large factor in customer purchase decisions tend to be more competitive than industries in which customers value other attributes more highly.

Although this depiction may sound like the description of a commodity industry versus a non-commodity industry, it is, in fact, a bit more subtle. Commercial aircraft and passenger cars are certainly more differentiated than lumps of coal or gallons of gasoline, but price nonetheless weighs heavily in the purchase decisions of buyers of aircraft and cars, because fairly good substitutes are easily available. If Airbus charges too much for an aircraft, such as the A350, an airline can buy as an alternative a Boeing 777 (a small amount of "path dependence" characterizes the airline industry, in that an airline with a large fleet of a particular Airbus model will be marginally more likely to stick with that model for a new purchase than it will be to buy a Boeing). If BMW's price for a four-door premium sedan rises too high, customers can switch to an alternative premium brand with similar features. Similar switching can be expected as a result of a unilateral price increase in the case of most industries in the "Weak Pricing Power" column of the two-factor analysis in Exhibit 8.

Contrast industries in software services that can be characterized by strong pricing power. Such software companies as Adobe, for example, sell a suite of products for creative professionals. Although Adobe's individual products do face competition, its successful transition to selling most of its products via its Creative Cloud has enabled the company to enjoy gross margins above 80%. In addition, the growth of digital companies and content bodes well for Adobe's pricing positioning in the industry.

Returning to a more capital-intensive industry, consider heavy-equipment manufacturers, such as Caterpillar, JCB, and Komatsu. A large wheel loader or combine harvester requires a large capital outlay, so price certainly plays a part in the buyers' decisions. However, other factors are important enough to customers to allow these companies a small amount of pricing power. Construction equipment is typically used as a complement to other gear on a large project, which means that downtime for repairs increases costs because, for example, hourly laborers must wait for a bulldozer to be fixed. Broken equipment is also expensive for agricultural users, who may have only a few days in which to harvest a season's crop. Because of the importance to users of their products' reliability and their large service networks—which are important "differentiators," or factors bestowing a competitive advantage—Caterpillar, Komatsu, and Deere have historically been able to price their equipment at levels that have generated solid returns on invested capital.

5.7. Industry Life Cycle

An industry's life-cycle position often has a large impact on its competitive dynamics, making this position an important component of the strategic analysis of an industry.

5.7.1. Description of an Industry Life-Cycle Model

Industries, like individual companies, tend to evolve over time and usually experience significant changes in the rate of growth and levels of profitability along the way. Just as an investment in an individual company requires careful monitoring, industry analysis is a continuous process to identify changes that may be occurring or likely to occur. A useful framework for analyzing the evolution of an industry is an industry life-cycle model, which identifies the sequential stages that an industry typically goes through. The five stages of an industry life-cycle model are embryonic, growth, shakeout, mature, and decline. Each stage is characterized by different opportunities and threats. Exhibit 13 shows the model as a curve illustrating the level and growth rate of demand at each stage.

EXHIBIT 13: An Industry Life-Cycle Model

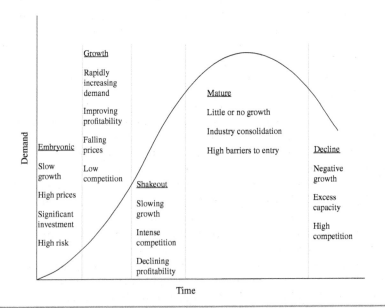

Source: Based on Figure 2.4 in Hill and Jones (2008).

5.7.1.1. Embryonic An embryonic industry is one that is just beginning to develop. For example, in 2014, the mobile food delivery industry was in the embryonic stage (it has grown to become a nearly US$15 billion industry in 2020), and in 1997, the global social media industry was just getting started. Characteristics of the embryonic stage include slow growth and high prices because customers tend to be unfamiliar with the industry's product and volumes are not yet sufficient to achieve meaningful economies of scale. Increasing product awareness and developing distribution channels are key strategic initiatives of companies during this stage. Substantial investment is generally required, and the risk of failure is high. A majority of startup companies do not succeed.

5.7.1.2. Growth A growth industry tends to be characterized by rapidly increasing demand, improving profitability, falling prices, and relativity low competition among companies in the industry. Demand is fueled by new customers entering the market, and prices fall as economies of scale are achieved and as distribution channels develop. The threat of new competitors entering the industry is usually highest during the growth stage, when barriers to entry are relatively low. Competition tends to be relatively limited, however, because rapidly expanding demand provides companies with an opportunity to grow without needing to capture market share from competitors. Industry profitability improves as volumes rise and economies of scale are attained.

5.7.1.3. Shakeout The shakeout stage is usually characterized by slowing growth, intense competition, and declining profitability. During the shakeout stage, demand approaches market saturation levels because few new customers are left to enter the market. Competition is intense as growth becomes increasingly dependent on market share gains. Excess industry capacity begins to develop as the rate at which companies continue to invest exceeds the overall growth of industry demand. In an effort to boost volumes to fill excess capacity, companies often cut prices, so industry profitability begins to decline. During the shakeout stage, companies increasingly focus on reducing their cost structure (restructuring) and building brand loyalty. Marginal companies may fail or merge with others.

5.7.1.4. Mature Characteristics of a mature industry include little or no growth, industry consolidation, and relatively high barriers to entry. Industry growth tends to be limited to replacement demand and population expansion because the market at this stage is completely saturated. As a result of the shakeout, mature industries often consolidate and become oligopolies. The surviving companies tend to have brand loyalty and relatively efficient cost structures, both of which are significant barriers to entry. During periods of stable demand, companies in mature industries tend to recognize their interdependence and try to avoid price wars. Periodic price wars do occur, however, most notably during periods of declining demand (such as during economic downturns). Companies with superior products or services are likely to gain market share and experience above-industry-average growth and profitability.

5.7.1.5. Decline During the decline stage, industry growth turns negative, excess capacity develops, and competition increases. Industry demand at this stage may decline for a variety of reasons, including technological substitution (for example, the newspaper industry has been declining for many years as more people turn to video platforms, the internet, and 24-hour cable news networks for information), social changes, and global competition. As demand falls, excess capacity in the industry forms and companies respond by cutting prices, which often leads to price wars. The weaker companies often exit the industry at this point, merge, or redeploy capital into different products and services.

When overall demand for an industry's products or services is declining, the opportunity for individual companies to earn above-average returns on invested capital tends to be less than when demand is stable or increasing, because of price cutting and higher per-unit costs as production is cut back. Exhibit 14 shows the life cycle stages for three representative industries.

EXHIBIT 14: Elements of a Strategic Analysis: Industry Life Cycle

	Branded Pharmaceuticals	Oil Services	Confections/Candy
Major Companies	Pfizer, Novartis, Merck, GSK plc	Schlumberger, Baker Hughes, Halliburton	Hershey, Mars/ Wrigley, Nestle
Life Cycle	*Mature*: Overall demand does not change greatly from year to year.	*Mature*: Demand does fluctuate with energy prices, but normalized revenue growth is only in the mid-single digits.	*Mature*: Growth is driven by population trends and pricing.

5.7.2. Using an Industry Life-Cycle Model

In general, new industries tend to be more competitive (with lots of players entering and exiting) than mature industries, which often have stable competitive environments and players that are more interested in protecting what they have than in gaining lots of market share. However, as industries move from maturity to decline, competitive pressures may increase again as industry participants perceive a zero-sum environment and fight over pieces of an ever-shrinking pie.

5.7.3. Relating Management Behavior to Industry Life Cycle

An important point for the analyst to think about is where a company is relative to where its industry sits in the life cycle. Companies in growth industries should be building customer loyalty as they introduce consumers to new products or services, building scale, and reinvesting heavily in their operations to capitalize on increasing demand. They are probably not focusing strongly on internal efficiency. Growth companies typically reinvest their cash flows in new products and product platforms rather than return cash flows to shareholders because these companies still have many opportunities to deploy their capital to make higher returns. Some may be able to sustain or even accelerate growth through innovation or by expansion into new markets.

Companies in mature industries are likely to be pursuing replacement demand or incremental demand rather than new buyers and are probably focused on extending successful product lines rather than introducing revolutionary new products. They are also probably focusing on cost rationalization and efficiency gains rather than on taking lots of market share. Importantly, these companies have fewer growth opportunities than in the previous stage and thus more limited avenues for profitably reinvesting capital, but they often have strong cash flows. Given their strong cash flows and relatively limited reinvestment opportunities, such companies should be, according to a common perspective, returning capital to shareholders via share repurchases or dividends.

5.7.4. Spotting Warning Signs

What can be a concern is a middle-aged company acting like a young growth company and pouring capital into projects with low return prospects in an effort to pursue size for its own sake. Many companies have a difficult time managing the transition from growth to maturity, and their returns on capital—and shareholder returns—may suffer until management decides to allocate capital in a manner more appropriate to the company's life-cycle stage.

5.7.5. Limitations of Industry Life-Cycle Analysis

Although models can provide a useful framework for thinking about an industry, the evolution of an industry does not always follow a predictable pattern. Various external factors that we will discuss in the subsequent sections influence life cycles. These include technological, demographic, social, environmental, or regulatory factors that may significantly affect the shape of the pattern, causing some stages to be longer or shorter than expected and, in certain cases, causing some stages to be skipped altogether. Technological changes may cause an industry to experience an abrupt shift from growth to decline, thus skipping the shakeout and mature stages. For example, the movie rental industry experienced rapid change as consumers switched from renting physical movies (on VHS tapes and DVDs) to on-demand services, such as downloading movies from the internet or through their cable providers.

Regulatory changes can also have a profound impact on the structure of an industry. A prime example is the deregulation of the telecommunications industry in the United States and Europe in the 1990s, which transformed a monopolistic industry into an intensely competitive one.

Social changes also have the ability to affect the profile of an industry. The casual dining industry has benefited over the past 30 years from the increase in the number of dual-income families in many large markets, who often have more income but less time to cook meals to eat at home. Thus, life-cycle models tend to be most useful for analyzing industries during periods of relative stability. They are less practical when the industry is experiencing rapid change over a short time period because of external or other special circumstances.

Another limiting factor of life-cycle models is that not all companies in an industry experience similar performance. The key objective for the analyst is to identify the potential winners while avoiding potential losers. Highly profitable companies can exist in competitive industries with below-average profitability—and vice versa, as shown by the cellular phone manufacturer Nokia for a number of years starting in the 1990s. It has been able to use its scale to generate levels of profitability that were well above average despite operating in a highly competitive industry. In contrast, despite the historically above-average growth and profitability of the software industry, countless examples exist of software companies that failed to ever generate a profit and eventually went out of business.

EXAMPLE 8   Industry Life Cycle

1. An industry experiencing slow growth and high prices is best characterized as being in the:
   A. mature stage.
   B. shakeout stage.
   C. embryonic stage.

Solution to 1:

C is correct. Both slow growth and high prices are associated with the embryonic stage. High price is not a characteristic of the mature or shakeout stage.

2. Which of the following statements about the industry life-cycle model is *least* accurate?
   A. The model is more appropriately used during a period of rapid change than during a period of relative stability.
   B. External factors may cause some stages of the model to be longer or shorter than expected, and in certain cases, a stage may be skipped entirely.
   C. Not all companies in an industry will experience similar performance, and very profitable companies can exist in an industry with below-average profitability.

Solution to 2:

A is correct. This statement is the least accurate. The model is best used during a period of relative stability rather than during a period of rapid change.

6. EXTERNAL INFLUENCES ON INDUSTRY

We now turn our attention to external factors that affect industries. We will explain macroeconomic, technological, demographic, governmental, social, and environmental influences.

6.1. Macroeconomic Influences

Trends in overall economic activity generally have significant effects on the demand for an industry's products or services. These trends can be cyclical (i.e., related to the changes in economic activity caused by the business cycle) or structural (i.e., related to enduring changes in the composition or magnitude of economic activity). Among the economic variables that usually affect an industry's revenues and profits are the following:

- GDP, either in current or constant currency (inflation-adjusted) terms;
- interest rates, which represent the cost of debt to consumers and businesses and are important ingredients in financial institutions' revenues and costs;
- the availability of credit, which affects business and consumer spending and financial solvency; and
- inflation, which reflects the changes in prices of goods and services and influences costs, interest rates, and consumer and business confidence.

6.2. Technological Influences

New technologies create new or improved products that can radically change an industry and can also change how other industries that use the products conduct their operations. Exhibit 15 provides an illustration of how innovation bringing new technologies changed the computer hardware and software industry.

EXHIBIT 15: Technological Influences

The computer hardware industry provides one of the best examples of how technological change can affect industries. The 1958 invention of the microchip (also known as an "integrated circuit") enabled the computer hardware industry to eventually create a new market of personal computing for the general public and radically extended the use of computers in business, government, and educational institutions.

Moore's law states that the number of transistors that can be inexpensively placed on an integrated circuit doubles approximately every two years. Several other measures of digital technology have improved at exponential rates related to Moore's law, including the size, cost, density, and speed of components. As a result of these trends, the computer hardware industry came to dominate the fields of hardware for word processing and many forms of electronic communication and home entertainment. The computing industry's integrated circuit innovation increased economies of scale and erected large barriers to new entrants because the capital costs of innovation and production became very high. Intel capitalized on both factors, which allowed it to garner an industry market leadership position and to become the dominant supplier of the PC industry's highest-value component (the microprocessor). Thus, Intel became dominant because of its cost advantage, brand power, and access to capital.

Along the way, the computer hardware industry was supported and greatly assisted by the complementary industries of computer software and telecommunications (particularly in regard to development of the internet); also important were other industries—entertainment (television, movies, games), retailing, and print media. Ever more powerful integrated circuits, advances in wireless technology, and the convergence of media, which the internet and new wireless technology have facilitated, continue to reshape the uses and the roles of PC hardware in business and personal life. In the middle of the 20th century, few people in the world would have imagined they would ever have any use for a home computer. Today, an estimated 4.3 billion people, or over half the world's population, have access to connected computing. For the United States, the estimate is at least 95% of the population; it is much less in emerging and underdeveloped countries. More than 8 billion mobile cellular telephone subscriptions exist in the world today.

Exhibit 16 explains how three representative industries are affected by technological change.

EXHIBIT 16: Technological Influences: Representative Industries

	Branded Pharmaceuticals	Oil Services	Confections/Candy
Technological Influences	*Medium/High*: Biologic (large-molecule) drugs are pushing new therapeutic boundaries, and many large pharmaceutical companies have a relatively small presence in biotech.	*Medium/High*: Industry is reasonably innovative, and players must reinvest in R&D to remain competitive. Temporary competitive advantages are possible via commercialization of new processes or exploitation of accumulated expertise.	*Very Low*: Innovation does not play a major role in the industry.

6.3. Demographic Influences

Changes in population size, in the distributions of age and gender, and in other demographic characteristics may have significant effects on economic growth and on the amounts and types of goods and services consumed.

The effects of demographics on industries are exemplified by the impact of Japan's aging population, which has one of the highest percentages of elderly residents (26% over the age of 65) and a very low birth rate. Japan's ministry of health estimates that by 2055, the percentage of the population over 65 will rise to 40% and the total population will fall by 25%. These demographic changes are expected by some observers to have negative effects on the overall economy because, essentially, they imply a declining workforce. However, some sectors of the economy stand to benefit from these trends—for example, the health care industry. Another example of demographic influence on an industry is the experience of "baby boomers" (those born in the years after World War II), who reached adulthood in significant numbers in the early 1970s, contributing to a strong demand for new housing throughout the 1970s and during 1995–2005 when their children reached adulthood.

6.4. Governmental Influences

Governmental influence on industries' revenues and profits is pervasive and important. In setting tax rates for corporations and individuals, governments affect profits and incomes, which, in turn, affect corporate and personal spending. Governments also set rules and regulations to protect consumers, employees, and the environment, affecting how companies operate, with implications for profitability. In addition, governments are also major purchasers of goods and services from a range of industries.

Often, governments exert their influence indirectly by empowering other regulatory or self-regulatory organizations (e.g., stock exchanges, medical associations, utility rate setters, and other regulatory commissions) to govern the affairs of an industry. By setting the terms of entry into various sectors, such as financial services and health care, and the rules that companies and individuals must adhere to in these fields, governments control the supply, quality, and nature of many products and services and the public's access to them. For example, in the financial industry, the acceptance of savings deposits from and the issuance of securities to the investing public are usually tightly controlled by governments and their agencies. This control is imposed through rules designed to protect investors from fraudulent operators and to ensure that investors receive adequate disclosure about the nature and risks of their investments. Exhibit 17 illustrates government influences on three representative industries.

EXHIBIT 17: Government Influences: Representative Industries

	Branded Pharmaceuticals	Oil Services	Confections/Candy
Government & Regulatory Influences	*Very High*: All drugs must be approved for sale by national safety regulators. Patent regimes may differ among countries. Also, health care is heavily regulated in most countries.	*Medium*: Regulatory frameworks can affect energy demand at the margin. Also, governments play an important role in allocating exploration opportunities to E&P companies, which can indirectly affect the amount of work flowing down to service companies.	*Low*: Industry is not regulated, but childhood obesity concerns in developed markets are a low-level potential threat. Also, high-growth emerging markets may block entry of established players into their markets, possibly limiting growth.

EXAMPLE 9   The Effects of Purchases by Government-Related Entities on the Aerospace Industry

The aerospace, construction, and firearms industries are prime examples of industries for which governments are major customers and whose revenues and profits are significantly—in some cases, predominantly—affected by their sales to governments. An example is Airbus, a major player in aerospace, defense, and related services with head offices in Paris and Ottobrunn, Germany. In 2017, Airbus generated revenues of €66.8 billion and employed an international workforce of about 130,000. Besides being a leading manufacturer of commercial aircraft, a business whose customers include government-owned airlines, Airbus also includes Airbus Military, providing tanker, transport, and mission aircraft; Airbus Helicopters SAS, the world's largest helicopter supplier; and EADS Astrium, the European leader in space programs, including Ariane and Galileo. Its Defence & Security Division is a provider of comprehensive systems solutions and makes Airbus the major partner in the Eurofighter consortium and a stakeholder in missile systems provider MBDA. These divisions are highly dependent on orders from governments.

6.5. Social Influences

Societal changes involving how people work, spend their money, enjoy their leisure time, and conduct other aspects of their lives can have significant effects on the sales of various industries.

Tobacco consumption in the United Kingdom provides a good example of the effects of social influences on an industry. Although the role of government in curbing tobacco advertising, legislating health warnings on the purchases of tobacco products, and banning smoking in public places (such as restaurants, bars, public houses, and transportation vehicles) probably has been the most powerful apparent instrument of changes in tobacco consumption, the forces underlying that change have really been social in nature. These forces are increasing consciousness on the part of the population of the damage to the health of tobacco users and those in their vicinity from smoking, the increasing cost to individuals and governments of the chronic illnesses caused by tobacco consumption, and the accompanying shift in public perception of smokers from socially correct to socially incorrect or even inconsiderate or reckless. As a result of these changes in society's views of smoking, cigarette consumption in the United Kingdom declined from 102.5 billion cigarettes in 1990 to less than 40.0 billion three decades later, placing downward pressure on tobacco companies' unit sales.

6.6. Environmental Influences

As industries continue to adapt to new technologies and strategies in order to compete and grow, the need to evaluate and mitigate environmental impact is an important influence. For example, climate change is shifting the way entire industries are perceived and evolving. With limited resources on our planet as a whole, climate change poses a real threat to many industries' growth and profitability that should be taken into consideration when evaluating external influences. These influences can be seen through three channels:

- consumer perception for certain brands, products, and services;
- increased government regulations and protections;
- potential disruptions to supply chains and the ability to operate, such as an increase in natural disasters or resource shortages in water or energy.

Take, for example, the agriculture industry. Global greenhouse gas emissions from agriculture, forestry, and other land use account for 25% of total carbon emissions globally. This is more than two times the pollution generated from all the cars on the planet. This factor and the rise of organic, natural, cruelty-free, and vegan foods will cause the agriculture industry to face strong environmental influences throughout the 21st century. The shift toward healthier and plant-based diets has become a major trend in the last 10 years. Organic food sales in the United States rose almost 6% in 2018 to reach $47.9 billion (according to the 2019 Organic Industry Survey).

Because of consumer awareness of climate change and a growing movement to protect animal rights, companies in the livestock industry could face significant reputational risk and disruption to their brands along with potential government intervention/fines. Public awareness of the environmental impact of raising livestock has been increasing—for example, that cattle are a significant source of methane (a more potent contributor to climate change than CO_2) and that cattle require very large quantities of land, fertilizer, water, and grain. Additionally, livestock treatment has been a huge concern and subject of debate among many organizations, including animal rights groups. As the trend toward ESG (environmental, social, and governance) and sustainable investing continues to grow, there is an increasing awareness among investors of the responsibility to work with food businesses to better ensure the mitigation of potential headline risk of animal cruelty and supply chain disruption from contaminated meat. Innovation in this space has evolved to include plant-based meat substitutes (e.g. Beyond Meat and Impossible Foods), which has become a multi-billion-dollar food category over the last decade.

EXAMPLE 11

1. Company A is a mining company with operations in several countries. Company B is a technology company providing video conferencing services. Company C is a consumer company, an apparel producer, with facilities in a number of Latin American and Asian countries. Which of the companies belongs to an industry most likely to be affected by environmental factors that analysts should evaluate?
   A. Company A
   B. Company B
   C. Company C

Solution to 1:
   A is correct. Environmental considerations should be incorporated in the industry analysis of Company A. It operates in a sector that has high exposure to greenhouse gas emissions, as well as water management and waste and hazardous materials management, which could incur additional costs to running businesses in this sector.

2. Which of the following statements best describes social influences that should be considered in evaluating the Consumer Goods industry?

Supply chain management, selling practices, and product labeling
Access and affordability, pricing policy
Impact of the industry on the environment

Solution to 2:

Statement 1 is correct. Statements 2 and 3 describe characteristics that, although important, are not considered to be of social nature.

3. Which of the following describes one of the ways governments influence large companies that produce and offer services relating to heating, air conditioning, and lighting systems?
   A.   Purchasing goods and services
   B.   Determining availability of credit
   C.   Providing raw materials

Solution to 3:

A is correct. Governments are a major buyer of goods and services. B is incorrect because governments do not normally provide credit to the industry. C is incorrect because the private sector provides raw materials to customers.

THE AIRLINE INDUSTRY: A CASE STUDY OF MANY INFLUENCES

The global airline industry exemplifies many of the concepts and influences we have discussed.

Life-Cycle Stage

The industry can be described as having some mature characteristics because average annual growth in global passenger traffic has remained relatively stable, growing at a single-digit rate for the first two decades of the 21st century, with the Asian and Middle Eastern markets growing faster than the more mature markets of North America and Europe.

Sensitivity to the Business Cycle

The airline industry is a cyclical industry; global economic activity produces swings in revenues and, especially, profitability, because of the industry's high fixed costs and operating leverage. In 2009, for example, global passenger traffic declined by approximately 3.5% and airlines lost close to US$11.0 billion, which was down from a global industry profit of US$12.9 billion in 2007. The industry tends to respond early to upward and downward moves in economic cycles; depending on the region, air travel changes at 1.5 times to 2.0 times GDP growth.

Regulation

The industry is highly regulated, with governments and airport authorities playing a large role in allocating routes and airport take-off and landing slots. Government agencies and the International Airline Transport Association set rules for aircraft and flight safety.

Product Differentiation and Customer Behavior

Airline customers tend to have low brand loyalty (except at the extremes of high and low prices and service); leisure travelers focus mainly on price, and business travelers focus mostly on schedules and service. Product and service differentiation at particular price points is low because aircraft, cabin configuration, and catering tend to be quite similar in most cases. For leisure travelers, the price competition is intense and is led by low-cost discount carriers, including Southwest Airlines in the United States, Ryanair in Europe, and Air Asia in Asia. For business travelers, the major scheduled airlines and a few service-quality specialists, such as Singapore Airlines, are the main contenders.

Technology and Costs

Fuel costs (typically more than 25% of total costs and highly volatile) and labor costs (around 10% of total costs) have been the focus of management cost-reduction efforts. The airline industry is highly unionized, and labor strikes have frequently been a source of costly disruptions to the industry. Technology and innovation have always played a major role, impacting fuel efficiency and operating costs. Technology also poses a threat to the growth of business air travel in the form of improved and widely adopted telecommunications—notably, videoconferencing and webcasting.

Social and Environmental Influences

Arguably, the airline industry has been a great force in shaping demography by permitting difficult-to-access geographical areas to be settled with large populations. At the same time, large numbers of post–World War II baby boomers have been a factor in generating growth in demand for air travel in the past half century. Environmental issues now play a role in the airline industry; carbon emissions, for example, have come under scrutiny by environmentalists and governments.

6.7. Industry Comparison

To illustrate how these elements might be applied, Exhibit 18 reproduces the factors discussed in stages and illustrated in the context of three representative industries.

EXHIBIT 18: Elements of a Strategic Analysis for Three Industries

	Branded Pharmaceuticals	Oil Services	Confections/Candy
Major Companies	Pfizer, Novartis, Merck, GSK plc	Schlumberger, Baker Hughes, Halliburton	Hershey, Mars/Wrigley, Nestle
Barriers to Entry	*Very High*: Substantial financial and intellectual capital required to compete effectively. A potential new entrant would need to create a sizable R&D operation, a global distribution network, and large-scale manufacturing capacity.	*Medium*: Technological expertise is required, but a high level of innovation allows niche companies to enter the industry and compete in specific areas.	*Very High*: Low financial or technological hurdles, but new players would lack the established brands that drive consumer purchase decisions.

	Branded Pharmaceuticals	Oil Services	Confections/Candy
Major Companies	Pfizer, Novartis, Merck, GSK plc	Schlumberger, Baker Hughes, Halliburton	Hershey, Mars/Wrigley, Nestle
Level of Concentration	*Concentrated*: A small number of companies control the bulk of the global market for branded drugs. Recent mergers have increased the level of concentration.	*Fragmented*: Although only a small number of companies provide a full range of services, many smaller players compete effectively in specific areas. Service arms of national oil companies may control significant market share in their own countries, and some product lines are concentrated in the mature US market.	*Very Concentrated*: The top four companies have a large proportion of global market share. Recent mergers have increased the level of concentration.
Impact of Industry Capacity	*Not Applicable*: Pharmaceutical pricing is primarily determined by patent protection and regulatory issues, including government approvals of drugs and of manufacturing facilities. Manufacturing capacity is of little importance.	*Medium/High*: Demand can fluctuate quickly depending on commodity prices, and industry players often find themselves with too few (or too many) employees on the payroll.	*Not Applicable*: Pricing is driven primarily by brand strength. Manufacturing capacity has little effect.
Industry Stability	*Stable*: The branded pharmaceutical market is dominated by major companies and consolidation via mega-mergers. Market shares shift quickly, however, as new drugs are approved and gain acceptance or lose patent protection.	*Unstable*: Market shares may shift frequently depending on technology offerings and demand levels.	*Very Stable*: Market shares change glacially slowly.
Life Cycle	*Mature*: Overall demand does not change greatly from year to year.	*Mature*: Demand does fluctuate with energy prices, but normalized revenue growth is only in the mid-single digits.	*Mature*: Growth is driven by population trends and pricing.
Price Competition	*Low/Medium*: In the United States, price is a minimal factor because of a consumer- and provider-driven, deregulated health care system. Price is a larger part of the decision process in single-payer systems, where efficacy hurdles are higher.	*High*: Price is a major factor in purchasers' decisions. Some companies have modest pricing power because of a wide range of services or best-in-class technology, but primary customers (major oil companies) can usually substitute with in-house services if prices are too high. Also, innovation tends to diffuse quickly throughout the industry.	*Low*: A lack of private-label competition keeps pricing stable among established players, and brand familiarity plays a much larger role in consumer purchase decisions than price.

	Branded Pharmaceuticals	Oil Services	Confections/Candy
Major Companies	Pfizer, Novartis, Merck, GSK plc	Schlumberger, Baker Hughes, Halliburton	Hershey, Mars/Wrigley, Nestle
Demographic Influences	*Positive*: Populations of developed markets are aging, which slightly increases demand.	*Not Applicable*	*Not Applicable*
Government & Regulatory Influences	*Very High*: All drugs must be approved for sale by national safety regulators. Patent regimes may differ among countries. Also, health care is heavily regulated in most countries.	*Medium*: Regulatory frameworks can affect energy demand at the margin. Also, governments play an important role in allocating exploration opportunities to E&P companies, which can indirectly affect the amount of work flowing down to service companies.	*Low*: Industry is not regulated, but childhood obesity concerns in developed markets are a low-level potential threat. Also, high-growth emerging markets may block entry of established players into their markets, possibly limiting growth.
Technological Influences	*Medium/High*: Biologic (large-molecule) drugs are pushing new therapeutic boundaries, and many large pharmaceutical companies have a relatively small presence in biotech.	*Medium/High*: Industry is reasonably innovative, and players must reinvest in R&D to remain competitive. Temporary competitive advantages are possible via commercialization of new processes or exploitation of accumulated expertise.	*Very Low*: Innovation does not play a major role in the industry.
Growth vs. Defensive vs. Cyclical	*Defensive*: Demand for most health care services does not fluctuate with the economic cycle, but demand is not strong enough to be considered "growth."	*Cyclical*: Demand is highly variable and depends on oil prices, exploration budgets, and the economic cycle.	*Defensive*: Demand for candy and gum is extremely stable.

Example 12 reviews some of the information presented in Exhibit 18.

EXAMPLE 12   External Influences

1. Which of the following industries is *most* affected by government regulation?
    A.   Oil services
    B.   Pharmaceuticals
    C.   Confections and candy

Solution to 1:

   B is correct. Exhibit 18 states that the pharmaceutical industry has a high amount of government and regulatory influences.

2. Which of the following industries is *least* affected by technological innovation?
   A. Oil services
   B. Pharmaceuticals
   C. Confections and candy

Solution to 2:

C is correct. Exhibit 18 states that innovation does not play a large role in the candy industry.

3. Which of the following statements about industry characteristics is *least* accurate?
   A. Manufacturing capacity has little effect on pricing in the confections/candy industry.
   B. The branded pharmaceutical industry is considered to be defensive rather than a growth industry.
   C. With respect to the worldwide market, the oil services industry has a high level of concentration with a limited number of service providers.

Solution to 3:

C is correct; it is a false statement. From a worldwide perspective, the industry is considered fragmented. Although a small number of companies provide the full range of services, competition by many smaller players occurs in niche areas. In addition, national oil service companies control significant market share in their home countries.

7. COMPANY ANALYSIS

Company analysis includes an analysis of the company's financial position, products and/or services, and **competitive strategy** (its plans for responding to the threats and opportunities presented by the external environment). Company analysis takes place after the analyst has gained an understanding of a company's external environment—the macroeconomic, demographic, governmental, technological, environmental, and social forces influencing the industry's competitive structure. The analyst should seek to determine whether the strategy is primarily defensive or offensive in its nature and how the company intends to implement the strategy.

Porter (2008) identified two chief competitive strategies: a low-cost strategy (cost leadership) and a product/service differentiation strategy:

- *Low-cost strategy*: Companies strive to become the low-cost producers and to gain market share by offering their products and services at lower prices than their competition while still making a profit margin sufficient to generate a superior rate of return based on the higher revenues achieved. Low-cost strategies may be pursued defensively to protect market positions and returns or offensively to gain market share and increase returns. Pricing also can be defensive (when the competitive environment is one of low rivalry) or aggressive (when rivalry is intense). In the case of intense rivalry, pricing may even become predatory—that is, aimed at rapidly driving competitors out of business at the expense of near-term profitability. The hope in such a strategy is that having achieved a larger market share, the company can later increase prices to generate higher returns than before. For example, the ride-sharing industry has produced fierce competition among companies that seek to capture market share by offering incentives and discount pricing for rides. Companies seeking to follow low-cost strategies must have tight cost controls, efficient operating and reporting systems, and appropriate managerial incentives. In addition, they must commit themselves to painstaking scrutiny of production systems and their labor forces and to low-cost designs and product distribution. In some cases, they must be able to invest in productivity-improving capital equipment and to finance that investment at a low cost of capital.

- *Differentiation strategies*: Companies attempt to establish themselves as the suppliers or producers of products and services that are unique either in quality, type, or means of distribution. To be successful, their price premiums must be above their costs of differentiation and the differentiation must be appealing to customers and sustainable over time. Corporate managers who successfully pursue differentiation strategies tend to have strong market research teams to identify and match customer needs with product development and marketing. Such a strategy puts a premium on employing creative and inventive people.

7.1. Elements That Should Be Covered in a Company Analysis

A thorough company analysis, particularly as presented in a research report, should

- provide an overview of the company (corporate profile), including a basic understanding of its businesses, investment activities, corporate governance, and perceived strengths and weaknesses;
- explain relevant industry characteristics;
- analyze the demand for the company's products and services;
- analyze the supply of products and services, which includes an analysis of costs;
- explain the company's pricing environment; and
- present and interpret relevant financial ratios, including comparisons over time and comparisons with competitors, using multi-year spreadsheets with historical and forecast data

Company analysis often includes forecasting the company's financial statements, particularly when the purpose of the analysis is to use a discounted cash flow method to value the company's common equity.

Exhibit 19 provides a checklist of points to cover in a company analysis. The list is not exhaustive and may need to be adapted to serve the needs of a particular company analysis.

EXHIBIT 19: A Checklist for Company Analysis

Corporate Profile
Company's major products & services & current position in industry & history
Company's product life-cycle stages
Research & development & capital expenditure activities past, present & planned

Governance Arrangements
- Board structure, composition, electoral system, anti-takeover provisions & other corporate governance issues plus insider ownership levels & changes
- Management strengths, weaknesses, compensation, turnover & corporate culture
- Labor relations, business ethics, anti-discrimination policy/diversity & inclusion initiatives
- Legal actions & the company's state of preparedness

Industry Characteristics
- Stage in its life cycle
- Business-cycle sensitivity or economic characteristics
- Typical product life cycles
- Brand loyalty, customer switching costs & intensity of competition
- Entry & exit barriers
- Industry supplier considerations
- Industry structure & concentration
- Opportunity to differentiate product/service & relative product/service price, cost & quality advantages/disadvantages
- Technologies used & resource management (energy, water & waste)
- Government regulation
- Ecological impacts & evaluation

Demand Analysis
- Sources of demand
- Product differentiation
- Past record, sensitivities & correlations with social, demographic, economic & other variables
- Outlook—short, medium & long term, including new product & business opportunities
- Selling practices & product labeling, access & affordability

Pricing analysis
- Past relationships among demand, supply & prices
- Significance of raw material & labor costs & the outlook for their cost & availability
- Outlook for selling prices, demand, & profitability (current & anticipated trends)

Supply Analysis
- Sources (concentration, competition & substitutes)
- Industry capacity outlook—short, medium & long term
- Ability to switch supplies
- Company's capacity & cost structure
- Import/export considerations
- Proprietary products or trademarks
- Labor practices

Financial Ratios and Measures
I. Activity Ratios (measuring efficiently):
- Days of sales outstanding (DSO), inventory on hand (DOH) & Days of payables outstanding (DPO)
II. Liquidity Ratios (ability to meet its short-term obligations)
- Current, quick & cash ratios
- Cash conversion cycle (DOH + DSO – DPO)
III. Solvency Ratios (the ability to meet obligations)
- Net debt to EBITDA, debt to capital or assets
- Financial leverage & interest cover ratio
- Contingent liabilities & non-arm's-length transactions
IV. Profitability Ratios
- Margins: gross, operating, pre-tax & net
- Returns: ROA, ROE & ROIC (net operating profits after tax/average invested capital)
V. Financial Statistics and Related Considerations (quantities & facts about a company's finances)
- Growth rates of net sales & gross profit
- EBITDA, net income, operating cash flow, EPS & operating cash flow per share & how cash flow relates to capital expenditures
- Expected rate of return on retained cash flow
- Debt maturities, ability to refinance or repay debt
- Dividend payout ratio
- Off-balance-sheet liabilities & contingent liabilities

Evaluation of past and current company performance and forecasting future cash flows and a company's prospects is a major topic that is the subject of extensive coverage elsewhere in the CFA Program curriculum. Here, we provide only a brief introduction.

To evaluate a company's performance, the key measures presented in the "checklist" in Exhibit 19 should be compared over time and between companies (particularly peer companies). The following formula can be used to analyze how and why a company's return on equity (ROE) differs from that of other companies or its own ROE in other periods by tracing the differences to changes in its profit margin, the productivity of its assets, or its financial leverage:

ROE = (Net profit margin: Net earnings/Net sales) × (Asset turnover: Net sales/Average total assets) × (Financial leverage: Average total assets/Average common equity).

The financial statements of a company over time provide numerous insights into the effects of industry conditions on its performance and the success or failure of its strategies. They also provide a framework for forecasting the company's operating performance when given the analyst's assumptions for numerous variables in the future. The financial ratios listed in Exhibit 19 are applicable to a wide range of companies and industries, but other statistics and ratios are often also used.

7.2. Spreadsheet Modeling

Spreadsheet modeling of financial statements to analyze and forecast revenues, operating and net income, and cash flows has become one of the most widely used tools in company analysis. Although spreadsheet models are a valuable tool for understanding past financial performance and forecasting future performance, the complexity of such models can at times be a problem. Because modeling requires the analyst to predict and input numerous items in financial statements, there is a risk of errors—either in assumptions made or in formulas in the model—which can compound, leading to erroneous forecasts. Yet, those forecasts may seem precise because of the sheer complexity of the model. The result is often a false sense of understanding and security on the part of those who rely on the models. To guard against this, before or after a model is completed, a "reality check" of the model is useful.

Such testing for reasonableness can be done by, first, asking what the few most important changes in income statement items are likely to be from last year to this year and the next year and, second, attempting to quantify the effects of these significant changes or "swing factors" on the bottom line. If an analyst cannot summarize in a few points what factors are realistically expected to change income from year to year and is not convinced that these assumptions are correct, then he or she does not really understand the output of the modeling efforts. In general, financial models should be in a format that matches the company's reporting of its financial results or supplementary disclosures or that can be accurately derived from these reports. Otherwise, there will be no natural reality check when the company issues its financial results and the analyst will not be able to compare his or her estimates with actual reported results.

EXAMPLE 13

1. An analyst makes the following statement:

"Analysis of a company's supply includes examination of labor relations; sources of and access to raw materials, including concentration of suppliers; and analysis of the company's production capacity."

The statement is:
A. correct.
B. incorrect because the analysis of supply should also include analysis of the stage in the product life cycle.
C. incorrect because the analysis of supply should consider the product's differentiating characteristics.

Solution to 1:
   A is correct. The statement accurately describes the analysis of a company's supply.

2. The challenge with using spreadsheet forecasting models stems from the fact that
A. the analyst may have a false sense of understanding the business.
B. spreadsheet models cannot be used to compare companies with their peer groups.
C. spreadsheet models require precise inputs.

Solution to 2:
   A is correct. B is incorrect because spreadsheet models are frequently used to compare companies. C is incorrect because although spreadsheet models require precise inputs, this requirement does not mean that they are not helpful.

8. SUMMARY

In this chapter, we have provided an overview of industry analysis and illustrated approaches that are widely used by analysts to examine an industry.

- Company analysis and industry analysis are closely interrelated. Company and industry analysis together can provide insight into sources of industry revenue growth and competitors' market shares and thus the future of an individual company's top-line growth and bottom-line profitability.
- Industry analysis is useful for
  - understanding a company's business and business environment,
  - identifying active equity investment opportunities,
  - formulating an industry or sector rotation strategy, and
  - portfolio performance attribution.

- The three main approaches to classifying companies are
  - products and/or services supplied,
  - business-cycle sensitivities, and
  - statistical similarities.

- A cyclical company is one whose profits are strongly correlated with the strength of the overall economy.
- A non-cyclical company is one whose performance is largely independent of the business cycle.

- Commercial industry classification systems include
  - The Global Industry Classification Standard (GICS)
  - The Industry Classification Benchmark (ICB)

- A limitation of current classification systems is that the narrowest classification unit assigned to a company generally cannot be assumed to constitute its peer group for the purposes of detailed fundamental comparisons or valuation.
- A peer group is a group of companies engaged in similar business activities whose economics and valuation are influenced by closely related factors.
- The steps in constructing a preliminary list of peer companies are as follows:
  - Examine commercial classification systems if available. These systems often provide a useful starting point for identifying companies operating in the same industry.
  - Review the subject company's annual report for a discussion of the competitive environment. Companies frequently cite specific competitors.
  - Review competitors' annual reports to identify other potential comparables.
  - Review industry trade publications to identify additional peer companies.
  - Confirm that each comparable or peer company derives a significant portion of its revenue and operating profit from a business activity similar to that of the subject company.

- Not all industries are created equal. Some are highly competitive, with many companies struggling to earn returns in excess of their cost of capital, and other industries have attractive characteristics that enable a majority of industry participants to generate healthy profits.
- Differing competitive environments are determined by the structural attributes of the industry. For this important reason, industry analysis is a vital complement to company analysis. The analyst needs to understand the context in which a company operates to fully understand the opportunities and threats that a company faces.
- The framework for strategic analysis known as "Porter's five forces" can provide a useful starting point. Porter maintained that the profitability of companies in an industry is determined by five forces: (1) the threat of new entrants, which, in turn, is determined by economies of scale, brand loyalty, absolute cost advantages, customer switching costs, and government regulation; (2) the bargaining power of suppliers, which is a function of the feasibility of product substitution, the concentration of the buyer and supplier groups, and switching costs and entry costs in each case; (3) the bargaining power of buyers, which is a function of switching costs among customers and the ability of customers to produce their own product; (4) the threat of substitutes; and (5) the intensity of rivalry among existing competitors, which, in turn, is a function of industry competitive structure, demand conditions, cost conditions, and the height of exit barriers.
- The concept of barriers to entry refers to the ease with which new competitors can challenge incumbents and can be an important factor in determining the competitive environment of an industry. If new competitors can easily enter the industry, the industry is likely to be highly competitive because incumbents that attempt to raise prices will be undercut by newcomers. As a result, industries with low barriers to entry tend to have low pricing power. Conversely, if incumbents are protected by barriers to entry, they may enjoy a more benign competitive environment that gives them greater

pricing power over their customers because they do not have to worry about being undercut by startups.

- Industry concentration is often, although not always, a sign that an industry may have pricing power and rational competition. Industry fragmentation is a much stronger signal, however, that the industry is competitive and pricing power is limited.

- The effect of industry capacity on pricing is clear: Tight capacity gives participants more pricing power because demand for products or services exceeds supply; overcapacity leads to price cutting and a highly competitive environment as excess supply chases demand. The analyst should think about not only current capacity conditions but also future changes in capacity levels—how long it takes for supply and demand to come into balance and what effect that process has on industry pricing power and returns.

- Examining the market share stability of an industry over time is similar to thinking about barriers to entry and the frequency with which new players enter an industry. Stable market shares typically indicate less competitive industries, whereas unstable market shares often indicate highly competitive industries with limited pricing power.

- An industry's position in its life cycle often has a large impact on its competitive dynamics, so it is important to keep this positioning in mind when performing strategic analysis of an industry. Industries, like individual companies, tend to evolve over time and usually experience significant changes in the rate of growth and levels of profitability along the way. Just as an investment in an individual company requires careful monitoring, industry analysis is a continuous process that must be repeated over time to identify changes that may be occurring.

- A useful framework for analyzing the evolution of an industry is an industry life-cycle model, which identifies the sequential stages that an industry typically goes through. The five stages of an industry life cycle according to the Hill and Jones model are
  - embryonic,
  - growth,
  - shakeout,
  - mature, and
  - decline.

- Price competition and thinking like a customer are important factors that are often overlooked when analyzing an industry. Whatever factors most influence customer purchasing decisions are also likely to be the focus of competitive rivalry in the industry. Broadly, industries for which price is a large factor in customer purchase decisions tend to be more competitive than industries in which customers value other attributes more highly.

- External influences on industry growth, profitability, and risk include
  - technology,
  - demographics,
  - government,
  - social factors, and
  - environmental factors.

- Company analysis takes place after the analyst has gained an understanding of the company's external environment and includes answering questions about how the company will respond to the threats and opportunities presented by the external environment. This intended response is the individual company's competitive strategy. The analyst should seek to determine whether the strategy is primarily defensive or offensive in its nature and how the company intends to implement it.

- Porter identified two chief competitive strategies:
  - A low-cost strategy (cost leadership) is one in which companies strive to become the low-cost producers and to gain market share by offering their products and services at lower prices than their competition while still making a profit margin sufficient to generate a superior rate of return based on the higher revenues achieved.
  - A product/service differentiation strategy is one in which companies attempt to establish themselves as the suppliers or producers of products and services that are unique either in quality, type, or means of distribution. To be successful, the companies' price premiums must be above their costs of differentiation and the differentiation must be appealing to customers and sustainable over time.

- A checklist for company analysis includes a thorough investigation of
  - the corporate profile,
  - industry characteristics,
  - demand for products/services,
  - supply of products/services,
  - pricing,
  - financial ratios, and
  - sustainability metrics.

- Spreadsheet modeling of financial statements to analyze and forecast revenues, operating and net income, and cash flows is one of the most widely used tools in company analysis. Spreadsheet modeling can be used to quantify the effects of the changes in certain swing factors on the various financial statements. The analyst should be aware that the output of the model will depend significantly on the assumptions that are made.

9. PRACTICE PROBLEMS

1. Which of the following is *least likely* to involve industry analysis?
   A. Sector rotation strategy
   B. Top-down fundamental investing
   C. Tactical asset allocation strategy

2. A sector rotation strategy involves investing in a sector by:
   A. making regular investments in it.
   B. investing in a pre-selected group of sectors on a rotating basis.
   C. timing investment to take advantage of business-cycle conditions.

3. Which of the following information about a company would *most likely* depend on an industry analysis? The company's:
   A. treatment of long-lived assets on its financial statements.
   B. competitive environment.
   C. trends in corporate expenses.

4. Which of the following is *not* a limitation of the cyclical/non-cyclical descriptive approach to classifying companies?
   A. A cyclical company may have a growth component in it.
   B. Business-cycle sensitivity is a discrete phenomenon rather than a continuous spectrum.
   C. A global company can experience economic expansion in one part of the world while experiencing recession in another part.

5. A cyclical company is *most likely* to:
   A. have low operating leverage.
   B. sell relatively inexpensive products.
   C. experience wider-than-average fluctuations in demand.

6. A company that is sensitive to the business cycle would *most likely*:
   A. not have growth opportunities.
   B. experience below-average fluctuation in demand.
   C. sell products that customers can purchase at a later date if necessary.

7. Which of the following factors would *most likely* be a limitation of applying business-cycle analysis to global industry analysis?
   A. Some industries are relatively insensitive to the business cycle.
   B. Correlations of security returns between different world markets are relatively low.
   C. One region or country of the world may experience recession while another region experiences expansion.

8. In which sector would a manufacturer of personal care products be classified?
   A. Health care
   B. Consumer staples
   C. Consumer discretionary

9. An automobile manufacturer is *most likely* classified in which of the following industry sectors?
   A. Consumer staples
   B. Industrial durables
   C. Consumer discretionary

10. Which of the following statements about commercial and government industry classification systems is *most* accurate?
    A. Many commercial classification systems include private for-profit companies.
    B. Both commercial and government classification systems exclude not-for-profit companies.
    C. Commercial classification systems are generally updated more frequently than government classification systems.

11. Which of the following statements about peer groups is *most* accurate?
    A. Constructing a peer group for a company follows a standardized process.
    B. Commercial industry classification systems often provide a starting point for constructing a peer group.
    C. A peer group is generally composed of all the companies in the most narrowly defined category used by the commercial industry classification system.

12. With regard to forming a company's peer group, which of the following statements is *not* correct?
    A. Comments from the management of the company about competitors are generally not used when selecting the peer group.
    B. The higher the proportion of revenue and operating profit of the peer company derived from business activities similar to those of the subject company, the more meaningful the comparison.
    C. Comparing the company's performance measures with those for a potential peer-group company is of limited value when the companies are exposed to different stages of the business cycle.

13. When selecting companies for inclusion in a peer group, a company operating in three different business segments would:
    A. be in only one peer group.
    B. possibly be in more than one peer group.
    C. not be included in any peer group.

14. An industry that *most likely* has both high barriers to entry and high barriers to exit is the:
    A. restaurant industry.
    B. advertising industry.
    C. automobile industry.

15. Which factor is *most likely* associated with stable market share?
    A. Low switching costs
    B. Low barriers to entry
    C. Slow pace of product innovation

16. Which of the following companies *most likely* has the greatest ability to quickly increase its capacity to offer goods or services?
    A. A restaurant
    B. A steel producer
    C. An insurance company

17. Which of the following life-cycle phases is typically characterized by high prices?
    A. Mature
    B. Growth
    C. Embryonic

18. In which of the following life-cycle phases are price wars *most likely* to be absent?
    A. Mature
    B. Decline
    C. Growth

19. When graphically depicting the life-cycle model for an industry as a curve, the variables on the axes are:
    A. price and time.
    B. demand and time.
    C. demand and stage of the life cycle.

20. Industry consolidation and high barriers to entry *most likely* characterize which life-cycle stage?
    A. Mature
    B. Growth
    C. Embryonic

21. Which of the following is *most likely* a characteristic of a concentrated industry?
    A. Infrequent, tacit coordination
    B. Difficulty in monitoring other industry members
    C. Industry members attempting to avoid competition on price

22. Which of the following industry characteristics is generally *least likely* to produce high returns on capital?
    A. High barriers to entry
    B. High degree of concentration
    C. Short lead time to build new plants

23. An industry with high barriers to entry and weak pricing power *most likely* has:
    A. high barriers to exit.
    B. stable market shares.
    C. significant numbers of issued patents.

24. Economic value is created for an industry's shareholders when the industry earns a return:
    A. below the cost of capital.
    B. equal to the cost of capital.
    C. above the cost of capital.

25. Which of the following industries is *most likely* to be characterized as concentrated with strong pricing power?
    A. Asset management
    B. Alcoholic beverages
    C. Household and personal products

26. A population that is rapidly aging would *most likely* cause the growth rate of the industry producing eyeglasses and contact lenses to:
    A. decrease.
    B. increase.
    C. not change.

27. If over a long period of time a country's average level of educational accomplishment increases, this development would *most likely* lead to the country's amount of income spent on consumer discretionary goods to:
    A. decrease.
    B. increase.
    C. not change.

28. If the technology for an industry involves high fixed capital investment, then one way to seek higher profit growth is by pursuing:
    A. economies of scale.
    B. diseconomies of scale.
    C. removal of features that differentiate the product or service provided.

29. With respect to competitive strategy, a company with a successful cost leadership strategy is *most likely* characterized by:
    A. a low cost of capital.
    B. reduced market share.
    C. the ability to offer products at higher prices than those of its competitors.

30. When conducting a company analysis, the analysis of demand for a company's product is *least likely* to consider the:
    A. company's cost structure.
    B. motivations of the customer base.
    C. product's differentiating characteristics.

31. Which of the following statements about company analysis is *most* accurate?
    A. The complexity of spreadsheet modeling ensures precise forecasts of financial statements.
    B. The interpretation of financial ratios should focus on comparing the company's results over time but not with competitors.
    C. The corporate profile would include a description of the company's business, investment activities, governance, and strengths and weaknesses.

CHAPTER 13

FINANCIAL STATEMENT MODELING

Matthew L. Coffina, CFA
Morningstar Investment Management LLC (USA)

Anthony M. Fiore, CFA
Silvercrest Asset Management (USA)

Antonius J. van Ooijen, MSc, CFA
APG Asset Management (Netherlands)

LEARNING OUTCOMES

The candidate should be able to:

- compare top-down, bottom-up, and hybrid approaches for developing inputs to equity valuation models
- compare "growth relative to GDP growth" and "market growth and market share" approaches to forecasting revenue
- evaluate whether economies of scale are present in an industry by analyzing operating margins and sales levels
- demonstrate methods to forecast the following costs: cost of goods sold, selling general and administrative costs, financing costs, and income taxes
- demonstrate methods to forecast non-operating items, financing costs, and income taxes
- describe approaches to balance sheet modeling
- demonstrate the development of a sales-based pro forma company model
- explain how behavioral factors affect analyst forecasts and recommend remedial actions for analyst biases
- explain how competitive factors affect prices and costs
- evaluate the competitive position of a company based on a Porter's five forces analysis
- explain how to forecast industry and company sales and costs when they are subject to price inflation or deflation
- evaluate the effects of technological developments on demand, selling prices, costs, and margins

- explain considerations in the choice of an explicit forecast horizon
- explain an analyst's choices in developing projections beyond the short-term forecast horizon

1. INTRODUCTION

Financial statement modeling is a key step in the process of valuing companies and the securities they have issued. We focus on how analysts use industry information and corporate disclosures to forecast a company's future financial results.

An effective financial statement model must be based on a thorough understanding of a company's business, management, strategy, external environment, and historical results. Thus, an analyst begins with a review of the company and its environment—its industry, key products, strategic position, management, competitors, suppliers, and customers. Using this information, an analyst identifies key revenue and cost drivers and assesses the likely impact of relevant trends, such as economic conditions and technological developments. An analyst's understanding of the fundamental drivers of the business and assessment of future events provide the basis for forecast model inputs. In other words, financial statement modeling is not merely a quantitative or accounting exercise, it is the quantitative expression of an analyst's expectations for a company and its competitive environment.

We begin our discussion with an overview of developing a revenue forecast. We then describe the general approach to forecasting each of the financial statements and demonstrate the construction of a financial statement model, including forecasted revenue, income statements, balance sheets, and statements of cash flows. Then, we describe five key behavioral biases that influence the modeling process and strategies to mitigate them. We then turn to several important topics on the effects of micro- and macroeconomic conditions on financial statement models: the impact of competitive factors on prices and costs, the effects of inflation and deflation, technological developments, and long-term forecasting considerations. The chapter concludes with a summary and practice problems.

Most of the examples and exhibits used throughout the chapter can be downloaded as a Microsoft Excel workbook. Each worksheet in the workbook is labeled with the corresponding example or exhibit number in the text.

1.1. Financial Statement Modeling: An Overview

Financial statement modeling generally begins with the income statement. The income statement is a logical starting point because most companies derive most of their value from future cash flow generation, determined primarily by the amount of future operating income generated by the business. Exceptions include banks and insurance companies, for which the value of existing assets and liabilities on the balance sheet might be more relevant to the companies' overall value than projected future income. The income statement also provides a useful starting point for modeling a company's balance sheet and cash flow statement.

1.1.1. Income Statement Modeling: Revenue

Companies receive revenue from multiple sources and can be analyzed by geographical source, business segment, or product line. In a geographic analysis, the analyst places a company's revenue into various geographic groupings, which might or might not be the same as the groupings provided by management in company disclosures. These groupings can be narrowly defined, such as by individual countries, or more broadly defined, such as by region of the world. A geographic analysis can be particularly useful for companies operating in multiple countries with different underlying growth rates or competitive dynamics. For example, a company's sales might be experiencing relatively slow growth in one region of the world and relatively fast growth in other regions. By examining each region of the world separately, analysts can enhance their understanding of overall growth.

Segment disclosures in companies' financial reports are often a rich source of information. Both International Financial Reporting Standards (IFRS) and US GAAP require issuers to disclose financial information for any operating segment whose revenue, operating income, or assets account for 10% or more of consolidated revenue, operating income, or assets. Disclosures, typically in the notes to financial statements, include how segments are defined; segment revenues, expenses, assets, and liabilities; and a reconciliation of segment results to consolidated results. In addition to the interim and annual financial reports issued by the company, important information can often be found in other company disclosures, such as press releases, presentations, and conference calls.

In a breakdown by segment, the analyst classifies a company's revenue into various business segments. Many companies operate in more than one industry or market niche with widely differing economics. Although information is often available for the different business segments, analysts should make an independent judgment about whether management's segmentation is relevant and material. Sometimes analysts can regroup reported information in a manner that helps make important points.

Finally, a product line analysis provides the most granular level of detail. A product line analysis is most relevant for a company with a manageably small number of products that behave differently but when combined, account for most of the company's sales.

Example 1 introduces the first of many examples and exhibits that we use. Please note that many numbers have been rounded; so, in replicating results based on the numbers given in the text and exhibits, small apparent discrepancies could reflect the rounding error.

EXAMPLE 1   Analysis of Revenue (1)

Novo Nordisk is a Denmark-based listed biopharmaceutical company. The company provides detailed disclosure of revenue along geographic, business segment, and product lines. All figures are in millions of Danish krone (DKK).

In its 2020 annual report, Novo Nordisk provided the following geographic breakdown of sales for the previous three years. The company also reported revenue in two business segments: Diabetes and Obesity Care and Biopharmaceuticals. Within each segment, disclosure on several individual product lines was also provided. Exhibit 1 and Exhibit 2 are in the Example1 sheet in the downloadable Microsoft Excel workbook.

EXHIBIT 1: Novo Nordisk's Sales by Geographic Region (DKK millions)

	2020	2019	2018
United States	57,824	57,846	54,488
Other North America	3,293	2,611	2,420
EMEA (Europe, Middle East, Africa)	34,297	32,208	29,226

	2020	2019	2018
China	14,084	12,844	11,285
Rest of world	17,448	16,512	14,412
Total net sales	126,946	122,021	111,831

EXHIBIT 2: Novo Nordisk's Sales by Segment and Product Line (DKK millions)

	2020	2019	2018
Modern insulins	47,677	50,657	50,391
Human insulin	8,873	9,036	9,265
Total insulin	56,550	59,693	59,656
GLP-1 analogs	41,831	33,221	26,129
Other Diabetes Care	4,031	4,247	4,250
Obesity Care	5,608	5,679	3,869
Total Diabetes and Obesity Care	108,020	102,840	93,904
Biopharmaceuticals	18,926	19,181	17,927
Total net sales	126,946	122,021	111,831

1. Modern insulins provide advantages over the more traditional human insulin, such as having a faster or longer-lasting effect on blood sugar. GLP-1 analogs are even newer products that help the human body produce more insulin. Compare Novo Nordisk's recent sales growth rate of its GLP-1 analogs with those of its modern insulins and human insulin products.

Solution to 1:
The growth rate of GLP-1 analogs sales was significantly higher than that for modern insulins and human insulin in 2020 and 2019. GLP-1 analogs sales grew 26% and 27% in 2020 and 2019, while modern insulins sales decreased by 6% in 2020 and grew 1% in 2019, and human insulin sales decreased by 2% in both 2020 and 2019.
The full calculations to support this solution are in the Example1 sheet in the downloadable Microsoft Excel workbook.

2. How did Novo Nordisk's sales breakdown by business segment (Diabetes and Obesity Care and Biopharmaceuticals) change from 2018 to 2020?

Solution to 2:
In the past two years, Novo Nordisk's sales breakdown by business segment changed slightly: Diabetes and Obesity Care increased from 84% to 85% of total net sales while Biopharmaceuticals decreased from 16% to 15% of total net sales.
The full calculations to support this solution are in the Example1 sheet in the downloadable Microsoft Excel workbook.

Once the analyst understands the important components of a company's revenue, they must decide whether to use a top-down, bottom-up, or hybrid approach to projecting future revenue. A **top-down approach** usually begins at the level of the overall economy. Forecasts can then be made at lower levels, such as sector, industry, and market for a specific product, to arrive at a revenue projection for the individual company. In contrast, a **bottom-up approach** begins at the level of the individual company or a unit within the company, such as individual product lines, locations, or business segments. Analysts then aggregate their projections for the individual products or segments to arrive at a forecast of total revenue for the company. Moreover, analysts also aggregate their revenue projections for individual companies to develop forecasts for a product market, industry, or the overall economy. A **hybrid approach** combines elements of both top-down and bottom-up analysis and can be useful for uncovering implicit assumptions or errors that could arise from using a single approach.

1.1.1.1. Top-Down Approaches to Modeling Revenue Two common top-down approaches to modeling revenue are "growth relative to GDP growth" and "market growth and market share."

   Growth relative to GDP growth approach: The analyst first forecasts the growth rate of nominal GDP. The analyst then considers how the growth rate of the specific company being examined will compare with nominal GDP growth. The analyst can use a forecast for real GDP growth to project volumes and a forecast for inflation to project prices. Analysts often think in terms of percentage point premiums or discounts derived from a company's position in the industrial life cycle (e.g., embryonic, growth, shakeout, mature, or decline) or business cycle sensitivity. Thus, an analyst's conclusion might be that a health care company's revenue will grow at a rate of 200 bps above the nominal GDP growth rate. The forecast could also be in relative terms. Thus, if GDP is forecast to grow at 4% and the company's revenue is forecast to grow at a 50% faster rate, the forecast percent change in revenue would be 4% $\times$ (1 + 0.50) = 6.0%, or 200 bps higher in absolute terms.

   Market growth and market share approach: The analyst first forecasts growth in a particular market. They then consider the company's current market share and how that share is likely to change over time. For example, if a company is expected to maintain an 8% market share of a given product market and the product market is forecast to grow from CNY144 billion to CNY154 billion in annual revenue, the forecast growth in company revenue is from a level of 8% $\times$ CNY144 billion = CNY11.5 billion to a level of 8% $\times$ CNY154 billion = CNY12.3 billion (considering this product market alone). If the product market revenue has a predictable relationship with GDP, regression analysis might be used to estimate the relationship.

1.1.1.2. Bottom-Up Approaches to Modeling Revenue Examples of bottom-up approaches to modeling revenue include the following:

- *Time series*: forecasts based on historical growth rates or time-series analysis.
- *Returns-based measure*: forecasts based on balance sheet accounts. For example, interest revenue for a bank can be calculated as loans multiplied by the average interest rate.
- *Capacity-based measure*: forecasts, for example, in retailing, based on same-store sales growth (for stores that have been open for at least 12 months) and sales related to new stores.

Time-series forecasts are among the simplest. For example, analysts might fit a trend line to historical data and then project sales over the desired time frame (e.g., using Excel's TREND formula). In such a case, analysts would be projecting historical growth rates to continue, but they might also use different assumptions—for example, they might project growth to decline linearly from current rates to some long-run rate. Note that time-series methods can also be used as tools in executing a top-down analysis, such as projecting GDP growth in a growth relative to GDP growth approach.

1.1.1.3. Hybrid Approaches to Modeling Revenue Hybrid approaches combine elements of both top-down and bottom-up analysis, and in practice, they are the most common approaches. For example, the analyst could use a market growth and market share approach to model individual product lines or business segments. Then, the analyst can aggregate the individual projections to arrive at a forecast for the overall company because the sum of forecast segment revenue equals the segment market size multiplied by the market share for all segments.

In a volume and price approach, the analyst makes separate projections for volumes (e.g., the number of products sold or the number of customers served) and average selling price. Depending on how these elements are forecast, this approach can be classified as top-down, bottom-up, or hybrid.

EXAMPLE 2   Analysis of Revenue (2)

Use the provided data as well as the data in Example 1 on Novo Nordisk to answer the following questions:

Xiaoping Wu is an equity analyst covering European pharmaceutical companies for his clients in China. Wu projects that global nominal GDP will grow 3% annually over the long run, based on 2% real growth and 1% inflation. The prevalence of diabetes is increasing globally because of increasingly unhealthy diets and sedentary lifestyles. As a result, Wu believes global sales of diabetes drugs will grow 100 bps faster than nominal GDP over the long run. Wu believes the revenue growth rate of Novo Nordisk's Diabetes and Obesity Care segment will decelerate linearly over four years to match the projected long-run growth rate of the diabetes drug market.

1. Is Wu using a top-down, bottom-up, or hybrid approach to modeling Novo Nordisk's revenue?

Solution to 1:

Wu's long-run revenue projections are based on Novo Nordisk's growth relative to nominal GDP growth, which is a top-down approach. However, his estimated growth rate is applied to only one of Novo Nordisk's segments (Diabetes and Obesity Care), indicating a hybrid approach. Wu's four-year forecasts are also based in part on the historical growth rate of the Diabetes and Obesity Care segment, which is a bottom-up approach. Wu is thus using a hybrid approach.

2. Based on Wu's projections for revenue growth, calculate the estimated revenue growth rate for the Diabetes and Obesity Care segment in 2021. Assume no impact from exchange rate changes.

Solution to 2:

The data in Example 1 indicate that Novo Nordisk's Diabetes and Obesity Care segment grew by 5% in 2020. Wu projects the long-run growth rate to be in line with the diabetes drug market growth at 4% (100 bps faster than GDP growth of 3%). The difference between the 2020 growth rate and the projected long-run growth rate is 1%

(= 5% – 4%), and Wu expects the modest deceleration in growth to occur linearly over four years, implying a reduction of 25 bps per year in the growth rate. The estimated growth rates by year are thus

$$2021 = 4.75\%$$

$$2022 = 4.5\%$$

$$2023 = 4.25\%$$

$$2024 = 4\%$$

Thereafter, 4%.

The estimated revenue growth rate for 2021 is 4.75%.

Helga Hansen is a buy-side analyst in Denmark. In 2021, Hansen was investigating Rybelsus, a Novo Nordisk product launched in 2019, in a class of diabetes drugs called GLP-1 analogs. As of 2021, Rybelsus is one of several GLP-1 analogs on the market, competing with Novo Nordisk's own Victoza and Ozempic, Eli Lilly's Trulicity, and exenatide (brands Byetta and Bydureon) by AstraZeneca. Rybelsus is the same drug compound as Ozempic but is a once-daily pill, unlike Ozempic and all other GLP-1 analogs, which are injectable drugs.

Eli Lilly and AstraZeneca reported global sales of their products in US dollars (USD). Hansen converted the companies' reported figures to Danish krone using annual average USD/DKK exchange rates to compile Exhibit 3, which shows annual sales of the GLP-1 analogs measured in millions of DKK. Exhibit 3 is in the Example2 sheet in the downloadable Microsoft Excel workbook.

EXHIBIT 3: GLP-1 Analog Sales, Annual (DKK millions)

Product	Company	2020	2019	2018
Victoza	Novo Nordisk	18,747	21,934	24,333
Ozempic	Novo Nordisk	21,211	11,237	1,796
Rybelsus	Novo Nordisk	1,873	50	0
Trulicity	Eli Lilly	33,135	27,533	20,215
Byetta and Bydureon	AstraZeneca	3,374	4,396	4,486

3. What was the growth rate in total GLP-1 analog sales in 2020?

Solution to 3:

Total GLP-1 analog sales in 2020 and 2019 were DKK78,340 million and DKK65,150 million, respectively. The growth rate of total GLP-1 analog sales in 2020 (78,340 – 65,150/65,150) was 20%.

The full calculations to support this solution are in the Example2 sheet in the downloadable Microsoft Excel workbook.

4. What percentage of GLP-1 analog sales growth in 2020 can be attributed to Rybelsus?

Solution to 4:

Total GLP-1 analog sales increased by DKK13,190 million in 2020. Rybelsus's sales increased by DKK1,823 million, which implies that Rybelsus's growth accounted for (1,823/13,190) ≈ 14% of GLP-1 analog sales growth.

The full calculations to support this solution are in the Example2 sheet in the downloadable Microsoft Excel workbook.

5. Hansen previously projected that the growth rate of the GLP-1 analog market would slow to 18% in 2020. She also expected Trulicity market share to fall by 5 percentage points. What was Hansen's estimate of 2020 Trulicity sales? How close was she to the actual result?

Solution to 5:

Based on 2019 sales of DKK65,150 million and a projected growth rate of 18%, Hansen projected the total GLP-1 analog sales to be DKK76,877 million in 2020. Trulicity's market share in 2019 was ~42%, which Hansen projected to fall by 5 percentage points, resulting in a ~37% market share in 2020. Hansen thus projected 2020 Trulicity sales to be DKK28,645 million. Actual Trulicity sales in 2020 were DKK33,135 million, so Hansen's estimate was too low by DKK4,490 million or 14%.

The full calculations to support this solution are in the Example2 sheet in the downloadable Microsoft Excel workbook.

6. Is Hansen's approach to modeling sales best described as bottom-up, top-down, or hybrid?

Solution to 6:

Hansen bases her estimates on market growth and market share, which would normally imply a top-down approach. The analysis, however, is applied to an individual product line, implying a bottom-up approach. Therefore, Hansen is using a hybrid approach.

2. INCOME STATEMENT MODELING: OPERATING COSTS

Disclosure about operating costs is frequently less detailed than disclosure about revenue. If relevant information is available, analysts might consider matching the cost analysis to the revenue analysis. For example, they might model costs separately for different geographic regions, business segments, or product lines. More frequently, analysts will be forced to consider costs at a more aggregated level than the level used to analyze revenue. Analysts should keep in mind their revenue analysis when deriving cost assumptions. For instance, if sales of a relatively low-margin product are expected to grow faster than those of a relatively high-margin product, analysts should project some level of overall margin deterioration, even if they are not certain about the precise margins earned on each product.

Once again, analysts can take a top-down, bottom-up, or hybrid view of costs. In a top-down approach, analysts might consider such factors as the overall level of inflation or industry-specific costs before making assumptions about the individual company. In contrast, in a bottom-up approach analysts would start at the company level, considering such factors as segment-level margins, historical cost growth rates, historical margin levels, or the costs of delivering specific products. A hybrid approach would incorporate both top-down and bottom-up elements.

When estimating costs, analysts should pay particular attention to fixed costs. Variable costs are directly linked to revenue, and they might be best modeled as a percentage of revenue or as projected unit volume multiplied by unit variable costs.

By contrast, fixed costs are not directly related to revenue; rather, they are related to investment in property, plant, and equipment (PP&E) and to total capacity. Practically, fixed costs might be assumed to grow at their own rate, based on an analysis of future PP&E and capacity growth. Analysts should determine whether, at its current level of output, the subject company has **economies of scale**, a situation in which average costs per unit of a good or service produced fall as volume rises. Gross and operating margins tend to be positively correlated with sales levels in an industry that enjoys economies of scale. Factors that can lead to economies of scale include high fixed costs, higher levels of production, greater bargaining power with suppliers, and lower per unit advertising expenses.

Analysts must also be aware of any uncertainty surrounding estimates of costs. For example, banks and insurance companies create reserves against estimated future losses, while companies with large pension plans have long-duration liabilities, the true costs of which might not be known for many years. A review of disclosures about reserving practices related to future obligations and pensions can be helpful in assessing whether cost estimates are reasonable. But most of the time, the external analyst has difficulty anticipating future revisions to cost estimates. Other aspects affecting the uncertainty of cost estimates include competitive factors and technological developments. This impact will be discussed in later sections.

EXAMPLE 3 Approaches to Modeling Operating Costs

CVS Health Corporation ("CVS"), Walgreens Boots Alliance Inc. ("Walgreens"), and Rite Aid Corporation ("Rite Aid") operate retail drugstores in the United States. There is reason to believe that economies of scale exist in the drugstore business. For example, larger drugstore companies might have the ability to spread fixed costs such as payroll and information technology (IT) across a greater amount of revenue, have greater bargaining leverage with distributors over the cost of pharmaceuticals, and negotiate better payment rates from health insurer customers than smaller drugstore companies. Some financial data from the US retail drugstore segment of CVS, Walgreens, and Rite Aid from fiscal year 2020 are presented in Exhibit 4.

EXHIBIT 4: 2020 Financial Results for CVS, Walgreens, and Rite Aid (US Retail Drugstore Segments) (FY2020, $ millions)

	CVS	Walgreens	Rite Aid
Revenues	91,198	107,701	16,365
Cost of goods sold	67,284	85,490	12,109
Selling, general, and administrative expenses	17,768	18,112	4,299
Operating income	6,146	4,099	−44
Same-store sales growth	5.60%	2.80%	3.50%
Number of stores	10,040	9,028	2,510

Customer service could be one driver of revenue for the retail drug business. Retail analysts commonly use a combination of qualitative and quantitative evidence to assess customer service. Qualitative evidence might come from personal store visits or customer surveys. Quantitative evidence might be based on such metrics as selling, general, and administrative (SG&A) expenses per store. Too little spending on SG&A might indicate that stores are under-resourced. Relatedly, same-store sales growth could be an indicator of customer satisfaction. Exhibit 5 shows annual same-store sales growth rates for the three companies from 2011 to 2020.

EXHIBIT 5: Annual Same-Store Sales Growth Rates: CVS, Walgreens, and Rite Aid

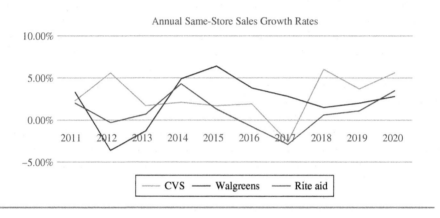

Use the data given to answer the following questions. Exhibits 4 and 5 are in the Example3 sheet in the downloadable Microsoft Excel workbook.

1. Based on the 2020 operating margins, is there evidence suggesting that economies of scale exist in the retail drugstore business? If so, are economies of scale realized in cost of goods sold or SG&A expenses?

Solution to 1:

Based on operating margins, economies of scale may be present, but whether they are is unclear. CVS and Walgreens are more than five times the size of Rite Aid by annual revenues and reported operating margins of 7% and 4%, respectively, versus less than 0% for Rite Aid. On the other hand, Walgreens is 18% larger by revenues than CVS yet has a significantly lower operating margin (4% versus 7%). Further research is required to uncover whether, for example, Walgreens and CVS have significant differences in prices, the mix of products sold, and so on.

If anywhere, economies of scale are evident in SG&A expenses. Both CVS and Walgreens have significantly lower SG&A expenses as a percentage of revenues (19% and 17%, respectively) than Rite Aid (26%), while gross margins appear unrelated to scale, given that CVS, Walgreens, and Rite Aid reported gross margins of 26%, 21%, and 26%, respectively.

The full calculations to support this solution are in the Example3 sheet in the downloadable Microsoft Excel workbook.

Marco Benitez is a United States–based equity analyst with an independent research firm. Benitez is researching service levels in the US drugstore industry.

2. Calculate and interpret the companies' SG&A expenses per store.

Solution to 2:

SG&A expenses per store for CVS and Rite Aid are similar, at USD1.8 and USD1.7 million, respectively, while Walgreens spent just over USD2 million per store. This comparison might indicate that Walgreens has service levels at its stores that are superior to those of CVS and Rite Aid or that its stores are in higher-cost (payroll and real estate) locations.

The full calculations to support this solution are in the Example3 sheet in the downloadable Microsoft Excel workbook.

3. Assuming that customer satisfaction is a driver of same-store sales growth, which company appears to have the most satisfied customer base?

Solution to 3:

Based on recent same-store sales growth rates, CVS appears to have the most satisfied customer base, followed by Walgreens. CVS's same-store sales growth rates have exceeded those of the others in each of the past three years. Over a longer time period, however, both CVS and Walgreens led in same-store sales growth in five of the past 10 years, though CVS's average same-store sales growth rate over the past 10 years is 54 bps higher than Walgreens'.

The full calculations to support this solution are in the Example3 sheet in the downloadable Microsoft Excel workbook.

4. Benitez projects that Rite Aid will increase its number of stores by 2% annually over the next three years. He believes SG&A expenses per store will increase 1% annually during this time. What is Benitez's projection for total SG&A expense in 2023?

Solution to 4:

Benitez projects Rite Aid's number of stores will be approximately 2,664 [$= 2,510 \times 1.02^3$] by the end of 2023. He projects that SG&A expenses per store will be USD1.76 million [$= 1.71 \times 1.01^3$]. He thus estimates total SG&A expenses to be USD4,701 million in 2023, which is approximately 9% higher than in fiscal 2020.

Jasmine Lewis is another United States–based equity analyst covering the retail drugstore industry. She is considering several approaches to forecasting operating costs for CVS, Walgreens, and Rite Aid. Classify each of the following as a bottom-up, top-down, or hybrid approach.

5. Lewis believes government health care programs in the United States will face budgetary pressures in the future, which will result in lower reimbursements for the retail drugstore industry. Lewis thinks this will lower all drugstores' gross margins.

Solution to 5:

This case describes a top-down approach because Lewis considers the overall industry environment before individual companies.

6. Lewis projects that Walgreens' historical rate of growth in SG&A expenses will continue for the next five years. But in the long run, he projects SG&A expenses to grow at the rate of inflation.

Solution to 6:

In this case, Lewis combines a bottom-up approach (projecting the historical rate of growth to continue) with a top-down approach (basing his long-run assumptions on the overall rate of inflation). Therefore, this is a hybrid approach.

7. To estimate Rite Aid's future lease expense, Lewis makes assumptions about store growth, the mix of owned and leased stores, and average lease expense per store.

Solution to 7:

This case describes a bottom-up approach because Lewis bases her forecasts on Rite Aid's historical experience.

3. MODELING OPERATING COSTS: COST OF GOODS SOLD AND SG&A

The cost of goods sold (COGS) is typically the single largest cost for companies that make and/or sell products. COGS includes the cost of producing, purchasing, and readying products for sale.

Because sales minus COGS equals gross profit (and gross margin is gross profit as a percentage of sales), COGS and gross profit vary inversely. Forecasting COGS as a percentage of sales and forecasting gross margin percentage are equivalent in that a value for one implies a value for the other.

Because COGS has a direct link with sales, forecasting this item as a percentage of sales is usually a good approach. Historical data on a company's COGS as a percentage of sales usually provide a useful starting point for estimates. For example, if a company is losing market share in a market in which the emergence of new substitute products is also putting the overall sector under pricing pressure, gross margins are likely to decline. But if the company is gaining market share because it has introduced new competitive and innovative products, especially if it has done so in combination with achieving cost advantages, gross margins are likely to improve.

COGS is typically a large cost, and so a small error in this item can have a material impact on the forecasted operating profit. Analysts should consider whether an analysis of these costs (e.g., by segment, by product category, or by volume and price components) is possible and improves forecasting accuracy. For example, some companies face fluctuating input costs that can be passed on to customers only with a time lag. Particularly for companies that have low gross margins, sudden shocks in input costs can affect operating profit significantly. A good example is the sensitivity of airlines' profits to unhedged changes in jet fuel costs. In these cases, a breakdown of both costs and sales into volume and price components is essential for developing short-term forecasts, even if analysts use the overall relationship between sales and input cost for developing longer-term forecasts.

EXAMPLE 4   The Effect of Prices and Costs on Gross Profit and Margin

Assume that a company's COGS as a percentage of sales equals 25%. If input costs double the following period, and the company can pass the entire increase on to its clients through a 25% price increase, COGS as a percentage of sales will increase (to 40%) because an equal absolute amount has been added to the numerator and to the denominator.

	Period 1	Period 2
Sales	100.0	125.0
COGS	25.0	50.0
Gross profit	75.0	75.0
COGS as % of sales	25%	40%
Gross margin %	75%	60%

Thus, although the absolute amount of gross profit will remain constant, the gross margin will decrease (from 75% to 60%).

Analysts should also consider the impact of a company's hedging strategy. For example, commodity-driven companies' gross margins almost automatically decline if input prices increase significantly because of variable costs increasing at a faster rate than revenue growth. Through various hedging strategies, a company can mitigate the impact on profitability. For example, brewers often hedge the cost of barley, a key raw material needed for brewing beer, one year in advance. Although companies usually do not disclose their hedging positions, their general strategy is often revealed in the footnotes of the annual report. Further, the negative impact of increasing sales prices on sales volume can be mitigated by a policy of gradual sales price increases. For example, if the brewer expects higher barley prices because of a bad harvest, the brewer can slowly increase prices to avoid a strong price jump next year.

Competitors' gross margins can also provide a useful cross check for estimating a realistic gross margin. Gross margin differences among companies within a sector should logically relate to differences in their business operations. For example, in the Netherlands, supermarket chain Albert Heijn has a higher gross margin in the very competitive grocery sector because it can leverage its dominant 35% market share to achieve savings in purchases; it also has the ability to make higher-margin private label products. All these competitive advantages contribute to its structurally higher gross margin within the grocery sector. But if a new large competitor emerges (e.g., through consolidation of the fragmented market), Albert Heijn's above-average gross margin could come under pressure.

Note that differences in competitors' gross margins do not always indicate a superior competitive position but could simply reflect differences in business models. For example, some companies in the grocery segment own and operate their own retail stores, whereas other companies operate as wholesalers with franchised retail operations. In the franchised retailing business model, most of the operating costs are incurred by the franchisee; the wholesaler offers products with only a small markup to these franchisees. Compared with a grocer with its own stores, a supermarket wholesaler will have a much lower gross margin.

The grocer with its own stores, however, will have much higher operating costs. Even though differences in business models can complicate direct comparisons, competitors' gross margins can nonetheless offer potentially useful insights.

3.1. SG&A Expenses

SG&A expenses are the other main type of operating costs. In contrast to COGS, SG&A expenses often have less of a direct relationship with revenues. As an illustration of the profit impact of COGS and SG&A, consider the historical case example of Thai cement and building materials company Siam Cement Group from 2017 to 2018. A summary of the company's key income statement items is shown in Exhibit 6.

EXHIBIT 6: Siam Cement Group 2017–18 Financials

| | 2017 (Baht billions) | 2018 (Baht billions) | Percent of Sales | | |
			YoY%	2017	2018
Net sales	450.92	478.44	6.1	100.0	100.0
COGS	349.31	383.46	9.8	77.5	80.1
Gross profit	101.61	94.98	–6.5	22.5	19.9
SG&A	52.58	55.09	4.8	11.7	11.5
Selected SG&A items:					
Salary and personnel expenses	24.24	23.98	–1.1	5.4	5.0
Freight costs	11.63	11.55	–0.7	2.6	2.4
Research and development	4.18	4.67	11.7	0.9	1.0
Promotion and advertising	2.62	2.58	–1.5	0.6	0.5
Operating income	49.03	39.89	–18.6	10.9	8.3

Note: "YoY%" means year-over-year percentage change.
Sources: Based on information in Siam Cement Group's annual reports.

As shown in the exhibit, Siam Cement was affected in 2018 by higher input costs that could not be fully passed on to customers. Consequently, despite sales growth of 6.1%, gross profit fell by 6.5% and gross margin declined. The company was able to limit its other operating costs; SG&A expenses grew 4.8%, declining slightly as a percentage of revenue. Operating income fell 18.6%. This contrasted with the company's experience in 2016, when lower input costs resulted in widening of the gross margin to 24.7% from 22.3% in 2015 (not shown in Exhibit 7).

Siam Cement's income statement illustrates that companies often disclose the different components of SG&A expenses. Siam Cement, for example, shows separate line items for several distribution cost items, such as freight and rental expenses, and a number of general and administrative expenses, such as depreciation, IT fees, professional fees, and research and development (R&D). Although SG&A expenses overall are generally less closely linked to revenue than COGS, certain expenses within SG&A could be more variable—more closely linked to revenue—than others. Specifically, selling and distribution expenses often have a large variable component and can be estimated, like COGS, as a percentage of sales. The largest component of selling expenses is often wages and salaries linked to sales. Therefore, selling expenses will usually increase with additional salespeople and/or an overall increase in wages and benefits for the sales force.

Other general and administrative expenses are less variable. Overhead costs for employees, for example, are more related to the number of employees at the head office and supporting IT and administrative operations than to short-term changes in the level of sales. R&D expense is another example of an expense that tends to fluctuate less than sales. Consequently, these expenses are more fixed in nature and tend to increase and decrease gradually over time compared with changes in the company's revenue.

In addition to analyzing the historical relationship between a company's operating expenses and sales, benchmarking a company against its competitors can be useful. By analyzing the cost structure of a company's competitors, the efficiency potential and margin potential of a specific company can be estimated. As a final measure, performing certain crosschecks within a forecast model can be useful, too. For example, in the supermarket sector, the projected floor square footage (or metric equivalent) underlying the revenue projections should match the floor space projections underlying the unit selling expense forecasts. Both sales and expense projections can be enhanced if the company provides a breakout of the product and/or geographical segments in the footnotes of its annual report.

EXAMPLE 5   L'Oréal's Operational Cost Structure versus Competitors

As shown in Exhibit 7, L'Oréal reported an EBIT (earnings before interest and taxes) margin of 18.6% in 2019, which makes it the most profitable company among a selection of beauty companies. However, the average EBIT margin of 19.6% for home and personal goods companies operating in mass markets is even greater than that of L'Oréal. Luxury goods companies tend to have higher gross margins, owing to higher prices, than mass market companies, but those margins are offset by higher "go to market" costs such as advertising and promotion (A&P) expenditures. With the exception of Avon, the business model of which is based on direct selling, A&P is substantially greater at the beauty companies than at the mass market producers.

L'Oréal is often considered a pure beauty company. But if the underlying business is examined in detail, the company's operations can be split 50/50 between a luxury beauty high-end business and a general consumer business. In the general consumer business, L'Oréal's products compete with those of such players as Colgate, Procter & Gamble, and Henkel in the mass market. Exhibit 7 presents relevant data and can also be found in the Example4 sheet in the downloadable Microsoft Excel workbook.

EXHIBIT 7: European and US Home and Personal Care Companies, Beauty vs. Mass Market Companies: Simplified and Common-Size Income Statement (2019)

Company	Sales (mlns)	Gross Margin	A&P %	SG&A/Other %	EBIT %
Beauty					
L'Oréal	€29,874	73.0%	30.8%	23.6%	18.6%
Estée Lauder	$14,863	77.2%	22.5%	37.1%	17.6%
Beiersdorf	€7,653	57.9%	34.8%	9.6%	13.5%

Company	Sales (mlns)	Gross Margin	A&P %	SG&A/Other %	EBIT %
Avon	$4,763	57.8%	1.5%	53.6%	2.6%
Beauty Average		66.5%	22.4%	31.0%	13.1%
Mass Market					
Colgate	$15,693	59.4%	10.8%	24.7%	23.9%
Reckitt Group	£12,846	60.5%	14.4%	19.9%	26.2%
Procter & Gamble	$67,684	48.6%	10.0%	18.2%	20.4%
Clorox	$6,214	43.9%	9.8%	16.0%	18.1%
Kimberly-Clark	$18,450	32.7%	4.1%	13.5%	15.1%
Henkel	€20,114	45.9%	N/A	31.9%	14.0%
Mass Market Average		48.5%	9.8%	20.7%	19.6%

Notes: The data for some of the companies listed in Exhibit 8 have been adjusted to reflect differences in accounting choices. For example, some of the consumer product companies include shipping and handling expenses in cost of sales, whereas others include these costs as a component of SG&A expenses.
Sources: Based on information in company reports.

1. Assuming the following information, what will L'Oréal's new operating margin be?

   • L'Oréal's beauty and mass market operations each represent half of revenues.

   • L'Oréal will be able to bring the overall cost structure of its mass market operations in line with the average of mass market companies (EBIT = 19.6%).

   • The cost structure of L'Oréal's beauty operations will remain stable (assumed EBIT = 18%).

Solution to 1:
   Operating margin will increase from 18.6% to 18.8%, which is 50% of 19.6% (mass market EBIT margin) plus 50% of 18% (assumed beauty EBIT margin).
   The full calculations to support this solution are in the Example4 sheet in the downloadable Microsoft Excel workbook.

2. What will happen to L'Oréal's EBIT margin if the company is able to adjust the operating cost structure of its mass market segment (50% of revenues) partly toward the average of its mass market peers but maintain its high gross margin? Assume the following:

   • The cost structure of half of the business, the beauty operations, will remain stable (EBIT margin = 18%).

   • L'Oréal's mass market operations will have a gross margin of 60.75% (the average of the current gross margin of 73% and the 48.5% reported by its mass market peers).

   • L'Oréal's mass market A&P costs will fall by half from 30.8% of sales to 15.4% of sales, while other mass market SG&A costs will remain at the corporate average.

Solution to 2:

EBIT margin will increase from 18.6% to 19.9%. The projected beauty EBIT is EUR2,689 million, while the projected mass market EBIT is EUR5,937 million, assuming mass market sales of EUR14,937 million, gross margin of 60.75%, A&P % of 15.4%, and SG&A/Other % of 23.6%.

The full calculations to support this solution are in the Example4 sheet in the downloadable Microsoft Excel workbook.

EXAMPLE 6   Analysis of the Consumer Goods Company Unilever

The consumer goods company Unilever reported an overall underlying operating margin of 18.4% in 2019. As shown in Exhibit 8 (see the Example5 sheet in the downloadable Microsoft Excel workbook), the operating margin is lowest in the fastest growing product category, home care products. The other parts of the business, personal care and foods categories, enjoy higher margins but are growing more slowly.

EXHIBIT 8: Unilever Revenue and Profit from Product Categories (€ millions, unless noted)

Segment	2019	2018	'19/'18 YoY	Avg Growth Rate 2017–2019
Beauty & Personal Care	21,868	20,624	6%	3%
Foods & Refreshments	19,287	20,227	–5%	–5%
Home Care	10,825	10,131	7%	3%
Total revenues	51,980	50,982	2%	0%
Underlying operating profit				
Beauty & Personal Care	4,960	4,543	9%	
Foods & Refreshments	3,382	3,576	–5%	
Home Care	1,605	1,344	19%	
Total	9,947	9,463	5%	
Underlying operating profit margin				
Beauty & Personal Care	22.7%	22.0%		
Foods & Refreshments	17.5%	17.7%		
Home Care	14.8%	13.3%		
Total	19.1%	18.6%		

Notes: Underlying operating profit is a non-IFRS operating profit measure, equal to IFRS operating profit adjusted for items such as restructuring costs.
Source: Based on Unilever's 2019 full-year and fourth quarter results.

1. Determine the estimated sales, operating profit, and operating profit margin by using the following two approaches: (A) Assume total sales growth of 2.0% and

overall underlying operating margin of 19.1% for the next five years, and (B) assume each individual segment's sales growth and underlying operating margin continue at the same rate reported in 2019. Which approach will result in a higher underlying estimated operating profit after five years?

Solution to 1:
Exhibit 9 shows that operating profit after five years will be EUR10,962 million under approach A and EUR11,549 million under approach B. The full calculations to support this solution are in the Example5 sheet in the downloadable Microsoft Excel workbook.

EXHIBIT 9: Sales and Operating Profit for Unilever, 2018–2023E (€ millions, unless noted)

Approach A	2019A	2020E	2021E	2022E	2023E	2024E
Total revenues	51,980	53,020	54,080	55,162	56,265	57,390
Growth rate		2.00%	2.00%	2.00%	2.00%	2.00%
Underlying operating profit	9,947	10,127	10,329	10,536	10,747	10,962
Growth rate		2%	2%	2%	2%	2%
Underlying operating profit margin	19.1%	19.1%	19.1%	19.1%	19.1%	19.1%

Approach B	2019A	2020E	2021E	2022E	2023E	2024E
Sales						
Beauty & Personal Care	21,868	23,187	24,586	26,069	27,641	29,308
Growth rate		6%	6%	6%	6%	6%
Foods & Refreshments	19,287	18,391	17,536	16,721	15,944	15,203
Growth rate		–5%	–5%	–5%	–5%	–5%
Home Care	10,825	11,567	12,359	13,205	14,110	15,077
Growth rate		7%	7%	7%	7%	7%
Total revenues	51,980	53,144	54,481	55,995	57,695	59,588
Margins						
Beauty & Personal Care	22.7%	22.7%	22.7%	22.7%	22.7%	22.7%
Foods & Refreshments	17.5%	17.5%	17.5%	17.5%	17.5%	17.5%
Home Care	14.8%	14.8%	14.8%	14.8%	14.8%	14.8%
Underlying operating profit						
Beauty & Personal Care	4,960	5,259	5,576	5,913	6,269	6,648
Foods & Refreshments	3,382	3,225	3,075	2,932	2,796	2,666
Home Care	1,605	1,715	1,832	1,958	2,092	2,235
Total	9,947	10,199	10,484	10,803	11,157	11,549

2. Compare and explain the results under the two alternative approaches (A and B) in Question 1.

Solution to 2:
Approach A assumes a constant 2.0% total sales growth rate and a stable 19.1% underlying operating margin. Therefore, the operating profit growth rate is in line with the revenue growth rate and constant at 2.0%, which therefore assumes no difference in growth rates and profitability of the segments. Approach B assumes growth rates of 6%, –5%, and 7% of sales for the Beauty & Personal Care, Foods & Refreshments,

and Home Care segments. This results in a faster overall compounded growth rate than with Approach A (3% versus 2%) and an annual increase, on average, in the total underlying operating profit margin of 6 bps due to the mix effect of different segment margins. In 2024E, Approach A yields an underlying operating profit margin of 19.1% compared with 19.4% for Approach B.

3. Assume Unilever can grow segment revenues over the next five years at the following rates: Beauty & Personal Care 3.0%, Foods & Refreshments 2.0%, and Home Care 4.0%. But underlying operating profit margins in Beauty & Personal Care will fall 20 bps annually for the next five years (because of high competition, limited growth, and costs resulting from the adoption of sustainable packaging), and operating profit margins in the Foods & Refreshments and Home Care segments will increase by 15 and 50 bps, respectively, each year for the next five years (helped by increasing demand for the company's products and better utilization of its factories). Calculate the overall underlying operating profit margin in each of the next five years.

Solution to 3:

As shown in Exhibit 10, the overall underlying operating profit margin improves from 19.1% in 2019 to 19.5% in 2024 because the margin decline in Beauty & Personal Care is more than offset by the margin increase in Foods & Refreshments and the faster growing Home Care segment. The full calculations to support this solution are in the Example5 sheet in the downloadable Microsoft Excel workbook.

EXHIBIT 10: Sales and Operating Profit for Unilever 2019–2024E (€ millions, unless noted)

	2019A	2020E	2021E	2022E	2023E	2024E
Sales						
Beauty & Personal Care	21,868	22,524	23,200	23,896	24,613	25,351
Growth rate		3%	3%	3%	3%	3%
Foods & Refreshments	19,287	19,673	20,066	20,468	20,877	21,294
Growth rate		2%	2%	2%	2%	2%
Home Care	10,825	11,258	11,708	12,177	12,664	13,170
Growth rate		4%	4%	4%	4%	4%
Total revenues	51,980	53,455	54,974	56,540	58,153	59,816
Margins						
Beauty & Personal Care	22.7%	22.5%	22.3%	22.1%	21.9%	21.7%
Foods & Refreshments	17.5%	17.7%	17.8%	18.0%	18.1%	18.3%
Home Care	14.8%	15.3%	15.8%	16.3%	16.8%	17.3%
Underlying operating profit						
Beauty & Personal Care	4,960	5,064	5,169	5,277	5,386	5,496
Foods & Refreshments	3,382	3,479	3,579	3,681	3,786	3,894
Home Care	1,605	1,725	1,853	1,988	2,131	2,282
Total	9,947	10,268	10,601	10,946	11,303	11,672
Margin	19.1%	19.2%	19.3%	19.4%	19.4%	19.5%

4. MODELING NON-OPERATING COSTS AND OTHER ITEMS

Line items on the income statement that appear below operating profit, such as interest income, interest expense, income taxes, noncontrolling interest, income from affiliates, and shares outstanding, also need to be modeled. The two most significant non-operating expenses in income statement modeling are financing expenses (i.e., interest) and taxes.

4.1. Financing Expenses

Financing expenses consist of interest income and interest expense, which are typically netted. Interest income depends on the amount of cash and investments on the balance sheet as well as the rates of return earned on investments. Interest income is a key component of revenue for banks and insurance companies, but it is generally less significant to non-financial companies. Interest expense depends on the level of debt on the balance sheet as well as the interest rate associated with the debt. Interest expense is typically presented net of interest income on the income statement, with the individual components disclosed in the notes to financial statements. Analysts should be aware of the effect of changing interest rates on the net interest expense and market value of company's debt.

When forecasting financing expenses, the capital structure of a company is a key determinant. For practical purposes, the debt level in combination with the interest rate are the main drivers in forecasting debt financing expenses. Usually, the notes to the financial statements provide detail about the maturity structure of the company's debt and the corresponding interest rates. This information can be used to estimate future financing expenses.

EXAMPLE 7   Interest Expense Calculations

Dutch grocer Ahold Delhaize, operating in several regions, has a debt structure with a relatively high amount of debt, primarily in the form of leases, as shown in Exhibit 11 (see the Example6 worksheet in the downloadable Microsoft Excel workbook).

EXHIBIT 11: Ahold's Debt, Interest Income, and Expense (€ millions)

	3 Jan. 2021	29 Dec. 2019	Average
Loans	3,863	3,841	3,852
Other non-current financial liabilities (primarily leases)	8,905	8,716	8,811
Current financial liabilities	2,386	3,257	2,822
Gross debt	15,154	15,814	15,484
Less: cash and cash equivalents	2,933	3,717	3,325
Net debt	12,221	12,097	12,159
Interest income	35	65	
Interest expense	138	175	
Net interest expense	103	110	

Source: Ahold Delhaize 2020 Annual Report.

> 1. Calculate the interest rate on the average gross debt and interest rate on the average cash position for the year ended 3 Jan. 2021.
>
> *Solution to 1:*
>   Interest rate on average gross debt is calculated as interest expense divided by average gross debt: (EUR138 million/EUR15,484 million) = 0.89% or 89 bps. The interest rate on average cash position is interest income divided by the average cash position (EUR35 million/EUR3,325 million) = 1.05%.
>
> 2. Calculate the interest rate on the average net debt, assuming the other financial income and expenses are not related to the debt or cash balances, for the year ended 3 Jan. 2021.
>
> *Solution to 2:*
>   The interest rate on the average net debt is calculated as net interest expense divided by average net debt (EUR103 million/EUR12,159 million) = 0.85% or 85 bps.

4.2. Corporate Income Tax

Income taxes are primarily determined by the geographic composition of profits and the tax rates in each geography but can also be influenced by the nature of a business. Some companies benefit from special tax treatment—for example, from R&D tax credits or accelerated depreciation of fixed assets. Analysts should also be aware of any governmental or business changes that can alter tax rates.

Differences in tax rates can be an important driver of value. Generally, there are three types of tax rates:

- The statutory tax rate, which is the corporate tax rate in the country in which the company is domiciled.
- The effective tax rate, which is calculated as the reported income tax expense amount on the income statement divided by the pre-tax income.
- The cash tax rate, which is the tax actually paid (cash tax) divided by pre-tax income.

Differences between cash taxes and reported taxes typically result from differences between financial accounting standards and tax laws and are reflected as a deferred tax asset or a deferred tax liability.

In forecasting tax expense and cash taxes, respectively, the effective tax rate and cash tax rate are key. A good understanding of their operational drivers and the financial structure of a company is useful in forecasting these tax rates.

Differences between the statutory tax rate and the effective tax rate can arise for many reasons. Tax credits, withholding tax on dividends, adjustments to previous years, and expenses not deductible for tax purposes are among the reasons for differences.

Effective tax rates can differ when companies are active outside the country in which they are domiciled. The effective tax rate becomes a blend of the different tax rates of the countries in which the activities take place in relation to the profit generated in each country. If a company reports a high profit in a country with a high tax rate and a low profit in a country with a low tax rate, the effective tax rate will be the weighted average of the rates and higher than the simple average tax rate of both countries.

In some cases, companies have also been able to minimize their taxes by using special purposes entities. For example, some companies create specialized financing and holding companies to minimize the amount of taxable profit reported in high tax rate countries. Although such actions could reduce the effective tax rate substantially, they also create risks if, for example, tax laws change.

In general, an effective tax rate that is consistently lower than statutory rates or the effective tax rates reported by competitors might warrant additional attention when forecasting future tax expenses. The notes on the financial statements should disclose other types of items, some of which could contribute to a temporarily high or low effective tax rate. The cash tax rate is used for forecasting cash flows, and the effective tax rate is relevant for projecting earnings on the income statement.

In developing an estimated tax rate for forecasts, analysts should adjust for any one-time events. If the income from equity-method investees is a substantial part of pre-tax income and also a volatile component of it, the effective tax rate excluding this amount is likely to be a better estimate for the future tax costs for a company. The tax impact from income from participations is disclosed in the notes on the financial statements.

Often, a good starting point for estimating future tax expense is a tax rate based on normalized operating income, before the results from associates and special items. This normalized tax rate should be a good indication of the future tax expense, adjusted for special items, in an analyst's earnings model.

Building a model allows the effective tax amount to be found in the profit and loss projections and the cash tax amount on the cash flow statement (or given as supplemental information). The reconciliation between the profit and loss tax amount and the cash flow tax figures should be the change in the deferred tax asset or liability.

EXAMPLE 8   Tax Rate Estimates

ABC, a hypothetical company, operates in Countries A and B. The tax rate in Country A is 40%, and the tax rate in Country B is 10%. In the first year, the company generates an equal amount of profit before tax in each country, as shown in Exhibit 12 (see the Example7 sheet in the downloadable Microsoft Excel workbook).

EXHIBIT 12: Tax Rates That Differ by Jurisdiction

	A	B	Total
Profit before tax	100	100	200
Effective tax rate	40%	10%	25%
Tax	40	10	50
Net profit	60	90	150

1. What will happen to the effective tax rate for the next three years if the profit before tax in Country A is stable but the profit before tax in Country B grows 15% annually?

Solution to 1:

   The effective tax rate will gradually decline because a higher proportion of profit will be generated in the country with the lower tax rate each year. In Exhibit 13, the effective tax rate declines from 25% in the beginning to 22% in the third year.

EXHIBIT 13: Worksheet for Problem 1

	Year			
	0	1	2	3
Profit before tax, Country A	100	100	100	100
Growth rate		0%	0%	0%
Profit before tax, Country B	100	115	132	152
Growth rate		15%	15%	15%
Total profit before tax	200	215	232	252
Effective tax rate, Country A	40%	40%	40%	40%
Effective tax rate, Country B	10%	10%	10%	10%
Total tax	50	52	53	55
Total effective tax rate	25%	24%	23%	22%

2. Evaluate the cash tax and effective tax rates for the next three years if the tax authorities in Country A allow some costs (e.g., accelerated depreciation) to be taken sooner for tax purposes. For Country A, the result will be a 50% reduction in taxes paid in the current year but an increase in taxes paid by the same amount in the following year (this happens each year). Assume stable profit before tax in Country A and 15% annual before-tax-profit growth in Country B.

Solution to 2:

   The combined cash tax rate (last line in Exhibit 14) will be 15% in the first year and then rebound in subsequent years. Only the rate for the first year will benefit from a tax deferral; in subsequent years, the deferral for a given year will be offset by the addition of the amount postponed from the previous year. The combined effective tax rate will be unaffected by the deferral. As shown in Exhibit 14, beginning with the second year, the combined cash tax and effective tax rates decline over time but remain identical to each other. The full calculations to support this solution are in the Example7 sheet in the downloadable Microsoft Excel workbook.

EXHIBIT 14: Worksheet for Problem 2

	Year			
	0	1	2	3
Profit before tax, Country A	100	100	100	100
Growth rate		0%	0%	0%
Profit before tax, Country B	100	115	132	152
Growth rate		15%	15%	15%
Total profit before tax	200	215	232	252

	Year			
	0	1	2	3
Effective tax rate, Country A	40%	40%	40%	40%
Effective tax rate, Country B	10%	10%	10%	10%
Total tax per income statement	50	52	53	55
Total effective tax rate	25%	24%	23%	22%
Cash taxes, Country A	20	40	40	40
Cash taxes, Country B	10	12	13	15
Total cash tax	30	52	53	55
Cash tax rate	15%	24%	23%	22%

3. Repeat the exercise of Problem 2, but now assume that Country B, rather than Country A, allows some costs to be taken sooner for tax purposes and that the tax effect described applies to Country B. Continue to assume stable profit before tax in Country A and 15% annual profit growth in Country B.

Solution to 3:

The combined effective tax rate is unchanged from Exhibits 15 and 16. Because of the growth assumed for Country B, however, the annual tax postponement will result in a lower cash tax rate in Country B than the effective tax rate in Country B. Consequently, as shown in Exhibit 15, the combined cash tax rate will be less than the effective tax rate.

EXHIBIT 15: Worksheet for Problem 3

	Year			
	0	1	2	3
Profit before tax, Country A	100	100	100	100
Growth rate		0%	0%	0%
Profit before tax, Country B	100	115	132	152
Growth rate		15%	15%	15%
Total profit before tax	200	215	232	252
Effective tax rate, Country A	40%	40%	40%	40%
Effective tax rate, Country B	10%	10%	10%	10%
Total tax per income statement	50	52	53	55
Total effective tax rate	25%	24%	23%	22%
Cash taxes, Country A	40	40	40	40
Cash taxes, Country B	5	11	12	14
Total cash tax	45	51	52	54
Cash tax rate	23%	24%	23%	22%

The next section addresses several points to note in modeling dividends, share count, and unusual expenses.

4.3. Income Statement Modeling: Other Items

A company's stated dividend policy helps in modeling future dividend growth. Analysts will often assume that dividends grow each year by a certain dollar amount or as a proportion of net income.

If a company shares an ownership interest in a business unit with a third party, the company might report minority interest expense or income from consolidated affiliates on its income statement. If a company owns more than 50% of an affiliate, it will generally consolidate the affiliate's results with its own and report the portion of income that does not belong to the parent company as minority interest. If a company owns less than 50% of an affiliate, it will not consolidate results but will report its share of income from the affiliate under the equity method. If the affiliate is profitable, minority interest would be reported as deduction from net income, whereas if a consolidated affiliate generates losses, minority interest would be reported as an addition to net income to shareholders. In either case, income or expense from these jointly owned businesses can be material.

Share count (shares issued and outstanding) is a key input in the calculation of an intrinsic value estimate and earnings per share. Share count changes for three primary reasons: dilution related to stock options, convertible bonds, and similar securities; issuance of new shares; and share repurchases. The market price of a stock is an important determinant of future share count changes, which can complicate their estimation. Projections for share issuance and repurchases should fit within the analyst's broader analysis of a company's capital structure.

Finally, unusual charges can be almost impossible to predict, particularly past the next couple of years. For this reason, analysts typically exclude unusual charges from their forecasts. But if a company has a habit of frequently classifying certain recurring costs as "unusual," analysts should consider some normalized level of charges in their model.

5. BALANCE SHEET AND CASH FLOW STATEMENT MODELING

Income statement modeling is the starting point for balance sheet and cash flow statement modeling. Analysts normally have a choice of whether to focus on the balance sheet or cash flow statement; the third financial statement will naturally result from the construction of the other two. Here, we focus on the balance sheet.

Some balance sheet line items—such as retained earnings—flow directly from the income statement, whereas other lines like working capital accounts—such as accounts receivable, accounts payable, and inventory—are very closely linked to income statement projections.

A common way to model working capital accounts is with efficiency ratios, as in Example 9.

EXAMPLE 9   Working Capital Forecasts with Efficiency Ratios

Exhibit 16 (see the Example8 sheet in the downloadable Microsoft Excel workbook) shows revenues, COGS, and year-end working capital account balances for YY Ltd., a fictional company, for years 1–3. Based on the data in the exhibit, answer questions 1–3.

EXHIBIT 16: YY Ltd. Financial Data, millions of CNY

	Year 1	Year 2	Year 3
Revenue	174,915	205,839	245,866
COGS	152,723	177,285	209,114
Accounts receivable	5,598	6,949	10,161
Inventory	29,481	32,585	41,671
Accounts payable	46,287	59,528	72,199

1. Calculate days sales outstanding, inventory days on hand, and days payable outstanding for years 1, 2, and 3, using year-end balances and assuming a 365-day fiscal year.

Solution to 1:

   Days sales outstanding is equal to accounts receivable/(revenues/365), inventory days on hand is equal to inventories/(COGS/365), and days payable outstanding is equal to accounts payable/(COGS/365). Using the data in Exhibit 16, the three ratios for years 1–3 are as follows. Full calculations to support this solution are in the Example8 sheet in the downloadable Microsoft Excel workbook

	Year 1	Year 2	Year 3
Days sales outstanding	12	12	15
Inventory days on hand	70	67	73
Days payable outstanding	111	123	126

2. Your colleague Liang forecasts revenue growth of 18%, 16%, and 13% and gross margins of 17%, 17%, and 16% in years 4, 5, and 6, respectively. Using Liang forecasts, calculate expected revenue and COGS in each of year 4, 5, and 6.

Solution to 2:

   Using Liang's forecasts for annual revenue growth and gross margins and the data in Exhibit 16, expected revenue and COGS for years 4–6 are as follows, shown in millions of CNY. Full calculations to support this solution are in the Example8 sheet in the downloadable Microsoft Excel workbook.

	Year (millions of CNY)					
	1	2	3	4	5	6
Revenue	174,915	205,839	245,866	290,122	336,541	380,292
Growth rate		18%	19%	18%	16%	13%
COGS	152,723	177,285	209,114	240,801	279,329	319,445
Gross margin	13%	14%	15%	17%	17%	16%

3. Liang forecasts that days sales outstanding, inventory days on hand, and days payable outstanding in years 4, 5, and 6 will remain the same as year 3 amounts. Using Liang's forecasts as well as forecasted revenue and COGS, calculate expected accounts receivable, inventory, and accounts payable year-end balances for each of years 4, 5, and 6.

Solution to 3:

Each of the efficiency ratios can be rearranged to yield working capital balances because we have values for two of the three variables in them: the efficiency ratios are assumed to remain constant from year 3 levels and the revenue and COGS variables have already been forecast.

Days sales outstanding is equal to accounts receivable/(revenues/365), thus, accounts receivable is equal to days sales outstanding × (revenues/365). Similarly, inventories is equal to inventory days on hand × (COGS/365) and accounts payable is equal to days payable outstanding × (COGS/365).

Using the data in Exhibit 16 and the revenue and COGS forecasts, year-end working capital account balances are as follows, shown in millions of CNY. Full calculations to support this solution are in the Example8 sheet in the downloadable Microsoft Excel workbook.

	Year (millions of CNY)					
	1	2	3	4	5	6
Revenue	174,915	205,839	245,866	290,122	336,541	380,292
COGS	152,723	177,285	209,114	240,801	279,329	319,445
Accounts receivable	5,598	6,949	10,161	11,990	13,908	15,716
Inventories	29,481	32,585	41,671	47,985	55,663	63,657
Accounts payable	46,287	59,528	72,199	83,139	96,442	110,292
Days sales outstanding	12	12	15	15	15	15
Inventory days on hand	70	67	73	73	73	73
Days payable outstanding	111	123	126	126	126	126

Working capital projections can be modified by both top-down and bottom-up considerations. In the absence of a specific opinion about working capital, analysts can look at historical efficiency ratios and project recent performance or a historical average to persist in the future, as in Example 8, which would be a bottom-up approach. Conversely, analysts might have a specific view of future working capital. For example, if they project economy-wide retail sales to decline unexpectedly, that could result in slower inventory turnover (higher inventory days on hand) across the retail sector. Because the analysts began with a forecast for a large sector of the economy, this would be considered a top-down approach.

Projections for long-term assets—such as PP&E and intangible assets—are less directly tied to the income statement for most companies. Net PP&E and intangible assets primarily change because of capital expenditures and depreciation and amortization, both of which are important components of the cash flow statement. Depreciation and amortization forecasts are usually based on historical depreciation, management's disclosures, and levels of long-term assets. Capital expenditure forecasts depend on the analysts' judgment of the future capacity expansion, which is generally driven by revenue growth and the business model. Capital expenditures can be thought of as including both **maintenance capital expenditures**, which are necessary to sustain the current business, and **growth capital expenditures**, which are needed to expand the business. All else being equal, maintenance capital expenditure forecasts should normally be higher than depreciation because of inflation.

Finally, analysts must make assumptions about a company's future capital structure. Leverage ratios—such as debt-to-capital, debt-to-equity, and debt-to-EBITDA—can be useful for projecting future debt and equity levels. Analysts should consider historical company practice, management's financial strategy, and the capital requirements implied by other model assumptions when projecting the future capital structure.

EXAMPLE 10   Balance Sheet Modeling

Exhibit 17 shows financial data for YY Ltd. related to its PP&E and intangible assets. Based on the data in Exhibit 17 and the data and analysis from Example 8, answer questions 1 and 2 (see the Example9 sheet in the downloadable Microsoft Excel workbook).

EXHIBIT 17: YY Ltd. Long-Term Asset Data, millions of CNY

	Year		
	1	2	3
PP&E, net	5,068	6,992	6,306
Goodwill	282	248	253
Intangible assets, net	1,779	1,424	4,013
Total fixed assets	7,129	8,664	10,572
Capital expenditures—PP&E	3,785	3,405	3,026
Capital expenditures—intangibles	333	142	3,310
Depreciation expense	220	324	518
Amortization expense	529	486	666

Note: PP&E and intangibles asset account balances were also affected each year by changes in exchange rates and by disposals, which are not shown in the exhibit. Assume that such effects are zero in years 4–6.

1. Using the data from Exhibits 17 and 18, calculate the following for years 1–3.

    o Capital expenditures (for both PP&E and intangibles) as a percentage of revenue.

    o Depreciation expense as a percentage of beginning of the year PP&E, net (for years 2 and 3).

    o Amortization expense as a percentage of beginning of the year intangible assets, net (for years 2 and 3).

Solution to 1:

Using the data from Example 8 and Exhibit 18, the following percentages were calculated. Full supporting calculations are in the Example9 sheet in the downloadable Microsoft Excel workbook.

	Year		
	1	2	3
Revenue	174,915	205,839	245,866
Capital expenditures—PP&E % of revenue	2.2%	1.7%	1.2%
Capital expenditures—intangibles % of revenue	0.2%	0.1%	1.3%
Depreciation % of beginning PP&E		6%	7%
Amortization % of beginning intangibles		27%	47%

2. Given the following assumptions and forecasted revenue from Example 8, calculate expected total fixed assets for years 4–6.

    • Capital expenditures for PP&E as a percentage of revenue to remain at the year 3 level

    • Capital expenditures for intangibles as a percentage of revenue to remain at the year 1 level

    • Goodwill to remain at the year 3 level

    • Depreciation and amortization expenses as a percentage of beginning of year PP&E, net, and intangible assets, net, to remain at year 3 levels.

    Exhibit 18 shows financial data for YY Ltd. related to its capital structure and profitability. Based on the data in Exhibit 18 and the data and analysis from Example 8, answer question 3 (see the Example9 sheet in the downloadable Microsoft Excel workbook).

EXHIBIT 18: YY Ltd. Debt and Profitability Data, millions of CNY

	Year		
	1	2	3
Gross debt	10,931	17,624	17,597
Revenue	174,915	205,839	245,866
EBITDA	9,304	12,343	14,190
EBITDA margin	5.3%	6.0%	5.8%

Solution to 2:

Using the data from Example 8 and Exhibit 18, total expected fixed assets for years 4–6 were calculated as CNY12,351 million; CNY15,179 million; and CNY18,662 million, respectively. PP&E, net, each year was calculated as the prior period balance plus capital expenditures minus depreciation expense. Intangible assets, net, each year was calculated in a similar fashion. Goodwill was held constant at CNY253 million. Full supporting calculations are in the Example9 sheet in the downloadable Microsoft Excel workbook.

	Year					
	1	2	3	4	5	6
Revenue	174,915	205,839	245,866	290,122	336,541	380,292
PP&E, net	5,068	6,992	6,306	9,410	12,854	16,583
Goodwill	282	248	253	253	253	253
Other intangible assets, net	1,779	1,424	4,013	2,688	2,072	1,827
Total fixed assets	7,129	8,664	10,572	12,351	15,179	18,662
Capital expenditures—PP&E	3,785	3,405	3,026	3,571	4,142	4,680
Capital expenditures—PP&E % of revenue	2.2%	1.7%	1.2%	1.2%	1.2%	1.2%
Capital expenditures—intangibles	333	142	3,310	552	641	724
Capital expenditures—intangibles % of revenue	0.2%	0.1%	1.3%	0.2%	0.2%	0.2%
Depreciation expense	220	324	518	467	697	952
Depreciation % of beginning PP&E		6%	7%	7%	7%	7%
Amortization expense	529	486	666	1,877	1,257	969
Amortization % of beginning Intangibles		27%	47%	47%	47%	47%

3. YY Ltd. management has a year 6 gross debt to EBITDA ratio target of 2.0.

   • Assuming an EBITDA margin of 6.0%, revenue forecasts from Example 8, and gross debt-to-EBITDA ratios of 1.25, 1.50, and 2.0 for years 4, 5, and 6, respectively, calculate expected gross debt for years 4–6.

   • Given the results of part A, how much incremental borrowing does the forecast imply from year 3 to year 6?

Solution to 3:

Gross debt of CNY21,579 million; CNY30,289 million; and CNY45,635 million are estimated for years 4–6 for YY Ltd. This forecast is found by first multiplying forecasted revenue by the forecasted EBITDA margin to calculate forecasted EBITDA. Then, the expected gross debt to EBITDA ratio is multiplied by the forecasted

EBITDA to calculate forecasted gross debt. Full supporting calculations are in the Example9 sheet in the downloadable Microsoft Excel workbook.

	Year					
	1	2	3	4	5	6
Gross debt	10,931	17,624	17,597	21,759	30,289	45,635
Revenue	174,915	205,839	245,866	290,122	336,541	380,292
EBITDA	9,304	12,343	14,190	17,407	20,192	22,818
EBITDA margin	5.3%	6.0%	5.8%	6.0%	6.0%	6.0%
Gross debt to EBITDA	1.17	1.43	1.24	1.25	1.50	2.00

Once projected income statements and balance sheets have been constructed, future cash flow statements can be projected. Analysts will normally make assumptions about how a company will use its future cash flows—whether for share repurchases, dividends, additional capital expenditures, acquisitions, and so on.

6. BUILDING A FINANCIAL STATEMENT MODEL

This section provides an example of building a financial statement model. The subject company is the Rémy Cointreau Group (Rémy), a French company that sells primarily spirits. After providing a brief overview of the company, we will focus primarily on the mechanics of constructing pro forma income statements, statements of cash flows, and balance sheets. Data sources for this example include the company's fiscal year ended 31 March 2021 and 2020 annual reports, the company's interim reports, and corresponding investor presentations for additional information on the underlying results of the respective divisions.

6.1. Company Overview

Rémy, whose reporting year ends 31 March, operates and reports three business segments:

1. Cognac. This division, composed primarily of Rémy Martin brand cognac, represented approximately 73% of FY2021 (year-end 31 March 2021) revenue and 94% of total current operating profit. Current operating profit is a non-IFRS measure reported by Rémy equal to IFRS operating profit excluding items related to discontinued brands or items deemed infrequent or immaterial, such as impairment or litigation provisions.
2. Liqueurs & Spirits. A diverse portfolio of spirits brands, the main brands in this segment are Cointreau, Metaxa, St-Rémy, Mount Gay, Bruichladdich, and The Botanist. The segment represented approximately 25% of FY2021 revenue and 14% of current operating profits.

3. Partner Brands. This segment includes other companies' brands that are marketed through Rémy's distribution network. They represented approximately 3% of FY2021 revenue and just under 0% of current operating profit, earning a slight operating loss in FY2021 of –EUR0.8 million. This division's importance has declined significantly over time as the company discontinued distribution ("partner brand") contracts.

Segment financial information is summarized in Exhibit 19. As shown, the company's largest business segment is also its most profitable: The Cognac segment earned a current operating profit margin of approximately 30% (= EUR221 million/EUR735 million) in fiscal year 2021. Exhibits 20–33 are in the downloadable Microsoft Excel workbook in a single worksheet titled Rémy. We strongly recommend following along with the Excel workbook and exploring the model construction in detail.

EXHIBIT 19: Analysis of Rémy's Turnover and Operating Profit

	FY2019	FY2020	FY2021
Revenue (€ millions)			
Cognac	774	736	735
Liqueurs & Spirits	264	262	248
Partner Brands	87	28	27
Total revenues	1,126	1,025	1,010
Current Operating Profit (€ millions)			
Cognac	236	200	221
Liqueurs & Spirits	39	38	33
Partner Brands	5	–2	–1
Holding/Corporate-level costs	–15	–20	–17
Total current operating profit	264	215	236
Current Operating Profit Margins			
Cognac	30.4%	27.1%	30.1%
Liqueurs & Spirits	14.7%	14.3%	13.3%
Partner Brands	5.6%	–6.2%	–3.0%
Holding/Corporate-level costs (% of total revenue)	–1.3%	–2.0%	–1.7%
Total current operating margin	23.5%	21.0%	23.4%

Source: Based on information in consolidated financial statements of Rémy Cointreau Group for year ended 31 March 2021 and 2020.

Construction of pro forma income statements, as Exhibit 20 illustrates, is composed of four forecasting steps: revenue, COGS, other operating expenses, and, finally, non-operating items.

EXHIBIT 20: Income Statement Forecast Process

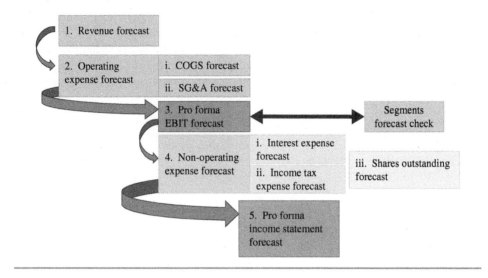

6.2. Revenue Forecast

The revenue forecasts use primarily a hybrid approach because trends in the individual segments (bottom-up) are combined with the overall cognac and spirits market development (top-down). For each segment, the change in revenue is driven by volume, price, and foreign currency estimates that are based on historical trends as adjusted for expected deviations from trend. Price changes refer not only to price changes for a single product but also to changes in price/mix, which are defined as changes in average prices that result from selling a different mix of higher- and lower-priced products. Changes in revenue attributable to volume or price/mix are organic growth and are shown separately from the impact of acquisitions and divestitures (scope change) and foreign exchange (forex impact in the model).

In the Cognac segment, historical volume growth is usually in the 4%–6% range. For future years, volume growth is expected to remain robust but be slower than the 9.1% achieved in 2021 as the global recovery from the COVID-19 pandemic and associated recession fades (volumes were down 10.1% in FY2020). The growing number of affluent Asian consumers will likely keep demand high, while developed market consumption is likely to be rather flat. In the model, the assumption is for 7% volume growth in 2022, declining to 6% in 2023 and 2024.

Price/mix contributed approximately 6.0%, 2.6%, and –5.4% to the Cognac segment revenue growth in FY2019, FY2020, and FY2021, respectively. Although the impact of price/mix on revenue growth has fluctuated in recent years, price/mix will likely remain a relatively significant contributor to revenue growth in the future given the favorable structure of the industry and the company's efforts to increase the share of revenues accounted for by what it calls "exceptional spirits" (those that cost more than USD50 per bottle and are seeing a 10% annual demand growth). A 4% price/mix contribution to revenue growth is assumed in 2022, with the trend maintained into 2023 and 2024. The combined projections for 2022 of 7%

volume growth and 4% price/mix impact results in overall organic revenue growth of 11.3%, calculated as $[(1 + 0.07) \times (1 + 0.04)] - 1$.

In addition to the impact of volume and price/mix, Rémy's revenues are affected by movements in exchange rates. Company disclosures indicate that more than 70% of revenues are realized outside the eurozone, whereas most of Rémy's production occurs within the eurozone. The model forecasts no foreign currency impact on revenue in the 2022–24 forecast period.

Exhibit 21 summarizes historical and projected information for the Cognac segment's revenue.

EXHIBIT 21: Historical and Projected Information for Cognac Segment Revenue

	FY2018	FY2019	FY2020	FY2021	FY2022E	FY2023E	FY2024E
Cognac Segment Revenues (€ million)	760	774	736	735	818	902	994
YoY%	7.4%	1.9%	−5.0%	−0.1%	11.3%	10.2%	10.2%
Volume growth %	6.0%	5.9%	−10.1%	9.1%	7.0%	6.0%	6.0%
Price/mix %	7.2%	6.0%	2.6%	−5.4%	4.0%	4.0%	4.0%
Organic growth %	13.6%	12.3%	−7.8%	3.2%	11.3%	10.2%	10.2%
Forex impact and scope change %	−5.8%	−4.0%	2.5%	−3.8%	0.0%	0.0%	0.0%
Effect of IFRS 15 adoption	0.0%	−6.0%	0.0%	0.0%	0.0%	0.0%	0.0%
YoY%	7.8%	2.3%	−5.3%	−0.6%	11.3%	10.2%	10.2%

Sources: Based on data from Rémy Cointreau Group and authors' analysis.

A similar analysis can be performed to project revenue for the other segments. Then, the amounts can be summed to derive projected consolidated revenue.

6.3. COGS

Rémy's gross margin has remained roughly flat from FY2018 (67.5%) to FY2021 (67.3%) as total sales have decreased modestly. Going forward, we project gross margin to increase by 100 bps in each of the next three years based on increasing total revenues, particularly from price/mix, which is strongly accretive to gross margin (see the previous section on "Revenue Forecast"). Management has set an FY2030 objective of a 72.0% gross margin, largely in line with our forecasts. Should revenue growth prove more (less) robust than our forecast, we expect more (less) gross margin accretion.

6.4. SG&A Expenses and Other Operating Expense

Distribution costs increased significantly over time, from 26.1% of revenue in FY2009 (not shown in the exhibits) to 38% in FY2018, and thereafter decreasing to 33.8% in FY2021. In particular, the setup of Rémy's distribution network in Asia increased the cost base. Rémy is very committed to its brand building and is also diversifying geographically. We estimate modest increases in distribution costs as a percentage of revenue, of 20 bps per year. Administrative costs as a percentage of revenue have increased from 8.1% to 10.1% as revenues have fallen, owing to the COVID-19 pandemic. However, the growth in absolute euro amounts has been modest, with costs of approximately EUR100 million in FY2019–FY2021. We expect 1% growth in administrative costs per year through FY2024E.

Other operating expense (income), composed primarily of provisions for impairments of intangible assets, restructurings, and divestiture gains, has fluctuated from –EUR2 million to EUR20 million from FY2018 to FY2021. Because we do not anticipate any transactions that would result in other operating expenses or income, we forecast zero for this line in the model.

Exhibit 22 provides a consolidated income statement for Rémy through the EBIT and EBIT margin line.

EXHIBIT 22: Consolidated Historical and Projected Income Statement (Operating) for Rémy Cointreau Group (€ millions, unless noted)

	FY2018	FY2019	FY2020	FY2021	FY2022E	FY2023E	FY2024E
Sales	1,127	1,126	1,025	1,010	1,095	1,181	1,275
Cost of sales	366	415	348	330	347	362	379
Gross profit	761	711	677	680	748	819	897
Gross margin	67.5%	63.1%	66.1%	67.3%	68.3%	69.3%	70.3%
Change in gross margin	0.8%	–4.4%	2.9%	1.3%	1.0%	1.0%	1.0%
Distribution costs	433	346	355	342	373	404	439
Distribution costs as % of sales	38.4%	30.7%	34.6%	33.8%	34.0%	34.2%	34.4%
Administrative expenses	92	101	107	103	104	105	106
Administrative expenses as % of sales	8.1%	8.9%	10.4%	10.1%	9.5%	8.9%	8.3%
Other operating expense (income)	13	–2	20	0	0	0	0
EBIT	223	266	196	236	272	310	352
EBIT margin	19.8%	23.6%	19.1%	23.3%	24.8%	26.2%	27.6%

Sources: Based on information from Rémy Cointreau Group and authors' analysis.

6.5. Operating Profit by Segment

In this section, we alternatively estimate operating profit and margin using a segment approach. Rémy discloses current operating profit for each of its segments as well as an operating cost at the corporate or holding company level. Recall that current operating profit is a non-IFRS measure that excludes certain items. These certain items are disclosed on Rémy's income statement as "Other operating expense (income)." Therefore, the sum of the segment current operating profit equals consolidated EBIT before other operating expense (income).

For the Cognac segment, the forecast of higher revenue growth, based partially on strong price/mix growth, assumes an improving product mix that will also result in a higher gross margin. But the benefit to gross margin will be somewhat mitigated by higher distribution costs. Thus, the expectation is that the Cognac segment's operating margin will increase to 33.4% by FY2024. As a benchmark, this forecast can be compared with the financial results reported by Hennessy (part of LVMH), another cognac brand. That company's operating margin in its Wine & Spirits segment in FY2017–2019 was 30%–32%, though that business has a significantly higher mix of lower-priced products with lower gross margins.

For the other segments, there is not much upside. In the Liqueurs & Spirits division, we assume operating margin to increase modestly to 13.6%. In total, Rémy Cointreau Group's consolidated operating margin is forecast to improve from 23.4% in FY2021 to 27.6% in FY2024, largely because of growth and margin improvement in the Cognac segment, the most profitable division, and leverage from that sales growth on corporate-level costs.

While a segment approach like Exhibit 23 can be used instead of a consolidated approach to forecasting revenue and operating profit, it is also commonly used as a "check" on the consolidated forecasts. This analysis revealed, for example, that the model relies significantly on margin improvement in the Cognac segment.

EXHIBIT 23: Historical and Projected Operating Profit by Segment for Rémy Cointreau Group

	FY2018	FY2019	FY2020	FY2021	FY2022E	FY2023E	FY2024E
Revenue (€ mlns)							
Cognac	760	774	736	735	818	902	994
Liqueurs & Spirits	267	264	262	248	251	253	256
Partner Brands	100	87	28	27	26	26	26
Total revenues	1,127	1,126	1,025	1,010	1,095	1,181	1,275
Current Operating Profit (€ mlns)							
Cognac	204	236	200	221	255	291	332
Liqueurs & Spirits	43	39	38	33	34	34	35
Partner Brands	5	5	−2	−1	−1	−1	−1
Holding/Corporate-level costs	−16	−15	−20	−17	−16	−15	−14
Total current operating profit	237	264	215	236	271	309	352
Current Operating Profit Margins							
Cognac	26.9%	30.4%	27.1%	30.1%	31.2%	32.3%	33.4%
Liqueurs & Spirits	16.0%	14.7%	14.3%	13.3%	13.4%	13.5%	13.6%
Partner Brands	5.3%	5.6%	−6.2%	−3.0%	−3.0%	−3.0%	−3.0%
Holding/Corporate-level costs	−1.4%	−1.3%	−2.0%	−1.7%	−1.5%	−1.3%	−1.1%
Total current operating profit	21.0%	23.5%	21.0%	23.4%	24.8%	26.2%	27.6%

Sources: Based on information from Rémy Cointreau Group and authors' analysis.

6.6. Non-Operating Items

Three types of non-operating line items are included in the model: finance expenses (i.e., interest expenses), income taxes, and shares outstanding.

Net finance cost on Rémy's income statement is interest expense on debt less interest income earned on cash and investments. Forecasting net finance cost, therefore, requires estimating the debt and cash positions and interest rates paid and earned.

Companies pay a fixed or variable interest rate on debt. If the interest rate is variable, the rate is typically determined by a market reference rate plus a credit spread. As shown in Exhibit 24, Rémy's interest expenses are fixed and calculated as 1.7% incurred on gross debt at the beginning of the period (EUR720 million at end of FY2020). Other financial expenses are assumed to be zero. Gross debt and the interest rate paid on it are estimated to remain flat from the year ended FY2021 level

Although interest income is typically forecasted after forecasting the cash position from the forecasted statement of cash flows, in this case we have simply estimated EUR0 in interest income through the model period; in each of FY2018–FY2021, annual interest income was EUR0, EUR0, EUR0.1, and EUR0.2 million, respectively, because Rémy maintains its liquidity in assets with zero or very low yields. For companies that own liquid assets with higher interest rates, or in higher interest rate environments, interest income should be forecast in the same manner as interest expense: forecasted cash and investments multiplied by a forecasted interest rate.

EXHIBIT 24: Debt Position and Financial Costs and Income for Rémy (€ millions, unless noted)

	FY2018	FY2019	FY2020	FY2021	FY2022E	FY2023E	FY2024E
Long-term financial debt	397	424	452	424	424	424	424
Short-term financial debt and ac-crued interest	73	98	268	92	92	92	92
Gross debt	470	522	720	515	515	515	515
Interest expense	14.5	13.7	12.9	12.1	8.7	8.7	8.7
Interest rate (on beginning balance)		2.9%	2.5%	1.7%	1.7%	1.7%	1.7%
Interest income	0.0	0.0	0.1	0.2	0.0	0.0	0.0
Net finance cost	14.5	13.7	12.8	11.9	8.7	8.7	8.7

Sources: Based on information from Rémy Cointreau Group and authors' analysis.

6.7. Corporate Income Tax Forecast

The French statutory tax rate at the time of analysis is 32%. Rémy Cointreau Group's effective tax rate has, over the longer run, been close to the statutory rate. Therefore, an estimated 32% effective tax rate is used in the forecast period. Rémy has no material minority interests in any of its subsidiaries.

6.8. Shares Outstanding

Shares outstanding to compute earnings per share (EPS) on the income statement are disclosed in two ways, both weighted averages throughout the fiscal year: basic and diluted.

Basic shares outstanding includes common equity securities outstanding, while diluted shares outstanding is a type of what-if analysis; it is basic shares outstanding plus the number of shares from the exercise or conversion of in-the-money instruments, less an assumed repurchase of those if-issued shares.

Typically, the two major factors that affect shares outstanding over time are share issuance related to equity-based compensation of employees (increases shares outstanding) and share repurchases (decreases shares outstanding). Less common but sometimes significant transactions that also affect shares outstanding include acquisitions financed with stock, secondary issuance, and conversions of preferred stock or other instruments to common stock.

Exhibit 25 shows beginning and ending basic shares outstanding for the past six fiscal years as well as the annual net amount of share repurchases and issuance, which were gathered from the statements of stockholders' equity and notes to financial statements. Additionally, the basic and diluted shares outstanding on the income statement used to calculate basic and diluted EPS (weighted averages) are shown and differed by approximately 2.6 million shares in each of the past five years.

EXHIBIT 25: Shares Outstanding for Rémy (€ millions, unless noted)

	FY2016	FY2017	FY2018	FY2019	FY2020	FY2021
Beginning basic shares outstanding	48.6	48.6	49.6	50.0	49.8	49.8
Share repurchases	−0.0	0.0	−0.3	−1.0	−0.0	0.0
Share issuance	0.0	1.0	0.7	0.8	0.1	0.4
Ending basic shares outstanding	48.6	49.6	50.0	49.8	49.8	50.3
Weighted average basic shares	48.6	49.1	49.8	50.1	49.8	50.1
Dilutive securities	0.1	2.7	2.6	2.6	2.6	2.6
Weighted average diluted shares	48.7	51.8	52.4	52.7	52.4	53.1

As evident in Exhibit 25, shares outstanding for Rémy have not changed materially in six years because the company does not pay significant share-based compensation nor has it repurchased shares. Additionally, management has not disclosed an intention to repurchase shares in the near term. Therefore, the model assumes that weighted average basic and diluted shares outstanding on the income statement remain flat at the FY2021 level.

6.9. Pro Forma Income Statement

Now with the forecast components in place, a consolidated pro forma income statement can be constructed, as shown in Exhibit 26. Although not presented on the face of the income statement as disclosed by the company, the calculation of EBITDA is shown after EBIT by adding depreciation and amortization expense from the statement of cash flows. It is not linked to other quantities on the income statement but merely shown as a useful profitability measure.

EXHIBIT 26: Consolidated Historical and Projected Income Statement for Rémy Cointreau Group (€ millions, unless noted)

	FY2018	FY2019	FY2020	FY2021	FY2022E	FY2023E	FY2024E
Sales	1,127	1,126	1,025	1,010	1,095	1,181	1,275
Cost of sales	366	415	348	330	347	362	379
Gross profit	761	711	677	680	748	819	897
Gross margin	67.5%	63.1%	66.1%	67.3%	68.3%	69.3%	70.3%
Change in gross margin	0.8%	−4.4%	2.9%	1.3%	1.0%	1.0%	1.0%
Distribution costs	433	346	355	342	373	404	439
Distribution costs as % of sales	38.4%	30.7%	34.6%	33.8%	34.0%	34.2%	34.4%
Administrative expenses	92	101	107	103	104	105	106
Administrative expenses as % of sales	8.1%	8.9%	10.4%	10.1%	9.5%	8.9%	8.3%
Other operating expense (income)	13	−2	20	0	0	0	0
EBIT	223	266	196	236	272	310	352
EBIT margin	19.8%	23.6%	19.1%	23.3%	24.8%	26.2%	27.6%
Depreciation and amortization (add-back)	22	30	33	34			
Depreciation and amortization as % of sales	1.9%	2.7%	3.3%	3.4%			
EBITDA	245	296	229	270			
EBITDA margin	21.7%	26.3%	22.3%	26.7%			
Net finance costs	15	14	13	12	9	9	9
Other financial expenses	8	19	15	3	0	0	0
Total financial expenses	22	33	28	15	9	9	9
Profit before tax	201	233	167	221	263	301	344
Income tax	54	68	61	78	84	96	110

	FY2018	FY2019	FY2020	FY2021	FY2022E	FY2023E	FY2024E
Effective tax rate	26.6%	29.0%	36.4%	35.1%	32.0%	32.0%	32.0%
Income from associates	1	−7	0	1	0	0	0
Profit from continuing operations	148	159	107	144	179	205	234
Profit from discontinued operations	0	0	6	0	0	0	0
Net profit for the year	148	159	113	144	179	205	234
YoY%		8%	−29%	27%	24%	14%	14%
EPS basic continuing operations	2.97	3.18	2.14	2.88	3.58	4.09	4.67
EPS diluted continuing operations	2.82	3.02	2.04	2.74	3.40	3.89	4.44
EPS basic total	2.97	3.18	2.27	2.88	3.58	4.09	4.67
EPS diluted total	2.82	3.02	2.16	2.74	3.40	3.89	4.44
Average number of shares, basic, mlns	49.8	50.1	49.8	50.1	50.1	50.1	50.1
Average number of shares, diluted, mlns	52.4	52.7	52.4	52.6	52.6	52.6	52.6

6.10. Pro Forma Statement of Cash Flows

The forecast statements of cash flows begin with forecasted net income and other amounts from the forecast income statement, and then typically require estimates for capital expenditures, depreciation and amortization, working capital, share-based compensation, dividends, and share repurchases. Once the forecasted income statements and statements of cash flows are completed, forecasting the balance sheet is largely a matter of properly linking the spreadsheet, as illustrated in Exhibit 27.

EXHIBIT 27: Statement of Cash Flows Projection Process

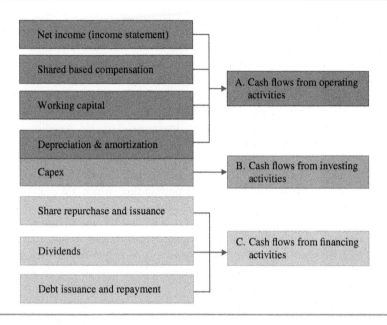

6.11. Capital Investments and Depreciation Forecasts

Capital investment, or capex, as a percentage of revenue was 5.3% in FY2021. Given the healthy volume growth prospects, we expect capex to remain at a modestly above historical average level of 5.0% of sales through FY2024. With Rémy's growing fixed asset base, it is logical that depreciation will increase. The model assumes that depreciation and amortization (D&A) is equal to 4.2% of prior year fixed assets, the average of the past three years. The breakdowns of capex and D&A are shown in Exhibit 28.

EXHIBIT 28: Capex, D&A Breakdowns

	2018	2019	2020	2021	2022E	2023E	2024E
D&A (€ millions)	22	30	33	34	36	36	37
As % of prior year fixed assets		4.0%	4.3%	4.2%	4.2%	4.2%	4.2%
Capex, PP&E and Intangibles (€ millions)	34	45	65	54	55	59	64
Capex as % of sales	3.0%	4.0%	6.3%	5.3%	5.0%	5.0%	5.0%
Capex/D&A ratio	1.6	1.5	1.9	1.6	1.5	1.6	1.7

Sources: Based on information from Rémy Cointreau Group and authors' analysis.

6.12. Working Capital Forecasts

We have assumed that working capital ratios will remain similar to what the company experienced in the FY2018–21 period. In Exhibit 29, we include only the relevant balance sheet items related to revenues and costs (i.e., inventories, accounts receivable, and accounts payable) and keep the other items constant. Rémy Cointreau Group had positive net working capital of 105% of its sales in fiscal year 2021. The largest working capital component is inventory because much of Rémy's cognac requires years of aging. Inventory days on hand in FY2021 was 1,493, which reflects an approximate 300-day increase owing to the volume slowdown during the COVID-19 pandemic. Inventory days are partially mitigated by extended payment terms to suppliers; days payable outstanding has averaged around 500 days since FY2018.

We model the working capital accounts by projecting working capital ratios (days of inventory, days sales outstanding, days payable outstanding) which are combined with the sales and cost of sales forecast to produce projected working capital accounts on the balance sheet. We expect inventory days to decline through FY2024 as the inventory increase that occurred during the COVID-19 pandemic is worked through, expect days sales outstanding to remain at FY2021 levels, and model days payable outstanding to decline back to an average level, again reflecting a normalization after the COVID-19 pandemic. As a result of the decrease in inventory days, the model projects a net positive contribution from working capital to the reconciliation of net income to cash flows from operations on the statement of cash flows, which is in stark contrast to prior years' negative contribution.

EXHIBIT 29: Working Capital Development for Rémy

	FY2018	FY2019	FY2020	FY2021	FY2022E	FY2023E	FY2024E
Inventories (€ millions)	1,170	1,246	1,364	1,493	1,426	1,340	1,245
Accounts receivable	210	271	199	158	171	185	200
Accounts payable	517	544	534	586	597	604	610
Working capital, net	863	973	1,029	1,065	1,000	922	835
% of sales	77%	86%	100%	105%	91%	78%	65%
Change in working capital		−110	−56	−36	64	79	87
Days inventories on hand	1,166	1,095	1,431	1,650	1,500	1,350	1,200
Days sales outstanding	68	88	71	57	57	57	57
Days payable outstanding	515	478	561	648	628	608	588

Sources: Based on information from Rémy Cointreau Group and authors' analysis.

6.13. Forecasted Cash Flow Statement

With net income, D&A, change in working capital, capex, and debt estimates already in place, the cash flow statement, shown in Exhibit 30 is almost automatically generated by linking the relevant lines on a spreadsheet. The three significant items left to forecast are share-based compensation, share repurchases or issuance, and dividends. Going forward, the model assumes flat share-based compensation, no share repurchases or issuance, and dividends paid equal to the FY2021 level through FY2024. Lines labeled "other" are aggregated and zeroed out going forward because they are immaterial, difficult to forecast, or both.

EXHIBIT 30: Projected Statement of Cash Flows for Rémy (€ millions)

	FY2018	FY2019	FY2020	FY2021	FY2022E	FY2023E	FY2024E
Net income (loss)	148	159	113	144	179	205	234
D&A	22	30	33	34	36	36	37
Share-based compensation	3	3	4	2	2	2	2
Investment in working capital	–7	–162	–72	–13	64	79	87
Other non-cash amounts	20	22	3	10	0	0	0
Cash flows from operations	185	53	81	177	281	322	360
Capex (PP&E and intangibles)	–34	–45	–65	–54	–55	–59	–64
Other investing activities	2	92	12	62	0	0	0
Cash flows from investments	–32	47	–53	8	–55	–59	–64
Debt issuance (repayment)	0	11	196	–246	0	0	0
Share issuance (repurchases)	–27	–104	–2	2	0	0	0
Dividends paid	–25	–9	–132	–10	–10	–10	–10
Cash flows from financing	–52	–102	62	–253	–10	–10	–10
FX translation effects	8	–6	1	–1	0	0	0
Net change in cash	109	–8	91	–68	217	254	287
Cash and equivalents, beginning	78	187	179	269	201	418	671
Cash and equivalents, end	187	179	269	201	418	671	958

Note: Apparent small discrepancies in addition reflect the effects of rounding error.
Sources: Based on information from Rémy Cointreau Group and authors' analysis.

6.14. Forecasted Balance Sheet

The forecasted balance sheet is given in Exhibit 31 and is based on the combination of the projected income statement (Exhibit 26), the projected statement of cash flows (Exhibit 30), and the historical starting balance sheet. The balance sheet items that were not specifically discussed are held constant, which preserves the accounting identity. For ease of presentation, the stockholders' equity lines (e.g., common stock, additional paid in capital, retained earnings, treasury shares, accumulated other comprehensive income) are aggregated. For each forecast period, common stockholders' equity is the prior year value plus net income and share-based compensation less dividends.

If each of the discussed lines is linked properly—and other lines are held constant from FY2021—the forecasted balance sheet should balance each year. Consult the Rémy worksheet in the downloadable Microsoft Excel workbook for greater detail.

EXHIBIT 31: Projected Balance Sheet for Rémy (€ millions)

	FY2018	FY2019	FY2020	FY2021	FY2022E	FY2023E	FY2024E
Cash and equivalents	186.8	178.6	269.4	201.0	418	671	958
Accounts receivable	210	271	199	158	171	185	200
Inventories	1,170	1,246	1,364	1,493	1,426	1,340	1,245
Other current assets	16	5	16	10	10	10	10
Total current assets	1,583	1,700	1,848	1,861	2,025	2,206	2,412
PP&E, intangibles, goodwill, net	752	785	808	845	864	887	913
Investment in associates	20	1	1	2	2	2	2
Other non-current assets	186	139	131	73	73	73	73
Total assets	2,542	2,625	2,789	2,781	2,964	3,168	3,400
Short-term/current debt	73	98	268	92	92	92	92
Accounts payable	517	544	534	586	597	604	610
Other current liabilities and accrued expenses	26	31	39	42	42	42	42
Total current liabilities	616	673	842	720	731	737	744
Long-term/non-current debt	397	424	452	424	424	424	424
Other non-current liabilities	121	102	92	88	88	88	88
Total common equity	1,407	1,425	1,403	1,548	1,720	1,918	2,144
NCI	1	1	1	1	1	1	1
Total equity and liabilities	2,542	2,625	2,789	2,781	2,964	3,168	3,400

Sources: Based on information from Rémy Cointreau Group and authors' analysis.

6.15. Valuation Model Inputs

In the previous sections, we have built a model that projects the income statement, cash flow statement, and balance sheet for Rémy Cointreau Group. This model is the starting point for most valuation models. Valuation estimates can be made based on a variety of metrics, including free cash flow, EPS, EBITDA, and EBIT. The company-specific inputs needed to build a discounted cash flow (DCF) to the firm model (to estimate enterprise value) are shown in Exhibit 32. All the variables are sourced from the forecasted income statements and statements of cash flows.

EXHIBIT 32: Calculating Free Cash Flow to the Firm as Basis for a DCF Valuation Model (€ millions)

	FY2021	FY2022E	FY2023E	FY2024E
EBIT	236	272	310	352
Taxes (32% tax rate)	−75	−87	−99	−113
After-tax EBIT	160	185	211	240
D&A	34	36	36	37
Change in working capital	−13	64	79	87
Capital expenditures	−54	−55	−59	−64
Free cash flow to the firm	127	230	267	300

Source: Based on the authors' analysis.

7. BEHAVIORAL FINANCE AND ANALYST FORECASTS

Studies have shown that experts in many fields persistently make forecasting errors arising from behavioral biases, and investment analysts' models of financial statements are in no way immune. To improve forecasts and the investment decisions based on them, analysts must be aware of the impact of biases and potential remedies for them. Five key behavioral biases that influence analyst forecasts are overconfidence, illusion of control, conservatism, representativeness, and confirmation bias.

7.1. Overconfidence in Forecasting

Overconfidence bias is a bias in which people demonstrate unwarranted faith in their own abilities. Studies have identified that 90 percent *confidence intervals* for forecasts, which should leave only 10% error rates, turn out to be wrong as much as 40% of the time (Russo and Schoemaker 1992). Studies have also suggested that individuals are more confident when making contrarian predictions that counter the consensus. That is, overconfidence arises more frequently when forecasting what others do not expect (Dunning, Griffin, Milojkovic, and Ross 1990).

To mitigate overconfidence bias, analysts should record and share their forecasts and review them regularly, identifying *both* the correct and incorrect forecasts they have made. Given the wide range of outcomes for most financial variables, an analyst will likely find that they have been wrong as much as or more often than they have been right. The goal is to recognize that forecast error rates are high, so mitigating actions that widen the confidence interval of forecasts should be taken. One such action is **scenario analysis**. By asking, "Where could I be wrong and by how much?," an analyst can generate different forecast scenarios.

EXAMPLE 11   Mitigating Overconfidence: Scenario Analysis for Rémy

In the earlier sections, a financial statement model was constructed for Rémy Cointreau Group that includes only one set of forecasted numbers, or one scenario. Creating several more scenarios is an important modeling step because the range of outcomes for the most important variable is wider than a single point.

Three important variables in the forecast of free cash flow are organic sales growth in the Cognac segment, EBIT margin, and net working capital as a percentage of sales. A benefit of the spreadsheet-driven model is that the forecasts can be easily modified to calculate different free cash flow estimates. The base case inputs and forecast for 2024E free cash flow to the firm, as well as figures for two different scenarios, are shown in Exhibit 33.

Alternative Scenario 1 assumes that the Cognac segment's organic growth remains the same as its FY2021 rate, an EBIT margin of 23.6%, where it was before the COVID-19 pandemic, and working capital of 86% of sales, also the pre-pandemic level from FY2019. Alternative Scenario 2 assumes the same Cognac segment organic growth rate as the base case but an EBIT margin of 25.0% and working capital of 90% of sales. This scenario reflects strong growth but a high level of reinvestment in sales and marketing costs and aged cognac inventory to support that growth.

As Exhibit 33 demonstrates, there is a wide range of free cash flow estimates for 2022E–2024E because of a wide range of reasonable inputs for key variables.

EXHIBIT 33: Calculating Free Cash Flow to the Firm as Basis for a DCF Valuation Model (€ millions)

	2022E	2023E	2024E
Base Case			
Cognac segment organic growth	11.3%	10.2%	10.2%
EBIT margin	24.8%	26.2%	27.6%
Working capital as % of sales	91%	78%	65%
Free cash flow to the firm est.	230	267	300
Alternative Scenario 1			
Cognac segment organic growth	4.0%	4.0%	4.0%
EBIT margin	23.6%	23.6%	23.6%
Working capital as % of sales	86%	86%	86%
Free cash flow to the firm est.	318	133	129
Alternative Scenario 2			
Cognac segment organic growth	11.3%	10.2%	10.2%
EBIT margin	25.0%	25.0%	25.0%
Working capital as % of sales	90%	90%	90%
Free cash flow to the firm est.	240	109	105

7.2. Illusion of Control

A bias often linked to overconfidence, illusion of control is a tendency to overestimate the ability to control what cannot be controlled and to take ultimately fruitless actions in pursuit of control. This bias often manifests in analysts' beliefs that forecasts can be rendered more accurate in two ways: by acquiring more information and opinions from experts and by creating more granular and complex models. Although additional information and complexity in model specification can improve forecasting accuracy, there are diminishing marginal returns. The amount of material information available for an investment is finite, and adding immaterial information will mislead. Complex models tend to be overfitted to historical data sets, which do not prove robust in a range of environments that include never-before-seen outliers. Excessive breadth of data and model complexity can also conceal assumptions and make updating forecasts upon the receipt of new information difficult. Finally, analysts face significant opportunity costs; additional hours modeling one company could mean that the analyst will examine fewer opportunities in total.

Beyond awareness of the bias and the recognition that uncertainty is an inherent characteristic in investments, illusion of control can be mitigated by restricting modeling variables to those that are regularly disclosed by the company, focusing on the most important or impactful variables, and speaking only with those who are likely to have unique or significant perspectives.

EXAMPLE 12   Illusion of Control: How Much Model Complexity?

Rémy Cointreau Group regularly reports revenues by segment and by geographic region (Europe/Middle East/Africa, the Americas, and Asia Pacific). It does not disclose segment revenue by geographic region (e.g., the Cognac segment revenue in the Asia Pacific region), nor does it disclose revenue by sales channel, such as retailers versus bars and restaurants, travel retail, and so on. In its quarterly earnings calls, however, the company often makes numerous references to segment growth rates in specific regions and growth rates of specific channels, even though the actual numbers are not disclosed. Such a practice is common, especially during the COVID-19 pandemic because large sales channel shifts occurred: travel retail in most regions experienced declines >90%, sales shifted from bars and restaurants to retailers for at-home consumption, and different geographies were affected by the pandemic at different times.

An analyst might be tempted to collect all these growth rates and other anecdotal figures that management discloses on its earnings calls and, perhaps by combining them with third-party estimates of sales, build an extensive revenue model for Rémy in which each segment is broken out into geographic regions and sales channels.

Although such an endeavor might be useful to set expectations and to monitor over time, building the revenue forecast in this way would introduce several problems and probably not materially improve accuracy. First, because the data used in the model are not regularly disclosed, there is no way to check actuals versus estimates. Second, model construction would take dozens of hours. Finally, and perhaps most importantly, whether the constituent small parts of such a model would be accurate is unclear, which would not make the consolidated revenue forecast any more accurate than a simpler model.

7.3. Conservatism Bias

Conservatism bias is a bias in which people maintain their prior views or forecasts by inadequately incorporating new information. This often happens in forecasting when an analyst does not update their forecasting after receiving conflicting information, such as disappointing earnings results or a competitor action. Although the most common form of conservatism is the reluctance to incorporate new negative information into a forecast, analysts could also fail to adequately incorporate positive information and thus have estimates that are too low. A different name for conservatism bias in this context is anchoring and adjustment, referring to an analyst using their prior estimates as an "anchor" that is subsequently adjusted. Although nothing is wrong with modifying a previous forecast, the previous forecast or anchor tends to exert significant influence; in other words, the adjustment is too small, and the updated forecast is too close to the previous forecast.

Conservatism bias can be mitigated by reviews of forecasts and models by an investment team at a regular interval, such as each quarter, and by creating flexible models with fewer variables, to make changing assumptions easier. Because conservatism bias is related to overconfidence and illusion of control, mitigating those biases can also serve to mitigate conservatism.

EXAMPLE 13   Conservatism Bias: Rémy Management Guidance for FY 2022

The base case forecasts in the Rémy Cointreau Group model call for organic revenue growth of 11.3% and net income growth of 24% in FY2022E over FY2021. However, during the earnings call for the fourth quarter of FY2021, Rémy management gave the following guidance for FY2022:

- "Fiscal year 2022 will be a strong year of growth and investment, and we are on track to achieve our 2030 [objectives of a 72% gross margin and 33% operating margin]."
- "Being ahead of [our] 2030 strategic plan and given the favorable environment, [we] have decided to revise up [our] strategic investments [in sales and marketing] to support brands through the recovery and boost their medium-term growth potential by developing brand awareness and attractiveness."
- Fiscal year 2022 will have "top-line and bottom-line growth in the mid-teens in organic terms."

Based on these comments, your colleague suggests revising the Rémy model slightly by reducing the operating margin forecast to reduce net income growth from 24% to 20%.

1. What behavioral bias does your colleague's suggestion exhibit, and what research or steps should be taken, if any, with respect to revising the Rémy model? Explain your answer.

Solution to 1:

Your colleague is exhibiting conservatism bias, or anchoring and adjustment; they are anchored to the prior forecast of 24% net income growth and not fully considering management's guidance on profitability.

Changing the model to follow the guidance without further consideration is not necessarily appropriate because results can and often do under- or outperform guidance. However, in this case, management guidance differs quite significantly from the FY2022E forecast on both sales growth and net income growth. As a first step, management's credibility should be assessed by examining the company's performance against management guidance in the past. Second, the guidance should be considered as a scenario in the scenario analysis, and the investment implications of that scenario should be examined; for example, if the company will in fact increase sales and profits at a mid-teens rate in FY2022, does that result in an investment decision? Finally, the performance of, and guidance provided by, other alcohol and spirits companies should be compared to these figures as a check for reasonableness.

7.4. Representativeness Bias

Representativeness bias refers to the tendency to classify information based on past experiences and known classifications. New information might resemble or seem representative of familiar elements already classified, but can in fact be very different and is better viewed from a different perspective. In these instances, the classification reflex can deceive, producing an incorrect understanding that biases all future thinking about the information. Base-rate neglect is a common form of representativeness bias in forecasting. In base-rate neglect, a phenomenon's rate of incidence in a larger population, or characteristics of a larger class to which a specific member belongs—its base rate—is neglected in favor of situation- or member-specific information. Considering the base rate is sometimes known as the "outside view," while the situation-specific is known as the "inside view."

For example, an analyst is modeling operating costs and margins for a biopharmaceutical company. The "inside view" approach would consider company-specific factors such as the types of drugs the company sells, the number of salespeople needed in each geography for each drug, and so on. The "outside view" approach would view the company as a member of the "biopharmaceuticals" industry, of which there are many others, and use industry or sector averages for gross margin, R&D expense as percentage of sales, and so on in the model.

Neither the outside nor inside view is superior; what makes for a superior forecast is considering both. One way of doing so is by starting with the base rate but determining which factors make the target company different from the base rate or class average and what the implications of those differences are, if any. For example, the analyst modeling the biopharmaceuticals company might start with industry averages in the model but change some of the variables to account for factors such as royalties versus product sales revenues, geographic composition of revenues, and whether the company is likely to face patent expirations on its products over the forecast period.

EXAMPLE 14 Considering Base Rates for Rémy

While constructing the Rémy model in the earlier section, little attention was given to comparable companies or to the broader industry to which Rémy belongs. In other words, the model was constructed primarily with the "inside view." In this example,

Rémy is put in the context of six other spirits-focused alcohol companies: Brown-Forman Corporation, Pernod Ricard SA, Davide Campari-Milano N.V., Diageo plc, Becle S.A.B de C.V. (Cuervo), and the Wine & Spirits segment of LVMH (LVMH W&S) for the last five most recently reported fiscal years at the time of analysis. The variable used for the industry comparison is the five-year average of EBIT margin because it is a key model input, and the profitability of an individual company is strongly influenced by industry profitability. Many of these peer companies are significantly larger by revenue than Rémy, which is useful because we have modeled Rémy becoming larger over time. The analysis for Exhibit 34 is included in the Exhibit34 worksheet in the downloadable Microsoft Excel workbook.

EXHIBIT 34: EBIT Margin Comparison of Spirits Companies, Last Five Reported Fiscal Years (€ millions)

| | EBIT margin | | | | |
	MRY-4	MRY-3	MRY-2	MRY-1	Most Recent Year (MRY)
Rémy	20%	20%	24%	19%	23%
Brown Forman	34%	32%	34%	32%	34%
Pernod	24%	25%	26%	26%	12%
Campari	22%	26%	25%	25%	17%
Diageo	27%	30%	30%	31%	18%
Cuervo	23%	26%	20%	18%	20%
LVMH W&S	31%	31%	32%	31%	29%
Peer average (ex Rémy)	27%	28%	28%	27%	22%
Peer five-year average (ex Rémy)	26%				

1. Evaluate the base case forecasts in the Rémy model as well as Rémy's management's FY2030 objective of a 33% operating margin considering the analysis in Exhibit 34.

Solution to 1:

The base case forecasts in the Rémy model are for EBIT margins of 24.8%, 26.2%, and 27.6% in FY2022E, FY2023E, and FY2024E, respectively. The most recently reported fiscal year(s) for most of the peer companies include the effect of deleveraging from sales declines associated with the COVID-19 pandemic. Aside from that, the base case forecasts are close to the peer average and by that measure appear reasonable, though they are substantially higher than the past five years of profitability for Rémy itself.

Rémy management's objective of 33% operating margin in 2030 appears high relative to those of its peers; only one company, Brown Forman, has achieved that level of profitability, on annual revenues ~3.0x that of Rémy. Industry-leading growth and profitability of Rémy's Cognac segment will be required to meet this objective.

7.5. Confirmation Bias

Confirmation bias is the tendency to look for and notice what confirms prior beliefs and to ignore or undervalue whatever contradicts them. A common manifestation of this bias among investment analysts is to structure the research process in pursuit of only positive news or certain criteria, or with a narrow scope. For example, an analyst might research a particular company but conduct only cursory research on its competitors and companies that offer substitute products. An analyst who has a positive view on a company might speak only to other analysts who share that view and the company's management, all of whom will likely tell the analyst what they want to hear and already know. Confirmation bias is closely related to overconfidence and representativeness biases.

The extent to which company management can be excessively optimistic is shown in Exhibit 35, which analyzes the annual report of a major European bank for 2007, published mere months before it entered bankruptcy and was nationalized.

Speaking with management is valuable given their role and should not be excluded from the research process, but analysts must be aware of management's inherent bias and seek differing perspectives, especially when examining a company with significant controversy. Two approaches to mitigating confirmation bias in the forecasting process are to speak to or read research from analysts with a negative opinion on the security under scrutiny and to seek perspectives from colleagues who are not economically or psychologically invested in the subject security.

EXHIBIT 35: Management Optimism

Consider this text analysis of the chairman's statement and business review in the 2007 annual report of a major European bank published in 2008, a few months before the bank was rescued by the government.

	Occurrences of		
Negative words		Positive words	
Disappoint/disappointed	0	Good	55
Bad/badly	0	Excellent	12
Poor	0	Success/successful	35
Weaker/weakening	7	Improvement	23
Slowdown	6	Strong/stronger/strongly	78

Source: Royal Bank of Scotland plc, Annual Report and Accounts 2007, SVM Analysis.

8. THE IMPACT OF COMPETITIVE FACTORS IN PRICES AND COSTS

One of the tools that analysts can use to think about how competition will affect financial results is Michael Porter's widely used "five forces" framework (see Porter 1980). The framework identifies five forces that affect the intensity of a company's competitive environment and thus cost and price projections. These forces include the following: threat of substitute products, intensity of rivalry among incumbent companies, bargaining power of suppliers, bargaining power of customers, and threat of new entrants.

The first force is the threat of substitute products. If numerous substitutes exist and switching costs are low, companies have limited pricing power. Conversely, if few substitutes exist and/or switching costs are high, companies have greater pricing power.

The second force is the intensity of rivalry among incumbent companies. Pricing power is limited in industries that are fragmented and that have limited growth, high exit barriers, high fixed costs, and basically identical product offerings.

The third force is the bargaining power of suppliers. Companies (and overall industries) whose suppliers have greater ability to increase prices and/or limit the quality and quantity of inputs face downward pressure on profitability. Suppliers' bargaining power is generally a function of relative size, the relative importance the supplier places on a particular product, and the availability of alternatives.

The fourth force is the bargaining power of customers. Companies (and overall industries) whose customers have greater ability to demand lower prices and/or control the quality and quantity of end products face downward pressure on profitability. Buyer power is the reverse of supplier power. Bargaining power of customers is generally lower in markets with a fragmented customer base, a non-standardized product, and high switching costs for the customer.

The fifth force is the threat of new entrants. Companies in industries in which the threat of new entrants is high because of the presence of above-market returns face downward pressure on profitability. In contrast, if there are barriers to entry, it could be costly for new competitors to enter a market. It is easier for incumbents to raise prices and defend their market position when barriers to entry are high.

8.1. Cognac Industry Overview

This industry overview will focus on the cognac industry because it is Rémy Cointreau Group's most important business segment, accounting for over 90% of total operating profit. (In practice, an analyst would also perform a similar industry analysis for the company's other major segments.) An important feature of the cognac market is that supply is limited and demand is growing. Supply is limited because the production of cognac, like that of champagne, is highly regulated, in this case through the Bureau National Interprofessionnel du Cognac. By regulation, cognac can be produced only in a limited geographic area, in and around the town of Cognac in southwest France. Furthermore, within the region, production volume is capped each year. Approximately 98% of production is exported. The cognac market is highly concentrated, with the top four players controlling 78% of world volume and 84% of global value. Rémy's market share is approximately 16% and 18% of global volume and value, respectively (*The Spirits Business*, June 2018). Demand for cognac has been growing because of increasing demand from Asia, particularly China and Singapore, more than offsetting a weakening European market. The global spirits market has grown more than 5% annually during the 2000–17 period (*Source:* IWSR drinks market analysis). Simultaneously, Rémy has also seen a product mix improvement because consumers increasingly prefer superior quality and more expensive cognac. Exhibit 36 summarizes Porter's five forces analysis of the cognac industry.

EXHIBIT 36: Porter's Five Forces Analysis of the Cognac Industry

Force	Degree	Factors to Consider
Threat of substitutes	Low	• Cognac consumers show brand loyalty and do not easily shift to other beverages or high-end spirits.
Rivalry	Low	• The market is consolidated, with four players controlling 78% of the world market in volume and 84% of global value. • Only the European market is fragmented, with less than half of the market controlled by the top four.
Bargaining power of suppliers	Low/ medium	• A large number of small independent vineyards supply inputs. • Most of the distillation is carried out by a large body of independent distillers that sell to the big houses.
Bargaining power of buyers	Low	• Premium beverages are sold primarily to wine and spirits retail outlets that do not coordinate purchasing. • Premium beverages are consumed primarily in small and fragmented on-premises outlets (restaurants, etc.).

Threat of new entrants	Low	• Producers have long-term contracts with suppliers in the Cognac area.
		• Barriers to entry are high.
		  o Building brands is difficult because they must have heritage/pedigree.
		  o A large capital investment is required to build an inventory with "aged" cognac and set up a distribution network.

In summary, the cognac market, Rémy's largest and most profitable operating segment, exhibits a favorable profitability profile. In addition to limited supply and growing demand, the industry faces a generally favorable situation with respect to substitutes, rivalry, suppliers, buyers, and potential new entrants.

Analysis of Anheuser-Busch InBev Using Porter's Five Forces

The competitive structure a company faces can vary among countries, with implications for modeling revenue growth, profit margins, capital expenditures, and return on investments. For example, Anheuser-Busch (AB) InBev, the largest global brewer, operates in many countries, two of which are the United Kingdom and Brazil, the world's third largest beer market. AB InBev's competitive position and prospects in the highly consolidated and growing Brazilian market are much more favorable than in the fragmented and declining UK market.

The Brazilian beer market is divided among four players. AmBev (AB InBev's subsidiary in Brazil, of which it owns a 61.9% stake) is the dominant brewer with an estimated 65% market share in 2018 versus 20% for Heineken and 12% for Petropolis, Brazil's largest privately owned brewing group. Helped by its dominant market position and strong distribution network, AmBev was able to report an EBITDA margin of nearly 50.4% in 2018 (ri.ambev.com.br), the highest in the global beer industry. The industry participants focus less on price competition and more on expanding distribution and "premiumization" (i.e., selling more expensive beers.) Although the

2015–18 time period saw challenging trading conditions due to subdued consumer demand, causing years of decline in the market by volume, Brazil is still considered a promising market. In this environment, an analyst would likely forecast solid revenue growth for AmBev. Exhibit 37 presents an analysis of the Brazilian beer market using Porter's five forces framework. Most of the competitive forces represent a low threat to profitability (consistent with AmBev's historical profitability), implying that analysts would most likely forecast continued above-average profitability.

EXHIBIT 37: Analysis of the Brazilian Beer Market Using Porter's Five Forces

Force	Degree	Factors to Consider
Threat of substitutes	Medium	• Beer consumers do not easily shift to other beverages, but such alternatives as wine and spirits are available. • Unlike in many other countries, the range of beers is relatively limited.
Rivalry	Low	• AmBev dominates the market with a 65% market share. Its economies of scale in production and distribution yield significant cost advantages relative to competition. • Price competition is limited because of AmBev's cost advantages and because of typically increasing beer volumes.
Bargaining power of suppliers	Low	• The primary inputs (water, hops, barley, and packaging) are basically commodities.
Bargaining power of buyers	Low	• Beer is mostly consumed in bars and restaurants. The owners of these outlets represent a large and highly fragmented group of beer buyers. • The supermarket industry in Brazil is relatively fragmented, and supermarkets are less likely to offer alternatives, such as private labels.
Threat of new entrants	Low	• New entrants face relatively high barriers to entry because of the high costs of building a brewery, establishing a national distribution network, and establishing a nationally known brand name.

The UK beer market is also divided among four players, but the competitive structure is totally different than in Brazil. The market is more fragmented, with smaller market shares held by the largest players. Heineken, MolsonCoors, AB InBev, and Carlsberg had market shares of 24% (adbrands.net), 18%, 18% (www.ab-inbev.com), and 11% (carlsberggroup.com), respectively, in 2018. Consequently, the British market has no dominant brewer. Given the high fixed costs of a brewery, declining volumes of UK beer consumption, and the highly consolidated customer base, which provides the clients with substantial purchasing power (particularly in the retail channels), price competition is usually intense. A gradual switch from drinking beer in pubs and restaurants ("on-trade") to consumption at home ("off-trade") is making brewers even more exposed to the bargaining power of the dominant retail supermarket (grocers) chains. Increasing taxes on beer and rents faced by pub landlords add to the burden faced by the industry, leading to a steady decline of Britain's pub industry. Profitability has been lower than the beer industry's global average; operating margins are believed to be less than 10%. In this kind of environment, analysts would most likely forecast only very cautious revenue growth, if any. Exhibit 38 presents an analysis of the UK beer market using Porter's five forces framework.

EXHIBIT 38: Analysis of the UK Beer Market Using Porter's Five Forces

Force	Degree	Factors to Consider
Threat of substitutes	Medium	• Beer consumers do not easily shift to other beverages, but such alternatives as wine, spirits, and cider are available.
Rivalry	High	• The market is relatively fragmented with no dominant market leader and large numbers of small breweries. • Declining beer volumes make price wars more likely.[a] • Brand loyalty is less developed because of the extensive range of alternative beers.
Bargaining power of suppliers	Low	• The primary inputs (water, hops, barley, and packaging) are basically commodities.
Bargaining power of buyers	High	• The large supermarket chains that dominate the grocery sector have significant bargaining power. • Large pub chains in the "on-trade" business (where beer is sold in pubs and restaurants) also have strong bargaining power.
Threat of new entrants	Low	• Barriers to entry are relatively high because of the high costs of building a brewery, establishing a national distribution network (particularly given the history of brewers owning pubs and bars), and establishing a nationally known brand. • Because the United Kingdom consists of islands, companies with breweries in other countries face higher transportation costs than existing participants.

[a] In some declining markets, companies focus on increasing prices to offset declining volumes, but in the case of beer, where the market is very fragmented and thus there is no price leadership, price increases are less feasible.

There is a distinction between Porter's five forces and other factors that can affect profitability, such as government regulation and taxes:

Industry structure, as manifested in the strength of the five competitive forces, determines the industry's long-run profit potential because it determines how the economic value created by the industry is divided.... Government is not best understood as a sixth force because government involvement is neither inherently good nor bad for industry profitability. The best way to understand the influence of government on competition is to analyze how specific government policies affect the five competitive forces. (Porter 2008, page 10)

EXAMPLE 15   EuroAlco case

In 20X2, EuroAlco was the beer market leader in Eurolandia (a fictional country) with 35% market share. The other large brewers held 15%, 15%, 10%, and 7% share, respectively. The Eurolandia market is considered a growth market. It historically had high overall alcohol consumption but a relatively low per capita consumption of beer, a product that is attracting interest from the growing, younger population and is further supported by increasing disposable incomes.

At the start of year 20X1, the Eurolandia government, in its fight to curb alcohol consumption, tripled the excise duty (a special tax) on beer from EUR0.3 per liter to EUR0.9 and announced that excise duty will further increase by EUR0.1 per liter.

In the following year, 20X2, EuroAlco made efforts to strengthen the position of the more expensive brands in its portfolio. These efforts led to a 20% increase in selling costs. Similar to most consumer staple companies, EuroAlco experienced higher production costs. Poor grain harvests put price pressure on buyers of almost all feedstocks, and rising oil prices resulted in higher packaging costs. In 20X2, competing companies were much more cautious with A&P spending than EuroAlco.

Two analysts research EuroAlco at the start of year 20X3. In making their EuroAlco forecasts, both analysts use market data and the published annual report from EuroAlco (see Exhibit 39 and/or the Example14 worksheet in the downloadable Microsoft Excel workbook). Based on the published data, they consider a number of scenarios and reach different conclusions.

EXHIBIT 39: EuroAlco Key Financial and Operational Data (€ millions)

				% Change	
	20X2	20X1	20X0	20X2/20X1	20X1/20X0
Retailer gross sales	11,504	10,248	9,180	12%	12%
Excise duty	2,900	2,520	900	15%	180%
As % of retail revenues	25%	25%	10%		
Value-Added-Tax, VAT (20%)	1,434	1,288	1,380	11%	−7%
Retailer net sales	7,170	6,440	6,900	11%	−7%
Typical retailer profit[a]	935	840	900	11%	−7%
As % of retailer net sales	13%	13%	13%		
Brewer net sales	6,235	5,600	6,000	11%	−7%
Key Financial Indicators					
Volume (mln hectoliters)	29	28	30	4%	−7%
Net sales	6,235	5,600	6,000	11%	−7%
Cost of sales	3,190	2,800	3,150	14%	−11%
Gross profit	3,045	2,800	2,850	9%	−2%
Selling expenses	2,088	1,680	1,650	24%	2%
Administrative expenses	145	140	150	4%	−7%
Operating profit	812	980	1,050	−17%	−7%

[a] This is the gross profit for retailers, companies that buy beer directly from the brewers and sell to end users.

	20X2	20X1	20X0	% Change	
				20X2/20X1	20X1/20X0
Average invested capital	3,000	3,000	3,100	0%	−3%
Gross margin	48.8%	50.0%	47.5%		
Selling expense %	33.5%	30.0%	27.5%		
Operating margin	13.0%	17.5%	17.5%		
Return on invested capital (pre-tax)	27%	33%	34%		
€ per hectoliter (hl)					
Retail price	397	366	306	8%	20%
Excise duty	100	90	30	11%	200%
VAT	49	46	46	7%	0%
Typical distributor profit	32	30	30	7%	0%
Brewer net sales	215	200	200	8%	0%
Cost of sales	110	100	105	10%	−5%
Gross profit	105	100	95	5%	5%
Selling expenses	72	60	55	20%	9%
Administrative expenses	5	5	5	0%	0%
Operating profit	28	35	35	−20%	0%

Note: Average invested capital includes debt and equity capital.

Both analysts assume that the government will impose a further increase in the excise duty (special tax on beer). They also assume that the excise duty increase will be borne by the consumers, who will face a 10% price increase that will allow the brewers to maintain their net (after-tax) revenues per hectoliter (hl). They assume that half the cost of sales is fixed per hectoliter and half is variable based on volume, that selling expenses will remain unchanged as a percentage of sales, and that administrative expenses are fixed.

1. Analyst A expects price elasticity of 0.8, indicating that volume will fall by 8% given the 10% retail price increase. Calculate the impact on operating profit and operating profit margin in 20X3 using Exhibit 40, which is also in the Example14 sheet in the downloadable Microsoft Excel workbook.

Solution to 1:

Exhibit 41 (see the Example14 worksheet in the downloadable Microsoft Excel workbook) shows the results for both analysts' projections. Analyst A predicts that operating profit will decrease by 25% to EUR608 in 20X3, resulting in an operating margin decline from 13.0% in 20X2 to 10.6% in 20X3. Analyst A calculates a revenue decline of 8% to EUR5,736 based on volume dropping by 8% and a constant price per hectoliter of EUR215. The decrease in volume reflects the price elasticity of 0.8 and the price increase of 10% as a result of the excise duty increase. COGS sold fell only 4% because part of the costs are fixed. COGS as the sum of fixed and variable costs is EUR1,595 + [26.68 (hl volume) × 55 (hl cost)] = EUR1,595 + 1,467 (ignoring rounding error) or EUR3,062. Analyst A predicts selling expenses will decline in line with sales by 8% and administrative costs will remain unchanged because of their fixed character in the short term.

2. Analyst B expects price elasticity of 0.5, indicating that volume will fall by 5% given the 10% retail price increase. Calculate the impact on operating profit and operating profit margin in 20X3 using Exhibit 40, which is also in the Example14 sheet in the downloadable Microsoft Excel workbook.

EXHIBIT 40: EuroAlco's Costs Structure for 20X2–20X3E (€ millions, unless noted)

		Analyst A		Analyst B	
	20X2	20X3E	YoY%	20X3E	YoY%
Volume (millions of hl)	29	26.7	–8.0%	27.6	–5.0%
Brewer net sales (€ per hl)	215				
Net sales	6,235				
Cost of sales	3,190				
Gross profit	3,045				
Gross margin	48.8%				
Selling expenses	2,088				
Administrative expenses	145	145		145	
Operating profit	812				
Operating profit margin	13.0%				
Cost of sales (fixed)	1,595	1,595		1,595	
Cost of sales (variable)	1,595				
Cost of sales (variable) per hl	55	55		55	
Selling expenses as % of sales	33.5%	33.5%		33.5%	

Solution to 2:

Analyst B forecasts that operating profit will decline by 16% to EUR684. Analyst B's calculations follow the same pattern as those of Analyst A, but Analyst B predicts a smaller, 5%, decline in volume. Analyst A's estimates are more pessimistic than those of Analyst B. Note that the net price per hectoliter for the brewer is held constant while the price for the consumer increased 10% as a result of the excise duty increase. Because of Analyst B's more optimistic volume forecast, fixed costs are spread over a higher level of sales than is the case for Analyst A. Consequently, Analyst B will have a higher operating margin estimate than Analyst A. However, both analysts are predicting a decline in operating margin in 20X3.

EXHIBIT 41: Analysts' Results for EuroAlco's Cost Structure and Projection (€ millions, unless noted)

		Analyst A		Analyst B	
	20X2	20X3E	YoY%	20X3E	YoY%
Volume (millions of hl)	29	26.7	–8%	27.6	–5%
Brewer net sales per hl	215	215	0%	215	0%

		Analyst A		Analyst B	
	20X2	20X3E	YoY%	20X3E	YoY%
Net sales	6,235	5,736	–8%	5,923	–5%
Cost of sales	3,190	3,062	–4%	3,110	–3%
Gross profit	3,045	2,674	–12%	2,813	–8%
Gross margin	48.8%	46.6%	–5%	47.5%	–3%
Selling expenses	2,088	1,921	–8%	1,984	–5%
Administrative expenses	145	145	0%	145	0%
Operating profit	812	608	–25%	684	–16%
Operating profit margin	13.0%	10.6%	–19%	11.6%	–11%
Cost of sales (fixed)	1,595	1,595	0%	1,595	0%
Cost of sales (variable)	1,595	1,467	–8%	1,515	–5%
Cost of sales (variable) per hl	55	55	0%	55	0%
Selling expenses as % of net sales	33.5%	33.5%	0%	33.5%	0%

3. Gross margin improved in 20X1 (50.0%) but fell in 20X2 (48.8%). Cost of sales was relatively high in 20X2 because of high barley costs, an important input for brewing beer. Assume that in 20X2, half of the cost of sales is fixed and half is based on volume. Of the variable part of the cost of sales, assume that half the amount is related to the barley price in 20X2. Barley prices increased 25% in 20X2. Consider a scenario where no additional taxes are imposed in 20X3, revenues and volumes remain stable, and barley prices return to their 20X1 level. Calculate EuroAlco's estimated gross **margin** for 20X3.

Solution to 3:

If barley prices return to their 20X1 level, they will decline 20% in 20X3. Because volumes are assumed to remain constant, other variable costs will not change. Gross profit in 20X2 was 48.8% of sales, which indicates the cost of sales was 51.2% (100% – 48.8%). Barley is 25% of the cost of sales (because barley represents half of variable costs, and variable cost of sales represents half of total cost of sales). Cost of sales is predicted to decline by 25% × 20% = 5%. New cost of sales will be 51.2% – (5% × 51.2%) or 48.6%. Consequently, gross margin is predicted to be 100% – 48.6% = 51.4% in 20X3. Compared with the gross margin of 48.8% in 20X2, gross margin is predicted to increase by 260 bps.

EXHIBIT 42: Gross Margin Analysis

	20X3	20X2	YoY%
Volume	29	29	0%
Revenue	6,235	6,235	0%
Cost of sales	3,031	3,190	–5%
Variable	1,436	1,595	–10%
Barley related	638	798	–20%
Not barley related	798	798	0%
Fixed	1,595	1,595	0%
Gross profit	3,205	3,045	5%
Gross margin	51.4%	48.8%	

4. EuroAlco's selling expenses increased from 30% of sales in 20X1 to 33.5% of sales in 20X2. Which competitive forces most likely influenced EuroAlco's significant increase in selling expenses?

Solution to 4:

Intra-industry rivalry and threat of substitutes most likely influenced EuroAlco's significant increase in selling costs. By spending more on advertising, EuroAlco wanted to enhance the brand loyalty of its products, thus improving its competitive position versus its brewer rivals and makers of other alcoholic beverages. Furthermore, buyers' bargaining power probably also influenced EuroAlco's increased spending to the extent that advertising creates demand by the ultimate consumer. Strong demand at the ultimate consumer level for EuroAlco's specific brands could enhance the company's bargaining position with its direct customers, the distributors who serve as intermediaries.

5. Retailers are the direct customers of brewers. They buy directly from the brewer and sell to the ultimate consumer. Analyst A expects that the increase in mass retailers in Eurolandia will cause brewers' margins to decline. He expects EuroAlco's operating margin will decrease from 13% in 20X2 to 8% in 20X6, with stable sales (EUR6,235 million) and an unchanged amount of average invested capital (EUR3,000 million). Analyst B also sees the increasing importance of the larger food retailers but expects that EuroAlco can offset potential pricing pressure by offering more attractive trade credit (e.g., allowing the retailers longer payment terms). He thinks operating margin can remain stable at 13% with no sales growth. Average invested capital (EUR3,000 million), however, will double because of the extra investments in inventory and receivables. Describe the analysts' expectations about the impact of large retailers on brewers in terms of Porter's five forces and return on invested capital (ROIC; pre-tax). Which of the two scenarios would be better for EuroAlco?

Solution to 5:

The increase in mass retailers in EuroAlco is expected to strengthen the bargaining power of buyers relative to brewers. According to Analyst A, this will lead to a lower operating margin of 8%, while Analyst B believes margins can be maintained if the company offers much more favorable credit terms reflected in doubling of invested capital. Analyst A expects operating profit on invested capital to fall from 27.1% (13% × EUR6,235/EUR3,000) to 16.6% (8% × EUR6,235/EUR3,000). Analyst B's assumptions indicate that the ROIC (operating profit divided by invested capital) in 20X2 of 27% will fall by half to 13.5% as the operating profit is earned on double the amount of invested capital (i.e., 13% × EUR6,235/EUR6,000). The scenario envisioned by Analyst A is better for EuroAlco. Full supporting calculations are in the Example14 worksheet in the downloadable Microsoft Excel workbook.

In summary, Porter's five forces framework and similar analytical tools can help analysts assess the relative profit potential of a company by helping them understand the company's industry and its position within that industry. Understanding the industry and competitive contexts of a company helps analysts estimate whether, for example, sales growth is likely to be relatively high or low (relative to history, relative to the overall growth in the economy or a sector, and/or relative to competing companies) and whether profit margins are likely to be relatively high or low (relative to historical profit margins and relative to competing companies). The process of incorporating an industry and competitive analysis into expectations for future financial performance requires judgment. Suppose analysts observe that a given company is the market leader in a moderately competitive industry with limited buyer and supplier power and relatively high barriers to entry. In broad terms, analysts might project that the company's future revenue growth will be in line with that of the overall industry and that its profit margins and ROIC might be somewhat higher than those of other companies in the industry. But there is no mechanical link between the analysts' observations and projecting the company's future sales growth and profit margin. Instead, the link is more subjective and probabilistic.

9. INFLATION AND DEFLATION

Inflation and deflation (i.e., the overall increase and decrease in the prices of goods and services) can significantly affect the accuracy of forecasts for a company's future revenue, profit, and cash flow. The impact of inflation or deflation on revenue and expenses differs from company to company. Even within a single company, the impact of inflation or deflation is generally different for revenue and expenses categories.

Some companies are better able to pass on higher input costs by raising the prices at which they sell their output. The ability to pass on price increases can be the result of, for example, strong branding (Coca-Cola) or proprietary technology (Apple). Companies that are well positioned to pass on price increases are, in turn, more likely to have higher and more stable profits and cash flow, relative to competitors.

We first consider the impact of inflation on sales and then on costs.

9.1. Sales Projections with Inflation and Deflation

The following analysis addresses the projection of industry sales and company sales in the presence of inflation.

9.1.1. Industry Sales and Inflation or Deflation

Most increases in the cost of inputs, such as commodities or labor, will eventually result in higher prices for end products. Industry structure can be an important factor in determining the relationship between increases in input costs and increases in the price of end products. For example, in the United States, the beer market is an oligopoly, with one player, AB InBev, controlling almost half of the market. Moreover, the three-tier structure of the US beer market, in which the producers (the brewers) must use a third party (the wholesalers) to get their products (beer) to the consumers (bars, restaurants, and retailers) results in a fragmented customer base because brewers are not allowed to deliver directly to the end consumer but rather must use wholesale distributors. These wholesalers often differ state by state. Large nationwide retailers, such as Wal-Mart, still must negotiate with several different wholesalers instead of using their dominant national market position to negotiate directly with the brewers. The industry structure in the United States has likely contributed to increases in beer prices roughly in line with the US Consumer Price Index. In other words, beer prices have generally risen during years of inflation in input costs and decreased when costs have eased (though there have been brief exceptional periods where the opposite has occurred). If necessary, US brewers have been able to increase prices to compensate for costs of inflation. In contrast, European beer companies distribute through a more concentrated customer base—namely, such dominant retail outlets as Carrefour, Tesco, and Ahold—which results in a weaker pricing position for the brewers. Also, the European market lacks an overall dominant brewer. As a result of the industry structure and the lack of underlying volume growth, changes in beer prices in Europe have been on average 100 bps less than customer inflation.

EXHIBIT 43: US General Inflation and Inflation in Beer Prices

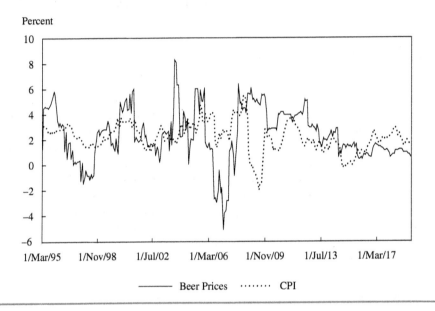

Source: US Bureau of Labor Statistics.

A company's efforts to pass on inflation through higher prices can have a negative impact on volume if the demand is price elastic, which is the case if cheaper substitutes are available. If selling prices could be increased 10% while maintaining unit sales volume to offset an increase of 10% in input costs, gross profit margin percentage would be the same but the absolute amount of gross profit would increase. In the short term, however, volumes will usually decline as a result of a price increase. The decline would depend not only on the price elasticity of demand but also on the reaction of competitors and the availability of substitutes. Lower input costs also make lower consumer prices possible. The first competitor to lower prices will usually benefit with an uptick in volume. Competitors react quickly, however, resulting in a short-term benefit. The price–volume trade-off can make accurate revenue projections difficult. In an inflationary environment, raising prices too late will result in a profit margin squeeze but acting too soon could result in volume losses. In a deflationary environment, lowering prices too soon will result in a lower gross margin, but waiting too long will result in volume losses.

In the highly competitive consumer goods market, pricing is strongly influenced by movements in input prices, which can account for half of the COGS. In some time periods, customers' price sensitivity has resulted in a strong inverse relationship between volume and pricing. For example, Exhibit 44 illustrates Unilever's annual underlying volume and price growth from 2001 to 2020. Increased input prices for packaging, wheat, and milk forced Anglo-Dutch consumer staple company Unilever to increase prices for its products significantly in 2008. Consequently, volumes deteriorated. But as raw material prices fell in 2009–2010, the company's prices were lowered and volumes recovered strongly. As the company started to increase prices in 2011, volume growth once again slowed. In 2016, the company faced challenging conditions in several emerging markets as currency-devaluation-led cost increases led to weaker volumes. Both volume and price growth have moderated to low-single digit growth rates, also exhibiting lower volatility.

EXHIBIT 44: Unilever Overall Revenue Growth by Percentage Change in Volume and Price

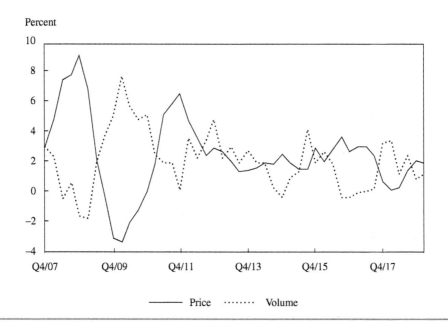

Sources: Unilever PLC filings.

9.1.2. Company Sales and Inflation or Deflation

Revenue projections in a model are based on the expected volume and price development. Forecasting revenue for a company faced with inflation in input costs requires some understanding of the price elasticity of the products, the different rates of cost inflation in the countries where the company is active, and, if possible, the likely inflation in costs relevant to a company's individual product categories. Pricing strategy and market position are also important.

The impact of higher prices on volume depends on the price elasticity of demand (i.e., how the quantity demanded varies with price). If demand is relatively price inelastic, revenues will benefit from inflation. If demand is relatively price elastic (i.e., elasticity is greater than unit price elasticity), revenue can decline even if unit prices are raised. For example, a regression of volume on food inflation in UK food stores from 1989 to 2012 (shown in Exhibit 45) gives a regression slope coefficient of –0.398. (For every increase by 1 percentage point in year-on-year food prices, year-on-year sales decreased by approximately 0.4%.)

An analyst covering UK food retailers can use this information when building forecast profit models. By assuming an expected level of food inflation, volume growth can be estimated and revenue calculated.

EXHIBIT 45: UK Relationship between Food Inflation and Volume, January 1989–February 2012

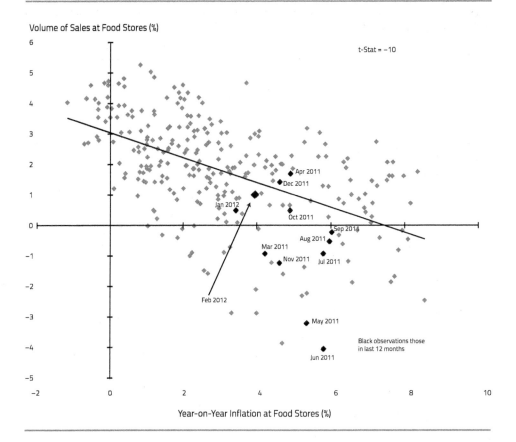

Source: Based on data from Datastream. Analysis is the authors'.

The expected pricing component for an international company should consider the geographic mix of its revenues to reflect different rates of inflation among countries. Of course, strategy and competitive factors, in addition to inflation in input costs, play roles in price setting.

AB InBev's volume growth and pricing have been more robust in emerging markets, for example, thanks to strong demand for its new beer products. The impact of inflation is also an important factor. In its Latin America South division, which then mainly consisted of Argentina, the brewer reported strong 24.7% organic revenue growth in 2011, of which only 2.1% was driven by volume and the remainder by price. As costs increased in line with revenues, operating margin remained more or less stable, and organic operating profit growth was high at 27%. With only a limited negative currency impact, reported operating profit increased 24% in US dollars.

High inflation in a company's export market relative to a company's domestic inflation rate generally implies that the export country's currency will come under pressure and any pricing gain could be wiped out by the currency losses. The strong pricing increases AB InBev reported in its Latin America South division were clearly driven by input price inflation. The absence of a negative currency impact should be seen as a positive surprise but not as a typical outcome. A country's currency will usually come under pressure and depreciate if high rates of inflation persist for an extended period.

Most analysts adjust for recent high inflation in foreign countries by assuming a normalized growth rate for both revenues and costs after one or two years. This constant currency growth rate is based on an underlying growth rate assumption for the business. This approach can understate revenues in the short term. Other analysts reflect in their forecasts the high impact of inflation on revenues and expense and adjust growth rates for the expected currency (interest rate parity) impact. This approach is also imperfect given the difficulty in projecting currency rates.

Identifying a company's major input costs provides an indication of likely pricing. For a specialist retail bakery chain, for example, the impact of increased grain prices will be more significant than for a diversified standard supermarket chain. Consequently, it seems logical that the bakery is likely to increase its prices by a higher percentage than the grocer in response to increased grain prices.

Company strategy is also an important factor. Faced with rising input prices, a company might decide to preserve its margins by passing on the costs to its customers, or it might decide to accept some margin reduction to increase its market share. In other words, the company could try to gain market share by not fully increasing prices to reflect increased costs. On the one hand, Sysco Company (the largest food distributor to restaurants and institutions in North America) has sometimes not passed on food price increases in recessionary conditions out of concern of not financially weakening already recession-affected customers (e.g., restaurants, private clubs, schools, nursing homes). On the other hand, in 2011 and 2012, the large French cognac houses substantially increased the prices of their products in China to reduce strong demand. Because older cognac generates a higher price, it can be more profitable to build an inventory of vintage cognac rather than maximizing short-term volumes.

EXAMPLE 16 Passing on Input Cost Increases or Not

Four food retail analysts are assessing the impact of a potential increase in input costs on the global supermarket chain Carrefour. In this hypothetical scenario, they believe that rising oil prices and packaging prices will affect many of the company's suppliers. They believe that Carrefour is likely to be confronted with 4% inflation in its COGS (with stable volume). The analysts have their own expectations about how the company will react. Exhibit 46 shows Carrefour's 2020 results, and Exhibit 47 shows the four analysts' estimates of input prices, volume growth, and pricing for the following year. Both exhibits are in the Example15 worksheet in the downloadable Microsoft Excel workbook.

EXHIBIT 46: Carrefour Data (€ millions, unless noted)

	2020
Total revenue	72,150
COGS	56,705
Gross profit	15,445
Gross margin	21.4%

Source: Based on data from Carrefour's annual report ("Universal Registration Document") for 2020.

EXHIBIT 47: Four Analysts' Estimates of Carrefour's Reaction to Inflation

	A	B	C	D
Price increase for revenues	0.00%	2.00%	3.00%	4.00%
Volume growth	5.00%	2.00%	1.00%	−4.00%
Total revenue growth	5.00%	4.04%	4.03%	−0.16%
Input costs increase	4.00%	4.00%	4.00%	4.00%

1. What are each analyst's predictions for gross profit and gross margin?

Solution to 1:

The results for each analyst are shown in Exhibit 48 and the Example15 worksheet in the downloadable Microsoft Excel workbook. For Analyst B, revenues increase 4% [= (1.02 × 1.02) − 1] and COGS 6.1% [= (1.02 × 1.04) − 1]. The difference between the calculated revenue and COGS is the new gross profit and gross margin is gross profit as a percentage of revenue.

EXHIBIT 48: Results for Analysts' Predictions (€ millions, unless noted)

	2020	Analyst A 2021E	YoY %	Analyst B 2021E	YoY %	Analyst C 2021E	YoY %	Analyst D 2021E	YoY %
Total revenue	72,150	75,758	5.0%	75,065	4%	75,058	4.0%	72,035	−0.2%
COGS	56,705	61,922	9.2%	60,153	6%	59,563	5.0%	56,614	−0.2%
Gross profit	15,445	13,836	− 10%	14,912	−3%	15,495	0%	15,420	−0.2%
Gross margin	21.4%	18.3%		19.9%		20.6%		21.4%	

2. Which analyst has the highest forecast for gross margin?

Solution to 2:

The highest gross margin is projected by Analyst D, who assumes that selling prices would increase by 4% to offset rising input costs and keep gross margin stable from the 2020 level.

3. Which analyst has the highest forecast for gross profit?

Solution to 3:

The highest gross profit is projected by Analyst D.

9.2. Cost Projections with Inflation and Deflation

The following analysis addresses the forecasting of industry and company costs in the presence of inflation and deflation.

9.2.1. Industry Costs and Inflation or Deflation

Familiarity with the specific purchasing characteristics of an industry can also be useful in forecasting costs. For example, long-term price-fixed forward contracts and hedges can delay the impact of price increases. Thus, an analyst forecasting costs for an industry in which companies customarily use such purchasing practices would incorporate any expected input price fluctuations more slowly than they would for an industry in which the participants do not use long-term contracts or hedges.

Monitoring the underlying drivers of input prices can also be useful in forecasting costs. For example, weather conditions can have a dramatic impact on the price of agricultural products and consequently on the cost base of industries that rely on them. An analyst observing a particular weather pattern might thus be able to incorporate this information into forecasts of costs.

How inflation or deflation affects an industry's cost structure depends on its competitive environment. For example, if the participants within the industry have access to alternative inputs or are vertically integrated, the impact of volatility in input costs can be mitigated. Jacobs Douwe Egberts (JDE) is a coffee company that has been facing high and volatile coffee prices. However, its coffee is a blend of different kinds of beans. By shifting the mix slightly, JDE can keep both taste and costs constant by reducing the amount of the more expensive types of coffee beans in the blend. But if all supplier countries significantly increase the price of coffee simultaneously, JDE cannot use blending as an offset and will be confronted with overall higher input costs. To sustain its profitability, JDE will have to increase its prices to its clients. But if competition from other companies, such as Nestlé (Nespresso, Dolce Gusto, Nescafe) makes it difficult to increase prices, JDE will have to look for alternatives if it wants to keep its profit margins stable. An easy solution for the short term could be reducing A&P spending, which usually improves profit. For the longer term, however, it could be harmful for revenues because the company's brand position could be weakened.

For example, in 2010, Russia experienced a heat wave that destroyed large parts of its grain harvest, causing prices for malting barley, a major input for beer, to increase significantly. Carlsberg, as the largest Russian brewer at that time, was particularly hard hit because it had to pay more for its Russian barley and also needed to import grain into the country, incurring additional transportation costs. By increasing imports from Western Europe, Carlsberg also pushed up barley prices in this region, affecting the cost base of other Western European brewers.

9.2.2. Company Costs and Inflation or Deflation

In forecasting a company's costs, it is often helpful to segment the cost structure by category and geography. For each item of cost, an assessment should be made about the impact of potential inflation and deflation on input prices. This assessment should take into account the company's ability to substitute cheaper alternatives for expensive inputs or to increase efficiency to offset the impact of increases in input prices. For example, although a jump in raw material prices in 2011 caused Unilever's and Nestlé's gross margins to fall sharply (by 110–170 bps), increases in operational efficiencies, such as reducing advertising spending, enabled both companies to achieve slightly higher overall operating profit margins that year. Example 17 shows the use of common size (percent-of-sales) analysis of inflation in input costs.

EXAMPLE 17 Inflation in Input Costs

Two fictional consumer staple companies—chocolate and sweets specialist "Choco A" and a food producer "Sweet B"—have costs that are constantly affected by inflation and deflation. Exhibit 49 (see the Example16 worksheet in the downloadable Microsoft Excel workbook) presents a common size analysis.

EXHIBIT 49: Common Size Analysis for Sweet B and Choco A

	Sweet B	Choco A
Net sales	100%	100%
COGS	50%	36%
Gross margin	50%	64%
SG&A	31%	47%
Depreciation	3%	4%
EBIT	16%	13%
Raw materials	22%	22%
Packaging	12%	10%
Other COGS	16%	4%
Total COGS	50%	36%

Assume inflation of 10% for all costs (except depreciation) and that the companies are not able to pass on this increase through higher prices (total revenues will remain constant).

1. Calculate the gross profit margin for each company. Which company will experience the greater reduction in gross profit margin?

Solution to 1:

The company with the higher COGS as a percent of net sales—equivalently, the lower gross margin—will experience the greater negative impact. Sweet B has a lower gross margin than Choco A: 50% compared with 64%, as shown in Exhibit 49. After the 10% increase in COGS to 1.10 × 50% = 55%, Sweet B's gross margin will fall to 45%, as shown in Exhibit 50. Sweet B's resulting gross margin of 45% represents a proportional decline of 10% from the initial value of 50%. In contrast, the proportional decline in Choco A's gross margin is approximately 4%/64% = 6%.

2. Calculate the operating profit margin for each company. Which company will experience the greater reduction in operating profit (EBIT) margin?

Solution to 2:

Choco A has higher overall costs than Sweet B, primarily as a consequence of its high SG&A expenses. Choco A's operating profit margin will drop to approximately 5%, as shown in Exhibit 51, representing a proportional decline of approximately 62% compared with a proportional decline of approximately 8%/16% = 50% for Sweet B.

3. Assume inflation of 10% only for the raw material costs (reflected in COGS) and that the companies are not able to pass on this increase through higher prices. Which company will be more affected negatively in terms of gross profit margin and operating profit margin?

Solution to 3:

The company with the higher raw material expense component will experience the more negative effect. In this case, raw materials represent 22% of net sales for both Sweet B and Choco A. Gross margin and operating margin will decline by 220 bps for both. This impact is more severe on gross margin on a relative basis for Sweet B (2.2%/50% = 4.4% decline) than for Choco A (2.2%/64% = 3.4% decline). But the relative effect on operating margin will be more severe for Choco A (2.2%/13% = 16.9% decline) than for Sweet B (2.2%/16% = 13.8%).

EXHIBIT 50: Effect of Cost Inflation

	All Costs (Except Depreciation) + 10%		Raw Materials + 10%	
	Sweet B	Choco A	Sweet B	Choco A
Net sales	100%	100%	100%	100%
COGS	55%	40%	52%	38%
Gross margin	45%	60%	48%	62%
SG&A	34%	52%	31%	47%
Depreciation	3%	4%	3%	4%
EBIT	8%	5%	14%	11%

10. TECHNOLOGICAL DEVELOPMENTS

Technological developments have the potential to change the economics of individual businesses and entire industries. Quantifying the potential impact of such developments on an individual company's earnings involves making certain assumptions about future demand. Such assumptions should be explored through scenario and/or **sensitivity analysis** so that a range of potential earnings outcomes can be considered. When a technological development results in a new product that threatens to cannibalize demand for an existing product, a unit forecast for the new product combined with an expected cannibalization factor can be used to estimate the impact on future demand for the existing product. When developing an estimate of the cannibalization factor, it might be useful to segment the market if the threat of substitution differs across segments.

Technological developments can affect demand for a product, the quantity supplied of a product, or both. When changes in technology lead to lower manufacturing costs, the supply curve will shift to the right as suppliers produce more of the product at the same price. Conversely, if technology results in the development of attractive substitute products, the demand curve will shift to the left. Consider the following historical example.

EXAMPLE 18   (Historical example)

Quantifying the Tablet Market's Potential to Cannibalize Demand for Personal Computers

---

The worldwide tablet market experienced a major technological development with the introduction of the Apple iPad tablet in April 2010, which was expected to have (and indeed did have) important implications for the manufacturers of desktop and laptop computers. A tablet promised to offer the capabilities of a portable personal computer (PC) with a touchscreen interface instead of a keyboard. Another distinguishing feature of tablets is that, unlike the majority of PCs that run on the Microsoft Windows platform, the then-new tablets would run on a non-Microsoft operating system, namely Apple's iOS and Google's Android. Given the tablet's ability to perform many of the most common tasks of a PC—including emailing, browsing the web, sharing photos, playing music, watching movies, playing games, keeping a calendar, and managing contacts—an analyst at that time might reasonably have wondered to what extent sales of tablets might cannibalize demand for PCs and the potential impact that might have on Microsoft's sales and earnings. Exhibit 52 (the Example17 worksheet in the downloadable Microsoft Excel workbook) presents one approach to answering these questions. It is set at the start of 2012, just over a year after the launch of the iPad. It is presented from the position of an analyst assessing the impact of the tablet on the PC market and Microsoft.

EXHIBIT 51: Unit and Revenue Projections ($ thousands, unless noted)

PRE-CANNIBALIZATION PC PROJECTIONS	FY2011	FY2012E	FY2013E	FY2014E	3-Year CAGR
Consumer PC shipments	170,022	174,430	184,120	193,811	4.5%
Non-consumer PC shipments	180,881	185,570	195,880	206,189	4.5%
Total global PC shipments	350,903	360,000	380,000	400,000	4.5%
% of which is consumer	48%	48%	48%	48%	
% of which is non-consumer	52%	52%	52%	52%	
Consumer tablet shipments	36,785	82,800	111,250	148,750	59.3%
Non-consumer tablet shipments	1,686	7,200	13,750	26,250	149.7%
Total global tablet shipments	38,471	90,000	125,000	175,000	65.7%
% of which is consumer	96%	92%	89%	85%	
% of which is non-consumer	4%	8%	11%	15%	
Cannibalization factor, consumer	30%	30%	30%	30%	
Cannibalization factor, non-consumer	10%	10%	10%	10%	
# of consumer PCs cannibalized by tablets	11,036	24,840	33,375	44,625	
# of non-consumer PCs cannibalized by tablets	169	720	1,375	2,625	
Total PCs cannibalized by tablets	11,204	25,560	34,750	47,250	
% of total PCs cannibalized by tablets	3.2%	7.1%	9.1%	11.8%	

POST-CANNIBALIZATION PC PROJECTIONS					
Consumer PC shipments	158,987	149,590	150,745	149,186	−2.1%
Non-consumer PC shipments	180,712	184,850	194,505	203,564	4.0%
Total global PC shipments	339,699	334,440	345,250	352,750	1.3%
Microsoft implied average selling price					
Consumer	$85	$85	$85	$85	
Non-consumer	$155	$155	$155	$155	
Revenue impact for Microsoft ($ millions)					
Consumer	938	2,111	2,837	3,793	
Non-consumer	26	112	213	407	
Total revenue impact	964	2,223	3,050	4,200	

Notes: CAGR is compound annual growth rate. Non-consumer includes enterprise, education, and government purchasers.

Sources: Based on data from Gartner, JPMorgan, Microsoft, and authors' analysis.

To begin, worldwide market shipments of PCs in FY2011 were 350.9 million units, and worldwide shipments of tablets were 38.5 million units (*Source:* Gartner Personal Computer Quarterly Statistics Worldwide Database). Shipments to consumers represented 96% of total tablet shipments during fiscal year 2011. Next, we estimate the magnitude of the potential substitution effect, or cannibalization factor, that tablets will have on the PC market. Because the cannibalization factor depends on many different variables, including user preferences, end-use application, and whether the purchaser already owns a PC, just to name a few, we use a range of potential estimates. Moreover, we also divide the worldwide PC market into consumer and non-consumer (enterprise, education, and government purchasers) because the degree of substitution is likely to differ between the two. For purposes of illustration, we assume a cannibalization factor of 30% for the consumer market and 10% for the non-consumer market in our base case scenario.

In addition, the base case scenario assumes that non-consumer adoption of tablets increases to 15% of the market from 4% in 2011. Moreover, although the composition of the global PC market is roughly evenly divided between consumers and non-consumers (48% and 52% in fiscal year 2011, respectively), the non-consumer segment is significantly more profitable for Microsoft because approximately 80% of the company's Office products are sold to enterprise, education, and government institutions. The average selling price (ASP) estimates are derived by dividing Microsoft's estimated average revenue for the prior three years by customer type by Microsoft's estimated PC shipments for each type of customer. By multiplying the projected number of PCs cannibalized by tablets by the estimated ASP, we are able to derive an estimate of the revenue impact for Microsoft. For example, in FY2012, it is projected that 24.8 million consumer PCs will be cannibalized by sales of tablets. With an average consumer ASP of USD85, this cannibalization implies a revenue loss for Microsoft of USD2.1 billion (24.8 million units × USD85 ASP per unit = USD2.1 billion).

Once the revenue impact has been projected, the next step is to estimate the impact of lower PC unit volumes on operating costs and margins. We begin by analyzing the cost structure of Microsoft and, more specifically, the breakdown between fixed and variable costs. Most software companies have a cost structure with a relatively high proportion of fixed costs and a low proportion of variable costs because costs related to product development and marketing (mostly fixed) are sunk and unrecoverable, whereas the cost of producing an additional copy of the software (mostly variable) is relatively low. Because very few, if any, companies provide an explicit breakdown of fixed versus variable costs, an estimate almost always needs to be made. One method is to use the formula

$$\%\Delta \text{ (Cost of revenue + Operating expense)}/\%\Delta \text{ revenue,}$$

where $\%\Delta$ is "percentage change in," used as a proxy for variable cost percentage. Another approach is to assign an estimate of the percentage of fixed and variable costs to the various components of operating expenses. Both approaches are illustrated in Exhibits 52 and 53 (see the Example17 worksheet in the downloadable Microsoft Excel workbook).

EXHIBIT 52: Estimation of Variable Costs for Microsoft, Method 1 ($ millions)

Selected Operating Segments	FY2009	FY2010	FY2011	FY2011/FY2009 Percentage Change
Revenue:				
Windows and Windows Live	15,563	18,792	18,778	
Microsoft business division	19,211	19,345	21,986	
Total segment revenue	34,774	38,137	40,764	17%
Operating expenses:				
Windows and Windows Live	6,191	6,539	6,810	
Microsoft business division	8,058	7,703	8,159	
Total operating expense	14,249	14,242	14,969	5%

%Variable cost estimate ≈ %Δ (Cost of revenue + Operating expense)/%Δ revenue ≈ 5%/17% ≈ **29%**.
   %Fixed cost ≈ 1 − %Variable cost ≈ 1 − 29% ≈ **71%**.

EXHIBIT 53: Estimation of Variable Costs for Microsoft, Method 2 ($ millions)

Operating Expenses	FY2009	FY2010	FY2011	FY2009– FY2011 Average	% of Total Op Expense	Estimated % of Cost Fixed	Fixed Cost Contribution
Cost of revenue (excl. depreciation)	10,455	10,595	13,577	11,542	29%	20%	6%
Depreciation expense	1,700	1,800	2,000	1,833	5%	100%	5%
Total cost of revenue	12,155	12,395	15,577	13,376	34%		10%
R&D	9,010	8,714	9,043	8,922	22%	100%	22%
Sales and marketing	12,879	13,214	13,940	13,344	34%	80%	27%
General and admin.	4,030	4,063	4,222	4,105	10%	100%	10%
Total operating expenses	38,074	38,386	42,782	39,747	100%		60%
Estimated percentage of Microsoft's total cost structure that is fixed:							70%

Note: Fiscal year ends in June.

Sources: Microsoft 2011 Form 10-K and authors' analysis.

As can be seen, Microsoft's cost structure appears to consist of approximately 70% fixed costs and 30% variable costs. Note, however, that a growing company like Microsoft will typically re-invest in PP&E to support future growth, so even those expenses that appear to be "fixed" will increase over time. To adjust for this expected growth in fixed costs, this example includes an assumption that the change in fixed costs will be half the rate of the change in sales. Variable costs are projected to change at the same rate as sales. As shown in Exhibit 54, after incorporating these assumptions into the projections, an assumed 7.0% compound annual growth rate (CAGR) in revenue through FY2014 would translate into a 10.6% CAGR in operating income $[(36,757/27,161)^{1/3} - 1 = 0.106$, or 10.6%]. In addition, these assumptions would result in an operating margin expansion of 410 bps over the same period (42.9% − 38.8% = 4.1%, or 410 bps) because of the significant amount of operating leverage that exists as a result of a relatively large fixed cost base. With the further assumptions of no change in other income, a constant effective tax rate, and no change in shares outstanding, the pre-cannibalization model, shown in Exhibit 54, results in projected revenue of USD85.7 billion, operating income of USD36.8 billion, an operating margin of 42.9%, and EPS that increases at a CAGR of 10.3% to USD3.62 in FY2014.

EXHIBIT 54: Microsoft Pre-Cannibalization EPS Projections ($ millions)

	FY2011	FY2012E	FY2013E	FY2014E	3-Year CAGR
Revenue	69,943	74,839	80,078	85,683	7.0%
YoY% change		7.0%	7.0%	7.0%	
Operating Expenses					
Fixed (70%)	29,947	30,996	32,080	33,203	3.5%
Variable (30%)	12,835	13,733	14,694	15,723	7.0%
Total operating expenses	42,782	44,729	46,775	48,926	4.6%
Operating income	27,161	30,110	33,303	36,757	10.6%
Operating margin	38.83%	40.23%	41.59%	42.90%	
Other income (expense)	910	910	910	910	
Pre-tax Income	28,071	31,020	34,213	37,667	
Provision for income taxes	4,921	5,438	5,998	6,603	
Effective tax rate	17.53%	17.53%	17.53%	17.53%	
Net income	23,150	25,582	28,215	31,064	
Weighted average shares outstanding, diluted	8,593	8,593	8,593	8,593	
Estimated EPS pre-cannibalization	$2.69	$2.98	$3.28	$3.62	10.3%

In the post-cannibalization scenario, as shown in Exhibit 55, revenue is reduced each year to reflect the expected impact from cannibalization. The expected impact of cannibalization results in a decrease in the CAGR of revenue over the period to 5.2%, down from 7.0% in the pre-cannibalization scenario. Given the reduction in revenue growth and holding the cost structure constant at 70/30 fixed versus variable costs, operating income growth slows to a CAGR of 8.0%, down from 10.6% in the pre-cannibalization scenario. Operating margin at the end of the period is reduced by approximately 100 bps from 42.9% to 41.9% because the company is unable to leverage its fixed cost base to the same degree as a result of slower revenue growth.

Overall, in the post-cannibalization scenario, Microsoft is expected to generate revenue of USD81.5 billion, operating income of USD34.2 billion, an operating margin of 41.9%, and EPS that increase at a CAGR of 7.7% to USD3.37 in FY2014. Thus, the cannibalization of PCs as a result of projected growth in the tablet market is expected to reduce the company's annual revenues in FY2014 by USD4.2 billion, operating income by USD2.6 billion, operating margins by 96 bps, and EPS by USD0.25.

EXHIBIT 55: Microsoft Post-Cannibalization EPS Projections, Base Case Scenario ($ millions, unless noted)

	FY2011	FY2012E	FY2013E	FY2014E	3-Year CAGR
Revenue	69,943	72,616	77,028	81,483	5.2%
YoY% change		3.8%	6.1%	5.8%	
Operating Expenses					
Fixed (70%)	29,947	30,520	31,447	32,356	2.6%
Variable (30%)	12,835	13,325	14,135	14,952	5.2%
Total operating expenses	42,782	43,845	45,581	47,308	3.4%
Operating income	27,161	28,771	31,446	34,175	8.0%
Operating margin	38.83%	39.62%	40.82%	41.94%	
Other income (expense)	910	910	910	910	
Pre-tax income	28,071	29,681	32,356	35,085	
Provision for income taxes	4,921	5,203	5,672	6,151	
Effective tax rate	17.53%	17.53%	17.53%	17.53%	
Net income	23,150	24,478	26,684	28,934	
Weighted average shares outstanding, diluted	8,593	8,593	8,593	8,593	
Estimated EPS post-cannibalization	$2.69	$2.85	$3.11	$3.37	7.7%
Estimated impact on operating margin		–61 bps	–76 bps	–96 bps	
Estimated impact on EPS		–$0.13	–$0.18	–$0.25	–2.6%

Estimating the Impact of Cannibalization

Answer the following questions using Exhibits 52 through 56 (see the Example17 worksheet in the downloadable Microsoft Excel workbook) on Microsoft:

1. Estimate post-cannibalization global PC shipments in FY2012 assuming a cannibalization factor of 40% for consumers and 15% for non-consumers.

Solution to 1:

The number of PCs cannibalized by tablets is equal to the product of the expected number of global tablet shipments, the percentage representation of each category, and the cannibalization factor for the category. Exhibit 51 shows that tablet shipments in

FY2012 are projected to be 90 million units. (90 million tablets × 92% consumer representation × 40% consumer cannibalization factor = 33.12 million consumer PCs cannibalized by tablets) + (90 million tablets × 8% non-consumer representation × 15% cannibalization = 1.08 million non-consumer PCs cannibalized by tablets) = 34.2 million total PCs cannibalized by tablets. Post-cannibalization shipments are equal to pre-cannibalization shipments minus expected cannibalization, or 360 million – 34.2 million = 325.8 million.

2. Using the results derived in Question 1, estimate the post-cannibalization revenue in FY2012 for Microsoft.

Solution to 2:

The estimated impact on revenue is equal to the product of the number of PCs cannibalized and the ASP. Using the results obtained in Question 1 and the ASP data contained in Exhibit 51, the expected revenue impact can be calculated as (33.12 million consumer PCs cannibalized by tablets × USD85 ASP = USD2.815 billion) + (1.08 million non-consumer PCs cannibalized by tablets × USD155 ASP = USD167.4 million) = USD2.983 billion total impact on revenue for Microsoft. Post-cannibalization revenue is equal to pre-cannibalization revenue minus the estimated impact on revenue from cannibalization, or USD74.839 billion – USD2.983 billion = USD71.856 billion.

3. Using the estimate for post-cannibalization revenue derived in Question 2 and the cost structure provided, estimate post-cannibalization operating income and operating margin in FY2012 for Microsoft. Assume that fixed costs change at half the rate of the change in sales.

Solution to 3:

EXHIBIT 56: Solution to Problem 3 ($ millions)

	FY2011	FY2012E	Notes
Revenue	69,943	71,856	Derived from Question 2
YoY%		2.74%	Rate of change in sales used to estimate operating expenses
Operating Expenses			
Fixed (70%)	29,947	30,357	Fixed costs change at half the rate of the change in sales, or 29,947 × (1 + 2.74%/2)
Variable (30%)	12,835	13,186	Variable costs change at the same rate as the change in sales, or 12,835 × (1 + 2.74%)
Total operating expenses	42,782	43,543	Although not shown, operating expenses include COGS
Operating income	27,161	28,314	Revenue minus total operating expense, or 71,856 – 43,543 = 28,313
Operating margin	38.8%	39.4%	Operating income divided by revenue, or 28,313/71,856 = 39.4%

Post-cannibalization operating income and operating margin in FY2012 for Microsoft are USD28,314 million and 39.4%, respectively.

4. Using the estimate for operating income derived in Question 3 and the data in the exhibits, calculate the expected post-cannibalization EPS in FY2012 for Microsoft. Assume that other income (expense), the effective tax rate, and the diluted weighted average shares outstanding provided for FY2011 remain constant in FY2012.

Solution to 4:

EXHIBIT 57: Solution to Problem 4 ($ millions, unless noted)

	FY2011	FY2012E	Notes
Revenue	69,943	71,856	
YoY%		2.74%	
Operating Expenses			
Fixed (70%)	29,947	30,357	
Variable (30%)	12,835	13,186	
Total operating expenses	42,782	43,543	
Operating income	27,161	28,314	
Operating margin	38.8%	39.4%	
Other income (expense)	910	910	
Pre-tax income	28,071	29,224	Operating income + Other income (expense), or 28,314 + 910 = 29,224
Provision for income taxes	4,921	5,123	Pre-tax Income × Effective tax rate, or 29,224 × 17.53% = 5,123
Effective tax rate	17.53%	17.53%	
Net income	23,150	24,101	Pre-tax income – Provision for income taxes, or 29,224 – 5,123 = 24,101
Weighted average shares outstanding, diluted	8,593	8,593	
Estimated EPS post-cannibalization	**$2.69**	**$2.80**	Net income/Wtd Avg Shs Out, or 24,101/8,593 = $2.80

Whenever one is estimating something that depends on many different variables that are difficult to measure, we recommend altering some of the assumptions to generate a range of estimates based on various scenarios. Thus, having developed a forecast under a base case cannibalization scenario, we are able to analyze the sensitivity of the results by altering the cannibalization assumptions. The base case scenario corresponds to the assumptions in the boxed center of the table in Exhibit 58. Exhibit 59 summarizes the results of bull and bear case scenarios, showing the estimated FY2014 EPS under alternative estimated cannibalization factors.

EXHIBIT 58: Estimated 2014 EPS Sensitivity to Changes in Cannibalization Rates

		Non-Consumer Cannibalization				
		0.0%	5.0%	10.0%	15.0%	20.0%
Consumer Cannibalization	15%	−$0.11	−$0.12	−$0.14	−$0.15	−$0.16
	20%	−$0.15	−$0.16	−$0.17	−$0.19	−$0.20
	25%	−$0.19	−$0.20	−$0.21	−$0.22	−$0.23
	30%	−$0.22	−$0.24	−$0.25	−$0.26	−$0.27
	35%	−$0.26	−$0.27	−$0.28	−$0.30	−$0.31
	40%	−$0.30	−$0.31	−$0.32	−$0.33	−$0.35
	45%	−$0.34	−$0.35	−$0.36	−$0.37	−$0.38

EXHIBIT 59: Post-Cannibalization EPS Projections for Bull and Bear Scenarios ($ millions, unless noted)

Bull Case Scenario (Cannibalization Factor: 15% Consumer/5% Non-Consumer)

	FY2011	FY2012E	FY2013E	FY2014E	3-Year CAGR
Revenue	69,943	73,728	78,553	83,583	6.1%
YoY%		5.4%	6.5%	6.4%	
Operating Expenses					
Fixed (70%)	29,947	30,758	31,764	32,781	3.1%
Variable (30%)	12,835	13,529	14,414	15,338	6.1%
Total operating expenses	42,782	44,287	46,179	48,119	4.0%
Operating income	27,161	29,441	32,374	35,464	9.3%
Operating margin	38.83%	39.93%	41.21%	42.43%	
Other income (expense)	910	910	910	910	
Pre-tax income	28,071	30,351	33,284	36,374	
Provision for income taxes	4,921	5,321	5,835	6,377	
Effective tax rate	17.53%	17.53%	17.53%	17.53%	
Net income	23,150	25,030	27,449	29,998	
Weighted average shares outstanding, diluted	8,593	8,593	8,593	8,593	
Estimated EPS post-cannibalization	**$2.69**	**$2.91**	**$3.19**	**$3.49**	**9.0%**

Bull Case Scenario (Cannibalization Factor: 15% Consumer/5% Non-Consumer)				
	FY2011	FY2012E	FY2013E	FY2014E	3-Year CAGR
Estimated impact on operating margin		–30 bps	–38 bps	–47 bps	
Estimated impact on EPS		**–$0.06**	**–$0.09**	**–$0.12**	**–1.3%**

Bear Case Scenario (Cannibalization Factor: 40% Consumer/20% Non-Consumer)				
	FY2011	FY2012E	FY2013E	FY2014E	3-Year CAGR
Revenue	69,943	71,801	75,869	79,812	4.5%
YoY%		2.7%	5.7%	5.2%	
Operating Expenses					
Fixed (70%)	29,947	30,345	31,205	32,016	2.3%
Variable (30%)	12,835	13,175	13,922	14,646	4.5%
Total operating expenses	42,782	43,521	45,127	46,661	2.9%
Operating income	27,161	28,280	30,742	33,151	6.9%
Operating margin	38.83%	39.39%	40.52%	41.54%	
Other income (expense)	910	910	910	910	
Pre-tax income	28,071	29,190	31,652	34,061	
Provision for income taxes	4,921	5,117	5,549	5,971	
Effective tax rate	17.53%	17.53%	17.53%	17.53%	
Net income	23,150	24,073	26,103	28,090	
Weighted average shares outstanding, diluted	8,593	8,593	8,593	8,593	
Estimated EPS post-cannibalization	**$2.69**	**$2.80**	**$3.04**	**$3.27**	**6.7%**
Estimated impact on operating margin		–85 bps	–107 bps	–136 bps	
Estimated impact on EPS		**–$0.18**	**–$0.25**	**–$0.35**	**–3.6%**

11. LONG-TERM FORECASTING

The choice of the forecast time horizon can be influenced by certain factors, including the investment strategy for which the security is being considered, the cyclicality of the industry, company-specific factors, and the analyst's employer's preferences. Most professionally managed investment strategies describe the investment time frame, or average holding period, in the stated investment objectives of the strategy; the time frame should ideally correspond with average annual turnover of the portfolio. For example, a stated investment time horizon of three to five years would imply average annual portfolio turnover between 20% and 33% (average holding period is calculated as one/portfolio turnover). The cyclicality of the industry could also influence the analyst's choice of time frame because the forecast period should be long enough to allow the business to reach an expected mid-cycle level of sales and profitability. Similar to cyclicality, various company-specific factors, including recent acquisition or restructuring activity, can influence the selection of the forecast period to allow enough time for the realization of the expected benefits from such activity to be reflected in the financial statements. In other cases, there might be no individual analyst choice in the sense that the analyst's employer has specified more or less fixed parameters. Much of the discussion so far has focused on various methods of forecasting a company's income statement, balance sheet, and cash flow for an explicit short-term forecast period. Although the underlying principles remain the same if one extends the time horizon, certain considerations and choices are available to the analyst when developing longer-term projections.

Longer-term projections often provide a better representation of the normalized earnings potential of a company than a short-term forecast, especially when certain temporary factors are present. **Normalized earnings** are the expected level of mid-cycle earnings for a company in the absence of any unusual or temporary factors that affect profitability (either positively or negatively). For example, at any given point in time, a company's profitability can be influenced by a number of temporary factors, including the stage in the business cycle, recent merger and acquisition activity, and restructuring activity. Similarly, normalized free cash flow can be defined as the expected level of mid-cycle cash flow from operations adjusted for unusual items just described less recurring capital expenditures. By extending the forecast period, an analyst is able to adjust for these unusual or temporary factors and derive an estimate of earnings that the company is likely to earn in a normal year. We will consider various alternatives for two aspects of long-term forecasting: revenue forecasts and terminal value.

As with most income statement projections, a long-term forecast begins with a revenue projection, with most of the remaining income statement items subsequently derived from the level or change in revenue. Revenue projection methods were covered earlier.

11.1. Case Study: Estimating Normalized Revenue

Exhibit 60 contains 10 years of historical revenue data and four years of estimated normalized data for Continental AG, a global automotive supplier. The accompanying bar chart in Exhibit 62 graphically depicts the data and includes a trend line based on a linear regression of the data. The numerical values for each point along the trend line can be found by using the TREND formula in Microsoft Excel. The TREND formula uses observations on the dependent variable (in this case revenue) and observations on the explanatory (time) variable to perform a linear regression by using least squares criterion to find the best fit. After computing the best fit regression model, the TREND formula returns predicted values associated with new points in time. The Exhibit60&61 worksheet in the downloadable Microsoft Excel workbook demonstrates the calculations used in the exhibits.

EXHIBIT 60: Historical and Estimated Revenue Data for Continental AG, 2011–2024E (€ billions)

€ blns	2011	2012	2013	2014	2015	2016	2017	2018	2019	2020	2021	2022	2023	2024
Revenue	30.5	32.7	33.3	34.5	39.2	40.6	44.0	44.4	44.5	37.7				
Normalized revenue	31.8	33.2	34.6	36.0	37.4	38.9	40.3	41.7	43.1	44.5	45.9	47.3	48.7	50.1
Percent above/ below trend	–4.1%	–1.4%	–3.7%	–4.2%	4.8%	4.4%	9.3%	–6.6%	3.3%	–15.2%				

Sources: Continental AG annual reports.

EXHIBIT 61: Historical and Estimated Revenue for Continental AG, 2011–2024E

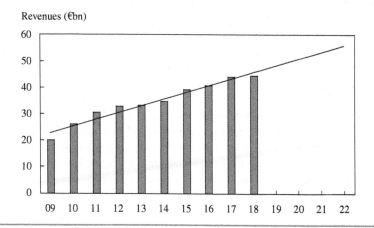

The "growth relative to GDP growth" and "market growth and market share" methods discussed earlier can also be applied to developing longer-term projections. Once a revenue projection has been established, previously described methods of forecasting costs can be used to complete the income statement, balance sheet, and cash flow statement.

If an analyst is creating a valuation model such as a DCF model, estimating a terminal value is required to capture the going-concern value of the company after the explicit forecast period. Certain considerations should be kept in mind when deriving the terminal value based on long-term projections.

First, an analyst should consider whether the terminal year free cash flow projection should be normalized before that cash flow is incorporated into a long-term projection. For example, if the explicitly forecasted terminal year free cash flow is "low" (e.g., because of business cycle reasons or capital investment projects), an adjustment to normalize the amount might be warranted. Second, an analyst should consider whether and how the future long-term growth rate will differ from the historical growth rate. For example, even some mature companies might be able to accelerate their long-term growth rate through product innovation and/or market expansion (e.g., Apple), whereas other seemingly well-protected "growers" could experience an unanticipated decline in their business as a result of technological change (e.g., Eastman Kodak Company, a global commercial printing and imaging company).

One of the greatest challenges facing the analyst is anticipating inflection points, when the future will look significantly different from the recent past. Most DCF models rely on a perpetuity calculation, which assumes that the cash flows from the last year of an explicit forecast grow at a constant rate forever. Because the perpetuity can account for a relatively large portion of the overall valuation of the company, it is critical that the cash flow used is representative of a "normalized" or "mid-cycle" result. If the analyst is examining a cyclical company, using a boom year as the starting point for the perpetuity could result in a grossly overstated valuation. Similarly, using a trough year could result in a valuation that is much too low.

Another important consideration is economic disruption. The economy can occasionally experience sudden, unprecedented changes that affect a wide variety of companies, such as the 2008 global financial crisis or the COVID-19 pandemic. Even a company with a sound strategy and solid operations can be thrown far off course by a sudden economic disruption, particularly if the company has a high degree of financial leverage.

Regulation and technology are also potential drivers of inflection points, and it is important for the analyst to keep a close eye on both. Government actions can have extreme, sudden, and unpredictable impacts on some businesses. Technological advances can turn fast-growing innovators obsolete in a matter of months. Both regulation and technology affect some industries more than others. Utilities experience intense regulation but might not see a significant technological change for decades. Semiconductor manufacturers must constantly keep up with new technology but experience relatively light regulation. Pharmaceutical manufacturers are heavily exposed to both regulation and technological advances.

Finally, long-term growth is a key input in the perpetuity calculation. Some companies and industries can grow faster than the overall economy for long periods of time, causing them to account for an increasing share of overall output. Examples include some technology companies, such as Tencent, Amazon, and Google. Other companies, such as those in the print media sector, are likely to grow slower than the overall economy or even shrink over time. Using an unrealistic long-term growth rate can put the analyst's valuation far off the mark.

EXAMPLE 19 Important Considerations When Making Assumptions

1. Turkish Airlines (THYAO.IS) operates in the highly cyclical global airline industry. Operating margins for 2011–2019 are shown in the following table and in the Example18 worksheet in the downloadable Microsoft Excel workbook.

	2011	2012	2013	2014	2015	2016	2017	2018	2019
Operating margin	1.0%	10.8%	6.5%	5.6%	8.6%	−2.9%	9.0%	9.9%	7.9%

1. On the basis of only the information in the table, which of the following operating margins would *most likely* be appropriate to use in a perpetuity calculation for Turkish Airlines to arrive at a reasonable intrinsic value estimate?
   A. 6.0%
   B. 9.0%
   C. 9.9%

Solution to 1:

A is correct. Because the airline industry is cyclical, an estimate of "mid-cycle" or "normalized" operating margin is necessary to estimate a perpetuity value. The nine-year average operating margin was 6.3%.

For each of the companies in the following problems, indicate which of the choices is *least likely* to cause a change in the company's outlook.

2. ABC Diesel (hypothetical company), a manufacturer of diesel-power trucks.
   A. Environmental regulations have been getting tighter in most regions, and consistent with past experience, the need to make the engines less polluting is expected to continue over the next several years.
   B. Consumers have started switching to trucks with electric engines, threatening ABC's historic strength in diesel engine trucks.
   C. ABC Diesel has formed a partnership with Electrico (hypothetical), a company involved in research and innovation in electric engines.

Solution to 2:

A is correct. Although it is important that environmental regulations have been getting stricter, this is consistent with past experience and so does not represent a turning point.

3. Abbott Laboratories, a diversified manufacturer of health care products, including medical devices.
   A. It has become more difficult for medical device manufacturers to receive regulatory approval for new products because of heightened safety concerns.
   B. A competitor has demonstrated favorable efficacy data on a medical device candidate that will compete with an important Abbott product.
   C. Management reiterates its long-standing approach to capital deployment.

Solution to 3:

C is correct. Management is sticking with its historical approach to capital deployment, so this does not represent a turning point.

4. Grupo Aeroportuario del Sureste, operator of nine airports in Mexico, especially in the tourist-heavy southeast.
   A. A technological advance will allow airlines to save 5% on fuel costs, but it is not expected to meaningfully alter passenger volumes. Similar developments in the past have benefited airlines but not airports, whose price per passenger is regulated.
   B. Global economic disruption has caused a sharp decline in international travel.
   C. Regulators will allow the construction of a new airport by a competitor in Grupo Aeroportuario del Sureste's service territory.

Solution to 4:

A is correct. Although the technological advance is good for the airlines, it will not have a meaningful effect on passenger volumes, which will likely prevent the airports from sharing in that benefit. In contrast, both B and C could have a significant impact on the long-run earnings power of Mexican airports.

5. LinkedIn, operator of an online social network for professionals and part of Microsoft Corporation, with limited investment needs and no debt.
   A. Facebook, another online social network, announces a plan to enhance its offerings in the professional category.
   B. Regulators announce an investigation of LinkedIn's privacy practices, which could result in significant changes to the service.
   C. The US Federal Reserve has just increased interest rates. Although this will raise borrowing costs, the rate increase is not expected to have a negative impact on the economy.

Solution to 5:

C is correct. Because LinkedIn carries no debt, it is unlikely that higher interest rates will cause a change in the company's outlook.

12. SUMMARY

Industry and company analysis are essential tools of fundamental analysis. The key points made include the following:

- Analysts can use a top-down, bottom-up, or hybrid approach to forecasting income and expenses. Top-down approaches usually begin at the level of the overall economy. Bottom-up approaches begin at the level of the individual company or unit within the company (e.g., business segment). Time-series approaches are considered bottom-up, although time-series analysis can be a tool used in top-down approaches. Hybrid approaches include elements of top-down and bottom-up approaches.
- In a "growth relative to GDP growth" approach to forecasting revenue, the analyst forecasts the growth rate of nominal gross domestic product and industry and company growth relative to GDP growth.
- In a "market growth and market share" approach to forecasting revenue, the analyst combines forecasts of growth in particular markets with forecasts of a company's market share in the individual markets.
- Operating margins that are positively correlated with sales provide evidence of economies of scale in an industry.
- Some balance sheet line items, such as retained earnings, flow directly from the income statement, whereas accounts receivable, accounts payable, and inventory are very closely linked to income statement projections.
- A common way to model working capital accounts is to use efficiency ratios.
- Return on invested capital (ROIC), defined as net operating profit less adjusted taxes divided by the difference between operating assets and operating liabilities, is an after-tax

measure of the profitability of investing in a company. High and persistent levels of ROIC are often associated with having a competitive advantage.

- Competitive factors affect a company's ability to negotiate lower input prices with suppliers and to raise prices for products and services. Porter's five forces framework can be used as a basis for identifying such factors.
- Inflation (deflation) affects pricing strategy depending on industry structure, competitive forces, and the nature of consumer demand.
- When a technological development results in a new product that threatens to cannibalize demand for an existing product, a unit forecast for the new product combined with an expected cannibalization factor can be used to estimate the impact on future demand for the existing product.
- Factors influencing the choice of the explicit forecast horizon include the projected holding period, an investor's average portfolio turnover, cyclicality of an industry, company-specific factors, and employer preferences.
- Key behavioral biases that influence analyst forecasts are overconfidence, illusion of control conservatism, representativeness, and confirmation bias.

13. PRACTICE PROBLEMS

The following information relates to questions 1–7

Angela Green, an investment manager at Horizon Investments, intends to hire a new investment analyst. After conducting initial interviews, Green has narrowed the pool to three candidates. She plans to conduct second interviews to further assess the candidates' knowledge of industry and company analysis.

Prior to the second interviews, Green asks the candidates to analyze Chrome Network Systems, a company that manufactures internet networking products. Each candidate is provided Chrome's financial information presented in Exhibit 1.

EXHIBIT 1: Chrome Network Systems Selected Financial Information ($ millions)

	Year-End		
	2017	2018	2019
Net sales	46.8	50.5	53.9
Cost of sales	18.2	18.4	18.8
Gross profit	28.6	32.1	35.1
SG&A expenses	19.3	22.5	25.1
Operating income	9.3	9.6	10.0
Interest expense	0.5	0.7	0.6
Income before provision for income tax	8.8	8.9	9.4
Provision for income taxes	2.8	2.8	3.1
Net income	6.0	6.1	6.3

Green asks each candidate to forecast the 2020 income statement for Chrome and to outline the key assumptions used in their analysis. The job candidates are told to include Horizon's economic outlook for 2020 in their analysis, which assumes nominal GDP growth of 3.6%, based on expectations of real GDP growth of 1.6% and inflation of 2.0%.

Green receives the models from each of the candidates and schedules second interviews. To prepare for the interviews, Green compiles a summary of the candidates' key assumptions in Exhibit 2.

EXHIBIT 2: Summary of Key Assumptions Used in Candidates' Models

Metric	Candidate A	Candidate B	Candidate C
Net sales	Net sales will grow at the average annual growth rate in net sales over the 2017–19 time period.	Industry sales will grow at the same rate as nominal GDP, but Chrome will have a 2 percentage point decline in market share.	Net sales will grow 50 bps slower than nominal GDP.
Cost of sales	The 2020 gross margin will be the same as the average annual gross margin over the 2017–19 time period.	The 2020 gross margin will decline as costs increase by expected inflation.	The 2020 gross margin will increase by 20 bps from 2019.
SG&A expenses	The 2020 SG&A/net sales ratio will be the same as the average ratio over the 2017–19 time period.	The 2020 SG&A will grow at the rate of inflation.	The 2020 SG&A/net sales ratio will be the same as the 2019 ratio.
Interest expense	The 2020 interest expense assumes the effective interest rate will be the same as the 2019 rate.	The 2020 interest expense will be the same as the 2019 interest expense.	The 2020 interest expense will be the same as the average expense over the 2017–19 time period.
Income taxes	The 2020 effective tax rate will be the same as the 2019 rate.	The 2020 effective tax rate will equal the blended statutory rate of 30%.	The 2020 effective tax rate will be the same as the average effective tax rate over the 2017–19 time period.

1. Based on Exhibit 1, which of the following provides the strongest evidence that Chrome displays economies of scale?
   A. Increasing net sales
   B. Profit margins that are increasing with net sales
   C. Gross profit margins that are increasing with net sales

2. Based on Exhibit 2, the job candidate *most likely* using a bottom-up approach to model net sales is:
   A. Candidate A
   B. Candidate B
   C. Candidate C

3. Based on Exhibit 2, the modeling approach used by Candidate B to project future net sales is *most accurately* classified as a:

    A. hybrid approach.

    B. top-down approach.

    C. bottom-up approach.

4. Based on Exhibits 1 and 2, Candidate C's forecast for cost of sales in 2020 is *closest* to:

    A. USD18.3 million.

    B. USD18.9 million.

    C. USD19.3 million.

5. Based on Exhibits 1 and 2, Candidate A's forecast for SG&A expenses in 2020 is *closest* to:

    A. USD23.8 million.

    B. USD25.5 million.

    C. USD27.4 million.

6. Based on Exhibit 2, forecasted interest expense will reflect changes in Chrome's debt level under the forecast assumptions used by:

    A. Candidate A.

    B. Candidate B.

    C. Candidate C.

7. Candidate B asks Green if she had additional information on Horizon's industry peers and competitors, to put the profitability estimates in a richer context. By asking for this additional information for their analysis, Candidate B is seeking to mitigate which behavioral bias?

    A. Illusion of control

    B. Base rate neglect

    C. Conservatism

The following information relates to questions 8–14

Nigel French, an analyst at Taurus Investment Management, is analyzing Archway Technologies, a manufacturer of luxury electronic auto equipment, at the request of his supervisor, Lukas Wright. French is asked to evaluate Archway's profitability over the past five years relative to its two main competitors, which are located in different countries with significantly different tax structures.

French begins by assessing Archway's competitive position within the luxury electronic auto equipment industry using Porter's five forces framework. A summary of French's industry analysis is presented in Exhibit 1.

Exhibit 1: Analysis of Luxury Electronic Auto Equipment Industry Using Porter's Five Forces Framework

Force	Factors to Consider
Threat of substitutes	Customer switching costs are high
Rivalry	Archway holds 60% of world market share; each of its two main competitors holds 15%
Bargaining power of suppliers	Primary inputs are considered basic commodities, and there are a large number of suppliers
Bargaining power of buyers	Luxury electronic auto equipment is very specialized (non-standardized)
Threat of new entrants	High fixed costs to enter industry

French notes that for the year just ended (2019), Archway's COGS was 30% of sales. To forecast Archway's income statement for 2020, French assumes that all companies in the industry will experience an inflation rate of 8% on the COGS. Exhibit 2 shows French's forecasts relating to Archway's price and volume changes.

EXHIBIT 2: Archway's 2020 Forecasted Price and Volume Changes

Average price increase per unit	5.00%
Volume growth	–3.00%

After putting together income statement projections for Archway, French forecasts Archway's balance sheet items. He uses Archway's historical efficiency ratios to forecast the company's working capital accounts.

Based on his financial forecast for Archway, French estimates a terminal value using a valuation multiple based on the company's average price-to-earnings multiple (P/E) over the past five years. Wright discusses with French how the terminal value estimate is sensitive to key assumptions about the company's future prospects. Wright asks French: "What change in the calculation of the terminal value would you make if a technological development that would adversely affect Archway was forecast to occur sometime beyond your financial forecast horizon?"

8. Which profitability metric should French use to assess Archway's five-year historic performance relative to its competitors?
   A. Current ratio
   B. Operating margin
   C. Return on invested capital

9. Based on the current competitive landscape presented in Exhibit 1, French should conclude that Archway's ability to:
   A. pass along price increases is high.
   B. demand lower input prices from suppliers is low.
   C. generate above-average returns on invested capital is low.

10. Based on the current competitive landscape presented in Exhibit 1, Archway's operating profit margins over the forecast horizon are *least likely* to:
    A. decrease.
    B. remain constant.
    C. increase.

11. Based on Exhibit 2, Archway's forecasted gross profit margin for 2020 is *closest* to:
    A. 62.7%.
    B. 67.0%.
    C. 69.1%.

12. French's approach to forecasting Archway's working capital accounts would be *most likely* classified as a:

   A. hybrid approach.

   B. top-down approach.

   C. bottom-up approach.

13. The *most appropriate* response to Wright's question about the technological development is to:

   A. increase the required return.

   B. decrease the price-to-earnings multiple.

   C. decrease the perpetual growth rate.

14. If the luxury electronic auto equipment industry is subject to rapid technological changes and market share shifts, how should French best adapt his approach to modeling?

   A. Examine base rates

   B. Speak to analysts who hold diverse opinions on the stock

   C. Forecast multiple scenarios

The following information relates to questions 15–21

Gertrude Fromm is a transportation sector analyst at Tucana Investments. She is conducting an analysis of Omikroon, N.V., a (hypothetical) European engineering company that manufactures and sells scooters and commercial trucks.

Omikroon's petrol scooter division is the market leader in its sector and has two competitors. Omikroon's petrol scooters have a strong brand name and a well-established distribution network. Given the strong branding established by the market leaders, the cost of entering the industry is high. But Fromm anticipates that small, inexpensive, imported petrol-fueled motorcycles could become substitutes for Omikroon's petrol scooters.

Fromm uses ROIC as the metric to assess Omikroon's performance.

Omikroon has just introduced the first electric scooter to the market at year-end 2019. The company's expectations are as follows:

- Competing electric scooters will reach the market in 2021.
- Electric scooters will not be a substitute for petrol scooters.
- The important research costs in 2020 and 2021 will lead to more efficient electric scooters.

Fromm decides to use a five-year forecast horizon for Omikroon after considering the following factors:

Factor 1 The annual portfolio turnover at Tucana Investments is 30%.

Factor 2 The electronic scooter industry is expected to grow rapidly over the next 10 years.

Factor 3 Omikroon has announced it would acquire a light truck manufacturer that will be fully integrated into its truck division by 2021 and will add 2% to the company's total revenues.

Fromm uses the base case forecast for 2020 shown in Exhibit 1 to perform the following sensitivity analysis:

- The price of an imported specialty metal used for engine parts increases by 20%.
- This metal constitutes 4% of Omikroon's cost of sales.
- Omikroon will not be able to pass on the higher metal expense to its customers.

EXHIBIT 1: Omikroon's Selected Financial Forecasts for 2020 Base Case (€ millions)

	Petrol Scooter Division	Commercial Truck Division	Electric Scooter Division	Total
Sales	99.05	45.71	7.62	152.38
Cost of sales				105.38
Gross profit				47.00
Operating profit				9.20

Omikroon will initially outsource its electric scooter parts. But manufacturing these parts in-house beginning in 2021 will imply changes to an existing factory. This factory cost EUR7 million three years ago and had an estimated useful life of 10 years. Fromm is evaluating two scenarios:

Scenario 1 Sell the existing factory for EUR5 million. Build a new factory costing EUR30 million with a useful life of 10 years.
Scenario 2 Refit the existing factory for EUR27 million.

15. Using Porter's five forces analysis, which of the following competitive factors is likely to have the *greatest* impact on Omikroon's petrol scooter pricing power?
    A. Rivalry
    B. Threat of substitutes
    C. Threat of new entrants

16. The metric used by Fromm to assess Omikroon's performance takes into account:
    A. degree of financial leverage.
    B. operating liabilities relative to operating assets.
    C. competitiveness relative to companies in other tax regimes.

17. Based on Omikroon's expectations, the gross profit margin of Omikroon's electric scooter division in 2021 is *most likely* to be affected by:
    A. competition.
    B. research costs.
    C. cannibalization by petrol scooters.

18. Which factor *best* justifies the five-year forecast horizon for Omikroon selected by Fromm?
    A. Factor 1
    B. Factor 2
    C. Factor 3

19. Fromm's sensitivity analysis will result in a decrease in the 2020 base case gross profit margin *closest to*:
    A. 0.55 percentage points.
    B. 0.80 percentage points.
    C. 3.32 percentage points.

20. Fromm's estimate of growth capital expenditure included in Omikroon's PP&E under Scenario 2 should be:

A. lower than under Scenario 1.

B. the same as under Scenario 1.

C. higher than under Scenario 1.

21. To validate the forecast for rapid growth in the electronic scooter market over the next 10 years, Fromm speaks to the management of Omikroon and investor relations of ZeroWheel, a competitor. Fromm might be subject to which behavioral bias?

A. Conservatism

B. Overconfidence

C. Confirmation

CHAPTER 14

CORPORATE RESTRUCTURINGS*

LEARNING OUTCOMES

The candidate should be able to:

- explain types of corporate restructurings and issuers' motivations for pursuing them
- explain the initial evaluation of a corporate restructuring
- demonstrate valuation methods for, and interpret valuations of, companies involved in corporate restructurings
- demonstrate how corporate restructurings affect an issuer's EPS, net debt to EBITDA ratio, and weighted average cost of capital
- evaluate corporate investment actions, including equity investments, joint ventures, and acquisitions
- evaluate corporate divestment actions, including sales and spin offs
- evaluate cost and balance sheet restructurings

1. INTRODUCTION

Corporate issuers change over time. While many changes are evolutionary, such as launching new products and expanding capacity, others involve more revolutionary changes to the legal and accounting structure of the issuer. The most well-known among these structural changes is acquisitions, in which one company buys another. Other well-known changes include divestitures and spin offs, in which an issuer sells or separates a segment of its business. Common features among these changes are that they tend to attract significant press and analyst attention and their announcement is associated with increased securities trading volume.

In this chapter, you will learn how to evaluate corporate restructurings from the perspective of an independent investment analyst. We begin our discussion in Section 2 with an overview of corporate restructurings, including putting these events in the context of the corporate life cycle, and corporate issuers' motivations for pursuing them. In Sections 3 and 4,

*CFA Institute would like to thank Rosita P. Chang, PhD, CFA, and Keith M. Moore, PhD, CFA for their contribution to this chapter, which includes material derived from Mergers and Acquisitions, CFA Level II, 2022. Rosita P. Chang, PhD, CFA, is at Shidler College of Business, University of Hawaii at Manoa (USA). Keith M. Moore, PhD, CFA (USA).

we discuss a three-step process for evaluating corporate restructurings as an investment analyst. Sections 5–7 demonstrate the evaluation process with case studies for each major type of corporate restructuring. The chapter concludes with a summary and practice problems.

2. CORPORATE EVOLUTION, ACTIONS, AND MOTIVATIONS

2.1. Corporate Life Cycle and Actions

Companies tend to follow a life cycle composed of four stages: start-up, growth, maturity, and decline. At each life-cycle stage, there is a corresponding revenue growth, profitability, and risk profile, which in turn generally determine the company's financing mix. A typical company's life cycle is illustrated in Exhibit 1.

EXHIBIT 1: Company Life Cycle

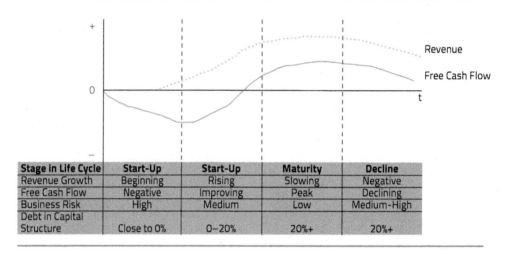

Stage in Life Cycle	Start-Up	Start-Up	Maturity	Decline
Revenue Growth	Beginning	Rising	Slowing	Negative
Free Cash Flow	Negative	Improving	Peak	Declining
Business Risk	High	Medium	Low	Medium-High
Debt in Capital Structure	Close to 0%	0–20%	20%+	20%+

    While it may be in investors' best interest for maturing companies to simply operate the business for maximum cash flow until returns fall below investors' required rate of return and then liquidate the firm, most corporate managers and boards take actions to change their destiny. We can group the kinds of changes corporate managers can make into three general categories: investment, divestment, and restructuring.

- Investment involves actions that increase the size of the company or the scope of its operations, thereby increasing revenue and perhaps revenue growth. In this chapter, we focus on external, or inorganic, growth through investment actions designed to increase revenues and improve margins. We do not look at investing in the existing business, or organic growth, through capital expenditures or research and development.
- Divestment involves actions that reduce a company's size or scope, typically by shedding slower-growing, lower-profitability, or higher-risk operations to improve the issuer's overall financial performance.

- Restructuring involves changes that do not alter the size or scope of the issuer but improve its cost and financing structure with the intention to increase growth, improve profitability, or reduce risks.

These three categories of changes, with an example of each, are shown in Exhibit 2.

EXHIBIT 2: Types of Corporate Structural Changes

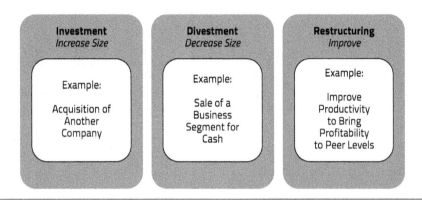

Most large corporate issuers are essentially portfolios of many diverse lines of business that often are in different stages of their life cycle and operate in different competitive environments. There are benefits to the individual business lines from common ownership and compatibility with other businesses, known as **synergies**. There can also be costs and inefficiencies, however, and some parts of the business might better fit in the hands of another corporate issuer or even operating as an independent company. Managers look to change the composition of the "corporate portfolio" in response to changing competitive conditions, limited synergies, poor profitability, or incompatibility with other businesses.

2.2. Motivations for Corporate Structural Change

An issuer's motivations to initiate a structural change can be issuer specific but can also be caused by broader macroeconomic or industry changes, known as top-down drivers, as shown in Exhibit 3.

EXHIBIT 3: Motivations for Corporate Structural Change

	Investment Actions	Divestment Actions	Restructuring Actions
Issuer-specific motivations	• Realize synergies • Increase growth • Improve capabilities or secure resources • Opportunity to acquire an undervalued target	• Focus operations and business lines • Valuation • Liquidity needs • Regulatory requirements	• Improve returns on capital • Financial challenges, including bankruptcy and liquidation
Top-down drivers	• High security prices • Industry shocks		

While issuer-specific motivations determine the type of action a corporate issuer may take, the response to top-down motivations span the three types of restructurings.

First, all types of changes have been found to be pro-cyclical, often coinciding with economic expansions and rising security prices and decreasing in recessions and when security prices are falling. From 2000 to 2019, the Boston Consulting Group (BCG) found that the correlation between the value of the MSCI World Index, a broad global equity market index, and the volume of corporate transactions was 0.80, as graphically shown in Exhibit 4 (Kengelbach, Gell, Keienburg, Degen, and Kim 2020).

EXHIBIT 4: Corporate Transactions and Equity Prices

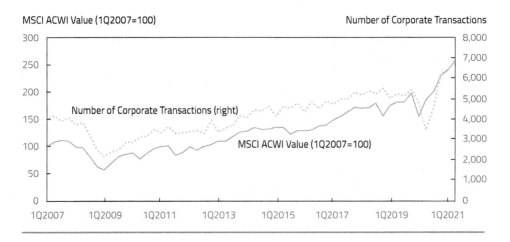

There are several possible explanations for the connection between asset prices and corporate transaction activity:

- *Greater CEO confidence.* High and rising security prices are associated with high and rising CEO confidence. While this explanation is controversial, it is likely true that CEOs take actions, especially large actions, only when they are confident about the future.
- *Lower cost of financing.* Lower interest rates (higher bond prices) and higher equity prices (lower equity risk premiums) result in lower interest expense and less dilution to existing shareholders from debt and equity-financed transactions, respectively.
- *Management and boards know that their stock is overvalued.* Higher equity valuations are beneficial for equity-financed acquisitions, sales, and spin offs. If a company believes its stock is overvalued, it can use these transactions to exchange overvalued stock and realize value.

While rarer, corporate transactions in periods of weak economic growth have been found to create more value, on average, than those in periods of strong economic growth. BCG found that "weak economy" deals are associated with a nearly 10% higher increase in shareholder return over three years than "strong economy" deals (Kengelbach, Keienburg, Gell, Nielsen, Bader, Degen, and Sievers 2019). In other words, in periods of economic stress and risk aversion, there are benefits to risk-taking.

Besides asset prices, empirical research also suggests that corporate restructuring activity tends to come in industry-specific waves during regulatory changes, technological changes, or changes in the growth rate of the industry, collectively known as **industry shocks**. Essentially, corporate issuers take action to adapt to disruptions in their competitive environment, which we will see through examples throughout this chapter.

2.3. Types of Corporate Restructurings

Within the general categories of investment, divestment, and restructuring, most corporate restructurings can be classified as one of nine specific types, as shown in Exhibit 5. Leveraged buyouts (LBOs) are a special type of restructuring that combines elements of each category.

EXHIBIT 5: Types of Corporate Restructurings

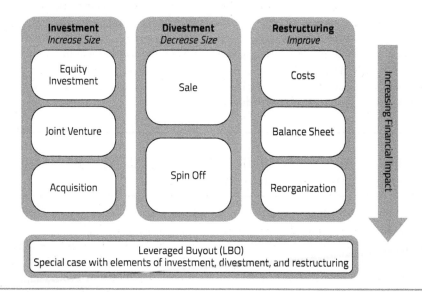

2.3.1. Investment Actions: Equity Investments, Joint Ventures, and Acquisitions

There are several common issuer-specific motivations for investment actions, including creating synergies, increasing growth, improving capabilities and access to resources, and finding undervalued investment opportunities.

Synergies refer to the combination of two companies being more valuable than the sum of the parts. Generally, synergies take the form of lower costs ("cost synergies") or increased revenues ("revenue synergies") through combinations that generate lower costs or higher revenues, respectively, than the sum of the separate companies.

Synergies in general and administrative costs, manufacturing and distribution expenses, research and development spending, and sales and marketing costs are typically achieved through economies of scale. Synergies in general and administrative expenses arise from the consolidation of redundant functions; for example, a company needs only one headquarters, support department, and executive management team. Synergies can also be created in manufacturing and distribution by increasing capacity utilization and route density if an acquirer and target have comparable products and customers.

Revenue synergies are typically created through economies of scope, such as the cross-selling of products to increase market share, or by increasing bargaining power with customers from reduced competition. For example, a bank that acquires an insurance company may directly market its newly acquired insurance products to its existing banking customers. In some industries, customers tend to prefer buying several products from the same company because it is easier to manage fewer relationships.

The desires for growth and for improving unique capabilities or securing resources are closely related to synergies. For instance, acquiring or investing in an established but faster-growing company can increase consolidated revenue growth. Since the 1980s, cross-border acquisitions have been a popular strategy for companies seeking to extend their market reach because in many parts of the world, waves of deregulation and privatizations of state-owned enterprises provided opportunities to acquire new manufacturing facilities, to enter into new foreign markets, and to find new sources of talent and production resources.

Moreover, a corporation may be dependent on another company for inputs or for distribution of its products. By acquiring that company, the acquirer will increase its vertical integration, which can result in lower costs and lower risks and provides a more compelling proposition to customers and investors. Such acquisitions can result in a competitive advantage for the acquirer and may reduce competition.

NVIDIA CORP. TO ACQUIRE ARM LTD. FROM SOFTBANK GROUP CORP. FOR GBP30.2 BILLION

On 13 September 2020, NVIDIA announced a definitive agreement under which it will acquire Arm Limited from SoftBank, its owner. NVIDIA is a US-based manufacturer of computer graphics processors, chipsets, and related multimedia software. Arm, a UK-based subsidiary of SoftBank, is focused on standards-based Internet of Things (IoT) devices and offers a free operating system that consolidates the fundamental building blocks of the IoT. SoftBank is a Japanese holding company engaged in the management of its group companies across multiple sectors.

NVIDIA will pay to SoftBank a total of USD21.5 billion in NVIDIA common stock and USD12 billion in cash, which includes USD2 billion payable at signing. At closing, NVIDIA will issue 44.3 million new shares to SoftBank.

In its press release, NVIDIA emphasized that "the combination brings together NVIDIA's leading AI computing platform with Arm's vast ecosystem to create the premier computing company for the age of artificial intelligence, accelerating innovation while expanding into large, high-growth markets. SoftBank will remain committed to Arm's long-term success through its ownership stake in NVIDIA, expected to be under 10%."

The proposed transaction is subject to regulatory approvals from the United Kingdom, China, the European Union, and the United States due to the expected impact of the acquisition on competition in the industry.

There are three types of investment actions:

- An **equity investment** refers to a company purchasing a material stake in another company's equity but less than 50% of its shares. The two companies maintain their independence, but the investor company has investment exposure to the investee and, in some cases depending on the size of the investment, can have representation on the investee's board of directors to influence operations. Equity investments are often made for one of several reasons: establishing a strategic partnership between companies, taking an initial step towards an eventual acquisition, or investing by an investor company into a company it believes is undervalued.
- In a **joint venture**, two or more companies form and jointly control a new, separate company to achieve a business objective. Each participant contributes assets, employees, know-how, or other resources to the joint venture company. The participants maintain their independence otherwise and continue to do business apart from the joint venture but share in the joint venture's profits or losses. Joint ventures are technically a type of equity investment (in a newly formed company) but are often larger than equity investments in several respects: size, operational control over joint venture, and time spent by management. A common use of joint ventures is conducting business in new markets; a company with a product or service will form a joint venture with another company with local business knowledge in a different, often international, market.
- An **acquisition** is when one company, the acquirer, purchases most or all of another company's, the target, shares to gain control of either an entire company, a segment of the other company, or a specific group of assets, in exchange for cash, stock, or the assumption of liabilities, alone or in combination. Once an acquisition is complete, the target ceases to exist as an independent company and becomes a subsidiary of the acquirer, and the acquirer will report a single set of financial statements that include the results of the target. Depending on the acquirer's integration approach, the management, operations, and resources across the companies will be consolidated. Each line on the financial statements (e.g., revenue, expenses, cash, cash flows from operations) is an aggregation of all consolidated subsidiaries of the issuer.

Acquisitions are distinct from equity investments and joint ventures because the acquirer acquires full control over the target and consolidates the financial statements, reflecting control.

2.3.2. Divestment Actions: Sales and Spin Offs

Motivations for divestment actions mirror those of investment actions because they represent a consolidation of the company's business. Common issuer-specific motivations to sell include focus, valuation, liquidity, and regulatory requirements.

Through either acquisitions or internal expansion over time, companies often operate across multiple different lines of business. Management may seek to improve performance by separating these businesses, either selling them to another company or spinning them off into independent companies. The source of performance improvement for the divested business may be increased management attention, focus, or effort and potential synergies with the acquirer.

Particularly in the case of spin offs, investors can be rewarded through increased stock prices that are tied directly to the performance of the specific business. Example 1 describes a divestment transaction intended to improve focus.

EXAMPLE 1   Daimler AG to Split into Daimler Truck and Mercedes-Benz

Until 2021, Daimler AG operated and reported in two business segments: Daimler Trucks & Buses and Mercedes-Benz Cars & Vans. In February 2021, Daimler AG announced that it will spin off Daimler Trucks & Buses into a separate Frankfurt-listed company and will rename itself (the remaining business segment) Mercedes-Benz, reflecting its focus on the car and van business that sells vehicles under that brand. The spin off will be effected by Daimler AG paying a stock dividend of newly created Daimler Trucks & Buses shares to Daimler AG shareholders, who will then own two separate types of shares: Daimler Trucks & Buses and Mercedes-Benz.

Ola Källenius, chairman of the Board of Management of Daimler AG, underlined that focus was the primary driver of the decision to split: "Mercedes-Benz Cars & Vans and Daimler Trucks & Buses are different businesses with specific customer groups, technology paths, and capital needs. Mercedes-Benz is the world's most valuable luxury car brand, offering the most desirable cars to discerning customers. Daimler Trucks & Buses supplies industry leading transportation solutions and services to customers. Both companies operate in industries that are facing major technological and structural changes. Given this context, we believe they will be able to operate most effectively as independent entities, equipped with strong net liquidity and free from the constraints of a conglomerate structure."

While an undervalued target is a motivation for an investment action, an overvalued target—or at least one with a potentially higher valuation than the parent company—is a motivation for a divestment action. Many large corporate issuers own businesses that could be valued more highly by the capital markets if they were independent instead of inside the parent company. An issuer trading at a valuation lower than the sum of its parts is said to have a **conglomerate discount**, which is generally the result of diseconomies of scale or scope, owing to a deficit in focus, management effort, or investment; due to incompatible businesses; or because the capital markets have overlooked the business and its prospects. Example 2 describes a divestment transaction intended to reduce the conglomerate discount and realize that value for its stakeholders.

EXAMPLE 2   Novartis AG Divestments

Like other major pharmaceutical companies, Novartis AG had a sprawling portfolio of health care businesses. In the years since the appointment of a new CEO in 2013, Novartis has made several large divestments: It divested its vaccines and over-the-counter pharmaceutical business to rival GlaxoSmithKline, sold its animal pharmaceuticals business to Eli Lilly, another rival, and spun off Alcon, its eye care business, as an independent SIX-listed company.

Alcon was spun off, via a stock dividend payable to Novartis AG shareholders, on 9 April 2019. At the time of the spin off, Alcon equity was valued at over 30 times its EPS, while Novartis AG's price-to-earnings ratio (P/E) was half that amount. Two years after the spin off, Alcon shares had appreciated by over 35% while Novartis AG shares were roughly flat, demonstrating that Alcon was more valuable outside of its parent than inside. Alcon was the market leader in eye care devices and supplies, a growing market that does not face significant patent expirations like biopharmaceuticals and that requires less R&D.

The two remaining common issuer-specific motivations for divestment actions—liquidity and regulatory requirements—represent situations where external circumstances force the issuer to act. Typically, unsustainable financial leverage prompts a corporate issuer to sell one or more of its businesses for cash and use these proceeds to reduce its leverage. Because these transactions are frequently made at comparatively lower valuations, they are advantageous to the acquirer. The same may hold true for divestments required by regulators to avoid anti-competitive conduct and to safeguard against corporations building cartels and monopolies that would undermine competition. Regulators may force divestments as a requirement for their approval of a pending acquisition. Similarly, courts may impose divestiture as a remedy in an antitrust legal proceeding.

There are two main form of divestments:

- A sale, also known as a **divestiture**, is the other side of an acquisition; the seller sells a company, segment of a company, or group of assets to an acquirer. Once complete, control of the target is transferred to the acquirer. After a sale, the seller is no longer exposed to the divested business, because it has been exchanged for cash. The logic of the transaction is for capital to be reallocated to a better use (or returned to shareholders or creditors) and for the seller and acquirer to focus on their strengths.
- A **spin off** is when a company separates a distinct part of its business into a new, independent company. The term "spin off" is used to describe both the transaction and the separated component, while the company that conducts the transaction and formerly owned the spin off is known as the parent. The goal of a spin off is to increase management and employee focus by separating distinct businesses, awarding employees with stock-based compensation that is more directly tied to their efforts, and to remove any lack of compatibilities between the parent and the company that was spun off. Upon completion, the two companies will be independent, with their own debt and equity securities, financial reporting, management, and so on.

The choice between selling and spinning off a business involves many variables, but valuation is often among the most significant. A business of moderate size with many potentially interested acquirers will often receive a higher valuation. In a spin off, the investor receives the divested business's equity and must value it and make an investment decision; the parent receives less in proceeds. Spin offs may take several quarters to complete as independent business operations are created and new management teams and separate functions, such as legal and finance, are put in place. Because spin offs reduce, rather than increase, concentration of market power, they typically do not face strict regulatory scrutiny.

2.3.3. Restructuring Actions: Cost and Balance Sheet Restructuring and Reorganization

There are two general types of issuer-specific motivations for restructuring actions: opportunistic improvement and forced improvement. Opportunistic improvement includes actions that alter the business model, trim the cost structure, or modify the composition of the balance sheet—all with the intention to improve returns on capital.

An example of opportunistic change to an existing business model is **franchising**, where an owner of an asset and associated intellectual property can divest the asset and license the intellectual property to a third-party operator. A well-known use of franchising is in restaurants, where a franchisor licenses intellectual property, including recipes, trademarks, and restaurant operating procedures, to third-party restaurant owner operators—franchisees— in exchange for royalties, typically in the mid-single digit range of percentage of restaurant sales. Franchisors, such as the restaurant chain McDonald's or the tutoring company Kumon, operate lean businesses with royalty income and a small, fixed cost base primarily composed of senior management, advertising, and product development. Franchisees operate the individual businesses independently under the franchisor's name and are subjected to meeting strict operational and business requirements under the franchisor's supervision and oversight. Because franchisors do not own stores or employ workers, they are shielded from store-level cost trends; franchising shifts away many business risks from the franchisors to the franchisees.

Forced improvements are actions taken to enhance returns on capital when profitability falls below investors' required rate of return. Several factors contribute to this happening, including insufficient effort by management, falling customer demand, a worsening competitive landscape, or increasing overcapacity. Three alternatives are available: cost restructuring, balance sheet restructuring, and reorganization.

- A **cost restructuring** refers to actions with the goal of reducing costs by improving operational efficiency and profitability, often to raise margins to a historical level or to those of comparable industry peers. Cost restructurings tend to follow periods of company underperformance and are often part of larger structural changes to focus the corporate issuer's operations, to realize synergies after an acquisition, or when there is a threat of activist investors or an unwelcome acquisition by another corporate issuer. Two common ways of reducing costs are **outsourcing** and **offshoring**.
  - A company outsourcing internal business services subcontracts specific, standardizable business processes, such as IT, call centers, HR, legal, and finance, to specialized third-party companies that can offer these services at lower costs through economies of scale from serving many clients. Manufacturing can also be outsourced; perhaps the best-known example is Apple outsourcing manufacturing of iPhones to Hon Hai Precision Ltd. Outsourcing reduces headcount, costs, and time spent on managerial oversight. Depending on what business processes are being outsourced, it can also free up expensive assets, such as office, manufacturing, and warehouse space, that can be disposed of or repurposed for alternative use. Apart from structural changes across the business, there are additional considerations, such as managing multiple contractual obligations with the outsourcing company that can introduce new risks in the decision to outsource.
  - Offshoring refers to relocating operations from one country to another, mainly to reduce costs through lower labor costs or to achieve economies of scale through centralization, while still maintaining operations within the corporation. Offshoring may include starting up a new subsidiary in a foreign country or creating a multi-location business model. Global companies, such as Genpact, have created a multi-location model in which certain core business services are offshored and centralized to specific countries and managed by the company.

Outsourcing and offshoring are often combined, where not only does a company outsource operations to another company but it also does so with foreign partners.

- A **balance sheet restructuring** alters the composition of the balance sheet by either shifting the asset composition, changing the capital structure, or both. On the assets side, most forms of restructuring involve selling assets to third parties for cash and concurrently entering into contractual agreements for their continued use. The seller reduces the risks of asset ownership, such as maintenance or obsolescence, but assumes other risks, such as higher, variable, and less predictable operating costs and lower revenues. Two common balance sheet restructuring transactions are sale leasebacks and dividend recapitalization.
    - In a **sale leaseback**, an asset owner sells an asset to a lessor for cash and immediately signs a lease agreement for its use, typically for the asset's remaining economic life. The result is that the asset owner receives cash up front, no longer owns the asset, yet, as the lessee, retains the right for future use. Typically, the annual lease expense is higher than the annual depreciation and amortization expense would have been because the lessor earns interest income from the transaction. Sometimes, when lessors can secure capital at lower cost, they can offer the lessee more attractive financing terms than the lessee could have obtained. Sale leasebacks are commonly used to secure liquidity on relatively short notice. Airlines used sale leasebacks during the COVID-19 pandemic to raise cash as their operations were suspended.
    - In a **dividend recapitalization**, the corporate issuer restructures the mix of debt and equity, typically from equity to debt through debt-financed dividends or share repurchases. The objective is to reduce the issuer's weighted average cost of capital by replacing expensive equity with cheaper debt. Because this recapitalization reduces the number of outstanding shares and the value of the corporation does not change, these transactions can increase the value to shareholders. While the strategy can be beneficial if interest rates are low, it can increase financial leverage significantly and is thus often used only by issuers with revenue and operating cash flow stability.

- In a **reorganization**, a court-supervised restructuring process available in some jurisdictions for companies facing insolvency, a bankruptcy court assumes control of the company and oversees an orderly negotiation process between the company and its creditors for asset sales, conversion of debt to equity, refinancing, and so on. The company's business operations typically continue as normal, and existing management remains in place throughout the process. Once the company reaches an agreement with its creditors on a reorganization plan, it needs to receive an approval from the bankruptcy court to exit from the process and begin its operations with a lighter debt burden. Sometimes reorganization is a strategic measure to renegotiate contracts with unfavorable terms. While the process can take years, in some cases, companies reach an agreement with creditors prior to filing a formal petition for reorganization to the bankruptcy court and can seek approval from the court quickly. There have been cases of reorganizations lasting less than 24 hours.

    The reorganization process is different from the liquidation process, which typically occurs when the reorganization process has failed to achieve its objectives and the company is still unable to pay its debts and meet its other contractual obligations. During the liquidation process, the bankruptcy court takes control of the corporation, divests these assets of the corporations, and then distributes proceeds to all creditors according to legal criteria.

EXAMPLE 3   Six Flags Inc. and Six Flags Entertainment Corp.

Six Flags Inc., an NYSE-listed owner and operator of amusement parks, began to struggle financially in 2006, as revenues stagnated and EBIT fell by 50% from 2005 because the company's operating expenses were primarily fixed. Its share price fell by almost 50%, closing in 2006 around USD5 per share.

Performance worsened in 2007, as revenues grew slightly but EBIT decreased by 34%, and the share price fell another 50%, closing around USD2.50. Standard & Poor's and Moody's downgraded the company's credit rating (though it was already speculative grade) because the company's net debt-to-EBITDA ratio increased to nearly 13× (see Exhibit 6). The United States, the company's primary operating region, entered a recession in late 2007, and credit markets seized, which was especially challenging for Six Flags because it was a highly levered company unable to refinance its debt and it faced a mandatory dividend payment on its preferred stock.

The company implemented an extensive cost restructuring program in 2008, which did improve profitability despite a 24% fall in revenue, but the company defaulted on its debt obligations by missing interest payments and preferred stock dividend payments. By early 2009, Six Flags shares had fallen below USD1.00, which triggered a delisting of its shares on the NYSE. Six Flags declared Chapter 11 (reorganization) bankruptcy on 13 June 2009, seeking an agreement with creditors to eliminate a significant amount of its debt, though its theme parks continued to operate.

EXHIBIT 6: Six Flags Inc. Net Debt and Net Debt to EBITDA, 2004–2008

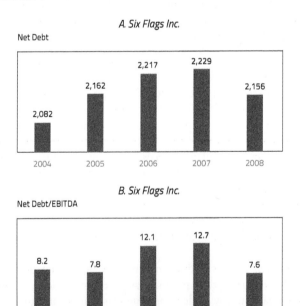

In May 2010, Six Flags and its bondholders reached an agreement and received approval from the bankruptcy court on a reorganization. The company's bondholders invested USD725 million in equity to recapitalize and convert over USD1 billion in existing debt to equity in the company. As a result, the bondholders would own virtually all of the equity and the company would emerge with USD784 million in net debt, a ratio of less than 3.0× expected EBITDA for 2010. Prior equityholders had lost their entire investment.

In June 2010, Six Flags shares were relisted on the NYSE under the same symbol but with a new company name, Six Flags Entertainment Corp.

2.3.4. Leveraged Buyouts

A special case of corporate restructuring is a **leveraged buyout (LBO)**, a series of actions that include investment, divestment, and restructuring. In an LBO, an acquirer uses a significant amount of debt to finance the acquisition of a target and then pursues restructuring actions, with the goal of exiting the target with a sale or public listing.

The term is reserved for leveraged acquisitions by investment funds led by a private equity general partner, with additional capital from limited partners that are often institutional investors, rather than acquisitions made by other corporate issuers. Often, funds that conduct LBOs are "buyout funds" that specialize in these transactions, because both investment and operational expertise are required. If the target is a listed company, an LBO may also be referred to as a "take-private" transaction, because the issuer's equity shifts from the public to the private market. The general and limited partners' investment returns are primarily a function of four variables: the purchase price, the amount of leverage, free cash flow (FCF) generated during the ownership period—which is often augmented by cost and balance sheet restructurings and used to pay down debt—and the exit price. After the exit, the target typically has a substantially more leveraged capital structure than prior to the LBO, as in the case in Example 4.

EXAMPLE 4   LBO of Hilton Hotels Corporation by Blackstone Group

In 2007, funds managed by the Blackstone Group acquired Hilton Hotels Corporation, an NYSE-listed global hotel and hospitality company in a transaction valued at approximately USD26 billion, with the Blackstone funds acquiring all outstanding shares of Hilton for USD47.50 per share, approximately USD20 billion in total, and assuming USD6 billion in existing Hilton debt. The Blackstone funds financed the cash portion of the transaction by borrowing USD14.5 billion and using 5.5 billion of equity.

Upon closing the acquisition at the end of 2007, Blackstone replaced the management and implemented a growth strategy, primarily through franchising. It also made several divestitures of highly priced, flagship properties.

In 2013, Hilton re-listed on the NYSE via an initial public offering. The trajectory of Hilton's long-term debt shows the effect of the leveraged buyout; long-term debt increased by a factor of 3 once it was taken private (see Exhibit 7). Blackstone funds used cash flows from operations to reduce indebtedness while Hilton was private, but it still returned to the public markets with a different capital structure.

EXHIBIT 7: Hilton Hotels Debt Position through Its LBO

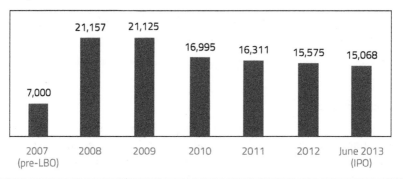

Blackstone funds did not sell any shares in the IPO; instead, Blackstone gradually sold its stake over 2013–2018, which resulted in significant gains as Hilton shares appreciated over that time. By 2018, 11 years after its initial investment, the funds had realized a cumulative net profit of over USD11 billion on the initial equity investment of USD5.5 billion.

EXAMPLE 5   Corporate Evolution and Actions

1. Explain what actions XYZ Ltd., a fictional company, might take in response to its declining revenue growth rates of 8%, 7%, 4%, 1%, and 1%, respectively, during the past five years.

Solution to 1:

XYZ Ltd. may make an investment in a faster-growing business, such as an acquisition, to accelerate its growth rate. If XYZ Ltd. operates multiple separable businesses with different growth rates, management may seek to divest those with growth rates below the consolidated rate to accelerate growth.

2. Instead of making an acquisition, a corporate issuer could invest internally via capital expenditures or R&D. Describe one possible advantage and one possible disadvantage of making an acquisition versus internal investment.

Solution to 2:

A potential advantage of an acquisition over internal investment is time to market for a new product. Internally developing and launching a new product, especially one with which the company lacks experience, may take significantly longer than acquiring a company already commercializing the product. A potential disadvantage of an acquisition is cost. Most companies are valued at prices greater than the replacement costs of their assets, and additionally, most acquisition values are greater than market valuations in the capital markets, reflecting a premium for control.

3. Identify which one of the following is *least likely* to be a motivation for divestment actions.
   A.   Increase revenue
   B.   Increase focus
   C.   Increase return on invested capital

Solution to 3:

A is correct. Divestment actions, including sales and spin offs, reduce the size of a company and its revenues. B is incorrect because divestments, by shrinking the number or scope of businesses in the corporate issuer, do increase focus. C is incorrect because divestments are often motivated by the desire to reduce capital investment in areas of low returns.

4. Recommend a corporate restructuring action for each condition in the *Conditions* column by selecting one of the actions in the *Corporate Restructuring Action* column.

Conditions	Corporate Restructuring Action
1. As a result of a significant downturn in commodity prices, an oil and gas producer faces negative cash flows from operations. The company has interest payments and debt maturities in the next 6 months.	A. Balance sheet restructuring
2. Slowing revenue growth, owing to its products reaching market share saturation in most markets	B. Reorganization
3. A company operates Segment A and Segment B. While Segment A is performing in line with expectations, Segment B revenue growth has declined, because of changes in its regulatory environment.	C. Acquisition
4. A company owns and operates 245 physiotherapy and sports medicine clinics. While the clinics are performing well, the business is capital and labor intensive because each clinic requires physical upkeep, capital equipment, and a skilled staff.	D. Spin off

Solution to 4:

B is correct. Reorganization is an appropriate action for companies facing significant debt levels that lack the financial wherewithal to service the debt. In reorganization, the company can negotiate adjusted debt payment plans with its creditors in an orderly fashion.

C is correct. An acquisition is a likely course of action for a company with slowing growth as it reaches maturity.

D is correct. Segments A and B have divergent performance and competitive landscapes. Unless there are significant synergies between the two, stakeholders may be better served if these businesses were separate rather than under the same ownership.

A is correct. The company should consider balance sheet restructuring, such as franchising the clinics to third-party owner operators—with the corporate entity retaining such functions as quality control, billing, marketing, and so on—or sale leasebacks of the fixed assets.

5. Identify the *most likely* reason for a corporate issuer to sell a segment of its business rather than spin it off.
   A. The issuer desires liquidity.
   B. The issuer operates capital-intensive, cyclical businesses.
   C. The issuer operates multiple businesses with varying revenue growth rates and risk profiles.

Solution to 5:
A is correct. A sale is the disposal of a segment in exchange for consideration, often cash consideration, while a spin off generally raises less liquidity because control is transferred to existing parent shareholders rather than sold. B is incorrect because capital intensity and cyclicality generally have no bearing on the choice of sale versus spin off. C is incorrect because this attribute is non-specific to sales or spin offs; it is an attribute that makes both options more logical.

6. What is the difference between a joint venture and an equity investment?

Solution to 6:
While the two share the same accounting treatment under IFRS and US GAAP, a joint venture is a specific type of equity investment, different from others in its formation, purpose, and governance.

	Joint Venture	Equity Investment
Formation	New legal entity formed when agreement is reached, and joint venture is financed	Investor acquires shares in existing investee company
Purpose	Specific—launch in new geography, new technology, etc.	General—investor company seeks exposure to investee
Governance	Controlled by participants by varying degrees	Investee maintains control over investee operations

7. Tyche, a fictional company, owns and operates 140 retail stores, including the real estate. As a result of a pandemic, Tyche's revenues and cash flows have declined severely, which may result in the inability to make interest and principal payments on its bonds and credit facility. Tyche management is considering selling the real estate for 40 of its stores to a commercial real estate investment fund and immediately leasing them (operating lease) for their remaining economic lives. Explain this type of action and its potential benefits and costs.

Solution to 7:

This is a balance sheet restructuring—more specifically, a sale-leaseback transaction. If completed, Tyche would receive cash from the sale and recognize a liability equal to the present value of future lease payments. Depreciation expense would be replaced with lease expense, which would include interest expense charged by the lessor. Potential benefits and costs of the sale leaseback versus asset ownership are as follows:

Benefits	Costs
Receive cash up front, to use for debt service	Lease expense includes interest expense, generally resulting in higher overall costs
Reduce costs of ownership, such as obsolescence and disposal	Increased indebtedness

8. Empirical research suggests that at least two-thirds of acquisitions fail to create meaningful value for acquirers. Explain why might this be the case.

Solution to 8:

The following are three common explanations for the failure of acquisitions to deliver meaningful value for acquirers:

1. Overpaying: While the target business and synergies associated with the acquisition may perform well, paying too great a price simply results in a negative net present value (NPV) transaction. In effect, value is transferred to the seller.
2. Under-realization of expected synergies: Acquisitions are often done with the assumption of greater revenue or greater profitability (lower costs) for the combined entity than for the two entities alone. Expected synergies are reflected, in part, in the acquisition price. These synergies can be overestimated, perhaps due to unrealistic assumptions.
3. Integration issues: Acquirers often change the business processes and resources of targets to match their existing processes. Additionally, target management is typically replaced. Such changes can result in the deterioration of the performance of the target.

AstraZeneca plc, an LSE-listed pharmaceutical company, announced its acquisition of Alexion Pharmaceuticals, a NASDAQ-listed biotechnology firm focused on therapeutics for rare diseases. AstraZeneca will pay USD60 in cash and 2.1243 AstraZeneca American Depositary Shares for each Alexion share, for a total consideration of USD39 billion, based on share prices just prior to the announcement.

AstraZeneca expects to realize annual recurring cost synergies of USD500 million (pre-tax), primarily from commercial and manufacturing efficiencies as well as savings in corporate costs. The achievement of the full USD500 million in synergies is expected by the end of the third year after the acquisition closes. AstraZeneca expects to incur cash costs in the first three years following the close of the transaction, reaching USD650 million in Year 3.

Prior to the acquisition announcement, expectations for revenues and total operating expenses for AstraZeneca and Alexion for the next three years are as shown in Exhibit 8.

EXHIBIT 8: AstraZeneca and Alexion Years 1–3 Figures, Prior to Acquisition (USD millions)

AstraZeneca	Year 1	Year 2	Year 3
Revenues	22,090	24,384	26,617
Operating expenses	16,418	17,948	19,277

Alexion	Year 1	Year 2	Year 3
Revenues	4,130	4,990	6,069
Operating expenses	1,952	2,201	2,646

9. Calculate the announced cost synergies as a percentage of Alexion's Year 3 standalone operating expenses.

Solution to 9:

By the end of the third year after the acquisition closes, AstraZeneca expects to realize USD500 million in synergies. As a standalone company, Alexion's total expected annual operating expenses are USD2,646 million. Therefore, cost synergies represent 500/2,646 = 19% of Alexion's standalone operating expenses.

10. Assuming synergies are realized in the amounts of USD166 million, USD333 million, and USD500 million in Years 1–3, respectively, and that cash costs of USD217 million, USD433 million, and USD650 million are incurred in Years 1–3, respectively, calculate expected operating income in each of Years 1–3 for the combination of AstraZeneca and Alexion.

Solution to 10:

Given the information in Exhibit 6 and the assumptions for the pace of synergies and cash costs associated with the combination, the process for forecasting operating income is as follows in Exhibit 9.

EXHIBIT 9: Combined AstraZeneca and Alexion Operating Income for Years 1–3

AstraZeneca + Alexion	Year 1	Year 2	Year 3
AstraZeneca Revenues	22,090	24,384	26,617
Plus: Alexion Revenues	4,130	4,990	6,069
Combined Revenues	26,220	29,374	32,686
AstraZeneca OpEx	16,418	17,948	19,277
Plus: Alexion OpEx	1,952	2,201	2,646
Minus: Synergies	(166)	(333)	(500)
Plus: One-Time Costs	217	433	650
Combined OpEx	18,421	20,249	22,073
Operating Income (Revenue minus OpEx)	7,799	9,125	10,613

11. Explain the impact of the acquisition of Alexion on AstraZeneca's revenue growth in Years 2 and 3 and its operating margin in Years 1–3.

Solution to 11:

Exhibit 10 shows AstraZeneca's revenue growth rate and operating margin prior to the acquisition for Years 1–3.

EXHIBIT 10: AstraZeneca Prior to Acquisition of Alexion

AstraZeneca	Year 1	Year 2	Year 3
Revenues	22,090	24,384	26,617
Growth Rate		10%	9%
Operating Expenses	16,418	17,948	19,277
Operating Income	5,672	6,436	7,340
Operating Margin	26%	26%	28%

Exhibit 11 shows AstraZeneca's revenue growth rate and operating margin after the acquisition for Years 1–3.

EXHIBIT 11: AstraZeneca after the Acquisition of Alexion

AstraZeneca	Year 1	Year 2	Year 3
Revenues	26,220	29,374	32,686
Growth Rate		12%	11%
Operating Expenses	18,421	20,249	22,073
Operating Income	7,799	9,125	10,613
Operating Margin	30%	31%	32%

As the exhibits show, the acquisition has positively impacted the revenue growth rate by approximately 200 bps in each of Years 2 and 3 and the operating margin by 400 bps–500 bps in Years 1–3. Even though cash costs associated with the acquisition exceeded the synergies, Alexion is a higher-margin, higher-growth business than AstraZeneca.

3. EVALUATING CORPORATE RESTRUCTURINGS

Investment analysts evaluate corporate restructurings in a process composed of three general steps before updating their investment thesis for the corporate issuer in light of the restructuring, as shown in Exhibit 12.

EXHIBIT 12: Evaluating a Corporate Structural Change

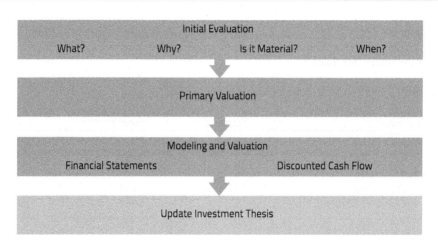

3.1. Initial Evaluation

An analyst's initial evaluation of a corporate restructuring involves answering four questions:

- What is happening?
- Why is it happening?
- Is it material?
- When is it happening?

Answering the first and second questions, covered in Section 2, typically involves reading the issuer's press release, securities filings, conference call transcripts, and relevant third-party research, if available. Once the relevant information is gathered, the analyst interprets the action and the issuer's motivations. Professional skepticism is required because management will virtually always frame restructuring positively.

The third question in the initial evaluation step is determining materiality. Analysts have finite time and must prioritize the most impactful announcements and focus on material changes. Materiality can be defined in this context along two dimensions: size and fit.

The larger a restructuring, the more likely it is to affect an issuer's future cash flows and financial position and thus its value. The size of a structural change can be measured in different ways for different types of restructurings. For restructuring involving a transaction, such as an acquisition, the value of the transaction (sum of cash paid, value of stock issued, and value of target's debt assumed) relative to the issuer's enterprise value (EV) is a good metric. For restructurings not involving a transaction, such as a cost restructuring, it is the scale of the intended action that is material—for instance, the announced cost reduction as a percentage of annual revenue or operating expenses. In any case, the size of the issuer matters: a EUR100 million acquisition may be large for one acquirer but small for another.

One rule of thumb for what constitutes a "large" acquisition is that the total transaction value exceeds 10% of the acquirer's enterprise value prior to the transaction. Most acquisitions (>95%) are under USD1 billion in value and over 80% of targets are private companies (source: Putz 2017). Therefore, for large-capitalization corporate issuers, most acquisitions are, in fact, immaterial.

Because an action of any size could signal a change in strategy or focus, an analyst should also assess how the current structural change fits in with earlier actions, previously announced strategies, and the analyst's own expectations for the issuer. For example, a company making a small acquisition of a company in a different industry or different business model could be interpreted as management changing its strategy or an admission, through their actions, that the issuer's existing business model has problems, as in the case in Example 6.

EXAMPLE 6   Farfetch Ltd. Acquires New Guards Groups

Farfetch Ltd. is a UK-based, publicly traded e-commerce company that primarily operates an online marketplace for branded luxury products. Luxury brands list their products and connect to consumers through Farfetch's website and mobile app but retain control over most of the sales process, such as product selection, pricing, promotions, and so on. Farfetch earns revenue through commissions on each sale.

In July 2019, Farfetch announced the acquisition of the privately held New Guards Groups, an apparel company that sells exclusively licensed luxury streetwear under the brand Off-White, for total consideration of USD704 million, which amounted to approximately 8% of Farfetch's total enterprise value just prior to the announcement.

Despite being relatively small financially, the acquisition was seen as a problem by investors, for two reasons: (1) It meant that Farfetch would start competing with sellers on its own platform by selling products itself, and (2) it represented a shift in business model away from an "asset-lite" online marketplace connecting third-party sellers to consumers towards an online retailer selling products under its own brands, with inventory risk and higher operating costs.

Farfetch shares, listed on the NYSE, fell 45% the day after the acquisition was announced.

A measure that is often used to judge all types of restructurings is the equity price returns on the day of the announcement; for a positive (negative) stock price reaction to the merger announcement on the day of the announcement, the merger is presumed to generate (decrease) value. However, research has cast doubt on the usefulness of this measure.

For instance, Rehm and West (2016) found no correlation between the announcement effects of a deal and its excess total return to shareholders two or more years later. More than half of the companies that initially saw negative price reactions were found to realize excess total shareholder returns over the longer term. Similarly, Ben-David, Bhattacharya, and Jacobsen (2020) reported that share price reaction on the announcement date has no correlation with transaction outcomes or future performance of an acquirer.

Finally, an important consideration in the initial evaluation is timing, because there is a substantial time delay, at least several quarters if not years, between the announcement of the transaction and its completion. The transaction is not reflected on the balance sheet of the acquirer until the date of closing, which is also when revenues, expenses, and cash flow effects are consolidated in the acquirer's financial statements. The length of the timeline is largely determined by the size and complexity of the transaction. For instance, a small-scale cost restructuring may take a matter of months to implement, and its effect would show up relatively quickly. But for a large acquisition or spin off, it may take over 12 months from announcement to the closing, on top of the time spent planning during the pre-announcement stage.

A key source of uncertainty in timing is the receipt of the required shareholder, creditor, and/or regulatory approvals. Depending on the corporate issuer's bylaws, shareholder approval may be required for a corporate transaction; typically, transactions large in scale and value must be approved by the shareholders. Additionally, most jurisdictions have antitrust laws and government authorities that enforce competition law. Approval from these authorities for acquisitions is typically a pre-requisite in all jurisdictions where the transacting entities conduct business. Transactions in some sectors tend to receive more scrutiny than others, particularly if they are perceived to affect geopolitical standing, industry competition, or employment levels.

Importantly, capital market participants discount the expected impact of a change (including the risk of it not closing) into security prices upon the announcement.

3.2. Preliminary Valuation

For restructurings that are material and involve transactions, an analyst will conduct a preliminary valuation of the target, typically using relative valuation methods to judge whether management uses stakeholder resources optimally to meet investors' required rate of return on capital. Three valuation methods analysts use in this step, often in combination, are comparable company analysis, comparable transaction analysis, and premium paid analysis. Discounted cash flow valuation will be discussed in the next step in the evaluation process with modeling.

3.2.1. Comparable Company Analysis

Comparable company analysis uses the valuation multiples of similar, listed companies to value a target. In this approach, the analyst first defines a set of other companies that are similar to the target under review.

Analysts often use a data aggregator, such as Bloomberg, FactSet, or Capital IQ, to create a set of comparable companies and transactions. The aggregator allows the user to specify time periods, the characteristics of the company, the involved parties, and the transaction (e.g., size, geography, form of payment). This set may include companies within the target's primary industry as well as companies in similar industries with similar financial characteristics, such as size, revenue growth rate, operating margin, and return on invested capital. The set should include as many similar companies as possible though not be diluted by dissimilar companies. A useful starting point for developing the comparable set is the company's peer group identified by management in its annual financial disclosures or provided by data aggregators.

Once a set of comparable companies is defined, the next step is to calculate valuation multiples and metrics based on the current market prices of the comparable companies. Common multiples used include enterprise value to EBITDA or sales, price to earnings, and, less commonly, enterprise value to free cash flow to the firm. Enterprise multiples are often used because they are less sensitive to differences in capital structure. An analyst may also use sector-specific valuation multiples, such as enterprise value to subscribers for technology companies, enterprise value to reserves for oil and gas companies, or enterprise value to funds from operations for real estate. Analysts typically then calculate the mean, median, and range for the chosen multiples and either compare those values for the target or apply the multiple to develop an estimated target value.

Comparable company analysis is more often employed for assessing the valuation of targets in spin offs than for acquisitions or sales because acquirers pay a premium for control; therefore, acquisition or sale multiples typically exceed trading multiples.

EXAMPLE 7 Spin Off Valuation

Wang, an analyst at Choice Fund covering the media and telecoms sector, has been asked to assess the valuation of a potential spin off by one of the companies owned by the fund.

The company operates and reports two segments: Connectivity and Media. Connectivity is a capital-intensive cable television and broadband distribution business, and Media produces and licenses television series, which are distributed to its Connectivity customers and other cable companies on traditional television, as well as to online video streaming companies. In the last 12 months, the company reported the following financial results.

Segment	Revenues (EUR mln)	EBITDA (EUR mln)
Connectivity	20,100	7,638
Media	8,000	2,000
Consolidated	28,100	9,638

The company is currently trading at an enterprise value of EUR96,380 million, or an EV/EBITDA multiple of 10.

A spin off of the Media segment has long been rumored, because it does not have material synergies with the Connectivity segment and has been under-invested in by the current management team, resulting in slower revenue growth than its peers.

1. If Wang finds that the median Connectivity and Media peers are trading at enterprise value-to-EBITDA multiples of 13 and 6, respectively, estimate whether a spin off of the Media segment has the potential to:
   A. decrease stakeholder value.
   B. increase stakeholder value.
   C. neither increase nor decrease stakeholder value.

Solution to 1:

B is correct. Multiplying the peer median EV/EBITDA multiples and last 12 months' segment EBITDA results in an estimated enterprise value of EUR111,294 million, which is more than 15% higher than the current enterprise value of EUR96,380 million. Based on this result, it seems that the market is undervaluing either the Connectivity segment, the Media segment, or both relative to peers. This may be justifiable, but we would need more information about peers and their prospects versus this company's prospects to evaluate it.

2. Explain why the Media segment might not be valued at the peer median multiple by market participants in a spin off.

Solution to 2:

Three general reasons for a different valuation from peers are differences in expected growth, differences in profitability, and differences in the risk profile. Relative to the median peer, the Media segment may differ on any or all these dimensions, particularly in profitability because the current management team has under-invested in the business; the period of under-investment may now necessitate a period of high investment, which would depress free cash flow.

3. The company incurs EUR250 million per year in corporate and headquarters operating costs. The company allocates the EUR250 million to the Connectivity and Media segments proportional to revenues. If the Media segment is spun off, estimate its annual EBITDA adjusted for the allocation of corporate and headquarters operating costs.

Solution to 3:

The Media segment accounted for 8,000/28,100 = 28.5% of the last 12 months' revenue. If the EUR250 million in corporate and headquarters operating costs are allocated based on its revenue contribution, then an allocation of 250 million × 28.5% = EUR71 million would be deducted from EBITDA, resulting in an adjusted figure of EUR2,000 million – EUR71 million = EUR1,929 million.

4. Wang's colleague suggests that a flaw in this analysis is that it fails to consider the capital structure of the Media segment if it's spun off; what if the parent transfers a significant amount of debt to it? Interpret the colleague's concern and justify the analysis.

Solution to 4:

While the amount of debt transferred to it and its capital structure generally will impact the equity and debt valuations of the Media segment if it's spun off, Wang's analysis is not specific to any capital structure, because Wang is using enterprise value multiples. However, Wang's colleague could be correct if leverage, for example, is substantially higher for the Media segment spin off than for its peers, which could increase its cost of capital and thus its overall enterprise value.

Advantages of Using Comparable Company Analysis

- This method provides a reasonable approximation of a target company's value relative to similar companies in the market. It assumes that "like" assets should be valued on a similar basis in the market.
- With this method, most of the required data are readily available.

- The estimates of value are derived directly from the market. This approach is unlike the discounted cash flow method, in which the value is determined based on many assumptions and estimates.

Disadvantages of Using Comparable Company Analysis

- A comparable set of listed companies, especially in a larger number of potential comparables, can be difficult to find or may not exist. This is especially true for large, industry-leading corporations that have unique business models. For example, Alphabet Inc., the NASDAQ-listed technology company, owns and operates YouTube, a leading social video platform. In 2020, YouTube earned USD19.8 billion in advertising revenues, making it one of the largest digital advertising companies in the world. Given its size, unique business model, and revenue growth rate over 30%, a peer group for YouTube would be challenging to construct if Alphabet were to spin it off.
- The method is sensitive to market mispricing. Suppose that all the comparable companies are currently overvalued by the market. A valuation relative to those companies may suggest a value that is too high, should the values be revised downward upon a correction.
- This approach yields an estimated *fairtrading* price for the target company. To estimate a fair *takeover* price, analysts must add an estimated takeover premium.

3.2.2. Comparable Transaction Analysis

Comparable transaction analysis is closely related to comparable company analysis, except that the analyst uses valuation multiples from historical acquisitions of similar targets rather than trading multiples of similar listed companies. Similar to comparable company analysis, an analyst would look to descriptive statistics, such as the mean, median, and range of valuation multiples, and apply professional judgment to estimate or evaluate a target's value.

Unlike comparable company analysis, the valuation multiples in comparable transaction analysis include takeover premiums, because they reflect historical acquisitions (sales).

EXAMPLE 8   Comparable Transaction Analysis

Joel Hofer, an investment analyst, is evaluating the price General Health Company paid to acquire Medical Services, Inc., of USD55.00 per share. He has already taken the initial step and assembled a sample of comparable transactions, all of which closed within the last two years. Details on the acquisition prices and relevant variables are shown in the following table.

Valuation Variable (USD)	Acquired Company 1	Acquired Company 2	Acquired Company 3
Acquisition share price	35.00	16.50	87.00
Earnings per share	2.12	0.89	4.37
Cash flow per share	3.06	1.98	7.95
Book value per share	9.62	4.90	21.62
Sales per share	15.26	7.61	32.66

The next step in the process is for Hofer to calculate the multiples at which each company was acquired:

Relative Valuation Ratio	Acquired Company 1	Acquired Company 2	Acquired Company 3	Mean
P/E	16.5	18.5	19.9	18.3
P/CF	11.4	8.3	10.9	10.2
P/BV	3.6	3.4	4.0	3.7
P/S	2.3	2.2	2.7	2.4

After reviewing the distribution of the various values around their respective means, Hofer is confident about using the mean value for each ratio because the range in values above and below the mean is reasonably small. Based on his experience with this industry, Hofer believes that cash flows are a particularly important predictor of value for these types of companies. Consequently, instead of finding an equally weighted average, Hofer has decided to weight the P/CF multiple higher (40%) than the others (20% each) for calculating a weighted average estimated price.

Target Company Valuation Variables

	Target Company (a)	Comparable Companies' Valuation Multiples	Mean Multiple Paid for Comparable Companies (b)	Estimated Takeover Value Based on Comparables (c = a × b)	Weight (d)	Weighted Estimates (e = c × d)
Earnings per share	USD2.62	P/E	18.3	47.95	20%	USD9.59
Cash flow per share	USD4.33	P/CF	10.2	44.17	40%	USD17.67
Book value per share	USD12.65	P/BV	3.7	46.81	20%	USD9.36
Sales per share	USD22.98	P/S	2.4	55.15	20%	USD11.03
Weighted average estimate	**USD47.65**					

In sum, Hofer estimated a fair takeover value for Medical Services, Inc., of USD47.65 per share, which is 13% below the price at which General Health Company acquired it. Based on Hofer's analysis, General Health Company overpaid.

Advantages of Using Comparable Transaction Analysis

- The value estimates come from actual transaction prices for similar targets. This approach is unlike the discounted cash flow method, in which the value is determined based on many assumptions and estimates.
- It is not necessary to separately estimate a takeover premium. The takeover premium is embedded in the comparable transaction multiples.

Disadvantages of Using Comparable Transaction Analysis

- The market for corporate control is illiquid. There may be no or few comparable transactions. In these cases, analysts may try to use data from similar or related industries. These derived values may not be accurate for the specific industry and may have to be adjusted.
- Historical valuation multiples reflect not only historical industry conditions, such as the industry growth rate and regulatory environment, but also historical macroeconomic conditions, such as the business cycle, interest rates, equity price levels, and tax rates, that can significantly influence transaction multiples. The analyst may need to exclude transactions before a certain date (e.g., prior to 10 years ago) or make adjustments to reflect changes in these conditions.
- There is a risk that past acquirers over- or underpaid. Transactions where there were multiple competing offers typically rachet up the final transaction price. The analyst should investigate the comparable transactions to better reconcile these valuations.

3.2.3. Premium Paid Analysis

To estimate or judge a sale value or acquisition price for a listed issuer, an analyst could also calculate an estimated **takeover premium**. This premium is the amount by which the per-share takeover price exceeds the unaffected price expressed as a percentage of the unaffected price and reflects the price of control, or the control premium—the amount shareholders require to relinquish their control of the company to the acquirer. For historical transactions, the premium is calculated as follows:

$$PRM = \frac{(DP - SP)}{SP},\qquad(1)$$

where
   PRM = takeover premium (as a percentage of stock price)
   DP = deal price per share of the target
   SP = unaffected stock price of the target

The analyst must be careful to exclude any pre-announcement increase in the price that may have occurred because of rumors in the press or speculation. Common approaches to control for this include using a share price from one week prior to the announcement or sometimes even longer, particularly if there were persistent rumors preceding the transaction, or a trading volume–weighted average price over a week- or month-long period.

To estimate a sale price using the premium paid analysis, the analyst will compile takeover premiums paid for companies like the target and calculate descriptive statistics, such as the mean, median, and range, in a similar fashion to comparable company and transaction analyses. The premium paid will vary by the same factors responsible for variation in valuation multiples: the target's outlook and risk profile. The annual median share price premium paid for acquisitions announced from 1990 to 2018, based on the premium to share price from the week prior to deal announcement, has been just over 30%, with a range of 20%–40% (Exhibit 13).

EXHIBIT 13: Average Annual Acquisition Premium Paid, 1990–2018

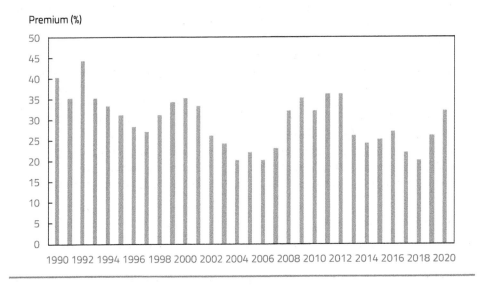

Source: Kengelbach, Keienburg, Gell, Nielsen, Bader, Degen, and Sievers 2019.

4. MODELING AND VALUATION

The next step of the evaluation process is estimating financial statements that include the effect of the restructuring, known as **pro forma financial statements**. Pro forma financial statements include important inputs for equity and credit evaluation, including revenue, EPS, the ratio of net debt to EBITDA, and free cash flow measures. The process for creating pro forma financial statements depends on the type of restructuring and situational specifics, which will be demonstrated in the case studies in Sections 4–6. As an initial example, the process for an acquisition is illustrated in the diagram in Exhibit 14.

EXHIBIT 14: Financial Modeling Steps for Acquisition

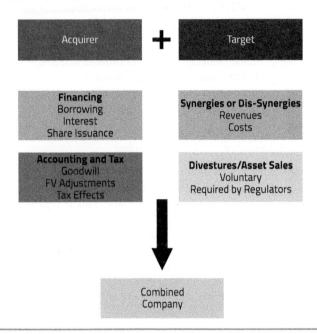

First, the financials for the acquirer and target are combined. Next, the effect of financing the transaction—debt issuance, increased interest expense, share issuance, lower cash—is included. Third, the effect of synergies or the lack of synergies and incompatibilities in forecasted revenues and costs is projected. Fourth, the effect of any divestitures, either voluntarily or involuntarily as required by regulators as a condition of approving the acquisition, are incorporated. Finally, adjustments are made for recognition of goodwill and the increase in the book value of the target's assets and liabilities to fair value.

An alternative presentation of these steps, in terms of how lines on the pro forma income statement (typically the first pro forma financial statement created) are estimated, is shown in Exhibit 15. After the pro forma financial statements are created, such ratios as EPS, net debt to EBITDA, and free cash flow are straightforward to calculate.

EXHIBIT 15: Pro Forma Income Statement (Acquisition) Modeling

Revenue	1. Combine acquirer and target revenues. 2. Add revenue synergies or subtract the cost of incompatible activities (dis-synergies).
Operating expenses	1. Combine acquirer and target operating expenses. 2. Subtract cost synergies or add the cost of incompatible activities (dis-synergies).
Depreciation and amortization	1. Combine acquirer and target depreciation and amortization. 2. Add amortization of acquired intangible assets.
Other expense or income	1. Combine acquirer and target other expense or income.

Interest expense   1. Start with current acquirer interest expense.
                              2. Add increased interest from new debt issuance and revised interest rate.

Income taxes   1. EBT-weighted average of tax rates of acquirer and target; estimate usually provided by issuers

Shares outstanding   1. Start with current acquirer shares outstanding
                             2. Add shares from any share issuance

4.1. Pro Forma Weighted Average Cost of Capital

While the pro forma financial statements contain most of the inputs needed for a discounted cash flow valuation model (unlevered or levered free cash flow), a key variable is the required rate of return to discount the pro forma free cash flows. This is typically estimated using a weighted average cost of capital (WACC) approach. Like the financial statements, WACC must be adjusted to reflect the anticipated corporate restructuring.

Recall that an issuer's cost of capital is a market-value weighted average of its cost of debt, equity, and other capital, as shown in Exhibit 16.

EXHIBIT 16: Weighted Average Cost of Capital Components

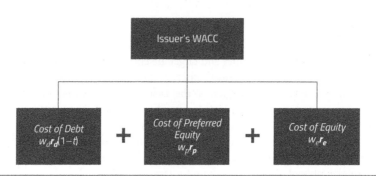

A restructuring can change both the weights of each type of capital (w_d, w_p, and w_e) in the capital structure and the costs of each type of capital (r_d, r_p, and r_e). The simplest example is an issuer acquiring a company for cash and financing it entirely with debt. If the equity price does not change materially, the capital structure will shift from equity to debt as debt increases (i.e., w_d increases and w_e decreases). Conversely, if an issuer sells a division for cash and uses that cash to retire debt, its capital structure will likely shift from debt to equity.

While changes in capital structure weights are straightforward, estimating the effect of a restructuring on the costs of debt and equity capital is more challenging. Recall that costs of capital are influenced by several factors and conditions both inside and outside the issuer, shown in Exhibit 17. Corporate restructurings change the costs of capital by changing these factors. For example, an acquisition that increases leverage and decreases profitability will generally result in an increase in the cost of capital.

EXHIBIT 17: Factors and Conditions Influencing Issuers' Costs of Capital

Factor/Condition	Primary Measures
Profitability	EBITDA or EBIT to sales
Volatility	Standard deviation of revenues
	Standard deviation of EBITDA
Leverage	Debt to EBITDA
Assets that can serve as collateral	Asset specificity, liquidity, active market for the asset
Prevailing interest rates	Market reference rates
	Corporate credit spreads

For this reason, it is common to see investment-grade issuers structure transactions to maintain their investment-grade rating and minimize their weighted average cost of capital. Moving from an investment-grade to a speculative-grade credit rating is empirically associated with a several hundred basis point increase in WACC (see Exhibit 18).

EXHIBIT 18: Median US Large-Cap WACC for Each Credit Rating Notch

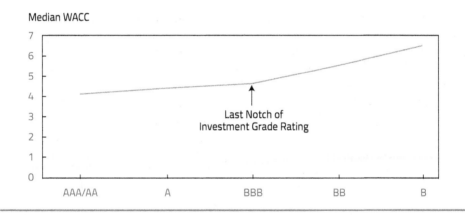

EXAMPLE 9   Competing Offers for Kansas City Southern

Kansas City Southern (KCS), an NYSE-listed railroad company, owns and operates railroads in the southern United States, northern Mexico, and Panama. In 2021, the company received acquisition offers from two Canada-based, TSX-listed railroad companies: Canadian Pacific Railway Limited (CP) and Canadian National Railway Company (CN). The table summarizes the terms of the two offers.

	CP	CN
Consideration:		
Offer price per KCS share, % premium	USD274 per share	USD325 per share
	23% premium	45% premium
Mix of consideration per KCS share	0.489 CP shares	1.129 CN shares
	USD90 in cash	USD200 in cash
Assumed KCS debt	USD3.8 billion	USD3.8 billion
Total consideration (enterprise value)	USD29 billion	USD33.6 billion
Financing:*		
New borrowings	USD8.6 billion	USD19 billion
Share issuance	44.5 million CP shares	103 million CN shares
Post-acquisition debt to EBITDA	4.0×	4.6×
Current KCS shareholders ownership of combined company	25%	12.6%

*The balance of financing is funded with cash on hand.

Following the close, CP expects its outstanding debt will be approximately USD20.2 billion and stated that they "remain committed to maintaining an investment-grade credit rating." CN expects its outstanding debt would be approximately USD33 billion after its acquisition but also remains committed to maintaining an investment-grade credit rating.

1. If, prior to the acquisition, CN has 713 million shares outstanding trading at USD105 per share, estimate how the weights of debt and equity in its capital structure would change after the acquisition closes as a result of an acquisition of KCS under the proposed terms, assuming a constant share price and that the book value of debt equals its market value.

Solution to 1:

Following the close of the acquisition, CN expects its outstanding debt to total USD33 billion, after assuming USD3.8 billion in existing KCS debt and issuing USD19 billion itself. Therefore, prior to the acquisition, CN had approximately (33 − 3.8 − 19) = USD10.2 billion in debt and (713 million shares outstanding × USD105 per share) = USD74.9 billion in equity, resulting in a mix of debt and equity of 12% and 88%, respectively.

After the acquisition, CN will have USD33 billion in debt and 816 (713 + 103) million shares outstanding, which, priced at USD105 per share, is USD85.7 billion in equity. The change in capital structure is shown in Exhibit 19.

EXHIBIT 19: CN Capital Structure before and after Proposed Acquisition of KCS

CN Capital Structure	Pre-Acquisition	Post-Acquisition
Debt %	12%	28%
Equity %	88%	72%

2. To increase the amount of the combined company that current KCS shareholders would own after the close, identify what change CN would have to make to the proportion of CN stock in its consideration.
   A. Increase
   B. Decrease
   C. Keep the same

Solution to 2:

A is correct. By issuing more CN stock to existing KCS stockholders, KCS stockholders would own more CN stock after the acquisition and, thus, own more of the combined company.

3. Identify CN's primary means of financing a higher amount of cash in the consideration versus CP's offer. CN plans to:
   A. offer a greater proportion of stock.
   B. issue a greater amount of debt.
   C. reduce operating expenses.

Solution to 3:

B is correct. By issuing a greater amount of debt and using the proceeds in its cash offer, CN's offer has a greater amount of cash in the consideration. A is incorrect because a greater proportion of stock would mean a lower proportion of cash in the consideration. C is incorrect because reducing operating expenses does not directly affect the mix of consideration offered.

4. Identify the *least* attractive element of CN's offer versus CP's offer, from the perspective of KCS shareholders.
   A. Higher proportion of cash in the consideration
   B. Higher total enterprise value
   C. Higher leverage for the combined company

Solution to 4:

C is correct. The higher leverage (4.6 versus 4.0 debt-to-EBITDA ratio) for the combined company is less attractive because it introduces higher credit risk and magnifies any downside risks, such as less-than-expected synergies or integration problems. Accordingly, the higher leverage may result in investors having higher required rates of return (higher cost of capital for the issuer).

5. If credit rating agencies were to warn CN that its investment-grade credit rating were in jeopardy, identify a modification that CN could make to its consideration or financing to bolster its credit rating.
   A. Borrow from credit facilities rather than issue bonds.
   B. Use a greater proportion of cash on hand.
   C. Use a greater proportion of stock.

Solution to 5:

C is correct. By using a greater proportion of stock in the consideration, less cash and therefore less debt issuance are needed to finance the acquisition. A is incorrect because the difference between bank debt and bond debt is immaterial to credit. B is incorrect because using cash on hand would have the same impact on net debt as borrowing.

You create a pro forma income statement for CN to evaluate the impact of its proposed acquisition of KCS. First, you compile forecasted income statements for the two companies on a standalone basis, shown in Exhibit 20 (see Example9 worksheet in the downloadable Microsoft Excel workbook).

EXHIBIT 20: CN and KCS Standalone Historical and Forecasted Summary Income Statements

	2019A	2020A	2021A	2022F	2023F	2024F
Canadian National						
Revenue	14,917	13,819	15,063	15,966	16,765	17,603
Operating expenses	(7,762)	(7,453)	(7,833)	(8,303)	(8,718)	(9,154)
D&A	(1,562)	(1,589)	(1,614)	(1,765)	(1,916)	(2,016)
Other income	374	321	353	353	353	353
Interest expense	(538)	(554)	(604)	(640)	(672)	(706)
Income taxes	(1,213)	(982)	(1,180)	(1,235)	(1,279)	(1,338)
Net income	4,216	3,562	4,185	4,376	4,533	4,742
Shares outstanding	723	713	713	710	707	704
Diluted EPS	5.83	5.00	5.87	6.16	6.41	6.74
Kansas City Southern						
Revenue	2,866	2,632	2,922	3,097	3,283	3,480
Operating expenses	(1,629)	(1,272)	(1,285)	(1,363)	(1,444)	(1,531)
D&A	(351)	(358	(380)	(403)	(427)	(452)
Other income	18	(29)	0	0	0	0
Interest expense	(116)	(151)	(154)	(163)	(161)	(165)
Income taxes	(248)	(204)	(276)	(292)	(313)	(333)
Net income	540	618	827	876	938	999
Shares outstanding	100	94	90	87	84	81
Diluted EPS	5.40	6.57	9.19	10.07	11.17	12.33

Based on the announcement and your own research, you make the following assumptions:

• The acquisition closes at the end of 2021, with 2022 a full year for the combined entity.

- CN announced that it expects to achieve annual cost synergies that reach USD1 billion by 2024; you assume that the synergies start at 1/3 of that in 2022, stepping up to 2/3 in 2023, and the full USD1 billion is achieved in 2024. There are no revenue synergies.
- The interest rate CN will pay on USD33 billion in outstanding debt—the amount it will have outstanding as of the acquisition closing—is 5.0%, and you assume CN's gross debt and interest rate remain constant to 2024.
- Amortization of acquired intangible assets is USD800 million per year from 2022 to 2024.
- Effective income tax rate is 22% from 2022 to 2024.

6. Given the information provided and the process outlined in Section 3, estimate a pro forma income statement, including diluted EPS, for CN.

Solution to 6:
Forecasted diluted EPS is USD5.24, USD5.89, and USD6.60 per share for fiscal years 2022, 2023, and 2024, respectively, as shown in Exhibit 21 (see Example9 worksheet in the downloadable Microsoft Excel workbook).

EXHIBIT 21: CN Pro Forma Income Statement, 2022–2024F

CN + KCS = New CN	2022F	2023F	2024F
CN revenue	15,966	16,765	17,603
KCS revenue	3,097	3,283	3,480
New CN revenue	19,063	20,047	21,083
CN operating expenses	8,303	8,718	9,154
KCS operating expenses	1,363	1,444	1,531
Synergies	(333)	(667)	(1,000)
New CN operating expenses	9,332	9,495	9,685
CN D&A	1,765	1,916	2,016
KCS D&A	403	427	452
Amortization of acquired intangible assets	800	800	800
New CN D&A	2,968	3,143	3,268
CN other income	(353)	(353)	(353)
KCS other income	0	0	0
New CN other income	(353)	(353)	(353)

CN + KCS = New CN	2022F	2023F	2024F
New CN interest expense	1,650	1,650	1,650
New CN income taxes	1,203	1,345	1,503
New CN net income	4,264	4,768	5,329
CN shares outstanding	710	707	704
CN shares issued	103	103	103
New CN shares outstanding	813	810	807
New CN diluted EPS	5.24	5.89	6.60

5. EVALUATING INVESTMENT ACTIONS

This section and the two that follow are composed of case studies of corporate restructurings based on real-world events and demonstrate the evaluation process, discussed in prior sections, undertaken by analysts upon their announcement. The case studies, primarily selected based on their real-world prevalence, expand on and provide context for the concepts introduced earlier.

5.1. Equity Investment

Example 10 describes a large, mature company that faces growth and regulatory challenges. As is common in these situations, the company seeks to improve its prospects by making an investment in a fast-growing competitor.

EXAMPLE 10   Dilmun Inc. and Spina Ltd.

Dilmun Inc., a fictional company, makes and sells traditional combustible cigarettes and cigars. Over the last 10 years, its sales volumes have declined annually by a mid- to high-single-digit rate, as the number of smokers in its major markets has dwindled, but strong pricing power has enabled the company to maintain stable revenues. Dilmun is the market share leader in its geographies and remains highly profitable, with operating margins exceeding 35% and returns on invested capital exceeding 30%.

In recent years, two trends have emerged that have challenged Dilmun, beyond the impact of declining volumes:

1. Some lawmakers have advocated limiting nicotine in tobacco products to non-addictive levels and banning menthol and other flavorings.
2. The proliferation of ESG-focused strategies by asset managers has pressured Dilmun's share price because Dilmun's business model scores low on social metrics. Additionally, shareholders have engaged with the company's board and management to change its products or business model to better align with ESG goals.

At the end of 20X3, Dilmun made the following announcement by press release:

Dilmun Inc. today announces it signed and closed a USD1.2 billion investment in, and service agreements with, Spina Ltd., a market leader in e-vapor. The investment and service agreements will accelerate Spina's strategy to switch smokers of traditional cigarettes to e-vapor products. Dilmun's investment represents a 30% interest in Spina equity, valuing the company at USD4.0 billion on an enterprise value basis. Spina will remain fully independent.

As part of the service agreements, Spina will have access to Dilmun's sales and marketing infrastructure, including

- premium shelf and display space at over 225,000 retail locations worldwide, up from less than 75,000 today, and
- marketing material inside of Dilmun-branded cigarette packs and access to contact information from customer loyalty programs.

While public health authorities recommend against the use of e-vapor products or any tobacco product, they have acknowledged their increased safety over traditional cigarettes.

"We are taking significant action to prepare for a future where adult smokers choose non-combustible products over cigarettes by investing in Spina, a market leader," said Dilmun's chairman and chief executive officer. "Lower-risk products are a promising way forward for all stakeholders. Today, we are making a significant investment toward that goal."

Dilmun will finance the transaction with borrowings on its credit facility, which has an interest rate of 600 bps, and expects to maintain its investment-grade credit rating. Spina intends to use the investment proceeds to support product development and marketing. Spina does not intend to pay dividends for the foreseeable future.

Summary historical and forecasted financial data for Dilmun Inc. and Spina Ltd., prior to the transaction, are shown in Exhibit 22 and Exhibit 23, which are also provided in the Example10 sheet in the downloadable Microsoft Excel workbook. Dilmun does not own any other equity method investments, and income (loss) from associates is reported as an operating item on its income statement. Dilmun expects amortization expense associated with the transaction, related to fair value adjustments of identifiable net assets, of USD10 million per year.

EXHIBIT 22: Dilmun Inc. Summary Financial Data (USD millions)

	20X1	20X2	20X3	20X4E
Net revenues	25,434	25,744	25,576	25,670
EBITDA	8,656	9,191	9,839	10,140
EBIT	8,406	8,941	9,589	9,890
Interest expense	(817)	(747)	(705)	(705)
Income tax expense	(1,594)	(1,721)	(1,866)	(1,929)
Net income	5,995	6,473	7,018	7,256
Diluted EPS	3.06	3.33	3.69	3.94
Diluted shares outstanding	1,960	1,943	1,901	1,840
Total debt	12,847	13,881	13,894	13,894
Cash and cash equivalents	4,878	4,569	1,253	2,000

EXHIBIT 23: Spina Ltd. Summary Financial Data (USD millions)

	20X1	20X2	20X3	20X4E
Net revenues	200	350	600	990
EBITDA	(300)	(400)	(400)	(350)
EBIT	(320)	(460)	(480)	(450)
Interest expense	0	0	0	0
Income tax expense	0	0	0	0
Net income (loss)	(320)	(460)	(480)	(450)
Diluted EPS	(0.37)	(0.53)	(0.56)	(0.52)
Diluted shares outstanding	860	860	860	860

1. Rather than this form of investment, identify other types of actions Dilmun could take with respect to Spina, and explain one advantage and one disadvantage of those alternatives, relative to the equity investment.

Solution to 1:

Two other types of actions Dilmun and Spina could have made to achieve similar objectives are acquisition and joint venture.

Alternative	Advantage vs. Equity Investment	Disadvantage vs. Equity Investment
Acquisition	• By acquiring control, Spina couldn't take actions that are against Dilmun's interest, such as sign other partnerships or reduce prices significantly.	• Substantially greater capital investment is required. If the target is risky, a smaller initial investment may be wise.
Joint Venture	• Dilmun and Spina would have governance representation, which reduces risks for Dilmun.	• A larger investment may be required, and Spina's independence may be an important element of its success to date.

2. Based on the information provided in the press release, explain both Dilmun's and Spina's motivations for this transaction.

Solution to 2:

Dilmun's motivations are investment exposure to a growing company and unique capabilities in the form of Spina's market-leading products. Dilmun is also seeking to diversify its business away from the declining (by volume) combustible cigarette market to an adjacent alternative that shares sales channels and customers.

Spina's motivations for entering the investment agreement are the synergies offered by the marketing agreement with Dilmun and the cash proceeds that enable it to increase investment to strengthen its position. The equity investment structure allows the current management and board to remain in control but benefit from the capabilities of a larger company.

3. Exhibit 24 shows current enterprise values and sales for the last 12 months for five listed companies comparable to Spina Ltd. Explain how the valuation multiple for Spina implied by the transaction differs from those for the comparable companies.

EXHIBIT 24: Comparable Company Analysis for Spina Ltd. (USD millions)

	Enterprise Value	Net Revenues (TTM)
Comparable A	1,211	269
Comparable B	821	82
Comparable C	973	191
Comparable D	768	157
Comparable E	1,346	224

Solution to 3:

The equity investment by Dilmun valued Spina Ltd. at USD4,000 billion, or an EV/Sales (trailing twelve months, or TTM) multiple of 6.7 (4,000/600 million in net revenues in 20X3). The EV/Sales (TTM) multiples of the comparables, including the median and average, are shown in Exhibit 25. The transaction multiple for Spina Ltd. was higher than both the peer median and average and is the second highest in the group, behind only Comparable B, valued at 10×.

EXHIBIT 25: EV/Sales Multiples of Comparables for Spina Ltd.

	Enterprise Value (USD mln)	Net Revenues (TTM)	EV/S
Comparable A	1,211	269	4.5
Comparable B	821	82	10.0
Comparable C	973	191	5.1
Comparable D	768	157	4.9
Comparable E	1,346	224	6.0
Median			5.1
Average			6.1

4. Discuss two potential reasons for the difference in valuation multiples for Spina Ltd. versus its comparables that should be investigated further.

Solution to 4:

Two potential reasons for the difference in valuation of Spina Ltd. versus its comparables that warrant further investigation are growth prospects and risk profile. On a standalone basis or by virtue of its partial ownership by and service agreement with Dilmun, Spina Ltd. may have faster revenue growth than its peers. Additionally, as a market leader with an established presence in the e-vapor category and the highest revenue, Spina likely has lower risk than its competitors, which may face significant problems as they scale.

5. Based on the information in the exhibits, estimate the effect of Dilmun's investment in Spina on Dilmun's debt-to-EBITDA ratio and its diluted EPS in 20X4E. Assume that Dilmun maintains its estimated effective tax rate.

Solution to 5:

As a result of the debt-financed investment in Spina, Dilmun's debt-to-EBITDA ratio in 20X4E will increase from 1.37 to 1.51 and its diluted EPS will decrease from USD3.94 to USD3.85 per share. Exhibit 26 shows the effect of the investment by reconciling the pre-investment to pro forma summary income statements. The investment reduces operating income by Dilmun's share of Spina's net loss (0.3 × 450 = 135) plus the amortization (10) associated with the investment and increases interest expense by an amount equal to the 600 bps in interest expense multiplied by the increase in debt. The dilutive effect on EPS is partially offset by tax effects.

EXHIBIT 26: Estimated Effect of Spina Investment on Dilmun Inc.

	Before Investment	Investment	After Investment
	20X4E	**20X4E**	**20X4E**
Net revenues	25,670	0	25,670
Income from associates		(145)	(145)
EBITDA	10,140	(145)	9,995
EBIT	9,890	(145)	9,745
Interest expense	(705)	(72)	(777)
Income tax expense	(1,929)	46	(1,883)
Net income	7,256	(171)	7,084
Diluted EPS	3.94	—	3.85
Diluted shares outstanding	1,840	—	1,840
Total debt	13,894	1,200	15,094
Cash and cash equivalents	2,000	0	2,000
Debt to EBITDA	1.37		1.51

5.2. Joint Venture

Example 11 shows a common joint venture arrangement: one company with a brand, technology, and know-how co-invests with a company in a foreign market that brings its established local market presence. This example also demonstrates an important step in the life cycle of many joint ventures: a partial buyout by one of the companies, which has significant financial statement impacts to both companies—particularly the acquirer, because the accounting model changes from the equity method to consolidation.

EXAMPLE 11   Opone-Hapalla Automotive Alliance SA

Opone SA, a fictional company headquartered in Brazil, designs, manufactures, and sells vehicles. While it sells some vehicles under its own brands, most of its business is a joint venture with Hapalla AG, named Opone-Hapalla Automotive Alliance SA (OHAA). OHAA was formed in 20X1 to make and sell Hapalla-branded vehicles in Latin America. Besides its participation in OHAA, Hapalla AG operates only in select European markets. OHAA has increased its annual vehicle sales volume from less than 10,000 in 20X1 to 1.5 million in 20X7. The joint venture has a contractually agreed-upon term of 25 years.

Opone SA and Hapalla AG disclose summary financial results and positions for OHAA in the notes to their financial statements and share equally in the joint venture's profit and loss, as well as any dividends paid. Exhibit 27 and Exhibit 28 (also in the Example 11 worksheet in the downloadable Microsoft Excel workbook) show summary financial data from Opone SA's 20X7 annual report and consensus forecast figures for 20X8E. OHAA is the only joint venture Opone SA has an investment in.

EXHIBIT 27: OHAA (Joint Venture) Summary Financial Data (BRL millions)

	20X5	20X6	20X7	20X8E
Net revenues	111,599	138,704	169,441	208,412
Profit after tax	10,476	12,491	15,267	18,757
Dividends paid	4,000	6,000	40,000	32,000
Cash and equivalents	60,418	62,537	32,461	12,653

EXHIBIT 28: Opone SA Summary Financial Data

	20X5	20X6	20X7	20X8E
Net revenues	5,305	4,377	3,862	3,910
Cost of sales	(5,119)	(4,091)	(3,788)	(3,793)
SG&A expense	(1,765)	(1,294)	(1,556)	(1,450)
Joint venture income	5,238	6,246	7,634	9,379
Interest expense	(138)	(114)	(95)	(95)
Income tax expense	(34)	(65)	(167)	(190)
Profit after tax	3,487	5,059	5,890	7,761
Cash flows from operations	(2,547)	(2,830)	(726)	(800)
Dividends received from joint venture	2,000	3,000	20,000	16,000
Capital expenditures	(624)	(461)	(795)	(560)
Free cash flow (non-IFRS measure)	(1,171)	(291)	18,479	14,640

1. Based on the information provided, explain how the OHAA joint venture is mutually beneficial for Opone SA and Hapalla AG.

Solution to 1:

The OHAA joint venture is clearly beneficial for Opone SA, because its income from the joint venture accounts for more than 100% of the company's net income; the company's other operations incur a net loss. The joint venture is beneficial for Hapalla AG because it enables the company to grow beyond its current markets and share the risks (and rewards) of international expansion with a partner that has an established presence in Latin America.

2. Exhibit 29 shows P/E and P/FCF valuation multiples for Opone SA and five listed comparable companies. Compare Opone SA's valuation to its comparables and explain why Opone SA's P/E differs significantly from its P/FCF multiple.

EXHIBIT 29: Comparable Company Analysis for Opone SA

	P/E (TTM)	P/FCF (TTM)
Comparable A	11	17
Comparable B	12	11
Comparable C	9	18
Comparable D	13	19
Comparable E	15	14
Opone SA	21	7

Solution to 2:

Exhibit 30 shows Opone SA's peer median and average P/E and P/FCF multiples. Opone SA is more expensive than peers in terms of P/E but far cheaper than peers on a P/FCF basis. The primary reason behind the difference in Opone SA's P/E and P/FCF multiples is that in 20X7, OHAA joint venture income recognized was less than 40% of dividends earned. Based on the financial data provided, it appears that OHAA has been reducing its cash balance through dividends that are well in excess of profits.

EXHIBIT 30: Comparable Company Analysis for Opone SA

	P/E (TTM)	P/FCF (TTM)
Comparable A	11	17
Comparable B	12	11
Comparable C	9	18
Comparable D	13	19
Comparable E	15	14
Median	12	17
Average	12	16
Opone SA	21	7

In the beginning of 20X8, Hapalla AG offered Opone SA BRL45 billion in cash to increase its stake in OHAA by 25% and replace the contractual term of 25 years with a perpetual agreement that Hapalla AG's interest in the joint venture would not exceed 75%.

3. If the OHAA joint venture has no debt, compare the valuation of OHAA implied by Hapalla AG's offer with those of comparable companies in Exhibit 29 on a P/E (TTM) basis.

Solution to 3:

Hapalla AG's offer of BRL45 billion to acquire a 25% interest in OHAA values OHAA at BRL180 billion (45/0.25) on an enterprise value basis, or BRL147,359 million in equity value after subtracting cash and cash equivalents at year-end 20X7. This equity value is 10.0× the joint venture's profit after tax in 20X7, which is 2.0 lower than the comparable company average and median of 12×.

4. If Opone SA were to accept Hapalla AG's offer at the beginning of 20X8, estimate the net effect of the transaction on Opone SA's 20X8 income statement based on Exhibit 28. Assume that Opone SA would account for its remaining interest in OHAA using the equity method, the carrying value of the OHAA joint venture interest on Opone SA's balance sheet as of 31 December 20X7 is BRL26 billion, and the effective tax rate is 10%.

Solution to 4:

The transaction would have two major effects. First, Opone SA would de-recognize half of its interest (BRL13 billion) from its balance sheet and recognize BRL45 billion in cash proceeds from the sale and a gain of (45 13 =) BRL32 billion. Second, the proportion of OHAA net income that Opone SA would recognize as joint venture income would fall from 50% to 25%. Exhibit 31 shows the effect of the transaction on the 20X8 income statement.

EXHIBIT 31: Pro Forma Opone SA Income Statement for Sale of Half of OHAA Joint Venture

	Before 20X8E	Transaction	After 20X8E
Net revenues	3,910	—	3,910
Cost of sales	(3,793)	—	(3,793)
SG&A expense	(1,450)	—	(1,450)
Joint venture income	9,379	(4,689)	4,689
Gain on sale	0	—	32,000
Interest expense	(95)	—	(95)
Income tax expense	(190)	—	(3,526)
Profit after tax	7,761		31,735

5. Describe the effect of the transaction on Hapalla AG's financial statements.

Solution to 5:
As of the date of the transaction close, Hapalla AG would change its accounting for OHAA from the equity method to consolidation and recognize a non-controlling interest that represents Opone SA's 25% interest. As a result, joint venture income will no longer be recognized while revenues, expenses, and other financial statement lines would, as of the close, reflect consolidated figures. On the balance sheet, Hapalla AG would de-recognize the joint venture investment and recognize OHAA's assets and liabilities, while reducing its cash balance for consideration transferred to Opone SA.

5.3. Acquisition

The next example illustrates an acquisition transaction, but unlike the prior Kansas City Southern example, the target is a segment of a company. While the financial statement impact is not categorically different for the acquirer, this type of transaction involves another party: a seller that continues to operate after the transaction. Example 12 is a common situation in which the seller is divesting a business segment to another company that is similar to the target but with much greater scale and focus. Additionally, the type of consideration transferred in this transaction results in the seller holding an equity investment in the acquirer.

EXAMPLE 12   Tulor to Acquire Retail Segment from Caracol Petroleum

Tulor Inc. is an Australian operator of convenience stores, including standalone corner shops, larger convenience stores, and stores with petroleum stations.

Caracol Petroleum is a global vertically integrated oil and gas company. Its Upstream operations focus on the exploration and production of oil and natural gas, its Downstream operations include several oil refineries, and its Retail business operates a large network of petroleum stations, all with convenience stores. As a result of a prolonged decline in oil prices and high financial leverage, Caracol Petroleum is seeking to improve its balance sheet and realize value for shareholders.

At the beginning of 20X2, Tulor and Caracol announced that the companies had reached an agreement in which Tulor would acquire the Retail segment of Caracol for AUD2 billion in cash and 80 million Tulor common shares for a total consideration of AUD3 billion, based on the unaffected share price prior to the announcement. Tulor and Caracol expect the transaction to close on 31 December 20X2.

Caracol will use the cash proceeds from the transaction to strengthen its balance sheet by retiring debt. Based on an effective tax rate of 18%, Caracol expects to receive after-tax cash proceeds of AUD1.6 billion, all of which will be used for debt retirement. In connection with the agreement, Caracol has agreed to not dispose of any Tulor shares for five years from the close of the acquisition.

Tulor intends to finance the cash portion of the consideration with cash on hand and by borrowing AUD1 billion from its credit facilities, which has already been committed by its lenders. Tulor intends to maintain an investment-grade credit rating.

Tulor expects to realize AUD125 million in EBITDA synergies by Year 3, primarily by expanding its private label products in the newly acquired stores, utilizing its scale in negotiating with suppliers, and closing unprofitable stores. Summary historical and consensus forecast financial data for Tulor and the Retail segment of Caracol are shown in Exhibit 32 and Exhibit 33, which are also included in the Example12 worksheet in the downloadable Microsoft Excel workbook.

EXHIBIT 32: Tulor Summary Financial Data (Pre-Acquisition)

	20X1	20X2	20X3E
Net revenues	19,896	20,891	21,726
Cost of sales	(15,121)	(15,835)	(16,447)
Operating expense	(3,183)	(3,343)	(3,476)
EBITDA	1,592	1,713	1,803
D&A	(597)	(627)	(652)
EBIT	995	1,086	1,152
Interest income	22	24	24
Interest expense	(370)	(388)	(401)
Income tax expense	(129)	(144)	(155)
Net income	517	578	620
Diluted EPS	0.80	0.89	0.96
Diluted shares outstanding	648	648	648
Cash and equivalents	4,400	4,800	4,800
Total debt	5,692	5,969	6,169

EXHIBIT 33: Caracol Petroleum, Retail Segment (Pre-Acquisition) Summary Financial Data

	20X1	20X2	20X3E
Net revenues	4,974	5,223	5,432
Cost of sales	(4,004)	(4,204)	(4,372)
Operating expense	(796)	(836)	(869)
EBITDA	174	183	190
D&A	(99)	(104)	(109)
EBIT	75	78	81

1. Explain Tulor's and Caracol's motivations for pursuing this transaction.

Solution to 1:

Tulor's motivations are two-fold: synergies and growth. By utilizing its superior scale (Tulor had a store footprint six times the size of Caracol's) and scope, Tulor expects to significantly increase Caracol's stores' annual EBITDA by the end of the third year after closing. This also results in a >15% increase in Tulor's EBITDA prior to the acquisition in three years, which is likely a rare opportunity in a mature industry, such as convenience stores; Tulor's revenues are growing at a low-single-digit rate.

Caracol's motivations to sell are to strengthen its balance sheet by using the proceeds to retire debt and, likely, to sharpen its focus on its Upstream and Downstream segments. Based on the significant synergies announced by Tulor, it's likely that Caracol is not the best owner for the Retail segment.

2. Evaluate the valuation implied by the purchase price against comparable companies based on the selected financial data for companies in Exhibit 34. Explain two reasons why the transaction multiple paid by Tulor (based on 20X2 EBITDA) may differ from the median comparable.

EXHIBIT 34: Comparable Company Analysis for Caracol Petroleum, Retail Segment

	Enterprise Value	EBITDA (TTM)
Comparable A	2,422	295
Comparable B	1,642	287
Comparable C	1,946	163
Comparable D	1,536	201
Comparable E	2,692	264

Solution to 2:

Exhibit 35 shows the EV/EBITDA of the median comparable and the implied multiple for Tulor's acquisition of Caracol Petroleum's Retail segment. While the median comparable trades at 8× 20X2 EBITDA, the acquisition multiple was double that, at 16×. There are two likely reasons for the much higher valuation in the acquisition: control and synergies.

The acquisition multiple includes a control premium paid by Tulor, while the trading multiples in comparable company analysis reflect only prices for non-controlling stakes. Control allows a buyer to make operational decisions, which in this case enables Tulor to realize significant synergies through its existing business.

If synergies of AUD125 million (in Year 3) are included in the analysis, the acquisition multiple falls to 10×, which is within the peer range.

EXHIBIT 35: Comparable Company Analysis—Caracol Petroleum, Retail Segment

	Enterprise Value	EBITDA (TTM)	EV/EBITDA
Comparable A	2,422	295	8
Comparable B	1,642	287	6
Comparable C	1,946	163	12
Comparable D	1,536	201	8
Comparable E	2,692	264	10
Median			8
Caracol Petroleum Retail	3,000	183	16
Caracol Petroleum Retail + Synergies		308	10

3. Estimate the impact of the transaction on Tulor's debt-to-EBITDA ratio and diluted EPS in 20X3, assuming the following:

   a. AUD42 million in cost synergies is realized,
   b. incremental amortization expense associated with fair value adjustments of identifiable net assets acquired is AUD200 million per year,
   c. Tulor earns 50 bps in annualized interest income on its cash and pays an interest rate of 650 bps on its debt, and
   d. the effective tax rate is 20%.

Solution to 3:

Based on the information and assumptions provided, compared to 20X3E estimates prior to the acquisition, the acquisition results in Tulor's diluted EPS decreasing by AUD0.26 per share, to 0.70, and its debt-to-EBITDA ratio increasing by 0.1×, to 3.5× EBITDA. While the acquisition increases EBITDA, it results in a decrease in income before taxes because of the incremental amortization expense and interest expense. The increase in shares outstanding from the equity portion of the consideration is alone responsible for a loss of AUD0.26 per share in EPS. The full analysis is shown in Exhibit 36.

EXHIBIT 36: Pro Forma Tulor Summary Income Statement

	Before 20X3E	Acquisition	After 20X3E
Net revenues	21,726	5,432	27,158
Cost of sales	(16,447)	(4,372)	(20,819)
Operating expense	(3,476)	(869)	(4,345)
Cost synergies	—	42	42
EBITDA	1,803	232	2,035
D&A	(652)	(309)	(960)
EBIT	1,152	(77)	1,075
Interest income	24	(5)	19
Interest expense	(401)	(60)	(461)
Income tax expense	(155)		(127)
Net income	620		506
Diluted EPS	0.96		0.70
Diluted shares outstanding	648	80	728
Cash and equivalents	4,800	(1,000)	3,800

	Before 20X3E	Acquisition	After 20X3E
Total debt	6,169	1,000	7,169
Debt to EBITDA	3.4		3.5

6. EVALUATING DIVESTMENT ACTIONS

Either through acquisitions or internal expansion over time, companies often become engaged in multiple businesses. Management may seek to improve performance by separating these businesses, either selling them to another company or spinning them off as independent companies.

While investment analysts often cannot fully evaluate a corporate restructuring until details are announced, companies sometimes publicly announce "strategic reviews" or similarly titled initiatives regarding a part of their business or its entirety before a specific restructuring action is taken and announced. The outcome of the review can vary, so analysts must estimate the potential impact of different scenarios and judge their likelihood. Market participants will often price in risk-adjusted estimates of actions when the strategic review is announced, so an investment perspective at the time of the strategic review is necessary.

Example 13 describes a strategic review intended to evaluate the focus of a company, any conglomerate discount that may exist, and possible actions to realize value for its stakeholders.

EXAMPLE 13   Benefit Ltd. Strategic Review

Benefit Ltd., a fictional company headquartered in Johannesburg, South Africa, sells consulting services and subscription-based human capital management software called BenefitsExchange. The company operates and reports two segments: Consulting and BenefitsExchange. Summary financial data for Benefit Ltd. for the last 12 months (LTM) and the prior-year period are shown in Exhibit 37, Exhibit 38, and Exhibit 39 (see Example13 worksheet in the downloadable Microsoft Excel workbook).

EXHIBIT 37: Benefit Ltd. Segment Data (ZAR millions)

Revenues	Prior-Year Period	Last 12 Months (LTM)
BenefitsExchange	55	75
Consulting	402	404
Total revenues	457	479

Segment EBITDA	Prior-Year Period	LTM
BenefitsExchange	(10)	(5)
Consulting	83	84
Total segment EBITDA	73	79

EXHIBIT 38: Benefit Ltd. Reconciliation of Segment EBITDA to Consolidated Net Income and EPS

	Prior-Year Period	LTM
Total segment EBITDA	73	79
D&A	(19)	(20)
Corporate/unallocated cost	(4)	(4)
EBIT	50	55
Other expense (income)	0	0
Interest expense	8	9
Income taxes	10	11
Net income	32	35
Shares outstanding	1,454	1,454
Diluted EPS (cents)	2.20	2.41

EXHIBIT 39: Benefit Ltd. Balance Sheets, Most Recent Quarter (MRQ) and Prior Year

	Prior Year	MRQ
Cash and equivalents	140	173
Other current assets	110	97
Total current assets	250	270
Non-current assets	540	590
Total assets	790	860
Current debt	20	20
Other current liabilities	110	120
Total current liabilities	130	140
Non-current debt	230	230
Other non-current liabilities	130	185
Total equity	300	305
Total liabilities and equity	790	860

While BenefitsExchange has grown at a rapid rate, Benefit Ltd. has significantly lagged its peers in share price performance over the last four years. Currently, the market values Benefit Ltd. at an enterprise value of ZAR1,437 million, or sales and EBITDA (last 12-month) multiples of 3 and 19, respectively.

Recently, an activist investor announced an 8% position in Benefit Ltd. equity and, in a public statement, expressed an interest in working with the company's management and board to improve stakeholder value. At the market close today, the company announced the following information in a press release.

Benefit Ltd. (Benefit) announced that its board of directors has initiated a comprehensive review of strategic alternatives to maximize stakeholder value. The board has formed a Strategic Review Committee, which is chaired by the independent director and includes Benefit's CEO.

"The board is committed to maximizing value and has initiated a comprehensive review of strategic alternatives, including selling or spinning off components of business, and a review of our strategic plans," said the independent director. "Benefit's management team and board have a strong track record of value creation."

No assurances can be given regarding the outcome or timing of the review process. Benefit does not intend to make any further public comment regarding the review until it has been completed or the company determines that disclosure is required or beneficial.

You believe there are two actions that management might take in its strategic review:

A. Sell the Consulting segment.
B. Spin off the Consulting segment (which would split the Consulting and BenefitsExchange businesses into separate companies).

Data on relative valuation for both the Consulting and BenefitsExchange segments are shown in Exhibit 40–Exhibit 42.

EXHIBIT 40: Consulting Segment, Comparable Company Data

Comparable Company	Market Cap	Cash	Debt	EBITDA (LTM)
Comparable A	1,459	13	146	159
Comparable B	2,477	461	220	319
Comparable C	788	89	92	66
Comparable D	1,402	340	348	235
Comparable E	2,770	241	113	330
Comparable F	2,934	440	498	299

EXHIBIT 41: Consulting Segment, Comparable Transaction Data

Comparable Transaction	Cash Paid	Value of Stock Issued	Net Debt (Cash) Assumed	Target EBITDA (LTM)
Comparable 1	791	0	118	101
Comparable 2	1,174	0	434	134
Comparable 3	578	84	(35)	87
Comparable 4	1,310	378	832	180

EXHIBIT 42: BenefitsExchange Segment, Comparable Company Analysis

Comparable Company	EV/Sales (LTM)	Sales Growth Rate (LTM)
Comparable A	20	55%
Comparable B	12	18%
Comparable C	11	22%
Comparable D	6	8%
Comparable E	15	35%

1. Based on Benefit Ltd.'s current valuation and that of its median peers, evaluate whether a conglomerate discount is present. Assume that corporate/unallocated costs are allocated to the Consulting segment.

Solution to 1:
Benefit Ltd.'s current enterprise value is ZAR1,437 million. To assess the conglomerate discount, we compare this valuation to a sum-of-the-parts valuation of its segments using comparable company analysis.

Comparable company analysis for the Consulting segment, shown in Exhibit 43, indicates that the median peer trades at an enterprise value-to-EBITDA multiple of 9.

EXHIBIT 43: Consulting Segment, Comparable Company Analysis

Comparable Company	Market Cap	Cash	Debt	EBITDA (LTM)	Enterprise Value	EV/EBITDA
Comparable A	1,459	13	146	159	1,592	10
Comparable B	2,477	461	220	319	2,236	7
Comparable C	788	89	92	66	791	12
Comparable D	1,402	340	348	235	1,410	6
Comparable E	2,770	241	113	330	2,642	8
Comparable F	2,934	440	498	299	2,992	10
					Median	9

Comparable company analysis for the BenefitsExchange segment, shown in Exhibit 44, indicates that the median peer trades at an enterprise value-to-sales multiple of 12.

EXHIBIT 44: BenefitsExchange Segment, Comparable Company Analysis

Comparable Company	EV/Sales (LTM)
Comparable A	20
Comparable B	12
Comparable C	11
Comparable D	6
Comparable E	15
Median	12

Applying these peer valuation multiples to Benefit Ltd.'s segment EBITDA, less corporate costs, results in an enterprise value of ZAR1,621 million and an implied conglomerate discount of ZAR184 million, as shown in Exhibit 45.

EXHIBIT 45: Benefit Ltd. Sum-of-the-Parts Valuation I

Consulting segment EBITDA	84
Corporate/unallocated cost	(4)
Consulting segment EBITDA	80
Peer median EV/EBITDA multiple	9
Enterprise value	721
BenefitsExchange segment sales	75
Peer median EV/S multiple	12
Enterprise value	900
Total est. enterprise value	1,621
Current trading EV	1,437
Conglomerate discount	184

2. The market's valuations of BenefitsExchange's peers seem to be sensitive to companies' sales growth rates. If the valuation multiple of the company with the closest sales growth rate to BenefitsExchange is used in the analysis from Question 1, what is the estimated conglomerate discount?

Solution to 2:

The BenefitsExchange sales growth rate for the last 12 months was $(75 - 55)/55 = 36.4\%$. The comparable company with the closest growth rate is Comparable E, which grew by 35% and trades at an enterprise value-to-sales multiple of 15. If this multiple is used in the sum-of-the-parts valuation of Benefit Ltd., the estimated conglomerate discount will increase from ZAR184 million to ZAR409 million, as shown in Exhibit 46.

EXHIBIT 46: Benefit Ltd. Sum-of-the-Parts Valuation II

Consulting segment EBITDA	84
Corporate/unallocated cost	(4)
Consulting segment EBITDA	80
Peer median EV/EBITDA multiple	9
Enterprise value	721
BenefitsExchange segment sales	75
EV/S multiple	15
Enterprise value	1,125
Total est. enterprise value	1,846
Current trading EV	1,437
Conglomerate discount	409

3. Benefit Ltd. receives only one bid from a competitor consulting company for its Consulting segment, for total consideration of ZAR800 million.

   a. Compare the bid to comparable transactions. Ignore corporate/unallocated costs.
   b. Compare the bid to the implied valuation of the Consulting segment in the current market value of Benefit Ltd., using the valuation of BenefitsExchange from Question 2.

Solution to 3:

This bid values the Consulting segment at an EV/EBITDA of approximately 10, while the median and average comparable stands at 11 (see Exhibit 47). Thus, the bid moderately undervalues the Consulting segment from this perspective.

EXHIBIT 47: Consulting Segment, Comparable Transaction Analysis

	Cash Paid	Value of Stock Issued	Net Debt (Cash) Assumed	Target EBITDA (LTM)	EV/EBITDA
Comparable 1	791	0	118	101	9
Comparable 2	1,174	0	434	134	12
Comparable 3	578	84	(35)	87	7
Comparable 4	1,310	378	832	180	14
				Median	11
				Mean	11
Consulting segment bid	800			84	10

If the enterprise value of BenefitsExchange is assumed to be ZAR1,125 million and Benefit Ltd. currently trades at an enterprise value of ZAR1,437 million, then the implied valuation of the Consulting segment is ZAR312 million (see Exhibit 48). The bid of ZAR800 million values the segment substantially higher (488 million).

EXHIBIT 48: Consulting Segment Bid vs. Current Implied Segment Valuation

Current Benefit Ltd. EV	1,437
BenefitsExchange segment sales	75
EV/S multiple	15
Est. enterprise value	1,125
Implied value of Consulting segment	312
Consulting segment bid	800
Premium to implied value	488

4. Assume Benefit Ltd. sells the Consulting segment for ZAR800 million in cash, transferring no cash or debt to the buyer, and reduces annualized corporate/unallocated operating costs by ZAR1 million and D&A expense by ZAR12 million. Additionally, assume Benefit Ltd., immediately upon receiving the proceeds, executes an accelerated share repurchase (ASR) for ZAR800 million, repurchasing 200 million shares.

Estimate the pro forma income statement for Benefit Ltd. for these transactions, using the LTM financial data provided. Assume a 0% effective tax rate.

Solution to 4:
As shown in Exhibit 49, the sale of the Consulting segment is dilutive to EPS, though the dilution is offset modestly by the using of the proceeds towards share repurchases.

EXHIBIT 49: Pro Forma Benefit Ltd. Income Statement

	LTM
BenefitsExchange EBITDA	(5)
Corporate unallocated costs	(4)
Effect of Consulting disposal	1
D&A	(20)
Effect of Consulting disposal	12
Pro forma EBIT	(16)
Other expense (income)	0
Interest expense	9
Income taxes	0
Pro forma net income	(25)
Shares outstanding	1,454
Effect of ASR	(200)
Pro forma shares outstanding	1,254
Pro forma diluted EPS (cents)	(1.99)

5. If a spin off of the Consulting segment were to be valued at an EV/EBITDA multiple of 13, discuss whether Benefit Ltd. should sell the Consulting segment for ZAR800 million or spin it off?

Solution to 5:
If a spin off were to be valued at an EV/EBITDA multiple of 13, Benefit Ltd. should spin off the segment rather than sell it because the sale price of ZAR800 million values the company at 10× EV/EBITDA, or 3× lower. However, an advantage of a sale is that the valuation is definitive. If the spin off is valued lower or there is a capital market correction, then the sale may be a better option.

7. EVALUATING RESTRUCTURING ACTIONS

Restructurings are challenging on many fronts, and so they are often prompted or forced on a company by external circumstances. The next example illustrates a cost restructuring that is prompted by two related external circumstances: (1) a rejected acquisition offer and (2) pressure from shareholders in response to that rejection. Example 14 also shows how there are multiple restructuring actions that can achieve the same objective: increased shareholder value.

EXAMPLE 14   Cyrene SARL Cost Restructuring

Cyrene SARL, a fictional European consumer goods company, received an unsolicited acquisition offer in 20X2 from a larger competitor that has a reputation for aggressive cost cutting. The offer valued Cyrene at a 20% premium, and Cyrene's share price appreciated 18% on the news. However, Cyrene's management and board flatly rejected the offer, releasing the following statement by press release: "This offer fundamentally undervalues Cyrene. We rejected the proposal because we see no merit for Cyrene's stakeholders. We do not see the basis for any further discussion." The competitor withdrew its bid, and Cyrene's share price fell by 3%.

Over the week following the bid and rejection, Cyrene management and board members held conversations with its large shareholders. Several large shareholders remarked that "for as long as you don't take actions to increase shareholder value, you are vulnerable to an acquirer who will."

Two weeks after the bid, Cyrene SARL announced the following by press release: "We are conducting a comprehensive review of our cost structure to accelerate delivery of shareholder value. Recent events have highlighted the need to quickly capture the value we see in the company. We expect the review to be completed in five weeks, after which time we will communicate further."

Summary financial data for the last 12 months for Cyrene and five other European consumer goods companies, including Competitor A, which made the initial offer to acquire Cyrene, are shown in Exhibit 50 (also in the Example14 worksheet in the downloadable Microsoft Excel workbook).

EXHIBIT 50: Summary Financial Data, European Consumer Goods (LTM; EUR millions)

	Total Assets	Revenues	EBIT	Revenue Growth Rate*	Debt as % of Assets
Competitor A	236,648	56,444	16,933	1.50%	44%
Competitor B	86,381	35,410	8,782	−2.00%	45%
Competitor C	127,940	91,187	15,867	1.00%	29%
Competitor D	101,450	25,896	5,257	0.00%	29%
Competitor E	66,477	27,808	5,228	2.50%	29%
Cyrene SARL	23,738	18,990	2,659	4.00%	20%

*CAGR for last three years.

1. Explain Cyrene's motivations for conducting a review of its cost structure. What did the large shareholders mean by their remark?

Solution to 1:

The large shareholders meant that another company could acquire Cyrene and cut costs (equivalently, realize operating cost synergies) and earn an attractive rate of return on the acquisition. By having below-average profitability, Cyrene is a potentially inexpensive target, after synergies, for an acquirer. By improving its profitability on its own now, as a standalone business, it can improve shareholder value and fend off an acquirer.

2. If Cyrene were to restructure to reach its peer median EBIT margin, calculate how much in annual operating expenses, in euros and as a percentage of its TTM operating expenses, would have to be eliminated.

Solution to 2:

Based on the data in Exhibit 50, the peer median EBIT margin is 20%. In the last 12 months, Cyrene reported sales and EBIT of EUR18,990 million and EUR2,659 million, respectively, implying operating expenses of EUR16,331 million. To reach the peer median EBIT margin of 20%, Cyrene would have to reduce its operating expenses by EUR1,139 million, or 7%.

3. Past cost restructuring programs by consumer goods companies have taken four years, on average, to achieve target profitability. Assuming the following, estimate Cyrene's EBIT and EBIT margin next year:

   a. Revenues grow by 3% annually.
   b. Cyrene incurs one-time costs associated with the restructuring of EUR1,250 million.
   c. EBIT margin increases towards the peer median, excluding the impact of one-time restructuring costs, in an even annual pace over four years.

Solution to 3:

Exhibit 51 shows the estimation of Cyrene's pro forma profitability for the restructuring plan, as outlined. If Cyrene's EBIT margin is to increase evenly over four years towards 20%, it will increase by (20% − 14%)/4 = 6%/4 = 1.5% each year. Revenue growth and margin expansion are more than offset in the next 12 months by the one-time restructuring costs.

EXHIBIT 51: Cyrene Pro Forma Profitability, NTM (EUR millions)

	LTM	NTM
Revenues	18,990	19,560
EBIT ex. restructuring costs	2,659	3,032
Margin	14.0%	15.5%
Restructuring costs	—	1,250
Pro forma EBIT	—	1,782
Margin	—	9.1%

4. Explain two risks for Cyrene for pursuing a cost restructuring like the one modeled in Question 3.

Solution to 4:

The first risk is decelerating revenue growth. Over the last three years, Cyrene has grown materially faster than its five competitors. A major cost reduction may result in cutting spending responsible for that growth, which may erase any value creation associated with the restructuring.

A second risk is political. Cost restructurings typically result in layoffs and the closures of facilities, which may result in pressure from government officials and the public. Cyrene is a consumer-facing company and can lose business or be the target of regulatory pressure that preempts the cost restructuring or results in less value creation than anticipated.

5. Cyrene operates and reports results for three segments: Household Goods, Beauty & Personal Care, and Food. Summary segment financial data for the last 12 months are presented in Exhibit 52. Your colleague has advocated that as an alternative to a cost restructuring, Cyrene could sell or spin off its Household Goods segment to improve profitability. Evaluate your colleague's proposal, and identify other information you need to fully evaluate the proposal.

EXHIBIT 52: Cyrene Segment Results, LTM (EUR millions)

	Revenues	EBIT	Revenue Growth Rate*
Household Goods	5,507	496	7%
Beauty & Personal Care	8,166	1,960	3%
Food	5,317	583	2%
Corporate/unallocated	—	(380)	
Total	18,990	2,659	4.00%
Margin		14.0%	

Solution to 5:

As Exhibit 53 shows, selling or spinning off the Household Goods segment would result in a pro forma EBIT and EBIT margin of EUR2,163 million and 16%, respectively. While the margin is 2 percentage points higher, total EBIT is 19% lower in this scenario.

EXHIBIT 53: Cyrene Pro Forma Segment Results, LTM (EUR millions)

	Revenues	EBIT	Revenue Growth Rate*
Beauty & Personal Care	8,166	1,960	3%
Food	5,317	583	2%
Corporate/unallocated	—	(380)	
Total	13,483	2,163	
Margin		16%	

To fully evaluate a cost restructuring versus a sale or spin off of the Household Goods segment, several additional analyses are necessary, including the following:

- Estimated valuation of the Household Goods segment in a sale or spin off versus the value it has to the current Cyrene enterprise value
- Benefits or costs to the remaining Cyrene business segments as a result of a separation
- Amount, if any, of corporate/unallocated costs that could be reduced in the event of a sale or a spin off
- Additional details of the cost restructuring to compare to a sale or a spin off (it may be the case that both a cost restructuring and sale or spin off could be pursued)

Most corporate restructurings aim for strategic focus and operational simplification. Often corporate issuers find themselves owning business units that would be better served by a different ownership or operating model or governance structure. Ideally, restructurings work towards that objective.

This is true not only for businesses within a corporate issuer but also for the assets that underlie them. A common balance sheet restructuring is the sale and immediate leasing of real estate owned by issuers for which real estate is not their core business to a company that does focus on real estate investments. Example 15 demonstrates this situation with a retailer that owns valuable commercial real estate: its distribution centers.

EXAMPLE 15   Kosala Corp. Balance Sheet Restructuring

Kosala Corp. is a global omnichannel retailer with physical stores and e-commerce operations on its own and on third-party websites. While it leases most of its retail stores and its headquarters, Kosala owns the real estate (land and buildings) associated with several distribution centers the company built many years ago and expanded over time. Because e-commerce has continued to grow at a rapid rate and land use is highly regulated, distribution centers and associated real estate are valued at attractive cap rates. (The cap rate is net operating income expressed as a percentage of a property's value and is a reciprocal of a valuation multiple.)

On 1 June 20X2, Kosala Corp. made the following announcement by press release.

Kosala Corp. announced today that its board of directors approved a strategic real estate plan to pursue a separation of substantially all of its distribution centers and related real estate assets. The separation would be achieved through a series of sale-leaseback transactions with real estate investment companies that specialize in distribution center properties.

The company's board reached this decision after an extensive real estate evaluation process, along with the support of its legal and financial advisers. This evaluation included asset suitability screening, market rent analysis on a property-by-property basis, and prospective portfolio quality and diversification analysis.

"This strategic real estate plan is the result of a comprehensive review of alternatives to best take advantage of our real estate portfolio," said the chairman and CEO of Kosala. "We appreciate the valuation differential between retailers and real estate. Importantly, we expect this real estate plan to create minimal operational distraction."

Under the plan, Kosala will sell some of its distribution centers and related real estate and lease them for 15-year terms with the option to extend the term. The company expects to receive cash proceeds of approximately CHF425 million, which will be used to retire approximately CHF215 million of debt and the remaining proceeds to repurchase 10 million common shares.

Annual rent expense for the leased assets will total CHF19 million. Kosala will continue to be responsible for maintenance, property taxes, and utilities and will generally be able to make modifications to the properties as business needs arise. The transaction values the assets at an average capitalization rate of 4.5%.

The company believes the pro forma capital structure following the transaction will enable it to receive an investment-grade credit rating, which will offer more attractive financing terms from its current speculative-grade rating. However, the company's credit rating is the responsibility of credit rating agencies, and no assurances can be made as to any changes.

Kosala expects the transaction, including the retirement of debt and the share repurchase, to be completed by the end of 20X2. Additional financial details are as follows:

- Expect to recognize a gain on asset sales of CHF200 million, to be amortized over 15 years.
- Incremental occupancy expense is CHF19 million per year.
- Depreciation expense savings are CHF30 million per year.
- Interest savings from the retirement of debt are CHF15 million per year.
- Because management cannot make any assurance regarding a change in the company's credit rating, further interest savings from a decrease in the company's cost of debt cannot be quantified at this time.
- Expect to recognize operating lease right-of-use asset and lease liabilities of CHF198 million.

1. Explain Kosala's motivation for this action.

Solution to 1:

Kosala's motivations are two-fold: to unlock the value in its real estate assets, a non-core business for the company with attractive valuations, and to improve its balance sheet by retiring debt and improving its credit rating, which will likely decrease its costs of capital.

2. The 25th, 50th, and 75th percentile cap rates for transactions for similarly situated properties and similar lease terms in the last five years were 3.0%, 5.5%, and 8.0%, respectively. Based on these figures, evaluate the valuation on a preliminary basis and identify two characteristics that may influence the cap rate for these transactions.

Solution to 2:

For leases in which the tenant bears operating costs and taxes, net operating income is generally equal to rent. Because the cap rate is a reciprocal of a valuation multiple, a lower cap rate implies a higher valuation and vice versa. For a seller (and future tenant), such as Kosala, a lower cap rate is desirable. The 4.5% cap rate in this transaction compares favorably to the descriptive statistics provided, because it is 100 bps below the median.

Two characteristics that may influence the cap rate for these transactions are the location of the property and its physical condition. Distribution centers near metropolitan centers are the most valuable, and one in good condition means that significant capital expenditures will not be required in the short run.

3. Based on the information provided and Exhibit 54, estimate Kosala's pro forma debt-to-EBITDA and interest coverage ratios for the announced transactions, assuming an effective tax rate of 25%.

EXHIBIT 54: Kosala Corp. Summary Financial Data (CHF millions)

	LTM (Pre-Transaction)
Net sales	5,323
Cost of sales	3,309
Gross margin	2,014
SG&A expenses	1,823
D&A expense	67
Operating profit	124
Interest expense	43
Income taxes	20
Net income	61
Diluted shares outstanding	97
Diluted EPS	0.63
Gross debt	615

Based on the information provided, Kosala's pro forma gross debt to EBITDA will decrease from 3.2 to 2.3 as a result of the transactions (see Exhibit 55; also in the Example15 worksheet in the downloadable Microsoft Excel workbook). Note that while depreciation expense decreases, amortization expense increases from the annual amortization of the gain on sale of the assets. Interest coverage (EBIT to interest expense) increases from 2.9 to 4.3.

EXHIBIT 55: Kosala Corp. Pro Forma Debt-to-EBITDA Analysis (CHF millions)

	LTM (Pre-Transaction)	Transaction	LTM (Pro Forma)
Net sales	5,323		5,323
Cost of sales	3,309		3,309
Gross margin	2,014		2,014
SG&A expenses	1,823	19	1,842

	LTM (Pre-Transaction)	Transaction	LTM (Pro Forma)
D&A expense	67	(17)	50
Operating profit	124		122
Interest expense	43	(15)	28
Income taxes	20		23
Net income	61		70
Diluted shares outstanding	97	(10)	87
Diluted EPS	0.63		0.81
Gross debt	615	(215)	400
Debt to EBITDA	3.2		2.3
EBIT to interest	2.9		4.3

4. Assuming credit ratings are primarily determined by interest coverage and debt-to-EBITDA ratios, estimate pro forma interest expense for Kosala using Exhibit 56. Assume that the spot Treasury rate at a similar tenor to Kosala's remaining indebtedness is 125 bps.

EXHIBIT 56: Corporate Credit Ratings and Spreads to Fundamentals

	AAA/AA	A	BBB	BB	B
Debt to EBITDA	0–1.0	1.0–1.5	1.6–2.3	2.4–3.5	3.6–4.5
EBIT interest coverage	>12	11.0–8.0	7.9–4.0	3.5–1.6	1.5–0.5
Average spread over Treasury	125	232	450	575	731

Solution to 4:

Pro forma for the transactions, Kosala's estimated debt-to-EBITDA and interest coverage ratios are 2.3× and 4.3×, respectively. This puts Kosala in the BBB credit rating range, which has an average spread over Treasuries of 450 bps. Given the Treasury rate of 125 bps, the pro forma interest rate is 575 bps. On gross debt of CHF400 million, pro forma interest expense is CHF23 million, which is CHF5 million less than prior to its credit rating upgrade and reduction in cost of debt.

8. SUMMARY

- Corporate issuers seek to alter their destiny, as described by the corporate life cycle, by taking actions known as restructurings.
- Restructurings include investment actions that increase the size and scope of an issuer's business, divestment actions that decrease size or scope, and restructuring actions that do not affect scope but improve performance.
- Investment actions include equity investments, joint ventures, and acquisitions. Investment actions are often made by issuers seeking growth, synergies, or undervalued targets.

- Divestment actions include sales and spin offs and are made by issuers seeking to increase growth or profitability or reduce risk by shedding certain divisions and assets.
- Restructuring actions, including cost cutting, balance sheet restructurings, and reorganizations, do not change the size or scope of issuers but are aimed at improving returns on capital to historical or peer levels.
- The evaluation of a corporate restructuring is composed of four phases: initial evaluation, preliminary evaluation, modeling, and updating the investment thesis. The entire evaluation is generally done only for material restructurings.
- The initial evaluation of a corporate restructuring answers the following questions: What is happening? When is it happening? Is it material? And why is it happening?
- Materiality is defined by both size and fit. One rule of thumb for size is that large actions are those that are greater than 10% of an issuer's enterprise value (e.g., for an acquisition, consideration in excess of 10% of the acquirer's pre-announcement enterprise value). Fit refers to the alignment between the action and an analyst's expectations for the issuer.
- Three common valuation methods for companies involved in corporate restructurings, during the preliminary valuation phase of the evaluation, are comparable company, comparable transaction, and premium paid analysis.
- Corporate restructurings must be modeled on the financial statements based on the situational specifics. Estimated financial statements that include the effect of a restructuring are known as pro forma financial statements.
- The weighted average cost of capital for an issuer is determined by the weights of different capital types and the constituent costs of capital. The costs of capital are influenced by both bottom-up and top-down drivers. Bottom-up drivers include stability, profitability, leverage, and asset specificity. Corporate restructurings affect the cost of capital by affecting these drivers.

9. PRACTICE PROBLEMS

The following information relates to questions 1–5

Jane Chang is an analyst at Alpha Fund covering the real estate and energy sectors. She and her colleague are analyzing two companies that are currently held by the fund.

The first company is Jupiter Corp., a publicly traded, national retail grocery store chain that has 2,800 physical stores. Jupiter leases most of its grocery stores and all five of its office locations that help the company achieve its core business of operating 50,000 square foot stores in all markets of the United States. Jupiter also owns the real estate (land and building) associated with 100 physical store locations. Jupiter recently announced that its board of directors approved a strategic real estate plan to pursue a separation of all its owned assets. The company currently has a speculative-grade credit rating.

The separation would be achieved through a series of sale-leaseback transactions with real estate investment trusts (REITs) that specialize in owning retail properties. Under the plan, Jupiter will sell its 100 owned grocery stores and lease them for 15-year terms with a combined annual rent expense of USD40 million. Jupiter expects to receive cash proceeds of approximately USD800 million from the property sales, which will be used to retire approximately USD600 million of debt and repurchase 4 million common shares.

Jupiter believes the pro forma capital structure following the transactions will enable it to receive an investment-grade credit rating. The sale-leaseback transactions value the 100 assets at an average capitalization rate of 5.50%. Based on Chang's colleague's research, the 25th, 50th, and 75th percentile cap rates for sale transactions for similarly situated properties and similar lease terms in the last three years were 5.00%, 5.50%, and 6.00%, respectively.

The second company is Saturn Corp., a publicly traded US energy company. Chang has been asked to assess the valuation of a potential spin off for this company. Saturn operates and reports three segments: Upstream, Midstream, and Downstream. In the last 12 months, the company reported the financial results shown in Exhibit 1.

EXHIBIT 1

Segment	EBITDA (USD Millions)
Upstream	14,400
Midstream	5,760
Downstream	3,840
Consolidated	24,000

Saturn is currently trading at an enterprise value of USD408,000 million, or an EV/EBITDA multiple of 17. A spin off of the Downstream segment has long been rumored because it has been under-invested in by the current management team, resulting in slower revenue growth than its peers. Chang finds that the median Upstream, Midstream, and Downstream peers are trading at enterprise value-to-EBITDA multiples of 19, 17, and 13, respectively.

During an internal discussion, Chang's colleague makes the following three statements about the comparable company analysis method:

Statement 1: The method is not sensitive to market mispricing.

Statement 2: The estimates of value are derived directly from the market.

Statement 3: The method provides a reasonable approximation of a target company's value relative to similar transactions in the market.

1. Jupiter's strategic real estate plan would be best characterized as a:
   A. reorganization.
   B. cost restructuring.
   C. balance sheet restructuring.

2. Which of the following statements about Jupiter's motivations for the strategic real estate plan is incorrect?
   A. The transactions will enable Jupiter to sell a non-core business.
   B. The transactions will allow Jupiter to unlock the value of its real estate assets.
   C. The expected change in Jupiter's credit rating after the transactions will increase the firm's costs of capital.

3. Which of the following statements *best* describes Jupiter's average capitalization rate for the sale-leaseback transactions? Jupiter's average capitalization rate:
   A. is supported by the comparable transactions.
   B. compares favorably to the comparable transactions.
   C. compares unfavorably to the comparable transactions.

4. Based on Exhibit 1 and the peer median EV/EBITDA multiples, Saturn's estimated enterprise value is *closest* to:
   A. USD392,000 million.
   B. USD408,000 million.
   C. USD421,440 million.

5. Which of Chang's colleague's three statements is correct?
   A. Statement 1
   B. Statement 2
   C. Statement 3

The following information relates to questions 6–10

Elaine Lee is an analyst at an investment bank covering the energy sector. She and her junior analyst are analyzing Stratton Oil Corporation.

Stratton Oil Corporation is a publicly traded, US-based energy company that just announced its acquisition of Midwest Oil Corporation, a smaller US-based energy company. Stratton will pay USD55 in cash and 2.25 Stratton shares for each Midwest share, for a total consideration of USD40 billion based on share prices just prior to the announcement. Stratton's current trading enterprise value just prior to the announcement was USD170 billion. Lee concludes that the acquisition does not signal a change in strategy or focus for Stratton.

Stratton expects to realize annual recurring cost synergies of USD350 million (pre-tax), primarily from efficiencies in oil exploration and production activities and savings in corporate costs. The achievement of the full USD350 million in synergies is expected by the end of the third year after the acquisition closes. Synergies are realized in the amounts of USD117 million, USD233 million, and USD350 million in Years 1–3, respectively, and cash costs of USD175 million, USD280 million, and USD395 million are incurred in Years 1–3, respectively.

Expectations for revenues and total operating expenses for Stratton and Midwest for the next three years prior to the acquisition announcement are shown in Exhibit 1.

EXHIBIT 1: Stratton and Midwest Year 1–3 Figures, Prior to Acquisition (USD millions)

Stratton	Year 1	Year 2	Year 3
Revenues	21,325	22,391	23,511
Operating expenses	16,525	17,351	18,219
Midwest			
Revenues	5,350	5,618	5,898
Operating expenses	3,050	3,203	3,363

Lee's junior analyst makes the following comment during a conversation with Lee:

The acquisition is considered immaterial in the initial evaluation step for Stratton because it does not signal a change in strategy or focus.

Stratton's offer valued Midwest at an enterprise value of USD40.6 billion, including USD4.3 billion of existing Midwest debt. To finance the consideration of USD55 in cash and

2.25 Stratton shares for each Midwest share, Stratton will issue 104 million new shares and raise approximately USD26 billion in new debt and fund the remainder with cash on hand. Following the close, Stratton expects its outstanding debt will be approximately USD62 billion. Prior to the acquisition, Stratton has 1.096 billion shares outstanding trading at USD125 per share. Lee wants to determine how much the weights of debt and equity in Stratton's capital structure will change assuming a constant share price and that the book value of debt equals its market value.

During an internal meeting, Lee asks if Stratton could have achieved its same goals by undertaking an equity investment or joint venture. In response, Lee's junior analyst makes the following three statements.

Statement 1: Acquisitions require substantially greater capital investments than equity investments.

Statement 2: Acquisitions and equity investments are similar in that they both allow the acquirer to gain control of the target.

Statement 3: Relative to joint ventures, equity investments provide more equal governance representation and require larger investments.

Lee conducted a sum-of-the-parts valuation of Stratton's three segments and calculated an estimated enterprise value of USD187 billion just prior to the announcement.

6. Based on Exhibit 1, the forecasted operating income in Year 3 for the combined Stratton and Midwest is *closest* to:
   A. USD7,432.
   B. USD7,782.
   C. USD8,177.

7. Lee's junior analyst's comment about materiality is:
   A. correct.
   B. incorrect because the acquisition is considered a small acquisition.
   C. incorrect because the acquisition represents more than 10% of Stratton's enterprise value prior to the transaction.

8. The weight of equity in Stratton's capital structure as a result of the acquisition of Midwest assuming Lee's two assumptions is closest to:
   A. 29%.
   B. 71%.
   C. 81%.

9. Which of Lee's junior analyst's three statements is correct?
   A. Statement 1
   B. Statement 2
   C. Statement 3

10. Stratton's estimated conglomerate discount just prior to the announcement is:
    A. –USD17 billion.
    B. USD0.
    C. USD17 billion.

ENVIRONMENTAL, SOCIAL, AND GOVERNANCE (ESG) CONSIDERATIONS IN INVESTMENT ANALYSIS

Deborah S. Kidd, CFA
CFA Institute (USA)

Young Lee, CFA, JD
MacKay Shields (USA and Europe)

Johan Vanderlugt
NN Investment Partners (Netherlands)[*]

LEARNING OUTCOMES

The candidate should be able to:

- describe global variations in ownership structures and the possible effects of these variations on corporate governance policies and practices
- evaluate the effectiveness of a company's corporate governance policies and practices
- describe how ESG-related risk exposures and investment opportunities may be identified and evaluated
- evaluate ESG risk exposures and investment opportunities related to a company

1. INTRODUCTION

Environmental, social, and governance (ESG) considerations are increasingly being integrated into investment analysis. Evaluating how ESG factors potentially affect a company may

---

[*] CFA Institute would like to thank Hardik Sanjay Shah, CFA, for his contributions to the 2022 update of this chapter.

provide analysts with a broader perspective on the risks and investment opportunities of a company's securities. Although corporate governance has long been recognized as having a significant impact on a company's long-term performance, investors have become increasingly concerned with environmental and social factors and how companies manage their resources and risk exposures that relate to such factors. Mismanagement of these resources has led to a number of high-profile corporate events that have negatively affected security prices. Increasingly stringent regulatory environments, potentially finite supplies of natural resources, and global trends toward energy conservation and waste reduction have led many investors to place greater emphasis on the management of environmental risks. Similarly, such issues as worker health and safety policies, community impact, and marketing practices have increased the visibility of how a company manages its social capital.

This chapter provides an overview of ESG considerations in investment analysis. Section 2 provides an overview of the global variations in corporate ownership structures, as well as how these ownership structures may affect corporate governance outcomes. In Section 3, we discuss company-specific factors that should be considered when evaluating corporate governance in the investment process. Section 4 discusses the identification of ESG-related risks and opportunities that are relevant to security analysis. Section 5 demonstrates the evaluation of ESG-related risks and opportunities through several examples. The chapter concludes with a summary of the key points and practice problems.

2. OWNERSHIP STRUCTURES AND THEIR EFFECTS ON CORPORATE GOVERNANCE

The global corporate governance landscape comprises a vast range of ownership structures that reflect unique economic, political, social, legal, and other forces in each country and/or region. Within any of these distinct ownership structures, one may find a variety of complex relationships involving shareholders and other stakeholders who have an interest in the company. Those other stakeholders include creditors, managers (executives), employees, directors, customers, suppliers, governments, and regulators. An understanding of the variation of ownership structures, the conflicts that arise within these structures, types of influential shareholders, and the effects of ownership structure on corporate governance are important considerations for analyzing corporate governance in the investment process.

2.1. Dispersed vs. Concentrated Ownership

Corporate ownership structures are generally classified as *dispersed*, *concentrated*, or a hybrid of the two. **Dispersed ownership** reflects the existence of many shareholders, none of which has the ability to individually exercise control over the corporation. In contrast, **concentrated ownership** reflects an individual shareholder or a group (called *controlling shareholders*) with the ability to exercise control over the corporation. In this context, a group is typically a family, another company (or companies), or a sovereign entity.

On a global basis, concentrated ownership structures are considerably more common than dispersed ownership structures. A global corporate governance report by the Organisation for Economic Co-operation and Development (OECD)[1] noted that 38 out

---

[1]OECD (2017).

of 47 jurisdictions analyzed have predominantly concentrated ownership structures. Among the other nine jurisdictions, four were characterized as having dispersed ownership structures (Australia, Ireland, the United Kingdom, and the United States) and five were characterized as having "hybrid" corporate ownership structures (Canada, Germany, Japan, the Netherlands, and Switzerland). The OECD's classification of corporate ownership structure by jurisdiction is shown in Exhibit 1.

EXHIBIT 1: Corporate Ownership Classifications

Jurisdictions with Concentrated Ownership	
Austria, Belgium, Brazil, Chile, China, Colombia, Czech Republic, Denmark, Estonia, Finland, France, Greece, Hungary, Iceland, India, Indonesia, Israel, Italy, Latvia, Mexico, New Zealand, Norway, Poland, Portugal, Russia, Singapore, Slovenia, South Africa, South Korea, Spain, Sweden, Turkey, United Arab Emirates	State ownership is characteristic of certain countries, such as China, Norway, and Sweden. In other countries, including Brazil, Mexico, Portugal, and South Korea, families are the predominant shareholders. Company groups are prevalent in a number of additional countries, such as India and Russia.

Jurisdictions with Dispersed Ownership	
Australia, Ireland, United Kingdom, United States	Among the largest companies in Australia, the majority of shares are held (albeit dispersed) by financial institutions. In Ireland, ownership shares tend to be widely dispersed, although there are a few family-controlled companies. Among UK companies, few have major shareholders owning 25% or more of shares. In the United States, ownership of public companies is generally characterized by dispersed shareholdings; listed companies are rarely under the control of a major shareholder.

Hybrid Jurisdictions	
Canada, Germany, Japan, Netherlands, Switzerland	In Canada, among the largest listed firms, a meaningful minority have controlling shareholders. In Germany, a significant number of companies are under "tight control," but in many cases shares are broadly distributed (especially for listed companies). In Japan, a small minority of listed companies have a shareholder that owns a majority of shares. The Netherlands has a more dispersed ownership structure than most continental European countries; however, when accounting for "trust offices," ownership is somewhat more concentrated. In Switzerland, the largest listed companies have more dispersed ownership than medium-sized and smaller companies.

Source: OECD (2017).

The degree of share ownership alone may not necessarily reflect whether the control of a company is dispersed or concentrated. This is true because controlling shareholders may be either **majority shareholders** (i.e., own more than 50% of a corporation's shares) or **minority shareholders** (i.e., own less than 50% of shares). In certain ownership structures, shareholders may have disproportionately high control of a corporation relative to their ownership stakes as a result of horizontal and/or vertical ownership arrangements. **Horizontal ownership** involves companies with mutual business interests (e.g., key customers or suppliers) that have cross-holding share arrangements with each other. This structure can help facilitate strategic alliances and foster long-term relationships among such companies. **Vertical ownership** (or pyramid ownership) involves a company or group that has a controlling interest in two or more holding companies, which in turn have controlling interests in various operating companies.

The existence of *dual-class* (or multiple-class) shares can also serve to disconnect the degree of share ownership from actual control. **Dual-class shares** grant one share class superior or sole voting rights, whereas the other share class has inferior or no voting rights. When used in connection with vertical ownership arrangements, the company or group at the top of the pyramid can issue to itself all or a disproportionately high number of shares with superior voting rights and thus maintain control of the operating companies with relatively fewer total shares of a company owned.

2.2. Conflicts within Different Ownership Structures

The type of corporate ownership structure affects corporate governance policies and practices because of the potentially different set of conflicts that may exist between shareholders and managers, as well as among shareholders themselves.

The combination of *dispersed* ownership and *dispersed* voting power is generally associated with shareholders who lack the power to exercise control over managers. These shareholders are referred to as *weak shareholders*, and such managers are referred to as *strong managers*. Under this combination, conflict between the shareholders and managers of a corporation may be significant. Shareholders are interested in maximizing shareholder value. There is a risk, however, that managers will seek to use a company's resources to pursue their own interests. In corporate governance, this conflict is known as a *principal–agent* problem. This problem can be mitigated if controlling shareholders are present because they may be able to control the board of directors (and, in turn, the appointment of managers) and have the incentive to monitor management.

The combination of *concentrated* ownership and *concentrated* voting power often results in controlling shareholders maintaining a position of power over both managers and minority shareholders; these controlling shareholders are referred to as *strong shareholders*, and such managers are referred to as *weak managers*. In this scenario, controlling shareholders can effectively monitor management because they are able to control the board of directors and, in turn, the appointment of managers. With concentrated ownership and concentrated voting power, however, controlling owners may also be able to allocate company resources to their own benefit at the expense of minority owners. This conflict is known as a *principal–principal* problem.

The combination of *dispersed* ownership and *concentrated* voting power generally leads to the principal–principal problem as well. The one difference, however, is that the strong controlling shareholders do not own a majority of the shares of a company. In this scenario, controlling shareholders with less than majority ownership can exert control over other minority owners through certain mechanisms, such as dual-class share structures and pyramid structures, and can also monitor management owing to their outsized voting power.

Finally, the combination of *concentrated* ownership and *dispersed* voting power arises when there are legal restrictions on the voting rights of large share positions, known as **voting caps**. A number of sovereign governments have imposed voting caps to deter foreign investors from obtaining controlling ownership positions in strategically important local companies.

EXAMPLE 1   Conflicts between Shareholders and Managers

1. The managers of Company A, a widely held conglomerate, collectively own approximately 30% of the outstanding shares. No other shareholder owns more than a 1% share. Each ownership share has equivalent voting rights. Describe the potential conflict between the shareholders and managers of Company A given its ownership structure and voting rights.

Solution to 1:

Company A has dispersed ownership and dispersed voting power. In this ownership structure, shareholders do not appear to have the ability to control or monitor managers; that is, there are weak shareholders and strong managers. In this case, a risk exists that managers may seek to use company resources to prioritize their own interests rather than to maximize shareholder value. This type of conflict is known as the *principal–agent* problem.

2.3. Types of Influential Shareholders

In different parts of the world, the types of corporate shareholders that have a significant influence on corporate governance vary. Each of these shareholder types possesses its own unique set of motivations, interests, and agendas. By identifying these shareholders, an investment analyst is in a position to further assess corporate governance risks.

2.3.1. Banks

In several regions, notably in Europe and Asia, banks often have considerable control over corporations with which they have a lending relationship as well as an equity interest. A conflict of interest could arise if banks have loan exposures to a corporation in addition to their equity investment. For example, if a bank has both a lending relationship with and an equity interest in a corporation, it could seek to influence the corporation to take out large loans, and perhaps on less favorable terms, to the potential detriment of other shareholders. In this situation, appropriate corporate governance controls could ensure that banks that are both creditors and investors appropriately balance their interests as lenders against their interests as shareholders.

2.3.2. Families

Family ownership is the predominant form of corporate structure in some parts of the world, notably Latin America and, to a slightly lesser extent, Asia and Europe. In some cases, also commonly in Latin America, individuals serve on the board of directors of multiple corporations. This situation, known as **interlocking directorates**, typically results in the same family or the same member of a corporate group controlling several corporations. A benefit of family control is lower risks associated with principal–agent problems as a result of families having concentrated ownership and management responsibility. Conversely, drawbacks of family ownership may include poor transparency, lack of management accountability, modest consideration for minority shareholder rights, and difficulty in attracting quality talent for management positions.

2.3.3. State-Owned Enterprises

State-owned enterprises (SOEs) often exist in corporate sectors that are strategically important to a sovereign government, have minimum initial or ongoing capital requirements that are beyond the private sector's funding ability, or provide certain products or services (e.g., power generation or health services) that the state believes should be provided at a certain price or minimum standard. Listed SOEs are partially owned by sovereign governments but also have shares traded on public stock markets. This structure is called a *mixed-ownership model*. This model tends to have lower market scrutiny of management than that of corporate ownership models, which have implicit or explicit state guarantees to prevent corporate bankruptcy. In some cases, SOEs may pursue policies that enhance social or public policy considerations at the expense of maximizing shareholder value.

2.3.4. Institutional Investors

In many countries, institutional investors—typically mutual funds, pension funds, insurance companies, and hedge funds—collectively represent a significant proportion of equity market ownership. Because these investors tend to have considerable resources and market expertise, they can use informed judgment in exercising their shareholder rights. In markets with widely dispersed ownership, institutional investors do not typically control a large enough ownership position to qualify as a controlling shareholder. Institutional investors can promote good corporate governance, however, by holding a company's board and management accountable when the board or management does not appear to be acting in the best interests of shareholders.

2.3.5. Group Companies

Some ownership structures, such as the previously mentioned horizontal and vertical ownership structures, may result in shareholders having disproportionately high control relative to their ownership stakes. Cross-holding share arrangements and long-term relationships between these group companies may restrict the potential for a transfer of share ownership—as well as create a potential obstacle for outsiders to purchase a significant portion of shares in companies. Without appropriate corporate governance policies/ procedures or regulatory protections, there is a greater risk that corporations controlled by groups engage in related-party transactions at the expense of minority shareholders. Examples of group companies are Samsung (South Korea), Sanwa (Japan), and Grupo Carso (Mexico).

2.3.6. Private Equity Firms

Private equity firms, notably those involved in venture capital and leveraged buyouts, are strategic owners that invest in privately owned companies or in public companies with the intent to take them private. Venture capital firms invest in the early stages of a company and provide oversight of portfolio companies. Similarly, leveraged buyout (LBO) firms typically have majority control in mature companies. The involvement of venture capital and LBO firms in the management of corporations may bring important changes to companies' corporate governance, such as the development of corporate codes and implementation of performance-based manager compensation.

2.3.7. Foreign Investors

Foreign investors, particularly when investing in emerging market countries, can have a significant influence on local companies when they own more shares than domestic investors own. Foreign investors from countries that have more stringent standards may demand higher levels of transparency and accountability. If a local company chooses to cross-list its shares in another country with greater transparency requirements and investor protections, local minority shareholders may benefit from the arrangement.

2.3.8. Managers and Board Directors

When managers and board directors are also shareholders of a company, they are known as **insiders**. As their ownership positions increase, insiders are more likely to dedicate company resources toward long-term profitability because their economic interests in the company have become more aligned with the interests of external shareholders. Large ownership positions, however, may also provide insiders with increased power and an accompanying desire to protect their own interests at the expense of other shareholders.

2.4. Effects of Ownership Structure on Corporate Governance

This subsection highlights the effects of ownership structures on corporate governance policies and practices. Key considerations include board independence; board structure; special voting arrangements; corporate governance codes, laws, and listing requirements; and stewardship codes.

2.4.1. Director Independence

Independent board directors (or independent board members) are defined as those with no material relationship with the company with regard to employment, ownership, or remuneration. The percentage of independent board directors tends to be higher in jurisdictions with generally dispersed ownership structures relative to those countries with generally concentrated ownership structures. Independent directors originated in dispersed ownership jurisdictions as a means to strengthen the board's monitoring role over managers. The proportion of independent directors on boards has increased over time amid regulatory responses to corporate scandals (e.g., the Enron Corporation scandal in the early 2000s).

Independent directors generally serve a narrower role in concentrated ownership structures than in dispersed ownership structures. For example, the United States requires that some committees (such as the audit, nomination, and compensation committees) be composed entirely of independent directors. Conversely, in most jurisdictions with concentrated ownership structures, nomination and remuneration committees are not mandatory; when these committees do exist, jurisdictions typically recommend that the committees be wholly or largely composed of independent directors. In short, the principal–agent problem is generally less of a concern in a concentrated ownership structure than in a dispersed ownership structure.

Almost all OECD countries have introduced a requirement or recommendation for the level of independent directors serving on boards. These requirements and recommendations vary by jurisdiction, however. Some countries impose or recommend a minimum number of independent directors (typically ranging from one to three), whereas others impose or recommend a minimum ratio of independent directors (typically ranging from 20% to 50% or greater).

2.4.2. Board Structures

A corporation's board of directors is typically structured as either one tier or two tier. A **one-tier board** structure consists of a single board of directors, composed of executive (internal) and non-executive (external) directors. A **two-tier board** structure consists of a supervisory board that oversees a management board. A one-tier board is the most common structure, but a number of jurisdictions mandate a two-tier board structure (e.g., Argentina, Germany, and Russia), whereas other jurisdictions offer the choice of a one-tier or two-tier board (e.g., Brazil and France). The supervisory board of a two-tier board can serve as a control function through activities such as inspecting the corporation's books and records, reviewing the annual report, overseeing the work of external auditors, analyzing information provided by the management board, and setting or influencing management compensation. In certain countries, such as Germany, the supervisory boards comprise representatives from key stakeholders, such as banks and labor or other groups.

2.4.3. Special Voting Arrangements

Several jurisdictions have special voting arrangements to improve the position of minority shareholders. For example, Brazil, India, Portugal, Turkey, Italy, Israel, and the United Kingdom have special arrangements that facilitate engagement of minority shareholders in board nomination and election processes. When a UK company has a controlling shareholder, a condition for obtaining a "premium listing" (i.e., meeting the United Kingdom's highest standards of regulation and corporate governance) on the London Stock Exchange is that independent directors must be separately approved by both the entire shareholder base and non-controlling shareholders.

2.4.4. Corporate Governance Codes, Laws, and Listing Requirements

Many countries have adopted national corporate governance codes in which companies disclose their adoption of recommended corporate governance practices or explain why they have not done so. In some jurisdictions, companies are required to go beyond this "comply or explain" approach. In Japan, for example, companies with no outside directors must justify why appointing outside directors is not appropriate. Some jurisdictions do not have national corporate governance codes but make use of company law or regulation (e.g., Chile) or stock exchange listing requirements (e.g., India) to achieve similar objectives.

2.4.5. Stewardship Codes

Many countries have introduced voluntary codes, known as *stewardship codes*, that encourage investors to exercise their legal rights and increase their level of engagement in corporate governance. In some cases, stewardship codes are not entirely voluntary. As an example, the UK Stewardship Code includes a duty for institutional investors to monitor the companies in which they invest and requires that UK asset managers investing in the shares of UK companies publish a "comply or explain" statement of commitment to the UK Stewardship Code.

3. EVALUATING CORPORATE GOVERNANCE POLICIES AND PROCEDURES

Effective corporate governance is critical for a company's reputation and competitiveness. Benefits of effective corporate governance may include higher profitability, growth in return on equity (or other return metrics), better access to credit, higher and sustainable dividends, favorable long-term share performance, and a lower cost of capital. In contrast, companies with ineffective corporate governance may experience reputational damage, reduced competitiveness, potential share price weakness/volatility, reduced profitability, and a higher cost of capital.

Corporate governance factors are often difficult to quantify. However, an understanding of these factors and their impact on governance policies and procedures can be important for investors to consider. Understanding the disclosed corporate governance policies and procedures is a key starting point for investors. Regular dialogue and engagement efforts with companies can help investors better understand corporate governance policies and procedures. In some situations, shareholder activism can be used to attempt to compel a company to act in a desired manner. **Shareholder activism** refers to strategies used by shareholders to attempt to compel a company to act in a desired manner.

The quality of corporate governance is typically reflected in a company's behavior in the market and toward its stakeholders. To that end, an evaluation of a corporation's board of directors is a starting point for investors. We discuss several of the considerations relating to boards of directors in this section. In addition, a company's policies regarding business ethics, bribery and corruption, whistleblower protection, and related-party transactions can help analysts evaluate a company's corporate governance. In practice, analysts typically adjust the risk premium (cost of capital) or credit spread of a company to reflect their assessment of corporate governance considerations.

3.1. Board Policies and Practices

A starting point for evaluating a board's effectiveness is its policies and practices. An oversight role is one aspect of a board's effectiveness—for example, whether the board is high-performing or dysfunctional. Each capital market is subject to different corporate governance issues, depending on its predominant ownership structure, history, legal environment, culture, and industry diversity. For example, boards of companies with concentrated family ownership structures and concentrated voting power may engage in related-party transactions that benefit family members or affiliates at the expense of outside shareholders.

3.1.1. Board of Directors Structure

Generally, when evaluating board structure, investors consider whether the organization and structure of the board—whether it is a one-tier or two-tier structure—provide sufficient oversight, representation, and accountability to shareholders. A related topic is "CEO duality," whereby the chief executive officer (CEO) also serves as chairperson of the board. CEO duality may raise concerns that the monitoring and oversight role of the board may be compromised relative to independent chairperson and CEO roles. When the chairperson is not independent or the role is combined, a company may appoint a lead independent director to help protect investor interests.

3.1.2. Board Independence

The independence of the directors, which we discussed previously, is a relevant consideration for investors. The absence or presence of a minority of independent directors is a negative aspect of corporate governance. Without independent directors, the potential exists for management to act in a self-serving manner. Consequently, a lack of independent directors on a board may increase investors' perception of the corporation's risk.

3.1.3. Board Committees

The number of board committees and how the committees operate are relevant considerations in an investor's analysis of governance. Committees vary by corporation and industry but generally include audit, governance, remuneration (or compensation), nomination, and risk and compliance committees. When evaluating a company's board committees, investors assess whether there are sufficiently independent committees that focus on key governance concerns, such as audit, compensation, and the selection of directors. The presence of non-independent committee members or executive directors may prompt the consideration of potential conflicts of interest or biases, such as those relating to compensation decisions (remuneration committee), management selection (nomination committee), and the integrity of financial reporting (audit committee).

3.1.4. Board Skills and Experience

The underlying skill set and experience of board directors are important investor considerations. A board with concentrated skills and experience may lack sufficient expertise to govern, as may a board with diverse skills and expertise that are not directly related to the company's core operations. In certain sectors/industries that rely on natural resources or face potentially large ESG risks, board members typically have expertise in environmental, climate, or social issues.

An issue related to skills and experience is board tenure. According to many corporate governance codes, a board director's tenure is considered long if it exceeds 10 years. Long tenure of a board member could be viewed positively or negatively. On the positive side, a board member with a long tenure may have a comprehensive understanding of how the corporation's business operates, as well as how effective company management has been during the director's tenure. On the negative side, long tenure may affect the independence of board members (i.e., they could be too closely aligned with management) or may result in directors being less willing to embrace changes in the corporation's business.

3.1.5. Board Composition

Board composition primarily reflects the number and diversity of directors, including their professional, cultural, and geographical background, as well as gender, age, and tenure. Boards with too many members or that lack diversity may govern less effectively than boards that are smaller or more diverse. For example, a board with long-tenured board members could become controlling, self-serving, or resistant to the introduction of new practices or policies that may benefit stakeholders.

3.1.6. Other Considerations in Board Evaluation

Board evaluation is necessary to maintain a company's competitive position and to meet the expectations of investors. Dimensions of the board evaluation process may include who evaluates the board, what should be evaluated, to whom the evaluation is targeted, and how the evaluation will be accomplished.

A board evaluation can be performed by the board itself (self-evaluation) or by an outsider on behalf of the board (external review). Some boards may decide to evaluate their performance on an "as needed" basis, whereas others will prefer to conduct a periodic external review. A board evaluation typically covers how the board performs its duties, its leadership, its structure (including the committees), and the interaction between board members and management (including culture). Apart from internal stakeholders, the evaluation may be targeted to the company's shareholders, regulators, or other external stakeholders.

EXAMPLE 2   Evaluating the Board of Directors

1. A junior analyst is analyzing the board of directors of Style, a fictional global clothing retailer based in Italy. Style was founded by the Donato family and is publicly traded. Style's 11-member board of directors has a chairperson—who is not the CEO—and two independent directors. Among the six non-independent directors, the Donato family accounts for four of them. All these family members have served on the board for at least 20 years. The gender and age characteristics of the board are both diverse, with women representing five of the board's directors—including its chair, Leila Donato—and the directors ranging in age from 35 to 75 years old.

   Describe considerations that the junior analyst would use in evaluating the effectiveness of Style's board of directors.

Solution to 1:
   The CEO and chairperson roles are separate for Style (no CEO duality), which can be considered a sign of effective corporate governance. In addition, the board appears to be diverse in terms of age and gender, which is typically considered a positive attribute. Conversely, board independence appears to be substandard: Only two board directors are independent, whereas four Donato family members, including the chairperson (Leila Donato), are board members. The tenure of the family board members is also likely to be considered a negative attribute (it far exceeds the typical 10 years).

3.2. Executive Remuneration

Executive remuneration involves such issues as transparency of compensation, performance criteria for incentive plans (both short term and long term), the linkage of remuneration with the company strategy, and the pay differential between the CEO and the average worker. When a corporation has a "say-on-pay" provision, shareholders can vote and/or provide feedback on remuneration issues. A clawback policy allows a company to recover previously paid remuneration if certain events, such as financial restatements, misconduct, breach of the law, or risk management deficiencies, are uncovered.

   There is increasing concern among investors regarding "excessive" remuneration, often represented by the ratio of CEO pay to average-worker pay. In evaluating a company's executive remuneration, investors typically consider whether the company's remuneration policies and practices provide appropriate incentives for management to drive the value of a corporation. Company disclosures such as those metrics (also known as key performance indicators, or KPIs) used in executive incentive plans may be useful tools for analysis.

3.3. Shareholder Voting Rights

Shareholder voting rights are important investor considerations. Under **straight voting** share structures, shareholders are granted the right of one vote for each share owned. Dual-class share structures differ from straight voting in that company founders and/or management typically have shares with more voting power than the class of shares available to the general public. That is, dual-class share structures—in contrast to the one share, one vote principle of straight voting—can benefit one group of shareholders over another. Because a potential conflict of interest may exist between minority shareholders and the company's founders and management (some of whom may also serve on the board of directors), it is important for investors to be aware of dual-class share structures when investing.

4. IDENTIFYING ESG-RELATED RISKS AND OPPORTUNITIES

A primary challenge when integrating ESG factors into investment analysis is identifying and obtaining information that is relevant and decision-useful. In practice, ESG-related data are generally obtained from publicly available corporate filings, documents, and communications such as corporate sustainability reports that may or may not be assured by a third party. Some of the challenges analysts face are related to inconsistent reporting of ESG information and metrics as well as the fact that the level of disclosure varies because most ESG-related disclosures are voluntary. ESG-related disclosure has generally increased over time, however, because of increased stakeholder and shareholder interest in understanding whether a company effectively manages its ESG risks and opportunities.

4.1. Materiality and Investment Horizon

When considering ESG factors in investment analysis, analysts need to evaluate the *materiality* of the underlying data. In an ESG context, materiality typically refers to ESG-related issues that are expected to affect a company's operations, its financial performance, and the valuation of its securities. In overall financial reporting, information is considered to be material if omission or misstatement of the information could influence users' decisions. Companies' as well as stakeholders' definitions of materiality in an ESG context may differ. Some companies may use the term "material" in emphasizing positive ESG information, although such information may have little impact on the company's operations or financial performance. In contrast, a company may minimize or not report negative ESG information that investors might consider material.

Analysts also consider their investment horizon and holding period when deciding which ESG factors to consider in their analysis, especially credit analysts, because of the different maturities of bonds. Some ESG issues may affect a company's performance in the short term, whereas other issues may be more long term in nature. It is important to note that the time horizon of ESG factors' impact can move from the long term to the short term and vice versa depending on a wide variety of external factors, such as a sudden change in regulation or an ESG-related controversy such as an oil spill. An investor with a short-term investment horizon may find that longer-term ESG issues can have little effect on a security's market value in the near term. Consider a manufacturing company operating in an industry that is expected to face stricter environmental regulations in the future. An investor with a short-term horizon may expect that the company's profitability will not be affected in the short term. An investor with a long-term horizon, however, may anticipate costly upgrades to plants and equipment or significant regulatory fines that are likely to reduce profitability over the longer term.

4.2. Relevant ESG-Related Factors

Corporate governance considerations, such as the structure of the board of directors, are often reasonably consistent across most companies, although best practices vary greatly regionally.

In contrast, there is no globally accepted best practice with regard to environmental and social considerations. When identifying a company's specific ESG risks and opportunities, analysts must determine the relevant factors that affect its industry. For example, energy companies are clearly more affected by environmental factors, whereas banking institutions are typically more affected by social factors (e.g., data security and privacy issues or customer satisfaction) than by environmental factors. Meanwhile, both industries are subject to governance factors. Once an analyst has determined which ESG-related factors are relevant to a company's industry, the analyst can identify applicable qualitative and quantitative data.

Approaches used to identify a company's (or industry's) ESG factors include (1) proprietary methods, (2) ratings and analysis from ESG data providers, and (3) not-for-profit industry initiatives and sustainability reporting frameworks. For example, Access to Nutrition Index evaluates the world's largest food and beverage manufacturers' policies and performance related to the most pressing nutrition challenges: obesity and undernutrition. Each of the above approaches can be used independently, or a combination of approaches can be used.

The first way of identifying company and industry ESG factors is the proprietary method approach. In this approach, analysts use their own judgment or their firm's proprietary tools to identify ESG information by researching companies, news reports, industry associations, environmental groups, financial markets, labor organizations, industry experts, and government organizations. Company-specific ESG data are generally publicly available from such sources as annual reports, corporate citizenship or sustainability reports, proxy reports, and regulatory filings (e.g., the annual 10-K report required by the US Securities and Exchange Commission). Company disclosures can generally be found on company websites.

Exhibit 2 illustrates an example of how management of one key ESG-related issue—climate change—is disclosed by City Developments Limited (CDL) in its sustainability report. Note that other real estate companies may report this information differently. In fact, ESG disclosures in general can range from minimal reporting to comprehensive data and information that span several pages, thus potentially creating comparability issues for analysts. As we discuss later in this section, a number of organizations and initiatives are working toward voluntary or mandatory standardization of various ESG-related metrics.

EXHIBIT 2: Climate Change Scenario Planning for City Developments Limited

Aligned with the recommendations of Task Force on Climate-related Financial Disclosures (TCFD) and Intergovernmental Panel on Climate Change (IPCC), CDL aims to better prepare its business for the potential financial impacts of both physical and transition risks of climate change.

CDL approached the study with two scenarios by 2030: one in which it assumed the world would decarbonize fast enough to meet the Paris Agreement's goal of limiting climate change to a global average surface temperature rise of 2C; and another scenario that used a more ambitious 1.5°C above pre-industrial level rise. A systematic and cohesive approach was used to holistically assess and quantify all potential impacts on CDL's selected portfolio from material climate-related risks and opportunities.

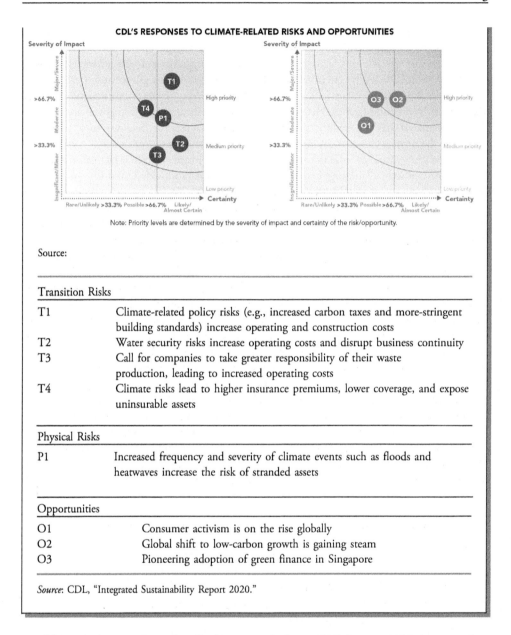

Note: Priority levels are determined by the severity of impact and certainty of the risk/opportunity.

Source:

Transition Risks	
T1	Climate-related policy risks (e.g., increased carbon taxes and more-stringent building standards) increase operating and construction costs
T2	Water security risks increase operating costs and disrupt business continuity
T3	Call for companies to take greater responsibility of their waste production, leading to increased operating costs
T4	Climate risks lead to higher insurance premiums, lower coverage, and expose uninsurable assets

Physical Risks	
P1	Increased frequency and severity of climate events such as floods and heatwaves increase the risk of stranded assets

Opportunities	
O1	Consumer activism is on the rise globally
O2	Global shift to low-carbon growth is gaining steam
O3	Pioneering adoption of green finance in Singapore

Source: CDL, "Integrated Sustainability Report 2020."

The second approach in identifying company/industry ESG factors—ESG data providers —involves the use of information supplied by an ESG data provider (vendor), such as MSCI or Sustainalytics. These vendors obtain publicly available corporate ESG disclosures and translate them into individual ESG analyses, scores, and/or rankings for each company in the vendor's universe, often with subjective assessments by ESG analysts. In addition, vendors may score and/or rank companies within their industries and provide detailed industry analyses relating to ESG considerations.

The third approach in identifying ESG factors involves the consideration of not-for-profit initiatives and sustainability reporting frameworks that provide data and insights on ESG issues. These include the International Integrated Reporting Council (IIRC), the Global Reporting Initiative (GRI), the Sustainable Accounting Standards Board (SASB), and the 2° Investing Initiative (2DII), to name a few. The IIRC is a coalition of industry participants that promotes a standardized framework of ESG disclosures in corporate reporting. The GRI has worked with various stakeholder groups to develop sustainability reporting standards. These standards include a list of business activity groups (industries) with relevant sustainability topics that correspond to each group. A GRI report excerpt relating to the consumer durables and household and personal products sector is shown in Exhibit 3. The exhibit indicates the proposed ESG-related topics for this sector as well as additional specifications on these topics, if available. The SASB seeks to promote uniform accounting standards for sustainability reporting. In doing so, it has developed the SASB Materiality Map, which lists relevant ESG-related, sector-specific factors that the organization and industry working groups deem to be material. Exhibit 4 displays a sample SASB Materiality Map that shows the key ESG factors (shaded boxes) for the health care sector.

As well as providing data and analysis, ESG service providers and not-for-profit initiatives provide a variety of tools to help integrate relevant ESG factors.

EXHIBIT 3: GRI Sustainability Topics—Consumer Durables and Household and Personal Products Sector

Category	Proposed Topic	Topic Specification (where applicable)
Environmental	Materials sourcing	Rare metals; Sourcing standards for raw materials; Sourcing standards on animal testing; Wood-based products from responsibly managed forests
	Product packaging	Not applicable
	Plastic use	Product and packaging
	Chemicals use	International and national chemical safe use regulations; Personal care products; Phthalates and parabens
	Energy efficiency of end products	Consumer electronics
	Life cycle assessment of products	Not applicable
	Product transport efficiency	Not applicable
Social	Migrant workers	Recruitment and employment
	Product safety	Personal care products—human health and the environment
	Transparent product information and labeling	Not applicable
	Access to products, technologies, and services	Consumers with disabilities
	Electronic waste (e-waste) management	Consumer awareness
	Product design	Eco-friendly personal care products
	Product innovation	Energy consumption, GHG emissions and packaging

Category	Proposed Topic	Topic Specification (where applicable)
Other	Corporate governance	Executive board compensation; Gender participation on governance bodies
	Supplier screening	Environmental and social standards in the supply chain

Source: GRI, "Sustainability Topics for Sectors: What Do Stakeholders Want to Know?" (2013).

EXHIBIT 4: SASB Materiality Map—Health Care Sector

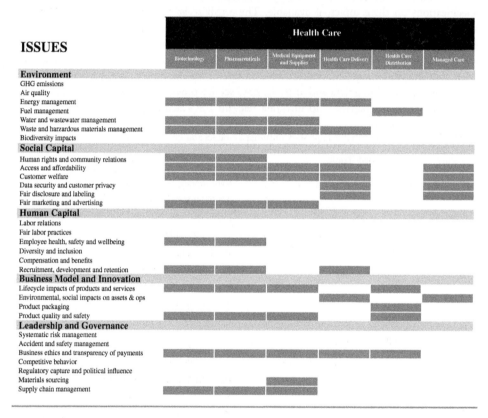

Source: Sustainability Accounting Standards Board.

From a risk/reward perspective, the use of **ESG integration**—the implementation of qualitative and quantitative ESG factors in traditional security and industry analysis as well as portfolio construction—typically differs for equity and fixed-income (debt) analysis. In equity analysis, ESG integration is used to both identify potential opportunities and mitigate downside risk, whereas in fixed-income analysis, ESG integration is generally focused on mitigating downside risk as the bond redeems at par on maturity.

The process of identifying and evaluating relevant ESG-related factors is reasonably similar for both equity and corporate credit analysis, because they share the same above-mentioned proprietary methods although material factors may differ based on relevance to credit. ESG integration techniques are also reasonably similar, such as adjustments to forecasted financial metrics and ratios, although the implication differs in practice.

In equity security analysis, ESG-related factors are often analyzed in the context of forecasting financial metrics and ratios, adjusting valuation model variables (e.g., discount rate), or using sensitivity and/or scenario analysis. For example, an analyst might increase her forecast of a hotel company's operating costs because of the impacts of excessive employee turnover—lost productivity, reduced customer satisfaction, and increased expenses for employee searches, temporary workers, and training programs. As another example, an analyst might choose to lower the discount rate for a snack food company that is expected to gain a competitive advantage by transitioning to a sustainable source of a key ingredient in its products.

In credit analysis, ESG factors may be integrated using internal credit assessments, forecasting financial ratios, and relative credit ranking of companies (or governments). In terms of valuation, relative value, spread, duration, and sensitivity/scenario analysis are often used. For example, an analyst may include the effect of lawsuits on the credit ratios, cash flow, or liquidity of a toy company. The same analyst may also estimate the potential for the credit spreads of the toy company's bonds to widen from these lawsuits. Generally speaking, the effect on the credit spreads of an issuer's debt obligations or its credit default swaps (CDSs) may differ depending on maturity. As a different example, consider an analyst who believes that a coal company faces long-term risk from potential **stranded assets**—that is, assets that are obsolete or not economically viable, often owing to changes in regulatory or government policy and/or shifts in demand. In this case, the analyst may believe that valuation of the coal company's 10-year-maturity notes would be considerably more negatively affected than its 1-year-maturity notes.

One particular type of bond an analyst might encounter is a **green bond**. The sidebar "Green Bonds" provides more detail about these securities and how investors typically analyze them. Increasingly, investors use scenario analysis and stress tests to assess the potential impact of key factors, such as physical risks of climate change.

GREEN BONDS

Green bonds are bonds in which the proceeds are designated by issuers to fund a specific project or portfolio of projects that have environmental or climate benefits. The first green bond, the Climate Awareness Bond, was issued by the European Investment Bank in 2007. Issuers have the primary decision for labeling their bonds "green." This decision is made in close cooperation with the lead underwriter. At a minimum level, issuers provide detail to the investors about the green eligibility criteria for the use of proceeds, in line with the Green Bond Principles (discussed in the next paragraph). Issuers are responsible for providing investors with details on the criteria used to classify the bonds as green and how the bond's proceeds are used. In some cases, issuers may commission independent reviews of the green criteria to provide investors with greater transparency. Issuers of green bonds typically incur additional costs related to the monitoring and reporting of the use of the bond's proceeds. However, these issuers may benefit from a more diversified investor base and potentially a new-issue premium if demand is strong.

The Green Bond Principles, a set of voluntary standards to guide issuers in the determination of labeling a bond as green, were developed in 2014 by a consortium of investment banks. Ongoing monitoring and further development of the Green Bond Principles is the responsibility of the International Capital Market Association, a global securities self-regulatory organization. As the green bond market has evolved, index providers, credit rating agencies, and the not-for-profit Climate Bonds Initiative have developed their own methodologies or standards to assess labeled green bonds. In addition, the European Commission is exploring the feasibility of imposing specific criteria that must be met for a bond to be labeled green.

Green bonds typically resemble an issuer's conventional bonds, with the exception that the bond proceeds are earmarked for green projects. Green bonds normally have the same credit ratings and bondholder recourse as conventional bonds of the same issuer (all else being equal). In addition to conventional or "plain vanilla" corporate bonds, other types of green bonds include project bonds, mortgage-backed and asset-backed securities, and municipal bonds. For example, the state of California's $300 million general obligation 2014 green bond issue is backed by the state's General Fund, just as California's other general obligation bonds are.

Because only the use of proceeds differs, the analysis and valuation of green bonds are essentially the same as those of conventional bonds. Some green bonds, however, may command a premium, or tighter credit spread, versus comparable conventional bonds because of market demand. One unique risk of green bonds is **greenwashing**, which is the risk that the bond's proceeds are not actually used for a beneficial environmental or climate-related project. Greenwashing can result in an investor overpaying for a bond (if the investor paid a premium for the bond's green feature) or holding a bond that does not satisfy a prescribed environmental or climate investment mandate. Liquidity risk may also be a consideration for green bonds, given that they are often purchased by buy-and-hold investors.

5. EVALUATING ESG-RELATED RISKS AND OPPORTUNITIES

By integrating ESG considerations into the investment process, investors can take a broader perspective of company and industry analysis. In this way, the potential effects of ESG factors on a company's financial statements and valuation can be assessed and, in turn, can help drive investment decisions. In this section, we discuss examples of how ESG considerations can be integrated into financial analysis and valuation, from both an equity and a corporate bond perspective.

5.1. ESG Integration

A typical starting point for ESG integration is the identification of material qualitative and quantitative ESG factors that pertain to a company or its industry. An analyst may evaluate these factors on both a historical and a forecast basis, as well as relative to a company's peers, and then make relevant adjustments to a company's financial statements or valuation. ESG-related adjustments to a company's income statement and cash flow statement typically relate to projected revenues, operating/non-operating costs, operating margins, earnings, capital expenditures, or other items. ESG-related adjustments to a company's balance sheet often reflect an analyst's estimate of impaired assets. For equities, valuation adjustments often include adjusting a company's cost of capital using the discount rate or a multiple of price or terminal value. For bonds, an analyst may adjust an issuer's credit spread or CDS to reflect anticipated effects from ESG considerations.

The use of qualitative and quantitative research, as well as securities valuation of equities and fixed income, are key elements of the "ESG Integration Framework" (see Exhibit 5). Portfolio construction, asset allocation, scenario analysis, and risk management form the remainder of this framework.

EXHIBIT 5: The ESG Integration Framework

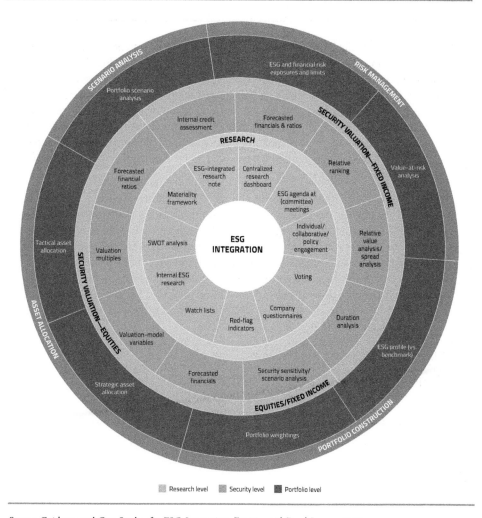

Source: Guidance and Case Studies for ESG Integration: Equities and Fixed Income, 2018

5.2. Examples of ESG Integration

This section provides examples of ESG integration for three fictitious companies in different industries: beverages, pharmaceuticals, and banks. For simplicity, each integration example focuses on either environmental, social, or governance factors—largely depending on which is most relevant for that company or its industry. Note that although specific industries are used in the examples, the underlying concepts can be applied to other industries as well. Finally, given the scope of this chapter, we focus on the *effects* of ESG integration on financial analysis and valuation rather than the computations involved.

EXAMPLE 3   ESG Integration—Environmental Factors (Beverage Company)

1. Based in the United States, Frizzle Drinks (Frizzle) is a fictitious non-alcoholic beverage company that ranks among the largest in the world. Frizzle operates in both developed and emerging markets, including countries where water is scarce. Frizzle is a significant user of water in its operations. Given that water is a key ingredient in Frizzle's beverages, the continued availability of water is critical to the company's manufacturing process. Because of its extensive use of water, Frizzle faces ongoing regulatory scrutiny for pollution and effects on climate change. Ultimately, how Frizzle conserves and manages its water usage has implications for product pricing and company/brand reputation.

   Sam Smith, CFA, is analyzing the effects of environmental factors on Frizzle's financial statements. Based on his research, Smith considers "water intensity" to be a key ESG metric for the beverage industry. Water intensity is defined as the ratio of total liters of water used per one liter of a beverage product. Exhibit 6 illustrates the trend of Frizzle's water intensity ratio from 2009 to 2021, as well as the consensus forecast ratio for the subsequent four years. Frizzle has steadily decreased its water usage over the past several years. From 2009 to 2021, its water intensity ratio declined by 27%. By the end of 2025(F), the company aims to reduce its water intensity by another 13%.

EXHIBIT 6: Water Intensity Ratio (in liters)

Note: (F) indicates forecast year.

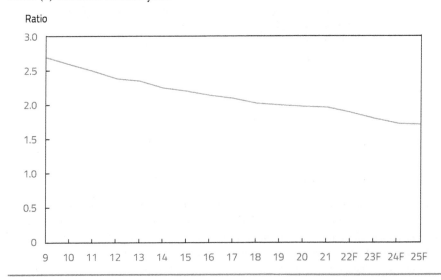

Exhibit 7 compares the year-over-year change in Frizzle's water intensity ratio with that of its peer group over the past three years. To facilitate comparison among companies of varying sizes, Smith normalized the reported water intensity ratios by calculating the water intensity ratio per $1 million of revenue. Exhibit 7 illustrates that Frizzle's water intensity has decreased considerably relative to its peers over the past few years, particularly in the last reported year, 2021.

EXHIBIT 7: Water Intensity Ratio Change per $1 Million of Revenue

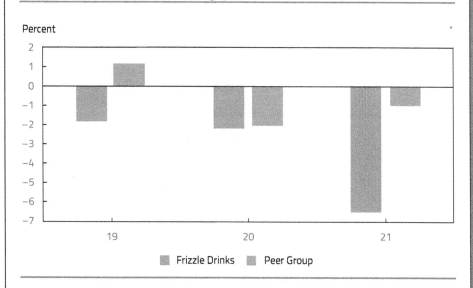

Next, Smith analyzes the effects of Frizzle's water intensity on its overall financial performance and compares it with the adjusted financial performance of its peers. As one example, Smith adjusts Frizzle's operating costs to account for the improved effects of water intensity (i.e., reduced usage). For the first projected year, 2022, Smith expects that Frizzle's cost of goods sold as a percentage of revenues (before any ESG adjustment) will be 40% and its peer group average will be 42%. For the same forecast period, Smith assumes that Frizzle's reduction in water intensity will result in a 1% reduction in its cost of goods sold/revenues, whereas the peer group average will remain the same. Exhibit 8 demonstrates this improvement in cost of goods sold/revenues on both an absolute and a relative basis. By extension, Exhibit 9 shows the absolute and relative improvement in Frizzle's gross margin (sales minus cost of goods sold) percentage.

EXHIBIT 8: Cost of Goods Sold as a Percentage of Revenue

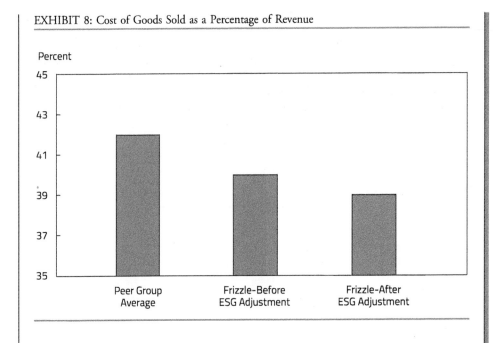

Percent

EXHIBIT 9: Gross Margin

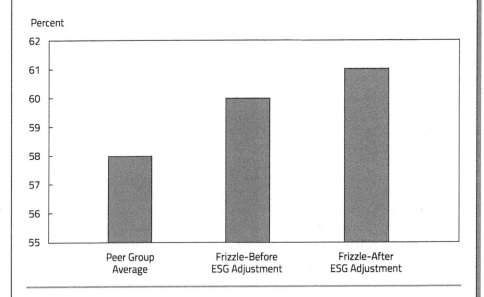

Percent

In the last step of the integration analysis, Smith incorporates Frizzle's adjusted financial performance in valuing Frizzle's stock, bonds, and, if applicable, CDSs. In this example, Smith judges that Frizzle's lower cost of goods sold from the adjustment would result in higher forecast earnings and, all else being equal, a theoretically higher fair value for Frizzle's stock. With respect to Frizzle's bonds and CDSs, Frizzle's operating cash flow would improve through a lower cost of goods sold. When assessing the credit spreads of Frizzle's bonds and/or CDSs, Smith will analyze whether the lower relative ESG risk is already reflected in current spread levels and adjust accordingly.

EXAMPLE 4   ESG Integration—Social Factors (Pharmaceutical Company)

1. Well Pharma (Well) is a fictitious European pharmaceutical company that manufactures drug products for autoimmune diseases and immune disorders. Over the last five years, Well has had the weakest track record among its peers in terms of product recalls and regulatory warning letters for manufacturing and marketing-related violations. Specifically, the company has been subject to four major drug quality and safety scandals arising from adverse side effects. These scandals have resulted in lost sales, multiple lawsuits, and significant fines. Business disruptions, lawsuits, and fines have reduced revenues and increased costs for the company.

As Well's experience shows, product quality is a material social factor for pharmaceutical companies in general. Smith assumes that a drug company's product quality is a combination of the factors shown in Exhibit 10.

EXHIBIT 10: Social Factors—Pharmaceuticals

Factor	Description
Product Quality Controversies	Have there been any controversies linked to the company's product or service quality and responsibility?
Regulatory Warning Letters	Number of regulatory warning letters received by the company
Product Recalls	Number and severity of product recalls (voluntary and involuntary)
Regulatory Fines	Level of fines imposed by regulator linked to poor product quality and/or irresponsible behavior
Product Quality Certifications Percentage	Percentage of plants certified according to a widely accepted product safety/quality standard (e.g., ISO 9001 or equivalent)

Exhibit 11 shows the number of regulatory warning letters received, as well as product and marketing controversies faced, by Well and several peers. As the graph shows, Well has received significantly more of these letters than its peers have.

EXHIBIT 11: Regulatory Warning Letters and Product Quality Controversies

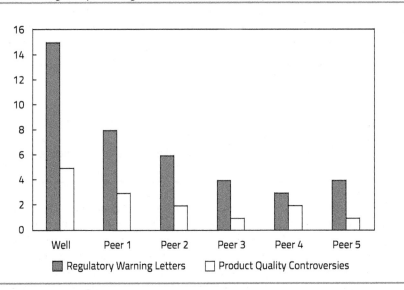

Exhibit 12 demonstrates how the factors listed in Exhibit 10 may affect the financial statements of Well and other pharmaceutical companies.

EXHIBIT 12: Social Factor Effects on Financial Performance

Factor	Financial Impact
Product Quality Controversies	Damage to brand value resulting in potential decrease in sales
Regulatory Warning Letters	Increased costs to comply with regulatory requirements
Product Recalls	Losses in sales revenue; increased costs of implementing product recalls
Regulatory Fines	Provisions for pharmaceutical sales returns and product-related litigation
Product Quality Certifications Percentage	Lower percentage increases risks of product quality issues, leading to product recalls and related costs

Based on these financial effects, Smith adjusts Well's projected revenues, operating expenses, and non-operating expenses. The nature of these financial statement adjustments will likely differ depending on whether Smith expects these product quality issues to be recurring or non-recurring in nature. Smith assumes that revenues will decrease by 2% over the next year because of existing product quality controversies. For operating expenses, Smith assumes that Well's cost of goods sold relative to revenues will increase by 1.3% to reflect product quality and additional investments in its manufacturing process. Exhibit 13 shows that Well's cost of goods sold as a percentage of revenues is in line with that of its peers, but the additional costs will increase this ratio well above that of the peer group. In addition to operating expenses, Smith forecasts that Well's non-operating expenses, such as restructuring charges, and other non-recurring costs will be an additional 4.5% of operating income. Exhibit 14 shows the current non-operating expense ratio for Well versus its peer group average, as well as the forecast amount.

EXHIBIT 13: Cost of Goods Sold as a Percentage of Revenue

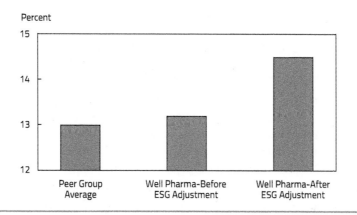

EXHIBIT 14: Non-Operating Expenses as a Percentage of Operating Income

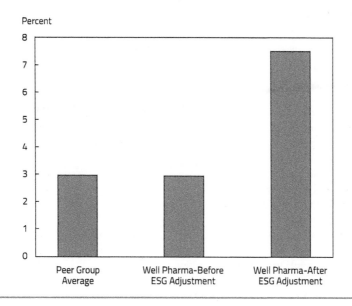

Smith believes that the valuation implications for Well's stock and bonds could be significant based on its poor product quality and safety track record. Expectations of

future poor performance could have a direct impact on earnings and cash flow to the detriment of both shareholders and bondholders. In addition, Smith believes there could be adverse valuation implications if investors view Well's brand value and reputation as impaired.

EXAMPLE 5   ESG Integration—Governance Factors (Bank Holding Company)

1. Sumiyoshi Banking Group (Sumiyoshi) is a fictitious Japanese bank holding company, with operations in Japan (80% of revenues), the United States, and Southeast Asia. Sumiyoshi's core businesses are commercial banking, leasing, securities, and consumer finance. As with most global banks, corporate governance reforms have become increasingly prominent for Sumiyoshi.

Smith has prepared Exhibit 15 to show how Sumiyoshi's board of directors compares with the majority of its domestic peer group, on the basis of governance factors discussed in Section 2 of this chapter.

EXHIBIT 15: Corporate Governance Factors—Banks

	Domestic Peer Group	Sumiyoshi Bank
Board type	Two tier	Two tier
Board size, no. of directors	13	14
Total assets/director	JPY14.9 million	JPY13.3 million
CEO duality	Yes	Yes
Independent chairperson	Yes	No
Board independence %	47%	36%
Board gender diversity	17% female; 83% male	7% female; 93% male
Directors with long tenure (>10 years)	0%	14%
Number of board committees	5	4
Audit, nomination, remuneration, and risk committees in place?	Yes	Yes
Additional board committees?	Yes, governance committee	No
Non-executive directors with industry executive experience/total independent directors	67%	20%
Short-term and long-term incentive plan metrics disclosed?	No	No

	Domestic Peer Group	Sumiyoshi Bank
Concentrated ownership	No single large shareholder	No single large shareholder
Say-on-pay provision	Yes	No
Straight voting	Yes	Yes
Dual-class shares	No	No

Smith notes that Sumiyoshi lags its peers in several elements of board composition, such as the lack of an independent chairperson, a lower level of board independence and diversity, fewer board members with industry executive experience, and a number of board directors with long tenures. In addition to board composition, Smith uses credit risk as a proxy for a bank's corporate governance risk. In particular, Smith reviews one key banking credit measure— non-performing loans (NPLs). NPLs are loans that are not current in paying the contractual amounts that are due (i.e., interest or principal payments).

Smith analyzes Sumiyoshi's credit risk by dividing its NPLs by the amount of its total loans outstanding. Smith estimates that Sumiyoshi's ratio of NPLs to total loans is 50 bps higher than its peer group average, reflecting Sumiyoshi's comparatively weaker credit/governance risk. To account for the effect of higher credit risk than that of its peers, Smith may increase the risk premium embedded in his valuation of Sumiyoshi's stock. When valuing Sumiyoshi's corporate bonds, Smith might increase the credit spread relative to peers embedded in the company's outstanding issues.

6. SUMMARY

- Shareholder ownership structures are commonly classified as dispersed, concentrated, or a hybrid of the two.
- Dispersed ownership reflects the existence of many shareholders, none of which, either individually or collectively, has the ability to exercise control over the corporation. Concentrated corporate ownership reflects an individual shareholder or a group (controlling shareholders) with the ability to exercise control over the corporation.
- Controlling shareholders may be either majority shareholders or minority shareholders.
- Horizontal ownership involves companies with mutual business interests that have cross-holding share arrangements with each other. Vertical (or pyramid) ownership involves a company or group that has a controlling interest in two or more holding companies, which in turn have controlling interests in various operating companies.
- Dual-class (or multiple-class) shares grant one or more share classes superior or even sole voting rights while other share classes have inferior or no voting rights.

- Types of influential owners include banks, families, sovereign governments, institutional investors, group companies, private equity firms, foreign investors, managers, and board directors.
- A corporation's board of directors is typically structured as either one tier or two tier. A one-tier board consists of a single board of directors, composed of executive (internal) and non-executive (external) directors. A two-tier board consists of a supervisory board that oversees a management board.
- CEO duality exists when the chief executive officer also serves as chairperson of the board.
- A primary challenge of integrating ESG factors into investment analysis is identifying and obtaining information that is relevant, comparable, and decision-useful.
- ESG information and metrics are inconsistently reported by companies, and such disclosure is voluntary, which provides additional challenges for analysts.
- In an ESG context, materiality typically refers to ESG-related issues that are expected to affect a company's operations or financial performance and the valuation of its securities.
- Corporate governance considerations, such as the structure of the board of directors, tend to be reasonably consistent across most companies. In contrast, environmental and social considerations often differ greatly.
- Analysts typically use three main sources of information to identify a company's (or industry's) ESG factors: (1) proprietary research, (2) ratings and analysis from ESG data providers, or (3) research from not-for-profit industry organizations and initiatives.
- In equity analysis, ESG integration is used to both identify potential opportunities and mitigate downside risk, whereas in fixed-income analysis, ESG integration is generally focused on mitigating downside risk.
- A typical starting point for ESG integration is the identification of material qualitative and quantitative ESG factors that pertain to a company or its industry.

7. PRACTICE PROBLEMS

The following information relates to questions 1–6

Theresa Blass manages the Toptier Balanced Fund (the Fund) and recently hired John Yorkton, a junior analyst, to help her research investment opportunities. Blass plans to integrate environmental, social, and governance (ESG) factors into her analysis. She is researching an equity investment in Titian International, a global steel producer. She asks Yorkton to identify ESG factors impacting Titian and estimate the equity valuation for the company. Yorkton uses proprietary methods to identify the ESG factors.

Yorkton points out that Titian's steel production is energy intensive and relies on coal in producing its main product, stainless steel. The firm's major customers are oil and gas firms using stainless steel in their drilling operations. Most of Titian's steel capacity is located in developing economies, where it currently faces few environmental regulations. Titian has a 10-member board with a chairperson and 5 independent members. The chairperson is not the CEO, and the board is diverse, with 6 women. The company has an excellent record on employee health and safety. In a discussion with Blass about ESG factors in investment analysis, Yorkton makes the following statements:

Statement 1
Material ESG information used in investment analysis is best obtained from the individual companies.

Statement 2
The level of disclosure varies among companies because these disclosures arc voluntary.
Statement 3
The time horizon has little effect on the materiality of the underlying ESG factors.

Yorkton integrates ESG factors into the equity valuation of Titian. He believes the company faces significant long-term risk due to regulatory changes regarding greenhouse gas emissions in the developing economies. These changes will have a negative impact on Titian's steel capacity and its production costs. Based on long-term forecasts from the International Energy Agency (IEA), Yorkton expects oil and natural gas demand to decline over the next decade, reducing oil company capital expenditures on exploration and drilling. He uses a discounted cash flow model to value Titian stock.

1. The potential problem with Yorkton's approach to identifying ESG factors is the:
    A. promotion of uniform accounting standards.
    B. subjective assessment of ESG scores and rankings.
    C. inconsistent reporting of ESG information and metrics among firms.

2. The most relevant industry risk factors affecting Titian are:
    A. social.
    B. governance.
    C. environmental.

3. Which of the statements made by Yorkton on ESG factors in investment analysis is correct?
    A. Statement 1
    B. Statement 2
    C. Statement 3

4. Titian faces long-term risk from _____ due to potential regulatory changes in the developing economies.

5. Yorkton's ESG integration approach is likely to impact equity valuation by:
    A. increasing revenues.
    B. raising the discount rate.
    C. reducing operating costs.

6. After integrating the ESG factors into the discounted cash flow model, the equity value of Titian is likely to:
    A. decrease.
    B. remain unchanged.
    C. increase.

The following information relates to questions 7–10

Emily Marker, CFA, is a fixed-income analyst for the Namsan Funds. Her supervisor asks her to identify ESG factors and value the corporate bonds of BR Hotels, a publicly traded boutique hotel company. Marker notes that BR Hotels is a "green hotel" company that prioritizes sustainability and has successfully reduced water and energy usage at its hotels. The founding family owns 55% of the outstanding shares. Each ownership share has equivalent voting rights. The board of directors of BR Hotels consists of 15 members, with independent

CEO and chairperson roles. The board includes one independent member and two women, and 20% of the board members have experience in the hotel industry.

BR Hotels has historically had a high labor turnover rate. Most of its workforce are paid at or near the minimum wage, and the company offers no health benefits. Marker and her supervisor discuss how BR Hotels will be affected by the expected passage of legislation raising the minimum wage and growing pressure to offer benefits. Marker integrates ESG factors in the investment valuation of BR Hotels' corporate bonds.

7. The potential conflict between or among shareholders and managers of BR Hotels can *best* be described as:
   A. voting caps.
   B. a principal-agent problem.
   C. a principal-principal problem.

8. BR Hotels' corporate governance risk is increased by:
   A. CEO duality.
   B. family control.
   C. the low percentage of independent board members.

9. The security analysis of BR Hotels is *most likely* focused on:
   A. mitigating downside risk.
   B. adjusting the discount rate.
   C. identifying potential opportunities.

10. After integrating the ESG factors, the credit spread on BR Hotels' bonds is *most likely* to:
   A. decrease.
   B. remain unchanged.
   C. increase.

CHAPTER 16

INTERCORPORATE
INVESTMENTS

Susan Perry Williams, CPA, CMA, PhD
Professor Emeritus at the McIntire School of Commerce, University of Virginia (USA)

Note: New rulings and/or pronouncements issued after the publication of the chapters in financial reporting and analysis may cause some of the information in these chapters to become dated. Candidates are expected to be familiar with the overall analytical framework contained in the study session chapters, as well as the implications of alternative accounting methods for financial analysis and valuation, as provided in the assigned chapters. Candidates are not responsible for changes that occur after the material was written.

LEARNING OUTCOMES

The candidate should be able to:

- describe the classification, measurement, and disclosure under International Financial Reporting Standards (IFRS) for 1) investments in financial assets, 2) investments in associates, 3) joint ventures, 4) business combinations, and 5) special purpose and variable interest entities
- compare and contrast IFRS and US GAAP in their classification, measurement, and disclosure of investments in financial assets, investments in associates, joint ventures, business combinations, and special purpose and variable interest entities
- analyze how different methods used to account for intercorporate investments affect financial statements and ratios

1. INTRODUCTION

Intercorporate investments (investments in other companies) can have a significant impact on an investing company's financial performance and position. Companies invest in the debt and equity securities of other companies to diversify their asset base, enter new markets, obtain competitive advantages, deploy excess cash, and achieve additional profitability. Debt securities include commercial paper, corporate and government bonds and notes, redeemable preferred stock, and asset-backed securities. Equity securities include common stock and non-redeemable preferred stock. The percentage of equity ownership a company acquires in an investee depends on the resources available, the ability to acquire the shares, and the desired level of influence or control.

The International Accounting Standards Board (IASB) and the US Financial Accounting Standards Board (FASB) worked to reduce differences in accounting standards that apply to the classification, measurement, and disclosure of intercorporate investments. The resulting standards have improved the relevance, transparency, and comparability of information provided in financial statements.

Complete convergence between IFRS accounting standards and US GAAP did not occur for accounting for financial instruments, and some differences still exist. The terminology used in this chapter is IFRS-oriented. US GAAP may not use identical terminology, but in most cases the terminology is similar.

This chapter is organized as follows: Section 2 explains the basic categorization of corporate investments. Section 3 describes reporting under IFRS 9, the IASB standard for financial instruments. Section 4 describes equity method reporting for investments in associates where significant influence can exist including the reporting for joint ventures, a type of investment where control is shared. Section 5 describes reporting for business combinations, the parent/subsidiary relationship, and variable interest and special purpose entities. A summary and practice problems conclude the chapter.

2. BASIC CORPORATE INVESTMENT CATEGORIES

In general, investments in marketable debt and equity securities can be categorized as 1) investments in financial assets in which the investor has no significant influence or control over the operations of the investee, 2) investments in associates in which the investor can exert significant influence (but not control) over the investee, 3) joint ventures where control is shared by two or more entities, and 4) business combinations, including investments in subsidiaries, in which the investor obtains a controlling interest over the investee. The distinction between investments in financial assets, investments in associates, and business combinations is based on the degree of influence or control rather than purely on the percent holding. However, lack of influence is generally presumed when the investor holds less than a 20% equity interest, significant influence is generally presumed between 20% and 50%, and control is presumed when the percentage of ownership exceeds 50%.

The following excerpt from Note 2 to the Financial Statements in the 2017 Annual Report of GlaxoSmithKline, a British pharmaceutical and healthcare company, illustrates the categorization and disclosure in practice:

> Entities over which the Group has the power to direct the relevant activities so as to affect the returns to the Group, generally through control over the financial and operating policies, are accounted for as subsidiaries.
>
> Where the Group has the ability to exercise joint control over, and rights to the net assets of, entities, the entities are accounted for as joint ventures. Where the Group has the ability to exercise joint control over an arrangement, but has rights to specified assets and obligations for specified liabilities of the arrangement, the arrangement is accounted for as a joint operation. Where the Group has the ability to exercise significant influence over entities, they are

accounted for as associates. The results and assets and liabilities of associates and joint ventures are incorporated into the consolidated financial statements using the equity method of accounting. The Group's rights to assets, liabilities, revenue and expenses of joint operations are included in the consolidated financial statements in accordance with those rights and obligations.

A summary of the financial reporting and relevant standards for various types of corporate investment is presented in Exhibit 1 (the headings in Exhibit 1 use the terminology of IFRS; US GAAP categorizes intercorporate investments similarly but not identically). The reader should be alert to the fact that value measurement and/or the treatment of changes in value can vary depending on the classification and whether IFRS or US GAAP is used. The alternative treatments are discussed in greater depth later in this chapter.

EXHIBIT 1: Summary of Accounting Treatments for Investments

	In Financial Assets	In Associates	Business Combinations	In Joint Ventures
Influence	Not significant	Significant	Controlling	Shared control
Typical percentage interest	Usually < 20%	Usually 20% to 50%	Usually > 50% or other indications of control	
US GAAP[b]	FASB ASC Topic 320	FASB ASC Topic 323	FASB ASC Topics 805 and 810	FASB ASC Topic 323
Financial Reporting	Classified as: • Fair value through profit or loss • Fair value through other comprehensive income • Amortized cost	Equity method	Consolidation	IFRS: Equity method
Applicable IFRS[a]	IFRS 9	IAS 28	IAS 27 IFRS 3 IFRS 10	IFRS 11 IFRS 12 IAS 28
US GAAP[b]	FASB ASC Topic 320	FASB ASC Topic 323	FASB ASC Topics 805 and 810	FASB ASC Topic 323

[a] IFRS 9 Financial Instruments; IAS 28 Investments in Associates; IAS 27 Separate Financial Statements; IFRS 3 Business Combinations; IFRS 10 Consolidated Financial Statements; IFRS 11 Joint Arrangements; IFRS 12, Disclosure of Interests in Other Entities.

[b] FASB ASC Topic 320 [Investments–Debt and Equity Securities]; FASB ASC Topic 323 [Investments–Equity Method and Joint Ventures]; FASB ASC Topics 805 [Business Combinations] and 810 [Consolidations].

3. INVESTMENTS IN FINANCIAL ASSETS: IFRS 9

Both IASB and FASB developed revised standards for financial investments. The IASB issued the first phase of their project dealing with classification and measurement of financial instruments by including relevant chapters in IFRS 9, *Financial Instruments*. IFRS 9, which replaces IAS 39, became effective for annual periods on 1 January 2018. The FASB's guidance relating to the accounting for investments in financial instruments is contained in ASC 825, *Financial Instruments*, which has been updated several times, with the standard being effective for periods after 15 December 2017. The resulting US GAAP guidance has many consistencies with IFRS requirements, but there are also some differences.

IFRS 9 is based on an approach that considers the contractual characteristics of cash flows as well as the management of the financial assets. The portfolio approach of the previous standard (i.e., designation of held for trading, available-for-sale, and held-to-maturity) is no longer appropriate, and the terms *available-for-sale* and *held-to-maturity* no longer appear in IFRS 9. Another key change in IFRS 9, compared with IAS 39, relates to the approach to loan impairment. In particular, companies are required to migrate from an incurred loss model to an expected credit loss model. This results in companies evaluating not only historical and current information about loan performance, but also forward-looking information.[1]

The criteria for using amortized cost are similar to those of the IAS 39 "management intent to hold-to-maturity" classification. Specifically, to be measured at amortized cost, financial assets must meet two criteria:[2]

1. A business model test:[3] The financial assets are being held to collect contractual cash flows; and
2. A cash flow characteristic test: The contractual cash flows are solely payments of principal and interest on principal.

3.1. Classification and Measurement

IFRS 9 divides all financial assets into two classifications—those measured at amortized cost and those measured at fair value. Under this approach, there are three different categories of measurement:

- Amortised cost
- Fair value through profit or loss (FVPL) or
- Fair Value through Other comprehensive income (FVOCI).

All financial assets are measured at fair value when initially acquired (which will generally be equal to the cost basis on the date of acquisition). Subsequently, financial assets are measured at either fair value or amortized cost. Financial assets that meet the two criteria above are generally measured at amortized cost. If the financial asset meets the criteria above

---

[1]Under US GAAP, requirements for assessing credit impairment are included in ASC 326, which is effective for most public companies beginning January 1, 2020.
[2]IFRS 9, paragraph 4.1.2.
[3]A business model refers to how an entity manages its financial assets in order to generate cash flows – by collecting contractual cash flows, selling financial assets, or both. (IFRS 9 Financial Instruments, Project Summary, July 2014.)

but may be sold, a "hold-to-collect and sell" business model, it may be measured at fair value through other comprehensive income (FVOCI). However, management may choose the "fair value through profit or loss" (FVPL) option to avoid an accounting mismatch.[4] An "accounting mismatch" refers to an inconsistency resulting from different measurement bases for assets and liabilities, i.e., some are measured at amortized cost and some at fair value. Debt instruments are measured at amortized cost, fair value through other comprehensive income (FVOCI), or fair value through profit or loss (FVPL) depending upon the business model.

Equity instruments are measured at FVPL or at FVOCI; they are not eligible for measurement at amortized cost. Equity investments held-for-trading must be measured at FVPL. Other equity investments can be measured at FVPL or FVOCI; however, the choice is irrevocable. If the entity uses the FVOCI option, only the dividend income is recognized in profit or loss. Furthermore, the requirements for reclassifying gains or losses recognized in other comprehensive income are different for debt and equity instruments.

EXHIBIT 2: Financial Assets Classification and Measurement Model, IFRS 9

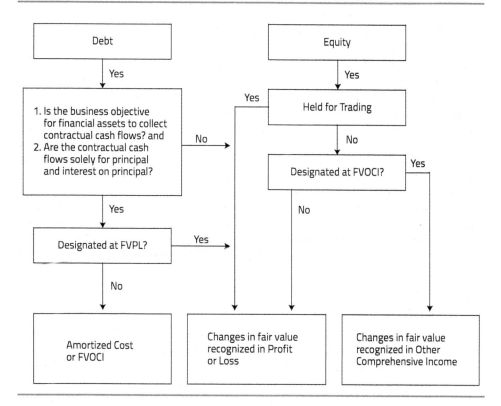

Financial assets that are derivatives are measured at fair value through profit or loss (except for hedging instruments). Embedded derivatives are not separated from the hybrid contract if the asset falls within the scope of this standard and the asset as a whole is measured at FVPL.

---

[4]IFRS 9, paragraph 4.1.5.

Exhibit 3 contains an excerpt from the 2017 Deutsche Bank financial statements that describes how financial assets and financial liabilities are determined, measured, and recognized on its financial statements.

EXHIBIT 3: Excerpt from Deutsche Bank's 2017 Financial Statements

Financial Assets

IFRS 9 requires that an entity's business model and a financial instrument's contractual cash flows will determine its classification and measurement in the financial statements. Upon initial recognition each financial asset will be classified as either fair value through profit or loss ("FVTPL"), amortized cost, or fair value through Other Comprehensive Income ("FVOCI"). As the requirements under IFRS 9 are different than the assessments under the existing IAS 39 rules, there will be some differences from the classification and measurement of financial assets under IAS 39, including whether to elect the fair value option on certain assets. The classification and measurement of financial liabilities remain largely unchanged under IFRS 9 from current requirements.

In 2015, the Group made an initial determination of business models and assessed the contractual cash flow characteristics of the financial assets within such business models to determine the potential classification and measurement changes as a result of IFRS 9. As a result of the initial analysis performed, in 2016 the Group identified a population of financial assets that are to be measured at either amortized cost or fair value through other comprehensive income, which will be subject to the IFRS 9 impairment rules. In 2017, the Group updated its business model assessments and completed outstanding classification decisions. On initial recognition of an equity investment not held for trading, the Group may, on an investment-by-investment basis, irrevocably elect to present subsequent fair value changes in OCI. The Group has not made any such elections. Where issued debt liabilities are designated at fair value, the fair value movements attributable to an entity's own credit risk will be recognized in Other Comprehensive Income rather than in the Statement of Income. The standard also allows the Group the option to elect to apply early the presentation of fair value movements of an entity's credit risk in Other Comprehensive Income prior to adopting IFRS 9 in full. The Group did not early adopt this requirement.

3.2. Reclassification of Investments

Under IFRS 9, the reclassification of equity instruments is not permitted because an entity's initial classification of FVPL and FVOCI is irrevocable. Reclassification of debt instruments is only permitted if the business model for the financial assets (objective for holding the financial assets) has changed in a way that significantly affects operations. Changes to the business model will require judgment and are expected to be very infrequent.

When reclassification is deemed appropriate, there is no restatement of prior periods at the reclassification date. For example, if the financial asset is reclassified from amortized cost to FVPL, the asset is then measured at fair value with any gain or loss immediately recognized in profit or loss. If the financial asset is reclassified from FVPL to amortized cost, the fair value at the reclassification date becomes the carrying amount.

In summary, the major changes made by IFRS 9 are:

- A business model approach to classification of debt instruments.
- Three classifications for financial assets:
  - Fair value through profit or loss (FVPL),
  - fair value through other comprehensive income (FVOCI), and
  - amortized cost.
- Reclassifications of debt instruments are permitted only when the business model changes.
- The choice to measure equity investments at FVOCI or FVPL is irrevocable.
- A redesign of the provisioning models for financial assets, financial guarantees, loan commitments, and lease receivables. The new standard moves the recognition criteria from an "incurred loss" model to an "expected loss" model. Under the new criteria, there is an earlier recognition of impairment—12 month expected losses for performing assets and lifetime expected losses for non-performing assets, to be captured upfront.[5]

Analysts typically evaluate performance separately for operating and investing activities. Analysis of operating performance should exclude items related to investing activities such as interest income, dividends, and realized and unrealized gains and losses. For comparative purposes, analysts should exclude non-operating assets in the determination of return on net operating assets. IFRS and US GAAP[6] require disclosure of fair value of each class of investment in financial assets. Using market values and adjusting pro forma financial statements for consistency improves assessments of performance ratios across companies.

4. INVESTMENTS IN ASSOCIATES AND JOINT VENTURES

Under both IFRS and US GAAP, when a company (investor) holds 20 to 50% of the voting rights of an associate (investee), either directly or indirectly (i.e., through subsidiaries), it is presumed that the company has (or can exercise) significant influence, but not control, over the investee's business activities.[7] Conversely, if the investor holds, directly or indirectly, less than 20% of the voting power of the associate (investee), it is presumed that the investor cannot exercise significant influence, unless such influence can be demonstrated. IAS 28 (IFRS) and FASB ASC Topic 323 (US GAAP) apply to most investments in which an investor has significant influence; they also provide guidance on accounting for investments in associates using the equity method.[8] These standards note that significant influence may be evidenced by

---

[5]IFRS 9, paragraphs 5.5.4, 5.5.5, 5.5.15, 5.5.16.

[6]IFRS 7 Financial Instruments: Disclosures and FASB ASC Section 320-10-50 [Investments–Debt and Equity Securities–Overall–Disclosure].

[7]The determination of significant influence under IFRS also includes currently exercisable or convertible warrants, call options, or convertible securities that the investor owns, which give it additional voting power or reduce another party's voting power over the financial and operating policies of the investee. Under US GAAP, the determination of an investor's voting stock interest is based only on the voting shares outstanding at the time of the purchase. The existence and effect of securities with potential voting rights are not considered.

[8]IAS 28 Investments in Associates and Joint Ventures and FASB ASC Topic 323 [Investments–Equity Method and Joint Ventures].

- representation on the board of directors;
- participation in the policy-making process;
- material transactions between the investor and the investee;
- interchange of managerial personnel; or
- technological dependency.

The ability to exert significant influence means that the financial and operating performance of the investee is partly influenced by management decisions and operational skills of the investor. The equity method of accounting for the investment reflects the economic reality of this relationship and provides a more objective basis for reporting investment income.

Joint ventures—ventures undertaken and controlled by two or more parties—can be a convenient way to enter foreign markets, conduct specialized activities, and engage in risky projects. They can be organized in a variety of different forms and structures. Some joint ventures are primarily contractual relationships, whereas others have common ownership of assets. They can be partnerships, limited liability companies (corporations), or other legal forms (unincorporated associations, for example). IFRS identify the following common characteristics of joint ventures: 1) A contractual arrangement exists between two or more venturers, and 2) the contractual arrangement establishes joint control. Both IFRS and US GAAP[9] require the equity method of accounting for joint ventures.[10]

Only under rare circumstances will joint ventures be allowed to use proportionate consolidation under IFRS and US GAAP. On the venturer's financial statements, proportionate consolidation requires the venturer's share of the assets, liabilities, income, and expenses of the joint venture to be combined or shown on a line-by-line basis with similar items under its sole control. In contrast, the equity method results in a single line item (equity in income of the joint venture) on the income statement and a single line item (investment in joint venture) on the balance sheet.

Because the single line item on the income statement under the equity method reflects the net effect of the sales and expenses of the joint venture, the total income recognized is identical under the two methods. In addition, because the single line item on the balance sheet item (investment in joint venture) under the equity method reflects the investors' share of the net assets of the joint venture, the total net assets of the investor is identical under both methods. There can be significant differences, however, in ratio analysis between the two methods because of the differential effects on values for total assets, liabilities, sales, expenses, etc.

4.1. Equity Method of Accounting: Basic Principles

Under the equity method of accounting, the equity investment is initially recorded on the investor's balance sheet at cost. In subsequent periods, the carrying amount of the investment is adjusted to recognize the investor's proportionate share of the investee's earnings or losses, and these earnings or losses are reported in income. Dividends or other distributions received

---

[9]Under US GAAP, ASC 323-10 provides guidance on the application of the equity method of accounting.
[10]IFRS 11, Joint Arrangements, classifies joint arrangements as either a joint operation or a joint venture. Joint ventures are arrangements wherein parties with joint control have rights to the net assets of the arrangement. Joint ventures are required to use equity method under IAS 28.

from the investee are treated as a return of capital and reduce the carrying amount of the investment and are not reported in the investor's profit or loss. The equity method is often referred to as "one-line consolidation" because the investor's proportionate ownership interest in the assets and liabilities of the investee is disclosed as a single line item (net assets) on its balance sheet, and the investor's share of the revenues and expenses of the investee is disclosed as a single line item on its income statement. (Contrast these disclosures with the disclosures on consolidated statements in Section 6.) Equity method investments are classified as non-current assets on the balance sheet. The investor's share of the profit or loss of equity method investments, and the carrying amount of those investments, must be separately disclosed on the income statement and balance sheet.

EXAMPLE 1   Equity Method: Balance in Investment Account

1. Branch (a fictitious company) purchases a 20% interest in Williams (a fictitious company) for €200,000 on 1 January 2016. Williams reports income and dividends as follows:

	Income	Dividends
2016	€200,000	€50,000
2017	300,000	100,000
2018	400,000	200,000
	€900,000	€350,000

Calculate the investment in Williams that appears on Branch's balance sheet as of the end of 2018.

Solution to 1:

Investment in Williams at 31 December 2018:

Initial cost	€200,000	
Equity income 2016	€40,000	= (20% of €200,000 Income)
Dividends received 2016	(€10,000)	= (20% of €50,000 Dividends)
Equity income 2017	€60,000	= (20% of €300,000 Income)
Dividends received 2017	(€20,000)	= (20% of €100,000 Dividends)
Equity income 2018	€80,000	= (20% of €400,000 Income)
Dividends received 2018	(€40,000)	= (20% of €200,000 Dividends)
Balance-Equity Investment	€310,000	= [€200,000 + 20% × (€900,000 − €350,000)]

This simple example implicitly assumes that the purchase price equals the purchased equity (20%) in the book value of Williams' net assets.

Using the equity method, the investor includes its share of the investee's profit and losses on the income statement. The equity investment is carried at cost, plus its share of post-acquisition income, less dividends received. The recorded investment value can decline as a result of investee losses or a permanent decline in the investee's market value. If the investment value is reduced to zero, the investor usually discontinues the equity method and does not record further losses. If the investee subsequently reports profits, the equity method is resumed after the investor's share of the profits equals the share of losses not recognized during the suspension of the equity method. Exhibit 4 contains excerpts from Deutsche Bank's 2017 annual report that describes its accounting treatment for investments in associates.

EXHIBIT 4: Excerpt from Deutsche Bank 2017 Annual Report

[From Note 01] Associates

An associate is an entity in which the Group has significant influence, but not a controlling interest, over the operating and financial management policy decisions of the entity. Significant influence is generally presumed when the Group holds between 20% and 50% of the voting rights. The existence and effect of potential voting rights that are currently exercisable or convertible are considered in assessing whether the Group has significant influence. Among the other factors that are considered in determining whether the Group has significant influence are representation on the board of directors (supervisory board in the case of German stock corporations) and material intercompany transactions. The existence of these factors could require the application of the equity method of accounting for a particular investment even though the Group's investment is less than 20% of the voting stock.

Investments in associates are accounted for under the equity method of accounting. The Group's share of the results of associates is adjusted to conform to the accounting policies of the Group and is reported in the Consolidated Statement of Income as Net income (loss) from equity method investments. The Group's share in the associate's profits and losses resulting from intercompany sales is eliminated on consolidation.

If the Group previously held an equity interest in an entity (for example, as available for sale) and subsequently gained significant influence, the previously held equity interest is remeasured to fair value and any gain or loss is recognized in the Consolidated Statement of Income. Any amounts previously recognized in other comprehensive income associated with the equity interest would be reclassified to the Consolidated Statement of Income at the date the Group gains significant influence, as if the Group had disposed of the previously held equity interest.

Under the equity method of accounting, the Group's investments in associates and jointly controlled entities are initially recorded at cost including any directly related transaction costs incurred in acquiring the associate, and subsequently increased (or decreased) to reflect both the Group's pro-rata share of the post-acquisition net income (or loss) of the associate or jointly controlled entity and other movements included directly in the equity of the associate or jointly controlled entity. Goodwill arising on the acquisition of an associate or a jointly controlled entity is included in the carrying value of the investment (net of any accumulated impairment loss). As goodwill is not reported separately it is not specifically tested for impairment. Rather, the entire equity method investment is tested for impairment at each balance sheet date.

If there is objective evidence of impairment, an impairment test is performed by comparing the investment's recoverable amount, which is the higher of its value in use and fair value less costs to sell, with its carrying amount. An impairment loss recognized in prior periods is only reversed if there has been a change in the estimates used to determine the investment's recoverable amount since the last impairment loss was recognized. If this is the case, the carrying amount of the investment is increased to its higher recoverable amount. The increased carrying amount of the investment in associate attributable to a reversal of an impairment loss shall not exceed the carrying amount that would have been determined had no impairment loss been recognized for the investment in prior years.

At the date that the Group ceases to have significant influence over the associate or jointly controlled entity the Group recognizes a gain or loss on the disposal of the equity method investment equal to the difference between the sum of the fair value of any retained investment and the proceeds from disposing of the associate and the carrying amount of the investment. Amounts recognized in prior periods in other comprehensive income in relation to the associate are accounted for on the same basis as would have been required if the investee had directly disposed of the related assets or liabilities.

[From Note 17] Equity Method Investments

Investments in associates and jointly controlled entities are accounted for using the equity method of accounting.

The Group holds interests in 77 (2016: 92) associates and 13 (2016: 14) jointly controlled entities. There are no individually material investments in associates and joint ventures.

Aggregated Financial Information on the Group's Share in Associates and Joint Ventures That Are Individually Immaterial (in €m)	Dec 31, 2017	Dec 31, 2016
Carrying amount of all associated that are individually immaterial to the Group	866	1,027
Aggregated amount of the Group's share of profit (loss) from continuing operations	141	183
Aggregated amount of the Group's share of post-tax profit (loss) from discontinued operations	0	0
Aggregated amount of the Group's share of other comprehensive income	(36)	11
Aggregated amount of the Group's share of total comprehensive income	105	194

It is interesting to note the explanations for the treatment of associates when the ownership percentage is less than 20% or is greater than 50%. The equity method reflects the strength of the relationship between the investor and its associates. In the instances where the percentage ownership is less than 20%, Deutsche Bank uses the equity method because it has significant influence over these associates' operating and financial policies either through its representation on their boards of directors and/or other measures. The equity method provides a more objective basis for reporting investment income than the accounting treatment for investments in financial assets because the investor can potentially influence the timing of dividend distributions.

5. AMORTIZATION OF EXCESS PURCHASE PRICE, FAIR VALUE OPTION, AND IMPAIRMENT

The cost (purchase price) to acquire shares of an investee is often greater than the book value of those shares. This is because, among other things, many of the investee's assets and liabilities reflect historical cost rather than fair value. IFRS allow a company to measure its property, plant, and equipment using either historical cost or fair value (less accumulated depreciation).[11] US GAAP, however, require the use of historical cost (less accumulated depreciation) to measure property, plant, and equipment.[12]

When the cost of the investment exceeds the investor's proportionate share of the book value of the investee's (associate's) net identifiable tangible and intangible assets (e.g., inventory, property, plant and equipment, trademarks, patents), the difference is first allocated to specific assets (or categories of assets) using fair values. These differences are then amortized to the investor's proportionate share of the investee's profit or loss over the economic lives of the assets whose fair values exceeded book values. It should be noted that the allocation is not recorded formally; what appears initially in the investment account on the balance sheet of the investor is the cost. Over time, as the differences are amortized, the balance in the investment account will come closer to representing the ownership percentage of the book value of the net assets of the associate.

IFRS and US GAAP both treat the difference between the cost of the acquisition and investor's share of the fair value of the net identifiable assets as goodwill. Therefore, any remaining difference between the acquisition cost and the fair value of net identifiable assets that cannot be allocated to specific assets is treated as goodwill and is not amortized. Instead, it is reviewed for impairment on a regular basis, and written down for any identified impairment. Goodwill, however, is included in the carrying amount of the investment, because investment is reported as a single line item on the investor's balance sheet.[13]

EXAMPLE 2   Equity Method Investment in Excess of Book Value

1. Blake Co. and Brown Co. are two hypothetical companies. Assume that Blake Co. acquires 30% of the outstanding shares of Brown Co. At the acquisition date, book values and fair values of Brown's recorded assets and liabilities are as follows:

---

[11]After initial recognition, an entity can choose to use either a cost model or a revaluation model to measure its property, plant, and equipment. Under the revaluation model, property, plant, and equipment whose fair value can be measured reliably can be carried at a revalued amount. This revalued amount is its fair value at the date of the revaluation less any subsequent accumulated depreciation

[12]Successful companies should be able to generate, through the productive use of assets, economic value in excess of the resale value of the assets themselves. Therefore, investors may be willing to pay a premium in anticipation of future benefits. These benefits could be a result of general market conditions, the investor's ability to exert significant influence on the investee, or other synergies.

[13]If the investor's share of the fair value of the associate's net assets (identifiable assets, liabilities, and contingent liabilities) is greater than the cost of the investment, the difference is excluded from the carrying amount of the investment and instead included as income in the determination of the investor's share of the associate's profit or loss in the period in which the investment is acquired.

	Book Value	Fair Value
Current assets	€10,000	€10,000
Plant and equipment	190,000	220,000
Land	120,000	140,000
	€320,000	€370,000
Liabilities	100,000	100,000
Net assets	€220,000	€270,000

Blake Co. believes the value of Brown Co. is higher than the book value of its identifiable net assets. They offer €100,000 for a 30% interest in Brown, which represents a €34,000 excess purchase price. The difference between the fair value and book value of the net identifiable assets is €50,000 (€270,000 – 220,000). Based on Blake Co.'s 30% ownership, €15,000 of the excess purchase price is attributable to the net identifiable assets, and the residual is attributable to goodwill. Calculate goodwill.

Solution to 1:

Purchase price	€100,000
30% of book value of Brown (30% × €220,000)	66,000
Excess purchase price	€34,000
Attributable to net assets	
Plant and equipment (30% × €30,000)	€9,000
Land (30% × €20,000)	6,000
Goodwill (residual)	19,000
	€34,000

As illustrated above, goodwill is the residual excess not allocated to identifiable assets or liabilities. The investment is carried as a non-current asset on the Blake's book as a single line item (Investment in Brown, €100,000) on the acquisition date.

5.1. Amortization of Excess Purchase Price

The excess purchase price allocated to the assets and liabilities is accounted for in a manner that is consistent with the accounting treatment for the specific asset or liability to which it is assigned. Amounts allocated to assets and liabilities that are expensed (such as inventory) or periodically depreciated or amortized (plant, property, and intangible assets) must be treated in a similar manner. These allocated amounts are not reflected on the financial statements of the investee (associate), and the investee's income statement will not reflect the necessary periodic adjustments. Therefore, the investor must directly record these adjustment effects by reducing the carrying amount of the investment on its balance sheet and by reducing the investee's profit recognized on its income statement. Amounts allocated to assets or liabilities that are not systematically amortized (e.g., land) will continue to be reported at their fair value as of the date the investment was acquired. As stated above, goodwill is included in the carrying amount of the investment instead of being separately recognized. It is not amortized because it is considered to have an indefinite life.

Using the example above and assuming a 10-year useful life for plant, property, and equipment and using straight-line depreciation, the annual amortization is as follows:

Account	Excess Price (€)	Useful Life	Amortization/Year (€)
Plant and equipment	9,000	10 years	900
Land	6,000	Indefinite	0
Goodwill	19,000	Indefinite	0

Annual amortization would reduce the investor's share of the investee's reported income (equity income) and the balance in the investment account by €900 for each year over the 10-year period.

EXAMPLE 3   Equity Method Investments with Goodwill

On 1 January 2018, Parker Company acquired 30% of Prince Inc. common shares for the cash price of €500,000 (both companies are fictitious). It is determined that Parker has the ability to exert significant influence on Prince's financial and operating decisions. The following information concerning Prince's assets and liabilities on 1 January 2018 is provided:

Prince, Inc.			
	Book Value	Fair Value	Difference
Current assets	€100,000	€100,000	€0
Plant and equipment	1,900,000	2,200,000	300,000
	€2,000,000	€2,300,000	€300,000
Liabilities	800,000	800,000	0
Net assets	€1,200,000	€1,500,000	€300,000

The plant and equipment are depreciated on a straight-line basis and have 10 years of remaining life. Prince reports net income for 2018 of €100,000 and pays dividends of €50,000. Calculate the following:

1. Goodwill included in the purchase price.

Solution to 1:

Purchase price	€500,000
Acquired equity in book value of Prince's net assets (30% × €1,200,000)	360,000
Excess purchase price	€140,000
Attributable to plant and equipment (30% × €300,000)	(90,000)
Goodwill (residual)	€50,000

2. Investment in associate (Prince) at the end of 2018.

Solution to 2:
    Investment in associate

Purchase price	€500,000
Parker's share of Prince's net income (30% × €100,000)	30,000
Dividends received (30% of €50,000)	(15,000)
Amortization of excess purchase price attributable to plant and equipment (€90,000 ÷ 10 years)	(9,000)
31 December 2018 balance in investment in Prince	€506,000

An alternate way to look at the balance in the investment account is that it reflects the basic valuation principle of the equity method. At any point in time, the investment account balance equals the investor's (Parker) proportionate share of the net equity (net assets at book value) of the investee (Prince) plus the unamortized balance of the original excess purchase price. Applying this principle to this example:

2018 Beginning net assets =	€1,200,000
Plus: Net income	100,000
Less: Dividends	(50,000)
2018 Ending net assets	€1,250,000
Parker's proportionate share of Prince's recorded net assets (30% × €1,250,000)	€375,000
Unamortized excess purchase price (€140,000 – 9,000)	131,000
Investment in Prince	€506,000

Note that the unamortized excess purchase price is a cost incurred by Parker, not Prince. Therefore, the total amount is included in the investment account balance.

5.2. Fair Value Option

Both IFRS and US GAAP give the investor the option to account for their equity method investment at fair value.[14] Under US GAAP, this option is available to all entities; however, under IFRS, its use is restricted to venture capital organizations, mutual funds, unit trusts, and similar entities, including investment-linked insurance funds.

Both standards require that the election to use the fair value option occur at the time of initial recognition and is irrevocable. Subsequent to initial recognition, the investment is reported at fair value with unrealized gains and losses arising from changes in fair value as well as any interest and dividends received included in the investor's profit or loss (income). Under the fair value method, the investment account on the investor's balance sheet does not reflect the investor's proportionate share of the investee's profit or loss, dividends, or other distributions. In addition, the excess of cost over the fair value of the investee's identifiable net assets is not amortized, nor is goodwill created.

5.3. Impairment

Both IFRS and US GAAP require periodic reviews of equity method investments for impairment. If the fair value of the investment is below its carrying value and this decline is deemed to be other than temporary, an impairment loss must be recognized.

Under IFRS, there must be objective evidence of impairment as a result of one or more (loss) events that occurred after the initial recognition of the investment, and that loss event has an impact on the investment's future cash flows, which can be reliably estimated. Because goodwill is included in the carrying amount of the investment and is not separately recognized, it is not separately tested for impairment. Instead, the entire carrying amount of the investment is tested for impairment by comparing its recoverable amount with its carrying amount.[15] The impairment loss is recognized on the income statement, and the carrying amount of the investment on the balance sheet is either reduced directly or through the use of an allowance account.

US GAAP takes a different approach. If the fair value of the investment declines below its carrying value *and* the decline is determined to be permanent, US GAAP[16] requires an impairment loss to be recognized on the income statement and the carrying value of the investment on the balance sheet is reduced to its fair value.

Both IFRS and US GAAP prohibit the reversal of impairment losses even if the fair value later increases.

Section 6 of this chapter discusses impairment tests for the goodwill attributed to a controlling investment (consolidated subsidiary). Note the distinction between the disaggregated goodwill impairment test for consolidated statements and the impairment test of the total fair value of equity method investments.

---

[14]IFRS 9 Financial Instruments. FASB ASC Section 825-10-25 [Financial Instruments–Overall–Recognition].

[15]Recoverable amount is the higher of "value in use" or net selling price. Value in use is equal to the present value of estimated future cash flows expected to arise from the continuing use of an asset and from its disposal at the end of its useful life. Net selling price is equal to fair value less cost to sell.

[16]FASB ASC Section 323-10-35 [Investments–Equity Method and Joint Ventures–Overall–Subsequent Measurement].

6. TRANSACTIONS WITH ASSOCIATES AND DISCLOSURE

Because an investor company can influence the terms and timing of transactions with its associates, profits from such transactions cannot be realized until confirmed through use or sale to third parties. Accordingly, the investor company's share of any unrealized profit must be deferred by reducing the amount recorded under the equity method. In the subsequent period(s) when this deferred profit is considered confirmed, it is added to the equity income. At that time, the equity income is again based on the recorded values in the associate's accounts.

Transactions between the two affiliates may be **upstream** (associate to investor) or **downstream** (investor to associate). In an upstream sale, the profit on the intercompany transaction is recorded on the associate's income (profit or loss) statement. The investor's share of the unrealized profit is thus included in equity income on the investor's income statement. In a downstream sale, the profit is recorded on the investor's income statement. Both IFRS and US GAAP require that the unearned profits be eliminated to the extent of the investor's interest in the associate.[17] The result is an adjustment to equity income on the investor's income statement.

EXAMPLE 4   Equity Method with Sale of Inventory: Upstream Sale

On 1 January 2018, Wicker Company acquired a 25% interest in Foxworth Company (both companies are fictitious) for €1,000,000 and used the equity method to account for its investment. The book value of Foxworth's net assets on that date was €3,800,000. An analysis of fair values revealed that all fair values of assets and liabilities were equal to book values except for a building. The building was undervalued by €40,000 and has a 20-year remaining life. The company used straight-line depreciation for the building. Foxworth paid €3,200 in dividends in 2018. During 2018, Foxworth reported net income of €20,000. During the year, Foxworth sold inventory to Wicker. At the end of the year, there was €8,000 profit from the upstream sale in Foxworth's net income. The inventory sold to Wicker by Foxworth had not been sold to an outside party.

1. Calculate the equity income to be reported as a line item on Wicker's 2018 income statement.

Solution to 1:

Equity Income

Wicker's share of Foxworth's reported income (25% × €20,000)	€5,000
Amortization of excess purchase price attributable to building, (€10,000 ÷ 20)	(500)
Unrealized profit (25% × €8,000)	(2,000)
Equity income 2018	€2,500

---

[17]IAS 28 Investments in Associates and Joint Ventures; FASB ASC Topic 323 [Investments–Equity Method and Joint Ventures].

2. Calculate the balance in the investment in Foxworth to be reported on the 31 December 2018 balance sheet.

Purchase price	€1,000,000
Acquired equity in book value of Foxworth's net assets (25% × €3,800,000)	950,000
Excess purchase price	€50,000
Attributable to:	
Building (25% × €40,000)	€10,000
Goodwill (residual)	40,000
	€50,000

Solution to 2:

Investment in Foxworth

Purchase price	€1,000,000
Equity income 2018	2,500
Dividends received (25% × €3,200)	(800)
Investment in Foxworth, 31 Dec 2018	€1,001,700
Composition of investment account:	
Wicker's proportionate share of Foxworth's net equity (net assets at book value)	€952,200
[25% × (€3,800,000 + (20,000 – 8,000) – 3,200)]	
Unamortized excess purchase price (€50,000 – 500)	49,500
	€1,001,700

EXAMPLE 5   Equity Method with Sale of Inventory: Downstream Sale

Jones Company owns 25% of Jason Company (both fictitious companies) and appropriately applies the equity method of accounting. Amortization of excess purchase price, related to undervalued assets at the time of the investment, is €8,000 per year. During 2017 Jones sold €96,000 of inventory to Jason for €160,000. Jason resold €120,000 of this inventory during 2017. The remainder was sold in 2018. Jason reports income from its operations of €800,000 in 2017 and €820,000 in 2018.

1. Calculate the equity income to be reported as a line item on Jones's 2017 income statement.

Solution to 1:

Equity Income 2017

Jones's share of Jason's reported income (25% × €800,000)	€200,000
Amortization of excess purchase price	(8,000)
Unrealized profit (25% × €16,000)	(4,000)
Equity income 2017	€188,000

Jones's profit on the sale to Jason = €160,000 – 96,000 = €64,000

Jason sells 75% (€120,000/160,000) of the goods purchased from Jones; 25% is unsold.

Total unrealized profit = €64,000 × 25% = €16,000

Jones's share of the unrealized profit = €16,000 × 25% = €4,000

Alternative approach:

Jones's profit margin on sale to Jason: 40% (€64,000/€160,000)

Jason's inventory of Jones's goods at 31 Dec 2017: €40,000

Jones's profit margin on this was 40% × 40,000 = €16,000

Jones's share of profit on unsold goods = €16,000 × 25% = €4,000

2. Calculate the equity income to be reported as a line item on Jones's 2018 income statement.

Solution to 2:

Equity Income 2018

Jones's share of Jason's reported income (25% × €820,000)	€205,000
Amortization of excess purchase price	(8,000)
Realized profit (25% × €16,000)	4,000
Equity income 2018	€201,000

Jason sells the remaining 25% of the goods purchased from Jones.

6.1. Disclosure

The notes to the financial statements are an integral part of the information necessary for investors. Both IFRS and US GAAP require disclosure about the assets, liabilities, and results of equity method investments. For example, in their 2017 annual report, within its note titled "Principles of Consolidation," Deutsche Bank reports that:

> Investments in associates are accounted for under the equity method of accounting. The Group's share of the results of associates is adjusted to conform to the accounting policies of the Group and is reported in the Consolidated Statement of Income as Net income (loss) from equity method investments. The Group's share in the associate's profits and losses resulting from intercompany sales is eliminated on consolidation.
>
> If the Group previously held an equity interest in an entity (for example, as available for sale) and subsequently gained significant influence, the previously held equity interest is remeasured to fair value and any gain or loss is recognized in the Consolidated Statement of Income. Any amounts previously recognized in other comprehensive income associated with the equity interest would be reclassified to the Consolidated Statement of Income at the date the Group gains significant influence, as if the Group had disposed of the previously held equity interest.
>
> Under the equity method of accounting, the Group's investments in associates and jointly controlled entities are initially recorded at cost including any directly related transaction costs incurred in acquiring the associate, and subsequently increased (or decreased) to reflect both the Group's pro-rata share of the post-acquisition net income (or loss) of the associate or jointly controlled entity and other movements included directly in the equity of the associate or jointly controlled entity. Goodwill arising on the acquisition of an associate or a jointly controlled entity is included in the carrying value of the investment (net of any accumulated impairment loss). As goodwill is not reported separately it is not specifically tested for impairment. Rather, the entire equity method investment is tested for impairment at each balance sheet date.

For practical reasons, associated companies' results are sometimes included in the investor's accounts with a certain time lag, normally not more than one quarter. Dividends from associated companies are not included in investor income because it would be a double counting. Applying the equity method recognizes the investor's full share of the associate's income. Dividends received involve exchanging a portion of equity interest for cash. In the consolidated balance sheet, the book value of shareholdings in associated companies is increased by the investor's share of the company's net income and reduced by amortization of surplus values and the amount of dividends received.

6.2. Issues for Analysts

Equity method accounting presents several challenges for analysis. First, analysts should question whether the equity method is appropriate. For example, an investor holding 19% of an associate may in fact exert significant influence but may attempt to avoid using the equity method to avoid reporting associate losses. On the other hand, an investor holding 25% of an associate may be unable to exert significant influence and may be unable to access cash flows, and yet may prefer the equity method to capture associate income.

Second, the investment account represents the investor's percentage ownership in the net assets of the investee company through "one-line consolidation." There can be significant assets and liabilities of the investee that are not reflected on the investor's balance sheet, which will significantly affect debt ratios. Net margin ratios could be overstated because income for the associate is included in investor net income but is not specifically included in sales. An investor may actually control the investee with less than 50% ownership but prefer the financial results using the equity method. Careful analysis can reveal financial performance driven by accounting structure.

Finally, the analyst must consider the quality of the equity method earnings. The equity method assumes that a percentage of each dollar earned by the investee company is earned by the investor (i.e., a fraction of the dollar equal to the fraction of the company owned), even if cash is not received. Analysts should, therefore, consider potential restrictions on dividend cash flows (the statement of cash flows).

7. ACQUISITION METHOD

Business combinations (controlling interest investments) involve the combination of two or more entities into a larger economic entity. Business combinations are typically motivated by expectations of added value through synergies, including potential for increased revenues, elimination of duplicate costs, tax advantages, coordination of the production process, and efficiency gains in the management of assets.[18]

Under IFRS, there is no distinction among business combinations based on the resulting structure of the larger economic entity. For all business combinations, one of the parties to the business combination is identified as the acquirer. Under US GAAP, an acquirer is identified, but the business combinations are categorized as merger, acquisition, or consolidation based on the legal structure after the combination. Each of these types of business combinations has distinctive characteristics that are described in Exhibit 5. Features of variable interest and special purpose entities are also described in Exhibit 5 because these are additional instances where control is exerted by another entity. Under both IFRS and US GAAP, business combinations are accounted for using the *acquisition method*.

EXHIBIT 5: Types of Business Combinations

Merger

The distinctive feature of a merger is that only one of the entities remains in existence. One hundred percent of the target is absorbed into the acquiring company. Company A may issue common stock, preferred stock, bonds, or pay cash to acquire the net assets. The net assets of Company B are transferred to Company A. Company B ceases to exist and Company A is the only entity that remains.

$$\text{Company A} + \text{Company B} = \text{Company A}$$

---

[18]IFRS 3, *Business Combinations*, revised in 2008 and FASB ASC Topic 805 [*Business Combinations*] provide guidance on business combinations.

Acquisition

The distinctive feature of an acquisition is the legal continuity of the entities. Each entity continues operations but is connected through a parent–subsidiary relationship. Each entity is an individual that maintains separate financial records, but the parent (the acquirer) provides consolidated financial statements in each reporting period. Unlike a merger or consolidation, the acquiring company does not need to acquire 100% of the target. In fact, in some cases, it may acquire less than 50% and still exert control. If the acquiring company acquires less than 100%, non-controlling (minority) shareholders' interests are reported on the consolidated financial statements.

$$\text{Company A} + \text{Company B} = (\text{Company A} + \text{Company B})$$

Consolidation

The distinctive feature of a consolidation is that a new legal entity is formed and none of the predecessor entities remain in existence. A new entity is created to take over the net assets of Company A and Company B. Company A and Company B cease to exist and Company C is the only entity that remains.

$$\text{Company A} + \text{Company B} = \text{Company C}$$

Special Purpose or Variable Interest Entities

The distinctive feature of a special purpose (variable interest) entity is that control is not usually based on voting control, because equity investors do not have a sufficient amount at risk for the entity to finance its activities without additional subordinated financial support. Furthermore, the equity investors may lack a controlling financial interest. The sponsoring company usually creates a special purpose entity (SPE) for a narrowly defined purpose. IFRS require consolidation if the substance of the relationship indicates control by the sponsor.

Under IFRS 10, *Consolidated Financial Statements* and SIC-12, *Consolidation-Special Purpose Entities*, the definition of control extends to a broad range of activities. The control concept requires judgment and evaluation of relevant factors to determine whether control exists. Control is present when 1) the investor has the ability to exert influence on the financial and operating policy of the entity; and 2) is exposed, or has rights, to variable returns from its involvement with the investee. Consolidation criteria apply to all entities that meet the definition of control.

US GAAP uses a two-component consolidation model that includes both a variable interest component and a voting interest (control) component. Under the variable interest component, US GAAP[19] requires the primary beneficiary of a variable interest entity (VIE) to consolidate the VIE regardless of its voting interests (if any) in the VIE or its decision-making authority. The primary beneficiary is defined as the party that will absorb the majority of the VIE's expected losses, receive the majority of the VIE's expected residual returns, or both.

In the past, business combinations could be accounted for either as a purchase transaction or as a uniting (or pooling) of interests. However, the use of the pooling accounting method for acquisitions is no longer permitted, and IFRS and US GAAP now

---

[19]FASB ASC Topic 810 [Consolidation].

require that all business combinations be accounted for in a similar manner. The *acquisition method* developed by the IASB and the FASB replaces the purchase method, and substantially reduces any differences between IFRS and US GAAP for business combinations.[20]

7.1. Acquisition Method

IFRS and US GAAP require the acquisition method of accounting for business combinations, although both have a few specific exemptions.

Under this approach, the fair value of the consideration given by the acquiring company is the appropriate measurement for acquisitions and also includes the acquisition-date fair value of any contingent consideration. Direct costs of the business combination, such as professional and legal fees, valuation experts, and consultants, are expensed as incurred.

The acquisition method (which replaced the purchase method) addresses three major accounting issues that often arise in business combinations and the preparation of consolidated (combined) financial statements:

- The recognition and measurement of the assets and liabilities of the combined entity;
- The initial recognition and subsequent accounting for goodwill; and
- The recognition and measurement of any non-controlling interest.

7.1.1. Recognition and Measurement of Identifiable Assets and Liabilities

IFRS and US GAAP require that the acquirer measure the identifiable tangible and intangible assets and liabilities of the acquiree (acquired entity) at fair value as of the date of the acquisition. The acquirer must also recognize any assets and liabilities that the acquiree had not previously recognized as assets and liabilities in its financial statements. For example, identifiable intangible assets (for example, brand names, patents, technology) that the acquiree developed internally would be recognized by the acquirer.

7.1.2. Recognition and Measurement of Contingent Liabilities[21]

On the acquisition date, the acquirer must recognize any contingent liability assumed in the acquisition if 1) it is a present obligation that arises from past events, and 2) it can be measured reliably. Costs that the acquirer expects (but is not obliged) to incur, however, are not recognized as liabilities as of the acquisition date. Instead, the acquirer recognizes these costs in future periods as they are incurred. For example, expected restructuring costs arising from exiting an acquiree's business will be recognized in the period in which they are incurred.

There is a difference between IFRS and US GAAP with regard to treatment of contingent liabilities. IFRS include contingent liabilities if their fair values can be reliably measured. US GAAP includes only those contingent liabilities that are probable and can be reasonably estimated.

---

[20]IFRS 10, Consolidated Financial Statements; IFRS 3, Business Combinations; FASB ASC Topic 805 [Business Combinations]; FASB ASC Topic 810 [Consolidations].

[21]A contingent liability must be recognized even if it is not probable that an outflow of resources or economic benefits will be used to settle the obligation.

7.1.3. Recognition and Measurement of Indemnification Assets

On the acquisition date, the acquirer must recognize an indemnification asset if the seller (acquiree) contractually indemnifies the acquirer for the outcome of a contingency or an uncertainty related to all or part of a specific asset or liability of the acquiree. The seller may also indemnify the acquirer against losses above a specified amount on a liability arising from a particular contingency. For example, the seller guarantees that an acquired contingent liability will not exceed a specified amount. In this situation, the acquirer recognizes an indemnification asset at the same time it recognizes the indemnified liability, with both measured on the same basis. If the indemnification relates to an asset or a liability that is recognized at the acquisition date and measured at its acquisition date fair value, the acquirer will also recognize the indemnification asset at the acquisition date at its acquisition date fair value.

7.1.4. Recognition and Measurement of Financial Assets and Liabilities

At the acquisition date, identifiable assets and liabilities acquired are classified in accordance with IFRS (or US GAAP) standards. The acquirer reclassifies the financial assets and liabilities of the acquiree based on the contractual terms, economic conditions, and the acquirer's operating or accounting policies, as they exist at the acquisition date.

7.1.5. Recognition and Measurement of Goodwill

IFRS allows two options for recognizing goodwill at the transaction date. The goodwill option is on a transaction-by-transaction basis. "Partial goodwill" is measured as the fair value of the acquisition (fair value of consideration given) less the acquirer's share of the fair value of all identifiable tangible and intangible assets, liabilities, and contingent liabilities acquired. "Full goodwill" is measured as the fair value of the entity as a whole less the fair value of all identifiable tangible and intangible assets, liabilities, and contingent liabilities. US GAAP views the entity as a whole and requires full goodwill.[22]

Because goodwill is considered to have an indefinite life, it is not amortized. Instead, it is tested for impairment annually or more frequently if events or circumstances indicate that goodwill might be impaired.

EXAMPLE 6   Recognition and Measurement of Goodwill

Acquirer contributes $800,000 for an 80% interest in Acquiree. The identifiable net assets have a fair value of $900,000. The fair value of the entire entity is determined to be $1 million.

	IFRS Partial Goodwill
Fair value of consideration	$800,000
80% of Fair value of identifiable net assets	720,000
Goodwill recognized	$80,000

---

[22]FASB ASC Topic 805 [Business Combinations].

	IFRS and US GAAP Full Goodwill
Fair value of entity	$1,000,000
Fair value of identifiable assets	900,000
Goodwill recognized	$100,000

7.1.6. Recognition and Measurement when Acquisition Price Is Less than Fair Value

Occasionally, a company faces adverse circumstances such that its market value drops below the fair value of its net assets. In an acquisition of such a company, where the purchase price is less than the fair value of the target's (acquiree's) net assets, the acquisition is considered to be a "bargain purchase" acquisition. IFRS and US GAAP require the difference between the fair value of the acquired net assets and the purchase price to be recognized immediately as a gain in profit or loss. Any contingent consideration must be measured and recognized at fair value at the time of the business combination. Any subsequent changes in value of the contingent consideration are recognized in profit or loss.

7.2. Impact of the Acquisition Method on Financial Statements, Post-Acquisition

Example 7 shows the consolidated balance sheet of an acquiring company after the acquisition.

EXAMPLE 7   Acquisition Method Post-Combination Balance Sheet

1. Franklin Company, a hypothetical company, acquired 100% of the outstanding shares of Jefferson, Inc. (another fictitious company) by issuing 1,000,000 shares of its €1 par common stock (€15 market value). Immediately before the transaction, the two companies compiled the following information:

	Franklin Book Value (000)	Jefferson Book Value (000)	Jefferson Fair Value (000)
Cash and receivables	€10,000	€300	€300
Inventory	12,000	1,700	3,000
PP&E (net)	27,000	2,500	4,500
	€49,000	€4,500	€7,800
Current payables	8,000	600	600
Long-term debt	16,000	2,000	1,800
	24,000	2,600	2,400
Net assets	€25,000	€1,900	€5,400

	Franklin Book Value (000)	Jefferson Book Value (000)	Jefferson Fair Value (000)
Shareholders' equity:			
Capital stock (€1 par)	€5,000	€400	
Additional paid in capital	6,000	700	
Retained earnings	€14,000	€800	

Jefferson has no identifiable intangible assets. Show the balances in the post-combination balance sheet using the acquisition method.

Solution to 1:
Under the acquisition method, the purchase price allocation would be as follows:

Fair value of the stock issued (1,000,000 shares at market value of €15)	€15,000,000
Book value of Jefferson's net assets	1,900,000
Excess purchase price	€13,100,000
Fair value of the stock issued	€15,000,000
Fair value allocated to identifiable net assets	5,400,000
Goodwill	€9,600,000

Allocation of excess purchase price (based on the differences between fair values and book values):

Inventory	€1,300,000
PP&E (net)	2,000,000
Long-term debt	200,000
Goodwill	9,600,000
	€13,100,000

Both IFRS and US GAAP record the fair value of the acquisition at the market value of the stock issued, or €15,000,000. In this case, the purchase price exceeds the book value of Jefferson's net assets by €13,100,000. Inventory, PP&E (net), and long-term debt are adjusted to fair values. The excess of the purchase price over the fair value of identifiable net assets results in goodwill recognition of €9,600,000.

The post-combination balance sheet of the combined entity would appear as follows:

Franklin Consolidated Balance Sheet (Acquisition Method) (000)	
Cash and receivables	€10,300
Inventory	15,000
PP&E (net)	31,500
Goodwill	9,600
Total assets	€66,400
Current payables	€8,600
Long-term debt	17,800
Total liabilities	€26,400
Capital stock (€1 par)	€6,000
Additional paid in capital	20,000
Retained earnings	14,000
Total stockholders' equity	€40,000
Total liabilities and stockholders' equity	€66,400

Assets and liabilities are combined using book values of Franklin plus fair values for the assets and liabilities acquired from Jefferson. For example, the book value of Franklin's inventory (€12,000,000) is added to the fair value of inventory acquired from Jefferson (€3,000,000) for a combined inventory of €15,000,000. Long-term debt has a book value of €16,000,000 on Franklin's pre-acquisition statements, and Jefferson's fair value of debt is €1,800,000. The combined long-term debt is recorded as €17,800,000.

Franklin's post-merger financial statement reflects in stockholders' equity the stock issued by Franklin to acquire Jefferson. Franklin issues stock with a par value of €1,000,000; however, the stock is measured at fair value under both IFRS and US GAAP. Therefore, the consideration exchanged is 1,000,000 shares at market value of €15, or €15,000,000. Prior to the transaction, Franklin had 5,000,000 shares of €1 par stock outstanding (€5,000,000). The combined entity reflects the Franklin capital stock outstanding of €6,000,000 (€5,000,000 plus the additional 1,000,000 shares of €1 par stock issued to effect the transaction). Franklin's additional paid in capital of €6,000,000 is increased by the €14,000,000 additional paid in capital from the issuance of the 1,000,000 shares (€15,000,000 less par value of €1,000,000) for a total of €20,000,000. At the acquisition date, only the acquirer's retained earnings are carried to the combined entity. Earnings of the target are included on the consolidated income statement and retained earnings only in post-acquisition periods.

In the periods subsequent to the business combination, the financial statements continue to be affected by the acquisition method. Net income reflects the performance of the combined entity. Under the acquisition method, amortization/depreciation is based on historical cost of Franklin's assets and the fair value of Jefferson's assets. Using Example 7, as Jefferson's acquired inventory is sold, the cost of goods sold would be €1,300,000 higher and depreciation on PP&E would be €2,000,000 higher over the life of the asset than if the companies had not combined.

8. THE CONSOLIDATION PROCESS

Consolidated financial statements combine the separate financial statements for distinct legal entities, the parent and its subsidiaries, as if they were one economic unit. Consolidation combines the assets, liabilities, revenues, and expenses of subsidiaries with the parent company. Transactions between the parent and subsidiary (intercompany transactions) are eliminated to avoid double counting and premature income recognition. Consolidated statements are presumed to be more meaningful in terms of representational faithfulness. It is important for the analyst to consider the differences in IFRS and US GAAP, valuation bases, and other factors that could impair the validity of comparative analyses.

8.1. Business Combination with Less Than 100% Acquisition

The acquirer purchases 100% of the equity of the target company in a transaction structured as a merger or consolidation. For a transaction structured as an acquisition, however, the acquirer does not have to purchase 100% of the equity of the target in order to achieve control. The acquiring company may purchase less than 100% of the target because it may be constrained by resources or it may be unable to acquire all the outstanding shares. As a result, both the acquirer and the target remain separate legal entities. Both IFRS and US GAAP presume a company has control if it owns more than 50% of the voting shares of an entity. In this case, the acquiring company is viewed as the parent, and the target company is viewed as the subsidiary. Both the parent and the subsidiary typically prepare their own financial records, but the parent also prepares consolidated financial statements at each reporting period. The consolidated financial statements are the primary source of information for investors and analysts.

8.2. Non-controlling (Minority) Interests: Balance Sheet

A non-controlling (minority) interest is the portion of the subsidiary's equity (residual interest) that is held by third parties (i.e., not owned by the parent). Non-controlling interests are created when the parent acquires less than a 100% controlling interest in a subsidiary. IFRS and US GAAP have similar treatment for how non-controlling interests are classified.[23] Non-controlling interests in consolidated subsidiaries are presented on the consolidated balance sheet as a separate component of stockholders' equity. IFRS and US GAAP differ, however, on the measurement of non-controlling interests. Under IFRS, the parent can measure the non-controlling interest at either its fair value (full goodwill method) or at the non-controlling interest's proportionate share of the acquiree's identifiable net assets (partial goodwill method). Under US GAAP, the parent must use the full goodwill method and measure the non-controlling interest at fair value.

Example 8 illustrates the differences in reporting requirements.

---

[23]IFRS 10, Consolidated Financial Statements and FASB ASC Topic 810 [Consolidation].

EXAMPLE 8   Non-Controlling Asset Valuation

On 1 January 2018, the hypothetical Parent Co. acquired 90% of the outstanding shares of the hypothetical Subsidiary Co. in exchange for shares of Parent Co.'s no par common stock with a fair value of €180,000. The fair market value of the subsidiary's shares on the date of the exchange was €200,000. Below is selected financial information from the two companies immediately prior to the exchange of shares (before the parent recorded the acquisition):

| | Parent Book Value | Subsidiary | |
		Book Value	Fair Value
Cash and receivables	€40,000	€15,000	€15,000
Inventory	125,000	80,000	80,000
PP&E (net)	235,000	95,000	155,000
	€400,000	€190,000	€250,000
Payables	55,000	20,000	20,000
Long-term debt	120,000	70,000	70,000
	175,000	90,000	90,000
Net assets	€225,000	€100,000	€160,000
Shareholders' equity:			
Capital stock (no par)	€87,000	€34,000	
Retained earnings	€138,000	€66,000	

1. Calculate the value of PP&E (net) on the consolidated balance sheet under both IFRS and US GAAP.

Solution to 1:
   Relative to fair value, the PP&E of the subsidiary is understated by €60,000. Under the acquisition method (IFRS and US GAAP), as long as the parent has control over the subsidiary (i.e., regardless of whether the parent had purchased 51% or 100% of the subsidiary's stock), it would include 100% of the subsidiary's assets and liabilities at fair value on the consolidated balance sheet. Therefore, PP&E on the consolidated balance sheet would be valued at €390,000.

2. Calculate the value of goodwill and the value of the non-controlling interest at the acquisition date under the full goodwill method.

Solution to 2:
   Under the full goodwill method (mandatory under US GAAP and optional under IFRS), goodwill on the consolidated balance sheet would be the difference between the total fair value of the subsidiary and the fair value of the subsidiary's identifiable net assets.

Fair value of the subsidiary	€200,000
Fair value of subsidiary's identifiable net assets	160,000
Goodwill	€40,000

The value of the non-controlling interest is equal to the non-controlling interest's proportionate share of the subsidiary's fair value. The non-controlling interest's proportionate share of the subsidiary is 10% and the fair value of the subsidiary is €200,000 on the acquisition date. Under the full goodwill method, the value of the non-controlling interest would be €20,000 (10% × €200,000).

3. Calculate the value of goodwill and the value of the non-controlling interest at the acquisition date under the partial goodwill method.

Solution to 3:
Under the partial goodwill method (IFRS only), goodwill on the parent's consolidated balance sheet would be €36,000, the difference between the purchase price and the parent's proportionate share of the subsidiary's identifiable assets.

Acquisition price	€180,000
90% of fair value	144,000
Goodwill	€36,000

The value of the non-controlling interest is equal to the non-controlling interest's proportionate share of the fair value of the subsidiary's identifiable net assets. The non-controlling interest's proportionate share is 10%, and the fair value of the subsidiary's identifiable net assets on the acquisition date is €160,000. Under the partial goodwill method, the value of the non-controlling interest would be €16,000 (10% × €160,000).

Regardless of which method is used, goodwill is not amortized under either IFRS or US GAAP but it is tested for impairment at least annually.

For comparative purposes, below is the balance sheet at the acquisition date under the full goodwill and partial goodwill methods.

Comparative Consolidated Balance Sheet at Acquisition Date: Acquisition Method

	Full Goodwill	Partial Goodwill
Cash and receivables	€55,000	€55,000
Inventory	205,000	205,000
PP&E (net)	390,000	390,000
Goodwill	40,000	36,000
Total assets	€690,000	€686,000
Payables	€75,000	€75,000
Long-term debt	190,000	190,000
Total liabilities	€265,000	€265,000

	Full Goodwill	Partial Goodwill
Shareholders' equity:		
Noncontrolling interests	€20,000	€16,000
Capital stock (no par)	€267,000	€267,000
Retained earnings	138,000	138,000
Total equity	€425,000	€421,000
Total liabilities and shareholders' equity	€690,000	€686,000

8.3. Non-controlling (Minority) Interests: Income Statement

On the income statement, non-controlling (minority) interests are presented as a line item reflecting the allocation of profit or loss for the period. Intercompany transactions, if any, are eliminated in full.

Using assumed data consistent with the facts in Example 8, the amounts included for the subsidiary in the consolidated income statements under IFRS and US GAAP are presented below. Income taxes are ignored in the table. In practice, however, non-controlling interest on the consolidated income statement is the non-controlling interest's share of the subsidiary's after-tax income.

	Full Goodwill	Partial Goodwill
Sales	€250,000	€250,000
Cost of goods sold	137,500	137,500
Interest expense	10,000	10,000
Depreciation expense	39,000	39,000
Income from continuing operations	€63,500	€63,500
Non-controlling interest (10%)	(6,350)	(6,350)
Consolidated net income to parent's shareholders	€57,150	€57,150

Income to the parent's shareholders is €57,150 using either method. This is because the fair value of the PP&E is allocated to non-controlling shareholders as well as to the controlling shareholders under the full goodwill and the partial goodwill methods. Therefore, the non-controlling interests will share in the adjustment for excess depreciation resulting from the €60,000 increase in PP&E. Because depreciation expense is the same under both methods, it results in identical net income to all shareholders, whichever method is used to recognize goodwill and to measure the non-controlling interest.

Although net income to parent's shareholders is the same, the impact on ratios would be different because total assets and stockholders' equity would differ.

Impact on Ratios

	Full Goodwill (%)	Partial Goodwill (%)
Return on assets	8.28	8.33
Return on equity	13.45	13.57

Over time, the value of the subsidiary will change as a result of net income and changes in equity. As a result, the value of the non-controlling interest on the parent's consolidated balance sheet will also change.

8.4. Goodwill Impairment

Although goodwill is not amortized, it must be tested for impairment at least annually or more frequently if events or changes in circumstances indicate that it might be impaired. If it is probable that some or all of the goodwill will not be recovered through the profitable operations of the combined entity, it should be partially or fully written off by charging it to an expense. Once written down, goodwill cannot be later restored.

IFRS and US GAAP differ on the definition of the levels at which goodwill is assigned and how goodwill is tested for impairment.

Under IFRS, at the time of acquisition, the total amount of goodwill recognized is allocated to each of the acquirer's cash-generating units that will benefit from the expected synergies resulting from the combination with the target. A cash-generating unit represents the lowest level within the combined entity at which goodwill is monitored for impairment purposes.[24] Goodwill impairment testing is then conducted under a one-step approach. The recoverable amount of a cash-generating unit is calculated and compared with the carrying value of the cash-generating unit.[25] An impairment loss is recognized if the recoverable amount of the cash-generating unit is less than its carrying value. The impairment loss (the difference between these two amounts) is first applied to the goodwill that has been allocated to the cash-generating unit. Once this has been reduced to zero, the remaining amount of the loss is then allocated to all of the other non-cash assets in the unit on a pro rata basis.

Under US GAAP, at the time of acquisition, the total amount of goodwill recognized is allocated to each of the acquirer's reporting units. A reporting unit is an operating segment or component of an operating segment that is one level below the operating segment as a whole. Goodwill impairment testing is then conducted under a two-step approach: identification of impairment and then measurement of the loss. First, the carrying amount of the reporting unit (including goodwill) is compared to its fair value. If the carrying value of the reporting unit exceeds its fair value, potential impairment has been identified. The second step is then performed to measure the amount of the impairment loss. The amount of the impairment loss is the difference between the implied fair value of the reporting unit's goodwill and its

---

[24] A cash-generating unit is the smallest identifiable group of assets that generates cash inflows that are largely independent of the cash inflows from other assets or groups of assets.

[25] The recoverable amount of a cash-generating unit is the higher of net selling price (i.e., fair value less costs to sell) and its value in use. Value in use is the present value of the future cash flows expected to be derived from the cash-generating unit. The carrying value of a cash-generating unit is equal to the carrying value of the unit's assets and liabilities including the goodwill that has been allocated to that unit.

carrying amount. The implied fair value of goodwill is determined in the same manner as in a business combination (it is the difference between the fair value of the reporting unit and the fair value of the reporting unit's assets and liabilities). The impairment loss is applied to the goodwill that has been allocated to the reporting unit. After the goodwill of the reporting unit has been eliminated, no other adjustments are made automatically to the carrying values of any of the reporting unit's other assets or liabilities. However, it may be prudent to test other asset values for recoverability and possible impairment.

Under both IFRS and US GAAP, the impairment loss is recorded as a separate line item in the consolidated income statement.

EXAMPLE 9   Goodwill Impairment: IFRS

1. The cash-generating unit of a French company has a carrying value of €1,400,000, which includes €300,000 of allocated goodwill. The recoverable amount of the cash-generating unit is determined to be €1,300,000, and the estimated fair value of its identifiable net assets is €1,200,000. Calculate the impairment loss.

Solution to 1:

Recoverable amount of unit	€1,300,000
Carrying amount of unit	1,400,000
Impairment loss	€100,000

The impairment loss of €100,000 is reported on the income statement, and the goodwill allocated to the cash-generating unit would be reduced by €100,000 to €200,000.

If the recoverable amount of the cash-generating unit had been €800,000 instead of €1,300,000, the impairment loss recognized would be €600,000. This would first be absorbed by the goodwill allocated to the unit (€300,000). Once this has been reduced to zero, the remaining amount of the impairment loss (€300,000) would then be allocated on a pro rata basis to the other non-cash assets within the unit.

EXAMPLE 10   Goodwill Impairment: US GAAP

1. A reporting unit of a US corporation (e.g., a division) has a fair value of $1,300,000 and a carrying value of $1,400,000 that includes recorded goodwill of $300,000. The estimated fair value of the identifiable net assets of the reporting unit at the impairment test date is $1,200,000. Calculate the impairment loss.

Solution to 1:
Step 1 – Determination of an Impairment Loss

Because the fair value of the reporting unit is less than its carrying book value, a potential impairment loss has been identified.

Fair value of unit: $1,300,000 < $1,400,000

Step 2 – Measurement of the Impairment Loss

Fair value of reporting unit	$1,300,000
Less: net assets	1,200,000
Implied goodwill	$100,000
Current carrying value of goodwill	$300,000
Less: implied goodwill	100,000
Impairment loss	$200,000

The impairment loss of $200,000 is reported on the income statement, and the goodwill allocated to the reporting unit would be reduced by $200,000 to $100,000.

If the fair value of the reporting unit was $800,000 (instead of $1,300,000), the implied goodwill would be a negative $400,000. In this case, the maximum amount of the impairment loss recognized would be $300,000, the carrying amount of goodwill.

9. FINANCIAL STATEMENT PRESENTATION

The presentation of consolidated financial statements is similar under IFRS and US GAAP. For example, selected financial statements for GlaxoSmithKline are shown in Exhibit 6 and Exhibit 7. GlaxoSmithKline is a leading pharmaceutical company headquartered in the United Kingdom.

The consolidated balance sheet in Exhibit 6 combines the operations of GlaxoSmithKline and its subsidiaries. The analyst can observe that in 2017 GlaxoSmithKline had investments in financial assets (other investments of £918,000,000 and liquid investments of £78,000,000), and investments in associates and joint ventures of £183,000,000. In 2017 GlaxoSmithKline did not acquire any additional companies, however, it made a number of small business disposals during the year for a net cash consideration of £342,000,000, including contingent consideration receivable of £86,000,000. In addition, during 2017 GlaxoSmithKline made cash investment of £15,000,000 in Associates and disposed of two associated for a cash consideration of £198,000,000.[26] The decrease in goodwill on the balance sheet reflects exchange adjustments

---

[26]Note 38: Acquisitions and Disposals, GlaxoSmithKline financial statements 2017.

recognized by GlaxoSmithKline due to the weakness of the functional currency of the parent (Pound Sterling). Note that GlaxoSmithKline has £6,172,000 in contingent consideration liabilities, which relate to future events such as development milestones or sales performance for acquired companies. Of the £6 billion total contingent liability, £1,076,000 is expected to be paid within one year in respect of the Novartis Vaccines business, which reached its sales milestone. The remaining contingent consideration, related to the acquisition of the Shionogi-ViiV Healthcare joint venture and Novartis Vaccines, is expected to be paid over a number of years.[27] The analyst can also note that GlaxoSmithKline is the parent company in a less than 100% acquisition. The minority interest of £3,557,000,000 in the equity section is the portion of the combined entity that accrues to non-controlling shareholders.

EXHIBIT 6: GlaxoSmithKline Consolidated Balance Sheet at 31 December 2017

	Notes	2017 £m	2016 £m
Non-current assets			
Property, plant and equipment	17	**10,860**	10,808
Goodwill	18	**5,734**	5,965
Other intangible assets	19	**17,562**	18,776
Investments in associates and joint ventures	20	**183**	263
Other investments	21	**918**	985
Deferred tax assets	14	**3,796**	4,374
Derivative financial instruments	42	**8**	—
Other non-current assets	22	**1,413**	1,199
Total non-current assets		**40,474**	42,370
Current assets			
Inventories	23	**5,557**	5,102
Current tax recoverable	14	**258**	226
Trade and other receivables	24	**6,000**	6,026
Derivative financial instruments	42	**68**	156
Liquid investments	31	**78**	89
Cash and cash equivalents	25	**3,833**	4,897
Assets held for sale	26	**113**	215
Total current assets		**15,907**	16,711
Total assets		**56,381**	59,081
Current liabilities			
Short-term borrowings	31	**(2,825)**	(4,129)
Contingent consideration liabilities	39	**(1,076)**	(561)
Trade and other payables	27	**(20,970)**	(11,964)

---

[27]The notes state that the amount included in the balance sheet is the present value of the expected contingent consideration payments, which have been discounted using a rate of 8.5%.

	Notes	2017 £m	2016 £m
Derivative financial instruments	42	**(74)**	(194)
Current tax payable	14	**(995)**	(1,305)
Short-term provisions	29	**(629)**	(848)
Total current liabilities		**(26,569)**	(19,001)
Non-current liabilities			
Long-term borrowings	31	**(14,264)**	(14,661)
Corporation tax payable	14	**(411)**	—
Deferred tax liabilities	14	**(1,396)**	(1,934)
Pensions and other post-employment benefits	28	**(3,539)**	(4,090)
Other provisions	29	**(636)**	(652)
Contingent consideration liabilities	39	**(5,096)**	(5,335)
Other non-current liabilities	30	**(981)**	(8,445)
Total non-current liabilities		**(26,323)**	(35,117)
Total liabilities		**(52,892)**	(54,118)
Net assets		**3,489**	4,963
Equity			
Share capital	33	**1,343**	1,342
Share premium account	33	**3,019**	2,954
Retained earnings	34	**(6,477)**	(5,392)
Other reserves	34	**2,047**	2,220
Shareholders' equity		**(68)**	1,124
Non-controlling interests		**3,557**	3,839
Total equity		**3,489**	4,963

The consolidated income statement for GlaxoSmithKline is presented in Exhibit 7. IFRS and US GAAP have similar formats for consolidated income statements. Each line item (e.g., turnover [sales], cost of sales, etc.) includes 100% of the parent and the subsidiary transactions after eliminating any **upstream** (subsidiary sells to parent) or **downstream** (parent sells to subsidiary) intercompany transactions. The portion of income accruing to non-controlling shareholders is presented as a separate line item on the consolidated income statement. Note that net income would be the same under IFRS and US GAAP.[28] The analyst will need to make adjustments for any analysis comparing specific line items that might differ between IFRS and US GAAP.

---

[28]It is possible, however, for differences to arise through the application of different accounting rules (e.g., valuation of fixed assets).

EXHIBIT 7: GlaxoSmithKline Consolidated Income Statement for the Year Ended 31 December 2017

	Notes	2017 Total £m	2016 £m	2015 £m
Turnover	6	**30,186**	27,889	23,923
Cost of sales		**(10,342)**	(9,290)	(8,853)
Gross profit		**19,844**	18,599	15,070
Selling, general and administration		**(9,672)**	(9,366)	(9,232)
Research and development		**(4,476)**	(3,628)	(3,560)
Royalty income		**356**	398	329
Other operating income	7	**(1,965)**	(3,405)	7,715
Operating profit	8	**4,087**	2,598	10,322
Finance income	11	**65**	72	104
Finance costs	12	**(734)**	(736)	(757)
Profit on disposal of interests in Associates		**95**	—	843
Share of after tax profits of associates and joint ventures	13	**13**	5	14
Profit before taxation		**3,525**	1,939	10,526
Taxation	14	**(1,356)**	(877)	(2,154)
Profit after taxation for the year		**2,169**	1,062	8,372
Profit/(loss) attributable to non-controlling interests		**637**	150	(50)
Profit attributable to shareholders		**1,532**	912	8,472
		2,169	1,062	8,372
Basic earnings per share (pence)	15	**31.4p**	18.8p	174.3p
Diluted earnings per share (pence)	15	**31.0p**	18.6p	172.3p

10. VARIABLE INTEREST AND SPECIAL PURPOSE ENTITIES

Special purpose entities (SPEs) are enterprises that are created to accommodate specific needs of the sponsoring entity.[29] The sponsoring entity (on whose behalf the SPE is created) frequently transfers assets to the SPE, obtains the right to use assets held by the SPE, or performs services for the SPE, while other parties (capital providers) provide funding to the SPE. SPEs can be a legitimate financing mechanism for a company to segregate certain activities and thereby reduce risk. SPEs may take the form of a limited liability company (corporation), trust, partnership, or unincorporated entity. They are often created with legal

---

[29]The term "special purpose entity" is used by IFRS and "variable interest entity" and "special purpose entity" is used by US GAAP.

arrangements that impose strict and sometimes permanent limits on the decision-making powers of their governing board or management.

Beneficial interest in an SPE may take the form of a debt instrument, an equity instrument, a participation right, or a residual interest in a lease. Some beneficial interests may simply provide the holder with a fixed or stated rate of return, while beneficial interests give the holder the rights or the access to future economic benefits of the SPE's activities. In most cases, the creator/sponsor of the entity retains a significant beneficial interest in the SPE even though it may own little or none of the SPE's voting equity.

In the past, sponsors were able to avoid consolidating SPEs on their financial statements because they did not have "control" (i.e., own a majority of the voting interest) of the SPE. SPEs were structured so that the sponsoring company had financial control over their assets or operating activities, while third parties held the majority of the voting interest in the SPE.

These outside equity participants often funded their investments in the SPE with debt that was either directly or indirectly guaranteed by the sponsoring companies. The sponsoring companies, in turn, were able to avoid the disclosure of many of these guarantees as well as their economic significance. In addition, many sponsoring companies created SPEs to facilitate the transfer of assets and liabilities from their own balance sheets. As a result, they were able to recognize large amounts of revenue and gains, because these transactions were accounted for as sales. By avoiding consolidation, sponsoring companies did not have to report the assets and the liabilities of the SPE; financial performance as measured by the unconsolidated financial statements was potentially misleading. The benefit to the sponsoring company was improved asset turnover, lower operating and financial leverage metrics, and higher profitability.

Enron, for example, used SPEs to obtain off-balance-sheet financing and artificially improve its financial performance. Its subsequent collapse was partly attributable to its guarantee of the debt of the SPEs it had created.

To address the accounting issues arising from the misuse and abuse of SPEs, the IASB and the FASB worked to improve the consolidation models to take into account financial arrangements where parties other than the holders of the majority of the voting interests exercise financial control over another entity. IFRS 10, *Consolidated Financial Statements*, revised the definition of control to encompass many special purpose entities. Special purpose entities involved in a structured financial transaction will require an evaluation of the purpose, design, and risks.

In developing new accounting standards to address this consolidation issue, the FASB used the more general term variable interest entity (VIE) to more broadly define an entity that is financially controlled by one or more parties that do not hold a majority voting interest. Therefore, under US GAAP, a VIE includes other entities besides SPEs. FASB ASC Topic 810 [*Consolidation*] provides guidance for US GAAP, which classifies special purpose entities as variable interest entities if:

1. total equity at risk is insufficient to finance activities without financial support from other parties, or
2. equity investors lack any one of the following:

    a. the ability to make decisions;
    b. the obligation to absorb losses; or
    c. the right to receive returns.

Common examples of variable interests are entities created to lease real estate or other property, entities created for the securitization of financial assets, or entities created for research and development activity.

Under FASB ASC Topic 810 [*Consolidation*], the primary beneficiary of a VIE must consolidate it as a subsidiary regardless of how much of an equity investment the beneficiary has in the VIE. The primary beneficiary (which is often the sponsor) is the entity that is expected to absorb the majority of the VIE's expected losses, receive the majority of the VIE's residual returns, or both. If one entity will absorb a majority of the VIE's expected losses and another unrelated entity will receive a majority of the VIE's expected residual returns, the entity absorbing a majority of the losses must consolidate the VIE. If there are non-controlling interests in the VIE, these would also be shown in the consolidated balance sheet and consolidated income statement of the primary beneficiary. ASC Topic 810 also requires entities to disclose information about their relationships with VIEs, even if they are not considered the primary beneficiary.

10.1. Securitization of Assets

Example 11 shows the effects of securitizing assets on companies' balance sheets.

EXAMPLE 11   Receivables Securitization

Odena, a (fictional) Italian auto manufacturer, wants to raise €55M in capital by borrowing against its financial receivables. To accomplish this objective, Odena can choose between two alternatives:

1. Borrow directly against the receivables; or
2. Create a special purpose entity, invest €5M in the SPE, have the SPE borrow €55M, and then use the funds to purchase €60M of receivables from Odena.

Using the financial statement information provided below, describe the effect of each alternative on Odena, assuming that Odena meets the definition of control and will consolidate the SPE.

Odena Balance Sheet

Cash	€30,000,000
Accounts receivable	60,000,000
Other assets	40,000,000
Total assets	€130,000,000
Current liabilities	€27,000,000
Noncurrent liabilities	20,000,000
Total liabilities	€47,000,000
Shareholder equity	€83,000,000
Total liabilities and equity	€130,000,000

Alternative 1:

Odena's cash will increase by €55M (to €85M) and its debt will increase by €55M (to €75M). Its sales and net income will not change.

Odena: Alternative 1 Balance Sheet

Cash	€85,000,000
Accounts receivable	60,000,000
Other assets	40,000,000
Total assets	€185,000,000
Current liabilities	€27,000,000
Noncurrent liabilities	75,000,000
Total liabilities	€102,000,000
Shareholder equity	€83,000,000
Total liabilities and equity	€185,000,000

Alternative 2:

Odena's accounts receivable will decrease by €60M and its cash will increase by €55 (it invests €5M in cash in the SPE). However, if Odena is able to sell the receivables to the SPE for more than their carrying value (for example, €65), it would also report a gain on the sale in its profit and loss. Equally important, the SPE may be able to borrow the funds at a lower rate than Odena, since they are bankruptcy remote from Odena (i.e., out of reach of Odena's creditors), and the lenders to the SPE are the claimants on its assets (i.e., the purchased receivables).

SPE Balance Sheet

Accounts receivable	€60,000,000
Total assets	€60,000,000
Long-term debt	€55,000,000
Equity	5,000,000
Total liabilities and equity	€60,000,000

Because Odena consolidates the SPE, its financial balance sheet would look like the following:

Odena: Alternative 2 Consolidated Balance Sheet

Cash	€85,000,000
Accounts receivable	60,000,000
Other assets	40,000,000
Total assets	€185,000,000
Current liabilities	€27,000,000

Noncurrent liabilities	75,000,000
Total liabilities	€102,000,000
Shareholder equity	€83,000,000
Total liabilities and equity	€185,000,000

Therefore, the consolidated balance sheet of Odena would look exactly the same as if it borrowed directly against the receivables. In addition, as a result of the consolidation, the transfer (sale) of the receivables to the SPE would be reversed along with any gain Odena recognized on the sale.

11. ADDITIONAL ISSUES IN BUSINESS COMBINATIONS THAT IMPAIR COMPARABILITY

Accounting for business combinations is a complex topic. In addition to the basics covered so far in this chapter, we briefly mention some of the more common issues that impair comparability between IFRS and US GAAP.

11.1. Contingent Assets and Liabilities

Under IFRS, the cost of an acquisition is allocated to the fair value of assets, liabilities, and contingent liabilities. Contingent liabilities are recorded separately as part of the cost allocation process, provided that their fair values can be measured reliably. Subsequently, the contingent liability is measured at the higher of the amount initially recognized or the best estimate of the amount required to settle. As mentioned previously, GlaxoSmithKline had approximately £6 billion in contingent liabilities in relation to a number of purchases for the year ended 31 December 2017, with the notes to the financial statements further stating that the £6 billion was the expected value of the contingent consideration payments, discounted at an appropriate discount rate. Contingent assets are not recognized under IFRS.

Under US GAAP, contractual contingent assets and liabilities are recognized and recorded at their fair values at the time of acquisition. Non-contractual contingent assets and liabilities must also be recognized and recorded only if it is "more likely than not" they meet the definition of an asset or a liability at the acquisition date. Subsequently, a contingent liability is measured at the higher of the amount initially recognized or the best estimate of the amount of the loss. A contingent asset, however, is measured at the lower of the acquisition date fair value or the best estimate of the future settlement amount.

11.2. Contingent Consideration

Contingent consideration may be negotiated as part of the acquisition price. For example, the acquiring company (parent) may agree to pay additional money to the acquiree's (subsidiary's) former shareholders if certain agreed upon events occur. These can include achieving specified sales or profit levels for the acquiree and/or the combined entity. Under both IFRS and US GAAP, contingent consideration is initially measured at fair value. IFRS and US GAAP classify contingent consideration as an asset, liability, or equity. In subsequent periods, changes in the fair value of liabilities (and assets, in the case of US GAAP) are recognized in the consolidated income statement. Both IFRS and US GAAP do not remeasure equity classified contingent consideration; instead, settlement is accounted for within equity.

11.3. In-Process R&D

IFRS and US GAAP recognize in-process research and development acquired in a business combination as a separate intangible asset and measure it at fair value (if it can be measured reliably). In subsequent periods, this research and development is subject to amortization if successfully completed (a marketable product results) or to impairment if no product results or if the product is not technically and/or financially viable.

11.4. Restructuring Costs

IFRS and US GAAP do not recognize restructuring costs that are associated with the business combination as part of the cost of the acquisition. Instead, they are recognized as an expense in the periods the restructuring costs are incurred.

12. SUMMARY

Intercompany investments play a significant role in business activities and create significant challenges for the analyst in assessing company performance. Investments in other companies can take five basic forms: investments in financial assets, investments in associates, joint ventures, business combinations, and investments in special purpose and variable interest entities. Key concepts are as follows:

- Investments in financial assets are those in which the investor has no significant influence. They can be measured and reported as

    - Fair value through profit or loss.
    - Fair value through other comprehensive income.
    - Amortized cost.

    IFRS and US GAAP treat investments in financial assets in a similar manner.
- Investments in associates and joint ventures are those in which the investor has significant influence, but not control, over the investee's business activities. Because the investor can exert significant influence over financial and operating policy decisions, IFRS and US GAAP require the equity method of accounting because it provides a more objective basis for reporting investment income.

    - The equity method requires the investor to recognize income as earned rather than when dividends are received.
    - The equity investment is carried at cost, plus its share of post-acquisition income (after adjustments) less dividends received.
    - The equity investment is reported as a single line item on the balance sheet and on the income statement.

- IFRS and US GAAP accounting standards require the use of the acquisition method to account for business combinations. Fair value of the consideration given is the appropriate measurement for identifiable assets and liabilities acquired in the business combination.
- Goodwill is the difference between the acquisition value and the fair value of the target's identifiable net tangible and intangible assets. Because it is considered to have an indefinite life, it is not amortized. Instead, it is evaluated at least annually for impairment. Impairment losses are reported on the income statement. IFRS use a one-step approach to determine and measure the impairment loss, whereas US GAAP uses a two-step approach.
- If the acquiring company acquires less than 100%, non-controlling (minority) shareholders' interests are reported on the consolidated financial statements. IFRS allows the non-controlling interest to be measured at either its fair value (full goodwill) or at the non-controlling interest's proportionate share of the acquiree's identifiable net assets (partial goodwill). US GAAP requires the non-controlling interest to be measured at fair value (full goodwill).
- Consolidated financial statements are prepared in each reporting period.
- Special purpose entities (SPEs) and variable interest entities (VIEs) are required to be consolidated by the entity, which is expected to absorb the majority of the expected losses or receive the majority of expected residual benefits.

13. PRACTICE PROBLEMS

The following information relates to questions 1–6

Burton Howard, CFA, is an equity analyst with Maplewood Securities. Howard is preparing a research report on Confabulated Materials, SA, a publicly traded company based in France that complies with IFRS 9. As part of his analysis, Howard has assembled data gathered from the financial statement footnotes of Confabulated's 2018 Annual Report and from discussions with company management. Howard is concerned about the effect of this information on Confabulated's future earnings.

Information about Confabulated's investment portfolio for the years ended 31 December 2017 and 2018 is presented in Exhibit 1. As part of his research, Howard is considering the possible effect on reported income of Confabulated's accounting classification for fixed income investments.

EXHIBIT 1: Confabulated's Investment Portfolio (€ Thousands)

Characteristic	Bugle AG	Cathay Corp	Dumas SA
Classification	FVPL	FVOCI	Amortized cost
Cost*	€25,000	€40,000	€50,000
Market value, 31 December 2017	29,000	38,000	54,000
Market value, 31 December 2018	28,000	37,000	55,000

* All securities were acquired at par value.

In addition, Confabulated's annual report discusses a transaction under which receivables were securitized through a special purpose entity (SPE) for Confabulated's benefit.

1. The balance sheet carrying value of Confabulated's investment portfolio (in € thousands) at 31 December 2018 is *closest* to:
   A. 112,000.
   B. 115,000.
   C. 118,000.

2. The balance sheet carrying value of Confabulated's investment portfolio at 31 December 2018 would have been higher if which of the securities had been reclassified as FVPL security?
   A. Bugle.
   B. Cathay.
   C. Dumas.

3. Compared to Confabulated's reported interest income in 2018, if Dumas had been classified as FVPL, the interest income would have been:
   A. lower.
   B. the same.
   C. higher.

4. Compared to Confabulated's reported earnings before taxes in 2018, if Dumas had been classified as an FVPL security, the earnings before taxes (in € thousands) would have been:
   A. the same.
   B. €1,000 lower.
   C. €1,000 higher.

5. Confabulated's reported interest income would be lower if the cost was the same but the par value (in € thousands) of:
   A. Bugle was €28,000.
   B. Cathay was €37,000.
   C. Dumas was €55,000.

6. Confabulated's special purpose entity is *most likely* to be:
   A. held off-balance-sheet.
   B. consolidated on Confabulated's financial statements.
   C. consolidated on Confabulated's financial statements only if it is a "qualifying SPE."

The following information relates to questions 7–11

Cinnamon, Inc. is a diversified manufacturing company headquartered in the United Kingdom. It complies with IFRS. In 2017, Cinnamon held a 19 percent passive equity ownership interest in Cambridge Processing. In December 2017, Cinnamon announced that it would be increasing its ownership interest to 50 percent effective 1 January 2018 through a cash purchase. Cinnamon and Cambridge have no intercompany transactions.

Peter Lubbock, an analyst following both Cinnamon and Cambridge, is curious how the increased stake will affect Cinnamon's consolidated financial statements. He asks Cinnamon's CFO how the company will account for the investment, and is told that the decision has not yet been made. Lubbock decides to use his existing forecasts for both companies' financial statements to compare the outcomes of alternative accounting treatments.

Lubbock assembles abbreviated financial statement data for Cinnamon (Exhibit 1) and Cambridge (Exhibit 2) for this purpose.

EXHIBIT 1: Selected Financial Statement Information for Cinnamon, Inc. (£ Millions)

Year Ending 31 December	2017	2018*
Revenue	1,400	1,575
Operating income	126	142
Net income	62	69
31 December	**2017**	**2018***
Total assets	1,170	1,317
Shareholders' equity	616	685

* Estimates made prior to announcement of increased stake in Cambridge.

EXHIBIT 2: Selected Financial Statement Information for Cambridge Processing (£ Millions)

Year Ending 31 December	2017	2018*
Revenue	1,000	1,100
Operating income	80	88
Net income	40	44
Dividends paid	20	22
31 December	**2017**	**2018***
Total assets	800	836
Shareholders' equity	440	462

* Estimates made prior to announcement of increased stake by Cinnamon.

7. In 2018, if Cinnamon is deemed to have control over Cambridge, it will *most likely* account for its investment in Cambridge using:
   A. the equity method.
   B. the acquisition method.
   C. proportionate consolidation.

8. At 31 December 2018, Cinnamon's total shareholders' equity on its balance sheet would *most likely* be:
   A. highest if Cinnamon is deemed to have control of Cambridge.
   B. independent of the accounting method used for the investment in Cambridge.
   C. highest if Cinnamon is deemed to have significant influence over Cambridge.

9. In 2018, Cinnamon's net profit margin would be *highest* if:
   A. it is deemed to have control of Cambridge.
   B. it had not increased its stake in Cambridge.
   C. it is deemed to have significant influence over Cambridge.

10. At 31 December 2018, assuming control and recognition of goodwill, Cinnamon's reported debt to equity ratio will *most likely* be highest if it accounts for its investment in Cambridge using the:
   A. equity method.
   B. full goodwill method.
   C. partial goodwill method.

11. Compared to Cinnamon's operating margin in 2017, if it is deemed to have control of Cambridge, its operating margin in 2018 will *most likely* be:
   A. lower.
   B. higher.
   C. the same.

The following information relates to questions 12–16

Zimt, AG is a consumer products manufacturer headquartered in Austria. It complies with IFRS. In 2017, Zimt held a 10 percent passive stake in Oxbow Limited. In December 2017, Zimt announced that it would be increasing its ownership to 50 percent effective 1 January 2018.

Franz Gelblum, an analyst following both Zimt and Oxbow, is curious how the increased stake will affect Zimt's consolidated financial statements. Because Gelblum is uncertain how the company will account for the increased stake, he uses his existing forecasts for both companies' financial statements to compare various alternative outcomes.

Gelblum gathers abbreviated financial statement data for Zimt (Exhibit 1) and Oxbow (Exhibit 2) for this purpose.

EXHIBIT 1: Selected Financial Statement Estimates for Zimt AG (€ Millions)

Year ending 31 December	2017	2018*
Revenue	1,500	1,700
Operating income	135	153
Net income	66	75
31 December	2017	2018*
Total assets	1,254	1,421
Shareholders' equity	660	735

* Estimates made prior to announcement of increased stake in Oxbow.

EXHIBIT 2: Selected Financial Statement Estimates for Oxbow Limited (€ Millions)

Year ending 31 December	2017	2018*
Revenue	1,200	1,350
Operating income	120	135
Net income	60	68
Dividends paid	20	22

31 December	2017	2018*
Total assets	1,200	1,283
Shareholders' equity	660	706

* Estimates made prior to announcement of increased stake by Zimt.

12. At 31 December 2018, Zimt's total assets balance would *most likely* be:
    A. highest if Zimt is deemed to have control of Oxbow.
    B. highest if Zimt is deemed to have significant influence over Oxbow.
    C. unaffected by the accounting method used for the investment in Oxbow.

13. Based on Gelblum's estimates, if Zimt is deemed to have significant influence over Oxbow, its 2018 net income (in € millions) would be *closest* to:
    A. €75.
    B. €109.
    C. €143.

14. Based on Gelblum's estimates, if Zimt is deemed to have joint control of Oxbow, and Zimt uses the proportionate consolidation method, its 31 December 2018 total liabilities (in € millions) will *most likely* be *closest* to:
    A. €686.
    B. €975.
    C. €1,263.

15. Based on Gelblum's estimates, if Zimt is deemed to have control over Oxbow, its 2018 consolidated sales (in € millions) will be *closest* to:
    A. €1,700.
    B. €2,375.
    C. €3,050.

16. Based on Gelblum's estimates, and holding the size of Zimt's ownership stake in Oxbow constant, Zimt's net income in 2018 will *most likely* be:
    A. highest if Zimt is deemed to have control of Oxbow.
    B. highest if Zimt is deemed to have significant influence over Oxbow.
    C. independent of the accounting method used for the investment in Oxbow.

The following information relates to questions 17–22

BetterCare Hospitals, Inc. operates a chain of hospitals throughout the United States. The company has been expanding by acquiring local hospitals. Its largest acquisition, that of Statewide Medical, was made in 2001 under the pooling of interests method. BetterCare complies with US GAAP.

BetterCare is currently forming a 50/50 joint venture with Supreme Healthcare under which the companies will share control of several hospitals. BetterCare plans to use the equity method to account for the joint venture. Supreme Healthcare complies with IFRS and will use the proportionate consolidation method to account for the joint venture.

Erik Ohalin is an equity analyst who covers both companies. He has estimated the joint venture's financial information for 2018 in order to prepare his estimates of each company's earnings and financial performance. This information is presented in Exhibit 1.

EXHIBIT 1: Selected Financial Statement Forecasts for Joint Venture ($ Millions)

Year ending 31 December	2018
Revenue	1,430
Operating income	128
Net income	62
31 December	**2018**
Total assets	1,500
Shareholders' equity	740

Supreme Healthcare recently announced it had formed a special purpose entity through which it plans to sell up to $100 million of its accounts receivable. Supreme Healthcare has no voting interest in the SPE, but it is expected to absorb any losses that it may incur. Ohalin wants to estimate the impact this will have on Supreme Healthcare's consolidated financial statements.

17. Compared to accounting principles currently in use, the pooling method BetterCare used for its Statewide Medical acquisition has *most likely* caused its reported:
    A. revenue to be higher.
    B. total equity to be lower.
    C. total assets to be higher.

18. Based on Ohalin's estimates, the amount of joint venture revenue (in $ millions) included on BetterCare's consolidated 2018 financial statements should be *closest* to:
    A. $0.
    B. $715.
    C. $1,430.

19. Based on Ohalin's estimates, the amount of joint venture net income included on the consolidated financial statements of each venturer will *most likely* be:
    A. higher for BetterCare.
    B. higher for Supreme Healthcare.
    C. the same for both BetterCare and Supreme Healthcare.

20. Based on Ohalin's estimates, the amount of the joint venture's 31 December 2018 total assets (in $ millions) that will be included on Supreme Healthcare's consolidated financial statements will be *closest* to:
   A. $0.
   B. $750.
   C. $1,500.

21. Based on Ohalin's estimates, the amount of joint venture shareholders' equity at 31 December 2018 included on the consolidated financial statements of each venturer will *most likely* be:
   A. higher for BetterCare.
   B. higher for Supreme Healthcare.
   C. the same for both BetterCare and Supreme Healthcare.

22. If Supreme Healthcare sells its receivables to the SPE, its consolidated financial results will *least likely* show:
   A. a higher revenue for 2018.
   B. the same cash balance at 31 December 2018.
   C. the same accounts receivable balance at 31 December 2018.

The following information relates to questions 23–29

John Thronen is an analyst in the research department of an international securities firm. Thronen is preparing a research report on Topmaker, Inc., a publicly-traded company that complies with IFRS. Thronen reviews two of Topmaker's recent transactions relating to investments in Blanco Co. and Rainer Co.

Investment in Blanca Co.

On 1 January 2016, Topmaker invested $11 million in Blanca Co. debt securities (with a 5.0% stated coupon rate on par value, payable each 31 December). The par value of the securities is $10 million, and the market interest rate in effect when the bonds were purchased was 4.0%. Topmaker designates the investment as held-to-maturity. On 31 December 2016, the fair value of the securities was $12 million.

Blanca Co. plans to raise $40 million in capital by borrowing against its financial receivables. Blanca plans to create a special purpose entity (SPE), invest $10 million in the SPE, have the SPE borrow $40 million, and then use the total funds to purchase $50 million of receivables from Blanca. Blanca meets the definition of control and plans to consolidate the SPE. Blanca's current balance sheet is presented in Exhibit 1.

EXHIBIT 1: Blanca Co. Balance Sheet at 31 December 2016 ($ millions)

Cash	20	Current liabilities	25
Accounts receivable	50	Noncurrent liabilities	30
Other assets	30	Shareholders' equity	45
Total assets	**100**	**Total liabilities and equity**	**100**

Investment in Rainer Co.

On 1 January 2016, Topmaker acquired a 15% equity interest with voting power in Rainer Co. for $300 million. Exhibit 2 presents selected financial information for Rainer on the acquisition date. Thronen notes that the plant and equipment are depreciated on a straight-line basis and have 10 years of remaining life. Topmaker has representation on Rainer's board of directors and participates in the associate's policy-making process.

EXHIBIT 2: Selected Financial Data for Rainer Co., 1 January 2018 (Acquisition Date) ($ millions)

	Book Value	Fair Value
Current assets	270	270
Plant and equipment	2,900	3,160
Total assets	3,170	3,430
Liabilities	1,830	1,830
Net assets	1,340	1,600

Thronen notes that, for fiscal year 2018, Rainer reported total revenue of $1,740 million and net income of $360 million, and paid dividends of $220 million.

Thronen is concerned about possible goodwill impairment for Topmaker due to expected changes in the industry effective at the end of 2017. He calculates the impairment loss based on selected data from the projected consolidated balance sheet data presented in Exhibit 3, assuming that the cash-generating unit and reporting unit of Topmaker are the same.

EXHIBIT 3: Selected Financial Data for Topmaker, Inc., Estimated Year Ending 31 December 2017 ($ millions)

Carrying value of cash-generating unit/reporting unit	15,200
Recoverable amount of cash-generating unit/reporting unit	14,900
Fair value of reporting unit	14,800
Identifiable net assets	14,400
Goodwill	520

Finally, Topmaker announces its plan to increase its ownership interest in Rainer to 80% effective 1 January 2018 and will account for the investment in Rainer using the partial goodwill method. Thronen estimates that the fair market value of the Rainer's shares on the expected date of exchange is $2 billion with the identifiable assets valued at $1.5 billion.

23. The carrying value of Topmaker's investment in Blanca's debt securities reported on the balance sheet at 31 December 2016 is:
   A. $10.94 million.
   B. $11.00 million.
   C. $12.00 million.

24. Based on Exhibit 1 and Blanca's plans to borrow against its financial receivables, the new consolidated balance sheet will show total assets of:
    A. $50 million.
    B. $140 million.
    C. $150 million.

25. Based on Exhibit 2, Topmaker's investment in Rainer resulted in goodwill of:
    A. $21 million.
    B. $60 million.
    C. $99 million.

26. Topmaker's influence on Rainer's business activities can be *best* described as:
    A. significant.
    B. controlling.
    C. shared control.

27. Using only the information from Exhibit 2, the carrying value of Topmaker's investment in Rainer at the end of 2016 is *closest* to:
    A. $282 million.
    B. $317 million.
    C. $321 million.

28. Based on Exhibit 3, Topmaker's impairment loss under IFRS is:
    A. $120 million.
    B. $300 million.
    C. $400 million.

29. Based on Thronen's value estimates on the acquisition date of 1 January 2018, the estimated value of the minority interest related to Rainer will be:
    A. $300 million.
    B. $400 million.
    C. $500 million.

The following information relates to questions 30–35

Percy Byron, CFA, is an equity analyst with a UK-based investment firm. One firm Byron follows is NinMount PLC, a UK-based company. On 31 December 2018, NinMount paid £320 million to purchase a 50 percent stake in Boswell Company. The excess of the purchase price over the fair value of Boswell's net assets was attributable to previously unrecorded licenses. These licenses were estimated to have an economic life of six years. The fair value of Boswell's assets and liabilities other than licenses was equal to their recorded book values. NinMount and Boswell both use the pound sterling as their reporting currency and prepare their financial statements in accordance with IFRS.

Byron is concerned whether the investment should affect his "buy" rating on NinMount common stock. He knows NinMount could choose one of several accounting methods to report the results of its investment, but NinMount has not announced which method it will use. Byron forecasts that both companies' 2019 financial results (excluding any merger accounting adjustments) will be identical to those of 2018.

NinMount's and Boswell's condensed income statements for the year ended 31 December 2018, and condensed balance sheets at 31 December 2018, are presented in Exhibits 1 and 2, respectively.

EXHIBIT 1: NinMount PLC and Boswell Company Income Statements for the Year Ended 31 December 2018 (£ millions)

	NinMount	Boswell
Net sales	950	510
Cost of goods sold	(495)	(305)
Selling expenses	(50)	(15)
Administrative expenses	(136)	(49)
Depreciation & amortization expense	(102)	(92)
Interest expense	(42)	(32)
Income before taxes	125	17
Income tax expense	(50)	(7)
Net income	75	10

EXHIBIT 2: NinMount PLC and Boswell Company Balance Sheets at 31 December 2018 (£ millions)

	NinMount	Boswell
Cash	50	20
Receivables—net	70	45
Inventory	130	75
Total current assets	250	140
Property, plant, & equipment—net	1,570	930
Investment in Boswell	320	—
Total assets	2,140	1,070
Current liabilities	110	90
Long-term debt	600	400
Total liabilities	710	490
Common stock	850	535
Retained earnings	580	45
Total equity	1,430	580
Total liabilities and equity	2,140	1,070

Note: Balance sheets reflect the purchase price paid by NinMount, but do not yet consider the impact of the accounting method choice.

30. NinMount's current ratio on 31 December 2018 *most likely* will be highest if the results of the acquisition are reported using:
    A. the equity method.
    B. consolidation with full goodwill.
    C. consolidation with partial goodwill.

31. NinMount's long-term debt to equity ratio on 31 December 2018 *most likely* will be lowest if the results of the acquisition are reported using:
    A. the equity method.
    B. consolidation with full goodwill.
    C. consolidation with partial goodwill.

32. Based on Byron's forecast, if NinMount deems it has acquired control of Boswell, NinMount's consolidated 2019 depreciation and amortization expense (in £ millions) will be *closest* to:
    A. 102.
    B. 148.
    C. 204.

33. Based on Byron's forecast, NinMount's net profit margin for 2019 *most likely* will be highest if the results of the acquisition are reported using:
    A. the equity method.
    B. consolidation with full goodwill.
    C. consolidation with partial goodwill.

34. Based on Byron's forecast, NinMount's 2019 return on beginning equity *most likely* will be the same under:
    A. either of the consolidations, but different under the equity method.
    B. the equity method, consolidation with full goodwill, and consolidation with partial goodwill.
    C. none of the equity method, consolidation with full goodwill, or consolidation with partial goodwill.

35. Based on Byron's forecast, NinMount's 2019 total asset turnover ratio on beginning assets under the equity method is *most likely*:
    A. lower than if the results are reported using consolidation.
    B. the same as if the results are reported using consolidation.
    C. higher than if the results are reported using consolidation.

GLOSSARY

Abandonment option   The option to terminate an investment at some future time if the financial results are disappointing.

Accredited investors   Those who are considered sophisticated enough to take greater risks and to have a reduced need for regulatory oversight and protection. In some jurisdictions, these investors are referred to as professional, eligible, or qualified investors.

Acquisition   When one company, the acquirer, purchases from the seller most or all of another company's (the target) shares to gain control of either an entire company, a segment of another company, or a specific group of assets in exchange for cash, stock, or the assumption of liabilities, alone or in combination. Once an acquisition is complete, the acquirer and target merge into a single entity and consolidate management, operations, and resources.

Activity ratios   Ratios that measure how well a company is managing key current assets and working capital over time.

Affiliate marketing   The generation of commission revenues for sales generated on other's websites.

Agency costs   Costs associated with conflicts of interest between principals and agents when a company is managed by non-owners. Agency costs result from the inherent conflicts of interest between managers and debtholders (referred to as agency costs of debt) and between managers and shareholders (referred to as agency costs of equity).

Aggregators   Similar to marketplaces, but the aggregator re-markets products and services under its own brand.

Asset beta   The unlevered beta, which reflects the business risk of the assets; the asset's systematic risk.

Asset-light business models   Business models that minimize required capital investment by shifting the ownership of high-cost assets to other firms.

Assignment of accounts receivable   The use of accounts receivable as collateral for a loan.

Asymmetric information   Also known as information asymmetry. The differential of information between corporate insiders and outsiders regarding the company's performance and prospects. Managers typically have more information about the company's performance and prospects than owners and creditors.

Auction/reverse auction models   Pricing models that establish prices through bidding (by sellers in the case of reverse auctions).

Balance sheet restructuring   Altering the composition of the balance sheet by either shifting the asset composition, changing the capital structure, or both.

Bond yield plus risk premium approach   An estimate of the cost of common equity that is produced by summing the before-tax cost of debt and a risk premium that captures the additional yield on a company's stock relative to its bonds. The additional yield is often estimated using historical spreads between bond yields and stock yields.

Bond yield plus risk premium (BYPRP) approach   An estimate of the cost of common equity that is produced by summing the before-tax cost of debt and a risk premium that captures the additional yield on a company's stock relative to its bonds.

Bonus issue of shares   A type of dividend in which a company distributes additional shares of its common stock to shareholders instead of cash.

Borrowed capital (debt)   Money that is lent by debtholders to a company.

Bottom-up approach   With respect to forecasting, an approach that usually begins at the level of the individual company or a unit within the company.

Breakeven point   Represents the price of the underlying in a derivative contract in which the profit to both counterparties would be zero.

Bundling   A pricing approach that refers to combining multiple products or services so that customers are incentivized or required to buy them together.

Business risk   The risk that the firm's operating results will fall short of expectations, independently of how the business is financed.

Buyback   A transaction in which a company buys back its own shares. Unlike stock dividends and stock splits, share repurchases use corporate cash.

Canceled shares   Shares that were issued, subsequently repurchased by the company, and then retired (cannot be reissued).

Cannibalization   Cannibalization occurs when an investment takes customers and sales away from another part of the company.

Capital allocation   The process that companies use for decision making on capital investments—those projects with a life of one year or longer.

Capital asset pricing model (CAPM)   A single factor model such that excess returns on a stock are a function of the returns on a market index.

Capital investment risk   The risk of sub-optimal investment by a firm.

Capital light   Also known as asset light. Capital-light businesses require little incremental investment in fixed assets or working capital to enable revenue growth.

Capital providers   Investors who provide capital proceeds to a company in return for holding the corporation's debt or equity securities. Equity investors are referred to as shareholders or owners, while debt investors are referred to as bondholders or debtholders.

Capital structure   The mix of debt and equity that a company uses to finance its business; a company's specific mix of long-term financing.

Cartel   Participants in collusive agreements that are made openly and formally.

Collaterals   Assets or financial guarantees underlying a debt obligation that are above and beyond the issuer's promise to pay.

Committed (regular) lines of credit   A bank commitment to extend credit; the commitment is considered a short-term liability and is usually in effect for 364 days (one day short of a full year).

Comparable company   A company that has similar business risk, usually in the same industry and preferably with a single line of business.

Competitive risk   The risk of a loss of market share or pricing power to competitors.

Complements   Goods that tend to be used together; technically, two goods whose cross-price elasticity of demand is negative.

Component cost of capital   The rate of return required by suppliers of capital for an individual source of a company's funding, such as debt or equity.

Concentrated ownership   Ownership structure consisting of an individual shareholder or a group (controlling shareholders) with the ability to exercise control over the corporation.

Confirmation bias   A belief perseverance bias in which people tend to look for and notice what confirms their beliefs, to ignore or undervalue what contradicts their beliefs, and to misinterpret information as support for their beliefs.

Conglomerate discount   When an issuer is trading at a valuation lower than the sum of its parts, which is generally the result of diseconomies of scale or scope or the result of the capital markets having overlooked the business and its prospects.

Constant dividend payout ratio policy   A policy in which a constant percentage of net income is paid out in dividends.

Consumer surplus   The difference between the value that a consumer places on units purchased and the amount of money that was required to pay for them.

Contribution margin The amount available for fixed costs and profit after paying variable costs; revenue minus variable costs.

Controlling shareholders A particular shareholder or group of shareholders holding a percentage of shares that gives them significant voting power.

Conventional cash flow pattern A conventional cash flow pattern is one with an initial outflow followed by a series of inflows.

Corporate governance The system of internal checks, balances, and incentives that exists to manage conflicting interests among a company's stakeholders.

Cost-based pricing Pricing set primarily by reference to the firm's costs.

Cost of capital (opportunity cost of funds) The cost of financing to a company; the rate of return that suppliers of capital require as compensation for their contribution of capital.

Cost of debt The required return on debt financing to a company, such as when it issues a bond, takes out a bank loan, or leases an asset through a finance lease.

Cost of equity The return required by equity investors to compensate for both the time value of money and the risk. Also referred to as the required rate of return on common stock or the required return on equity.

Cost of preferred stock The cost to a company of issuing preferred stock; the dividend yield that a company must commit to pay preferred stockholders.

Cost restructuring Actions to reduce costs by improving operational efficiency and profitability, often to raise margins to a historical level or to those of comparable industry peers.

Cost structure The mix of a company's variable costs and fixed costs.

Country risk premium (CRP) The additional return required by investors to compensate for the risk associated with investing in a foreign country relative to the investor's domestic market.

Country risk rating (CRR) The rating of a country based on many risk factors, including economic prosperity, political risk, and ESG risk.

Cournot assumption Assumption in which each firm determines its profit-maximizing production level assuming that the other firms' output will not change.

Covenants The terms and conditions of lending agreements that the issuer must comply with; they specify the actions that an issuer is obligated to perform (affirmative covenant) or prohibited from performing (negative covenant).

Credit spread The compensation for the risk inherent in a company's debt security.

Creditworthiness The perceived willingness and ability of the borrower to pay its debt obligations in a timely manner; it represents the ability of a company to withstand adverse impacts on its cash flows.

Cross-price elasticity of demand The percentage change in quantity demanded for a given percentage change in the price of another good; the responsiveness of the demand for Product A that is associated with the change in price of Product B.

Crowdsourcing A business model that enables users to contribute directly to a product, service, or online content.

Cumulative preferred stock Preferred stock that requires that the dividends be paid in full to preferred stock owners for any missed dividends prior to any payment of dividends to common stock owners.

Cumulative voting A voting process whereby shareholders can accumulate and vote all their shares for a single candidate in an election, as opposed to having to allocate their voting rights evenly among all candidates.

Customer concentration risk The risk associated with sales dependent on a few customers.

Debt-rating approach A method for estimating a company's before-tax cost of debt based on the yield on comparably rated bonds for maturities that closely match that of the company's existing debt.

Debt tax shield The tax benefit from interest paid on debt being tax-deductible from income, equal to the marginal tax rate multiplied by the value of the debt.

Degree of financial leverage (DFL) The ratio of the percentage change in net income to the percentage change in operating income; the sensitivity of the cash flows available to owners when operating income changes.

Degree of operating leverage (DOL) The ratio of the percentage change in operating income to the percentage change in units sold; the sensitivity of operating income to changes in units sold.

Degree of total leverage The ratio of the percentage change in net income to the percentage change in units sold; the sensitivity of the cash flows to owners to changes in the number of units produced and sold.

Direct listing (DL) A process whereby a company becomes public by listing on an exchange and shares are sold by existing shareholders.

Direct sales A sales strategy used by businesses to sell directly to the end customer, which bypasses ("disintermediates") the distributor or retailer.

Dispersed ownership Ownership structure consisting of many shareholders, none of which has the ability to individually exercise control over the corporation.

Disruption When new or potential competitors using new technology or business models take market share rather than known or established competitors using established business models.

Divestiture When a seller sells a company, segment of a company, or group of assets to an acquirer. Once complete, control of the target is transferred to the acquirer.

Dividend A distribution paid to shareholders based on the number of shares owned.

Dividend coverage ratio The ratio of net income to dividends.

Dividend discount model (DDM) The model of the value of stock that is the present value of all future dividends, discounted at the required return on equity.

Dividend imputation tax system A taxation system that effectively assures corporate profits distributed as dividends are taxed just once and at the shareholder's tax rate.

Dividend payout ratio The ratio of cash dividends paid to earnings for a period.

Dividend policy The strategy a company follows with regard to the amount and timing of dividend payments.

Dividend recapitalization Restructuring the mix of debt and equity, typically shifting the capital structure from equity to debt through debt-financed share repurchases. The objective is to reduce the issuer's weighted average cost of capital by replacing expensive equity with cheaper debt by purchasing equity from shareholders using newly issued debt.

Dividend yield Annual dividends per share divided by share price.

Double taxation system Corporate earnings are taxed twice when paid out as dividends. First, corporate pretax earnings are taxed regardless of whether they will be distributed as dividends or retained at the corporate level. Second, dividends are taxed again at the individual shareholder level.

Downstream A transaction between two related companies, an investor company (or a parent company) and an associate company (or a subsidiary) such that the investor company records a profit on its income statement. An example is a sale of inventory by the investor company to the associate or by a parent to a subsidiary company.

Drag on liquidity When receipts (inflows) lag, creating pressure from the decreased available funds.

Drop shipping Often used in e-commerce, when goods are delivered directly from manufacturer to end customer, enabling the marketer to avoid taking the goods into inventory.

Dual-class shares Shares that grant one share class superior or even sole voting rights, whereas the other share class has inferior or no voting rights.

Dynamic pricing A pricing approach that charges different prices at different times. Specific examples include off-peak pricing, "surge" pricing, and "congestion" pricing.

Economic costs All the remuneration needed to keep a productive resource in its current employment or to acquire the resource for productive use; the sum of total accounting costs and implicit opportunity costs.

Economic profit Equal to accounting profit less the implicit opportunity costs not included in total accounting costs; the difference between total revenue (TR) and total cost (TC). Also called *abnormal profit* or *supernormal profit*.

Economies of scale A situation in which average costs per unit of good or service produced fall as volume rises. In reference to mergers, the savings achieved through the consolidation of operations and elimination of duplicate resources.

Elasticity The percentage change in one variable for a percentage change in another variable; a general measure of how sensitive one variable is to a change in the value of another variable.

Engagement/active ownership An ESG investment approach that uses shareholder power to influence corporate behavior through direct corporate engagement (i.e., communicating with senior management and/or boards of companies), filing or co-filing shareholder proposals, and proxy voting directed by ESG guidelines.

Equity investment A company purchasing another company's equity but less than 50% of its shares. The two companies maintain their independence, but the investor company has investment exposure to the investee and, in some cases depending on the size of the investment, can have representation on the investee's board of directors to influence operations.

Equity risk premium The expected return on equities minus the risk-free rate; the premium that investors demand for investing in equities.

Equity risk premium (ERP) Compensation for bearing market risk.

ESG An acronym that encompasses environmental, social, and governance factors.

ESG integration An ESG investment approach that focuses on systematic consideration of material ESG factors in asset allocation, security selection, and portfolio construction decisions for the purpose of achieving the product's stated investment objectives. Used interchangeably with **ESG investing**.

ESG risk The risk associated with environmental, social, and governance–related factors.

Ex-dividend Trading ex-dividend refers to shares that no longer carry the right to the next dividend payment.

Ex-dividend date The first date that a share trades without (i.e., "ex") the right to receive the declared dividend for the period.

Execution risk The risk that management will be unable to do what is needed to deliver the expected results.

Externality An effect of a market transaction that is borne by parties other than those who transacted.

Extra dividend A dividend paid by a company that does not pay dividends on a regular schedule, or a dividend that supplements regular cash dividends with an extra payment.

Factor betas An asset's sensitivity to a particular factor; a measure of the response of return to each unit of increase in a factor, holding all other factors constant.

Factoring arrangement When a company sells its accounts receivable to a lender (known as a factor) who assumes responsibility for the credit-granting and collection process.

Factor risk premiums The expected return in excess of the risk-free rate for a portfolio with a sensitivity of 1 to one factor and a sensitivity of 0 to all other factors. Also called factor price.

Fama–French models Factor models that explain the drivers of returns related to three, four, or five factors.

Finance lease A type of lease that is more akin to the purchase or sale of the underlying asset.

Finance (or capital) lease A lease that is viewed as a financing arrangement.

Financial distress Heightened uncertainty regarding a company's ability to meet its various obligations because of diminished earnings power or actual current losses.

Financial leverage The use of fixed sources of capital, such as debt, relative to sources without fixed costs, such as equity.

Financial risk The risk arising from a company's capital structure and, specifically, from the level of debt and debt-like obligations.

First-degree price discrimination Where a monopolist is able to charge each customer the highest price the customer is willing to pay.

Fixed costs Costs that remain at the same level regardless of a company's level of production and sales.

Fixed price tender offer Offer made by a company to repurchase a specific number of shares at a fixed price that is typically at a premium to the current market price.

Fixed-rate perpetual preferred stock Nonconvertible, noncallable preferred stock that has a fixed dividend rate and no maturity date.

Flotation cost Fees charged to companies by investment bankers and other costs associated with raising new capital.

Forward-looking estimates Estimates based on current and expectations. Also referred to as ex ante estimates.

Fractionalization The creation of value by selling something in parts.

Franchising An owner of an asset and associated intellectual property divests the asset and licenses intellectual property to a third-party operator (franchisee) in exchange for royalties. Franchisees operate under the constraints of a franchise agreement.

Franking credit A tax credit received by shareholders for the taxes that a corporation paid on its distributed earnings.

Free cash flow hypothesis The hypothesis that higher debt levels discipline managers by forcing them to make fixed debt service payments and by reducing the company's free cash flow.

Freemium pricing A pricing approach that allows customers a certain level of usage or functionality at no charge. Those who wish to use more must pay.

Game theory The set of tools decision makers use to incorporate responses by rival decision makers into their strategies.

General partner Individual(s) in a limited partnership responsible for managing the business with unlimited liability.

Global CAPM (GCAPM) A single-factor model with a global index representing the single factor.

Gordon growth model A DDM that assumes dividends grow at a constant rate into the future.

Green bond Bonds in which the proceeds are designated by issuers to fund a specific project or portfolio of projects that have environmental or climate benefits.

Green finance A type of finance that addresses environmental concerns while achieving economic growth.

Green loans Any loan instruments made available exclusively to finance or re-finance, in whole or in part, new and/or existing eligible green projects. Green loans are commonly aligned in the market with the Green Loan Principles.

Greenmail The purchase of the accumulated shares of a hostile investor by a company that is targeted for takeover by that investor, usually at a substantial premium over market price.

Greenwashing The risk that a green bond's proceeds are not actually used for a beneficial environmental or climate-related project.

Growth capital expenditures Capital expenditures needed for expansion.

Growth option The option to make additional investments in a project at some future time if the financial results are strong. Also called an *expansion option*.

Hidden revenue business models Business models that provide services to users at no charge and generate revenues elsewhere.

Historical equity risk premium approach An estimate of a country's equity risk premium that is based on the historical averages of the risk-free rate and the rate of return on the market portfolio.

Horizontal demand schedule Implies that at a given price, the response in the quantity demanded is infinite.

Horizontal ownership Companies with mutual business interests (e.g., key customers or suppliers) that have cross-holding share arrangements with each other.

Hostile takeover   An attempt by one entity to acquire a company without the consent of the company's management.

Hurdle rate   The rate of return that a project's IRR must exceed for the project to be accepted by the company.

Hybrid approach   With respect to forecasting, an approach that combines elements of both top-down and bottom-up analyses.

Idiosyncratic risk premium (IRP)   The additional return required for bearing company-specific risks.

Impact investing   Investment approach that seeks to achieve targeted social or environmental objectives along with measurable financial returns through engagement with a company or by direct investment in projects or companies.

Impairment of capital rule   A legal restriction that dividends cannot exceed retained earnings.

Income elasticity of demand   A measure of the responsiveness of demand to changes in income, defined as the percentage change in quantity demanded divided by the percentage change in income.

Incremental borrowing rate (IBR)   The rate of interest that the lessee would have to pay to borrow using a collateralized loan over the same term as a lease.

Incremental cash flow   The net cash flow that is realized because of a decision; the changes or increments to cash flows resulting from a decision or action.

Indenture   A written contract between a lender and borrower that specifies the terms of the loan, such as interest rate, interest payment schedule, or maturity.

Independent board directors   Directors with no material relationship with the company with regard to employment, ownership, or remuneration.

Independent projects   Independent projects are capital investments whose cash flows are independent of each other.

Industry risk premium (IP)   The additional return that is required to bear industry-specific risk.

Industry risks   Risks that apply to all competitors in the same industry and include risk factors likely to affect the overall level of demand, pricing, and profitability in the industry.

Industry shocks   Unexpected changes to an industry from regulations or the legal environment, technology, or changes in the growth rate of the industry.

Initial public offering (IPO)   A process used by companies to raise capital and offer shares to the public for the first time.

Insiders   Corporate managers and board directors who are also shareholders of a company.

Intangible assets   Assets without a physical form, such as patents and trademarks.

Interlocking directorates   Corporate structure in which individuals serve on the board of directors of multiple corporations.

Internal rate of return   The discount rate that makes net present value equal 0; the discount rate that makes the present value of an investment's costs (outflows) equal to the present value of the investment's benefits (inflows).

International CAPM (ICAPM)   A two-factor model with a global index and a wealth-weighted currency index.

Joint venture   Two or more companies form and control a new, separate company to achieve a business objective. Each participant contributes assets, employees, know-how, or other resources to the joint venture company. The participants maintain their independence otherwise and continue to do business apart from the joint venture, but they share in the joint venture's profits or losses.

Law of diminishing returns   The smallest output that a firm can produce such that its long run average costs are minimized.

Lean startups   A form of asset-light business model that attempts to outsource as many functions as possible in order to minimize both capital investment and fixed operating expenses.

Leasing   The right to use an asset for a specified time, without ownership rights, for a fee.

Leverage   A measure for identifying a potentially influential high-leverage point.

Leveraged buyout (LBO) An acquirer (typically an investment fund specializing in LBOs) uses a significant amount of debt to finance the acquisition of a target and then pursues restructuring actions, with the goal of exiting the target with a sale or public listing.

Licensing arrangements The right to produce a product or have access to intangible assets using someone else's brand name in return for a royalty (often a percentage of revenues).

Limited partners The partners in a limited partnership who cannot lose more than their investment in the partnership due to having limited liability.

Limited partnership A special form of partnership in which there is at least one general partner with unlimited liability and responsibility for management of the business. The remaining limited partners have limited liability in the business.

Liquidating dividend A dividend that is a return of capital rather than a distribution from earnings or retained earnings.

Liquidation To sell the assets of a company, division, or subsidiary piecemeal, typically because of bankruptcy; the form of bankruptcy that allows for the orderly satisfaction of creditors' claims after which the company ceases to exist.

Liquidity The extent to which a company is able to meet its short-term obligations using cash flows and those assets that can be readily transformed into cash.

Liquidity management The company's ability to generate cash when needed, at the lowest possible cost.

Liquidity ratios Financial ratios measuring the company's ability to meet its short-term obligations to creditors as they come due.

Macro risk The risk from political, economic, legal, and other institutional risk factors that impact all businesses in an economy, a region, or a country.

Maintenance capital expenditures Capital expenditures needed to maintain operations at the current level.

Majority shareholders Shareholders that own more than 50% of a corporation's shares.

Management buyout (MBO) A process used to take a public company private, involving significant amounts of debt to finance the acquisition by members of the company's current management team.

Marginal value curve A curve describing the highest price consumers are willing to pay for each additional unit of a good.

Market conditions Interest rates, inflation rates, and other economic characteristics that comprise the macroeconomic environment.

Market model A regression model with the return on a stock as the dependent variable and the returns on a market index as the independent variable.

Marketplace businesses Businesses that create networks of buyers and sellers without taking ownership of the goods during the process.

Matrix pricing Process of estimating the market discount rate and price of a bond based on the quoted or flat prices of more frequently traded comparable bonds.

Minority shareholders Particular shareholders or a block of shareholders holding a small proportion of a company's outstanding shares, resulting in a limited ability to exercise control in voting activities.

Monopolistic competition Highly competitive form of imperfect competition; the competitive characteristic is a notably large number of firms, while the monopoly aspect is the result of product differentiation.

Monopoly In pure monopoly markets, there are no substitutes for the given product or service. There is a single seller, which exercises considerable power over pricing and output decisions.

Mutually exclusive projects Mutually exclusive projects compete directly with each other. For example, if Projects A and B are mutually exclusive, you can choose A or B but you cannot choose both.

Nash equilibrium When two or more participants in a non-cooperative game have no incentive to deviate from their respective equilibrium strategies given their opponent's strategies.

Negative screening An ESG investment style that focuses on the exclusion of certain sectors, companies, or practices in a fund or portfolio on the basis of specific ESG criteria.

Net present value The present value of an investment's cash inflows (benefits) minus the present value of its cash outflows (costs).

Network effects The increase in value or utility for some services and products as more users join and wider adoption occurs.

Non-bank lenders Unlike typical banks, which make loans and take deposits, these lenders only make loans and may provide specific financial services to targeted consumers and firms such as mortgage services, lease financing, and venture capital.

Nonconventional cash flow pattern In a nonconventional cash flow pattern, the initial outflow is not followed by inflows only, but the cash flows can flip from positive (inflows) to negative (outflows) again or even change signs several times.

Nonprofit corporations (Nonprofits) Corporations formed with the specific purpose of promoting a public benefit, religious benefit, or charitable mission. The motive of nonprofits is not expressly profit driven.

Normalized earnings The expected level of mid-cycle earnings for a company in the absence of any unusual or temporary factors that affect profitability (either positively or negatively).

Offshoring Refers to relocating operations from one country to another, mainly to reduce costs through lower labor costs or to achieve economies of scale through centralization, but still maintaining operations within the corporation.

Oligopoly Market structure with a relatively small number of firms supplying the market.

Omnichannel A distribution strategy that integrates both digital and physical sales channels, so that both can be used together to complete a sale.

One-tier board Board structure consisting of a single board of directors, composed of executive (internal) and non-executive (external) directors.

Operating breakeven The number of units produced and sold at which the company's operating profit is zero (revenues = operating costs).

Operating lease A type of lease that is more akin to the rental of the underlying asset.

Operating leverage The sensitivity of a firm's operating profit to a change in revenues.

Operating risk The risk attributed to the operating cost structure, in particular the use of fixed costs in operations; the risk arising from the mix of fixed and variable costs; the risk that a company's operations may be severely affected by environmental, social, and governance risk factors.

Opportunity cost Reflects the foregone opportunity of investing in a different asset. It is typically denoted by the risk-free rate of interest, r.

Optimal capital structure The capital structure at which the value of the company is maximized.

Optional product pricing A pricing approach that applies when a customer buys additional services or product features, either at the time of purchase or afterward.

Outsourcing Shifting internal business services to a subcontractor that can offer services at lower costs by scaling to serve many clients.

Ownership capital (equity) Money invested by the owners of the company.

Partnership agreement A legal document used in a partnership business structure that details how much of the business each partner owns, how the profits are to be shared, and what the duties are of each partner.

Pay-in-advance A business model that requires payment from customers before a product or service is delivered, in order to reduce or eliminate the need for working capital.

Payout policy The principles by which a company distributes cash to common shareholders by means of cash dividends and/or share repurchases.

Payouts Cash dividends and the value of shares repurchased in any given year.

Pecking order theory The theory that managers consider how their actions might be interpreted by outsiders and thereby order their preferences for various forms of corporate financing. Forms of financing that are least visible to outsiders (e.g., internally generated funds) are most preferable to managers, and those that are most visible (e.g., equity) are least preferable.

Peer company See *comparable company*.

Penetration pricing A discount pricing approach used when a firm willingly sacrifices margins in order to build scale and market share.

Perfect capital markets Markets in which, by assumption, there are no taxes, transaction costs, or bankruptcy costs and in which all investors have equal ("symmetric") information.

Perfect competition A market structure in which the individual firm has virtually no impact on market price, because it is assumed to be a very small seller among a very large number of firms selling essentially identical products.

Per unit contribution margin The amount that each unit sold contributes to covering fixed costs—that is, the difference between the price per unit and the variable cost per unit.

Pet projects Investments in which influential managers want the corporation to invest. Often, unfortunately, pet projects are selected without undergoing normal capital allocation analysis.

Positive screening An ESG implementation approach that seeks to identify the most favorable companies and sectors based on ESG considerations. Also called *best-in-class*.

Price discrimination A pricing approach that charges different prices to different customers based on their willingness to pay.

Priced risk Risk for which investors demand compensation for bearing (e.g., equity risk, company-specific factors, macroeconomic factors).

Price elasticity of demand Measures the percentage change in the quantity demanded, given a percentage change in the price of a given product.

Price-setting option The option to adjust prices when demand varies from what is forecast.

Price takers Producers that must accept whatever price the market dictates.

Price-to-earnings ratio (P/E) The ratio of share price to earnings per share.

Principal–agent relationship A relationship in which a principal hires an agent to perform a particular task or service; also known as an *agency relationship*.

Private label or "contract" manufacturers Manufacturers that produce goods to be marketed by others.

Private placement memorandum (PPM) A legal document used in the purchase of private company shares that describes the business, the terms of the offering, and the risks involved in making an investment in the company. Also termed an offering memorandum.

Production-flexibility option The option to alter production when demand varies from what is forecast.

Product market risk The risk that the market for a new product or service will fall short of expectations.

Pro forma financial statements Financial statements that include the effect of a corporate restructuring.

Project sequencing To defer the decision to invest in a future project until the outcome of some or all of a current investment is known. Investments are sequenced over time, so that making an investment creates the option to invest in future projects.

Proxy contest Corporate takeover mechanism in which shareholders are persuaded to vote for a group seeking a controlling position on a company's board of directors.

Proxy voting A process that enables shareholders who are unable to attend a meeting to authorize another individual to vote on their behalf.

Pull on liquidity When disbursements (outflows) are paid too quickly or trade credit availability is limited, requiring companies to expend funds before they receive funds from sales that could cover the liability.

Rate implicit in the lease (RIIL) The discount rate that equates the present value of the lease payment with the fair value of the leased asset, considering also the lessor's direct costs and the present value of the leased asset's residual value.

Razors-and-blades pricing A pricing approach that combines a low price on a piece of equipment and high-margin pricing on repeat-purchase consumables.

Recency bias The behavioral tendency to place more relevance on recent events.

Recurring revenue/subscription pricing A pricing approach that enables customers to "rent" a product or service for as long as they need it.

Reorganization A court-supervised restructuring process available in some jurisdictions for companies facing insolvency from burdensome debt levels. A bankruptcy court assumes control of the company and oversees an orderly negotiation process between the company and its creditors for asset sales, conversion of debt to equity, refinancing, and so on.

Required rate of return on equity The minimum rate of return required by an investor to invest in an asset, given the asset's riskiness. Also known as the required return on equity.

Responsible investing A broad (umbrella) term to describe investing that incorporates environmental, social, and governance factors into investment decisions.

Return on capital employed Operating profit divided by capital employed (debt and equity capital).

Return on invested capital A measure of the profitability of a company relative to the amount of capital invested by the equity- and debtholders.

Reverse stock split A reduction in the number of shares outstanding with a corresponding increase in share price, but no change to the company's underlying fundamentals.

Revolving credit agreements (also known as revolvers) The most reliable form of short-term bank borrowing facilities; they are in effect for multiple years (e.g., three to five years) and can have optional medium-term loan features.

Risk-based models Models of the return on equity that identify risk factors or drivers and sensitivities of the return to these factors.

Risk-free rate The minimum rate of return expected on a security that has no default risk.

Sale-leaseback A situation in which a company sells the building it owns and occupies to a real estate investor and the company then signs a long-term lease with the buyer to continue to occupy the building. At the end of the lease, use of the property reverts to the landlord.

Sales risk The uncertainty regarding the price and number of units sold of a company's products.

Say on pay A process whereby shareholders may vote on executive remuneration (compensation) matters.

Scenario analysis A technique for exploring the performance and risk of investment strategies in different structural regimes.

Second-degree price discrimination When the monopolist charges different per-unit prices using the quantity purchased as an indicator of how highly the customer values the product.

Secured ("asset-based") loans Loan that are backed by specific, secured company assets.

Sensitivity analysis Analysis that shows the range of possible outcomes as specific assumptions are changed.

Shadow banking Lending by financial institutions that are not regulated as banks.

Shareholder activism Strategies used by shareholders to attempt to compel a company to act in a desired manner.

Share repurchase A transaction in which a company buys back its own shares. Unlike stock dividends and stock splits, share repurchases use corporate cash.

Size premium (SP) Additional return compensation for bearing the additional risk associated with smaller companies.

Socially responsible investing (SRI) Investing in assets and companies with favorable profiles or attributes based on the investor's social, moral, or faith-based beliefs.

Sovereign yield spread The spread between the yield on a foreign country's sovereign bond and a similar-maturity domestic sovereign bond.

Special dividend A dividend paid by a company that does not pay dividends on a regular schedule, or a dividend that supplements regular cash dividends with an extra payment.

Special purpose acquisition company (SPAC) A publicly listed shell company, also referred to as a "blank check" company, that exists solely for the purpose of acquiring an unspecified private company sometime in the future.

Specific-company risk premium (SCRP) Additional return required by investors for bearing non-diversifiable company-specific risk.

Spin off When a company separates a distinct part of its business into a new, independent company. The term is used to describe both the transaction and the separated component, while the company that conducts the transaction and formerly owned the spin off is known as the parent.

Split-rate tax system In reference to corporate taxes, a split-rate system taxes earnings to be distributed as dividends at a different rate than earnings to be retained. Corporate profits distributed as dividends are taxed at a lower rate than those retained in the business.

Stable dividend policy A policy in which regular dividends are paid that reflect long-run expected earnings. In contrast to a constant dividend payout ratio policy, a stable dividend policy does not reflect short-term volatility in earnings.

Stackelberg model A prominent model of strategic decision making in which firms are assumed to make their decisions sequentially.

Staggered boards Board-related election process whereby directors are typically divided into multiple classes that are elected separately in consecutive years—that is, one class every year.

Stakeholder management The identification, prioritization, and understanding of the interests of stakeholder groups and managing the company's relationships with these groups.

Static trade-off theory of capital structure A theory pertaining to a company's optimal capital structure. The optimal level of debt is found at the point where additional debt would cause the costs of financial distress to increase by a greater amount than the benefit of the additional tax shield.

Stock dividend A type of dividend in which a company distributes additional shares of its common stock to shareholders instead of cash.

Straight debt Debt with no embedded options.

Straight voting A shareholder voting process in which shareholders receive one vote for each share owned.

Stranded assets Assets that are obsolete or not economically viable.

Substitutes Said of two goods or services such that if the price of one increases, the demand for the other tends to increase, holding all other things equal (e.g., butter and margarine).

Sunk cost A cost that has already been incurred.

Supply chain The sequence of processes involved in the creation and delivery of a physical product to the end customer, both within and external to a firm, regardless of whether those steps are performed by a single firm.

Survey approach An estimate of the equity risk premium that is based on estimates provided by a panel of finance experts.

Survivorship bias The exclusion of poorly performing or defunct companies from an index or database, biasing the index or database toward financially healthy companies.

Sustainability linked loans These are any types of loan instruments and/or contingent facilities (such as bonding lines, guarantee lines, or letters of credit) that incentivize the borrower's achievement of ambitious, pre-determined sustainability performance objectives.

Sustainable investing Investing in assets and companies based on their perceived ability to deliver value by advancing economic, environmental, and social sustainability.

Switching barriers Factors that make it more difficult or more costly to switch suppliers.

Synergies The combination of two companies being more valuable than the sum of the parts. Generally, synergies take the form of lower costs ("cost synergies") or increased revenues ("revenue synergies") through combinations that generate lower costs or higher revenues, respectively.

Takeover premium The amount by which the per-share takeover price exceeds the unaffected price expressed as a percentage of the unaffected price. It reflects the amount shareholders require to relinquish their control of the company to the acquirer.

Tangible assets Identifiable, physical assets such as property, plant, and equipment.

Target capital structure A company's chosen proportions of debt and equity.

Target payout ratio A strategic corporate goal representing the long-term proportion of earnings that the company intends to distribute to shareholders as dividends.

Tender offer A public offer whereby the acquirer invites target shareholders to submit ("tender") their shares in return for the proposed payment.

Thematic investing An investment approach that focuses on companies within a specific sector or following a specific theme, such as energy efficiency or climate change.

Third-degree price discrimination When the monopolist segregates customers into groups based on demographic or other characteristics and offers different pricing to each group.

Tiered pricing A pricing approach that charges different prices to different buyers, commonly based on volume purchased.

Top-down approach With respect to forecasting, an approach that usually begins at the level of the overall economy. Forecasts are then made at more narrowly defined levels, such as sector, industry, and market for a specific product.

Total cost of ownership The aggregate direct and indirect costs associated with owning an asset over its life span.

Trade credit A spontaneous form of credit in which a purchaser of the goods or service is financing its purchase by delaying the date on which payment is made.

Treasury shares/stock Shares that were issued and subsequently repurchased by the company.

Two-tier board Board structure consisting of a supervisory board that oversees a management board.

Uncommitted lines of credit The least reliable form of bank borrowing in which a bank offers, without formal commitment, a line of credit for an extended period of time but reserves the right to refuse any request for its use.

Unit economics The expression of revenues and costs on a per-unit basis.

Upstream A transaction between two related companies, an investor company (or a parent company) and an associate company (or a subsidiary company) such that the associate company records a profit on its income statement. An example is a sale of inventory by the associate to the investor company or by a subsidiary to a parent company.

Value added resellers Businesses that distribute a product and also handle more complex aspects of product installation, customization, service, or support.

Value-based pricing Pricing set primarily by reference to the value of the product or service to customers.

Value chain The systems and processes within a firm that create value for its customers.

Value proposition The product or service attributes valued by a firm's target customer that lead those customers to prefer that firm's offering.

Variable costs Costs that fluctuate with the level of production and sales.

Vertical demand schedule Implies that some fixed quantity is demanded, regardless of price.

Vertical ownership Ownership structure in which a company or group that has a controlling interest in two or more holding companies, which in turn have controlling interests in various operating companies.

Voting caps Legal restrictions on the voting rights of large share positions.

Web-based lenders Lenders that operate primarily on the internet, offering loans in relatively small amounts, typically to small businesses in need of cash.

Weighted average cost of capital A weighted average of the after-tax required rates of return on a company's common stock, preferred stock, and long-term debt, where the weights are the fraction of each source of financing in the company's target capital structure.

Weighted average cost of capital (WACC) A weighted average of the after-tax required rates of return on a company's common stock, preferred stock, and long-term debt, where the weights are the fraction of each source of financing in the company's target capital structure.

Working capital management The management of a company's short-term assets (such as inventory) and short-term liabilities (such as money owed to suppliers).

Yield-to-maturity Annual return that an investor earns on a bond if the investor purchases the bond today and holds it until maturity. It is the discount rate that equates the present value of the bond's expected cash flows until maturity with the bond's price. Also called *yield-to-redemption* or *redemption yield*.

REFERENCES

Amendments to Rules Governing the Investment Company Act of 1940, 17 CFR Part 270, July 2004.

American Management Association. 1960. "Executive Committee Control Charts." *AMA Management Bulletin*, No. 6: 22.

Anderson, Miranda, and David Gardiner. 2006. *Climate Risk and Energy in the Auto Sector: Guidance for Investors and Analysts on Key Off-Balance Sheet Drivers*. Thousand Oaks, CA: Ceres.

Armitage, Seth. 2000. "The Direct Costs of UK Rights Issues and Open Offers." *European Financial Management*, Vol. 6, No. 1: 57–68.

Baker, Malcolm, and Jeffrey Wurgler. 2004. "A Catering Theory of Dividends." *Journal of Finance*, Vol. 59, No. 3: 1125–1165.

Bancel, Franck, and Usha Mittoo. 2004. "The Determinants of Capital Structure Choice: A Survey of European Firms." *Financial Management*, Vol. 44, No. 4.

Bauer, Rod, and Nadja Guenster. 2003. "Good Corporate Governance Pays Off!: Well-Governed Companies Perform Better on the Stock Market." Working paper.

Blume, Marshall. 1971. "On the Assessment of Risk." *Journal of Finance*, Vol. 26, No. 1: 1–10.

Brav, Alon, John Graham, Campbell Harvey, and Roni Michaely. 2005. "Payout Policy in the 21st Century." *Journal of Financial Economics*, Vol. 77, No. 3: 483–527.

Brealey, Richard, Stewart Myers, and Alan Marcus. 2007. *Fundamentals of Corporate Finance*. New York: McGraw-Hill Irwin.

Brounen, Dirk, Abe de Jong, and Kees Koedijk. 2004. "Corporate Finance in Europe: Confronting Theory with Practice." *Financial Management*, Vol. 33, No. 4: 71–101.

Brown, Lawrence D., and Marcus Caylor. 2004. "Corporate Governance Study: The Correlation Between Corporate Governance and Company Performance." Institutional Shareholder Services. www.tkyd.org/files/downloads/corporate_governance_study_104.pdf (accessed February 1, 2008).

Bruner, Robert F. 2005. *Deals from Hell: M&A Lessons That Rise above the Ashes*. Hoboken, NJ: John Wiley & Sons.

Bruner, Robert F., Robert M. Conroy, Wei Li, Elizabeth O'Halloran, and Miquel Palacios Lleras. 2003. *Investing in Emerging Markets*. Charlottesville, VA: AIMR Research Foundation.

Bühner, Thomas, and Christoph Kaserer. 2002. "External Financing Costs and Economies of Scale in Investment Banking: The Case of Seasoned Equity Offerings in Germany." *European Financial Management*, Vol. 9, No. 2: 249–253.

Chance, Don M. 2003. *Analysis of Derivatives for the CFA Program*. Charlottesville, VA: Association for Investment Management and Research.

Chetty, Raj, and Emmanuel Saez. 2004. "Do Dividends Respond to Taxes? Preliminary Evidence from the 2003 Dividend Tax Cut." National Bureau of Economic Research, working paper 10572.

Claessens, Stijn, Simeon Djankov, and Titiana Nenova. 2001. "Corporate Risk around the World." In *Financial Crises in Emerging Markets*. Reuven Glick, Ramon Moreno, and Mark Speigel, editors. New York: Cambridge University Press.

Copeland, Thomas E., J. Fred Weston, and Kuldeep Shastri. 2005. *Financial Theory and Corporate Policy*, 4th edition. Old Tappan, NJ: Pearson/Addison Wesley.

Copeland, Tom, Tim Koller, and Jack Murrin. 2000. *Valuation: Measuring and Managing the Value of Companies*, 3rd edition. New York: John Wiley & Sons.

Cornell, Bradford. 2009. "Stock Repurchases and Dividends: Trade-Offs and Trends." *Dividends and Dividend Policy*. H. Kent Baker, editor. Hoboken, NJ: John Wiley & Sons.

Corporate Governance of Listed Companies: A Manual for Investors, The. 2005. Charlottesville, VA: CFA Institute Centre for Financial Market Integrity.

Damodaran, Aswath. 1999. "Estimating Equity Risk Premiums." New York University working paper.

Damodaran, Aswath. 2001. *Corporate Finance*. New York: John Wiley & Sons.

Damodaran, Aswath. 2003. "Measuring Company Exposure to Country Risk: Theory and Practice." New York University working paper.

Daves, Phillip R., Michael C. Ehrhardt, and Robert A. Kunkel. 2000. "Estimating Systematic Risk: The Choice of Return Interval and Estimation Period." *Journal of Financial and Strategic Decisions*, Vol. 13, No. 1: 7–13.

DeAngelo, Harry, Linda DeAngelo, and Douglas Skinner. 1986. "Reversal of Fortune: Dividend Signals and the Disappearance of Sustained Earnings Growth." *Journal of Financial Economics*, Vol. 40, No. 3: 341–371.

DeAngelo, Harry, Linda DeAngelo, and Douglas Skinner. 2004. "Are Dividends Disappearing? Dividend Concentration and the Consolidation of Earnings." *Journal of Financial Economics*, Vol. 72, No. 3: 425–456.

Demirguc-Kunt, Asli, and Voljislav Maksimovic. 1998. "Law, Finance, and Company Growth." *Journal of Finance*, Vol. 53, No. 6: 2107–2137.

Demirguc-Kunt, Asli and Voljislav Maksimovic. 1999. "Institutions, Financial Markets, and Company Debt Maturity." *Journal of Financial Economics*, Vol. 54, No. 3: 295–336.

Dimson, Elroy, Paul Marsh, and Mike Staunton. 2003. "Global Evidence on the Equity Risk Premium." *Journal of Applied Corporate Finance* (Fall): 27–38.

Domowitz, Ian, Jack Glen, and Ananth Madhavan. 2000. "International Evidence on Aggregate Corporate Financing Decisions." Pennsylvania State University working paper.

Edmondson, Gail. 2004. "How Parmalat Went Sour." *BusinessWeek* (July 12).

Edwards, Edgar O., and Philip W. Bell. 1961. *The Theory and Measurement of Business Income*. Berkeley: University of California Press.

Elton, Edward, and Martin Gruber. 1970. "Marginal Tax Rates and the Clientele Effect." *Review of Economics and Statistics*, Vol. 52, No. 1: 68–74.

Erb, Claude, Campbell R. Harvey, and Tadas Viskanta. 1996. "Expected Returns and Volatility in 135 Countries." *Journal of Portfolio Management*.

Ezzell, John R., and R. Burr Porter. 1976. "Flotation Costs and the Weighted Average Cost of Capital." *Journal of Financial and Quantitative Analysis*, Vol. 11, No. 3: 403–413.

Fabozzi, Frank. 2004. *Fixed Income Analysis for the Chartered Financial Analyst® Program*, 2nd edition. Charlottesville, VA: CFA Institute.

Fama, Eugene, and Kenneth French. 1992. "The Cross-Section of Expected Stock Returns." *Journal of Finance*, Vol. 47, No. 2: 427–465.

Fama, Eugene, and Kenneth French. 2001. "Disappearing Dividends: Changing Firm Characteristics or Lower Propensity to Pay?" *Journal of Financial Economics*, Vol. 60, No. 1: 3–43.

Fama, Eugene, and Kenneth French. 2004. "The Capital Asset Pricing Model: Theory and Evidence." *Journal of Economic Perspectives*, Vol. 18, No. 3: 25–46.

Fan, J. P. H., Sheridan Titman, and Garry J. Twite. 2004. "An International Comparison of Capital Structure and Debt Maturity Choices." European Finance Association 2003 Annual Conference Paper No. 769.

Ferris, Stephen, Narayanan Jayaraman, and Sanjiv Sabherwal. 2009. "Catering Effects in Corporate Dividend Policy: The International Evidence." *Journal of Banking and Finance*, Vol. 33, No. 9: 1730–1738.

Ferris, Stephen, Nilanjan Sen, and Emre Unlu. 2009. "An International Analysis of Dividend Payment Behavior." *Journal of Business Finance & Accounting*, Vol. 36, Nos. 3–4: 496–522.

Filbeck, Greg. 2009. "Asymmetric Information and Signaling Theory." *Dividends and Dividend Policy*. H. Kent Baker, editor. Hoboken, NJ: John Wiley & Sons.

Fisher, Irving. 1930. *The Theory of Interest.* New York: Macmillan.

Gaughan, Patrick A. 2002. *Mergers, Acquisitions, and Corporate Restructurings*, 3rd edition. Hoboken, NJ: John Wiley & Sons.

Gill, Amar. 2001. "Corporate Governance in Emerging Markets—Saints and Sinners: Who's Got Religion?" CLSA Emerging Markets, *CG Watch* research report (April).

Gitman, Lawrence, and V. Mercurio. 1982. "Cost of Capital Techniques Used by Major U.S. Firms: Survey and Analysis of Fortune's 1000." *Financial Management*, Vol. 14, No. 4.

Glader, Paul, Eleanor Laise, and E. S. Browning. 2009. "GE Joins Parade of Deep Dividend Cuts." *Wall Street Journal* (28 February 2009): A1.

Gompers, Paul A., Joy L. Ishii, and Andrew Metrick. 2003. "Corporate Governance and Equity Prices." *Quarterly Journal of Economics*, Vol. 118, No. 1: 107–155.

Gordon, Myron J. 1962. *The Investment, Financing, and Valuation of the Corporation.* Homewood, IL: Irwin.

Gordon, Myron. 1963. "Optimal Investment and Financing Policy." *Journal of Finance*, Vol. 18, No. 2: 264–272.

Grace, Kerry, and Rob Curran. 2009. "Stock Buybacks Plummet." *Wall Street Journal* (27 March 2009): C9.

Graham, Benjamin, and David L. Dodd. 1934. *Security Analysis.* New York: McGraw-Hill.

Graham, Benjamin, David Dodd, Sidney Cottle, and Charles Tatham. 1962. *Security Analysis*, 4th edition. New York: McGraw-Hill.

Graham, John, and Campbell Harvey. 2001. "The Theory and Practice of Corporate Finance: Evidence from the Field." *Journal of Financial Economics*, Vol. 60, Nos. 2–3: 187–243.

Graham, John, and Campbell Harvey. 2002. "How Do CFOs Make Capital Budgeting and Capital Structure Decisions?" *Journal of Applied Corporate Finance*, Vol. 15, No. 1: 8–22.

Grinblatt, Mark, Ronald Masulis, and Sheridan Titman. 1984. "The Valuation Effects of Stock Splits and Stock Dividends." *Journal of Financial Economics*, Vol. 13, No. 4: 461–490.

Grullon, Gustavo, and Roni Michaely. 2002. "Dividends, Share Repurchases, and the Substitution Hypothesis." *Journal of Finance*, Vol. 57, No. 4: 1649–1684.

Hall, Martin. 2003. "A/R Outsourcing: Coming of Age in the New Millennium." *Business Credit* (February): 1–2.

Hamada, Robert. 1972. "The Effect of the Firm's Capital Structure on the Systematic Risk of Common Stocks." *Journal of Finance*, Vol. 27, No. 2: 435–452.

Hansen, Robert, Raman Kumar, and Dilip Shome. 1994. "Dividend Policy and Corporate Monitoring: Evidence from the Regulated Electric Utility Industry." *Financial Management*, Vol. 23, No. 1: 16–22.

Harvey, Campbell R. 2001. "The International Cost of Capital and Risk Calculator." Duke University working paper.

Harvey, Campbell R., Karl V. Lins, and Andrew H. Roper. 2004. "The Effect of Capital Structure When Expected Agency Costs Are Extreme." *Journal of Financial Economics*, Vol. 74, No. 1: 3–30.

He, Wei. 2009. "Dividend Reinvestment Plans." In *Dividends and Dividend Policy.* H. Kent Baker, editor. Hoboken, NJ: John Wiley & Sons.

Healy, P., and K. Palepu. 1988. "Earnings Information Conveyed by Dividend Initiations and Omissions." *Journal of Financial Economics*, Vol. 21, No. 2: 149–175.

Hirshleifer, Jack. 1958. "On the Theory of Optimal Investment Decisions." *Journal of Political Economy*, Vol. 66, No. 4: 329–352.

Ibbotson, Roger G., Paul D. Kaplan, and James D. Peterson. 1997. "Estimates of Small Stock Betas Are Much Too Low." *Journal of Portfolio Management*, Vol. 23, No. 4: 104–111.

Jensen, Michael C. 1969. "The Performance of Mutual Funds in the Period 1945–1964." *Journal of Finance.* Vol. 23, No. 2: 389–416.

Jensen, Michael C. 1986. "Agency Costs of Free Cash Flow, Corporate Finance, and Takeovers." *American Economic Review*, Vol. 76, No. 2: 323–329.

Jensen, Michael C., and William H. Meckling. 1976. "Theory of the Company: Managerial Behavior, Agency Costs, and Ownership Structure." *Journal of Financial Economics*, Vol. 3, No. 4: 305–360.

Kaserer, Christoph, and Fabian Steiner. 2004. "The Cost of Raising Capital—New Evidence from Seasoned Equity Offerings in Switzerland." Technische Universität München working paper (February).

Koller, T., M. Goedhart, and D. Wessels. 2005. *Valuation: Measuring and Managing the Value of Companies*, 4th edition. Hoboken, NJ: John Wiley & Sons.

Lease, Ronald, Kose John, Avner Kalay, Uri Loewenstein, and Oded Sarig. 2000. *Dividend Policy: Its Impact on Firm Value*. Boston, MA: Harvard Business School Press.

Lee, Inmoo, Scott Lochhead, Jay R. Ritter, and Quanshui Zhao. 1996. "The Costs of Raising Capital." *Journal of Financial Research*, Vol. 19, No. 1: 59–74.

Lintner, John. 1956. "Distribution of Incomes of Corporations among Dividends, Retained Earnings, and Taxes." *American Economic Review*, Vol. 46: 97–113.

Lintner, John. 1962. "Dividends, Earnings, Leverage, Stock Prices and the Supply of Capital to Corporations." *Review of Economics and Statistics*, Vol. 44, No. 3: 243–269.

Madden, Ian. 2008. "High Dividend Stocks: Proceed with Caution." www.kbcam.com/newsand pressdivplus.jsp.

Maremont, Mark, and Laurie Cohen. 2002. "How Tyco's CEO Enriched Himself." *The Wall Street Journal* (August 7).

Mariscal, Jorge O., and Rafaelina M. Lee. 1993. "The Valuation of Mexican Stocks: An Extension of the Capital Asset Pricing Model." New York: Goldman Sachs.

Markon, Jerry, and Robert Frank. 2002. "Five Adelphia Officials Arrested on Fraud Charges." *Wall Street Journal* (July 25): A3.

Marshall, Alfred. 1892. *Elements of Economics of Industry*, Book 2, Chapter 12, Sections 3 and 4. New York: Macmillan.

Materiality of Social, Environmental and Corporate Governance Issues to Equity Pricing: 11 Sector Studies by Brokerage House Analysts, The. 2004. New York: United Nations Environmental Programme Finance Initiative (UNEP FI), Asset Management Working Group.

Megginson, William J. 1997. *Corporate Finance Theory*. Reading, MA: Addison-Wesley.

Mian, Shehzad L., and Clifford W. Smith. 1992. "Accounts Receivable Management Policy: Theory and Evidence." *Journal of Finance*, Vol. 47, No. 1: 169–200.

Miles, James A., and John R. Ezzell. 1980. "The Weighted Average Cost of Capital, Perfect Capital Markets, and Project Life: A Clarification." *Journal of Financial and Quantitative Analysis*, Vol. 15, No. 3: 719–730.

Miller, Merton H. 1977. "Debt and Taxes." *Journal of Finance*, Vol. 32, No. 2: 261–275.

Miller, Merton H., and Franco Modigliani. 1961. "Dividend Policy, Growth, and the Valuation of Shares." *Journal of Business*, Vol. 34, No. 4: 411–433.

Modigliani, Franco, and Merton H. Miller. 1958. "The Cost of Capital, Corporation Finance, and the Theory of Investment." *American Economic Review*, Vol. 48, No. 3: 261–297.

Modigliani, Franco, and Merton H. Miller. 1963. "Corporate Income Taxes and the Cost of Capital: A Correction." *American Economic Review*, Vol. 54, No. 3: 433–443.

Mukherjee, Tarun. 2009. "Agency Costs and the Free Cash Flow Hypothesis." *Dividends and Dividend Policy*. H. Kent Baker, editor. Hoboken, NJ: John Wiley & Sons.

Myers, Stewart, and Nicholas Majluf. 1984. "Corporate Financing and Investment Decisions When Firms Have Information That Investors Do Not Have." *Journal of Financial Economics*, Vol. 13, No. 2: 187–221.

New York Society of Securities Analysts. 2003. Corporate Governance Handbook. New York City.

Nofsinger, John, and Kenneth Kim. 2003. *Infectious Greed*. Upper Saddle River, NJ: Prentice-Hall Financial Times.

Oded, Jacob, and Allen Michel. 2008. "Stock Repurchases and the EPS Enhancement Fallacy." *Financial Analysts Journal*, Vol. 64, No. 4: 62–75.

Parrino, Robert, and David Kidwell. 2009. *Fundamentals of Corporate Finance*. Hoboken, NJ: John Wiley & Sons.

Peterson, Pamela P., and David R. Peterson. 1996. *Company Performance and Measures of Value Added.* Charlottesville, VA: The Research Foundation of the ICFA.

Pinto, Jerald E., Elaine Henry, Thomas R. Robinson, and John D. Stowe. 2010. *Equity Asset Valuation,* 2nd edition. Hoboken, NJ: John Wiley & Sons.

Powers, William C., Jr., Raymond S. Troubh, and Herbert S. Winokur, Jr. 2002. Report of Investigation by the Special Investigative Committee of the Board of Directors of Enron Corp. (February 1). Collingdale, PA: Diane Pub. Co.

Rajan, Raghuram G., and Luigi Zingales. 1995. "What Do We Know about Capital Structure? Some Evidence from International Data." *Journal of Finance,* Vol. 50, No. 5: 1421–1460.

Reilly, Frank, and Keith Brown. 2003. *Investment Analysis and Portfolio Management,* 7th edition. Mason, OH: South-Western.

Roll, Richard. 1986. "The Hubris Hypothesis on Corporate Takeovers." *Journal of Business,* Vol. 59, No. 2: 176–216.

Ross, Stephen. 1977. "The Determination of Financial Structure: The Incentive-Signaling Approach." *Bell Journal of Economics,* Vol. 8, No. 1: 23–40.

Sabri, Nidal Rashid. 2003. "Using Treasury 'Repurchase' Shares to Stabilize Stock Markets," *International Journal of Business,* Vol. 8, No. 4.

Sears, Steven M. 2009. "The Fortunes of Reversals." *Barron's* (3 August): M10.

Shefrin, Hersh, and Meir Statman. 1984. "Explaining Investor Preference for Cash Dividends." *Journal of Financial Economics,* Vol. 13, No. 2: 253–282.

Siegel, Jeremy J. 2005. "Perspectives on the Equity Risk Premium." *Financial Analysts Journal,* Vol. 61, No. 6: 61–73.

Smith, Clifford, Jr., and Jerold Warner. 1979. "On Financial Contracting: An Analysis of Bond Covenants." *Journal of Financial Economics,* Vol. 7, No. 2: 117–161.

Solnik, Bruno, and Dennis McLeavey. 2004. *International Investments,* 5th edition. Reading, MA: Addison-Wesley.

Stewart, G. Bennett. 1991. *The Quest for Value.* New York: HarperCollins.

Thomas, Landon, Jr. 2004a. "Regulators Said to Be Focusing on Board's Vote for Grasso Pay." *The New York Times* (March 26).

Thomas, Landon, Jr. 2004b. "Saying Grasso Duped Big Board, Suit Seeks Return of $100 Million." *New York Times* (May 25).

Vermaelen, Theo. 2005. *Share Repurchases.* Hanover, MA: Now Publishers.

Von Eije, Henk, and William L. Megginson. 2008. "Dividends and Share Repurchases in the European Union." *Journal of Financial Economics,* Vol. 89, No. 2: 347–374.

Weston, J. Fred, and Samuel C. Weaver. 2001. *Mergers & Acquisitions.* New York: McGraw-Hill.

Weston, J. Fred, Kwang S. Chung, and Susan E. Hoag. 1990. *Mergers, Restructuring, and Corporate Control.* Upper Sadde River, NJ: Prentice-Hall.

White, Gerald I., Ashwinpaul C. Sondhi, and Dov Fried. 2003. *The Analysis and Use of Financial Statements,* 3rd edition. Hoboken, NJ: John Wiley & Sons.

ABOUT THE AUTHORS

Raj Aggarwal, CFA, is the Frank C. Sullivan Professor of International Business and Finance at the University of Akron in Ohio. Prior to his current position, he was the Firestone Chair in Corporate Finance at Kent State University and the Mellen Chair in Finance at John Carroll University. He has also taught at Harvard University, the University of Michigan, and the University of South Carolina. He serves as a director of Ancora Mutual Funds, Manco/Henkel AC, and the Financial Executives Research Foundation, a division of Financial Executives International.

He is an author of texts and widely cited scholarly books and papers and ranked highly in studies of academic contributions in finance and international business. He has been an officer of professional associations, such as the Financial Management Association, and is a graduate of Leadership Cleveland and a member of the Union Club.

Rosita P. Chang, CFA, is Professor of Finance and the codirector of the Asia Pacific Financial Markets (FIMA) Research Center at the Shidler College of Business, University of Hawaii at Manoa. Her research has appeared in the *Journal of Finance, Journal of International Business Studies, Journal of Financial Services Research*, and the *Pacific Basin Finance Journal*, among others. In addition, she has conducted commissioned studies for international institutions such as the Organisation for Economic Cooperation and Development (OECD), United Nations Industrial Development Organization, Securities & Futures Commission of Hong Kong, and several Asian stock exchanges. Her current research interests include issues related to Chinese capital markets, financial services industry, and market microstructure.

Dr. Chang received her BA from Mills College and her MBA and PhD from the University of Pittsburgh. She has been a CFA charterholder since 1984 and served as an independent trustee for Zurich Scudder Investments, Inc., from 1995 to 2001.

Catherine Clark, CFA, was a Vice President at Bankers Trust and Reich & Tang, where she was a securities analyst and portfolio manager. Ms. Clark received her BA degree in economics from the University of Washington in 1972 and MBA degree from New York University in 1975. She has been a CFA charterholder since 1979 and has been an active volunteer with CFA Institute for more than 20 years.

Michelle R. Clayman, CFA, is the founder, Managing Partner, and Chief Investment Officer of New Amsterdam Partners LLC, an institutional money management firm in New York. Ms. Clayman received a degree in philosophy, politics, and economics from Oxford University in England and an MBA from Stanford University, California. She has been a CFA charterholder since 1983. Ms. Clayman sits on the boards of the Society of Quantitative Analysts (of which she is a past President) and the Institute for Quantitative Research in Finance.

Yves Courtois, CFA, is a Corporate Finance Partner at KPMG in Luxembourg, where he leads the corporate finance, private equity, and valuation practices. He is cohead of KPMG's Global Valuation Institute and a member of KPMG's Global Valuation committee. He has extensive cross-border work experience in Europe and in the United States. He is currently head of the valuation and alternative investments advisory groups in Luxembourg and is an accredited valuer within the KPMG global corporate finance network. His other key areas of expertise include M&A, due diligence, financial risk management, and structuring. He is a frequent speaker at alternative investment funds industry forums on private equity, hedge funds, and valuation. He has worked on a wide range of projects with CFA Institute, including a webcast and CFA curriculum development. He received his BSBA degree from Solvay Business School in Brussels in 1995 and an MS degree in accountancy from Katholieke Universiteit Leuven in Belgium in 1996. He is also a Chartered Market Technician.

Pamela Peterson Drake, CFA, is Department Head and J. Gray Ferguson Professor of Finance at James Madison University. Professor Peterson Drake received her PhD from the University of North Carolina at Chapel Hill and taught at Florida State University and Florida Atlantic University before joining James Madison University. She has been a CFA charterholder since 1992. Professor Peterson Drake is author and coauthor of a number of books, including the *Basics of Finance, Analysis of Financial Statements*, and *Financial Management and Analysis*, all with Frank J. Fabozzi. Professor Peterson Drake has authored or coauthored monographs and a number of chapters in books, as well as published numerous articles in academic and practitioner journals.

Martin S. Fridson, CFA, is Global Credit Strategist at BNP Paribas Investment Partners. He is "perhaps the most well-known figure in the high-yield world," according to *Investment Dealers' Digest*. Over a 25-year span with brokerage firms including Salomon Brothers, Morgan Stanley, and Merrill Lynch, he became known for his innovative work in credit analysis and investment strategy. He has served as president of the Fixed Income Analysts Society, governor of the Association for Investment Management and Research (now CFA Institute), and director of the New York Society of Security Analysts. In 2000, *The Green Magazine* called Fridson's *Financial Statement Analysis* "one of the most useful investment books ever." The Financial Management Association International named Fridson the Financial Executive of the Year in 2002. In 2000, he became the youngest person ever inducted into the Fixed Income Analysts Society Hall of Fame. Fridson received his BA cum laude in history from Harvard College and his MBA from Harvard Business School.

Jacques R. Gagne, CFA, is director of asset and risk management at *La société de l'assurance automobile du Québec*, in Quebec City. Previously, he had been Vice President at the Quebec Pension Board and director of financial planning at the Quebec Ministry of Finance. He also has 10 years of experience as a pension consulting actuary. Mr Gagné received his B.SC degree (mathematics) from McGill University in 1966, became a fellow of the Society of Actuaries and of the Canadian Institute of Actuaries in 1975, and has been a CFA charterholder since 1995.

Cynthia Harrington, CFA, is Principal in an executive coaching and business process consulting firm specializing in the asset management sector, applying behavioral finance. She has written extensively on investment theory, accounting practices, and behavioral and neuro economics. She was a Contributing Editor for *Accounting Today*, and has written over 450 articles that appear in national publications, including *Bloomberg Wealth Manager, Entrepreneur Magazine, Fraud Magazine, CFA Magazine, Journal of Accountancy*, and *Financial Engineering News*. She is a coauthor of the "Financial Statement Fraud" course for the Association of Certified Fraud Examiners. Prior to her writing career in 1999, she was President/ Owner/CIO of *Harrington Capital Management, Ltd.*, an SEC-registered value style asset management company catering to high-net-worth individuals and small institutions. She holds a BA from St. Olaf College. She is a certified fraud examiner (CFE) and a member of the

ACFE. Ms. Harrington has been a CFA charterholder since 1993 and served on the Board of Trustees of the CFALA Charitable Foundation and on the board of the Applied Behavioral Finance Group.

Kenneth Kim is an Associate Professor of Finance at the State University of New York at Buffalo. At SUNY-Buffalo, Dr. Kim teaches corporate finance and international corporate finance to MBA students. During 1998 and 1999, Dr. Kim worked as a senior financial economist at the U.S. Securities and Exchange Commission in Washington, DC, where he worked on a wide variety of corporate finance and governance issues, including mergers and acquisitions regulations. His primary research interests include corporate finance and corporate governance. He has been published in the *Journal of Finance*, the *Journal of Business*, the *Journal of Corporate Finance*, and the *Journal of Banking and Finance*, among other leading journals. Dr. Kim is also a coauthor of *Infectious Greed* and the textbooks *Corporate Governance* and *Global Corporate Finance*. Dr. Kim has also won numerous awards for teaching.

Adam Kobor, CFA, is a Principal Portfolio Manager at the World Bank Treasury. Mr. Kobor is responsible for the development of asset allocation strategies and managing mortgage-backed securities portfolios. Prior to joining the Investment Management Department in 2008, he worked for the Quantitative Strategies, Risk & Analytics Department for six years. His responsibilities included preparing strategic asset allocation recommendations for several internal and external clients, as well as developing quantitative financial models. Prior to joining the bank, he was a risk analyst at the National Bank of Hungary. He holds a PhD from the Budapest University of Economic Sciences, and he is a CFA charterholder. He is author and coauthor of several publications, and he speaks at conferences.

Gene C. Lai is Safeco Distinguished Professor of Insurance and Chairperson of the Department of Finance and Management Science at Washington State University. Professor Lai received his bachelor's degree in economics from National Chengchi University in Taiwan, his master's degree in decision science from Georgia State University in 1981, and his PhD in risk management and insurance and finance from the University of Texas at Austin in 1987. His publications have appeared in *The Journal of Risk and Insurance* and *Journal of Banking and Finance*, among others. Dr. Lai serves as associate editor for many journals, including *Journal of Risk and Insurance*. He is President of the American Risk and Insurance Association and past president of the Western Risk and Insurance Association and was a board member of the Asia-Pacific Risk and Insurance Association.

Rebecca T. McEnally, CFA, until her retirement in 2008, was Director, Capital Markets Policy, with the Capital Markets Policy Group for the CFA Centre for Financial Market Integrity. She was responsible for financial reporting and capital markets advocacy efforts of the CFA Centre and appeared on behalf of the members of CFA Institute before regulatory authorities, legislative bodies, professional associations, and the general public in both the United States and abroad to further the CFA Institute mandate to improve corporate financial reporting and disclosure. Prior to joining CFA Institute, Dr. McEnally taught financial reporting and financial statement analysis at various universities, including the University of North Carolina at Chapel Hill, the Stern School of Business at New York University, and the School of Management at Boston University. She has published a number of articles, monographs, and books, and she has served as a consultant on accounting and finance to financial institutions in the United States, Europe, and Asia.

Keith M. Moore, CFA, is Managing Director of MKM Partners' Event-Driven group. Prior to joining MKM Partners in December 2009, Mr. Moore served as Kellner DiLeo & Company's Co-Chief Investment Officer, Portfolio Manager of the KDC Merger

Arbitrage Fund, and Director of Risk Management. His arbitrage career spans research, trading, and portfolio management at Neuberger & Berman; Donaldson, Lufkin & Jenrette; and Jupiter Capital. A former Assistant Professor of economics and finance at St. John's University and Adjunct Professor at the University of Rhode Island and New York University, Mr. Moore has earned numerous academic awards and honors. He holds a BS and a PhD from the University of Rhode Island and an MBA from New York University. He has been a CFA charterholder since 1982.

Gregory Noronha, CFA, is Professor of Finance at the University of Washington's Tacoma campus, where he currently teaches classes in business finance and investment valuation to both undergraduate and MBA students. He has held previous academic appointments at Arizona State University and Old Dominion University. Mr. Noronha earned a BSE in naval architecture and marine engineering from the University of Michigan and an MBA and PhD in finance from Virginia Tech. His research has focused on the areas of corporate finance and investments, and he has published articles in the *Journal of Finance, Journal of Banking and Finance,* and *Financial Analysts Journal,* among others. Mr. Noronha earned the CFA charter in 1999 and has served CFA Institute in a variety of volunteer roles. He served as Education Chair of the Phoenix Society of Financial Analysts and is currently a member of the Seattle CFA Society.

Edgar A. Norton, CFA, is professor of finance at the College of Business at Illinois State University. He has authored or coauthored more than 30 papers that have been published in journals and conference proceedings, as well as presented at international, national, and regional conferences. He is coauthor of several textbooks, including *Investments; Finance: An Introduction to Institutions, Investments, and Management; Foundations of Financial Management;* and *Economic Justice in Perspective: A Book of Readings.* Mr. Norton has served on the board of directors and as president of the Midwest Finance Association; on the board of the Financial Planning Association of Illinois; and on the board of the ISU Credit Union. He has served CFA Institute for many years in a number of capacities.

Kenneth L. Parkinson is managing director of Treasury Information Services, a consulting and publishing firm. He has been a visiting and adjunct associate professor at Stern Graduate School of Business at New York University, where he teaches courses in working capital management, corporate finance, and corporate treasury practices. Mr. Parkinson actively consults with corporations of all sizes on treasury management projects and is a frequent speaker at major industry conferences and seminars as well as private training sessions for certification candidates. He is the author or coauthor of several texts and a frequent author of articles in trade magazines. Previously, Mr. Parkinson was director of treasury operations at RCA Corporation, managing treasury and banking activities worldwide. He holds a BS from Penn State and an MBA from Wharton Graduate School and is a permanently certified cash manager (CCM).

John D. Stowe, CFA, is the O'Bleness Professor of Finance at Ohio University. Prior to joining Ohio University, he was head, Curriculum Development at CFA Institute and also a Director of Exam Development. Before joining CFA Institute in 2003, he was finance professor, department head, and associate dean at the University of Missouri-Columbia. In addition to *Equity Asset Valuation,* he is coauthor of *Corporate Financial Management.* He has published professional and academic articles in finance journals such as the *Journal of Finance, Journal of Financial and Quantitative Analysis, Financial Management, Journal of Portfolio Management,* and others. He received his BA degree from Centenary College and his PhD from University of Houston. He became a CFA charterholder in 1995 and has since served the

CFA Program in a number of volunteer capacities. He has been a member of the St. Louis and Cleveland CFA societies.

George H. Troughton, CFA, is Professor Emeritus of Finance at California State University, Chico. He holds an AB degree from Brown, an MBA from Columbia, and a PhD from the University of Massachusetts, Amherst. He began his career as an investment analyst at Lehman Brothers and Scudder, Stevens & Clark in New York. He was professor of finance at Babson College before moving to Chico, California. Mr. Troughton has been an active participant in the CFA Program for more than 20 years. At CFA Institute, he was awarded the C. Stewart Sheppard Award in 1999 and the Donald L. Tuttle Award in 2004. He is a member of the Phoenix CFA Society.

ABOUT THE CFA PROGRAM

The Chartered Financial Analyst® designation (CFA®) is a globally recognized standard of excellence for measuring the competence and integrity of investment professionals. To earn the CFA charter, candidates must successfully pass through the CFA Program, a global graduate-level self-study program that combines a broad curriculum with professional conduct requirements as preparation for a wide range of investment specialties.

Anchored by a practice-based curriculum, the CFA Program is focused on the knowledge identified by professionals as essential to the investment decision-making process. This body of knowledge maintains current relevance through a regular, extensive survey of practicing CFA charterholders across the globe. The curriculum covers 10 general topic areas, ranging from equity and fixed-income analysis to portfolio management to corporate finance—all with a heavy emphasis on the application of ethics in professional practice. Known for its rigor and breadth, the CFA Program curriculum highlights principles common to every market so that professionals who earn the CFA designation have a thoroughly global investment perspective and a profound understanding of the global marketplace.

www.cfainstitute.org

INDEX

Page numbers followed by e refer to exhibits

Abandonment options, 131, 743
Abbott Laboratories, 474
AC (average cost), 413–414
Accounts payable, 83
Accounts receivable:
    assignment of, 743
    and internal financing, 84
Accounts receivable turnover, 100e
Accredited investors, 16, 743
Acquisitions:
    as business combinations, 710e
    defined, 743
    evaluating, 636–640
    financial modeling steps for, 621e
    as investment action, 599
Acquisition method, 709–716
Active ownership, 74–75, 76e, 747
Activision Blizzard, 458e
Activist shareholders, 54
Activity ratios, 100, 743
Adidas, 364
Adobe, 475
Aerospace industry, 483
Affiliates, 525
Affiliate marketing, 375, 743
Agency costs:
    defined, 743
    and dividends, 317–319
    and financial distress, 166
    and pecking order theory, 172–174
    and shareholder and manager/director
        relationships, 44
Aggregators, 375
    data, 614
    defined, 743
    in hotel and travel industry, 378
AGMs (annual general meetings), 52
Agriculture industry, 484
Ahold Delhaize, 520–521
Airbnb, 143, 378
Airbus, 470, 475, 483
Airline industry, 149–150, 404, 485–486
AirTran Airways, 423

Alcon, 600–601
Alexion Pharmaceuticals, 609–611
Alibaba, 317, 375
Alphabet Inc., 617
Alternatives, considering, 125
Amazon, 47, 367, 376, 397, 582
American Airlines, 149–150
Amortization, of excess purchase price, 702–704
Anchoring and adjustment, 548
Anheuser-Busch (AM) InBev, 553–555, 561, 564–565
Annual general meetings (AGMs), 52
Apple, 317, 397, 570, 582, 602
Apple Computer, 232
Archer Daniels Midland, 443
Arithmetic mean return, 269–270
Arm Ltd., 598
ASC 825 *Financial Instruments, 692*
ASEAN (Association of Southeast Asian Nations),
    423
ASML Holdings NV, 464
Assets:
    and capital structure, 142–143
    contingent, 729–730
    and cost of capital, 255
    identifiable, 712
    indemnification, 712
    intangible (*see* Intangible assets)
    liquidating, 96
    ownership of, 143
    securitization of, 727–729
    and short-term financing, 103
    stranded, 754
    tangible (*see* Tangible assets)
Asset-backed loans, 86, 753
Asset beta:
    defined, 743
    estimating, 233
    and MM propositions, 161–162
Asset-light business models, 143, 380, 743
Assets:
    financial, 692–695, 712
    fungible, 142
    liquid, 84–85
    marketable, 156–157
    stranded, 70, 675

Assignment of accounts receivable, 86, 743
Associates:
    disclosure and transactions with, 705–709
    intercorporate investments in, 695–700
Association of Southeast Asian Nations (ASEAN), 423
AstraZeneca plc, 507–508, 609–611
Asymmetric information:
    and agency costs, 172–174
    defined, 743
    and signaling, 313–314
AT&T, 443
Auction models, 367, 743
Audi, 66
Audit committees, 57
Automobile industry, 399, 438
Average cost (AC), 413–414
Avon, 516e
Awin, 375

Balance sheets:
    acquisition method on, 714–716
    consolidated, 723–725
    income statement modeling, 525–531, 543–544
    noncontrolling interests, 717–719
    and restructuring actions, 601–605
Balance sheet restructuring, 603, 743
Balwani, Ramesh, 64
Bancel, Franck, 239
Banks:
    as influential shareholders, 663
    as stakeholders, 38
Bank debt, 263–264
Bank financing, 85–86
Bank of America Corporation, 343e
Bankruptcy, 212–213
    Chapter 7 liquidation, 212
    Chapter 11 reorganization, 212, 213
    and liquidity sources, 96
    as risk of poor corporate governance, 66
Barriers to entry, 468–469, 486e
Base rates, 549–550
BASF, 443
BCG (Boston Consulting Group), 596
Becle S.A.B. de C.V. (Cuervo), 550
Beer industry, 553–555, 561–562
Behavioral finance and analyst forecasts, 545–551
Beiersdorf, 515e
Beta:
    asset, 161–162, 743
    estimating, 232–236
    factor, 283, 747
Bezos, Jeff, 47
Bias:
    about capital, 125
    confirmation, 277, 551, 744
    conservatism, 548–549

illusion of control, 547
overconfidence, 545–546
recency, 277, 752
representativeness, 549–550
survivorship, 754
Blackstone Group, 605–606
Bloomberg, 614
BMW, 475
Board committees, 56–60, 62, 668
Board composition, 668
Boards of directors:
    independent, 749
    as influential shareholders, 665
    manager and board relationships, 49
    one-tier boards, 666
    policies and practices of, 667–669
    staggered boards, 39, 754
    as stakeholders, 38–39
    structure of, 666
    two-tier boards, 666
    two-tiered boards, 755
Boeing, 470, 475
Bonds, green, 75, 675–676, 748
Bondholders:
    conflicts of interests between shareholders
        and, 31
    equity and debt risk–return profiles, 25–28
    as stakeholders, 38
Bond indentures, 55–56, 318
Bond yield plus risk premium (BYPRP) approach:
    for cost of equity, 231–232, 280–281
    defined, 743
Bonus issues of shares, 307–309, 743
Booking.com, 378
Book value:
    investment in excess of, 700–702
    market value vs., 169–170
Book value per share (BVPS), 337
Borrowed capital, 9, 335–336, 744. See also Debt
Boston Consulting Group (BCG), 596
Boston Scientific, 474
Bottom-up approach, 505–506, 744
Bottom-up company specific factors, 254–259
Brazil, 553–554
Breakeven points, 208–211, 214, 744
Brookstone, 213
Brounen, Dirk, 240
Brown-Forman Corporation, 550
BT Group Plc, 316
Buffett, Warren, 114, 125
Build-up approach, 286–287
Bundling, 367, 744
Business combinations:
    with impaired comparability, 729–730
    with less than 100% acquisition, 716
    types of, 710e–711e

Business cycle:
  airline industry, 485
  and capital structure, 149–150
  in industry analysis, 488*e*
  and similar companies, 454–455
Business environment, understanding, 452
Business growth, 112–113
Business liability, 8
Business life cycle:
  and capital structure, 151–157
  of corporations, 20–23
Business maintenance, 111–112
Business model characteristics, 141–144
Business models, 359–383
  asset-light, 743
  elements of, 359–373
  financial implications for, 378–383
  types of, 373–378
Business risk, 192–193, 383–391
  company-specific risk as, 387–389
  components of, 385*e*
  defined, 385, 744
  and financial risk, 389–391
  industry risk as, 386–387
  macro risk, financial risk, and, 384–386
Business structures, 2–12
  corporations, 5–11
  general partnerships, 3–4
  limited liability companies, 5–11
  limited partnerships, 4–5
  sole proprietorships, 2–3
Buybacks, 332, 744. *See also* share repurchases
BVPS (book value per share), 337
BYPRP, *see* Bond yield plus risk premium approach

Cable television, 397
Callability, 256
Cambridge Analytica, 72
Canadian National Railway Company, 623–628
Canadian Pacific Railway Limited, 623–627
Canceled shares, 332, 744
Cannibalization, 117–118, 570–579, 744
Capabilities, of business, 370–372
Capacity-based measure forecasts, 505
Capital:
  access to, 16*e*
  availability of, 251
  bias related to, 125
  borrowed, 9, 335–336, 744 (*See also* Debt)
  debt, 212
  equity, 212
  estimating proportions of, 171–172
  ownership, 9, 751
  working (*see* Working capital)
Capital allocation:
  corporate use of, 126–129
  defined, 744

  pitfalls in, 125–126
  principles of, 116*e*
  process, 114–119
Capital asset pricing model (CAPM):
  for cost of capital, 239–240
  for cost of equity, 228–231, 282, 294
  defined, 744
  expanded CAPM, 285–286
  global CAPM, 288, 289, 748
  international CAPM, 288–289, 749
Capital expenditures:
  growth, 748
  maintenance, 750
Capital financing, 8–9
Capital gains, 324
Capital-intensive businesses, 156–157
Capital investment risk, 389, 744
Capital investments, 109–133
  capital allocation pitfalls, 125–126
  capital allocation process, 114–119
  corporate use of capital allocation, 126–129
  income statement modeling, 541
  investment decision criteria in, 119–124
  real options in, 129–132
  types of, 110–114
Capital IQ, 614
Capital leases, 264, 747
Capital light, 153–154, 157, 744
Capital providers, 9, 744
Capital structure, 139–183
  and company life cycle, 151–157
  defined, 139–140, 744
  factors affecting, 140–151
  Modigliani–Miller propositions, 157–167
  optimal, 167–174, 751
  policies and guidelines influencing, 146–147
  and stakeholders interests, 174–182
  static trade-off theory of, 754
  target, 167–174, 221, 250, 754
CAPM, *see* Capital asset pricing model
Carlsberg, 554, 567–568
Carnegie, Andrew, 433
Carrefour, 565–567
Carrillion PLC, 166
Cartels, 429, 433, 744
Cash conversion cycle, 100*e*
Cash dividends, 305
Cash flow(s):
  discounted cash flow model, 544–545
  free, 96
  free cash flow to equity, 348–351
  incremental, 117, 749
  operating, 83
Cash flow patterns:
  conventional, 745
  nonconventional, 751
Cash flow sensitivity, 141–142

Cash flow statement modeling, 525–531, 542–543
Cash flow volatility, 254–255
Cash management, 96
Cash ratio, 100*e*
Cash tax rate, 521
Caterpillar, 475, 476
CEO duality, 667
Chamberlin, Edward H., 398
Channels, 362–365
Cisco, 317
Citigroup Inc., 343*e*
City Developments Limited, 671–672
Civil law, 62–63
CJ Affiliate, 375
Climate Action 100+, 74–75
Clorox, 516*e*
Cluster analysis, 456
Coca-Cola, 398
Cognac industry, 552, 553*e*
COGS, *see* Cost of goods sold
Colgate, 515, 516*e*
Collaterals, 56, 744
Collusion:
    factors for successful, 429–430
    oligopoly markets with and without, 423
Commercial aircraft market, 470, 475
Commercial industry classification systems, 457–461
Commercial paper, short-term, 87
Committed (regular) lines of credit, 85, 744
Common equity, 87
Common law, 62–63
Communication services/telecommunication sector, 459*e*
Company analysis, 452, 489–493
Company costs, 568–569
Company sales, 563–565
Company specific factors:
    affecting business models, 380–383
    bottom-up, in cost of capital, 254–259
Company-specific risks, 387–389
Company strategy, 565
Company valuation, 190
Comparability, impaired, 729–730
Comparable companies, 233, 614–617, 744
Comparable transaction analysis, 617–619
Compensation committees, 58–59
Competition:
    among incumbent companies, in Porter's five
        forces model, 552
    among retail businesses, 213
    and business models, 380
    imperfect, 421
    and industry risk, 386
    monopolistic (*see* Monopolistic competition)
    non-price, 399
    perfect (*see* Perfect competition)
    price, 475–476, 487*e*
    prices and costs related to, 551–561

Competitive Advantage (Porter), 371
Competitive risk, 388, 744
Competitive strategy, 489–490
Competitive Strategy (Porter), 400–401
Complements, 407, 744
Component cost of capital, 220, 744
Computer hardware industry, 481
Concentrated industries, 470–471
Concentrated ownership, 45, 46*e*, 660–662, 744
Concentration ratio, 444–445
Confirmation bias, 277, 551, 744
Conflicts of interest:
    between debt and equity, 175–180
    equity vs. debt, 31
    within ownership structures, 662–663
Conglomerate discount, 600, 744
Conservatism bias, 548–549
Consolidated balance sheets, 723–725
Consolidated Financial Statements (IFRS 10), 711,
    726
Consolidated income statements, 725
Consolidated-Special Purpose Entities (SIC-12), 711
Consolidation, 710*e*
Consolidation (FASB ASC Topic 810), 727
Consolidation process, 716–722
Constant dividend payout ratio policy, 327, 329–
    331, 744
Consumer discretionary sector, 458*e*
Consumer staples sector, 458*e*
Consumer surplus, 408–410, 440–442, 744
Continental AG, 580–581
Contingent assets, 729–730
Contingent consideration, 730
Contingent liabilities, 712, 729–730
Contracts:
    and dividend policies, 325–326
    employment, 60
    negotiating debt, 96
Contract manufacturers, 374, 752
Contribution margin, 195–196, 745
Controlling shareholders:
    controlling and minority shareholder relationships,
        44–48
    defined, 45, 745
    as majority or minority shareholders, 661
Control systems, weak, 63–65
Conventional cash flow patterns, 118, 745
Convertibility, 257
Corporate actions, 594–595
Corporate governance, 36–69
    defined, 51, 745
    in ESG integration, 684–685
    evaluating policies and procedures for, 666–670
    overview of, 51–52
    and ownership structures, 660–666
    relationships in, 41–51
    risks and benefits related to, 63–69

stakeholder groups, 36–41
stakeholder risk management, 51–69
Corporate governance codes, 61, 666
Corporate income tax:
  income statement modeling, 537
  in income statement modeling, 521–524
Corporate investments, 690–691
Corporate life cycle, 594–595
Corporate reporting, 52, 56
Corporate restructuring, 593–654
  corporate life cycle and actions, 594–595
  evaluating, 611–620
  evaluating divestment actions, 640–646
  evaluating investment actions, 628–640
  evaluating restructuring actions, 647–653
  modeling and valuation, 620–628
  motivations for, 595–597
  types of, 597–611
Corporate structures, 2–23
  business structures, 2–12
  exchange listing and share ownership transfer, 13–15
  going public from private, 18–20
  life cycle of corporations, 20–23
  share issuance, 15–18
Corporate takeovers, 55
Corporate tax rate, 146
Corporate transaction activity, 596
Corporations, 5–11
  business liability, 8
  capital allocation used by, 126–129
  capital financing, 8–9
  for-profits, 6–7
  legal identity of, 7
  life cycle of, 20–23
  nonprofit, 6, 751
  owner–operator separation in, 7–8
  private for-profits, 7
  public for-profits, 7
  taxation, 10–11
Costs. *See also specific types*
  effects of, on gross profit and margin, 513
  impact of competitive factors in prices and, 551–561
  of restructuring and reorganization, 601–605
Cost advantages, 388
Cost-based pricing, 366, 745
Costco Wholesale Corporation, 101
Cost of capital, 219–241, 249–300
  in capital allocation, 117
  case studies, 293–300
  component, 744
  cost of common equity, 228–232
  cost of debt, 223–226
  cost of equity, 279–292
  cost of preferred stock, 226–227
  defined, 220, 745

ERP, 268–278
  estimating beta, 232–236
  estimating cost of debt, 261–267
  factors related to, 250–261
  flotation costs, 237–239
  methods for estimating, 239–240
  and MM propositions with taxes, 163–165
  taxes and, 222–223
Cost of common equity, 228–232
Cost of debt, 223–226
  and corporate governance, 66–67
  defined, 249, 745
  estimating, 261–267
  and internal forecasting, 126
  and taxes, 238e
Cost of equity, 228–232, 279–292
  defined, 249, 745
  and flotation costs, 238
  and internal forecasting, 126
  and taxes, 238e
Cost of goods sold (COGS):
  income statement modeling, 533
  and inflation and deflation, 563–565
  operating cost modeling, 512–514
Cost of preferred stock, 226–227, 745
Cost projections, 567–569
Cost restructuring, 602–603, 745
Cost structure, 191, 193, 745
Country risk, 252
Country risk premium (CRP), 266, 287–290, 745
Country risk rating (CRR), 266, 745
Cournot, Augustin, 425
Cournot assumption, 425–428, 745
Covenants, 55, 745
COVID-19 pandemic, 149–150
Credit, 98
Credit analysis:
  ESG considerations in, 73, 675
Creditors:
  risk management related to, 55–56
  risks of, 211–213
  shareholder interests vs., 49
  as stakeholders, 38
Creditor committees, 56
Credit policies, changes in, 95
Credit spread, 250, 745
Creditworthiness, 85–86, 103, 745
Cross-price elasticity of demand, 406–407, 745
Cross-sectional regression analysis, 444
Crowdsourcing, 376, 378, 745
CRP, *see* Country risk premium
CRR (country risk rating), 266, 745
Cuervo (Becle S.A.B. de C.V.), 550
Cumulative preferred stock, 257, 745
Cumulative voting, 53, 745
Current income, 324
Current ratio, 99e

Customers:
  bargaining power of, in Porter's five forces model, 552
  behavior of, 486
  in business model, 361–362
  governments as, 483
  and stakeholder risk management, 60–61
  as stakeholders, 40
  variety preferred by, 421
Customer concentration risk, 254, 745
CVS Health Corporation, 509–512
Cyclical companies, 454–455
Cyclicality, 386

Daimler AG, 101, 600
Damodaran, Aswath, 288
Danielsson, Anders, 321–322
Data aggregators, 614
Data privacy, 71–72
Davide Campari-Milano N.V., 550
Days inventory outstanding, 100e
Days payable outstanding, 100e
Days sales outstanding, 100e
DCF (discounted cash flow) model, 544–545
DDM, see Dividend discount model
De Beers Consolidated Mines Limited, 434
Debt. See also Cost of debt
  ability to support, 142
  bank, 263–264
  as borrowed capital, 9
  conflicts of interest between equity and, 31
  distressed, 179
  fixed-rate, 225
  floating-rate, 225
  leveraging role of, 204–205
  long-term, 87
  nonrated, 226
  non-traded, 262–263
  with optionlike features, 225–226
  straight, 262, 754
  traded, 262
Debt capital, 212
Debt claims, 24e
Debt contracts, negotiating, 96
Debt default, 66
Debtholders, 38
Debt-rating approach, 224–225, 745
Debt ratings, third-party, 148–149
Debt risk–return profiles, 25–30
Debt tax shield, 163, 745
Decision-making, ineffective, 63–65
Decline corporation stage, 21
Decline industry stage, 477–478
Deere, 476
Default risk, 66–67
Defensive industries, 454–455
Defined, 752
Deflation, 561–569

Degree of financial leverage (DFL), 201–205, 207, 214, 746
Degree of operating leverage (DOL), 194–201, 207, 214, 746
Degree of total leverage (DTL), 205–208, 214, 746
De Jong, Abe, 240
Delta Air Lines, 200, 423
Demand:
  cannibalization of, 570–577
  factors affecting, 406–408
  in monopolistically competitive markets, 419–420
  in monopoly markets, 435–436
  in oligopoly markets, 423–425
  in perfectly competitive markets, 401–403
  price elasticity of, 403–406
  and technological developments, 570
Demand curves, 412–413
Demographics, 379, 482, 488e
Denso Corporation, 318
Depreciation, 541
Deutsche Bank, 694, 698e–700e, 708
DFL, see Degree of financial leverage
Diageo plc, 550
Dieselgate, 66
Differentiation:
  airline industry, 486
  and market structure, 399
  in monopolistic competition, 418–419, 421
Differentiation strategies, 490
Digital marketing, 374
Dimson, Elroy, 230
Direct listing (DL), 19, 746
Direct negotiation:
  share repurchases by, 333, 339
Directors:
  independence of, 665, 667
  interests of, 181–182
Directorates, interlocking, 663, 749
Direct sales, 363, 364e, 746
Disclosures, 705–709
Disclosure requirements, 16–17
Discounted cash flow (DCF) model, 544–545
Dispersed ownership, 44, 45e, 660–662, 746
Disruptions:
  and competitive risk, 388
  defined, 746
  in long-term forecasting, 582
Distressed debt, 179
Divestitures, 601, 746
Divestment actions:
  evaluating, 640–646
  types of, 599–601
Dividends, 304–332
  analysis of dividend safety, 347–351
  cash, 305
  defined, 304, 746
  dividend policy theories, 311–313

extra, 305–307, 747
factors affecting dividend policy, 319–327
irregular, 305–307
liquidating, 307, 750
payout policies, 327–332
regular cash, 305
share repurchases vs., 339–347
signaling, 313–319
special, 305–307, 753
stock, 307–309, 754
valuation equivalence of, 338–339
Dividend coverage ratio, 347–351, 746
Dividend discount model (DDM):
for cost of equity, 279–280
defined, 746
for ERP, 273–274, 277
Dividend imputation tax system, 323, 746
Dividend payout ratio, 306–307, 746
Dividend policy(-ies), 306–307
decision-making related to, 345–347
defined, 746
factors affecting, 319–327
stable, 327–331, 754
Dividend policy theories, 311–313
Dividend recapitalization, 603, 746
Dividend safety, 347–351
Dividend yield, 309, 746
DL (direct listing), 19, 746
DOL, *see* Degree of operating leverage
Dollar Shave Club, 368
Double taxation system, 323–324
defined, 746
Dow Corning Corporation, 213
Dow Jones, 457
Downstream, 705, 707–708, 725, 746
Drag on liquidity, 98–99, 746
Drop shipping, 364, 746
DTL, *see* Degree of total leverage
Dual-class shares, 47–48
defined, 746
and ownership structure, 662
and voting, 669–670
DuPont, 407
DuPont equation, 93
Dutch auctions, 333
Dynamic pricing, 367, 746

Earnings:
and capital structure, 141–142
as company specific factor, 254–255
expected volatility of future, 321
normalized, 580, 751
revenues and operating, 200, 201e
Earnings per share (EPS):
investment decisions based on, 126
and share repurchases, 335–337
Eastman Kodak Company, 582

eBay, 317, 375
Eberhard, Martin, 1
EBIT, 145
EBITDA, 145
E-commerce business models, 375
Econometric approaches, 444
Economic conditions, 378–379
Economic costs, 411, 746
Economic profits, 411, 747
Economies of scale, 509, 747
eDreams, 378
Effective tax rate, 521, 522
Efficiency ratios, 526–527
EGMs (extraordinary general meetings), 52
Elasticity, 194, 747
Elasticity of demand, 403–406
Electric utilities, 319
Eli Lilly, 507–508, 600
Elucida Oncology, 234–235
Embryonic industries, 477
Emissions, toxic, 71
Empire building, 43
Employees, 40, 60
Employee stock ownership plans (ESOPs), 60
Employment contracts, 60
Energy sector, 459e
Engagement ownership, 74–75, 76e, 747
Enron Corporation, 665, 726
Enterprise value, 14–15
Entity relationships, 17e
Entrants, threat of new, 552
Entrenchment, 43
Entry, barriers to, 468–469
Environmental, social, and governance (ESG)
considerations, 69–77, 659–686
evaluating corporate governance policies and
procedures, 666–670
evaluating ESG-related risks and opportunities,
676–685
factors in, 70–72
identifying ESG-related risks and opportunities,
670–676
for industries, 484
in investment analysis, 69–73
investment approaches including, 73–77
ownership structures and corporate governance,
660–666
in stakeholder theory, 37
Environmental considerations:
airline industry, 486
in ESG integration, 70–71, 678–681
influence of, on industry, 483–485
EPS, *see* Earnings per share
Equifax Inc., 71–72
Equity:
common, 87
conflicts of interest between debt and, 31

long-term, 87
    as ownership capital, 9, 751
Equity analysis, 72
Equity beta, 162
Equity capital, 212
Equity claims, 24e
Equity indexes, 268
Equity investments:
    defined, 747
    evaluating, 628–632
    as investment action, 599
Equity method of accounting, 697–709
Equity risk premium (ERP), 229–231, 250, 268–
    278, 747
Equity risk–return profiles, 25–30
ERP, see Equity risk premium
ESG, 747. See also Environmental, social, and
    governance considerations
ESG integration, 74, 76e, 674–685, 747
ESG risk, 389, 747
ESOPs (employee stock ownership plans), 60
ESPN, 397
Estée Lauder, 515e
Etsy, 375
Ex ante estimates, 272
Excessive risk taking, 43–44
Excess purchase price, amortization of, 702–704
Exchange listing, 13–15
Ex-dividend, 304, 747
Ex-dividend date, 304, 747
Execution risk, 388–389, 747
Executive remuneration, 669
Expanded CAPM, 285–286
Expansion projects, 112–113
Expected volatility of future earnings, 321
Expedia, 378
External factors:
    affecting business models, 378–379
    affecting capital structure, 149–151
    on industries, 480–489
    top-down, in cost of capital, 251–253
External financing, 82, 85–89
    capital markets, 87
    financial intermediaries, 85–86
Externality, 117–118, 747
Extra dividends, 305–307, 747
Extraordinary general meetings (EGMs), 52

Facebook, 72
Factor beta, 283, 747
Factoring arrangement, 86, 747
Factor risk premiums, 283, 300, 747
FactSet, 614
Fairtrading prices, 617
Fair value:
    acquisition price less than, 713–714
    financial assets measured at, 693

Fair value option, 704
Fair value through other comprehensive income
    (FVOCI), 693–695
Fair value through profit or loss (FVPL), 693–695
Fama–French five-factor model (FF5), 283, 294
Fama–French models, 282–284, 747
Fama–French three-factor model, 282–283
Families, as shareholders, 663–664
Farfetch Ltd., 613
FASB (U.S. Financial Accounting Standards Board),
    690, 692
FASB ASC Topic 323, 696
FASB ASC Topic 810 (Consolidation), 727
FCFE (free cash flow to equity), 348–351
FF5 (Fama–French five-factor model), 283, 294
Finance leases, 226, 264, 747
Financial assets, 692–695, 712
Financial distress:
    defined, 747
    MM propositions and costs of, 165–167
    and static trade-off theory, 168e
Financial flexibility, 321–322
Financial Instruments (ASC 825), 692
Financial Instruments (IFRS 9), 692–695
Financial intermediaries, 85–86
Financial leverage:
    as company specific factor, 254
    and cost of capital, 256
    defined, 747
    and financial risk, 385
    increasing, with share repurchases, 341–342
    measuring, 390–391
Financial liabilities, 712
Financial options, 130
Financial risk, 201–205
    and business risk, 389–391
    and corporate governance, 66–69
    defined, 201, 385–386, 747
    macro risk, business risk, and, 384–386
Financial sector, 459e
Financial services sector, 373
Financial statements:
    pro forma, 752
    and share repurchases, 334–337
Financial statement modeling, 501–585
    balance sheet and cash flow statement modeling,
        525–531
    behavioral finance and analyst forecasts, 545–551
    building a model, 531–545
    impact of competitive factors in prices and costs,
        551–561
    income statement modeling, 508–512
    inflation and deflation, 561–569
    long-term forecasting, 580–584
    non-operating costs modeling, 520–525
    operating costs modeling, 512–519
    technological developments, 570–579

Financial statement presentation, 723–725
Financing:
  growth company, 154
  and life cycle, 20*e*, 22*e*
  start-up, 153
Financing expenses, 520–521
Financing options:
  flexibility of, 103
  working capital, 82–89
First-degree price discrimination, 440, 748
Fixed costs, 189, 191, 196, 197, 199, 509, 748
Fixed-income analysis, 72
Fixed operating costs, 194
Fixed price tender offers, 333, 748
Fixed-rate debt, 225
Fixed-rate perpetual preferred stock, 226, 748
Flexibility options, 131
Floating-rate debt, 225
Flotation costs, 237–239, 312, 324, 748
Ford Motor Company, 318
Foreign investors, 665
For-profit corporations, 6–7
Forward-looking approach, to ERP, 268, 272–277
Forward-looking estimates, 272, 748
Fractionalization, 368, 377, 748
Fragmented industries, 470–471
Franchising:
  as alternative to ownership, 368
  as business model, 375
  defined, 748
  in hotel and travel industry, 377
  as restructuring action, 602
Franking credit, 323, 748
Free cash flow, 96
Free cash flow hypothesis, 173, 748
Free cash flow to equity (FCFE), 348–351
Freemium pricing, 367, 748
Friedman, Thomas J., 396
FTSE Russell, 457
Functional separation, 377
Fundamental options, 131
Fungible assets, 142
Future earnings, expected volatility of, 321
FVOCI (fair value through other comprehensive
  income), 693–695
FVPL (fair value through profit or loss), 693–695

Game theory, 428, 748
Gary, Elbert, 433
GCAPM (global CAPM), 288, 289, 748
General Electric, 443
General partners (GPs), 4–5, 748
General partnerships, 3–4
Genpact, 602
Geographic analysis, 502–503
Geometric mean return, 269–270
GICS (Global Industry Classification Standard), 454, 457

GIIN (Global Impact Investing Network), 75
GlaxoSmithKline, 600, 690, 723–725
Global CAPM (GCAPM), 288, 289, 748
Global Impact Investing Network (GIIN), 75
Global Industry Classification Standard (GICS), 454,
  457
Global Reporting Initiative (GRI), 77, 673
Global Sustainable Investment Alliance (GSIA), 77
Globus Maritime Ltd, 310–311
Going concern projects, 111
Goodwill:
  impairment of, 720–722
  investments with, 703–704
  recognition and measurement of, 713
Google, 360, 396, 397, 582
Google Maps, 376
Gordon growth model, 273, 748
Governance committees, 57–58
Governments:
  as customers, 483
  influence of, on industry, 482–483, 488*e*
  monopolies controlled by, 434–435, 439–440, 442
  and stakeholder risk management, 61–63
  as stakeholders, 40
Government franchises, 442
Government regulations, 61
GPs (general partners), 4–5, 748
Graham, John, 239, 240
Green Bond Principles, 675–676
Green bonds, 75, 675–676, 748
Green finance, 75–76, 748
Green loans, 75–76, 748
Greenmail, 333, 748
Greenwashing, 676, 748
GRI (Global Reporting Initiative), 77, 673
Grinold-Kroner model, 274–275
Gross margin, 513–514
Gross profit, 513
Group companies, 664
Groupe Eurotunnel, 314
Growth businesses, 153–154
Growth capital expenditures, 528, 748
Growth company financing, 154
Growth cyclical companies, 455
Growth industries, 455, 477
Growth options, 131, 748
Growth relative to GDP growth approach, 505
Growth stage, 21
Grupo Aeroportuario del Sureste, 583–584
Grupo Carso, 664
Gruppo Hera, 327–328
GSIA (Global Sustainable Investment Alliance), 77
GSK plc, 454, 464

Harley-Davidson, 419
Harvey, Campbell, 239, 240
HBO, 397

Health care sector, 459e, 674e
Heavy-equipment market, 475–476
Heineken, 553, 554
Henkel, 515, 516e
Herfindahl, O. C., 445
Herfindahl–Hirschman Index (HHI), 387, 445–446
Hewlett-Packard Company (HP), 462
Hewlett-Packard Enterprise (HPE), 462
hhgregg, 213
HHI (Herfindahl–Hirschman Index), 387, 445–446
Hidden revenue business models, 367–368, 748
Hilton Hotels Corporation, 605–606
Hilton Hotels & Resorts, 377
Hirschman, A. O., 445
Historical approach, to ERP, 268–272
Historical equity risk premium approach, 230, 748
Historical rates of return, 231
Holiday Inn, 377
Holmes, Elizabeth, 64
Home Depot, 470
Home improvement market, 470
Home sharing, 378
Honeywell, 443
Hon Hai Precision Ltd., 602
Horizontal demand schedules, 405, 748
Host Hotels & Resorts, 377
Hostile takeovers, 55, 749
Hotel and travel industry, 376–378, 391
HP (Hewlett-Packard Company), 462
HPE (Hewlett-Packard Enterprise), 462
HP Inc., 462
Huawei, 367
Hurdle rate, 123, 749
Hurricane Katrina, 473
Hybrid approach, 505, 506, 749
Hybrid business models, 376
Hyundai, 365

IAS 28, 696
IAS 39, 692
IASB (International Accounting Standards Board), 690, 692
IBM, 71
IBR (incremental borrowing rate), 264, 749
ICAPM (international CAPM), 288–289, 749
ICB (Industry Classification Benchmark), 454, 457–458
ICMA (International Capital Market Association), 75, 675–676
Idea generation, 115
Identifiable assets and liabilities, 712
Idiosyncratic risk premium (IRP), 250, 749
IFRS, see International Financial Reporting Standards
IFRS 9 Financial Instruments, 692–695
IFRS 10 Consolidated Financial Statements, 711, 726
IFRS 11, Joint Arrangements, 696n10
IIRC (International Integrated Reporting Council), 673

IKEA, 360
Illusion of control, 547
Impact investing, 75, 76e, 749
Impairment:
    of goodwill, 720–722
    in intercorporate investments, 704–705
Impairment of capital rule, 325, 749
Imperfect competition, 421
Income elasticity of demand, 406, 749
Income statements:
    consolidated, 725
    noncontrolling interests, 719–720
Income statement modeling:
    non-operating costs, 520–525
    operating costs, 508–512
    revenue analysis, 502–508
Incremental borrowing rate (IBR), 264, 749
Incremental cash flow, 117, 749
Indemnification assets, 712
Indentures, 318, 749
Independent board directors, 665, 667, 749
Independent projects, 119, 749
Industrials sector, 459e
Industry(-ies), defining, 387, 453
Industry analysis, 452–489
    external influences on industry, 480–489
    identifying similar companies, 453–456
    industry classification systems, 457–465
    process of, 465–480
    uses of, 452–453
Industry capacity, 472–473, 487e
Industry Classification Benchmark (ICB), 454, 457–458
Industry classification systems, 453–454, 457–465
Industry concentration, 470–472, 487e
Industry costs:
    and business models, 379
    with inflation and deflation, 567–568
Industry life cycle, 476–480, 485, 487e
Industry risk premium (IP), 284–285, 749
Industry risks, 386–387, 749
Industry sales, 561–563
Industry sectors:
    and capital structure, 150–151
    in industry classification schemes, 453
    variations between, 157
Industry shocks, 597, 749
Industry structure, 386–387
Inelastic demand, 404
Inflation:
    and capital allocation, 129
    cost projections with, 567–569
    in financial statement modeling, 561–569
    sales projections with, 561–567
Influential shareholders, 663–665
Information:
    asymmetric, 172–174, 313–314, 743

signaled by dividend decisions, 313–317
Information technology sector, 459e
Infrastructure, 434–435
Initial public offerings (IPOs), 12, 19, 749
Innovation:
    in business models, 374
    and perfectly competitive markets, 418
In-process R&D, 730
Insiders, 665, 749
Institutional investors, 664
Intangible assets:
    and capital structure, 142
    and cost of capital, 255
    defined, 749
Intel Corporation, 443, 464
InterContinental Hotels & Resorts, 376
Intercorporate investments, 689–731
    acquisition method, 709–716
    amortization of excess purchase price, 702–704
    in associates and joint ventures, 695–700
    business combinations with impaired
        comparability, 729–730
    consolidation process, 716–722
    corporate investment categories, 690–691
    fair value option, 704
    in financial assets, 692–695
    financial statement presentation, 723–725
    impairment in, 704–705
    transactions with associates and disclosure, 705–
        709
    variable interest and special purpose entities, 726–
        729
Interlocking directorates, 663, 749
Internal factors, affecting capital structure, 141–144
Internal financing, 82–85
Internal forecasting errors, 126
Internal rate of return (IRR), 119, 122–124, 749
International Accounting Standards Board (IASB),
    690, 692
International Capital Market Association (ICMA),
    75, 675–676
International CAPM (ICAPM), 288–289, 749
International considerations:
    for cost of debt, 266
    in cost of equity, 287–290
International Financial Reporting Standards (IFRS),
    692
    acquisition method, 710, 711–713
    consolidated financial statements, 725
    consolidation, 716, 717, 719
    contingent assets and liabilities, 729–730
    contingent consideration, 730
    disclosures, 708
    excess purchase price, 700–701
    fair value option, 704
    impairment, 704–705
    impairment of goodwill, 720–722

in-process R&D, 730
investment in financial assets, 692–695
investments in associates and joint ventures, 695–
    696
restructuring costs, 730
transactions with associates and disclosures, 705
US GAAP and, 690
International Integrated Reporting Council (IIRC),
    673
Intuit, 376
Inventory:
    as liquid asset, 84–85
    and liquidity, 98
Inventory turnover, 100e
Investing:
    impact, 75, 76e, 749
    responsible, 73, 753
    socially responsible, 73, 753
    sustainable, 73, 754
    thematic, 74, 76e, 755
    value-based vs. values-based, 73
Investments. *See also specific types*
    approaches including ESG considerations, 73–77
    dividends and opportunities for, 320–321
    identifying opportunities for, 452–453
    reclassification of, 693–695
Investment actions:
    evaluating, 628–640
    types of, 597–599
Investment analysis:
    in capital allocation, 115
    ESG considerations in, 69–73
Investment committees, 60
Investment decision criteria:
    for capital allocation, 126
    in capital investments, 119–124
Investment horizon, 670
Investors:
    accredited, 16, 743
    equity and debt risk–return profiles, 25–28
    foreign, 665
    institutional, 664
IP (industry risk premium), 284–285, 749
IPOs, *see* Initial public offerings
IRP (idiosyncratic risk premium), 250, 749
IRR, *see* Internal rate of return
Irregular dividends, 305–307
Issuer-specific motivations, 595e, 596
ITOCHU Corporation, 342–343

Jacobs Douwe Egberts (JDE), 567
Japan, 482
JCB, 475
JD.com, 317
JDE (Jacobs Douwe Egberts), 567
Jensen, Michael, 173
Johnson & Johnson, 474

Joint Arrangements (IFRS 11), 696n10
Joint ventures:
   defined, 749
   evaluating, 632–636
   intercorporate investments in, 695–700
   as investment action, 599
JP Morgan Chase and Co., 343*e*

Kansas City Southern, 623–628
Kimberly-Clark, 516*e*
Kinked demand curves, 424–425
Kitov Pharma, 310
Koedijk, Kees, 240
Kohl's Corporation, 101–102
Komatsu, 475, 476
Kumon, 602

Labor laws, 60
Lam Research Corporation, 464
Law of diminishing returns, 413–414, 749
LBOs, *see* Leveraged buyouts
Leadbit, 375
Lean startups, 380, 749
Leases:
   and cost of debt, 226, 264–266
   finance or capital, 226, 264, 747
   operating, 226, 751
Leasing, 368, 749
Least squares regression, 200
Legal considerations:
   and business models, 379
   and cost of capital, 252
   in dividend policies, 325–326
   for short-term financing, 103
Legal identity, of corporations, 7
Legal risks, 65–66
Legal systems:
   common law vs. civil law, 62–63
   labor laws, 60
Lenders:
   non-bank, 86, 751
   and owners, 23–31
   private, as stakeholders, 38
   seniority and security of, 180
   web-based, 86, 755
Leverage:
   company value and, 190
   components of, 390*e*
   defined, 189, 213–214, 749
   degree of operating leverage (*see* Degree of
      operating leverage)
   degree of total leverage (*see* Degree of total leverage)
   effect of, on equity beta, 162
   existing, 144–149
   financial (*see* Financial leverage)
   and management stock options, 181–182
   measures of, 189–214

   operating (*see* Operating leverage)
   peer firm, 150–151
   risk and, 192–205, 211–213
   and stakeholder relationships, 50–51
   total, 205–208
Leveraged buyouts (LBOs), 22–23, 605–606, 750
Liabilities:
   contingent, 712, 729–730
   identifiable, 712
   recognition and measurement of financial, 712
Libor (London Interbank Offered Rate), 86
Licensing arrangements, 368, 374–375, 750
Life cycle, *see* Business life cycle; Corporate life cycle;
      Industry life cycle
Limited companies, 5. *See also* limited liability
      companies (LLCs)
Limited liability companies (LLCs), 5–11
Limited partners (LPs), 4–5, 750
Limited partnerships, 4–5, 750
Linear business models, 375
Lines of credit, 85–86, 98, 744
Lintner, John, 328
Liquid assets, 84–85
Liquidating dividends, 307, 750
Liquidation, 212, 603, 750
Liquidity, 89–105
   and cost of capital, 255
   defined, 95, 750
   drag on, 746
   estimating costs of, 97
   evaluating short-term financing choices, 103–105
   measuring, 99–102
   primary sources of, 96
   secondary sources of, 96
   short-term funding and, 89–99
   working capital and, 89–95
Liquidity management, 95, 750
Liquidity ratios, 99–102, 750
Listing requirements, 666
LLCs (limited liability companies), 5–11
Loans:
   green, 75–76, 748
   secured or asset-backed, 86, 753
   sustainability linked, 75–76, 754
Location, in business models, 374
London Interbank Offered Rate (Libor), 86
Long-run equilibrium:
   in monopolistic competition, 421–422
   in monopoly markets, 442–443
   in oligopoly markets, 433
   in perfectly competitive markets, 416–418
Long-term capacity, 472
Long-term debt and equity, 87
Long-term forecasting, 580–584
Long-term growth and demand outlook, 387
Long-term risk-free rate proxy, 270*e*
L'Oréal, 515–517

Low-cost strategy, 489–490
Lowe's, 470
Loyalty programs, 377
LPs (limited partners), 4–5, 750
Lufthansa AG, 149–150
LVMH W&S, 550

Macroeconomic influences, on industry, 480
Macroeconomic modeling, 274–275, 277
Macro risk, 384–386, 750
Maintenance capital expenditures, 528, 750
Majority shareholders, 661, 750
Management buyouts (MBOs), 22–23, 750
Management stock options, 181–182
Manager and board relationships, 49
Managers and management:
    and industry life cycle, 478
    as influential shareholders, 665
    interests of, 181–182
    manager and board relationships, 49
    optimism of, 551
    in ownership structures, 662–663
    risk management related to, 56–60
    shareholder and manager/director relationships,
        42–44
    as stakeholders, 39
Marginal cost (MC), 413–414
Marginal value curves, 409, 750
Marketable assets, 156–157
Marketable securities, 85
Market capitalization, 14–15
Market conditions:
    and capital structure, 149–150
    defined, 750
    as top-down external factor, 251–252
Market growth and market share approach, 505
Marketing:
    affiliate, 375, 743
    digital, in business models, 374
Market model, 282, 750
Marketplace businesses, 375, 750
Market power, 443–446
Market share stability, 474–475, 487e
Market structures, 395–447
    analysis of, 395–401
    consumer surplus, 408–410
    Cournot assumption, 425–428
    elasticity of demand, 403–406
    factors affecting demand, 406–408
    identification of, 443–446
    monopolistic competition, 418–422
    monopoly markets, 434–440, 442–443
    Nash equilibrium, 428–431
    oligopoly and pricing strategies, 422–425
    oligopoly markets, 431–433
    perfect competition, 401–403
    perfectly competitive markets, 410–418

    price discrimination and consumer surplus, 440–442
Market value, 169–170
Marriott, 368, 377
Marsh, Paul, 230
MasterCard, 468
Materiality, 670
Materials sector, 458e
Matrix pricing, 225, 750
Mature businesses:
    and business models, 380
    as life cycle stage, 154–156
Mature industry stage, 477
Maturity stage, 21
MBOs (management buyouts), 22–23, 750
MC (marginal cost), 413–414
McDonald's, 143, 602
Medtronic, 474
Mercado Libre, 375
Mercedes-Benz, 600
Merck & Co., 234–235
Mergers, 710e
Metal mesh devices, 474
Microsoft, 317, 318, 397, 435, 572–575
Miller, Merton, 157, 311
Mimicking, costs of, 315
Minority interests, 717–720
Minority shareholders:
    controlling and minority shareholder relationships,
        44–48
    as controlling shareholders, 661
    defined, 45, 750
Mittoo, Usha, 239
Mixed-ownership models, 664
MM Proposition I:
    with taxes, 163
    without taxes, 159
MM Proposition II:
    with taxes, 164
    without taxes, 160–162
MM propositions (MM), *see* Modigliani–Miller
    propositions
Modigliani, Franco, 157, 311
Modigliani–Miller (MM) propositions, 157–167
    MM Proposition I without taxes, 159
    MM Proposition I with taxes, 163
    MM Proposition II without taxes, 160–162
    MM Proposition II with taxes, 164
    with taxes, 163
MolsonCoors, 554
Monitoring, in capital allocation, 115–116
Monopolistic competition:
    defined, 398, 750
    long-run equilibrium in, 421–422
    market structures, 400e, 418–422
    short-run equilibrium in, 420e
Monopoly(-ies):
    defined, 750

as market structure, 398, 400*e*
natural, 434–435, 439–440, 442
and network effect, 435
regulations related to, 435, 442
in utility industry, 434–435
Monopoly markets:
long-run equilibrium in, 442–443
market structures, 434–440, 442–443
Moore's law, 481
Morgan, J. P., 433
MSCI, 457
Multi-sided network effects, 375
Musk, Elon, 1
Mutually exclusive projects, 119, 750

Nash, John, 428
Nash equilibrium, 428–431, 750
Natural monopolies, 434–435, 439–440, 442
Negative screening, 74, 76*e*, 751
Negotiation, share repurchases by, 333, 339
Nestlé, 567, 568
Netflix, 367, 397
Net income:
investment decisions based on, 126
operating income and, 202
NetJets, 368
Net present value (NPV), 119–122
and capital investments, 129
defined, 751
investment decisions based on, 126
and stock prices, 128
Network effects:
in business models, 374
and competitive advantage, 388
defined, 751
and monopolies, 435
and platform business models, 375
New Guards Groups, 613
Nine West, 213
Nishiyama Onsen Keiunkan (hotel), 376
Nokia, 479
Nomination committees, 59
Non-bank lenders, 86, 751
Noncontrolling interests, 717–720
Nonconventional cash flow patterns, 118, 751
Non-cumulative preferred stock, 257
Non-cyclical companies, 454–455
Non-operating costs modeling, 520–525, 537
Non-price competition, 399
Nonprofit corporations, 6, 751
Non-profit organizations, 41
Nonpublic companies, 233–236
Nonrated debt, 226
Non-traded debt, 262–263
Normalized earnings, 580, 751
Normalized revenue, 580–584
Novartis AG, 454, 463–464, 600–601

Novo Nordisk, 503–504, 506–508
NPV, *see* Net present value
Number of days of inventory, 100*e*
Number of days of payables, 100*e*
Number of days of receivables, 100*e*
NuvoMedia, 1
NVIDIA Corp., 598

Oath, 397
OECD, *see* Organisation for Economic Co-operation and Development
Offshoring, 602–603, 751
Oligopoly(-ies):
defined, 398, 751
market structures, 400*e*
and pricing strategies, 422–425
Oligopoly markets:
Cournot assumption, 425–428
market structures, 431–433
Nash equilibrium, 428–431
Omnichannel, 364, 751
One-sided network effects, 375
One-tier boards, 666, 751
Online travel agencies (OTAs), 377–378
OPEC cartel, 423, 430
Operating breakeven points, 208–211, 214, 751
Operating cash flows, 83
Operating costs:
fixed, 196, 197, 199
income statement modeling, 533–535
in income statement modeling, 508–512
variable, 196, 197, 199
Operating costs modeling, 512–519
Operating earnings, 200, 201*e*
Operating income:
changes in, 196
defined, 195
elasticity of, 194
financial risk and, 201–205
net income and, 202
revenues and, 200, 201*e*
sales risk and, 193–194
Operating leases, 226, 751
Operating leverage, 199, 205–208
and capital structure, 141–142
as company-specific risk, 389
defined, 751
measuring, 390–391
Operating lines of credit, 86
Operating performance, 65
Operating profit by segment, 535–536
Operating risk, 194–201, 751
Operational risk, 63–65
Opportunity costs, 411, 751
Optimal capital structure, 167–174, 751
Optimal price:
in monopolistically competitive markets, 420

in monopoly markets, 438–440
in oligopoly markets, 432–433
Optional product pricing, 367, 751
Optionlike features, debt with, 225–226
Oracle Corporation, 314, 317
Organisation for Economic Co-operation and
     Development (OECD), 51, 75, 660–661
Organization, of business, 370–372
Ørsted, 117
Orthopedic devices, 474
OTAs (online travel agencies), 377–378
Output:
     in monopolistically competitive markets, 420
     in monopoly markets, 438–440
     in oligopoly markets, 432–433
Outsourcing:
     in business models, 374
     defined, 751
     to reduce costs, 602, 603
Overconfidence, in forecasting, 545–546
Owner–operator relationships, 7–8
Owners:
     risks of, 211–213
Owners, risks of, 211–213
Ownership:
     alternatives to, 368
     of assets, 143
     of assets, 143
     concentrated, 45, 46e, 660–662, 744
     dispersed, 44, 45e, 660–662, 746
     engagement, 74–75, 76e
     engagement or active, 74–75, 76e, 747
     horizontal, 662, 748
     in income statement modeling, 525
     lenders and owners, 23–31
     mixed-ownership models, 664
     total cost of, 366, 755
     vertical, 662, 755
Ownership capital, 9, 751
Ownership structures, 660–666

Partners:
     general, 4–5, 748
     limited, 4–5, 750
Partnerships:
     general, 3–4
     limited, 4–5, 750
Partnership agreements, 3, 751
Pay-in-advance, 380, 751
Payless, 213
Payouts, 348–349, 751
Payout policies, 304, 327–332, 751
PayPal, 458e
Pecking order theory, 172–174, 751
Peer companies, 233. *See also* comparable companies
Peer firm leverage, 150–151
Peer groups, constructing, 462–465

Peloton Interactive, 458e
Penetration pricing, 367, 752
P/E (price-to-earnings) ratio, 308, 752
Perfect capital markets:
     defined, 752
     and dividend policy, 311
     and MM propositions, 158
     value of firm in, 162
Perfect competition:
     defined, 397–398, 752
     market structures, 400e, 401–403
Perfectly competitive markets:
     long-run equilibrium in, 416–418
     market structures, 410–418
     optimal price and output in, 411–415
Performance attribution, 453
Pernod Ricard SA, 550
Personal computer market, 570–577
Per unit contribution margin, 196, 752
Pet projects, 125–126, 752
Petropolis, 553
Pfizer Inc., 454, 464
Pharmaceuticals, 463–464
Physical capacity, 473
Platform business models, 375
Political considerations, 379
Ponemon Institute, 71
Porter, Michael, 371, 400–401, 467, 489, 551
Porter's five forces, 400–401, 467, 551–561
Portfolio performance attribution, 453
Positive screening, 74, 76e, 752
Post-audits, 115–116
PPMs (private placement memorandums), 16,
     752
Preferred shareholders, interests of, 180
Preferred stock:
     cost of, 226–227, 745
     cumulative, 257, 745
     cumulative vs. non-cumulative, 257
     fixed-rate perpetual, 748
Premium paid analysis, 619–620
Prices:
     effects of, on gross profit and margin, 513
     impact of competitive factors in costs and, 551–
        561
Price competition, 475–476, 487e
Price discrimination, 366–367
     and consumer surplus, 440–442
     defined, 752
     first-degree, 440, 748
     second-degree, 440, 753
     third-degree, 440–441, 755
Priced risk, 229, 752
Price elasticity of demand, 403–406, 752
Price leaders, 431–432
Price-setting option, 131, 752
Price takers, 399, 752

Price-to-earnings (P/E) ratio, 308, 752
Price wars, 423–424
Pricing:
  in business model, 365–368
  cost-based, 366, 745
  dynamic, 367, 746
  freemium, 367, 748
  matrix, 225, 750
  for multiple products, 367
  optional product, 367, 751
  penetration, 367, 752
  for rapid growth, 367–368
  razors-and-blades, 367, 752
  recurring revenue, 368, 753
  regulated, by government, 439–440
  strategies for, 422–425
  subscription, 368, 753
  tiered, 366, 755
  two-part tariff pricing, 441–442
  value-based, 366, 755
PRI (Principles for Responsible Investment)
      Initiative, 77
Principal–agent relationships, 41–42, 662, 752
Principal business activity, 454
Principles for Responsible Investment (PRI)
      Initiative, 77
Privacy, of data, 71–72
Private companies, 284–287
Private corporations, 12–23
Private equity firms, 664
Private for-profit corporations, 7
Private label manufacturers, 374, 752
Private lenders, 38
Private placement memorandums (PPMs), 16, 752
Procter & Gamble, 515, 516e
Products, identifying similar companies by, 453–454
Product differentiation:
  airline industry, 486
  in monopolistic competition, 418–419
Production-flexibility option, 131, 132, 752
Product line analysis, 503
Product market risk, 388, 752
Profitability:
  in business model, 372
  and cost of capital, 256
  degree of operating leverage and, 198e
Pro forma financial statements, 620–628, 752
Pro forma income statement, 538–540
Pro forma statement of cash flows, 540–541
Pro forma weighted average cost of capital, 622–623
Project sequencing, 119, 752
Proxy contests, 55, 752
Proxy voting, 53, 752
Public companies, 232–233
Public corporations, 12–23
Public debtholders, 38. See also Bondholders
Public for-profit corporations, 7

Pull on liquidity, 98–99, 752
Putability, 256–257

Qtel, 47
Quick ratio, 99e

Radio Shack, 213
Rate implicit in the lease (RIIL), 264, 752
Razors-and-blades pricing, 367, 752
Ready cash balances, 96
Real estate sector, 459e
Real options, in capital investments, 129–132
Receivables:
  securitization of, 727–729
  uncollected, 98
Recency bias, 277, 752
Reckitt Group, 516e
Reclassification, of investments, 694–695
Recoverable amount, 705n15
Recurring revenue pricing, 368, 753
Registration, of corporations, 16–17
Regression analysis, 444
Regular cash dividends, 305
Regular lines of credit, 85, 744
Regulations:
  airline industry, 485
  government, 61
  and industry life cycle, 479
  influence of, on industry, 482, 488e
  and long-term forecasting, 582
  related to monopolies, 435, 442
  related to pricing, 439–440
Regulatory/compliance projects, 111–112
Regulatory considerations:
  and business models, 379
  and capital structure, 150
  and cost of capital, 252
  for short-term financing, 103
Regulatory risks, 65–66
Reinsurance market, 473
Relevancy, of ESG considerations, 69–70
Remuneration, executive, 669
Remuneration committees, 58–59
Remuneration plans, 58–59
Rémy Cointreau, 531–550, 552
Reorganization, 603, 753
Representativeness bias, 549–550
Reputational risks, 65–66
Required rate of return, 117
Required rate of return on equity, 249, 279–292.
      See also Cost of equity
  defined, 753
Responsible investing, 73, 753
Restructuring, costs of, 730. See also Corporate
      restructuring
Restructuring actions:
  evaluating, 647–653

types of, 601–605
Retail businesses, competition among, 213
Return on capital employed, 753
Return on equity (ROE):
    increasing, with share repurchases, 342–343
    investment decisions based on, 126
    leveraging and, 204e–205e
Return on invested capital (ROIC), 126–128, 753
Returns-based measure forecasts, 505
Revenues:
    and capital structure, 141–142
    as company specific factor, 254–255
    income statement modeling, 502–508, 533–534
    normalized, 580–584
    operating earnings and, 200, 201e
    synergies in, 598
Revenue models, 366–368
Reverse auction models, 367, 743
Reverse stock splits, 310–311, 753
Revolving credit agreements, 86, 753
Rhone-Poulenc, 443
RIIL (rate implicit in the lease), 264, 752
Risk(s). *See also* Business risk; Financial risk
    business, 192–193, 744
    capital investment, 389, 744
    company-specific, 387–389
    competitive, 388, 744
    country, 252
    of creditors and owners, 211–213
    as cumulative, 386
    customer concentration, 254, 745
    default, 66–67
    ESG, 389, 747
    ESG-related, 72–73
    execution, 388–389, 747
    industry, 386–387, 749
    legal, 65–66
    leverage and, 192–205, 211–213
    macro, 384–386, 750
    operating, 194–201, 751
    of owners, 211–213
    priced, 229, 752
    product market, 388, 752
    regulatory, 65–66
    reputational, 65–66
    sales, 192–194, 254
Risk-based models, 281–284, 753
Risk committees, 59
Risk-free rate, 250, 270, 753
Rite Aid Corporation, 509–512
Robinson, Joan, 398
Roche, 443
Roche Holding AG, 454, 464
ROE, *see* Return on equity
ROIC (return on invested capital), 126–128, 753
Rolex, 435

Russell 1000 Index, 344–345
Russell Investments, 457

Sale-leaseback, 603, 753
Sales:
    company, 563–565
    direct, 363, 364e, 746
    industry, 561–563
Sales projections, 561–567
Sales risk, 192–194, 254, 753
Samsung, 664
Sanofi S.A., 454, 464
Sanwa, 664
SASB (Sustainability Accounting Standards Board), 77
SASB (Sustainable Standards Board), 673, 674e
Satellite television, 397
Say on pay, 59, 753
Scale, in hotel and travel industry, 376
Scenario analysis, 545–546, 753
Schneider Electric SA, 310
Schumpeter, Joseph A., 417–418, 421
Schwab, Charles M., 433
SCRP (specific-company risk premium), 284–286, 753
Scrutiny, adequate, 65
SDGs (Sustainable Development Goals), 75
Second-degree price discrimination, 440, 753
Sector demand, 379
Secured loans, 86, 753
Securitization, of assets, 727–729
Security:
    of data, 71–72
    of lenders, 180
Security(-ies):
    features embedded in, 256–258
    risk of, 201
Segment disclosures, 503, 532
Semi-conductor industry, 464–465
Seniority, of lenders, 180
Sensitivity analysis, 570, 753
Services, identifying similar companies by, 453–454
SG&A expenses, 514–519, 534–535
Shadow banking, 251, 753
Shakeout industry stage, 477
Shares:
    bonus issues of, 743
    canceled, 744
    cost to acquire, 700
    dual-class, 746
Share buybacks, 154–155. *See also* Share repurchases
Share classes, 257
Shareholders, 38
    conflicts of interests between bondholders and, 31
    controlling, 44–48, 745
    creditor interests vs., 49
    equity and debt risk–return profiles, 25–28
    influential, 663–665

majority, 750
minority, 44–48, 750
preferences of, 324
risk management related to, 52–55
shareholder and manager/director relationships, 42–44
Shareholder activism, 54, 62, 667, 753
Shareholder and manager/director relationships, 42–44
Shareholder derivative lawsuits, 54–55
Shareholder meetings, 52–53
Shareholder theory, 37
Shareholder voting rights, 669–670
Share issuance, 15–18
Share ownership transfer, 13–15
Share repurchases, 332–337
defined, 753
dividends vs., 339–347
valuation equivalence of, 338–339
Shares outstanding:
income statement modeling, 537–538
in income statement modeling, 525
Shipping:
drop, 746
Short-run equilibrium, 420e
Short-term capacity, 472
Short-term commercial paper, 87
Short-term financing choices, 103–105
Short-term funding, 89–96
Short-term rental services, 378
Short-term risk-free rate proxy, 270e
Siam Cement Group, 514
SIC-12 Consolidated-Special Purpose Entities, 711
Siegel, Jeremy, 230
Signaling, 172–174, 313–319
Similar companies, identifying, 453–456
Singha Co., 423
Six Flags Entertainment Corp., 604–605
Six Flags Inc., 604–605
Size, of company, 103
Size premium (SP), 284–285, 753
Sizing options, 131
Skanska AB, 321–322
Smith & Nephew, 474
Social considerations:
airline industry, 486
and business models, 379
in ESG integration, 681–684
and industry life cycle, 479
influence of, on industry, 483
Social factors, 71–72
Socially responsible investing (SRI), 73, 753
Social media, 61
SOEs (state-owned enterprises), 664
SoftBank Group Corp., 598
Software service market, 475
Sole proprietorships, 2–3

Southwest Airlines, 149–150
Sovereign yield spread, 287, 753
SP (size premium), 284–285, 753
SPACs (special purpose acquisition companies), 19, 753
Special dividends, 305–307, 753
Specialization, 377
Special purpose acquisition companies (SPACs), 19, 753
Special purpose entities (SPEs), 711e, 726–729
Special purpose vehicles (SPVs), 86
Specific-company risk premium (SCRP), 284–286, 753
SPEs (special purpose entities), 711e, 726–729
Spin offs:
defined, 754
as divestment action, 601
valuation of, 615–616
Split-rate tax system, 324, 754
Spotify, 375
Spreadsheet modeling, 492–493
SPVs (special purpose vehicles), 86
SRI (socially responsible investing), 73, 753
Stable dividend policy, 327–331, 754
Stackelberg model, 430–431, 754
Staggered boards, 39, 754
Stakeholders, interests of, 174–182
Stakeholder groups, 36–41, 175e
Stakeholder management, 52, 754
Stakeholder risk management, 51–69
Stakeholder theory, 37
Standard & Poor's, 457
StarHub, 351
Startups:
lean, 380, 749
in life cycles of corporations, 21
as life cycle stage, 152–153
Start-up financing, 153
State-owned enterprises (SOEs), 664
Static trade-off theory of capital structure, 167, 168e, 754
Statistical similarities, of companies, 456
Statutory tax rate, 521, 522
Staunton, Mike, 230
Stewardship codes, 666
Stock dividends, 307–309, 754
Stock options, 181–182
Stock performance, 67
Stock prices, 128
Stock repurchases, 154–155. See also Share repurchases
Stock splits, 309–311, 753
Straight debt, 262, 754
Straight voting, 46, 669, 754
Stranded assets, 70, 675, 754
Strategic analysis, 467–468, 486e–488e
Strategic games, 430

Stryker, 474
Subscription pricing, 368, 753
Substitutes, 407, 552, 754
Sunk costs, 117, 754
Suppliers:
  bargaining power of, in Porter's five forces model, 552
  and stakeholder risk management, 60–61
  as stakeholders, 40
Supply:
  in monopolistically competitive markets, 420
  in monopoly markets, 436–438
  in perfectly competitive markets, 416
Supply chains, 371, 754
Surplus cash, 335
Survey approach, 231, 754
Survey-based estimates:
  for ERP, 272, 277
Survivorship bias, 754
Sustainability Accounting Standards Board (SASB), 77
Sustainability linked loans, 75–76, 754
Sustainable Development Goals (SDGs), 75
Sustainable investing, 73, 754
Sustainable Standards Board (SASB), 673, 674e
Switching barriers, 388, 754
Synergies, 595, 597–598, 754
Synthetic credit ratings, 262–263, 299, 300e
Sysco Company, 565

Tablet market, 570–577
Taiwan Semiconductor Manufacturing Company Ltd. (TSMC), 464–465
Takeover premium, 619, 754
Takeover prices, 617
Take-private transactions, 605
Tangible assets:
  and capital structure, 142
  and cost of capital, 255
  defined, 754
Target capital structure, 167–174, 221, 250, 754
Target Corporation, 101
Target payout ratio, 328, 329, 754
Target weights, 170–172
Tarpenning, Marc, 1
Taxes:
  breakeven points and, 209n7
  corporate tax rate, 146
  corporations, 10–11
  and cost of capital, 222–223, 252
  and cost of debt, 224, 225, 238e
  and cost of equity, 238e
  dividend imputation tax system, 323, 746
  and dividend policy, 313, 322–324, 340
  double taxation system, 323–324, 746
  income statement modeling, 537
  in income statement modeling, 521–524

MM Proposition I without, 159
MM Proposition II without, 160–162
MM propositions with, 163–165
and share repurchases, 340
split-rate tax system, 324, 754
Technological developments:
  in financial statement modeling, 570–579
  and long-term forecasting, 582
Technological influences, on industry, 480–481, 486, 488e
Telephone industry, 438, 443
Television broadcasting, 397
Telstra, 316
Tencent, 305–306, 582
Tender offers, 55, 755
Tesla, 1–2, 361, 362, 365, 366, 369, 371, 372, 376
ThaiBev, 423
Thematic investing, 74, 76e, 755
Theranos Inc., 64
Thinly traded companies, 233–236
Third-degree price discrimination, 440–441, 755
Third-party debt ratings, 148–149
Tiered pricing, 366, 755
Time periods, in historical approach to ERP, 269
Time-series forecasts, 505–506
Timing options, 130
Tobacco consumption, 483
Top-down approach, 504–505, 755
Top-down drivers, 595e, 596
Top-down external factors, 251–253
Total cost of ownership, 366, 755
Total leverage, 205–208
Toxic emissions, 71
Toys R Us, 213
Trade credit, 755
Traded debt, 262
Traditional channel strategy, 363, 364e
Transparency, 52, 56
Treasury shares/stocks, 332, 755
TREND formula, 580–581
Tripadvisor.com, 376, 378
Trip.com, 378
TSMC (Taiwan Semiconductor Manufacturing Company Ltd.), 464–465
Turkish Airlines, 582–583
2019 Cost of a Data Breach Report (IBM and Ponemon Institute), 71
2° Investing Initiative (2DII), 673
Two-part tariff pricing, 441–442
Two-sided network effects, 375
Two-tier boards, 666, 755

Uber, 143, 375, 458e
Uncollected receivables, 98
Uncommitted lines of credit, 85, 755
UNEP FI (United Nations Environment Programme Finance Initiative), 77

Unequal voting rights, 47–48
Unilever, 517–519, 563, 568
Unions, 60
Unitary elastic demand, 404
Unit economics, 372, 755
United Kingdom, 554–555
United Nations Environment Programme Finance
    Initiative (UNEP FI), 77
United States Steel Corporation (US Steel), 433
Unusual charges, 525
Upstream, 705–707, 725, 755
U.S. Bankruptcy Code:
    Chapter 7 liquidation, 212
    Chapter 11 reorganization, 212, 213
U.S. equity risk premium, 230
U.S. Financial Accounting Standards Board (FASB),
    690, 692
U.S. GAAP:
    acquisition method, 710, 711–713
    consolidated financial statements, 725
    consolidation, 716, 717, 719
    contingent assets and liabilities, 730
    contingent consideration, 730
    disclosures, 708
    excess purchase price, 700–701
    fair value option, 704
    IFRS and, 690
    impairment, 704, 705
    impairment of goodwill, 720–722
    in-process R&D, 730
    investment in financial assets, 692
    investments in associates and joint ventures, 695–
        696
    restructuring costs, 730
    transactions with associates and disclosures, 705
    variable interest entities, 727
U.S. Supreme Court, 407
US Steel (United States Steel Corporation), 433
Utilities sector, 459e
Utility industry, 319, 434–435, 439

Vale, 71
Valeant Pharmaceuticals International Inc., 127–128
Valuation:
    and corporate governance, 67
    corporate restructuring, 620–628
    and corporate restructuring, 614–620
    in perfection capital markets, 162
Valuation models, 544–545
Value added resellers, 375, 755
Value-based investing, 73
Value-based pricing, 366, 755
Value chains, 371–372, 387, 755
Value propositions, 368–370, 755
Values-based investing, 73

Variable costs, 191, 196, 197, 199, 755
Variable interest entities (VIEs), 711, 711e, 726–729
Variable operating costs, 194
Vertical demand schedule, 405
Vertical demand schedules, 755
Vertical ownership, 662, 755
VIEs, see Variable interest entities
Visa, 468
Volatility, of future earnings, 321
Volkswagen, 66
Volume growth, 564
Voting:
    cumulative, 53, 745
    proxy, 53, 752
    special voting arrangements, 666
    straight, 46, 669, 754
Voting caps, 662, 755
Voting rights:
    as investor consideration, 669–670
    unequal, 47–48
Vrbo, 378

WACC, see Weighted average cost of capital
Walgreens Boots Alliance Inc., 509–512
Walmart, 101, 200, 201e, 561
Wataniya, 47
Waze, 376
Web-based lenders, 86, 755
WeChat, 375
Weibo, 317
Weighted average cost of capital (WACC), 117
    computing, 221–222
    defined, 221, 249, 755
    factors considered in determining, 259e
    pro forma, 622–623
    and target weights, 170–172
WeWork, 368
Whole Foods Market, 310
Wikipedia, 376
Working capital, 81–95
    financing options, 82–89
    forecasting, with efficiency ratios, 526–527
    income statement modeling, 542
    liquidity, short-term funding needs, and, 89–95
Working capital management, 81, 89–93, 94e,
    755
The World Is Flat (Friedman), 396
Wyndham Destinations, 377

Yield-to-maturity (YTM), 223–224
    and cost of debt, 262
    defined, 755
YouTube, 617

Zimmer Biomet, 474

CFA Institute
+ Wiley
= Success

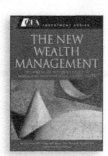
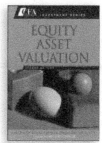

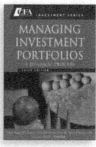

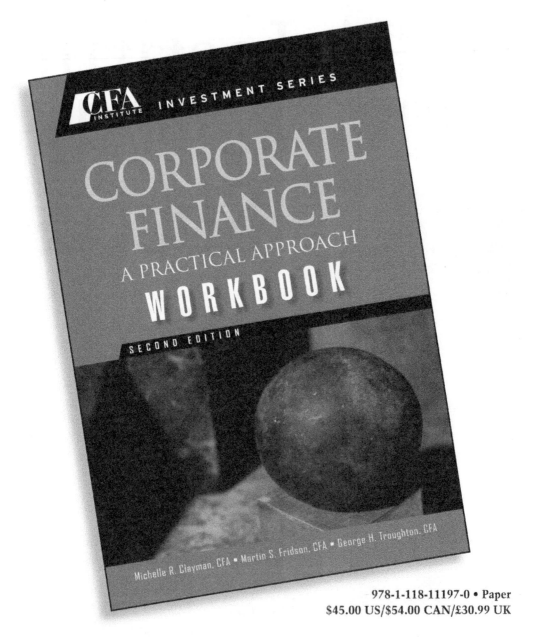